PrincetonReview.com

W9-BSE-600

THE BEST 379 COLLEGES

2015 Edition

By Robert Franek, Kristen O'Toole, David Soto,
and The Staff of The Princeton Review

2015 Edition

PENGUIN RANDOM HOUSE

The Princeton Review
24 Prime Parkway, Suite 201
Natick, MA 01760
E-mail: editorialsupport@review.com

ISBN 978-0-8041-2479-9

Senior VP—Publisher: Robert Franek
Editorial Director: Kristen O'Toole
Director of Content Development: David Soto
Student Survey Manager: Stephen Koch
Production: Best Content Solutions, LLC
Production Editor: Melissa Duclos-Yourdon

Printed in the United States of America on partially recycled paper.

Editorial

Robert Franek, SVP, Publisher
Selena Coppock, Managing Editor
Kristen O'Toole, Editorial Director
Calvin Cato, Editor
Meave Shelton, Editor
Alyssa Wolff, Editorial Assistant

Random House Publishing Team

Tom Russell, Publisher
Alison Stoltzfus, Publishing Manager
Ellen L. Reed, Production Manager
Dawn Ryan, Managing Editor
Kristin Lindner, Production Supervisor
Andrea Lau, Designer

ACKNOWLEDGMENTS

Each year we assemble an awe-inspiringly talented group of colleagues who work together to produce our guidebooks; this year is no exception. Everyone involved in this effort—authors, editors, data managers, production specialists, and designers—goes above and beyond to make *The Best 379 Colleges* an exceptional student resource guide. This new edition gives prospective college students what they really want: The most honest, accessible, and pertinent information about the colleges they are considering attending.

My sincere thanks go to the many who contributed to this tremendous project. I know our readers will benefit from our collective efforts to collect the opinions of current students at the outstanding schools we profile. A special thank you goes to our authors, Jen Adams, Andrea Kornstein, Lincoln Michel, and Julie Doherty-Meade, for their dedication in poring through tens of thousands of surveys to produce the campus culture narratives of each school profiled. Thanks to Chris Koch for checking student quotes. Very special thanks goes to Kristen O'Toole for her editorial commitment and vision. A warm and special thank you goes to our Student Survey Manager, Stephen Koch, who continues to work in partnership with school administrators and students alike. My continued thanks go to our data collection master, David Soto, for his successful efforts in collecting and accurately representing the statistical data that appear with each college profile. The enormousness of this project and its deadline constraints could not have been realized without the calm presence of Scott Harris of Best Content Solutions and production editor Melissa Duclos-Yourdon—their dedication, focus, and attention to detail continue to impress and remind me of what a pleasure it is to work on this project each year. Special thanks also go to Jeanne Krier, our Random House publicist, for the dedicated work she has done on this book and the overall series since its inception. Jeanne continues to be my trusted colleague, media advisor, and friend. I would also like to make special mention of Tom Russell and Alison Stoltzfus, our Random House publishing team, for their continuous investment and faith in our ideas. Last, I thank my TPR Partner Team, Deborah Ellinger, Scott Kirkpatrick, Michael Bleyhl, John Kelley, and Paul Kanarek for their confidence in me and my content team and for their commitment to providing students the resources they need to find the right fit school for them. Again, to all who contributed so much to this publication, thank you for your efforts; they do not go unnoticed.

Robert Franek
Senior VP—Publisher
Lead Author—*The Best 379 Colleges*

DOONESBURY   **By Garry Trudeau**

CONTENTS

PART I: INTRODUCTION

Getting into Selective Colleges: A Guide for High School Students

What we've put together in this book is a guide to the nation's 379 most academically outstanding institutions so that you can be informed about the unique opportunities these schools offer and what it's really like to be a student at them. As selective as you'll be about choosing the right college for you, know that many of the colleges we profile will be selective in choosing the students right for them. While some of the schools you'll read about here admit upwards of eighty percent of their applicants, the majority have many more applicants than they have seats to fill, and some admit less than ten percent of the students who apply. That means—depending on which colleges you're pinning your hopes on attending—you are likely going to have to put quite a bit of effort into getting in. High grades in challenging courses are just the beginning!

If you're like most of the two million high school students who apply to college each year, you're probably wondering what college admissions officers are really looking for in an applicant. What exactly does it take to get into college? What can I do to make my application stand out? Once I get accepted, how do I know which college is best for me?

In order to get you started on the road to a successful application, we're going to give you a few goals, suggestions, and tips for checkpoints along the way. This brief primer will help you know what you should be doing year by year in high school to prepare yourself for admission to your "best" college.

6 STEPS TO GETTING INTO COLLEGE

Sure, high school is supposed to be fun, but putting some effort into your schoolwork and extracurricular experiences can make applying to your choice colleges a lot less stressful. Though it might sound like boring advice, the following steps are extremely important!

1. Work hard for good grades.

2. Enroll in challenging courses.

3. Spend time preparing for the ACT or SAT and SAT Subject Tests.

4. Polish your writing skills.

5. Establish relationships with teachers and advisors who can write strong letters of recommendation for you.

6. Get involved in some activities, community service, or work experiences that will enable you to show your values, talents, and skills.

NEED MORE HELP?

For more information on how you can make the most of your high school years and turn those experiences into a successful college application, check out our offering of college admissions books at PrincetonReviewBooks.com.

Freshman Year

Getting a good start is the best way to get a strong finish! You don't want to have to play catch-up during your junior and senior years when you're supposed to be focusing on bigger things. During your freshman year, make sure you concentrate on your studies and work hard to earn good grades. Get to know your teachers and ask for their help if you are having trouble in a subject—as well as if you just really enjoy it and want to learn more. They'll most certainly want to help you do your best. If there is an honor roll at your school, make it a goal to get on it. And if your grades are so good that you qualify for membership in the National Honor Society, pat yourself on the back and don't think twice about accepting the invitation to join. Make it a point to meet your guidance counselor so you can begin pinpointing colleges you may be interested in and studying for the courses and admission tests they require. The great thing about freshman year is that you have plenty of time to focus on projects that can make your admissions applications during your senior year look the best they can. Make sure you take hold of that opportunity!

> "During your freshman year, make sure you concentrate on your studies and work hard to earn good grades."

Read a Good Book! (or two)

Strong vocabulary and reading skills are essential to doing well on the SAT and ACT (and most tests you'll take for that matter—even math tests require good reading skills!). By cracking open a few good books, you can do some early prep for both tests. Here are some books we love by interesting authors. Not only will you learn some stuff by reading them, but we think you'll love them too!

- *The Curious Incident of the Dog in the Night-Time: A Novel* by Mark Haddon

- *A Heartbreaking Work of Staggering Genius* by Dave Eggers

- *Life of Pi* by Yann Martel

- *Reading Lolita in Tehran* by Azar Nafisi

- *White Teeth* by Zadie Smith

Another Good Book

For extra practice building your vocabulary, check out our book *SAT Power Vocab*. It has nearly 1,600 words, including our "SAT Hit Parade": words appearing most frequently on the SAT.

Sophomore Year

As a sophomore, you'll need to stay focused on your studies. If you didn't earn strong grades during your freshman year, start doing so this year. Scope out the Advanced Placement courses that are offered at your school. You'll want to sign up for as many AP courses as you can reasonably take, starting in your junior year. During sophomore year, you'll also want to choose one or more extracurriculars that interest you. Admissions officers tell us they look favorably on involvement in student government, student newspaper, community service, and sports. What you don't want to do is overload your schedule with activities just to rack up a long list of extracurriculars. Colleges would much rather see you focus on a few worthwhile extracurriculars than divide your time among a bunch of different activities that you're not passionate about. Your sophomore year is when you'll have an opportunity to take the PSAT. Given every October, the PSAT is a shortened version of the SAT. It is used to predict how well you will do on the SAT, and it determines eligibility for National Merit Scholarships. While your PSAT scores won't count until you retake the test in your junior year, you should approach this as a test run for the real thing, because the real thing is coming, and it's coming fast. Sophomore year will be over before you know it, and you'll soon have to step it up and be running strong in the critical part of the race to reach the application finish line.

> "Colleges would much rather see you focus on a few worthwhile extracurriculars than divide your time among a bunch of different activities that you're not passionate about."

What Should You Do This Summer?

Ahhh, summer. The possibilities seem endless. You can get a job, intern, travel, study, volunteer, or do nothing at all. Here are a few ideas to get you started:

- **Go to college:** No, not for real. However, you can participate in summer programs at colleges and universities at home and abroad. Programs can focus on anything from academics (stretch your brain by taking an intensive science or language course) to sports to admissions guidance. This is also a great opportunity to explore college life firsthand, especially if you get to stay in a dorm. Summer is also a time when families on vacations can squeeze in a college visit while they're in "the neighborhood." Even if classes aren't in session when you are able to tour a campus, the more colleges you can visit the better informed your final college choice will be.

- **Prep for the PSAT, SAT, or ACT:** So maybe it's not quite as adventurous as trekking around Patagonia for the summer (it's also not as expensive!) or as cool as learning to slam dunk at basketball camp, but hey, there's nothing adventurous or cool about being rejected from your top-choice college because of unimpressive test scores. Plus, you'll be ahead of the game if you can return to school with much of your PSAT, SAT, and ACT preparation behind you.

- **Research scholarships:** College is expensive. While you should never rule out a school based on cost, the more scholarship money you can secure beforehand, the more college options you will have. You'll find loads of info on financial aid and scholarships (including a scholarship search tool) on our site, PrincetonReview.com.

Get Help

Admissions officers will want to see that you've earned high grades in challenging classes. The Princeton Review's *Cracking the AP Exam* series offers test-prep guides to the most popular AP subject tests to help give you a leg up on passing the exams. High AP scores can boost your chances of admission; plus they are used for placement in college courses and for awarding college credit (ka-ching! ka-ching!). We also offer *Cracking the PSAT/NMSQT*, which has two full-length practice tests and tips on how to score your best on the test. And a great vocabulary will help you with both AP classes and the PSAT, so sign up for lots of help on PrincetonReview.com.

Junior Year

Your junior year is going to be exciting and challenging and extremely important in your academic career. You'll start the year off by taking the PSAT in October. High PSAT scores in junior year qualify you for the National Merit Scholarship competition. To become a finalist, you also need great grades and a recommendation from your school. It's critical that your junior-year grades be solid. When colleges look at your transcripts, they put a heavy emphasis on junior-year grades. Decisions are made before admissions officers see your second-semester, senior-year grades and possibly before they see your first-semester, senior-year grades! During your junior year, you'll probably take the SAT or ACT test for the first time. Most colleges require scores from one of these tests for admission and/or scholarship award decisions. Also take time during your junior year to research colleges, and, if possible, visit schools high on your "hopes" list. When researching colleges, you'll want to consider a variety of factors besides whether or not you can get in, including location, school size, majors or programs offered that interest you, and cost and availability of financial aid. It helps to visit schools because it's the best way to learn whether a school may be right for you. If you can schedule an interview with an admissions officer during your visit, it may help him or her discover how right you may be for the school.

The SAT is Changing

The SAT is undergoing its biggest change in 30 years. The Redesigned SAT is expected to debut in March of 2016 and will impact students who will graduate high school in the class of 2017 and younger. The content on the Redesigned SAT will be very similar to that which is on the ACT. The major difference is in how the concepts are tested and the steps students will have to take to solve problems correctly.

Some students may find the Redesigned SAT more friendly:

- There will not be a penalty for wrong answers, so students won't have to worry about losing points for guessing incorrectly.

- There will be only 4 answer choices instead of 5.

- Students may be more familiar with some of the vocabulary tested, but they will need to know multiple definitions of those words.

Some students may find some of the changes more challenging:

- Questions will require multiple steps to get to an answer.

- The reading passages will include complex structure and vocabulary.

- Foundational math skills will be more important.

- Reasoning and critical thinking skills will be paramount.

- There will be fewer sections on the Redesigned Test, but they will be longer in time than the current SAT.

This remains a very coachable test for which students need to prepare. Stay on top of new test information as it is released by visiting PrincetonReview.com/SATchanges/.

Senior Year

It's finally here! Senior year! It's now time to get serious about pulling everything together on your applications. Deadlines will vary from school to school, and you will have a lot to keep track of, so make checklists of what's due when. If you're not happy with your previous SAT scores, you should take the October SAT. If you still need to take any SAT Subject Tests, now's the time.

When you ask teachers to write recommendations for you, give them everything they need. Tell them your application deadline and include a stamped, addressed envelope, or directions on how to submit the recommendation online, and be sure to send them a thank-you note after you know the recommendation was turned in.

Your essay, on the other hand, is the one part of your application you have total control over. Don't repeat information from other parts of your application. And by all means, proofread! You'll find more than 100 actual essays by students who got into great colleges plus tips from 19 admissions officers on what they look for (and what peeves them the most) about college applicants' essays in our book, *College Essays That Made a Difference*.

If you have found the school of your dreams and you're happy with your grades and test scores, consider filing an early decision application. Many selective colleges commit more than half of their admissions spots to early decision applicants. To take this route, you must file your application in early November (Note: you can apply for early decision to only one college.). By mid-December, you'll find out whether you got in—but there's a catch. If you're accepted early decisions to a college, you cannot apply to other colleges. This means that you won't have financial aid offer from other colleges to consider. If the early decision college accepts you, be prepared to attend it and to accept its financial aid award (if you applied for aid). An early decision application is considered a binding one. Another option which is not binding is an early action application. At colleges that offer this route, students can apply early (usually November) and receive admissions decisions early (usually January/February), but the accepted student does not have to commit to attend the college and s/he has until May 1st to reply. Regardless of which route you decide to take, have a backup plan. Make sure you apply to at least one safety school—one that you feel confident you can get into and, if cost is a factor, one that you can afford.

We know how exciting but stressful the final decision can be. If you're having a difficult time choosing between two colleges, try to visit each of them one more time. Can you imagine yourself walking around that campus, building a life in that community, and establishing friendships with those people? Finally, decide and be happy. Don't forget to thank your recommenders and tell them where you'll be going to school. Some of the best times of your life await!

Some of Our Other Helpful Books

Our book *If the U Fits: Expert Advice on Finding the Right College and Getting Accepted* is full of advice from the admissions counselors at our partner Collegewise on finding the right school for you and putting your best foot forward on your applications. It's packed with strategies for essays and interviews, and tips for maintaining your sanity during the application process!

The Princeton Review's *Paying for College Without Going Broke* is the only annually updated guide to financial aid that has detailed, line-by-line strategies for completing the highly complicated FAFSA for the upcoming school year (as well as the CSS/PROFILE form) to one's best advantage. It explains how the financial aid process works and reveals strategies—all legal—for maximizing your eligibility for aid. Authored by Kal Chany, one of the nation's most widely sourced experts on college funding, it also includes annually updated information on education tax breaks, college savings programs, and student and parent loans.

Check out Kal Chany's "26 Tips for Getting Financial Aid . . ." on pages 7–8.

K & W Guide to College Programs & Services for Students with Learning Disabilities or Attention Deficit/Hyperactivity Disorder profiles 350 schools highly recommended for such students. It includes strategies to help them successfully apply to the best programs for their needs, plus advice from specialists in the field of learning disabilities.

Is a College's Cost a Key Concern?

We say it over and over: Never rule out applying to a college because of its "sticker" price. Many schools are very generous with their financial aid, and it can cost less to attend an expensive private college than an inexpensive public university. Our book, *The Best Value Colleges* profiles 75 public and 75 private colleges we selected for their excellent academics combined with generous financial aid and/or relatively low cost of attendance. You'll also find a list of our 150 "best value" schools list in this book on page 54. (Also note our ranking list, "Great Financial Aid," on page 41: it names the top twenty schools at which students we surveyed were happiest with their financial aid awards.) Be sure to check our unique Financial Aid Rating scores in the school profiles in this book (see page 29 to learn how we tally these ratings). We also offer an index of colleges in this book sorted by tuition. You'll find it on page 826.

And on page 822 you'll also find an index of schools in the book by location.

26 Tips for Getting Financial Aid, Scholarships, and Grants and for Paying Less for College

by Kalman A. Chany, author of *Paying for College Without Going Broke*

(Random House/Princeton Review Books)

Getting financial aid

1. Learn how financial aid works. The more and the sooner you know about how need-based aid eligibility is determined, the better you can take steps to maximize such eligibility.

2. Apply for financial aid no matter what your circumstances. Some merit-based aid can only be awarded if the applicant has submitted financial aid application forms.

3. Don't wait till the student is accepted to apply for financial aid. Do it when applying for admission.

4. Complete all the required aid applications. All students seeking aid must submit the FAFSA (Free Application for Federal Student Aid); other forms may also be required. Check with each college to see what's required and when.

5. Get the best scores you can on the SAT or ACT. They are used not only in decisions for admission but they can also impact financial aid. If your scores and other stats exceed the school's admission criteria, you are likely to get a better aid package than a marginal applicant.

6. Apply strategically to colleges. Your chances of getting aid will be better at schools that have generous financial aid budgets. (Check the "Best Value Colleges" list and Financial Aid Ratings for schools in this book and on princetonreview.com.)

7. Don't rule out any school as too expensive. A generous aid award from a pricey private school can make it less costly than a public school with a lower sticker price.

8. Take advantage of education tax benefits. A dollar saved on taxes is worth the same as a dollar in scholarship aid. Look into Coverdells, 529 Plans, education tax credits, and loan deductions.

Scholarships and grants

9. Get your best possible score on the PSAT: It is the National Merit Scholarship Qualifying Test and also used in the selection of students for other scholarships and recognition programs.

10. Check your eligibility for grants and scholarships from your state. Some (but not all) states will allow you to use such funds out of state.

11. Look for scholarships locally. Find out if your employer offers scholarships or tuition assistance plans for employees or family members. Also look into scholarships from your community groups and high school, as well as your church, temple, or mosque.

12. Look for outside scholarships realistically: they account for less than five percent of aid awarded. Research them at princetonreview.com or other free sites. Steer clear of scholarship search firms that charge fees and "promise" scholarships.

Paying for college

13. Start saving early when the student is an infant. Too late? Start now. The more you save, the less you'll have to borrow.

14. Invest wisely. Considering a 529 plan? Compare your own state's plan which may have tax benefits with other states' programs. Get info at savingforcollege.com.

15. If you have to borrow, first pursue federal education loans (Perkins, Stafford, PLUS). Avoid private loans at all costs.

16. Never put tuition on a credit card. The debt is more expensive than ever given recent changes to interest rates and other fees some card issuers are now charging.

17. Try not to take money from a retirement account or 401(k) to pay for college. In addition to likely early distribution penalties and additional income taxes, the higher income will reduce your aid eligibility.

Paying less for college

18. Attend a community college for two years and transfer to a pricier school to complete the degree. Plan ahead: Be sure the college you plan to transfer to will accept the community college credits.

19. Look into "cooperative education" programs. Over 900 colleges allow students to combine college education with a job. It can take longer to complete a degree this way. But graduates generally owe less in student loans and have a better chance of getting hired.

20. Take as many AP courses as possible and get high scores on AP exams. Many colleges award course credits for high AP scores. Some students have cut a year off their college tuition this way.

21. Earn college credit via "dual enrollment" programs available at some high schools. These allow students to take college level courses during their senior year.

22. Earn college credits by taking CLEP (College-Level Examination Program) exams. Depending on the college, a qualifying score on any of the thirty-three CLEP exams can earn students three to twelve college credits. (See Princeton Review's Cracking the CLEP-5th Edition.)

23. Stick to your college and your major. Changing colleges can result in lost credits. Aid may be limited/not available for transfer students at some schools. Changing majors can mean paying for extra courses to meet requirements.

24. Finish college in three years if possible. Take the maximum number of credits every semester, attend summer sessions, and earn credits via online courses. Some colleges offer three-year programs for high-achieving students.

25. Let Uncle Sam pay for your degree. ROTC (Reserve Officer Training Corps) programs available from U.S. Armed Forces branches (except the Coast Guard) offer merit-based scholarships up to full tuition via participating colleges in exchange for military service after you graduate.

26. Better yet: Attend a tuition-free college. Check out the nine institutions in this book on the "Tuition-Free Schools Honor Roll" list on p. 53.

Great Schools for 20 of the Most Popular Undergraduate Majors

Worried about having to declare a major on your college application? Relax. Most colleges won't require you to declare a major until the end of your sophomore year, giving you plenty of time to explore your options. However, problems may arise if you are thinking about majoring in a program that limits its enrollment—meaning that if you don't declare that major early on, you might not get into that program at a later date.

On the flip side, some students declare a major on their application because they believe it will boost their chances of gaining admission. This can be problematic, however, if you later decide to change your major. It involves switching from one school within the college to another (e.g., from the school of arts and sciences to the school of business, for example), it can be difficult.

Never choose a college solely on the prestige of a particular program. College will expose you to new and exciting learning experiences. (Choosing a school based on program availability is a different story.) You may also want to investigate opportunities to design your own major. A commitment to a major would limit you in many ways.

How Did We Compile These Lists?

Each year we collect data from more than 2,000 colleges on the subject of—among many other things—undergraduate academic offerings. We ask colleges not only to report which undergraduate majors they offer, but also which of their majors have the highest enrollment and the number of bachelor's degrees each school awarded in these areas. The list below identifies (in alphabetical order) twenty of the forty "most popular" majors that the schools responding to our survey reported to us. We also conduct our own research on college majors. We look at institutional data, and we consult with our in-house college admissions experts as well as our National College Counselor Advisory Board (whom we list on pages 829–830) for their input on schools offering great programs in these majors. We thank them and all of the guidance counselors, college admissions counselors, and education experts across the country whose recommendations we considered in developing these lists. Of the nearly 3,000 four-year colleges across the United States, those on these lists represent only a snapshot of the many offering great programs in these majors. Use our lists as a starting point for further research.

Great Schools for Accounting Majors

- Alfred University
- Auburn University
- Babson College
- Baylor University
- Birmingham-Southern College
- Boston College
- Boston University
- Brigham Young University (UT)
- Bucknell University
- Calvin College
- Claremont McKenna College
- Clemson University
- College of Charleston
- Cornell University
- DePaul University
- Drexel University
- Duquesne University
- Elon University
- Emory University
- Fordham University
- Georgetown University
- Indiana University—Bloomington
- Iowa State University
- James Madison University
- Le Moyne College
- Lehigh University
- Marquette University
- Michigan State University
- New York University
- Northeastern University
- Pennsylvania State University—University Park
- Pepperdine University
- Rider University
- Rochester Institute of Technology
- Seton Hall University
- Suffolk University
- Temple University
- Texas A&M University—College Station
- University of Houston
- University of Illinois at Urbana-Champaign
- University of Michigan—Ann Arbor
- University of Pennsylvania
- University of Southern California
- The University of Texas at Austin
- The University of Texas at Dallas

Great Schools for Agriculture Majors

- Angelo State University
- Arizona State University
- Auburn University
- Berea College
- California State University, Stanislaus
- Clemson University
- College of the Atlantic
- College of the Ozarks
- Colorado State University
- Cornell University
- Green Mountain College
- Iowa State University
- Kansas State University
- Louisiana State University
- Michigan State University
- North Carolina State University
- Ohio State University
- Pennsylvania State University—University Park
- Prescott College
- Purdue University—West Lafayette
- Texas A&M University—College Station
- Texas Christian University
- Truman State University
- Tuskegee University
- University of Arizona
- University of Arkansas—Fayetteville
- University of California—Davis
- University of Florida
- University of Georgia
- University of Hawaii—Manoa
- University of Idaho
- University of Illinois at Urbana-Champaign
- University of Kentucky
- University of Maine
- University of Maryland—College Park
- University of Massachusetts Amherst
- University of Missouri—Columbia
- University of Nebraska—Lincoln
- University of Tennessee
- The University of Vermont
- University of Wisconsin—Madison
- University of Wyoming
- Washington State University
- West Virginia University

Great Schools for Biology Majors

- Agnes Scott College
- Albion College
- Austin College
- Allegheny College
- Baylor University
- Brandeis University
- Carleton College
- Christopher Newport University
- Colby College
- Cornell University
- Drexel University
- Duke University
- Guilford College
- Harvard College
- Haverford College
- Howard University
- Illinois Wesleyan University
- Indiana University—Bloomington
- Johns Hopkins University
- Louisiana State University
- Loyola University—Chicago
- Massachusetts Institute of Technology
- Millsaps College
- Mount Holyoke College
- The Ohio State University—Columbus
- Ohio University—Athens
- Pomona College
- Reed College
- Rice University
- Swarthmore College
- Temple University
- Texas A&M University—College Station
- United States Coast Guard Academy
- University of California—Davis
- University of California—San Diego
- The University of Chicago
- University of Dallas
- University of Delaware
- University of Denver
- University of Houston
- University of New Mexico
- University of the Pacific
- Wofford College
- Xavier University of Louisiana

Great Schools for Business/Finance Majors

- Arizona State University
- Babson College
- Bentley University
- Boston College
- Bryant University
- Carnegie Mellon University
- Champlain College
- Christopher Newport University
- City University of New York—Baruch College
- City University of New York—Brooklyn College
- Cornell University
- DePaul University
- Emory University
- Florida State University
- Indiana University—Bloomington
- Iowa State University
- Lehigh University
- Massachusetts Institute of Technology
- Miami University (OH)
- Michigan State University
- New York University
- Northwestern University
- Ohio University—Athens
- Portland State University
- Rice University
- Roanoke College
- Seattle University
- University of California—Berkeley
- University of California—Los Angeles
- The University of Chicago
- University of Florida
- University of Houston
- University of Illinois at Urbana-Champaign
- University of Michigan—Ann Arbor
- University of Notre Dame
- University of Pennsylvania
- University of Richmond
- University of Southern California
- The University of Texas at Austin

Great Schools for Communications Majors

- Baylor University
- Boston College
- Boston University
- Bradley University
- City University of New York—
  Hunter College
- Clemson University
- College of Charleston
- Cornell University
- Denison University
- DePaul University
- Duquesne University
- Eckerd College
- Elon University
- Emerson College
- Fairfield University
- Fordham University
- Gonzaga University
- Gustavus Adolphus College
- Hollins University
- Indiana University—Bloomington
- Iowa State University
- Ithaca College
- James Madison University
- Lake Forest College
- Loyola University—New Orleans
- Michigan State University
- Muhlenberg College
- New York University
- Northwestern University
- Pepperdine University
- Quinnipiac University
- Ripon College
- Salisbury University
- Seton Hall University
- St. John's University (NY)
- Stanford University
- Suffolk University
- Syracuse University
- University of California—San Diego
- University of California—Santa Barbara
- University of Iowa
- University of Maryland—College Park
- University of Southern California
- The University of Texas at Austin
- The University of Texas at Dallas
- University of Utah
- University of Virginia
- Washington University in St. Louis

Great Schools for Computer Science/Computer Engineering Majors

- Auburn University
- Boston University
- Bradley University
- Brown University
- California Institute of Technology
- Carnegie Mellon University
- Champlain College
- Clemson University
- Drexel University
- Florida State University
- George Mason University
- Georgia Institute of Technology
- Gonzaga University
- Hampton University
- Harvey Mudd College
- Illinois Institute of Technology
- Iowa State University
- Johns Hopkins University
- Lehigh University
- Massachusetts Institute of Technology
- Michigan State University
- Missouri University of Science and Technology
- New Jersey Institute of Technology
- Northeastern University
- Northwestern University
- Pennsylvania State University—University Park
- Princeton University
- Rice University
- Rensselaer Polytechnic Institute
- Roanoke College
- Rochester Institute of Technology
- Seattle University
- Stanford University
- State University of New York
  at Binghamton
- Texas A&M University—College Station
- United States Air Force Academy
- University of Arizona
- University of California—Berkeley
- University of California—Los Angeles
- University of California—Riverside
- University of Illinois at Urbana-Champaign
- University of Maryland—Baltimore County
- University of Massachusetts Amherst
- University of Michigan—Ann Arbor
- University of Washington
- Worcester Polytechnic Institute

Great Schools for Criminology Majors

- American University
- Auburn University
- Florida State University
- Guilford College
- Indiana University of Pennsylvania
- North Carolina State University
- The Ohio State University—Columbus
- Ohio University—Athens
- Quinnipiac University
- Suffolk University
- University of Delaware
- University of Denver
- University of Maryland—College Park
- University of Miami
- University of New Hampshire
- University of South Florida
- University of Utah
- Valparaiso University
- Virginia Wesleyan College
- Whittier College

Great Schools for Education Majors

- Auburn University
- Barnard College
- Bucknell University
- City University of New York—Brooklyn College
- City University of New York—Hunter College
- Colgate University
- College of the Ozarks
- The College of William & Mary
- Columbia University
- Cornell College
- Cornell University
- Duquesne University
- Elon University
- Gonzaga University
- Goucher College
- Hillsdale College
- Indiana University—Bloomington
- Knox College
- Loyola Marymount University (CA)
- Marquette University
- McGill University
- Miami University (OH)
- Monmouth University (NJ)
- Nazareth College
- New York University
- Northeastern University
- Northwestern University
- The Ohio State University—Columbus
- Prescott College
- Simmons College
- Skidmore College
- Smith College
- Trinity University (TX)
- University of Maine
- University of Mississippi
- The University of Montana—Missoula
- Vanderbilt University
- Villanova College
- Wagner College
- Wellesley College
- Westminster College (PA)
- William Jewell College
- Xavier University (OH)

Great Schools for Engineering Majors

- California Institute of Technology
- Carnegie Mellon University
- Columbia University
- The Cooper Union for the Advancement of Science and Art
- Cornell University
- Drexel University
- Duke University
- Franklin W. Olin College of Engineering
- Georgia Institute of Technology
- Harvard College
- Harvey Mudd College
- Illinois Institute of Technology
- Johns Hopkins University
- Massachusetts Institute of Technology
- Missouri University of Science and Technology
- Montana Tech of the Univ. of Montana
- Pennsylvania State University—University Park
- Princeton University
- Purdue University—West Lafayette
- Rensselaer Polytechnic Institute
- Stanford University
- Stevens Institute of Technology
- Texas A&M University—College Station
- United States Merchant Marine Academy
- University of California—Berkeley
- University of California—Los Angeles

- The University of Texas at Austin
- University of Wisconsin—Madison
- Virginia Tech
- Webb Institute
- Worcester Polytechnic Institute

Great Schools for English Literature and Language Majors

- Amherst College
- Auburn University
- Bard College (NY)
- Barnard College
- Bates College
- Bennington College
- Boston College
- Brown University
- Bryn Mawr College
- City University of New York—
    Hunter College
- Claremont McKenna College
- Clemson University
- Colby College
- Colgate University
- Columbia University
- Cornell University
- Dartmouth College
- Denison University
- Duke University
- Emory University
- Fordham University
- George Mason University
- Gettysburg College
- Gordon College
- Grinnell College
- Harvard College
- Johns Hopkins University
- Kalamazoo College
- Kenyon College
- Marlboro College
- Oberlin College
- Pitzer College
- Pomona College
- Princeton University
- Reed College
- Rice University
- Sewanee—The University of the South
- Smith College
- Stanford University
- St. Mary's College of Maryland
- State University of New York—
    University at Albany
- Syracuse University
- Tufts University
- University of California—Berkeley
- The University of Chicago
- University of Michigan—Ann Arbor
- The University of North Carolina at Asheville
- University of Notre Dame
- University of Utah
- Vassar College
- Washington University in St. Louis
- Wellesley College
- Williams College
- Yale University

Great Schools for Environmental Studies Majors

- Allegheny College
- Bates College
- Bowdoin College
- Catawba College
- Colby College
- College of the Atlantic
- Colorado College
- Dickinson College
- Eckerd College
- Emory University
- The Evergreen State College
- Green Mountain College
- Harvard College
- Hobart and William Smith Colleges
- Juniata College
- Middlebury College
- New College of Florida
- Northeastern University
- Occidental College
- Pitzer College
- Pomona College
- Portland State University
- Prescott College
- Sewanee—The University of the South
- Sonoma State University
- State University of New York at Binghamton
- State University of New York—College of
    Environmental Science and Forestry
- University of California—Berkeley
- University of California—Santa Cruz

- University of Colorado—Boulder
- University of Idaho
- The University of Montana—Missoula
- University of New Hampshire
- The University of North Carolina at Asheville
- The University of North Carolina at Chapel Hill
- University of Oregon
- University of Redlands
- University of the Pacific
- The University of Vermont
- Warren Wilson College
- Washington College

Great Schools for Health Services Majors

- Bellarmine University
- Boston University
- Clemson University
- The College of Idaho
- College of the Ozarks
- Creighton University
- Drexel University
- Duquesne University
- Fairfield University
- Gettysburg College
- Gustavus Adolphus College
- Hampton University
- Howard University
- Ithaca College
- Johns Hopkins University
- Kalamazoo College
- Loyola University—Chicago
- Marywood University
- Monmouth University (NJ)
- Nazareth College
- Northeastern University
- Ohio University—Athens
- Purdue University—West Lafayette
- Quinnipiac University
- Sacred Heart University
- Saint Anselm College
- Saint Louis University
- Seton Hall University
- Simmons College
- State University of New York— Stony Brook University
- Stephens College
- Suffolk University
- Texas A&M University—College Station
- Texas Christian University
- Tulane University
- University of Alabama at Birmingham
- University of Central Florida
- University of Cincinnati
- University of Florida
- University of Houston
- University of Miami
- University of Oklahoma
- University of Utah
- Wagner College
- Washington University in St. Louis
- Westminster College (UT)
- Wheaton College (IL)
- William Jewell College

Great Schools for History Majors

- Bates College
- Bowdoin College
- Brown University
- Centre College
- Colgate University
- College of the Holy Cross
- The College of Wooster
- Columbia University
- Davidson College
- Drew University
- Furman University
- Georgetown University
- Grinnell College
- Hampden-Sydney College
- Harvard College
- Haverford College
- Hillsdale College
- Kenyon College
- Marlboro College
- Oberlin College
- Princeton University
- Ripon College
- Trinity College (CT)
- Tulane University
- University of Virginia
- Wabash College
- Williams College
- Yale University

Great Schools for Journalism Majors

- American University
- Arizona State University
- Auburn University
- Ball State University
- Boston University
- Bowling Green State University
- Carleton College
- Duke University
- Emerson College
- The George Washington University
- Hampton University
- Howard University
- Indiana University—Bloomington
- Iowa State University
- Ithaca College
- Kansas State University
- Loyola University—New Orleans
- Michigan State University
- New York University
- Northwestern University
- Ohio University—Athens
- Pennsylvania State University—University Park
- St. Bonaventure University
- State University of New York— Stony Brook University
- Syracuse University
- Temple University
- The University of Alabama—Tuscaloosa
- University of Arizona
- University of Florida
- University of Georgia
- University of Kansas
- University of Kentucky
- University of Idaho
- University of Illinois at Urbana-Champaign
- University of Iowa
- University of Maryland—College Park
- University of Minnesota—Twin Cities
- University of Mississippi
- University of Missouri—Columbia
- The University of Montana—Missoula
- University of Nebraska—Lincoln
- The University of North Carolina at Chapel Hill
- University of Oklahoma
- University of Oregon
- University of Southern California
- The University of Texas at Austin
- University of Wisconsin—Madison
- Washington State University

Great Schools for Marketing and Sales Majors

- Babson College
- Baylor University
- Bentley College
- Duquesne University
- Fairfield University
- Hofstra University
- Indiana University—Bloomington
- Iowa State University
- James Madison University
- Miami University (OH)
- Providence College
- Seattle University
- Siena College
- Syracuse University
- Texas A&M University—College Station
- University of Central Florida
- University of Michigan—Ann Arbor
- University of Mississippi
- University of Pennsylvania
- University of South Florida
- The University of Texas at Austin

Great Schools for Mathematics Majors

- Agnes Scott College
- Bowdoin College
- Bryant University
- Bryn Mawr College
- California Institute of Technology
- Carleton College
- College of the Holy Cross
- The College of Idaho
- Grinnell College
- Hamilton College
- Hampton University
- Harvard College
- Harvey Mudd College
- Haverford College
- Macalester College
- Massachusetts Institute of Technology
- Randolph College
- Reed College
- Rice University
- St. Lawrence University
- St. Olaf College
- State University of New York—University at Albany
- United States Coast Guard Academy
- The University of Chicago
- University of Rochester
- Wabash College

Great Schools for Mechanical Engineering Majors

- Auburn University
- Bradley University
- California Institute of Technology
- Clarkson University
- Colorado State University
- The Cooper Union for the Advancement of Science and Art
- Drexel University
- Franklin W. Olin College of Engineering
- Georgia Institute of Technology
- Grove City College
- Harvey Mudd College
- Illinois Institute of Technology
- Iowa State University
- Lehigh University
- Massachusetts Institute of Technology
- New Jersey Institute of Technology
- North Carolina State University
- Purdue University—West Lafayette
- Rochester Institute of Technology
- Rose-Hulman Institute of Technology
- Stanford University
- State University of New York— University at Buffalo

Great Schools for Nursing Majors

- Angelo State University
- Baylor University
- Bellarmine University
- Calvin College
- The Catholic University of America
- Drexel University
- Duquesne University
- Fairfield University
- Florida Southern College
- Indiana University of Pennsylvania
- Loyola University—Chicago
- Montana Tech of the University of Montana
- Ohio Northern University
- Saint Louis University
- Texas Christian University
- The University of Alabama—Tuscaloosa
- University of Pennsylvania
- University of Wyoming
- Valparaiso University
- Villanova University
- Washington State University
- Xavier University (OH)

Great Schools for Political Science/Government Majors

- American University
- Amherst College
- Bard College (NY)
- Bates College
- Bowdoin College
- Brigham Young University (UT)
- Bryn Mawr College
- Carleton College
- Claremont McKenna College
- College of the Holy Cross
- Columbia University
- Davidson College
- Dickinson College
- Drew University
- Furman University
- George Mason University
- The George Washington University
- Georgetown University
- Gettysburg College
- Gonzaga University
- Harvard College
- Kenyon College
- Macalester College
- Princeton University
- Stanford University
- Swarthmore College
- Syracuse University
- University of Arizona
- University of California—Berkeley
- University of California—Los Angeles
- University of Washington
- Vassar College
- Yale University

Great Schools for Psychology Majors

- Albion College
- Bates College
- Carnegie Mellon University
- Christopher Newport University
- Clark University
- Colorado State University
- Columbia University
- Cornell University
- Dartmouth College
- Duke University
- George Mason University
- Gettysburg College
- Harvard College
- James Madison University
- Lewis & Clark College
- Loyola University—Chicago
- New York University
- Pitzer College
- Portland State University
- Princeton University
- Roanoke College
- Smith College
- Stanford University
- University of California—Davis
- University of California—Los Angeles
- University of California—Riverside
- University of California—Santa Barbara
- University of California—Santa Cruz
- University of Houston
- University of Michigan—Ann Arbor
- University of Southern California
- The University of Texas at Austin
- University of Utah
- Washington University in St. Louis
- Yale University

A Note About Campus Safety

Safety on and around college campuses should be a key concern among applicants. In particular, rising sexual assault statistics on campuses have recently warranted increased advocacy and the creation of a White House task force focused on addressing this issue with the seriousness it demands. We encourage applicants, as part of their search for their best-fit college, to ask questions about safety during campus visits, read news coverage of the local area, and to visit the Clery Center for Security on Campus online at clerycenter.org. For most of the colleges we profile on PrincetonReview.com we include links to the school's individual Clery Report. Colleges and universities in the United States are required to disclose information about crime on and round campuses, and the U.S. Department of Education makes these reports publicly available at studetnaid.ed.gov. We provide additional, up-to-date resources on this subject at PrincetonReview.com/Safety.

How and Why
We Produce This Book

This Year's Edition

In the twenty-two years since the first edition of this book, our *Best Colleges* guide has grown considerably. We've added more than 150 colleges to the guide and deleted several along the way. How we choose the schools for the book, and how we produce it, however, has not changed significantly over the years (with the exception of how we conduct our student survey—more on this follows).

To determine which schools will be in each edition, we don't use mathematical calculations or formulas. Instead we rely on a wide range of input, both quantitative and qualitative. Every year we collect data from more than 2,000 colleges that we use for *The Complete Book of Colleges* and *The Best Value Colleges*, this book, and our web-based profiles of schools. We visit dozens of colleges and meet with their admissions officers, deans, presidents, and college students. We talk with hundreds of high school counselors, parents, and students. Colleges also submit information to us requesting consideration for inclusion in the book. As a result, we are able to maintain a constantly evolving list of colleges to consider adding to the book. Any college we add to the guide, however, must agree to support our efforts to survey its students via our anonymous student survey. (Sometimes a college's administrative protocols will not allow it to participate in our student survey; this has caused some academically outstanding schools to be absent from the guide.) Finally, we work to ensure that our roster of colleges in the book presents a wide representation of institutions by region, character, and type. Here you'll find profiles of public and private schools, Historically Black Colleges and Universities, men's and women's colleges, science- and technology-focused institutions, nontraditional colleges, highly selective schools, and some with virtually open-door admissions policies.

For this year's edition, we added eight schools to the guide: Assumption College, Coe College, College of St. Benedict/Saint John's University, Gordon College, Randolph-Macon College, Siena College, State University of New York—College of Environmental Science and Forestry, and University of Louisville.

Our ranking lists in this edition are based on our surveys of 130,000 students attending the 379 colleges in the book. We surveyed about 343 students per campus on average, though that number varies depending on the size of the student population. We've surveyed anywhere from twenty-some students at Deep Springs College (100 percent of the all-male student body) to more than 1,000 collegians at such colleges as Drexel University, Clemson University, and the United States Military Academy.

All of the institutions in this guide are academically terrific in our opinion. The 379 schools featured—our picks of the cream of the crop colleges and universities—comprise only the top 14 percent of the approximately 2,800 four-year colleges in the nation. Not every college will appeal to every student, but that is the beauty of it. These are all very different schools with many different and wonderful things to offer. We hope you will use this book as a starting point (it will certainly give you a snapshot of what life is like at these schools), but not as the final word on any one school. Check out other resources. Visit as many colleges as you can. Talk to students at those colleges—ask what they love and what bothers them most about their schools. Finally, form your own opinions about the colleges you are considering. At the end of the day, it's what YOU think about the schools that matters most, and that will enable you to answer that all-important question: "Which college is best for me?"

> "We worked to create a guide that would help people who couldn't always get to the campus nonetheless get in-depth campus feedback to find the schools best for them."

The History of This Book

When we published the first edition of this book in 1992, there was a void in the world of college guides (hard to believe, but true!). No publication provided college applicants with statistical data from colleges that covered academics, admissions, financial aid, and student demographics along with narrative descriptions of the schools based on comprehensive surveys of students attending them. Of course, academic rankings of colleges had been around for some time. They named the best schools on hierarchical lists, from 1 to 200 and upwards, some in tiers. Their criteria factored in such matters as faculty salaries, alumni giving, and peer reviews (i.e., what college administrators thought of the schools that, in many cases, they competed with for students). But no ranking publication was surveying students at these terrific colleges about their experiences on campus—both inside and outside the classroom. We created our first *Best Colleges* guide to address that void. It was born out of one very obvious omission in college guide publishing and two very deep convictions we held then and hold even more strongly today:

- One: The key question for students and parents researching colleges shouldn't be "What college is best, academically?" The thing is, it's not hard to find academically great schools in this country. (There are hundreds of them.) The key question—and one that is truly tough to answer—is "What is the best college for me?"

- Two: We believe the best way for students and parents to know if a school is right—and ultimately best—for them is to visit it. Travel to the campus, get inside a residence hall, audit a class, browse the town and—most importantly—talk to students attending the school. In the end it's the school's customers—its students—who are the real experts about a particular college. Only they can give you the most candid and informed feedback on what life is really like on the campus.

Guided by these convictions, we worked to create a resource that would help give applicants up-to-date stats and facts, plus "straight from the campus" student feedback from a wide range of colleges to find the schools best for them. We culled an initial list of 250 academically great schools, based on our own college knowledge and input from fifty independent college counselors. We gathered institutional data from those schools and surveyed 30,000 students attending them (about 120 per campus on average). We wrote the school profiles, incorporating school data and extensive quotes from surveyed students, and we compiled for the book more than sixty ranking lists of top twenty schools in various categories based on our surveys of students at the schools.

With support from more than a million students who've participated in our student surveys over the years, and administrators at nearly 400 colleges, we're pleased to offer what we continue to believe is the most substantive resource you can find to know which of these 379 schools may be best for you.

About Our Student Survey for Our *Best Colleges* Books

Surveying tens of thousands of students on hundreds of campuses has been a mammoth undertaking since we initiated this project in 1992. For more than ten years, our survey was entirely a paper survey. We worked with school administrators to set up tables in centrally-trafficked locations on their campuses at which students filled out the surveys. To reach a range of students, freshmen to seniors, this process sometimes took place over several days and at various on-campus locations. That process yielded about 125 surveys per college.

However, the launch of our online survey more than a decade ago made our survey process more efficient, secure, and representative. Our student survey is also now a continuous process. Students from all schools in the book can participate in our survey online at any time during the academic year at http://survey.review.com. (However, our site will accept only one survey from a student per academic year per school. (It's not possible to "stuff" the ballot box, as it were). In addition to those surveys we receive from students on an ongoing basis, we also conduct "formal" surveys of students at each school in the book at least once every three years. (We conduct these more often than once every three years if the colleges request that we do so (and we can accommodate that request) or we deem it necessary.)

How do we do conduct those "formal" surveys? First, we notify our administrative contacts at the schools we plan to survey. We depend upon these contacts for assistance in informing the student body of our survey (although we also get the word out to students about our survey via other channels independent of the schools). An increasing number of schools have chosen to send an e-mail to the entire student body about the availability of our online survey; in such cases this has yielded robust response rates. Our average number of student surveys (per college) is now 343 students per campus (and at some schools we hear from more than 3,000 students).

Surveys we receive from students outside of their schools' normal survey cycles are always factored into the subsequent year's ranking calculations, so our pool of student survey data is continuously refreshed.

The survey has more than eighty questions divided into four sections: "About Yourself," "Your School's Academics/Administration," "Students," and "Life at Your School." We ask about all sorts of things, from "How many out-of-class hours do you spend studying each day?" to "How do you rate your campus food?" Most questions offer students a five-point grid on which to indicate their answer choices (headers may range from "Excellent" to "Awful"). Eight questions offer students the opportunity to expand on their answers with narrative comment. These essay-type responses are the sources of the student quotations that appear in the school profiles. Once the surveys have been completed and responses stored in our database, every college is given a score (similar to a grade point average) for its students' answers to each question. This score enables us to compare students' responses to a particular question from one college to the next. We use these scores as an underlying data point in our calculation of the ratings in the profile sidebars and the ranking lists in the section of the book titled "School Rankings and Lists."

Once we have the student survey information in hand, we write the college profiles. Student quotations in each profile are chosen because they represent the sentiments expressed by the majority of survey respondents from the college; or, they illustrate one side or another of a mixed bag of student opinion, in which case there will also appear a counterpoint within the text. In order to guard against producing a write-up that's off the mark for any particular college, we send our administrative contact at each school a copy of the profile we intend to publish prior to its publication date, with ample opportunity to respond with corrections, comments, and/or outright objections. In every case in which we receive requests for changes, we take careful measures to review the school's suggestions against the student survey data we collected and make appropriate changes when warranted.

How This Book is Organized

Each of the colleges and universities in this book has its own two-page profile. To make it easier to find and compare information about the schools, we've used the same profile format for every school. Look at the sample pages below: Each profile has nine major components. First, at the very top of the profile you will see the school's address, telephone, and fax numbers for the admissions office, the telephone number for the financial aid office, and the school's website and/or e-mail address. Second, there are two sidebars (the narrow columns on the outside of each page, which consist mainly of statistics) divided into the categories of Campus Life, Academics, Selectivity, and Financial Facts. Third, there are four headings in the narrative text: Students Say, Admissions, Financial Aid, and From the Admissions Office. Here's what you'll find in each part:

The Sidebars

The sidebars contain various statistics culled from our surveys of students attending the school and from questionnaires that school administrators complete at our request in the fall of each year. Keep in mind that not every category will appear for every school—in some cases the information is not reported or not applicable. We compile the eight ratings—Quality of Life, Fire Safety, Green Rating, Academic, Profs Interesting, Profs Accessible, Admissions Selectivity, and Financial Aid—listed in the sidebars based on the results from our student surveys and/or institutional data we collect from school administrators.

These ratings are on a scale of 60–99. If a 60* (60 with an asterisk) appears as any rating for any school, it means that the school reported so few of the rating's underlying data points by our deadline that we were unable to calculate an accurate rating for it. (These measures are outlined in the ratings explanation below.) Be advised that because the Admissions Selectivity Rating is a factor in the computation that produces the Academic Rating, a school that has 60* (60 with an asterisk) as its Admissions Selectivity Rating will have an Academic Rating that is lower than it should be. Also bear in mind that each rating places each college on a continuum for purposes of comparing colleges within this edition only. Since our ratings computations may change from year to year, it is invalid to compare the ratings in this edition to those that appear in any prior or future edition.

Finally, these ratings are quite different from the ranking lists that appear in Part 2 of the book, "School Rankings and Lists." The ratings are numerical measures that show how a school "sizes up," if you will, on a fixed scale. Our sixty-two ranking lists report the top twenty (or in some cases bottom twenty) schools of the 379 in the book (not of all schools in the nation) in various categories. They are based on our surveys of students at the schools and/or institutional data. We don't rank the schools in the book 1 to 379 hierarchically. Here is what each heading in the sidebar tells you, in order of their appearance:

Quality of Life Rating

On a scale of 60–99, this rating is a measure of how happy students are with their campus experiences outside the classroom. To compile this rating, we weighed several factors, all based on students' answers to questions on our survey. They included the students' assessments of: their overall happiness; the beauty, safety, and location of the campus; comfort of dorms; quality of food; ease of getting around campus and dealing with administrators; friendliness of fellow students; and the interaction of different student types on campus and within the greater community.

> "Ratings are quite different from the ranking lists. The ratings are numerical measures that show how a school 'sizes up,' if you will, on a fixed scale. Our sixty-two ranking lists report the top twenty (or in some cases bottom twenty) schools of the 379 in the book (not of all schools in the nation) in various categories."

Fire Safety Rating

On a scale of 60–99, this rating measures how well prepared a school is to prevent or respond to campus fires, specifically in residence halls. We asked schools several questions about their efforts to ensure fire safety for campus residents. We developed the questions in consultation with the Center for Campus Fire Safety (www.campusfiresafety.org). Each school's responses to seven questions were considered when calculating its Fire Safety Rating. They cover:

1. The percentage of student housing sleeping rooms protected by an automatic fire sprinkler system with a fire sprinkler head located in the individual sleeping rooms.

2. The percentage of student housing sleeping rooms equipped with a smoke detector connected to a supervised fire alarm system.

3. The number of malicious fire alarms that occur in student housing per year.

4. The number of unwanted fire alarms that occur in student housing per year.

5. The banning of certain hazardous items and activities in residence halls, like candles, smoking, halogen lamps, etc.

6. The percentage of student housing fire alarm systems that, if activated, result in a signal being transmitted to a monitored location, where security investigates before notifying the fire department.

7. The percentage of student housing fire alarm systems that, if activated, result in a signal being transmitted immediately to a continuously monitored location.

Schools that did not report answers to a sufficient number of questions receive a Fire Safety Rating of 60* (60 with an asterisk). You can also find Fire Safety Ratings for our best 379 colleges (and several additional schools) in *The Complete Book of Colleges*, 2014 Edition. On page 53 of this book, you'll find a list of the schools with 99 (the highest score) Fire Safety Ratings.

Green Rating

We asked all the schools we collect data from annually to answer a number of questions that evaluate the comprehensive measure of their performance as an environmentally aware and responsible institution. The questions cover: 1) whether students have a campus quality of life that is both healthy and sustainable; 2) how well a school is preparing students not only for employment in the clean energy economy of the twenty-first century, but also for citizenship in a world now defined by environmental challenges; and 3) how environmentally responsible a school's policies are.

Additionally, The Princeton Review, the Association for the Advancement of Sustainability in Higher Education (AASHE), and *Sierra* magazine, have collaborated on an effort to streamline the reporting process for institutions that choose to participate in various higher education sustainability assessments. The intent of this initiative is to reduce and streamline the amount of time campus staff spend tracking sustainability data and completing related surveys.

To address this issue these groups worked to establish the Campus Sustainability Data Collector (CSDC). The CSDC was based off of the STARS Reporting Tool and was available for all schools (free of charge) who wanted to submit data to these groups in one single survey. For our most recent collection, the CSDC was replaced with the launch of STARS 2.0. The new version of STARS offers a basic level of access at no cost to institutions.

Please find more information here:

http://www.princetonreview.com/green-data-partnership/

Each school's responses to ten questions were considered when calculating The Princeton Review's Green Rating.

They include:

1. The percentage of food expenditures that go toward local, organic, or otherwise environmentally preferable food.

2. Whether the school offers programs including mass transit programs, bike sharing, facilities for bicyclists, bicycle and pedestrian plan, car sharing, carpool discount, carpool/vanpool matching, cash-out of parking, prohibiting idling, local housing, telecommuting, and condensed work week.

3. Whether the school has a formal committee that is devoted to advancing sustainability on campus.

4. Whether school buildings that were constructed or underwent major renovations in the past three years are LEED certified.

5. The schools overall waste-diversion rate.

6. Whether the school offers at least one sustainability-focused undergraduate major, degree program, or equivalent.

7. Whether the school's students graduate from programs that include sustainability as a required learning outcome or include multiple sustainability learning outcomes.

8. Whether the school has a formal plan to mitigate its greenhouse gas emissions.

9. What percentage of the school's energy consumption is derived from renewable resources.

10. Whether the school employs a dedicated full-time (or full-time equivalent) sustainability officer.

Colleges that did not supply answers to a sufficient number of the green campus questions for us to fairly compare them to other colleges receive a Green Rating of 60*. On page 53 of this book and on our website at www.princetonreview.com/green-honor-roll, you'll find a list of the schools with 99 (the highest score) Green Ratings.

> Check out our free downloadable resource, The Princeton Review's *Guide to 332 Green Colleges* at www.princetonreview.com/green-guide.

Type of school
Whether the school is public or private.

Affiliation
Any religious order with which the school is affiliated.

Environment
Whether the campus is located in an urban, suburban, or rural setting.

Total undergrad enrollment
The total number of degree-seeking undergraduates who attend the school.

"% male/female" through "# countries represented"
Demographic information about the full-time undergraduate student body, including male to female ratio, ethnicity, and the number of countries represented by the student body. Also included are the percentages of the student body who are from out of state, attended a public high school, freshmen living on campus, and belong to Greek organizations.

Survey Says . . .
A snapshot of key results of our student survey. This list names survey topics about which the body of students we surveyed at the school—as a group—showed a statistically higher consensus of opinion in their answers to our questions on those topics (as compared with their answers to questions on other topics). See the end of this section for a detailed explanation of items on the list.

Academic Rating
On a scale of 60–99, this rating is a measure of how hard students work at the school and how much they get back for their efforts. The rating is based on results from our surveys of students and data we collect from administrators. Factors weighed included how many hours students reported that they study each day outside of class, students' assessments of their professors' teaching abilities and of their accessibility outside the classroom and the quality of students the school attracts as measured by admissions statistics.

% of students returning for sophomore year
The percentage of degree-seeking freshmen returning for sophomore year.

4-year graduation rate
The percentage of degree-seeking undergraduate students graduating in four years or less.

6-year graduation rate
The percentage of degree-seeking undergraduate students graduating within six years.

Calendar

The school's schedule of academic terms. A "semester" schedule has two long terms, usually starting in September and January. A "trimester" schedule has three terms, one usually beginning before Christmas and two after. A "quarterly" schedule has four terms, which go by very quickly: the entire term, including exams, usually lasts only nine or ten weeks. A "4-1-4" schedule is like a semester schedule, but with a month-long term in between the fall and spring semesters. (Similarly, a "4-4-1" has a short term following two longer semesters.) It is always best to call the admissions office for details.

Student/faculty ratio

The ratio of full-time undergraduate instructional faculty members to all undergraduates.

Profs interesting rating

On a scale of 60–99, this rating is based on levels of surveyed students' agreement or disagreement with the statement: "Your instructors are good teachers."

Profs accessible rating

On a scale of 60–99, this rating is based on levels of surveyed students' agreement or disagreement with the statement: "Your instructors are accessible outside the classroom."

Most common regular class size; Most common lab size

The most commonly occurring class size for regular courses and for labs/discussion sections.

Most popular majors

The majors with the highest enrollments at the school.

Admissions Selectivity Rating

On a scale of 60–99, this rating is a measure of how competitive admission is at the school. This rating is determined by several factors, including the class rank of entering freshmen, test scores, and percentage of applicants accepted.

% of applicants accepted

The percentage of applicants to whom the school offered admission.

% of acceptees attending

The percentage of accepted students who eventually enrolled at the school.

accepting a place on wait list

The number of students who decided to take a place on the wait list when offered this option.

admitted from wait list

The percentage of applicants who opted to take a place on the wait list and were subsequently offered admission. These figures will vary tremendously from college to college, and should be a consideration when deciding whether to accept a place on a college's wait list.

of early decision applicants

The number of students who applied under the college's early decision or early action plan.

accepted early decision

The percentage of early decision or early action applicants who were admitted under this plan. By the nature of these plans, the vast majority who are admitted ultimately enroll.

Range SAT Critical Reading, Range SAT Math, Range SAT Writing, Range ACT Composite

The average and the middle fifty percent range of test scores for entering freshmen.

Don't be discouraged from applying to the school of your choice even if your combined SAT scores are 80 or even 120 points below the average, because you may still have a chance of getting in. Remember that many schools value other aspects of your application (e.g., your grades, how good a match you make with the school) more heavily than test scores.

Minimum TOEFL

The minimum test score necessary for entering freshmen who are required to take the TOEFL (Test of English as a Foreign Language). Most schools will require all international students or non-native English speakers to take the TOEFL in order to be considered for admission.

Average HS GPA

The average grade point average of entering freshman. We report this on a scale of 1.0–4.0 (occasionally colleges report averages on a 100 scale, in which case we report those figures). This is one of the key factors in college admissions.

% graduated top 10%, top 25%, top 50% of class

Of those students for whom class rank was reported, the percentage of entering freshmen who ranked in the top tenth, quarter, and half of their high school classes.

Early decision/action deadlines

The deadline for submission of application materials under the early decision or early action plan.

Early decision, early action, priority, and regular admission deadlines

The dates by which all materials must be postmarked (we suggest "received in the office") in order to be considered for admission under each particular admissions option/cycle for matriculation in the fall term.

Early decision, early action, priority, and regular admission notification

The dates by which you can expect a decision on your application under each admissions option/cycle.

Nonfall registration

Some schools will allow incoming students to register and begin attending classes at times other than the fall term, which is the traditional beginning of the academic calendar year. Other schools will allow you to register for classes only if you can begin in the fall term. A simple "yes" or "no" in this category indicates the school's policy on nonfall registration.

Applicants also look at

These lists are based on information we receive directly from the colleges. Admissions officers are annually given the opportunity to review and suggest alterations to these lists for their schools, as most schools track as closely as they can other schools to which applicants they accepted applied, and whether the applicants chose their school over the other schools, or vice versa.

Financial Aid Rating

On a scale of 60–99, this rating is a measure of the financial aid the school awards and how satisfied students are with the aid they receive. It is based on school-reported data on financial aid and students' responses to the survey question, "If you receive financial aid, how satisfied are you with your financial aid package?" On page 53 of this book you'll find a list of the schools with 99 (the highest score) Financial Aid Ratings.

Annual in-state tuition

The tuition at the school, or for public colleges, the cost of tuition for a resident of the school's state. Usually much lower than out-of-state tuition for state-supported public schools.

Annual out-of-state tuition

For public colleges, the tuition for a non-resident of the school's state. This entry appears only for public colleges, since tuition at private colleges is generally the same regardless of state of residence.

Required fees

Any additional costs students must pay beyond tuition in order to attend the school. These often include fitness center fees and the like. A few state schools may not officially charge in-state students tuition, but those students are still responsible for hefty fees.

Tuition and fees

In cases when schools do not report separate figures for tuition and required fees, we offer this total of the two.

Comprehensive fee

A few schools report one overall fee that reflects the total cost of tuition, room and board, and required fees. If you'd like to see how this figure breaks down, we recommend contacting the school.

Room and board

Estimated annual room and board costs.

Books and supplies

Estimated annual cost of necessary textbooks and/or supplies.

% needy frosh receiving need-based scholarship or grant aid

The percentage of all degree-seeking freshmen who were determined to have need and received any need-based scholarship or grant.

% needy UG receiving need-based scholarship or grant aid

The percentage of all degree-seeking undergraduates who were determined to have need and received any need-based scholarship or grant.

% needy frosh receiving non-need-based scholarship or grant aid

The percentage of all degree-seeking freshmen, determined to have need, receiving any non-need based scholarship or grant aid.

% needy ugrads receiving non-need-based scholarship or grant aid

The percentage of all degree-seeking undergraduates, determined to have need, receiving any non-need based scholarship or grant aid.

% needy frosh receiving need-based self-help aid

The percentage of all degree-seeking freshmen, determined to have need, who received any need-based self-help aid.

% needy ugrads receiving need-based self-help aid

The percentage of all degree-seeking undergraduates, determined to have need, who received any need-based self-help aid.

% frosh receiving any financial aid

The percentage of all degree-seeking freshmen receiving any financial aid (need-based, merit-based, gift aid).

% UG receiving any financial aid

The percentage of all degree-seeking undergraduates receiving any financial aid (need-based, merit-based, gift aid).

% UG borrow to pay for school

The percentage who borrowed at any time through any loan programs (institutional, state, Federal Perkins, Federal Stafford Subsidized and Unsubsidized, private loans that were certified by your institution, etc., exclude parent loans). Includes both Federal Direct Student Loans and Federal Family Education Loans (prior to the FFEL program ending in June 2010).

% frosh and ugrad need fully met

The percentage of needy degree-seeking students whose needs was fully met (excludes PLUS loans, unsubsidized loans, and private alternative loans).

Average % of frosh and upgrad need met

On average, the percentage of need that was met of students who were awarded any need-based aid. Excludes any aid that was awarded in excess of need as well as any resources that were awarded to replace EFC (PLUS loans, unsubsidized loans, and private alternative loans).

Average Indebtedness

The average per-borrower cumulative undergraduate indebtedness of those who borrowed at any time through any loan programs (institutional, state, Federal Perkins, Federal Stafford Subsidized and Unsubsidized, private loans that were certified by your institution, etc.; exclude parent loans).

Nota Bene: The statistical data reported in this book, unless otherwise noted, was collected from the profiled colleges from the fall of 2013 through the spring of 2014. In some cases, we were unable to publish the most recent data because schools did not report the necessary statistics to us in time, despite our repeated outreach efforts. Because the enrollment and financial statistics, as well as application and financial aid deadlines, fluctuate from one year to another, we recommend that you check with the schools to make sure you have the most current information before applying.

Students Say

This section shares the straight-from-the-campus feedback we get from the school's most important customers: The students attending them. It summarizes the opinions of freshman through seniors we've surveyed and it includes direct quotes from scores of them. When appropriate, it also incorporates statistics provided by the schools. The Students Say section is divided into three subsections: Academics, Life, and Student Body. The Academics section describes how hard students work and how satisfied they are with the education they are getting. It also often tells you which programs or academic departments students rated most favorably and how professors interact with students. Student opinion regarding administrative departments also works its way into this section. The Life section describes life outside the classroom and addresses questions ranging from "How comfortable are the dorms?" to "How popular are fraternities and sororities?" In this section, students describe what they do for entertainment both on-campus and off, providing a clear picture of the social environment at their particular school. The Student Body section will give you the lowdown on the types of students the school attracts and how the students view the level of interaction among various groups, including those of different ethnic, socioeconomic, and religious backgrounds.

All quotations in these sections are from students' responses to open-ended questions on our survey. We select quotations based on the accuracy with which they reflect overall student opinion about the school as conveyed in the survey results.

Admissions

This section lets you know which aspects of your application are most important to the admissions officers at the school. It also lists the high school curricular prerequisites for applicants, which standardized tests (if any) are required, and special information about the school's admissions process (e.g., Do minority students and legacies, for example, receive special consideration? Are there any unusual application requirements for applicants to special programs?).

Financial Aid

Here you'll found out what you need to know about the financial aid process at the school, namely what forms you need and what types of merit-based aid and loans are available. Information about need-based aid is contained in the financial aid sidebar. This section includes specific deadline dates for submission of materials as reported by the colleges. We strongly encourage students seeking financial aid to file all forms—federal, state, and institutional—carefully, fully, and on time.

The Inside Word

This section gives you the inside scoop on what it takes to gain admission to the school. It reflects our own insights about each school's admissions process and acceptance trends. (We visit scores of colleges each year and talk with hundreds of admissions officers in order to glean this info.) It also incorporates information from institutional data we collect and our surveys over the years of students at the school.

From the Admissions Office

This section presents the key things the school's admissions office would like you to know about their institution. For schools that did not respond to our invitation to supply text for this space, we excerpted an appropriate passage from the school's catalog, web site, or other admissions literature. For this section, we also invited schools to submit a brief paragraph explaining their admissions policies regarding the SAT (especially the Writing portion of the exam) and the SAT Subject Tests. We are pleased that nearly every school took this opportunity to clarify its policies as we know there has been some student and parent confusion about how these scores are evaluated for admission.

Survey Says

Our Survey Says list, located in the Campus Life sidebar on each school's two-page spread, is based entirely on the results of our student survey. In other words, the items on this list are based on the opinions of the students we surveyed at those schools (not on any quantitative analysis of library size, endowment, etc.). These items reveal popular or unpopular trends on campus for the purpose of providing a snapshot of life on that campus only. The appearance of a Survey Says item in the sidebar does not reflect the popularity of that item relative to its popularity among the student bodies at other schools. To ascertain the relative popularity of certain items/trends on campus, see the appropriate ranking (e.g., for the Survey Says item

"Career Services are Great," see the "Best Career Services" ranking). Some of the terms that appear on the Survey Says list are not entirely self-explanatory; these terms are defined below.

Different types of students interact: We asked students whether students from different class and ethnic backgrounds interacted frequently and easily. When students' collective response is "yes," the heading "Different types of students interact" appears on the list. When the collective student response indicates there are not many interactions between students from different class and ethnic backgrounds, the phrase "Students are cliquish" appears on the list. Note: This topic is not based on demographic data about the student body.

No one cheats: We asked students how prevalent cheating is at their school. If students reported cheating to be rare, the term "No one cheats" shows up on the list.

Students are happy: This category reflects student responses to the question "Overall, how happy are you?"

Students are very religious or Students aren't religious: We asked students how religious students are at their school. Their responses are reflected in this category.

Diverse student types on campus: We asked students whether their student body is made up of a variety of ethnic groups. This category reflects their answers to this question. This heading shows up as "Diversity lacking on campus" or "Diverse student types on campus." It does not reflect any institutional data on this subject.

Students get along with local community: This category reflects student responses to a question concerning how well the student body gets along with residents of the college town or community.

Career services are great: This category reflects student opinion on the quality of career/job placement services on campus.

About Our College Ranking Lists

Finding a college that has terrific academics is easy. There are hundreds of academically great colleges out there. Their campus cultures, student bodies, and school offerings, however, differ widely. Finding the academically great school that is right for you is the tough part. Hence, we compile not one ranking list but sixty-two unique lists, each one reporting the top twenty (or in some cases bottom twenty) schools from our *Best Colleges* book in a specific category.

None of our lists are based on what we think of the schools (though members of the media, the public, and school administrators mistakenly credit or blame us for the results, saying "According to The Princeton Review, X school is the best in the nation for…" or "The Princeton Review ranks Y school the tenth most…."). In fact, the only thing we say is that all of the 379 colleges in this book are outstanding (hence, the "Best" designation). It's what students think of their schools—how they rate various aspects of their colleges' offerings and what they report to us about their campus experiences—that results in a school's appearance on our ranking lists.

Here you won't find the colleges in the book ranked hierarchically, 1 to 379. We think such lists—particularly those driven by and perpetuating a "best academics" mania—are not useful for the people they are supposed to serve (college applicants). More and more college administrators—including several at schools ranked high on these lists—agree. In fact, the primary reason we developed this book was to give applicants and parents better and broader information that will help them winnow a list of colleges right for them.

About 80 percent of the schools in our book end up on one or more of the lists in each edition. To college officials happy about the lists their schools are on, we say don't thank us, we're just the messengers. To college officials unhappy about the lists their schools are on (and unsurprisingly, it is mainly they who claim our student survey has no validity), we say don't blame us, we're just the messengers.

All of these ranking lists are based entirely on students' answers to questions on our surveys (e.g., our "Best Campus Food" list and inverse list, "Is it Food?" are each based on the single survey question, "How do you rate your campus food?") or students' answers to a combination of survey questions (e.g., our "Party Schools" list and our inverse list, "Stone-Cold Sober Schools" are each based on students' answers to survey questions concerning the use of alcohol and drugs on their campuses, the popularity of the frat/sorority scene on their campuses, and the number of hours they say they study each day outside of class time).

Each list covers one of many aspects of a college's character that can be helpful in deciding if it's the right or wrong place for an individual student. The lists report on a wide range of issues that may be important, either singly or, more likely, in combination. Our ranking lists cover: financial aid, campus facilities and amenities, extracurriculars, town-gown relations, the student body's political leanings, social life, race/class relations, LGBT-friendly (or not so friendly) atmosphere, career services, athletic facilities, and more.

> "It's what students think of their schools—how they rate various aspects of their colleges' offerings and what they report to us about their campus experiences—that results in a school's appearance on our ranking lists."

In 2013 we added our newest ranking list category: "Best Science Lab Facilities."

The ranking list category that media covers the most (though it appears fifty-eighth among the lists in our "School Rankings and Lists" section, and is only referenced briefly in our press materials) is the "Party Schools" list. It's even been the subject of a Doonesbury cartoon (which appears on the frontispiece of this book) as well as a USA TODAY editorial in which the paper commended us for reporting the list, calling it "a public service." Our "Party Schools" list draws a wide range of reaction every year. Some students complain that their college didn't make the list, while others are irate because their college did. One reporter from the *Washington Post* whose alma mater was number one on the list several years back wrote a column in which he argued that the ranking was grossly undeserved: He had recently visited his campus and pronounced the then current student body lame as "partiers" compared to the revelers of his day.

Many incorrectly assume that an institution that shows up on the "Party Schools" list is not an advisable college to attend. We recommend all 379 schools in this book as outstanding institutions at which to earn one's college degree. But just as the schools on our "LGBT-Unfriendly" list may not be ideal campuses for gay students, the schools on our "Party Schools" list may not be ideal for students seeking a campus at which the use of alcohol and drugs and the frat/sorority scene is, well, less exuberant.

On the other hand, no one should make the mistake of assuming that the colleges and universities that don't show up on our "Party Schools" list are in any way insulated from the influences of alcohol and drugs on their campuses. An oft-quoted Harvard University School of Public Health study published in 2000 found that (then) 45 percent of undergraduates, in general, had engaged in binge drinking (consuming five or more alcoholic beverages in one sitting for men, four drinks or more for women).[1] These facts are alarming, as they should be. College administrators face tremendous challenges in creating and enforcing campus alcohol and drug use/abuse policies. Many struggle with problems resulting from the prevalence of bars and liquor stores near their campuses; at some universities that have appeared on our "Party Schools" list there are more than 100 such establishments within a few miles from the campus. "Dry campus" policies often exacerbate the problem, driving drinking off-campus, making it even more dangerous for students.

Despite the claims of some administrators at colleges that have repeatedly made our "Party School" list that our reporting this list promotes drinking on campuses (a group of such administrators receiving funding through the American Medical Association to address their campus alcohol problems made the news several years back with this claim, after which USA TODAY published the editorial praising our ranking as a "public service"), we neither encourage nor discourage students who wish to drink. None of our lists promote behavior: They report on it. What we promote is information.

What we do say to college students—as we have said in this very section of this book for more than 15 years—is this: If you're going to drink, do it safely, smartly, responsibly, and legally. If you're going off campus to drink, don't drive back drunk—get a designated driver. Don't let a peer situation (fraternity rush, etc.) put you in jeopardy—it's simply not worth it. Don't use alcohol or drugs as a badge of your coolness—there's not much of a fine line between someone who's socially engaging and someone who's totally disengaging because he or she has performed a chemical auto-lobotomy. Last, don't simply take responsibility for yourself; remember to keep an eye on your friends, and never leave them passed out and alone.

---

1 Harvard University School of Public Health. *"College Student Binge Drinking Rates Remain High Despite Efforts by School Administrations." www.hsph.harvard.edu/news/press-releases/2000-releases/press03142000.html.*

Finally, we would like to thank all the college officials, college counselors, advisors, students, and parents, who have made this annual guide possible by supporting us these past 22 years. Our ranking lists have, collectively, been based tallies of more than 2 million students. To all students who have completed our past surveys and to all who will do so this year, we say thanks. Your input is vital to our publication of this book. We know that it has helped students find great colleges perfect for them, and it has brought to the colleges in our book many outstanding applicants who otherwise may not have considered applying to or attending these institutions.

WE WANT TO HEAR FROM YOU

To all of our readers, we welcome your feedback on how we can continue to improve this guide. We hope you will share with us your comments, questions, and suggestions. Please contact us at editorialsupport@review.com. We welcome it.

To college applicants, we wish you all the best in your college search. And when you get to your campuses and settle in to your college life, come back to us online; participate in our survey for this book at http://survey.review.com. Let your honest comments about your schools guide prospective students who want your help answering the $64,000 question (goodness knows, the sticker price at some schools may be that high or even higher!): "Which is the best college for me?"

PART 2

School Rankings and Lists

We present our 62 "Top 20" ranking lists in eight categories.

Schools by Type

Under each list heading, we tell you the survey question or assessment that we used to tabulate the list. We tally student responses to several questions on our survey for our lists "Best Classroom Experience," "Best Quality of Life," and the five lists in our Schools by Type rankings (including our "Party Schools" and "Stone-Cold Sober Schools" lists). Be aware that all of our 62 ranking lists are based entirely on our student surveys. They do not reflect our opinions of the schools. They are entirely the result of what students attending these schools tell us about them: It's how students rate their own schools and what they report to us about their campus experiences at them that make our ranking lists so unusual. After all, what better way is there to judge a school than by what its customers—its students—say about it?

Honor Rolls

Best Value Colleges List

ACADEMICS/ADMINISTRATION

Best Classroom Experience

Based on a combination of survey questions concerning teachers, classroom/lab facilities, classes attended, and amount of in-class discussion

1. Bard College
2. Franklin W. Olin College of Engineering
3. Reed College
4. Bennington College
5. Swarthmore College
6. Whitman College
7. Thomas Aquinas College
8. Grinnell College
9. Wabash College
10. Mount Holyoke College
11. Middlebury College
12. Sarah Lawrence College
13. Hamilton College
14. United States Military Academy
15. Scripps College
16. University of Richmond
17. Claremont McKenna College
18. The University of Chicago
19. Haverford College
20. Kenyon College

Students Study the Most

How many out-of-class hours do you spend studying each day?

1. Harvey Mudd College
2. California Institute of Technology
3. Franklin W. Olin College of Engineering
4. Reed College
5. Middlebury College
6. Swarthmore College
7. Massachusetts Institute of Technology
8. Marlboro College
9. Carleton College
10. Princeton University
11. Gettysburg College
12. The Cooper Union for the Advancement of Science and Art
13. Grinnell College
14. Carnegie Mellon University
15. Harvard College
16. The University of Chicago
17. Cornell University
18. Haverford College
19. Worcester Polytechnic Institute
20. Wellesley College

Students Study the Least
How many out-of-class hours do you spend studying each day?

1. Monmouth University (NJ)
2. University of Mississippi
3. National University of Ireland, Maynooth
4. Trinity College Dublin
5. Manhattanville College
6. West Virginia University
7. University of New Orleans
8. DePaul University
9. City University of New York—Queens College
10. University of Central Florida
11. Flagler College
12. University of South Carolina—Columbia
13. Florida State University
14. University of Maryland, College Park
15. University of Iowa
16. University of Tampa
17. Indiana University of Pennsylvania
18. St. John's University (NY)
19. Champlain College
20. James Madison University

Professors Get High Marks
Are your instructors good teachers?

1. Reed College
2. Bennington College
3. College of the Atlantic
4. Franklin W. Olin College of Engineering
5. Swarthmore College
6. St. John's College (NM)
7. Bard College at Simon's Rock
8. Hillsdale College
9. Bard College
10. Middlebury College
11. Sarah Lawrence College
12. Marlboro College
13. Harvey Mudd College
14. Ripon College
15. Wellesley College
16. Claremont McKenna College
17. Carleton College
18. Wabash College
19. Whitman College
20. Randolph College

Professors Get Low Marks
Are your instructors good teachers?

1. New Jersey Institute of Technology
2. United States Merchant Marine Academy
3. Stevens Institute of Technology
4. Howard University
5. State University of New York—Stony Brook University
6. California Institute of Technology

7. Hampton University
8. McGill University
9. Tuskegee University
10. Illinois Institute of Technology
11. University of Connecticut
12. Rutgers, The State University of New Jersey—New Brunswick
13. University of Hawaii—Manoa
14. University of California—San Diego
15. University of California—Los Angeles
16. City University of New York—Baruch College
17. University of Louisville
18. University of Rhode Island
19. University of California—Davis
20. University of North Dakota

Most Accessible Professors
Are your instructors accessible outside the classroom?

1. United States Military Academy
2. Claremont McKenna College
3. St. John's College (NM)
4. Webb Institute
5. Swarthmore College
6. Bennington College
7. Bard College
8. Hillsdale College
9. College of the Holy Cross
10. Grinnell College
11. Hamilton College
12. Whitman College
13. Centre College
14. Wake Forest University
15. College of the Atlantic
16. The College of Idaho
17. Scripps College
18. Sweet Briar College
19. Beloit College
20. United States Naval Academy

Least Accessible Professors
Are your instructors accessible outside the classroom?

1. McGill University
2. United States Merchant Marine Academy
3. New Jersey Institute of Technology
4. Howard University
5. Hampton University
6. University of Hawaii—Manoa
7. Portland State University
8. Trinity College Dublin
9. St. John's University (NY)
10. University of California—Los Angeles
11. University of California—San Diego
12. State University of New York—Stony Brook University

13. University of Massachusetts Amherst
14. University of California—Berkeley
15. Manhattanville College
16. Stevens Institute of Technology
17. Marywood University
18. City University of New York—
    Queens College
19. Drexel University
20. University of Minnesota—Twin Cities

Best Science Lab Facilities
Based on students' assessment of science lab facilities

1. California Institute of Technology
2. St. Olaf College
3. University of Richmond
4. United States Naval Academy
5. Pomona College
6. Middlebury College
7. Bowdoin College
8. Harvey Mudd College
9. Grinnell College
10. Washington University in St. Louis
11. Colgate University
12. Franklin W. Olin College of Engineering
13. Wheaton College (IL)
14. Lehigh University
15. Union College (NY)
16. Smith College
17. The University of Chicago
18. Whitman College
19. Beloit College
20. Swarthmore College

Most Popular Study Abroad Program
How popular is studying abroad at your school?

1. Goucher College
2. Worcester Polytechnic Institute
3. Kalamazoo College
4. Centre College
5. Susquehanna University
6. Dartmouth College
7. Union College (NY)
8. University of Dallas
9. Elon University
10. Tufts University
11. Austin College
12. University of Delaware
13. University of Denver
14. The George Washington University
15. Syracuse University
16. Pitzer College
17. Trinity College (CT)
18. Skidmore College
19. DePauw University
20. College of Saint Benedict/
    Saint John's University

Best Health Services
Based on students' assessments of student health services/facilities on campus

1. Pennsylvania State University—
   University Park
2. University of Central Florida
3. University of California—Davis
4. University of Wisconsin—Madison
5. United States Military Academy
6. University of Arizona
7. University of California—Los Angeles
8. Calvin College
9. Whitman College
10. The University of Texas at Austin
11. Mills College
12. University of Pittsburgh—
    Pittsburgh Campus
13. Rice University
14. The College of Idaho
15. Villanova University
16. North Carolina State University
17. University of Oregon
18. University of Alabama at Birmingham
19. University of Georgia
20. University of Louisville

Best Career Services
Based on students' rating of campus career/job-placement services

1. Northeastern University
2. Pennsylvania State University—
   University Park
3. Claremont McKenna College
4. Bentley University
5. Clemson University
6. University of Richmond
7. Wabash College
8. Southwestern University
9. Washington University in St. Louis
10. University of Florida
11. Kansas State University
12. Southern Methodist University
13. Sweet Briar College
14. Villanova University
15. Stevens Institute of Technology
16. Lafayette College
17. Franklin W. Olin College of Engineering
18. Barnard College
19. Connecticut College
20. Wake Forest University

Best College Library
Based on students' assessment of library facilities

1. The University of Chicago
2. Yale University
3. United States Military Academy
4. Stanford University
5. Columbia University
6. Emory University
7. Hampden-Sydney College
8. Whitman College
9. Vassar College
10. Harvard College
11. West Virginia University
12. Pennsylvania State University—University Park
13. Middlebury College
14. Colgate University
15. Bentley University
16. University of Wisconsin—Madison
17. Wellesley College
18. Brigham Young University (UT)
19. Illinois Wesleyan University
20. Lehigh University

This Is a Library?
Based on students' assessment of library facilities

1. Clarkson University
2. United States Merchant Marine Academy
3. Bradley University
4. Marywood University
5. United States Coast Guard Academy
6. Salisbury University
7. Bard College at Simon's Rock
8. Duquesne University
9. University of Dallas
10. Prescott College
11. William Jewell College
12. New Jersey Institute of Technology
13. Tuskegee University
14. Washington College
15. University of Denver
16. Montana Tech of the Univ. of Montana
17. Stevens Institute of Technology
18. Juniata College
19. University of Hawaii—Manoa
20. Drexel University

Great Financial Aid
Based on students' assessments of how satisfied they are with their financial aid package

1. Pomona College
2. Swarthmore College
3. Princeton University
4. University of Virginia
5. Yale University
6. Vassar College

7. Rice University
8. Claremont McKenna College
9. Columbia University
10. New College of Florida
11. Franklin W. Olin College of Engineering
12. Thomas Aquinas College
13. Trinity College (CT)
14. Reed College
15. Stanford University
16. City University of New York—Hunter College
17. University of Richmond
18. The Cooper Union for the Advancement of Science and Art
19. College of the Atlantic
20. Vanderbilt University

Financial Aid Not So Great
Based on students' assessments of how satisfied they are with their financial aid package

1. Spelman College
2. Pennsylvania State University—University Park
3. New York University
4. University of Delaware
5. State University of New York—Purchase College
6. Suffolk University
7. Quinnipiac University
8. State University of New York—University at Albany
9. State University of New York at Binghamton
10. Hampton University
11. Duquesne University
12. University of Rhode Island
13. University of Missouri
14. University of Illinois at Urbana-Champaign
15. Hofstra University
16. University of Mary Washington
17. Christopher Newport University
18. The University of Vermont
19. Howard University
20. University of Pittsburgh—Pittsburgh Campus

Best-Run Colleges
Overall, how smoothly is your school run?

1. Elon University
2. Claremont McKenna College
3. United States Coast Guard Academy
4. Pomona College
5. Bowdoin College
6. United States Naval Academy
7. Wheaton College (IL)

8. Stanford University
9. Brigham Young University (UT)
10. Washington University in St. Louis
11. Princeton University
12. United States Military Academy
13. University of Scranton
14. Kansas State University
15. Rice University
16. Centre College
17. Yale University
18. Vanderbilt University
19. College of the Ozarks
20. Pennsylvania State University—University Park

Administrators Get Low Marks
Overall, how smoothly is your school run?

1. United States Merchant Marine Academy
2. Wells College
3. New Jersey Institute of Technology
4. Hampton University
5. New York University
6. Whittier College
7. Tuskegee University
8. Manhattanville College
9. University of Rhode Island
10. Howard University
11. University of Hawaii—Manoa
12. Warren Wilson College
13. Prescott College
14. Illinois Institute of Technology
15. Moravian College
16. The Catholic University of America
17. Stevens Institute of Technology
18. State University of New York—Purchase College
19. Marywood University
20. University of Californi—Berkeley

Their Students Love These Colleges
Overall, how satisfied are you with your school?

1. Claremont McKenna College
2. Clemson University
3. Virginia Tech
4. Pomona College
5. Vanderbilt University
6. Franklin W. Olin College of Engineering
7. Villanova University
8. Scripps College
9. Rice University
10. Washington University in St. Louis
11. College of the Atlantic
12. Bowdoin College
13. Whitman College
14. Stanford University
15. University of Wisconsin—Madison
16. Miami University

17. Brandeis University
18. Saint Michael's College
19. Haverford College
20. Florida State University

QUALITY OF LIFE

Happiest Students
Overall, how happy are you?

1. Vanderbilt University
2. Claremont McKenna College
3. Clemson University
4. Tulane University
5. Virginia Tech
6. Rice University
7. Kansas State University
8. Bowdoin College
9. Vassar College
10. Hillsdale College
11. Whitman College
12. The College of Idaho
13. University of California—Santa Barbara
14. Yale University
15. Wheaton College (IL)
16. Wesleyan University
17. Pomona College
18. Washington University in St. Louis
19. Franklin W. Olin College of Engineering
20. Auburn University

Least Happy Students
Overall, how happy are you?

1. Marywood University
2. United States Merchant Marine Academy
3. New Jersey Institute of Technology
4. University of Hawaii—Manoa
5. Manhattanville College
6. Illinois Institute of Technology
7. Duquesne University
8. Suffolk University
9. United States Naval Academy
10. Clarkson University
11. State University of New York—Stony Brook University
12. Alfred University
13. United States Military Academy
14. Indiana University of Pennsylvania
15. United States Coast Guard Academy
16. University of New Orleans
17. City University of New York—Baruch College
18. The University of South Dakota
19. The Catholic University of America
20. Montana Tech of the Univ. of Montana

Most Beautiful Campus
Based on students' rating of campus beauty

1. Colgate University
2. Pepperdine University
3. Rhodes College
4. Sweet Briar College
5. Scripps College
6. Rollins College
7. Southern Methodist University
8. University of Mississippi
9. Princeton University
10. Florida Southern College
11. University of San Diego
12. Union College (NY)
13. Wellesley College
14. Hanover College
15. Vassar College
16. Kenyon College
17. Ohio University—Athens
18. Agnes Scott College
19. Lewis & Clark College
20. University of Richmond

Least Beautiful Campus
Based on students' rating of campus beauty

1. University of Dallas
2. New Jersey Institute of Technology
3. Harvey Mudd College
4. State University of New York—Purchase College
5. Drexel University
6. Rutgers, The State University of New Jersey—New Brunswick
7. Xavier University of Louisiana
8. Clarkson University
9. United States Merchant Marine Academy
10. Illinois Institute of Technology
11. The University of Tennessee at Knoxville
12. City University of New York—Baruch College
13. University of New Orleans
14. Prescott College
15. Montana Tech of the Univ. of Montana
16. Case Western Reserve University
17. The University of Texas at Dallas
18. University of Maryland, Baltimore County
19. State University of New York at Binghamton
20. Rochester Institute of Technology

Easiest Campus to Get Around
Based on students' assessments of ease of getting around their campus

1. Wabash College
2. New College of Florida
3. Webb Institute
4. Whitman College

5. Franklin W. Olin College of Engineering
6. St. John's College (NM)
7. Rollins College
8. Thomas Aquinas College
9. Macalester College
10. Saint Michael's College
11. Centre College
12. Dartmouth College
13. Harvey Mudd College
14. Austin College
15. Franklin & Marshall College
16. Loyola University New Orleans
17. Truman State University
18. Skidmore College
19. Westminster College of Salt Lake City
20. Lawrence University

Best Campus Food
Based on students' rating of campus food

1. Virginia Tech
2. University of Massachusetts Amherst
3. Cornell University
4. Bowdoin College
5. St. Olaf College
6. James Madison University
7. Washington University in St. Louis
8. Bryn Mawr College
9. College of the Atlantic
10. St. Anselm College
11. Skidmore College
12. Wheaton College (IL)
13. Tufts University
14. Seattle University
15. Claremont McKenna College
16. Bates College
17. Boston University
18. Dartmouth College
19. Goucher College
20. University of Notre Dame

Is It Food?
Based on students' rating of campus food

1. United States Merchant Marine Academy
2. St. John's College (NM)
3. New College of Florida
4. Juniata College
5. Drew University
6. Bard College at Simon's Rock
7. Fordham University
8. Berea College
9. Catawba College
10. The Catholic University of America
11. Southwestern University
12. Hollins University
13. Ohio Northern University
14. Emerson College

15. Denison University
16. Randolph-Macon College
17. The Evergreen State College
18. Xavier University of Louisiana
19. Coe College
20. Austin College

Best College Dorms
Based on students' rating of dorm comfort

1. Washington University in St. Louis
2. Loyola University Maryland
3. Franklin W. Olin College of Engineering
4. Smith College
5. Scripps College
6. Bennington College
7. Bowdoin College
8. Trinity University
9. Bryn Mawr College
10. Sweet Briar College
11. Christopher Newport University
12. The George Washington University
13. Pomona College
14. The University of Chicago
15. Skidmore College
16. Mount Holyoke College
17. Bentley University
18. Emory University
19. Champlain College
20. State University of New York—College of Environmental Science and Forestry

Is That a Dorm?
Based on students' rating of dorm comfort

1. United States Merchant Marine Academy
2. College of the Ozarks
3. United States Coast Guard Academy
4. Alfred University
5. Hampton University
6. Prescott College
7. United States Military Academy
8. Tuskegee University
9. Manhattanville College
10. Xavier University of Louisiana
11. State University of New York—Purchase College
12. New Jersey Institute of Technology
13. University of Miami
14. United States Naval Academy
15. Whittier College
16. University of Washington
17. University of Idaho
18. Cornell College
19. Rider University
20. University of Wyoming

Best Quality of Life
Based on The Princeton Review's Quality of Life Rating (page 25)

1. Bowdoin College
2. Rice University
3. Kansas State University
4. Claremont McKenna College
5. Virginia Tech
6. Tulane University
7. Southern Methodist University
8. Dartmouth College
9. Whitman College
10. Vanderbilt University
11. Washington University in St. Louis
12. Franklin W. Olin College of Engineering
13. Wheaton College (IL)
14. College of the Atlantic
15. Scripps College
16. Loyola University New Orleans
17. Auburn University
18. Stanford University
19. Agnes Scott College
20. Middlebury College

POLITICS

Most Conservative Students
Based on students' assessment of their personal political views

1. Texas A&M University—College Station
2. Thomas Aquinas College
3. Grove City College
4. College of the Ozarks
5. University of Dallas
6. United States Merchant Marine Academy
7. Auburn University
8. Hampden-Sydney College
9. Brigham Young University (UT)
10. Hillsdale College
11. Wofford College
12. Clemson University
13. United States Military Academy
14. Wheaton College (IL)
15. United States Naval Academy
16. United States Coast Guard Academy
17. Gordon College
18. Angelo State University
19. Kansas State University
20. Baylor University

Most Liberal Students
Based on students' assessment of their personal political views

1. Sarah Lawrence College
2. Warren Wilson College
3. Bennington College
4. Bard College
5. Marlboro College
6. College of the Atlantic
7. Beloit College
8. Reed College
9. New College of Florida
10. Smith College
11. Macalester College
12. Skidmore College
13. Grinnell College
14. Pitzer College
15. Mills College
16. Vassar College
17. Occidental College
18. The Evergreen State College
19. Lewis & Clark College
20. Swarthmore College

Most Politically Active Students
How popular are political/activist groups?

1. The George Washington University
2. Grinnell College
3. United States Military Academy
4. Vassar College
5. Wellesley College
6. Amherst College
7. New College of Florida
8. Claremont McKenna College
9. Georgetown University
10. American University
11. Warren Wilson College
12. The University of Chicago
13. Macalester College
14. Bard College
15. Bard College at Simon's Rock
16. United States Naval Academy
17. University of Maryland, College Park
18. Hampden-Sydney College
19. Reed College
20. New York University

Election? What Election?
How popular are political/activist groups?

1. Ohio Northern University
2. Becker College
3. University of Tampa
4. Assumption College
5. Villanova University
6. Indiana University of Pennsylvania
7. Alfred University

8. Marywood University
9. Wagner College
10. The University of Montana
11. City University of New York—Baruch College
12. Monmouth University (NJ)
13. University of California—Davis
14. Nazareth College
15. The University of South Dakota
16. Sacred Heart University
17. University of Scranton
18. Colorado State University
19. University of the Pacific
20. State University of New York—College of Environmental Science and Forestry

DEMOGRAPHICS

Lots of Race/Class Interaction
Do different types of students (black/white, rich/poor) interact frequently and easily?

1. George Mason University
2. Loyola University New Orleans
3. Bard College at Simon's Rock
4. Swarthmore College
5. City University of New York—Hunter College
6. University of Miami
7. City University of New York—Brooklyn College
8. Claremont McKenna College
9. Rice University
10. City University of New York—Queens College
11. University of Redlands
12. St. Mary's College of Maryland
13. Mills College
14. St. John's College (NM)
15. University of Houston
16. Randolph College
17. Harvey Mudd College
18. Knox College
19. Suffolk University
20. Babson College

Little Race/Class Interaction
Do different types of students (black/white, rich/poor) interact frequently and easily?

1. Furman University
2. Trinity College (CT)
3. Gettysburg College
4. The Catholic University of America
5. Miami University
6. Villanova University
7. Illinois Wesleyan University

8. Boston College
9. Providence College
10. Lehigh University
11. Rhodes College
12. Bucknell University
13. Skidmore College
14. United States Merchant Marine Academy
15. Southern Methodist University
16. University of Notre Dame
17. University of San Diego
18. Colgate University
19. Duquesne University
20. Fairfield University

LGBT-Friendly
Do students, faculty and administrators treat
all persons equally, regardless of their sexual
orientation and gender identity/expression?

1. Stanford University
2. Oberlin College
3. Emerson College
4. Smith College
5. Warren Wilson College
6. Bryn Mawr College
7. University of Wisconsin-Madison
8. Franklin W. Olin College of Engineering
9. New College of Florida
10. Pitzer College
11. Carleton College
12. Sarah Lawrence College
13. Yale University
14. New York University
15. Macalester College
16. Bard College
17. Prescott College
18. Grinnell College
19. Vassar College
20. Rice University

LGBT-Unfriendly
Do students, faculty and administrators treat
all persons equally, regardless of their sexual
orientation and gender identity/expression?

1. College of the Ozarks
2. Grove City College
3. Wheaton College (IL)
4. Brigham Young University (UT)
5. Hampden-Sydney College
6. Wake Forest University
7. Pepperdine University
8. Wofford College
9. University of Notre Dame
10. Calvin College
11. Baylor University
12. The Catholic University of America
13. Auburn University
14. The University of Tennessee at Knoxville

15. Gordon College
16. Hillsdale College
17. Indiana University of Pennsylvania
18. Trinity College (CT)
19. Texas A&M University—College Station
20. University of Mississippi

Most Religious Students
Are students very religious?

1. Brigham Young University (UT)
2. Thomas Aquinas College
3. Wheaton College (IL)
4. Hillsdale College
5. Gordon College
6. Grove City College
7. University of Dallas
8. College of the Ozarks
9. Texas A&M University—College Station
10. Calvin College
11. Baylor University
12. Auburn University
13. Pepperdine University
14. Clemson University
15. Furman University
16. The Catholic University of America
17. Marquette University
18. Creighton University
19. Spelman College
20. Tuskegee University

Least Religious Students
Are students very religious?

1. Vassar College
2. Lewis & Clark College
3. Pomona College
4. Reed College
5. Bard College
6. Bennington College
7. Sarah Lawrence College
8. Skidmore College
9. Emerson College
10. Bard College at Simon's Rock
11. Marlboro College
12. Prescott College
13. The Evergreen State College
14. University of California—Santa Barbara
15. Beloit College
16. Pitzer College
17. California Institute of Technology
18. Macalester College
19. State University of New York—
    Purchase College
20. Kalamazoo College

TOWN LIFE

College City Gets High Marks
Based on students' assessment of the surrounding city or town

1. Boston University
2. Tulane University
3. DePaul University
4. New York University
5. The George Washington University
6. Southern Methodist University
7. City University of New York—Hunter College
8. Columbia University
9. College of Charleston
10. Northeastern University
11. University of San Diego
12. Suffolk University
13. Georgetown University
14. Stevens Institute of Technology
15. University of Kansas
16. University of San Francisco
17. Barnard College
18. The Cooper Union for the Advancement of Science and Art
19. Champlain College
20. Illinois Institute of Technology

College City Gets Low Marks
Based on students' assessment of the surrounding city or town

1. New Jersey Institute of Technology
2. Tuskegee University
3. United States Coast Guard Academy
4. University of the Pacific
5. Albion College
6. United States Military Academy
7. Wheaton College (MA)
8. Wabash College
9. Ohio Northern University
10. Bates College
11. Vassar College
12. Hofstra University
13. Hillsdale College
14. Wittenberg University
15. College of the Holy Cross
16. DePauw University
17. Truman State University
18. Beloit College
19. Hampden-Sydney College
20. Baylor University

Town-Gown Relations Are Great
Do students get along well with members of the local community?

1. Clemson University
2. Virginia Tech
3. Saint Michael's College
4. Gordon College
5. Kansas State University
6. Loyola University New Orleans
7. Texas A&M University—College Station
8. Auburn University
9. University of Mississippi
10. Agnes Scott College
11. College of the Ozarks
12. Ripon College
13. Franklin W. Olin College of Engineering
14. The University of North Carolina at Asheville
15. Brigham Young University (UT)
16. St. Anselm College
17. United States Naval Academy
18. Wheaton College (IL)
19. Westminster College (PA)
20. Washington State University

Town-Gown Relations Are Strained
Do students get along well with members of the local community?

1. Trinity College (CT)
2. Duke University
3. Lehigh University
4. Bates College
5. Bennington College
6. The College of Wooster
7. New Jersey Institute of Technology
8. Sarah Lawrence College
9. Albion College
10. Colorado College
11. Wheaton College (MA)
12. Franklin & Marshall College
13. Johns Hopkins University
14. Providence College
15. The College of New Jersey
16. College of the Holy Cross
17. Vassar College
18. Dickinson College
19. The Catholic University of America
20. United States Merchant Marine Academy

EXTRACURRICULARS

Best Athletic Facilities
Based on students' rating of campus athletic facilities

1. University of Illinois at Urbana-Champaign
2. Macalester College
3. West Virginia University
4. Kenyon College
5. Loyola University Maryland
6. United States Military Academy

7. Southern Methodist University
8. Ohio University—Athens
9. Pennsylvania State University—University Park
10. University of South Carolina—Columbia
11. University of Richmond
12. George Mason University
13. Grinnell College
14. University of Louisville
15. University of Arizona
16. Georgia Institute of Technology
17. University of Alabama at Birmingham
18. Bucknell University
19. University of Florida
20. Providence College

Students Pack the Stadiums
How popular are intercollegiate sports?

1. University of Kansas
2. Clemson University
3. Syracuse University
4. Pennsylvania State University—University Park
5. University of Arizona
6. University of Notre Dame
7. The University of North Carolina at Chapel Hill
8. University of Southern California
9. Auburn University
10. University of Connecticut
11. Kansas State University
12. West Virginia University
13. University of Iowa
14. University of Oklahoma
15. Gonzaga University
16. University of Oregon
17. Florida State University
18. Texas A&M University—College Station
19. University of Louisville
20. University of Florida

There's a Game?
How popular are intercollegiate sports?

1. Bennington College
2. College of the Atlantic
3. Prescott College
4. Reed College
5. Franklin W. Olin College of Engineering
6. Barnard College
7. St. John's College (NM)
8. Thomas Aquinas College
9. Spelman College
10. Marlboro College
11. New College of Florida
12. Sarah Lawrence College
13. Champlain College
14. Carnegie Mellon University

15. State University of New York—Purchase College
16. The Evergreen State College
17. City University of New York—Hunter College
18. Case Western Reserve University
19. Stephens College
20. The University of Texas at Dallas

Everyone Plays Intramural Sports
How popular are intramural sports?

1. United States Military Academy
2. Clemson University
3. Gonzaga University
4. Pennsylvania State University—University Park
5. Grove City College
6. Whitman College
7. Wabash College
8. United States Naval Academy
9. Providence College
10. Gettysburg College
11. United States Coast Guard Academy
12. Florida Southern College
13. Colorado College
14. Florida State University
15. University of Notre Dame
16. Kansas State University
17. Washington State University
18. University of Nebraska—Lincoln
19. Ripon College
20. University of Colorado—Boulder

Nobody Plays Intramural Sports
How popular are intramural sports?

1. College of the Atlantic
2. Stephens College
3. Wells College
4. Prescott College
5. New College of Florida
6. Reed College
7. Manhattanville College
8. Sarah Lawrence College
9. The Cooper Union for the Advancement of Science and Art
10. Emerson College
11. Hollins University
12. Bard College at Simon's Rock
13. Bennington College
14. New Jersey Institute of Technology
15. Howard University
16. Mount Holyoke College
17. Spelman College
18. Marlboro College
19. Barnard College
20. Simmons College

Best College Radio Station
How popular is the radio station?

1. Hofstra University
2. Ithaca College
3. St. Bonaventure University
4. Emerson College
5. Syracuse University
6. Fordham University
7. DePauw University
8. Union College (NY)
9. Rochester Institute of Technology
10. The College of Wooster
11. Knox College
12. University of Puget Sound
13. Guilford College
14. Howard University
15. Manhattanville College
16. Suffolk University
17. Denison University
18. Illinois Wesleyan University
19. Chapman University
20. Michigan Technological University

Best College Newspaper
How do you rate your campus newspaper?

1. Yale University
2. Syracuse University
3. Cornell University
4. University of California—Los Angeles
5. Loyola University New Orleans
6. Pennsylvania State University—University Park
7. Tufts University
8. West Virginia University
9. The University of North Carolina at Chapel Hill
10. University of Wisconsin—Madison
11. University of Kansas
12. University of Florida
13. University of South Carolina—Columbia
14. Wagner College
15. St. Bonaventure University
16. Howard University
17. Boston College
18. The University of Vermont
19. Dartmouth College
20. University of Iowa

Best College Theater
How do you rate college's theater productions?

1. Wagner College
2. Carnegie Mellon University
3. Yale University
4. Bennington College
5. Emerson College
6. Ithaca College

7. Drew University
8. Fordham University
9. Vassar College
10. Northwestern University
11. Indiana University—Bloomington
12. Stephens College
13. Elon University
14. Kenyon College
15. State University of New York—Purchase College
16. Randolph College
17. Nazareth College
18. Knox College
19. Juniata College
20. Westminster College (PA)

SOCIAL SCENE

Lots of Greek Life
How popular are fraternities/sororities?

1. Transylvania University
2. Gettysburg College
3. Southern Methodist University
4. DePauw University
5. Dartmouth College
6. Miami University
7. Bucknell University
8. Syracuse University
9. University of Illinois at Urbana-Champaign
10. Lehigh University
11. Union College (NY)
12. Vanderbilt University
13. Florida Southern College
14. Pennsylvania State University—University Park
15. Wofford College
16. Howard University
17. University of Iowa
18. University of Mississippi
19. Wake Forest University
20. Rhodes College

Lots of Beer
How widely used is beer?

1. Pennsylvania State University—University Park
2. University of Florida
3. Florida State University
4. Syracuse University
5. University of Wisconsin—Madison
6. Ohio University—Athens
7. Lehigh University
8. University of Illinois at Urbana-Champaign

9. University of Iowa
10. Bucknell University
11. West Virginia University
12. University of California—Santa Barbara
13. Colby College
14. Bates College
15. Hamilton College
16. University of Delaware
17. University of Georgia
18. Miami University
19. St. Bonaventure University
20. Kenyon College

Got Milk?
How widely used is beer?

1. Brigham Young University (UT)
2. City University of New York—Brooklyn College
3. College of the Ozarks
4. Wheaton College (IL)
5. Gordon College
6. Wesleyan College
7. Grove City College
8. Spelman College
9. Xavier University of Louisiana
10. City University of New York—City College
11. City University of New York—Queens College
12. City University of New York—Baruch College
13. Calvin College
14. Mills College
15. Howard University
16. Thomas Aquinas College
17. Pepperdine University
18. Berea College
19. Agnes Scott College
20. Tuskegee University

Lots of Hard Liquor
How widely used is hard liquor?

1. University of Iowa
2. Syracuse University
3. Providence College
4. Tulane University
5. University of Georgia
6. University of California—Santa Barbara
7. Connecticut College
8. Colgate University
9. Wake Forest University
10. University of Wisconsin—Madison
11. University of Illinois at Urbana-Champaign
12. Ohio University—Athens
13. West Virginia University
14. DePauw University
15. University of Florida

16. Lehigh University
17. Boston College
18. Miami University
19. Pennsylvania State University—University Park
20. Bucknell University

Scotch and Soda, Hold the Scotch
How widely used is hard liquor?

1. Brigham Young University (UT)
2. College of the Ozarks
3. Wheaton College (IL)
4. Grove City College
5. Gordon College
6. City University of New York—Brooklyn College
7. Wesleyan College
8. City University of New York—Queens College
9. City University of New York—City College
10. Christopher Newport University
11. City University of New York—Baruch College
12. University of California—Riverside
13. California State University, Stanislaus
14. Xavier University of Louisiana
15. The University of Texas at Dallas
16. University of Houston
17. The Cooper Union for the Advancement of Science and Art
18. St. John's University (NY)
19. Becker College
20. United States Naval Academy

Reefer Madness
How widely used is marijuana?

1. Skidmore College
2. Eckerd College
3. The Evergreen State College
4. University of Colorado—Boulder
5. Ithaca College
6. The University of Vermont
7. University of Oregon
8. Sarah Lawrence College
9. Pitzer College
10. University of California—Santa Cruz
11. University of California—Santa Barbara
12. State University of New York—Purchase College
13. Colorado College
14. Guilford College
15. Lewis & Clark College
16. Emerson College
17. Reed College
18. Syracuse University
19. University of Wisconsin—Madison
20. Marlboro College

Don't Inhale

How widely used is marijuana?

1. United States Coast Guard Academy
2. Brigham Young University (UT)
3. United States Military Academy
4. United States Naval Academy
5. United States Merchant Marine Academy
6. Thomas Aquinas College
7. College of the Ozarks
8. Wheaton College (IL)
9. City University of New York—Brooklyn College
10. Grove City College
11. Hillsdale College
12. Wesleyan College
13. Calvin College
14. United States Air Force Academy
15. City University of New York—Baruch College
16. City University of New York—City College
17. City University of New York—Queens College
18. Agnes Scott College
19. Webb Institute
20. Gordon College

SCHOOLS BY TYPE

Party Schools

Based on a combination of survey questions concerning the use of alcohol and drugs, hours of study each day, and the popularity of the Greek system

1. Syracuse University
2. University of Iowa
3. University of California—Santa Barbara
4. West Virginia University
5. University of Illinois at Urbana-Champaign
6. Lehigh University
7. Pennsylvania State University—University Park
8. University of Wisconsin-Madison
9. Bucknell University
10. University of Florida
11. Miami University
12. Florida State University
13. Ohio University—Athens
14. DePauw University
15. University of Georgia
16. University of Mississippi
17. Tulane University
18. The University of Vermont
19. University of Oregon
20. University of Delaware

Stone-Cold Sober Schools

Based on a combination of survey questions concerning the use of alcohol and drugs, hours of study each day, and the popularity of the Greek system

1. Brigham Young University (UT)
2. Wheaton College (IL)
3. United States Military Academy
4. Calvin College
5. Thomas Aquinas College
6. College of the Ozarks
7. Gordon College
8. Grove City College
9. United States Coast Guard Academy
10. City University of New York—Brooklyn College
11. City University of New York—City College
12. Wesleyan College
13. United States Naval Academy
14. Franklin W. Olin College of Engineering
15. City University of New York—Queens College
16. Mills College
17. St. Olaf College
18. University of Houston
19. Nazareth College
20. University of Dallas

Jock Schools

Based on a combination of survey questions concerning the popularity of intercollegiate sports, intramural sports, and the Greek system

1. Auburn University
2. Clemson University
3. Wabash College
4. University of Missouri
5. Kansas State University
6. Florida State University
7. Virginia Tech
8. University of Kansas
9. Pennsylvania State University—University Park
10. University of Connecticut
11. University of Florida
12. Purdue University—West Lafayette
13. University of Nebraska—Lincoln
14. University of Arizona
15. Union College (NY)
16. Villanova University
17. The University of Tennessee at Knoxville
18. University of South Carolina—Columbia
19. University of Louisville
20. North Carolina State University

Future Rotarians and Daughters of the American Revolution

Based on a combination of survey questions concerning the political persuasion, the use of drugs, the popularity of student government, and the level of acceptance of the gay community on campus

1. Grove City College
2. Hillsdale College
3. College of the Ozarks
4. Brigham Young University (UT)
5. Wheaton College (IL)
6. University of Dallas
7. United States Naval Academy
8. Thomas Aquinas College
9. Gordon College
10. Texas A&M University—College Station
11. United States Merchant Marine Academy
12. United States Military Academy
13. Auburn University
14. United States Coast Guard Academy
15. Calvin College
16. Clemson University
17. Baylor University
18. United States Air Force Academy
19. Pepperdine University
20. Wofford College

Birkenstock-Wearing, Tree-Hugging, Clove-Smoking Vegetarians

Based on a combination of survey questions concerning the political persuasion, the use of drugs, the popularity of student government, and the level of acceptance of the gay community on campus

1. Skidmore College
2. Sarah Lawrence College
3. Reed College
4. Bennington College
5. Oberlin College
6. Vassar College
7. Bard College
8. Pitzer College
9. Guilford College
10. Lewis & Clark College
11. University of Puget Sound
12. Emerson College
13. New College of Florida
14. State University of New York—Purchase College
15. Warren Wilson College
16. Grinnell College
17. Green Mountain College
18. Occidental College
19. The University of Vermont
20. Eckerd College

Deep Springs Honor Roll

Since Deep Springs is a two-year college (and the only one in *The Best 379 Colleges*), we remove it from our rankings tallies in order to avoid comparing "apples and oranges." Instead we present this list of some ranking categories in which Deep Springs ranks high (or low, as it were) among the best colleges in our book.

Students Study the Most
Professors Get High Marks
Most Accessible Professors
This is a Library?
Best Run Colleges
Most Beautiful Campus
Best Campus Food
Most Liberal Students
Least Religious Students
Got Milk?
Scotch and Soda, Hold the Scotch
Don't Inhale
Stone-Cold Sober Schools
Great Financial Aid
Lots of Race/Class Interaction

THE PRINCETON REVIEW'S "FINANCIAL AID RATING," "FIRE SAFETY RATING," AND "GREEN RATING" HONOR ROLLS

We salute theses schools that received a 99 (the highest score) in the tallies for our "Financial Aid," "Fire Safety," and "Green" Ratings—three of eight ratings on some of the school profiles in this book as well as in *The Complete Book of Colleges*, 2015 Edition, and at www.PrincetonReview.com. Our school ratings are numerical scores (Note: They are not ranking lists) that show how a school "sizes up" on a fixed scale. They are comparable to grades and based primarily on institutional data we collect directly from the colleges.

Financial Aid Honor Roll

Schools are listed in alphabetical order. See page 29 for information on how our "Financial Aid Rating" is determined.

Claremont McKenna College
Colgate University
Franklin W. Olin College of Engineering
Haverford College
Pomona College
Princeton University
Reed College
Thomas Aquinas College
Trinity College (CT)
Vanderbilt University
Vassar College
Yale University

Fire Safety Honor Roll

Schools are listed in alphabetical order. See page 25 for information on how our "Fire Safety Rating" is determined.

Bay Path College*
Bentley University
City University of New York—
  Hunter College
City University of New York—
  Queens College
DePaul University
Duquesne University
Five Towns College*
Florida College*
Husson University*
Kennesaw State University*
Lincoln University (MO)*
Loyola University New Orleans
Mercy College*
Milwaukee School of Engineering*
Montana Tech of the University of Montana
Montclair State University*
New Jersey Institute of Technology
Susquehanna University
Sweet Briar College
The Citadel, The Military College
  of South Carolina*
University of Maine at Farmington*
University of Maine—Fort Kent*
University of Minnesota, Morris*
The University of North Carolina at Pembroke*

Schools marked with an asterisk do not appear in the *Best 379 Colleges*. You can find those school profiles in *The Complete Book of Colleges*, 2015 Edition.

Green Honor Roll

Schools are listed in alphabetical order. See page 26 for information on how our "Green Rating" is determined.

American University
Colgate University
Colorado State University
Columbia University
Cornell University
Dickinson College
Georgia Institute of Technology
Green Mountain College
Harvard University
Iowa State University
Lewis & Clark College
Portland State University
Santa Clara University
Stanford University
State University of New York—Stony Brook University
University of California, Irvine*
University of California, Santa Barbara
University of Colorado at Colorado Springs
University of Illinois, Urbana-Champaign
University of Massachusetts Amherst
University of New Hampshire
University of Vermont
University of Victoria*
University of Washington

Tuition-Free Schools Honor Roll

The following schools have been excluded from our ranking lists dealing with financial aid:

Berea College
College of the Ozarks
Deep Springs College
United States Air Force Academy
United States Coast Guard Academy
United States Merchant Marine Academy
United States Military Academy
United States Naval Academy
Webb Institute

We commend these schools on their ability to do the seemingly impossible: not charge tuition. While some charge students for room and board and other fees, the overall cost of attendance at these schools is very low, and at some schools: free! (Note: We do not include these schools in our ranking lists dealing with financial aid, since they would have an unfair advantage over schools that charge even a moderate tuition.)

The Princeton Review collaborated with USA TODAY to bring you this list of 150 Best Value Colleges in February 2014. We selected the 150 schools—75 private and 75 public—based on 30 factors covering academics, costs, and financial aid. We reported the two lists in alphabetical order and named the top 10 ranking schools in each group. For more information on this project, visit us online at www.PrincetonReview.com/best-value-colleges.aspx. At USA TODAY's site, you can find information about each school with an exclusive analysis in an interactive database and map at www.usatoday.com/news/education/best-value-colleges. For detailed profiles of all these great schools, see our companion book, *The Best Value Colleges: The 150 Best-Buy Schools and What It Takes to Get In.*

Top 75 Private

Amherst College (#9)
Bard College
Barnard College
Bates College
Boston College
Bowdoin College
Brandeis University
Brown University
Bryn Mawr College
Bucknell University
California Institute of Technology
Carleton College
Centre College
Claremont McKenna College
Colby College
Colgate University
College of the Atlantic
College of the Holy Cross
Colorado College
Columbia University
Connecticut College
The Cooper Union for the Advancement of (#6)
Cornell University
Dartmouth College
Davidson College
Denison University
DePauw University
Duke University
Emory University
Franklin W. Olin College of Engineering
Georgetown University
Gettysburg College
Grinnell College
Hamilton College
Harvard College (#2)
Harvey Mudd College
Haverford College
Hillsdale College
Johns Hopkins University
Kenyon College
Lafayette College
Macalester College
Massachusetts Institute of Technology (#8)
Middlebury College
Mount Holyoke College

Northwestern University
Occidental College
Pitzer College
Pomona College (#10)
Princeton University (#5)
Reed College
Rhodes College
Rice University
Scripps College
Skidmore College
Smith College
St. Olaf College
Stanford University
Swarthmore College (#3)
Thomas Aquinas College
Trinity College (CT)
The University of Chicago
University of Notre Dame
University of Pennsylvania
University of Richmond
Vanderbilt University
Vassar College (#7)
Wabash College
Wake Forest University
Washington University in St. Louis
Wellesley College
Wesleyan University
Whitman College
Williams College (#1)
Yale University (#4)

Top 75 Public

Appalachian State University
California State University—Long Beach
Christopher Newport University
City University of New York—Baruch College
Brooklyn College, City University of New York
City University of New York—City College
City University of New York—Hunter College
City University of New York—Queens College
Clemson University
The College of New Jersey
The College of William & Mary (#8)
Florida State University
Georgia Institute of Technology
Indiana University Bloomington

Iowa State University
James Madison University
Longwood University
Louisiana State University—Baton Rouge
New College of Florida (#2)
North Carolina State University (#4)
Purdue University—West Lafayette
Radford University
Salisbury University
Southern Utah University
St. Mary's College of Maryland
State University of New York at Binghamton (Binghamton University) (#10)
State University of New York—College of Environmental Science and Forestry
State University of New York at Geneseo
State University of New York—Oswego
State University of New York at Purchase College
State University of New York—Stony Brook University
State University of New York—University at Buffalo
Texas A&M University—College Station
Truman State University (#9)
University of Arkansas—Fayetteville
University of California—Berkeley
University of California—Davis
University of California—Irvine
University of California—Los Angeles (#6)
University of California—Riverside
University of California—San Diego
University of California—Santa Barbara
University of California—Santa Cruz
University of Central Florida
University of Colorado Boulder
University of Delaware
University of Florida (#7)
University of Georgia
University of Houston
University of Illinois at Urbana Champaign
University of Maryland—Baltimore County
University of Maryland—College Park
University of Massachusetts Amherst
University of Michigan—Ann Arbor (#5)
University of Minnesota—Twin Cities
University of Missouri—Kansas City
University of Nebraska—Lincoln
University of New Orleans
The University of North Carolina at Asheville
The University of North Carolina at Chapel Hill (#1)
University of North Carolina—Wilmington

University of North Florida
University of Oklahoma
University of Pittsburgh—Pittsburgh Campus
University of South Florida
The University of Tennessee
The University of Tennessee at Martin
The University of Texas at Austin
The University of Texas at Dallas
University of Virginia (#3)
University of Washington
University of Wisconsin—Eau Claire
University of Wisconsin—Madison
Virginia Tech
Worcester State University

Top 10 Private Schools
1. Williams College
2. Harvard College
3. Swarthmore College
4. Yale University
5. Princeton University
6. The Cooper Union for the Advancement of
7. Vassar College
8. Massachusetts Institute of Technology
9. Amherst College
10. Pomona College

Top 10 Public Schools
1. The University of North Carolina at Chapel Hill
2. New College of Florida
3. University of Virginia
4. North Carolina State University
5. University of Michigan—Ann Arbor
6. University of California—Los Angeles
7. University of Florida
8. The College of William & Mary
9. Truman State University
10. State University of New York at Binghamton (Binghamton University)

Schools marked with an asterisk do not appear in *The Best 379 Colleges.* You can find those school profiles in *The Complete Book of Colleges,* 2015 Edition.

PART 3

THE BEST
379 COLLEGES

AGNES SCOTT COLLEGE

141 EAST COLLEGE AVENUE, DECATUR, GA 30030-3770 • ADMISSIONS: 404-471-6285 • FAX: 404-471-6414

STUDENTS SAY ". . ."

Academics

Agnes Scott College is a tiny women's liberal arts college that is "all about creating intelligent, confident, well rounded women." With just 900 or so students, there is a pervasively "caring and intellectual atmosphere" at a school that students claim is "dedicated to the enrichment of young women's lives." "Agnes Scott College is a school that focuses on education and experience for women who have any size plan, big or small, for their lives."

The "phenomenal" professors at Agnes Scott are "indescribably amazing." Their passion for the subjects they teach "shines through in everything that they do." If a student shows that they are trying, but still not grasping the material, then the professors will usually go out of their way to help. "Every professor that I have had has encouraged students to meet them if they have any questions," says a junior. "You can get to know your professors personally." Discussion is encouraged, and the classroom is "a place where you can speak your mind and actually be heard by your professors and peers." "Every day my thought process is challenged and I learn more about myself and how the world functions," says a history major. Most classes require papers rather than exams, which students find "challenging and more rewarding."

There are "rich opportunities as a consequence of small size" (such as extra tutoring on writing skills and "great opportunities for networking"), and "students get opportunities that most graduate students exclusively get at other universities." In addition, the financial aid is "exceptional" and the administration "actually listens to the students and tries to improve" when issues are raised, and "you can complain directly to the person in charge."

Life

This "fun, quirky little college" provides "a very safe space that is conducive for learning." "People study very hard here which encourages you to study hard as well," says a student. With the honor code in place (everyone must sign upon matriculation), "We don't have to worry about anyone taking our things when we're not looking or while we're asleep. We all look out for one another."

While academics and extracurriculars dominate the week, Scotties let their hair down on weekends. There is "a very modern artsy feel to this city [Decatur] and school," which is "close enough to Atlanta to enjoy the nightlife, and far enough to enjoy nature." "Many music groups come to Atlanta when they're on tour," and students also go to nearby shops, open mics, and museums, or to parties at other colleges or (occasionally) on campus ("where Emory, Morehouse, and Georgia Tech boys are invited"). "We have friends here of course, but we all go out off campus when wanting to hang out or do something fun," says a student.

Students universally agree that there needs to be "better dining hall food," and some say that the Wellness Center is "slightly unorganized" and "isn't as helpful as it should be." Luckily, "there are a lot of nice restaurants within the walk."

Student Body

The "smart, ambitious women" who attend Agnes Scott are a "hodgepodge," as the school "truly invests in diversity." "You would be hard pressed not to fit in somewhere," says a student. This "sisterhood of women...are willing to help" and are "very assertive" and "not afraid to speak their minds." Everyone here is "almost always active in something (not restricted to just sports)" and LGBT support and membership are big. While everyone is "friendly and open-minded," most everyone is "at least somewhat feministic" and "very liberal."

FINANCIAL AID: 404-471-6395 • E-MAIL: ADMISSION@AGNESSCOTT.EDU • WEBSITE: WWW.AGNESSCOTT.EDU

THE PRINCETON REVIEW SAYS

Admissions

Very important factors considered include: Class rank, GPA, rigor of secondary school record, application essay, recommendation(s), talent/ability, character/personal qualities. *Important factors considered include:* extracurricular activities, volunteer work, work experience. *Other factors considered include:* Standardized test scores, first generation, geographical residence, interview, racial/ethnic status, state residency, alumni/ae relations, level of applicant's interest. SAT or ACT considered if submitted; SAT and SAT Subject Tests or ACT required for some; ACT with Writing component required. TOEFL required of all international applicants. *Academic units recommended:* 4 English; 3 mathematics; 2 science; (2 science lab); 2 social studies; 2 foreign language; 2 history.

Financial Aid

Students should submit: FAFSA. Regular filing deadline is 5/1. The Princeton Review suggests that all financial aid forms be submitted as soon as possible after January 1. *Need-based scholarships/grants offered:* Federal Pell, SEOG, State scholarships/grants, private scholarships, the school's own gift aid. *Loan aid offered:* Direct Subsidized Stafford Loans, Direct Unsubsidized Stafford Loans, Direct PLUS loans. Federal Work-Study Program available. Institutional employment available. Off-campus job opportunities are excellent.

The Inside Word

Agnes Scott waives the application fee for those who apply online; all it will cost you is your time. Take the time to craft a solid application if you want to be considered seriously, as this is a very competitive school where admissions officers give each candidate a very careful look. A strong application that creates a compelling portrait may well overcome moderate shortcomings in high school grades or test scores, especially if bolstered by an enthusiastic interview during a campus visit.

THE SCHOOL SAYS ". . ."

From the Admissions Office

"Spend four years with brilliant women who won't suffer fools, stand for injustice or tolerate prejudice; with confident women who never settle; with women who question, confront and debate.

"Study with professors who will help you when you call, push you to the limits and then challenge you again.

"Gain experience through research projects, internships with *Fortune* Global 500 companies and nonprofits big and small and explore the world through study abroad and service opportunities.

"Read as widely as possible; write as much as you can; discuss and debate until your mind is ready to fall apart at the seams. Even then you'll make connections between and across everything you're studying.

"After four years at Agnes Scott College, you will not be the same. You will be a better you: more reflective, more intelligent, more cultured, more prepared for the world. The question isn't whether Agnes Scott women are ready for the world, but whether the world is ready for Agnes Scott women.

"If you've read this far, why not visit campus? We'd love to meet you and show you our world. Schedule a campus tour at agnesscott.edu/visit."

SELECTIVITY

Admissions Rating	88
# of applicants	1,340
% of applicants accepted	67
% of acceptees attending	28

FRESHMAN PROFILE

Range SAT Critical Reading	500–660
Range SAT Math	510–650
Range SAT Writing	520–640
Range ACT Composite	22–28
Average HS GPA	3.59
% graduated top 10% of class	40
% graduated top 25% of class	67
% graduated top 50% of class	91

DEADLINES

Early action	
Deadline	11/15
Notification	12/15
Regular	
Priority	3/1
Nonfall registration?	Yes

APPLICANTS ALSO LOOK AT AND OFTEN PREFER
University of Georgia; Georgia State University

AND SOMETIMES PREFER
Georgia Institute of Technology

AND RARELY PREFER
Mercer University

FINANCIAL FACTS

Financial Aid Rating	86
Annual tuition	$35,742
Room and board	$10,850
Required fees	$240
Books and supplies	$1,000
% needy frosh rec. need-based scholarship or grant aid	100
% needy UG rec. need-based scholarship or grant aid	100
% needy frosh rec. non-need-based scholarship or grant aid	22
% needy UG rec. non-need-based scholarship or grant aid	23
% needy frosh rec. need-based self-help aid	86
% needy UG rec. need-based self-help aid	90
% frosh rec. any financial aid	100
% UG rec. any financial aid	99
% UG borrow to pay for school	63
Average cumulative indebtedness	$30,139
% frosh need fully met	32
% ugrads need fully met	23
Average % of frosh need met	87
Average % of ugrad need met	87

ALBION COLLEGE

611 East Porter, Albion, MI 49224 • Admissions: 517-629-0321 • Fax: 517-629-0569

STUDENTS SAY ". . ."

Academics

Armed with a "great reputation" and a "small-town feeling," Albion College provides undergraduates with a "rigorous but rewarding" academic experience replete with "huge opportunities." Students here truly appreciate that Albion works diligently to foster an environment that "encourages questions [and] thinking" all the while aiming to "provide personal attention to each student." While the college certainly offers a "great liberal arts education," undergrads are especially quick to highlight the strong science, premed, and business programs. Indeed, students like to boast that Albion "has a very high rate of students being accepted into medical school." And business majors point to the Gerstacker Institute for Business and Management, which allows students to "gain real-world experience" and even the potential to walk away with "a job offer." Of course, regardless of discipline or department, Albion undergrads are full of praise for their teachers. As one thrilled student eagerly shares, "The professors care about their students' success and are always there to help." Importantly, they are "very knowledgeable in their material and try to make sure you learn as much as possible." Further, they are "easily approachable," "extremely passionate about their work," and always "available for discussions." As one content undergrad sums up, "I would say that the overall experience has been great, and I couldn't be more pleased with my decision to attend Albion College."

Life

While Albion students are often quite "studious" during the week, once the weekend rolls around they certainly know how to get "crazy [and] exciting." Fortunately, there "is almost always something going on on campus." Indeed, the "Union Board plans lots of free activities, concerts, comedians, etc." Moreover, those interested in the party scene will be delighted to discover that fraternities and sororities are very popular at Albion. As one thrilled undergrad notes, "Greek life is fantastic. It really is the cornerstone of our campus. Every weekend there is a party or something going on at the fraternities. Whether you are into drinking or not, the guys there know how to have a good time." While students bemoan the fact that "there's not much to do in the city of Albion," they do take solace in finding other off campus options. As another satisfied student reveals, "Bigger cities like Jackson and Battle Creek are only a fifteen- or twenty-minute drive away, so if you're looking for a day at a mall, that's always an option. Plus, the college sponsors sending buses and vans to take students to places like Ann Arbor or Lansing. Generally you can find something to do."

Student Body

At first glance, Albion College appears to be "a microcosm of upper-class metro-Detroit and Chicago." Therefore, it's not surprising that a "slightly right-leaning, white, and Greek-loving [student body seems to be] the norm." However, those seeking more diversity should fear not! One student assures us, "I have met anarchists and proud communists. There is a mix, but you have to dig for it." Beyond race and political affiliation, undergrads here find their peers to be "serious about school but also very fun and friendly." Moreover, they are "bright individuals that want to succeed" and certainly people who "value their education." They also seem to have "a million interests," which they vigorously pursue through a number of extracurricular activities and programs. As one socially satisfied undergrad sums up, "I think there is a club or niche here where everyone can find a group of people they fit in with. I truthfully would feel comfortable sitting down at a table with anyone of my classmates in the cafeteria and having lunch with them."

FINANCIAL AID: 517-629-0440 • E-MAIL: ADMISSION@ALBION.EDU • WEBSITE: WWW.ALBION.EDU

THE PRINCETON REVIEW SAYS

Admissions

Very important factors considered include: GPA, rigor of secondary school record. *Important factors considered include:* Class rank, standardized test scores, application essay, recommendation(s). *Other factors considered include:* Extracurricular activities, interview, racial/ethnic status, talent/ability, volunteer work, work experience, alumni/ae relations, character/personal qualities. SAT or ACT required; SAT and SAT Subject Tests or ACT considered if submitted; ACT with Writing component recommended. TOEFL required of all international applicants. *Academic units recommended:* 4 English; 4 mathematics; 3 science; (2 science lab); 2 social studies; 2 foreign language.

Financial Aid

Students should submit: FAFSA. The Princeton Review suggests that all financial aid forms be submitted as soon as possible after January 1. *Need-based scholarships/grants offered:* Federal Pell, SEOG, State scholarships/grants, private scholarships, the school's own gift aid. *Loan aid offered:* Direct Subsidized Stafford Loans, Direct Unsubsidized Stafford Loans, Direct PLUS loans, Federal Perkins Loans. Federal Work-Study Program available. Institutional employment available. Off-campus job opportunities are fair.

The Inside Word

Albion's growing reputation means that earning a coveted acceptance letter is no easy feat. Academic success takes precedence, and applicants should have taken a challenging high school curriculum including a handful of honors and advanced placement courses. Of course, admissions officers are also concerned about maintaining a vibrant community, so careful attention will also be paid to essays and extracurricular activities.

THE SCHOOL SAYS "..."

From the Admissions Office

"As an Albion student, you'll be equipped to make an impact. You'll be prepared to go on to the nation's top graduate and professional schools and to assume leadership roles in the sciences and medicine, business, law, education, the arts, and social services. To do that, your education will take you beyond the classroom, beyond our campus, and beyond conventional thinking. It will help you discover what you're meant to do with your life. And it will prepare you to live it well. Through the Albion Advantage, you'll develop practical knowledge and purposeful direction to equip you to succeed.

"You'll identify your goals through a four-year individualized career plan and build a strong foundation in the liberal arts. You'll sharpen your career focus and develop skills through internships and other real-world, hands-on experiences like those in our prestigious institutes in business, public policy and service, sustainability and the environment, education, and pre-medicine and the sciences. Your creativity and curiosity may be satisfied through a multitude of research experiences available as early as your freshman year through our Foundation for Undergraduate Research, Scholarship and Creative Activity and the Prentiss M. Brown Honors Program.

"On our residential campus, you can choose from more than 100 campus organizations catering to a wide range of interests. Our athletic teams regularly head to NCAA Division III postseason play, and our equestrian team members compete regionally and nationally.

"Check us out online at www.albion.edu or visit us to learn if Albion will be right for you."

SELECTIVITY

Admissions Rating	80
# of applicants	4,430
% of applicants accepted	56
% of acceptees attending	14

FRESHMAN PROFILE

Range SAT Critical Reading	520–580
Range SAT Math	510–590
Range ACT Composite	22–28
Minimum paper TOEFL	550
Average HS GPA	3.50
% graduated top 10% of class	21
% graduated top 25% of class	52
% graduated top 50% of class	84

DEADLINES

Early action	
Deadline	12/1
Notification	1/15
Regular	
Priority	12/1
Nonfall registration?	Yes

APPLICANTS ALSO LOOK AT AND OFTEN PREFER

University of Michigan——Ann Arbor; Michigan State University; Kalamazoo College

AND RARELY PREFER

Alma College

FINANCIAL FACTS

Financial Aid Rating	81
Annual tuition	$35,454
Room and board	$10,144
Required fees	$412
Books and supplies	$900
% needy frosh rec. need-based scholarship or grant aid	100
% needy UG rec. need-based scholarship or grant aid	100
% needy frosh rec. non-need-based scholarship or grant aid	98
% needy UG rec. non-need-based scholarship or grant aid	93
% needy frosh rec. need-based self-help aid	83
% needy UG rec. need-based self-help aid	86
% frosh rec. any financial aid	98
% UG rec. any financial aid	98
% UG borrow to pay for school	67
Average cumulative indebtedness	$37,191
% frosh need fully met	26
% ugrads need fully met	20
Average % of frosh need met	85
Average % of ugrad need met	81

ALFRED UNIVERSITY

ALUMNI HALL, ONE SAXON DRIVE, ALFRED, NY 14802-1205 • ADMISSIONS: 607-871-2115 • FAX: 607-871-2198

STUDENTS SAY " . . ."

Academics

Alfred University is a small school with an impressive range of world-class majors. The school is known for its "excellent art program," particularly its ceramics and glass majors, as well as for its engineering and psychology programs. While some students at Alfred focus only on their majors, students happily report that there are a "variety of academic opportunities" and that it's "easy to take subjects outside your major." This is appreciated by many, including one art student who likes that Alfred offers "other majors versus a traditional art [school] setting. If I had decided to change majors, Alfred has almost every opportunity." Alfred's "outstanding, talented, dedicated" faculty is one of its biggest draws. An English writing student gushes that professors "bring a level of vibrancy and academic encouragement through enthusiasm to the classroom." "The professors are always pushing you to reach your full potential" and are "always willing to put time into student independent projects." Students also rave about the small classes sizes. "It is the closest to one-on-one teaching you can get," a clinical and counseling psychology major notes, and "The classroom size is perfect for a more personalized education."

Life

Alfred's "beautiful," "small" campus and its "somewhat rural location" are big draws for students looking for a quieter academic experience with a strong "sense of community." Of course, its location means the weather isn't exactly tropical. One student notes that it can feel like "it's basically winter here for about 80 percent of the school year, and it snows constantly." Luckily, "There is always something to do on weekends and week days," for distraction, such as "student club productions…and fundraisers and an excellent selection of movies shown on campus." On top of that, "There are so many clubs and options that you can find something to do," and "Every sports team is supported, and superfans are at every event." "The facilities are amazing," particularly the "great" art buildings and the engineering facilities. Alfred's "strong equestrian program" and barn are also a big draw. Students find some of Alfred's dorms to be "pretty outdated," and there's a bit of grumbling about the "hit-or-miss" and "expensive" dining facilities.

Student Body

Alfred has a "warm" atmosphere, and "You can't go down the street without receiving a smile." Students are "friendly, outgoing, and involved," and many do community service work and are active in one of Alfred's many clubs or organizations. The prominent art school means that there's a large presence of creative types on campus, and the equally prominent engineering school ensures a good mix of personalities. One student notes, "A pretty significant gap between the prevalent, spunky art students and the more reclusive engineers," but another adds that this means students are "well-acquainted with people from a variety of studies and backgrounds and with a variety of interests." Most people believe that "everyone finds their own little niche," but they appreciate that it "definitely does not mean they stay there—you are allowed to float between everything." In fact, "More often than not, you'll see engineers rubbing elbows with philosophy majors and artists chilling with math and chemistry majors."

ALFRED UNIVERSITY

FINANCIAL AID: 607-871-2159 • E-MAIL: ADMISSIONS@ALFRED.EDU • WEBSITE: WWW.ALFRED.EDU

THE PRINCETON REVIEW SAYS

Admissions

Very important factors considered include: Class rank, GPA, rigor of secondary school record, extracurricular activities, character/personal qualities. *Important factors considered include:* Standardized test scores, application essay, recommendation(s), volunteer work, work experience. *Other factors considered include:* First generation, interview, racial/ethnic status, talent/ability, level of applicant's interest. SAT or ACT required; ACT with or without Writing component accepted. TOEFL required of all international applicants. *Academic units required:* 4 English; . *Academic units recommended:* 4 English; 4 mathematics; 3 science; (3 science lab); 3 social studies; 1 foreign language.

Financial Aid

Students should submit: FAFSA, Institution's own financial aid form, State aid form, Noncustodial PROFILE, Business/Farm Supplement. Regular filing deadline is 3/15. The Princeton Review suggests that all financial aid forms be submitted as soon as possible after January 1. *Need-based scholarships/grants offered:* Federal Pell, SEOG, State scholarships/grants, private scholarships, the school's own gift aid. *Loan aid offered:* Direct Subsidized Stafford Loans, Direct Unsubsidized Stafford Loans, Direct PLUS loans, Federal Perkins Loans, College/university loans from institutional funds. Federal Work-Study Program available. Institutional employment available. Off-campus job opportunities are poor.

The Inside Word

Alfred is a fine university with a solid local reputation. The allure for arts students is obvious—Alfred's programs in the arts are especially well-regarded—and as a result, competition is fiercest among applicants for these programs. A killer portfolio, even more than great grades and standardized test scores, is your most likely ticket in. Competition for the engineering school is also tight. Applicants will need to have thrived in a rigorous high school program.

THE SCHOOL SAYS "..."

From the Admissions Office

"The admissions process at Alfred University is the foundation for the personal attention each student can expect during their time at AU. Each applicant is evaluated individually and receives genuine, individual care and consideration.

"The best way to discover all Alfred University has to offer is to come to campus. We truly have something for everyone with more than fourty courses of study, twenty-one NCAA Division III sports and two IHSA sports and over eighty student-run clubs and organizations. You can tour campus; meet current students, faculty, coaches and staff; attend a class; and eat in our dining hall—experience firsthand what life at AU is like.

"Alfred University is a place where students are free to pursue their interests—all of them—no matter how varied or different. Academics, athletics, co-ops, study abroad, internships, special interests—they're all part of what makes you who you are and who you are going to become."

SELECTIVITY

Admissions Rating	75
# of applicants	3,417
% of applicants accepted	70
% of acceptees attending	22
# offered a place on the wait list	91
% accepting a place on wait list	36
% admitted from wait list	33
# of early decision applicants	49
% accepted early decision	92

FRESHMAN PROFILE

Range SAT Critical Reading	490–590
Range SAT Math	510–610
Range SAT Writing	460–570
Range ACT Composite	22–27
Minimum paper TOEFL	550
Minimum web-based TOEFL	213
Average HS GPA	3.18
% graduated top 10% of class	16
% graduated top 25% of class	43
% graduated top 50% of class	84

DEADLINES

Early decision	
Deadline	12/1
Notification	12/15
Regular	
Priority	2/1
Deadline	8/1
Nonfall registration?	Yes

APPLICANTS ALSO LOOK AT AND OFTEN PREFER
Rochester Institute of Technology; Clarkson University

AND SOMETIMES PREFER
State University of New York—University at Buffalo; Ithaca College

AND RARELY PREFER
Hartwick College

FINANCIAL FACTS

Financial Aid Rating	80
Annual tuition	$27,824
Room and board	$11,618
Required fees	$950
Books and supplies	$1,150
% needy frosh rec. need-based scholarship or grant aid	100
% needy UG rec. need-based scholarship or grant aid	99
% needy frosh rec. non-need-based scholarship or grant aid	78
% needy UG rec. non-need-based scholarship or grant aid	62
% needy frosh rec. need-based self-help aid	90
% needy UG rec. need-based self-help aid	89
% frosh rec. any financial aid	92
% UG rec. any financial aid	90
% UG borrow to pay for school	82
Average cumulative indebtedness	$33,467
% frosh need fully met	11
% ugrads need fully met	14
Average % of frosh need met	87
Average % of ugrad need met	83

ALLEGHENY COLLEGE

ALLEGHENY COLLEGE, MEADVILLE, PA 16335 • ADMISSIONS: 814-332-4351 • FAX: 814-337-0431

CAMPUS LIFE
Quality of Life Rating	77
Fire Safety Rating	74
Green Rating	97
Type of school	Private
Affiliation	United Methodist
Environment	Town

STUDENTS
Total undergrad enrollment	2,126
% male/female	46/54
% from out of state	46
% frosh from public high school	83
% frosh live on campus	99
% ugrads live on campus	90
# of fraternities (% ugrad men join)	5 (31)
# of sororities (% ugrad women join)	5 (33)
% African American	4
% Asian	3
% Caucasian	80
% Hispanic	6
% Native American	<1
% international	2
# of countries represented	41

SURVEY SAYS . . .
Political activism is unpopular or nonexistent
Lab facilities are great
Career services are great
Students are friendly
Athletic facilities are great

ACADEMICS
Academic Rating	93
% students returning for sophomore year	85
% students graduating within 4 years	74
% students graduating within 6 years	79
Calendar	Semester
Student/faculty ratio	12:1
Profs interesting rating	90
Profs accessible rating	92

Most classes have 10–19 students.
Most lab/discussion sessions have
20–29 students.

MOST POPULAR MAJORS
psychology; biology; economics

STUDENTS SAY ". . ."

Academics

Allegheny College in western Pennsylvania is a school "where people exude passion about what they are involved in," and the curriculum is "all about applying your knowledge to your experiences." The school allows students to combine completely unrelated majors and minors (in fact, it requires both), which means students "practically create [their] own education," and a student has "the freedom to dabble in my many areas of interest." "Allegheny students are known for their 'unusual combinations' of interests such as a major in biology and a minor in dance," explains a student. This "unique and valuable educational experience" provided by a school that "truly cares about the learning process" is a boon to students looking to forge any path in life (as well as those who are unsure), and the small population means that there are "many researching opportunities." "Faculty members reach out to students about internship and research opportunities often."

The "amazing," "very passionate" professors "go above and beyond to make sure their students understand the material." Professors are "great about teaching the material to you in a variety of ways until you understand." "I have never once felt dumb or like I couldn't handle something after getting help one on one," says a student. "I love my professors. I consider some of them to be friends, and most of them to be mentors," says another. Professors focus on student contribution "in and out of the classroom," so there are lectures, but students are the main focus. If you would rather have peers look at your work, then "there are plenty of consultants and tutors who are more than willing to help." The "workload is large," and the academics are demanding, but "the school is very understanding of how special and different each student is and tries to help each student excel in their own way."

Life

Attending Allegheny "is a lot of work," but "there is still time to be social and make the best friends of your life." "It can get wild on weekends," but for the most part people "are very studious during the week," and "students care for their grades." With so much leeway in academic studies, it's not surprising that the administration is concerned with "making sure that there is a place for everyone." Student activities are well-organized and plentiful, and the school works just as hard at "promoting [a] statement of community." The school organizes many late night activities: "We always have some type of performer, like comedians, musicians, or magicians." "There is a place for everyone with the different clubs and organizations on campus," says a student. "If you get involved enough, you'll rarely have a boring moment," says a student. The "mutual respect [among] students, faculty, and the administration" feeds into the overall happy satisfaction with life, and "Most students find their area either through work, class, sports, or clubs." Greek life is healthy here, but not overpowering. Some say that food services "are repetitive and not very good"; luckily, the green, scenic campus "has many open spaces," and the school's commitment toward sustainability has always been apparent.

Student Body

Allegheny's strong emphasis on community invites "very diverse" students who are "completely accepting and understanding of everyone's needs, interests, and feelings." Upperclassmen are "really welcoming to freshmen," and "the importance of being unique" is stressed from the get-go. Everyone is fun loving, but "always knows when to stop socializing and get to work." This "mixed bag" all get along well, but "we usually have at least a tiny nerdy side." Cliques aren't that common among this group of 2,100 "liberal, idealistic, and global thinkers," and though students normally find their niche within the first three semesters, they "are always eager to meet new people and do new things." Students say that there "is a lot of support to help minority students fit in."

FINANCIAL AID: 800-835-7780 • E-MAIL: ADMISSIONS@ALLEGHENY.EDU • WEBSITE: WWW.ALLEGHENY.EDU

THE PRINCETON REVIEW SAYS

Admissions

Very important factors considered include: Class rank, GPA, rigor of secondary school record. *Important factors considered include:* Standardized test scores, extracurricular activities, interview, recommendation(s), character/personal qualities, level of applicant's interest. *Other factors considered include:* Application essay, first generation, geographical residence, racial/ethnic status, talent/ability, volunteer work, work experience, alumni/ae relations. SAT or ACT required; ACT with Writing component recommended. TOEFL required of all international applicants. *Academic units required:* 4 English; 3 mathematics; 3 science; 3 social studies; 2 foreign language; 1 academic elective.

Financial Aid

Students should submit: FAFSA. The Princeton Review suggests that all financial aid forms be submitted as soon as possible after January 1. *Need-based scholarships/grants offered:* Federal Pell, SEOG, State scholarships/grants, private scholarships, the school's own gift aid. *Loan aid offered:* Direct Subsidized Stafford Loans, Direct Unsubsidized Stafford Loans, Direct PLUS loans, Federal Perkins Loans. Federal Work-Study Program available. Institutional employment available. Off-campus job opportunities are excellent.

The Inside Word

A whopping 70 percent of Allegheny's student body is in the top 25 percent of their class. The typical admit here has solid high school grades in a demanding curriculum and above-average standardized test scores. The school's stellar admissions officers are known to take the time to get to know applicants' full profiles and prove to be strong advocates for students during the admissions process.

THE SCHOOL SAYS "..."

From the Admissions Office

"Allegheny is the premier college in the country for students with 'Unusual Combinations' of interests and talents. Students develop combinations of majors and minors in areas that may, at first glance, seem unrelated: biology and economics; political science and music; history and psychology. There is an abiding passion for learning and life and shared inquiry that spans individuals as well as areas of study. Building on a combination of academic disciplines and passions, every student completes a comprehensive Senior Project. This significant piece of original scholarly work has a creative, analytical or experimental focus and the experience culminates with an oral defense in front of faculty experts and mentors. The project demonstrates the skills most prized by employers and graduate schools: the ability to complete a major assignment, to work independently, to analyze and synthesize information and to write and speak persuasively. Exploring academic disciplines from multiple perspectives leads students to extraordinary outcomes. Biochemistry majors highlight their skills learned in communication arts to start marketing careers at the Environmental Protection Agency. English majors collaborate with our pre-health advisors and enjoy acceptance rates to graduate and medical schools between 80 and 100 percent—twice the national average. Over and over again, we hear from leaders in business, government, medicine, education and community service that the future belongs to individuals who are innovators, inventors, and big picture thinkers, those who think both analytically and creatively. It is this preparation for the global marketplace that Allegheny is known for providing."

SELECTIVITY

Admissions Rating	89
# of applicants	4,512
% of applicants accepted	65
% of acceptees attending	21
# offered a place on the wait list	174
% accepting a place on wait list	100
% admitted from wait list	4
# of early decision applicants	125
% accepted early decision	45

FRESHMAN PROFILE

Range SAT Critical Reading	530–640
Range SAT Math	540–650
Range SAT Writing	520–630
Range ACT Composite	23–29
Minimum paper TOEFL	550
Minimum web-based TOEFL	80
Average HS GPA	3.74
% graduated top 10% of class	41
% graduated top 25% of class	70
% graduated top 50% of class	95

DEADLINES

Early decision	
Deadline	11/15
Notification	12/15
Regular	
Deadline	2/15
Notification	4/1
Nonfall registration?	Yes

APPLICANTS ALSO LOOK AT AND OFTEN PREFER

Boston University; Bucknell University; Kenyon College; University of Rochester; Denison University

AND SOMETIMES PREFER

The College of Wooster; Skidmore College; Gettysburg College; Dickinson College

FINANCIAL FACTS

Financial Aid Rating	87
Annual tuition	$40,260
Room and board	$10,320
Required fees	$400
Books and supplies	$1,000
% needy frosh rec. need-based scholarship or grant aid	100
% needy UG rec. need-based scholarship or grant aid	100
% needy frosh rec. non-need-based scholarship or grant aid	21
% needy UG rec. non-need-based scholarship or grant aid	16
% needy frosh rec. need-based self-help aid	82
% needy UG rec. need-based self-help aid	86
% frosh rec. any financial aid	100
% UG rec. any financial aid	99
% frosh need fully met	38
% ugrads need fully met	32
Average % of frosh need met	91
Average % of ugrad need met	88

AMERICAN UNIVERSITY

4400 MASSACHUSETTS AVENUE, NORTHWEST, WASHINGTON, D.C. 20016-8001 • ADMISSIONS: 202-885-6000 • FAX: 202-885-1025

CAMPUS LIFE

Quality of Life Rating	87
Fire Safety Rating	74
Green Rating	99
Type of school	Private
Affiliation	Methodist
Environment	Metropolis

STUDENTS

Total undergrad enrollment	6,830
% male/female	39/61
% from out of state	81
% frosh live on campus	98
# of fraternities (% ugrad men join)	11 (21)
# of sororities (% ugrad women join)	12 (19)
% African American	6
% Asian	6
% Caucasian	57
% Hispanic	10
% Native American	<1
% international	7
# of countries represented	114

SURVEY SAYS . . .
Career services are great
Students love Washington, DC
Great off-campus food
Political activism is popular
Internships widely available
Students environmentally aware
Campus feels safe

ACADEMICS

Academic Rating	82
% students returning for sophomore year	88
% students graduating within 4 years	76
% students graduating within 6 years	80
Calendar	Semester
Student/faculty ratio	12:1
Profs interesting rating	79
Profs accessible rating	74

MOST POPULAR MAJORS
international relations; business/commerce;
mass communication/media studies

STUDENTS SAY ". . ."

Academics
American University exploits its Washington, D.C., location—that facilitates a strong faculty, prestigious guest lecturers, and "a wealth of internship opportunities"—to offer "incredibly strong programs" in political science and international relations. "The poli-sci kids are all going to be president one day, and the international studies ones are all going to save the world," a student insists. The school of communication also excels, and the school works hard to accommodate "interdisciplinary majors and the opportunities associated with studying them," which include "taking advantage of the resources of the city. The school values learning out of the classroom as much as learning in the classroom." As you might expect from a school with a strong international relations program, "AU's study abroad program is one of the best." Although AU "does not have the automatically recognizable prestige of nearby Georgetown," that's not necessarily a drawback; on the contrary, "the administration and professors go out of their way to ensure a great academic experience," in part because the school is trying to "climb in the rankings and gain recognition as one of the nation's top universities." However, some concede, "The university could improve programs in other fields, aside from its specialties in international studies, public affairs, business, and communication."

Life
"The greatest strength of AU is the activity level both politically and in the community," students tell us, noting that the most recent election the campus "was a proxy holy war…Whether it was signs in windows, talk in the class or in the hallways, t-shirts, or canvassing in Metro-accessible Virginia, students on both sides took November 4 religiously." As one student explains, "Let's put it this way: A politician who comes to campus is likely to draw about 90 percent of the student population [and] an AU basketball game, about 9 [percent]." Students get involved in the community through "campus outreach by student-run organizations," which many see as "the school's greatest asset." The typical undergrad is "incredibly engaged and active…Students seek internships in every line of work, becoming actively involved in a field of interest before graduation." When it's time to relax, "Washington, D.C., offers limitless opportunities to explore." Many "enjoy partying and hanging out off-campus and on campus (even though AU is a 'dry campus')," but there are also "a lot of people who don't drink and have a very good time just using what D.C. has to offer: museums, restaurants, parks, cinemas, theaters, and shops." As one student sums it up: "The city is the school's greatest resource. You will never run out of things to do in Washington."

Student Body
AU attracts a crowd that "tends to be very ideologically driven." "Liberals run the show," most here agree, although they add that "Plenty of students don't fit this mold, and I've never seen anyone rejected for what they believe." The campus "is very friendly to those with alternative lifestyles (GLBT, vegetarian, green-living, etc.)," but students with more socially conservative inclinations note that "while AU boasts about the many religious groups on campus, there is still a general antipathy toward piety." The perception that some departments outshine others is reflected in the way students perceive each other; one says, "You have the political studies know-it-alls, the international studies student who thinks he is going to save the world, the artsy film/communication students, and the rest [who] are unhappy students who couldn't get into George Washington or Georgetown."

FINANCIAL AID: 202-885-6100 • E-MAIL: ADMISSIONS@AMERICAN.EDU • WEBSITE: WWW.AMERICAN.EDU

THE PRINCETON REVIEW SAYS

Admissions

Very important factors considered include: GPA, rigor of secondary school record, level of applicant's interest. *Important factors considered include:* Standardized test scores, application essay, extracurricular activities, recommendation(s), volunteer work, character/personal qualities. *Other factors considered include:* First generation, geographical residence, racial/ethnic status, talent/ability, work experience, alumni/ae relations. SAT or ACT required; ACT with Writing component required. TOEFL required of all international applicants. *Academic units required:* 4 English; 3 mathematics; 3 science; (2 science lab); 2 social studies; 2 foreign language; 3 academic electives. *Academic units recommended:* 4 mathematics; 4 science; 4 social studies; 3 foreign language; 4 academic electives.

Financial Aid

Students should submit: FAFSA, CSS/Financial Aid PROFILE. Regular filing deadline is 2/15. The Princeton Review suggests that all financial aid forms be submitted as soon as possible after January 1. *Need-based scholarships/grants offered:* Federal Pell, SEOG, State scholarships/grants, private scholarships, the school's own gift aid. *Loan aid offered:* Direct Subsidized Stafford Loans, Direct Unsubsidized Stafford Loans, Direct PLUS loans, Federal Perkins Loans, College/university loans from institutional funds. Applicants will be notified of awards beginning 4/1. Federal Work-Study Program available. Institutional employment available. Off-campus job opportunities are excellent.

The Inside Word

Despite strong competition from other area powerhouses, American sees a strong application pool that allows it to be very selective. Admissions rates have declined significantly in recent years. In addition to asking students to indicate their intended field of study, the university is also interested in clear demonstrations of interest on the part of applicants.

THE SCHOOL SAYS " . . ."

From the Admissions Office

"A college centered research university, American's rigorous curriculum challenges you to combine serious theoretical study with meaningful, real-world learning experiences. Whatever major you choose, you will acquire a solid foundation in liberals arts while pursuing in-depth study in your chosen field. You won't be confined to a single course of study or even be limited to traditional learning venues and methodologies. We encourage you to learn in every imaginable way—across disciplines, departments, and schools. Beyond that, we offer innovative programs that take you out of the classroom and into the realm of experience. Washington, D.C. is a laboratory for learning. Few locations can compare when it comes to internships of global importance. AU places special emphasis on balancing classroom time with active learning and application of knowledge. Eighty-eight percent of responding graduates held one or more internships. For all who participate, internships provide a firm foundation in both academic and practical achievement. Our post-graduation census of 2012 graduates (with a response rate of 81 percent) speak to excellent post-graduation outcomes: Nine out of ten (89 percent) 2012 AU grads were employed, enrolled in graduate school, or both, within six months of graduation. Almost half (48.9 percent) of those working secured jobs before completing their degrees. Nine out of ten (92 percent) new AU grads who work hold a position related to their degree or career objective. Experience and networks prove valuable: Nine out of ten students who interned or studied abroad were employed or enrolled in grad school within six months. Of those who are working or in graduate school, 92 percent had internships and 61 percent studied abroad while at American."

SELECTIVITY

Admissions Rating	95
# of applicants	17,545
% of applicants accepted	41
% of acceptees attending	21
# offered a place on the wait list	1,465
% accepting a place on wait list	64
% admitted from wait list	0
# of early decision applicants	968
% accepted early decision	67

FRESHMAN PROFILE

Range SAT Critical Reading	590–690
Range SAT Math	570–660
Range SAT Writing	580–680
Range ACT Composite	26–30
Minimum paper TOEFL	550
Average HS GPA	3.74
% graduated top 10% of class	47
% graduated top 25% of class	78
% graduated top 50% of class	96

DEADLINES

Early decision	
Deadline	1/15
Notification	2/15
Regular	
Deadline	1/15
Notification	4/1
Nonfall registration?	Yes

APPLICANTS ALSO LOOK AT AND OFTEN PREFER

The George Washington University; Georgetown University; Brown University; Tufts University; Boston College; The College of William & Mary; Harvard College

AND SOMETIMES PREFER

Boston University; New York University

AND RARELY PREFER

Northeastern University; Fordham University

FINANCIAL FACTS

Financial Aid Rating	82
Annual tuition	$41,316
Required fees	$517
Books and supplies	$800
% needy frosh rec. need-based scholarship or grant aid	90
% needy UG rec. need-based scholarship or grant aid	77
% needy frosh rec. non-need-based scholarship or grant aid	32
% needy UG rec. non-need-based scholarship or grant aid	34
% needy frosh rec. need-based self-help aid	92
% needy UG rec. need-based self-help aid	91
% UG borrow to pay for school	44
Average cumulative indebtedness	$32,000
% frosh need fully met	34
% ugrads need fully met	18
Average % of frosh need met	84
Average % of ugrad need met	69

ANGELO STATE UNIVERSITY

ASU STATION #11014, SAN ANGELO, TX 76909-1014 • ADMISSIONS: 325-942-2041 • FAX: 325-942-2078

CAMPUS LIFE

Quality of Life Rating	78
Fire Safety Rating	94
Green Rating	79
Type of school	Public
Environment	City

STUDENTS

Total undergrad enrollment	5,503
% male/female	46/54
% from out of state	3
% frosh from public high school	96
% frosh live on campus	73
% ugrads live on campus	32
# of fraternities (% ugrad men join)	3 (8)
# of sororities (% ugrad women join)	2 (7)
% African American	8
% Asian	1
% Caucasian	55
% Hispanic	30
% Native American	<1
% international	3
# of countries represented	24

SURVEY SAYS . . .
Lots of conservative students
Athletic facilities are great
Intramural sports are popular

ACADEMICS

Academic Rating	73
% students returning for sophomore year	55
% students graduating within 4 years	12
% students graduating within 6 years	28
Calendar	Semester
Student/faculty ratio	18:1
Profs interesting rating	75
Profs accessible rating	75

Most classes have 20–29 students.
Most lab/discussion sessions have fewer than 10 students.

MOST POPULAR MAJORS
multi-/interdisciplinary studies; business administration and management; health professions

STUDENTS SAY ". . ."

Academics

A formidable player in the Texas Tech University System, Angelo State offers students a "very affordable" education coupled with a "wide range of degree programs." Importantly, a "small-town feel" permeates the campus, and students are quick to assert that "you're not just a number at Angelo." While the university has a handful of great departments, undergrads here are especially quick to highlight the stellar biology, nursing, physical therapy, and music programs. Like many schools, the quality of professors can run the gamut. Fortunately, as one undergrad happily shares, the vast majority are "brilliant, energetic, and inspiring." Indeed, they're "enthusiastic about their subjects" and "genuinely care about their students." And while they "have high success standards, [they] are also willing to do almost anything to help you meet those standards." Another student elaborates, "Angelo State's faculty is very dedicated to their students and to helping us grow. There is never a need to hesitate to ask a question, or to speak with a professor one on one for better understanding." Finally, one extremely content student sums up the Angelo State experience with the confident assertion, "I feel like I am receiving the best education money can buy!"

Life

Undergrads at Angelo State proudly proclaim that their campus is "always alive and buzzing." The university sponsors a number of events that "range from movie marathons to Monopoly, Texas Hold'em, and Call of Duty tournaments." One happy undergrad eagerly adds to the list, "On campus, there are many activities to get involved as for example, intramural sports, video games available in main lobbies at each dorm, a renovated…[rec center] with new equipment. There are also many events on campus sponsored by a student council and they bring comedians, singers, and other fun activities." A fellow student interjects, "The combination of the brand new fitness center with the popular intramural activities has made this a very active campus, where physical education and team sports are very popular." Hometown San Angelo is "relatively small" and "conservative." However, "Plenty of good restaurants" are available along with bowling, shopping, and movies. Lastly, when students are itching to get away, they can easily explore all that Texas has to offer. As one eager undergrad elaborates, "The good news is that we are centrally located. Because we are only about three or four hours from Lubbock, San Antonio, Austin, or the DFW area, most students plan multiple trips to these areas throughout the semester."

Student Body

When asked to describe their peers, the first adjective that leaps out of the mouths of Angelo State students is "friendly." Indeed, most students "seem outgoing and involved in many different activities around school or in the community." In addition, they're "down-to-earth" and aim to "balance [their] social life with making good grades." As one ecstatic student gushes, "I haven't spoken with a student that has found a place where he/she has not felt welcome." Indeed, we are assured, "To fit in, all you have to do is get involved in something—that way the different networks of friends are available to you and you get to know a lot of people." Finally, it should be noted that the university also has a decent number of returning students, and most report a seamless transition. As one student shares, "Nontraditional students blend in quite well. I have a family and live off campus, but I feel very comfortable in the classroom and interacting with all students and professors."

FINANCIAL AID: 325-942-2246 • E-MAIL: ADMISSIONS@ANGELO.EDU • WEBSITE: WWW.ANGELO.EDU

THE PRINCETON REVIEW SAYS

Admissions

Very important factors considered include: Class rank, standardized test scores. *Important factors considered include:* Rigor of secondary school record. *Other factors considered include:* GPA, SAT or ACT required; ACT with or without Writing component accepted. TOEFL required of all international applicants. *Academic units recommended:* 4 English; 4 mathematics; 4 science; 2 foreign language; 1 visual/performing arts.

Financial Aid

Students should submit: FAFSA. The Princeton Review suggests that all financial aid forms be submitted as soon as possible after January 1. *Need-based scholarships/grants offered:* Federal Pell, SEOG, State scholarships/grants, private scholarships, the school's own gift aid, federal nursing scholarships. *Loan aid offered:* Direct Subsidized Stafford Loans, Direct Unsubsidized Stafford Loans, Direct PLUS loans, Federal Perkins Loans, Federal Nursing Loans, State Loans, College/university loans from institutional funds. Federal Work-Study Program available. Institutional employment available. Off-campus job opportunities are good.

The Inside Word

The admissions criteria for Angelo State are fairly straightforward. Applicants must have successfully completed a rigorous college prep program and, depending on where their class ranking falls, meet specific standardized test requirements. Those who don't meet the minimum requirements might still be admitted on a conditional basis.

THE SCHOOL SAYS "..."

From the Admissions Office

"Angelo State University remains an affordable institution with a superb record of sending graduates on to success in business, agribusiness, health care, and education as well as in medical, law, and professional school. ASU maintains strong academic programs in traditional fields, such as physics, biology, mathematics, education, business, agriculture, and nursing, while developing innovative offerings like the computer science department's computer gaming design sequence, ranked by The Princeton Review as one of the top fifty in the nation.

"Because of strong academics and a substantial gift aid program, including the Carr Scholarship Program, which annually awards scholarships totaling approximately $4 million, ASU remains one of the top educational values in Texas. About 73 percent of ASU students receive gift aid, financial support which does not have to be repaid to the university. ASU targets students with minimum scores of 980 SAT and 21 ACT for gift aid. Additionally, ASU offers its Carr Blue and Gold Guarantee program for students from low income families.

"Because of its low eighteen to one student/faculty ratio and individualized instruction, ASU attracts many first-generation students, who benefit from special programs and scholarships. A quarter of the student body is Hispanic, enhancing the university's overall diversity. Comprehensive academic advising and numerous opportunities for international study enhance the college experience on the 268-acre Angelo State campus known for its safety and modern academic, residential and recreational facilities."

SELECTIVITY

Admissions Rating	69
# of applicants	2,599
% of applicants accepted	80
% of acceptees attending	58

FRESHMAN PROFILE

Range SAT Critical Reading	420–520
Range SAT Math	440–540
Range ACT Composite	18–23
Minimum paper TOEFL	550
Minimum web-based TOEFL	213
% graduated top 10% of class	11
% graduated top 25% of class	35
% graduated top 50% of class	73

DEADLINES

Regular	
Deadline	8/27
Nonfall registration?	Yes

FINANCIAL FACTS

Financial Aid Rating	74
Annual In-state tuition	$4,700
Annual out-of-state tuition	$15,560.40
Room and board	$7,756
Required fees	$2,942
Books and supplies	$1,200
% needy frosh rec. need-based scholarship or grant aid	77
% needy UG rec. need-based scholarship or grant aid	65
% needy frosh rec. non-need-based scholarship or grant aid	61
% needy UG rec. non-need-based scholarship or grant aid	38
% needy frosh rec. need-based self-help aid	74
% needy UG rec. need-based self-help aid	77
% frosh rec. any financial aid	87
% UG rec. any financial aid	81
% UG borrow to pay for school	58
Average cumulative indebtedness	$25,728
% frosh need fully met	16
% ugrads need fully met	13
Average % of frosh need met	76
Average % of ugrad need met	65

ARIZONA STATE UNIVERSITY

PO Box 870112, Tempe, AZ 85287-0112 • Admissions: 480-965-7788 • Fax: 480-965-3610

CAMPUS LIFE
Quality of Life Rating	76
Fire Safety Rating	88
Green Rating	97
Type of school	Public
Affiliation	No Affiliation
Environment	Metropolis

STUDENTS
Total undergrad enrollment	61,815
% male/female	50/50
% from out of state	28
% frosh live on campus	73
% ugrads live on campus	20
# of fraternities (% ugrad men join)	34 (6)
# of sororities (% ugrad women join)	25 (7)
% African American	5
% Asian	6
% Caucasian	58
% Hispanic	20
% Native American	2
% international	5
# of countries represented	119

SURVEY SAYS . . .
Great library
Internships are widely available
Great off-campus food
Lots of beer drinking
Hard liquor is popular
Everyone loves the Sun Devils
Student publications are popular

ACADEMICS
Academic Rating	76
% students returning for sophomore year	84
% students graduating within 4 years	37
% students graduating within 6 years	59
Calendar	Semester
Student/faculty ratio	20:1
Profs interesting rating	71
Profs accessible rating	71

Most classes have 10–19 students.
Most lab/discussion sessions have 20–29 students.

MOST POPULAR MAJORS
psychology; interdisciplinary studies; communications and media studies

STUDENTS SAY ". . ."

Academics
Arizona State University's "greatest strength is the great depth of its faculty and wealth of opportunities offered to students." Many students say they chose ASU because it "offers a huge range of classes and majors at a reasonable cost for in-state students." Students also say the university provides "the best of both worlds: a large research university and an honors program tailored for individual needs." The Honors College and The Walter Cronkite School of Journalism and Mass Communication stand out as notable programs that offer "targeted education." A marketing management major says "Even though ASU is considered to be a 'party school,' it only is if...you choose." Many ASU students agree, believing they get from the university what they put into it, reporting, "A large number of students truly care about the education they are receiving." At ASU, "class size can range from 15 to 440 students," while "for the most part, ASU is home to engaging professors that are genuinely concerned with the success of their students."

Life
At ASU, "there is always something happening on campus," and students say, "ASU is all about diversity and open doors; there are a million distinct opportunities to get involved in whatever you're passionate about." Many rave, "Campus life is amazing. There is always something to do, someone to hang out with, or places to be," adding, "The weather is nice enough to sit outside and study a lot." A kinesiology major says, "The overall culture is very Southern California," but "the west side of campus has more of a Portland feel, which is more individual and artsy. It all depends on where you decide to get plugged in." Many students praise ASU's dedication to "pursuing new ways to become more sustainable and encouraging 'going green' throughout campus, classrooms, and offices," though some would like to see more parking and stronger technology infrastructure. Others complain that ASU needs to "improve in advising and the overall process of changing a major," and say, "The red tape can be very frustrating, especially as a new student."

Student Body
With an enrollment of more than 50,000 undergraduates, "It's hard to define typical" when it comes to describing the ASU student body. "Due to the huge student population size and plethora of social events and organizations, any student can find a niche and a group of people with similar interests." Students are unconcerned about ASU's historical reputation: "We are known as a party school everywhere else but here...if you spend time on campus you realize there are many more students that are all about getting involved and learning as much as they can than there are kids that just want to go to college to party." Other students say, "Even the party kids care about their grades," and the typical student is "laid-back but invested in their future." One political science major jokes, "I would say the hardest part for students fitting in is dealing with the heat." Most agree, "The 'dry campus' rules are *far* from followed, and even for those who don't break those rules, there are places right across the street for students to drink at their leisure," adding, "Tempe is great—if you're in college," and "Tempe has many fun activities both indoors and outdoors, depending on the weather! From hiking to biking, all kinds of sports, going downtown and being around the museums and history, to having a good time hanging out with friends on Mill Avenue."

FINANCIAL AID: 480-965-3355 • E-MAIL: ADMISSIONS@ASU.EDU • WEBSITE: WWW.ASU.EDU

THE PRINCETON REVIEW SAYS
Admissions
Very important factors considered include: Class rank, GPA, standardized test scores. *Important factors considered include:* Rigor of secondary school record. *Other factors considered include:* State residency, SAT or ACT recommended; SAT and SAT Subject Tests or ACT required for some; ACT with or without Writing component accepted. TOEFL required of all international applicants. *Academic units required:* 4 English; 4 mathematics; 3 science; (3 science lab); 1 social studies; 2 foreign language; 1 history.

Financial Aid
Students should submit: FAFSA. The Princeton Review suggests that all financial aid forms be submitted as soon as possible after January 1. *Need-based scholarships/grants offered:* Federal Pell, SEOG, State scholarships/grants, private scholarships, the school's own gift aid, United Negro College Fund. *Loan aid offered:* Direct Subsidized Stafford Loans, Direct Unsubsidized Stafford Loans, Direct PLUS loans, Federal Perkins Loans, State Loans. Federal Work-Study Program available. Institutional employment available. Off-campus job opportunities are good.

The Inside Word
ASU clearly outlines all the requirements for admission on its website. The applications of students who do not meet all the requirements go under "individual review" and are carefully evaluated by the admissions team. Students interested in Barrett, The Honors College may apply for admission only after submitting an application to ASU.

THE SCHOOL SAYS " . . ."
From the Admissions Office
"ASU is breaking down the walls of the traditional academic experience to increase the impact of education and research in local and global communities. As the New American University, ASU is committed to interdisciplinary connections, academic excellence, and societal impact. We are bold and forward-thinking, and we see challenges as opportunities.

"With 300-plus undergraduate majors, ASU is a learning environment where personal expression is valued as much as research and discovery. ASU champions intellectual and cultural diversity and welcomes students from all fifty states and 120-plus nations. Our distinguished faculty receives prestigious honors including the Nobel Prize and membership in the National Academies. Student achievements include Goldwater, Rhodes, Marshall, and Fulbright scholars.

"ASU has four unique campuses in metropolitan Phoenix. State-of-the-art living and learning facilities are found at ASU's Downtown Phoenix campus. The campus creates strong learning and career connections for 10,000-plus students with media, health care, corporate, and government organizations.

"The Polytechnic campus, located in Mesa, Arizona, is home to 3,500-plus students who are exploring professional and technical programs. Thousands of square feet of new laboratory space make way for project-based learning.

"ASU welcomes 48,500-plus students studying at the historic Tempe campus. The Sun Devils athletic complex, performing arts facilities, and high-tech research space create a dynamic and engaging learning environment.

"At the West campus in northwest Phoenix, ASU offers business, education, and interdisciplinary arts and science programs to 3,500-plus students. The campus's award-winning architecture and lush landscaping are designed to create a close-knit learning community."

SELECTIVITY
Admissions Rating	80
# of applicants	35,294
% of applicants accepted	76
% of acceptees attending	38

FRESHMAN PROFILE
Range SAT Critical Reading	480–610
Range SAT Math	500–630
Range ACT Composite	21–27
Minimum paper TOEFL	500
Minimum web-based TOEFL	61
Average HS GPA	3.39
% graduated top 10% of class	28
% graduated top 25% of class	56
% graduated top 50% of class	85

APPLICANTS ALSO LOOK AT AND OFTEN PREFER
University of Arizona; Northern Arizona University

AND SOMETIMES PREFER
University of California--Los Angeles; Universitiy of Southern California

DEADLINES
Regular	
Priority	2/1
Nonfall registration?	Yes

FINANCIAL FACTS
Financial Aid Rating	75
Annual in-state tuition	$9,484
Annual out-of-state tuition	$23,136
Room and board	$9,340
Required fees	$518
Books and supplies	$1,040
% needy frosh rec. need-based scholarship or grant aid	98
% needy UG rec. need-based scholarship or grant aid	91
% needy frosh rec. non-need-based scholarship or grant aid	11
% needy UG rec. non-need-based scholarship or grant aid	8
% needy frosh rec. need-based self-help aid	59
% needy UG rec. need-based self-help aid	73
% frosh rec. any financial aid	92
% UG rec. any financial aid	84
% UG borrow to pay for school	57
Average cumulative indebtedness	$21,371
% frosh need fully met	21
% ugrads need fully met	17
Average % of frosh need met	65
Average % of ugrad need met	57

ASSUMPTION COLLEGE

500 SALISBURY STREET, WORCESTER, MA 01609-1296 • ADMISSIONS: 508-767-7285 • FAX: 508-799-4412

STUDENTS SAY ". . ."

Academics

Located in the liberal arts college haven of Worcester, MA, Assumption College is "a tight knit, faith-based community where everyone is part of a family." The small school focuses on "educating aware and prospective young adults to become active and productive members of society while maintaining human core values" through "service, meaningful discussions, and liberal arts classes." Assumption is definitely all about education ("especially if you are a science major"), but there is also "a big push for sports" at this Division II school, and perhaps as a result the college's sense of community is "amazing." "We are one school, we are Assumption," says a student. The "beyond helpful" professors here are "engaging," "approachable," and "have a diversity of teaching styles," as well as being "willing to talk to you whenever you need it and [caring] about your well-being." They "bring their personal experiences into the classroom" to make studies "interesting and enjoyable," and the application of the liberal arts curriculum to small classes means that students "receive a greater impact" from their learning. "The professors here at Assumption all love what they do and it is obvious in the classroom," says a junior. However, some do admit that the school is "limited on the number of courses offered" which "can make getting into classes a little difficult." This "very welcoming and inclusive institution" focuses on giving its student every resource possible to help them succeed and be happy; tutoring is provided at the academic center, campus jobs are "abundant," and the Career and Internship Center admirably aids students in finding jobs after graduation. "Guidance counselors, teachers, [and] coaches are truly a blessing to have at this college," says a student. Overall, Assumption "helps foster well rounded, creative, intelligent and caring young adults to be successful and morally sound in their future endeavors."

Life

Life at Assumption is great. It's "easy to meet new people" and "there is a great sense of belonging." "Assumption does a great job of getting people involved one way or another," says a student. The "beautiful, diverse and secured campus" is "easily recognizable" from brochures, and those who get to take advantage of it "are very invested in academics, sports, extracurriculars, and social experiences." There is always an activity going on and "always something to do if you want to get off campus" in the college town of Worcester. Housing is guaranteed all four years and around 90% of students choose to take advantage of this, but "weekends can be dead sometimes" when students leave campus.

The school is "strict as far as drinking goes": Make no mistake, Assumption is "a VERY Catholic school" that "has a very conservative feel." This doesn't mean there's not fun to be had; though during the week "everyone is either in the library or involved in clubs/sports," once Thursday hits "upperclassmen flock to Leits off campus while underclassmen stick to their dorms." "Friday and Saturday are the go to nights for parties" for those that choose to so; however, a large majority go to the events the campus activities board puts on "like BINGO Nights, movie nights, trivia, [and] family feud." "They are really fun and have some amazing prizes like iPads, TV's, etc." says a student.

Student Body

Though there's a lack of socioeconomic diversity—"generally middle class Caucasians that are heterosexual"—students can be separated into "student-athletes and non-student-athletes." Most students "come from Catholic upbringings or have attended Catholic school but are not necessarily religious." New England preppy is a classic style; girls are usually seen in "leggings, Ugg boots, a North Face jacket." People here are "generally happy" and "very sociable and approachable" in all aspects of the college; everyone is "courteous and [will] hold doors open or lend you a calculator in class if your forgot yours." Overall, the student body "is like no other": People "genuinely care about each other and it makes for a wonderful experience."

FINANCIAL AID: 508-767-7158 • E-MAIL: ADMISS@ASSUMPTION.EDU • WEBSITE: WWW.ASSUMPTION.EDU

THE PRINCETON REVIEW SAYS

Admissions

Very important factors considered include: GPA, rigor of secondary school record. *Important factors considered include:* Essay, interview, recommendation(s), volunteer work, level of applicant's interest. *Other factors considered include:* Class rank, standardized test scores, extracurricular activities, first generation, racial/ethnic status, talent/ability, alumni/ae relations, character/personal qualities. SAT or ACT considered if submitted; ACT with or without Writing component accepted. TOEFL required of all international applicants. *Academic units required:* 4 English; 3 mathematics; 2 science; 2 foreign language; 2 history; 5 academic electives.

Financial Aid

Students should submit: FAFSA. Regular filing deadline is 2/15. The Princeton Review suggests that all financial aid forms be submitted as soon as possible after January 1. *Need-based scholarships/grants offered:* Federal Pell, SEOG, State scholarships/grants, private scholarships, the school's own gift aid. *Loan aid offered:* Direct Subsidized Stafford Loans, Direct Unsubsidized Stafford Loans, Direct PLUS loans, Federal Perkins Loans, State Loans, College/university loans from institutional funds. Federal Work-Study Program available. Institutional employment available. Off-campus job opportunities are good.

The Inside Word

Around three-quarters of those who apply to Assumption are admitted; keeping in mind that the applicant pool is somewhat self-selective, average students shouldn't have a hard time getting in. Assumption uses the Common Application and submitting standardized test scores is optional.

THE SCHOOL SAYS "..."

From the Admissions Office

"Students flourish at Assumption College. Established in 1904 by the Augustinians of the Assumption, the College is a Catholic coeducational institution known for its classic liberal arts curriculum and strong programs in business and professional studies. Approximately 2,000 undergraduates choose among 42 majors and 47 minors, gaining the depth and breadth of knowledge that is the foundation of lifelong success. The educational experience is grounded in the Catholic intellectual tradition, which cultivates both the intellect and personal values and the academic atmosphere is marked by individual attention and the quest for excellence. Undergraduates and graduate students engage with a highly credentialed faculty and staff in a thriving community that fosters critical intelligence, thoughtful citizenship and compassionate service. With a student/faculty ratio of just 12:1, Assumption's professors challenge students to ask questions, find their answers and grow intellectually, socially and spiritually. Students gain important professional experience through our internship program and independent research projects. Ninety-nine percent of our Class of 2013 was employed or in graduate school within six months of graduation."

"Assumption's beautiful 185-acre campus is situated in a residential neighborhood minutes from downtown Worcester, Massachusetts, (including a campus in Rome, Italy) and 90 percent of the College's undergraduate population lives on campus, with housing guaranteed all four years. The campus is lively seven days a week with academic programming, activities sponsored by student clubs and organizations, community service opportunities, campus ministry programs; and intercollegiate, intramural and club sports. The College's state-of-the-art recreation center supports the well-being of all students."

SELECTIVITY
Admissions Rating	72
# of applicants	4,659
% of applicants accepted	74
% of acceptees attending	15
# offered a place on the wait list	368
% accepting a place on wait list	31
% admitted from wait list	11

FRESHMAN PROFILE
Range SAT Critical Reading	510–595
Range SAT Math	510–620
Range ACT Composite	23–27
Minimum paper TOEFL	550
Minimum web-based TOEFL	80
Average HS GPA	3.32
% graduated top 10% of class	10
% graduated top 25% of class	40
% graduated top 50% of class	79

DEADLINES
Early action	
Deadline	11/1
Notification	12/15
Regular	
Deadline	2/15
Nonfall registration?	Yes

FINANCIAL FACTS
Financial Aid Rating	78
Annual tuition	$34,475
Required fees	$500
Books and supplies	$1,000
% needy frosh rec. need-based scholarship or grant aid	100
% needy UG rec. need-based scholarship or grant aid	100
% needy frosh rec. non-need-based scholarship or grant aid	11
% needy UG rec. non-need-based scholarship or grant aid	12
% needy frosh rec. need-based self-help aid	83
% needy UG rec. need-based self-help aid	84
% frosh rec. any financial aid	99
% UG rec. any financial aid	98
% UG borrow to pay for school	79
Average cumulative indebtedness	$33,481
% frosh need fully met	16
% ugrads need fully met	18
Average % of frosh need met	73
Average % of ugrad need met	74

AUBURN UNIVERSITY

108 Mary Martin Hall, Auburn, AL 36849-5149 • Admissions: 334-844-4080 • Fax: 334-844-6436

CAMPUS LIFE
Quality of Life Rating	98
Fire Safety Rating	80
Green Rating	91
Type of school	Public
Affiliation	No Affiliation
Environment	Town

STUDENTS
Total undergrad enrollment	19,761
% male/female	51/49
% from out of state	37
% frosh from public high school	86
% frosh live on campus	69
% ugrads live on campus	21
# of fraternities (% ugrad men join)	30 (25)
# of sororities (% ugrad women join)	17 (43)
% African American	7
% Asian	2
% Caucasian	85
% Hispanic	3
% Native American	1
% international	1
# of countries represented	83

SURVEY SAYS . . .
Lots of conservative students
Students are happy
Lab facilities are great
Career services are great
School is well run
Students are friendly
Students get along with local community
Students love Auburn, AL
Campus feels safe
Lots of beer drinking
Everyone loves the Tigers
Frats and sororities are popular
Alumni active on campus
Active student government

ACADEMICS
Academic Rating	76
% students returning for sophomore year	89
% students graduating within 4 years	38
% students graduating within 6 years	68
Calendar	Semester
Student/faculty ratio	18:1
Profs interesting rating	74
Profs accessible rating	78

Most classes have 20–29 students.
Most lab/discussion sessions have 20–29 students.

MOST POPULAR MAJORS
mechanical engineering; business administration and management; secondary education

STUDENTS SAY ". . ."

Academics
Auburn University is a traditional Southern school full of Southern hospitality that provides a surprisingly "family-like atmosphere" for a school of 25,000 and an unsurprising level of school spirit. "Auburn people are proud to be Auburn people," says a student. Such a large student body has the power to enact change, and the school actually listens to the constant desire "to improve academically, to make the campus safer and the facilities better, to improve the aesthetic appeal of the campus, and to address student demands." "Auburn has really accessible faculty and administration that care if the students here succeed." With this constant growth added to longstanding tradition, the university is "all about the Auburn family—whether it's football games, student organizations, or academics, we're all in it together!" Along with its generous scholarships, the school's reputable honors program and veterinary and engineering schools are also big draws, but "there's a major for everyone." "I'll be the first one to tell you that Auburn engineers are some of the best you'll ever have the pleasure of working with," says an engineering student. Some professors are "amazing," and "Others are less than that," but students are generally satisfied. "For the most part, my professors have been extremely intelligent people who further my knowledge and are able to increase my interest in subjects I might not have had interest in," says a student. The faculty emphasizes "not the course material, but how to apply what we learn in the classroom to real-life issues and to look beyond just knowing but understanding." Finally, the research at Auburn is "top-notch." Regardless of your area of study, the school provides "many services to help you achieve the goal you are trying to accomplishment."

Life
Auburn is "a big school in a small college town, where the people are friendly and love their football." On this "nice comfortable campus," everyone is "amiable, outgoing, and pleasant," and "there are so many groups and ways to get involved that it's almost ridiculous. If you can think of it, you can find a class or club about it!" As one student lovingly puts it, "Auburn creates a sense of family during the first few months after moving away from your biological family, and it lasts through life." To say "Auburn football is popular" is to make the understatement of the century; "Football is religion at Auburn," and students say, "If you don't like Auburn football at least a little, you might have trouble finding friends to do things with on a Saturday!" UPC at Auburn "provides many events around campus that are free to students for students to have fun," and people often "go to fraternity parties or downtown" from Wednesday to Saturday. The nearby arboretum and Chewacla Park are "nice places to go" for hiking, camping, and outdoor activities.

Student Body
Though the school was once mainly populated by Alabamans, "Auburn is becoming more diverse," and a large percentage are from out-of-state (though still mainly the South), so "it's not hard to fit in...because you meet people that came from areas just like you." There are also a fair number of legacy Tigers here who are carrying on family tradition: "I was born an Auburn Tiger...my doorbell at home plays the Auburn fight song, and I was also grounded for a week in high school for saying 'roll tide' to my father. He said it was disrespectful," one student says. Typical students "tend to look like they are in fraternities or sororities—even if they aren't in them" (though about a third of students are). Most students "have good values and aren't prejudiced toward anyone in particular," and there are so many types of people and groups that "it is practically impossible to not find somewhere you fit in."

AUBURN UNIVERSITY

FINANCIAL AID: 334-844-4634 • E-MAIL: ADMISSIONS@AUBURN.EDU • WEBSITE: WWW.AUBURN.EDU

THE PRINCETON REVIEW SAYS

Admissions

Very important factors considered include: GPA, standardized test scores, application essay. *Important factors considered include:* Rigor of secondary school record, extracurricular activities, first generation, geographical residence, state residency, talent/ability, volunteer work, work experience, alumni/ae relations, character/personal qualities, level of applicant's interest. *Other factors considered include:* Recommendation(s). SAT or ACT required; ACT with Writing component required. TOEFL required of all international applicants. *Academic units required:* 4 English; 3 mathematics; 2 science; (1 science lab); 3 social studies. *Academic units recommended:* (2 science lab); 4 social studies; 1 foreign language.

Financial Aid

Students should submit: FAFSA. The Princeton Review suggests that all financial aid forms be submitted as soon as possible after January 1. *Need-based scholarships/grants offered:* Federal Pell, SEOG, State scholarships/grants, private scholarships, the school's own gift aid. *Loan aid offered:* Direct Subsidized Stafford Loans, Direct Unsubsidized Stafford Loans, Direct PLUS loans, Federal Perkins Loans, Federal Nursing Loans, College/university loans from institutional funds. Federal Work-Study Program available. Institutional employment available. Off-campus job opportunities are good.

The Inside Word

Auburn admissions officers have more than 15,000 applications to sort through each year. Applicants meeting certain baseline GPA, curricular, and standardized test score levels are admitted by rule. Applicants who fall far short of these baselines are nearly always rejected, except for those with unique talents and traits that will contribute substantially to campus life. Letters of recommendation, essays, and extracurricular activities are the make-or-break point for borderline candidates. Applicants' test scores must be submitted directly from the testing agencies.

THE SCHOOL SAYS "..."

From the Admissions Office

"Auburn University is a comprehensive land-grant university serving Alabama and the nation. The university is especially charged with the responsibility of enhancing the economic, social, and cultural development of the state through its instruction, research, and extension programs. In all of these programs, the university is committed to the pursuit of excellence. The university assumes an obligation to provide an environment of learning in which the individual and society are enriched by the discovery, preservation, transmission, and application of knowledge; in which students grow intellectually as they study and do research under the guidance of competent faculty; and in which the faculty develop professionally and contribute fully to the intellectual life of the institution, community, and state. This obligation unites Auburn University's continuing commitment to its land-grant traditions and the institution's role as a dynamic and complex, comprehensive university."

SELECTIVITY

Admissions Rating	81
# of applicants	15,745
% of applicants accepted	83
% of acceptees attending	29

FRESHMAN PROFILE

Range SAT Critical Reading	520–620
Range SAT Math	540–650
Range SAT Writing	510–620
Range ACT Composite	24–30
Minimum paper TOEFL	550
Minimum web-based TOEFL	79
Average HS GPA	3.74
% graduated top 10% of class	29
% graduated top 25% of class	60
% graduated top 50% of class	86

DEADLINES

Early action	
Deadline	10/1
Notification	10/15
Regular	
Priority	2/1
Deadline	6/1
Notification	2/15
Nonfall registration?	Yes

APPLICANTS ALSO LOOK AT AND SOMETIMES PREFER

University of Florida; University of Georgia; University of Alabama—Tuscaloosa; Clemson University; Georgia Institute of Technology; University of Mississippi

FINANCIAL FACTS

Financial Aid Rating	70
Annual in-state tuition	$8,256
Annual out-of-state tuition	$24,768
Room and board	$11,552
Required fees	$1,596
Books and supplies	$1,200
% needy frosh rec. need-based scholarship or grant aid	86
% needy UG rec. need-based scholarship or grant aid	73
% needy frosh rec. non-need-based scholarship or grant aid	11
% needy UG rec. non-need-based scholarship or grant aid	8
% needy frosh rec. need-based self-help aid	66
% needy UG rec. need-based self-help aid	79
% frosh rec. any financial aid	49
% UG rec. any financial aid	45
% UG borrow to pay for school	41
Average cumulative indebtedness	$26,990
% frosh need fully met	15
% ugrads need fully met	14
Average % of frosh need met	49
Average % of ugrad need met	45

AUSTIN COLLEGE

900 North Grand Ave, Suite 6N Sherman, TX 75090-4400 • Admissions: 903-813-3000 • Fax: 903-813-3198

CAMPUS LIFE

Quality of Life Rating	82
Fire Safety Rating	74
Green Rating	83
Type of school	Private
Affiliation	Presbyterian
Environment	Town

STUDENTS

Total undergrad enrollment	1,208
% male/female	49/51
% from out of state	9
% frosh from public high school	84
% frosh live on campus	98
% ugrads live on campus	81
# of fraternities (% ugrad men join)	6 (19)
# of sororities (% ugrad women join)	6 (22)
% African American	6
% Asian	15
% Caucasian	58
% Hispanic	16
% Native American	1
% international	3
# of countries represented	9

SURVEY SAYS . . .
Students are happy
Internships are widely available
Students are friendly
Easy to get around campus

ACADEMICS

Academic Rating	89
% students returning for sophomore year	83
% students graduating within 4 years	62
% students graduating within 6 years	73
Calendar	4/1/4
Student/faculty ratio	12:1
Profs interesting rating	95
Profs accessible rating	92

Most classes have 10–19 students.
Most lab/discussion sessions have 10–19 students.

MOST POPULAR MAJORS
biology; business, psychology

STUDENTS SAY ". . ."

Academics

"Individual attention" is the name of the game at Austin College. Indeed, the small size of the school allows for a lot of "one-on-one interaction" and provides students with "many opportunities to get involved on campus." Additionally, students are grateful that Austin seems to maintain a healthy financial aid office. A psychology major concurs stating, "This college was very generous in helping fund my education." Undergrads are also excited about Austin's "excellent study abroad program." As one thrilled biology major brags, "I have already traveled to Trinidad for three weeks and I am planning to study in Cuba for three weeks as well as a semester abroad in Australia." Students also rave about the college's "GREAT pre-medicine program," "strong Japanese program" and excellent five year education program. Importantly, undergrads find their professors to be "very accessible." They are generally "willing to help and give us opportunities to advance ourselves outside the classroom as well as inside the classroom." Moreover, professors are "devoted to teaching their students how to think, not memorize." Finally, they "encourage their students to engage the material and ask meaningful questions."

Life

Despite its small size, Austin College is certainly a hotbed of activity. Truly, there are a myriad of clubs and events from which to choose. As one amazed senior shares, "I have played in a woodwind ensemble, done swing dancing and English country dancing, [attended] theater performances, art displays, choir, band and symphony concerts." She continues gushing, "There [have even been] mini carnivals with rock walls, live music, food, and inflatable race courses." And undergrads here are quick to tip their (metaphorical) hats to the Campus Activities Board (CAB) which "[throws] events almost every day." These might include "making wax hands…[and] pumpkin painting." Additionally, "CAB also hosts bigger events such as Kangapalooza where the college brings in three bands to play for the student body." While there are plenty of school events, a handful of students feel that "house parties sponsored by Greek groups are usually what encompass social life at Austin." Some students itching to get off campus are dismayed by hometown Sherman which doesn't seem to offer much beyond "Target and a few book stores." However, others insist there is more than meets the eye. As an optimistic international relations major sums up, "At first, Sherman seemed really small to a big city girl like me. But it really grows on you and now I love it! There are lots of great little hole-in-the-wall restaurants with awesome food. And if you need some city time, Dallas is about an hour away!"

Student Body

Undergrads here emphatically insist that "there is no typical student at AC." As one biology major explains, "Personalities range from frat-tastic jock to the gothic president of the English Country Dancing club." Fortunately, most everyone is "very welcoming." Indeed, "the environment here is so warm and friendly that the students easily fit in." Nevertheless, despite the reported uniqueness of the student body, there are some commonalities to be found. For starters, most undergrads here are "motivated in their studies" as well as "engaged in other extracurricular activities." Many students also describe their peers as "laid back," "pretty liberal" and "open minded." Of course, Austin does net "a lot of local Texas kids." However, there are definitely "some foreign students thrown in [there]" and students appreciate the diversity they bring to campus. And if you're still wary, this junior is moved to assuage your fears, "After coming to campus it doesn't take long to realize that even though most of us call Texas home, we are in no way defined by the Texas stereotype. Don't be deceived; the differences in socio-economic status, religion, political beliefs, and general perspective on life could not be more varied."

FINANCIAL AID: 903-813-2900 • E-MAIL: ADMISSION@AUSTINCOLLEGE.EDU • WEBSITE: WWW.AUSTINCOLLEGE.EDU

THE PRINCETON REVIEW SAYS

Admissions

Very important factors considered include: GPA, rigor of secondary school record. *Important factors considered include:* Class rank, standardized test scores, application essay, extracurricular activities, recommendation(s), talent/ability, character/personal qualities. *Other factors considered include:* First generation, geographical residence, interview, racial/ethnic status, state residency, volunteer work, work experience, alumni/ae relations, religious affiliation. SAT or ACT required; ACT with Writing component required. TOEFL required of all international applicants. *Academic units required:* 4 English; 3 mathematics; 3 science; (2 science lab); 2 social studies; 2 foreign language; 1 academic elective; 1 visual/performing arts. *Academic units recommended:* 4 English; 4 mathematics; 4 science; (3 science lab); 3 social studies; 3 foreign language; 2 visual/performing arts.

Financial Aid

Students should submit: FAFSA. The Princeton Review suggests that all financial aid forms be submitted as soon as possible after January 1. *Need-based scholarships/grants offered:* Federal Pell, SEOG, State scholarships/grants, private scholarships, the school's own gift aid. *Loan aid offered:* Direct Subsidized Stafford Loans, Direct Unsubsidized Stafford Loans, Direct PLUS loans, Federal Perkins Loans, State Loans. Federal Work-Study Program available. Institutional employment available. Off-campus job opportunities are good.

The Inside Word

Austin College takes a holistic approach to the admissions game. Indeed, the school does its best to get a feel for who each applicant is beyond his or her GPA and test scores. Therefore, expect your recommendations, extracurricular activities, and essay to be heavily vetted. Additionally, the college is impressed with students who challenge themselves academically. Admissions officers are frequently more impressed with a B in an honors course than an A in a standard college prep class.

THE SCHOOL SAYS "..."

From the Admissions Office

"If you want to be anonymous, choose a different school. But if you dream of connecting with others, exploring the world, and discovering more about yourself, then Austin College is exactly where you belong.

"Learning happens in classroom discussions led by talented professors, dedicated to teaching and passionate about their work, who act as partners in education with students. Faculty and students often work together in research projects and learning opportunities in which sometimes the answers discovered aren't as important as the process of inquiry and discovery.

"Students come to Austin College for exceptional academic offerings in more than forty-five areas of study in the humanities, sciences, and social sciences. Among 2012 graduates, 83 percent completed an internship as career preparation. More than 40 percent of first-year alumni attend graduate school; graduates enjoy an 80 percent acceptance rate into healthcare programs, with the highest numbers going to medical school, and law school applicants also are successful. Within five years of graduation, 63 percent of alumni begin graduate or professional studies. Many graduates receive prestigious honors like Fulbright grants or Teach for America positions.

"Few schools the size of Austin College offer a greater emphasis on all things global. Within the Class of 2012, for example, 78 percent of students had at least one international study experience, either during January Term or a semester abroad program. For the past decade, an average 70 percent of graduates have had an international experience."

SELECTIVITY

Admissions Rating	89
# of applicants	3,138
% of applicants accepted	59
% of acceptees attending	12
# offered a place on the wait list	9
% accepting a place on wait list	56
% admitted from wait list	40

FRESHMAN PROFILE

Range SAT Critical Reading	540–660
Range SAT Math	560–670
Range SAT Writing	520–630
Range ACT Composite	23–27
Minimum paper TOEFL	550
Minimum web-based TOEFL	213
Average HS GPA	3.56
% graduated top 10% of class	35
% graduated top 25% of class	74
% graduated top 50% of class	95

DEADLINES

Early action	
Deadline	1/15
Notification	3/1
Regular	
Priority	1/15
Deadline	5/1
Nonfall registration?	Yes

APPLICANTS ALSO LOOK AT AND OFTEN PREFER

Trinity University, Southwestern University

AND SOMETIMES PREFER

Baylor University; Texas A&M University—College Station; Texas Christian University

AND RARELY PREFER

Hendrix College; University of Dallas

FINANCIAL FACTS

Financial Aid Rating	86
Annual tuition	$34,655
Room and board	$11,503
Required fees	$185
Books and supplies	$1,250
% needy frosh rec. need-based scholarship or grant aid	100
% needy UG rec. need-based scholarship or grant aid	99
% needy frosh rec. non-need-based scholarship or grant aid	15
% needy UG rec. non-need-based scholarship or grant aid	73
% needy frosh rec. need-based self-help aid	75
% needy UG rec. need-based self-help aid	75
% frosh rec. any financial aid	100
% UG rec. any financial aid	100
% frosh need fully met	21
% ugrads need fully met	22
Average % of frosh need met	83
Average % of ugrad need met	77

BABSON COLLEGE

231 FOREST STREET, BABSON PARK, MA 02457 • ADMISSION: 781-239-5522 • FAX: 781-239-4006

CAMPUS LIFE

Quality of Life Rating	93
Fire Safety Rating	77
Green Rating	95
Type of school	Private
Affiliation	No Affiliation
Environment	Village

STUDENTS

Total undergrad enrollment	2,106
% male/female	55/45
% from out of state	78
% frosh live on campus	100
% ugrads live on campus	81
# of fraternities (% ugrad men join)	3 (14)
# of sororities (% ugrad women join)	3 (18)
% African American	4
% Asian	12
% Caucasian	39
% Hispanic	10
% Native American	<1
% international	26
# of countries represented	72

SURVEY SAYS . . .
Students are happy
Classroom facilities are great
School is well run
Great financial aid
Great off-campus food
Campus feels safe
Active student government
Active minority support groups

ACADEMICS

Academic Rating	95
% students returning for sophomore year	95
% students graduating within 4 years	84
% students graduating within 6 years	91
Calendar	Semester
Student/faculty ratio	15:1
Profs interesting rating	94
Profs accessible rating	91
Most classes have 30–39 students.	

MOST POPULAR MAJORS
business administration and management

STUDENTS SAY ". . ."

Academics

An AASCB-accredited business school with both graduate and undergraduate programs, Babson College "aims to create future leaders" through an "innovative curriculum" emphasizing "entrepreneurial thought and action." In the first year, incoming "freshman essentially take the same core classes," which include the yearlong Foundations of Management and Entrepreneurship course. "Class size is generally between 20–60 students," which means there is plenty of opportunity for group work and discussion (here, attendance and participation are often factored into your final grade). "Engaging and approachable," professors not only "encourage creativity" but "express a genuine concern for student learning." In fact, "most professors are quick to give out their numbers/Skypes and are available at odd hours, even when they are not on campus." Relying heavily on "case-based learning," Babson professors "had successful business careers" before joining the faculty, and "the material that we learn in the classroom is applicable to the current business world." At the same time, the school maintains a "great sense of corporate social responsibility," making Babson an appropriate choice for students with diverse career goals, from future bankers to start-up visionaries. Here, you'll meet "students who are heavily invested in starting their own businesses...while others are studying how environmental justice and conservationism plays a role in the corporate world and how environmentalism is evolving in the business world." Savvy business students see a good return on investment at Babson. Despite the wavering economy, one student states that "Over 99 percent of Babson students either have a job or are pursuing higher education six months after graduation." Plus, "students have direct access to all of the Babson alumni, who are always helpful."

Life

Outside the classroom, Babson's serious overachievers "get involved with the campus in as many ways as possible—Greek life, athletics, special interest groups, community service organizations"—with many holding leadership positions in at least one of those activities, often as early as freshman year. Highly career-focused, "Students constantly think about landing an internship or being the best candidate for employment," while some "come to Babson having already started several ventures and then go on to run several more while in school." Busy as they are, most undergrads also maintain a vibrant social life. Come the weekend, students flock to "themed parties" and fraternity shindigs, or gather at the "pub on campus," a popular destination for students over 21. That said, "while there are a good number of parties on-campus, it's not so prevalent that students feel pressured to drink to have a good time or fit in." From campus, the school operates "shuttles into Boston that go up until 2:00 A.M. on the weekends," letting students spend the day in the city without driving.

Student Body

You'll find a few predominant "types" on campus—"wealthy international students," New England prep-school graduates, athletes—though students say Babson is a "diverse" school, "with about 30 percent of the student body coming from outside of the United States." Some Babson undergraduates are "taking on a lot of loans to come here," but students notice that most of their classmates "come from affluent families" and favor a "preppy" style ("not a lot of interesting tattoos, piercings, multicolored hair, etc."). Movers and shakers, "people are very social" at Babson, and most "have large networks of friends." It's worth noting, however, that "students at Babson are very focused on building connections with as many people as possible and act in a more professional manner than the typical college student." On that note, Babson undergrads are "passionate about business," and they are all "very motivated and driven to succeed" in their chosen field. In short, "Babson College attracts creative, hardworking, extremely passionate individuals that want to turn their passions into businesses."

FINANCIAL AID: 781-239-4015 • E-MAIL: UGRADADMISSION@BABSON.EDU • WEBSITE: WWW.BABSON.EDU

THE PRINCETON REVIEW SAYS

Admissions

Very important factors considered include: Class rank, GPA, rigor of secondary school record, standardized test scores, application essay, extracurricular activities, recommendation(s), character/personal qualities. *Other factors considered include:* First generation, geographical residence, interview, racial/ethnic status, state residency, talent/ability, volunteer work, work experience, alumni/ae relations, level of applicant's interest. SAT or ACT required. TOEFL required of all international applicants. *Academic units required:* 4 English; 4 mathematics; 3 science; 4 social studies; 4 foreign language.

Financial Aid

Students should submit: FAFSA, CSS/Financial Aid PROFILE, Noncustodial PROFILE. Regular filing deadline is 2/15. The Princeton Review suggests that all financial aid forms be submitted as soon as possible after January 1. *Need-based scholarships/grants offered:* Federal Pell, SEOG, State scholarships/grants, private scholarships, the school's own gift aid. *Loan aid offered:* Direct Subsidized Stafford Loans, Direct Unsubsidized Stafford Loans, Direct PLUS loans, Federal Perkins Loans, State Loans, College/university loans from institutional funds. Applicants will be notified of awards beginning 4/1. Federal Work-Study Program available. Institutional employment available. Off-campus job opportunities are good.

The Inside Word

Babson's national profile is ascending quickly and prospective students can expect admissions standards to likewise rise in the upcoming years. Students are evaluated based on a variety of factors, including academic performance (a GPA between B-plus and A-minus is average for incoming students), standardized test scores, and leadership experience. The school considers writing ability a strong indicator of preparedness for college; proceed accordingly.

THE SCHOOL SAYS "..."

From the Admissions Office

"Nationally recognized as the number one school in entrepreneurship for seventeen years, Babson College defines entrepreneurship education for the world. Our learning concepts provide students with the ability to adapt to ever-changing business environments, the experience to hit the ground running upon graduation, and the know-how to discover opportunities that will create economic and social value everywhere. We believe, as do our graduates and their employers, in the value of an integrated approach combined with experiential education. As a business school where one-half of the classes are in liberal arts, Babson emphasizes creativity, innovation, and risk-taking as essential to learning the foundation of business.

"Babson's close-knit community provides students with the opportunity to form close relationships with faculty and staff. An average class size of twenty-nine and student/faculty ratio of fifteen to one allow faculty to serve as role models and mentors committed to helping our students grow. With about 85 percent holding a doctoral degree, these accomplished business executives, authors, entrepreneurs, scholars, researchers, and artists bring an intellectual diversity and real-world experience that adds depth to Babson's programs. Most importantly, faculty members teach 100 percent of the courses.

"At Babson, students receive a world-class education that is innovative and creative, yet practical. They study business, learn about leadership, and undertake a transformative life experience preparing them to create an authentic, powerful brand of success. Our students make friends, find mentors, and develop long-lasting relationships that will thrive long after graduation."

SELECTIVITY

Admissions Rating	96
# of applicants	6,086
% of applicants accepted	28
% of acceptees attending	28
# offered a place on the wait list	1,359
% accepting a place on wait list	37
% admitted from wait list	5
# of early decision applicants	339

% ACCEPTED EARLY DECISION 44 FRESHMAN PROFILE

Range SAT Critical Reading	550–640
Range SAT Math	610–700
Range SAT Writing	580–670
Range ACT Composite	26–29
Minimum paper TOEFL	600
Minimum web-based TOEFL	100

DEADLINES

Early decision	
Deadline	11/1
Notification	12/15
Early action	
Deadline	11/1
Notification	1/1
Regular	
Priority	11/1
Deadline	1/1
Notification	4/1
Nonfall registration?	Yes

FINANCIAL FACTS

Financial Aid Rating	92
Annual tuition	$45,120
Room and board	$14,494
Required fees	$0
Books and supplies	$1,020
% needy frosh rec. need-based scholarship or grant aid	90
% needy UG rec. need-based scholarship or grant aid	91
% needy frosh rec. non-need-based scholarship or grant aid	12
% needy UG rec. non-need-based scholarship or grant aid	12
% needy frosh rec. need-based self-help aid	88
% needy UG rec. need-based self-help aid	88
% frosh rec. any financial aid	53
% UG rec. any financial aid	50
% UG borrow to pay for school	44
Average cumulative indebtedness	$33,258
% frosh need fully met	48
% ugrads need fully met	48
Average % of frosh need met	96
Average % of ugrad need met	96

BARD COLLEGE (NY)

OFFICE OF ADMISSIONS, ANNANDALE-ON-HUDSON, NY 12504 • ADMISSIONS: 845-758-7472 • FAX: 845-758-5208

CAMPUS LIFE

Quality of Life Rating	77
Fire Safety Rating	86
Green Rating	92
Type of school	Private
Affiliation	No Affiliation
Environment	Rural

STUDENTS

Total undergrad enrollment	1,955
% male/female	44/56
% from out of state	65
% frosh from public high school	60
% frosh live on campus	9
% ugrads live on campus	73
% African American	6
% Asian	4
% Caucasian	62
% Hispanic	2
% Native American	1
% international	11
# of countries represented	60

SURVEY SAYS . . .
Lots of liberal students
Political activism is popular
Students are happy
Lab facilities are great
Class discussions encouraged
No one cheats
Students aren't religious
Campus feels safe
Lots of beer drinking
Theater is popular
Active minority support groups

ACADEMICS

Academic Rating	98
% students returning for sophomore year	87
% students graduating within 4 years	60
% students graduating within 6 years	74
Calendar	Semester
Student/faculty ratio	10:1
Profs interesting rating	99
Profs accessible rating	99
Most classes have 10–19 students.	

MOST POPULAR MAJORS
English language and literature;
social sciences; visual and performing arts

STUDENTS SAY ". . ."

Academics
Bard College is private, liberal arts institution located in the Hudson Valley that boasts a strong arts focus and a dedication to civic engagement locally, nationally, and worldwide in ways that "are unheard of for an institution of this size." The school's "amazing commitment to the arts" and "the variety of people and opinions and attitudes that are available" truly make Bard "a place to think," and the liberal arts atmosphere encourages students to consider their interests from many perspectives. "Bard is about questioning the fundamental assumptions of your existence in society," says one particularly philosophical student. Professors here are "incredibly intelligent" individuals, who despite being high up in their fields "are very down-to-earth and funny," and they are "extremely interested in their students' academic happiness and welfare." Even in lecture-based classes, discussion is abundant, making for a "really fun classroom environment." "We listen and respond to each other's opinions often, and we are encouraged to speak up in class." In turn, students feel personally committed to what they are learning about, instead of just being in class to get the credit or the grade. "Being here makes me feel as if I am gaining not only knowledge, but also maturity and the capacity for critical thought," says a student. The school has a unique system for declaring your major called "moderation" in which students gradually focus their studies and independent work on one or more areas throughout their four years; this "encourages the student to really think hard about what they choose to major in, and ultimately what they're passionate about." "It made me take a deep breath in the middle of college and figure out what really got me excited, and pursue it because of that passion," says one student.

Life
The "low-key atmosphere" at this thought center is echoed by its serene, idyllic surroundings. "We wake up to look at the mountains. We dance till the cows come home," says a student. There is "an obvious community" at Bard that stretches from the classroom to extracurriculars, and "students generally don't separate their social lives from their academic interests." "We get into heated debates on thought experiments," says a student. "It's common to talk about academics at a party on the weekends, and that doesn't feel weird at all." Bard students love to plan events, and these are not limited to the school's "famous dinner parties"; on any given weekend, there is "a plethora of student theater productions, garage band shows, dances, dinner parties, dorm activities, club meetings, magazine release parties, cozy gatherings, off-campus ragers, [and] more dinner parties." People also tend to be politically and socially active, and the care for the environment and for getting involved locally is "impressive." "We live for today and for generations ahead," says a student.

Student Body
Bard students are "eccentric intellectuals" who "like pontificating about anything and everything." Most students are "incredibly interested in an area of study outside of their major," and they are "united by a belief that whatever we are studying is personally important to us and makes us into who we are." "Everyone is a walking contradiction and not what you expect when you look at them," says a student. Pretty much each person you will encounter has a specific academic interest, or a special skill, or a unique background. "We are hipsters, hippies, yuppies, nerds, dorks, freaks, dweebs, and socially awkward—the best people you'll ever meet—kind of kids."

FINANCIAL AID: 845-758-7526 • E-MAIL: ADMISSION@BARD.EDU • WEBSITE: WWW.BARD.EDU

THE PRINCETON REVIEW SAYS

Admissions

Very important factors considered include: GPA, rigor of secondary school record, application essay, extracurricular activities, recommendation(s), talent/ability, character/personal qualities. *Important factors considered include:* Volunteer work, work experience. *Other factors considered include:* Class rank, standardized test scores, first generation, geographical residence, interview, racial/ethnic status, state residency, alumni/ae relations, level of applicant's interest, religious affiliation. SAT and SAT Subject Tests or ACT considered if submitted; ACT with or without Writing component accepted. TOEFL required of all international applicants. *Academic units recommended:* 4 English; 4 mathematics; 4 science; (3 science lab); 4 social studies; 4 foreign language; 4 history.

Financial Aid

Students should submit: FAFSA, CSS/Financial Aid PROFILE, State aid form, Noncustodial PROFILE, Business/Farm Supplement. Regular filing deadline is 2/15. The Princeton Review suggests that all financial aid forms be submitted as soon as possible after January 1. *Need-based scholarships/grants offered:* Federal Pell, SEOG, State scholarships/grants, private scholarships, the school's own gift aid. *Loan aid offered:* Direct Subsidized Stafford Loans, Direct Unsubsidized Stafford Loans, Direct PLUS loans, Federal Perkins Loans, College/university loans from institutional funds. Applicants will be notified of awards beginning 4/1. Federal Work-Study Program available. Institutional employment available. Off-campus job opportunities are good.

The Inside Word

Bard receives more than enough applications from students with the academic credentials to gain admission (ten times more than it can accept each year), so the school has the luxury of focusing on matchmaking. The goal is to find students who can handle the independence allowed here and who will thrive in an intellectually intensive environment. The school requires two application essays; expect both to be very carefully scrutinized by the admissions office.

THE SCHOOL SAYS "..."

From the Admissions Office

"An alliance with Rockefeller University, the renowned graduate scientific research institution, gives Bardians access to Rockefeller's professors and laboratories and to places in Rockefeller's Summer Research Fellows Program. Almost all our math and science graduates pursue graduate or professional studies; 90 percent of our applicants to medical and health professional schools are accepted.

"The Globalization and International Affairs (BGIA) Program is a residential program in the heart of New York City that offers undergraduates a unique opportunity to undertake specialized study with leading practitioners and scholars in international affairs and to gain internship experience with international-affairs organizations. Topics in the curriculum include human rights, international economics, global environmental issues, international justice, managing international risk, and writing on international affairs, among others. Internships/tutorials are tailored to students' particular fields of study.

"Civic engagement has become a large and growing part of student life at Bard, with a high percentage of students participating in a wide variety of local, national, and international programs sponsored by the college or initiated by students.

"Beyond the central campus, Bard has created global programs and satellite campuses from Berlin to the West Bank, offering students unique opportunities for study abroad and making Bard's student body strongly international."

SELECTIVITY

Admissions Rating	95
# of applicants	5,466
% of applicants accepted	38
% of acceptees attending	24
# offered a place on the wait list	404
% accepting a place on wait list	71
% admitted from wait list	31

FRESHMAN PROFILE

Range SAT Critical Reading	600–710
Range SAT Math	570–670
Minimum paper TOEFL	600
Minimum web-based TOEFL	250
Average HS GPA	3.50
% graduated top 10% of class	58
% graduated top 25% of class	92
% graduated top 50% of class	99

DEADLINES

Early action	
Deadline	11/1
Notification	1/1
Regular	
Deadline	1/1
Notification	4/1
Nonfall registration?	No

APPLICANTS ALSO LOOK AT AND OFTEN PREFER

Amherst College; Brown University; Yale University; Harvard College

AND SOMETIMES PREFER

Boston University; Vassar College; Reed College; New York University; Oberlin College

AND RARELY PREFER

Sarah Lawrence College; Skidmore College; Ithaca College; Hampshire College; Macalester College

FINANCIAL FACTS

Financial Aid Rating	90
Annual tuition	$45,730
Room and board	$13,502
Required fees	$640
Books and supplies	$950
% needy frosh rec. need-based scholarship or grant aid	98
% needy UG rec. need-based scholarship or grant aid	98
% needy frosh rec. non-need-based scholarship or grant aid	0
% needy UG rec. non-need-based scholarship or grant aid	0
% needy frosh rec. need-based self-help aid	85
% needy UG rec. need-based self-help aid	78
% frosh rec. any financial aid	73
% UG rec. any financial aid	70
% UG borrow to pay for school	47
Average cumulative indebtedness	$25,664
% frosh need fully met	60
% ugrads need fully met	52
Average % of frosh need met	84
Average % of ugrad need met	80

BARD COLLEGE AT SIMON'S ROCK (MA)

84 ALFORD ROAD, GREAT BARRINGTON, MA 01230 • ADMISSIONS: 413-528-7312 • FAX: 413-528-7334

CAMPUS LIFE
Quality of Life Rating	78
Fire Safety Rating	93
Green Rating	60*
Type of school	Private
Affiliation	No Affiliation
Environment	Village

STUDENTS
Total undergrad enrollment	344
% male/female	42/58
% from out of state	88
% frosh from public high school	71
% frosh live on campus	93
% ugrads live on campus	94
% African American	7
% Asian	6
% Caucasian	57
% Hispanic	2
% Native American	0
% international	10
# of countries represented	15

SURVEY SAYS . . .
Political activism is popular
Students are happy
Class discussions encouraged
No one cheats
Diverse student types on campus
Students aren't religious
Great off-campus food
Campus feels safe
Active minority support groups

ACADEMICS
Academic Rating	99
% students returning for sophomore year	68
% students graduating within 4 years	21
% students graduating within 6 years	28
Calendar	Semester
Student/faculty ratio	6:1
Profs interesting rating	99
Profs accessible rating	97

Most classes have 10–19 students.
Most lab/discussion sessions have 10–19 students.

MOST POPULAR MAJORS
visual and performing arts;
multi-/interdisciplinary studies;
social sciences

STUDENTS SAY ". . ."

Academics

There's no one else doing what Bard College at Simon's Rock is doing. The small, selective "early college" aims "to create a good experience for passionate younger students" through small class sizes, engaging class discussion, and "catering to each student as an individual." All 400 Simon's Rock students come to this "haven for young, bright minds" after tenth or eleventh grade in high school, and while half of the students receive an associate's degree after two years and transfer to other institutions, others moderate into the Simon's Rock B.A. program. The small size of the school "allows for almost unlimited rule-bending, as long as it is beneficial," and the "ability to create your own major" is one of the most lauded academic aspects. "No one has ever told me that a project wasn't my place because I'm an undergrad or that I couldn't do something because there wasn't enough oversight," says a student. "I have been constantly encouraged to pursue my interests by way of independent research, tutorials, internships, etc., and given support at every step of the way."

The school's "idyllic location" in the middle of the Berkshire Mountains provides the perfect level of seclusion for students who mean to get down to business with their studies, and "the professors here make the difficulty and volume of course work worth it." "They are what is amazing about this school." There will be a lot of writing for any class, but "pretty much all the professors are more than happy to help outside of the classroom." "My chemistry professor became upset when she realized that she wouldn't be able to teach a class for a week due to break," says one student. Classes are very oriented around discussion, typically are less than twenty students, and "nothing's off the tradition for questioning and examination." Though all who attend here admit that it is "definitely not a walk in the park," they agree that "you will learn an incredible amount and be prepared for the future."

Life

Because it is an early college, the administration "is more strict about normal college pasttimes (partying, etc.)," but most students spend time hanging out with friends on campus, or going into town (though "there is very little to do" there). "We're far from a party school, but we make our own fun," says a student of the dry campus. People's hobbies "tend toward the academic and/or geeky," and "fun is a *Doctor Who* viewing party or rehearsing for *Rocky Horror*." "It's not uncommon to go to the dining hall and discuss the anti-feminism of *Twilight* at one table, Occupy Wall Street at another table, and tell chemistry puns at another table." (Though, the food doesn't have many fans: "Each day I feel as if the dining hall food is progressively getting worse.") Many students here study abroad during their junior years, and student activities are instigated and run by students, "which means that if you want to start a club or activity group, you're given full support." Mainly, Rockers "spend a significant portion of our time studying. We think about work and talk about work."

Student Body

Students come from every end of the spectrum, but they are all here for the same reason: "We were ready to learn, and we weren't going to let a high school diploma stand in our way." The student body is "99 percent genius"; this is a "liberal, open-minded, bright, precocious" group full of "rigor and self-determination." Most of the incoming students are sixteen or seventeen years of age, but "They can still obtain a bachelor's degree in four years, just like at most other undergraduate schools." This is truly a "ragtag bunch of future political workers and the ragtag misfits from high school mixed in with some cool (albeit tough) professors." "I would say there is relatively little pressure to fit in at all, since a lot of us are high school misfits in the first place," says a student. Unsurprisingly, "You get to know your fellow students very well, as the size of the school is very small."

BARD COLLEGE AT SIMON'S ROCK (MA)

FINANCIAL AID: 413-528-7297 • E-MAIL: ADMIT@SIMONS-ROCK.EDU • WEBSITE: WWW.SIMONS-ROCK.EDU

THE PRINCETON REVIEW SAYS

Admissions

Very important factors considered include: GPA, rigor of secondary school record, application essay, interview, talent/ability. *Important factors considered include:* Recommendation(s), character/personal qualities. *Other factors considered include:* Class rank, standardized test scores, extracurricular activities, first generation, volunteer work, work experience, alumni/ae relations, level of applicant's interest. SAT and SAT Subject Tests or ACT considered if submitted; ACT with or without Writing component accepted. TOEFL required of all international applicants. *Academic units recommended:* 2 English; 2 mathematics; 2 science; 2 social studies; 2 foreign language; 2 history.

Financial Aid

Students should submit: FAFSA, CSS/Financial Aid PROFILE, State aid form, Noncustodial PROFILE. The Princeton Review suggests that all financial aid forms be submitted as soon as possible after January 1. *Need-based scholarships/grants offered:* Federal Pell, SEOG, State scholarships/grants, private scholarships, the school's own gift aid. *Loan aid offered:* Direct Subsidized Stafford Loans, Direct Unsubsidized Stafford Loans, Direct PLUS loans, Federal Perkins Loans. Federal Work-Study Program available. Institutional employment available. Off-campus job opportunities are good.

The Inside Word

Because Simon's Rock boasts healthy application numbers, it's in a position to concentrate on matchmaking. To that end, admissions officers seek students with independent and inquisitive spirits. Applicants who exhibit academic ambition while extending their intellectual curiosity beyond the realm of the classroom are particularly appealing. Successful candidates typically have several honors and advanced placement courses on their transcripts, as well as strong letters of recommendation and well-written personal statements. An interview is required for all applicants.

THE SCHOOL SAYS "..."

From the Admissions Office

"Bard College at Simon's Rock is the only four-year college of the liberal arts and sciences specifically designed to provide bright, highly motivated students with the opportunity to begin college in a residential environment immediately after the tenth or eleventh grade.

"Approximately half of our students transfer after the sophomore year and complete their junior and senior years of college elsewhere. The most common transfer destinations are Bard College, Brown University, Cornell University, New York University, Smith College, Stanford University, University of California—Berkeley, and University of Chicago. For those who choose to complete the BA at Simon's Rock, the graduation rate exceeds 90 percent."

SELECTIVITY

Admissions Rating	90
# of applicants	218
% of applicants accepted	92
% of acceptees attending	72

FRESHMAN PROFILE

Range SAT Critical Reading	690–750
Range SAT Math	600–710
Range SAT Writing	620–710
Range ACT Composite	24–27
Minimum paper TOEFL	600
Minimum web-based TOEFL	250
Average HS GPA	3.71
% graduated top 10% of class	46
% graduated top 25% of class	67
% graduated top 50% of class	89

DEADLINES

Regular	
Priority	2/1
Deadline	5/1
Nonfall registration?	Yes

FINANCIAL FACTS

Financial Aid Rating	76
Annual tuition	$45,618
Room and board	$12,690
Required fees	$1,695
Books and supplies	$1,000
% needy frosh rec. need-based scholarship or grant aid	97
% needy UG rec. need-based scholarship or grant aid	88
% needy frosh rec. non-need-based scholarship or grant aid	0
% needy UG rec. non-need-based scholarship or grant aid	0
% needy frosh rec. need-based self-help aid	76
% needy UG rec. need-based self-help aid	71
% frosh rec. any financial aid	90
% UG rec. any financial aid	86
% UG borrow to pay for school	56
Average cumulative indebtedness	$28,175
% frosh need fully met	14
% ugrads need fully met	13
Average % of frosh need met	76
Average % of ugrad need met	75

BARNARD COLLEGE

3009 BROADWAY, NEW YORK, NY 10027 • ADMISSIONS: 212-854-2014 • FAX: 212-854-6220

STUDENTS SAY " . . ."

Academics

Barnard is a small school, an urban school, a resource-rich school, a school that "offers so many opportunities." In some ways, Barnard College combines all the desirable traits one would want from an all-women's liberal arts college. Located in New York City, here "you get the best of both worlds," both a "small academic setting" as well as having "full access to the Ivy League institution (Columbia University) right across the street." The school's size means it "provides a small, close community" where students will "see familiar faces often." Among those familiar faces are the professors themselves, who are "really engaging and make the material approachable and interesting." Classes are a mix between lectures and discussions, and even in the larger classes professors "definitely make time for students to come talk to them." Students say educators here are adept at "creating an environment to learn from and be inspired by classmates through the discussions held." The "phenomenal" education experience at Barnard may be "challenging and very stressful" at times, but students are "so grateful" for those challenges. And while the school itself may be small, "you can cross Broadway and feel that large, Ivy League University feel." Graduates from Barnard should expect to experience a "transition from a young female college student to an adjusted global citizen."

Life

Finding things to do at Barnard? "It's easy—we live in New York." When you live in "one of the greatest cities on Earth," you are "open to a wide range of things to do such as shows, film festivals, amazing restaurants, etc." As one student puts it, while there is a thriving party scene on campus, "put down your vodka and go to the Met." Students even enjoy free admission to many such attractions. But while the opportunities for entertainment and cultural activities are limitless in a city like New York—the museums, sports venues, book stores, music venues, cultural centers and more are too numerous to list— "a lot of fun events take place on campus." There are a number of clubs on campus, busy students often spend time "just chilling" because "everyone is working or going to office hours, or pursuing an internship, a personal job, etc.," and neighboring Columbia offers a "phenomenal Greek life" for those interested in that scene. No matter their chosen form of distraction from school work and extracurriculars, students here "are intensely dedicated to pursuing their interests, whether that be artistic, academic, pre-professional, or athletic ones."

Student Body

Finding a single trait to define a school full of "cool, creative, confident, well-spoken, and determined" women who are "aware that [they are] in the cosmopolitan NYC" may seem difficult, but the repeated refrain of students makes it clear that there is something that unites Barnard students: They are ambitious. These are "driven, intelligent" women who are "extremely interested, dedicated, and passionate about something." What that something may be varies— "biology, dance, theatre, architecture, economics, or international relations" and more—but the "strong, powerful, intelligent personalities" make them who they are. These "motivated individuals" sometimes "have a tendency to overload," but "all Barnard women are very proactive and use all resources available…to achieve their goals." That said, while students here are "ambitious, driven, and hard workers," it is "not at the cost of physical or mental health: they know how to have fun, too." Barnard women tend to be well-dressed and embrace the cosmopolitan side of New York City. One student comments, "I know of very few students here who feel they don't fit in or haven't found their niche," and maybe that is because a Barnard student is one who is "smart, independent, and ready to take on the world."

FINANCIAL AID: 212-854-2154 • E-MAIL: ADMISSIONS@BARNARD.EDU • WEBSITE: WWW.BARNARD.EDU

THE PRINCETON REVIEW SAYS

Admissions

Very important factors considered include: GPA, rigor of secondary school record, application essay, extracurricular activities, recommendation(s), character/personal qualities. *Important factors considered include:* Class rank, standardized test scores, talent/ability, volunteer work. *Other factors considered include:* First generation, geographical residence, interview, racial/ethnic status, work experience, alumni/ae relations, level of applicant's interest. SAT and SAT Subject Tests or ACT required; ACT with Writing component required. TOEFL required of all international applicants. *Academic units recommended:* 4 English; 3 mathematics; 3 science; (2 science lab); 3 foreign language.

Financial Aid

Students should submit: FAFSA, CSS/Financial Aid PROFILE, State aid form, Noncustodial PROFILE. Regular filing deadline is 2/15. The Princeton Review suggests that all financial aid forms be submitted as soon as possible after January 1. *Need-based scholarships/grants offered:* Federal Pell, SEOG, State scholarships/grants, private scholarships, the school's own gift aid. *Loan aid offered:* Direct Subsidized Stafford Loans, Direct Unsubsidized Stafford Loans, Direct PLUS loans, Federal Perkins Loans. Applicants will be notified of awards beginning 3/31. Federal Work-Study Program available. Institutional employment available. Off-campus job opportunities are excellent.

The Inside Word

Barnard may have a highly competitive selection process—indeed, early decision applications have increased dramatically in recent years—but you wouldn't know it based on the admissions staff, who are surprisingly open and accessible. It comes as no surprise that the admission committee's expectations are high, given the school's long and impressive tradition of excellence, but those expectations reflect a genuine interest in who potential students are and what's on their minds.

THE SCHOOL SAYS ". . ."

From the Admissions Office

"Barnard College is a small, distinguished liberal arts college for women that is partnered with Columbia University and located in the heart of New York City. Barnard students are wide ranging in their interests and passions, but they also share in a distinctive experience that creates an enduring bond: they live and learn in an environment where women always come first, where they're surrounded by other smart and inspiring women, and where they have access to a wide array of opportunities, both on and off campus. The Barnard community thrives on high expectations. By setting rigorous academic standards and giving students the support they need to meet those standards, Barnard enables them to discover their own capabilities.

"The college enrolls women from all over the United States and around the world. More than forty countries, including Australia, Brazil, China, Denmark, France, India, Morocco, Russia, Turkey, and Zimbabwe are represented in the student body. Students pursue their academic studies in more than forty majors and are able to cross register at Columbia University. Students may participate in Division I Varsity Columbia University athletic teams, in more than thirty club sports, and in a wide variety of intramural sports, and have access to over 500 student clubs and organizations at Barnard and Columbia.

"Applicants for the entering class must submit scores from the SAT Reasoning test and two SAT Subject Tests of their choice, or the ACT with the writing component."

SELECTIVITY

Admissions Rating	98
# of applicants	5,606
% of applicants accepted	21
% of acceptees attending	50
# offered a place on the wait list	1,207
% accepting a place on wait list	53
% admitted from wait list	6
# of early decision applicants	599
% accepted early decision	43

FRESHMAN PROFILE

Range SAT Critical Reading	620–730
Range SAT Math	620–710
Range SAT Writing	650–740
Range ACT Composite	28–32
Minimum paper TOEFL	600
Minimum web-based TOEFL	250
Average HS GPA	3.86
% graduated top 10% of class	79
% graduated top 25% of class	98
% graduated top 50% of class	100

DEADLINES

Early decision	
Deadline	11/15
Notification	12/15
Regular	
Deadline	1/1
Notification	4/1
Nonfall registration?	Yes

APPLICANTS ALSO LOOK AT AND OFTEN PREFER

Yale University; University of Pennsylvania; Harvard College; Brown University; Columbia University

AND SOMETIMES PREFER

Tufts University; Northwestern University; Princeton University; Wesleyan University; Wellesley College; Stanford University; The University of Chicago

AND RARELY PREFER

Boston College; Bryn Mawr College; Fordham University; Vassar College; University of California—Berkeley

FINANCIAL FACTS

Financial Aid Rating	95
Annual tuition	$44,300
Room and board	$14,660
Required fees	$1,740
% needy frosh rec. need-based scholarship or grant aid	97
% needy UG rec. need-based scholarship or grant aid	98
% needy frosh rec. need-based self-help aid	100
% needy UG rec. need-based self-help aid	100
% frosh rec. any financial aid	54
% UG rec. any financial aid	50
% UG borrow to pay for school	45
Average cumulative indebtedness	$18,815
% frosh need fully met	100
% ugrads need fully met	100
Average % of frosh need met	100
Average % of ugrad need met	100

BATES COLLEGE

23 CAMPUS AVENUE, LEWISTON, ME 04240 • ADMISSIONS: 207-786-6000 • FAX: 207-786-6025

CAMPUS LIFE

Quality of Life Rating	87
Fire Safety Rating	95
Green Rating	87
Type of school	Private
Affiliation	No Affiliation
Environment	Town

STUDENTS

Total undergrad enrollment	1,753
% male/female	47/53
% from out of state	89
% frosh from public high school	53
% frosh live on campus	100
% ugrads live on campus	92
% African American	4
% Asian	4
% Caucasian	74
% Hispanic	5
% Native American	<1
% international	6
# of countries represented	71

SURVEY SAYS . . .

Students are happy
Students are friendly
Students environmentally aware
Great food on campus
Lots of beer drinking

ACADEMICS

Academic Rating	94
% students returning for sophomore year	95
% students graduating within 4 years	85
% students graduating within 6 years	88
Calendar	Semester
Student/faculty ratio	10:1
Profs interesting rating	94
Profs accessible rating	94

Most classes have fewer than 10 students.
Most lab/discussion sessions have 20–29 students.

MOST POPULAR MAJORS

political science; psychology; history

STUDENTS SAY ". . ."

Academics

A "small liberal arts college," nestled in Maine, Bates College is dedicated to "empowering its students environmentally, academically, and socially." The "picturesque" campus offers the traditional New England atmosphere but "with its own personality." Students are drawn to the "warmth and friendliness of students and teachers, the political awareness of students on campus, and high quality academics!" They describe Bates as "a community of learners who care deeply about doing what [they] love in and outside of the classroom, be it service-learning in the Lewiston schools, adventuring in the outdoors, canvassing for an upcoming election, braving the puddle jump during Winter Carnival, or playing sports with [their] friends." If that isn't enough to draw people there, then consider the "community atmosphere, amazing food, supportive professors, beautiful campus, [the] many activities to be involved in, and grounded students." The athletics program is popular. "Most people play a sport of some kind, whether it's intramural or varsity." One student commends the many options for travel and studying abroad. "I have been to China, Vietnam, and Spain through Bates, and I cherish those opportunities." Professors are "very passionate about helping you succeed and are always willing to meet with you outside of class if you have any questions. Academics are challenging (in a good way!) and help you develop as a writer, thinker, and leader." Another student points out that "Bates focuses on writing skills" and nearly every member of the senior class writes a senior thesis. With all this praise, there are a few complaints about some facilities. "The science labs are a little behind the times," and students tell us that renovations to some of the older buildings would be welcome.

Life

The college's setting, in Lewiston, Maine, near Auburn, is quintessential Maine. Bates is located in a medium sized city, but "The school is amazing at arranging things to go on every week and even on the weekends. Concerts, shows, visiting artists, and movie showings are just a few things that are offered regularly." Students show an interest in the off-campus community. "Bates is extremely involved in Lewiston and Auburn through a myriad of social service and community learning opportunities. Almost every Bates student will volunteer in Lewiston/Auburn before they graduate, and everyone loves it," confirms a student. "Outside of the classroom, there is a strong sense of community that comes from the many events that various groups on campus hold." The atmosphere at Bates lends itself to "a lot of smaller parties," and "there are dances just about every weekend," and over 100 clubs. Also, at Bates, "People think a lot about the outdoors." "When it's warmer in the spring and fall everyone goes to a nearby lake or hangs out outside a lot playing Ultimate Frisbee or other active games. In the winter many students go skiing on the weekends or during the week if there is a great snow storm." Definitely not to be overlooked is the food, which, unlike the fare at a majority of college campuses, Bates students call "amazing."

Student Body

People who come to Bates are "very engaged and excited to be here." One student describes the majority of students as "upper-middle-class Caucasian with a major in the humanities and a more left-wing political view." But that may be changing. Another student says, "The diversity at Bates has improved dramatically—even having been here just three years. There has been a lot of successful attention put toward expanding diversity on campus." Some may "wish there were more social diversity," but another student does not see a problem. "There are cliques, but they are not exclusive." Whichever group a person may be part of, "the concerns and needs of individual students are never ignored." Together, Bates students are "one strong and open community bonding, growing, and sharing over the course of a four-year education."

FINANCIAL AID: 207-786-6096 • E-MAIL: ADMISSION@BATES.EDU • WEBSITE: WWW.BATES.EDU

THE PRINCETON REVIEW SAYS

Admissions

Very important factors considered include: Class rank, GPA, rigor of secondary school record, application essay, extracurricular activities, recommendation(s), talent/ability, character/personal qualities, level of applicant's interest. *Important factors considered include:* Interview. *Other factors considered include:* Standardized test scores, first generation, geographical residence, racial/ethnic status, state residency, volunteer work, work experience, alumni/ae relations. SAT and SAT Subject Tests or ACT considered if submitted; ACT with or without Writing component accepted. TOEFL required of all international applicants. *Academic units required:* 4 English; 3 mathematics; 3 science; (2 science lab); 3 social studies; 2 foreign language; 3 history. *Academic units recommended:* 4 English; 4 mathematics; 4 science; (3 science lab); 4 social studies; 4 foreign language; 4 history.

Financial Aid

Students should submit: FAFSA, CSS/Financial Aid PROFILE, Noncustodial PROFILE. Regular filing deadline is 2/15. The Princeton Review suggests that all financial aid forms be submitted as soon as possible after January 1. *Need-based scholarships/grants offered:* Federal Pell, SEOG, State scholarships/grants, private scholarships, the school's own gift aid. *Loan aid offered:* Direct Subsidized Stafford Loans, Direct Unsubsidized Stafford Loans, Direct PLUS loans, Federal Perkins Loans, State Loans Applicants will be notified of awards beginning 4/1. Federal Work-Study Program available. Institutional employment available. Off-campus job opportunities are good.

The Inside Word

Bates looks for students who challenge themselves in the classroom and beyond. A student's academic rigor, essays, and recommendations may be even more important than his or her GPA and test scores. Interviews are strongly encouraged, and candidates who opt out of these face-to-face meetings may place themselves at a disadvantage.

THE SCHOOL SAYS "..."

From the Admissions Office

"Bates College is widely recognized as one of the finest liberal arts colleges in the nation. The curriculum and faculty challenge students to develop the essential skills of critical assessment, analysis, expression, aesthetic sensibility, and independent thought. Founded by abolitionists in 1855, Bates graduates have always included men and women from diverse ethnic and religious backgrounds. Bates highly values its study abroad programs, unique calendar (4-4-1), and the many opportunities available for one-on-one collaboration with faculty through seminars, research, service-learning, and the capstone experience of senior thesis. Co-curricular life at Bates is rich; most students participate in club or varsity sports; many participate in performing arts; and almost all students participate in one of more than 110 student-run clubs and organizations. More than two-thirds of alumni enroll in graduate study within ten years.

"The Bates College Admission Staff reads applications very carefully; the high school record and the quality of writing are of particular importance. Applicants are strongly encouraged to have a personal interview, either on campus or with an alumni representative. Students who choose not to interview may place themselves at a disadvantage in the selection process. Bates offers tours, interviews, and information sessions throughout the summer and fall. Drop-ins are welcome for tours and information sessions. Please call ahead to schedule an interview. At Bates, the submission of standardized testing (the SAT, SAT Subject Tests, and the ACT) is not required for admission. After two decades of optional testing, our research shows no differences in academic performance and graduation rates between submitters and nonsubmitters."

SELECTIVITY

Admissions Rating	97
# of applicants	4,906
% of applicants accepted	27
% of acceptees attending	39
# offered a place on the wait list	1,599
% accepting a place on wait list	20
% admitted from wait list	22
# of early decision applicants	527
% accepted early decision	46

FRESHMAN PROFILE

Range SAT Critical Reading	630–720
Range SAT Math	630–710
Range SAT Writing	643–720
Range ACT Composite	30–32
% graduated top 10% of class	45
% graduated top 25% of class	71
% graduated top 50% of class	94

DEADLINES

Early decision	
Deadline	11/15
Notification	12/20
Regular	
Deadline	1/1
Notification	4/1
Nonfall registration?	Yes

APPLICANTS ALSO LOOK AT AND OFTEN PREFER

Dartmouth College; Brown University; Williams College

AND SOMETIMES PREFER

Bowdoin College; Middlebury College; Wesleyan University

AND RARELY PREFER

Bucknell University; Connecticut College; Trinity College (CT)

FINANCIAL FACTS

Financial Aid Rating	95
Annual tuition	$45,380
Room and board	$13,300
Required fees	$270
Books and supplies	$1,750
% needy frosh rec. need-based scholarship or grant aid	92
% needy UG rec. need-based scholarship or grant aid	91
% needy frosh rec. non-need-based scholarship or grant aid	0
% needy UG rec. non-need-based scholarship or grant aid	0
% needy frosh rec. need-based self-help aid	82
% needy UG rec. need-based self-help aid	89
% frosh rec. any financial aid	42
% UG rec. any financial aid	42
% UG borrow to pay for school	40
Average cumulative indebtedness	$24,515
% frosh need fully met	97
% ugrads need fully met	97
Average % of frosh need met	100
Average % of ugrad need met	100

BAYLOR UNIVERSITY

ONE BEAR PLACE #97056, WACO, TX 76798-7056 • ADMISSIONS: 254-710-3435 • FAX: 254-710-3436

STUDENTS SAY ". . ."

Academics

Located deep in the heart of Texas, Baylor is an educational powerhouse that helps undergraduates "achieve their academic potential" while simultaneously "guiding [and fostering] their moral and Christian values." The university seamlessly "integrates faith and learning" while providing an "uncommonly warm and open environment for any student." Yes, despite the fact that Baylor "is a big school," it still manages to maintain a "small community feel." And this sentiment clearly extends to the classroom. Undergrads gleefully explain that their professors "are always willing to help." What's more, "they actually care about you as an individual and they want you to succeed." One astounded freshman shares, "I heard during orientation that professors are known to invite their students to their home for dinner. I assumed this was mainly in upper-level classes. As a first semester freshman I've already had three offers." Of course, this friendliness doesn't mean that instructors go easy on their students. We've been assured that Baylor academics are "challenging." Thankfully, these professors also know how to make courses "fun and interesting." And they deliver "lectures [that] are understandable, realistic and applicable to both exams and real life." All in all, as another impressed freshman concludes, "Baylor is a school that pushes its students to grow, both intellectually and in their faith, in order to help them pursue the ultimate purpose for their life."

Life

Undergrads at Baylor are quite adept at finding "a good balance" between academics and social life. While they certainly take their schoolwork seriously, many students are quick to take advantage of opportunities outside the classroom as well. For starters, the university has a fairly sporty community and athletic events are quite popular on campus. As one sophomore business major shares, "Football games and tailgating are a must and the basketball games are fun too." Greek life is fairly active and fraternities and sororities certainly "have a strong presence." Many undergrads here are drawn to community service as well. One impressed freshman relays, "Volunteering is a big thing at Baylor, and many of the student organizations actively help out in the community." Undergrads also love the fact that there's "a bowling alley on campus," as well as "cheap movies" continually being screened. Baylor also hosts a number of great events such as "socials, dances...farmers markets, etc." Of course, there's plenty of adventure to be had when students are itching to get off-campus for a bit. For example, Baylor is located near a national park where students love to go for "hammocking, mountain biking, and hiking." And hometown Waco is "just an hour away from both Austin and Dallas so it's easy to make a weekend trip."

Student Body

When it comes to the typical Baylor student, it's probably not terribly surprising to learn that majority is "most likely Christian." These "bright" and "studious" undergrads are not wholly defined by their faith, however, and many happily report that their peers are "eager to engage with...people of differing convictions." Indeed, a handful of undergrads asserts that "diversity is welcome and appreciated." Of course, that would be expected from a "respectful" and "courteous" student body. As one junior tells us, "There are so many different people here that summing us all up is impossible. Everyone can find someone who absolutely adores them and they become best friends. It's not hard to make friends at all." Hence, Baylor's "outgoing" undergrads seem to "have no problem adapting to college life and responsibilities."

FINANCIAL AID: 254-710-2611 • E-MAIL: ADMISSIONS@BAYLOR.EDU • WEBSITE: WWW.BAYLOR.EDU

THE PRINCETON REVIEW SAYS

Admissions

Very important factors considered include: Class rank, rigor of secondary school record, standardized test scores. *Important factors considered include:* GPA. *Other factors considered include:* Application essay, extracurricular activities, interview, recommendation(s), talent/ability, volunteer work, alumni/ae relations, character/personal qualities, level of applicant's interest. SAT or ACT required; ACT with Writing component required. TOEFL required of all international applicants. *Academic units required:* 4 English; 4 mathematics; 4 science; (2 science lab); 2 social studies; 2 foreign language; 1 history.

Financial Aid

Students should submit: FAFSA. The Princeton Review suggests that all financial aid forms be submitted as soon as possible after January 1. *Need-based scholarships/grants offered:* Federal Pell, SEOG, State scholarships/grants, private scholarships, the school's own gift aid. *Loan aid offered:* Direct Subsidized Stafford Loans, Direct Unsubsidized Stafford Loans, Direct PLUS loans, Federal Perkins Loans, Federal Nursing Loans, State Loans. Applicants will be notified of awards beginning 3/1. Federal Work-Study Program available. Institutional employment available. Off-campus job opportunities are good.

The Inside Word

Securing admission to Baylor is no proverbial walk in the park. Beyond assessing GPA, class rank and standardized test scores, admissions officers closely analyze applications to find students who demonstrate intellectual drive and curiosity. Moreover, they want undergrads who value their faith, demonstrate a commitment to service and a deep desire to become a Baylor Bear. We should also note that certain schools/programs (ex. School of Engineering and Computer Science) maintain additional requirements. Be sure to thoroughly investigate.

THE SCHOOL SAYS "..."

From the Admissions Office

"Baylor University is a Christian university in the Baptist tradition and is affiliated with the Baptist General Convention of Texas. As the oldest continually operating institution of higher learning in the state, Baylor's founders sought to establish a college dedicated to Christian principles, superior academics, and a shared sense of community. Students come from all fifty states and more than eighty foreign countries. Baylor's nationally recognized academic divisions offer 144 undergraduate degree programs, seventy-six master's degree programs, and thirty-three doctoral degree programs. Baylor ranks in the top 10 percent of colleges and universities participating in the National Merit Scholarship program. Baylor is one of the select 10 percent of U.S. colleges and universities with a Phi Beta Kappa chapter. Baylor's undergraduate programs emphasize the central importance of vocation (calling) and service in students' lives, helping them explore their value and role in society. Baylor is a charter member of the Independent 529 Tuition Plan, a prepaid college tuition plan. Baylor's tuition is one of the lowest of any major private university in the Southwest and one of the least expensive in the nation. Approximately 90 percent of Baylor students receive student financial assistance. The approximately 1,000-acre main campus adjoins the Brazos River near downtown Waco, a Central Texas city of 120,000 people."

SELECTIVITY

Admissions Rating	90
# of applicants	29,249
% of applicants accepted	57
% of acceptees attending	19
# offered a place on the wait list	4,727
% accepting a place on wait list	22
% admitted from wait list	56

FRESHMAN PROFILE

Range SAT Critical Reading	550–660
Range SAT Math	570–670
Range SAT Writing	530–640
Range ACT Composite	24–29
Minimum paper TOEFL	540
Minimum web-based TOEFL	207
% graduated top 10% of class	42
% graduated top 25% of class	75
% graduated top 50% of class	97

DEADLINES

Early action	
Deadline	11/1
Notification	1/15
Regular	
Deadline	2/1
Notification	3/15
Nonfall registration?	Yes

FINANCIAL FACTS

Financial Aid Rating	75
Annual tuition	$34,480
Room and board	$10,708
Required fees	$3,840
Books and supplies	$1,250
% needy frosh rec. need-based scholarship or grant aid	98
% needy UG rec. need-based scholarship or grant aid	95
% needy frosh rec. non-need-based scholarship or grant aid	96
% needy UG rec. non-need-based scholarship or grant aid	90
% needy frosh rec. need-based self-help aid	82
% needy UG rec. need-based self-help aid	82
% frosh need fully met	14
% ugrads need fully met	14
Average % of frosh need met	64
Average % of ugrad need met	62

BECKER COLLEGE

61 Sever Street, Worcester, MA 01609 • Admissions: 508-373-9400 • 508-890-1500

STUDENTS SAY ". . ."

Academics

The mission of Becker College is to deliver a "transformational learning experience—anchored by academic excellence, social responsibility, and creative expression." Becker offers "the ability to pursue unique interests such as veterinary science, animal care, game design, criminal justice, and interior design" in a "calm, friendly environment" that is "flexible with the needs of different students." "I really like how small the campus was and how personal the classes are," says one new student, with another adding how this closeness lets you "know and interact with your professor on a higher level." Professors "do their best to adapt to student's individual learning styles," and the teaching environment lends itself to undergraduates being "able to ask questions and really understand what you are being taught." "If I have anything to add or feel differently about a topic I do not hesitate to bring it up. Never has it been ill received." One student admires how "the teachers show respect for their students which in turn makes me want to produce better work." Undergraduates here are comfortable asking instructors for assistance with things, such as "recommendations, internship assistance, and advice regarding graduate options." Providing a hands-on education is paramount at Becker. For instance, a veterinary clinic and kennel on campus provide "the opportunity for animal care majors to work hands on with live animals." For game design majors, the school sponsors "gamer fairs and competitions," as well as provides "networking opportunities with worker[s] in the video game industry." "The academic experience overall has been…relevant and current." Becker strives diligently to prepare students for the challenges of life in today's global society.

Life

There are two distinctive campuses, located six miles apart. The first is in Worcester, "a great college city," situated amidst New England's second-largest urban center. Students are often in the "Hawk's Nest" which is "a hangout spot" amidst tree-lined streets sporting Victorian-style homes. Leicester is the second campus, in a country town adjacent to an historic village green. This rural setting provides space for athletic team facilities and for the animal sciences programs. With a free shuttle service, students move easily between locations. Becker "offers plenty of student activities to make the campus more of a family and make students feel comfortable." There is a wide range of cultural, social, and recreational options available, being in a metropolitan area. Undergrads "love to go on the Boston and New York City trips," which may include Bruins, Celtics, and Red Sox games. "The Shoppes at Blackstone Valley are only twenty minutes away," and "Spring Carnival is another huge event for our College." For fun closer to campus, students commonly "have house parties. We do not have frats and sororities."

Student Body

Becker undergraduates find the appearance of campus pleasant, "keeping the old world charm but still maintaining a professional look." The environment is "nice, and laid-back;" students are "friendly and accepting" and "treat others with respect." "It's very easy to get around, and it's very easy to fit in." "Typical" students are involved in sports or clubs. "Student-athletes are very popular. Most students interact based on their program, class schedule, interests, and specific sport." "Our school is all about sports, game design, nursing, and vet science." There is a great commitment to diversity; Becker is "a school that teaches everyone how to be a global citizen and how to interact within a community." "Work-study opportunities that pertain to the person's academic major" are also common.

FINANCIAL AID: 508-373-9440 • E-MAIL: ADMISSIONS@BECKER.EDU • WEBSITE: WWW.BECKER.EDU

THE PRINCETON REVIEW SAYS

Admissions

Very important factors considered include: GPA, rigor of secondary school record, standardized test scores. *Important factors considered include:* Class rank, recommendation(s). *Other factors considered include:* Application essay, extra-curricular activities, interview, volunteer work, work experience, alumni/ae relations, level of applicant's interest, TOEFL required of all international applicants. *Academic units recommended:* 4 English; 3 mathematics; 3 science; (2 science lab); 2 social studies; 2 foreign language; 2 history.

Financial Aid

Students should submit: FAFSA, Institution's own financial aid form, State aid form. The Princeton Review suggests that all financial aid forms be submitted as soon as possible after January 1. *Need-based scholarships/grants offered:* Federal Pell, SEOG, State scholarships/grants, private scholarships, the school's own gift aid. *Loan aid offered:* Direct Subsidized Stafford Loans, Direct Unsubsidized Stafford Loans, Direct PLUS loans, State Loans. Federal Work-Study Program available. Institutional employment available. Off-campus job opportunities are good.

The Inside Word

The admissions process is personal and unique for each applicant, although Becker College reviews both the SAT and ACT college entrance examinations, as well as advanced placement examination scores if applicable. Recommendations and essays are also taken heavily into consideration. Becker seeks to enroll applicants with not only impressive high school transcripts, but those wanting to contribute to the greater good, both locally and globally.

THE SCHOOL SAYS "..."

From the Admissions Office

"Becker College offers forty academic programs, including a choice of twenty-nine bachelor degree programs and extensive adult learning programs. Becker College students are engaged socially, academically, and athletically. Our students receive a transformational learning experience that prepares them to thrive, contribute to, and lead in a global society. We emphasize global citizenship: knowledge of other world regions and cultures, familiarity with international issues, and cultivating skills to work effectively in cross-cultural environments. These skills are learned while engaging in all aspects of the college—from academics, community service, and student leadership, to campus activities, clubs, and social interaction. We also are committed to preparing students to be world ready for the rapidly changing and complex job market by offering unique, trans-disciplinary career pathways and learning experiences, and we are proud of our 99% placement rate for employment or further study.

"Our admissions process reflects the Becker College philosophy that each student is a unique individual. Because of this, our requirements allow you to put your best foot forward and provide as much information as possible about who you are, what you hope to accomplish during your time at Becker College, and what you hope to do upon graduation.

"The admissions process is personal and unique for each applicant. To be considered for admission, applicants must submit a completed application along with an official high school transcript and official SAT/ACT test score results. Transfer students must submit an official college transcript. Admission requirements vary by program.

"Due to the rigorous admission standards for many of our programs, the most academically qualified applicants will be selected for admission."

SELECTIVITY

Admissions Rating	71
# of applicants	3,936
% of applicants accepted	63
% of acceptees attending	15

FRESHMAN PROFILE

Range SAT Critical Reading	450–550
Range SAT Math	440–570
Range SAT Writing	430–520
Minimum paper TOEFL	550
Average HS GPA	3.02
% graduated top 10% of class	7
% graduated top 25% of class	26
% graduated top 50% of class	57

DEADLINES

Early action	
Deadline	11/15
Notification	12/15
Regular	
Priority	2/15
Nonfall registration?	Yes

FINANCIAL FACTS

Financial Aid Rating	70
Annual tuition	$301,320
Room and board	$12,000
Required fees	$1,550
Books and supplies	$960
% needy frosh rec. need-based scholarship or grant aid	78
% needy UG rec. need-based scholarship or grant aid	66
% needy frosh rec. non-need-based scholarship or grant aid	100
% needy UG rec. non-need-based scholarship or grant aid	88
% needy frosh rec. need-based self-help aid	96
% needy UG rec. need-based self-help aid	95
% frosh rec. any financial aid	95
% UG rec. any financial aid	88
% UG borrow to pay for school	94
Average cumulative indebtedness	$43,238
% frosh need fully met	9
% ugrads need fully met	7
Average % of frosh need met	61
Average % of ugrad need met	58

BELLARMINE UNIVERSITY

2001 NEWBURG ROAD, LOUISVILLE, KY 40205 • ADMISSIONS: 502-272-8131 • TOLL-FREE: 800-274-4723 • FAX: 502-272-8002

STUDENTS SAY " . . . "

Academics

Bellarmine University is a "high-energy school completely focused on academics," with a faculty and staff that are "willing to go beyond the call of duty all in the name of your education." The school has a good amount of prestige in Kentucky (and to some extent, the country) and encourages critical thinking, teaching others, and "building a strong, involved community." Many of its students consider it "a friendly stepping stone to higher education," and the school continues to improve existing schools and programs (both physical and internal aspects), and to add innovative new ones. As it stands, the "self-directed research opportunities" and sense of community are "absolutely incredible" here. Students admire the school's integrity and dedication to its students' well-being, citing as a main strength its "ability to provide an avenue for every individual to express themselves and to receive the most from their education."

Professors "love their students" and "will do whatever it takes to help them succeed." "Not only are they experts in their field, but they truly care about your learning and whether you are getting the most out of the class possible," says a student. Small class sizes "maximize participation and professor involvement with the student." With so much support from faculty (who are all "readily available for assistance outside of class"), there are "a lot of opportunities for growth," as well as for help on homework, papers, and exams. "I can even wake up for my 8:00 A.M. classes because they are that interesting," says a student.

The administration is similarly "more than helpful." "I've been able to obtain great leadership roles on campus that will help me in the future," says a student. The school's Freshman Orientation process—in which new students go on a retreat before classes start to meet other classmates—also helps to make "anyone and everyone who comes to campus feel welcome." "I've learned many new ways of seeing things, i.e., culturally, critically, etc.," says a student.

Life

Located "in the heart of a beautiful city" (Louisville, Kentucky), Bellarmine "revolves around a community." "I chose Bellarmine because it has the atmosphere of an intimate school, but is in a city-like area," says a student. Also, the campus, located on a giant hill, is "gorgeous," which "makes studying anywhere on campus easy." There are "so many" cute little shops and unique restaurants within walking distance, and "the big city of Louisville offers theaters, baseball, and pretty much everything else you could want!"

Almost 50 percent of the students are commuters with a few nontraditional students sprinkled in, but there are many clubs and activities for these students to get involved in so they can find their niche. "There are always events on campus," says a student. School-hosted events around town "are a weekly thing." As for fun, students here are "just like every other college student—working hard on the weekdays and trying to have fun on the weekends!" The Greek life at BU consists of one fraternity and one sorority but there are no houses so "most evening and weekend shenanigans happen off campus at house parties and bars for those old enough." If there is a complaint, it's that the food in the dining halls "could use some work."

Student Body

This "very friendly" bunch of students has typically "always been in good academic standing," and the students are "full of school spirit and eager to meet new people in classes." A wide variety of personalities exist on campus, and "nobody appears ashamed to be themselves by openly expressing their personality and views." International students in particular are "highly welcomed." The "rigorous" nursing program at Bellarmine is well-regarded, so there are a large number of nursing students on campus. Though the school can be a "little cliquey"—"they don't call it the 'high school on the hill' for nothing"—it's nothing too terrible. "It seems like everyone knows everyone," says a student. "No one feels like a total stranger."

BELLARMINE UNIVERSITY

FINANCIAL AID: 502-452-8124 • E-MAIL: ADMISSIONS@BELLARMINE.EDU • WEBSITE: WWW.BELLARMINE.EDU

THE PRINCETON REVIEW SAYS

Admissions

Very important factors considered include: GPA, rigor of secondary school record, standardized test scores, recommendation(s), character/personal qualities, level of applicant's interest. *Important factors considered include:* Class rank, extracurricular activities. *Other factors considered include:* Application essay, first generation, geographical residence, interview, racial/ethnic status, state residency, talent/ability, volunteer work, work experience, alumni/ae relations. SAT or ACT required; ACT with or without Writing component accepted. TOEFL required of all international applicants. *Academic units required:* 4 English; 3 mathematics; 3 science; (2 science lab); 2 social studies; 2 foreign language; 1 history; 5 academic electives. *Academic units recommended:* 4 English; 4 mathematics; 4 science; (2 science lab); 3 social studies; 2 foreign language; 2 history; 7 academic electives.

Financial Aid

Students should submit: FAFSA. The Princeton Review suggests that all financial aid forms be submitted as soon as possible after January 1. *Need-based scholarships/grants offered:* Federal Pell, SEOG, State scholarships/grants, private scholarships, the school's own gift aid. *Loan aid offered:* Direct Subsidized Stafford Loans, Direct Unsubsidized Stafford Loans, Direct PLUS loans. Applicants will be notified of awards beginning 3/15. Federal Work-Study Program available. Institutional employment available. Off-campus job opportunities are excellent.

The Inside Word

Admissions at Bellarmine University is competitive. However, much like their mission statement, Bellarmine's admissions committee views applicants' profiles from a composite perspective and is looking for a well-rounded candidate whose qualifications reflect more than the sum total of a GPA and test scores. Recommendations and personal statements—which present a stronger picture of the students' educational goals—volunteer experiences, and extracurricular commitments, hold significant weight. Candidates with strong grades and diverse interests are likely to earn acceptance.

THE SCHOOL SAYS "..."

From the Admissions Office

"Bellarmine University prepares students for success through a liberal arts education, combined with training for mastery in a specialized area. We offer more than fifty majors in the arts and sciences, humanities, education, communication, business, environmental studies, nursing and health science, plus graduate programs in nursing, education, physical therapy, business and communication. We engage students in state-of-the-art classrooms and expand their horizons through internship and study abroad opportunities. Bellarmine delivers this world-class education just five miles from downtown Louisville, the nation's sixteenth largest city. The 144-acre campus is set in a safe, historic and eclectic neighborhood, and features a fitness center, tennis courts, athletic fields and two new dining halls. With more than fifty clubs and organizations, twenty NCAA Division II athletic teams, plus Division I men's lacrosse, Bellarmine offers a variety of recreational opportunities for all students. Students who reside on campus also find a Bellarmine difference in the living arrangements. From traditional residence halls to apartment-style and suite living arrangements, students have many housing options to choose from; the newest residence halls surround a Tuscan-style piazza. As Bellarmine attracts more residential students, the university has created more gathering spaces for them, such as the café on the ground floor of the Siena Primo residence hall. New learning communities cater to residents and commuters alike, offering opportunities for focused, collaborative studies on topics such as leadership, healthcare, science and technology."

SELECTIVITY
Admissions Rating	76
# of applicants	4,160
% of applicants accepted	95
% of acceptees attending	17

FRESHMAN PROFILE
Range SAT Critical Reading	490–590
Range SAT Math	490–590
Range ACT Composite	22–27
Minimum paper TOEFL	550
Minimum web-based TOEFL	213
Average HS GPA	3.52
% graduated top 10% of class	25
% graduated top 25% of class	54
% graduated top 50% of class	82

DEADLINES
Early action	
Deadline	11/1
Notification	11/15
Regular	
Priority	2/1
Deadline	8/15
Nonfall registration?	Yes

FINANCIAL FACTS
Financial Aid Rating	78
Annual tuition	$34,900
Room and board	$10,700
Required fees	$1,390
Books and supplies	$692
% needy frosh rec. need-based scholarship or grant aid	100
% needy UG rec. need-based scholarship or grant aid	97
% needy frosh rec. non-need-based scholarship or grant aid	32
% needy UG rec. non-need-based scholarship or grant aid	29
% needy frosh rec. need-based self-help aid	67
% needy UG rec. need-based self-help aid	64
% frosh rec. any financial aid	100
% UG rec. any financial aid	98
% UG borrow to pay for school	72
Average cumulative indebtedness	$28,071
% frosh need fully met	19
% ugrads need fully met	18
Average % of frosh need met	76
Average % of ugrad need met	73

BELOIT COLLEGE

700 COLLEGE STREET, BELOIT, WI 53511 • ADMISSIONS: 608-363-2500 • FAX: 608-363-2075

STUDENTS SAY ". . ."

Academics

Beloit College is a small, liberal arts institution with "phenomenal academics" where "people are committed to their work out of passion, not out of pressure." As one student notes, "It's more about the community than competitiveness." Another says, "I was most impressed by an emphasis on actual learning as opposed to stiff competition or an exclusive focus on getting grades." A "vibrant, interesting, idiosyncratic place," where "every person is full of little surprises," the school promotes interdisciplinary learning and practical experience. "Education becomes a collaborative and collective experience here." Beloit attempts to "strike an optimal balance between freedom and guidance." Students can create a path that works best for them, as there is "flexibility in everything from class schedules to meal plans. You can customize your experience at Beloit to fit your needs." This creativity also applies to the actual educational process, since "you can learn in whatever way is best for you; teachers mold their lessons to the needs of the students." At the same time, "professors here aren't going to stand up there and feed you information." Interactivity is encouraged, and Beloit's intimate class sizes "usually have a good discussion portion for students to think critically and develop their own ideas." "Professors have lectures, but they really want the students to lead conversations." The ability to work closely with professors is highly prized at Beloit. As one student enthuses, "the personal attention has helped me to 'come out of my shell' and become a confident member of our academic community." Beloit provides excellent support services outside of the classroom as well; "our Liberal Arts in Practice Center and the Office of International Education are great at providing information and support for internships, volunteer opportunities, and study abroad." "My academic experience has been exploratory and invaluable."

Life

"Beloit College graciously takes the stance that its students are adults," and this is evident in their alcohol "philosophy," as well as the setup of residential living. "Many people do look out for each other and tend to be fairly responsible." Students mention that "you are responsible for yourself, and the school is there to help you when you need it," although the alcohol policy at Beloit "has definitely gotten stricter in recent years." Undergrads looking for alternative entertainment need not venture far. Dance parties are prevalent, and "the most popular ones are at Greek houses." "Student Activities hosts shuttles to the movies on Friday nights and to restaurants on Sundays," and "Our Programming Board does an excellent job bringing entertainment to campus." There are frequent lectures from visiting speakers, and two museums. Students enjoy "going to see Voodoo Barbie, our outrageously hilarious improv group," and "events like Folk N' Blues Festival and Apple Day are looked forward to all year." The on-campus bar C-Haus is "always a good place to catch great live music, have a beer, play some pool, or grab some late night snacks." The campus has good proximity to outlying Chicago, Madison, and Milwaukee, and "the parks and forests surrounding Beloit are very nice."

Student Body

According to one undergraduate, "The student body is definitely not homogeneous, save for the liberal bent." Another likes that "at Beloit you are respected for your individuality and your contribution to the community." Beloiters "come in all races, nationalities, social classes, religions, sexual orientations, body types, and hair colors (including pink and blue)." "Our director of spiritual life has made a large impact on incorporating and talking about faith, religion, and spirituality." "The student body has become increasingly more accepting." The social environment is "low-pressure," and being "genuine" is important here. "The best way to fit in is to be yourself; students here do not go for fakes."

FINANCIAL AID: 608-363-2663 • E-MAIL: ADMISS@BELOIT.EDU • WEBSITE: WWW.BELOIT.EDU

THE PRINCETON REVIEW SAYS

Admissions

Very important factors considered include: GPA, rigor of secondary school record, application essay, recommendation(s). *Important factors considered include:* Class rank, standardized test scores, talent/ability. *Other factors considered include:* Extracurricular activities, first generation, interview, volunteer work, work experience, alumni/ae relations, character/personal qualities, level of applicant's interest. SAT or ACT required; ACT with or without Writing component accepted. TOEFL required of all international applicants. *Academic units recommended:* 4 English; 4 mathematics; 3 science; (2 science lab); 4 social studies; 2 foreign language.

Financial Aid

Students should submit: FAFSA, Institution's own financial aid form. Regular filing deadline is 3/1. The Princeton Review suggests that all financial aid forms be submitted as soon as possible after January 1. *Need-based scholarships/grants offered:* Federal Pell, SEOG, State scholarships/grants, private scholarships, the school's own gift aid. *Loan aid offered:* Direct Subsidized Stafford Loans, Direct Unsubsidized Stafford Loans, Direct PLUS loans, Federal Perkins Loans, College/university loans from institutional funds. Federal Work-Study Program available. Institutional employment available. Off-campus job opportunities are good.

The Inside Word

Beloit seeks to evaluate the entire student when considering potential for admission—from grades and test scores, to essays and recommendations, to personality and strength of character. This holistic approach to assessment leads Beloit to seek students with not only impressive high school transcripts, but those who possess a strong sense of responsibility and show the capacity for leadership.

THE SCHOOL SAYS ". . ."

From the Admissions Office

"Beloiters spend four years challenged to explore their passions, excel in their studies, and apply the lessons of the classroom to the larger world, in their careers, and in service to others. That focus—putting the liberal arts into practice—has long set this college and its graduates apart. Study abroad, internships, research, service, and work opportunities are typical examples of the ways the Beloit experience extends beyond the classroom. Beloit students are more apt to value learning for its own sake and at the same time, understand the connection between college and the rest of their lives as citizens of the world.

"Beloit College uses the Common Application exclusively. Although students must submit test scores from the ACT or SAT, standardized test scores are less important than the strength of the academic program and performance, the essays, and recommendations. Beloit offers one binding early decision plan with a deadline of November 1 and notification by November 30; and two nonbinding early action plans with deadlines of either November 1 or December 1; notification is six weeks hence. Applicants who wish to be considered for merit scholarships are urged to apply under one of the early action plans. The preferred deadline for regular decision applicants in January 15."

SELECTIVITY

Admissions Rating	88
# of applicants	2,253
% of applicants accepted	68
% of acceptees attending	20
# offered a place on the wait list	40
% accepting a place on wait list	28
% admitted from wait list	27

FRESHMAN PROFILE

Range SAT Critical Reading	550–710
Range SAT Math	540–660
Range ACT Composite	24–30
Minimum paper TOEFL	550
Minimum web-based TOEFL	213
Average HS GPA	3.43
% graduated top 10% of class	29
% graduated top 25% of class	61
% graduated top 50% of class	89

DEADLINES

Early decision	
Deadline	11/1
Notification	11/30
Early action	
Deadline	12/1
Notification	1/15
Regular	
Priority	1/15
Nonfall registration?	Yes

APPLICANTS ALSO LOOK AT AND OFTEN PREFER
Carleton College

AND SOMETIMES PREFER
Grinnell College; Macalester College

AND RARELY PREFER
Ripon College; University of Illinois at Urbana-Champaign; Lewis & Clark College; University of Wisconsin-Madison

FINANCIAL FACTS

Financial Aid Rating	87
Annual tuition	$42,220
Room and board	$7,470
Required fees	$280
Books and supplies	$1,000
% needy frosh rec. need-based scholarship or grant aid	100
% needy UG rec. need-based scholarship or grant aid	100
% needy frosh rec. non-need-based scholarship or grant aid	15
% needy UG rec. non-need-based scholarship or grant aid	16
% needy frosh rec. need-based self-help aid	85
% needy UG rec. need-based self-help aid	84
% frosh rec. any financial aid	96
% UG rec. any financial aid	95
% UG borrow to pay for school	67
Average cumulative indebtedness	$29,306
% frosh need fully met	17
% ugrads need fully met	19
Average % of frosh need met	87
Average % of ugrad need met	86

BENNINGTON COLLEGE

OFFICE OF ADMISSIONS, BENNINGTON, VT 05201-6003 • ADMISSIONS: 802-440-4312 • FAX: 802-440-4320

STUDENTS SAY ". . ."

Academics

One big draw to Bennington College is its "Field Work Term program, where students intern every year for seven weeks to gain practical experience related to their academic interests." This mandatory program provides a "real-world" opportunity many students appreciate. "It's a huge advantage upon graduation, because with a degree from Bennington, you automatically have four internships or jobs on your résumé—and that's only if you do absolutely nothing during summers." An even bigger draw for some students may be Bennington's Plan Process. "Bennington's greatest strength is the opportunity that it gives its students to design our own educations, that we are encouraged to study what we are truly passionate about." This is ideal for students without a clear career focus, as well as those who are "frustrated with the "core requirements" style of education that high school shuttled [them] through" and want to "personally craft your own education tailored to your interests." As one student explains, "I had no idea what I wanted to do or what I wanted to study. I needed to be free to explore however I please." A flexible academic plan and yearly internships mean "students are constantly revisiting and reevaluating the questions of 'What do I want to study and why?'" Students are given "not only the freedom to explore a wide range of disciplines but the ability to discover and study [their] passions in depth." Bennington's professors received high praise. "The professors here are universally outstanding. Because of Bennington's teacher-practitioner model, which requires professors to be active professionals in their fields of instruction, students at Bennington are privy to professors who not only are immensely knowledgeable in their fields, but are also so excited to teach about them." "Most professors treat you as a future colleague rather than a student, which helps foster the experience of learning a skill or ability to analyze." The school's small size has a lot of benefits: "Classes are mostly discussion-based, small, and seminar style. Lectures are kept to a strict minimum, and classes are rarely more than twenty people." But being small "can occasionally impact the curriculum—for example, few art history classes being offered one term. However, Bennington tries to accommodate this, and thus I took a private art history tutorial with a professor instead."

Life

Life at Bennington "centers around work," which is fine with students since "it's work we really enjoy." Located in an "absolutely, positively stunning" and "very cozy" campus in the small town of Bennington, Vermont, students spend a lot of time on school grounds. The "unique housing" where students "live in houses instead of dorms" builds a "strong community." The arts are very popular on campus. "There's always a concert, or an opening, or a show going on somewhere, and we like to support each other by going to as many events as we can." "Dance, live music, and drama are really well attended here because the work that goes up is just so good." Some students find transportation a challenge; "People do make it to Boston and New York City for performances and weekend getaways, though the surrounding area is much more accessible." "Outside of campus one can walk around the quaint town with lots of shops and restaurants." "We also go out for dinner a lot at local restaurants." "Students love eating and cooking together. The atmosphere is pretty relaxed and conversational."

Student Body

Bennington students are "a body of individuals." They are "hipsters, artists, and the next generation of geniuses having a good time and doing real, amazing things in the world." They are "driven and passionate about their work," and "everyone here is so amazing and artistic." "Students tend to be pretty liberal, open, and tolerant. Most students genuinely care about their studies, and they pride themselves on their intellectual nature and academic successes. Most students are artistically aware, and they enjoy discussing literature, film, music, etc." Although "it's not a super diverse place ethnically or politically, in terms of diversity of interests, it's wonderful." "Everyone truly wants to be here and is engaged in their work."

FINANCIAL AID: 802-440-4325 • E-MAIL: ADMISSIONS@BENNINGTON.EDU • WEBSITE: WWW.BENNINGTON.EDU

THE PRINCETON REVIEW SAYS

Admissions

Very important factors considered include: Class rank, GPA, rigor of secondary school record, application essay, extracurricular activities, interview, recommendation(s), talent/ability, character/personal qualities. *Other factors considered include:* Standardized test scores, first generation, geographical residence, racial/ethnic status, volunteer work, work experience, alumni/ae relations, level of applicant's interest. SAT and SAT Subject Tests or ACT considered if submitted; ACT with or without Writing component accepted. TOEFL required of all international applicants. *Academic units recommended:* 4 English; 4 mathematics; 3 science; 4 social studies; 2 foreign language; 4 history.

Financial Aid

Students should submit: FAFSA, Institution's own financial aid form, CSS/Financial Aid PROFILE, Noncustodial PROFILE. Regular filing deadline is 2/15. The Princeton Review suggests that all financial aid forms be submitted as soon as possible after January 1. *Need-based scholarships/grants offered:* Federal Pell, SEOG, State scholarships/grants, private scholarships, the school's own gift aid. *Loan aid offered:* Direct Subsidized Stafford Loans, Direct Unsubsidized Stafford Loans, Direct PLUS loans, College/university loans from institutional funds. Applicants will be notified of awards beginning 4/1. Federal Work-Study Program available. Institutional employment available. Off-campus job opportunities are good.

The Inside Word

Bennington students need to be academically accomplished, driven, and self-directed to handle the academic freedom granted by the curriculum. The admissions office seeks all these qualities in applicants and, because of the school's prestige, typically finds them in all admitted students. A campus visit isn't required but is strongly recommended as an excellent way to demonstrate your interest in the school and to provide admissions officers with the personal contact they prefer in evaluating candidates.

THE SCHOOL SAYS "..."

From the Admissions Office

"At Bennington, your education is unified and fueled by your intellect and imagination, guided by a rigorous and ongoing conversation with your faculty, and shaped by your experience working in the world each year. Bennington is the only college to require that its students spend a term—every year—at work in the world. And its new Center for the Advancement of Public Action provides a unique opportunity for students to explore how the questions that matter to them come together with the questions that matter to the world. Rooted in an abiding faith in the talent, imagination, and responsibility of the individual, Bennington invites students to pursue and shape their own intellectual inquiries and, in doing so, to discover the profound interconnection of things.

"Submission of standardized test scores (the SAT, SAT Subject Tests, or the ACT) is optional."

SELECTIVITY

Admissions Rating	92
# of applicants	1,236
% of applicants accepted	63
% of acceptees attending	25
# offered a place on the wait list	175
% accepting a place on wait list	87
% admitted from wait list	18
# of early decision applicants	50
% accepted early decision	42

FRESHMAN PROFILE

Range SAT Critical Reading	620–720
Range SAT Math	560–660
Range SAT Writing	610–700
Range ACT Composite	26–30
Minimum paper TOEFL	577
Minimum web-based TOEFL	233
Average HS GPA	3.53
% graduated top 10% of class	35
% graduated top 25% of class	67
% graduated top 50% of class	93

DEADLINES

Early decision	
Deadline	11/15
Notification	12/20
Early action	
Deadline	12/1
Notification	2/1
Regular	
Deadline	1/3
Notification	4/1
Nonfall registration?	Yes

APPLICANTS ALSO LOOK AT AND OFTEN PREFER
Bard College

AND SOMETIMES PREFER
Lewis & Clark College

FINANCIAL FACTS

Financial Aid Rating	83
Annual tuition	$44,490
Room and board	$13,190
Required fees	$1,150
Books and supplies	$1,000
% needy frosh rec. need-based scholarship or grant aid	99
% needy UG rec. need-based scholarship or grant aid	98
% needy frosh rec. non-need-based scholarship or grant aid	16
% needy UG rec. non-need-based scholarship or grant aid	7
% needy frosh rec. need-based self-help aid	81
% needy UG rec. need-based self-help aid	89
% frosh rec. any financial aid	95
% UG rec. any financial aid	90
% UG borrow to pay for school	68
Average cumulative indebtedness	$25,716
% frosh need fully met	19
% ugrads need fully met	12
Average % of frosh need met	82
Average % of ugrad need met	80

BENTLEY UNIVERSITY

175 FOREST STREET, WALTHAM, MA 02452 • ADMISSIONS: 781-891-2244 • FAX: 781-891-3414

CAMPUS LIFE

Quality of Life Rating	90
Fire Safety Rating	99
Green Rating	97
Type of school	Private
Affiliation	No Affiliation
Environment	Town

STUDENTS

Total undergrad enrollment	4,172
% male/female	60/40
% from out of state	53
% frosh from public high school	65
% frosh live on campus	97
% ugrads live on campus	78
# of fraternities (% ugrad men join)	8 (10)
# of sororities (% ugrad women join)	4 (17)
% African American	3
% Asian	8
% Caucasian	61
% Hispanic	7
% Native American	<1
% international	15
# of countries represented	90

SURVEY SAYS . . .
Students are happy
Classroom facilities are great
Career services are great
Internships are widely available
School is well run
Dorms are like palaces
Campus feels safe
Athletic facilities are great
Lots of beer drinking

ACADEMICS

Academic Rating	80
% students returning for sophomore year	94
% students graduating within 4 years	81
% students graduating within 6 years	87
Calendar	Semester
Student/faculty ratio	14:1
Profs interesting rating	81
Profs accessible rating	85

Most classes have 30–39 students.

MOST POPULAR MAJORS
marketing; accounting; finance

STUDENTS SAY "..."

Academics
Bentley University's business-focused classes are taught by "real-life business men and women that bring their experiences from the real world into the classroom." The business education here is "well-rounded," and offers "connections to many alumni throughout the state," prompting one student to offer their reason for choosing the school: "Since I wanted to pursue a career, Bentley would offer me the best testing grounds to try every kind of major." The Boston area school's reputation is a good one, carried far and wide by students who "believe that I'm getting a great education that will be extremely beneficial to me in the future." This education is led by a team of professors who are "very engaged in their fields and are often around after hours to help you understand concepts. Although they take their research seriously, they do not view themselves as the keepers of the knowledge that you must bow before to earn an education." Indeed, "most professors want you to do well, so that creates an environment where you feel more inclined to comment and ask questions." Students find that not only are professors easily accessible, so are their fellow students thanks to "small class sizes" and "discussion-based classes." One student remarked that professors try "to get all students involved in their discussions. They enjoy team projects, which is a great way to learn the material and meet new people."

Life
Students at Bentley are serious about education, but they are also a group who "work hard during the week and play hard on the weekends." Most agree that "life here at Bentley is good." Team sports and trips into Boston fill weekend time for many. "Ultimate Frisbee seems to be like a strange cult on campus, which is pretty cool actually. People take the sport very seriously." However, the Division I school does not offer club teams for sports in which it has a varsity team, so in those cases students must make their own fun. Trips into Boston include all that you would expect from the city—a thriving night life, historic pubs, museums, professional sports, and more. Students "enjoy the free shuttle to Harvard Square, [so] they can access Boston very easily." Waltham itself "doesn't have much," though you can find "great restaurants" in town. There are also a wealth of clubs and the Greek system to keep students involved. Failing all that, "at night most of the parties are in dorms, as most students live on campus," though they are "relatively tame" when compared to party-notorious schools. All in all, "Life at Bentley can be hard or very easy, depending on how you set yourself up. You could cruise by taking easy classes, relaxing and enjoying college years, or pursue as many opportunities as you would like—and there are a lot."

Student Body
Though unrelated, think of Bentley University's student body as being not too far removed from the car of the same name. The typical student is a "wealthy individual who has a family background in business," usually "an upper middle class Caucasian from the New England area." Which isn't to say that no one else can fit in. Students here "are instantly integrated into the culture and build lasting relationships from the start," which takes place largely because "everyone is VERY friendly, and that is one of the reasons I chose to attend Bentley." Indeed, "students here are relatively preppy but everyone seems to get along no matter what their background is," a group who are "very academically conscious, so they fit together well." Perhaps that is because there is a common tie that binds: No matter their background, those who attend Bentley are "business-minded, determined and motivated student who works hard and pushes other around them to do better." As one student sums it up, "Most students are easy-going but driven towards their goals as well. Despite the diversity, students get along with each other very well."

FINANCIAL AID: 781-891-3441 • E-MAIL: UGADMISSION@BENTLEY.EDU • WEBSITE: WWW.BENTLEY.EDU

THE PRINCETON REVIEW SAYS

Admissions

Very important factors considered include: GPA, rigor of secondary school record, standardized test scores. *Important factors considered include:* Application essay, extracurricular activities, recommendation(s), talent/ability, volunteer work, work experience, character/personal qualities. *Other factors considered include:* Class rank, first generation, geographical residence, interview, racial/ethnic status, state residency, alumni/ae relations, level of applicant's interest. SAT or ACT required; SAT and SAT Subject Tests or ACT considered if submitted; ACT with Writing component required. TOEFL required of all international applicants. *Academic units required:* 4 English; 4 mathematics; 3 science; (3 science lab); 3 social studies; 3 foreign language. *Academic units recommended:* 4 English; 4 mathematics; 3 science; (3 science lab); 3 social studies; 3 foreign language.

Financial Aid

Students should submit: FAFSA, CSS/Financial Aid PROFILE, Noncustodial PROFILE, Business/Farm Supplement. Regular filing deadline is 2/1. The Princeton Review suggests that all financial aid forms be submitted as soon as possible after January 1. *Need-based scholarships/grants offered:* Federal Pell, SEOG, State scholarships/grants, private scholarships, the school's own gift aid. *Loan aid offered:* Direct Subsidized Stafford Loans, Direct Unsubsidized Stafford Loans, Direct PLUS loans, Federal Perkins Loans, State Loans. Applicants will be notified of awards beginning 4/1. Federal Work-Study Program available. Institutional employment available. Off-campus job opportunities are good.

The Inside Word

If you're thinking about stacking your senior year electives with business classes in order to impress the Bentley admissions office, think again. Taking a broad array of classes that will challenge your skills, at AP level if possible, is your best approach. Whether in English, history/social sciences, math, lab sciences, and foreign language, admissions wants to see academic diversity. And be sure your grades and test scores are up to snuff, because you'll have plenty of competition.

THE SCHOOL SAYS ". . ."

From the Admissions Office

"Bentley is an internationally recognized business university known for integrating business with the arts and sciences. Students learn in an unmatched collection of high-tech learning labs and benefit from close working relationships with faculty who collaborate across disciplines. Bentley students are highly sought after by today's leading organizations because of their classwork with corporate clients, service-learning projects and valuable internship experiences. In its 2013 "Best Undergraduate Business Schools" issue, Bloomberg BusinessWeek ranks Bentley 20th among the country's top undergraduate business programs.

"More than 95 percent of 2013 graduates were employed or enrolled in graduate school within six months of commencement. Their median annual salary was more than $50,000. This success was recognized by the Princeton Review in 2014 as Bentley was ranked number three nationally for "Best Career Services."

"Approximately 97 percent of freshmen live on campus. Students live and learn in a diverse environment that prepares them to thrive in today's diverse work world. International students representing nearly 100 countries are part of the Bentley community. There are more than 100 student organizations, as well as abundant intramurals, recreational sports, and twenty-three varsity teams in NCAA Divisions I and II. Bentley's location in Waltham, Massachusetts— minutes from Boston—puts the city's many resources within easy reach. Bentley's free shuttle makes regular trips to Harvard Square in Cambridge, just a subway ride from the heart of Boston. Boston also offers students many opportunities for internships and jobs after graduation."

SELECTIVITY	
Admissions Rating	93
# of applicants	7,493
% of applicants accepted	44
% of acceptees attending	30
# offered a place on the wait list	1,000
% accepting a place on wait list	31
% admitted from wait list	18
# of early decision applicants	169
% accepted early decision	60

FRESHMAN PROFILE	
Range SAT Critical Reading	540–630
Range SAT Math	600–680
Range SAT Writing	550–650
Range ACT Composite	26–30
Minimum paper TOEFL	577
Minimum web-based TOEFL	233

DEADLINES	
Early decision	
Deadline	11/15
Early action	
Deadline	11/15
Notification	2/7
Regular	
Deadline	1/15
Nonfall registration?	Yes

APPLICANTS ALSO LOOK AT AND SOMETIMES PREFER

Babson College; Boston College; Boston University; Bryant University; Northeastern University; University of Massachusetts Amherst; Villanova University

FINANCIAL FACTS	
Financial Aid Rating	89
Annual tuition	$39,600
Room and board	$13,445
Required fees	$1,510
Books and supplies	$1,200
% needy frosh rec. need-based scholarship or grant aid	98
% needy UG rec. need-based scholarship or grant aid	97
% needy frosh rec. non-need-based scholarship or grant aid	14
% needy UG rec. non-need-based scholarship or grant aid	12
% needy frosh rec. need-based self-help aid	96
% needy UG rec. need-based self-help aid	96
% frosh rec. any financial aid	75
% UG rec. any financial aid	73
% UG borrow to pay for school	58
Average cumulative indebtedness	$31,208
% frosh need fully met	34
% ugrads need fully met	34
Average % of frosh need met	95
Average % of ugrad need met	94

BEREA COLLEGE

CPO 2220, BEREA, KY 40404 • ADMISSIONS: 859-985-3500 • FAX: 859-985-3512

STUDENTS SAY "..."

Academics

Kentucky's Berea College is one of the nation's few entirely tuition-free private colleges, providing a liberal arts education "to those who otherwise couldn't afford college but who are deserving of the opportunity." Berea is "truly a different world when it comes to the atmosphere of the college," and the "wonderful opportunity" offered to students is truly appreciated. The school takes a "holistic approach" to education and "expects a lot from students both in and outside of class," including labor (everyone is required to work at least 10 hours per week) and convocations.

Professors take an active role in helping students learn: "If you miss a class, professors will email you to find out why." They "care about not just your learning but also about who you are as an individual" and "lively and passionate about their subjects, and it is very evident within their classrooms." "I've never felt more challenged than when I stepped foot in a Berea classroom," says a junior. The small student-to-faculty ratio gives professors the opportunity to get to know their students, and "[allows] them to adapt to their students' needs."

Dating back to 1855, the college is "very deeply rooted in Appalachian culture and history, but unafraid to address issues outside of that." The school gives low income students the opportunity to pursue higher education while participating in a labor program, and so "produces well-rounded, hardworking students fully prepared for grad school or the workforce." "If the labor program is used to its fullest extent, each student has the opportunity to graduate with a fantastic résumé and many network connections," says a sophomore. It also offers "a huge scholarship to study abroad," of which many students take advantage.

Life

"Berea is a calm place" and "there isn't much going on unless you make something happen." Students are quite busy with studying and work, so "naps are rare" and "we usually don't sleep in because there is just so much to do." Most students are taking a full course load and then doing at least one or two extracurricular activities as well. "The town life is simply atrocious" but on campus, "student organizations are constantly holding events to keep Berea students occupied and having fun," including "movie nights, game nights, dances, [and] bowling." Heritage activities, such as Contra dancing, are big.

The town of Richmond is just a 15 minute drive away (there is also a campus shuttle, and Lexington is a bit further), so getting out of small town life for some shopping or restaurant dining "is a must" from time to time. It is illegal to sell alcohol in the town of Berea, and it is against school rules to have alcohol on campus, so "there isn't a big party scene." There also happen to be "a lot of couples on campus," and "people take relationships seriously" here.

Student Body

Berea students are "creative" and "incredibly resilient" and almost every one "comes from the Appalachian region [and] limited resources." Many tend to be first generation college students, and "most student's priorities are not in having the best material items or joining the best sorority." The most typical thing you'll see is "an overworked, but generally content student shuffling between classes and work." Also, "the one thing that ties us all together is the fact that we had to work so hard to get into Berea," says a freshman ("You have to be either an outright nerd or a secret nerd to get [here]"). As some have noticed, there "seems to be a great divide between traditional students and non-traditional."

FINANCIAL AID: 859-985-3310 • E-MAIL: ADMISSIONS@BEREA.EDU • WEBSITE: WWW.BEREA.EDU

THE PRINCETON REVIEW SAYS

Admissions

Very important factors considered include: Interview. *Important factors considered include:* Class rank, GPA, rigor of secondary school record, standardized test scores, application essay, character/personal qualities. *Other factors considered include:* Extracurricular activities, first generation, geographical residence, racial/ethnic status, recommendation(s), state residency, talent/ability, volunteer work, work experience, level of applicant's interest. SAT or ACT required; ACT with or without Writing component accepted. TOEFL required of all international applicants. *Academic units recommended:* 4 English; 3 mathematics; 2 science; (2 science lab); 2 social studies; 2 foreign language.

Financial Aid

Students should submit: FAFSA. Regular filing deadline is 3/1. The Princeton Review suggests that all financial aid forms be submitted as soon as possible after January 1. *Need-based scholarships/grants offered:* Federal Pell, SEOG, State scholarships/grants, private scholarships, the school's own gift aid. *Loan aid offered:* Direct Subsidized Stafford Loans, Direct Unsubsidized Stafford Loans, Direct PLUS loans, Federal Perkins Loans, College/university loans from institutional funds. Federal Work-Study Program available.

Inside Word

The full-tuition scholarship that every student receives understandably attracts a lot of applicants. Competition among candidates is intense. To make matters worse, you may be too wealthy to get admitted here. Berea won't admit students whose parents can afford to send them elsewhere. Financially qualified applicants should apply as early as possible.

THE SCHOOL SAYS "..."

From the Admissions Office

"Founded in 1855 by ardent abolitionists, Berea College was the first racially integrated coeducational college in the South. Over the past 150 years, Berea has evolved into one of the most distinctive colleges in the United States. Serving students primarily from the Appalachian region, Berea College seeks to serve students who possess great academic promise but have access to limited financial resources. Berea provides an inviting and personal educational experience, evidenced in part by an eleven to one student/faculty ratio and extensive, faculty-led advising and orientation programs.

"In support of students with limited financial resources, every enrolling student receives a full-tuition scholarship, a laptop computer, as well as a paid on-campus job. Students may use earnings from their jobs to assist with their portion of room, board, and fee charges; books and supplies; and other personal expenses. Any remaining housing, meals, and fee charges are covered through scholarships and grant-based aid.

"As a result of this combination of academic reputation and generous financial assistance, Berea attracts many more applicants than are able to be accepted, so admission is competitive. The best means of improving the chances for admission is to complete the application process as early as possible, preferably by October 31 of the senior year."

SELECTIVITY

Admissions Rating	91
# of applicants	1,606
% of applicants accepted	34
% of acceptees attending	72

FRESHMAN PROFILE

Range SAT Critical Reading	510–630
Range SAT Math	513–610
Range SAT Writing	483–610
Range ACT Composite	22–26
Minimum paper TOEFL	500
Minimum web-based TOEFL	173
Average HS GPA	3.42
% graduated top 10% of class	25
% graduated top 25% of class	73
% graduated top 50% of class	95

DEADLINES

Regular	
Deadline	4/30
Nonfall registration?	No

FINANCIAL FACTS

Financial Aid Rating	84
Annual tuition	$0
% needy frosh rec. need-based scholarship or grant aid	100
% needy UG rec. need-based scholarship or grant aid	100
% needy frosh rec. non-need-based scholarship or grant aid	0
% needy UG rec. non-need-based scholarship or grant aid	0
% needy frosh rec. need-based self-help aid	100
% needy UG rec. need-based self-help aid	100
% frosh rec. any financial aid	100
% UG rec. any financial aid	100
% UG borrow to pay for school	67
Average cumulative indebtedness	$6,652
% frosh need fully met	0
% ugrads need fully met	0
Average % of frosh need met	96
Average % of ugrad need met	92

BOSTON COLLEGE

140 COMMONWEALTH AVENUE, CHESTNUT HILL, MA 02467-3809 • ADMISSIONS: 617-552-3100 • FAX: 617-552-0798

STUDENTS SAY "..."

Academics

Boston College, a small Jesuit school on the outskirts of Boston, "is all about educating the person as a whole." Its strong core curriculum ensures all students receive a "well-rounded" liberal arts education regardless of their chosen major. Boston College's well-respected education and business school attract a lot of students, and there are many other strong programs, including English and communication. Students think Boston College is a "great experience academically" and gush about their "phenomenal professors." A secondary education major student says, "Boston College's professors are truly exceptional and are devoted to undergraduate learning." They're "engaging, challenging, and understanding, [and] are genuinely interested in the student as a whole person." Boston College's "prestigious" academics come with "high expectations," but if students need help professors are "easily accessible outside of classes." Students "feel prepared for whatever is next" and note that their "well-connected" teachers and strong alumni network help with the job search. One student, who was drawn to Boston College because of its stellar reputation, finds it "even better than expected." Another adds, "I have always revered Boston College's academic and athletic reputation, and coming here, I have not been disappointed."

Life

Boston College's "gorgeous campus" and "perfect'" suburban location has created a very rich campus life and given the school a "strong community feel." There's "a superb sense of school spirit, which truly sets it apart." One students raves, "There is just so much school spirit and love for the university!" Boston College's "incredible sports teams" are well-supported by "superfans at every event." "There is also a large service component," to life at Boston College, which allows students "to serve the community in Boston and communities all around the world." Boston College offers a "plethora of extracurricular activities," and students think "there's a club or group for everyone here." The school has "great facilities" and "state-of-the-art resources." Dorms are generally well-reviewed, though students think the housing lottery could be more "fair." Students often go into Boston for all of its entertainment and cultural activities but are happy to return to their "close-knit college" where they "feel very at home."

Student Body

Boston College has gotten some flak for its "preppy," "white," and "homogenous" student body, and a communication student admits, "The school's nickname as 'J. Crew U.' isn't entirely unwarranted." Boston College could definitely use "greater racial diversity," but one student says that each year "the student body becomes more and more diverse." A student double-majoring in economics and German says, "Once you've settled in you'll find that it's not at all difficult to find a group of friends" no matter who you are. "There is a large religious/spiritual community," because of the school's Jesuit affiliation, but "it is only one group of many." Boston College's Division I ranking means there are plenty of athletes and sports fans. Students warn that Boston College is "not the place to go to class in your pajamas." People, particularly women, are "very well-dressed" and "stylish." Students say their peers are "really ambitious" and "hardworking." "The majority of students seem intelligent and academically driven as well as dedicated to and passionate about one or more extracurricular activities." Though people at Boston College are "academically oriented," they're "also into having a good time, and "have a work hard, play hard mentality." There's a moderate amount of drinking on campus and off, but students say that no matter what, everyone "definitely [has] school as a top priority."

FINANCIAL AID: 617-552-3300 • WEBSITE: WWW.BC.EDU

THE PRINCETON REVIEW SAYS

Admissions

Very important factors considered include: GPA, rigor of secondary school record, standardized test scores. *Important factors considered include:* Class rank, application essay, extracurricular activities, recommendation(s), talent/ability, volunteer work, alumni/ae relations, character/personal qualities, religious affiliation. *Other factors considered include:* First generation, racial/ethnic status, work experience. SAT and SAT Subject Tests or ACT required; ACT with Writing component required. TOEFL required of all international applicants. *Academic units recommended:* 4 English; 4 mathematics; 4 science; (4 science lab); 4 social studies; 4 foreign language; 4 history.

Financial Aid

Students should submit: FAFSA, CSS/Financial Aid PROFILE, Noncustodial PROFILE, Business/Farm Supplement. The Princeton Review suggests that all financial aid forms be submitted as soon as possible after January 1. *Need-based scholarships/grants offered:* Federal Pell, SEOG, State scholarships/grants, private scholarships, the school's own gift aid. *Loan aid offered:* Direct Subsidized Stafford Loans, Direct Unsubsidized Stafford Loans, Direct PLUS loans, Federal Perkins Loans, Federal Nursing Loans, State Loans. Applicants will be notified of awards beginning 4/1. Federal Work-Study Program available. Institutional employment available. Off-campus job opportunities are good.

The Inside Word

Boston College is one of many selective schools that eschew set admissions formulae. While a challenging high school curriculum and strong test scores are essential for any serious candidate, the college seeks students who are passionate and make connections between academic pursuits and extracurricular activities. The application process should reveal a distinct, mature voice and a student whose interest in education goes beyond the simple desire to earn an A.

THE SCHOOL SAYS ". . ."

From the Admissions Office

"Boston College students achieve at the highest levels with honors including two Rhodes scholarship winners, 173 Fulbrights, four Marshalls, nine Goldwaters, fifteen Beckmans, and six Truman Postgraduate Fellowship Programs. Junior Year Abroad and Scholar of the College Program offer students flexibility within the curriculum. Facilities opened in the past ten years include Stokes Hall, Merkert Chemistry Center, Higgins Hall (housing the Biology and Physics departments), three new residence halls, the Yawkey Athletics Center, the Vanderslice Commons Dining Hall, the Hillside Cafe, and a state-of-the-art library. Students enjoy the vibrant location in Chestnut Hill with easy access to the cultural and historical richness of Boston.

"Boston College requires freshman applicants to take the SAT with writing (or the ACT with the writing exam required). Two SAT Subject Tests are required; students are encouraged to take Subject Tests in fields in which they excel."

SELECTIVITY
Admissions Rating	97
# of applicants	24,538
% of applicants accepted	32
% of acceptees attending	28
# offered a place on the wait list	6,000
% accepting a place on wait list	54
% admitted from wait list	9

FRESHMAN PROFILE
Range SAT Critical Reading	620–710
Range SAT Math	650–740
Range SAT Writing	640–730
Range ACT Composite	30–33
Minimum paper TOEFL	600
Minimum web-based TOEFL	250
% graduated top 10% of class	81
% graduated top 25% of class	97
% graduated top 50% of class	99

DEADLINES
Early action	
Deadline	11/1
Notification	12/25
Regular	
Deadline	1/1
Notification	4/15
Nonfall registration?	Yes

APPLICANTS ALSO LOOK AT AND OFTEN PREFER
Harvard College; Brown University; University of Pennsylvania; Yale University

AND SOMETIMES PREFER
Georgetown University; Cornell University; University of Notre Dame; New York University

AND RARELY PREFER
Boston University; Villanova University; Northeastern University; Fordham University

FINANCIAL FACTS
Financial Aid Rating	94
Annual tuition	$44,870
Room and board	$12,884
Required fees	$752
Books and supplies	$1,000
% needy frosh rec. need-based scholarship or grant aid	89
% needy UG rec. need-based scholarship or grant aid	88
% needy frosh rec. non-need-based scholarship or grant aid	2
% needy UG rec. non-need-based scholarship or grant aid	2
% needy frosh rec. need-based self-help aid	96
% needy UG rec. need-based self-help aid	94
% frosh rec. any financial aid	63
% UG rec. any financial aid	68
% UG borrow to pay for school	49
Average cumulative indebtedness	$20,601
% frosh need fully met	100
% ugrads need fully met	100
Average % of frosh need met	100
Average % of ugrad need met	100

BOSTON UNIVERSITY

233 BAY STATE ROAD, BOSTON, MA 02215 • ADMISSIONS: 617-353-2300 • FAX: 617-353-9695

CAMPUS LIFE

Quality of Life Rating	95
Fire Safety Rating	61
Green Rating	87
Type of school	Private
Affiliation	No Affiliation
Environment	Metropolis

STUDENTS

Total undergrad enrollment	16,460
% male/female	40/60
% from out of state	74
% frosh from public high school	60
% frosh live on campus	99
% ugrads live on campus	75
# of fraternities (% ugrad men join)	11 (5)
# of sororities (% ugrad women join)	10 (15)
% African American	3
% Asian	13
% Caucasian	47
% Hispanic	9
% Native American	<1
% international	16
# of countries represented	133

SURVEY SAYS . . .
Students are happy
Students love Boston, MA
Great food on campus
Great off-campus food
Athletic facilities are great
Hard liquor is popular

ACADEMICS

Academic Rating	87
% students returning for sophomore year	93
% students graduating within 4 years	80
% students graduating within 6 years	84
Calendar	Semester
Student/faculty ratio	13:1
Profs interesting rating	82
Profs accessible rating	83

Most classes have 10–19 students.
Most lab/discussion sessions have 20–29 students.

MOST POPULAR MAJORS
communications; engineering; business administration and management

STUDENTS SAY ". . ."

Academics
Long recognized for offering both the breadth of a large research university and the depth of a private college, the "various schools and colleges within Boston University provide students with access to almost every imaginable program of study." In keeping with this, students report a wide variety of majors and concentrations, naming standout programs in engineering, education, and business administration. Professors are praised as much as is students' ability to choose them: BU professors are both "actively pursuing research in their field" and "engaging partners in my academic experience," and students find that professors' "interesting backgrounds...fuel class discussions in a variety of academic areas." Undergraduates also love the university's "location" as an "urban campus" in Boston's Back Bay, and benefit distinctly from BU's "opportunity access" when it comes to job placement. As a private university with a large student body, BU students also become the beneficiaries of the institution's "wealth," calling the experience one of "big campus resources with a small campus feel." The faculty and administration "are constantly striving to be better for the student's benefit" in delivering BU's unique curriculum, which is "equal parts liberal arts education and pre-professional experience." The university emphasizes "study abroad" and "research opportunities," which further broaden the possibilities of a BU education. Perhaps ideal for the student who desires a wide variety of choices in order to discover what comes next, "the range and diversity of opportunities at Boston University allows you to Be You."

Life
Continuing the theme of wide-ranging options, BU undergraduates divulge that student "life at BU is anything you want it to be." Because of BU's location in "the heart of Boston," "the city itself is like our campus", and BU undergrads can mingle freely with Boston's many other college students students in nearby Cambridge, Somerville, Allston and Brookline. Students are rarely bored because "there's always something interesting going on on- and off-campus": campus life boasts "a lot of clubs and activities to get involved in," as well as "house parties," "BU hockey games," and "frat parties," while students' access to Boston spans everything from "a run along the Charles River" to "shopping on Newbury or in Harvard Square" to frequenting "plays and ballets and museums" and the many local "clubs and bars." Students strive to maximize the best of both sides of BU life, "prid[ing] themselves on being able to find balance in living strong academic lives and exciting social lives as well." Students seem satisfied with the choices they do end up making, reporting that BU life is "wonderful" and that "there is more to do than you will be able to find the time for."

Student Body
"There is a great sense of diversity, yet an overwhelming feeling of unity" within BU's large but closely connected undergraduate population. Students strongly resist the idea of a "typical student," asserting that "originality is valued highly at BU," as is "diversity of thought." "Because we are an international university," many students point out, "the student body is vastly diverse." Students have "a wide range of interests both inside and outside the classroom," and characterize themselves as "motivated, culturally-aware, intelligent, adventurous," "driven and involved," and "very passionate." BU undergrads find their peers "intellectually stimulating in conversations" and tend to group, as in most college experiences, around shared interests and experiences. One student echoes many of her classmates this way: "My life at BU is quite packed because I chose to make it that way."

FINANCIAL AID: 617-353-4176 • E-MAIL: ADMISSIONS@BU.EDU • WEBSITE: WWW.BU.EDU

THE PRINCETON REVIEW SAYS

Admissions

Very important factors considered include: Rigor of secondary school record. *Important factors considered include:* Class rank, GPA, standardized test scores, application essay, recommendation(s). *Other factors considered include:* Extracurricular activities, first generation, geographical residence, racial/ethnic status, state residency, talent/ability, volunteer work, work experience, alumni/ae relations, character/personal qualities, level of applicant's interest. SAT or ACT required; SAT and SAT Subject Tests or ACT considered if submitted; ACT with Writing component required. TOEFL required of all international applicants. *Academic units required:* 4 English; 3 mathematics; 3 science; (3 science lab); 3 social studies; 2 foreign language; 3 history. *Academic units recommended:* 4 English; 4 social studies; 4 history.

Financial Aid

Students should submit: FAFSA, CSS/Financial Aid PROFILE, Noncustodial PROFILE. Regular filing deadline is 2/15. The Princeton Review suggests that all financial aid forms be submitted as soon as possible after January 1. *Need-based scholarships/grants offered:* Federal Pell, SEOG, State scholarships/grants, private scholarships, the school's own gift aid. *Loan aid offered:* Direct Subsidized Stafford Loans, Direct Unsubsidized Stafford Loans, Direct PLUS loans, Federal Perkins Loans, State Loans. Federal Work-Study Program available. Institutional employment available. Off-campus job opportunities are excellent.

The Inside Word

BU can afford to stay competitive, and they strongly emphasize high school academic performance as the key indicator of a student's admissibility to the university. BU values students who take on a challenging high school curriculum (especially AP and IB classes, or whatever the most challenging courseload available is). The personal essay, recommendations, extracurricular activities, and standardized test scores (SAT or ACT plus SAT Writing) are also important factors in assessing applicants. Several undergraduate courses of study (mostly in medicine and the arts) require specific standardized test supplements; prospective students are encouraged to read BU's admissions requirements carefully before applying.

THE SCHOOL SAYS "..."

From the Admissions Office

"Boston University is a world-recognized, private teaching and research university committed to excellence in undergraduate education. It is ranked in the top 4 percent of universities in the nation by *U.S. News & World Report*. Students study with distinguished faculty that include Fulbright Scholars, Pulitzer Prize winners, MacArthur Fellows, Nobel Prize winners, and a former Poet Laureate. In nine undergraduate schools and colleges, BU offers students more than 250 programs of study, cutting-edge research with faculty mentors, internships in the United States and abroad, and one of the nation's most extensive study abroad programs. Housing is guaranteed for four years in a variety of on-campus residences, including high-rise buildings and historic brownstones. BU students are engaged with their campus community through over 500 student organizations, club and intramural sports, and twenty-three NCAA Division I sports teams. Students experience the city of Boston as an extension of campus for study, internships, employment, and cultural and recreational activities.

"BU requires freshman applicants to take the SAT or the ACT (with Writing). Students applying to the Accelerated Medical or Dental Programs are required to submit Subject Tests in chemistry, math (Level 2), and a foreign language (recommended). Candidates for the College of Fine Arts must present a portfolio or participate in an audition."

SELECTIVITY

Admissions Rating	95
# of applicants	52,705
% of applicants accepted	37
% of acceptees attending	20
# offered a place on the wait list	5,055
% accepting a place on wait list	48
% admitted from wait list	3
# of early decision applicants	1,496
% accepted early decision	40

FRESHMAN PROFILE

Range SAT Critical Reading	570–670
Range SAT Math	620–720
Range SAT Writing	600–690
Range ACT Composite	27–31
Minimum web-based TOEFL	215
Average HS GPA	3.59
% graduated top 10% of class	58
% graduated top 25% of class	89
% graduated top 50% of class	99

DEADLINES

Early decision	
Deadline	11/1
Notification	12/15
Regular	
Priority	11/1
Deadline	1/1
Notification	4/1
Nonfall registration?	Yes

APPLICANTS ALSO LOOK AT AND OFTEN PREFER
University of Southern California; New York University; The George Washington University

AND SOMETIMES PREFER
Boston College; Cornell University; Syracuse University; Tufts University

AND RARELY PREFER
University of Massachusetts Amherst

FINANCIAL FACTS

Financial Aid Rating	90
Annual tuition	$45,686
Room and board	$14,030
Required fees	$978
Books and supplies	$1,000
% needy frosh rec. need-based scholarship or grant aid	94
% needy UG rec. need-based scholarship or grant aid	95
% needy frosh rec. non-need-based scholarship or grant aid	36
% needy UG rec. non-need-based scholarship or grant aid	25
% needy frosh rec. need-based self-help aid	88
% needy UG rec. need-based self-help aid	90
% frosh rec. any financial aid	61
% UG rec. any financial aid	61
% UG borrow to pay for school	58
Average cumulative indebtedness	$37,694
% frosh need fully met	54
% ugrads need fully met	46
Average % of frosh need met	92
Average % of ugrad need met	89

BOWDOIN COLLEGE

5000 COLLEGE STATION, BRUNSWICK, ME 04011-8441 • ADMISSIONS: 207-725-3100 • FAX: 207-725-3101

CAMPUS LIFE

Quality of Life Rating	99
Fire Safety Rating	89
Green Rating	92
Type of school	Private
Affiliation	No Affiliation
Environment	Village

STUDENTS

Total undergrad enrollment	1,789
% male/female	50/50
% from out of state	89
% frosh from public high school	51
% frosh live on campus	100
% ugrads live on campus	92
% African American	5
% Asian	7
% Caucasian	64
% Hispanic	12
% Native American	<1
% international	5
# of countries represented	34

SURVEY SAYS . . .
Students are happy
Classroom facilities are great
Lab facilities are great
School is well run
No one cheats
Students are friendly
Students environmentally aware
Great food on campus
Great off-campus food
Dorms are like palaces
Campus feels safe
Easy to get around campus
Athletic facilities are great
Lots of beer drinking
Everyone loves the Polar Bears
Student publications are popular
Alumni active on campus

ACADEMICS

Academic Rating	97
% students returning for sophomore year	97
% students graduating within 4 years	88
% students graduating within 6 years	93
Calendar	Semester
Student/faculty ratio	9:1
Profs interesting rating	95
Profs accessible rating	96

Most classes have 10–19 students.
Most lab/discussion sessions have 10–19 students.

MOST POPULAR MAJORS
political science; economics; mathematics

STUDENTS SAY "..."

Academics

From the "academic rigor" to the "laid-back attitude of the people" and "the beautiful Maine scenery," Bowdoin is a small liberal arts college that packs a considerable punch. Tucked away in the quaint town of Brunswick, Bowdoin provides students with an "extremely high quality of education" and "amazing resources." Moreover, there's a "tangible sense of community" and the campus resonates with a "friendly vibe." The college also does "a great job of maintaining a culture that is not based on competition, but collaboration." While there are certainly a number of great departments, both the science and government programs have an especially stellar reputation. And when it comes to the classroom, it's obvious that "professors at Bowdoin are very passionate about the classes that they teach." Students greatly appreciate that they are "easily accessible by e-mail, during office hours and even on weekends." And though professors here are known to be "tough," undergrads admit that they are "pushed academically in the best possible ways." Further, professors truly "want you to learn and they want to get to know you." Indeed, as one freshman brags, "Bowdoin is a place where taking your professors to lunch is the norm." Overall, as one content sophomore rhapsodizes, "Stepping on to the Bowdoin campus, it's hard to not get genuinely excited about all of the academic, social and cultural opportunities that await you."

Life

Undergrads at Bowdoin are pretty frank about the fact that "life during the week is consumed by work." As a sophomore reveals, "People are very focused on their studies, and academics always come first." Fortunately, even the most studious undergrads here find the time to kick back every once in awhile. And there are plenty of activities and events of which to take advantage. For example, "Every weekend there are film screenings, speakers or miscellaneous activities sponsored by ResLife or student groups." Additionally, "athletics are popular, as are the music groups [and] the outing club is another major draw [as well]." And a satisfied freshman adds, "Last weekend we had a 'Zombie Run' for Halloween [and] there was a Hunger Games competition earlier in the year." While Bowdoin doesn't have Greek life, "house parties are a big thing." These can typically be found "every Friday and Saturday [night]." However, one knowledgeable senior clarifies by saying these are "mostly [attended] by first-years and sophomores. Juniors and seniors typically spend time with friends, some choosing to drink in a smaller and quieter atmosphere." When students are eager to get off campus, they frequently take advantage of Maine's outdoor splendor. There's "sea kayaking, white-water kayaking/rafting, surfing, hiking, backpacking, skiing, sailing [and] rocking climbing, among other [activities]." Those students looking for a more relaxing outing can head to nearby Portland or Freeport for shopping and dining. Finally, we'd be remiss if we didn't point out that undergrads are content to hang around the dining halls simply because, "the food is AMAZING."

Student Body

Many undergrads here agree that there's a perception that Bowdoin attracts a lot of "wasp-y, wealthy, preppy, upper-middle class" students. However, they just as fiercely assert that if you look beyond these superficial characterizations, you'll discover "a wide spread of personalities and student types." And, more importantly, they insist that across the board their peers are "extremely nice and welcoming." They also define their fellow students as "intelligent," "outdoorsy" and "fairly left-wing politically." Additionally, "almost everyone either plays a sport or works out regularly and is involved in too many extracurricular activities for their own good." It also seems as though "each student has [his/her] own special talent, interest [or] hobby." As one senior explains, "I love that everyone has their own nerdy passion for some random subject—Japanese architecture, genetics, medieval women, food justice, etc." Perhaps this sagacious junior describes the Bowdoin social experience best, "I think that as long as students come to Bowdoin being willing and open to meeting lots of people, they will have no trouble finding a loyal group of friends whom they will want to stay in contact with long after they graduate."

FINANCIAL AID: 207-725-3273 • E-MAIL: ADMISSIONS@BOWDOIN.EDU • WEBSITE: WWW.BOWDOIN.EDU

THE PRINCETON REVIEW SAYS

Admissions

Very important factors considered include: Class rank, GPA, rigor of secondary school record, application essay, extracurricular activities, recommendation(s), talent/ability, character/personal qualities. *Important factors considered include:* Standardized test scores, first generation, alumni/ae relations. *Other factors considered include:* Geographical residence, interview, racial/ethnic status, state residency. SAT and SAT Subject Tests or ACT considered if submitted; ACT with or without Writing component accepted. TOEFL required of all international applicants. *Academic units recommended:* 4 English; 4 mathematics; 4 science; (3 science lab); 4 social studies; 4 foreign language.

Financial Aid

Students should submit: FAFSA, CSS/Financial Aid PROFILE, Noncustodial PROFILE, Business/Farm Supplement. Regular filing deadline is 2/15. The Princeton Review suggests that all financial aid forms be submitted as soon as possible after January 1. *Need-based scholarships/grants offered:* Federal Pell, SEOG, State scholarships/grants, private scholarships, the school's own gift aid. *Loan aid offered:* Direct Subsidized Stafford Loans, Direct Unsubsidized Stafford Loans, Federal Perkins Loans, State Loans. Applicants will be notified of awards beginning 4/5. Federal Work-Study Program available. Institutional employment available. Off-campus job opportunities are good.

The Inside Word

Securing admission to Bowdoin is no easy feat. Competition is definitely fierce and it's imperative that applicants be near the top of their class. Admissions officers do take a holistic approach carefully analyzing academic success, course levels, school/community involvement, academic potential, writing samples, recommendations and character. Candidates who think Bowdoin might be their top choice are encouraged to apply early decision.

THE SCHOOL SAYS "..."

From the Admissions Office

"A Bowdoin education is best summed up by 'The Offer of the College':"

To be at home in all lands and all ages;
To count Nature a familiar acquaintance,
And Art an intimate friend;
To gain a standard for the appreciation of others' work
And the criticism of your own;
To carry the keys of the world's library in your pocket,
And feel its resources behind you in whatever task you undertake;
To make hosts of friends...
Who are to be leaders in all walks of life;
To lose yourself in generous enthusiasms
And cooperate with others for common ends—
This is the offer of the college for the best four years of your life."

Adapted from the original 'Offer of the College'
by William DeWitt Hyde
President of Bowdoin College 1885–1917"

SELECTIVITY

Admissions Rating	99
# of applicants	7,052
% of applicants accepted	15
% of acceptees attending	47
# of early decision applicants	865
% accepted early decision	26

FRESHMAN PROFILE

Range SAT Critical Reading	680–760
Range SAT Math	680–750
Range SAT Writing	690–770
Range ACT Composite	30–33
Minimum paper TOEFL	600
Minimum web-based TOEFL	250
Average HS GPA	3.80
% graduated top 10% of class	83
% graduated top 25% of class	94
% graduated top 50% of class	100

DEADLINES

Early decision	
Deadline	11/15
Notification	12/15
Regular	
Deadline	1/1
Notification	4/5
Nonfall registration?	No

APPLICANTS ALSO LOOK AT

AND OFTEN PREFER
Brown University; Dartmouth College; Harvard College; Princeton University; Stanford University; Yale University

AND SOMETIMES PREFER
Amherst College; Williams College

AND RARELY PREFER
Middlebury College; Tufts University; Wesleyan University

FINANCIAL FACTS

Financial Aid Rating	97
Annual tuition	$45,004
Room and board	$12,388
Required fees	$442
Books and supplies	$816
% needy frosh rec. need-based scholarship or grant aid	100
% needy UG rec. need-based scholarship or grant aid	100
% needy frosh rec. non-need-based scholarship or grant aid	0
% needy UG rec. non-need-based scholarship or grant aid	0
% needy frosh rec. need-based self-help aid	86
% needy UG rec. need-based self-help aid	87
% frosh rec. any financial aid	50
% UG rec. any financial aid	48
% UG borrow to pay for school	31
Average cumulative indebtedness	$21,292
% frosh need fully met	100
% ugrads need fully met	100
Average % of frosh need met	100
Average % of ugrad need met	100

BRADLEY UNIVERSITY

1501 WEST BRADLEY AVENUE, PEORIA, IL 61625 • ADMISSIONS: 309-677-1000 • FAX: 309-677-2797

CAMPUS LIFE

Quality of Life Rating	78
Fire Safety Rating	84
Green Rating	60*
Type of school	Private
Affiliation	No Affiliation
Environment	City

STUDENTS

Total undergrad enrollment	4,872
% male/female	47/53
% from out of state	12
% frosh from public high school	82
% frosh live on campus	92
% ugrads live on campus	66
# of fraternities (% ugrad men join)	16 (33)
# of sororities (% ugrad women join)	11 (31)
% African American	7
% Asian	4
% Caucasian	80
% Hispanic	6
% Native American	<1
% international	1
# of countries represented	34

SURVEY SAYS . . .

Students are friendly
Athletic facilities are great
Frats and sororities are popular

ACADEMICS

Academic Rating	80
% students returning for sophomore year	86
% students graduating within 4 years	53
% students graduating within 6 years	75
Calendar	Semester
Student/faculty ratio	12:1
Profs interesting rating	79
Profs accessible rating	87
Most classes have 10–19 students.	

MOST POPULAR MAJORS

mechanical engineering; family practice nursing; communications; communications

STUDENTS SAY ". . ."

Academics

Academically, Bradley provides "the resources of a large university with the familiarity that comes from a small liberal arts school." The goal is to provide students with a hands-on learning environment and to prepare them for the world beyond college. In addition to the traditional liberal arts and sciences, academic programs include business, communication, education, engineering, fine and performing arts, and health sciences. Unique programs include entrepreneurship, health science with a direct entry to the Doctorate of Physical Therapy, interactive media, and sports communication. A recent graduate shares her experience, saying, "While Bradley offers the academic choices of a larger university, it also provides students the guidance and mentoring of faculty that only a smaller university can provide." "Ninety-five percent of graduates begin work, graduate school, or other postgraduate experiences of their choice within six months of graduation. I knew I would be prepared and pointed in the right direction." Bradley University provides advantages normally only seen in larger schools with the community and personal attention only a smaller school can deliver.

Life

"It is just the right size. I never imagined myself in a huge university. I like having the ability to meet with my teachers regularly." Another student echoes that sentiment, and adds, "There is always something to do on campus and plenty of activities to become involved in." Located in a residential neighborhood on the west bluff of the Illinois River, the eighty-five-acre campus of Bradley University is just one mile from downtown Peoria, Illinois. The distinctive feel of Bradley comes from a blend of large school opportunities with the quality, and personal attention of a small, private college. A current student tells us, "Bradley is a small-scale school with a big personality and something for everyone." What endears the university to most students is that it is able to provide the resources of a large university and the connections to big cities such as Chicago and St. Louis while maintaining the familiarity that comes from a small, liberal arts school. Bradley is all about community, and students tell us that the greatest strength is "the amount of activities and organizations on campus."

Student Body

One of our interviewees provided an interesting insight, saying, "Students here are normal, kind of boring, but beneath all that is a potential for anything, greatness. There are phenomenal opportunities to volunteer and help people here. Bradley is a community of good people who are respectful and awesome." Another student shares, "Everyone is really involved. I am extremely busy but not overwhelmed. Bradley creates several activities for students to [enjoy]. For fun I mainly hang with friends on campus and go off campus." Another perspective comes from this commuter, "I think life on campus was great, now I live off-campus as an upperclassman. The time that I was on campus I felt that there were various activities to attend on the weekends if we wanted to but a lot of us just hung out together in the dorms." Back on campus, a junior tells us, "Bradley offers a great deal of free and alcohol-free activities that can take the place of partying for those interested. That being said, Bradley is in no way a party school. While there are occasions when the festivities get wild, I would never describe anything as 'out of control.'" Another student explains the Bradley "balance" this way: "Life at school is great…People are still very determined to do well in school, to get their degree, and to get a great job upon graduation."

FINANCIAL AID: 309-677-3089 • E-MAIL: ADMISSIONS@BRADLEY.EDU • WEBSITE: WWW.BRADLEY.EDU

THE PRINCETON REVIEW SAYS

Admissions

Very important factors considered include: GPA, rigor of secondary school record. *Important factors considered include:* Class rank, standardized test scores. *Other factors considered include:* Application essay, extracurricular activities, first generation, geographical residence, interview, racial/ethnic status, recommendation(s), talent/ability, volunteer work, work experience, alumni/ae relations, character/personal qualities, level of applicant's interest. SAT or ACT required; ACT with or without Writing component accepted. TOEFL required of all international applicants. *Academic units required:* 4 English; 3 mathematics; 2 science; (2 science lab); 2 social studies. *Academic units recommended:* 5 English; 4 mathematics; 3 science; (3 science lab); 3 social studies; 2 foreign language; 2 history.

Financial Aid

Students should submit: FAFSA. The Princeton Review suggests that all financial aid forms be submitted as soon as possible after January 1. *Need-based scholarships/grants offered:* Federal Pell, SEOG, State scholarships/grants, private scholarships, the school's own gift aid. *Loan aid offered:* Direct Subsidized Stafford Loans, Direct Unsubsidized Stafford Loans, Direct PLUS loans, Federal Perkins Loans, Federal Nursing Loans. Federal Work-Study Program available. Institutional employment available.

The Inside Word

With much regional appeal, the vast majority of students at Bradley originate from Illinois. With an active eye toward broadening the student body's geographic demographics, the school presents an opportunity for out-of-staters seeking to attend an excellent university without having to endure the grueling admissions process of many private universities. Above-average students should find that gaining admission here is a relatively painless experience.

THE SCHOOL SAYS "..."

From the Admissions Office

"Bradley is a private, independent university in Peoria, Illinois, offering 6,000 students a world-class education linking academic excellence, experiential learning and leadership development with an entrepreneurial spirit in more than 100 academic programs.

"Great academic variety leads to choices of majors, minors and graduate programs that are uncommon at most private universities. Bradley's size allows for access to a combination of resources not available at most small colleges and personal attention not commonly found at larger universities.

"Located less than three hours from Chicago, St. Louis, and Indianapolis, the eighty-five-acre park-like campus is located in a historic residential neighborhood just one mile from downtown Peoria; the largest metropolitan area in downstate Illinois.

"Bradley students develop leadership skills in more than 240 student organizations with more than sixty dedicated to leadership and community service. Students may also participate in the national champion speech team, fraternities and sororities, NCAA Division I sports, and more than a dozen diverse religious organizations.

"At Bradley, career development begins in a student's first year. This career development approach leads to 95 percent placement of graduates who accept jobs, positions in graduate school, or other postgraduate experiences within six months of graduation.

"National college guides rank Bradley among the top schools in the nation for academic quality and value. Guidebooks also note mentoring of students by faculty, access to quality facilities, and hand's-on learning among Bradley's greatest strengths. The Princeton Review rates Bradley's entrepreneurship program and video game design programs as among the top in the nation."

SELECTIVITY

Admissions Rating	87
# of applicants	7,562
% of applicants accepted	63
% of acceptees attending	21

FRESHMAN PROFILE

Range SAT Critical Reading	520–660
Range SAT Math	510–650
Range SAT Writing	520–620
Range ACT Composite	23–28
Minimum paper TOEFL	550
Minimum web-based TOEFL	197
Average HS GPA	3.69
% graduated top 10% of class	35
% graduated top 25% of class	69
% graduated top 50% of class	94

DEADLINES

Regular	
Priority	2/1
Nonfall registration?	Yes

APPLICANTS ALSO LOOK AT AND OFTEN PREFER

Purdue University—West Lafayette; University of Illinois at Urbana-Champaign

AND SOMETIMES PREFER

DePaul University; Marquette University; Loyola The University of Chicago; Augustana College (IL); Illinois Wesleyan University; Saint Louis University

AND RARELY PREFER

Illinois State University; University of Missouri; University of Iowa; Iowa State University

FINANCIAL FACTS

Financial Aid Rating	73
Annual tuition	$29,320
Room and board	$9,050
Required fees	$344
Books and supplies	$1,200
% needy frosh rec. need-based scholarship or grant aid	97
% needy UG rec. need-based scholarship or grant aid	95
% needy frosh rec. non-need-based scholarship or grant aid	10
% needy UG rec. non-need-based scholarship or grant aid	8
% needy frosh rec. need-based self-help aid	98
% needy UG rec. need-based self-help aid	97
% frosh rec. any financial aid	97
% UG rec. any financial aid	94
% frosh need fully met	14
% ugrads need fully met	14
Average % of frosh need met	67
Average % of ugrad need met	62

BRANDEIS UNIVERSITY

415 SOUTH STREET, WALTHAM, MA 02454-9110 • ADMISSIONS: 781-736-3500 • FAX: 781-736-3536

CAMPUS LIFE

Quality of Life Rating	91
Fire Safety Rating	93
Green Rating	88
Type of school	Private
Affiliation	No Affiliation
Environment	City

STUDENTS

Total undergrad enrollment	3,603
% male/female	43/57
% from out of state	73
% frosh from public high school	65
% frosh live on campus	98
% ugrads live on campus	79
% African American	5
% Asian	12
% Caucasian	50
% Hispanic	7
% Native American	<1
% international	15
# of countries represented	92

SURVEY SAYS . . .
Lots of liberal students
Students are happy
Lab facilities are great
Students are friendly
Diverse student types on campus
Students get along with local community
Students involved in community service
Students environmentally aware
Great off-campus food
Theater is popular
Active minority support groups

ACADEMICS

Academic Rating	89
% students returning for sophomore year	93
% students graduating within 4 years	86
% students graduating within 6 years	90
Calendar	Semester
Student/faculty ratio	10:1
Profs interesting rating	88
Profs accessible rating	85
Most classes have 10–19 students.	

MOST POPULAR MAJORS
biology; economics; psychology

STUDENTS SAY ". . ."

Academics
Located in the Boston area, Brandeis is a private liberal arts research university that has "a little bit of everything." The school "gives students the freedom to explore both in and outside of the classroom" It has a (rightful) reputation for tough academics, particularly in the sciences, and this "pays off. Employers, grad schools, and certainly medical schools, know how tough the academics are." The school puts "a great importance on social justice and community," the latter of which "is unmatched" elsewhere. Academics at Brandeis are "stimulating," and even though a few professors at times can be "inconsistent and unreliable," the faculty on the whole is "extremely dedicated to their subjects" and "truly there for the students." "As a first-year student I was part of a class that was invited to the professor's house for a Thanksgiving pot luck dinner," says one. Getting some sort of outside help is necessary for the sciences, as "classes are often curved, and the competition is tough," but luckily professors are all available, and "all of the introductory classes break down into small groups once a week." People "care about their studies, but the atmosphere isn't competitive." Along with "plenty of scientific research opportunities" for such a small school, many students "find it difficult to choose classes because of all of the awesome course descriptions." Student services have expanded in recent years, and the Hiatt Career Center now offers "Graduate School Thursdays, alumni shadowing, mock interviews, and career fairs specifically themed toward 'green jobs,' government forums, and other student interests." Independence is a huge part of a Brandeis student's life, and the administration is good about "letting students take charge of their own educations." "We create our own experiences: independent study, clubs, and committees. Students own their experiences," says one student. "It is a wonderfully unique college experience with some of the nicest—and occasionally strangest—people you will ever meet."

Life
Because the school is situated in a small city immediately outside of college-rich Boston, it's able to have "sprawling lawns and an atmosphere of community and openness" while still being accessible to an urban cultural center. There is a "massive amount of extracurricular activities," so "there is always something to do," including a "Cheese Club that provides free cheese tasting," "arts outlets," and numerous organizations that place a "strong emphasis on volunteerism and social justice." "This is…a tremendous place to explore your passions—religiously, socially, and academically," says a student. There are "a ton" of theater, a cappella, and improv groups on campus, and if the campus events aren't enough to satiate your appetite for fun, "there are always ways to go and support other extracurricular groups on campus and see what they're all about." Housing and dining services are considered by students to be the most frustrating aspects of the school; students say a few of the dorms are "rundown and need renovation," and one student warns, "If athletics are the center of your universe, then do not go to Brandeis."

Student Body
There are "few social lines that define the student body" at Brandeis, and "a lot of social life revolves around club life." Students are active here, and "it's not unheard of to find a neuroscience major who juggles DJing on WBRS, skydiving, and student government." This "intellectual and exciting" crew includes a "strong Jewish community," and almost everyone is "nerdy in a very, very cool way." People here are "really quirky and different," and most have secondary pursuits or hobbies outside of academics. "Whatever the students' passions and skills might be, everyone is incredibly motivated and driven toward achievement." Everyone is "fairly studious and encourages each other to study and do their best." Students seem to be friendly without fail. "If you stand in one place for too long on campus, you'll immediately find students approaching you asking if you're lost and how they can help," says a student.

FINANCIAL AID: 781-736-3700 • E-MAIL: ADMISSIONS@BRANDEIS.EDU • WEBSITE: WWW.BRANDEIS.EDU

THE PRINCETON REVIEW SAYS

Admissions

Very important factors considered include: Class rank, GPA, rigor of secondary school record, character/personal qualities. *Important factors considered include:* Application essay, extracurricular activities, recommendation(s), talent/ability, volunteer work, work experience, level of applicant's interest. *Other factors considered include:* Standardized test scores, first generation, geographical residence, interview, racial/ethnic status, state residency, alumni/ae relations. TOEFL required of all international applicants. *Academic units recommended:* 4 English; 4 mathematics; 4 science; (2 science lab); 4 social studies; 4 foreign language.

Financial Aid

Students should submit: FAFSA, CSS/Financial Aid PROFILE, State aid form, Noncustodial PROFILE. Regular filing deadline is 2/1. The Princeton Review suggests that all financial aid forms be submitted as soon as possible after January 1. *Need-based scholarships/grants offered:* Federal Pell, SEOG, State scholarships/grants, private scholarships, the school's own gift aid. *Loan aid offered:* Direct Subsidized Stafford Loans, Direct Unsubsidized Stafford Loans, Direct PLUS loans, Federal Perkins Loans, State Loans, College/university loans from institutional funds. Applicants will be notified of awards beginning 4/1. Federal Work-Study Program available. Institutional employment available.

The Inside Word

Admissions standards have risen at all top schools, and Brandeis is no exception: If you expect to get in here, you've got your work cut out for you. Your application should give evidence of both the ability and enthusiasm to handle demanding academics. A clear demonstration of writing ability will also help a lot.

THE SCHOOL SAYS "..."

From the Admissions Office

"Education at Brandeis is personal, combining the intimacy of a small liberal arts college and the intellectual power of a large research university. Classes are small and are taught by professors, 95 percent of whom hold the highest degree in their fields. They give students personal attention in state-of-the-art resources, giving them the tools to succeed in a variety of postgraduate endeavors.

"This vibrant, free-thinking, intellectual university was founded in 1948. Brandeis University reflects the values of the first Jewish Supreme Court Justice Louis Brandeis, which are passion for learning, commitment to social justice, respect for creativity and diversity, and concern for the world.

"Brandeis has an ideal location on the commuter rail right outside of downtown Boston; state-of-the-art sports facilities; and internships that complement interests in law, medicine, government, finance, business, and the arts.

"Brandeis meets 100 percent of demonstrated need for all admitted students."

SELECTIVITY

Admissions Rating	97
# of applicants	9,496
% of applicants accepted	37
% of acceptees attending	24
# offered a place on the wait list	1,405
% accepting a place on wait list	44
% admitted from wait list	7
# of early decision applicants	544
% accepted early decision	45

FRESHMAN PROFILE

Range SAT Critical Reading	600–710
Range SAT Math	630–760
Range SAT Writing	620–720
Range ACT Composite	28–32
Minimum paper TOEFL	600
Minimum web-based TOEFL	100
Average HS GPA	3.87
% graduated top 10% of class	65
% graduated top 25% of class	89
% graduated top 50% of class	99

DEADLINES

Early decision	
Deadline	11/1
Notification	12/15
Regular	
Deadline	1/1
Notification	4/1
Nonfall registration?	Yes

FINANCIAL FACTS

Financial Aid Rating	86
Annual tuition	$44,380
Room and board	$12,714
Required fees	$1,726
Books and supplies	$1,000
% needy frosh rec. need-based scholarship or grant aid	97
% needy UG rec. need-based scholarship or grant aid	95
% needy frosh rec. non-need-based scholarship or grant aid	6
% needy UG rec. non-need-based scholarship or grant aid	5
% needy frosh rec. need-based self-help aid	90
% needy UG rec. need-based self-help aid	93
% frosh rec. any financial aid	69
% UG rec. any financial aid	65
% UG borrow to pay for school	60
Average cumulative indebtedness	$28,647
% frosh need fully met	36
% ugrads need fully met	23
Average % of frosh need met	95
Average % of ugrad need met	90

BRIGHAM YOUNG UNIVERSITY (UT)

A-153 ASB, PROVO, UT 84602-1110 • ADMISSIONS: 801-422-2507 • FAX: 801-422-0005

STUDENTS SAY ". . ."

Academics

Brigham Young University is a Mormon school that's "all about putting religion and education together" and learning "about secular subjects through spiritual eyes." The school provides a "high-quality" education in a "challenging" academic atmosphere. Students at Brigham Young strive for academic excellence. As one student explains, "Brigham Young pushes us to realize that our 'best' can be a lot better than we ever dreamed, and I love that!" The school offers a wide range of majors, and its education, business, and mathematics programs get great reviews, as does their language program. Classes are generally a "healthy mix of discussion and lecture," and the education classes in particular have "a lot of group work." The school doesn't focus only on classroom learning, however. "Hands-on experience, internships, and study abroad are highly encouraged," and many students take advantage of these opportunities. There are also "tons of undergraduate research opportunities." Professors are "passionate about what they're teaching," and they "really care about their students' success." Another adds, "Professors really do take a genuine interest in their students," and "The vast majority are also very willing to help out students individually." While students at Brigham Young appreciate the academic attention they receive from professors, they also like that it "is committed to spiritual and academic learning for the benefit and betterment of everyone" and that they're being taught to "pursue lifelong learning and service."

Life

Students at Brigham Young love the "atmosphere of spirituality that unites everyone" and "the kindness of those around you." Brigham Young provides a "safe environment," but students "still get to have real-world experiences." Recreationally, "There are multiple clubs across campus to fit the taste of different people," "tons of…performing events," and "fun student body activities, which are cheap." There are also "exceptional weekly devotions and forums." Brigham Young's athletics are well-supported and are a place where "students love to have fun." Students rave about the library and the "Adlab," but more than anything they appreciate that there are "good people everywhere you go."

Student Body

Brigham Young has an extremely conservative "Honor Code" derived from the Mormon Church that requires, among other things, abstinence from drugs, alcohol, tobacco, coffee, and tea, as well as "inappropriate" "sexual activity, including sex outside of marriage and homosexuality." The Honor Code is a plus for students seeking a like-minded peer group, such as this art education student who "didn't want to have to worry about walking in on my roommate sleeping with someone or have to hold her head up while she was puking her guts out into the toilet." The Honor Code also demands honesty and respect for others, which means the student body is "friendly, outgoing," and "concerned for others." Students are "smart and very confident in their intelligence," as well as "hardworking" and "goal-oriented." Mormon traditions mean that 25 percent of students are married, and people appreciate that "the school caters…really well to the average Latter-day Saint student coming in and working with those wanting to get married [or] go on missions." Marriage is definitely on many people's minds. A family studies major notes, "We are constantly encouraged to date." People generally think that "students mesh together well and it is easy to make new friends," though one concedes, "I can see how it could be hard to fit in if you are not used to the Mormon culture or beliefs."

FINANCIAL AID: 801-422-4104 • E-MAIL: ADMISSIONS@BYU.EDU • WEBSITE: WWW.BYU.EDU

THE PRINCETON REVIEW SAYS

Admissions

Very important factors considered include: GPA, rigor of secondary school record, standardized test scores, interview, character/personal qualities, religious affiliation. *Important factors considered include:* Application essay, extracurricular activities, racial/ethnic status, recommendation(s), volunteer work. *Other factors considered include:* First generation, geographical residence, state residency, talent/ability, work experience, level of applicant's interest. SAT or ACT required; ACT with Writing component recommended. TOEFL required of all international applicants. *Academic units recommended:* 4 English; 4 mathematics; 3 science; 2 foreign language; 2 history.

Financial Aid

Students should submit: FAFSA. The Princeton Review suggests that all financial aid forms be submitted as soon as possible after January 1. *Need-based scholarships/grants offered:* Federal Pell, private scholarships, the school's own gift aid. *Loan aid offered:* Direct Subsidized Stafford Loans, Direct Unsubsidized Stafford Loans, Direct PLUS loans.

The Inside Word

An applicant pool of more than 10,000 necessitates a reliance on numbers, especially during the first round of cuts. Much of the matchmaking done at other schools isn't necessary here, as a highly self-selecting applicant pool typically precludes those who would make a poor fit. Still, admissions officers want to see at least respect (if not reverence) for LDS principles, without which survival here would be difficult indeed.

THE SCHOOL SAYS "..."

From the Admissions Office

"The mission of Brigham Young University—founded, supported, and guided by The Church of Jesus Christ of Latter-day Saints—is to assist individuals in their quest for perfection and eternal life. That assistance should provide a period of intensive learning in a stimulating setting where a commitment to excellence is expected and the full realization of human potential is pursued. All instruction, programs, and services at BYU, including a wide variety of extracurricular experiences, should make their own contribution toward the balanced development of the total person. Such a broadly prepared individual will not only be capable of meeting personal challenge and change but will also bring strength to others in the tasks of home and family life, social relationships, civic duty, and service to mankind.

"Freshman applicants are required to take either the ACT (with the optional writing section) or the SAT. The highest composite score will be used in admissions decisions."

SELECTIVITY

Admissions Rating	95
# of applicants	11,603
% of applicants accepted	49
% of acceptees attending	78

FRESHMAN PROFILE

Range SAT Critical Reading	570–680
Range SAT Math	580–680
Range ACT Composite	26–31
Minimum paper TOEFL	500
Minimum web-based TOEFL	173
Average HS GPA	3.80
% graduated top 10% of class	54
% graduated top 25% of class	85
% graduated top 50% of class	97

DEADLINES

Notification	2/28
Nonfall registration?	Yes

APPLICANTS ALSO LOOK AT AND SOMETIMES PREFER
University of Utah

FINANCIAL FACTS

Financial Aid Rating	67
Annual tuition	$9,700
Room and board	$7,250
Required fees	$0
Books and supplies	$992
% needy frosh rec. need-based scholarship or grant aid	51
% needy UG rec. need-based scholarship or grant aid	77
% needy frosh rec. non-need-based scholarship or grant aid	63
% needy UG rec. non-need-based scholarship or grant aid	43
% needy frosh rec. need-based self-help aid	28
% needy UG rec. need-based self-help aid	33
% frosh rec. any financial aid	53
% UG rec. any financial aid	64
% UG borrow to pay for school	30
Average cumulative indebtedness	$15,769
% frosh need fully met	1
% ugrads need fully met	1
Average % of frosh need met	30
Average % of ugrad need met	34

BROWN UNIVERSITY

PO Box 1876, Providence, RI 02912 • Admissions: 401-863-2378 • Fax: 401-863-9300

STUDENTS SAY ". . ."

Academics

Known for its somewhat unconventional (but still highly regarded) approaches to life and learning, Brown University remains the slightly odd man out of the Ivy League, and the school wouldn't have it any other way. The school's willingness to employ and support different, methods such as the shopping period, the first two weeks of the semester where anyone can drop into any class to "find out if it's something they're interested in enrolling in," or the *Critical Review*, a student publication that produces reviews of courses based on evaluations from students who have completed the course, is designed to treat students "like an adult" through "freedom and choice." This open-minded environment allows them "to practice passion without shame or fear of judgment," the hallmark of a Brown education. Even if students do find themselves exploring the wrong off-the-beaten path, "There are multitudes of built-in support measures to help you succeed despite any odds." Even grades are a non-issue here, "except amongst paranoid premeds."

Professors are mostly hits with a few misses, but there are "amazing professors in every department, and they're not hard to find"; it's just "up to students to find the teaching styles that work for them." "Academics at Brown are what you make of them," and even though students are diligent in their academic pursuits and feel assured they're "getting a wonderful education with the professors," most agree that their education is "really more about the unique student body and learning through active participation in other activities." The administration gets cautiously decent reviews for their accessibility and general running of the school, but it also gets scolded for getting "distracted by the long term." The president, however, is absolutely loved by students for being "an incredible person with a great vision for the school."

Life

Thinking—yes, thinking—and discussing take up a great deal of time at Brown. "People think about life, politics, society at large, global affairs, the state of the economy, developing countries, animals, plants, rocket science, math, poker, each other, sex, sexuality, the human experience, gender studies, what to do with our lives, etc.," says a senior anthropology major. "Most people here don't go home that often," and like any school, "there are people who go out five nights a week and people who go out five nights a semester." "Alcohol and weed are pretty embedded in campus life," and most parties are dorm room events, even though partying "never gets in the way of academics or friendship. If you don't drink/smoke, that's totally cool." There's also plenty of cultural activities, such as indie bands, student performances, jazz, swing dancing, and speakers. Themed housing (art house, tech house, interfaith house) and co-ops are also popular social mediators.

Student Body

It's a pretty unique crowd here, where "athletes, preps, nerds, and everyone in between come together" because they "love learning for the sake of learning, and [they] love Brown equally as much." "The 'mainstream' is full of people who are atypical in sense of fashion, taste in music, and academic interests," says a junior. Unsurprisingly, everyone here's "very smart," as well as "very quirky and often funny," and "a great [number] are brilliant and passionate about their interests;" "most have interesting stories to tell." People here are "curious and open about many things," which is perhaps why sexual diversity is a "strong theme" among Brown interactions and events. The overall culture "is pretty laid-back and casual," and "most of the students are friendly and mesh well with everyone."

FINANCIAL AID: 401-863-2721 • E-MAIL: ADMISSION_UNDERGRADUATE@BROWN.EDU • WEBSITE: WWW.BROWN.EDU

THE PRINCETON REVIEW SAYS

Admissions

Very important factors considered include: Class rank, GPA, rigor of secondary school record, standardized test scores, application essay, recommendation(s), talent/ability, character/personal qualities. *Important factors considered include:* Extracurricular activities. *Other factors considered include:* First generation, geographical residence, interview, racial/ethnic status, state residency, volunteer work, work experience, alumni/ae relations. SAT and SAT Subject Tests or ACT required; ACT with Writing component required. TOEFL required of all international applicants. *Academic units required:* 4 English; 3 mathematics; 3 science; (2 science lab); 3 foreign language; 2 history; 1 academic elective. *Academic units recommended:* 4 English; 4 mathematics; 4 science; (3 science lab); 4 foreign language; 2 history; 1 academic elective; 1 visual/performing arts.

Financial Aid

Students should submit: FAFSA, CSS/Financial Aid PROFILE, Noncustodial PROFILE. Regular filing deadline is 3/1. The Princeton Review suggests that all financial aid forms be submitted as soon as possible after January 1. *Need-based scholarships/grants offered:* Federal Pell, SEOG, State scholarships/grants, private scholarships, the school's own gift aid. *Loan aid offered:* Direct Subsidized Stafford Loans, Direct Unsubsidized Stafford Loans, Direct PLUS loans, Federal Perkins Loans, College/university loans from institutional funds Applicants will be notified of awards beginning 4/1. Federal Work-Study Program available. Institutional employment available. Off-campus job opportunities are excellent.

The Inside Word

The cream of just about every crop applies to Brown. Gaining admission requires more than just a superior academic profile from high school. Some candidates, such as the sons and daughters of Brown graduates (who are admitted at virtually double the usual acceptance rate), have a better chance for admission than most others. Minority students benefit from some courtship, particularly once admitted. Ivies like to share the wealth and distribute offers of admission across a wide range of constituencies. Candidates from states that are overrepresented in the applicant pool, such as New York, have to be particularly distinguished in order to have the best chance at admission. So do those who attend high schools with many seniors applying to Brown, as it is rare for several students from any one school to be offered admission.

THE SCHOOL SAYS "..."

From the Admissions Office

"Brown University is the nation's seventh oldest institution of higher education and the third oldest in New England. Since 1764, Brown has offered the best in liberal arts education, leading-edge scholarship and research, and opportunities for community-based service learning. Its flexible undergraduate curriculum involves more than 6,000 students in the design of their own studies, with nearly eighty concentrations in forty-four different academic areas and the option of independent study. The Warren Alpert Medical School of Brown University, Rhode Island's only medical school, provides more than 400 students with medical instruction and clinical training at seven Brown-affiliated hospitals in and around Providence. Brown is one of eight members of the Ivy League."

SELECTIVITY

Admissions Rating	99
# of applicants	28,919
% of applicants accepted	9
% of acceptees attending	58
# of early decision applicants	3,015
% accepted early decision	19

FRESHMAN PROFILE

Range SAT Critical Reading	660–760
Range SAT Math	670–780
Range SAT Writing	670–770
Range ACT Composite	29–34
Minimum paper TOEFL	600
Minimum web-based TOEFL	250
% graduated top 10% of class	94
% graduated top 25% of class	98
% graduated top 50% of class	100

DEADLINES

Early decision	
Deadline	11/1
Notification	12/15
Regular	
Deadline	1/1
Notification	4/1
Nonfall registration?	No

APPLICANTS ALSO LOOK AT AND OFTEN PREFER

Princeton University; Yale University; Stanford University; Harvard College

AND SOMETIMES PREFER

Columbia University; Dartmouth College; University of Pennsylvania; Duke University

AND RARELY PREFER

Bowdoin College; Tufts University; Georgetown University; Oberlin College

FINANCIAL FACTS

Financial Aid Rating	91
Annual tuition	$44,608
Required fees	$1,004
Books and supplies	$1,404
% needy frosh rec. need-based scholarship or grant aid	97
% needy UG rec. need-based scholarship or grant aid	95
% needy frosh rec. non-need-based scholarship or grant aid	0
% needy UG rec. non-need-based scholarship or grant aid	0
% needy frosh rec. need-based self-help aid	82
% needy UG rec. need-based self-help aid	88
% frosh rec. any financial aid	65
% UG rec. any financial aid	57
% UG borrow to pay for school	35
Average cumulative indebtedness	$24,382
% frosh need fully met	100
% ugrads need fully met	100
Average % of frosh need met	100
Average % of ugrad need met	100

BRYANT UNIVERSITY

1150 DOUGLAS PIKE, SMITHFIELD, RI 02917-1291 • ADMISSIONS: 401-232-6100 • FAX: 401-232-6731

CAMPUS LIFE

Quality of Life Rating	79
Fire Safety Rating	91
Green Rating	76
Type of school	Private
Affiliation	No Affiliation
Environment	Village

STUDENTS

Total undergrad enrollment	3,263
% male/female	59/41
% from out of state	87
% frosh from public high school	71
% frosh live on campus	94
% ugrads live on campus	81
# of fraternities (% ugrad men join)	5 (6)
# of sororities (% ugrad women join)	4 (8)
% African American	4
% Asian	4
% Caucasian	74
% Hispanic	6
% Native American	<1
% international	7
# of countries represented	73

SURVEY SAYS . . .

Career services are great
Campus feels safe
Lots of beer drinking
Hard liquor is popular

ACADEMICS

Academic Rating	80
% students returning for sophomore year	90
% students graduating within 4 years	78
% students graduating within 6 years	82
Calendar	Semester
Student/faculty ratio	16:1
Profs interesting rating	74
Profs accessible rating	79

Most classes have 30–39 students.
Most lab/discussion sessions have fewer than 10 students.

MOST POPULAR MAJORS
finance; accounting; marketing

STUDENTS SAY ". . ."

Academics

Rhode Island's Bryant University may offer an attractive "balance between business-focus and liberal arts–focus," but the school's reputation is primarily built on its robust business education. Most professors here "bring a lot of real-world experience in their field to the classroom" and hands-on experience that "provides you with a sense of how business operates." Bryant's "small size" means students will get "personal academic attention"—students consistently brag that "professors are highly accessible outside of the classroom and very passionate about what they teach"—but that does not mean those attending will have an easy time. The school's "rigorous curriculum" can be "a little stringent, especially for majors like accounting and international business," making educators who "clearly love the subject matter and the students" a key to success. Most students praise the faculty, saying "they make learning here interesting rather than a chore." Also appealing to students is the "close-knit community feel." The "engaging and dedicated faculty" lead the way, but that torch is also kept aflame by students who "are so willing to contribute to our 'student community' here."

Life

"Work hard during the week and party hard on the weekends" seems to be a common statement among students, who fill weeks with studying and weekends with themed parties, trips to Providence or Boston, or an array of school clubs and organizations. For those students who enjoy the focus on community service at Bryant—and there are many of them—groups give students "the opportunity to be give back to the community constantly, take on leadership roles, and make a ton of great friends." There is also an active Greek community on campus, as well as varsity sports. In addition, "intramural and club sports are also big on campus for recreational activity." However, the career-oriented student body means that "there are a number of students who don't do much besides go to class." Still, "People at Bryant do like to work hard, but they also do play hard." Overall, "those who do well are those who can strike that balance easily and recognize when work needs to be done."

Student Body

Students at Bryant tend to be "career-orientated and very focused on succeeding." "The typical Bryant student is from an upper-middle-class New England family, majoring in business," so while the school "does have a growing number of liberal arts majors," as well as "international and multicultural students," the general student population can seem, according to one student's cynical assessment, "rich, spoiled, and white." Most, however, do not have that cynical a view. "Every student feels welcome," others note, and "groups are pretty open, and it's easy to make friends." Most say it is easy to fit in here. "There are cliques like with any school, but you tend to find your niche group after freshman year." The campus places "less importance on athletes," so the "typical student is very involved and committed to academic work." Those attending Bryant tend to "aspire to go into finance, accounting, and/or work in a large banking/insurance/technology company after graduation." That said, many students say there is a growing diversity in the focus of the student population, including "students who aspire to go into a wider variety of fields after graduation."

BRYANT UNIVERSITY

FINANCIAL AID: 401-232-6020 • E-MAIL: ADMISSION@BRYANT.EDU • WEBSITE: WWW.BRYANT.EDU

THE PRINCETON REVIEW SAYS

Admissions

Very important factors considered include: GPA, rigor of secondary school record. *Important factors considered include:* Class rank, standardized test scores, application essay, recommendation(s). *Other factors considered include:* Extracurricular activities, first generation, geographical residence, interview, racial/ethnic status, state residency, talent/ability, volunteer work, work experience, alumni/ae relations, character/personal qualities, level of applicant's interest. SAT or ACT considered if submitted; ACT with or without Writing component accepted. TOEFL required of all international applicants. *Academic units required:* 4 English; 4 mathematics; 2 science; (2 science lab); 2 foreign language; 2 history. *Academic units recommended:* 4 English; 4 mathematics; 3 science; (2 science lab); 2 foreign language; 3 history.

Financial Aid

Students should submit: FAFSA. Regular filing deadline is 2/15. The Princeton Review suggests that all financial aid forms be submitted as soon as possible after January 1. *Need-based scholarships/grants offered:* Federal Pell, SEOG, State scholarships/grants, private scholarships, the school's own gift aid. *Loan aid offered:* Direct Subsidized Stafford Loans, Direct Unsubsidized Stafford Loans, Direct PLUS loans, Federal Perkins Loans. Applicants will be notified of awards beginning 3/24. Federal Work-Study Program available. Institutional employment available. Off-campus job opportunities are fair.

The Inside Word

The common wisdom is that liberal arts and business educations are not compatible. Bryant University seeks to change that thinking, and its reputation seems to indicate it is succeeding. Business-focused students who do not want to give up educational opportunities in other areas should have Bryant on their short list—especially considering that Bryant boasts an impressive 98 percent job-placement rate.

THE SCHOOL SAYS ". . ."

From the Admissions Office

"Bryant delivers an exceptional education for success in an age of unlimited global opportunity. The undergraduate curriculum is nationally recognized for innovation. From the very first semester, you'll find that Bryant's interdisciplinary studies and engaged learning are designed with your success in mind. Our world-class professors integrate theoretical and applied concepts in a broad range of majors from accounting to sociology, all complemented by rich co-curricular opportunities. A Bryant education speaks for itself – 98 percent of our students are employed or enrolled in graduate school within six months of Commencement.

"At Bryant, you will discover your passion and create your own path as you develop the knowledge, skills, credentials, and qualities of character to become an active contributor who thinks in a global context. Uniquely dedicated to the integration of business and the liberal arts, and committed to an educational experience that blends knowledge and practice, Bryant students choose from more than 100 courses of study.

"From attending a Bulldogs football game to practicing for a business competition, our students participate in more than 100 organizations and clubs.

"A globally focused education includes a diverse student body from 85 countries and 33 states.

"Our stunning, 428-acre campus in Smithfield, Rhode Island, is just 15 minutes from downtown Providence, an hour from Boston, and three hours from New York City."

SELECTIVITY

Admissions Rating	79
# of applicants	6,013
% of applicants accepted	77
% of acceptees attending	19
# offered a place on the wait list	97
# of early decision applicants	181
% accepted early decision	76

FRESHMAN PROFILE

Range SAT Critical Reading	510–590
Range SAT Math	540–630
Range SAT Writing	500–590
Range ACT Composite	23–27
Minimum paper TOEFL	550
Minimum web-based TOEFL	80
Average HS GPA	3.32
% graduated top 10% of class	18
% graduated top 25% of class	50
% graduated top 50% of class	88

DEADLINES

Early decision	
Deadline	11/15
Notification	12/16
Early action	
Deadline	12/2
Notification	1/15
Regular	
Deadline	2/3
Notification	3/23
Nonfall registration?	Yes

APPLICANTS ALSO LOOK AT AND OFTEN PREFER
Babson College; Bentley University; Boston University
AND SOMETIMES PREFER
Provdence College; Fairfield University
AND RARELY PREFER
Quinnipiac University; Stonehill College

FINANCIAL FACTS

Financial Aid Rating	80
Annual tuition	$38,199
Room and board	$14,102
Required fees	$375
Books and supplies	$1,300
% needy frosh rec. need-based scholarship or grant aid	78
% needy UG rec. need-based scholarship or grant aid	85
% needy frosh rec. non-need-based scholarship or grant aid	64
% needy UG rec. non-need-based scholarship or grant aid	39
% needy frosh rec. need-based self-help aid	84
% needy UG rec. need-based self-help aid	87
% frosh rec. any financial aid	79
% UG rec. any financial aid	87
% UG borrow to pay for school	88
Average cumulative indebtedness	$44,580
% frosh need fully met	50
% ugrads need fully met	50
Average % of frosh need met	52
Average % of ugrad need met	53

BRYN MAWR COLLEGE

101 NORTH MERION AVENUE, BRYN MAWR, PA 19010-2859 • ADMISSIONS: 610-526-5152 • FAX: 610-526-7471

STUDENTS SAY ". . ."

Academics

Bryn Mawr is all about "empowering women to achieve their dreams." The school has a "reputation for strong academics," and students confirm that work there's "no joke." Bryn Mawr is a small college, which means small classes. One student reports that most of hers have "around ten people," and another says her largest lecture class had forty students. This leads to "deep discussions [and] meaningful relationships [being] formed with peers and colleagues." Classes are "very interactive," and "great student-teacher relationships [are] established by the way classes are conducted." The faculty is "amazing and no doubt brilliant," and "They go a long way to make sure you don't only feel like students but also like a mini-family." An East Asian studies student says she feels "comfortable talking to faculty members/professors about anything." Students think one of the best parts about Bryn Mawr is the "amazing academic opportunities within the tri-co," and the "Quaker consortium": agreements that allow students to take classes at Haverford, Swarthmore, and the University of Pennsylvania. All of these great attributes combine to make Bryn Mawr a fantastic college experience. As one student puts it, Bryn Mawr "compels me to be extraordinary in an environment of equally extraordinary students."

Life

Academics are the focus of life at Bryn Mawr, but that doesn't mean students are "a bunch of nuns who sit around studying all day." "We do a lot of studying," a student explains, "but we also enjoy our time here." Not only are there "tons of school-sponsored activities," but there are opportunities to "go to a big party with tons of dancing and tons of people," at Bryn Mawr or at Haverford. "Meals here are really important," adds a student. "Dinner can be the only time we'll see each other, [which] can easily go on for an hour and a half." Bryn Mawr's "amazing food" probably has something to do with that. Bryn Mawr has an "absolutely beautiful campus," with great facilities, including a new gym with an "Olympic-sized swimming pool…TVs, large windows…and state-of-the-art machines that are built for women." Though Bryn Mawr has a suburban location, "The proximity and ease in traveling to Philadelphia, New York, and Washington, DC, is beyond fantastic." Students love Bryn Mawr's traditions, two of which are the Self-Government Association and the Honor Code. The Self-Government Association, the oldest student government in America, "allows…students to have an input on many aspects of how the college is run." The Honor Code, which every student must sign, emphasizes respect and integrity. The code creates "a strong community" and a safe one. One student says, "I don't lock my door!" Another adds, "You could lose a ring anywhere on campus and just send an e-mail out to the student body and have it back in the next few hours."

Student Body

"There is no typical student," at Bryn Mawr, "aside from women with a passion for learning and a commitment to excellence." A German student reports, "The variety of people here is enormous," and this "creates the…uniqueness that Bryn Mawr prides itself on." People's thoughts on racial diversity, however, "are kind of conflicting." One student explains, "Coming from a big city…Bryn Mawr did not seem very diverse, but my roommate came from a very small town and thought Bryn Mawr was extremely diverse." What students do agree on is that they're "friendly and welcoming," "creative," and "a little quirky." Though the intense workload means students are "very interested in… academics and work hard to get good grades," they "are also social" and "take time to build up strong friendships with other students." Students at Bryn Mawr really respect each other's individuality and love that their peers "have a purposive direction in regards to what they want to do with their future."

FINANCIAL AID: 610-526-5245 • E-MAIL: ADMISSIONS@BRYNMAWR.EDU • WEBSITE: WWW.BRYNMAWR.EDU

THE PRINCETON REVIEW SAYS

Admissions

Very important factors considered include: Rigor of secondary school record, GPA recommendation(s). *Important factors considered include:* Application essay, extracurricular activities, character/personal qualities. *Other factors considered include:* Class rank, standardized test scores, first generation, geographical residence, interview, racial/ethnic status, talent/ability, volunteer work, work experience, alumni/ae relations. SAT or ACT considered if submitted; ACT with or without Writing component accepted. TOEFL required of all international applicants. *Academic units recommended:* 4 English; 3 mathematics; 2 science; (1 science lab); 2 social studies; 3 foreign language; 2 history; 2 academic electives.

Financial Aid

Students should submit: FAFSA, CSS/Financial Aid PROFILE. Regular filing deadline is 3/1. The Princeton Review suggests that all financial aid forms be submitted as soon as possible after January 1. *Need-based scholarships/grants offered:* Federal Pell, SEOG, State scholarships/grants, the school's own gift aid. *Loan aid offered:* Direct Subsidized Stafford Loans, Direct Unsubsidized Stafford Loans, Direct PLUS loans, Federal Perkins Loans. Applicants will be notified of awards beginning 3/23.

The Inside Word

Bryn Mawr's student body is among the academically best in the nation. Outstanding preparation for graduate study draws an applicant pool that's well-prepared and intellectually curious. Interviews are strongly recommended but not required. If you're still unsure of how to stand out in the crowd, take advantage of Bryn Mawr's numerous on-campus and online opportunities to connect with current students.

THE SCHOOL SAYS "..."

From the Admissions Office

"Bryn Mawr's extraordinary academics, vibrant and diverse community, and focus on global leadership prepare students to challenge convention and take their places in the world. Every year 1,300 women from around the world gather on the college's historic campus to study with leading scholars, conduct advanced research, and expand the boundaries of what is possible. Consistently producing outstanding scholars, Bryn Mawr is ranked among the top fifteen of all colleges and universities in percentage of graduates who go on to earn a PhD, and is considered excellent preparation for the nation's top law, medical and business schools. More than 500 students collaborate with faculty on independent projects every year, and to augment an already strong curriculum, students may choose from more than 5,000 courses offered through nearby Haverford and Swarthmore colleges, as well as the University of Pennsylvania.

"Minutes outside of Philadelphia and only two hours by train from New York City and Washington, D.C., Bryn Mawr is recognized by many as one of the most stunning college campuses in the United States.

"The SAT, SAT Subject Tests and ACT test scores will be considered if submitted. TOEFL scores must be submitted by all students for whom English is not the primary language of instruction."

SELECTIVITY

Admissions Rating	95
# of applicants	2,708
% of applicants accepted	40
% of acceptees attending	34
# offered a place on the wait list	642
% accepting a place on wait list	52
% admitted from wait list	7
# of early decision applicants	234
% accepted early decision	52

FRESHMAN PROFILE

Range SAT Critical Reading	600–710
Range SAT Math	610–760
Range SAT Writing	620–720
Range ACT Composite	27–32
Minimum paper TOEFL	600
Minimum web-based TOEFL	250
% graduated top 10% of class	65
% graduated top 25% of class	93
% graduated top 50% of class	99

DEADLINES

Early decision	
Deadline	11/15
Notification	12/15
Regular	
Deadline	1/15
Notification	4/1
Nonfall registration?	No

APPLICANTS ALSO LOOK AT AND OFTEN PREFER

University of Pennsylvania; Brown University; Harvard College

AND SOMETIMES PREFER

Smith College; Swarthmore College; Wellesley College; Mount Holyoke College; Scripps College; Haverford College

AND RARELY PREFER

Vassar College; Oberlin College

FINANCIAL FACTS

Financial Aid Rating	97
% needy frosh rec. need-based scholarship or grant aid	100
% needy UG rec. need-based scholarship or grant aid	99
% needy frosh rec. non-need-based scholarship or grant aid	6
% needy UG rec. non-need-based scholarship or grant aid	4
% needy frosh rec. need-based self-help aid	95
% needy UG rec. need-based self-help aid	96
% frosh rec. any financial aid	76
% UG rec. any financial aid	76
% UG borrow to pay for school	61
Average cumulative indebtedness	$21,017
% frosh need fully met	100
% ugrads need fully met	100
Average % of frosh need met	100
Average % of ugrad need met	100

BUCKNELL UNIVERSITY

OFFICE OF ADMISSION, 1 DENT DRIVE, LEWISBURG, PA 17837 • ADMISSIONS: 570-577-3000 • FAX: 570-577-3538

CAMPUS LIFE

Quality of Life Rating	84
Fire Safety Rating	90
Green Rating	98
Type of school	Private
Affiliation	No Affiliation
Environment	Village

STUDENTS

Total undergrad enrollment	3,498
% male/female	48/52
% from out of state	76
% frosh from public high school	63
% frosh live on campus	100
% ugrads live on campus	86
# of fraternities (% ugrad men join)	11 (44)
# of sororities (% ugrad women join)	9 (41)
% African American	3
% Asian	4
% Caucasian	79
% Hispanic	5
% Native American	<1
% international	5
# of countries represented	50

SURVEY SAYS . . .
Classroom facilities are great
Lab facilities are great
Career services are great
Campus feels safe
Athletic facilities are great
Lots of beer drinking
Hard liquor is popular
Frats and sororities are popular
Alumni active on campus

ACADEMICS

Academic Rating	94
% students returning for sophomore year	94
% students graduating within 4 years	87
% students graduating within 6 years	91
Calendar	Semester
Student/faculty ratio	9:1
Profs interesting rating	88
Profs accessible rating	93
Most classes have 10–19 students.	
Most lab/discussion sessions have 10–19 students.	

MOST POPULAR MAJORS
psychology; economics; biology

STUDENTS SAY ". . ."

Academics

Armed with a great reputation, Bucknell is a small university that still manages to provide a "large amount of resources and opportunities." Surrounded by a "beautiful" campus, undergrads happily become part of a "strong, spirited community." Moreover, students here truly appreciate that the university "places a large emphasis on [both] undergraduate learning and preparation for graduate school." Among the many great disciplines Bucknell offers, students are especially quick to highlight the "extremely strong language, international relations, and science departments, [along with the] engineering and management schools." Undergrads also give their professors high marks, citing them as "extremely engaging," "very knowledgeable," and "deeply involved in their areas of study." One pleased Bucknellian elaborates, "I am extremely lucky in that all of my professors are fantastic! In fact, my organic chemistry professor changed my outlook on organic chemistry as a whole. In high school, chemistry was my least favorite subject. Now, however, I look forward to that class every week!" Professors here are also lauded for being highly "accessible" and always "willing and excited to meet students outside of class." Another contented student adds, "Professors devote themselves tirelessly to their students; they are available at a moment's notice and genuinely enjoy interaction with their students both in and outside of the classroom. They seek to become lifelong friends and mentors." Finally, as one student succinctly puts it, "Bucknell provides a student lifestyle that is welcoming, active, and challenging."

Life

Undergrads at Bucknell seem to unanimously agree that most everyone here adopts a "work hard, play hard" mentality. Indeed, "During the week, students are very focused on their work." However, once the weekend rolls around, "everyone lets loose." Of course, no matter the day of the week, the university is always buzzing with activity. The campus "hosts a lot of events such as BU After Dark and the Spring/Fall Semester Concert." In addition, "the school does a wonderful job of bringing in a lot of diverse and interesting speakers." One pleased undergrad interjects sharing, "There are lots of concerts either for free or for minimal price. The music is [of] all sorts. It can be either Tchaikovsky or Wiz Khalifa. There is a Craft Center that provides all kinds of art supplies. I go there almost every Friday and either play with clay, do something on potter's wheel, or do a stained glass." Sporting events (intramurals and varsity alike) are also quite popular. As another student reveals, "We have a lot of pride for our teams and love to go to the home games on the weekends." Greek life tends to "dominate the social scene here," and the vast majority of students can be found "partying at the frats" during the weekend. However, for those wary of the Greek lifestyle, rest assured, you'll still enjoy your time at Bucknell. As an undergrad confidently states, "If you don't want to go Greek, no worries. My roommate is not in a sorority, and she loves Bucknell just as much as I do!"

Student Body

At first glance, the typical Bucknell undergrad could be described as "upper-middle-class and white." Further, "preppy" is certainly the look that permeates this campus; as one student sharply notes, "I have never seen so many Sperry's in my life!" However, though some do acknowledge that "there is a lack of diversity," they quickly follow up this assertion by stating, "Everyone is very open-minded and accepting of people with different backgrounds." More importantly, if you push past the exterior, you'll discover a student body that's "smart and eager to learn" as well as "outgoing and friendly to anyone they come in contact with." And perhaps best of all, "The typical student also loves Bucknell and could never see themselves anywhere else."

FINANCIAL AID: 570-577-1331 • E-MAIL: ADMISSIONS@BUCKNELL.EDU • WEBSITE: WWW.BUCKNELL.EDU

THE PRINCETON REVIEW SAYS
Admissions

Very important factors considered include: Class rank, GPA, rigor of secondary school record, standardized test scores, application essay, talent/ability, character/personal qualities. *Important factors considered include:* Extracurricular activities, recommendation(s), volunteer work, work experience, level of applicant's interest. *Other factors considered include:* First generation, geographical residence, racial/ethnic status, alumni/ae relations, religious affiliation. SAT or ACT required; ACT with Writing component recommended. TOEFL required of all international applicants. *Academic units required:* 4 English; 3 mathematics; 2 science; 2 social studies; 2 foreign language; 2 history; 1 academic elective. *Academic units recommended:* 4 English; 4 mathematics; 2 science; (2 science lab); 2 social studies; 4 foreign language; 2 history; 1 academic elective.

Financial Aid

Students should submit: FAFSA, CSS/Financial Aid PROFILE, Noncustodial PROFILE. Regular filing deadline is 1/15. The Princeton Review suggests that all financial aid forms be submitted as soon as possible after January 1. *Need-based scholarships/grants offered:* Federal Pell, SEOG, State scholarships/grants, private scholarships, the school's own gift aid. *Loan aid offered:* Direct Subsidized Stafford Loans, Direct Unsubsidized Stafford Loans, Direct PLUS loans, Federal Perkins Loans. Applicants will be notified of awards beginning 4/1. Federal Work-Study Program available. Institutional employment available. Off-campus job opportunities are poor.

The Inside Word

Securing admission to Bucknell is no easy feat. Admissions officers are looking for candidates who excel both inside the classroom and with extracurriculars. The university strives to achieve a complete picture of every candidate so rest assured all application facets will be considered.

THE SCHOOL SAYS "..."
From the Admissions Office

"Bucknell combines the personal experience of a small liberal arts college with the breadth and opportunity typically found at larger research universities. With a low student/faculty ratio, students gain exceptional hands-on experience, working closely with faculty in an environment enhanced by first-class academic, residential, and athletic facilities. Together, the College of Arts and Sciences and the College of Engineering offer more than 50 majors and 65 minors. Learning opportunities permeate campus life in and out of the classroom and across the disciplines. For example, engineering students participate in music ensembles, theater productions, and poetry readings, while arts and sciences students take engineering courses, conduct scientific research in the field, and produce distinctive creative works. Students also pursue their interests in more than 150 organizations and through athletic competition in the prestigious Division I Patriot League. These activities constitute a comprehensive approach to learning that teaches students how to think critically and develop their leadership skills so that they are prepared to make a difference locally, nationally, and globally."

SELECTIVITY
Admissions Rating	96
# of applicants	7,947
% of applicants accepted	30
% of acceptees attending	40
# offered a place on the wait list	1,881
% accepting a place on wait list	43
% admitted from wait list	5
# of early decision applicants	817
% accepted early decision	52

FRESHMAN PROFILE
Range SAT Critical Reading	580–680
Range SAT Math	620–720
Range SAT Writing	600–690
Range ACT Composite	27–32
Minimum paper TOEFL	600
Average HS GPA	3.54
% graduated top 10% of class	62
% graduated top 25% of class	87
% graduated top 50% of class	98

DEADLINES
Early decision	
Deadline	11/15
Notification	12/20
Regular	
Deadline	1/15
Notification	4/1
Nonfall registration?	No

APPLICANTS ALSO LOOK AT AND OFTEN PREFER
Boston College; Cornell University; Tufts University; University of Pennsylvania; University of Virginia

AND SOMETIMES PREFER
Boston University; Colgate University; Pennsylvania State University—University Park; University of Rochester

AND RARELY PREFER
Lafayette College; Lehigh University; Northeastern University; University of Richmond; Villanova University

FINANCIAL FACTS
Financial Aid Rating	94
Annual tuition	$48,234
Books and supplies	$900
% needy frosh rec. need-based scholarship or grant aid	92
% needy UG rec. need-based scholarship or grant aid	92
% needy frosh rec. non-need-based scholarship or grant aid	22
% needy UG rec. non-need-based scholarship or grant aid	16
% needy frosh rec. need-based self-help aid	100
% needy UG rec. need-based self-help aid	100
% frosh rec. any financial aid	62
% UG rec. any financial aid	61
% UG borrow to pay for school	54
Average cumulative indebtedness	$22,500
% frosh need fully met	90
% ugrads need fully met	92
Average % of frosh need met	95
Average % of ugrad need met	95

CALIFORNIA INSTITUTE OF TECHNOLOGY

1200 EAST CALIFORNIA BOULEVARD, PASADENA, CA 91125 • ADMISSIONS: 626-395-6341 • FAX: 626-683-3026

STUDENTS SAY ". . ."

Academics

Beyond arguably one of the most rigorous undergraduate educations in science out there, Caltech is a small, tight-knit community that is "geared towards training tomorrow's leaders and pioneers in the field of science." There may be a heavy emphasis on scientific learning and research, but "not to the point where students can do nothing else," as the core curriculum "exposes each student to a broad range of subjects" beyond the stereotypical fare. At Caltech, passionate researchers "work together to solve the problems of tomorrow, while enjoying great weather." Or to put it in the parlance of collegiate times: "Cross collaboration of ideas and ingenuity leads to epic-ness!" Academics are understandably "intense" at Caltech: "The work can be hell but you'll love what you learn." Fortunately, "classes are small and it's often easy to form tight bonds with the professors." The quality of teaching can vary— "Just because they're Nobel Prize winners, does not make them good lecturers"—but the extremely low student to faculty ratio "makes it easier to interact on a personal basis with professors." "My academic experience here has been an extremely difficult whirlwind of humbling and fascinating knowledge," says a student. Much learning is done through the homework sets, on which students are encouraged to collaborate. The dedication Caltech has for training the researchers of tomorrow is renowned, and is evident in the accessibility to research for all students, even freshmen. The academic experience isn't just in the classroom; there are "lots of funding opportunities (for instance, the Housner and the MHF) for projects outside of the classroom." "One professor took me on for research after freshman year (we formulated an improved way to rank basketball players and teams), and I'm very good friends with him in what is now my junior year," says a mathematics major. Undergraduate student representation and self-government are happily welcomed here, and the school "really cares about the undergrads and wants to keep us happy." The school also does "a really good job of keeping students occupied and entertained while at the same time cramming a ridiculous amount of information into our heads."

Life

Modeled after the Oxford college system (and "very similar to Harry Potter"), the Caltech house system is the basis for undergraduate life, offering both a place to live and a social center for students. Freshmen are placed into one of eight houses after the first week of school, and "immediately are integrated into a close social network/safety net. Basically each student automatically gets ~100 friends." Each house has "a slightly different culture, and most people find that they identify strongly with at least one of the cultures"; as one student says, "My house has a tool room and turned down the housing office's offer to buy us a TV," says a senior electrical engineering major. In keeping with the one big happy family vibe, "undergraduates and grad students play Frisbee together, students and faculty play together in music groups, grad students go to undergraduate parties…and the students have a lot of unexploited trust from the faculty because of the Honor Code." Caltech has lots of fun traditions such as Halloween, when students "freeze pumpkins in liquid nitrogen and drop them off of Millikan library as a 'pumpkin-drop experiment.'" However, some feel that some of the new administrators "are trying to circumvent various student traditions and freedoms." The cherry on top of the Caltech sundae is "the fantastic SoCal weather, which is hard to beat anywhere in the world." Time is at a premium, but students "take trips to the beach and LA over the weekend; during the week, "[problem] sets and extracurriculars keep us pretty close to campus."

Student Body

"Everyone knows each other" at this "beautiful, small campus," and there's "no way around it": students here are "smart" and "nerdier than average," but "there is a wide range in personality within the student body." Most everyone has "an odd sense of humor and a serious hobby, whether it be MineCraft, building lasers, or rock climbing." There is "complete trust within the student body" at Caltech, and the house system provides "a family-like support network for students," which is a welcome respite from "extreme academic pressures."

FINANCIAL AID: 626-395-6280 • E-MAIL: UGADMISSIONS@CALTECH.EDU • WEBSITE: ADMISSIONS.CALTECH.EDU

THE PRINCETON REVIEW SAYS

Admissions

Very important factors considered include: Rigor of secondary school record. *Important factors considered include:* Class rank, GPA, standardized test scores, application essay, extracurricular activities, recommendation(s), character/personal qualities. *Other factors considered include:* First generation, racial/ethnic status, talent/ability, volunteer work, work experience, alumni/ae relations. SAT or ACT required; ACT with or without Writing component accepted. *Academic units required:* 3 English; 4 mathematics; 2 science; (1 science lab); 1 social studies; 1 history. *Academic units recommended:* 4 English; 4 science; 3 social studies; 3 foreign language; 1 history.

Financial Aid

Students should submit: FAFSA, Institution's own financial aid form, CSS/Financial Aid PROFILE, State aid form, Noncustodial PROFILE, Business/Farm Supplement. The Princeton Review suggests that all financial aid forms be submitted as soon as possible after January 1. *Need-based scholarships/grants offered:* Federal Pell, SEOG, State scholarships/grants, private scholarships, the school's own gift aid. *Loan aid offered:* Direct Subsidized Stafford Loans, Direct Unsubsidized Stafford Loans, Direct PLUS loans, Federal Perkins Loans, College/university loans from institutional funds. Applicants will be notified of awards beginning 4/1. Federal Work-Study Program available. Institutional employment available.

The Inside Word

Each Caltech application receives more than one read before it's presented to the admissions committee. This ensures that all candidates receive a thorough evaluation. The school values the unique drive and energy of its current students and desires applicants who display a similar combination of creativity and intellect. Stellar academic credentials are a must, and prospective students must display an aptitude for math and science.

THE SCHOOL SAYS " . . ."

From the Admissions Office

"Admission to the freshman class is based on many factors—some quantifiable, some not. What you say in your application is important! We do not offer interviews as part of the application, meaning that your essays and recommendation letters are particularly substantial in our review, especially given that faculty serve on the admissions committee. High school academic performance is very important, as is a demonstrated interest in math, science, and/or engineering. We are also interested in your character, maturity, and motivation, and we're proud of a selection process that incorporates all these aspects into each individual and thorough review. If you have any questions about the process or about Caltech in general, write us a letter or give us a call. We'd like to hear from you!

"Freshman applicants must submit scores from either the SAT or ACT. All applicants must submit the SAT Math II Subject exam, as well as one of the science subject exams (either biology, chemistry. or physics.)"

SELECTIVITY

Admissions Rating	99
# of applicants	5,535
% of applicants accepted	11
% of acceptees attending	42
# offered a place on the wait list	550
% accepting a place on wait list	79
% admitted from wait list	0

FRESHMAN PROFILE

Range SAT Critical Reading	720–800
Range SAT Math	770–800
Range SAT Writing	720–790
Range ACT Composite	33–35
% graduated top 10% of class	97
% graduated top 25% of class	100
% graduated top 50% of class	100

DEADLINES

Early action	
Deadline	11/1
Notification	12/15
Regular	
Deadline	1/3
Notification	3/15
Nonfall registration?	No

APPLICANTS ALSO LOOK AT AND OFTEN PREFER
Massachusetts Institute of Technology

AND SOMETIMES PREFER
Princeton University; Stanford University; Harvard College

AND RARELY PREFER
Rensselaer Polytechnic Institute; Virginia Tech

FINANCIAL FACTS

Financial Aid Rating	97
Annual tuition	$41,790
Room and board	$12,918
Required fees	$1,572
Books and supplies	$1,323
% needy frosh rec. need-based scholarship or grant aid	100
% needy UG rec. need-based scholarship or grant aid	100
% needy frosh rec. non-need-based scholarship or grant aid	1
% needy UG rec. non-need-based scholarship or grant aid	2
% needy frosh rec. need-based self-help aid	63
% needy UG rec. need-based self-help aid	70
% frosh rec. any financial aid	60
% UG rec. any financial aid	60
% UG borrow to pay for school	40
Average cumulative indebtedness	$15,090
% frosh need fully met	100
% ugrads need fully met	100
Average % of frosh need met	100
Average % of ugrad need met	100

CALIFORNIA STATE UNIVERSITY, STANISLAUS

ONE UNIVERSITY CIRCLE, TURLOCK, CA 95382 • ADMISSIONS: 209-667-3070 • FAX: 209-667-3788

CAMPUS LIFE

Quality of Life Rating	76
Fire Safety Rating	95
Green Rating	72
Type of school	Public
Affiliation	No Affiliation
Environment	City

STUDENTS

Total undergrad enrollment	7,751
% male/female	36/64
% from out of state	0
% frosh from public high school	95
% frosh live on campus	21
% ugrads live on campus	7
# of fraternities (% ugrad men join)	6 (7)
# of sororities (% ugrad women join)	9 (6)
% African American	3
% Asian	11
% Caucasian	28
% Hispanic	45
% Native American	<1
% international	2
# of countries represented	22

SURVEY SAYS . . .
Lab facilities are great
Great library
Students are friendly

ACADEMICS

Academic Rating	71
% students returning for sophomore year	87
% students graduating within 4 years	18
% students graduating within 6 years	52
Calendar	Semester
Student/faculty ratio	21:1
Profs interesting rating	69
Profs accessible rating	68

Most classes have 20–29 students.
Most lab/discussion sessions have
20–29 students.

MOST POPULAR MAJORS
business/commerce; psychology; liberal arts

STUDENTS SAY ". . ."

Academics

One of the members of California's noted state university system, Stanislaus "provides affordable education" that focuses on helping students prepare for their careers with a "professional, yet laid-back demeanor." This is "a great environment to be a part of," and the school "wants you to succeed, and they give you the info you need to succeed." Many of the students here live nearby, and the in-state tuition offers "rigorous" academics and "a great place to meet mentors and learn different approaches to life." Professors get mixed but mainly positive reviews; "some are excellent…go above and beyond," and are "wonderful at helping the students as much as they can," but others are just "fair," and "some should not be teaching." Registration could use some rejiggering; students say that the registration priority needs to change each semester, and the more popular departments could use "more of the same classes offered every semester, with multiple sections." Still, for higher-level classes, "small class sizes where you are able to get a lot of help from professors" are a huge boon. Nursing and business are some of "the strongest subjects that come out of here," and it is "very inexpensive for a fully accredited business degree" relative to many other schools. In developing well-prepared students, Stanislaus personnel are "attentive" on all fronts. "Very rarely are any of your classes taught by a graduate student or someone without a PhD," says a student. The accessibility of departments and staff is "always very easy," and "they are very informative with upcoming changes or events." Job placement is a huge end goal for Stanislaus, and "helping students (especially veterans) during these rough economic times is a priority at CSU Stanislaus."

Life

Though Stanislaus offers "scenery as beautiful and varied as the students" and "awesome" weather, popular complaints are that "buildings need updating" and "there are too many geese on the grounds." The university's efforts to provide "a ton of organizations on campus" give the commuter students "a college experience like that of any other student living on campus." "It's nice that the school recognizes that we need a break sometimes and promote being a healthy individual, both mind and body," says one student. Events are regularly held in the quad, "student-run shows [such] as dance-offs or karaoke," and "music concerts are regularly held throughout the semesters, usually featuring guest artists or students." Turlock is "not the biggest town," but there is "easy access to the freeway," and local events and great places "keep everyone occupied." On campus, "There are lounges that you can play pool, darts, video games, etc.," and "Greek life is well-supported." The many commuter students mean that resident community on campus is "small and tightly knit"; there are a fair number of nontraditional students here as well, and they have no problems getting by. "I am an older student, and life on campus is great; everybody accepts me as just another student working toward my degree," one says.

Student Body

Perhaps due to the focus on future careers here, students are "motivated and excited to be at school." "I think we all know that with every class session we are that much closer to graduation," says one. Because the campus is so small, "A big portion of the student life is also Greek." Diversity is "rich" here, and there are "many different ethnicities and culture from all over." Though everyone is friendly and "easygoing," "Typical students keep to themselves but does not hesitant to help another student if he or she asks for it," but even those who want to "can fit in almost anywhere, as most groups found around campus are very accepting."

FINANCIAL AID: 209-667-3336 • E-MAIL: OUTREACH_HELP_DESK@CSUSTAN.EDU • WEBSITE: WWW.CSUSTAN.EDU

THE PRINCETON REVIEW SAYS

Admissions

Very important factors considered include: GPA, rigor of secondary school record, standardized test scores. *Important factors considered include:* Class rank. *Other factors considered include:* SAT or ACT required for some; ACT with or without Writing component accepted. TOEFL required of all international applicants. *Academic units required:* 4 English; 3 mathematics; 2 science; (2 science lab); 1 social studies; 2 foreign language; 1 history; 1 academic elective; 1 visual/performing arts.

Financial Aid

The Princeton Review suggests that all financial aid forms be submitted as soon as possible after January 1. Federal Work-Study Program available. Institutional employment available. Off-campus job opportunities are good.

The Inside Word

Like most state schools, CSU Stanislaus admissions practices are fairly straightforward. The university adheres to the eligibility index as defined by the California state system, so applicants who meet GPA and standardized test score minimums are automatically granted admission. Out-of-state candidates face more stringent requirements, as do those applying for highly competitive majors and programs.

THE SCHOOL SAYS "..."

From the Admissions Office

"For over fifty years, California State University, Stanislaus, has welcomed students from California's Central Valley and around the world. CSU Stanislaus continues to distinguish itself as an institution that provides top-quality degree programs with a high level of personal attention, offering over 100 undergraduate programs; twenty-five graduate programs, including a doctorate in educational leadership; seven credential programs; and six certificate programs. With a student-to-faculty ratio of 21 to 1, CSU Stanislaus demonstrates its commitment to individualized instruction over the more common lecture-hall style of many larger universities. The university enjoys an ideal location in the Northern San Joaquin Valley, a short distance from the San Francisco Bay Area, Monterey, Big Sur, the Sierra Nevada Mountains and the state capital of Sacramento. The main campus is located in the city of Turlock, a community that prides itself on its small-town atmosphere, clean living space, excellent schools and low crime rate. Degree programs in these disciplines have earned specialized accreditation: art, business administration, education, genetic counseling, music, nursing, psychology, public administration, social work and theater. The College of Business Administration and the College of Education have also earned prestigious state and national accreditation. More than $52 million in merit- and need-based grants and scholarships was awarded for the 2012–13 school year. Approximately 83 percent of undergraduates receive need-based aid and more than $87 million in total financial assistance is awarded annually."

SELECTIVITY

Admissions Rating	69
# of applicants	5,804
% of applicants accepted	74
% of acceptees attending	29

FRESHMAN PROFILE

Range SAT Critical Reading	400–510
Range SAT Math	410–510
Range SAT Writing	400–500
Range ACT Composite	16–22
Minimum paper TOEFL	500
Minimum web-based TOEFL	173
Average HS GPA	3.26

DEADLINES

Regular	
Priority	11/30
Deadline	11/30
Nonfall registration?	Yes

FINANCIAL FACTS

Financial Aid Rating	65
Annual in-state tuition	$5,472
Annual out-of-state tuition	$16,632
Room and board	$9,200
Required fees	$1,214
Books and supplies	$1,760
% frosh rec. any financial aid	84
% UG rec. any financial aid	83

CALVIN COLLEGE

3201 BURTON STREET SOUTHEAST, GRAND RAPIDS, MI 49546 • ADMISSIONS: 616-526-6106 • FAX: 616-526-6777

STUDENTS SAY ". . ."

Academics

Nestled in the heart of Grand Rapids, Calvin College manages to seamlessly integrate "Christian faith and learning." While Christian principles certainly permeate the campus, students stress that "religion [isn't] forced." Rather, the college simply "encourage[s] spiritual growth and provide[s] opportunities for spiritual, social, physical, and mental development." And though the academics are rigorous, undergrads have the benefit of learning in an "incredibly supportive and collaborative community." Students here also appreciate Calvin's emphasis on both "social justice and sustainability." Moreover, the college maintains a liberal arts focus and undergrads can explore numerous disciplines. Many individuals are especially quick to highlight the "amazing" science, education, and accounting programs. No matter their chosen courses of study, Calvin undergrads are likely to have great classroom experiences. As one nursing student brags, "The professors are what makes this school. They know everyone by name and help you to succeed." Additionally, undergrads make sure to note that their teachers "are engaged with the material while also being aware of individual student needs." A biochemistry major wholeheartedly agrees stating, "The professors are all very passionate about their field and they pass that on to the students." Importantly, students also find their instructors to be "very intelligent and well respected, but also very down-to-earth." As this satisfied literature major succinctly states, "I would say that faculty/student relationship is probably one of my favorite parts of Calvin."

Life

Life at Calvin is always abuzz with activity. As one sophomore psychology major shares, "The college puts on more than enough programs for students to attend during the weekend." For example, "carnivals and game nights...are pretty well attended and are an easy way for college students to have fun." Students also love taking in part in annual traditions such as "Jump into the Frozen Pond" which happens every February. We're even told that "you get a golden towel if you do it all four years!" Aside from testing their mettle in the cold, many undergrads also enjoy participating in dorm events like "floor dates" wherein "a given girl floor and guy floor do something together to get to know each other." Concerts are a fairly common occurrence as well—"FUN, Switchfoot, [and] Regina Spektor have all come in recent years." Students interested in a school with a hearty drinking culture might do best to look elsewhere, though. As one freshman reveals, "People more prone to partying seem frustrated with the campus' dry policies." However, he does quickly follow up by assuring they do "manage with off-campus events." And, of course, Grand Rapids offers "plenty of bars and clubs" for students of age.

Student Body

Students here readily admit that the typical Calvin undergrad can be easily categorized as "white, upper-middle class, [of] Dutch [ancestry], and part of the Christian Reformed Church." Indeed, not surprisingly, most Calvin students would describe themselves as religious or "spiritual." However, a knowledgeable senior insists that, "We aren't limited by the fact that we are Christian, and being Christian doesn't make us all the same." In fact, "a great variety of students all with their different styles and personalities" can be found wandering Calvin's campus. A fellow senior stresses that, "Calvin does a great job at recruiting students of different ethnic cultures and countries. Diversity is something that Calvin is very proud of!" One music education major agrees, stating, "There are a variety of people here: sporty people, nerds, musical people, math and science people, dancers, environmentally conscious people, etc." Thankfully, most students can also be described as "warm and welcoming," so "new students always seem to fit right in!"

FINANCIAL AID: 800-688-0122 • E-MAIL: ADMISSIONS@CALVIN.EDU • WEBSITE: WWW.CALVIN.EDU

THE PRINCETON REVIEW SAYS

Admissions

Very important factors considered include: GPA, rigor of secondary school record, standardized test scores, religious affiliation. *Important factors considered include:* Application essay, extracurricular activities, recommendation(s), character/personal qualities. *Other factors considered include:* Class rank, volunteer work, work experience, level of applicant's interest. SAT or ACT required for some; ACT with or without Writing component accepted. TOEFL required of all international applicants. *Academic units required:* 3 English; 3 mathematics; 2 science; 2 social studies; 3 academic electives. *Academic units recommended:* 4 English; 3 mathematics; 2 science; (1 science lab); 3 social studies; 2 foreign language; 3 academic electives.

Financial Aid

Students should submit: FAFSA. The Princeton Review suggests that all financial aid forms be submitted as soon as possible after January 1. *Need-based scholarships/grants offered:* Federal Pell, SEOG, State scholarships/grants, private scholarships, the school's own gift aid. *Loan aid offered:* Direct Subsidized Stafford Loans, Direct Unsubsidized Stafford Loans, Direct PLUS loans, Federal Perkins Loans, State Loans, College/university loans from institutional funds. Federal Work-Study Program available. Institutional employment available. Off-campus job opportunities are excellent.

The Inside Word

Admissions officers at Calvin are interested in candidates who will flourish within the school's academic and social community. Just as importantly, they seek applicants who are looking to deepen and affirm their faith. The college accepts roughly 75 percent of their applicant pool so students who maintain solid transcripts should not have too much difficulty getting in, though bear in mind that high acceptance rate is partially due to the self-selecting nature of Calvin's applicant cohort.

THE SCHOOL SAYS "..."

From the Admissions Office

"Calvin's respected faculty, innovative core curriculum, and well-qualified student body come together in an environment that links intellectual freedom with a heart for service. Calvin's 400-acre campus is home to nearly 4,000 students and 380 professors who chose Calvin because of its international reputation for academic excellence combined with faith-shaped learning.

"Calvin students come from near and far, with a record-setting 2010–2011 class that included 10 percent international students and nearly 12 percent racial or ethnic minorities. Calvin encourages students to explore all things and offers nearly 100 majors, minors, and accredited professional programs to choose among.

"Quality teaching and accessibility to students are considered top priorities by faculty members. More than 82 percent of Calvin professors hold the highest degree in their field, the student/faculty ratio is eleven to one, and the average class size is twenty-two. In the past four years, Calvin has produced seven Fulbright Scholars. Calvin professors lead thirteen different semester-long study abroad programs and more than thirty January interim courses that take students into other countries and cultures. The Open Doors report of the Institute for International Education consistently ranks Calvin among the top five baccalaureate colleges for the number of students who complete a short-term study abroad.

"Before they graduate, more than 80 percent of Calvin students report having at least one internship, a great way for students to try their individual gifts in the workplace while gaining professional experience. In a survey of recent graduates, nearly 100 percent of responders report that they had either secured a job or begun graduate school within six months of graduation. Calvin is among the top 5 percent of four-year private colleges in the number of graduates who go on to earn a PhD."

SELECTIVITY

Admissions Rating	85
# of applicants	4,001
% of applicants accepted	70
% of acceptees attending	36

FRESHMAN PROFILE

Range SAT Critical Reading	518–650
Range SAT Math	530–660
Range ACT Composite	23–29
Minimum paper TOEFL	550
Average HS GPA	3.66
% graduated top 10% of class	30
% graduated top 25% of class	55
% graduated top 50% of class	82

DEADLINES

Regular	
Deadline	8/15
Nonfall registration?	Yes

APPLICANTS ALSO LOOK AT AND OFTEN PREFER

Wheaton College (IL)

AND SOMETIMES PREFER

University of Michigan—Ann Arbor; Grand Valley State University

AND RARELY PREFER

Western Michigan University; Michigan State University

FINANCIAL FACTS

Financial Aid Rating	76
Annual tuition	$28,025
Room and board	$9,335
Required fees	$225
Books and supplies	$1,050
% needy frosh rec. need-based scholarship or grant aid	100
% needy UG rec. need-based scholarship or grant aid	99
% needy frosh rec. non-need-based scholarship or grant aid	10
% needy UG rec. non-need-based scholarship or grant aid	8
% needy frosh rec. need-based self-help aid	93
% needy UG rec. need-based self-help aid	92
% frosh rec. any financial aid	97
% UG rec. any financial aid	95
% UG borrow to pay for school	65
Average cumulative indebtedness	$34,978
% frosh need fully met	15
% ugrads need fully met	15
Average % of frosh need met	74
Average % of ugrad need met	70

CARLETON COLLEGE

100 SOUTH COLLEGE STREET, NORTHFIELD, MN 55057 • ADMISSIONS: 507-222-4190 • TOLL FREE: 800-995-2275 • FAX: 507-222-4526

CAMPUS LIFE

Quality of Life Rating	94
Fire Safety Rating	67
Green Rating	94
Type of school	Private
Affiliation	No Affiliation
Environment	Village

STUDENTS

Total undergrad enrollment	2,023
% male/female	47/53
% from out of state	79
% frosh from public high school	60
% frosh live on campus	100
% ugrads live on campus	96
% African American	4
% Asian	9
% Caucasian	66
% Hispanic	6
% Native American	<1
% international	9
# of countries represented	42

SURVEY SAYS . . .

Lots of liberal students
Students always studying
Students are happy
Classroom facilities are great
Lab facilities are great
School is well run
No one cheats
Students are friendly
Students environmentally aware
Campus feels safe
Athletic facilities are great
Lots of beer drinking
Hard liquor is popular
Very little drug use

ACADEMICS

Academic Rating	99
% students returning for sophomore year	96
% students graduating within 4 years	90
% students graduating within 6 years	92
Calendar	Trimester
Student/faculty ratio	9:1
Profs interesting rating	98
Profs accessible rating	97

Most classes have 10–19 students.
Most lab/discussion sessions have
10–19 students.

MOST POPULAR MAJORS

political science/international relations;
biology; economics

STUDENTS SAY ". . ."

Academics

Students seeking a "top-notch" and "cooperative…learning environment that challenges students without leaving them overwhelmed" will find a happy home at Carleton College, an extremely rigorous liberal arts school characterized by what students call "collaborative academia." The "phenomenal" professors, in particular, who "focus on teaching" rather than on research and "seek out…personal relationships with all of their students" are a huge draw. As one undergraduate says, "One of my biology professors got an ovation at the end of the last class of the term." Class sizes have fewer than twenty-five students, with the exception of introductory science classes, and as one student explains, professors "have answered my e-mails past midnight and been available in their offices past 10:00 P.M." Carleton also supports its students with "a plethora of resources" like "a really cool system that gives science, math, and many social science classes student tutors or 'prefects' who have already taken the class and are available for group or one-on-one help" and the Math Skills Center, which "provides tutoring, homework help, and a great space to study." The school could "get better about supporting students in the arts," but "most professors are very open to pursuing independent studies with students who choose a particular subject that is not offered." Carleton has also opened the new Weitz Center for Creativity as part of an expanding arts program.

Life

While "quaint," Northfield and its "coffee shops, thrift stores, random little bookstores and art shops, [and] restaurants" are "minutes away," Carleton life, or "the famous Carleton Bubble," centers around a balance between "study hard, party hard," and it's "pretty easy to get completely wrapped in what's happening on campus." Weekends bustle with activity since "people go a little bit insane from overwork during the week," and as one student put it, "I often find myself attending a concert at the Cave, the student pub; going to a show one of my friends wrote at the Little Nourse Theater; taking a quick trip to the cities for Mall of America or an uptown excursion; or, most likely, having a surprisingly engaging and deep intellectual discussion with some friends at a party on a Friday night." Intramural sports such as broomball and ultimate Frisbee are "freakishly popular," and "campus traditions are rich and plentiful." Another "huge draw is the Arboretum, an 800-acre forest where students go for runs, go snow-shoeing, or have camp fires"; there is also always the option to "bake cookies at Dacie Moses house." In terms of the party scene, "you can usually find somewhere to do it," and "there's a pretty good gradient—some people live substance free, some people drink heavily every weekend, but most people are somewhere in between." As one student says, "Whichever path you choose, you're bound to make friends."

Student Body

"Quirky," "passionate," and "nerdy" are a few words undergraduates fondly use to describe the community at Carleton. As one student explains, "Due to some sort of unexplainable Carleton magic, a motley crew of odd, but intelligent and disciplined individuals come together at Carleton for an excellent and challenging four years." Another student describes her reasons for choosing Carleton: "Almost everyone is friendly—and I don't mean that only groups of people are friendly, I mean that practically any individual you could come across has this desire in them to learn in a positive environment, which I think is so intense that it translates into sharing that desire with others through encouragement and assistance." The student body reflects geographic diversity but could improve on reflecting more "diversity with political and social backgrounds." Still, "People are very self-aware, but not self-centered," and "The best part about that is that they all keep really open minds."

FINANCIAL AID: 507-222-4138 • E-MAIL: ADMISSIONS@CARLETON.EDU • WEBSITE: WWW.CARLETON.EDU

THE PRINCETON REVIEW SAYS

Admissions

Very important factors considered include: Class rank, GPA, rigor of secondary school record. *Important factors considered include:* Standardized test scores, application essay, extracurricular activities, racial/ethnic status, recommendation(s), talent/ability, volunteer work, work experience, alumni/ae relations, character/personal qualities. *Other factors considered include:* First generation, geographical residence, interview, state residency. SAT or ACT required; ACT with Writing component required. TOEFL required of all international applicants. *Academic units recommended:* 4 English; 3 mathematics; 3 science; (1 science lab); 3 social studies; 3 foreign language.

Financial Aid

Students should submit: FAFSA, CSS/Financial Aid PROFILE, Noncustodial PROFILE. Regular filing deadline is 2/15. The Princeton Review suggests that all financial aid forms be submitted as soon as possible after January 1. *Need-based scholarships/grants offered:* Federal Pell, SEOG, State scholarships/grants, private scholarships, the school's own gift aid. *Loan aid offered:* Direct Subsidized Stafford Loans, Direct Unsubsidized Stafford Loans, Direct PLUS loans, Federal Perkins Loans, State Loans, College/university loans from institutional funds, Applicants will be notified of awards beginning 4/1. Federal Work-Study Program available.

The Inside Word

Gaining admission to Carleton is highly competitive. While it is possible to get in without stellar high school grades and test scores if you show tremendous promise or have an exceptional talent, most successful applicants demonstrate all of these qualities. High school records are weighed most heavily here; standardized test scores and your personal essay are also very important. Interviews may not be required, but they are recommended. We encourage you to sit for one, even if you can't schedule a campus visit; local reps are usually available to interview you in or near your hometown.

THE SCHOOL SAYS "..."

From the Admissions Office

"In an annual college freshmen survey, Carleton students identify themselves as everything from conservatives to liberals, with a majority of them falling in the moderate to liberal range. Although individualistic and energetic Carls take their academics seriously, they don't take themselves seriously. Participation in athletics, theater or music, religious events, or dining hall discussions marks the Carleton experience. The college recently opened two new LEED-certified, environmentally friendly residence halls and the new Weitz Center for Creativity, 134,000 square feet of performance, rehearsal, exhibition, teaching, and collaboration space. With nearly three-fifths of the student body receiving need-based grant aid, there is a broad socioeconomic representation across the student body. Eight percent of all students are international, and 21 percent come from traditionally underrepresented groups, and about 8 percent are first-generation students. A look at majors in the past decade shows that graduates cover all areas, with about one-third of them in each of the following: math/science, humanities and arts, and social sciences. More than two-thirds of all students will spend time earning class credits off campus; Carleton participates in programs worldwide from Asia to Africa. You can scuba dive off the Great Barrier Reef or walk the Great Wall of China. Within ten years of graduating, about 75 percent of alumni pursue graduate or professional degrees. Carleton ranks third among liberal arts colleges in the number of PhDs earned by its alumni."

SELECTIVITY

Admissions Rating	98
# of applicants	7,045
% of applicants accepted	21
% of acceptees attending	36
# offered a place on the wait list	1,424
% accepting a place on wait list	34
% admitted from wait list	0
# of early decision applicants	727
% accepted early decision	31

FRESHMAN PROFILE

Range SAT Critical Reading	660–750
Range SAT Math	680–770
Range SAT Writing	660–750
Range ACT Composite	29–33
Minimum paper TOEFL	600
Minimum web-based TOEFL	250
% graduated top 10% of class	79
% graduated top 25% of class	96
% graduated top 50% of class	100

DEADLINES

Early decision	
Deadline	11/15
Notification	12/15
Regular	
Deadline	1/15
Notification	3/30
Nonfall registration?	No

APPLICANTS ALSO LOOK AT AND OFTEN PREFER
Williams College; Yale University

AND SOMETIMES PREFER
Washington University in St. Louis

AND RARELY PREFER
Oberlin College; Macalester College

FINANCIAL FACTS

Financial Aid Rating	98
Annual tuition	$47,736
Room and board	$12,366
% needy frosh rec. need-based scholarship or grant aid	100
% needy UG rec. need-based scholarship or grant aid	100
% needy frosh rec. non-need-based scholarship or grant aid	18
% needy UG rec. non-need-based scholarship or grant aid	16
% needy frosh rec. need-based self-help aid	98
% needy UG rec. need-based self-help aid	98
% frosh rec. any financial aid	57
% UG rec. any financial aid	55
% UG borrow to pay for school	45
Average cumulative indebtedness	$18,000
% frosh need fully met	100
% ugrads need fully met	100
Average % of frosh need met	100
Average % of ugrad need met	100

CARNEGIE MELLON UNIVERSITY

5000 FORBES AVENUE, PITTSBURGH, PA 15213 • ADMISSIONS: 412-268-2082 • FAX: 412-268-7838

CAMPUS LIFE
Quality of Life Rating	87
Fire Safety Rating	94
Green Rating	96
Type of school	Private
Affiliation	No Affiliation
Environment	Metropolis

STUDENTS
Total undergrad enrollment	6,223
% male/female	57/43
% from out of state	82
% frosh live on campus	99
% ugrads live on campus	38
# of fraternities	14
# of sororities	10
% African American	5
% Asian	23
% Caucasian	36
% Hispanic	7
% Native American	<1
% international	19
# of countries represented	114

SURVEY SAYS . . .
Lab facilities are great
Campus feels safe
Theater is popular

ACADEMICS
Academic Rating	90
% students returning for sophomore year	94
% students graduating within 4 years	74
% students graduating within 6 years	88
Calendar	Semester
Student/faculty ratio	13:1
Profs interesting rating	75
Profs accessible rating	86

Most classes have 10–19 students.
Most lab/discussion sessions have 20–29 students.

MOST POPULAR MAJORS
computer science; engineering; electrical and computer engineering

STUDENTS SAY ". . ."

Academics

The dedicated students at Carnegie Mellon range from the hard-core engineers to the artsiest of drama students (making it "a breeding ground for interdisciplinary collaboration"); however, the school's motto—"My heart is in the work"—rings true for all "because of the amount of schoolwork that is required." The school, envisioned by Andrew Carnegie in 1900, gives students the opportunity to become experts in their chosen field while studying a broad range of course work across disciplines. The difficulty of the classes and high expectations from your professors "push you to do your best work. You really do learn in every aspect of academics." "We are in it together to defeat the class rather than ourselves," says a student. The interdisciplinary environment that the school crafts is backed by the tremendous resources afforded students in whatever they choose, and the school "practically throws opportunities (internships, guidance)" at students. Though the course work is admittedly "stressful," the professors "care immensely about their students," and the "we're all in it together" mantra is a universal refrain. "Academically, you get challenged, but so does everyone else, so the work-heavy culture becomes a social thing," says a student. Though there "have been a few 'ehh' professors," for the most part, they are "extremely vested" in students' learning and "have always been accessible and eager to help with whatever [students] need." Much as its mission statement promises, CMU "provides excellent preparation for your future, especially the career center." The residence life staff, RAs, and housefellows are also "really committed to improving the social aspects of college." For those who know what they want, there are "unlimited opportunities to pursue your passions." "It is nice to know I will get a good degree, but that it is also unique to me," says a student.

Life

"Most of the students here really push themselves to the max," and most social activity "is based off of academics." "Everyone can find a little niche to fit into and thrive in because there are just so many opportunities to take advantage of." Despite the number of hours spent hitting the books, CMU has a decidedly non-competitive atmosphere: "It's not about being THE best, it's about giving the best performance." Discussions "are just at a higher level," and if students have to work late into a Friday evening, then so be it. "Still, everyone appreciates down time." The mix of student interests and majors provides a curious but totally harmonious balance at every turn: "Carnegie Mellon is the only place where you will see engineers working while an art installation goes in above their heads." Most here "have extremely full plates and are very dedicated to a variety of clubs and interests," but "not everyone is very social." "They say you get to pick two: sleep, good grades, or a social life," goes the mantra. Still, in their spare time, "there is a massive video game 'community,'" and the popular Greek life "is very different here than at a lot of schools, and it is a great way to open up lots of experiences." The Pittsburgh location offers a "safe campus...but it is still within a city that offers many things to do," including free entry into all museums, "great restaurants, and sports teams."

Student Body

There is "no race, religion or special interest [that] takes up more than half" of Carnegie Mellon students; basically, "a few crazy people, a bunch of eccentric people, and a ton of great people rule this place." Everybody is "quirky in an endearing way," and "there is literally a niche for anything someone could want." "We're all weird in our own way—we're either a scientist or artist so we can seem a strange bunch...eventually the labels artist or scientist fades, and you become friends with people from all over campus," says a student. Basically, all are "closet nerds," "insanely driven," and "all have hidden talents"; however, one common bond abides: "A typical student gets *Monty Python* jokes."

FINANCIAL AID: 412-268-8186 • E-MAIL: UNDERGRADUATE-ADMISSIONS@ANDREW.CMU.EDU • WEBSITE: WWW.CMU.EDU

THE PRINCETON REVIEW SAYS

Admissions

Important factors considered include: Class rank, GPA, rigor of secondary school record, standardized test scores, application essay, extracurricular activities, first generation, interview, recommendation(s), talent/ability, volunteer work, work experience, alumni/ae relations, character/personal qualities, level of applicant's interest. *Other factors considered include:* SAT or ACT required; ACT with Writing component required. TOEFL required of all non-native English speakers. *Academic units required:* 4 English; 4 mathematics; 3 science; (3 science lab); 2 foreign language; 3 academic electives. *Academic units recommended:* 4 English; 4 mathematics; 3 science; (3 science lab); 2 foreign language; 4 academic electives.

Financial Aid

Students should submit: FAFSA, CSS/Financial Aid PROFILE. Regular filing deadline is 5/1. The Princeton Review suggests that all financial aid forms be submitted as soon as possible after January 1. *Need-based scholarships/grants offered:* Federal Pell, SEOG, State scholarships/grants, private scholarships, the school's own gift aid. *Loan aid offered:* Direct Subsidized Loans, Direct Unsubsidized Loans, Direct PLUS loans, Federal Perkins Loans. Applicants will be notified of awards beginning 3/15. Federal Work-Study Program avaiable. Institutional employment available. Off-campus job opportunities are good.

The Inside Word

Don't be misled by Carnegie Mellon's acceptance rate. Although relatively high for a university of this caliber, the applicant pool is fairly self-selecting. If you haven't loaded up on demanding courses in high school, you're not likely to be a serious contender. The admissions office explicitly states that it doesn't use formulas when making decisions. That said, a record of strong academic performance in the area of your intended major is key. Each of the school's six undergraduate colleges has varying academic and testing requirements; the various majors in the College of the Fine Arts can also require an additional essay, portfolio, or audition.

THE SCHOOL SAYS "..."

From the Admissions Office

"If you're looking for an intellectual environment that blends academic and artistic richness with classroom innovation, explore Carnegie Mellon. Consistently ranked as a top twenty-five institution, Carnegie Mellon is world-renowned for its unique approach to education and research. Left-brain and right-brain thinking unite within our collaborative culture, and is the foundation of learning at Carnegie Mellon. As a student, you will acquire a depth and breadth of knowledge while sharpening your problem-solving, critical thinking, creative and quantitative skills. You will develop sound critical judgment, resourcefulness and professional ethics through a collaborative and hands-on education. As a graduate, you will be one of the innovative leaders and problem-solvers of tomorrow.

"While a Carnegie Mellon education is marked by a strong focus on fundamental and versatile problem-solving skills in a particular discipline, your talents and interests don't remain confined to one area. The university respects academic diversity and provides opportunities for you to explore more than one field of study. Carnegie Mellon consists of seven colleges (six undergraduate): Carnegie Institute of Technology (engineering), College of Fine Arts, Dietrich College of Humanities and Social Sciences (combining liberal arts education with professional specializations), Tepper School of Business, Mellon College of Science, the School of Computer Science, and the Heinz College. Here, music, molecular science, acting, analysis, opera and organic chemistry weave in and out of the lives and minds of Carnegie Mellon students on a daily basis.

"The university's 150-acre main campus is located in the Oakland area of Pittsburgh, five miles from downtown."

SELECTIVITY

Admissions Rating	98
# of applicants	18,884
% of applicants accepted	25
% of acceptees attending	30
# offered a place on the wait list	4,843
% accepting a place on wait list	38
% admitted from wait list	5
# of early decision applicants	1,083
% accepted early decision	33

FRESHMAN PROFILE

Range SAT Critical Reading	640–740
Range SAT Math	700–790
Range SAT Writing	650–750
Range ACT Composite	30–34
Minimum paper TOEFL	600
Minimum web-based TOEFL	250
Average HS GPA	3.72
% graduated top 10% of class	80
% graduated top 25% of class	96
% graduated top 50% of class	99

DEADLINES

Early decision	
Deadline	11/1
Notification	12/15
Regular	
Deadline	1/1
Notification	4/15
Nonfall registration?	No

FINANCIAL FACTS

Financial Aid Rating	79
Annual tuition	$48,030
Room and board	$12,400
Required fees	$992
Books and supplies	$2,400
% needy frosh rec. need-based scholarship or grant aid	95
% needy UG rec. need-based scholarship or grant aid	95
% needy frosh rec. non-need-based scholarship or grant aid	36
% needy UG rec. non-need-based scholarship or grant aid	35
% needy frosh rec. need-based self-help aid	96
% needy UG rec. need-based self-help aid	95
% frosh rec. any financial aid	51
% UG rec. any financial aid	45
% UG borrow to pay for school	43
Average cumulative indebtedness	$30,798
% frosh need fully met	27
% ugrads need fully met	28
Average % of frosh need met	84
Average % of ugrad need met	82

CASE WESTERN RESERVE UNIVERSITY

WOLSTEIN HALL, CLEVELAND, OH 44106-7055 • ADMISSIONS: 216-368-4450 • FAX: 216-368-5111

CAMPUS LIFE

Quality of Life Rating	75
Fire Safety Rating	76
Green Rating	95
Type of school	Private
Affiliation	No Affiliation
Environment	Metropolis

STUDENTS

Total undergrad enrollment	4,551
% male/female	55/45
% from out of state	64
% frosh from public high school	70
% frosh live on campus	97
% ugrads live on campus	89
# of fraternities (% ugrad men join)	16 (40)
# of sororities (% ugrad women join)	8 (37)
% African American	5
% Asian	19
% Caucasian	54
% Hispanic	5
% Native American	<1
% international	8
# of countries represented	36

SURVEY SAYS . . .
Lab facilities are great
Great off-campus food
Great library

ACADEMICS

Academic Rating	84
% students returning for sophomore year	94
% students graduating within 4 years	65
% students graduating within 6 years	80
Calendar	Semester
Student/faculty ratio	10:1
Profs interesting rating	71
Profs accessible rating	75

Most classes have 10–19 students.
Most lab/discussion sessions have 20–29 students.

MOST POPULAR MAJORS
bioengineering; biology; psychology

STUDENTS SAY ". . ."

Academics

If you want a school "huge" in research, then CWRU may be the choice for you. This "hidden gem" in Cleveland, Ohio, "deserves at least a second look." At CWRU, you have "the chance to do research [in] a world-class medical school," to take part in one of the "strong engineering programs with numerous undergraduate research opportunities," to participate in an "aerospace program connected to NASA," or to gain "clinical experience in [a] hospital setting" during a nursing program freshman year. "You can study almost anything, get involved in just about any type of research, and you aren't limited by what's available. The only limit you have is what you can imagine." this "midsize school" is for serious, "intellectual individuals looking to pursue a first-class education." CWRU is "a very self-starting campus, so if you are not used to some degree of independence, you might be in over your head." However, "this school has a lot of resources, both materials and people, for students to utilize and grab on to, especially when they're struggling." "Professors are "great," although there may be a "couple of exceptions." Some "aren't quite as entertaining as others, but they are all passionate about what they teach." One fourth-year student comments, "[My] professors have become personal friends and mentors who guide me in cutting-edge research. This provides me with an unbeatable education." Another student says, "The professors I have had are absolutely amazing. They come from various backgrounds. I have had a history professor who is a former chemist for the FDA, a political science professor who is a former employee of the United Nations, and a geology professor who is an Antarctic researcher. The professors are all extremely approachable, very kind, and highly accessible, and they make the students an enormous part of their lives."

Life

Due to the high academic standards, "Life here can be stressful at times, but there is always a support group of close and understanding friends or faculty to help you through it." "There are plenty of service groups and even a service fraternity. There are political activism clubs, musical groups, theater groups, Greek chapters, and so much more." "Greek Life is not at all like the stereotype, but it instead aims for community involvement, better academics, and creating a home away from home." Weekends offer many choices for entertainment. "There are parties, which are fun, but they're not too excessive at Case." "Student affairs groups on campus provide a pretty nice variety of events in which students may participate, ranging from skiing or skydiving, to free Cleveland Orchestra tickets or on campus concerts." Students find there "is a ton to do downtown, as well as in the areas around campus." Explorations include "visiting all the different museums, the aquarium, botanical gardens, an Indians or Browns game, [or] one of the many restaurants." Not all students are comfortable with transportation options to explore Cleveland in the evenings, as it "can get sketchy at night."

Student Body

CWRU "attracts a very diverse group of students" who are "extremely intelligent and know exactly what they want to do with their life and understand that education is the key to their future." Students "come from all different parts of the country, and world, yet still interact very well with one another." They "work hard for good grades," and "most (if not all) are focused on individual improvement and achievement, and not on beating everyone else." So although they are competitive with themselves, they are "helpful to one another." "Most…are over-achievers, but it's hard to meet someone who is over-competitive. Most people are friendly and hard workers." Since "most students were the nerd in high school," "dorkiness (e.g., *Lord of the Rings* obsessions) is highly accepted here." With fellow classmates it's "easy to talk about technical things that would have been difficult to discuss with most people off-campus."

CASE WESTERN RESERVE UNIVERSITY

FINANCIAL AID: 216-368-4530 • E-MAIL: ADMISSION@CASE.EDU • WEBSITE: WWW.CASE.EDU

THE PRINCETON REVIEW SAYS

Admissions

Very important factors considered include: Class rank, GPA, rigor of secondary school record, standardized test scores, extracurricular activities. *Important factors considered include:* Application essay, interview, recommendation(s), talent/ability, volunteer work, work experience, character/personal qualities, level of applicant's interest. *Other factors considered include:* First generation, racial/ethnic status, alumni/ae relations. SAT or ACT required; ACT with Writing component required. TOEFL required of all international applicants. *Academic units required:* 4 English; 3 mathematics; 3 science; (2 science lab); 3 social studies; 2 foreign language. *Academic units recommended:* 4 mathematics; (3 science lab); 4 social studies; 3 foreign language.

Financial Aid

Students should submit: FAFSA, Institution's own financial aid form, CSS/Financial Aid PROFILE. Regular filing deadline is 5/15. The Princeton Review suggests that all financial aid forms be submitted as soon as possible after January 1. *Need-based scholarships/grants offered:* Federal Pell, SEOG, State scholarships/grants, private scholarships, the school's own gift aid. *Loan aid offered:* Direct Subsidized Stafford Loans, Direct Unsubsidized Stafford Loans, Direct PLUS loans, Federal Perkins Loans, College/university loans from institutional funds. Federal Work-Study Program available. Institutional employment available. Off-campus job opportunities are excellent.

The Inside Word

CWRU faces tough competition from similar schools and handles it well as both the number of overall applications and out-of-state applications has increased substantially over the past decade, indicating an improving national profile. As a result, CWRU grows ever more selective. CWRU uses a "single-door" admissions policy, meaning that once you're admitted you can change your intended major without having to reapply, even if it means switching schools (for example, switching from the School of Engineering to the School of Management).

THE SCHOOL SAYS "..."

From the Admissions Office

"Challenging and innovative academic programs, next-level technology, experiential learning, real-world environments, and faculty mentors are at the core of the Case Western Reserve University experience. CWRU's faculty challenges and supports motivated students, and its partnerships with world-class cultural, educational, and scientific institutions ensure that your education extends beyond the classroom. CWRU offers more than seventy-five majors and minors and a single-door admission policy; once admitted to CWRU, you can major in any of our programs, or double and even triple major in several of them. Our student/faculty ratio, among the best in the nation, allows students to have close interaction with professors. Co-ops, internships, study abroad, and other opportunities bring theory to life in amazing settings, and 66 percent of students participate in research and independent study. SAGES, CWRU's four-year undergraduate core curriculum, connects students with faculty, peers and the community through small seminars that explore effective communication and analytical skills, and culminates in a Senior Capstone project. With 85 percent of students living on campus, CWRU has a residential feel unique to urban universities. First-year students live together in one of three themed residential colleges that involve resources from across Northeast Ohio: Cedar (arts), Juniper (world culture), Magnolia (sustainability), and Mistletoe (leadership through service). Admission Counselors consider all sections of the SAT, taking the best score for each section from multiple dates. The SAT (or ACT with writing) is used for evaluating applications for admission (and not used for course placement purposes)."

SELECTIVITY

Admissions Rating	95
# of applicants	18,418
% of applicants accepted	42
% of acceptees attending	16
# offered a place on the wait list	6,651
% accepting a place on wait list	45
% admitted from wait list	16

FRESHMAN PROFILE

Range SAT Critical Reading	600–720
Range SAT Math	670–760
Range SAT Writing	620–710
Range ACT Composite	29–33
Minimum paper TOEFL	577
Minimum web-based TOEFL	213
% graduated top 10% of class	67
% graduated top 25% of class	92
% graduated top 50% of class	99

DEADLINES

Early action	
Deadline	11/1
Notification	12/15
Regular	
Deadline	1/15
Notification	3/20
Nonfall registration?	Yes

APPLICANTS ALSO LOOK AT AND OFTEN PREFER

Northwestern University; Washington University in St. Louis

AND SOMETIMES PREFER

University of Pittsburgh—Pittsburgh Campus; Boston University; Carnegie Mellon University; The Ohio State University—Columbus

AND RARELY PREFER

Pennsylvania State University—University Park; University of Rochester; Purdue University—West Lafayette

FINANCIAL FACTS

Financial Aid Rating	93
Annual tuition	
% needy frosh rec. need-based scholarship or grant aid	100
% needy UG rec. need-based scholarship or grant aid	99
% needy frosh rec. non-need-based scholarship or grant aid	97
% needy UG rec. non-need-based scholarship or grant aid	86
% needy frosh rec. need-based self-help aid	75
% needy UG rec. need-based self-help aid	82
% frosh rec. any financial aid	84
% UG rec. any financial aid	87
% UG borrow to pay for school	60
Average cumulative indebtedness	$34,998
% frosh need fully met	70
% ugrads need fully met	75
Average % of frosh need met	88
Average % of ugrad need met	84

CATAWBA COLLEGE

2300 West Innes Street, Salisbury, NC 28144 • Admissions: 704-637-4402 • Fax: 704-637-4222

STUDENTS SAY ". . ."

Academics

Catawba College sports "a small, close-knit community where you can really get to know your professors and your fellow classmates." The school is known especially for its "high-ranking theater program and the hugely growing music program" as well as its athletics. Don't let its small size fool you, as "big things come in small packages." "Class sizes are small in order for you to receive as much of a personalized education as possible." "Excellent financial aid" attracts many students, although some feel the university isn't doing enough to "increase scholarships to match rising tuition." Catawba is particularly strong for "highly focused programs (theater [and] music in particular)." The honors program also gets high marks among students. "I can get whatever educational experience I make for myself here, especially because of the diversity of the honors program courses." Some students feel that the facilities could be improved. "While our computer labs are good, I feel like that Catawba's computer centers and facilities are not as advanced and developed as [at] other schools." "Most of the professors here really care about the students" and "know your name as well as your interests." As "a melting pot with many opportunities if you reach out for them," Catawba is "a place where you can truly discover who you are through exposure to a variety of thoughts and perspectives."

Life

Life on Catawba campus is driven by the school's strong athletics, theater, and music programs. Students tend to be "busy, busy, busy. Everyone is active. Campus clubs are huge, and there is a school-sponsored event every weekend." There are frequent sporting events, "theater and music performances," and other activities sponsored by the school or clubs. "The students focus a lot on their activities," one student says. "For instance, my life centers around rehearsal for the many performances by the Catawba Singers. The same goes for the theater department as well as athletics." Another student describes life: "My life at school? Class, work in the theater, homework, sleep, rinse, repeat," but also notes that "other students have more free time." "There are usually campus-wide events on the weekends that generally have very high turnouts." When asked what the school could improve on, the chorus responds unanimously: "Food! The food is pretty bad. We pay a lot of money to be here, and our food is sometimes not edible." Consequently, many students leave campus to "go to downtown Salisbury or Charlotte for shopping, restaurants, and clubbing." Note that Catawba does impose an age limit for students to live off campus, although it was recently "lowered to twenty-one."

Student Body

The student body is divided clearly into "three types of students. The athletes are a large part of the student population. The theater and music students make up the next largest population. Then there is the other category." "We all identify with a category," one student explains, "but that does not mean that we are always divided this way." Others see the campus fairly divided, with the three sections busy in their own work. "Athletes don't go to theater, and theater students don't go to sporting events" although "generally everyone mixes because of our general education classes, so no one really stands out." Students "are either athletes, all about education, or theater/music kids. They all do their own thing, and it works." Most students are from the area, but "33 percent of Catawba students are from out of state." Otherwise, it's "difficult to describe the typical student, because there is such diversity at Catawba College." "Catawba has almost anyone you can imagine, it's a wide array of different cultures of people that go here."

FINANCIAL AID: 704-637-4416 • E-MAIL: ADMISSION@CATAWBA.EDU • WEBSITE: WWW.CATAWBA.EDU

THE PRINCETON REVIEW SAYS

Admissions

Very important factors considered include: GPA, first generation, geographical residence, interview, talent/ability, character/personal qualities. *Important factors considered include:* Rigor of secondary school record, standardized test scores, extracurricular activities, recommendation(s), state residency, volunteer work, alumni/ae relations. *Other factors considered include:* Class rank, work experience, level of applicant's interest, ACT with Writing component recommended. TOEFL required of all international applicants. *Academic units required:* 4 English; 3 mathematics; 3 science; 3 social studies. *Academic units recommended:* 2 foreign language.

Financial Aid

Students should submit: FAFSA, State aid form. The Princeton Review suggests that all financial aid forms be submitted as soon as possible after January 1. *Need-based scholarships/grants offered:* Federal Pell, SEOG, State scholarships/grants, private scholarships, the school's own gift aid. *Loan aid offered:* William D. Ford Federal Direct Loans (subsidized and unsubsidized), Direct PLUS loans, Federal Perkins Loans, State Loans, College/university loans from institutional funds. Federal Work-Study Program available. Institutional employment available. Off-campus job opportunities are good.

The Inside Word

Since Catawba competes for students with several top regional schools, it's willing to take a chance on students who may not make the cut at Davidson, Chapel Hill, or Duke. Students who may not have been the highest achievers in high school but are ready to excel at the college level should put Catawba on their list. For students of all stripes with an interest in theater or music, Catawba demands consideration.

THE SCHOOL SAYS "..."

From the Admissions Office

"Catawba College prepares students for rewarding lives and careers helping them reach their highest potential as individuals. This attractive campus is centrally located in Salisbury, North Carolina, a short drive away from the mountains and Atlantic beaches. The community possesses a rich past and commitment to preserving its cultural and historic charm. In contrast, just forty-five minutes away is the much faster pace of Charlotte, North Carolina where shopping, transportation, and entertainment of all kinds are readily available.

"On campus, students study and socialize in a small college setting that offers strong traditions, excellent facilities, and beautiful surroundings. The high standards of quality set by Catawba's academic programs are matched by equally demanding sports and co-curricular programs. Students describe the community as caring and personable. They are also highly involved in campus activities ranging from the performing arts to homecoming and travel abroad. Faculty and staff are described by students as being important mentors. Whether in a state-of-the-art environmental science facility, attractive music and theatrical performance center, classroom, or one of the college's first-class athletic facilities, students report they feel as if they are among family when on campus.

"Perhaps the most important testimony to the attractiveness of Catawba is found in the words of its graduates who report numerous successful careers and rich memories of their time at school.

"Students applying for admission to Catawba College can apply test optional if they have a cumulative grade point average of a 3.25. Students interested in this option and those who meet the GPA requirement, must submit an Extracurricular & Leadership form found on the Catawba College website. For those students submitting test scores, Catawba accepts both ACT and SAT (students must submit the writing score of the SAT and ACT). Catawba does super score."

SELECTIVITY

Admissions Rating	89
# of applicants	3,226
% of applicants accepted	41
% of acceptees attending	26

FRESHMAN PROFILE

Range SAT Critical Reading	420–540
Range SAT Math	430–550
Range ACT Composite	18–23
Minimum web-based TOEFL	197
% graduated top 10% of class	11
% graduated top 25% of class	22
% graduated top 50% of class	39

DEADLINES

Regular	
Priority	8/1
Nonfall registration?	Yes

APPLICANTS ALSO LOOK AT AND SOMETIMES PREFER

Appalachian State University; The University of North Carolina at Chapel Hill

AND RARELY PREFER

North Carolina State University; The University of North Carolina at Greensboro

FINANCIAL FACTS

Financial Aid Rating	78
Annual tuition	$27,360
Room and board	$9,890
Books and supplies	$1,400
% needy frosh rec. need-based scholarship or grant aid	81
% needy UG rec. need-based scholarship or grant aid	85
% needy frosh rec. non-need-based scholarship or grant aid	99
% needy UG rec. non-need-based scholarship or grant aid	82
% needy frosh rec. need-based self-help aid	73
% needy UG rec. need-based self-help aid	79
% frosh rec. any financial aid	99
% UG rec. any financial aid	99
% UG borrow to pay for school	77
Average cumulative indebtedness	$30,662
% frosh need fully met	20
% ugrads need fully met	15
Average % of frosh need met	77
Average % of ugrad need met	74

THE CATHOLIC UNIVERSITY OF AMERICA

OFFICE OF UNDERGRADUATE ADMISSIONS, WASHINGTON, D.C. 20064 • ADMISSIONS: 202-319-5305 • FAX: 202-319-6533

STUDENTS SAY " . . ."

Academics

Located in our vibrant capital city, The Catholic University of America undoubtedly provides undergrads with a "wonderful campus in a great location." Impressively, "despite being in such a big city, there's a great community feel to the school that you can't ignore when visiting it." Of course, this prime location in Northeast D.C. is heaven for political junkies and "perfect for internships" as well. Moreover, students truly appreciate that the university manages to deftly balance a "wonderful academic experience" with a "strong focus on our spiritual development." Though one senior follows up by assuring us that for "those that are not interested in pursuing their faith, it is not forced upon them." Inside the classroom, students find their professors to be "very passionate about what they are teaching." Importantly, they "want to see their students do well" and make a concerted effort to "get to know each and every [one]." Undergrads at CUA also appreciate the fact that their professors have "an immense amount of real life experience." Many students find that this translates into "unbelievable [opportunities] to network with employers." And as one satisfied philosophy major succinctly states, "I have learned so much here and I feel that my intellect has been challenged." What more could you ask of your higher education experience?

Life

With a bustling campus life and Washington, D.C., as their playground, undergrads at CUA "can [never] really be bored." To begin with, "there are so many clubs and organizations that you can get involved in, or volunteer with." One senior concurs, excitedly stating that, "there are ALWAYS opportunities to volunteer, so many of us take part in Habitat for Humanity or homeless food runs or even visiting the nearby nursing home." Further, students can mingle with their peers at numerous university-sponsored events such as "Luaupalooza, midnight pancake breakfasts, Thanksgiving potlucks, university-wide masses [and] multiple Christmas events." Of course, it's also common for students to simply kick back and "hang out in each others' dorms and watch movies or TV shows on Netflix and play video games." Undergrads openly admit that there is a definitely a drinking culture here and "many students enjoy going out to party on the weekends, mostly bars and clubs but [there] are occasional house parties." Fortunately, there isn't much pressure and students can easily abstain. Finally, undergrads love the fact that D.C. is so accessible, especially given that "we live right off of the metro." As an English major shares, "The city offers endless opportunities for a Friday night date, a plunge into museum culture, a dinner with girlfriends, or even the simplicity of walking and enjoying the vibrancy of town."

Student Body

When asked to describe the typical student, some CUA undergrads quickly spout that many of their peers seem to "[hail] from New Jersey [or] Philadelphia" and that they're often seen sporting "J. Crew, Vineyard Vines [and] Ralph Lauren." However, a handful of other undergrads counter that "for such a small school, we have a pretty diverse student body." Certainly, while it's not surprising that "there are plenty of religious people," students steadfastly assert that you'll also find "a lot of party-goers, athletes, LGBT students, and politically active and engaged people." A contented junior explains, "You really find a nice mix of people here and while people tend to stick to their group of friends, people know each other and are quite friendly." And a pleased sophomore interjects, "There's a strong All-American vibe on campus. People are pretty preppy, but there's definitely a strong trendy, urban population." And fortunately, overall, "students are pretty happy." A few people do caution that "there's a slight divide between 'God Squad' and the big partiers, but everyone else mostly fits in the middle and enjoys it." Finally, one proud psychology major shares, "Even students who would probably be outcasts at other colleges are shown kindness and welcomed into various groups of friends."

FINANCIAL AID: 202-319-5307 • E-MAIL: CUA-ADMISSIONS@CUA.EDU • WEBSITE: WWW.CUA.EDU

THE PRINCETON REVIEW SAYS

Admissions

Very important factors considered include: GPA, rigor of secondary school record, recommendation(s), volunteer work, character/personal qualities, level of applicant's interest. *Important factors considered include:* Standardized test scores, application essay, extracurricular activities, first generation, talent/ability. *Other factors considered include:* Class rank, geographical residence, interview, work experience, alumni/ae relations. SAT or ACT required; ACT with Writing component required. TOEFL required of all international applicants. *Academic units recommended:* 4 English; 3 mathematics; 3 science; (1 science lab); 4 social studies; 2 foreign language.

Financial Aid

Students should submit: FAFSA. Regular filing deadline is 4/10. The Princeton Review suggests that all financial aid forms be submitted as soon as possible after January 1. *Need-based scholarships/grants offered:* Federal Pell, SEOG, State scholarships/grants, private scholarships, the school's own gift aid. *Loan aid offered:* Direct Subsidized Stafford Loans, Direct Unsubsidized Stafford Loans, Direct PLUS loans, Federal Perkins Loans, Federal Nursing Loans. Federal Work-Study Program available. Institutional employment available. Off-campus job opportunities are good.

The Inside Word

The Catholic University of America's admissions process is fairly standard. Certainly, the admissions committee carefully assesses your GPA and the rigor of your course load. However, you must not slack on the other facets of your app as close attention is given to your personal statement and recommendations. Your extracurricular involvement is also vetted and the university is especially on the lookout for candidates dedicated to community service.

THE SCHOOL SAYS " . . ."

From the Admissions Office

"The Catholic University of America's friendly atmosphere, rigorous academic programs, and emphasis on time-honored values attract students from all fifty states and more than eighty foreign countries. Its 180-acre, tree-lined campus is only ten minutes from the Capitol building. Distinguished as the national university of the Catholic Church in the United States, CUA is the only institution of higher education established by the U.S. Catholic bishops; however, students from all religious traditions are welcome. CUA offers undergraduate degrees in seventy-four major areas in nine schools of study. Students enroll into the School of Arts and Sciences, Social Work, Architecture, Nursing, Engineering, Music, Business and Economics, Philosophy or Professional Studies. Additionally, CUA students can concentrate in areas of preprofessional study including law, dentistry, medicine, or veterinary studies.

"With Capitol Hill, the Smithsonian Institution, NASA, the Kennedy Center, and the National Institutes of Health among the places students obtain internships, firsthand experience is a valuable piece of the experience that CUA offers.

"Numerous students also take the opportunity in their junior year to study abroad at one of Catholic's forty-eight different semester programs. Political science majors even have the opportunity to do a Parliamentary Internship in either England or Ireland. With the campus just minutes away from downtown via the Metrorail rapid transit system, students enjoy a residential campus in an exciting city of historical monuments, theaters, festivals, ethnic restaurants, and parks.

"Matriculating students should submit the SAT Subject Test: Foreign Language exam if they plan to continue studying that language at CUA."

SELECTIVITY
Admissions Rating	83
# of applicants	6,298
% of applicants accepted	60
% of acceptees attending	22

FRESHMAN PROFILE
Range SAT Critical Reading	500–610
Range SAT Math	510–610
Range ACT Composite	22–27
Minimum paper TOEFL	550
Minimum web-based TOEFL	213
Average HS GPA	3.33

DEADLINES
Early action	
Deadline	11/15
Notification	12/15
Regular	
Deadline	2/15
Nonfall registration?	Yes

APPLICANTS ALSO LOOK AT AND OFTEN PREFER
Boston College; University of Notre Dame

AND SOMETIMES PREFER
University of Virginia

AND RARELY PREFER
Fordham University; American University; The George Washington University

FINANCIAL FACTS
Financial Aid Rating	85
Annual tuition	$38,000
Room and board	$14,326
Required fees	$526
Books and supplies	$1,440
% needy frosh rec. need-based scholarship or grant aid	99
% needy UG rec. need-based scholarship or grant aid	97
% needy frosh rec. need-based self-help aid	84
% needy UG rec. need-based self-help aid	86
% frosh rec. any financial aid	94
% UG rec. any financial aid	91
% frosh need fully met	41
% ugrads need fully met	42
Average % of frosh need met	79
Average % of ugrad need met	77

CENTENARY COLLEGE OF LOUISIANA

PO Box 41188, Shreveport, LA 71134-1188 • Admissions: 318-869-5131 • Fax: 318-869-5005

CAMPUS LIFE

Quality of Life Rating	80
Fire Safety Rating	70
Green Rating	60*
Type of school	Private
Affiliation	Methodist
Environment	Metropolis

STUDENTS

Total undergrad enrollment	689
% male/female	44/56
% from out of state	34
% frosh live on campus	77
% ugrads live on campus	56
# of fraternities	5
# of sororities	2
% African American	13
% Asian	3
% Caucasian	72
% Hispanic	5
% Native American	1
% international	3
# of countries represented	12

SURVEY SAYS . . .
Students are friendly
Frats and sororities are popular
Active student government

ACADEMICS

Academic Rating	88
% students returning for sophomore year	69
% students graduating within 4 years	43
% students graduating within 6 years	56
Calendar	Semester
Student/faculty ratio	9:1
Profs interesting rating	91
Profs accessible rating	86

Most classes have fewer than 10 students.
Most lab/discussion sessions have 10–19 students.

STUDENTS SAY "..."

Academics
As a small, private college with fewer than 1,000 students, Centenary College doesn't need to exaggerate the personal attention it can (and does) offer its undergraduates. "I have texted a pictured of my homework to one of my professors and they helped explain how to find the answer." Over and over again, students name their professors' close attention as the key to their success and satisfaction at Centenary: echoing the sentiment of many others, one says "the professors are the best part of Centenary." The faculty "wants to stay connected to their students", is "exciting and animated", "eager to help you succeed in their classes", and "extremely dedicated." The small class sizes are popular with both the "exceptionally supportive" faculty and the students, which fosters "a lot of personal attention as well as responsibility to show up to class." "Centenary is a small liberal arts school where the teachers know your name and are passionate about your success." However, slackers need not apply: "Most professors demand a lot out of students. There is no such thing as an easy class." The Centenary experience is also one that's well-oriented toward the future, and students praise their "easy access to the experiences I need for my major." They feel that Centenary's strength is founded on the "commitment it takes to its students" and that undergraduates "are the most important aspect" of the faculty and administration's pursuit of continuing excellence. "Centenary students pursue a personalized education" that is perhaps best encapsulated this way: "Small classes, passionate professors."

Life
Centenary's size as an "intimate and quaint campus" dominates students' depictions of their social life as much as it does their academic experience. The campus is "a close community and family" with "a plethora of organizations that allow for leadership opportunities", as well as "a surprisingly good Greek life for our size." Students are both academically serious and down for some good fun: "During the week students are always on top of school, come Thursday-Sunday it's all about the parties, frats and drinking, and Sunday is recovery and homework day." Politically, the student body is "pretty evenly split between liberal and conservative", though since the school is "United Methodist affiliated," there is a Christian emphasis on producing "moral, caring, and wise leaders." Many students participate in Centenary's "variety of sports, intramural or varsity," but non-athletes find plenty of social opportunities in the "alternative hang outs in dorm lobbies or at the religious life center, theatre, or library." Students love the "close-knit" vibe on campus, without feeling claustrophobic, reporting that undergrads "are quite close to each other here and it's easy to become fast friends with most anybody, so plenty of good old fashioned hanging out goes on."

Student Body
Centenary students "love to try new things", are "generally accepting of others", and "very committed to their interests." In terms of dividing their time between work and play, they're "highly involved socially and academically," and "able to balance both very well." Undergrads "have many interests and are encouraged to explore them together" "in a way that makes the whole campus hum harmoniously." They're happy on campus, reflecting that "Centenary campus life always has something going on" and that "overall life is pretty great at Centenary." When they want something different, there are also opportunities to "go off-campus to the Boardwalk or other places around Shreveport/Bossier" or enjoy "the local movie theater or shopping in downtown Shreveport." Students also let their minds take them to new frontiers, and depict that it's "usual to find people clustered talking about the problems of the world and offering ways to solve them." More than anything, Centenary students seem to like and value each other, and find their peers "becoming friends for life."

FINANCIAL AID: 318-869-5137 • E-MAIL: ADMISSIONS@CENTENARY.EDU • WEBSITE: WWW.CENTENARY.EDU

THE PRINCETON REVIEW SAYS

Admissions

Very important factors considered include: Class rank, GPA, rigor of secondary school record, standardized test scores, application essay. *Important factors considered include:* extracurricular activities, recommendation(s), volunteer work. *Other factors considered include:* Interview, talent/ability, alumni/ae relations, character/personal qualities, religious affiliation. SAT or ACT required; ACT with or without Writing component accepted. TOEFL required of all international applicants. *Academic units recommended:* 4 English; 3 mathematics; 3 science; 3 social studies; 2 foreign language.

Financial Aid

Students should submit: FAFSA. The Princeton Review suggests that all financial aid forms be submitted as soon as possible after January 1. *Need-based scholarships/grants offered:* Federal Pell, SEOG, State scholarships/grants, private scholarships, the school's own gift aid. *Loan aid offered:* Direct Subsidized Stafford Loans, Direct Unsubsidized Stafford Loans, Direct PLUS loans, Federal Perkins Loans. Federal Work-Study Program available. Institutional employment available. Off-campus job opportunities are good.

The Inside Word

Centenary prides itself on assessing applicants through a "holistic" review process that includes standard factors like GPA, high school courseload, a personal essay, recommendations, and especially a demonstrated record of balancing academic and extracurricular commitments. The school will accept applications after its February 15 deadline, but students seeking financial aid are strongly encouraged to apply by or before that deadline.

THE SCHOOL SAYS "..."

From the Admissions Office

"Just as a student's four-year experience at Centenary will be very personalized, so too is the application process. We pride ourselves on treating each applicant as an individual. We encourage all interested students to visit us—not only so they can see our campus and get a sense of the atmosphere, but also to provide us the opportunity to meet and get to know them.

"Consider Centenary for a life-changing experience. Our professors value your ideas and contributions and are passionate about teaching. We consider the Centenary Experience to be more than just a degree. You will live in a comprehensive learning environment that features connections to your academic, social, personal, and residential lives.

"Our students work and live within a strong community to create personalized, distinctive experiences, and enjoy a vibrant college life and graduate from Centenary prepared for their professional and personal lives.

"First-year applicants must submit either ACT or SAT scores. We recommend, but do not require, the ACT writing component."

SELECTIVITY

Admissions Rating	89
# of applicants	933
% of applicants accepted	64
% of acceptees attending	26

FRESHMAN PROFILE

Range SAT Critical Reading	490–620
Range SAT Math	430–780
Range ACT Composite	23–28
Minimum paper TOEFL	550
Minimum web-based TOEFL	213
Average HS GPA	3.53
% graduated top 10% of class	32
% graduated top 25% of class	89
% graduated top 50% of class	97

DEADLINES

Early action	
Deadline	12/15
Regular	
Priority	2/15
Deadline	8/1
Notification	9/1
Nonfall registration?	Yes

FINANCIAL FACTS

Financial Aid Rating	83
Annual tuition	$30,740
Room and board	$9,620
Required fees	$0
Books and supplies	$1,200
% needy frosh rec. need-based scholarship or grant aid	100
% needy UG rec. need-based scholarship or grant aid	99
% needy frosh rec. non-need-based scholarship or grant aid	27
% needy UG rec. non-need-based scholarship or grant aid	20
% needy frosh rec. need-based self-help aid	73
% needy UG rec. need-based self-help aid	74
% UG borrow to pay for school	50
Average cumulative indebtedness	$21,820
% frosh need fully met	29
% ugrads need fully met	20
Average % of frosh need met	77
Average % of ugrad need met	74

CENTRE COLLEGE

600 WEST WALNUT STREET, DANVILLE, KY 40422 • ADMISSIONS: 859-238-5350 • FAX: 859-238-5373

CAMPUS LIFE

Quality of Life Rating	91
Fire Safety Rating	67
Green Rating	67
Type of school	Private
Affiliation	Presbyterian
Environment	Village

STUDENTS

Total undergrad enrollment	1,372
% male/female	49/51
% from out of state	46
% frosh from public high school	79
% frosh live on campus	100
% ugrads live on campus	98
# of fraternities	6
# of sororities	4
% African American	5
% Asian	2
% Caucasian	83
% Hispanic	2
% Native American	0
% international	4
# of countries represented	11

SURVEY SAYS . . .

Students are happy
Classroom facilities are great
Lab facilities are great
School is well run
No one cheats
Students are friendly
Campus feels safe
Easy to get around campus
Athletic facilities are great
Very little drug use
Active student government

ACADEMICS

Academic Rating	95
% students returning for sophomore year	90
% students graduating within 4 years	80
% students graduating within 6 years	82
Calendar	4/1/4
Student/faculty ratio	10:1
Profs interesting rating	96
Profs accessible rating	98

Most classes have 10–19 students.
Most lab/discussion sessions have
10–19 students.

MOST POPULAR MAJORS

economics; history; Spanish language
and literature

STUDENTS SAY ". . ."

Academics

Centre College offers "a genuine, personal, practical education in all areas of life." Its "small classes" are focused and challenging, "and students definitely spend a lot of time studying, reading, and writing papers." An international studies student comments, "I find myself working harder than I ever thought possible...I feel so accomplished at the end of each semester." Students are taught by "extremely passionate and dedicated professors." Teachers are "kind, supportive, caring, and are always available for help outside the classroom," and they make "an effort to work one-on-one with you if necessary." One of Centre's goals is "preparing students to be actively engaged global citizens," and there's "a big movement on getting out of the classroom with the community-based learning." "If a professor doesn't require that kind of learning," a student explains, "then they almost always will still make connections outside the classroom whether to real life or to other classes." Centre has an impressively strong study abroad program, and about 85 percent of their students take advantage of it. One student says, "You are guaranteed the chance to have an internship and study abroad." Students love this combination of global, local, and personal learning. One proudly says that Centre "looks toward the future...of our world and the need for students to be prepared for it...Centre has and will continue to prepare me for what comes next in my journey."

Life

Centre College has an active campus life. Fraternities and sororities have a big presence and host a lot of parties. One student says, "There are a lot of students who are involved in Greek life, but there are a fair amount who are not involved in any way." Another adds, "There has been a significant development in alternative organizations, such as the Art House for drama, music, and art majors." There's also the "philanthropic coed fraternity Alpha Phi Omega," which "provides a very different, positive experience for...students who prefer to focus on service and forming strong friendships rather than partying." The Student Activities Council also organizes a lot of events, including "midnight movies." The small, picturesque town of Danville is "very much a college town." "New restaurants and bars have been opening, which is making Danville a little more exciting," but students admit that overall "there isn't much to do off campus." However, "there is so much going on at campus" that students "don't ever want to leave."

Student Body

Centre College's small student body and rural setting lend it a "welcoming atmosphere" and help create a "close-knit community." Students are "kind, respectful, and friendly to peers, professors, and administrators alike." Students are "hyper-involved," either in athletics, Greek life, the many "clubs and organizations," or all three. Students may "work hard all week," but they still find time to "attend club meetings, support their friends in sporting events, relax in the campus center...attend sorority/fraternity activities, and attend events." The stereotype of the Centre student is one who is "white," "Southern," and "middle- or upper-class," but many insist that Centre's student body has "changed dramatically." One student says, "I believe that Centre has lived up to its mission of improving racial diversity on campus." They add, "The number of African American, international, and Hispanic students has increased dramatically." Students admit, "Centre is quite cliquish," but say, "People always find their own place." One student explains, "During the week people tend to stick to their groups," but "barriers break down on weekends."

CENTRE COLLEGE

FINANCIAL AID: 859-238-5365 • E-MAIL: ADMISSION@CENTRE.EDU • WEBSITE: WWW.CENTRE.EDU

THE PRINCETON REVIEW SAYS

Admissions

Very important factors considered include: GPA, rigor of secondary school record. *Important factors considered include:* Class rank, standardized test scores, application essay. *Other factors considered include:* Extracurricular activities, first generation, geographical residence, interview, racial/ethnic status, recommendation(s), state residency, talent/ability, volunteer work, work experience, alumni/ae relations, character/personal qualities, level of applicant's interest. SAT or ACT required; ACT with Writing component recommended. TOEFL required of all international applicants. *Academic units required:* 4 English; 3 mathematics; 2 science; (2 science lab); 1 social studies; 2 foreign language; 1 history. *Academic units recommended:* 4 mathematics; 4 science; 2 social studies; 4 foreign language; 2 history.

Financial Aid

Students should submit: FAFSA, Institution's own financial aid form. Regular filing deadline is 1/31. The Princeton Review suggests that all financial aid forms be submitted as soon as possible after January 1. *Need-based scholarships/grants offered:* Federal Pell, SEOG, State scholarships/grants, private scholarships, the school's own gift aid. *Loan aid offered:* Direct Subsidized Stafford Loans, Direct Unsubsidized Stafford Loans, Direct PLUS loans, Federal Perkins Loans, College/university loans from institutional funds. Applicants will be notified of awards beginning 3/19. Federal Work-Study Program available. Institutional employment available. Off-campus job opportunities are fair.

The Inside Word

Centre's small but very capable student body reflects solid academic preparation from high school. If you're ranked in the top quarter of your graduating class and have taken challenging courses throughout your high school career, you should have smooth sailing through the admissions process. Those who rank below the top quarter or who have inconsistent academic transcripts will find entrance here more difficult and may benefit from an interview.

THE SCHOOL SAYS "..."

From the Admissions Office

"Centre College offers its students a world of opportunities, highlighted by the nation's premier study abroad program. Approximately 85 percent of students study abroad at least once. CentreTerm programs explore an ever-increasing number of countries in January; in 2014, they include Burma, China, France, Guatemala, India, New Zealand, Rwanda, Spain, Thailand, and Uganda In addition, there are nine permanent, semester-long residential programs: England, Scotland, Northern Ireland, France, Spain, Yucatan, China, and Japan. Centre's personalized approach means that most international study includes at least one Centre professor. Study abroad is so important that it is a component of the Centre Commitment: study abroad, an internship or research experience, and graduation in four years—guaranteed, or Centre will provide up to one more year of tuition for free.

"Centre's stellar academic reputation and exceptional commitment to remaining affordable lead to extraordinary success for our students: entrance to top graduate and professional schools, prestigious undergraduate and postgraduate fellowships (Rhodes, Fulbright, Goldwater), and rewarding jobs. (On average, 97 percent are employed or in advanced study within ten months of graduation.)

"Centre is a place where important conversations occur—in and out of the classroom. In 2012, for the second time in a dozen years, Centre's Norton Center for the Arts was the setting for the nation's only vice presidential debate. Even in years without a vice presidential debate, the Norton Center features an amazing array of high-profile arts performances and speakers, including the legendary Vienna Philharmonic, country music icon Dolly Parton, and Nobel prize–winner Elie Wiesel."

SELECTIVITY

Admissions Rating	92
# of applicants	2,533
% of applicants accepted	69
% of acceptees attending	22
# offered a place on the wait list	178
% accepting a place on wait list	21
% admitted from wait list	26
# of early decision applicants	115
% accepted early decision	70

FRESHMAN PROFILE

Range SAT Critical Reading	550–670
Range SAT Math	560–680
Range SAT Writing	550–670
Range ACT Composite	26–31
Minimum paper TOEFL	580
Average HS GPA	3.70
% graduated top 10% of class	52
% graduated top 25% of class	81
% graduated top 50% of class	96

DEADLINES

Early decision	
Deadline	12/1
Notification	12/3
Early action	
Deadline	12/1
Notification	1/15
Regular	
Deadline	1/15
Notification	3/31
Nonfall registration?	No

APPLICANTS ALSO LOOK AT AND OFTEN PREFER
Davidson College

AND SOMETIMES PREFER
Kenyon College; Furman University

AND RARELY PREFER
University of Louisville

FINANCIAL FACTS

Financial Aid Rating	85
Annual tuition	$36,000
Room and board	$9,100
Required fees	$0
Books and supplies	$1,400
% needy frosh rec. need-based scholarship or grant aid	100
% needy UG rec. need-based scholarship or grant aid	100
% needy frosh rec. non-need-based scholarship or grant aid	0
% needy UG rec. non-need-based scholarship or grant aid	0
% needy frosh rec. need-based self-help aid	62
% needy UG rec. need-based self-help aid	69
% frosh rec. any financial aid	97
% UG rec. any financial aid	96
% UG borrow to pay for school	56
Average cumulative indebtedness	$25,269
% frosh need fully met	28
% ugrads need fully met	26
Average % of frosh need met	84
Average % of ugrad need met	83

CHAMPLAIN COLLEGE

163 SOUTH WILLARD STREET BOX 670, BURLINGTON, VT 05402-0670 • ADMISSIONS: 802-860-2727 • FAX: 802-860-2767

CAMPUS LIFE

Quality of Life Rating	96
Fire Safety Rating	96
Green Rating	93
Type of school	Private
Affiliation	No Affiliation
Environment	Town

STUDENTS

Total undergrad enrollment	2,067
% male/female	61/39
% from out of state	70
% frosh from public high school	85
% frosh live on campus	90
% ugrads live on campus	40
% African American	1
% Asian	2
% Caucasian	69
% Hispanic	2
% Native American	<1
% international	<1
# of countries represented	23

SURVEY SAYS . . .

Students are happy
Classroom facilities are great
Career services are great
Class discussions encouraged
Students are friendly
Students get along with local community
Students love Burlington, VT
Great off-campus food

ACADEMICS

Academic Rating	83
% students returning for sophomore year	76
% students graduating within 4 years	52
% students graduating within 6 years	65
Calendar	Semester
Student/faculty ratio	14:1
Profs interesting rating	95
Profs accessible rating	87

Most classes have 10–19 students.
Most lab/discussion sessions have fewer than 10 students.

MOST POPULAR MAJORS

business/commerce; intermedia/multimedia; game and interactive media design

STUDENTS SAY ". . ."

Academics

Both Champlain students and the studies they pursue are "professional" and "career minded," and name Champlain's "high job placement rate" as a primary reason for choosing the college. "Networking and the emphasis on internships at Champlain leads to a great deal of job placements relevant to your chosen major after (or before!) graduation," extols one student. Students love the "small class sizes," which "allows for a more personalized educational experience, where students are seen as unique individuals instead of numbers." They're also crazy about Champlain's "upside-down curriculum," which uniquely allows undergraduates "to take major classes in your first year": "I could begin major related work on the first day." Game design, digital filmmaking, psychology, and marketing are all offered as majors, distinguishing Champlain's available courses of study to many applicants, with its "strong focus on major specific skills, and field-applicable classwork." Professors nurture "an innovative and interactive classroom with hands on experience" and "an integration of personalized education and real world problem solving." Champlain works hard to produce graduates who know "how to survive and thrive in the business world" and "reach their highest level of satisfaction": "Champlain wants to make sure you're doing what you love and that you can continue doing what you love long after you've graduated." This career-conscious education is animated by Champlain's "invested, passionate, and dedicated" professors, who "know your name," are "enthusiastic about the students' education," and "have an extraordinary amount of experience in their field." In addition to academic curricula, Champlain's "LEAD program readies students for outside life," teaching life skills such as "financial sophistication" and fostering a "strong sense of community." Champlain's greatest academic strength lies in "Excellent professors, innovative classes," and an "inviting small-classroom environment."

Life

The small liberal arts college in cozy Burlington, Vermont, has a heavy academic focus on the video game industry, and skiing and gaming figure prominently into Champlain's social life. As "the major surrounding schools in the area," UVM and St. Michael's, "are also packed with students," "student activities are always available" such as "skiing or boarding, biking, hiking, movies, plays, clubs and bars." Students love Burlington—an "amazing college town"—and enjoy the shops and nightlife of Church Street. Both Champlain and Burlington "heavily promote sustainable living" and as such, students learn "an incredible amount about how to help and be aware of my community and ecosystem." For the dedicated skier/student, Champlain IDs will nab you discounted ski passes in the area, and "snow dictates class attendance in the spring." Overall, the outdoorsy will find plenty to love about Champlain: "There is the lake to kayak at, beaches to swim in, farms to berry/apple/pumpkin pick, amazing mountains to ski and snowboard, and so much more!" Indoors, the "laid-back" social atmosphere tends toward "play[ing] video games rather often," and there are "always events around campus, whether it's going to the Grind for talent or seeing a musical performance in the auditorium."

Student Body

Champlain's student population is summed up by one as, "Snowboarders and hardcore gamers everywhere." It's a self-selective, "open-minded" population that's passionately adored by those who know what to expect: students "fit in well if they have researched the college before coming, as it is a small community within a larger community." There are "lots of gamers/geeks, lots of hippies," and due to the wintry climate, one student quips that the typical Champlain undergrad is "a very warm kind person at heart and someone that is bundled up out in the cold." Another summarizes Champlain undergrads as "earthy, like winter sports, artsy, outgoing, and always looking for new opportunities." Champlain "is split into game majors and non-game majors," but as a whole, students are "very noticeably goal oriented" and "very interactive, conversational, and friendly" within their close-knit community. They enjoy the social opportunities afforded by Burlington and Champlain, but "are also serious about doing big things and going far in life."

FINANCIAL AID: 802-860-2730 • E-MAIL: ADMISSION@CHAMPLAIN.EDU • WEBSITE: WWW.CHAMPLAIN.EDU

THE PRINCETON REVIEW SAYS

Admissions

Very important factors considered include: GPA, rigor of secondary school record, application essay, first generation, talent/ability, alumni/ae relations. *Important factors considered include:* Class rank, standardized test scores, extracurricular activities, recommendation(s), character/personal qualities. *Other factors considered include:* geographical residence, interview, volunteer work, work experience, level of applicant's interest. SAT or ACT required; ACT with or without Writing component accepted. TOEFL required of all international applicants. *Academic units required:* 4 English; 3 mathematics; 3 science; (2 science lab); 4 history; 4 academic electives. *Academic units recommended:* 4 mathematics; 4 science; (3 science lab); 2 social studies; 2 foreign language.

Financial Aid

Students should submit: FAFSA, Institution's own financial aid form, State aid form, Noncustodial PROFILE. The Princeton Review suggests that all financial aid forms be submitted as soon as possible after January 1. *Need-based scholarships/grants offered:* Federal Pell, SEOG, State scholarships/grants, private scholarships, the school's own gift aid. *Loan aid offered:* Federal Perkins Loans. Federal Work-Study Program available. Institutional employment available. Off-campus job opportunities are good.

The Inside Word

Like many colleges and universities in the digital age, Champlain now offers the common application; however, don't neglect Champlain's special supplement to the application, which allows you an opportunity to detail just what you'd contribute to, and get out of, the Champlain community. For the BFA or BS programs in graphic design, game design, digital filmmaking, professional writing, game art and animation, and creative media, prospective students must submit a portfolio of relevant creative work. Champlain looks closely at the rigor of prospectives' high school course load, and specifically states that they prefer students to take a challenging, full course load senior year.

THE SCHOOL SAYS "..."

From the Admissions Office

"Preparing students for the opportunities and challenges of an increasingly competitive world is not negotiable for us. When a student graduates from Champlain College, they can be confident that they are not only career-ready, but also life-ready.

"Students at Champlain College are immediately immersed in their prospective major and real-life internships via the Upside-Down Curriculum; they are challenged to think critically and further develop communication and writing abilities from the nationally acclaimed liberal arts core; and they will gain important skills such as financial sophistication, career management, and other life-building knowledge. It is an academic experience that is unparalleled, and our graduates are experiencing the benefits the day after graduation.

"However, in addition to academic preparation, going to college is about experiences, and there is no better college town in the East than Burlington, Vermont. Whether your interests are snowboarding and skiing, art and culture, music and expression, volunteering and community-building, or anything else, Burlington, Vermont, and our amazing campus have it covered. Champlain College students reside in historic Victorian mansions that overlook one of the country's most amazing natural vistas and are only steps from downtown Burlington.

"A Champlain College student is a student that feels optimistic about the future because she is taking control of it. It is a college environment of enrichment, support, and activity, and continually asks the question, what do you need to be successful upon graduation?

"We hope you can visit us soon and get a taste of the Champlain experience."

SELECTIVITY

Admissions Rating	72
# of applicants	3,077
% of applicants accepted	85
% of acceptees attending	25
# offered a place on the wait list	27
% accepting a place on wait list	52
% admitted from wait list	79
# of early decision applicants	321
% accepted early decision	77

FRESHMAN PROFILE

Range SAT Critical Reading	500–610
Range SAT Math	490–590
Range ACT Composite	20–25
Minimum paper TOEFL	500
Minimum web-based TOEFL	173
% graduated top 10% of class	11
% graduated top 25% of class	35
% graduated top 50% of class	70

DEADLINES

Early decision	
Deadline	11/15
Notification	12/15
Regular	
Deadline	1/31
Notification	12/15
Nonfall registration?	Yes

APPLICANTS ALSO LOOK AT AND OFTEN PREFER

University of Vermont; University of Massachusetts Amherst; University of New Hampshire

AND SOMETIMES PREFER

Rochester Institute of Technology; Ithaca College; Drexel University; Quinnipiac University; St. Michael's College

FINANCIAL FACTS

Financial Aid Rating	72
Annual tuition	$31,250
Room and board	$13,500
Required fees	$140
Books and supplies	$1,000
% needy frosh rec. need-based scholarship or grant aid	74
% needy UG rec. need-based scholarship or grant aid	74
% needy frosh rec. non-need-based scholarship or grant aid	2
% needy UG rec. non-need-based scholarship or grant aid	2
% needy frosh rec. need-based self-help aid	92
% needy UG rec. need-based self-help aid	92
% frosh rec. any financial aid	90
% UG rec. any financial aid	83
% frosh need fully met	19
% ugrads need fully met	21
Average % of frosh need met	58
Average % of ugrad need met	63

CHAPMAN UNIVERSITY

One University Drive, Orange, CA 92866 • Admissions: 714-997-6711 • Fax: 714-997-6713

STUDENTS SAY ". . ."

Academics

Orange County's Chapman University boasts "a more personalized education" of a style "you can't find at any other university," according to students, who say the "personal relationship with your professors" and "greater opportunity to meet one-on-one with your professors" thanks to "small class sizes" sets it apart from other West Coast schools. Sure, the location is a big draw, but so is the "emphasis on personalized education," which aims to "aid students in becoming global citizens, productive workers, and [have] positive impacts in the world." The "amazing and very informative" professors here make classes "engaging" and provide an education "that motivates students to go for their dreams." Indeed, "Professors will go out of their way to get to know students and make sure they are doing well in the class." These educators "bring real experiences into the classrooms," which give students "real-life case studies," and they "assist with networking opportunities." Students agree, "Professors at Chapman are really here to see their students succeed." A few students complain, "Sometimes adjunct faculty are not asked back," which means "it is difficult to keep connections with professors who you never see again." While "there are a few professors who are not as engaging, for the most part all of my teachers have been interesting and have really had a desire to help me learn in whatever way is best for me."

Life

Chapman is in Orange County, California, so Disneyland, Los Angeles, gorgeous West Coast beaches, and more are all seemingly right around the corner. That means it is no surprise that "Chapman students believe in a work hard, play hard mentality." Students here "don't only excel in the classroom, but they like to have a good time." And it's easy to have a good time here. After all, "with so many entertainment venues nearby, in addition to on-campus events, students can always find something to do." The play-hard attitude doesn't necessarily mean your stereotypical, beer-chugging frat party, however. "Because there are a lot of families that live here in the area, it can be difficult for 'typical college parties' to exist." When it comes to things to do, Disneyland, Disneyland, and Disneyland ends up on a lot of lists. "I go frequently," one student notes, "and quite a few Chapman students are employed there." Some say they get a year pass and go as many as five times a week. But the Mouse is only one of many things to do here. "There is never a boring weekend," students say. "We have so many options available including, the beach, Disneyland, or things on campus—from movie nights to open mic nights in the student union to concerts."

Student Body

You had better be ready to socialize if you decide on Chapman, because "the typical student at Chapman is friendly, social, and active." Students are "very busy and pretty involved and committed to their interests" and "are usually very involved in multiple activities and very passionate and excited to be here." In many cases, "Students are leaders on our campus and dedicated to their passions." A willingness to interact is a major factor for those attending this school. "If students are willing to get involved, there is always a place for them to fit in." It's not always easy, but as one student notes, "I would say there is a niche for everyone; it might take a while to find it, though." In addition to sociability, embracing diversity is also a common trait here. The typical person on campus is someone "who is passionate and accepting." Students say, "There is no discrimination here; everyone accepts everyone." The bottom line: "If you are willing to adopt the SoCal lifestyle, Chapman is for you. If you don't like being out and about, constantly in a social situation, Chapman may not feel like home."

FINANCIAL AID: 714-997-6741 • E-MAIL: ADMIT@CHAPMAN.EDU • WEBSITE: WWW.CHAPMAN.EDU

THE PRINCETON REVIEW SAYS

Admissions

Very important factors considered include: Class rank, GPA, rigor of secondary school record, standardized test scores, application essay, character/personal qualities. *Important factors considered include:* Extracurricular activities, talent/ability, volunteer work. *Other factors considered include:* First generation, geographical residence, interview, racial/ethnic status, recommendation(s), state residency, work experience, alumni/ae relations. SAT or ACT required; ACT with Writing component required. TOEFL required of all international applicants. *Academic units required:* 2 English; 2 mathematics; 2 science; (1 science lab); 3 social studies; 2 foreign language. *Academic units recommended:* 4 English; 4 mathematics; 4 science; (1 science lab); 4 social studies; 4 foreign language.

Financial Aid

Students should submit: FAFSA, State aid form. The Princeton Review suggests that all financial aid forms be submitted as soon as possible after January 1. *Need-based scholarships/grants offered:* Federal Pell, SEOG, State scholarships/grants, private scholarships, the school's own gift aid. *Loan aid offered:* Direct Subsidized Stafford Loans, Direct Unsubsidized Stafford Loans, Federal Perkins Loans. Federal Work-Study Program available. Institutional employment available. Off-campus job opportunities are excellent.

Inside Word

No need to decode arcane admissions formulas or race in your application before everyone else. There is no trick into getting into Chapman other than this: Be as well-rounded a person as possible, with a strong focus on service to your community. This will show that you're a good fit for the school's "global responsibility" program. The approach makes getting accepted tough, but that hasn't slowed down the ceaseless flow of applications, applications that keep coming in despite stiff competition from other California schools.

THE SCHOOL SAYS "..."

From the Admissions Office

"During our more than 150-year history, Chapman has evolved from a small, traditional liberal arts college into a vibrant and comprehensive midsized university distinguished for its extraordinary blend of liberal arts, science, and professional curriculum, including nationally recognized programs in athletic training, film and television production, business and economics, dance, music, theatre, writing, and teacher education. At Chapman, learning extends well beyond the classroom—our central Orange County, California, location offers countless cultural, educational, and career opportunities. Additionally, the temperate climate allows for a dynamic, outdoor-oriented lifestyle.

"Chapman's environment is involving, and we seek students who are willing to enter an atmosphere of healthy competition where their talents will be nurtured and actualized to the fullest—whether in the classroom, on the stage, or on the athletic field. We encourage prospective students to thoroughly investigate our fine balance of liberal arts and professional learning, so they may make a fully informed decision about 'fit' with regard to their personalities and that of the University.

"Chapman is a member of the Common Application group. Applicants for freshman admission to Chapman University will be required to submit scores from either the SAT or the ACT including the ACT writing section."

SELECTIVITY

Admissions Rating	94
# of applicants	11,750
% of applicants accepted	45
% of acceptees attending	25
# offered a place on the wait list	1,390
% accepting a place on wait list	27
% admitted from wait list	24

FRESHMAN PROFILE

Range SAT Critical Reading	550–640
Range SAT Math	570–660
Range SAT Writing	560–650
Range ACT Composite	24–29
Minimum paper TOEFL	550
Minimum web-based TOEFL	213
Average HS GPA	3.68
% graduated top 10% of class	48
% graduated top 25% of class	93
% graduated top 50% of class	98

DEADLINES

Early action	
Deadline	11/1
Notification	1/10
Regular	
Deadline	1/15
Nonfall registration?	Yes

APPLICANTS ALSO LOOK AT AND OFTEN PREFER

Loyola Marymount University; University of San Diego; University of California Los Angeles; University of Southern California, New York University

AND SOMETIMES PREFER

Pepperdine University

FINANCIAL FACTS

Financial Aid Rating	81
Annual tuition	$44,710
Room and board	$12,954
Required fees	$683
Books and supplies	$1,560
% needy frosh rec. need-based scholarship or grant aid	90
% needy UG rec. need-based scholarship or grant aid	88
% needy frosh rec. non-need-based scholarship or grant aid	74
% needy UG rec. non-need-based scholarship or grant aid	62
% needy frosh rec. need-based self-help aid	88
% needy UG rec. need-based self-help aid	91
% UG borrow to pay for school	63
Average cumulative indebtedness	$27,268
% frosh need fully met	10
% ugrads need fully met	11
Average % of frosh need met	78
Average % of ugrad need met	75

CHRISTOPHER NEWPORT UNIVERSITY

1 AVENUE OF THE ARTS, NEWPORT NEWS, VA 23606-2998 • ADMISSIONS: 757-594-7015 • FAX: 757-594-7333

CAMPUS LIFE

Quality of Life Rating	88
Fire Safety Rating	95
Green Rating	70
Type of school	Public
Affiliation	No Affiliation
Environment	City

STUDENTS

Total undergrad enrollment	5,083
% male/female	43/57
% from out of state	7
% frosh from public high school	15
% frosh live on campus	96
% ugrads live on campus	73
# of fraternities	9
# of sororities	8
% African American	8
% Asian	2
% Caucasian	75
% Hispanic	5
% Native American	<1
% international	<1
# of countries represented	34

SURVEY SAYS . . .

Classroom facilities are great
Students are friendly
Dorms are like palaces
Campus feels safe
Athletic facilities are great

ACADEMICS

Academic Rating	81
% students returning for sophomore year	84
% students graduating within 4 years	57
% students graduating within 6 years	66
Calendar	Semester
Student/faculty ratio	16:1
Profs interesting rating	86
Profs accessible rating	89
Most classes have 10–19 students.	

MOST POPULAR MAJORS

psychology; biology; speech communications
and rhetoric

STUDENTS SAY " . . ."

Academics

Christopher Newport was an English seaman and captain of "the largest of the three ships that brought the Jamestown settlers to the New World." Over 400 years later, Christopher Newport University "is Virginia's up and coming prestigious university," providing "a private school education and experience at a public school cost." "CNU is the perfect size" at "just over 5,000 students." Students enjoy "close relationships between teachers and students" and "small classes and easily accessible professors." Most of the professors "are enthusiastic about their material" and "will work you until you sweat...but this is not necessarily a bad thing." CNU is a university where "professors actually HAVE office hours in which you can see them without appointment to receive extra help." As is true at any school, "some are better than others." One English major says that while the professors are "very approachable" and "care about the students," "I can't say I've had very many who just strike me with awe and inspiration." Students have positive things to say about the administration and the "interactive president" who "runs CNU with excellence." "From the deans to the custodial staff, everyone at CNU is held to a high standard and each seems to genuinely enjoy his/her job." Students rave about the weather, the "absolutely beautiful" campus, and the "always delicious" dining hall food. Students do feel the dining food, while tasty, can be "overpriced" and the dining facilities are "a tad small" and "crowded." Some students feel the school could add more majors, but note "every year CNU seems to be adding more." Perhaps that's because "CNU's motto is 'Students first'" and responds to student needs. From the "friendly atmosphere" and "amazing professors" to the "good financial aid" and "great classes," CNU is a school that feels like a "second home" while also being "a gateway to opportunities in all areas of life."

Life

CNU students are very active on campus and "almost every student is involved in some type of club or organization." "We have SO MANY clubs (literally more than 200) and students are always creating new clubs," meaning "there is something for everyone." "From a capella to ballroom dancing to ping pong to politics or finance, you are actually going to find something (or many things!) that you love," one student explains. CNU is a dry campus, which means there is no alcohol allowed on campus, even for students who are over 21. So unlike a lot of universities, "the party scene isn't exactly a big part of college life," although students note that "drinking is somewhat common off campus." "The Greek presence at CNU is very widespread," and "the school does an excellent job of getting speakers and events on campus." "There isn't much to do in the town on weekends" so "for fun people go to CNU hockey games, Virginia Beach (40 minutes away), beaches on the James River near campus (5 minutes away), house parties, concerts at the Norva in Norfolk...[participate in] intramural sports, and hundreds of clubs." Overall, students are happy with life on CNU's "beautiful campus." Life is "laid back" and fosters a "unique and positive culture." "I am able to see new faces every day, but still see friendly faces in the crowd as well," one student says.

Student Body

The number one description of students at CNU is "friendly." This is a school where "people will always find something in common with one another" and people form "intentional relationships that last a lifetime." The typical student is a "studious, middle class Caucasian; friendly, sociable," and many are "rich white kids from NOVA [who] love big white columns." Although "there needs to be greater diversity at the university," "CNU is not Pleasantville, we have plenty of diversity in socioeconomic backgrounds, styles, and ways of thinking." One student warns that "atheist/agnostic" students might find an "overbearing prevalence of Christian organizations." Other students love the "strong moral values" on campus and say, "People of all different races, religions, and interests interact on a daily basis." Students here care "about their academic career" and "are very friendly and always willing to help others." At the end of the day, "everyone here is really cool and everyone is so nice!"

FINANCIAL AID: 757-594-7170 • E-MAIL: ADMIT@CNU.EDU • WEBSITE: WWW.CNU.EDU

THE PRINCETON REVIEW SAYS

Admissions

Very important factors considered include: GPA, rigor of secondary school record. *Important factors considered include:* Class rank, standardized test scores, application essay, extracurricular activities, interview, recommendation(s), talent/ability, character/personal qualities, level of applicant's interest. *Other factors considered include:* First generation, geographical residence, state residency, volunteer work, work experience, alumni/ae relations. SAT or ACT required for some; ACT with or without Writing component accepted. TOEFL required of all international applicants. *Academic units required:* 4 English; 4 mathematics; 4 science; 4 social studies; 3 foreign language; 2 academic electives; 1 visual/performing arts. *Academic units recommended:* 4 English; 4 mathematics; 4 science; (3 science lab); 4 social studies; 3 foreign language; 2 academic electives; 1 visual/performing arts.

Financial Aid

Students should submit: FAFSA. The Princeton Review suggests that all financial aid forms be submitted as soon as possible after January 1. *Need-based scholarships/grants offered:* Federal Pell, SEOG, State scholarships/grants, private scholarships, the school's own gift aid. *Loan aid offered:* Direct Subsidized Stafford Loans, Direct Unsubsidized Stafford Loans, Direct PLUS loans. Federal Work-Study Program available. Institutional employment available. Off-campus job opportunities are good.

The Inside Word

Alongside the Honors Program, CNU boasts a unique President's Leadership Program for "high achieving students identified for their academic and leadership potential." Interviews are required for both programs. Christopher Newport University is one of the more selective universities in the state, so students will want to bring their A game to their applications.

THE SCHOOL SAYS " . . ."

From the Admissions Office

"Christopher Newport University wants you to thrive academically. Even more so, we want you to lead a life of significance. That's why our undergraduate experience—one that combines cutting-edge academics, stellar leadership opportunities, and high-impact service initiatives—inspires great leaders for the twenty-first century.

"Honoring the best of the liberal arts and sciences, our curriculum shapes hearts and minds for a lifetime of service. We seek students of honor who will make the world a better place. Fifty percent of our students score between 1140 and 1200 on the SAT (critical reading and math), and students must live on campus through their junior year. Our contemporary, state-of-the-art residential facilities win rave reviews from students and parents alike.

"Here you will study alongside distinguished professors, and over the last five years, we have added more than 100 tenure-track Ph.D.s to our faculty. Outside the classroom, you will gain hands-on experience through internships with top organizations like NASA and the Thomas Jefferson National Accelerator Facility.

"At CNU, you will enjoy countless opportunities to develop leadership skills. Make an impact through the President's Leadership Program; design a challenging curriculum in the Honors Program; team with faculty on groundbreaking research; take your studies overseas by studying abroad; and share your talents through 200-plus student organizations. We are also home to one of the most successful NCAA Division III programs in the nation with student-athletes who excel both in the classroom and on the field of play.

"Explore our campus further to discover opportunities as rich as your imagination."

SELECTIVITY

Admissions Rating	83
# of applicants	7,016
% of applicants accepted	59
% of acceptees attending	31
# offered a place on the wait list	1,639
% accepting a place on wait list	32
% admitted from wait list	26
# of early decision applicants	476
% accepted early decision	72

FRESHMAN PROFILE

Range SAT Critical Reading	540–630
Range SAT Math	530–620
Range ACT Composite	23–28
Average HS GPA	3.70
% graduated top 10% of class	20
% graduated top 25% of class	53
% graduated top 50% of class	91

DEADLINES

Early decision	
Deadline	11/15
Notification	12/15
Early action	
Deadline	12/1
Notification	1/15
Regular	
Priority	12/1
Deadline	2/1
Nonfall registration?	Yes

APPLICANTS ALSO LOOK AT AND OFTEN PREFER
The College of William & Mary; University of Virginia

AND SOMETIMES PREFER
George Mason University; James Madison University; Virginia Tech

FINANCIAL FACTS

Financial Aid Rating	83
Annual in-state tuition	$6,520
Annual out-of-state tuition	$16,024
Room and board	$9,958
Required fees	$4,572
Books and supplies	$1,159
% needy frosh rec. need-based scholarship or grant aid	70
% needy UG rec. need-based scholarship or grant aid	71
% needy frosh rec. non-need-based scholarship or grant aid	98
% needy UG rec. non-need-based scholarship or grant aid	66
% needy frosh rec. need-based self-help aid	79
% needy UG rec. need-based self-help aid	85
% frosh rec. any financial aid	81
% UG rec. any financial aid	70
% UG borrow to pay for school	56
Average cumulative indebtedness	$22,967
% frosh need fully met	62
% ugrads need fully met	49
Average % of frosh need met	74
Average % of ugrad need met	69

CITY UNIVERSITY OF NEW YORK—BARUCH COLLEGE

UNDERGRADUATE ADMISSIONS, 151 EAST 25TH STREET, NEW YORK, NY 10010 • ADMISSIONS: 646-312-1400 • FAX: 646-312-1363

CAMPUS LIFE

Quality of Life Rating	70
Fire Safety Rating	60*
Green Rating	61
Type of school	Public
Affiliation	No Affiliation
Environment	Metropolis

STUDENTS

Total undergrad enrollment	13,698
% male/female	52/48
% from out of state	3
% frosh from public high school	90
% frosh live on campus	9
% ugrads live on campus	2
# of fraternities (% ugrad men join)	9 (1)
# of sororities (% ugrad women join)	7 (1)
% African American	10
% Asian	35
% Caucasian	29
% Hispanic	13
% Native American	<1
% international	12
# of countries represented	164

SURVEY SAYS . . .

Political activism is unpopular or nonexistent
Students love New York, NY
Very little drug use

ACADEMICS

Academic Rating	74
% students returning for sophomore year	88
% students graduating within 4 years	39
% students graduating within 6 years	67
Calendar	Semester
Student/faculty ratio	16:1
Profs interesting rating	66
Profs accessible rating	68

Most classes have 20–29 students.
Most lab/discussion sessions have
 20–29 students.

MOST POPULAR MAJORS
accounting; finance

STUDENTS SAY ". . ."

Academics

Baruch College consists of three schools, and although its Weissman School of Arts and Sciences and School of Public Affairs are both strong, it's the Zicklin School of Business that garners nearly all the attention here (as well over three-quarters of the student body). Zicklin offers a "very demanding business-oriented program that provides a great education in an overcrowded environment" where "it's very easy to get lost," but just as easy for go-getters to access "unparalleled internships, career, and networking opportunities to major global companies' headquarters." Because New York City is a worldwide finance capital, Baruch's connections and internships provide "a gateway to the world of finance," and it is for this reason—as well as for the fact that "tuition is about one-fourth what it is at NYU," making it "the best college value in New York City"—that students flock to Baruch. Students warn that you must be willing to "put 110 percent into your studies and take advantage of the NYC network and Starr Career Development Center" to reap all available benefits here. Those who make the effort will discover a career office that "works tirelessly to prepare its students for the working world. Not only do they offer workshops on how to make yourself an attractive candidate, they also offer counseling and even résumé reviews to make sure your résumé is perfect, as well as mock interviews that help you analyze your strengths and weaknesses as an interviewer."

Life

Baruch is a collection of six buildings scattered over four city blocks. Most of the action centers around the seventeen-story Newman Vertical Campus facility, which is "beautiful" but "does not offer a lot of things to do" between classes. Furthermore, the mostly residential area surrounding the school offers "few places you can hang out at, especially when you have huge breaks between classes." Although the building is fairly new, "the escalators almost never work," and the elevators "are always as packed as the commute on the train." Many here grumpily opt for the stairway. School-related extra-curriculars are hampered by the lack of a "real campus" and by the fact that many students are commuters who work part time. Some get involved in community service and/or major-related clubs and organizations, but anyone coming here for a traditional college experience will be sorely disappointed. However access to New York City, for most, more than compensates for this drawback.

Student Body

The "hardworking" student body at Baruch could well be "the most diverse university in the country." It's the sort of place where "you can eat samosas on Tuesday, mooncakes on Wednesday, and falafel on Thursdays for free because of all the cultural events that are held." Students brag that "hundreds of countries are represented in our student body" and note that "the one common thread would be we are mostly business-oriented and have jobs/internships outside of school." While students get along well in class, outside the classroom they can be "very cliquey." One student explains, "If you know people from your high school, you stick with them; if you're a foreign student you stick with others from your home country. Otherwise you get the cold shoulder." Because "the school puts tremendous pressure on grades," most students are "extremely stressed."

CITY UNIVERSITY OF NEW YORK—BARUCH COLLEGE

FINANCIAL AID: 646-312-1360 • E-MAIL: ADMISSIONS@BARUCH.CUNY.EDU • WEBSITE: WWW.BARUCH.CUNY.EDU

THE PRINCETON REVIEW SAYS

Admissions

Very important factors considered include: GPA, rigor of secondary school record, standardized test scores, *Important factors considered include:* Application essay, recommendation(s). *Other factors considered include:* Extracurricular activities, interview, talent/ability, work experience, character/personal qualities. SAT or ACT required; ACT with or without Writing component accepted. TOEFL required of all international applicants. *Academic units required:* 4 English; 3 mathematics; 2 science; (2 science lab); 4 social studies; 2 foreign language. *Academic units recommended:* 4 mathematics; 2 foreign language; 1 academic elective.

Financial Aid

Students should submit: FAFSA, State aid form. The Princeton Review suggests that all financial aid forms be submitted as soon as possible after January 1. *Need-based scholarships/grants offered:* Federal Pell, SEOG, State scholarships/grants, Private scholarships, the school's own gift aid. *Loan aid offered:* Direct Subsidized Stafford Loans, Direct Unsubsidized Stafford Loans, Direct PLUS loans, Federal Perkins Loans. Federal Work-Study Program available. Institutional employment available. Off-campus job opportunities are excellent.

The Inside Word

Baruch's business school greatly upgrades the school's profile in its hallmark academic field. Admissions have grown steadily more competitive since, especially for students seeking undergraduate business degrees. Today, Baruch receives nearly ten applications for every slot in its freshman class. Your math scores on standardized tests count more heavily here than verbal scores.

THE SCHOOL SAYS "..."

From the Admissions Office

"Baruch College is in the heart of New York City. As an undergraduate, you will join a vibrant learning community of students and scholars in the middle of an exhilarating city full of possibilities. Baruch is a place where theory meets practice. You can network with city leaders; secure business, cultural, and nonprofit internships; access the music, art, and business scene; and meet experts who visit our campus. You will take classes that bridge business, arts, science, and social policy, learning from professors who are among the best in their fields. One third of our freshmen participate in learning communities, which offer incoming students small, interdisciplinary classes and an opportunity to get to know our faculty through class room discussion and planned field trips throughout the city. Baruch offers thirty-one majors and fifty-five minors in three schools: the School of Public Affairs, the Weissman School of Arts and Science, and the Zicklin School of Business. Highly qualified undergraduates may apply to the Baruch College Honors program, which offers scholarships, small seminars and honors courses. Students may also study abroad through programs in more than thirty countries. Our seventeen-floor Newman Vertical Campus serves as the college's hub. Here you will find the atmosphere and resources of a traditional college campus, but in a lively urban setting. Our classrooms have state-of-the-art technology, and our library was named the top college library in the nation. Baruch also has a simulated trading floor for students who are interested in Wall Street. You can also enjoy a three-level athletics and recreation complex, which features a twenty-five-meter indoor pool as well as a performing arts complex. In 2013, Baruch College opened the 25th Street Pedestrian Plaza, providing outdoor space for major student actives like Freshmen Convocation, Winter Carnival and Spring Fling, as well as an informal setting for students to gather on a nice day.The college is now offering housing at 1760 3rd Avenue (in Manhattan, on the Upper East Side). The state-of-the-art residences are equipped with a concierge, high tech gym, laundry facility that texts when your clothes are dry, and a very chill lounge to study or relax with your friends. The building is just blocks away from Central Park, the Whitney Museum, and Serendipity. Baruch's selective admission standards, strong academic programs, top national honors, as well as its internship and job-placement opportunities make it an exceptional educational value."

SELECTIVITY
Admissions Rating	93
# of applicants	19,423
% of applicants accepted	27
% of acceptees attending	24

FRESHMAN PROFILE
Range SAT Critical Reading	530–630
Range SAT Math	600–700
Minimum paper TOEFL	550
Minimum web-based TOEFL	80
Average HS GPA	3.21
% graduated top 10% of class	41
% graduated top 25% of class	70
% graduated top 50% of class	89

DEADLINES
Early decision	
Deadline	12/13
Notification	1/7
Regular	
Priority	12/1
Deadline	2/1
Notification	5/1
Nonfall registration?	Yes

APPLICANTS ALSO LOOK AT AND OFTEN PREFER
CUNY Brooklyn College; CUNY Queens College

AND SOMETIMES PREFER
State University of New York at Albany; CUNY Hunter College

FINANCIAL FACTS
Financial Aid Rating	75
Annual in-state tuition	$6,030
Annual out-of-state tuition	$16,050
Required fees	$531
Books and supplies	$1,248
% needy frosh rec. need-based scholarship or grant aid	100
% needy UG rec. need-based scholarship or grant aid	99
% needy frosh rec. non-need-based scholarship or grant aid	6
% needy UG rec. non-need-based scholarship or grant aid	3
% needy frosh rec. need-based self-help aid	22
% needy UG rec. need-based self-help aid	34
% frosh rec. any financial aid	67
% UG rec. any financial aid	53
% UG borrow to pay for school	20
Average cumulative indebtedness	$9,949
% frosh need fully met	18
% ugrads need fully met	17
Average % of frosh need met	71
Average % of ugrad need met	64

CITY UNIVERSITY OF NEW YORK—BROOKLYN COLLEGE

2900 BEDFORD AVENUE, BROOKLYN, NY 11210 • ADMISSIONS: 718-951-5001 • FAX: 718-951-4506

CAMPUS LIFE
Quality of Life Rating	72
Fire Safety Rating	60*
Green Rating	83
Type of school	Public
Affiliation	No Affiliation
Environment	Metropolis

STUDENTS
Total undergrad enrollment	12,625
% male/female	41/59
% from out of state	2
% frosh from public high school	81
% frosh live on campus	0
% ugrads live on campus	0
# of fraternities (% ugrad men join)	7 (3)
# of sororities (% ugrad women join)	9 (3)
% African American	22
% Asian	17
% Caucasian	38
% Hispanic	18
% Native American	<1
% international	3
# of countries represented	150

SURVEY SAYS . . .
Great library
Athletic facilities are great
Very little drug use

ACADEMICS
Academic Rating	76
% students returning for sophomore year	86
% students graduating within 4 years	24
% students graduating within 6 years	51
Calendar	Semester
Student/faculty ratio	16:1
Profs interesting rating	68
Profs accessible rating	68
Most classes have 20–29 students.

MOST POPULAR MAJORS
business administration and management;
accounting; psychology

STUDENTS SAY ". . ."
Academics
Brooklyn College "is the perfect representative of Brooklyn as a borough and [of] success in the community," an institution that, like its home borough, "educates its students in an environment that reflects diversity, opportunity (study abroad, research, athletics, employment), and support." "Lauded as one of the best senior colleges in CUNY" and boasting "a beautiful campus," Brooklyn College entices a lot of bright students looking for an affordable, quality, undergraduate experience as well as some attracted by the school's relatively charitable admissions standards. It's easier to get in here than to stay in; Brooklyn College is "an academically challenging and rigorous school" that "feels a lot more competitive than one would anticipate." Professors "are fabulous" and "really passionate about the subjects that they teach and their students' career paths," although there are some "grumpy and nasty professors" that might best be avoided. Students are especially sanguine about special programs here, such as the various honors programs, in which "you will meet tons of highly intelligent people. Honors classes boast very good in-class discussions and highly vibrant, enthusiastic students. Non-honors classes are more run-of-the-mill but still very good academically." The school also works hard to provide "constant and innumerable job opportunities available to students and the Magner Center, which helps students find jobs and internships, and [to] help them prepare for the real world through résumé writing workshops [and] job interview workshops." There are also "many financial awards available."

Life
"Apart from all the clubs and athletics on campus, most people come for class and then leave" at Brooklyn College because "we are a commuter school, so it has to be this way. All social activities happen off campus." There are "pretty nice places to hang out around campus for the occasional coffee," and "there are a lot of student organizations and a lot of activities done to help enhance student life on campus," but the "immediate surroundings of the Brooklyn College campus are generally not where you would want to stay for hours," and "on weekends the campus usually is dead." That said, "the campus is quite beautiful, and the quad during spring time is usually a nice place to sit and relax." Furthermore, "New York City hotspots are a twenty- to forty-minute [subway] ride away," and Brooklyn itself is "a great place to live" where "there are always fun things happening."

Student Body
"The typical student at Brooklyn College is hardworking, from the NY metro area, and a commuter." Many "hold part-time jobs and pay at least part of their own tuition, so they are usually in a rush because they have a lot more responsibility on their shoulders than the average college student." Like Brooklyn itself, "the student body is very diversified," with everyone from "an aspiring opera singer to quirky film majors to single mothers looking for a better life for their children," and so "no student can be described as being typical. Everyone blends in as normal, and little segregation is noticed (if it exists)." Students here represent more than 100 nations and speak nearly as many languages. There are even students "that come from Long Island to North Carolina, from Connecticut to even Hong Kong."

CITY UNIVERSITY OF NEW YORK—BROOKLYN COLLEGE

FINANCIAL AID: 718-951-5051 • E-MAIL: ADMINQRY@BROOKLYN.CUNY.EDU • WEBSITE: WWW.BROOKLYN.CUNY.EDU

THE PRINCETON REVIEW SAYS

Admissions

Very important factors considered include: GPA, rigor of secondary school record, standardized test scores. *Other factors considered include:* SAT or ACT required; SAT and SAT Subject Tests or ACT considered if submitted; ACT with or without Writing component accepted. TOEFL required of all international applicants. *Academic units recommended:* 4 English; 3 mathematics; 3 science; 4 social studies; 3 foreign language; 4 academic electives.

Financial Aid

Students should submit: FAFSA, State aid form. The Princeton Review suggests that all financial aid forms be submitted as soon as possible after January 1. *Need-based scholarships/grants offered:* Federal Pell, SEOG, State scholarships/grants, private scholarships, the school's own gift aid. *Loan aid offered:* Direct Subsidized Stafford Loans, Direct Unsubsidized Stafford Loans, Direct PLUS loans, Federal Perkins Loans. Federal Work-Study Program available. Institutional employment available. Off-campus job opportunities are excellent.

The Inside Word

Brooklyn College doesn't set the bar inordinately high; students with less-than-stellar high school records can receive a chance to prove themselves here. Once they get in, though, they had better be prepared to work; Brooklyn College typically loses about 20 percent of its freshman class each year, and six-year graduation rates rarely exceed 50 percent. Getting into Brooklyn College is one thing; surviving its academic challenges is a whole other thing entirely.

THE SCHOOL SAYS "..."

From the Admissions Office

"Brooklyn College is a premier public liberal arts college. For the last five years it has been consistently designated as one of America's Best Value Colleges by The Princeton Review and, in 2009, was cited as one of the top fifty Best Value Public Colleges in the nation. Respected nationally for its rigorous academic standards, the college has increased both the size and academic quality of its student body. It takes pride in such innovative programs as its award-winning Freshman Year College; the Honors Academy, which houses six programs for high achievers; and its nationally recognized core curriculum. Its School of Education is ranked among the top twenty in the country for graduates who go on to be considered among the best teachers in New York City. Brooklyn College's strong academic reputation has attracted an outstanding faculty of nationally renowned teachers and scholars. Among the awards they have won are Pulitzers, Guggenheims, Fulbrights, and many National Institutes of Health grants.

"The student body consists of more than 16,000 undergraduate and graduate students who represent the ethnic and cultural diversity of the borough. The college's accessibility by subway or bus allows students to further enrich their educational experience through New York City's many cultural events and institutions. In recent years, student achievements have been acknowledged with Fulbright and Truman Scholarships and an Emmy Award. In 2010 we received our third Rhodes Scholarship in eleven years.

"The Brooklyn College campus, considered to be among the most beautiful in the nation, is in the midst of an ambitious program of expansion and renewal. A new residence hall has opened two blocks from the campus. It includes such amenities as single, as well as shared, rooms, Wi-Fi throughout, community lounges, a fitness center, and kitchenettes in every room. The dazzling library is the most technologically advanced educational and research facility in the CUNY system. Opened in 2009, the West Quad Building has state-of-the-art student services and is home to the physical education department. A separate fitness center, basketball and handball courts, and a competition pool is open for use by students and staff. Ground has been broken for a new performing arts center, followed in the coming years with a new science complex."

SELECTIVITY

Admissions Rating	88
# of applicants	20,145
% of applicants accepted	34
% of acceptees attending	18

FRESHMAN PROFILE

Range SAT Critical Reading	470–570
Range SAT Math	510–600
Minimum paper TOEFL	500
Minimum web-based TOEFL	173
Average HS GPA	3.28
% graduated top 10% of class	18
% graduated top 25% of class	50
% graduated top 50% of class	77

DEADLINES

Regular	
Priority	2/1
Nonfall registration?	Yes

FINANCIAL FACTS

Financial Aid Rating	92
Annual in-state tuition	$6,030
Required fees	$505
Books and supplies	$1,304
% needy frosh rec. need-based scholarship or grant aid	72
% needy UG rec. need-based scholarship or grant aid	86
% needy frosh rec. non-need-based scholarship or grant aid	26
% needy UG rec. non-need-based scholarship or grant aid	28
% needy frosh rec. need-based self-help aid	70
% needy UG rec. need-based self-help aid	79
% frosh rec. any financial aid	77
% UG rec. any financial aid	78
% UG borrow to pay for school	46
Average cumulative indebtedness	$11,000
% frosh need fully met	73
% ugrads need fully met	81
Average % of frosh need met	91
Average % of ugrad need met	92

CITY UNIVERSITY OF NEW YORK—CITY COLLEGE

160 CONVENT AVENUE, WILLE ADMINISTRATION BUILDING, NEW YORK, NY 10031 • ADMISSIONS: 212-650-6977 • FAX: 212-650-6417

STUDENTS SAY ". . ."

Academics

As the first school of the City University of New York system, CCNY "stands for growth, education, and creativity." Many students choose the school due to its "astonishingly low cost" and proximity to home, and its practicality is backed up by "rigorous academic programs." "I fell in love with the school during open house, and it's the exact way I imagined after enrolling," says a student. The university has also made substantial new investments in science and medicine, and it is the only public college in New York City to offer engineering and architecture degrees, which is a huge draw for the school (but there is "no coddling here in the engineering school," warns one student). A "multitude" of classes are taught by "awesome professors with experience and wonderful careers" who "are available outside of the class" and "exhibit great love for the materials they teach." Generally, professors "go above and beyond" to ensure that students are able to grasp what they are learning. "My professors devote time and effort to making sure students understand the material being taught," confirms a student. The diversity in the student body, as well as the faculty and administration, "is profound," which "helps many people interact with different people from different cultures and come together to get through each semester in college." No matter their background, all here "take our education and future careers seriously." "There are a lot of talented people in the school overall," says a student, not to mention the "strong ties to research collaborators and institutions." Professors "will make you learn and work for the A," but "It has overall been a very rewarding experience," according to a student.

Life

Since so many students work and live full lives outside of classes, most students commute home each night. "The campus is nice, and there's a lot to do, but there's very little 'campus life,'" according to one student. CCNY has "amazing events," but "sometimes it's hard to partake due to our employment and fiscal priorities." The clubs "are always having shows, fairs, and other types of events offered to all students." People are "very respectful and helpful," and "a new student will always be able to find help." The library and cafeteria are both popular hangout spots, and "there is a gym, both for workout and for sports." Let's also not forget where the school is located: "It isn't hard to find fun around New York City." Harlem "is very historic," and "there are great places to eat around City College." The radio station WCCR "always has a ton of people having fun, hanging out, and playing music."

Student Body

The diversity at CCNY is not just ethnic—it is also political, economic, academic, age, and every other means of categorization—which means that there is no typical student. This large group of "diverse students seeking excellence" all feel like they fit in because "we each have something to bring to the table." On any average day, "You can walk through the college and see people of all ages and races interacting with each other." Students "live busy lives," and the vast majority "works and goes to school at the same time." Most students are commuters, and many are "immigrant or come from an immigrant family," but "most identify first and foremost as New Yorkers." Many subscribe to clubs and other extracurriculars "to fit in and make friends." Most CCNY students are not looking for the "typical college experience," but rather are interested "in the intellectual and emotional growth that comes with higher education."

FINANCIAL AID: 212-650-5819 • E-MAIL: ADMISSIONS@CCNY.CUNY.EDU • WEBSITE: WWW.CCNY.CUNY.EDU

THE PRINCETON REVIEW SAYS

Admissions

Very important factors considered include: GPA, rigor of secondary school record. *Important factors considered include:* Standardized test scores. *Other factors considered include:* Application essay, recommendation(s). SAT or ACT required. TOEFL required of all international applicants. *Academic units recommended:* 4 English; 3 mathematics; 2 science; (2 science lab); 4 social studies; 3 foreign language; 1 visual/performing arts.

Financial Aid

Students should submit: FAFSA, State aid form. The Princeton Review suggests that all financial aid forms be submitted as soon as possible after January 1. *Need-based scholarships/grants offered:* Federal Pell, SEOG, State scholarships/grants, the school's own gift aid. *Loan aid offered:* Direct Subsidized Stafford Loans, Direct Unsubsidized Stafford Loans, Direct PLUS loans. Federal Work-Study Program available. Institutional employment available. Off-campus job opportunities are fair.

The Inside Word

CUNY—City College is one of the toughest CUNY schools get into, with an admissions rate of about 33 percent (some schools and programs within can be lower). Selective freshman programs—such as the honors college—may require a supplemental paper application, letters of recommendation, and/or a personal statement. The good news is that students can apply online to as many as six CUNY colleges with one application.

THE SCHOOL SAYS "..."

From the Admissions Office "City is an old school with new ideas. Founded in 1847, we take pride in our tradition, eagerly embrace the present, and ride the cutting edge of the future. CCNY has one of the most diverse student bodies in any college of America, and is a mirror image of New York City. Our mission emphasizes access and excellence in undergraduate and graduate education and research, and opportunities for internships and study abroad abound. Whether you are looking for preparation for an exciting career or graduate and doctoral studies, City College offers the path to your future. We offer over 100 undergraduate and graduate degrees in architecture, education, engineering, the arts and humanities, the social sciences and science, as well as a unique BS/MD program. High achieving students interested in any discipline also may have the opportunity to participate including the Macaulay Honors College and the CCNY Honors Program.

"We are seeking students who will thrive at City both academically and personally, while contributing to the community inside and outside of the classroom. Candidates will be considered on the basis of overall strength of academic preparation (a minimum of sixteen academic units must have been completed), grades in individual subjects, overall high school average, and SAT or ACT scores. Applicants who have taken the General Equivalency Diploma (GED) examination must submit test scores and can be eligible provided they have attained a score of at least 3250 or higher. City College admits a small number of academically exceptional high school students upon the completion of their high school junior year. Students enter as matriculated students into the college's Honors program. Applicants generally are from the upper 10 percent of their high school class.

"All freshmen applying to The Bernard and Anne Spitzer School of Architecture are required to submit a Creative Challenge form; freshmen applying to The Grove School of Engineering are required to submit a supplemental application form; and freshmen applying to the Sophie Davis School of Biomedical Education are required to submit two separate applications."

SELECTIVITY

Admissions Rating	85
# of applicants	26,628
% of applicants accepted	34
% of acceptees attending	16

FRESHMAN PROFILE

Range SAT Critical Reading	450–510
Range SAT Math	520–580
RMinimum paper TOEFL	500
Minimum web-based TOEFL	61

DEADLINES

Regular	
Priority	2/1
Nonfall registration?	Yes

FINANCIAL FACTS

Financial Aid Rating	82
Annual in-state tuition	$6,030
Annual out-of-state tuition	$12,840
Required fees	$410
Books and supplies	$1,304
% needy frosh rec. need-based scholarship or grant aid	93
% needy UG rec. need-based scholarship or grant aid	95
% needy frosh rec. non-need-based scholarship or grant aid	49
% needy UG rec. non-need-based scholarship or grant aid	11
% needy frosh rec. need-based self-help aid	31
% needy UG rec. need-based self-help aid	98
% frosh rec. any financial aid	88
% UG rec. any financial aid	84
% UG borrow to pay for school	22
Average cumulative indebtedness	$16,842
% frosh need fully met	60
% ugrads need fully met	89
Average % of frosh need met	87
Average % of ugrad need met	82

CITY UNIVERSITY OF NEW YORK—HUNTER COLLEGE

695 PARK AVENUE, ROOM N203, NEW YORK, NY 10065 • ADMISSIONS: 212-772-4490 • FAX: 212-650-3472

STUDENTS SAY ". . ."

Academics

Hunter boasts an "outstanding" reputation based in part on its ability to offer "a solid education at an affordable price" and "exposure to New York City." Students who like to challenge the status quo will find a home here. In Hunter classrooms, "diversity of thought is not only tolerated, but encouraged." Those classes can be "very tough," forcing students to "work hard to keep good grades." Some students groan that professors here "teach at a fast pace," but students who pay attention will find that their educators generally "know the subjects that they are teaching very well." While there are some "very tedious professors," most students find that professors are "intellectually challenged by brilliant instructors." A few students wish there were more tenured professors on staff and say that part-time educators "would care more if they were paid more." Yet many departments win praise, including the "highly respected" psychology department, which is "affiliated with most of the prestigious hospitals in New York City," as well as challenging English and nursing programs. Maybe most important is that students will get a sense for what their education will mean outside of school. These professors "bring to the table their vast experiences in their field of expertise and have never hesitated to educate on what to expect when we are outside of the classroom, often offering a practical aspect to what in many classrooms are strictly academic discussions."

Life

On one hand, being located in Manhattan means that Hunter has immediate access to almost anything in arts, culture, music, and nightlife that an urban adventurer can imagine. On the other hand, "Hunter is largely a commuter school, so there is not much campus life at night or on the weekends," a situation one student calls "miserable." Students won't get a typical college life here. "Nobody lives on campus at Hunter," and "most people who attend school at Hunter work part-time or full-time, have apartments, pay bills, and go to school full-time." That is not to say there is no excitement at Hunter. You just "have to make an effort for things to happen and to gather people because they need to make time from their schedules to meet up." Those who put in the effort will find that the city is their oyster. One student notes that whether it is food or music or entertainment, "anything that's not academic-related you can find easily from blocks away," while another notes, "New York is a tourist haven," so there is no shortage of things to do. But again, it won't come to you. Be prepared to make things happen. "The only way to make friends is to dorm (which is nearly impossible) or to hang around campus joining fraternities and clubs." If you're a commuter student or work full-time, as many Hunter students do, "socializing is nearly impossible."

Student Body

New York City is one of the most diverse metropolitan areas in the world, so it should come as no surprise that "there is no typical student at Hunter." This cultural melting pot of a region means "the diversity here is real and comes in all forms, most especially diversity of thought and opinion." One student notes that "all of my classrooms contain a mix of every ethnicity and nationality, all ages, all types of people." Even with this wide array of cultures, "somehow, [students] all manage to fit in and get along with one another." Students here also vary wildly in age, with older attendees common in most classrooms. "Most students work full- or part-time while juggling a full-time schedule," which can make it "extremely difficult to make friends, because it's a commuter school." This also means that "there's little sense of school identity." However, for those who involve themselves with other students, "as long as you are not too shy, it is easy to make friends around here."

CITY UNIVERSITY OF NEW YORK—HUNTER COLLEGE

FINANCIAL AID: 212-772-4820 • E-MAIL: ADMISSIONS@HUNTER.CUNY.EDU • WEBSITE: WWW.HUNTER.CUNY.EDU

THE PRINCETON REVIEW SAYS

Admissions

Very important factors considered include: GPA, rigor of secondary school record, standardized test scores, application essay, level of applicant's interest. *Other factors considered include:* SAT or ACT required. TOEFL required of all international applicants. *Academic units required:* 2 English; 2 mathematics; 1 science; (1 science lab). *Academic units recommended:* 4 English; 3 mathematics; 2 science; 4 social studies; 2 foreign language; 1 academic elective; 1 visual/performing arts.

Financial Aid

Students should submit: FAFSA, State aid form. The Princeton Review suggests that all financial aid forms be submitted as soon as possible after January 1. *Need-based scholarships/grants offered:* Federal Pell, State scholarships/grants, the school's own gift aid. *Loan aid offered:* Direct Subsidized Stafford Loans, Direct Unsubsidized Stafford Loans, Direct PLUS loans, Federal Perkins Loans, State Loans, College/university loans from institutional funds. Federal Work-Study Program available. Institutional employment available. Off-campus job opportunities are fair.

The Inside Word

Getting into Hunter is consistently getting harder, with the admissions office getting in excess of 30,000 applications a year. Applicants should be prepared to present strong grades that meet the school's admissions formula. (Hunter officials do not divulge the formula.) Programs fill up fast, so applying early is essential. Wait too long and thousands of students will have gotten in line in front of you.

THE SCHOOL SAYS "..."

From the Admissions Office

"Located in the heart of Manhattan, Hunter offers students the stimulating learning environment and career-building opportunities you might expect from a college that's been a part of the world's most exciting city since 1870. The largest college in the City University of New York, Hunter pulses with energy. Hunter's vitality stems from a large, highly diverse faculty and student body. Its schools—Arts and Sciences, Education, Nursing, Social Work and Public Health—provide an affordable first-rate education. Undergraduates have extraordinary opportunities to conduct high level research with renowned faculty, and to participate in credit-bearing internships in media, the arts, government and many other fields. The college's high standards and special programs ensure a challenging education. Several specialized programs for first-year students keep classmates together as they pursue courses in the liberal arts, pre–health science, pre-nursing, premed, or honors. A range of honors programs is available for students with strong academic records, including the highly competitive tuition-free Macaulay Honors College for entering freshmen and the Thomas Hunter Honors Program, which offers small classes with personalized mentoring by outstanding faculty. Qualified students also benefit from Hunter's participation in minority science research and training programs, the prestigious Andrew W. Mellon Minority Undergraduate Program, and many other passports to professional success.

"Applicants for the entering class are required to take either the SAT or the ACT."

SELECTIVITY

Admissions Rating	86
# of applicants	30,708
% of applicants accepted	31
% of acceptees attending	21

FRESHMAN PROFILE

Range SAT Critical Reading	520–620
Range SAT Math	550–650
Minimum paper TOEFL	500
Minimum web-based TOEFL	173

DEADLINES

Regular	
Deadline	3/15
Nonfall registration?	Yes

FINANCIAL FACTS

Financial Aid Rating	79
Annual out-of-state tuition	$15,300
Required fees	$399
Books and supplies	$1,248
% needy frosh rec. need-based scholarship or grant aid	89
% needy UG rec. need-based scholarship or grant aid	82
% needy frosh rec. non-need-based scholarship or grant aid	82
% needy UG rec. non-need-based scholarship or grant aid	13
% needy frosh rec. need-based self-help aid	21
% needy UG rec. need-based self-help aid	22
% frosh rec. any financial aid	91
% UG rec. any financial aid	94
% UG borrow to pay for school	71
Average cumulative indebtedness	$13,000
% frosh need fully met	22
% ugrads need fully met	14
Average % of frosh need met	73
Average % of ugrad need met	72

CITY UNIVERSITY OF NEW YORK—QUEENS COLLEGE

65-30 KISSENA BOULEVARD, QUEENS, NY 11367 • ADMISSIONS: 718-997-5600 • FAX: 718-997-5617

STUDENTS SAY ". . ."

Academics

As a senior college of the City University of New York, Queens College is an educational institution for locals. The large, diverse university sits upon eighty acres in the middle of Flushing, and offers (mainly locals and commuters) the chance to get a degree that is "affordable without sacrificing proper education." One enamored senior describes it poetically: "A green bedding of low-cost tuition and the strong roots of the administrators, faculty, and stuff holding up the dozens of 'club' trees surrounded by a heavy sprinkling of diverse people makes QC the most beautiful school in NY: both literally and figuratively."

Most professors here are "caring and devoted teachers," but "you always have a few in the bunch per year that give you a real headache." However, "when chosen wisely, the professors can be the most wonderful part of your education at QC." There are "opportunities for growth inside and outside the classroom" for those that seek them, and "the environment is very inviting" for those that just want to try their hand. Most professors use effective teaching techniques that "help students understand and learn through not only lecture style classes but observation and demonstration," as do the "many resources and challenging science courses" provided by the school.

"Courses are topical and abundant," and the administration is refreshingly receptive to new ideas; "when students want to bring change to an area for improvement, it usually happens." "Student counseling services" and the Macaulay Honors College both get singled out for being excellent. All in all, Queens College gives a student body that is "extremely diverse... in every way" (including "many students who would be unable to afford college otherwise") the opportunity for an education.

Life

Students love "the school culture, events, students, and wifi accessibility all over campus!" The school opened its first residence hall (the Summit Apartments) in 2009, which means that only around 500 students have on-campus housing and are often on the go; everyone is typically "running around campus like busy bees with places to go and things to do." "You go to class, maybe stay for a few other errands, or maybe a break in between classes, and then you go home," says a junior. There are some students who just go to class and leave campus, but then "there are others who socialize and are active in campus organizations" or sports teams, of which there are more than one hundred (though no football). "Many people find their place in clubs and other extracurricular activities," says a student. Compared to many other schools, the QC population is "more familiar with the local area around the school since many of us do live off campus."

People are happy with the "nice facilities" at the university, including the "gym and the pool." For fun, the school offers various events like "readings and plays and concerts to attend," as well as "small carnivals or festivities on the main campus with various games like laser tag or rock climbing" for those who are children at heart. There are many restaurants and cafes located on campus, giving students a place to rest their weary head in between classes.

Student Body

The "various backgrounds of different students/faculty make for an eye opening cultural experience." Many students are the first generation in their family to get college educated, and "most students here know a second/third language." This is "very accepted and liked in the college because Queens, our borough, is the most ethnically diverse county in all the United States." Most people here are commuters, and so a typical student is "hardworking" and "usually going to school [while] having some sort of a part-time job on the side." "It isn't uncommon to see students who are, for the most part, self-sufficient financially."

CITY UNIVERSITY OF NEW YORK—QUEENS COLLEGE

FINANCIAL AID: 718-997-5123 • E-MAIL: VINCENT.ANGRISANI@QC.CUNY.EDU • WEBSITE: WWW.QC.CUNY.EDU

THE PRINCETON REVIEW SAYS

Admissions

Very important factors considered include: GPA, rigor of secondary school record, standardized test scores. *Other factors considered include:* SAT or ACT required; ACT with or without Writing component accepted. TOEFL required of all international applicants. *Academic units required:* 4 English; 3 mathematics; 2 science; (2 science lab); 4 social studies; 3 foreign language. *Academic units recommended:* 3 science; (3 science lab).

Financial Aid

Students should submit: FAFSA, Institution's own financial aid form, State aid form. The Princeton Review suggests that all financial aid forms be submitted as soon as possible after January 1. *Need-based scholarships/grants offered:* Federal Pell, SEOG, State scholarships/grants, private scholarships, the school's own gift aid. *Loan aid offered:* Direct Subsidized Stafford Loans, Direct Unsubsidized Stafford Loans, Direct PLUS loans, Federal Perkins Loans. Federal Work-Study Program available. Institutional employment available. Off-campus job opportunities are good.

The Inside Word

Minority enrollment has declined at CUNY in the past several years, partially as a result of changes to admissions criteria and stiffer competition for minority applicants. The school would love to boost its numbers, meaning that qualified minority students could be able to finagle a pretty nice financial aid package here, making an already economical situation even more affordable.

THE SCHOOL SAYS "..."

From the Admissions Office

"At Queens College, you will engage the world of ideas with faculty and students from the world over, prepare for your career, and enjoy the many activities our beautiful, seventy-seven-acre campus has to offer. And with the opening of the Summit Apartments—our first residence hall—you'll find a place to enjoy everything that comes with a college residential experience.

"Since 1937, we've provided a premier liberal arts education to talented students. From graduate and undergraduate degrees, a variety of honors and pre-professional programs to research and real work internship opportunities, you'll find countless ways to realize your potential under the guidance of our award-winning, dedicated faculty. We offer nationally recognized programs—such as our Aaron Copland School of Music—in many fields. And we're also the ideal choice for aspiring teachers, preparing more future educators than any college in the tristate area.

"Located only minutes from Manhattan, our campus boasts a traditional quad overlooking the skyline. You'll find a stimulating and welcoming environment here, with a bustling student union, an impressive arts center, and opportunities to participate in dozens of clubs and sports. (We're the only City University of New York college to participate in Division II.) Campus-wide Wi-Fi, computer kiosks, and cybercafes keep you informed and in touch. And best of all, as part of CUNY, we can offer all this at an affordable cost. To apply for fall 2015, submit your application online along with your SATs comprising critical reading, writing, and math."

SELECTIVITY

Admissions Rating	84
# of applicants	18,518
% of applicants accepted	36
% of acceptees attending	20

FRESHMAN PROFILE

Range SAT Critical Reading	477–570
Range SAT Math	540–610
Range SAT Writing	460–570
Minimum paper TOEFL	500
Minimum web-based TOEFL	173

DEADLINES

Regular	
Priority	2/1
Nonfall registration?	Yes

FINANCIAL FACTS

Financial Aid Rating	93
Annual in-state tuition	$6,030
Annual out-of-state tuition	$14,850
Required fees	$477
Books and supplies	$1,248
% needy frosh rec. need-based scholarship or grant aid	79
% needy UG rec. need-based scholarship or grant aid	82
% needy frosh rec. non-need-based scholarship or grant aid	38
% needy UG rec. non-need-based scholarship or grant aid	16
% needy frosh rec. need-based self-help aid	26
% needy UG rec. need-based self-help aid	36
% frosh rec. any financial aid	69
% UG rec. any financial aid	48
% UG borrow to pay for school	45
Average cumulative indebtedness	$20,000
% frosh need fully met	63
% ugrads need fully met	79
Average % of frosh need met	95
Average % of ugrad need met	95

CLAREMONT McKENNA COLLEGE

888 COLUMBIA AVENUE, CLAREMONT, CA 91711 • ADMISSIONS: 909-621-8088 • FAX: 909-621-8516

STUDENTS SAY ". . ."

Academics
Students at Claremont McKenna really love their school. With its "phenomenal academics," "brilliant professors," "amazing career services center," and "perfect weather," it's no wonder CMC students are "the happiest students in America." Claremont McKenna is known for its government and economics majors, but philosophy, international relations, and the joint sciences program also get high marks. CMC is a part of the Claremont College Consortium, so if students are looking for something that CMC doesn't have, they can probably find it at one of the four affiliated schools. Students rave about Claremont's emphasis on "professionalism" and all of the "great research and internship opportunities." The workload is heavy, and professors set "high expectations," so "students spend their weeks slaving over their papers, books, readings, research projects, problem sets, etc." Despite the intense workload, students love their professors. "Professors are absolute geniuses in their field," one student gushes. They're "helpful and encouraging," "incredibly accessible," and even "willing to Skype on the weekends to answer questions." "This sounds corny," one student admits, "this really is a place where professors become like family." Students spend a "good deal of out-of-classroom time" with their teachers. "Professors and students are so close that it might be considered creepy to outsiders," but students aren't too worried about creeping anyone out because they know how good they've got it. "When you take both academics and quality of life into account," a cognitive neuroscience major says, "I can't believe I almost went to an Ivy over this place."

Life
Life is good at Claremont McKenna. The "constantly beaming California sun and the close vicinity to both mountains and beaches" mean students spend their time outdoors when they can. But even when students are lounging in the sun or playing Frisbee, they're not really taking a break. The "conversation doesn't end in the classroom," a student explains, and the "intellectual culture… really allows for twenty-four-hour learning." While Claremont McKenna has the campus and "community-life and identity of a small school" it "still [has] the resources of the other four C's." Even without the other schools students feel "completely pampered" because "the school cares about its students so much." A Spanish major says, "The relationship between the students and the administration is excellent here," and the "student government and Dean of Students Office…subsidize incredible off-campus trips and on-campus parties." One of the best things about Claremont McKenna is the Marian Miner Cook Atheneum, which hosts prestigious guest lecturers four nights a week. One student wisely asks, "Where else could you have dinner with Jesse Jackson, Mitt Romney, etc.?" Partying is definitely a part of life here, and a student admits that if you don't drink, it could be "easy to feel left out." However, students agree, "There's a niche for everyone, and the welcoming, accepting atmosphere makes fitting in easy."

Student Body
"Claremont McKenna doesn't accept students who aren't amazing." "Amazing" means a "really smart" person who's "incredibly motivated and career-driven" and "loves drinking and partying." It's "a tight-knit community of driven, competitive, and intelligent people who know how to be successful and have a great time." "A lot of kids are political and well-informed"; most are "active on campus," very into sports, and involved with internships or clubs. But even though the environment is "academically strict, the students…rarely fit the 'nerdy' stereotype." Students are extremely well-rounded; they "know how to lead a discussion…clock hours in the library, play a varsity or club sport, and hold a leadership position in a club or organization," and they also know how to throw "a great party on Saturday night."

CLAREMONT MCKENNA COLLEGE

FINANCIAL AID: 909-621-8356 • E-MAIL: ADMISSION@CMC.EDU • WEBSITE: WWW.CMC.EDU

THE PRINCETON REVIEW SAYS

Admissions

Very important factors considered include: Class rank, GPA, rigor of secondary school record, standardized test scores, extracurricular activities, recommendation(s), character/personal qualities. *Important factors considered include:* Application essay, talent/ability. *Other factors considered include:* First generation, geographical residence, interview, racial/ethnic status, volunteer work, work experience, alumni/ae relations. SAT or ACT required; ACT with Writing component required. TOEFL required of all international applicants. *Academic units required:* 4 English; 3 mathematics; 2 science; (2 science lab); 1 social studies; 3 foreign language; 1 history. *Academic units recommended:* 4 English; 4 mathematics; 3 science; (3 science lab); 1 social studies; 3 foreign language; 1 history.

Financial Aid

Students should submit: FAFSA, CSS/Financial Aid PROFILE, State aid form, Noncustodial PROFILE, Business/Farm Supplement. Regular filing deadline is 2/1. The Princeton Review suggests that all financial aid forms be submitted as soon as possible after January 1. *Need-based scholarships/grants offered:* Federal Pell, SEOG, State scholarships/grants, private scholarships, the school's own gift aid. *Loan aid offered:* Direct Subsidized Stafford Loans, Direct Unsubsidized Stafford Loans, Direct PLUS loans, Federal Perkins Loans, College/university loans from institutional funds. Applicants will be notified of awards beginning 4/1. Federal Work-Study Program available. Institutional employment available. Off-campus job opportunities are excellent.

The Inside Word

Although applicants have to possess exemplary academic qualifications to gain admission to Claremont McKenna, the importance of making a good match shouldn't be underestimated. Colleges of such small size and selectivity devote much more energy to determining whether the candidate as an individual fits instead of whether a candidate has the appropriate test scores.

THE SCHOOL SAYS "..."

From the Admissions Office

"CMC offers a first-rate liberal arts education where students can acquire a broad experience across a range of disciplines from the humanities to the social sciences to the sciences, but where they can also pursue an unusually rich spectrum of courses in economics, public affairs, and international relations. CMC's mission is clear: To educate students for meaningful, productive, and responsible lives of leadership. By combining the intellectual breadth of liberal arts with the more pragmatic concerns of public affairs, CMC students gain the vision, skills, and values necessary for leadership in all sectors of society.

"Applicants must take the SAT Reasoning Test or ACT with writing. We will use the highest scores from the SAT or ACT. SAT Subject Tests are not required unless home-schooled."

SELECTIVITY

Admissions Rating	98
# of applicants	5,058
% of applicants accepted	14
% of acceptees attending	42
# offered a place on the wait list	549
% accepting a place on wait list	43
% admitted from wait list	23
# of early decision applicants	535
% accepted early decision	28

FRESHMAN PROFILE

Range SAT Critical Reading	650–750
Range SAT Math	660–760
Range SAT Writing	660–740
Range ACT Composite	29–32
Minimum paper TOEFL	600
Minimum web-based TOEFL	250
% graduated top 10% of class	63
% graduated top 25% of class	93
% graduated top 50% of class	100

DEADLINES

Early decision	
Deadline	11/1
Notification	12/15
Regular	
Deadline	1/2
Notification	4/1
Nonfall registration?	No

APPLICANTS ALSO LOOK AT AND OFTEN PREFER

Harvard College; Princeton University; Stanford University; Yale University

AND SOMETIMES PREFER

Amherst College; Dartmouth College; Georgetown University; Pomona College

AND RARELY PREFER

Pitzer College; Tufts University; University of Southern California

FINANCIAL FACTS

Financial Aid Rating	99
Annual tuition	$45,380
Room and board	$14,385
Required fees	$245
Books and supplies	$900
% needy frosh rec. need-based scholarship or grant aid	100
% needy UG rec. need-based scholarship or grant aid	100
% needy frosh rec. non-need-based scholarship or grant aid	11
% needy UG rec. non-need-based scholarship or grant aid	9
% needy frosh rec. need-based self-help aid	87
% needy UG rec. need-based self-help aid	79
% frosh rec. any financial aid	49
% UG rec. any financial aid	47
% UG borrow to pay for school	31
Average cumulative indebtedness	$23,179
% frosh need fully met	100
% ugrads need fully met	100
Average % of frosh need met	100
Average % of ugrad need met	100

CLARKSON UNIVERSITY

HOLCROFT HOUSE, POTSDAM, NY 13699 • ADMISSIONS: 315-268-6480 • FAX: 315-268-7647

STUDENTS SAY ". . ."

Academics

Located in the wilds of northern New York, Clarkson University is best known for its strong business and engineering programs, and its exceptional record of career placement for graduates thanks to its "amazing reputation with a large range of companies." The science and tech programs "prepare engineering-centric minds for the future of the ever-advancing technological world," and the school is constantly "keeping a responsible eye on ways to positively influence a 'green' and sustainable future." A competitive Honors Program and excellent scholarships only sweeten the deal. As one sophomore puts it, "Golden Knights = Golden Education."

The classes are undoubtedly tough, but professors "are always available for extra help." These teachers "have been in their field for years and try to give you the best information they can." "Many of my professors have become advisers, friends, and great mentors," says one student. "A lot of the math and science professors are foreign" and can be hard to understand, but "the TAs are usually very good" and the higher level courses in particular "really show the brilliance of the staff here." The curriculum is "challenging" and goes beyond theory to real world application, and everything is taught through the lens of the "sustainability mindset." The workload is "heavy," but you "always have something applicable to take from every class."

Clarkson being a medium-sized school, "you meet tons of people and get to form good connections with most," and the excellent alumni network is buoyed by the many internships and co-ops that are readily available. "I know that if I obtain a degree I will have little to no trouble getting a job," says a civil engineering major. Facilities are the source of many complaints here, as "nearly all of the academic and recreational buildings could use a major overhaul."

Life

Clarkson is "a good size—not so small as to be clique-y, not so big that you get lost among thousands of other students," and there are several nearby schools that help to diversify the faces students see each day. Though it's proximate to Canada and the Adirondacks, there is "not much to do in Potsdam" for fun without "freezing to death in the cold weather," so "most entertainment lies in campus attractions and campus organizations." People partake in a lot of winter sports such as hiking and skiing, or they "just stay in and play Cards Against Humanity, or rent an academic building and watch a movie on the big screen."

For a STEM major there is "much pressure put on you by the workload," so students study for the most of the week—"sleepless nights are commonplace and being in more clubs than you should be able to handle is normal"—then decompress with "sports, clubs or other activities in their free time." There is "a good attempt at late night programs by res life, but often times you'll end up at a party." Greek life "thrives on weekends" and the Division I hockey games are "a great event where the whole community—both school and town—gather together and cheer as loudly as possible."

Student Body

The "small town atmosphere" of Clarkson is home to a group of "strongly motivated" students and people who "are always there by your side trying to push you to always do your best." The number of students creates a community where "everyone seems to know one another and you rarely see a unknown face." Though the majority of students fit the description "nerdy white male," Clarkson is a "very academically and socially diverse" school for its size; "you don't always have to hang out with the 'smart' people, but you aren't surrounded by dumb people either." Religion rarely matters; "whether you're a PS4, XBox One, PC, or Nintendo player is much more important." "We're all a little quirky here," confesses one student.

FINANCIAL AID: 315-268-6480 • E-MAIL: ADMISSION@CLARKSON.EDU • WEBSITE: WWW.CLARKSON.EDU

THE PRINCETON REVIEW SAYS

Admissions

Very important factors considered include: GPA, rigor of secondary school record. *Important factors considered include:* Class rank, standardized test scores, extracurricular activities, recommendation(s), volunteer work. *Other factors considered include:* Application essay, first generation, talent/ability, work experience, alumni/ae relations, character/personal qualities, level of applicant's interest. SAT or ACT required; ACT with or without Writing component accepted. TOEFL required of all international applicants. *Academic units required:* 4 English; 3 mathematics; 1 science. *Academic units recommended:* 4 mathematics; 4 science.

Financial Aid

Students should submit: FAFSA, State aid form. Regular filing deadline is 3/1. The Princeton Review suggests that all financial aid forms be submitted as soon as possible after January 1. *Need-based scholarships/grants offered:* Federal Pell, SEOG, State scholarships/grants, private scholarships, the school's own gift aid. *Loan aid offered:* Direct Subsidized Stafford Loans, Direct Unsubsidized Stafford Loans, Direct PLUS loans, Federal Perkins Loans, College/university loans from institutional funds. Federal Work-Study Program available. Institutional employment available. Off-campus job opportunities are excellent.

The Inside Word

Clarkson wants students with a strong background in science and math who also have a curiosity for applying technology and science in the real world. Show them that you're interested in being involved outside the classroom. Students with solid transcripts will have a good shot at admission. Serious candidates should interview anyway; if you have a strong application and strong desire to come here, it could help you get some scholarship money.

THE SCHOOL SAYS "..."

From the Admissions Office

"Clarkson University is the institution of choice for 3,500 enterprising students from diverse backgrounds who embrace challenge and thrive in a rigorous, highly collaborative learning environment. Our 640-wooded-acre campus is adjacent to the six-million-acre Adirondack Park, which offers exceptional outdoor recreation and a living laboratory for field research and environmental studies.

"Clarkson's programs in engineering, business, the sciences, liberal arts, and the health professions emphasize team-based learning as well as immersion in sustainability principles, creative problem solving and leadership skills. Clarkson is also on the leading edge of today's emerging technologies and fields of study offering innovative, boundary-spanning degree programs in engineering and management, digital arts and sciences, and environmental science and policy, among others.

"At Clarkson, students and faculty work closely together in a supportive and personalized environment. Students are encouraged to participate in faculty-mentored research projects from their first year, and to take advantage of co-ops and study abroad programs. Our collaborative and hands-on approach to education translates into remarkably successful careers and meaningful contributions to society; our placement rates into students' career choice are among the highest in the country. Alumni experience accelerated career growth. One in five alumni are already a CEO, president, or vice president of a company.

"Applicants are required to take the ACT with writing section optional or the SAT. We will use the student's best scores from either test. SAT Subject Tests are recommended but not required."

SELECTIVITY

Admissions Rating	89
# of applicants	6,747
% of applicants accepted	64
% of acceptees attending	18
# offered a place on the wait list	159
% accepting a place on wait list	11
% admitted from wait list	82
# of early decision applicants	200
% accepted early decision	60

FRESHMAN PROFILE

Range SAT Critical Reading	520–620
Range SAT Math	570–670
Range SAT Writing	500–600
Range ACT Composite	24–28
Minimum paper TOEFL	550
Minimum web-based TOEFL	213
Average HS GPA	3.60
% graduated top 10% of class	40
% graduated top 25% of class	76
% graduated top 50% of class	96

DEADLINES

Early decision	
Deadline	12/1
Notification	1/1
Regular	
Deadline	1/15
Nonfall registration?	Yes

APPLICANTS ALSO LOOK AT AND OFTEN PREFER
Rensselaer Polytechnic Institute; Rochester Institute of Technology, Syracuse University

AND SOMETIMES PREFER
Northeastern University; St. Lawrence University; Worcester Polytechnic Institute

AND RARELY PREFER
Cornell University; Drexel University; Ithaca College; University of Rochester

FINANCIAL FACTS

Financial Aid Rating	86
Annual tuition	$41,690
Room and board	$13,440
Required fees	$840
Books and supplies	$1,416
% needy frosh rec. need-based scholarship or grant aid	99
% needy UG rec. need-based scholarship or grant aid	99
% needy frosh rec. non-need-based scholarship or grant aid	14
% needy UG rec. non-need-based scholarship or grant aid	11
% needy frosh rec. need-based self-help aid	84
% needy UG rec. need-based self-help aid	85
% frosh rec. any financial aid	98
% UG rec. any financial aid	98
% UG borrow to pay for school	83
Average cumulative indebtedness	$27,835
% frosh need fully met	18
% ugrads need fully met	16
Average % of frosh need met	89
Average % of ugrad need met	90

CLEMSON UNIVERSITY

105 SIKES HALL, CLEMSON, SC 29634-5124 • ADMISSIONS: 864-656-2287 • FAX: 864-656-2464

CAMPUS LIFE
Quality of Life Rating	97
Fire Safety Rating	93
Green Rating	80
Type of school	Public
Affiliation	No Affiliation
Environment	Village

STUDENTS
Total undergrad enrollment	15,697
% male/female	54/46
% from out of state	29
% frosh from public high school	89
% frosh live on campus	98
% ugrads live on campus	41
# of fraternities (% ugrad men join)	26 (14)
# of sororities (% ugrad women join)	17 (27)
% African American	6
% Asian	2
% Caucasian	84
% Hispanic	2
% Native American	<1
% international	1
# of countries represented	84

SURVEY SAYS . . .
Lots of conservative students
Students are happy
Career services are great
Internships are widely available
School is well run
Students are friendly
Students get along with local community
Students involved in community service
Great off-campus food
Campus feels safe
Athletic facilities are great
Lots of beer drinking
Everyone loves the Tigers
Intramural sports are popular
Alumni active on campus
Active student government

ACADEMICS
Academic Rating	83
% students returning for sophomore year	90
% students graduating within 4 years	54
% students graduating within 6 years	80
Calendar	Semester
Student/faculty ratio	18:1
Profs interesting rating	81
Profs accessible rating	89

Most classes have 10–19 students.
Most lab/discussion sessions have 10–19 students.

MOST POPULAR MAJORS
engineering; business/commerce; biology

STUDENTS SAY "..."

Academics
Located in South Carolina, legendary sports stronghold Clemson University is "all about supporting its academics as well as its athletic teams." This public university is an AACC school that can provide "many opportunities to each student, no matter the major." The "incredible energy" surrounding Clemson academics, sports, and culture yields "a ton of school spirit," and it is apparent from the first step on campus that "the students love Clemson, and professors love Clemson students." The size and Southern charm offer students the best of both worlds: the "friendly atmosphere of a small town college, with the advantages and opportunities of a huge university," including study abroad, myriad research opportunities, and Division I athletics. "No other place makes a student feel so instantly welcomed and at home while making you feel like you are a part of something bigger than yourself." Most of the professors are "very engaging" and "supportive advisers" who relate interesting real-life examples to their lectures. "Professors are willing to delve deep into subjects that they are interested in and love student input and involvement," says a student. They are "lively and make the material interesting to learn" and "put teaching first," and the resulting atmosphere is "enriching and expansive." There is no competitive streak among students, only a desire to succeed, and the whole campus is "full of encouragement, support, and building relationships with those around you." Unsurprisingly, the school is "full of traditions," and it has "a great balance between sports, organizations, and study." The Clemson alumni network is internationally strong. "Clemson is one big family; [you] immediately bond with other Clemson people you meet around the world," one student says. "There is something in these hills that is something special, and you will know it immediately once you become a member of the Clemson Family."

Life
One of the greatest strengths of Clemson University is its heritage, which "resonates with any person who has ever had the privilege to call this campus home." The school is all about uniting 15,500 strangers into "a supportive family grounded in a shared passion for excellence." "Students at Clemson are very interested in Clemson," says a student. "What I mean by that is the students create their own lives and communities within the school." There are "plenty of opportunities" to become involved and active on campus, whether "through sports or academic organizations." Greek life is also "rather popular," but not every student joins. Study abroad is strongly encouraged, and "almost every student does some sort of study abroad." The school is nestled next to the mountains, and "there are a ton of trails owned by Clemson University" for students to hike and bike. Varsity sports are massively well-attended, and intramural sports are "huge"; "There are always pickup games on Bowman Field." On weekends, many students go downtown to the bars, "where there is a smaller, intimate setting, but still fun and exciting."

Student Body
While the majority of students are Southern and white, students of all backgrounds are bonded "by their sheer love of Clemson." The school spirit bleeds into everyone's demeanor, and this overwhelmingly happy and "very active" bunch "honestly try to include and befriend everyone." They are "very friendly, family oriented, athletic, and well put together." Many are also religious ("mostly Christian") and "go on mission trips and volunteer locally in the community." Most students here are down with Clemson athletics and "are willing to cheer for whatever sport is going on."

FINANCIAL AID: 864-656-2280 • E-MAIL: CUADMISSIONS@CLEMSON.EDU • WEBSITE: WWW.CLEMSON.EDU

THE PRINCETON REVIEW SAYS

Admissions

Very important factors considered include: Class rank, GPA, rigor of secondary school record, standardized test scores, state residency. *Important factors considered include:* alumni/ae relations. *Other factors considered include:* Application essay, extracurricular activities, recommendation(s), talent/ability. SAT or ACT required; ACT with Writing component required. TOEFL required of all international applicants. *Academic units required:* 4 English; 3 mathematics; 3 science; (3 science lab); 3 social studies; 3 foreign language; 1 history; 2 academic electives. *Academic units recommended:* 4 mathematics; (4 science lab).

Financial Aid

Students should submit: FAFSA. The Princeton Review suggests that all financial aid forms be submitted as soon as possible after January 1. *Need-based scholarships/grants offered:* Federal Pell, SEOG, State scholarships/grants, private scholarships, the school's own gift aid, federal nursing scholarships. *Loan aid offered:* Direct Subsidized Stafford Loans, Direct Unsubsidized Stafford Loans, Direct PLUS loans, Federal Perkins Loans, State Loans, College/university loans from institutional funds. Federal Work-Study Program available. Institutional employment available. Off-campus job opportunities are fair.

The Inside Word

With its Southern charm, competitive Division I athletics, and Greek life, Clemson will be an ideal fit for many types of students. But don't think that Clemson doesn't take its academics seriously. Admissions are competitive, and a good GPA and test scores will be needed for all who apply. For the SAT, the middle 50 percent of recently admitted students have test scores ranging from 1160 to 1310 (not including the writing section). For the ACT, the middle 50 percent score range is 26 to 30 for the composite.

THE SCHOOL SAYS "..."

From the Admissions Office

"One of the country's most selective public research universities, Clemson University was founded with a mission to be a high seminary of learning dedicated to teaching, research, and service. Nearly 120 years later, these three concepts remain at the heart of this university and provide the framework for an exceptional educational experience for Clemson students.

"At Clemson, professors take the time to get to know students and to explore innovative ways of teaching. Exceptional teaching is one reason Clemson's retention and graduation rates rank among the highest in the country among public universities. Exceptional teaching is also why Clemson continues to attract an increasingly talented student body. The class rank and SAT scores of Clemson's incoming freshman are among the highest of the nation's public research universities.

"Clemson offers over 250 student clubs and organizations; the spirit that students show for this university is unparalleled.

"Midway between Charlotte, North Carolina, and Atlanta, Georgia, Clemson University is located on 1,400 acres of beautiful rolling hills within the foothills of the Blue Ridge Mountains and along the shores of Lake Hartwell.

"Applicants are required to take the SAT or the ACT with the writing section. The best combined scores from SAT test will be used in the admissions process. We do not, however, combine sub scores from the ACT in order to create a new composite score."

SELECTIVITY

Admissions Rating	93
# of applicants	17,016
% of applicants accepted	60
% of acceptees attending	29
# offered a place on the wait list	1,395
% accepting a place on wait list	50
% admitted from wait list	42

FRESHMAN PROFILE

Range SAT Critical Reading	550–650
Range SAT Math	590–680
Range ACT Composite	25–30
Minimum paper TOEFL	550
Minimum web-based TOEFL	213
Average HS GPA	4.18
% graduated top 10% of class	48
% graduated top 25% of class	80
% graduated top 50% of class	97

DEADLINES

Regular	
Priority	12/1
Deadline	5/1
Nonfall registration?	Yes

APPLICANTS ALSO LOOK AT AND SOMETIMES PREFER

Georgia Institute of Technology; University of Virginia; University of Georgia

AND RARELY PREFER

Auburn University; Florida State University; North Carolina State University; University of Maryland; College Park; University of South Carolina—Columbia; College of Charleston

FINANCIAL FACTS

Financial Aid Rating	76
Annual in-state tuition	$13,382
Annual out-of-state tuition	$30,826
Room and board	$8,142
Books and supplies	$1,112
% needy frosh rec. need-based scholarship or grant aid	35
% needy UG rec. need-based scholarship or grant aid	42
% noedy frosh rec. non-need-based scholarship or grant aid	86
% needy UG rec. non-need-based scholarship or grant aid	67
% needy frosh rec. need-based self-help aid	61
% needy UG rec. need-based self-help aid	71
% frosh rec. any financial aid	87
% UG rec. any financial aid	71
% UG borrow to pay for school	50
Average cumulative indebtedness	$25,826
% frosh need fully met	28
% ugrads need fully met	22
Average % of frosh need met	64
Average % of ugrad need met	55

COE COLLEGE

1220 First Avenue NE, Cedar Rapids, IA 52402 • Admissions: 319-399-8500 • Fax: 319-399-8816

STUDENTS SAY ". . ."

Academics

Located in Cedar Rapids, Iowa, Coe College is a small school with a "tight-knit community feel" that provides "something different for everyone." "Coe has a very warm and friendly atmosphere" that works for "the betterment of each individual Kohawk through experiences, in and out of the classroom, as well as creating a mature adult prepared for the 'real-world.'" Students who need financial help shouldn't worry, because the "financial aid rocks!" Students love "the small class sizes that allow you to have a personable experience with each of your professors." The "small teacher/student ratio" also comes with "excellent, intelligent, helpful, and caring professors" who "all have great abundances of knowledge and all teach in different ways." "I honestly have not had a bad instructor," a chemistry major tells us. "They give you their home phone and cell phone numbers and invite you to call them. No teaching assistants here." A sociology student boasts of "relationships with my professors, and [I] feel that they invest in me and want me to succeed." Although the students rate their professors highly, they didn't feel the same way about the classrooms the professors teach in. "Our academic buildings and dorms are really run down," one student says. Others claimed the college "needs faster Internet." For many, the school is "an ideal size." "Big without being too big." One student lists Coe's strengths up as "the small class sizes, the community atmosphere, the involvement of students, study abroad programs, physics, and athletics." Coe has "the ability [to make] literally anyone feel comfortable."

Life

Although Coe is located in Iowa's second largest city, the college has a four-year residency requirement, and "people often fall victim to the 'Coe bubble,'" one student warns. "A lot of people are not familiar with the city and refuse to venture out. Most people I know enjoy alcohol on the weekends." While Coe isn't located "in the best neighborhood to go out in, we do have bars that are within blocks from our campus [that] are attended a lot on the weekends by students." Like many colleges, drinking is a common social activity. "In all honesty, Coe's students typically do drink alcohol—both on campus and off campus at the Cedar Rapids bars." However, other students see a variety of activities available. "There are parties, lots of video games, people playing intramural sports, Friday after class events…something for everyone." "For fun students go to SAC events like free midnight movies, tie-dying, dance socials in the pub, quarter bowling night, ice skating." The school hosts a regular talent show, Blindspot, which is so named because it's "open for students to perform without judgment." When asked what the school could improve on, the students were unanimous in their complaint: "The food is something we all wish would improve." To compound matters, "students are required to have a meal plan," and there aren't many options for "alternative diets such as vegan and vegetarian."

Student Body

"About one-third of [Coe's] student body is athletes," but "there really isn't a particular social group or type of personality that this school is known for, so it's easy to fit in with one—or any—group on campus." "The average students are exactly that: average," a student explains. "It is a very typical representation of the Midwest. There are very few students (I'd say less than ten people in the entire population on campus) [who] do not truly fit in anywhere." "While Greek organizations maintain a significant presence in numbers," Greek life doesn't dominate the school: "They don't organize for significant events or provide any clear distinction from other students." Students at Coe "are friendly," a trait helped by an "orientation [that] creates a forced interaction [and] gets people mingling." "There is not a typical student at Coe," one student says, "because each student is treated uniquely and takes a unique set of classes."

FINANCIAL AID: 319-399-8540 • E-MAIL: ADMISSION@COE.EDU • WEBSITE: WWW.COE.EDU

THE PRINCETON REVIEW SAYS

Admissions

Very important factors considered include: GPA, standardized test scores. *Important factors considered include:* Class rank, application essay, recommendation(s). *Other factors considered include:* Rigor of secondary school record, extracurricular activities, first generation, interview, racial/ethnic status, talent/ability, volunteer work, alumni/ae relations, character/personal qualities, level of applicant's interest. SAT or ACT required; ACT with or without Writing component accepted. TOEFL required of all international applicants. *Academic units recommended:* 4 English; 3 mathematics; 3 science; (1 science lab); 3 social studies; 2 foreign language; 2 academic electives.

Financial Aid

Students should submit: FAFSA. The Princeton Review suggests that all financial aid forms be submitted as soon as possible after January 1. *Need-based scholarships/grants offered:* Federal Pell, SEOG, State scholarships/grants, private scholarships, the school's own gift aid. *Loan aid offered:* Direct Subsidized Stafford Loans, Direct Unsubsidized Stafford Loans, Direct PLUS loans, Federal Perkins Loans, College/university loans from institutional funds. Federal Work-Study Program available. Institutional employment available. Off-campus job opportunities are excellent.

The Inside Word

About 400 new students begin their college journey at Coe College each fall, and classes average a mere sixteen students. Despite its small size, Coe has the largest undergraduate writing center in the country, and many students enjoy its help. If you're seeking an intimate college experience with quality academics—Coe is one of the smallest colleges to contain a Phi Beta Kappa chapter—you would do well to consider Coe.

THE SCHOOL SAYS "..."

From the Admissions Office

"A Coe education begins to pay off right away. In fact, ninety-eight percent of last year's graduating class was either working or in graduate school within six months of graduation. One reason our graduates do so well is the Coe Plan—a step-by-step sequence of activities designed to prepare our students for life after Coe. This required sequence stretches from the first-year seminar to community service, issue dinners, career planning seminars, and the required hands-on experience. The hands-on component may be satisfied through an internship, research, practicum, or study abroad. One student lived with a Costa Rican family while she studied the effects of selective logging on rain forest organisms. Others have interned at places like Warner Brothers in Los Angeles and the Chicago Board of Trade. Still others combine travel with an internship or student teaching for an unforgettable off-campus experience. Coe College is one of the few liberal arts institutions in the country to require hands-on learning for graduation."

SELECTIVITY	
Admissions Rating	87
# of applicants	2,972
% of applicants accepted	62
% of acceptees attending	21

FRESHMAN PROFILE	
Range SAT Critical Reading	493–693
Range SAT Math	495–670
Range SAT Writing	458–660
Range ACT Composite	23–28
Minimum paper TOEFL	520
Minimum web-based TOEFL	173
Average HS GPA	3.62
% graduated top 10% of class	31
% graduated top 25% of class	61
% graduated top 50% of class	91

DEADLINES	
Early action	
Deadline	12/10
Notification	1/20
Regular	
Priority	12/10
Deadline	3/1
Nonfall registration?	Yes

**APPLICANTS ALSO LOOK AT
AND OFTEN PREFER**
Luther College

AND SOMETIMES PREFER
Cornell College; Drake University

FINANCIAL FACTS	
Financial Aid Rating	85
% needy frosh rec. need-based scholarship or grant aid	100
% needy UG rec. need-based scholarship or grant aid	100
% needy frosh rec. non-need-based scholarship or grant aid	16
% needy UG rec. non-need-based scholarship or grant aid	15
% needy frosh rec. need-based self-help aid	82
% needy UG rec. need-based self-help aid	81
% frosh rec. any financial aid	99
% UG rec. any financial aid	99
% UG borrow to pay for school	74
Average cumulative indebtedness	$31,660
% frosh need fully met	21
% ugrads need fully met	20
Average % of frosh need met	86
Average % of ugrad need met	82

COLBY COLLEGE

4000 MAYFLOWER HILL, WATERVILLE, ME 04901-8848 • ADMISSIONS: 207-859-4800 • FAX: 207-859-4828

STUDENTS SAY ". . ."

Academics

An absolute gem of Maine's private, liberal arts colleges, Colby College is a "fun and smart community" that places an emphasis on internationalism and study abroad. The school's "homey environment" offers "phenomenal academics in a unique setting," and small, discussion-oriented classes encourage teacher-student collaboration outside the classroom. "I love the opportunities that I have been afforded in my major, and I have gotten a lot of great opportunities to do outside research," says a student. With so many chances for students and professors to team up "to create positive relationships and fantastic work," faculty will "do anything they can to help out a student with a project or internship if the student shows initiative." There are a few complaints about the quality of visiting professors, but for the most part, teachers are "experienced, personable, and passionate," and students recognize how professors go out of their way to make sure students "receive individualized academic attention." "It is easy to see what professors are truly interested in and how they apply that interest to the courses they teach," says a student. There is a "varying course selection" for students to round out their education, as Colby is "all about creating people who are great at thinking." "If you want to coast through college, this is not the right school," one student says. Students have involvement "in all spheres of the college," and the inclusive community "fosters growth academically, emotionally, and socially by giving its students an ability to play a large role in shaping the college and its direction." There are tons of ways for students to get involved and to have an impact on the campus, simply because "it's small enough to do that." Unfortunately, several students note that the "communication between the administration and the student body is severely lacking."

Life

Everyone at Colby "works very hard," weekdays and weekends alike. It is a "very campus-oriented life style," and students generally stay on campus for activities such as dances and "a lot of partying on the weekends." People "do almost constantly stress about work," but they know that Friday and Saturday is a deserved break. "Most people drink, but there isn't so much drug use"; "Sunday is a big study day," regardless. The campus culture is "dominated" with athletic teams: the "Mule Mob," the student fan section, is always "loud and enthusiastic" at this Division III school's games. People are "fairly to really outdoorsy"; students "love to ski on weekends in the winter" or go to the nearby lake. The spring is "the best for barbecues and hanging outside on the various quads." Meals are a key component of social interaction at Colby; very often "you'll see big groups of friends having leisurely meals together on the weekends." "Gotta love the dining halls and finding all my people there to have deliciously long chats over food," says a student. Plenty of people take advantage of being in Maine, and "without too much effort, you can spend a day on the coast or in the mountains regardless of the season," activities made easier by Colby's popular "outing club." Often, people "take trips down to Freeport, go skiing at Sugarloaf, or go hiking." Additionally, the college organizes "many activities and concerts," and many people "pass through the student union and see people in the 'spa' (cafe on campus)."

Student Body

Everyone at Colby is "really involved," whether in classes, community service, athletics, extracurriculars or clubs, and the typical student is "on some sort of athletic team, is a member of at least two campus clubs, [and] loves the outdoors." These "amiable, enthusiastic," students are often from a "New England background." While more than half the student body hails from outside New England, some with they saw more diversity on campus. Students are "genuinely open to learning at Colby," and most everyone here is "friendly and hardworking," though they also "like to go out."

FINANCIAL AID: 207-859-4832 • E-MAIL: ADMISSIONS@COLBY.EDU • WEBSITE: WWW.COLBY.EDU

THE PRINCETON REVIEW SAYS

Admissions

Very important factors considered include: GPA, rigor of secondary school record, standardized test scores, recommendation(s), character/personal qualities. *Important factors considered include:* Class rank, application essay, extracurricular activities, racial/ethnic status, talent/ability. *Other factors considered include:* first generation, geographical residence, interview, state residency, volunteer work, work experience, alumni/ae relations, level of applicant's interest. SAT or SAT Subject Tests or ACT considered if submitted; ACT with Writing component recommended. TOEFL required of all international applicants. *Academic units recommended:* 4 English; 3 mathematics; 2 science; (2 science lab); 2 social studies; 3 foreign language.

Financial Aid

Students should submit: FAFSA, CSS/Financial Aid PROFILE, Business/Farm Supplement, federal tax returns, W-2s. Regular filing deadline is 2/1. The Princeton Review suggests that all financial aid forms be submitted as soon as possible after January 1. *Need-based scholarships/grants offered:* Federal Pell, SEOG, State scholarships/grants, private scholarships, the school's own gift aid. *Loan aid offered:* Direct Subsidized Stafford Loans, Direct Unsubsidized Stafford Loans, Direct PLUS loans, Federal Perkins Loans, State Loans. Applicants will be notified of awards beginning 4/1. Federal Work-Study Program available. Institutional employment available. Off-campus job opportunities are poor.

The Inside Word

Colby continues to be both very selective and successful in converting admits to enrollees, which makes for a perpetually challenging admissions process. Currently, less than 30 percent of applicants are accepted (more than 60 percent of which graduated in the top 10 percent of their class), so hit those books and ace those exams to stand a fighting chance. One thing that could set you apart from the pack? An interest in other cultures. Two-thirds of Colby students study abroad—in fact, for some degrees it's required.

THE SCHOOL SAYS "..."

From the Admissions Office

"Colby is one of only a handful of liberal arts colleges that offer world-class academic programs, leadership in internationalism, a close-knit community, and rich opportunities after graduation. On one of the nation's most beautiful campuses, Colby provides students opportunities for civic engagement in Maine and around the world. Students' access to Colby's outstanding faculty is extraordinary, and the college is a leader in undergraduate research and project-based learning. The Colby museum's extraordinary art collection is a magnet for art loves and a resource for students in courses across the curriculum. The challenging academic experience is complemented by a collaborative campus atmosphere and vibrant community life enhanced by more than 100 student-run organizations, more than fifty athletic and recreational choices, and extensive leadership and volunteer opportunities.

"Colby graduates succeed. At graduation, 78 percent of seniors are employed, admitted to grad school, or have received full-time fellowships (three year average). They earn places at the best medical schools and research universities, law and business programs, financial firms, in the arts, government service, social service, education, and nonprofit organizations. And they are inspired leaders in their communities. An environmental leader, Clby achieved carbon neutrality in 2013 and won one of the earliest Senator Paul Simon Awards for Internationalizaing the Campus, in 2005. Colby replaced loans in its financial aid packages with grants, making it possible for all students to graduate without college-loan debt. Applicants must submit SAT or ACT scores or SAT Subject Tests in three different subject areas; the choice is up to each applicant. The optional ACT writing test is recommended."

SELECTIVITY

Admissions Rating	97
# of applicants	5,234
% of applicants accepted	29
% of acceptees attending	32
# offered a place on the wait list	1,161
% accepting a place on wait list	43
% admitted from wait list	2
# of early decision applicants	527
% accepted early decision	53

FRESHMAN PROFILE

Range SAT Critical Reading	610–710
Range SAT Math	630–720
Range SAT Writing	610–710
Range ACT Composite	29–32
% graduated top 10% of class	65
% graduated top 25% of class	88
% graduated top 50% of class	99

DEADLINES

Early decision	
Deadline	11/15
Notification	12/15
Regular	
Deadline	1/1
Notification	4/1
Nonfall registration?	Yes

APPLICANTS ALSO LOOK AT AND OFTEN PREFER

Amherst College; Bowdoin College; Dartmouth College; Middlebury College, Williams College, Brown University; Princeton University; Cornell University; Harvard College

AND SOMETIMES PREFER

Bates College; Boston College; Colgate University; Hamilton College; Vassar College

AND RARELY PREFER

Skidmore College; University of Vermont; Franklin & Marshall College

FINANCIAL FACTS

Financial Aid Rating	97
Annual tuition	$43,840
Room and board	$11,750
Required fees	$1,920
Books and supplies	$700
% needy frosh rec. need-based scholarship or grant aid	100
% needy UG rec. need-based scholarship or grant aid	99
% needy frosh rec. non-need-based scholarship or grant aid	2
% needy UG rec. non-need-based scholarship or grant aid	2
% needy frosh rec. need-based self-help aid	72
% needy UG rec. need-based self-help aid	80
% frosh rec. any financial aid	44
% UG rec. any financial aid	42
% UG borrow to pay for school	34
Average cumulative indebtedness	$24,453
% frosh need fully met	100
% ugrads need fully met	99
Average % of frosh need met	100
Average % of ugrad need met	100

COLGATE UNIVERSITY

13 OAK DRIVE, HAMILTON, NY 13346 • ADMISSIONS: 315-228-7401 • FAX: 315-228-7544

STUDENTS SAY ". . ."

Academics

Colgate University is known for its "very rigorous academic curriculum" and "invaluable" professors who "are the glue that hold the university together." Many students say they chose Colgate because they wanted "a small liberal arts school that had the opportunities and resources of a larger institution" combined with a "heavily involved alumni network" that "makes the Colgate connection a truly valuable resource." All agree that, at Colgate, you're "more than just a number" and say, "There is no [shortage] of caring professors that are meaningfully invested in your academic success." As intimidating as it might seem to have, "internationally influential" professors, a history and political science double major assures that "classes are enjoyable and the professors are accessible." A junior adds, "One of the wonderful things about Colgate is that these relationships start as early as freshman year. Students do not have to wait until their senior year to build fantastic relationships with the faculty." However, another student grumbles, "Course selection is very stressful, and freshmen often get slighted." Any complaints about the faculty centered on "teaching styles" not meshing with individual students' "learning style." "However, there are a plethora of resources available to students to succeed despite any of their problems." "Colgate allowed me to become the person I always wanted to be, but didn't know I was capable of being," sings one senior whose sentiment is widely echoed.

Life

Colgate University "has an amazing campus with people who work hard and have goals but also know how to have a really fun time." Students say the campus is "breathtaking," and they value "its small size and intimate nature." A philosophy major says, "Colgate is great because you can't walk 200 feet without out a professor, student, or faculty member acknowledging you by name, yet you're constantly meeting new people and having new experiences. There is never a dull moment at Colgate." Students say, "Colgate strives for the perfect combination of academics and extracurriculars," and they feel the university "does a great job at helping us balance those and gives us opportunities to get involved in all the groups and events around campus." In addition to a plethora of clubs, students are actively involved in Greek life and Division I athletics. A junior says, "I loved how Colgate was located in the middle of nowhere" because "everything revolved around the campus," but in case you're worried about isolation, another student adds, "Colgate brings a lot of interesting speakers to the campus, which helps provide for a more rounded liberal arts experience." Students praise the administration, saying, "It is easy for students to contact the administration and thus have their voices directly heard by the community. The president holds drop-in office hours for students every week and takes notes on what students say during the session."

Student Body

Colgate boasts a "happy and enthusiastic student body" with a typical student that 'is athletic, smart, engaged, and down to earth." They "enjoy having fun, but spend time in the library as well.'" Many say "the typical Colgate student is a preppy New Englander, who can be found almost always wearing Patagonia and Sperrys." However, this stereotype seems to be becoming less apt as there is "great diversity under the surface." As long as students are "not afraid to do what they love, they will find their niche and fit in." Fraternities and sororities as well as partying in general are popular: "Greek life does have a huge presence in the social life at Colgate," but "it is not exclusive to just those who are members." Most students mentioned the recent changes in the school's alcohol policies. Some tout it as the impetus for "initiatives to expand the amount of alternatives to partying on weekends." Others cited it as "the biggest issue on campus right now" between the students and administration. Despite the "country club atmosphere," a computer science major says, "When you're stranded in Hamilton, New York, for four years you'll inevitably end up fitting in regardless whether you are the typical student or not."

FINANCIAL AID: 315-228-7431 • E-MAIL: ADMISSION@COLGATE.EDU • WEBSITE: WWW.COLGATE.EDU

THE PRINCETON REVIEW SAYS

Admissions

Very important factors considered include: Class rank, GPA, rigor of secondary school record. *Important factors considered include:* Standardized test scores, application essay, extracurricular activities, recommendation(s), talent/ability, character/personal qualities. *Other factors considered include:* first generation, geographical residence, racial/ethnic status, volunteer work, work experience, alumni/ae relations. SAT or ACT required; ACT with or without Writing component accepted. TOEFL required of all international applicants. *Academic units required:* 4 English; 3 mathematics; 3 science; (2 science lab); 3 social studies; 3 foreign language. *Academic units recommended:* 4 English; 4 mathematics; 4 science; (4 science lab); 4 social studies; 4 foreign language.

Financial Aid

Students should submit: CSS/Financial Aid PROFILE, Noncustodial PROFILE. Regular filing deadline is 1/15. The Princeton Review suggests that all financial aid forms be submitted as soon as possible after January 1. *Need-based scholarships/grants offered:* Federal Pell, SEOG, State scholarships/grants, the school's own gift aid. *Loan aid offered:* Direct Subsidized Stafford Loans, Direct Unsubsidized Stafford Loans, Direct PLUS loans, Federal Perkins Loans. Applicants will be notified of awards beginning 3/26. Federal Work-Study Program available. Institutional employment available. Off-campus job opportunities are fair.

The Inside Word

Admission to this Upstate New York gem is some of the most competitive around. You will need to arm yourself with excellent scores, grades, recommendations, and extracurricular activities. However, Colgate is also looking for that extra ingredient which might not translate from the common app alone and is always seeking increased diversity across the board.

THE SCHOOL SAYS "..."

From the Admissions Office

"Colgate provides an environment where students can appreciate, celebrate, and learn about their own cultures as well as those of the people around them. The class of 2017 represents one of Colgate's most diverse class years yet. Of the class of 2017, 28.7 percent self-identified as being from multicultural backgrounds, and 11 percent are international students. Colgate's student body also includes students from forty-eight states, the District of Columbia, and forty-seven countries. Students and faculty alike are drawn to Colgate by the quality of its academic programs. Faculty initiative has given the university a rich mix of learning opportunities that includes a liberal arts core, fifty-three academic concentrations, and a wealth of Colgate faculty-led, off-campus study programs in the United States and abroad. But there is more to Colgate than academic life, including a full complement of living options set within a campus described as one of the most beautiful in the country. The new Trudy Fitness Center is an integral component of Colgate's Wellness Initiative, which encourages healthy, purposeful, and balanced lifestyles within the community. A center for community service builds upon the tradition of Colgate students interacting with the surrounding community in meaningful ways. Colgate students become extraordinarily devoted alumni, contributing significantly to career networking and exploration programs on and off campus. For students in search of a busy and varied campus life, Colgate is a place to learn and grow."

SELECTIVITY

Admissions Rating	97
# of applicants	8,375
% of applicants accepted	26
% of acceptees attending	34
# offered a place on the wait list	1,734
% accepting a place on wait list	51
% admitted from wait list	7
# of early decision applicants	795
% accepted early decision	47

FRESHMAN PROFILE

Range SAT Critical Reading	620–720
Range SAT Math	650–730
Range ACT Composite	30–32
Average HS GPA	3.66
% graduated top 10% of class	76
% graduated top 25% of class	93
% graduated top 50% of class	99

DEADLINES

Early decision	
Deadline	11/15
Notification	12/15
Regular	
Deadline	1/15
Notification	4/1
Nonfall registration?	No

APPLICANTS ALSO LOOK AT AND OFTEN PREFER

Cornell University; Middlebury College; Georgetown University, Dartmouth College

AND SOMETIMES PREFER

Boston College; Hamilton College; University of Rochester; New York University

AND RARELY PREFER

Bucknell University; University of Vermont; Villanova University; Lafayette College

FINANCIAL FACTS

Financial Aid Rating	99
Annual tuition	$46,060
Room and board	$11,510
Required fees	$320
Books and supplies	$1,100
% needy frosh rec. need-based scholarship or grant aid	100
% needy UG rec. need-based scholarship or grant aid	98
% needy frosh rec. non-need-based scholarship or grant aid	100
% needy UG rec. non-need-based scholarship or grant aid	100
% needy frosh rec. need-based self-help aid	82
% needy UG rec. need-based self-help aid	80
% frosh rec. any financial aid	41
% UG rec. any financial aid	42
% UG borrow to pay for school	34
Average cumulative indebtedness	$18,719
% frosh need fully met	100
% ugrads need fully met	100
Average % of frosh need met	100
Average % of ugrad need met	100

COLLEGE OF THE ATLANTIC

105 EDEN STREET, BAR HARBOR, ME 04609 • ADMISSIONS: 207-288-5015 • FAX: 207-288-4126

STUDENTS SAY ". . ."

Academics
College of the Atlantic is a small liberal arts college in Bar Harbor, on Mount Desert Island, Maine, that its students think of as a "progressive educational experiment that broadens perspective." The college offers the sole major of "human ecology," which allows students to design their own majors around classes they wish to take. Each student can "mix-and-match interests and connect them to one another in a way that works and matters" to them. The population of the school is fairly small, with the student body being less than 400 individuals. The average class size is around twelve students, which affords students the kind of one-on-one attention that they love. Some have a little trouble getting in to the classes they want, but most students find that any of their professors "have impressive credentials with diverse backgrounds." Students also find that professors "are extremely passionate" and expect their students to have the same passion. With that kind of attention in class, students agree that it is "rare to graduate without having had dinner at a professor's house at least once." Many find by the time they graduate that they have "several brilliant mentors" in their professors. The motto of the school is "life changing, world changing" and many find that motto pervades the "stimulating academic experience" at College of the Atlantic.

Life
Because each person is taught that "voices and actions count," most students tend to focus on the sustainability efforts within campus and participate in one of the college's many groups. The college allows students to "give faculty reviews" and "even [participate] in the hiring of the staff," making them even more active players in their education. Most students tend to be "outdoorsy," and being on an island just off the coast, there is plenty for students to do. Given that the campus is adjacent to Acadia National park, many cite "hiking, biking, canoeing, kayaking, contradancing, sailboating, and more" as just a few of the many options. There is also "a lot to do on-campus with student art installations," and two of the most recent additions to campus include a student-built "greenhouse at Beech Hill Farm" and "a root cellar." The "very small town" of Bar Harbor attracts many students on the weekends who are looking for a break from campus.

Student Body
One thing is for sure about College of the Atlantic, most students consider themselves "fairly liberal" and "very individualistic." Some are a little put off by the latter saying "at times it seems like an almost requirement," but most seem to love the idea that they have opportunities to express themselves. One student says, "We wear plaid. We play music. We swim in the ocean in the middle of winter," a statement that most students would seem to agree sums up a good deal of the student population. Despite focusing on individualism, most everyone agrees that the entirety of the student body is "respectful, supportive, and passionate" about their fellow students. There is a "friendly" nature that pervades the population, and that sort of friendly nature, "makes up for [its] small size."

FINANCIAL AID: 207-288-5015 • E-MAIL: INQUIRY@COA.EDU • WEBSITE: WWW.COA.EDU

THE PRINCETON REVIEW SAYS

Admissions

Very important factors considered include: Rigor of secondary school record, application essay, recommendation(s). *Important factors considered include:* Class rank, GPA, extracurricular activities, interview, talent/ability, volunteer work, work experience, character/personal qualities. *Other factors considered include:* Standardized test scores, first generation, geographical residence, racial/ethnic status, state residency, alumni/ae relations, level of applicant's interest. SAT and SAT Subject Tests or ACT considered if submitted; ACT with or without Writing component accepted. TOEFL required of all international applicants. *Academic units required:* 4 English; 3 mathematics; 2 science; (2 science lab); 2 social studies. *Academic units recommended:* 4 mathematics; 3 science; 2 foreign language; 2 history; 1 academic elective.

Financial Aid

Students should submit: FAFSA, Institution's own financial aid form, Noncustodial PROFILE, Business/Farm Supplement. Regular filing deadline is 2/15. The Princeton Review suggests that all financial aid forms be submitted as soon as possible after January 1. *Need-based scholarships/grants offered:* Federal Pell, SEOG, State scholarships/grants, private scholarships, the school's own gift aid. *Loan aid offered:* Direct Subsidized Stafford Loans, Direct Unsubsidized Stafford Loans, Direct PLUS loans, Federal Perkins Loans. Applicants will be notified of awards beginning 4/1. Federal Work-Study Program available. Off-campus job opportunities are good.

The Inside Word

Don't let COA's high acceptance rate fool you: the self-selecting applicant pool is comprised of dedicated and successful students. Standardized test scores are optional, but encouraged for applicants from nontraditional programs or alternative grading systems. Visit the school's website for inspirational personal statement prompts.

THE SCHOOL SAYS "..."

From the Admissions Office

"College of the Atlantic is a small, intellectually challenging college on Mount Desert Island, Maine. We look for students seeking a rigorous, hands-on, self-directed academic experience. Come for a visit, and you will begin to understand that COA's unique approach to education, governance and community life extends throughout its structure. Resolutely value centered and interdisciplinary—there are no departments and no majors, COA sees its mission as preparing people to become independent thinkers, to challenge conventional wisdom, to deal with pressing global change—both environmental and social—and to be passionately engaged in transforming the world around them into a better place.

"College of the Atlantic does not require standardized testing as part of the application process. Learning and intelligence can be gauged in many ways; standardized test scores are just one of many measures. If an applicant chooses to submit standardized test scores for consideration, the SAT, SAT Subject Tests, or ACT scores are all acceptable."

SELECTIVITY

Admissions Rating	86
# of applicants	455
% of applicants accepted	73
% of acceptees attending	31
# of early decision applicants	47
% accepted early decision	79

FRESHMAN PROFILE

Range SAT Critical Reading	580–690
Range SAT Math	530–640
Range SAT Writing	580–650
Range ACT Composite	25–33
Minimum paper TOEFL	567
Minimum web-based TOEFL	227
Average HS GPA	3.56
% graduated top 10% of class	10
% graduated top 25% of class	69
% graduated top 50% of class	95

DEADLINES

Early decision	
Deadline	12/1
Notification	12/15
Regular	
Deadline	2/15
Notification	4/1
Nonfall registration?	Yes

APPLICANTS ALSO LOOK AT AND OFTEN PREFER
Bowdoin College; Middlebury College

AND SOMETIMES PREFER
Hampshire College; Colby College

AND RARELY PREFER
Green Mountain College; University of Maine; Warren Wilson College; Marlboro College; University of Vermont

FINANCIAL FACTS

Financial Aid Rating	92
Annual tuition	$39,942
Room and board	$9,300
Required fees	$549
Books and supplies	$600
% needy frosh rec. need-based scholarship or grant aid	99
% needy UG rec. need-based scholarship or grant aid	97
% needy frosh rec. non-need-based scholarship or grant aid	0
% needy UG rec. non-need-based scholarship or grant aid	1
% needy frosh rec. need-based self-help aid	99
% needy UG rec. need-based self-help aid	96
% frosh rec. any financial aid	98
% UG rec. any financial aid	97
% UG borrow to pay for school	61
Average cumulative indebtedness	$19,285
% frosh need fully met	41
% ugrads need fully met	42
Average % of frosh need met	95
Average % of ugrad need met	95

COLLEGE OF CHARLESTON

66 GEORGE STREET, CHARLESTON, SC 29424 • ADMISSIONS: 843-953-5670 • FAX: 843-953-6322

STUDENTS SAY ". . ."

Academics

Situated on a "beautiful, historic campus" in one of the South's most charming cities, it's no wonder that College of Charleston has such satisfied undergraduates. Indeed, students report that a "welcoming" vibe permeates the school and it's truly evident that the "supportive staff [want] to see...their students [succeed]." Many undergraduates also appreciate that the school is generous with scholarships and provides "lots of opportunities for travel and research." Students benefit from "small class sizes" and "a student-teacher ratio of 16:1." By and large, professors here are quite "passionate about their subject [matter]" and their enthusiasm is often infectious. Most instructors "encourage discussion" and seem to really "love student involvement both inside and outside of the classroom." Undergrads also happily report that many professors make themselves "accessible" and are "happy to talk to any students who are interested in their class." And one political science major even brags that "every teacher I've had has known the name of every student." Finally, this blissful sophomore concludes, "The College of Charleston consistently provides great academics, meaningful experiences to engage with the city, and fantastic people who want to do fantastic things."

Life

Life at College of Charleston is simultaneously "stressful [and] fun." Therefore, these undergrads very quickly adopt the work-hard-play-hard mentality so popular among college students everywhere. Thankfully, there's plenty to take advantage of when they want to kick back. To begin with, fraternities and sororities are "a big part of campus life." Indeed, "people are always excited for Greek events; although only 20 percent of [undergrads] are active members it [still maintains a visible] presence." Moreover, students admit that C of C does have a healthy drinking culture. As one political science major shares, "House parties in cramped historic homes are popular, as are the bars downtown." However, a psychology major quickly follows up by emphatically stating, "While there are quite a few parties that go on, none are really out of hand. People stay safe and watch out for each other mostly." Of course, opportunities and activities outside of the party scene abound. Students with a penchant for the outdoors can enjoy "going to the beach, kayaking, sailing, rock climbing, surfing, and hiking." And the "Cougar Activities Board always [hosts] great [events]." Finally, students simply adore their adopted hometown. "There's so much history here in Charleston, you're guaranteed to learn something new all the time." The city is also home to "hundreds of renowned restaurants" and many "festival, concert" and "shopping" options.

Student Body

When walking around C of C's campus, one could easily be forgiven for thinking that the typical student here is "a young white female who comes from a wealthy family and is into sorority life." However, don't be fooled! The college is actually home to "a wide array of people from different places in life." A sophomore tells us, "We have a diverse student body of preppy southern belles, hipsters, sorority girls, frat stars, skater boys, and beach bums." Indeed, there's a range of personalities, "and you can find someone like you." Importantly, looking beyond stereotypes and broad social categorization, the College of Charleston seems to attract a student body that's "smart, well-rounded, and willing to work hard." And while "there are definitely cliques," many undergrads are able to hop around differing social groups with ease. Perhaps this can be attributed to the fact that, "in general, the typical student absorbs the Charleston spirit: they're friendly, open, and generally happy."

FINANCIAL AID: 843-953-5540 • E-MAIL: ADMISSIONS@COFC.EDU • WEBSITE: WWW.COFC.EDU

THE PRINCETON REVIEW SAYS

Admissions

Very important factors considered include: GPA, rigor of secondary school record, standardized test scores, state residency. *Important factors considered include:* Class rank, first generation, talent/ability, character/personal qualities. *Other factors considered include:* Application essay, extracurricular activities, geographical residence, racial/ethnic status, recommendation(s), volunteer work, work experience, level of applicant's interest. SAT or ACT required; ACT with or without Writing component accepted. TOEFL required of all international applicants. *Academic units required:* 4 English; 4 mathematics; 3 science; (3 science lab); 2 social studies; 3 foreign language; 1 history; 3 academic electives. *Academic units recommended:* 4 English; 4 mathematics; 2 history; 1 computer science.

Financial Aid

Students should submit: FAFSA. The Princeton Review suggests that all financial aid forms be submitted as soon as possible after January 1. *Need-based scholarships/grants offered:* Federal Pell, SEOG, State scholarships/grants, private scholarships, the school's own gift aid. *Loan aid offered:* Direct Subsidized Stafford Loans, Direct Unsubsidized Stafford Loans, Direct PLUS loans, Federal Perkins Loans. Federal Work-Study Program available. Institutional employment available. Off-campus job opportunities are fair.

The Inside Word

When it comes to assessing applicants, admissions officers at the College of Charleston try to take the holistic approach shared by many liberal arts schools. Of course, a candidate's GPA, standardized tests and class rank hold the most weight. Successful applicants are typically in the top 20 percent of their class and consistently earn A's and B's. Beyond academics, leadership and extracurricular experience will also help bolster an application. Above all, the admissions committee wants students who will contribute to a vibrant campus life.

THE SCHOOL SAYS ". . ."

From the Admissions Office

"To succeed in our increasingly complex world, college graduates must be able to think creatively, explore new ideas, compete, collaborate, and meet the challenges of our global society. At the College of Charleston, students find out about themselves, their lives and the lives of others. They discover how to shape their future, and they prepare to create change and opportunity.

"Founded in 1770, the College of Charleston's mission is to provide students with a first-class education in the arts and sciences, education and business. Students have 130 majors and minors from which to choose—and they often choose to combine several—and complement their academic courses with overseas study, research and internships for a truly customized education.

"Approximately 10,000 undergraduates choose the college for its small-college feel blended with the advantages and diversity of an urban, mid-sized university. The College, home to students from forty-nine states and sixty-two countries, provides a creative and intellectually stimulating environment where students are challenged and guided by a committed and caring full-time faculty of 565 distinguished teacher-scholars, all in an incomparable historic setting.

"The city of Charleston serves as a living and learning laboratory for student experiences in business, science, teaching, the humanities, languages and the arts. At the same time, students and faculty are engaged with the community in partnerships to improve education, enhance the business community and enrich the overall quality of life in the region.

"In the great liberal arts tradition, a College of Charleston education focuses on discovery and personal growth, as well as preparation for life, work and service to our society."

SELECTIVITY

Admissions Rating	88
# of applicants	11,532
% of applicants accepted	72
% of acceptees attending	25
# offered a place on the wait list	484
% accepting a place on wait list	54
% admitted from wait list	24

FRESHMAN PROFILE

Range SAT Critical Reading	530–630
Range SAT Math	520–610
Range ACT Composite	23–27
Minimum paper TOEFL	570
Minimum web-based TOEFL	230
Average HS GPA	3.90
% graduated top 10% of class	26
% graduated top 25% of class	34
% graduated top 50% of class	92

DEADLINES

Early action	
Deadline	11/1
Regular	
Priority	2/1
Deadline	4/1
Nonfall registration?	Yes

APPLICANTS ALSO LOOK AT AND OFTEN PREFER

University of Virginia; The University of North Carolina at Chapel Hill; University of Georgia

AND SOMETIMES PREFER

University of South Carolina—Columbia; James Madison University; Furman University; Clemson University; Tulane University

AND RARELY PREFER

Auburn University; Appalachian State University

FINANCIAL FACTS

Financial Aid Rating	71
Annual in-state tuition	$10,230
Annual out-of-state tuition	$26,694
Required fees	$260
Books and supplies	$1,186
% needy frosh rec. need-based scholarship or grant aid	68
% needy UG rec. need-based scholarship or grant aid	66
% needy frosh rec. non-need-based scholarship or grant aid	67
% needy UG rec. non-need-based scholarship or grant aid	41
% needy frosh rec. need-based self-help aid	69
% needy UG rec. need-based self-help aid	78
% frosh rec. any financial aid	48
% UG rec. any financial aid	46
% UG borrow to pay for school	46
Average cumulative indebtedness	$23,357
% frosh need fully met	21
% ugrads need fully met	19
Average % of frosh need met	56
Average % of ugrad need met	57

COLLEGE OF THE HOLY CROSS

ADMISSIONS OFFICE, ONE COLLEGE STREET, WORCESTER, MA 01610-2395 • ADMISSIONS: 508-793-2443 • FAX: 508-793-3888

CAMPUS LIFE

Quality of Life Rating	77
Fire Safety Rating	95
Green Rating	92
Type of school	Private
Affiliation	Roman Catholic
Environment	City

STUDENTS

Total undergrad enrollment	2,875
% male/female	50/50
% from out of state	63
% frosh from public high school	49
% frosh live on campus	100
% ugrads live on campus	92
% African American	4
% Asian	5
% Caucasian	68
% Hispanic	11
% Native American	<1
% international	1
# of countries represented	20

SURVEY SAYS . . .

Students are happy
Lab facilities are great
School is well run
Students are friendly
Students involved in community service
Lots of beer drinking
Hard liquor is popular
Alumni active on campus
Active student government

ACADEMICS

Academic Rating	96
% students returning for sophomore year	95
% students graduating within 4 years	89
% students graduating within 6 years	91
Calendar	Semester
Student/faculty ratio	10:1
Profs interesting rating	96
Profs accessible rating	99

Most classes have 10–19 students.
Most lab/discussion sessions have 10–19 students.

MOST POPULAR MAJORS

psychology; economics; political science

STUDENTS SAY ". . ."

Academics

This small, Jesuit liberal arts school in Massachusetts operates under a selfless mission statement of "men and women for others." The school's strong academic tradition marries with "countless opportunities to learn through internships, speaker series," "strong student life," and "small classes" to focus on shaping the student as a whole person. Academics at Holy Cross are "rigorous, and the main priority of students on campus"; a caring faculty and administration foster "an incredible learning environment for students," and through their experiences, students receive "a broad-based foundation to be successful in variety of careers." "From the acceptance letter alone, I knew that my entire application was read thoroughly and that my character was closely examined," says one happy student. At Holy Cross, "you're more than just a number in the classroom and on the field." Professors here are "dedicated to creating an exciting learning environment." They are "always accessible and more than happy to help," and they "get to know you on an individual and personal level." Students are encouraged "to reflect on their experiences and continue to better himself/herself as a whole person." "There are endless opportunities despite the fact that it is a small college," one student says. "It is a place where like in the parable of the mustard seed one can grow." In addition to a "fantastic alumni network" spread across several fields in various industries, there is a strong science program that includes plenty of research opportunities. The college "demands enormous amounts of work from its students, but puts them in a great position to succeed." "Holy Cross equips their students with an intangible set of skills that not only prepares them for a job, but for life," says a student.

Life

Holy Cross has "a multitude" of groups and activities available to its students, as well as a plethora of community service opportunities. Everyone loves "going to sporting events, especially football and basketball." Though the "exceptionally beautiful" campus has a lot of fans, all agree that the college "could update some of the residence halls" and could provide more dining options. The community among freshmen dorms is "outstanding," and "many of the friends you make your first year will stay with you for years to come." During the week and on Sundays, "people take their work very seriously," and the library is generally pretty full, but parties are popular on weekends, and "that nerdy chem major you see working hard all week can turn into the girl riding the mechanical bull at a local bar." For those who choose to abstain from the party circuit, "SGA-sponsored events such as karaoke or dances are a blast." Worcester is a fun little town (and Boston a free weekend shuttle ride away), and the restaurants in the area are "amazing."

Student Body

Many students here are "preppy" and from New England, and most all of this "uncommonly friendly" lot is "studious with an activity or two that defines their interests and what they do during the weekend"; in fact, it is rare "to find someone with no extracurricular responsibilities." Everyone tends to be "very put together" and "generally articulate," and "there is a tremendous sense of community." Surface diversity is lacking, but there is "a diverse set of interests" among the whole student body. In general, "all love being here." "If you want to do well academically, have fun on the weekend…study hard and play hard, then you will fit in at Holy Cross."

FINANCIAL AID: 508-793-2265 • E-MAIL: ADMISSIONS@HOLYCROSS.EDU • WEBSITE: WWW.HOLYCROSS.EDU

THE PRINCETON REVIEW SAYS

Admissions

Very important factors considered include: Rigor of secondary school record, interview, recommendation(s). *Important factors considered include:* Class rank, GPA, application essay, extracurricular activities, character/personal qualities. *Other factors considered include:* Standardized test scores, first generation, geographical residence, racial/ethnic status, state residency, talent/ability, volunteer work, work experience, alumni/ae relations, level of applicant's interest, religious affiliation. SAT and SAT Subject Tests or ACT considered if submitted; ACT with or without Writing component accepted. TOEFL required of all international applicants. *Academic units recommended:* 4 English; 4 mathematics; 4 science; (2 science lab); 2 social studies; 4 foreign language; 2 history.

Financial Aid

Students should submit: FAFSA, CSS/Financial Aid PROFILE, Noncustodial PROFILE, Business/Farm Supplement. Regular filing deadline is 2/1. The Princeton Review suggests that all financial aid forms be submitted as soon as possible after January 1. *Need-based scholarships/grants offered:* Federal Pell, SEOG, State scholarships/grants, private scholarships, the school's own gift aid. *Loan aid offered:* Direct Subsidized Stafford Loans, Direct Unsubsidized Stafford Loans, Direct PLUS loans, Federal Perkins Loans. Applicants will be notified of awards beginning 4/1. Federal Work-Study Program available. Institutional employment available. Off-campus job opportunities are fair.

The Inside Word

Admission to Holy Cross is competitive; therefore, a demanding high school course load is required to be a viable candidate. The college values effective communication skills—it thoroughly evaluates each applicant's personal statement and short essay responses. Interviews are important, especially for those applying early decision. Students who graduate from a Jesuit high school might find themselves at a slight advantage.

THE SCHOOL SAYS ". . ."

From the Admissions Office

"When applying to Holy Cross, two areas deserve particular attention. First, the essay should be developed thoughtfully, with correct language and syntax in mind. That essay reflects for the Board of Admissions how you think and how you can express yourself. Second, activity beyond the classroom should be clearly defined. Since Holy Cross [has only] 2,800 students, the chance for involvement/participation is exceptional. The board reviews many applications for academically qualified students. A key difference in being accepted is the extent to which a candidate participates in-depth beyond the classroom—don't be modest; define who you are.

"Standardized test scores (i.e., SAT, SAT Subject Tests, and ACT) are optional. Students may submit their scores if they believe the results paint a fuller picture of their achievements and potential, but those students who don't submit scores will not be at a disadvantage in admissions decisions."

SELECTIVITY

Admissions Rating	96
# of applicants	7,115
% of applicants accepted	33
% of acceptees attending	31
# offered a place on the wait list	1,382
% accepting a place on wait list	22
% admitted from wait list	11
# of early decision applicants	522
% accepted early decision	67

FRESHMAN PROFILE

Range SAT Critical Reading	610–690
Range SAT Math	610–700
Range SAT Writing	610–700
Range ACT Composite	28–31
Minimum paper TOEFL	550
Minimum web-based TOEFL	213
% graduated top 10% of class	57
% graduated top 25% of class	90
% graduated top 50% of class	100

DEADLINES

Early decision	
Deadline	12/15
Regular	
Deadline	1/15
Nonfall registration?	No

APPLICANTS ALSO LOOK AT AND OFTEN PREFER

Boston College; University of Notre Dame; Georgetown University

AND SOMETIMES PREFER

Villanova University; Boston University

FINANCIAL FACTS

Financial Aid Rating	93
Annual tuition	$45,080
Room and board	$12,350
Required fees	$612
Books and supplies	$700
% needy frosh rec. need-based scholarship or grant aid	75
% needy UG rec. need-based scholarship or grant aid	75
% needy frosh rec. non-need-based scholarship or grant aid	2
% needy UG rec. non-need-based scholarship or grant aid	2
% needy frosh rec. need-based self-help aid	76
% needy UG rec. need-based self-help aid	79
% frosh rec. any financial aid	59
% UG rec. any financial aid	60
% UG borrow to pay for school	59
Average cumulative indebtedness	$30,880
% frosh need fully met	100
% ugrads need fully met	100
Average % of frosh need met	100
Average % of ugrad need met	100

THE COLLEGE OF IDAHO

2112 CLEVELAND BOULEVARD, CALDWELL, ID 83605-4432 • ADMISSIONS: 208-459-5305 • FAX: 208-459-5757

CAMPUS LIFE

Quality of Life Rating	97
Fire Safety Rating	83
Green Rating	73
Type of school	Private
Affiliation	No Affiliation
Environment	Town

STUDENTS

Total undergrad enrollment	1,030
% male/female	42/58
% from out of state	15
% frosh live on campus	96
% ugrads live on campus	62
# of fraternities (% ugrad men join)	3 (20)
# of sororities (% ugrad women join)	4 (23)
% African American	1
% Asian	3
% Caucasian	55
% Hispanic	14
% Native American	1
% international	10
# of countries represented	46

SURVEY SAYS . . .

Students are happy
Students are friendly
Diverse student types on campus
Great food on campus
Campus feels safe
Easy to get around campus
Lots of beer drinking
Very little drug use
Active student government
Active minority support groups

ACADEMICS

Academic Rating	91
% students returning for sophomore year	83
% students graduating within 4 years	50
% students graduating within 6 years	64
Calendar	Semester
Student/faculty ratio	12:1
Profs interesting rating	95
Profs accessible rating	98

Most classes have 10–19 students.
Most lab/discussion sessions have
10–19 students.

MOST POPULAR MAJORS

biology; business administration and
management; psychology

STUDENTS SAY " . . ."

Academics

A small liberal arts school, The College of Idaho is "like a diamond in the rough." Students tell us, "You'd be surprised at the very high quality this little school offers!" The small class sizes and low student-to-teacher ratio promote the school's emphasis on "individual learning" and a "personalized education plan." The academic experience at The College of Idaho is "incredibly rigorous but also very rewarding." Though the school has a "well-developed" liberal arts core, students also describe the biology and premed programs as "fantastic." Courses are "challenging," "fascinating," and "great preparation for both graduate school and the professional world." The small school environment provides a "sense of community" and allows students to develop "strong working relationships" with their professors. Students tell us their professors are "attentive," "very accessible," and "passionate about what they teach." One graduating senior described the school as "an academic gold mine of some of the most published and highly regarded professors and researchers in the field." The "personal teaching" approach the professors at The College of Idaho take makes them "consistently recognized nationally and internationally for their contributions to the academic community and to their students." The administration is "involved with the students" and "effective" though "the professors are what make The College of Idaho great." Also great is the fact that the school is "cost competitive" and offers "generous scholarships." As one freshman tells us, "My school is way more than a place for me to learn. My teachers have become more like guardians for my education, and my peers…my second family."

Life

Life in Caldwell can be "pretty quiet" but Boise, the capital, is only about a thirty-minute drive away, and the school regularly hosts trips into the city. However, the campus "strives" and "mostly succeeds" in making up for the town by sponsoring many activities on campus. A student tells us, "On campus there is always something going on…I rarely have a night where there isn't something that I could do for fun." The College of Idaho offers a variety of extracurricular activities. The school's Program Council "puts on great events all year long." Such events as movie and bowling nights are open to all students and are often offered free of charge. Students at The College of Idaho also tend to be very interested in clubs and club-sponsored events. With a multitude of clubs to join, there is a club "for all personality types." One student tells us, "Whether it is attending a theater or band concert, an athletic event, or a club meeting, there are plenty of ways to get involved." Students describe their school life as "great overall," and because the school is so small, "any major campus-sponsored activity brings us all together as one, giant, friendly social club."

Student Body

Students tell us, The College of Idaho has "students from many walks of life" and a "student body full of individuals." While a majority of the student body is "white, middle-class, and right out of high school," students at The College of Idaho promote an "atmosphere of learning from others no matter their background." Many students tell us that there really isn't a "typical student," which isn't so surprising given its large international student population. Each student at The College of Idaho is "an active participant in the campus community." One junior tells us students are, "overly involved" and "extremely busy with clubs, campus activities, athletics, and academics." Students are "hardworking but social," "intelligent," and "well-rounded." According to one sophomore, "though [we are all] different, the commonality of going to C of I brings us together."

FINANCIAL AID: 208-459-5307 • E-MAIL: ADMISSION@COLLEGEOFIDAHO.EDU • WEBSITE: WWW.COLLEGEOFIDAHO.EDU

THE PRINCETON REVIEW SAYS

Admissions

Very important factors considered include: GPA, standardized test scores. *Important factors considered include:* Application essay, recommendation(s), alumni/ae relations, level of applicant's interest. *Other factors considered include:* Class rank, rigor of secondary school record, extracurricular activities, interview, talent/ability, volunteer work, work experience, character/personal qualities. SAT or ACT required; ACT with Writing component required. TOEFL required of all international applicants. *Academic units recommended:* 4 English; 4 mathematics; 3 science; 4 social studies; 3 foreign language.

Financial Aid

Students should submit: FAFSA, Institution's own financial aid form. The Princeton Review suggests that all financial aid forms be submitted as soon as possible after January 1. *Need-based scholarships/grants offered:* Federal Pell, SEOG, State scholarships/grants, private scholarships, the school's own gift aid. *Loan aid offered:* Direct Subsidized Stafford Loans, Direct Unsubsidized Stafford Loans, Direct PLUS loans, Federal Perkins Loans. Federal Work-Study Program available. Off-campus job opportunities are good.

The Inside Word

The admissions committee at The College of Idaho is looking for students who have taken high school seriously. Candidates who demonstrate reasonable academic success and a variety of extracurricular activities will be handed the keys to a quality academic program and a unique college experience, one that stresses self-confidence and social responsibility.

THE SCHOOL SAYS "..."

From the Admissions Office

"The school's distinctive PEAK Curriculum enables students to graduate in four years with one major and three minors spread across four academic peaks: the natural sciences, humanities and fine arts, social sciences and a professional field. Within the campus community is the opportunity to create classroom opportunities for students that span the globe—both technologically and geographically. Here, students are just as apt to attend a biology class on campus as they are to hike in the nearby Owyhee or Sawtooth Mountains to carry out field research. During the college's four-week winter term, approximately 15 percent of the students are emailing friends and family from such locales as Australia, Israel, France, Ireland, England, Peru, and or Mexico while taking part in faculty-led, multidisciplinary trips. International students from fifty-three different countries comprise 9 percent of the student body. Students are invited to visit the campus and the admissions counselors, either in person or online.

"C of I requires all admission candidates (who have not reached sophomore status in college) to submit either the SAT or the ACT with the writing component. The College of Idaho will consider all scores. There is no SAT Subject Test requirement, but scores will be considered as part of a holistic evaluation."

SELECTIVITY

Admissions Rating	80
# of applicants	1,388
% of applicants accepted	65
% of acceptees attending	32

FRESHMAN PROFILE

Range SAT Critical Reading	470–630
Range SAT Math	480–600
Range SAT Writing	460–600
Range ACT Composite	22–27
Minimum paper TOEFL	550
Average HS GPA	3.64
% graduated top 10% of class	25
% graduated top 25% of class	56
% graduated top 50% of class	88

DEADLINES

Early action	
Deadline	11/15
Notification	12/15
Regular	
Priority	2/15
Deadline	7/15
Nonfall registration?	Yes

APPLICANTS ALSO LOOK AT AND OFTEN PREFER

Gonzaga University; Brigham Young University (UT); University of Idaho; Idaho State University; Boise State University

FINANCIAL FACTS

Financial Aid Rating	87
Annual tuition	$23,300
Room and board	$8,551
Required fees	$755
Books and supplies	$1,200
% needy frosh rec. need-based scholarship or grant aid	100
% needy UG rec. need-based scholarship or grant aid	100
% needy frosh rec. non-need-based scholarship or grant aid	100
% needy UG rec. non-need-based scholarship or grant aid	100
% needy frosh rec. need-based self-help aid	81
% needy UG rec. need-based self-help aid	81
% frosh rec. any financial aid	99
% UG rec. any financial aid	100
% UG borrow to pay for school	55
Average cumulative indebtedness	$27,008
% frosh need fully met	17
% ugrads need fully met	17
Average % of frosh need met	94
Average % of ugrad need met	93

THE COLLEGE OF NEW JERSEY

PO BOX 7718, EWING, NJ 08628-0718 • ADMISSIONS: 609-771-2131 • FAX: 609-637-5174

STUDENTS SAY ". . ."

Academics

The College of New Jersey is a small public college dedicated to education and to the pursuit of passions, all at an affordable price. Each of TCNJ's "excellent" seven schools offers "an awesome range of classes to choose from" (it is "one of the best schools in the area for future teachers," in particular), and the academic environment "is an open and honest one." On top of all that, "the campus is gorgeous, the students are friendly, and you can't beat the price!" "The College of New Jersey is a community unlike any I have ever been a part of; everyone is proud to be a part of and to contribute to the TCNJ culture," says a satisfied student.

Professors are always available in and out of the "small classes," and they "are truly interested in the progress and well-being of their students." Though the classes for liberal learning requirements are "stressful," teachers want their students to do well and "are eager to help and answer questions." "There has never been a moment where I have felt unsupported in my academic endeavors or felt that I could not reach out for help," says a student. A few students warn that some requirements become hard to fill because "there are only a few options that fit the topic, and everyone is trying to get into those classes."

One of TCNJ's greatest strengths is the Freshman Year Seminar Program. Freshman students choose a class that they are interested in (ranging from "a class on Bruce Springsteen, to one about *Harry Potter,* to one about the meaning of life"), and then live on a floor with all of the students in that class. "This is a wonderful opportunity to build community and to ensure that students are surrounded by people with similar interests and academic goals."

Life

Life at TCNJ is "calm and enjoyable." Students refer to the school as an "island of suburban housing," which works well in terms of building community, but the atmosphere does tend to cut students off from the outside world (especially freshmen, who aren't allowed cars). Students keep busy with their studies, organizations, and "many great events the school hosts," but "they also enjoy spending time with friends and having a good time together." "A lot of people party. A lot of people don't party. Most people love it here," sums up a student simply. While the local origins of the students means that some students do go home on weekends, "almost every weekend, the school organizes a trip to nearby Princeton, NYC, or Philadelphia" for those who stick around. "The school actually sends out a weekly calendar listing all of the events being held on campus that week," says a student. Students do warn about housing; as selection for upper-class housing is done strictly by a lottery system, "several do not get housing" each year, and some of the freshmen that do get their guaranteed housing find that their dorms are "ancient, dirty, and falling apart."

Student Body

People "are serious about their education here," and students describe themselves as "quite diverse." There is "always a group for somebody": "I don't know anyone that feels like they don't fit in, and if they do feel that way, it's because they aren't putting in the effort to do so," says a student. Everyone is on campus for a reason, whether it's major-/career-specific or "simply to gain leadership or life experiences," and all are "self-motivated, personable, and goal-oriented." While students are accepting of minorities, "the majority is most certainly still white." On the whole, "students are very happy and friendly and therefore make it much easier to fit in and make friends."

FINANCIAL AID: 609-771-2211 • E-MAIL: TCNJINFO@TCNJ.EDU • WEBSITE: WWW.TCNJ.EDU

THE PRINCETON REVIEW SAYS

Admissions

Very important factors considered include: Class rank, rigor of secondary school record, standardized test scores, extracurricular activities, volunteer work. *Important factors considered include:* Application essay, geographical residence, recommendation(s), state residency, talent/ability, character/personal quali- ties. *Other factors considered include:* GPA, first generation, racial/ethnic status, work experience, alumni/ae relations, level of applicant's interest. SAT or ACT required; ACT with or without Writing component accepted. TOEFL required of all international applicants. *Academic units required:* 4 English; 4 mathemat- ics; 4 science; (2 science lab); 2 social studies; 2 foreign language.

Financial Aid

Students should submit: FAFSA, State aid form. Regular filing deadline is 10/1. The Princeton Review suggests that all financial aid forms be submitted as soon as possible after January 1. *Need-based scholarships/grants offered:* Federal Pell, SEOG, State scholarships/grants, private scholarships, the school's own gift aid, federal nursing scholarships. *Loan aid offered:* Direct Subsidized Stafford Loans, Direct Unsubsidized Stafford Loans, Direct PLUS loans, Federal Perkins Loans, Federal Nursing Loans. Federal Work-Study Program available. Institutional employment available. Off-campus job opportunities are excellent.

The Inside Word

TCNJ accepts a high percentage of its 10,000 applicants, but that figure is deceiving; this is a self-selecting applicant pool, and those with no chance of acceptance simply don't bother. Admissions are as competitive as you would expect at a school that offers state residents a small-college experience and a highly respected degree for bargain-basement prices. TCNJ's admissions staff examines every component of a student's application, but none more carefully than the high school transcript. Students should apply a soon as possible once the application becomes available.

THE SCHOOL SAYS "..."

From the Admissions Office

"The College of New Jersey is one of the United States' great higher education success stories. With a long history as New Jersey's preeminent teacher of teachers, the college has grown into a new role as educator of the nation's best students in a wide range of fields. The College of New Jersey has created a culture of constant questioning—a place where knowledge is not merely received but reconfigured. In small classes, students and faculty members collaborate in a rewarding process: As they seek to understand fundamental principles, apply key concepts, reveal new problems, and pursue new lines of inquiry, students gain a fluency of thought in their disciplines. The college's 289-acre tree-lined campus is a union of vision, engineering, beauty, and func- tionality. Neoclassical Georgian Colonial architecture, meticulous landscaping, and thoughtful design merge in a dynamic system, constantly evolving to meet the needs of TCNJ students. About half of TCNJ's entering class will be aca- demic scholars, with large numbers of National Merit finalists and semifinalists. The College of New Jersey is bringing together the best ideas from around the nation and building a new model for public undergraduate education on one campus."

SELECTIVITY

Admissions Rating	94
# of applicants	11,145
% of applicants accepted	43
% of acceptees attending	29
# offered a place on the wait list	1,598
% accepting a place on wait list	33
% admitted from wait list	7
# of early decision applicants	560
% accepted early decision	61

FRESHMAN PROFILE

Range SAT Critical Reading	550–660
Range SAT Math	580–680
Range SAT Writing	560–670
Minimum paper TOEFL	550
% graduated top 10% of class	84
% graduated top 25% of class	89
% graduated top 50% of class	99

DEADLINES

Early decision	
Deadline	11/15
Notification	12/15
Regular	
Priority	11/15
Deadline	1/15
Nonfall registration?	Yes

APPLICANTS ALSO LOOK AT AND OFTEN PREFER

New York University; Rutgers- The State University of New Jersey—New Brunswick; University of Delaware; Villanova University

AND SOMETIMES PREFER

Boston University; Pennsylvania State University—University Park

AND RARELY PREFER

Stevens Institute of Technology; Bucknell University; Loyola University Maryland

FINANCIAL FACTS

Financial Aid Rating	69
Annual in-state tuition	$10,355
Annual out-of-state tuition	$20,760
Room and board	$11,343
Required fees	$4,375
Books and supplies	$1,200
% needy frosh rec. need-based scholarship or grant aid	36
% needy UG rec. need-based scholarship or grant aid	39
% needy frosh rec. non-need-based scholarship or grant aid	40
% needy UG rec. non-need-based scholarship or grant aid	32
% needy frosh rec. need-based self-help aid	63
% needy UG rec. need-based self-help aid	74
% frosh rec. any financial aid	70
% UG rec. any financial aid	62
% UG borrow to pay for school	60
Average cumulative indebtedness	$32,362
% frosh need fully met	16
% ugrads need fully met	15
Average % of frosh need met	43
Average % of ugrad need met	48

COLLEGE OF THE OZARKS

OFFICE OF ADMISSIONS, POINT LOOKOUT, MO 65726 • ADMISSIONS: 417-690-2636 • FAX: 417-335-2618

CAMPUS LIFE

Quality of Life Rating	88
Fire Safety Rating	81
Green Rating	65
Type of school	Private
Affiliation	Interdenominational
Environment	Rural

STUDENTS

Total undergrad enrollment	1,513
% male/female	47/53
% from out of state	16
% frosh from public high school	76
% frosh live on campus	89
% ugrads live on campus	81
% African American	1
% Asian	1
% Caucasian	93
% Hispanic	2
% Native American	1
% international	2
# of countries represented	25

SURVEY SAYS . . .

Lots of conservative students
School is well run
Great financial aid
Students are friendly
Students are very religious
Students get along with local community
Campus feels safe
Very little drug use

ACADEMICS

Academic Rating	81
% students returning for sophomore year	85
% students graduating within 4 years	49
% students graduating within 6 years	64
Calendar	Semester
Student/faculty ratio	15:1
Profs interesting rating	80
Profs accessible rating	78

Most classes have 10–19 students.
Most lab/discussion sessions have
10–19 students.

MOST POPULAR MAJORS
elementary education; business
administration and management; agricultural
business

STUDENTS SAY " . . ."

Academics
The appeal of College of the Ozarks is simple: "It's a tuition-free, small, Christ-oriented college!" Students come here so they can "graduate debt-free" and get "a free education consisting of hard work and Christian qualities." The school's slogan is "Hard Work U," and students are expected to work hard while receiving a "Christian education" in a "positive environment." The school "works to instill patriotic, academic, Christian, cultural, and vocational morals to all students." An example is how "we are strongly encouraged to respect war veterans and thank them for their service as much as possible." C of O is about "hard work and God!!!" This can sometimes come at a price, as students suggest there could be "more tolerance for those who think differently." "It seems that some of the new policies and expectations aim to isolate the school from mainstream higher education and I don't agree with that," a Mathematics and Computer Science major says. Students who share the school's values will find "a great place to receive an amazing education, form lifelong relationships, and deepen [their] faith." C of O professors are "dedicated, intelligent leaders" who "are challenging, but willing to help each student understand in a way that works best for them." "I am willing to brag on for hours on most of my professors," and English major says. "I have never had professors more eager to teach not have I had professors so eager to help you succeed," says another student. Overall, "College of the Ozarks cares for nothing but its students" and focuses on making them "well rounded citizens rather than making money." One happy Business Administration major explains their decision to attend this way: "As soon as I came through the gates, I saw how beautiful it was. On our tour, EVERYTHING exceeded my expectations. That's when I knew College of the Ozarks was where I wanted to be."

Life
Students enjoy the "safety and the strictness of an alcohol-free campus." As a Christian school, "we have really strict policies about alcohol and drugs" and "although some students party, most do not." Instead, students "participate in school activities or clubs for fun" and "spend any free time outdoors playing games when the weather is nice." The school works hard to organize events on campus "such as dances, competitions, and a variety of other student events." "The school is constantly planning hay rides, drive in movies, and other events," a Nursing student explains. As a school with a strongly religious student body, many students participate in "Bible studies either on or off campus." "Come midnight campus is like a ghost town," perhaps in part because "many students hold jobs in addition to their 'on-campus 15-hour-a-week job.'" While "some of the buildings are very old and sketchy," "in a few years that won't be the case because they have plans of renovation and construction." Students really love "the week-long freshman orientation," which leaves incoming students "familiar with the whole campus/campus opportunities" as well as giving them "a solid group of friends." Another student explains that "this entire place is one huge family and you are never bored."

Student Body
The typical C of O student is "hard working," "white, traditional," and a "Christian conservative." "Most of our students" come from a "mid-western small town," especially around the Ozarks. "Students fit in by being hard workers" and are frequently described as "very friendly." "Very laid-back, but very driven; an interesting dynamic," one student explains. Since students come from "a similar background" they "have no reason to disagree with one another." This means that the school luckily "doesn't have a lot of drama." On the other hand, "C of O is NOT diverse at all," and "one of the most conservative places you will find in the [United States]." The traditional religious values mean "a typical student at C of O is responsible and respectful to authority" while following "high moral standards." If you share those values, you'll find fellow students who are "very friendly, polite, eager to serve and help, and well informed." "There isn't your typical separation of upper and lower class men," one student explains. "It is a privilege to get into this college and we treat everyone like they deserve to be here."

FINANCIAL AID: 417-690-3292 • E-MAIL: ADMISS4@COFO.EDU • WEBSITE: WWW.COFO.EDU

THE PRINCETON REVIEW SAYS

Admissions

Very important factors considered include: Class rank, rigor of secondary school record, interview, character/personal qualities. *Important factors considered include:* GPA, standardized test scores, geographical residence, recommendation(s), volunteer work, work experience, level of applicant's interest. *Other factors considered include:* Extracurricular activities, first generation, state residency, talent/ability, alumni/ae relations, religious affiliation. SAT or ACT required; ACT with or without Writing component accepted. TOEFL required of all international applicants. *Academic units required:* 4 English; 3 mathematics; 2 science; (1 science lab); 3 history. *Academic units recommended:* 3 social studies; 2 foreign language; 3 academic electives.

Financial Aid

Students should submit: FAFSA. The Princeton Review suggests that all financial aid forms be submitted as soon as possible after January 1. *Need-based scholarships/grants offered:* Federal Pell, SEOG, State scholarships/grants, private scholarships, the school's own gift aid. *Loan aid offered:* Applicants will be notified of awards beginning 7/1. Federal Work-Study Program available. Off-campus job opportunities are excellent.

The Inside Word

C of O was founded "to provide the advantages of a Christian education for youth of both sexes, especially those found worthy, but who are without sufficient means to procure such training." The tuition-free education, which requires students to work fifteen hours a week on campus, means that applicants will need to demonstrate their financial need. The school's slogan of "Hard Work U" is not an empty phrase. Applicants will want to showcase a hard work ethic when applying.

THE SCHOOL SAYS "..."

From the Admissions Office

"College of the Ozarks is unique because of its no-tuition, work-study program, but also because it strives to educate the head, the heart, and the hands. At C of O, there are high expectations of students—the college stresses character development as well as study and work. An education from 'Hard Work U.' offers many opportunities, not the least of which is the chance to graduate debt-free. Life at C of O isn't all hard work and no play, however. There are many opportunities for fun. The nearby resort town of Branson, Missouri, offers ample opportunities for recreation and summer employment, and Table Rock Lake, only a few miles away, is a terrific spot to swim, sun, and relax. Numerous on-campus activities such as Mudfest, Luau Night, dances, and holiday parties give students lots of chances for fun without leaving the college. At 'Hard Work U.,' we work hard, but we know how to have fun, too.

"Applicants are required to submit scores from the ACT or the SAT. We will use the student's best scores from either test. Writing scores are not required."

SELECTIVITY

Admissions Rating	90
# of applicants	3,050
% of applicants accepted	12
% of acceptees attending	96
# offered a place on the wait list	785
% accepting a place on wait list	99
% admitted from wait list	0

FRESHMAN PROFILE

Range SAT Critical Reading	510–560
Range SAT Math	450–548
Range SAT Writing	495–548
Range ACT Composite	20–25
Minimum paper TOEFL	550
Minimum web-based TOEFL	213
Average HS GPA	3.63
% graduated top 10% of class	19
% graduated top 25% of class	50
% graduated top 50% of class	94

DEADLINES

Regular	
Priority	2/15
Nonfall registration?	No

APPLICANTS ALSO LOOK AT AND OFTEN PREFER
Missouri State University

AND SOMETIMES PREFER
Southwest Baptist University

FINANCIAL FACTS

Financial Aid Rating	90
Annual tuition	$0
Room and board	$6,200
Required fees	$430
Books and supplies	$800
% needy frosh rec. need-based scholarship or grant aid	100
% needy UG rec. need-based scholarship or grant aid	100
% needy frosh rec. non-need-based scholarship or grant aid	9
% needy UG rec. non-need-based scholarship or grant aid	12
% needy frosh rec. need-based self-help aid	91
% needy UG rec. need-based self-help aid	88
% frosh rec. any financial aid	100
% UG rec. any financial aid	100
% UG borrow to pay for school	13
Average cumulative indebtedness	$6,424
% frosh need fully met	18
% ugrads need fully met	28
Average % of frosh need met	82
Average % of ugrad need met	84

COLLEGE OF SAINT BENEDICT/SAINT JOHN'S UNIVERSITY

37 SOUTH COLLEGE AVE, ST. JOSEPH, MN 56374 • ADMISSIONS: 320-363-5055 • FAX: 320-363-5650

CAMPUS LIFE

Quality of Life Rating	89
Fire Safety Rating	91
Green Rating	92
Type of school	Private
Affiliation	Roman Catholic
Environment	Village

STUDENTS

Total undergrad enrollment	3,922
% male/female	48/52
% from out of state	17
% frosh from public high school	73
% frosh live on campus	100
% ugrads live on campus	87
% African American	3
% Asian	4
% Caucasian	81
% Hispanic	5
% Native American	1
% international	5
# of countries represented	31

SURVEY SAYS . . .

Political activism is unpopular or nonexistent
Students are happy
Career services are great
Students are friendly
Great food on campus
Alumni active on campus

ACADEMICS

Academic Rating	87
% students returning for sophomore year	87
% students graduating within 4 years	73
% students graduating within 6 years	81
Calendar	Semester
Student/faculty ratio	12:1
Profs interesting rating	85
Profs accessible rating	87

Most classes have 10–19 students.
Most lab/discussion sessions have 10–19 students.

MOST POPULAR MAJORS

global business leadership; biology; English language and literature

STUDENTS SAY " . . ."

Academics

Minnesota's College of Saint Benedict (for women) and Saint John's University (for men) are two Catholic liberal arts colleges that share one academic program and classes, but retain separate dorms, campuses, and traditions. Students come to this "beautiful, friendly environment" and leave with "a well-rounded education...ready to take on the world." The Benedictine values "are upheld by every student in everyday life" and help breed graduates that are "all about service and making an impact in the world." "This school is a must for any student who wants to feel accepted and a part of a rich community, while at the same time receiving an education that is second to none," says one junior.

Professors truly take to heart the feedback they receive from their students, are "extremely dedicated and passionate," and "are willing to work...on projects outside of class even if it means extra work for them." They "are interested in us figuring things out for ourselves" and are "big on [students] being prepared for class so more time can be spend discussing or practicing material instead of lecturing." The ultimate testament to faculty involvement: "At CSB/SJU, I have never had a professor that has struggled to know my name (besides the fact that I am a twin)." Discussion is "lively" (particularly in upper division courses), and students "are offered many great opportunities to further our experiences and education." The open environment "does what it can to help students feel comfortable and learn."

The school provides "excellent scientific and business opportunities" and "endless connections with not only other schools across the nation, but.... across the world" that aid in post-undergraduate employment or continued education opportunities. The "incredible" study abroad program sees a large number of students take advantage of it at some point in their college careers.

Life

The school "really makes sure your transition into your first semester runs smoothly" and that students "have a lot of options for meeting new people." The Student Activities and Leadership Development Office plans "large campus events such as orientation and Thanksgiving dinners," and also has an "inspired leaders series" of after-hours classes taught by professors that promote leadership on campus. On weekends, students often take adventure trips (like "California Surfing trips, Boundary Waters canoe trips, and Colorado climbing trips") with the school's Peer Resource Program.

School pride is "ridiculous" at CSB/SJU and athletic events "are the high points for entertainment," especially against rival St. Thomas. For fun, students take advantage of the school's "rich recreational abilities" both in the arboretum and on nearby waterways, where "ice fishing, fishing, hiking, and hanging out at the beach are popular." "The warm months of the year are awesome with the lake/raft open. It feels like a summer camp," says a student. Many students "do go out on the weekends" to parties or bars, but there is an "outstanding campus programming board" that plans events every weekend on campus as an alternative to drinking. "As long as you can step out that door and make good use of your time, you'll have an amazing time," assures a sophomore.

Student Body

Most of the "Johnnies" and "Bennies" here are "from Minnesota or the surrounding states," are "hard-working, fun-loving," and "believe in the importance of education." Not surprisingly, the majority are Catholic and take "'Minnesota Nice' to a whole new level": "Expect to have doors open for you [and] people smile and greet you on occasion when you're passing by." People have no trouble finding a friend group with related interests via "the many clubs and activities that are offered." "Everyone fits like a puzzle piece" and students "commonly have social issues that they are passionate about, such as gender equality, sustainability, [or] health and wellness."

COLLEGE OF SAINT BENEDICT/SAINT JOHN'S UNIVERSITY

FINANCIAL AID: 320-363-5388 • E-MAIL: ADMISSIONS@CSBSJU.EDU • WEBSITE: WWW.CSBSJU.EDU

THE PRINCETON REVIEW SAYS

Admissions

Very important factors considered include: GPA, rigor of secondary school record, standardized test scores, application essay. *Important factors considered include:* Extracurricular activities, recommendation(s). *Other factors considered include:* Class rank, first generation, geographical residence, interview, racial/ethnic status, talent/ability, volunteer work, work experience, alumni/ae relations, character/personal qualities. SAT or ACT required; ACT with or without Writing component accepted. TOEFL required of all international applicants. *Academic units required:* 4 English; 3 mathematics; 2 science; (2 science lab); 2 social studies; 4 academic electives. *Academic units recommended:* 2 foreign language.

Financial Aid

Students should submit: FAFSA, Institution's own financial aid form. The Princeton Review suggests that all financial aid forms be submitted as soon as possible after January 1. *Need-based scholarships/grants offered:* Federal Pell, SEOG, State scholarships/grants, private scholarships, the school's own gift aid. *Loan aid offered:* Direct Subsidized Stafford Loans, Direct Unsubsidized Stafford Loans, Direct PLUS loans, Federal Perkins Loans, State Loans. Federal Work-Study Program available. Institutional employment available Off-campus job opportunities are fair.

The Inside Word

Students with decent grades and a few extracurricular activities that "show promise of community contribution" shouldn't have any problem getting into CSB/SJU. While you may apply to CSB/SJU using the Common Application, the school suggests using the CSBSJU GET INspired application.

THE SCHOOL SAYS ". . ."

From the Admissions Office

"The College of Saint Benedict (CSB), for women, and Saint John's University (SJU), for men, are nationally recognized Catholic liberal arts colleges and ranked as two of the top three Catholic colleges in the nation. They share one academic program, and students attend classes together on both campuses. This integrated learning experience combines a challenging academic program with extensive opportunities for international study, leadership, service learning, spiritual growth and cultural and athletic involvement. Our partnership of two nationally leading institutions gives students the educational opportunities and choices of a large university and the individual attention and community of a premier small college experience. We provide students access to the resources of not one, but two nationally leading liberal arts colleges through a common undergraduate curriculum, identical degree requirements, and a single academic calendar. Students from both colleges attend all classes and activities together on two campuses. We are committed to the development of the whole person, meeting the unique needs of both women and men in single-gender and co-educational experiences – experiences that could not be provided by traditional single-sex colleges and would not typically be provided by co-educational colleges. The colleges are part of a centuries-old Benedictine tradition of faith, learning, and community. Hospitality, community, stewardship and service to the common good are bedrock Benedictine values expressed throughout the curriculum and the co-curriculum. We are part of a Catholic intellectual tradition committed to openness, intellectual inquiry, and the lively engagement of faith and reason. The colleges are committed to global learning and connection. We provide international study programs on six continents and are annually ranked among the top three baccalaureate colleges nationally in the number of students completing semester-long study abroad. More than half of all students study abroad before they graduate – an international study participation rate significantly higher than the national average for liberal arts colleges. More than 200 academic courses have an international component or global emphasis. One-third of our faculty has led a study abroad program. We enroll nearly 150 students from more than 30 countries, creating an enriching and culturally diverse global experience on campus. CSB/SJU annually rank first or second among Minnesota's private colleges for the number of undergraduate international students."

SELECTIVITY

Admissions Rating	79
# of applicants	3,824
% of applicants accepted	75
% of acceptees attending	36

FRESHMAN PROFILE

Range SAT Critical Reading	470–600
Range SAT Math	475–620
Range ACT Composite	23–28
Minimum paper TOEFL	500
Minimum web-based TOEFL	190
Average HS GPA	3.59
% graduated top 10% of class	28
% graduated top 25% of class	62
% graduated top 50% of class	89

DEADLINES

Early action	
Deadline	11/15
Notification	12/15
Regular	
Priority	11/15
Nonfall registration?	Yes

APPLICANTS ALSO LOOK AT AND OFTEN PREFER

Gustavus Adolphus College; University of Minnesota—Twin Cities; University of St. Thomas

FINANCIAL FACTS

Financial Aid Rating	89
Annual tuition	$36,986
Room and board	$9,644
Required fees	$940
Books and supplies	$1,000
% needy frosh rec. need-based scholarship or grant aid	98
% needy UG rec. need-based scholarship or grant aid	97
% needy frosh rec. non-need-based scholarship or grant aid	97
% needy UG rec. non-need-based scholarship or grant aid	93
% needy UG rec. need-based self-help aid	91
% frosh rec. any financial aid	96
% UG rec. any financial aid	94
% UG borrow to pay for school	67
Average cumulative indebtedness	$37,692
% frosh need fully met	49
% ugrads need fully met	39
Average % of frosh need met	93
Average % of ugrad need met	88

THE COLLEGE OF WILLIAM & MARY

OFFICE OF ADMISSIONS, PO BOX 8795, WILLIAMSBURG, VA 23187-8795 • ADMISSIONS: 757-221-4223 • FAX: 757-221-1242

CAMPUS LIFE

Quality of Life Rating	93
Fire Safety Rating	77
Green Rating	85
Type of school	Public
Affiliation	No Affiliation
Environment	Village

STUDENTS

Total undergrad enrollment	6,129
% male/female	45/55
% from out of state	32
% frosh from public high school	~70
% frosh live on campus	100
% ugrads live on campus	72
# of fraternities (% ugrad men join)	17 (16)
# of sororities (% ugrad women join)	13 (22)
% African American	7
% Asian	6
% Caucasian	59
% Hispanic	9
% Native American	<1
% international	4
# of countries represented	54

SURVEY SAYS . . .

Students are happy
Lab facilities are great
Career services are great
No one cheats
Students are friendly
Diverse student types on campus
Students involved in community service
Great off-campus food
Campus feels safe
Athletic facilities are great
Very little drug use

ACADEMICS

Academic Rating	91
% students returning for sophomore year	96
% students graduating within 4 years	85
% students graduating within 6 years	91
Calendar	Semester
Student/faculty ratio	12:1
Profs interesting rating	89
Profs accessible rating	91

Most classes have students.

STUDENTS SAY ". . ."

Academics

Students at The College of William & Mary are extraordinarily happy with their overall experience and with their academics in particular. One student sums up the school's vibe by saying, "William & Mary achieves a remarkable balance between the dynamic, progressive academics of a liberal arts college and the strong sense of history and tradition one would expect from America's second-oldest school." "There are endless and amazing" opportunities here, with an emphasis on undergraduate research that makes W&M unique among small liberal arts schools. "Professors will engage you outside of the classroom and give you the opportunity to conduct your own research project, even in a non-science curriculum." Many "are often in newspapers and magazines and have relevant and copious work experience in the subjects they're teaching." Across the board, "professors are one of the best things about W&M." They "are always accessible for extra help," and "they also really take the time to get to know their students outside of the classroom." In the classroom, "William & Mary professors truly know how to balance lecture with discussion. Especially in traditionally lecture-based subjects, like history, professors devote a lot of class time to discussion to understand what students think." Slackers take note: "Professors expect a lot of work outside of class," and "classes usually require a good amount of reading, especially for the humanities." All this hard work is very rewarding, though, with many upperclassmen and graduating seniors expressing how well-prepared they feel for the "real-world," and one student says that the professors "have upended the way I thought about their subject, opening completely new veins of inquiry."

Life

When students describe campus life at W&M, the word community comes up—a lot. And this community "is made up of incredibly involved, dedicated, and supportive students who have big dreams and big fun," who say: "We study hard, but we know how to have fun, too." Alma Mater Productions (AMP), the college programming board, "sponsors a lot of different events that are well-attended, including…comedians, music artists, movies, etc." Student organizations are also very strong, from intramural sports, some form of which "almost everyone plays," to arts organizations such as "the William & Mary Symphony Orchestra, three university choirs, the Middle Eastern Music Ensemble, an Early Music Ensemble, an Appalachian string band, a small chamber orchestra, eleven a cappella groups and…two all-student theater companies." "On the weekends, there is always a party to go to" and "the Greek community is very inclusive." Off campus, students enjoy the charms of Colonial Williamsburg, theme park Busch Gardens, Jamestown Beach on the James River, and "great outlet shopping!" Despite a few gripes about parking (which are common on a small campus), students are generally happy with their facilities, with the library and the business school receiving special mention.

Student Body

Students are quick to note that there's a generalization that the "T.W.A.M.P., or Typical William & Mary Person…is the person [who] does all their reading, shows up to class every day, and is a nerd," but most are equally quick to cast this stereotype aside. The real T.W.A.M.P., they tell us, is "open-minded, outgoing, charismatic, driven, dedicated, caring, and unique." The school is full of "well-rounded people who are in touch with their inner nerd," and "intellectual people who care about the world find the zaniest ways to have fun." "Students fit in many social circles," and students credit the close bonding that happens in freshmen dorms for this inclusivity. "You will often see the members of the football team in the library as much as any other student," and "everyone is involved with at least one other thing outside of class, and often…about ten other things." "Students are an eclectic bunch united by our thirst for knowledge and overwhelming Tribe Pride."

THE COLLEGE OF WILLIAM & MARY

FINANCIAL AID: 757-221-2420 • E-MAIL: ADMISSION@WM.EDU • WEBSITE: WWW.WM.EDU

THE PRINCETON REVIEW SAYS

Admissions

Very important factors considered include: Class rank, GPA, rigor of secondary school record, standardized test scores, application essay, extracurricular activities, recommendation(s), state residency, talent/ability, volunteer work, work experience, character/personal qualities. *Other factors considered include:* First generation, geographical residence, interview, racial/ethnic status, alumni/ae relations. SAT or ACT required; ACT with or without Writing component accepted. TOEFL required of all international applicants. *Academic units recommended:* 4 English; 4 mathematics; 4 science; (3 science lab); 4 social studies; 4 foreign language.

Financial Aid

Students should submit: FAFSA, CSS/Financial Aid PROFILE. Regular filing deadline is 3/1. The Princeton Review suggests that all financial aid forms be submitted as soon as possible after January 1. *Need-based scholarships/grants offered:* Federal Pell, SEOG, State scholarships/grants, private scholarships, the school's own gift aid. *Loan aid offered:* Direct Subsidized Stafford Loans, Direct Unsubsidized Stafford Loans, Direct PLUS loans, Federal Perkins Loans. Federal Work-Study Program available. Institutional employment available. Off-campus job opportunities are excellent.

The Inside Word

The volume of applications at W&M is extremely high; thus, admission is ultra-competitive. Only very strong students from out of state should apply. The large applicant pool necessitates a labor-intensive candidate evaluation process; each admissions officer reads roughly 150 application folders per week during the peak review season. But this is one admissions committee that moves fast without sacrificing a thorough holistic review. There probably isn't a tougher public college admissions committee in the country.

THE SCHOOL SAYS "..."

From the Admissions Office

"William & Mary is the nation's second-oldest college and preeminent small public university. Yes, we have one of the lowest student/faculty ratio (twelve to one) of any public university. We're also known for having one of the most successful undergraduate business programs in the United States, a model United Nations team that perennially vies for the world championship, and extensive opportunities for undergraduate research. Students at William & Mary follow in the footsteps of alumni ranging from Thomas Jefferson, James Monroe, and John Tyler to Comedy Central's Jon Stewart, Academy Award nominee Glenn Close, Chancellor and former Secretary of Defense Robert Gates, and Super Bowl-winning Pittsburg Steeler's coach Mike Tomlin. In short, William & Mary offers a top-rated educational experience at a comparatively low cost and in the company of interesting people from a broad variety of backgrounds. If you are an academically strong, involved student looking for a challenge in a great campus community, William & Mary may well be the place for you."

SELECTIVITY

Admissions Rating	97
# of applicants	13,660
% of applicants accepted	32
% of acceptees attending	33
# offered a place on the wait list	3,518
% accepting a place on wait list	44
% admitted from wait list	10
# of early decision applicants	1,167
% accepted early decision	48

FRESHMAN PROFILE

Range SAT Critical Reading	630–740
Range SAT Math	620–720
Range SAT Writing	620–720
Range ACT Composite	28–32
Minimum paper TOEFL	600
Minimum web-based TOEFL	250
Average HS GPA	4.00
% graduated top 10% of class	79
% graduated top 25% of class	97
% graduated top 50% of class	100

DEADLINES

Early decision	
Deadline	11/1
Notification	12/1
Regular	
Deadline	1/1
Notification	4/1
Nonfall registration?	No

APPLICANTS ALSO LOOK AT AND SOMETIMES PREFER

Duke University; Georgetown University; University of Virginia; The University of North Carolina at Chapel Hill; Cornell University; Princeton University; Dartmouth College; Vanderbilt University

FINANCIAL FACTS

Financial Aid Rating	77
Annual in-state tuition	$10,428
Annual out-of-state tuition	$32,816
Room and board	$9,622
Required fees	$5,035
Books and supplies	$1,200
% needy frosh rec. need-based scholarship or grant aid	67
% needy UG rec. need-based scholarship or grant aid	75
% needy frosh rec. non-need-based scholarship or grant aid	42
% needy UG rec. non-need-based scholarship or grant aid	31
% needy frosh rec. need-based self-help aid	60
% needy UG rec. need-based self-help aid	66
% frosh rec. any financial aid	54
% UG rec. any financial aid	53
% UG borrow to pay for school	41
Average cumulative indebtedness	$24,344
% frosh need fully met	22
% ugrads need fully met	25
Average % of frosh need met	73
Average % of ugrad need met	75

THE COLLEGE OF WOOSTER

847 COLLEGE AVENUE, WOOSTER, OH 44691 • ADMISSIONS: 330-263-2322 • FAX: 330-263-2621

STUDENTS SAY " . . . "

Academics

The College of Wooster is small, personable "tight-knit community" that offers "a truly stellar education" to those who attend. Mentoring is a huge focal point of Wooster's academics, and the "resources are endless" for those looking to take advantage of things like "numerous opportunities for research and internships." Independent study is a highlight of the undergraduate experience, and the school "teaches research and how to apply skills learned to the outside world." This "very open school" challenges its student to succeed both in and out of the class-room, and "the staff pushes [the college] to change with the times in the class-room and around the campus."

Professors at Wooster are "hidden gems" who are all "very passionate about their subjects" and their goal "to shape their students into lifelong learners." "It's as if your professor is your colleague on your quest for eternal knowledge," says a freshman. These intimate ties between student and professor are "what makes Wooster such an incredible place." "My professors, both past and present, know more than just my name," says a student. "My success is a product of my profes-sor's enthusiasm towards their subject matter and our futures," says another. The work may be "challenging," but it "teaches students how to write exceptionally," and there is "plenty of help from professors, TAs, [and] peer tutoring." "Collaborative work and experience" are stressed, and classes are set up "in a way that allows people to learn from their peers as well as their professors."

Research plays a "huge" role at Wooster, especially with senior year Independent Study, when students are given the opportunity to work with a faculty mentor on a project in any topic they are passionate about—and "they can do so much with it." The institution is also aware of the effort that students must put in to have success and "is realistic in its expectations for students' learning." "Wooster is a community of learners working together to help one another reach their full potential and goals," says a sophomore chemistry major.

Life

"The character of the campus community is friendly beyond measure" at this "dazzling" campus. People are usually "busy in the library doing homework or working on their Independent Studies," but everyone finds time for (typically multiple) extracurriculars, which "run the gamut of recreational pastimes." "We have just as many students in our music ensembles as we do that play sports," says a student. People enjoy using the weekends to relieve the stress of a rigorous academic schedule, and the majority enjoy "social drinking" at the fraternity or program houses, or going to the on-campus club called "the Underground" on Friday nights.

For those who choose not to party, there are "many other recreational activities for those who are not in sports or who do not enjoy drinking," and the college "is very good at bringing in entertainment," such as "comedians, professional music artists, and forum speakers which are all free to students ." A student run weekly flyer, *The Pot*, helps "keep students up to date on all of the campus events hap-pening." A lot of the time, though, "students will just hang out together and relax."

Student Body

"The life force of this school is really our fantastic student body," says a student. This "unparalleled" community is made up of "quite a range of people," but most are "quirky," "friendly," "open-minded," and "liberal." It's also a "very involved" student body ("school spirit is huge at Wooster"), so a typical COW kid "tends to be in a hodgepodge of sports, clubs, music groups, etc. that suit their fancy." There are "very few social cliques" and everyone is friendly and "willing to inter-act with one another." Students here are "very accepting of different personalities, beliefs, and ways of life."

FINANCIAL AID: 800-877-3688 • E-MAIL: ADMISSIONS@WOOSTER.EDU • WEBSITE: WWW.WOOSTER.EDU

THE PRINCETON REVIEW SAYS

Admissions

Very important factors considered include: GPA, rigor of secondary school record. *Important factors considered include:* Class rank, standardized test scores, application essay, extracurricular activities, recommendation(s), character/personal qualities, level of applicant's interest. *Other factors considered include:* First generation, geographical residence, interview, racial/ethnic status, state residency, talent/ability, volunteer work, work experience, alumni/ae relations. SAT or ACT required; ACT with Writing component recommended. TOEFL required of all international applicants. *Academic units required:* 4 English; 3 mathematics; 3 science; (2 science lab); 3 social studies; 2 foreign language; 1 academic elective.

Financial Aid

Students should submit: FAFSA, Institution's own financial aid form, CSS/Financial Aid PROFILE. The Princeton Review suggests that all financial aid forms be submitted as soon as possible after January 1. *Need-based scholarships/grants offered:* Federal Pell, SEOG, State scholarships/grants, private scholarships, the school's own gift aid. *Loan aid offered:* Direct Subsidized Stafford Loans, Direct Unsubsidized Stafford Loans, Direct PLUS loans, Federal Perkins Loans. Applicants will be notified of awards beginning 3/15. Federal Work-Study Program available. Institutional employment available. Off-campus job opportunities are good.

The Inside Word

The College of Wooster is a small, selective liberal arts school in a region of the country where there are quite a few small, selective liberal arts schools. For the most part, only solid students get past the gatekeepers here, and you should expect a thorough review of your application. Nevertheless, the admit rate is high. Stiff competition from similar institutions means the school will occasionally admit students who don't have stellar academic records.

THE SCHOOL SAYS "..."

From the Admissions Office

"The College of Wooster is America's premier college for mentored undergraduate research. Our mission is to graduate educated, not merely trained, people; to produce responsible, independent thinkers, rather than specialists in any given field. Our commitment to independence is especially evident in IS, the college's distinctive program in which every senior works one-to-one with a faculty mentor to complete a project in the major. IS comes from 'independent study,' but, in reality, it is an intellectual collaboration of the highest order and permits every student the freedom to pursue something in which he or she is passionately interested. IS is the centerpiece of an innovative curriculum. More than just the project itself, the culture that sustains IS—and, in turn, is sustained by IS—is an extraordinary college culture. The same attitudes of student initiative, openness, flexibility, and individual support enrich every aspect of Wooster's vital residential college life."

SELECTIVITY

Admissions Rating	92
# of applicants	5,583
% of applicants accepted	56
% of acceptees attending	18
# offered a place on the wait list	632
% accepting a place on wait list	14
% admitted from wait list	30
# of early decision applicants	117
% accepted early decision	71

FRESHMAN PROFILE

Range SAT Critical Reading	550–670
Range SAT Math	550–660
Range SAT Writing	560–650
Range ACT Composite	25–30
Minimum web-based TOEFL	81
Average HS GPA	3.66
% graduated top 10% of class	40
% graduated top 25% of class	73
% graduated top 50% of class	92

DEADLINES

Early decision	
Deadline	11/1
Notification	11/15
Early action	
Deadline	11/15
Notification	12/31
Regular	
Deadline	2/15
Notification	4/1
Nonfall registration?	Yes

FINANCIAL FACTS

Financial Aid Rating	92
Annual tuition	$41,300
Room and board	$9,920
Required fees	$380
Books and supplies	$1,000
% needy frosh rec. need-based scholarship or grant aid	97
% needy UG rec. need-based scholarship or grant aid	98
% needy frosh rec. non-need-based scholarship or grant aid	16
% needy UG rec. non-need-based scholarship or grant aid	11
% needy frosh rec. need-based self-help aid	80
% needy UG rec. need-based self-help aid	85
% frosh rec. any financial aid	99
% UG rec. any financial aid	98
% UG borrow to pay for school	61
Average cumulative indebtedness	$26,891
% frosh need fully met	55
% ugrads need fully met	54
Average % of frosh need met	95
Average % of ugrad need met	93

COLORADO COLLEGE

14 EAST CACHE LA POUDRE STREET, COLORADO SPRINGS, CO 80903 • ADMISSIONS: 719-389-6344 • FAX: 719-389-6816

CAMPUS LIFE

Quality of Life Rating	83
Fire Safety Rating	93
Green Rating	94
Type of school	Private
Affiliation	No Affiliation
Environment	Metropolis

STUDENTS

Total undergrad enrollment	2,025
% male/female	45/55
% from out of state	81
% frosh live on campus	100
% ugrads live on campus	76
# of fraternities (% ugrad men join)	3 (9)
# of sororities (% ugrad women join)	3 (11)
% African American	2
% Asian	4
% Caucasian	70
% Hispanic	9
% Native American	<1
% international	6
# of countries represented	57

SURVEY SAYS . . .

Students are happy
Students are friendly
Students environmentally aware
Lots of beer drinking
Hard liquor is popular
Intramural sports are popular

ACADEMICS

Academic Rating	96
% students returning for sophomore year	96
% students graduating within 4 years	79
% students graduating within 6 years	87
Calendar	Semester
Student/faculty ratio	10:1
Profs interesting rating	94
Profs accessible rating	89
Most classes have 10–19 students.	

MOST POPULAR MAJORS
biology; economics; sociology

STUDENTS SAY ". . ."

Academics

Colorado College has a unique program that breaks the school year into eight segments, or blocks, of three-and-a-half weeks each. Students take a single course during each block. And unsurprisingly, it's hugely popular. Students "love the block plan," calling it "an incredible way to learn" and a system that will "help you become who you always wanted to be, or someone better." All this is moved along by "incredible" professors who are "extremely smart in their academic area and make it really interesting and fun to learn more about what they do and know." In fact, one student suggests, professors are "the reason to go to CC." They are "absolutely amazing," some of the "most interesting people I have ever met, and they remember their students because classes aren't 700 people large." Classrooms are generally discussion-based, but that doesn't make this "academically rigorous" school easy. "Because you meet for three-plus hours a day, every day, there is no slacking," students note. "Professors hold students to a high standard, and most often, students rise to meet them."

Life

Intellectual activity, outdoor adventures, and learning on a "beautiful campus" are the rule of the day here. But it's with a reward in mind. CC students are "working hard as hell so we can party hard as hell." Make no mistake, however, education is most important to CC students. The school is a "constant sprint of academics, and during whatever free time we have, an intense pursuit of fun of all kinds." When it comes to activities, this college offers what you'd expect from a school in Colorado. Students "do outdoor activities such as skiing, snowboarding, and hiking," and "if it's a sunny day we read, tan, or play Frisbee, maybe slack line." It ranges from the sublime—"student body events" and "the many, many clubs and intramurals on campus"—to the ridiculous, such as "naked hot springs, river rafting, hiking the sand dunes," and "crazy athletic things (like the incline) along with normal athletic things like skiing and snowboarding." You don't even have to go far to find the outdoors. "There are millions of hikes around campus," one student points out, and "at around 3:00 P.M. when sports practices start, you are bound to see at least fifteen CC students run by you on the creek trail next to the fields."

Student Body

The "well-off, white, socially conscious" students of Colorado College tend to be "laid-back, intelligent, and very opinionated." Most of all, students are "really intense about all the things they care about," whether it is the outdoor adventure so popular among students here, environmental awareness, social causes, or just plain having fun. Students disinclined to seek adventure may find themselves in the minority, as most "are very outdoorsy and like to ski, rock climb, and camp." The "generally leftist" student body also enjoys "unique intellectual discussion," often centered around "community service or sustainability efforts," environmental causes, and more. That might lead one to believe pretentiousness is common, but students say this group is "super intelligent" yet "down-to-earth." That's because CC students know life is an adventure. The typical students are "invested in their education but also like to have fun." And when they throw themselves into something, whether for business in pleasure, they go all the way. "One of the big things we have in common is that we are all passionate about something. We exude passion and make sure to include that passion in all that we do at CC."

FINANCIAL AID: 719-389-6651 • E-MAIL: ADMISSION@COLORADOCOLLEGE.EDU • WEBSITE: WWW.COLORADOCOLLEGE.EDU

THE PRINCETON REVIEW SAYS

Admissions

Very important factors considered include: Rigor of secondary school record. *Important factors considered include:* Class rank, GPA, standardized test scores, application essay, extracurricular activities, interview, recommendation(s). *Other factors considered include:* First generation, racial/ethnic status, talent/ability, volunteer work, work experience, alumni/ae relations, character/personal qualities, level of applicant's interest, religious affiliation. SAT and SAT Subject Tests or ACT required for some; ACT with or without Writing component accepted. *Academic units required:* 4 English; . *Academic units recommended:* 4 English.

Financial Aid

Students should submit: FAFSA, CSS/Financial Aid PROFILE, Noncustodial PROFILE. Regular filing deadline is 3/1. The Princeton Review suggests that all financial aid forms be submitted as soon as possible after January 1. *Need-based scholarships/grants offered:* Federal Pell, SEOG, State scholarships/grants, private scholarships, the school's own gift aid. *Loan aid offered:* Direct Subsidized Stafford Loans, Direct Unsubsidized Stafford Loans, Direct PLUS loans, Federal Perkins Loans. Applicants will be notified of awards beginning 3/15. Federal Work-Study Program available. Institutional employment available. Off-campus job opportunities are good.

The Inside Word

Colorado College's block program means admissions officers are looking for some very specific traits in applicants, seeking students who are best suited for this nontraditional college structure. Students who have taken demanding course loads in high school will get their attention, especially if supplemented by activities and extracurriculars that go hand-in-hand with their in-class work. And more so than in many other schools, the application essay is genuinely important at CC. Strong writing skills and an interest in guiding the course of your own education are a must.

THE SCHOOL SAYS ". . ."

From the Admissions Office

"Students enter Colorado College for the opportunity to study intensely in small learning communities. Groups of students work closely with one another and faculty in discussion-based classes and hands-on labs. CC encourages a well-rounded education, combining the academic rigor of a traditional liberal arts college, with the focus and flexibility of the block plan. Rich programs in athletics, community service, student government, and the arts balance an engaged student life. The college encourages students to push themselves academically, and many continue their studies at the best graduate and professional schools in the nation. Because 81 percent of students study abroad while at CC, the college has been recognized as a national leader in international education. The block plan allows classes to incorporate field study into the curriculum, whether studying winter field ecology at the CC Cabin or Dante and Michelangelo in Italy. Its location at the base of the Rockies makes CC a great choice for students who enjoy backpacking, hiking, climbing, and skiing.

"Colorado College adopted a flexible testing policy, beginning with the 2015 class. We require that applicants submit either the SAT Reasoning Test or ACT or elect a third option, including three exams of the applicant's choice, chosen from a list of acceptable exams."

SELECTIVITY

Admissions Rating	97
# of applicants	5,780
% of applicants accepted	22
% of acceptees attending	41
# offered a place on the wait list	872
% accepting a place on wait list	30
% admitted from wait list	16
# of early decision applicants	610
% accepted early decision	33

FRESHMAN PROFILE

Range SAT Critical Reading	610–710
Range SAT Math	610–720
Range SAT Writing	620–700
Range ACT Composite	27–32
% graduated top 10% of class	66
% graduated top 25% of class	94
% graduated top 50% of class	99

DEADLINES

Early decision	
Deadline	11/15
Notification	12/15
Early action	
Deadline	11/15
Notification	12/20
Regular	
Priority	1/15
Deadline	1/15
Notification	4/1
Nonfall registration?	Yes

FINANCIAL FACTS

Financial Aid Rating	96
Annual tuition	$46,000
Room and board	$10,752
Required fees	$410
Books and supplies	$1,256
% needy frosh rec. need-based scholarship or grant aid	95
% needy UG rec. need-based scholarship or grant aid	94
% needy frosh rec. non-need-based scholarship or grant aid	58
% needy UG rec. non-need-based scholarship or grant aid	55
% needy frosh rec. need-based self-help aid	90
% needy UG rec. need-based self-help aid	89
% frosh rec. any financial aid	53
% UG rec. any financial aid	56
% UG borrow to pay for school	30
Average cumulative indebtedness	$20,566
% frosh need fully met	98
% ugrads need fully met	99
Average % of frosh need met	100
Average % of ugrad need met	100

COLORADO STATE UNIVERSITY

1062 CAMPUS DELIVERY, FORT COLLINS, CO 80523-1062 • ADMISSIONS: 970-491-6909 • FAX: 970-491-7799

CAMPUS LIFE

Quality of Life Rating	93
Fire Safety Rating	77
Green Rating	99
Type of school	Public
Affiliation	No Affiliation
Environment	City

STUDENTS

Total undergrad enrollment	22,565
% male/female	49/51
% from out of state	19
% frosh live on campus	97
% ugrads live on campus	25
# of fraternities (% ugrad men join)	21 (7)
# of sororities (% ugrad women join)	16 (11)
% African American	2
% Asian	2
% Caucasian	74
% Hispanic	10
% Native American	<1
% international	3
# of countries represented	77

SURVEY SAYS . . .

Political activism is unpopular or nonexistent
Students are happy
Students are friendly
Students get along with local community
Students love Fort Collins, CO
Great off-campus food
Athletic facilities are great
Student publications are popular

ACADEMICS

Academic Rating	77
% students returning for sophomore year	87
% students graduating within 4 years	38
% students graduating within 6 years	65
Calendar	Semester
Student/faculty ratio	17:1
Profs interesting rating	76
Profs accessible rating	76

Most classes have 10–19 students.
Most lab/discussion sessions have
20–29 students.

MOST POPULAR MAJORS

business administration and management;
biology; mechanical engineering

STUDENTS SAY " . . ."

Academics

Colorado State University provides its 30,000 students with numerous academic resources that guide them toward academic success. Even in light of its size, there is "open communication" between students and the administration, and "the institution strives to prepare students with hands-on experience while they are students so they can be prepared in the real world." This "hidden gem" offers a "wonderful education, friendly people, and awesome culture," along with "excellent" green efforts, a strong engineering program, and myriad research opportunities. CSU also cares about its students becoming active members in the community ("Social responsibility, ethics, and sustainability play a large part in our education at CSU," one student says), and the school is quite connected with its hometown of Fort Collins.

Most professors are "willing to help you however way they can"; their feedback is "honest and beneficial for students." "Our professors genuinely care, and they leave their legacy on campus by helping students network and make an impact in the community," says a student. For those in need of extra assistance, there is free tutoring offered for classes in the College of Natural Sciences and College of Liberal Arts. Even though it is a large campus, the school has "so many ways to meet people and create communities on campus that really help you succeed." Green is god here; no matter what aspect of the university you look at, "everyone is concerned with how their actions affect the environment," and "many majors look toward educating their students about job opportunities in the green job force." As for the working world, "an education at CSU is valued and therefore opens up many career opportunities." The college also "does a great job or bringing resources to campus through speakers, panels, and career fairs."

Life

"People enjoy each other here; they enjoy life here." "Bike-friendly" Fort Collins offers a "big-city, small-town life that is green but not pretentious." When everyone is done with the various meetings they have that evening, they "most likely enjoy some great food in our Old Town then head to the nice nightlife in the area." "Fort Collins is such a fun town with fabulous food and many things to do. There is always something to do around here: go to a concert, go shopping, spend a day in the mountains," says a student. "Living in Colorado encourages us to be better students so we can go outside and enjoy why we live in this beautiful state." People are "definitely more outdoors-oriented"; year-round sports are expected—on the weekends "lots of people will rock-climb, trail-run, bike, ski, snowboard, or ice-climb"—and "the gym is always busy." Once in a while, students go to Denver or Boulder "just to try something new," such as malls, the aquarium, or attending sports games—though CSU football gets some criticism from students due to its performance. Basically, life is "usually hectic, yet productive."

Student Body

CSU is "probably the friendliest campus I visited," according to many students. Rams are "chill and outgoing," "well-rounded, physically fit," and "place an emphasis on grades." They are "laid-back but serious about studies," and they "want to succeed, but also like to have fun outside of class." Most are "generally very involved either in the campus community or the Fort Collins community whether it is with service, jobs, or community events." Everyone here "finds their comfort zone in some way or another, and it seems to work for everyone."

COLORADO STATE UNIVERSITY

FINANCIAL AID: 970-491-6321 • E-MAIL: ADMISSIONS@COLOSTATE.EDU • WEBSITE: WWW.COLOSTATE.EDU

THE PRINCETON REVIEW SAYS

Admissions

Very important factors considered include: GPA, rigor of secondary school record. *Important factors considered include:* Class rank, standardized test scores, application essay, recommendation(s). *Other factors considered include:* Extracurricular activities, first generation, geographical residence, talent/ability, volunteer work, work experience, alumni/ae relations, character/personal qualities. SAT or ACT required; ACT with or without Writing component accepted. TOEFL required of all international applicants. *Academic units required:* 4 English; 4 mathematics; 3 science; (2 science lab); 2 social studies; 1 foreign language; 1 history; 2 academic electives. *Academic units recommended:* 4 English; 4 mathematics; 3 science; (2 science lab); 2 social studies; 2 foreign language; 1 history; 2 academic electives.

Financial Aid

Students should submit: FAFSA. The Princeton Review suggests that all financial aid forms be submitted as soon as possible after January 1. *Need-based scholarships/grants offered:* Federal Pell, SEOG, State scholarships/grants, private scholarships, the school's own gift aid. *Loan aid offered:* Direct Subsidized Stafford Loans, Direct Unsubsidized Stafford Loans, Direct PLUS loans, Federal Perkins Loans. Federal Work-Study Program available. Institutional employment available. Off-campus job opportunities are excellent.

The Inside Word

Colorado State University admits about nine out of ten applicants; the primary task of its admissions office is to determine who not to admit. Certain majors and programs are more competitive and impose additional admissions qualifications. Art and design programs, for example, require a portfolio review; programs in art, biomedical sciences, business, computer science, engineering, and technical journalism impose higher GPA and standardized test score floors than the school's other programs.

THE SCHOOL SAYS "..."

From the Admissions Office

"As one of the nation's premier research universities, Colorado State offers more than 150 undergraduate programs of study in eight colleges. Students come here from fifty states and eighty-five countries, and they appreciate the quality and breadth of the university's academic offerings. But Colorado State is more than just a place where students can take their scholarship to the highest level. It's also a place where they can gain invaluable experience in the fields of their choice, whether they're immersing themselves in professional internships, studying on the other side of the globe or teaming up with faculty on groundbreaking research projects. In addition to an outstanding experiential learning environment, Colorado State students enjoy a sense of community that's unusual for a large university. They develop meaningful relationships with faculty members who bring out their best work, and they live and learn with diverse peers who value their ideas and expand their perspectives. These types of connections lead to countless opportunities for social networking and professional accomplishments. By the time our students graduate from Colorado State, they have the knowledge, practical experience, and interpersonal skills they need to make a significant contribution to their world.

"Although academic performance is a primary factor in admissions decisions, Colorado State's holistic review process also recognizes personal qualities and experiences that have the potential to enrich the university and the Fort Collins community. To apply, students may submit the Common Application or the Colorado State University application for admission."

SELECTIVITY

Admissions Rating	78
# of applicants	17,970
% of applicants accepted	77
% of acceptees attending	32

FRESHMAN PROFILE

Range SAT Critical Reading	510–620
Range SAT Math	510–630
Range ACT Composite	22–27
Minimum paper TOEFL	450
Minimum web-based TOEFL	45
Average HS GPA	3.61
% graduated top 10% of class	22
% graduated top 25% of class	52
% graduated top 50% of class	88

DEADLINES

Early action	
Deadline	12/1
Notification	2/1
Regular	
Priority	2/1
Deadline	2/1
Nonfall registration?	Yes

APPLICANTS ALSO LOOK AT AND OFTEN PREFER

Arizona State University; University of Colorado—Boulder; University of Denver; University of Oregon; University of Arizona

FINANCIAL FACTS

Financial Aid Rating	70
Annual in-state tuition	$7,494
Annual out-of-state tuition	$23,347
Room and board	$10,776
Required fees	$1,819
Books and supplies	$1,126
% needy frosh rec. need-based scholarship or grant aid	72
% needy UG rec. need-based scholarship or grant aid	69
% needy frosh rec. non-need-based scholarship or grant aid	0
% needy UG rec. non-need-based scholarship or grant aid	0
% needy frosh rec. need-based self-help aid	68
% needy UG rec. need-based self-help aid	75
% frosh rec. any financial aid	70
% UG rec. any financial aid	71
% UG borrow to pay for school	54
Average cumulative indebtedness	$23,726
% frosh need fully met	12
% ugrads need fully met	9
Average % of frosh need met	71
Average % of ugrad need met	67

COLUMBIA UNIVERSITY

212 HAMILTON HALL MC 2807, NEW YORK, NY 10027 • ADMISSIONS: 212-854-2522 • FAX: 212-894-1209

CAMPUS LIFE

Quality of Life Rating	91
Fire Safety Rating	61
Green Rating	99
Type of school	Private
Affiliation	No Affiliation
Environment	Metropolis

STUDENTS

Total undergrad enrollment	6,084
% male/female	52/48
% from out of state	77
% frosh from public high school	57
% frosh live on campus	100
% ugrads live on campus	94
# of fraternities	17
# of sororities	11
% African American	11
% Asian	22
% Caucasian	36
% Hispanic	13
% Native American	2
% international	13
# of countries represented	97

SURVEY SAYS . . .

Easy to get around campus
Great library
Students love New York, NY
Great off-campus food
Campus feels safe
Students are happy
Student publications are popular
Political activism is popular

ACADEMICS

Academic Rating	93
% students returning for sophomore year	99
% students graduating within 4 years	88
% students graduating within 6 years	96
Calendar	Semester
Student/faculty ratio	6:1
Profs interesting rating	76
Profs accessible rating	76

Most classes have students.

MOST POPULAR MAJORS

political science; English language
and literature; engineering

STUDENTS SAY "..."

Academics

At Columbia, you are in a "fantastic city" where "everyone loves learning." "Columbia should be considered by students who are willing to develop a breadth of knowledge before specializing, as it actively encourages intellectualism and academic excellence in every form." The fact that this "great" school is located "in the heart of New York City" is a big draw for the majority of Columbia University students. "You can't beat the location." It "offers unlimited resources." "There are many opportunities, and it is such a diverse community of unique individuals." The "highly prestigious name" is also a draw for students to gain "access to great liberal arts academics while still attaining a technical degree." As one student explains, "I get to take everything from art history to music to physics, even though I'm majoring in something completely different." Many students note the strength of the school's teachings, which "value intellectualism over single-minded preprofessionalism, and the Core Curriculum ensures that students can understand and analyze the foundations of Western thought and contemporary society." For the most part, classes are "thought-provoking," and "professors are invested in the students and are extremely accessible." One student complains, "I don't like the fact that I have graduate students teaching some of my intro classes." Another student confesses, "Not every class has been a home run, but the ones that have been truly knock it out of the park." Good grades take some hard work. "Although it is difficult to get an A, it is definitely not uncommon." There is room for improvement in dealing with administration. "The red tape is awful, but the individual employees are all wonderful." To stay aligned with today's fast-growing technological needs, Columbia "should probably get better Wi-Fi Internet access in the library and dorms."

Life

Life at Columbia University has "boundless opportunities" both on and off campus. New York City is "vibrant" and "exciting" and "is the best resource ever. There's always something to do, and all you have to do is get on the [subway]." Among other things, students at Columbia can "take advantage of the arts programs in that they get discounted tickets to Broadway shows, operas, and concerts." As much as "people love to take advantage of the activities in the city," they "are also very passionate about events on campus. Performances by student groups are very popular, and it is also very common to just hang out in a suite with a group of friends watching movies and playing board games!" The "huge" campus also offers an "innumerable amount of sports games" as well as a satisfactory amount of parties, "either in dorms or at local bars." It is "by no means a party school, though; most people don't go out on week nights." For many, "it is the perfect balance of a social and academic life."

Student Body

Students describe Columbia as "a school made up of smart, witty, ironic, slightly cynical people." "The average Columbia student also has a wide range of interests. This is not the type of school where science majors are only interested in science or humanities majors are only interested in the humanities." It's a school where "students tend to be globally aware and academically strong; but there are extremes in both directions." "There is no one way to be a Columbian" because "students fit in by being unique and outstanding in something." Here, "being normal is frowned upon." Coming from varying "backgrounds, communities, and cultures," students at Columbia seem united in their "intellectual curiosity and desire to do something positive with their education." The "unparalleled" student body "encompasses multiple political views." "Students fit in by learning to accept that they are different and that others may disagree with them on any number of issues." One student opines, "Because the right-wing portion of the student body is a minority, it is also more outspoken and thus pretty visible on campus." Another comments, "Being religious and/or conservative on this campus is tough." "In terms of socioeconomic status, ethnicity, religion, age, and sexual preference, this school has everything. You will never feel as if you don't belong." A student sums up the general thought by saying, "We fit in because of our diversity."

FINANCIAL AID: 212-854-3711 • WEBSITE: WWW.STUDENTAFFAIRS.COLUMBIA.EDU/ADMISSIONS

THE PRINCETON REVIEW SAYS

Admissions

Very important factors considered include: Class rank, GPA, rigor of secondary school record, standardized test scores, application essay, first generation, recommendation(s), character/personal qualities, level of applicant's interest. *Important factors considered include:* Extracurricular activities, talent/ability. *Other factors considered include:* Geographical residence, interview, racial/ethnic status, volunteer work, work experience, alumni/ae relations. SAT and SAT Subject Tests or ACT required; ACT with Writing component required. TOEFL required of all international applicants. *Academic units recommended:* 4 English; 4 mathematics; 4 science; (4 science lab); 4 foreign language; 4 history; 4 academic electives.

Financial Aid

Students should submit: FAFSA, CSS/Financial Aid PROFILE, Noncustodial PROFILE. Regular filing deadline is 3/1. The Princeton Review suggests that all financial aid forms be submitted as soon as possible after January 1. *Need-based scholarships/grants offered:* Federal Pell, SEOG, State scholarships/grants, private scholarships, the school's own gift aid. *Loan aid offered:* Direct Subsidized Stafford Loans, Direct Unsubsidized Stafford Loans, Direct PLUS loans, Federal Perkins Loans, College/university loans from institutional funds. Applicants will be notified of awards beginning 4/1. Federal Work-Study Program available. Institutional employment available. Off-campus job opportunities are excellent.

The Inside Word

There's no magic formula or pattern to guide students who are seeking admission to Columbia University. Excellent grades in rigorous classes may not be enough, and many great candidates are rejected each year. Admissions officers take a holistic approach to evaluating applications, and they pay extra attention to personal accomplishments in non-academic activities as they look to build a diverse class that will greatly contribute to the university.

THE SCHOOL SAYS "..."

From the Admissions Office

"Columbia maintains an intimate college campus within one of the world's most vibrant cities. After a day exploring New York City you come home to a traditional college campus within an intimate neighborhood. Nobel Prize–winning professors will challenge you in class discussions and meet one-on-one afterward. The Core Curriculum attracts intensely free-minded scholars, and connects all undergraduates. Science and engineering students pursue cutting-edge research in world-class laboratories with faculty members at the forefront of scientific discovery. Classroom discussions are only the beginning of your education. Ideas spill out from the classrooms, electrifying the campus and Morningside Heights. Friendships formed in the residence halls solidify during a game of Frisbee on the South Lawn or over bagels on the steps of Low Library. From your first day on campus, you will be part of our diverse community.

"Columbia offers extensive need-based financial aid and meets the full need of every student admitted as a first-year with grants instead of loans. Parents with calculated incomes below $60,000 are not expected to contribute any income or assets to tuition, room, board and mandatory fees and families with calculated incomes between $60,000 and $100,000 and with typical assets have a significantly reduced contribution. Parents earning over $100,000 can still qualify for significant financial aid. To support students pursuing study abroad, research, internships and community service opportunities, Columbia offers the opportunity to apply for additional funding and exemptions from academic year and summer work expectations. A commitment to diversity—of every kind—is a long-standing Columbia hallmark. We believe cost should not be a barrier to pursuing your educational dreams."

SELECTIVITY

Admissions Rating	99
# of applicants	33,531
% of applicants accepted	7
% of acceptees attending	61
# of early decision applicants	3,126

FRESHMAN PROFILE

Range SAT Critical Reading	700–780
Range SAT Math	700–790
Range SAT Writing	690–780
Range ACT Composite	32–34
Minimum paper TOEFL	600
Minimum web-based TOEFL	250

DEADLINES

Early decision	
Deadline	11/1
Notification	12/15
Regular	
Deadline	1/1
Notification	4/1
Nonfall registration?	No

APPLICANTS ALSO LOOK AT AND OFTEN PREFER

Massachusetts Institute of Technology; Yale University; Stanford University; Harvard College

AND SOMETIMES PREFER

University of Pennsylvania; Princeton University

AND RARELY PREFER

Brown University; Cornell University; Dartmouth College; New York University

FINANCIAL FACTS

Financial Aid Rating	96
Annual tuition	$46,846
Room and board	$11,978
Required fees	$2,813
Books and supplies	$3,028
% needy frosh rec. need-based scholarship or grant aid	95
% needy UG rec. need-based scholarship or grant aid	96
% needy frosh rec. non-need-based scholarship or grant aid	1
% needy UG rec. non-need-based scholarship or grant aid	1
% needy frosh rec. need-based self-help aid	76
% needy UG rec. need-based self-help aid	85
% frosh need fully met	100
% ugrads need fully met	100
Average % of frosh need met	100
Average % of ugrad need met	100

CONNECTICUT COLLEGE

270 MOHEGAN AVENUE, NEW LONDON, CT 06320 • ADMISSIONS: 860-439-2200 • FAX: 860-439-4301

STUDENTS SAY "..."

Academics
Located in eastern Connecticut, the picturesque Connecticut College is a classic private New England liberal arts school that shows a "great commitment to being sustainable, to promoting community service, and to learning." The college provides "great academic, extracurricular, and athletic opportunities to all students," and the "beloved" honor code makes for "a close-knit, supportive community." A strong focus on interdisciplinary education, small classes, and self-scheduled exams give students the autonomy to truly tailor their learning around their interests. The academics are "rigorous but continuously relevant, interesting, and enlightening." Most classes are discussion-based, which "allows students to express their own opinions while hearing from their fellow students and professors." Though there are a few bad apples, most professors are always accessible ("especially outside of their office hours") and are "constantly bringing learning outside of the classroom, whether it be within a residence hall, a restaurant, museum, or gallery downtown, or within their own homes." "All of my professors are incredibly engaging and obviously here to excite students about their studies," says a student. Other high points include the "approachability of the staff," excellent career office and internship opportunities, and strong residential programs and academic centers that "help students with a myriad of topics." Connecticut College assures that no student will go through school with "your typical major/minor pairing"; with certificate programs, tons of research opportunities, independent studies and more, every student "has a completely unique and entirely interdisciplinary experience here."

Life
"Life as a student is all about balancing your school work with your extracurricular activities and choosing which events you want to attend," says one. The residential programs lay a great groundwork for student life, and much of the fun on campus "is through social events through the dorms." It helps that "everyone knows one another—between offices, custodial staff, campus safety, and students." There are a wide range of activities to get involved with (everything from athletics, to arts, to activism, to community service, etc.), as well as "numerous faculty-led discussions and speakers every week." Most activities that take place on campus make it "lively and interesting." The campus as a whole is "very friendly, and you are always surrounded by familiar faces," though the relationship with the town of New London is "something that can always be improved upon." For fun, students "attend each others' events, attend social functions in the student center, grab some coffee at one of our coffee shops, and generally hang out with each other." The library is "a very social place during the week," and though students work very hard, they "know how to have a good time on the weekends"—every Saturday there is a well-attended dance put on by the Student Activities Council. Day trips to Boston and New York are also common.

Student Body
Many students at Conn are generally "smart, probably upper-class, well-dressed, and white," though the school "embraces diversity." The common theme among all Conn students in "their active involvement both on campus and off and their desire to be challenged is all aspects of their educations." Students fit in by "showing an interest in their studies, but also carrying on an active social life." It is fairly easy to find one's niche within the community, and "while it might take a semester to become adjusted, there are many groups, teams, and other resources...that help freshmen find a place here."

FINANCIAL AID: 860-439-2058 • E-MAIL: ADMISSION@CONNCOLL.EDU • WEBSITE: WWW.CONNCOLL.EDU

THE PRINCETON REVIEW SAYS

Admissions

Very important factors considered include: Class rank, GPA, rigor of secondary school record, character/personal qualities. *Important factors considered include:* Application essay, extracurricular activities, interview, racial/ethnic status, recommendation(s), talent/ability, volunteer work, work experience. *Other factors considered include:* Standardized test scores, first generation, geographical residence, state residency, alumni/ae relations, level of applicant's interest, religious affiliation. SAT and SAT Subject Tests or ACT considered if submitted; ACT with or without Writing component accepted. TOEFL required of all international applicants. *Academic units required:*

Financial Aid

Students should submit: FAFSA, CSS/Financial Aid PROFILE, Noncustodial PROFILE. Regular filing deadline is 2/1. The Princeton Review suggests that all financial aid forms be submitted as soon as possible after January 1. *Need-based scholarships/grants offered:* Federal Pell, SEOG, State scholarships/grants, the school's own gift aid. *Loan aid offered:* Direct Subsidized Stafford Loans, Direct Unsubsidized Stafford Loans, Direct PLUS loans, Federal Perkins Loans. Applicants will be notified of awards beginning 4/1. Federal Work-Study Program available. Institutional employment available. Off-campus job opportunities are good.

The Inside Word

Connecticut College is the archetypal selective New England college, and admissions officers are judicious in their decisions. Competitive applicants will have pursued a demanding course load in high school. Admissions officers look for students who are curious and who thrive in challenging academic environments. Since Connecticut College has a close-knit community, personal qualities are also closely evaluated, and interviews are important.

THE SCHOOL SAYS "..."

From the Admissions Office

"Nearly 1,900 students from more than forty states and seventy countries bring their diverse talents, experiences and ambitions to a beautiful hilltop campus overlooking Long Island Sound. Here they find intellectual challenge, a community that supports student initiative, and a unique internship program that sets the stage for life after college.

"Connecticut College has all the hallmarks of the best liberal arts colleges: small classes; stellar teaching; close faculty-student relationships; more than 40 majors in the arts, sciences, humanities and social sciences; and plentiful co-curricular activities.

"What sets this college apart is its active, outward-focused vision of 'liberal arts in action.' Interdisciplinary classes, programs, centers and majors foster critical thinking and problem solving. Students connect theory to the real world via community service, community learning, student-faculty research, international experiences and campus leadership. More than half of students study away during their four years, and more than 70 percent do a College-funded summer internship in the United States or abroad. Preparation for the internship begins in the first year, and, for many recent graduates, shapes job, grad school and career choices.

"Liberal arts in action also means living under a ninety-two-year-old Honor Code, with self-scheduled exams, a student-run Honor Council, and a student voice in campus decision making. The campus community is close and supportive; there is no Greek life. About 30 percent of students are varsity athletes competing in the New England Small College Athletic Conference (NCAA Division III) with Amherst, Bates, Bowdoin, Colby, Hamilton, Middlebury, Trinity, Tufts, Wesleyan and Williams."

SELECTIVITY

Admissions Rating	96
# of applicants	4,837
% of applicants accepted	36
% of acceptees attending	29
# offered a place on the wait list	1,152
% accepting a place on wait list	18
% admitted from wait list	15
# of early decision applicants	416
% accepted early decision	64

FRESHMAN PROFILE

Range SAT Critical Reading	620–710
Range SAT Math	615–700
Range SAT Writing	640–725
Range ACT Composite	28–31
Minimum paper TOEFL	600
Minimum web-based TOEFL	250
% graduated top 10% of class	56
% graduated top 25% of class	95
% graduated top 50% of class	100

DEADLINES

Early decision	
Deadline	11/15
Notification	12/15
Regular	
Deadline	1/1
Notification	3/31
Nonfall registration?	No

APPLICANTS ALSO LOOK AT AND OFTEN PREFER

Bates College; Bowdoin College; Colby College; Hamilton College; Middlebury College; Tufts University; Vassar College; Wesleyan University

AND SOMETIMES PREFER

Trinity College (CT)

AND RARELY PREFER

Skidmore College

FINANCIAL FACTS

Financial Aid Rating	95
Annual tuition	$45,765
Room and board	$12,695
Required fees	$320
Books and supplies	$1,000
% needy frosh rec. need-based scholarship or grant aid	93
% needy UG rec. need-based scholarship or grant aid	94
% needy frosh rec. non-need-based scholarship or grant aid	0
% needy UG rec. non-need-based scholarship or grant aid	0
% needy frosh rec. need-based self-help aid	90
% needy UG rec. need-based self-help aid	89
% frosh rec. any financial aid	48
% UG rec. any financial aid	50
% UG borrow to pay for school	50
Average cumulative indebtedness	$23,558
% frosh need fully met	100
% ugrads need fully met	100
Average % of frosh need met	100
Average % of ugrad need met	100

THE COOPER UNION FOR THE ADVANCEMENT OF SCIENCE AND ART

30 COOPER SQUARE, NEW YORK, NY 10003 • ADMISSIONS: 212-353-4120 • FAX: 212-353-4342

STUDENTS SAY "..."

Academics

Gifted students clamor for a spot at The Cooper Union for the Advancement of Science and Art. The universal "full-tuition scholarships" have been one of the school's major selling points. However, the rigorous and "very reputable" academic programs are the main reason to attend this unique New York City college. "An institution of the highest caliber," Cooper Union has a narrow academic focus, conferring degrees only in fine arts, architecture, and engineering. Cooper Union's "engineering program is considered one of the best in the nation"; there are "plenty of opportunities for independent study in your field," and "lab facilities are incredible." Individual learning is emphasized, and the student-to-teacher ratio is excellent: "The freshman year courses have about twenty to twenty-five students in each, while the courses in later years have as few as five students in a class." When it comes to the teaching staff, adjunct faculty gets mixed reviews, while "full-time professors are really great. They have great experience, like what they do, like the students, [and] are really accessible and happy to help." "Professors vary widely in their teaching methods"; yet most are "very accessible, friendly, [and] expect a high level of quality for work." Unfortunately, if you don't like your instructor, you're out of luck because "there are only a few professors in each department, meaning students have the same professor over and over again."

Life

Located in New York City's East Village, Cooper Union offers "an opportunity to live in one of the most energetic and dynamic cities in the world." Unfortunately, "There isn't time for anything other than your classes" at Cooper Union. To meet the school's high academic demands and "spine-breaking workload," "the typical schedule for any Cooper student who hopes to survive is go to class, study and do homework, sleep for a few hours, and repeat." At Cooper Union, there are few Greek organizations, no dormitories for upperclassmen, and "no recreational facilities or cafeterias on campus." Students are the first to admit that "the social life is rather limited" and "weekends are more often spent in the lab or library than at parties." However, those who make time for a little recreation say, "There are plenty of parties happening in the Village and at NYU that students can attend"— not to mention, plenty of "comedy clubs, movies, bowling, lounges, and bars" throughout New York City. Art students, though also self-professed workaholics, may also make time to "go to art openings of fellow students, professors, and friends, party, [or] play a lot of music." However, most students say that when they "sacrifice a few hours of sleep to do something enjoyable, it usually includes just hanging out with friends."

Student Body

Cooper Union's campus is largely comprised of "three distinct types of students," each delineated by major field: art, architecture, and engineering. Typical art students are "alternative kids" with the "just-rolled-out-of-bed look" while future architects are "very sleek" and fashionable, but "never leave their studio." The more "socially awkward" engineers are also largely like minds. One says, "If you have some obscure technological passion, someone in the engineering school is guaranteed to be as passionate." According to some, "Artists hang out with artists, engineers with engineers, architects with architects." However, most Cooper Union students laugh off stereotypes, telling us the school is filled with "very unique, interesting people," eager to learn and cross-pollinate between departments. A current student reassures us, "Of course, the odds are high that a group of electrical engineers will end up talking about video games, but there seems to be a broad spectrum of personalities present here." Across the board, students in every major are serious about their studies, and most of Cooper's selective admits are "super intelligent, super creative, and/or just super hardworking."

THE COOPER UNION FOR THE ADVANCEMENT OF SCIENCE AND ART

FINANCIAL AID: 212-353-4130 • E-MAIL: ADMISSIONS@COOPER.EDU • WEBSITE: WWW.COOPER.EDU

THE PRINCETON REVIEW SAYS

Admissions

Very important factors considered include: GPA, rigor of secondary school record, standardized test scores, talent/ability, level of applicant's interest. *Important factors considered include:* Application essay, extracurricular activities, character/personal qualities. *Other factors considered include:* Class rank, first generation, interview, racial/ethnic status, recommendation(s), volunteer work, work experience. SAT or ACT required; SAT and SAT Subject Tests or ACT required for some; ACT with Writing component recommended. TOEFL required of all international applicants. *Academic units required:* 4 English; 1 mathematics; 1 science; 1 social studies; 1 history; 8 academic electives. *Academic units recommended:* 4 English; 4 mathematics; 4 science; (3 science lab); 4 social studies; 2 foreign language.

Financial Aid

Students should submit: FAFSA, CSS/Financial Aid PROFILE. Regular filing deadline is 6/1. The Princeton Review suggests that all financial aid forms be submitted as soon as possible after January 1. *Need-based scholarships/grants offered:* Federal Pell, SEOG, State scholarships/grants, private scholarships, the school's own gift aid. *Loan aid offered:* Direct Subsidized Stafford Loans, Direct Unsubsidized Stafford Loans, Direct PLUS loans, Federal Perkins Loans, College/university loans from institutional funds. Applicants will be notified of awards beginning 6/1. Federal Work-Study Program available. Institutional employment available. Off-campus job opportunities are excellent.

The Inside Word

The admission rate to Cooper Union is extremely competitive. In recent years, only about 8 percent of applicants have been accepted to the undergraduate program. The fine arts (BFA) program is usually the most competitive of Cooper's three schools, though all admits must be academically accomplished and top of their high school class. Depending on whether you plan to pursue engineering, art, or architecture, admissions requirements and applications deadlines vary.

THE SCHOOL SAYS " . . ."

From the Admissions Office

"Each of Cooper Union's three schools, architecture, art, and engineering, adheres strongly to preparation for its profession and is committed to a problem-solving philosophy of education in a unique, scholarly environment. A rigorous curriculum and group projects reinforce this unique atmosphere in higher education and contribute to a strong sense of community and identity in each school. With McSorley's Ale House and the Joseph Papp Public Theatre nearby, Cooper Union remains at the heart of the city's tradition of free speech, enlightenment, and entertainment. Cooper's Great Hall has hosted national leaders, from Abraham Lincoln to Booker T. Washington, from Mark Twain to Samuel Gompers, from Susan B. Anthony to Betty Friedan, and more recently, President Bill Clinton and President Barack Obama.

"In fall of 2009, we opened the doors of our new academic building. Designed by Pritzker Prize–winning architect, Thom Mayne, the new building was designed to enhance and encourage more interaction between students in all three schools.

"We're seeking students who have a passion to study our professional programs. Cooper Union students are independent thinkers, following the beat of their own drum. Many of our graduates become world-class leaders in the disciplines of architecture, fine arts, design, and engineering.

"For art and architecture applicants, SAT scores are considered after the home test and portfolio work. For engineering applicants, high school grades and the SAT and SAT Subject Test scores are the most important factors considered in admissions decisions. Currently, we do not use the writing section of the SAT to assist in making admissions decisions. We expect to revisit that policy as more data is available in the near future."

SELECTIVITY

Admissions Rating	98
# of applicants	3,193
% of applicants accepted	8
% of acceptees attending	75
# offered a place on the wait list	135
% accepting a place on wait list	89
% admitted from wait list	10
# of early decision applicants	666
% accepted early decision	15

FRESHMAN PROFILE

Range SAT Critical Reading	610–710
Range SAT Math	610–780
Range SAT Writing	610–730
Range ACT Composite	28–33
Minimum paper TOEFL	600
Minimum web-based TOEFL	250
Average HS GPA	3.60
% graduated top 10% of class	92
% graduated top 25% of class	95
% graduated top 50% of class	96

DEADLINES

Early decision	
Deadline	12/1
Notification	12/23
Regular	
Priority	12/1
Deadline	1/1
Notification	4/1
Nonfall registration?	No

APPLICANTS ALSO LOOK AT AND OFTEN PREFER
Columbia University; Cornell University; Massachusetts Institute of Technology

AND SOMETIMES PREFER
Carnegie Mellon University; Duke University

AND RARELY PREFER
Rochester Institute of Technology

FINANCIAL FACTS

Financial Aid Rating	92
Annual tuition	$39,600
Room and board	$15,000
Required fees	$1,800
Books and supplies	$1,600
% needy frosh rec. need-based scholarship or grant aid	100
% needy UG rec. need-based scholarship or grant aid	100
% needy frosh rec. non-need-based scholarship or grant aid	100
% needy UG rec. non-need-based scholarship or grant aid	100
% needy frosh rec. need-based self-help aid	81
% needy UG rec. need-based self-help aid	82
% frosh rec. any financial aid	100
% UG rec. any financial aid	100
% UG borrow to pay for school	27
Average cumulative indebtedness	$16,640
% frosh need fully met	81
% ugrads need fully met	57
Average % of frosh need met	92
Average % of ugrad need met	91

CORNELL COLLEGE

600 FIRST STREET SW, MOUNT VERNON, IA 52314-1098 • ADMISSIONS: 319-895-4215 • FAX: 319-895-4451

CAMPUS LIFE

Quality of Life Rating	73
Fire Safety Rating	72
Green Rating	70
Type of school	Private
Affiliation	Methodist
Environment	Rural

STUDENTS

Total undergrad enrollment	1,122
% male/female	45/55
% from out of state	82
% frosh live on campus	100
% ugrads live on campus	92
# of fraternities (% ugrad men join)	7 (25)
# of sororities (% ugrad women join)	8 (33)
% African American	5
% Asian	3
% Caucasian	65
% Hispanic	13
% Native American	1
% international	6
# of countries represented	17

SURVEY SAYS . . .

Lots of beer drinking
No one cheats
Students are friendly
Students get along with local community
Theater is popular

ACADEMICS

Academic Rating	92
% students returning for sophomore year	83
% students graduating within 4 years	64
% students graduating within 6 years	67
Calendar	Block
Student/faculty ratio	11:1
Profs interesting rating	90
Profs accessible rating	96

Most classes have 10–19 students.

MOST POPULAR MAJORS
economics; psychology; biochemistry

STUDENTS SAY ". . ."

Academics

Cornell College, a small liberal arts school in Iowa, employs a unique one-course-at-a-time program, allowing students to focus on just one course (or "block") each month, providing an "intense, thorough, and complete immersion." Though students agree that this "series of experiences" "doesn't give you any time to think about anything but the class you're in right then," it allows for personalized curricula design, and areas like the humanities "work perfectly with the block plan." Students also "always know when to find people," which makes it easy to get together. Some classes may not be the most challenging, but "upper-level courses are very engaging and fulfilling." "You could have hours and hours of homework one block and practically none the next," says a student. The block plan makes it very easy to gain off-campus field experience or do international study, and it's "easier to try off-campus opportunities." Administration is generally "excellent at taking a personal interest in each student," though some note, "There is not much transparency at the administrative level," which can be "out of touch" at times. The registrar is "the most dreaded office on campus," with residence life a close second. On the classroom side, professors "know how to motivate and encourage their students," and though "you may get a bad apple maybe once a year," they're "not only knowledgeable but dedicated." "The personal attention you can receive from any given professor, if you seek them out, is especially rewarding," says a student. All in all, students love the block structure and the sense of community it creates, as "no matter what it is you may want to do, you can find someone to do it with you." One student claims he "cannot imagine learning any other way."

Life

Since Cornell is very campus-focused (you "rarely see students venture past the edge of campus"), the school makes sure there's a large variety of campus organizations and "many events going on almost every weekend." Though there's definitely a "small-town quiet," Cedar Rapids and Iowa City are both only a twenty-minute drive away, and "ice climbing, rock-climbing, paddling, and hiking" are popular outdoor pastimes. It's also "fairly easy to start up a new club or group." In addition, the school provides winter and spring breaks as well as five "block breaks," which last four and a half days and give students the opportunity to travel, go skiing or camping, and so on. The cold weather can cause problems here, in both a locked-in feel and the possibility for accidents, and students are encouraged to "bring snow boots!" Many here tend to have a love-hate relationship with sports; while athletics are a huge boon, "the athletes and the non-athletes are seldom friends." Much like the curriculum, lunchtimes are pretty unique, and students all eat in a common cafeteria, naturally falling into a somewhat "high school" habit of eating at the same tables every day. Most people stay on campus for entertainment and socializing, "creating a cohesive community." Parties do take place on weekends, and "drinking is popular on campus but never forced," but in general, "people are more interested in just having a good conversation with their peers."

Student Body

There's "a great diversity of interests" in people who attend Cornell, and the "super busy" students have a hard time defining a more common characteristic than the fact that almost all are driven and involved. Some division into typical groups does occur—"the cafeteria design and Greek life are very conducive to this problem"—but "even group to group there is always mingling because you never know who will be in your next class." Since the classes are so small and "you see the same people four hours a day for three and a half weeks," people are generally accepting, and "you have to be really, really strange here to stick out." As one freshman says, "The only intolerance I've seen is toward the consistently indolent."

FINANCIAL AID: 319-895-4216 • E-MAIL: ADMISSIONS@CORNELLCOLLEGE.EDU • WEBSITE: WWW.CORNELLCOLLEGE.EDU

THE PRINCETON REVIEW SAYS

Admissions

Very important factors considered include: GPA, rigor of secondary school record, character/personal qualities. *Important factors considered include:* Class rank, application essay, extracurricular activities, recommendation(s), talent/ability, volunteer work, work experience. *Other factors considered include:* Standardized test scores, first generation, geographical residence, interview, racial/ethnic status, state residency, alumni/ae relations, level of applicant's interest. SAT or ACT required; ACT with or without Writing component accepted. TOEFL required of all international applicants. *Academic units recommended:* 4 English; 3 mathematics; 3 science; 3 social studies; 2 foreign language; 1 academic elective.

Financial Aid

Students should submit: FAFSA. The Princeton Review suggests that all financial aid forms be submitted as soon as possible after January 1. *Need-based scholarships/grants offered:* Federal Pell, SEOG, state scholarships/grants, private scholarships, the school's own gift aid. *Loan aid offered:* Direct Subsidized Stafford Loans, Direct Unsubsidized Stafford Loans, Direct PLUS loans, Federal Perkins Loans, institutional loans. Federal Work-Study Program available. Institutional employment available. Off-campus job opportunities are fair.

The Inside Word

Given Cornell's relatively unique approach to study, it's no surprise that the admissions committee here focuses attention on both academic and personal strengths. Cornell's small, highly self-selected applicant pool is chock-full of students with solid self-awareness, motivation, and discipline.

THE SCHOOL SAYS ". . ."

From the Admissions Office

"Cornell College, a highly selective liberal arts college in Mount Vernon, Iowa, is recognized as one of 40 colleges featured in Colleges That Change Lives. Characterized by the life-changing academic immersion of its One Course At A Time curriculum, this distinctive approach allows students to focus on a single academic subject per 3.5 week block. It lays the foundation for a student's entire Cornell education through transformative intellectual partnerships and close-knit learning communities that bring out the best in our ambitious students. The One Course curriculum mirrors the pace of most working environments where employees are expected to handle tight deadlines and high expectations on every project, every day. Since there is never more than one course to focus on, faculty can take entire classes on field trips for a day or an entire block. Cornell's residential campus attracts a student body from 47 states and 17 foreign countries. Together, they experience a vast array of off-campus opportunities designed to take them into the world to fulfill their academic and personal goals, as well as a lineup of speakers and entertainment options that brings the world to them. Cornell College is frequently cited as a "Best Buy." Ninety-three percent of Cornell graduates complete their degrees in four years, and 55 percent go on to complete an advanced degree.

SELECTIVITY

Admissions Rating	91
# of applicants	2,498
% of applicants accepted	59
% of acceptees attending	18
# offered a place on the wait list	81
% accepting a place on wait list	65
% admitted from wait list	62
# of early decision applicants	123
% accepted early decision	17

FRESHMAN PROFILE

Range SAT Critical Reading	520–670
Range SAT Math	510–650
Range SAT Writing	510–630
Range ACT Composite	23–29
Minimum paper TOEFL	550
Minimum web-based TOEFL	213
Average HS GPA	3.54
% graduated top 10% of class	39
% graduated top 25% of class	69
% graduated top 50% of class	90

DEADLINES

Early decision	
Deadline	11/1
Notification	12/15
Early action	
Deadline	12/1
Notification	2/1
Regular	
Priority	12/1
Deadline	2/1
Nonfall registration?	Yes

APPLICANTS ALSO LOOK AT AND SOMETIMES PREFER

Beloit College; Coe College; Colorado College; Knox College; Kalamazoo College

FINANCIAL FACTS

Financial Aid Rating	88
Annual tuition	$37,275
Room and board	$8,500
Required fees	$225
Books and supplies	$1,114
% needy frosh rec. need-based scholarship or grant aid	100
% needy UG rec. need-based scholarship or grant aid	100
% needy frosh rec. non-need-based scholarship or grant aid	92
% needy UG rec. non-need-based scholarship or grant aid	87
% needy frosh rec. need-based self-help aid	86
% needy UG rec. need-based self-help aid	85
% frosh rec. any financial aid	99
% UG rec. any financial aid	97
% UG borrow to pay for school	78
Average cumulative indebtedness	$26,252
% frosh need fully met	28
% ugrads need fully met	27
Average % of frosh need met	93
Average % of ugrad need met	85

CORNELL UNIVERSITY

UNDERGRADUATE ADMISSIONS, 410 THURSTON AVENUE, ITHACA, NY 14850 • ADMISSIONS: 607-255-5241 • FAX: 607-255-0659

CAMPUS LIFE

Quality of Life Rating	94
Fire Safety Rating	78
Green Rating	99
Type of school	Private
Affiliation	No Affiliation
Environment	Town

STUDENTS

Total undergrad enrollment	14,309
% male/female	49/51
% from out of state	64
% frosh live on campus	100
% ugrads live on campus	55
# of fraternities	47)
# of sororities	18)
% African American	6
% Asian	16
% Caucasian	43
% Hispanic	11
% Native American	<1
% international	9
# of countries represented	77

SURVEY SAYS . . .
Students are happy
Classroom facilities are great
Lab facilities are great
Career services are great
Internships are widely available
Great food on campus
Great off-campus food
Lots of beer drinking
Frats and sororities are popular
Student publications are popular
Alumni active on campus

ACADEMICS

Academic Rating	92
% students returning for sophomore year	97
% students graduating within 4 years	87
% students graduating within 6 years	93
Calendar	Semester
Student/faculty ratio	9:1
Profs interesting rating	79
Profs accessible rating	75

Most classes have 10–19 students.
Most lab/discussion sessions have
10–19 students.

MOST POPULAR MAJORS
agricultural economics; agricultural engineering; mechanical engineering; biology; biomedical science; economics

STUDENTS SAY ". . ."

Academics

The westernmost of the Ivies, Cornell University provides its students with a prestigious education, paired with "an unwavering commitment to leave a positive impact on the world." The school is "more than a bunch of books and exams—it's an experience that challenges students to break free from their comfort zones." Seven different undergraduate colleges (including one of the premier Hotel Administration schools in the nation) "really make it feel small and specialized," and "top notch faculty." The university is "a place where any person can find instruction in any study (and it won't feel like work)," as it allows its students to explore any kind of interest they may have (ranging from Punk Rock as a literary genre to particle physics) while "also offering an incredible amount of depth within each department." There are endless opportunities to "pursue other topics, enhance your knowledge of things that you're already interested in, and try completely random things that you'd never even heard of before." Professors are "experts in their field, almost always conducting their own research, and are enthusiastic about passing their knowledge on to their students."

"[Since] being in Ithaca, you're kind of in the middle of nowhere," there are plenty of reasons to focus on your studies, but "Cornell as an administration keeps the faculty, research, and access to the most recent information so up-to-date that this campus is as connected as any place in the world." Between balancing those amazing resources and the community feel, the Cornell bigwigs get a lot of applause, as they have "proven time and time again that they care, both on an individual and system-wide level." Great internships, a strong alumni network, and "boundless opportunities after graduation" round out the "definition of amazing" that is Cornell University. "I was intimidated to go here, but now I will say that I cannot imagine going anywhere else," says a junior.

Life

As they say, "Ithaca is gorges," so hiking and outdoor activities are big pastimes. The "absolutely gorgeous campus" in the Finger Lakes region allows students to "truly, purely enjoy their time here" by "experiencing the natural beauties of Upstate New York, along with the eccentricity of surrounding town." "I think it sums up the Cornell experience to say that at dinner a few nights ago, our conversation included the presidential debate, Macbeth, sex, cantaloupes, sex WITH cantaloupes, drone strikes in Pakistan, the iPhones, and invasive parasitic species in Southeast Asia," says a freshman. The school's infrastructure is "intense"—"we have our own dairy so that we can make our own milk, for goodness' sake"—and "there's just so much going on at every moment [that] the hard part is choosing what it is you want to do." Many admit that various aspects of Cornell life can cause stress—the upperclass housing lottery, course enrollment system, workload, and difficulty studying abroad all get singled out—but students are able to discern when to kick back and enjoy themselves. Fun can range anywhere from "an awesome party in Collegetown to a movie night in the dorm while ordering insomnia cookies," but "it's definitely acceptable to turn down weekend plans because you have too much work to do."

Student Body

With so many different colleges within Cornell, there is "a plethora of diverse students" here, but the underlying commonality between all students is "ambition and ability." "From farm kids and pre-med students to engineers and hotelies, Cornell is home to all sorts of students," says one. "You'll find yourself with a roommate who was on Team USA, a friend who was a firefighter, and a classmate who's backpacked around the world." The integration of people with eclectic interests "[inspires] others to become active students," which is easily enough done at a university with hundreds upon hundreds of student organizations. "Everyone's smart and that's just accepted," but "a competitive environment isn't created." Cornellians are "very committed to academics but always know how to put books aside and relax." Most do research and volunteer work, and many "are involved in some form of Greek life."

CORNELL UNIVERSITY

FINANCIAL AID: 607-255-5147 • E-MAIL: ADMISSIONS@CORNELL.EDU • WEBSITE: WWW.CORNELL.EDU

THE PRINCETON REVIEW SAYS

Admissions

Very important factors considered include: GPA, rigor of secondary school record, standardized test scores, application essay, extracurricular activities, recommendation(s), talent/ability, character/personal qualities. *Important factors considered include:* Class rank. *Other factors considered include:* First generation, geographical residence, interview, racial/ethnic status, state residency, volunteer work, work experience, alumni/ae relations. SAT or ACT required; ACT with Writing component required. TOEFL required of all international applicants. *Academic units required:* 4 English; 3 mathematics. *Academic units recommended:* 3 science; (3 science lab); 3 social studies; 3 foreign language; 3 history.

Financial Aid

Students should submit: FAFSA, Institution's own financial aid form, CSS/Financial Aid PROFILE, Noncustodial PROFILE, Business/Farm Supplement. Regular filing deadline is 2/15. The Princeton Review suggests that all financial aid forms be submitted as soon as possible after January 1. *Need-based scholarships/grants offered:* Federal Pell, SEOG, State scholarships/grants, private scholarships, the school's own gift aid. *Loan aid offered:* Direct Subsidized Stafford Loans, Direct Unsubsidized Stafford Loans, Direct PLUS loans, Federal Perkins Loans, College/university loans from institutional funds. Applicants will be notified of awards beginning 4/1. Federal Work-Study Program available. Institutional employment available. Off-campus job opportunities are fair.

The Inside Word

Gaining admission to Cornell is a tough coup regardless of your intended field of study, but some of the university's seven schools are more competitive than others. If you're thinking of trying to "backdoor" your way into one of the most competitive schools—by gaining admission to a less competitive one, then transferring after one year—be aware that you will have to resubmit the entire application and provide a statement outlining your academic plans. It's not impossible to accomplish, but Cornell works hard to discourage this sort of maneuvering.

THE SCHOOL SAYS "..."

From the Admissions Office

"Cornell University, an Ivy League school and land-grant college located in the scenic Finger Lakes region of central New York, provides an outstanding education to students in seven small to midsize undergraduate colleges: Agriculture and Life Sciences; Architecture, Art, and Planning; Arts and Sciences; Engineering; Hotel Administration; Human Ecology; and Industrial and Labor Relations. Cornellians come from all fifty states and more than 120 countries, and they pursue their academic goals in more than 100 departments. The College of Arts and Sciences, one of the smallest liberal arts schools in the Ivy League, offers more than forty majors, most of which rank near the top nationwide. Applied programs in the other six colleges also rank among the best in the world. "Other special features of the university include a world-renowned faculty; over 4,000 courses available to all students; an extensive undergraduate research program; superb research, teaching, and library facilities; a large, diverse study abroad program; and more than 800 student organizations and thirty-four varsity sports. Cornell's campus is one of the most beautiful in the country; students pass streams, rocky gorges, and waterfalls on their way to class. First-year students make their home on North Campus, a living-learning community that features a special advising center, faculty-in-residence, a fitness center, and traditional residence halls as well as theme-centered buildings such as Ecology House. Cornell University invites applications from all interested students and uses the Common Application exclusively with a short required Cornell Supplement. Students applying for admissions will submit scores from the SAT or ACT (with writing). We also require SAT Subject Tests. Subject test requirements are college-specific."

SELECTIVITY

Admissions Rating	98
# of applicants	39,999
% of applicants accepted	16
% of acceptees attending	52
# offered a place on the wait list	3,144
% accepting a place on wait list	63
% admitted from wait list	9
# of early decision applicants	4,203
% accepted early decision	30

FRESHMAN PROFILE

Range SAT Critical Reading	640–740
Range SAT Math	680–780
Range ACT Composite	30–34
Minimum paper TOEFL	600
% graduated top 10% of class	87
% graduated top 25% of class	98
% graduated top 50% of class	99

DEADLINES

Early decision	
Deadline	11/1
Regular	
Deadline	1/2
Nonfall registration?	No

FINANCIAL FACTS

Financial Aid Rating	96
Annual tuition	$45,130
Room and board	$13,680
Required fees	$228
Books and supplies	$850
% needy frosh rec. need-based scholarship or grant aid	98
% needy UG rec. need-based scholarship or grant aid	97
% needy frosh rec. non-need-based scholarship or grant aid	0
% needy UG rec. non-need-based scholarship or grant aid	0
% needy frosh rec. need-based self-help aid	85
% needy UG rec. need-based self-help aid	90
% frosh rec. any financial aid	48
% UG rec. any financial aid	49
% UG borrow to pay for school	45
Average cumulative indebtedness	$20,557
% frosh need fully met	100
% ugrads need fully met	100
Average % of frosh need met	100
Average % of ugrad need met	100

CREIGHTON UNIVERSITY

2500 CALIFORNIA PLAZA, OMAHA, NE 68178 • ADMISSIONS: 402-280-2703 • FAX: 402-280-2685

CAMPUS LIFE

Quality of Life Rating	86
Fire Safety Rating	90
Green Rating	90
Type of school	Private
Affiliation	Roman Catholic
Environment	Metropolis

STUDENTS

Total undergrad enrollment	3,942
% male/female	40/60
% from out of state	70
% frosh from public high school	48
% frosh live on campus	95
% ugrads live on campus	62
# of fraternities (% ugrad men join)	5 (37)
# of sororities (% ugrad women join)	7 (37)
% African American	2
% Asian	9
% Caucasian	74
% Hispanic	7
% Native American	<1
% international	2
# of countries represented	45

SURVEY SAYS . . .

Students are happy
Career services are great
Students are friendly
Students get along with local community
Students involved in community service
Great off-campus food
Athletic facilities are great
Everyone loves the Bluejays

ACADEMICS

Academic Rating	87
% students returning for sophomore year	91
% students graduating within 4 years	67
% students graduating within 6 years	76
Calendar	Semester
Student/faculty ratio	11:1
Profs interesting rating	83
Profs accessible rating	84

Most classes have 10–19 students.
Most lab/discussion sessions have fewer than 10 students.

MOST POPULAR MAJORS
nursing; biology; psychology

STUDENTS SAY "..."

Academics

The voices echoing from this Omaha school are resoundingly pleased with their choice to attend "a great Jesuit university focused on academics and creating well-rounded students." Students are also active outside the classroom, getting "involved" in the campus and local community, and the school makes sure it churns a student out as a complete package: "academically, socially, culturally, faith-filled, and service-oriented." Creighton wants to form students who are driven inside the classroom but "want to find deeper meanings in all that they do to enact change in the world." Though classes are tough, the typical class size is small, which "makes discussion possible in nearly every class." Likewise, professors are extraordinarily helpful and "know how to present material in an interesting manner for the most part." Professors are all "exceptional" and really run the gamut "from quirky nerds to outspoken rebels to hilarious Jesuit priests." Many students come here for medical school, allied health, or business school. There are also a variety of services offered, such as a tutoring program called "The Study," where students get help from other students on a one-on-one basis. "Students at Creighton learn to enjoy the process, rather than just the product," says one. Both the teaching staff and administration are highly accessible; office hours don't seem to stop, and every Wednesday morning the much-loved president has breakfast with a different group of students to listen to their concerns and to talk about how life at Creighton is going. "At Creighton students come first, and it is as simple as that!" chirps a happy junior.

Life

"While academics are a huge part of our schooling, they are not all-encompassing," says a student. Community service happily takes up a lot of students' time, and there are fall break and spring break service trips all over the United States. Sports, both intercollegiate and intramural, are huge on and off campus; Omaha and the Old Market have plenty of music venues, bowling, shopping, and restaurants (a good thing, because the food at Creighton is universally despised and "needs to be improved drastically"). Students would like to see some more options for getting off campus, though; the difficulty and cost of living off campus means on-campus housing is in high demand. The Greek community at Creighton "is not as intense as at state schools," but students in sororities or fraternities hold many leadership positions on campus. Weeknights are mainly for studying, but house parties are available on weekends, and "the bar scene is where many students spend their nights off." The school and student government do an excellent job of providing plenty of activities that are enjoyed by all, such as ice skating, weekly movies, and "mock TV shows like the 'Price is Right,'" and no one has any problem with peer pressure. "It is very easy to be productive and involved but still be able to find time for fun," says a biology and Spanish major.

Student Body

The typical student is white and from the Midwest, and most are "outgoing and friendly," which is probably why atypical students have no problems fitting in. And the "old brick road that runs down the middle of campus (called the mall) provides excellent opportunities to meet new people." "It doesn't matter where you came from or why you're here" as "most students have the same values, which allows the community to feel connected." "Everyone is interconnected through someone; there are very few degrees of separation between individuals," one student says, though others claim that there's no shortage of cliques. Creighton students are incredibly balanced in their work and play and are "over-the-top involved" with activities and community service while maintaining full academic loads. The school is very involved in study abroad programs, so there are a fair number of international students in each class. "I've never been in a place where so many people will hold the door open for me to walk through, if that gives any indication of the type of student here," says a student.

FINANCIAL AID: 402-280-2731 • E-MAIL: ADMISSIONS@CREIGHTON.EDU • WEBSITE: WWW.CREIGHTON.EDU

THE PRINCETON REVIEW SAYS

Admissions

Very important factors considered include: GPA, rigor of secondary school record. *Important factors considered include:* Standardized test scores, application essay. *Other factors considered include:* Class rank, extracurricular activities, first generation, racial/ethnic status, recommendation(s), talent/ability, volunteer work, character/personal qualities, level of applicant's interest. SAT or ACT required; ACT with or without Writing component accepted. TOEFL required of all international applicants. *Academic units required:* 4 English; 3 mathematics; 2 science; (1 science lab); 2 social studies; 2 foreign language; 3 academic electives. *Academic units recommended:* 4 English; 4 mathematics; 3 science; (1 science lab); 3 social studies; 3 foreign language; 1 history; 3 academic electives.

Financial Aid

Students should submit: FAFSA, Institution's own financial aid form. The Princeton Review suggests that all financial aid forms be submitted as soon as possible after January 1. *Need-based scholarships/grants offered:* Federal Pell, SEOG, State scholarships/grants, private scholarships, the school's own gift aid, federal nursing scholarships. *Loan aid offered:* Direct Subsidized Stafford Loans, Direct Unsubsidized Stafford Loans, Direct PLUS loans, Federal Perkins Loans, Federal Nursing Loans. Federal Work-Study Program available. Institutional employment available. Off-campus job opportunities are excellent.

The Inside Word

Creighton's lack of name recognition and its location can handicap its search for quality students, occasionally forcing the school to lower the bar to fill its incoming classes, so the school's loss could well be your gain. For those comfortable in a Jesuit school, Creighton offers bright, hardworking students a great opportunity at a quality education.

THE SCHOOL SAYS "..."

From the Admissions Office

"Students come to Creighton University for the opportunities of a lifetime. Creighton's nine schools and colleges deliver powerful education that connects renowned programs in arts and sciences, law and business with eight health professions programs (dentistry, medicine, nursing, pharmacy, occupational and physical therapy, public health and emergency medical services) all on the same walkable campus. Creighton's rigorous academics and commitment to Jesuit, Catholic ideals and values create an environment that fosters academic excellence, social justice and personal growth. More than 8,000 undergraduate, graduate and professional students come to Creighton each year to find their place in the world through lives of leadership and service.

"Creighton's 4,000+ undergraduates find new possibilities through personalized advising, a strong focus on leadership skills and opportunities for undergraduate research. The Center for Undergraduate Research and Scholarship (CURAS) ensures that undergraduates work directly with faculty researchers, present at national conferences and publish in scholarly journals. And not all learning takes place in the classroom or lab. Creighton business students find abundant internship opportunities (the University is within walking distance of five Fortune 500 company headquarters) and all Creighton students find life-changing experiences through community service opportunities. (Last year, they contributed 389,000 volunteer hours!)

"At Creighton, you get it all—national professors of the year; a 96 percent placement rate within eight months of graduation; an 11:1 student-to-faculty ratio; 70+ undergraduate majors; 161 partner universities in 53 countries; BIG EAST athletic competition; 200+ clubs and organizations and more—because Creighton University is the complete package."

SELECTIVITY

Admissions Rating	88
# of applicants	5,336
% of applicants accepted	77
% of acceptees attending	24

FRESHMAN PROFILE

Range SAT Critical Reading	520–640
Range SAT Math	540–660
Range SAT Writing	500–620
Range ACT Composite	24–30
Minimum paper TOEFL	550
Minimum web-based TOEFL	80
Average HS GPA	3.75
% graduated top 10% of class	40
% graduated top 25% of class	68
% graduated top 50% of class	93

DEADLINES

Regular	
Priority	12/1
Deadline	2/15
Nonfall registration?	Yes

APPLICANTS ALSO LOOK AT AND OFTEN PREFER

University of Notre Dame

AND SOMETIMES PREFER

Fordham University; University of Denver; University of Nebraska—Lincoln; Villanova University

AND RARELY PREFER

University of Nebraska at Omaha, Loyola University of Chicago, Regis College

FINANCIAL FACTS

Financial Aid Rating	90
Annual tuition	$33,796
Room and board	$9,996
Required fees	$1,564
Books and supplies	$1,200
% needy frosh rec. need-based scholarship or grant aid	100
% needy UG rec. need based scholarship or grant aid	98
% needy frosh rec. non-need-based scholarship or grant aid	100
% needy UG rec. non-need-based scholarship or grant aid	84
% needy frosh rec. need-based self-help aid	70
% needy UG rec. need-based self-help aid	80
% frosh rec. any financial aid	99
% UG rec. any financial aid	97
% UG borrow to pay for school	62
Average cumulative indebtedness	$35,510
% frosh need fully met	32
% ugrads need fully met	39
Average % of frosh need met	87
Average % of ugrad need met	88

DARTMOUTH COLLEGE

6016 McNUTT HALL, HANOVER, NH 03755 • ADMISSIONS: 603-646-2875 • FAX: 603-646-1216

CAMPUS LIFE
Quality of Life Rating	99
Fire Safety Rating	84
Green Rating	92
Type of school	Private
Affiliation	No Affiliation
Environment	Village

STUDENTS
Total undergrad enrollment	4,276
% male/female	50/50
% from out of state	97
% frosh from public high school	55
% frosh live on campus	100
% ugrads live on campus	88
# of fraternities (% ugrad men join)	17 (47)
# of sororities (% ugrad women join)	11 (46)
% African American	6
% Asian	14
% Caucasian	46
% Hispanic	7
% Native American	2
% international	8
# of countries represented	70

SURVEY SAYS . . .
Political activism is popular
Students are happy
Classroom facilities are great
Lab facilities are great
Internships are widely available
School is well run
Students are friendly
Students get along with local community
Great food on campus
Dorms are like palaces
Campus feels safe
Easy to get around campus
Athletic facilities are great
Lots of beer drinking
Frats and sororities are popular
Student publications are popular
Alumni active on campus

ACADEMICS
Academic Rating	97
% students returning for sophomore year	98
% students graduating within 4 years	87
% students graduating within 6 years	95
Calendar	Quarter
Student/faculty ratio	8:1
Profs interesting rating	93
Profs accessible rating	95
Most classes have 10–19 students.	

MOST POPULAR MAJORS
economics; psychology; political science

STUDENTS SAY ". . ."

Academics

Tucked away in bucolic New Hampshire, Dartmouth College manages to strike a nice "balance between the intimacy of a college [and] the opportunity of a university." Students feel fortunate that the administration places an "emphasis on pursuing passions, and making the college experience your own." And while Dartmouth certainly maintains a "competitive" atmosphere, students here truly appreciate that "no one really talks about their grades openly." Indeed, it's "generally understood that everyone is smart." A neuroscience major tells us that academically, "Dartmouth puts a huge focus on the undergraduate students, and I have found my professors to be available and engaging in nearly every instance. My classes are all challenging, but they are very discussion based and tend to be small, which keeps me working hard and interested in the material." And an impressed Middle Eastern studies major interjects, "I came to Dartmouth for the professors, but they were far beyond anything I could have hoped for. Not only are they great lecturers and accomplished scholars, they go out of their way to be available outside of the classroom, and to forge relationships beyond what is expected or necessary." When it comes down to it, "Dartmouth is considered to be a combination of Hogwarts and Disney World because it is known for its community and intelligent students and faculty, who also are personable and know how to have fun."

Life

There's no getting around it; at Dartmouth, the "Greek system is the main source of social activity." However, if you're wary of fraternities and sororities, fret not. A biology major reveals that a "very large percentage of students are involved which makes the Greek houses quite diverse and representative of the student body as a whole." Indeed, fraternities "are very inclusive" and while students definitely drink "there really isn't any pressure to." Further, plenty of social options exist beyond the party scene. "On any given night, you can do anything from see a hockey game to the early premiere of some cool new movie at the Hop[kins Center for the Arts], you can go to a dance party or just play cards or jam out on guitar or something... there are so many options to do whatever you're interested in doing." Dartmouth undergrads also love convening with nature. "Outdoorsy activities are huge here. The Appalachian Trail literally runs right through our campus. The Dartmouth Outing Club is the oldest and largest college outing club, and many students (even students who never did so before college) get involved with hiking, canoeing, rock climbing, and so forth." And a philosophy major concludes, "Whether it's skating on Occom Pond, going on a hike, going kayaking, apple picking, thrift shopping... there are boundless opportunities to do anything that interests you, and it means that whatever you're doing in your free time is always something really awesome."

Student Body

Undergrads here emphatically insist that it's "hard to define a typical student because at Dartmouth literally every type of person is represented." Of course, if pressed, they might reluctantly admit that the average student comes across as "preppy, academically goal oriented but also extremely social." And, as you might expect, undergrads also report that their peers are certainly very "smart." Fortunately, they "do not boast about their intellectual capacity." A happy senior tells us that "the common denominator is that Dartmouth students are very involved." Indeed, "Whether it's with a club sports team, a cappella group, community service project, academic research, or a Greek house, Dartmouth students manage to do a lot of things in the course of the day." One incredulous sophomore concurs, adding that his friends "are always studying and participating in some extracurricular activity and you wonder how they have time to sleep and then you will see them out at a frat too. Then they show up at class the next morning with all of the work completed and they seem like a magician." Finally a junior concludes, "It's a small enough school that there is a sense of community that's always present, but large enough that everyone can find their own niche and their own area of the school and the community that caters to them perfectly."

FINANCIAL AID: 800-443-3605 • E-MAIL: ADMISSIONS.REPLY@DARTMOUTH.EDU • WEBSITE: WWW.DARTMOUTH.EDU

THE PRINCETON REVIEW SAYS

Admissions

Very important factors considered include: Class rank, GPA, rigor of secondary school record, standardized test scores, application essay, extracurricular activities, recommendation(s), character/personal qualities. *Important factors considered include:* Talent/ability, volunteer work. *Other factors considered include:* First generation, geographical residence, interview, racial/ethnic status, work experience, alumni/ae relations. SAT or ACT required; ACT with Writing component required. TOEFL required of all international applicants. *Academic units recommended:* 4 English; 4 mathematics; 4 science; 4 social studies; 4 foreign language.

Financial Aid

Students should submit: FAFSA, CSS/Financial Aid PROFILE, Noncustodial PROFILE, Business/Farm Supplement. Regular filing deadline is 2/1. The Princeton Review suggests that all financial aid forms be submitted as soon as possible after January 1. *Need-based scholarships/grants offered:* Federal Pell, SEOG, State scholarships/grants, private scholarships, the school's own gift aid. *Loan aid offered:* Direct Subsidized Stafford Loans, Direct Unsubsidized Stafford Loans, Direct PLUS loans, Federal Perkins Loans, Federal Nursing Loans, State Loans, College/university loans from institutional funds. Applicants will be notified of awards beginning 4/2. Federal Work-Study Program available. Institutional employment available. Off-campus job opportunities are excellent.

The Inside Word

Competition to secure a coveted acceptance letter from Dartmouth is fierce. After all, the majority of admitted students are in the top of their respective high school classes. Therefore, academic success is mandatory for any serious contender as is a schedule chock-full of honors, AP and/or IB courses. Of course, admissions officers are looking for well-rounded students so extracurricular activities, personal statements and recommendations will also be closely assessed. Finally, it's important to know that Dartmouth is a need-blind institution.

THE SCHOOL SAYS ". . ."

From the Admissions Office

"With its focus on undergraduate education and a flexible year-round academic calendar that encourages travel and research, Dartmouth is uniquely positioned to help students pursue their interests, prepare for a career and make an impact on the world. All classes are taught by members of the faculty, over 1,000 students per year pursue independent study for credit, and almost two-thirds of students participate in study abroad programs.

"Dartmouth opened the Class of 1978 Life Sciences Center in the fall of 2011, and the Black Family Visual Arts Center is opening in the fall of 2012. These new facilities are designed to expand Dartmouth's commitment to undergraduate research and further the college's collaboration between faculty and students.

"On campus, students participate in nearly 400 student organizations, including thirty-four intercollegiate varsity teams, over forty different community service projects, and more than fifty performing groups. Dartmouth's hometown of Hanover offers an active political scene, a vibrant arts community, and unparalleled outdoors and recreational opportunities (including our own ski mountain!).

"To help all Dartmouth students take advantage of the Dartmouth Experience, the college practices need-blind admission for all applicants, meets the full demonstrated need for all admitted students, and offers free tuition and no loan requirements for all students whose annual family incomes are below $100,000.

"Dartmouth's admissions process is designed to identify students who will thrive in a challenging and flexible academic environment, who value community, and who will take advantage of the college's undergraduate focus."

SELECTIVITY	
Admissions Rating	99
# of applicants	22,428
% of applicants accepted	10
% of acceptees attending	48
# offered a place on the wait list	1,681
% accepting a place on wait list	57
% admitted from wait list	10
# of early decision applicants	1,574
% accepted early decision	29

FRESHMAN PROFILE	
Range SAT Critical Reading	680–780
Range SAT Math	680–780
Range SAT Writing	680–780
Range ACT Composite	30–34
Minimum paper TOEFL	600
Minimum web-based TOEFL	250
% graduated top 10% of class	98
% graduated top 25% of class	97
% graduated top 50% of class	100

DEADLINES	
Early decision	
Deadline	11/1
Notification	12/15
Regular	
Deadline	1/1
Notification	4/10
Nonfall registration?	No

FINANCIAL FACTS	
Financial Aid Rating	97
Annual tuition	$46,764
Room and board	$13,839
Required fees	$1,344
Books and supplies	$1,176
% needy frosh rec. need-based scholarship or grant aid	91
% needy UG rec. need-based scholarship or grant aid	93
% needy frosh rec. non-need-based scholarship or grant aid	0
% needy UG rec. non-need-based scholarship or grant aid	0
% needy frosh rec. need-based self-help aid	89
% needy UG rec. need-based self-help aid	92
% frosh rec. any financial aid	67
% UG rec. any financial aid	54
% UG borrow to pay for school	38
Average cumulative indebtedness	$15,671
% frosh need fully met	100
% ugrads need fully met	100
Average % of frosh need met	100
Average % of ugrad need met	100

DAVIDSON COLLEGE

PO BOX 7156, DAVIDSON, NC 28035-7156 • ADMISSIONS: 704-894-2230 • FAX: 704-894-2016

CAMPUS LIFE

Quality of Life Rating	82
Fire Safety Rating	60*
Green Rating	85
Type of school	Private
Affiliation	Presbyterian
Environment	Village

STUDENTS

Total undergrad enrollment	1,782 % male/
female	50/50
% from out of state	77
% frosh from public high school	44
% frosh live on campus	100
% ugrads live on campus	92
# of fraternities	8 (
# of sororities	6 (
% African American	7
% Asian	5
% Caucasian	69
% Hispanic	6
% Native American	1
% international	5
# of countries represented	42

SURVEY SAYS . . .
No one cheats
Lab facilities are great
School is well run
Students are friendly
Students get along with local community
Campus feels safe
Students environmentally aware
Students involved in community service

ACADEMICS

Academic Rating	93
% students returning for sophomore year	96
% students graduating within 4 years	92
% students graduating within 6 years	95
Calendar	Semester
Student/faculty ratio	10:1
Profs interesting rating	92
Profs accessible rating	94
Most classes have 10–19 students.	
Most lab/discussion sessions have 10–19 students.	

MOST POPULAR MAJORS
biology; political science; psychology

STUDENTS SAY ". . ."

Academics
This small school north of Charlotte, North Carolina, cultivates an environment "that is very open to change and improvement" and empowers students to "be better people and make a difference in the world." The administration works hard to create an on-campus community and constantly makes efforts "to support and improve Davidson," all while keeping students happy and their minds full. "I have never witnessed people so eager to come do their job every day. [Professors] are almost too willing to help," says a student. There is also a trickle-down effect because even the student body is supportive and "eager to watch you succeed." The school offers a classic liberal arts education, encouraging students to take classes in all areas, and "all of these people come out smarter than they came in." "If I could spend twenty years being educated by this administration and these professors, I would," says a very happy junior. School is the number one priority for all of the students here, and while academics are all-consuming, time-wise, they are also "fascinating and rewarding." Without a doubt, Davidson is a tough school—"99 percent of us left our 4.0 GPAs back in high school," claims a student—and professors don't believe in grade inflation or curving grades, but they do readily make themselves available outside of class for help or discussion. There is a lot of work, but it "is accompanied by even more resources with which it can be successfully managed." One student testimonial: "My calculus teacher last semester has office hours in the student union, and he invited the whole class over to his house for chicken dinner—twice!" The dedication of the staff is contagious, and "though the work is rigorous, time spent in school never feels wasted."

Life
Davidson "possesses an intense study culture, and people hit the books regularly; it's cool to be smart." One of the many wonderful things about Davidson "is that academics voluntarily leave the classroom." "It's not uncommon to hear people discussing their current academic topics at lunch or in the gym." Basketball is a huge common ground for the student body at large; "Everyone enjoys being a part of the underdog/Cinderella story." Weeks are devoted to study, as well as extra-curricular activities—"you see your friends because you are doing homework together or eating meals together, not because you're vegging out." Of course, even Davidson students need to kick back, and there are always plenty of parties to be found on the weekends. Fraternities and eating houses (the Davidson version of sororities) are popular. Fortunately, "There really is no pressure to drink. You can go out and dance and have a great time or have movie nights with friends," says a student. The combination of the idyllic atmosphere and the workload "can make it hard to stay up-to-date on current events, yet most students remain well-informed."

Student Body
Davidson is "an amalgamation of all types of people, religiously, ethnically, politically, economically, etc.," all "united under the umbrella of intellectual curiosity" and their devotion to the school as a community. The typical Davidson student is "probably white," but in the past few years, admissions has been making progress in racially diversifying the campus, which students agree upon as necessary. Though there are plenty of Southern, preppy, athletic types to fit the brochure examples, there are many niches for every type of "atypical" student. "There are enough people that one can find a similar group to connect with, and there are few enough people that one ends up connecting with dissimilar [people] anyway," says a student. Everyone here is smart and well-rounded; admissions "does a good job...so if you're in you'll probably make the cut all the way through the four years." Most students have several extracurriculars to round out their free time, and they have a healthy desire to enjoy themselves when the books shut. "During the week we work hard. On the weekends we play hard. We don't do anything halfway," says a senior. Though the majority of students lean to the left, there's a strong conservative contingent, and there are no real problems between the two.

DAVIDSON COLLEGE

FINANCIAL AID: 704-894-2232 • E-MAIL: ADMISSION@DAVIDSON.EDU • WEBSITE: WWW.DAVIDSON.EDU

THE PRINCETON REVIEW SAYS

Admissions

Very important factors considered include: Rigor of secondary school record, first generation, recommendation(s), volunteer work, character/personal qualities, level of applicant's interest. *Important factors considered include:* Standardized test scores, application essay, extracurricular activities, interview, talent/ability. *Other factors considered include:* Class rank, GPA, alumni/ae relations. SAT or ACT required; SAT and SAT Subject Tests or ACT recommended; ACT with or without Writing component accepted. TOEFL required of all international applicants. *Academic units required:* 4 English; 3 mathematics; 2 science; 2 foreign language. *Academic units recommended:* 4 mathematics; 4 science; 4 foreign language.

Financial Aid

Students should submit: FAFSA, CSS/Financial Aid PROFILE, Noncustodial PROFILE, Business/Farm Supplement. Regular filing deadline is 2/15. The Princeton Review suggests that all financial aid forms be submitted as soon as possible after January 1. *Need-based scholarships/grants offered:* Federal Pell, SEOG, State scholarships/grants, private scholarships, the school's own gift aid. *Loan aid offered:* Direct Subsidized Stafford Loans, Direct Unsubsidized Stafford Loans, Direct PLUS loans. Applicants will be notified of awards beginning 4/1. Federal Work-Study Program available. Institutional employment available. Off-campus job opportunities are excellent.

The Inside Word

The combination of Davidson's low acceptance rate and high yield really packs a punch. Prospective applicants beware: Securing admission at this prestigious school is no easy feat. Admitted students are typically at the top of their high school classes and have strong standardized test scores. Candidates with leadership experience generally garner the favor of admissions officers. The college takes its honor code seriously and, as a result, seeks out students of demonstrated reputable character.

THE SCHOOL SAYS " . . ."

From the Admissions Office

"Davidson College is one of the nation's premier academic institutions, a college of the liberal arts and sciences respected for its intellectual vigor, the high quality of its faculty and students, and the achievements of its alumni. Davidson is distinguished by its strong honor code, close collaboration between professors and students, an environment that encourages both intellectual growth and community service, and a commitment to international education. Davidson places great value on student participation in extracurricular activities, intercollegiate athletics, and intramural sports. The college has a strong regional identity, grounded in traditions of civility and mutual respect, and has historic ties to the Presbyterian Church. The college has a strong commitment to making a Davidson education affordable. The college doesn't include student loans in its financial aid packages. Through the Davidson Trust, 100 percent of demonstrated financial need for domestic student is met with a combination of grants and student employment.

"Applicants are required to complete and submit scores from the SAT and/or the ACT. SAT Subject Tests (mathematics and one of your choice) are recommended. Davidson will utilize the scores that place the student in the greatest possible light."

SELECTIVITY

Admissions Rating	97
# of applicants	4,745
% of applicants accepted	26
% of acceptees attending	40
# of early decision applicants	617
% accepted early decision	41

FRESHMAN PROFILE

Range SAT Critical Reading	630–730
Range SAT Math	600–710
Range SAT Writing	610–710
Range ACT Composite	29–33
Minimum paper TOEFL	600
Minimum web-based TOEFL	250
Average HS GPA	3.98
% graduated top 10% of class	64
% graduated top 25% of class	91
% graduated top 50% of class	100

DEADLINES

Early decision	
Deadline	11/15
Notification	12/15
Regular	
Deadline	1/2
Notification	4/1
Nonfall registration?	No

APPLICANTS ALSO LOOK AT AND OFTEN PREFER
Princeton University; Swarthmore College; Williams College; Stanford University, Duke University; Dartmouth College

AND SOMETIMES PREFER
Vanderbilt University; University of Virginia; The University of North Carolina at Chapel Hill;

AND RARELY PREFER
Colgate University; Emory University; Furman University; Wake Forest University

FINANCIAL FACTS

Financial Aid Rating	91
Annual tuition	
% needy frosh rec. need-based scholarship or grant aid	98
% needy UG rec. need-based scholarship or grant aid	99
% needy frosh rec. non-need-based scholarship or grant aid	17
% needy UG rec. non-need-based scholarship or grant aid	14
% needy frosh rec. need-based self-help aid	60
% needy UG rec. need-based self-help aid	68
% frosh rec. any financial aid	45
% UG rec. any financial aid	46
% UG borrow to pay for school	22
Average cumulative indebtedness	$25,075
% frosh need fully met	100
% ugrads need fully met	100
Average % of frosh need met	100
Average % of ugrad need met	100

DEEP SPRINGS COLLEGE

APPLICATIONS COMMITTEE, DYER, NV 89010 • ADMISSIONS: 760-872-2000 • FAX: 760-872-4466

CAMPUS LIFE

Quality of Life Rating	97
Fire Safety Rating	82
Green Rating	60*
Type of school	Private
Affiliation	No Affiliation
Environment	Rural

STUDENTS

Total undergrad enrollment	25
% male/female	100/0
% from out of state	80
% frosh from public high school	50
% frosh live on campus	100
% ugrads live on campus	100
% Caucasian	44
% Hispanic	0
% Native American	0
% international	4
# of countries represented	3

SURVEY SAYS . . .

Lots of liberal students
Students always studying
Internships are widely available
Class discussions encouraged
School is well run
Great financial aid
No one cheats
Students are friendly
Diverse student types on campus
Students aren't religious
Students get along with local community
Students involved in community service
Great food on campus
Dorms are like palaces
Very little drug use

ACADEMICS

Academic Rating	99
% students returning for sophomore year	92
Calendar	Semester
Student/faculty ratio	4:1
Profs interesting rating	99
Profs accessible rating	99
Most classes have fewer than 10 students.	

MOST POPULAR MAJORS
liberal arts and sciences

STUDENTS SAY ". . ."

Academics

The "three pillars" of a Deep Springs education—"labor, academics, and self-governance"—combine to produce "unparalleled challenges" that run the gamut "from fixing a hay baler in the middle of the night to puzzling over a particularly difficult passage of Hegel." That's what the twenty-six men who attend Deep Springs tell us. These unique undergraduates basically run their own school, work the ranch where it is located, and complete a rigorous curriculum, an itinerary that "creates an environment of intense growth and responsibility." Class work occurs in a seminar format in which "the distinction between teacher and student becomes fuzzy [because] everyone is equally invested, thoughtful, and engaged." Composition and public speaking are the only required courses; all others are chosen by the student body and taught by a faculty of three long-term professors (one each in the humanities, social sciences, and natural sciences) and three visiting scholars or artists. The system relies on a commitment to self-determination, which means "the smoothness with which many programs run depends largely on the kind of responsibility students take. Sometimes students do a good job taking care of administrative tasks, sometimes a worse job. It's all part of the educational experience." While the size of the school inevitably means that "lab and library facilities are not what they might be," students tell us that the overall Deep Springs experience compensates for any shortcomings. As one student explains, "through intense academics and running the college administratively and practically, we receive an unprecedented education in citizenship of a conscious human being."

Life

Deep Springs is totally unlike other colleges in terms of the everyday life of a student," because "no one drinks, everyone helps run the ranch in some way, and no one can be totally self-absorbed (unless he's out hiking in the desert)." Instead, students immerse themselves in the Deep Springs way. As one student explains, "The Deep Springs program is our whole life. The intellectual questions we're asking and the labor we're doing is all bound up with our identity." Students spend their free time "thinking about intellectual things: moral issues, politics, and the community. 'Fun' is hard to come by, and one has to learn how to enjoy people, work, and engagement." Students do occasionally take a break, however; "on weekends in the rumpus room of the dorm, you can find a group of motley adventurers engaged in a Dungeons & Dragons quest or a pack of students watching 'Gossip Girl.' You'll find even more people scoffing at such pedantry and watching arty French movies," and "communal soccer is excellent…we even play in the snow." Also, occasionally "we have dance parties called 'boojies,'" and "we do some other strange things for fun, like sledding naked down 800-foot-tall sand dunes in neighboring Eureka Valley." Undergrads concede that Deep Springs "life can be intense. Students usually are utterly exhausted. But most of the time we know that something good is coming out of this," and that keeps undergrads energized and motivated.

Student Body

"Having only twenty-eight students makes it even harder to characterize the 'typical' Deep Springer," students understandably warn, but they add that "we're all very able and driven, but in our own ways, not in the way that most Ivy League students are. Deep Springs isn't a stepping stone to the world of white-collar work but an end in itself that we all pursue with all our hearts. So I guess the typical student has a healthy disgust for the pedagogy of most other universities." Undergrads are also predictably "intelligent, motivated, and responsible," as they "must demonstrate depth of thought to be accepted" to the school. As one student puts it, "The typical student at Deep Springs is committed to the life of the intellect and committed to finding education in our labor program. Most of the students here believe that a life of service, informed by discourse and labor, is a necessary notion to understand in today's world."

FINANCIAL AID: 760-872-2000 • E-MAIL: APCOM@DEEPSPRINGS.EDU • WEBSITE: WWW.DEEPSPRINGS.EDU

THE PRINCETON REVIEW SAYS

Admissions

Very important factors considered include: Application essay, interview, character/personal qualities, level of applicant's interest. *Important factors considered include:* GPA, rigor of secondary school record, extracurricular activities, volunteer work, work experience. *Other factors considered include:* Class rank, standardized test scores, racial/ethnic status, recommendation(s), talent/ability. SAT or ACT required.

Financial Aid

Students should submit: The Princeton Review suggests that all financial aid forms be submitted as soon as possible after January 1.

The Inside Word

Students will be hard-pressed to find a school with a more personal or thorough application process than Deep Springs. Given the intimate and collegial atmosphere of the school, matchmaking is the top priority. Candidates are evaluated by a body composed of students, faculty, and staff members. The application is writing intensive; finalists are expected to spend several days on campus, during which they will undergo a lengthy interview.

THE SCHOOL SAYS "..."

From the Admissions Office

"Founded in 1917, Deep Springs College lies isolated in a high desert valley of eastern California, thirty miles from the nearest town. Its enrollment is limited to twenty-eight students, each of whom receives a full scholarship that covers tuition and room and board, and is valued at more than $50,000 per year. Students engage in rigorous academics, govern themselves, and participate in the operation of our cattle and alfalfa ranch. After two years, students generally transfer to other schools to complete their studies. Students regularly transfer to Harvard, The University of Chicago, and Brown, but also choose Cornell, Columbia, Stanford, Swarthmore, University of California—Berkeley, and Yale.

In the past five years Deep Springers have won the following national scholarship competitions:

- The Jack Kent Cooke Scholarship (2)
- The Barry M. Goldwater Scholarship (1)
- The Rhodes Scholarship (1)
- The Harry S. Truman Scholarship (5)
- The Morris Udall Scholarship (1)"

SELECTIVITY

Admissions Rating	99
# of applicants	170
% of applicants accepted	7
% of acceptees attending	100
# offered a place on the wait list	3
% accepting a place on wait list	100
% admitted from wait list	0

FRESHMAN PROFILE

Range SAT Critical Reading	750–800
Range SAT Math	700–800
% graduated top 10% of class	83
% graduated top 25% of class	93
% graduated top 50% of class	100

DEADLINES

Regular	
Deadline	11/15
Notification	4/15
Nonfall registration?	No

APPLICANTS ALSO LOOK AT AND RARELY PREFER

Swarthmore College; Brown University; Yale University; Stanford University; Cornell University; University of California—Berkeley; The University of Chicago; Harvard College

FINANCIAL FACTS

Financial Aid Rating	60*
Annual tuition	$0
Room and board	$0
Books and supplies	$1,200
% frosh rec. any financial aid	100
% UG rec. any financial aid	100
% UG borrow to pay for school	0
Average cumulative indebtedness	$0
Average % of frosh need met	0
Average % of ugrad need met	0

DENISON UNIVERSITY

BOX H, GRANVILLE, OH 43023 • ADMISSIONS: 740-587-6276 • FAX: 740-587-6306

STUDENTS SAY ". . ."

Academics

For those seeking out "a small, liberal arts school with quality academics as well as a penchant for producing students who are well-rounded citizens," Denison University deserves a closer look. The school is "set in a beautiful and very safe town" in rural Ohio and offers "an intelligent and welcoming community ready and willing to help others" as well as "a great support system." Denison offers a campus filled with "continuous construction of new facilities" where "students have diverse opportunities to explore their talents and improve their skills through campus jobs, clubs, internships, and the election of double majors and minors that don't necessarily fit together." "The classes are challenging," and "the academics are competitive and foster interesting class selection." One student also admits, "General education requirements, although somewhat tedious, provide opportunities for students to grow in areas that they normally would not consider investing their time in."

The crown jewels of the school's academic life seem to be the professors who are "tough, but usually fair." One student raves, "At Denison, we have professors that can make a poem out of a picture and a mountain out of a math problem. We are so privileged to be surrounded by scholars who are passionate about teaching and learning what they love." Students get a chance to form close bonds with their professors thanks to the "small student-to-faculty ratio" as well as the high accessibility of the professors outside of the classroom. According to one student, "As far as professor availability goes, I see my professors on campus so often that I'm starting to suspect they sleep in their offices..." Students keep it all in perspective and recognize that "although academics are certainly important here, Denison teaches you how to shape what you know so that you become a more curious, passionate, and interesting individual."

Life

"Life here is a big blur of class, athletics, parties, and down time." That seems to be the general consensus among students at this school. In other words, "whether you enjoy sports, Greek life, service or quidditch it can all be found at Denison!" Students highlight that "There's a good party scene, largely dominated by fraternities, but there are more and more non-Greek options" and "at least 50 percent of the campus is out partying on any given Friday or Saturday night." Offering another perspective, one student notes, "Parties happen every weekend, but there are plenty of people who prefer to chill with friends in the dorm rooms and just watch movies." For those interested in exploring life off campus, "Granville is small but cute, [and] there's plenty to eat at a good price," and "some cute shops." "Many also choose Columbus for clubbing, the alternative and bucolic Homestead for random parties, or even the Broadway area in Granville for dining in the ten-ish big restaurant options, drinking at Brew's, or just studying in River Road or Village Coffee Co. coffee shops. Whit's Frozen Custard is great too."

Student Body

Denison students generally agree that "we have a reputation as a WASP-y, East-Coast-in-Ohio school, but that is slowly changing." And while many students at Denison can be described as "tall, good-looking, and dressed in Vineyard Vines, J. Crew, or RL," one student explains, "At first, most students will feel like preppy New Englanders, but if you don't conform to this image it's still easy to find friends." This would include the environmentalists who "are a pretty big presence on campus now." At Denison, many seem to agree, "Students are also extremely involved, almost everyone is involved in at least two to three clubs or activities, and many people hold some sort of leadership role." Ultimately, "Denison is a place for real people who love caring about each other and learning, [and] if you don't like having a close-knit group of people there to support you, then don't go to Denison."

FINANCIAL AID: 800-336-4766 • E-MAIL: ADMISSIONS@DENISON.EDU • WEBSITE: WWW.DENISON.EDU

THE PRINCETON REVIEW SAYS

Admissions

Very important factors considered include: GPA, rigor of secondary school record, application essay, recommendation(s), religious affiliation. *Important factors considered include:* Extracurricular activities, interview, talent/ability, level of applicant's interest. *Other factors considered include:* Class rank, standardized test scores, first generation, geographical residence, racial/ethnic status, state residency, volunteer work, work experience, alumni/ae relations, character/personal qualities. SAT or ACT considered if submitted; ACT with or without Writing component accepted. TOEFL required of all international applicants. *Academic units required:* 4 English; 4 mathematics; 4 science; 2 social studies; 3 foreign language; 1 history; 1 academic elective.

Financial Aid

Students should submit: FAFSA. The Princeton Review suggests that all financial aid forms be submitted as soon as possible after January 1. *Need-based scholarships/grants offered:* Federal Pell, SEOG, State scholarships/grants, private scholarships, the school's own gift aid. *Loan aid offered:* Direct Subsidized Stafford Loans, Direct Unsubsidized Stafford Loans, Direct PLUS loans, Federal Perkins Loans, College/university loans from institutional funds. Applicants will be notified of awards beginning 3/28. Federal Work-Study Program available. Institutional employment available. Off-campus job opportunities are fair.

The Inside Word

Admission to Denison is pretty straightforward. The school "suggests" an interview, meaning you should do one if at all possible. It's a great way to demonstrate your interest in the school, which improves your chances of admission, especially if your grades, test scores, and overall profile put you on the admit/reject borderline.

THE SCHOOL SAYS ". . ."

From the Admissions Office

"At the top of the winding drive that takes you to Denison's hilltop campus overlooking the Welsh Hills and the village of Granville, you'll discover the perfect college setting. Founded in 1831, Denison focuses on the success of its students, who typically come from all 50 states and dozens of countries.

"You'll find them strolling down Chapel Walk, playing Frisbee on the Common, grabbing some coffee in Doane Library, or heading into the newly expanded Mitchell Athletics Center. They're all here, hanging out together, because Denison is a completely residential college, featuring 10 modern apartment-style halls for upperclass students.

"Denison is known for the learning partnership it fosters between students and professors. The faculty, who are brilliant scholars, teachers and mentors, thrive on collaboration with their students through joint research, small seminars and lively discussions in and outside the classroom. Denison offers 48 courses of study, eleven pre-professional programs and bachelor's degrees in science, art and fine arts. Beyond Denison's rigorous and relevant liberal arts curriculum, students are involved in community service, student government, varsity and intramural sports, honor societies and social groups. Denisonians develop leadership skills through some 180 student-run organizations. The Career Exploration and Development office helps to prepare students for a wide range of careers and advanced study following graduation. In addition, the college's acclaimed internship program and its impressive alumni network allow students to choose from hundreds internship opportunities in real-world settings. Denison offers a test-optional application process for high-achieving students and practices need-blind admissions policies."

SELECTIVITY

Admissions Rating	92
# of applicants	4,757
% of applicants accepted	50
% of acceptees attending	27
# offered a place on the wait list	207
% accepting a place on wait list	83
% admitted from wait list	1
# of early decision applicants	192
% accepted early decision	79

FRESHMAN PROFILE

Range SAT Critical Reading	720–600
Range SAT Math	680–600
Range ACT Composite	31–27
Minimum paper TOEFL	599
Minimum web-based TOEFL	213
Average HS GPA	3.50
% graduated top 10% of class	49
% graduated top 25% of class	39
% graduated top 50% of class	12

DEADLINES

Early decision	
Deadline	11/15
Regular	
Deadline	1/15
Notification	3/15
Nonfall registration?	No

APPLICANTS ALSO LOOK AT AND OFTEN PREFER

University of Michigan—Ann Arbor; University of Richmond

AND SOMETIMES PREFER

Kenyon College; Oberlin College; Boston College; Vanderbilt University; Northwestern University; Gettysburg College

AND RARELY PREFER

Case Western Reserve University; Bucknell University; DePauw University; Dickinson College; Miami University; Ohio Wesleyan University; The College of Wooster; The Ohio State University—Columbus

FINANCIAL FACTS

Financial Aid Rating	91
Annual tuition	$42,990
Room and board	$10,760
Required fees	$920
% needy frosh rec. need-based scholarship or grant aid	100
% needy UG rec. need-based scholarship or grant aid	100
% needy frosh rec. non-need-based scholarship or grant aid	93
% needy UG rec. non-need-based scholarship or grant aid	90
% needy frosh rec. need-based self-help aid	73
% needy UG rec. need-based self-help aid	77
% frosh rec. any financial aid	97
% UG rec. any financial aid	96
% frosh need fully met	48
% ugrads need fully met	28
Average % of frosh need met	97
Average % of ugrad need met	96

DePaul University

ONE EAST JACKSON BOULEVARD, CHICAGO, IL 60604-2287 • ADMISSIONS: 312-362-8300 • FAX: 312-362-5749

CAMPUS LIFE

Quality of Life Rating	92
Fire Safety Rating	99
Green Rating	92
Type of school	Private
Affiliation	Roman Catholic
Environment	Metropolis

STUDENTS

Total undergrad enrollment	16,120
% male/female	46/54
% from out of state	20
% frosh from public high school	77
% frosh live on campus	71
% ugrads live on campus	16
# of fraternities	10
# of sororities	16
% African American	8
% Asian	7
% Caucasian	56
% Hispanic	17
% Native American	<1
% international	3
# of countries represented	84

SURVEY SAYS . . .

Classroom facilities are great
Students love Chicago, IL
Great off-campus food
Athletic facilities are great

ACADEMICS

Academic Rating	78
% students returning for sophomore year	85
% students graduating within 4 years	54
% students graduating within 6 years	70
Calendar	Quarter
Student/faculty ratio	16:1
Profs interesting rating	79
Profs accessible rating	76

Most classes have 20–29 students.
Most lab/discussion sessions have 20–29 students.

MOST POPULAR MAJORS

psychology; accounting; finance

STUDENTS SAY ". . ."

Academics

DePaul University's urban setting means this Chicago school is "all about integrating the opportunities of the city into the classroom," offering students "the essentials in order for a student to succeed in the business field." Here, the "dedicated" teaching staff's "extensive experience outside of the classroom… really brings valuable information into the classroom." That experience proves beneficial to career-focused students because it "encourages students to become critical life thinkers so that they are not just prepared for a job, but have the skills to become present in all life decisions." This real-world focus in classroom studies and its "extensive school of commerce curriculum" is part of what has given DePaul a "strong academic reputation." Internship and career-placement opportunities both during school and after graduation result in, according to some graduates, students who are "some of the hardest working and driven college students around." The multiple colleges of DePaul University "stress engaging with other students, working collaboratively, combining previous knowledge with new learning, and being an active participant in one's education." Students praise the easy access provided by the urban setting and its accompanying public transportation, and like the "practical real world experience" brought to the table by the educators here—though some note "there are ones that are tougher graders," so applicants should be prepared to work.

Life

The school's location in downtown Chicago, one of the largest and most vibrant cities in the United States, means that "there is a plethora of choices of things to do" and plenty of transportation to get to them. Students "are always going to the museums, the art institute, Navy pier, shopping on Michigan Ave, the zoo, the beach, etc.," and "in the summer the outdoor concerts and food tasting events take over Grant Park." Throw in "the lakefront, bars and restaurants, sports teams (pro and collegiate)," along with "cultural venues [and] free public events," and it's no wonder students say they "never get bored." Sports fanatics will especially find more than enough to keep themselves busy outside of class. If the wealth of riches that is Chicago professional sports is not enough—the Bulls, Blackhawks, White Sox, Cubs, and Bears all play here—"having DePaul in the Big East conference brings great college basketball to Chicago," too. For those who prefer to stay on campus in this "simply amazing" city, DePaul has a strong Greek scene. The bottom line is, life at DePaul is all about location, location, location, so "the internships, classes, and social life are centered around the city."

Student Body

There is no nailing down the typical DePaul student. "It's like a melting pot of experience and people from all over the world that come to be a part of the DePaul environment," a "unique blend of all kinds of students" who are "like a giant mixed bag of Jelly Bellys…every student is so different you have a little bit of everything." One student goes so far as to suggest it's "possibly the most diverse school in the country." Though attendees "come from all walks of life" and "individuality is promoted strongly," virtually anyone "can fit in easily if they want." "Every student has a place where they feel comfortable," one student says, "and it is hard to find a student that doesn't fit in here." If there is a tie that binds, it is that DePaul students are "kind and friendly," "outgoing and respectful," a group who "study hard to get where they're going but still find time to socialize." Hard work is a common trait. "The majority of students seem to hold outside employment," a student notes, "which brings a strong real world emphasis to the class from staff and students alike." But hard workers aside, the typical DePaul student? "There is no typical anything."

Financial Aid: 312-362-8091 • E-mail: admission@depaul.edu • Website: www.depaul.edu

THE PRINCETON REVIEW SAYS

Admissions

Very important factors considered include: GPA, rigor of secondary school record, standardized test scores, application essay. *Important factors considered include:* Class rank, extracurricular activities, recommendation(s), talent/ability, volunteer work, work experience, character/personal qualities, level of applicant's interest. *Other factors considered include:* First generation, geographical residence, interview, racial/ethnic status, state residency, alumni/ae relations, religious affiliation, SAT or ACT recommended; ACT with or without Writing component accepted. TOEFL required of all international applicants. *Academic units required:* 4 English; 3 mathematics; 3 science; (2 science lab). *Academic units recommended:* 4 English; 3 mathematics; 3 science; (2 science lab); 2 foreign language.

Financial Aid

Students should submit: FAFSA. The Princeton Review suggests that all financial aid forms be submitted as soon as possible after January 1. *Need-based scholarships/grants offered:* Federal Pell, SEOG, State scholarships/grants, private scholarships, the school's own gift aid. *Loan aid offered:* Direct Subsidized Stafford Loans, Direct Unsubsidized Stafford Loans, Direct PLUS loans, Federal Perkins Loans. Federal Work-Study Program available. Institutional employment available. Off-campus job opportunities are excellent.

The Inside Word

DePaul's reputation as one of the most diverse schools in the country is not mere hyperbole, it's a truth expressed by student after student, and by the actions of the administration itself. The school actively seeks out minority students both as freshmen and transfers, and in an effort to surmount tuition-related obstacles works with local community colleges so students can meet their requirements at a lower cost before transferring to DePaul.

THE SCHOOL SAYS "..."

From the Admissions Office

"The nation's largest Catholic university, DePaul University is nationally recognized for its innovative academic programs that embrace a comprehensive learn-by-doing approach. DePaul has two residential locations and four commuter locations in the suburbs. The Lincoln Park campus is located in one of Chicago's most exciting neighborhoods, filled with theaters, cafés, clubs, and shops. It is home to DePaul's College of Liberal Arts and Sciences, the School of Education, the Theater School, and the School of Music. New buildings on the thirty-six-acre campus include residence halls, a science building, a student recreational facility, and the student center, which features a café where students can gather with friends. The Loop location, located in Chicago's downtown—a world-class center for business, government, law, and culture—is home to DePaul's Driehaus College of Business; College of Law; School of Computer Science, Telecommunications, and Information Systems; School for New Learning; and School of Accountancy and Management Information Systems."

SELECTIVITY

Admissions Rating	85
# of applicants	19,957
% of applicants accepted	60
% of acceptees attending	20

FRESHMAN PROFILE

Range SAT Critical Reading	530–630
Range SAT Math	520–630
Range ACT Composite	23–28
Minimum paper TOEFL	550
Minimum web-based TOEFL	213
Average HS GPA	3.65
% graduated top 10% of class	25
% graduated top 25% of class	57
% graduated top 50% of class	89

DEADLINES

Early action	
Deadline	11/15
Notification	1/15
Regular	
Priority	11/15
Deadline	2/1
Notification	3/15
Nonfall registration?	Yes

FINANCIAL FACTS

Financial Aid Rating	80
Annual tuition	$33,390
Room and board	$12,103
Required fees	$600
Books and supplies	$1,134
% needy frosh rec. need-based scholarship or grant aid	85
% needy UG rec. need-based scholarship or grant aid	84
% needy frosh rec. non-need-based scholarship or grant aid	87
% needy UG rec. non-need-based scholarship or grant aid	55
% needy frosh rec. need-based self-help aid	69
% needy UG rec. need-based self-help aid	77
% frosh rec. any financial aid	98
% UG rec. any financial aid	83
% UG borrow to pay for school	61
Average cumulative indebtedness	$26,848
% frosh need fully met	12
% ugrads need fully met	11
Average % of frosh need met	66
Average % of ugrad need met	92

DePauw University

204 East Seminary, Greencastle, IN 46135 • Admissions: 765-658-4006 • Fax: 765-658-4007

STUDENTS SAY ". . ."

Academics

Serious-minded students are drawn to DePauw University for its "small classes," "encouraging" professors, and the "individual academic attention" they can expect to receive. Academically, DePauw is "demanding but rewarding," and "requires a lot of outside studying and discipline" in order to keep up. Professors' "expectations are very high," which means "you can't slack off and get good grades." Be prepared to pull your "fair share of all-nighters." Fortunately, DePauw professors are more than just stern taskmasters. Though they pile on the work, they "are always helpful and available" to students in need. When things get overwhelming, "they are very understanding and will cut you a break if you really deserve" it. As a result, students come to know their professors "on a personal level," making DePauw the kind of school where it is "common [for students] to have dinner at a professor's house." Beyond stellar professors, DePauw's other academic draws include "extraordinary" study abroad opportunities and a "wonderful" alumni network great for "connections and networking opportunities." Alums also "keep our endowment pretty high, making it easy for the school to give out merit scholarships," which undergraduates appreciate. Student opinion regarding the administration ranges from ambivalent to slightly negative. One especially thorny issue is class registration; you "rarely" get into all the classes you want.

Life

Few schools are as Greek as DePauw, but students are quick to point out that "it is by no means *Animal House*." The Greek system here is more holistic than that. It "promotes not only social activities but also philanthropic events." That's not to say there aren't lots of frat parties here. There are. But "the administration has cracked down big time" on the larger frat parties, and "now there are just small parties in apartments and dorms." One recently issued rule is that freshmen "will not be allowed on Greek property until after rush, which is the first week of second semester." In addition to administrative regulation, students exercise their own self-restraint; for the typical undergraduate, "the week is mostly reserved for studying." Beyond the frats and sororities, "there is always a theater production, athletic event, or organization-sponsored event going on," and popular bands occasionally perform on campus. It's a good thing so much is happening at the school because off-campus entertainment options are scarce: "If there is really any fun to be had, it's not in Greencastle." The situation could be greatly improved if there were just a few "more restaurants and stores in the town or a nearby town." As things stand, however, students "have to go to Indianapolis (forty-five miles) to go shopping, watch a good movie, eat at a good restaurant, etc."

Student Body

The typical DePauw student is "upper middle class," "a little preppy, a little athletic," and "hardworking;" students "[party] hard on weekend," and "usually become[s] involved with the Greek system." Students describe their peers as "driven" and wearing "polos and pearls." They "have all had multiple internships, international experience, and [have held] some type of leadership position." Though these folks may seem "overcommitted," they "always get their work done." For those who don't fit this mold, don't fret; most students seem to be "accepting of the different types" of people on campus. Diversity on campus is augmented through the school's partnership with the Posse Foundation, which brings in urban (though not necessarily minority) "students from Chicago and NYC every year." These students are described as "leaders on campus" and "take real initiative to hold their communities together."

FINANCIAL AID: 765-658-4030 • E-MAIL: ADMISSION@DEPAUW.EDU • WEBSITE: WWW.DEPAUW.EDU

THE PRINCETON REVIEW SAYS

Admissions

Very important factors considered include: GPA, rigor of secondary school record, standardized test scores. *Important factors considered include:* Class rank, application essay, recommendation(s). *Other factors considered include:* Extracurricular activities, first generation, geographical residence, interview, state residency, talent/ability, volunteer work, work experience, alumni/ae relations, character/personal qualities, level of applicant's interest. SAT or ACT required; SAT and SAT Subject Tests or ACT considered if submitted; ACT with or without Writing component accepted. TOEFL required of all international applicants. *Academic units recommended:* 4 English; 4 mathematics; (2 science lab).

Financial Aid

Students should submit: FAFSA, CSS/Financial Aid PROFILE. Regular filing deadline is 3/1. The Princeton Review suggests that all financial aid forms be submitted as soon as possible after January 1. *Need-based scholarships/grants offered:* Federal Pell, SEOG, State scholarships/grants, private scholarships, the school's own gift aid. *Loan aid offered:* Direct Subsidized Stafford Loans, Direct Unsubsidized Stafford Loans, Direct PLUS loans, Federal Perkins Loans, College/university loans from institutional funds. Federal Work-Study Program available. Institutional employment available. Off-campus job opportunities are fair.

The Inside Word

Prospective applicants should not be deceived by DePauw's high acceptance rate. The students who are accepted and choose to enroll here have the academic goods to justify their admission. Many of them are accepted by more "competitive" schools and still choose DePauw. DePauw's generous financial aid packages have a lot to do with students' choice to enroll.

THE SCHOOL SAYS ". . ."

From the Admissions Office

"DePauw University is nationally recognized for intellectual and experiential challenges that link liberal arts education with life's work, preparing graduates for uncommon professional success, service to others and personal fulfillment. DePauw graduates count among their ranks a Nobel Laureate, a vice president and United States congressman, Pulitzer Prize-winning and Newbery Award-winning authors, and a number of CEOs and humanitarian leaders. Our students demonstrate a love for learning, a willingness to serve others, the reason and judgment to lead, an interest in engaging worlds and cultures unknown to them, the courage to question their assumptions and a strong commitment to community. Pre-professional and career exploration are encouraged through Winter Term, when more than 700 students pursue their own off-campus experiential learning opportunities. Other innovative programs include Honor Scholars, Environmental Fellows, Media Fellows and Science Research Fellows, affording selected students additional seminar and internship opportunities. The University offers a new approach to music education in the entrepreneurial 21CM program in the School of Music.

"Freshman applicants are required to submit scores of the writing section of the SAT or the ACT."

SELECTIVITY

Admissions Rating	93
# of applicants	5,204
% of applicants accepted	60
% of acceptees attending	21
# of early decision applicants	61
% accepted early decision	92

FRESHMAN PROFILE

Range SAT Critical Reading	520–650
Range SAT Math	550–680
Range SAT Writing	530–630
Range ACT Composite	25–30
Minimum web-based TOEFL	90
Average HS GPA	3.75
% graduated top 10% of class	49
% graduated top 25% of class	78
% graduated top 50% of class	100

DEADLINES

Early decision	
Deadline	11/1
Notification	12/1
Early action	
Deadline	12/1
Notification	1/15
Deadline	1/15
Notification	1/1
Regular	
Deadline	2/1
Nonfall registration?	Yes

APPLICANTS ALSO LOOK AT AND OFTEN PREFER
Indiana University—Bloomington; Vanderbilt University; University of Notre Dame; Northwestern University

AND SOMETIMES PREFER
University of Illinois at Urbana-Champaign; Miami University; Denison University

AND RARELY PREFER
Hanover College

FINANCIAL FACTS

Financial Aid Rating	89
Annual tuition	$42,050
Room and board	$11,200
Required fees	$696
Books and supplies	$750
% needy frosh rec. need-based scholarship or grant aid	100
% needy UG rec. need-based scholarship or grant aid	100
% needy frosh rec. non-need-based scholarship or grant aid	27
% needy UG rec. non-need-based scholarship or grant aid	22
% needy frosh rec. need-based self-help aid	67
% needy UG rec. need-based self-help aid	74
% UG borrow to pay for school	55
Average cumulative indebtedness	$22,755
% frosh need fully met	33
% ugrads need fully met	29
Average % of frosh need met	87
Average % of ugrad need met	87

DICKINSON COLLEGE

PO Box 1773, Carlisle, PA 17013-2896 • Admissions: 717-245-1231 • Fax: 717-245-1442

CAMPUS LIFE

Quality of Life Rating	72
Fire Safety Rating	80
Green Rating	99
Type of school	Private
Affiliation	No Affiliation
Environment	City

STUDENTS

Total undergrad enrollment	2,352
% male/female	44/56
% from out of state	77
% frosh from public high school	60
% frosh live on campus	100
% ugrads live on campus	95
# of fraternities	4
# of sororities	5
% African American	4
% Asian	2
% Caucasian	76
% Hispanic	6
% Native American	<1
% international	7
# of countries represented	44

SURVEY SAYS . . .
Lab facilities are great
Lots of beer drinking
Great library

ACADEMICS

Academic Rating	89
% students returning for sophomore year	90
% students graduating within 4 years	83
% students graduating within 6 years	85
Calendar	Semester
Student/faculty ratio	9:1
Profs interesting rating	89
Profs accessible rating	87
Most classes have 10–19 students.	

MOST POPULAR MAJORS
political science; international business and management; biology

STUDENTS SAY ". . ."

Academics
Many students cite Dickinson's unique combination of being a small liberal arts institution with a global perspective as their reason for coming here. There's a host of study abroad options, and "it's assumed that most juniors will go abroad." Students who have attended large universities while studying abroad come to appreciate Dickinson's "small class sizes," which "allow professors to get to know their students." "Professors are tremendously accessible" and are "always willing to find a way to help students achieve their goals and meet their potential." "They come with all sorts of life experiences and connections in their respective fields to get students to interact with people in the areas they are studying." Classes are often "discussion-based, and [they] really give you an opportunity to engage and grow into the topic," though a few students wish lab science classes were more accessible to non-majors. "Class materials are very well-chosen, and professors are always passionate about their subjects." While some students gripe about the administration's "superficial changes" and "red tape," many more praise it as accessible and "forward-thinking"—this praise tends to come from students who chose Dickinson in part for its recently adopted emphasis on "promoting sustainable and green lifestyles."

Life
Descriptions of student life at Dickinson vary widely—suggesting a lot of options. While many students subscribe to the "work hard, play hard" philosophy, "the campus has a pretty good social life that does not involve alcohol." "The college's Event Advisory Board makes the plans readily available through e-mail and paper posts for every weekend. These lists are typically pretty extensive as there are many options to do for fun around campus." Sports are very popular, and many students note that participation in a campus group, whether it's a team, club, or Greek organization, is integral to social life. Some feel there's a bit of pressure for men to go Greek, but those who have chosen non-Greek life are generally happy, and for fun they "participate in Dickinson-sponsored dances and events and hang out with friends." Students are satisfied overall with their campus and facilities, and note that the library and cafeteria can be social hotbeds, though many wish for more meal options (one student suggests "the cafeteria should give up cooking fish."). Though small hometown Carlisle "isn't for everyone," "there are quite a few good restaurants within easy walking distance of campus," and the Carlisle Theater "brings in independent films and those sponsored by community groups and offers excellent discounts to students." "There is also a shuttle service that takes students anywhere in the town of Carlisle from 9:00 P.M. to 3:00 A.M."

Student Body
"The typical Dickinson student is outgoing, balanced, and engaged," and "because it's such a small community most people find their niche or group fairly easily." "while some report "most students are pretty preppy," "upper-middle-class," from the Northeast, and "are really fit, go to the gym a lot, [and] play a lot of sports," we also hear that "the beauty of Dickinson is that there is no 'typical' student. Everyone is here to become more globally aware and educated." Dickinson's emphasis on global perspectives and a strong international studies program draw "a lot of international [students], so there is good cultural diversity." "There are different crowds. There is a faction that parties all the time, and there is a faction that is heavily involved in academics, extracurriculars, and community service." "Involved" and "engaged" are two words that come up a lot: "Joining clubs and extracurricular activities is a great way to meet people, and there are plenty of them!"

DICKINSON COLLEGE

FINANCIAL AID: 717-245-1308 • E-MAIL: ADMISSIONS@DICKINSON.EDU • WEBSITE: WWW.DICKINSON.EDU

THE PRINCETON REVIEW SAYS

Admissions

Very important factors considered include: GPA, rigor of secondary school record, application essay, extracurricular activities, recommendation(s), talent/ability, volunteer work, character/personal qualities, level of applicant's interest. *Important factors considered include:* Class rank, standardized test scores, geographical residence, interview, racial/ethnic status, state residency, work experience, alumni/ae relations. *Other factors considered include:* First generation. SAT and SAT Subject Tests or ACT considered if submitted; ACT with or without Writing component accepted. TOEFL required of all international applicants. *Academic units required:* 4 English; 3 mathematics; 3 science; (2 science lab); 2 social studies; 2 foreign language; 2 academic electives. *Academic units recommended:* 3 foreign language.

Financial Aid

Students should submit: FAFSA, CSS/Financial Aid PROFILE, State aid form, Noncustodial PROFILE. Regular filing deadline is 2/1. The Princeton Review suggests that all financial aid forms be submitted as soon as possible after January 1. *Need-based scholarships/grants offered:* Federal Pell, SEOG, State scholarships/grants, private scholarships, the school's own gift aid. *Loan aid offered:* Direct Subsidized Stafford Loans, Direct Unsubsidized Stafford Loans, Direct PLUS loans, Federal Perkins Loans, College/university loans from institutional funds. Applicants will be notified of awards beginning 3/20. Federal Work-Study Program available. Institutional employment available. Off-campus job opportunities are good.

The Inside Word

The applicant pool for small liberal arts colleges has become increasingly competitive in recent years, and Dickinson is no exception. For admission here, you'll want to be the stereotypical well-rounded student, with a solid GPA in challenging classes, and broad extracurricular involvement.

THE SCHOOL SAYS "..."

From the Admissions Office

"Dickinson is a nationally recognized liberal arts college chartered in 1783 in Carlisle, Pennsylvania. Devoted to its revolutionary roots, the college maintains the mission of founder Benjamin Rush—to provide a useful education in the liberal arts and sciences. Dickinson has a robust academic program, offering forty-three majors plus minors, certificates, independent research, and internships. Our innovative programs range from neuroscience to security studies, and develop intellectual independence by actively engaging in research, fieldwork, lab work in state-of-the-art science programs and other experiential opportunities. Dickinson's global curriculum includes international business and management, international studies, thirteen languages, and many globally oriented courses. Dickinson offers one of the world's most respected study abroad programs, and more than half of Dickinson's students study in more than forty programs in twenty-five countries on six continents. Dickinson is recognized as a leader among educational institutions committed to sustainability and green initiatives. The Center for Sustainability Education integrates sustainability into its academics, facilities, operations, and campus culture. Dickinson has received the highest awards from the Association for the Advancement of Sustainability in Higher Education, Sierra Club, Sustainable Endowments Institute, The Princeton Review, and Second Nature. Dickinson alumni are at the top of their fields as business leaders, professional artists and writers, sports agents and athletes, doctors and researchers. And many of them used their liberal arts foundation to forge their own paths. Our graduate school partnerships enable our students to enter top programs with greater ease and reflect the high regard in which Dickinson is held."

SELECTIVITY
Admissions Rating	94
# of applicants	5,826
% of applicants accepted	44
% of acceptees attending	24
# offered a place on the wait list	774
% accepting a place on wait list	34
% admitted from wait list	4
# of early decision applicants	401
% accepted early decision	69

FRESHMAN PROFILE
Range SAT Critical Reading	590–675
Range SAT Math	600–690
Range SAT Writing	590–680
Range ACT Composite	27–31
% graduated top 10% of class	46
% graduated top 25% of class	78
% graduated top 50% of class	93

DEADLINES
Early decision	
Deadline	11/15
Notification	12/15
Early action	
Deadline	12/1
Notification	2/1
Regular	
Deadline	2/1
Notification	3/20
Nonfall registration?	No

APPLICANTS ALSO LOOK AT AND OFTEN PREFER
Colby College; Colgate University; Connecticut College; Franklin & Marshall College

AND SOMETIMES PREFER
American University; Bucknell University; Gettysburg College; Hamilton College; Kenyon College; Lafayette College; Skidmore College; Trinity College

FINANCIAL FACTS
Financial Aid Rating	92
Annual tuition	$47,242
Room and board	$11,972
Required fees	$450
Books and supplies	$1,050
% needy frosh rec. need-based scholarship or grant aid	96
% needy UG rec. need-based scholarship or grant aid	97
% needy frosh rec. non-need-based scholarship or grant aid	6
% needy UG rec. non-need-based scholarship or grant aid	7
% needy frosh rec. need-based self-help aid	91
% needy UG rec. need-based self-help aid	90
% frosh rec. any financial aid	76
% UG rec. any financial aid	75
% UG borrow to pay for school	55
Average cumulative indebtedness	$24,739
% frosh need fully met	72
% ugrads need fully met	62
Average % of frosh need met	98
Average % of ugrad need met	96

DREW UNIVERSITY

OFFICE OF COLLEGE ADMISSIONS, MADISON, NJ 07940-1493 • ADMISSIONS: 973-408-3739 • FAX: 973-408-3068

CAMPUS LIFE

Quality of Life Rating	75
Fire Safety Rating	97
Green Rating	95
Type of school	Private
Affiliation	Methodist
Environment	Village

STUDENTS

Total undergrad enrollment	1,453
% male/female	38/62
% from out of state	31
% frosh from public high school	66
% frosh live on campus	87
% ugrads live on campus	77
% African American	11
% Asian	5
% Caucasian	56
% Hispanic	14
% Native American	<1
% international	3
# of countries represented	24

SURVEY SAYS . . .
Theater is popular
Frats and sororities are unpopular
or nonexistent
Student publications are popular

ACADEMICS

Academic Rating	85
% students returning for sophomore year	76
% students graduating within 4 years	65
% students graduating within 6 years	69
Calendar	Semester
Student/faculty ratio	10:1
Profs interesting rating	83
Profs accessible rating	83

Most classes have 10–19 students.
Most lab/discussion sessions have
10–19 students.

MOST POPULAR MAJORS
political science; English; psychology

STUDENTS SAY "..."

Academics

Drew University features three major draws, according to current students: a gorgeous campus, a prime location (less than an hour from New York City by train), and strong academics. As at many schools, "some majors…are stronger than others," and introductory classes tend to be large lectures, but "class sizes, especially in upper-level courses, are generally small," which allows for "meaningful discussions." Though some say the administration "tends to be aloof," this obviously isn't a problem with the faculty. Students say professors are "very approachable, accommodating, and enthusiastic about what they teach." "They are quite engaging…have PhDs in the field that they teach, and…seem genuinely interested in helping us improve." "They're always there when students want extra help and are very understanding." One happy English major tells us, "My professors have really encouraged me to pursue the most out of my education here. One provided me with the opportunity to read my original poetry in NYC with distinguished poets. Another has influenced my decision to write a senior thesis. Within my major, I feel like part of a family. All of my professors know me, and I think they truly care about my performance." A neuroscience major raves, "Science professors will be acting out the material or showing demos of the material." Study abroad opportunities also abound, and the proximity to New York City gives students amazing internship opportunities.

Life

Life at Drew is typical of life on other small, Northeastern campuses, with a balanced blend of school-sponsored events, student clubs, and "of course, like any other college, students drink and party once the weekend comes, but it's not the only focus here." Students also enjoy heading off campus to nearby Morristown, and "trips to NYC are funded to go to museums, the outlet mall, basketball games, etc." Also on campus is the Shakespeare Theatre of New Jersey, and students are happy to take advantage of work-study opportunities there, as well as performances. On campus, there are a lot of "activities—at least one every night," and "facilities and living councils are constantly making improvements." "Students tend to try and get their money's worth by participating in as many opportunities as they can," and whether it's "environmental film screenings, a lecture by Anderson Cooper, or free food from the Polish Culture Club, there is always something you can become involved in." "There are lots of alcohol-free events planned for the weekends," "for example, sometimes performers like musicians or comedians come and perform, or sometimes there are guests." Club Drew, "a club [night] once a month on campus with a DJ," is well-attended.

Student Body

"A typical student at Drew is smart, driven," and "hardworking, but still parties at least once a week." "Talkative," "outgoing," and "social" also come up a lot when Drew students describe themselves. While some say "the typical Drew student is white, American, [and] from the East Coast," "we have an abundance of students from diverse ethnic backgrounds," and "there's a lot of different types of people, from jocks to hipsters." "There are jocks, theater junkies, musicians, premed students, international students, political science enthusiasts, and everything else." "It's mind-boggling how different the... undergraduates are," but "with an outstanding number of clubs and other social groups, literally any student can find a group of people to click with," and students suggest "to get the best experience out of Drew…you need to get involved."

FINANCIAL AID: 973-408-3112 • E-MAIL: CADM@DREW.EDU • WEBSITE: WWW.DREW.EDU

THE PRINCETON REVIEW SAYS

Admissions

Very important factors considered include: GPA, rigor of secondary school record. *Important factors considered include:* Standardized test scores, application essay, extracurricular activities, recommendation(s), talent/ability, character/personal qualities. *Other factors considered include:* Class rank, interview, racial/ethnic status, volunteer work, work experience, alumni/ae relations, level of applicant's interest. SAT or ACT required; ACT with or without Writing component accepted. TOEFL required of all international applicants. *Academic units recommended:* 4 English; 3 mathematics; 2 science; 2 social studies; 2 foreign language; 2 history; 3 academic electives.

Financial Aid

Students should submit: FAFSA. Regular filing deadline is 2/15. The Princeton Review suggests that all financial aid forms be submitted as soon as possible after January 1. *Need-based scholarships/grants offered:* Federal Pell, SEOG, State scholarships/grants, private scholarships, the school's own gift aid. *Loan aid offered:* Direct Subsidized Stafford Loans, Direct Unsubsidized Stafford Loans, Direct PLUS loans, State Loans. Federal Work-Study Program available. Institutional employment available. Off-campus job opportunities are fair.

The Inside Word

Drew takes a holistic approach to evaluating applications, so you definitely want to showcase more than just your GPA (though that's also important). Drew's applicant pool has grown significantly in recent years, so presenting yourself as not only a great student but also a great fit with the school will help you stand out from the pack.

THE SCHOOL SAYS "..."

From the Admissions Office

"Drew offers what few liberal arts colleges can: an intimate, stimulating community on a bucolic campus that is fully plugged into New York City. Drew is small enough so that professors know you and your dreams, but like urban schools in NYC, it calls the United Nations, Wall Street and the world mecca of contemporary art home. Drew is also building on its long legacy of globalism by admitting an ever larger number of international students. Living and studying amid a mélange of cultures gives our students a distinct advantage in highly connected global workplace.

"'We Deliver Full-Impact Learning' is how Drew describes its innovative and thoughtful approach to education. To better yourself, we believe, is to better the world. Drew makes its commitment clear: we offer four-year scholarships to Civic Scholars, students who, regardless of major, choose to graduate as civic leaders. Students can also find their place in the world by shadowing physicians in a busy emergency room; traveling extensively abroad; interning at a comedy club in Manhattan; spending intense, life-changing summers in Drew labs; or being a Baldwin Honor Scholar.

After graduation, Full-Impact Learning also enables your greatest success. Drew alumni are readily accepted into elite graduate schools and hired at major corporations and financial firms, in public service, in the arts, in science and, of course, in education."

SELECTIVITY

Admissions Rating	80
# of applicants	3,430
% of applicants accepted	77
% of acceptees attending	15
# of early decision applicants	133
% accepted early decision	53

FRESHMAN PROFILE

Range SAT Critical Reading	490–610
Range SAT Math	500–610
Range SAT Writing	500–610
Range ACT Composite	21.5–27
Minimum paper TOEFL	550
Minimum web-based TOEFL	213
Average HS GPA	3.40
% graduated top 10% of class	31
% graduated top 25% of class	62
% graduated top 50% of class	89

DEADLINES

Early decision	
Deadline	12/1
Notification	12/16
Regular	
Deadline	2/15
Nonfall registration?	Yes

FINANCIAL FACTS

Financial Aid Rating	78
Annual tuition	$42,936
Room and board	$11,944
Required fees	$1,132
Books and supplies	$1,128
% needy frosh rec. need-based scholarship or grant aid	100
% needy UG rec. need-based scholarship or grant aid	100
% needy frosh rec. non-need-based scholarship or grant aid	9
% needy UG rec. non-need-based scholarship or grant aid	8
% needy frosh rec. need-based self-help aid	78
% needy UG rec. need-based self-help aid	83
% frosh rec. any financial aid	98
% UG rec. any financial aid	95
% UG borrow to pay for school	70
Average cumulative indebtedness	$25,526
% frosh need fully met	17
% ugrads need fully met	16
Average % of frosh need met	75
Average % of ugrad need met	76

DREXEL UNIVERSITY

3141 CHESTNUT STREET, PHILADELPHIA, PA 19104 • ADMISSIONS: 215-895-2400 • FAX: 215-895-1285

STUDENTS SAY ". . ."

Academics

By far the biggest draw for students seems to be Drexel University's cooperative education program that "gives students the opportunity to gain hands-on experience and develop professionally in their field of study." The co-op program is "an amazing experience" and "really sets [Drexel] apart." The program "offers real-world work experience and contacts at up to three local and/or national companies before graduation—and in this economy, it's all in who you know!" The co-op really helps students get "an excellent job after graduation." "Drexel University has diversified from its roots," and the school is "no longer being about just engineering. [Drexel] has set out to educate students to prepare them for careers in all industries." Students enjoy a "great campus location" in Philadelphia and "prides itself on innovative technologies that value sustainability, progressive learning that encourages constant change, and opportunities for invaluable experience." Although most of the professors "are very knowledgeable in their field" and offer "hands-on learning combined with direct application," many students say that "too many professors speak English as a second language" and "have difficulty communicating to their students." Students also pinpoint the "red tape" and "bureaucracy" as frustrating, saying that it bogs down the school. "Drexel is unfortunately run too much like a business sometimes," one student explains. "It can be difficult to get through the red tape that ties up departments." Some students also see the tuition as "outrageous." Although "some facilities are old and need work," Drexel is good about "dumping money into improving facilities" and most are "top-quality." One student proudly says, "Drexel is a great school," and it "is only going upward from here."

Life

Drexel University is located "right in the heart" of Philadelphia, one of the country's largest and most vibrant cities. Consequently, much of student life involves exploring this unique city. "It is so easy to learn how to use the subway and go into the heart of the city. It's so much fun to check out new locations, go shopping, and try out some of the best restaurants in town." Students love "the comedy club in center city [and] the bars in Old City," and they often head to a "Phillies, Flyers, or 76ers game." "The music scene in Philadelphia is great," and "the Philadelphia Museum of Art is just a twenty-minute walk from campus." In addition to having the entire city of Philadelphia at your disposal, the University of Pennsylvania is "right across the street." "If you're into partying, there's always a party going on, if not, head over to UPenn or Temple," one student advises. On campus, "Greek life is a big part of Drexel's community." If there's a downside to Drexel life, it's that there's "very little school spirit." "The basketball team is all the school spirit that exists; there isn't any besides that," a student explains. But as soon as you step off campus, "there are countless other things to do too, like museums, operas, and musicals."

Student Body

"There is no such thing as a typical Drexel student," one student declares. "Our campus is incredibly diverse in every way." "Drexel is a mixing bowl" and "very multicultural." "Everyone is different, and we all interact with each other and fit in [with] all different groups." "There are so many different people from everywhere, and it's amazing. Black, white, gay, straight: it just makes the college life here diverse and exciting." "Most students get involved in one or more student organizations" to fit in. Students are also very hardworking and "busy with classes and studies." "Everyone is focused on careers after college, but people still like to have fun on the weekends." "We're generally pretty mellow people," a chemical engineering student explains. "[We] work hard, but don't get too uptight about grades and classes."

FINANCIAL AID: 215-895-1600 • E-MAIL: ENROLL@DREXEL.EDU • WEBSITE: WWW.DREXEL.EDU

THE PRINCETON REVIEW SAYS

Admissions

Very important factors considered include: Class rank, GPA, rigor of secondary school record, standardized test scores. *Important factors considered include:* Application essay, recommendation(s), character/personal qualities. *Other factors considered include:* Extracurricular activities, talent/ability, volunteer work, work experience, alumni/ae relations, level of applicant's interest. SAT or ACT required; ACT with or without Writing component accepted. TOEFL required of all international applicants. *Academic units required:* 3 mathematics; 1 science; (1 science lab). *Academic units recommended:* 1 foreign language.

Financial Aid

Students should submit: FAFSA. The Princeton Review suggests that all financial aid forms be submitted as soon as possible after January 1. *Need-based scholarships/grants offered:* Federal Pell, SEOG, State scholarships/grants, private scholarships, the school's own gift aid. *Loan aid offered:* Federal Perkins Loans, college/university loans from institutional funds. Federal Work-Study Program available.

The Inside Word

Drexel University's nationally recognized co-op program provides unique hands-on experience for students with companies in and around Philadelphia to help them in their post-college employment. Given the current state of the economy, that's a huge boost for prospective applicants, especially in the engineering fields that Drexel still specializes in.

THE SCHOOL SAYS ". . ."

From the Admissions Office

"Drexel University has maintained a reputation for academic excellence since its founding in 1891. Through Drexel Co-op, students have the opportunity to test-drive their degree in paid full-time positions where they can earn up to 18 months of workplace experience before graduation with employers such as Fortune 500 companies, major pharmaceutical companies, and top design firms, as well as nonprofit agencies and government organizations. More than 1,500 employers in 33 states and 40 international locations participate in the Drexel Co-op program. The average six-month co-op salary is more than $16,000.

"Drexel offers more than 80 undergraduate majors and over 20 accelerated degree programs. Accelerated degree options include the BA/BS/JD in law; BA/BS/MD in medicine; BS/DPT in physical therapy; BS/MS in computing and informatics; and BS/MBA in business.

"Qualified students can apply to the Honors program, which is open to students in every academic discipline. The Honors program offers special living communities designed for the exceptional student and opportunities for social activities, traveling, and independent projects. The STAR (Students Tackling Advanced Research) Scholars program invites qualified students to participate in faculty-mentored research projects in their chosen fields as early as the freshman year.

"Drexel also has an active Study Abroad program in more than two dozen countries around the world. Freshman Frontiers: First Term in Dublin, Drexel's newest option for studying abroad, is a selective program that enables students in qualifying majors to study at the Dublin Business School and School of Arts for the first term of their freshman year."

SELECTIVITY

Admissions Rating	85
# of applicants	40,586
% of applicants accepted	75
% of acceptees attending	10

FRESHMAN PROFILE

Range SAT Critical Reading	540–640
Range SAT Math	580–680
Range SAT Writing	530–640
Range ACT Composite	24–29
Minimum paper TOEFL	550
Minimum web-based TOEFL	213
Average HS GPA	3.60
% graduated top 10% of class	34
% graduated top 25% of class	65
% graduated top 50% of class	92

DEADLINES

Early action	
Deadline	11/1
Notification	12/15
Regular	
Deadline	1/15
Nonfall registration?	Yes

FINANCIAL FACTS

Financial Aid Rating	74
Annual tuition	$33,800
Room and board	$14,175
Required fees	$2,290
Books and supplies	$2,000
% needy frosh rec. need-based scholarship or grant aid	99
% needy UG rec. need-based scholarship or grant aid	93
% needy frosh rec. non-need-based scholarship or grant aid	15
% needy UG rec. non-need-based scholarship or grant aid	8
% needy frosh rec. need-based self-help aid	81
% needy UG rec. need-based self-help aid	90
% frosh rec. any financial aid	94
% UG rec. any financial aid	89
% UG borrow to pay for school	73
Average cumulative indebtedness	$35,082
% frosh need fully met	40
% ugrads need fully met	31
Average % of frosh need met	61
Average % of ugrad need met	56

DUKE UNIVERSITY

2138 CAMPUS DRIVE, DURHAM, NC 27708-0586 • ADMISSIONS: 919-684-3214 • FAX: 919-681-1661

CAMPUS LIFE

Quality of Life Rating	70
Fire Safety Rating	60*
Green Rating	97
Type of school	Private
Affiliation	Methodist
Environment	City

STUDENTS

Total undergrad enrollment	6,493
% male/female	50/50
% from out of state	87
% frosh from public high school	65
% frosh live on campus	100
% ugrads live on campus	81
# of fraternities	21
# of sororities	14
% African American	10
% Asian	21
% Caucasian	46
% Hispanic	6
% Native American	1
% international	8
# of countries represented	89

SURVEY SAYS . . .

Political activism is unpopular or nonexistent
Students are happy
Great library
Lots of beer drinking
Hard liquor is popular
Everyone loves the Blue Devils
Frats and sororities are popular
Student publications are popular

ACADEMICS

Academic Rating	87
% students returning for sophomore year	97
% students graduating within 4 years	87
% students graduating within 6 years	94
Calendar	Semester
Student/faculty ratio	7:1
Profs interesting rating	77
Profs accessible rating	74

Most classes have 10–19 students.
Most lab/discussion sessions have
10–19 students.

MOST POPULAR MAJORS

psychology; public policy; economics

STUDENTS SAY " . . ."

Academics

Duke University is "all about academic excellence complemented by highly competitive Division I sports and an enriching array of extracurricular activities," making the university "an exciting, challenging, and enjoyable place to be." Undergraduates choose Duke because they "are passionate about a wide range of things, including academics, sports, community service, research, and fun." And because the school seems equally committed to accommodating all of those pursuits; as one student puts it, "Duke is for the Ivy League candidate who is a little bit more laid-back about school and overachieving (but just a bit) and a lot more into the party scene." Academics "are very difficult in the quantitative majors (engineering, math, statistics, economics, premed)" and "much easier in the non-quantitative majors," but there's an "across-the-board excellence in all departments from humanities to engineering." In all areas, there's a "supportive environment in which the faculty, staff, and students are willing to look out for the other person and help them succeed." It's the norm to have large study groups, and "the review sessions, peer tutoring system, writing center, and academic support center are always helpful when students are struggling with anything from math homework to creating a résumé." Professors' "number-one priority is teaching undergraduates," and their love of discussion means they "would rather that the students lead the class as opposed to them leading the class." "There are a few who make me want to stay at Duke forever," says a student. Because "the school has a lot of confidence in its students," it offers them "seemingly limitless opportunities."

Life

Life at Duke "is very relaxed," and "you can either be a part of nothing, or you can be so over-committed that it's not even funny." Because "the student union and other organizations provide entertainment all the time, from movies to shows to campus-wide parties," there's "a wealth of on-campus opportunities to get involved." Indeed, weekends are for relaxing, and "people usually stay on campus for fun," because hometown Durham "has a few quirky streets and squares with restaurants, shops, clubs, etc., but to really do much you have to go to Raleigh or Chapel Hill," each twenty to thirty minutes away by car. The perception that "Durham is pretty dangerous" further dampens students' enthusiasm for the city. Undergrads' fervor for Blue Devils sports, on the other hand, can be boundless; sports, "especially basketball, are a huge deal here," and undergrads "will paint themselves completely blue and wait in line on the sidewalk in K-ville for three days to jump up and down in Cameron Indoor Stadium." Greek life "plays a big role in the social scene here," but "almost all the parties are open, so it definitely isn't hard to get into a party." Though it's a "very party-heavy school," a lot of people "just do their own thing—have a movie night, go exploring, go skiing or to the beach for a weekend." Still, the social scene can be "a little too intense" at times.

Student Body

The typical Duke student "is someone who cares a lot about his or her education but at the same time won't sacrifice a social life for it." Life involves "getting a ton of work done first and then finding time to play and have fun." The typical student here is studious but social, athletic but can never be seen in the gym, job hunting but not worrying, and so on and so forth." Everyone is "incredibly focused," but "that includes social success as well." Students tend to be "focused on graduating and obtaining a lucrative and prosperous career," and although they "go out two to three times a week," they're "always looking polished." An "overwhelming number" are athletes, "not just varsity athletes…but athletes in high school or generally active people. Duke's athletic pride attracts this kind of person." The student body "is surprisingly ethnically diverse, with a number of students of Asian, African, and Hispanic descent," and "every type of person finds a welcoming group where he or she fits in."

FINANCIAL AID: 919-684-6225 • E-MAIL: UNDERGRAD-ADMISSIONS@DUKE.EDU • WEBSITE: WWW.DUKE.EDU

THE PRINCETON REVIEW SAYS

Admissions

Very important factors considered include: Rigor of secondary school record, standardized test scores, application essay, extracurricular activities, recommendation(s), talent/ability. *Important factors considered include:* Character/personal qualities. *Other factors considered include:* Class rank, GPA, geographical residence, interview, racial/ethnic status, state residency, volunteer work, work experience, alumni/ae relations. SAT and SAT Subject Tests or ACT required. *Academic units recommended:* 4 English; 4 mathematics; 4 science; 4 social studies; 4 foreign language.

Financial Aid

Students should submit: FAFSA, CSS/Financial Aid PROFILE, Noncustodial PROFILE, Business/Farm Supplement. Regular filing deadline is 3/1. The Princeton Review suggests that all financial aid forms be submitted as soon as possible after January 1. *Need-based scholarships/grants offered:* Federal Pell, SEOG, State scholarships/grants, private scholarships, the school's own gift aid. *Loan aid offered:* Direct Subsidized Stafford Loans, Direct Unsubsidized Stafford Loans, Direct PLUS loans, Federal Perkins Loans, College/university loans from institutional funds. Applicants will be notified of awards beginning 4/1. Federal Work-Study Program available. Institutional employment available. Off-campus job opportunities are good.

The Inside Word

Duke is an extremely selective undergraduate institution, which affords the school the luxury of rejecting many qualified applicants. You'll have to present an exceptional record just to be considered; to make the cut, you'll have to impress the admissions office that you can contribute something unique and valuable to the incoming class. Being one of the best basketball players in the nation (male or female) helps a lot, but even athletes have to show academic excellence to get in the door here.

THE SCHOOL SAYS "..."

From the Admissions Office

"Duke University offers an interesting mix of tradition and innovation, undergraduate college and major research university, Southern hospitality and international presence, and athletic prowess and academic excellence. Students come to Duke from all over the United States and the world and from a range of racial, ethnic, and socioeconomic backgrounds. They enjoy contact with a world-class faculty through small classes and independent study. More than forty majors are available in the arts and sciences and engineering; arts and sciences students may also design their own curriculum through Program II. Certificate programs are available in a number of interdisciplinary areas. Special academic opportunities include the Focus Program and seminars for first-year students, study abroad, study at the Duke Marine Laboratory and Duke Primate Center, the Duke in New York and Duke in Los Angeles arts programs, and several international exchange programs. While admission to Duke is highly selective, applications of U.S. citizens and permanent residents are evaluated without regard to financial need and the university pledges to meet 100 percent of the demonstrated need of all admitted U.S. students and permanent residents. A limited amount of financial aid is also available for foreign citizens, and the university will meet the full demonstrated financial need for those admitted students as well.

"Applicants must take either the ACT with the writing exam, or the SAT plus two SAT Subject Tests (mathematics Subject Test required for applicants to the Pratt School of Engineering)."

SELECTIVITY

Admissions Rating	99
# of applicants	30,374
% of applicants accepted	13
% of acceptees attending	42
# of early decision applicants	2,533
% accepted early decision	26

FRESHMAN PROFILE

Range SAT Critical Reading	670–760
Range SAT Math	690–790
Range SAT Writing	680–780
Range ACT Composite	30–34
% graduated top 10% of class	90
% graduated top 25% of class	98
% graduated top 50% of class	100

DEADLINES

Early decision	
Deadline	11/1
Notification	12/15
Regular	
Deadline	1/2
Notification	4/1
Nonfall registration?	No

APPLICANTS ALSO LOOK AT AND OFTEN PREFER

Princeton University; Yale University; Stanford University; Harvard College

AND SOMETIMES PREFER

University of Pennsylvania; Brown University; Cornell University; Dartmouth College

AND RARELY PREFER

Georgetown University; University of Virginia; The University of North Carolina at Chapel Hill; Northwestern University

FINANCIAL FACTS

Financial Aid Rating	91
Annual tuition	$44,020
Room and board	$12,902
Required fees	$1,356
Books and supplies	$1,300
% needy frosh rec. need-based scholarship or grant aid	95
% needy UG rec. need-based scholarship or grant aid	95
% needy frosh rec. non-need-based scholarship or grant aid	10
% needy UG rec. non-need-based scholarship or grant aid	7
% needy frosh rec. need-based self-help aid	83
% needy UG rec. need-based self-help aid	89
% UG borrow to pay for school	39
Average cumulative indebtedness	$19,506
% frosh need fully met	100
% ugrads need fully met	100
Average % of frosh need met	100
Average % of ugrad need met	100

DUQUESNE UNIVERSITY

600 FORBES AVENUE, PITTSBURGH, PA 15282 • ADMISSIONS: 412-396-6222 • FAX: 412-396-6223

CAMPUS LIFE

Quality of Life Rating	82
Fire Safety Rating	99
Green Rating	71
Type of school	Private
Affiliation	Roman Catholic
Environment	Metropolis

STUDENTS

Total undergrad enrollment	5,944
% male/female	41/59
% from out of state	25
% frosh live on campus	92
% ugrads live on campus	61
# of fraternities (% ugrad men join)	7 (17)
# of sororities (% ugrad women join)	11 (24)
% African American	4
% Asian	2
% Caucasian	84
% Hispanic	3
% Native American	<1
% international	4
# of countries represented	77

SURVEY SAYS . . .

Students love Pittsburgh, PA
Athletic facilities are great
Great off-campus food

ACADEMICS

Academic Rating	77
% students returning for sophomore year	88
% students graduating within 4 years	66
% students graduating within 6 years	76
Calendar	Semester
Student/faculty ratio	15:1
Profs interesting rating	74
Profs accessible rating	78

Most classes have 10–19 students.
Most lab/discussion sessions have
20–29 students.

MOST POPULAR MAJORS
nursing; pharmacy; accounting

STUDENTS SAY ". . ."

Academics

Duquesne University in Pittsburgh is a Catholic University that focuses on "guiding students to be involved, seek their interests, and be constructive members of society." With around 6,000 undergraduates and a "culturally-rich urban setting" in "the heart of the city," students get a personalized experience in "an enriching environment in which students are encouraged to think critically and act deliberately."

The school's cosmopolitan location also means that students in the university's strong business program are given access to "professionals with actual business experience, not just theory." "My professors know what they are teaching and do so with enthusiasm," says a freshman of a school where "the small student body makes it easier to interact with professors and staff." No matter which of the approximately 80 majors one chooses, there is an "emphasis put on challenging the mainstream discourse." Professors are "varied" in their teaching styles; some "are strict and assign hours of homework," while others "are laid back and focus more on the students' understanding." There are also "very helpful" tutoring services available.

The eye to a well-rounded future is also a strength of the school, and the faculty maintain "a lot of connections with people to help [students] with jobs after graduation," making sure that all who matriculate are educated "in multiple facets for the field they plan to enter." "A significant portion of my professors really care and want to make sure their students succeed and are always sending me emails about internship and job opportunities pertaining to my major," says one junior. "Even the deans and department chairs" are easily accessible, and "love to get to know their students personally."

Life

There is "an excellent orientation program for new students" (and a pre-orientation for commuters), who turn to one of the "million and one ways for people to get involved" to find friends and support. Some admit that "school spirit is lacking" in some areas (particularly athletics), and "a lot of students go to Pitt or CMU on the weekends." Because most of the freshmen and sophomore class are required to live on campus, "many interactions happen on campus," but the dorms "are outdated, except for one new building for a select few upperclassmen."

The "secluded campus'" location "is part of Pittsburgh and at the same time, it is its own neighborhood." Downtown Pittsburgh (especially the nearby South Side) is a short distance away and "there's a lot of places to go eat, shop, or go for a run." The weekends "are somewhat dominated by pot/alcohol, but there are still plenty of people who refrain from using them." "I enjoy attending the NiteSpot events such as first run movies, scavenger hunts, and bingo nights. There is always something to do!" says one such student. There are no Greek houses at Duquesne, though Greek life does exist and is "particularly strong."

Student Body

Most students are "upper-middle class," "white," and a "jock or a prep," but "no judgment is passed" on anyone of different backgrounds or style. The guy to girl ratio is heavy on the girl side, and "attractive" ones at that ("very few wear sweatpants to class"). Though cliques do form, they are not inclusive and "all students fit in with all types of other students." Everyone is "pretty chill and communicative," "laid back and super friendly," and a "smart kid who sometimes likes to have fun on the weekends." A lot of people here are also "really into working out, usually done at the Power Center gym.

FINANCIAL AID: 412-396-6607 • E-MAIL: ADMISSIONS@DUQ.EDU • WEBSITE: WWW.DUQ.EDU

THE PRINCETON REVIEW SAYS

Admissions

Very important factors considered include: GPA, rigor of secondary school record, standardized test scores, application essay, recommendation(s). *Important factors considered include:* Extracurricular activities, interview, talent/ability, volunteer work, character/personal qualities. *Other factors considered include:* First generation, racial/ethnic status, work experience, alumni/ae relations, level of applicant's interest. SAT or ACT required; SAT and SAT Subject Tests or ACT considered if submitted; ACT with or without Writing component accepted. *Academic units recommended:* 4 English; 2 mathematics; 2 science; 2 social studies; 2 foreign language; 4 academic electives.

Financial Aid

Students should submit: FAFSA, Institution's own financial aid form. Regular filing deadline is 5/1. The Princeton Review suggests that all financial aid forms be submitted as soon as possible after January 1. *Need-based scholarships/grants offered:* Federal Pell, SEOG, State scholarships/grants, private scholarships, the school's own gift aid, United Negro College Fund. *Loan aid offered:* Direct Subsidized Stafford Loans, Direct Unsubsidized Stafford Loans, Direct PLUS loans, Federal Perkins Loans, Federal Nursing Loans. Federal Work-Study Program available. Institutional employment available. Off-campus job opportunities are good.

The Inside Word

Duquesne recommends that all prospective students to complete a college preparatory curriculum in high school and provide a personal essay and recommendation. Most programs require a minimum GPA of 3.0 and minimum SAT score of 1000 (Math and Critical Reading) or ACT score of 22 for admission (some programs, including those in health sciences, require higher GPA and test scores). A student's academic record and test scores are two primary factors considered in awarding merit scholarships.

THE SCHOOL SAYS " . . ."

From the Admissions Office

"Duquesne University is a private, Catholic institution long known for its rich, diverse liberal arts studies and schools of pharmacy, law, sciences, music, education, nursing, business, health sciences and leadership. Founded in 1878 by the Congregation of the Holy Spirit (the Spiritans), Duquesne University has grown to become an educational and economic powerhouse that serves more than 10,000 students across 10 schools of study. Our students enjoy a secure 50-acre campus and can take advantage of a variety of opportunities for athletics and arts, as well as nearly 200 student organizations. Approximately 4,000 students live in seven residence halls. Campus amenities include the multi-level Power Center, which houses a recreation and fitness center, a Barnes & Noble bookstore with a Starbucks café, and The Red Ring, a full-service restaurant. In an ecumenical atmosphere open to diversity, students of all races, cultures and religious traditions are valued and supported. Located just steps away from downtown Pittsburgh, Duquesne University is readily accessible to the business, entertainment and shopping centers of the city. The university's central location also provides a perfect laboratory for off-campus learning and community service. Duquesne students gain practical experience through fieldwork, research projects and internships at Pittsburgh's major corporations and health care systems."

SELECTIVITY

Admissions Rating	81
# of applicants	6,793
% of applicants accepted	74
% of acceptees attending	31
# of early decision applicants	205
% accepted early decision	60

FRESHMAN PROFILE

Range SAT Critical Reading	510–600
Range SAT Math	520–610
Range SAT Writing	500–600
Range ACT Composite	22–27
Minimum paper TOEFL	575
Minimum web-based TOEFL	90
Average HS GPA	3.66
% graduated top 10% of class	27
% graduated top 25% of class	60
% graduated top 50% of class	89

DEADLINES

Early decision	
Deadline	11/1
Notification	12/15
Early action	
Deadline	12/1
Notification	1/15
Regular	
Priority	11/1
Deadline	7/1
Nonfall registration?	Yes

APPLICANTS ALSO LOOK AT AND OFTEN PREFER

Pennsylvania State University—University Park; University of Pittsburgh—Pittsburgh Campus; Temple University

AND SOMETIMES PREFER

West Virginia University; Gannon University; Robert Morris University; Saint Vincent College

FINANCIAL FACTS

Financial Aid Rating	76
Annual tuition	$28,913
Room and board	$10,632
Required fees	$2,472
Books and supplies	$1,000
% needy frosh rec. need-based scholarship or grant aid	99
% needy UG rec. need-based scholarship or grant aid	97
% needy frosh rec. non-need-based scholarship or grant aid	98
% needy UG rec. non-need-based scholarship or grant aid	93
% needy frosh rec. need-based self-help aid	87
% needy UG rec. need-based self-help aid	86
% frosh rec. any financial aid	100
% UG rec. any financial aid	97
% UG borrow to pay for school	80
Average cumulative indebtedness	$26,119
% frosh need fully met	24
% ugrads need fully met	25
Average % of frosh need met	88
Average % of ugrad need met	77

ECKERD COLLEGE

4200 FIFTY-FOURTH AVENUE SOUTH, ST. PETERSBURG, FL 33711 • ADMISSIONS: 727-864-8331 • FAX: 727-866-2304

CAMPUS LIFE
Quality of Life Rating	82
Fire Safety Rating	73
Green Rating	87
Type of school	Private
Affiliation	Presbyterian
Environment	City

STUDENTS
Total undergrad enrollment	1,813
% male/female	40/60
% from out of state	78
% frosh live on campus	98
% ugrads live on campus	85
% African American	2
% Asian	1
% Caucasian	79
% Hispanic	8
% Native American	1
% international	5
# of countries represented	35

SURVEY SAYS . . .
Students are friendly
Students environmentally aware
Lots of beer drinking
Hard liquor is popular

ACADEMICS
Academic Rating	84
% students returning for sophomore year	83
% students graduating within 4 years	60
% students graduating within 6 years	66
Calendar	4/1/4
Student/faculty ratio	12:1
Profs interesting rating	85
Profs accessible rating	84

Most classes have 20–29 students.
Most lab/discussion sessions have 20–29 students.

MOST POPULAR MAJORS
environmental studies; marine biology; psychology

STUDENTS SAY ". . ."

Academics
Located on Florida's Gulf Coast in St. Petersburg, Eckerd College is a small liberal arts college that prepares students to be "well-rounded, educated people for the 'real world', rather than for just one job." Indeed, 40 percent of all students will go on to pursue advanced degrees, and the school's "academics are top notch and continue to impress," particularly the constantly expanding, "hands on" science department, which "really flourishes." Also of note is the study abroad program, of which many students take advantage.

Eckerd is "all about having small class sizes in order to maximize learning and personal connections to professors." Professors are "always approachable on an academic and personal level" and "make the classes fun and interesting." There is a "level of genuine care" from the teachers; according to a senior, "If I have a question, it gets answered, simple as that." "Not once has an email been ignored that I have sent to a professor," echoes a junior. Class discussion is very important (many classes have a sizeable participation grade), and faculty encourages opposing views, creating "an environment where it is easy for everybody to openly express their opinions without judgment."

The mentor program assigns students to professors in the field of their major(s), their job being "to help guide the student through choosing classes and registration, or anything else." The "quirky" liberal arts curriculum turns out graduates that "are not pigeonholed into the skills associated with their major, but [who] have developed a wide range of abilities which make them attractive to employers."

Life
The school's heartstoppingly beautiful location on the waterfront gives it a feel of being "like summer camp with an enriching academic experience"; as a senior asks (rhetorically): "How can you beat a dorm that overlooks the bay?" The dorms "are beautiful so there is no need to live off campus," and the school's yellow bike program allows students to "just pick up the yellow bikes and ride wherever you need" (though some students think there should "more dedication through internal action to the environmental principles it espouses").

There are "eclectic options of student activities" at Eckerd, and since there is no Greek life, the Campus Activities crew is allotted "a crazy amount of money to have fun events on campus, such as cookouts, dances, casino nights, and an actual carnival brought onto campus." Obviously marine activities are popular, and for fun, people "go to the beach, go downtown, [and borrow] paddleboards/kayaks at the waterfront." People love to go to downtown St. Pete, and there are many famous restaurants nearby (good thing, as the cafeteria food is "definitely our weakest point," according to many students).

There's a definite party streak here, and "pot and beer are not strangers to Eckerd parties," which typically take place outside. Still, it's "a very no-pressure environment" for those who choose not to partake, and "there is a very 'free as a bird' mentality'" here so "people rarely feel trapped." Life at this school is generally relaxed but busy. It matches the atmosphere of the location," says a freshman.

Student Body
This "barefooted and brainy" brood "has a wide variety of students who all fit different niches." "It isn't unheard of to see people in 3-piece suits sitting with what we might call modern-day hippies," says a student. The "very relaxed" crowd adopts a "laid back Florida attitude," and every student is "friendly, approachable and has a general positive attitude about being here at Eckerd." Most everyone is "pretty liberal" and "has a strong interest in environmental sustainability."

FINANCIAL AID: 727-864-8854 • E-MAIL: ADMISSIONS@ECKERD.EDU • WEBSITE: WWW.ECKERD.EDU

THE PRINCETON REVIEW SAYS

Admissions

Very important factors considered include: GPA, rigor of secondary school record. *Important factors considered include:* Standardized test scores, application essay, extracurricular activities, interview, recommendation(s), talent/ability, character/personal qualities. *Other factors considered include:* Class rank, first generation, volunteer work, work experience, alumni/ae relations, level of applicant's interest. SAT or ACT required; ACT with or without Writing component accepted. *Academic units recommended:* 4 English; 3 mathematics; 3 science; (2 science lab); 2 social studies; 2 foreign language; 1 history; 3 academic electives.

Financial Aid

Students should submit: FAFSA. The Princeton Review suggests that all financial aid forms be submitted as soon as possible after January 1. *Need-based scholarships/grants offered:* Federal Pell, SEOG, State scholarships/grants, private scholarships, the school's own gift aid. *Loan aid offered:* Direct Subsidized Stafford Loans, Direct Unsubsidized Stafford Loans, Direct PLUS loans, Federal Perkins Loans, College/university loans from institutional funds. Federal Work-Study Program available. Institutional employment available. Off-campus job opportunities are excellent.

The Inside Word

Most of the applicants Eckerd admits come from the top quarter of their high school classes. However, competition from other small liberal arts schools of roughly the same caliber or better is stiff. As a result, Eckerd is a relatively easy admit for B-plus students with decent standardized test scores (the school gives more weight in its decisions to courses and grades than to SAT and ACT scores, however). The admissions process here is rolling, which means that applying early will help your chances. Eckerd can afford to be more selective later on in the admissions cycle, especially for candidates who profess an interest in its most esteemed programs (for example, marine science), so those with serious interest should consider Eckerd's early admission policy.

THE SCHOOL SAYS "..."

From the Admissions Office

"Eckerd, a coeducational college of liberal arts and sciences, has a diverse student body from forty-eight states and thirty-three countries. Located on 188 acres of waterfront property in St. Petersburg, Florida, we take advantage of our spectacular mile of campus waterfront along the Gulf of Mexico for outdoor laboratories in biology, marine science and environmental studies as well as for an array of intramural, club and intercollegiate sports and water recreation. Offerings in the arts and humanities, including lectures and classes by Nobel Prize-winner Elie Wiesel, inspire creativity and foster critical thinking and self-awareness.

"Eckerd is dedicated to minimizing its operational footprint and maximizing sustainable practices. Eckerd's Community Garden contributes to our 'Eat Local' initiative, and our Yellow Community Bike Program is designed to increase bicycle use on campus and decrease car traffic. In addition to being "green," Eckerd students are service-oriented, volunteering more than 70,000 hours annually in the Tampa Bay community and across the globe.

"Eckerd's innovative 4-1-4 calendar gives students the opportunity to study abroad during the January Winter Term or semester-long programs. Nearly 70 percent of our graduates have spent at least one term overseas, many at Eckerd study centers in London, China and Latin America.

"A recent successful fundraising campaign made it possible for a renaissance in the sciences at Eckerd. In addition to the new, 55,000 square-foot James Center for Molecular and Life Sciences, the college is significantly upgrading equipment, labs and classrooms for the environmental studies, math, physics, computer science and behavioral sciences departments. We venture together in the Eckerd experience to think beyond the conventional questions, methods and solutions. At Eckerd College, we ThinkOUTside."

SELECTIVITY

Admissions Rating	80
# of applicants	3,509
% of applicants accepted	72
% of acceptees attending	18
# offered a place on the wait list	47

FRESHMAN PROFILE

Range SAT Critical Reading	520–620
Range SAT Math	510–600
Range ACT Composite	23–28
Minimum paper TOEFL	550
Average HS GPA	3.34

DEADLINES

Early action	
Deadline	11/15
Notification	12/15
Regular	
Nonfall registration?	Yes

FINANCIAL FACTS

Financial Aid Rating	82
Annual tuition	$37,046
Room and board	$10,144
Required fees	$316
Books and supplies	$1,200
% needy frosh rec. need-based scholarship or grant aid	100
% needy UG rec. need-based scholarship or grant aid	100
% needy frosh rec. non-need-based scholarship or grant aid	0
% needy UG rec. non-need-based scholarship or grant aid	0
% needy frosh rec. need-based self-help aid	100
% needy UG rec. need-based self-help aid	100
% frosh rec. any financial aid	97
% UG rec. any financial aid	95
% UG borrow to pay for school	59
Average cumulative indebtedness	$32,605
% frosh need fully met	15
% ugrads need fully met	16
Average % of frosh need met	86
Average % of ugrad need met	86

ELON UNIVERSITY

100 CAMPUS DRIVE, ELON, NC 27244-2010 • ADMISSIONS: 336-278-3566 • FAX: 336-278-7699

STUDENTS SAY " . . ."

Academics

If you ask Elon undergrads to capture the essence of their university with one turn of phrase, they'll likely report that it's all about "big-school opportunities with a small-school community." Happily expounding, students are also quick to underscore that "the hard work that Elon puts into giving its students a hands-on, experiential learning environment is recognized from day one." Further, students here appreciate the numerous opportunities for study abroad along with the "small class sizes and individual attention." What's more, Elon's "personable," "engaging" professors are both "enthusiastic about their fields and helping students." They truly "want their students to succeed both in and out of the classroom." Undergrads also value the care and concern the administration shows to students, which extends to even the top brass. As one incredulous student shares, "Our president opens his home to the student body around the holidays, provides us with food on the school's dime, and stands in a holiday hat to take pictures with students that are placed on a holiday card and sent home." It's no wonder this fellow undergrad concludes by simply stating, "I felt an instant comfort when I stepped on campus. At other schools I really felt like a visitor, but at Elon I felt like I belonged there."

Life

Undergrads at Elon certainly know how to "keep themselves busy." Indeed it's difficult to find someone who isn't juggling academics with a myriad of extra-curricular activities. In addition, many students "choose to participate in Greek life, which tends to run the social scene. On the weekends, students go out to the bars in the town or to parties at various off-campus houses." While some claim that those not in the party scene "often feel like [they] are in a minority," others assure us, "There's a lot to do around here, even if you don't drink." As one undergrads explains, "Oftentimes my friends and I will play Frisbee, climb the magnolia trees on campus, have movie nights, play video games, just hang out." Of course, there are also plenty of school-sponsored events to enjoy. Another student adds, "Our Student Union Board holds free events all the time like bingo, movies on the lawn, concerts, midnight meals, and even a hypnotist show. I always have options for something fun to do!" Locally, there are "a lot of great restaurants in the area that range from diner-style places to really authentic Indian and Korean restaurants, so there is a lot of choice. [Certainly,] going out for dinner is a common social activity." Further, students also value Elon's location, which "allows you to get to Raleigh, Chapel Hill, or Greensboro in less than an hour."

Student Body

On the surface, the typical Elon undergrad appears to be "preppy, white, and from a well-off family, [and he or she] probably [attended] a private high school." However, if you're willing to look beyond the "Lily and Southern Tide" exterior, you're sure to discover a student body that's "cordial," "highly motivated," "driven, and engaged." Indeed, on this "hardworking" campus, you'll find students are "passionate about their studies" and "take their schooling very seriously." Leadership is another big attribute that's tossed around as most students are "on the executive board of an organization or more than one organization, and [they are] heavily focused on self-improvement." Perhaps more importantly, undergrads at Elon also report that their peers are "compassionate" and "open and willing to talk and help anybody." Finally, as one content undergrad sums up her campus, "Students fit in by getting involved. Whether it's Greek life, sports, or clubs, I think there is something for everyone."

FINANCIAL AID: 336-278-7640 • E-MAIL: ADMISSIONS@ELON.EDU • WEBSITE: WWW.ELON.EDU

THE PRINCETON REVIEW SAYS

Admissions

Very important factors considered include: GPA, rigor of secondary school record, standardized test scores, application essay. *Important factors considered include:* extracurricular activities, recommendation(s), talent/ability, volunteer work, work experience, alumni/ae relations. *Other factors considered include:* Class rank, first generation, geographical residence, racial/ethnic status, state residency, character/personal qualities, level of applicant's interest. SAT or ACT required; ACT with Writing component required. TOEFL required of all international applicants. *Academic units required:* 4 English; 3 mathematics; 3 science; (1 science lab); 1 social studies; 2 foreign language; 2 history. *Academic units recommended:* 4 English; 4 mathematics; 3 science; (1 science lab); 1 social studies; 3 foreign language; 2 history.

Financial Aid

Students should submit: FAFSA, Institution's own financial aid form, CSS/Financial Aid PROFILE. The Princeton Review suggests that all financial aid forms be submitted as soon as possible after January 1. *Need-based scholarships/grants offered:* Federal Pell, SEOG, State scholarships/grants, private scholarships, the school's own gift aid. *Loan aid offered:* Direct Subsidized Stafford Loans, Direct Unsubsidized Stafford Loans, Direct PLUS loans, Federal Perkins Loans. Federal Work-Study Program available. Institutional employment available. Off-campus job opportunities are good.

The Inside Word

Over the years, securing admittance to Elon has become an increasingly challenging feat. To be successful, it's important to have chosen a rigorous high school curriculum. Indeed, candidates must have gone beyond the basic college prep classes offered. In addition, admissions officers seek out students who have demonstrated leadership savvy. Finally, students looking to transfer should know that the greatest weight will be placed on completed college course work.

THE SCHOOL SAYS "..."

From the Admissions Office

"Elon offers the resources of a university in a close-knit community atmosphere. The university's 5,599 undergraduates choose from more than 60 majors. Graduate programs are offered in business administration, law, education, interactive media, physical therapy and physician assistant studies. The National Survey of Student Engagement recognizes Elon among the nation's most effective universities in promoting hands-on learning. Academic and co-curricular activities are seamlessly blended, especially in the Elon Experiences: study abroad, internships, service, leadership and undergraduate research. Participation is among the highest in the nation; 72 percent of graduating seniors have studied abroad, 87 percent have internship experiences and 85 percent have participated in service. Elon's 4-1-4 academic calendar allows students to devote January to global study or to explore innovative on-campus courses. Elon's historic 620-acre campus is recognized as one of the most beautiful in the country. New additions include two major residential neighborhoods – the Global Neighborhood and The Station at Mill Point; the Gerald L. Francis Center, home of the School of Health Sciences; the three-story Elon Town Center, which includes Elon's Barnes & Noble bookstore, a pizzeria and ice cream shop; the international themed Lakeside Dining Hall, including the Winter Garden Café food court; and Alumni Field House and Hunt Softball Park for Elon's NCAA Division I Phoenix athletics. The athletics programs compete in the Colonial Athletic Association. Freshman applicants are required to take the SAT (or the ACT with the writing section). The best critical reading, math, and writing scores from either test will be used."

SELECTIVITY

Admissions Rating	91
# of applicants	9,949
% of applicants accepted	54
% of acceptees attending	27
# offered a place on the wait list	3,072
% accepting a place on wait list	37
% admitted from wait list	2
# of early decision applicants	484
% accepted early decision	85

FRESHMAN PROFILE

Range SAT Critical Reading	540–630
Range SAT Math	540–610
Range SAT Writing	540–640
Range ACT Composite	25–29
Minimum paper TOEFL	550
Minimum web-based TOEFL	213
Average HS GPA	3.96
% graduated top 10% of class	26
% graduated top 25% of class	63
% graduated top 50% of class	92

DEADLINES

Early decision	
Deadline	11/1
Notification	12/1
Early action	
Deadline	11/10
Notification	12/20
Regular	
Priority	11/1
Deadline	1/10
Notification	3/15
Nonfall registration?	Yes

APPLICANTS ALSO LOOK AT AND OFTEN PREFER

The University of North Carolina at Chapel Hill; Wake Forest University

AND SOMETIMES PREFER

North Carolina State University; University of Maryland; College Park; University of Richmond

FINANCIAL FACTS

Financial Aid Rating	69
Annual tuition	$29,750
Required fees	$399
Books and supplies	$900
% needy frosh rec. need-based scholarship or grant aid	84
% needy UG rec. need-based scholarship or grant aid	89
% needy frosh rec. non-need-based scholarship or grant aid	40
% needy UG rec. non-need-based scholarship or grant aid	42
% needy frosh rec. need-based self-help aid	79
% needy UG rec. need-based self-help aid	81
% frosh rec. any financial aid	67
% UG rec. any financial aid	64
% UG borrow to pay for school	44
Average cumulative indebtedness	$28,327
Average % of frosh need met	57
Average % of ugrad need met	62

EMERSON COLLEGE

120 BOYLSTON STREET, BOSTON, MA 02116-4624 • ADMISSIONS: 617-824-8600 • FAX: 617-824-8609

CAMPUS LIFE

Quality of Life Rating	81
Fire Safety Rating	83
Green Rating	73
Type of school	Private
Affiliation	No Affiliation
Environment	Metropolis

STUDENTS

Total undergrad enrollment	3,454
% male/female	41/59
% from out of state	75
% frosh from public high school	70
% frosh live on campus	99
% ugrads live on campus	48
# of fraternities	4
# of sororities	3
% African American	3
% Asian	5
% Caucasian	62
% Hispanic	8
% Native American	<1
% international	3
# of countries represented	45

SURVEY SAYS . . .

Students aren't religious
Students love Boston, MA
Great off-campus food
College radio is popular
Theater is popular

ACADEMICS

Academic Rating	78
% students returning for sophomore year	88
% students graduating within 4 years	74
% students graduating within 6 years	78
Calendar	Semester
Student/faculty ratio	13:1
Profs interesting rating	82
Profs accessible rating	70

Most classes have 10–19 students.
Most lab/discussion sessions have 10–19 students.

MOST POPULAR MAJORS
cinematography; theater

STUDENTS SAY ". . ."

Academics

"Perfectly situated in the heart of Boston," Emerson's campus sits "in close proximity to a plethora of other academic institutions and culture." Emerson is "the number one school for film/television/media production." The combination of a "very active" alumni network and plentiful "industry connections" greatly help students in their post-college careers. Emerson fosters a "creative atmosphere" where people have "passion for [their] craft" and "strive to do their best." As one student puts it, "Emerson is a specialized school for people who are passionate and know exactly what they want to do with that passion." The faculty and students are "creative and professional," and the experience of attending Emerson "is like a mini version of what the film industry or the business world looks like." In general, "the facilities are awesome, especially the TV studios." However, the most common complaint was the state of the dining facilities, with feedback ranging from "not very good" to "makes me feel sick every time." Students also wish there were "more study abroad programs." Academics are "very hands-on rather than learning theory." The professors "are knowledgeable and passionate about their crafts," and have plenty of experience "working in their field of study." As with any school, "professors obviously vary depending on the subject," however, the school's size makes it "pretty easy to avoid the bad professors just through word of mouth." Overall, "Emerson is an inclusive, accepting, and progressive school that fosters creativity and provides a positive environment to learn and grow." As one happy student declares, "Emerson College is the greatest decision I have ever made!"

Life

Emerson does not have a "normal campus where kids walk around in their pjs." Students here are constantly active. "Life at school is a combination of running to classes, running to projects, and running to clubs," one student reports. "No matter what your major is, there's an abundance of extracurricular opportunities" and the "clubs and organizations are awesome and incredibly professional." The college puts on "a lot of activities on weekends on campus," and students here are "very social beings and love to get involved in everything - from summer internships to student orgs to the Quidditch World Cup team." Due to Emerson's "extremely strict rules regarding drugs and alcohol," "you have to take a train to get to any parties." Luckily, "Emerson is right in the middle of Boston" providing "many opportunities to experience the real world, see live music, study in the park, go to a free movie pre-screening, eat out, [or] explore new neighborhoods."

Student Body

Emerson students are "creative, innovative, friendly, and passionate." Although students say racial diversity could be improved, the school is "very LGBTQ friendly" and has a "large LGBT community." The most common word used to describe students was "hipster," specifically "hipsters who have a love affair with cigarettes and black coffee." This can make some non-hipster students feel "out of place," but most students "are friendly and are very open-minded." There is also a strong "nerdy" vibe to campus. "I have not met anybody who hates Doctor Who," one student says. Another describes the student body as "artsy, nerdy, funny, weird, cool, hipster, chill, creative, smart... the list is endless. We all fit in." Despite the "very artsy" student body and general "liberal" views, students can be "apathetic and uninformed when it comes to politics." One thing is for sure though, the students at Emerson "work hard." A visual media arts major even declares them "the most dedicated and ambitious students of all time." Since "everyone here does cool things," when you attend Emerson your creative sparks fly and "you too will begin to do cool things."

THE PRINCETON REVIEW SAYS

Admissions

Very important factors considered include: GPA, standardized test scores. *Important factors considered include:* Class rank, rigor of secondary school record, application essay, extracurricular activities, recommendation(s), talent/ability, character/personal qualities. *Other factors considered include:* First generation, geographical residence, racial/ethnic status, volunteer work, work experience, alumni/ae relations. SAT or ACT required; ACT with Writing component required. TOEFL required of all international applicants. *Academic units required:* 4 English; 3 mathematics; 3 science; 3 social studies; 3 foreign language. *Academic units recommended:* 4 English; 3 mathematics; 3 science; 3 social studies; 3 foreign language; 4 academic electives.

Financial Aid

Students should submit: FAFSA, CSS/Financial Aid PROFILE, Noncustodial PROFILE, Business/Farm Supplement. The Princeton Review suggests that all financial aid forms be submitted as soon as possible after January 1. *Need-based scholarships/grants offered:* Federal Pell, SEOG, State scholarships/grants, private scholarships, the school's own gift aid. *Loan aid offered:* Federal Perkins Loans, State Loans. Applicants will be notified of awards beginning 4/1. Federal Work-Study Program available. Institutional employment available. Off-campus job opportunities are excellent.

The Inside Word

From its location in Boston's theatre district to its large alumni network of arts workers, Emerson is the perfect school for students interested in theater, television, or the arts. Jobs and internship opportunities abound in those fields, helping students jumpstart their careers upon graduation. If you are applying in cinematography or the performing arts, be prepared to complete an artistic review with your application.

THE SCHOOL SAYS "..."

From the Admissions Office

"Founded in 1880, Emerson is one of the premier colleges in the country for communication and the arts. Students may choose from more than two-dozen undergraduate and graduate programs supported by state-of-the-art facilities and a nationally renowned faculty. The campus is home to WERS-FM, the oldest noncommercial radio station in Boston; the historic 1,200-seat Cutler Majestic Theatre; and *Ploughshares*, the award winning literary journal for new writing.

"Located on Boston Common in the heart of the city's Theatre District, the campus is walking distance from the Massachusetts State House, Chinatown, and historic Freedom Trail. More than half the students reside on-campus, some in special learning communities such as the Writers' Block and Digital Culture Floor. There is also a fitness center, athletic field, and new gymnasium and campus center.

"Emerson has nearly eighty student organizations and performance groups as well as fifteen NCAA teams, student publications, and honor societies. The college also sponsors programs in Los Angeles and Washington, D.C.; study abroad in the Netherlands, Taiwan, and Czech Republic; and course cross-registration with the six-member Boston ProArts Consortium.

"Students have access to outstanding facilities, including sound treated television studios, digital editing and audio post-production suites. An eleven-story performance and production center houses a theater design/technology center, makeup lab, and costume shop. There are seven programs to observe speech and hearing therapy, a professional marketing focus group room, and digital newsroom, and new performance development center with a sound stage, scene shop, black box, and film screening room."

SELECTIVITY

Admissions Rating	94
# of applicants	6,943
% of applicants accepted	42
% of acceptees attending	26
# offered a place on the wait list	2,089
% accepting a place on wait list	38
% admitted from wait list	13

FRESHMAN PROFILE

Range SAT Critical Reading	570–670
Range SAT Math	540–640
Range SAT Writing	580–670
Range ACT Composite	24–29
Minimum paper TOEFL	550
Minimum web-based TOEFL	213
Average HS GPA	3.59
% graduated top 10% of class	42
% graduated top 25% of class	77
% graduated top 50% of class	98

DEADLINES

Early action	
Deadline	11/1
Notification	12/15
Regular	
Deadline	1/5
Notification	4/1
Nonfall registration?	Yes

APPLICANTS ALSO LOOK AT AND OFTEN PREFER
New York University

AND SOMETIMES PREFER
Ithaca College; University of Southern California

AND RARELY PREFER
Syracuse University; Boston University

FINANCIAL FACTS

Financial Aid Rating	89
Annual tuition	$29,408
Room and board	$12,280
Required fees	$672
Books and supplies	$800
% needy frosh rec. need-based scholarship or grant aid	84
% needy UG rec. need-based scholarship or grant aid	79
% needy frosh rec. non-need-based scholarship or grant aid	4
% needy UG rec. non-need-based scholarship or grant aid	3
% needy frosh rec. need-based self-help aid	84
% needy UG rec. need-based self-help aid	94
% frosh rec. any financial aid	63
% UG rec. any financial aid	61
% UG borrow to pay for school	59
Average cumulative indebtedness	$15,262
% frosh need fully met	55
% ugrads need fully met	56
Average % of frosh need met	89
Average % of ugrad need met	90

EMORY UNIVERSITY

EMORY UNIVERSITY, BOISEUILLET JONES CENTER, ATLANTA, GA 30322 • ADMISSIONS: 404-727-6036 • FAX: 404-727-4303

STUDENTS SAY " . . ."

Academics

As one of the South's premier universities, Emory University provides students with "a rigorous academic environment [where students] are provided with the necessary skills to be successful." Emphasis on a liberal arts education coupled with a "plethora of opportunities including location in Atlanta, proximity to graduate programs, and many ethically engaged programs" make this university a reputed destination for students who are "proactive" and "very involved high achievers." For the many who are interested in "some sort of pre-professional path," Emory has an "excellent science program (for premed or research interests)" and "one of the top undergraduate business programs in the country." Students note, however, that there is no engineering school. "Access to resources such as internships, research, volunteering, [and] alumni relations" is one of Emory's greatest assets, second only to its "excellent and engaged" faculty. Professors are "knowledgeable and relevant to their fields," and as one sophomore put it, "After two years, there has only been one class that I did not feel was worth my time." Emory is seen as "a school where academic inquiry thrives" and where "academically curious students [are encouraged] to go out into the community and serve others." While "it's a hefty price for education," the financial aid department, which sometimes "lacks efficiency," compensates with scholarships and "comprehensive financial aid" packages.

Life

Emory strikes "the perfect balance between social and academic life" where students "work and play hard but are committed to whatever they are part of." "There is a lot of support from upperclassmen and residence life...to guide underclassmen to activities that fit them," and people tend to participate in "activities that are sponsored by university organizations," such as student concerts, movies on campus, and intramurals. Describing university culture as "social but also academically competitive," students are "always in the library" during the week, and on weekends they take advantage of the scarce free time and opportunities for fun. As one student says, "The fraternities are a popular destination for underclassmen, especially freshman...there is definitely a population of non-drinkers and party animals." With the school's "beautiful campus," there are "many great outdoor areas to go relax...The gym, the WoodPec, is...conveniently located right in the center of campus, so people go there often to rock-climb together, play sports such as tennis, badminton or racquetball together." Of course, if you've exhausted activities on campus, students have access to the "so many things to do in Atlanta, which makes it a great city in which to attend college." One student also makes note of "Emory's talent for pulling in famous speakers in such a way that students get to really interact with them...my friend spent his twentieth birthday having dinner with Salman Rushdie at his house."

Student Body

"Community" is the word that undergrads use to describe the student body at Emory University. Due to the fact that the typical student is "very involved," "driven and motivated," and committed to "mutual learning," "you interact with different people in the different organizations you are a part of, [and] there are several students who are a part of a cultural, religious or ethnic clubs different from their own cultural, religious, or ethnic backgrounds." Students cite "diversity in terms of race, religion, and socioeconomic conditions" as a great asset, although some students also feel that Emory attracts "wealthy, white, prep-school kids" from cities "up north like Chicago, Boston, or NYC." Due to an "alternative school spirit" rooted less in sports and more in the fact that "students are very proud to go to Emory," students here are "friendly and engaged," and the "overly competitive and ambitious are few in number."

FINANCIAL AID: 404-727-6039 • E-MAIL: ADMISS@EMORY.EDU • WEBSITE: WWW.EMORY.EDU

THE PRINCETON REVIEW SAYS

Admissions

Very important factors considered include: GPA, rigor of secondary school record, standardized test scores, extracurricular activities, character/personal qualities. *Important factors considered include:* Class rank, application essay, recommendation(s), talent/ability, volunteer work, level of applicant's interest. *Other factors considered include:* First generation, geographical residence, interview, racial/ethnic status, state residency, work experience, alumni/ae relations. SAT or ACT required; SAT and SAT Subject Tests or ACT considered if submitted; ACT with Writing component required. TOEFL required of all international applicants. *Academic units recommended:* 4 English; 4 mathematics; 4 science; (2 science lab); 2 social studies; 4 foreign language; 2 history; 1 visual/performing arts.

Financial Aid

Students should submit: FAFSA, CSS/Financial Aid PROFILE, Noncustodial PROFILE. Regular filing deadline is 3/1. The Princeton Review suggests that all financial aid forms be submitted as soon as possible after January 1. *Need-based scholarships/grants offered:* Federal Pell, SEOG, private scholarships, the school's own gift aid. *Loan aid offered:* Direct Subsidized Stafford Loans, Direct Unsubsidized Stafford Loans, Direct PLUS loans, Federal Perkins Loans, Federal Nursing Loans, College/university loans from institutional funds. Applicants will be notified of awards beginning 4/1. Federal Work-Study Program available. Institutional employment available. Off-campus job opportunities are good.

The Inside Word

Over the past few years, early decision applicants to Emory have risen drastically, creating a quandary for aspiring Emory students: Do they join the growing early applicant crowd, which presumably increases the likelihood of admission, or do they take their chances with regular admission? "The good news?" Emory financial aid has traditionally met 100 percent of applicants' demonstrated need.

THE SCHOOL SAYS ". . ."

From the Admissions Office

"Emory is an inquiry-driven, ethically engaged, and diverse community whose members work collaboratively for positive transformation in the world through courageous leadership in teaching, research scholarship, health care, and social action. The university is internationally recognized for its outstanding liberal arts colleges, superb professional schools, and leading health care system. Emory is noted as one of the most diverse selective universities in the country.

"Emory offers a distinctive undergraduate experience with programs in the humanities, sciences, business, and nursing allowing students to explore their interests and talents in the classroom and in the field. Entering freshman may apply to Emory College, a four-year liberal arts education within the heart of a major research university. Students may also apply to Oxford College where student spend the first two years on Emory's original campus thirty-eight miles east of Atlanta. Emory provides a rich setting for learning from excellent teaching in small classes to lectures from prominent scholars to opportunities for study abroad, research, and internships.

"Emory students balance hard work with having fun. With 70 percent of students living on campus, the community is enhanced by a close-knit living environment. The campus life thrives on constant activity, and students are encouraged to get involved, share opinions, and flourish. Emory is a dynamic place that is constantly in a state of sustainable growth and improvement. Take a look at all Emory has to offer—you'll see why Emory students feel inspired to do more with what they learn here."

SELECTIVITY

Admissions Rating	98
# of applicants	17,678
% of applicants accepted	26
% of acceptees attending	29

FRESHMAN PROFILE

Range SAT Critical Reading	610–710
Range SAT Math	650–760
Range SAT Writing	630–730
Range ACT Composite	29–32
Minimum paper TOEFL	600
Minimum web-based TOEFL	250
Average HS GPA	3.75
% graduated top 10% of class	75
% graduated top 25% of class	94
% graduated top 50% of class	98

DEADLINES

Early decision	
Deadline	11/1
Notification	12/15
Regular	
Deadline	1/15
Notification	4/1
Nonfall registration?	No

APPLICANTS ALSO LOOK AT AND OFTEN PREFER

Washington University in St. Louis; Duke University; The University of North Carolina at Chapel Hill; Georgia Institute of Technology; Vanderbilt University

AND SOMETIMES PREFER

Dartmouth College; Wake Forest University; Amherst College; Boston University

AND RARELY PREFER

Drexel University; DePauw University; Providence College

FINANCIAL FACTS

Financial Aid Rating	95
Annual tuition	$42,400
Room and board	$12,000
Required fees	$580
Books and supplies	$1,100
% needy frosh rec. need-based scholarship or grant aid	94
% needy UG rec. need-based scholarship or grant aid	96
% needy frosh rec. non-need-based scholarship or grant aid	13
% needy UG rec. non-need-based scholarship or grant aid	14
% needy frosh rec. need-based self-help aid	90
% needy UG rec. need-based self-help aid	91
% frosh rec. any financial aid	55
% UG rec. any financial aid	54
% UG borrow to pay for school	42
Average cumulative indebtedness	$28,076
% frosh need fully met	100
% ugrads need fully met	100
Average % of frosh need met	100
Average % of ugrad need met	100

THE EVERGREEN STATE COLLEGE

2700 EVERGREEN PARKWAY NORTHWEST, OLYMPIA, WA 98505 • ADMISSIONS: 360-867-6170 • FAX: 360-867-5114

CAMPUS LIFE

Quality of Life Rating	79
Fire Safety Rating	84
Green Rating	92
Type of school	Public
Affiliation	No Affiliation
Environment	City

STUDENTS

Total undergrad enrollment	4,017
% male/female	46/54
% from out of state	24
% frosh live on campus	74
% ugrads live on campus	20
% African American	5
% Asian	2
% Caucasian	66
% Hispanic	7
% Native American	2
% international	<1
# of countries represented	22

SURVEY SAYS . . .
Lots of liberal students
Students aren't religious
Students environmentally aware

ACADEMICS

Academic Rating	75
% students returning for sophomore year	74
% students graduating within 4 years	43
% students graduating within 6 years	57
Calendar	Quarter
Student/faculty ratio	23:1
Profs interesting rating	91
Profs accessible rating	70
Most classes have 20–29 students.	

MOST POPULAR MAJORS
social sciences; liberal arts; natural sciences

STUDENTS SAY " . . ."

Academics

"Keeping education in its purest form alive and well in the heart of the Northwest," The Evergreen State College offers "a unique approach" to academics. The school provides an "interactive environment—with a diverse, enriching learning method," which allows students "to focus on [their] passions and explore them in detail." Everyone creates their own educational paths and directs the pace of their own learning. As a few students say admiringly, "I feel a sense of freedom with the academics at Evergreen." "I have more power as a student." Greatly appreciated is the flexibility found within the curriculum. "I was excited about building my own major." "No self-motivated student will leave Evergreen unsatisfied." Students work collaboratively here and support one another in their endeavors. "It's not about grades or competition; it's about self-improvement and personal fulfillment." Evaluations are used to view student progress, with "interdisciplinary education over declared majors" being the focus. "Your classes are all interconnected, so it's easy to link what you're doing into a defined path." "My transcript says more about me than A's, B's, and C's possibly could." "The philosophy...definitely lowers the stress I experience around academics." Professors assist students in innumerable ways and are "very intimately involved in the educations of their students." "At Evergreen, in order to have a great experience you need to be able to talk to your professors and engage with them." "I have not met a professor yet who was not willing to rework their mode of teaching to better serve the class." The educational atmosphere is highly interactive. Most every student "actively engages the material with field work, undergraduate research, and extended trips." "Class time is spent doing workshops, seminars, or a led discussion where everyone participates." "Even the science programs involve large portions of discussion and peer collaboration." As one undergraduate describes slyly, "My professors have been A++, if Evergreen assigned grades."

Life

Evergreen has a "booming extracurricular life"; students enjoy the "thriving local art and music scene, very hip and fresh," in Olympia as well as easily accessible Seattle or Portland. "The Flaming Eggplant, the student-run cafe, is simply the cheapest and most delicious place on the planet," as well as a very popular hangout. The Student Activities office has no shortage of options for undergraduates here, with "more than fifty different clubs and student groups." Physical activity is popular, and the recreational center has racquetball, a pool, a rock-climbing wall, and various places to exercise. There is "no shortage of local hiking, backpacking, and biking opportunities." "Hikes in the woods, down to the beach, or up to the bluff are very common as well as late-night stargazing." The physical surroundings are viewed with much admiration at Evergreen. "Our campus is set back in this magical forest with these winding paths down to the beach. There are tree forts, giant sculptures, dream catchers in the trees, hidden drum circles, and music everywhere." As one student describes fondly, "To me, it is reminiscent of Thoreau's solitude in nature."

Student Life

The "kindness and awareness of the community" is frequently said by students to be one of the most valued aspects of their experience here. "Articulate" and "inquisitive" undergraduates are evident in large numbers. "Students tend to be very politically aware and active with very liberal points of view" and are "mostly peaceful relaxed people" amidst an "open-minded social environment." The dorms are divided into different themes, and "the residential staff is professional and keeps the housing community functioning and safe." "The campus police are pretty awesome people," as well. Evergreen is respected by students throughout the college for its "forward-thinking" administration and faculty, with a "dedication to sustainability" being clearly evident around the campus.

FINANCIAL AID: 360-867-6205 • E-MAIL: ADMISSIONS@EVERGREEN.EDU • WEBSITE: WWW.EVERGREEN.EDU

THE PRINCETON REVIEW SAYS

Admissions

Other factors considered include: SAT or ACT required; ACT with or without Writing component accepted. TOEFL required of all international applicants. *Academic units required:* 4 English; 3 mathematics; 2 science; (2 science lab); 3 social studies; 2 foreign language; 1 academic elective.

Financial Aid

Students should submit: FAFSA. The Princeton Review suggests that all financial aid forms be submitted as soon as possible after January 1. *Need-based scholarships/grants offered:* Federal Pell, SEOG, State scholarships/grants, private scholarships, the school's own gift aid. *Loan aid offered:* Direct Subsidized Stafford Loans, Direct Unsubsidized Stafford Loans, Direct PLUS loans, Federal Perkins Loans, College/university loans from institutional funds. Federal Work-Study Program available. Institutional employment available. Off-campus job opportunities are good.

The Inside Word

Students at Evergreen are commonly some of the strongest performers from their high schools, although the admissions department considers a variety of traits from applicants (including strength of character) when considering prospective undergraduates. The school's unique and self-directed academic curriculum favors those students who can adequately handle the responsibility of creating and developing their own educational path.

THE SCHOOL SAYS "..."

From the Admissions Office

"Evergreen is a public liberal arts and sciences college nationally recognized for its full-time interdisciplinary studies programs. Students work closely with faculty to study an issue or theme from the perspective of several academic disciplines. They apply what's learned to real world issues, complete projects in groups, and discuss concepts in seminars that typically involve a faculty member and twenty to twenty-five students. The emphasis on seminars, interdisciplinary problem solving, and collaboration means students are well prepared for graduate school and the world of work. Our students tend to be politically active, environmentally savvy, and more concerned about social justice than competition and personal gain.

"All applicants are encouraged to complete a Free Application for Federal Student Aid (FAFSA). Evergreen's priority financial aid deadline is March 1, though applicants may submit the form later and may be awarded aid if funds are still available.

"Freshman applicants are required to submit test scores from either the SAT or ACT tests. The student's best composite score will be used in the admissions process."

SELECTIVITY

Admissions Rating	65
# of applicants	1,583
% of applicants accepted	97
% of acceptees attending	33

FRESHMAN PROFILE

Range SAT Critical Reading	500–630
Range SAT Math	450–580
Range SAT Writing	460–590
Range ACT Composite	20–27
Minimum paper TOEFL	550
Minimum web-based TOEFL	213
Average HS GPA	3.02
% graduated top 10% of class	10
% graduated top 25% of class	23
% graduated top 50% of class	54

DEADLINES

Regular	
Priority	2/1
Nonfall registration?	Yes

APPLICANTS ALSO LOOK AT AND OFTEN PREFER

University of Washington; University of Oregon

AND SOMETIMES PREFER

University of California—Santa Cruz; Hampshire College; Seattle University

AND RARELY PREFER

Warren Wilson College; Lewis & Clark College

FINANCIAL FACTS

Financial Aid Rating	69
Annual in-state tuition	$7,833
Annual out-of-state tuition	$19,920
Room and board	$9,492
Required fees	$839
Books and supplies	$1,026
% needy frosh rec. need-based scholarship or grant aid	65
% needy UG rec. need-based scholarship or grant aid	77
% needy UG rec. non-need-based scholarship or grant aid	1
% needy frosh rec. need-based self-help aid	68
% needy UG rec. need-based self-help aid	77
% frosh rec. any financial aid	59
% UG rec. any financial aid	63
% UG borrow to pay for school	51
Average cumulative indebtedness	$19,401
% frosh need fully met	11
% ugrads need fully met	9
Average % of frosh need met	59
Average % of ugrad need met	63

FAIRFIELD UNIVERSITY

1073 North Benson Road, Fairfield, CT 06824-5195 • Admissions: 203-254-4100 • Fax: 203-254-4199

CAMPUS LIFE

Quality of Life Rating	84
Fire Safety Rating	87
Green Rating	82
Type of school	Private
Affiliation	Roman Catholic-Jesuit
Environment	Town

STUDENTS

Total undergrad enrollment	3,721
% male/female	40/60
% from out of state	69
% frosh from public high school	56
% frosh live on campus	94
% ugrads live on campus	80
% African American	3
% Asian	2
% Caucasian	72
% Hispanic	8
% Native American	<1
% international	2
# of countries represented	30

SURVEY SAYS . . .

Students are happy
Great off-campus food
Campus feels safe
Lots of beer drinking
Hard liquor is popular
Active student government

ACADEMICS

Academic Rating	86
% students returning for sophomore year	87
% students graduating within 4 years	79
% students graduating within 6 years	82
Calendar	Semester
Student/faculty ratio	11:1
Profs interesting rating	83
Profs accessible rating	84

Most classes have 20–29 students.
Most lab/discussion sessions have fewer than 10 students.

MOST POPULAR MAJORS

nursing; accounting; communication

STUDENTS SAY " . . ."

Academics

Fairfield University, founded in 1942, is "a promising young institution short on tradition and diversity, but big on community, cross-disciplinary academics" and "educating the whole person: body, mind, and spirit." This Jesuit institution is based in "an amazing little New England town an hour outside of New York City." "It was everything I wanted in my school," a happy biology student testifies. "Small class size, beautiful campus, approachable professors—it's perfect." The school has a strong "commitment to the Jesuit values," a "friendly atmosphere," and a small size that means you'll "see so many familiar faces every day." Fairfield works hard to prepare "its students for life after college with the tools inherent in a Jesuit education." Students found the professors to be "amazingly engaging and knowledgeable." They're "experienced veterans in their fields of study" who have "actual industry, practical, real-world experience. This gives the students real insight into what a career actually is." Thanks to the small size, professors are "very accessible and tend to truly care about their students." One religious studies student sums up the Fairfield experience as being "about community—between the encouragement to get involved, living and learning communities, and its dedication to service, Fairfield is about forming and improving its own community and the greater community around it."

Life

Although some students can "get stuck in the 'Fairfield bubble,'" New Haven and "New York City [are] not that far away," and "it's easy to get on the train and go to the city if you want real fun." On campus, "students attend parties on the weekends, concerts on campus, or local concerts." The convenient location "enables students to visit other schools as well." "Townhouse parties are the biggest things for the weekend," and going to the "beach is always fun once the weather gets warmer in the spring." "FUSA (Fairfield University Student Association) plans activities for every night of the week (games, speakers, late night food, etc.)." "The extracurricular activities the school provides for its students are really a great diversion from school work when you've had a stressful day!" If there's one downside to campus life, it seems to be "the food in the cafeteria," which was frequently derided, as well as the definite "lack of school spirit." Although one student proclaimed: "We learn and live together; we are Stags!" "Overall, it's a laid-back school with nightlife, and I like it that way, nothing really wild."

Student Body

Fairfield students are typically "white, middle- or upper-class students," who are "usually devoted to studies as well as serving the community and others." However, many students feel the school "should improve in recruiting a more diverse student body." "Perhaps the downfall of Fairfield is that the student population seems pretty homogeneous," one student explains. "White and wealthy would be a fitting description for most. However, diversity is an initiative the university is working on." In particular, "socioeconomic differences are very clearly defined." "Although it is not very diverse, most students are open to people of different backgrounds, and joining clubs or other teams is an easy way to make friends and fit in." One student points out that, while the school isn't racially diverse, that doesn't mean the school isn't accepting: "Being a minority here, I think the openness to minorities is undervalued. Everyone here is accepting, and though there are some things that could be improved upon, it is a very good school to belong." As for fashion, Fairfield "has the 'J. Crew U.' reputation" for a reason. "The typical student owns a Northface, was really good at some sport back in high school, owns some articles of Polo, is moderately attractive, and enjoys a weekend of partying." However, while "everyone always looks put together...no one is going over the top—we do have to go to class."

FINANCIAL AID: 203-254-4125 • E-MAIL: ADMIS@FAIRFIELD.EDU • WEBSITE: WWW.FAIRFIELD.EDU

THE PRINCETON REVIEW SAYS

Admissions

Very important factors considered include: GPA, rigor of secondary school record, application essay, recommendation(s). *Important factors considered include:* Extracurricular activities, first generation, interview, talent/ability, volunteer work, work experience, character/personal qualities, level of applicant's interest. *Other factors considered include:* Class rank, standardized test scores, geographical residence, racial/ethnic status, alumni/ae relations. SAT and SAT Subject Tests or ACT considered if submitted; ACT with or without Writing component accepted. TOEFL required of all international applicants. *Academic units required:* 4 English; 3 mathematics; 3 science; (2 science lab); 2 social studies; 2 foreign language; 2 history. *Academic units recommended:* 4 mathematics; 4 foreign language.

Financial Aid

Students should submit: FAFSA, CSS/Financial Aid PROFILE, Noncustodial PROFILE, Business/Farm Supplement. Regular filing deadline is 2/15. The Princeton Review suggests that all financial aid forms be submitted as soon as possible after January 1. *Need-based scholarships/grants offered:* Federal Pell, SEOG, State scholarships/grants, private scholarships, the school's own gift aid, federal nursing scholarships. *Loan aid offered:* Direct Subsidized Stafford Loans, Direct Unsubsidized Stafford Loans, Direct PLUS loans, Federal Perkins Loans, Federal Nursing Loans. Applicants will be notified of awards beginning 4/1. Federal Work-Study Program available. Institutional employment available. Off-campus job opportunities are good.

The Inside Word

Steady increases in the number of admission applications have nicely increased selectivity in recent years. Fairfield's campus and central location, combined with improvements to the library, campus center, classrooms, athletic facilities, and campus residencies, make this a campus worth seeing.

THE SCHOOL SAYS "..."

From the Admissions Office

"Fairfield University welcomes students of unique promise into a learning and living community that will give them a solid intellectual foundation and the confidence they need to reach their individual goals. Students at Fairfield benefit from the deep-rooted Jesuit commitment to education of the whole person— mind, body, and spirit, and our admission policies are consistent with that mission. When considering an applicant, Fairfield looks at measures of academic achievement, students' curricular and extracurricular activities, their life skills and accomplishments, and the degree to which they have an appreciation for Fairfield's mission and outlook. In keeping with its holistic review process, Fairfield is a test optional institution. Students choosing not to submit test scores do not have to submit any additional documents, but are encouraged to schedule a campus interview. Fairfield University students are challenged to be creative and active members of a community in which diversity is encouraged and honored. The university community is committed to excellence in educating, serving, inspiring and training students in a wide variety of disciplines and fields. Students can complement their classroom performance with a rich array of study abroad, internship and research opportunities. Our location is ideal, offering a picturesque 200-acre campus in the coastal community of Fairfield, Connecticut, just an hour away from the cultural, intellectual and economic opportunities of New York City. On campus, students participate in a vast array of activities, including varsity and intramural athletics, performing arts groups and an extremely active student government. All of this prepares our graduates for a rich and fulfilling future, whether students pursue a career, service opportunities or graduate study. In our most recent survey of graduates of the Class of 2013 six months after graduation, 98 percent of students were employed full time, in graduate school or pursuing a service opportunity."

SELECTIVITY

Admissions Rating	84
# of applicants	9,582
% of applicants accepted	70
% of acceptees attending	14
# offered a place on the wait list	1,745
% accepting a place on wait list	28
% admitted from wait list	14
# of early decision applicants	93
% accepted early decision	62

FRESHMAN PROFILE

Range SAT Critical Reading	540–620
Range SAT Math	550–630
Range SAT Writing	550–640
Range ACT Composite	24–28
Minimum paper TOEFL	550
Minimum web-based TOEFL	80
Average HS GPA	3.38

DEADLINES

Early decision	
Deadline	11/15
Notification	1/1
Early action	
Deadline	11/1
Notification	1/1
Regular	
Priority	11/15
Deadline	1/15
Notification	4/1
Nonfall registration?	Yes

APPLICANTS ALSO LOOK AT AND OFTEN PREFER
Boston College

AND SOMETIMES PREFER
College of the Holy Cross; Villanova University; Boston University

FINANCIAL FACTS

Financial Aid Rating	81
Annual tuition	$42,320
Room and board	$12,930
Required fees	$600
Books and supplies	$1,150
% needy frosh rec. need-based scholarship or grant aid	87
% needy UG rec. need-based scholarship or grant aid	89
% needy frosh rec. non-need-based scholarship or grant aid	90
% needy UG rec. non-need-based scholarship or grant aid	70
% needy frosh rec. need-based self-help aid	79
% needy UG rec. need-based self-help aid	85
% frosh rec. any financial aid	87
% UG rec. any financial aid	85
% UG borrow to pay for school	65
Average cumulative indebtedness	$28,918
% frosh need fully met	18
% ugrads need fully met	13
Average % of frosh need met	87
Average % of ugrad need met	87

FLAGLER COLLEGE

74 KING STREET, ST. AUGUSTINE, FL 32085-1027 • ADMISSIONS: 800-304-4208 • FAX: 904-826-0094

CAMPUS LIFE

Quality of Life Rating	86
Fire Safety Rating	85
Green Rating	73
Type of school	Private
Affiliation	No Affiliation
Environment	Town

STUDENTS

Total undergrad enrollment	2,839
% male/female	41/59
% from out of state	38
% frosh from public high school	78
% frosh live on campus	94
% ugrads live on campus	36
% African American	4
% Asian	1
% Caucasian	76
% Hispanic	8
% Native American	<1
% international	3
# of countries represented	39

SURVEY SAYS . . .

Great off-campus food
Students love St. Augustine, FL
Frats and sororities are unpopular
or nonexistent
Very little drug use

ACADEMICS

Academic Rating	78
% students returning for sophomore year	67
% students graduating within 4 years	44
% students graduating within 6 years	58
Calendar	Semester
Student/faculty ratio	16.5:1
Profs interesting rating	80
Profs accessible rating	77

Most classes have 20–29 students.

MOST POPULAR MAJORS

business/commerce; psychology; education

STUDENTS SAY ". . ."

Academics

For those seeking "an excellent education in a beautiful location," Flagler College is a small comprehensive liberal arts school in Florida that offers a "comfortable atmosphere," "tons of history and culture," and "a perfect ratio of professors to student." The school's strong education program is a huge draw here, but there are plenty of other strong programs in Flagler's twenty-five available majors. Hard workers get noticed, and there are plenty of opportunities to excel outside of the classroom, which "has been the most valuable aspect," according to one student.

The faculty here is "extremely enthusiastic about their jobs" and "very knowledgeable in their fields," though "there are a few that I don't think have real direction," says a student. Nevertheless, most are "always willing to meet and discuss work outside of the classroom," and the fact that "it is pretty easy to get to know the professors within your major on a personal basis makes things a lot easier and comfortable." This close-knit community breeds an environment where every person actively wants "to share experiences and knowledge with the faculty and other students." Class time is treated as an "intellectual journey," wherein one main question or discussion topic is introduced, and students explore every aspect of it using the professor as the tour guide. "This system the professors at Flagler College have evokes curiosity from all students, leaving very little room for confusion."

Aside from the "ample help from teachers," the "personable" administration is "good at communicating to all students via school e-mail." The attendance policy can be tough on some students—"you only get a certain number of absences, excused or unexcused, before you get dropped from a course"—but most still know that this tough love is in place to help students be "encouraged in a way that leads to excellent work." The best classes are the ones with eight or so people in them, as "you really lean on each other throughout the semester."

Life

Life is "pretty chill at Flagler," where "homework usually isn't too bad most of the time." As far as making friends, this "relaxed," happy lot has no problems. "Attend a few of the many social activities that Flagler College offers. It's really easy to make friends there!" suggests one student. On the first Friday of the month, all the art galleries "throw their doors wide open and serve treats," and the "casual and quaint" tourist-centric town of St. Augustine "is an awesome place to spend your time, walking around, going out to eat, and doing a little bit of shopping." Campus activities tend to "die around 7:00 P.M.," and many students tend to live nearby off campus (due to Flagler College residential rules, which restrict interdorm visiting, drugs, and alcohol).

Sunny days mean "the pool and West lawn are the places to be," and on weekends, "many times we drive to Jacksonville and go out at night there." Biking, beach volleyball, and walking along the sand dunes are just some of the beachy pastimes here, where "the beach mentality triumphs, including surfer culture." The campus itself "is beautiful, we sometimes even compare it to Hogwarts," says a student.

Student Body

Your typical Flagler student is "easygoing and very laid-back" ("How can you not be with the beach five miles away?" asks a student) as well as "super nice and friendly." It's not difficult to fit in at Flagler College, because "there is a crowd for everybody, despite the small size of the student body," even if this student body as a whole is a bit "homogenous." All students provide different viewpoints and "seem to be very respectful of others' views." There are quite a few surfers and artistic types, and even these groups are "very motivated and ready to broaden their education."

FINANCIAL AID: 904-819-6225 • E-MAIL: ADMISS@FLAGLER.EDU • WEBSITE: WWW.FLAGLER.EDU

THE PRINCETON REVIEW SAYS

Admissions

Very important factors considered include: Rigor of secondary school record. *Important factors considered include:* GPA, standardized test scores, application essay, extracurricular activities, recommendation(s), talent/ability, alumni/ae relations, character/personal qualities. *Other factors considered include:* Class rank, first generation, geographical residence, interview, racial/ethnic status, state residency, volunteer work, level of applicant's interest. SAT or ACT required; ACT with Writing component recommended. TOEFL required of all international applicants. *Academic units required:* 4 English; 3 mathematics; 2 science; (1 science lab); 3 social studies; 1 history; 2 academic electives. *Academic units recommended:* 4 English; 4 mathematics; 3 science; (2 science lab); 3 social studies; 2 foreign language; 2 history; 2 academic electives; 1 computer science; 1 visual/performing arts.

Financial Aid

Students should submit: FAFSA, state aid form. The Princeton Review suggests that all financial aid forms be submitted as soon as possible after January 1. *Need-based scholarships/grants offered:* Federal Pell, SEOG, State scholarships/grants, private scholarships, the school's own gift aid. *Loan aid offered:* Direct Subsidized Stafford Loans, Direct Unsubsidized Stafford Loans, Direct PLUS loans, Federal Perkins Loans. Federal Work-Study Program available. Institutional employment available. Off-campus job opportunities are excellent.

The Inside Word

Several high-profile programs, a desirable location, and a small, incoming freshman class all conspire to drive down Flagler's admissions rate. Still, Flagler is not top-tier when it comes to selectivity, and strong candidates should meet little resistance from the admissions office. About half of the incoming freshmen graduated in the top quarter of their classes, so make sure you build a strong application with harder courses and strong grades.

THE SCHOOL SAYS "..."

From the Admissions Office

"Flagler College is an independent, four-year, coeducational, residential institution located in picturesque St. Augustine. A famous historic tourist center in northeast Florida, it is located to the south of Jacksonville and north of Daytona Beach. Flagler students have ample opportunity to explore the rich cultural heritage and international flavor of St. Augustine, and there's always time for a relaxing day at the beach, about four miles from campus. The annual cost for tuition, room, and board at Flagler is about the same as state universities. The small student body helps to keep one from becoming 'just a number.' Flagler serves a predominately full-time student body and seeks to enroll students who can benefit from the type of educational experience the college offers. Because of the college's mission and distinctive characteristics, some students may benefit more from an educational experience at Flagler than others. The college's admission standards and procedures are designed to select from among the applicants those students most likely to succeed academically, to contribute significantly to the student life program at Flagler, and to become graduates of the college. Flagler College provides an exceptional opportunity for a private education at an extremely affordable cost.

"All applicants to Flagler College must submit either their SAT or ACT scores."

SELECTIVITY

Admissions Rating	60*
# of applicants	5,396
% of applicants accepted	50
% of acceptees attending	26
# offered a place on the wait list	474
% accepting a place on wait list	27
% admitted from wait list	24
# of early decision applicants	459
% accepted early decision	57

FRESHMAN PROFILE

Minimum paper TOEFL	550
Minimum web-based TOEFL	213

DEADLINES

Early decision	
Deadline	11/1
Notification	12/15
Regular	
Priority	1/15
Deadline	3/1
Notification	3/30
Nonfall registration?	Yes

APPLICANTS ALSO LOOK AT AND RARELY PREFER

Florida Southern College; Eckerd College

FINANCIAL FACTS

Financial Aid Rating	71
Annual tuition	$16,180
Room and board	$8,780
Books and supplies	$1,100
% needy frosh rec. need-based scholarship or grant aid	97
% needy UG rec. need-based scholarship or grant aid	96
% needy frosh rec. non-need-based scholarship or grant aid	6
% needy UG rec. non-need-based scholarship or grant aid	7
% needy frosh rec. need-based self-help aid	82
% needy UG rec. need-based self-help aid	81
% frosh rec. any financial aid	61
% UG rec. any financial aid	64
% UG borrow to pay for school	69
Average cumulative indebtedness	$27,408
% frosh need fully met	14
% ugrads need fully met	15
Average % of frosh need met	59
Average % of ugrad need met	59

FLORIDA SOUTHERN COLLEGE

111 LAKE HOLLINGSWORTH DRIVE, LAKELAND, FL 33801 • ADMISSIONS: 800-274-4131 • FAX: 863-680-4120

CAMPUS LIFE

Quality of Life Rating	80
Fire Safety Rating	87
Green Rating	78
Type of school	Private
Affiliation	Methodist
Environment	City

STUDENTS

Total undergrad enrollment	2,162
% male/female	41/59
% from out of state	36
% frosh from public high school	81
% frosh live on campus	94
% ugrads live on campus	79
# of fraternities (% ugrad men join)	7 (36)
# of sororities (% ugrad women join)	6 (33)
% African American	6
% Asian	2
% Caucasian	73
% Hispanic	9
% Native American	<1
% international	6
# of countries represented	40

SURVEY SAYS . . .

Everyone loves the Mocsie
Intramural sports are popular
Frats and sororities are popular

ACADEMICS

Academic Rating	81
% students returning for sophomore year	78
% students graduating within 4 years	48
% students graduating within 6 years	58
Calendar	Semester
Student/faculty ratio	14:1
Profs interesting rating	83
Profs accessible rating	78
Most classes have 10–19 students.	
Most lab/discussion sessions have 10–19 students.	

MOST POPULAR MAJORS

business administration and management; biology; psychology

STUDENTS SAY " . . ."

Academics

Though it might sound like a cliché, Florida Southern takes great pains to assure that students here "are not just a number." As one astonished freshman excitedly reveals, "The faculty knew my name before I even committed to going here!" And with the college's "absolutely gorgeous campus" and "friendly atmosphere" it's no wonder that Florida Southern undergrads are so content. Armed with an "excellent reputation," FSC offers students a very "personalized education." Indeed, the "small class sizes… really [allow you to] get to know everyone, even in your gen ed. and freshman [courses]." And, importantly, "the school provides so many opportunities to get involved and find things that you are truly interested in." Students speak glowingly about their professors who manage to "really bring the subjects [they teach] to life." Many also stress that their professors are truly "dedicated to helping you succeed and make time in their busy schedules to help you with whatever you need." A religion major gushes, "I have had professors sit down and work with me to get papers and assignments accomplished as well as checking on me when they know that I have been going through a tough time." Finally, one pleased senior sums up, "When I came to Florida Southern, I felt like I had found the place I could truly call home."

Life

By and large, students feel that life at Florida Southern "is pretty laid back." Though undergrads are definitely quite diligent about their studies, they manage to hit a good work/life balance. This is partially due to the fact that they're privy to "a beautiful campus that promotes a very relaxing environment. There are great places around campus where you can kick back and relax a little; for example, [there's] a Zen garden, the library, student lounges, and stress relieving activities in the career center." Certainly, there are also a number of organizations in which to join/participate. As one freshman expounds, "There are plenty of groups for every kind of interest: political groups, religious groups…pre-professional groups, sports teams. There's almost always something to do." Further, the campus activities committee (known as ACE) continually sponsors "fun events such as a foam party, dances and comedians." For those concerned and/or curious about the drinking culture, FSC "technically [maintains] a 'dry' campus." However, "most students like to go to the local bar to dance and drink." Additionally, "Greek life is very important to most students." Beyond the campus, undergrads also love to take advantage of FSC's location in central Florida. For example, the college is "close to Disney World and Universal Studios/Islands of Adventure. [Additionally] there are water parks, including Wet 'n' Wild and Adventure Island." And, of course, hometown Lakeland offers "shopping and movies…right down the road!"

Student Body

No matter the adjectives employed to describe their peers, most FSC undergrads agree that they joined "a wonderful community of students." As one satisfied freshman explains, "All the students are pretty cool. Everyone gets along for the most part. You start to recognize faces just from walking around campus and exchange 'hello's' even if you have never had a conversation." However, some students do bemoan the fact that it often feels as though everyone "is in a sorority or fraternity or [an] athlete." As another freshman puts it, "You constantly get asked if you're rushing." Fortunately, others counter that, "It is difficult to not find a 'place' at FSC." A business administration student assures us that, "independents are also able to form their own identity here." Moreover, a sagacious senior shares, "There is no criteria for what a student at FSC is, really. There is just that cohesive family feeling that you get when you walk on campus that does not depend on who you are or what you believe." Finally, perhaps nothing unites this student body more than the fact that "we all…complain about the lack of parking on a regular basis."

FINANCIAL AID: 863-680-4140 • E-MAIL: FSCADM@FLSOUTHERN.EDU • WEBSITE: WWW.FLSOUTHERN.EDU

THE PRINCETON REVIEW SAYS

Admissions

Very important factors considered include: GPA, rigor of secondary school record. *Important factors considered include:* Standardized test scores, application essay, extracurricular activities, recommendation(s), talent/ability, character/personal qualities, level of applicant's interest. *Other factors considered include:* Class rank, first generation, interview, volunteer work, work experience, alumni/ae relations. SAT or ACT required; ACT with or without Writing component accepted. TOEFL required of all international applicants. *Academic units required:* 4 English; 3 mathematics; 2 science; (2 science lab); 3 social studies; 3 history; 1 academic elective. *Academic units recommended:* 2 foreign language.

Financial Aid

Students should submit: FAFSA, Institution's own financial aid form. Regular filing deadline is 7/1. The Princeton Review suggests that all financial aid forms be submitted as soon as possible after January 1. *Need-based scholarships/grants offered:* Federal Pell, SEOG, State scholarships/grants, private scholarships, the school's own gift aid, federal nursing scholarships. *Loan aid offered:* Direct Subsidized Stafford Loans, Direct Unsubsidized Stafford Loans, Direct PLUS loans, Federal Perkins Loans. Federal Work-Study Program available. Institutional employment available. Off-campus job opportunities are good.

The Inside Word

Grades and test scores are the most important admission criteria here, but extra-curricular activities, community service, and leadership experience also count for a lot. Admissions officers are on the lookout for applicants who demonstrate intellectual curiosity and a desire to succeed both inside the classroom and out. Without a doubt, the strongest candidates are those who have challenged themselves by taking honors, advanced placement or IB courses.

THE SCHOOL SAYS "..."

From the Admissions Office

"Florida Southern is a friendly, vibrant, and energetic campus, offering dynamic engaged learning opportunities that include guaranteed internships, student-faculty collaborative research and performance, service learning, and study abroad. An innovative program—the Junior Journey—guarantees all students the opportunity to study domestically or overseas during their junior year at no cost for the trip other than minimal course credit charges. FSC offers more than fifty majors in fields such as art, biology, business, chemistry, communication, education, marine biology, music and theater performance, nursing, and psychology. Pre-professional programs include pre-medicine, pre-pharmacy, pre-dentistry, and pre-law. The college is known for its great faculty, small classes (thirteen to one student/faculty), and personalized attention. The college has a state-of-the art technology center, as well as contemporary residence halls with scenic views of Lake Hollingsworth. Our involved student population enjoys rich and varied student life programming that includes championship NCAA Division II events in nineteen sports, intramurals, more than eighty clubs and organizations, an extensive Greek system, and an elaborate and diverse selection of weekend activities. The college's popular lakefront program features free kayaks, canoes, and paddleboats. FSC is home to the world's largest single-site collection of structures designed by Frank Lloyd Wright, which provides a stunning setting for living and academic learning communities. Ninety-six percent of graduates report landing jobs in their fields or continuing their studies at top-tier graduate and professional schools within six months of graduation."

SELECTIVITY

Admissions Rating	85
# of applicants	4,963
% of applicants accepted	50
% of acceptees attending	26
# of early decision applicants	78
% accepted early decision	64

FRESHMAN PROFILE

Range SAT Critical Reading	500–590
Range SAT Math	510–590
Range SAT Writing	480–580
Range ACT Composite	23–27
Minimum paper TOEFL	550
Minimum web-based TOEFL	213
Average HS GPA	3.62
% graduated top 10% of class	20
% graduated top 25% of class	56
% graduated top 50% of class	81

DEADLINES

Early decision	
Deadline	12/1
Notification	12/15
Regular	
Priority	3/1
Nonfall registration?	Yes

FINANCIAL FACTS

Financial Aid Rating	79
% needy frosh rec. need-based scholarship or grant aid	100
% needy UG rec. need-based scholarship or grant aid	98
% needy frosh rec. non-need-based scholarship or grant aid	61
% needy UG rec. non-need-based scholarship or grant aid	68
% needy frosh rec. need-based self-help aid	9
% needy UG rec. need-based self-help aid	28
% frosh rec. any financial aid	99
% UG rec. any financial aid	98
% UG borrow to pay for school	75
Average cumulative indebtedness	$33,191
% frosh need fully met	29
% ugrads need fully met	26
Average % of frosh need met	75
Average % of ugrad need met	73

FLORIDA STATE UNIVERSITY

PO Box 3062400, Tallahassee, FL 32306-2400 • Admissions: 850-644-6200 • Fax: 850-644-0197

CAMPUS LIFE
Quality of Life Rating	84
Fire Safety Rating	79
Green Rating	91
Type of school	Public
Affiliation	No Affiliation
Environment	City

STUDENTS
Total undergrad enrollment	32,086
% male/female	45/55
% from out of state	10
% frosh from public high school	84
% frosh live on campus	75
% ugrads live on campus	20
# of fraternities (% ugrad men join)	30 (27)
# of sororities (% ugrad women join)	27 (35)
% African American	8
% Asian	3
% Caucasian	67
% Hispanic	17
% Native American	<1
% international	1
# of countries represented	142

SURVEY SAYS . . .
Students are happy
School is well run
Students are friendly
Great off-campus food
Athletic facilities are great
Lots of beer drinking
Everyone loves the Seminoles
Intramural sports are popular
Frats and sororities are popular
Alumni active on campus
Active student government
Active minority support groups

ACADEMICS
Academic Rating	76
% students returning for sophomore year	92
% students graduating within 4 years	57
% students graduating within 6 years	77
Calendar	Semester
Student/faculty ratio	26:1
Profs interesting rating	77
Profs accessible rating	77
Most classes have 20–29 students.	
Most lab/discussion sessions have 20–29 students.	

MOST POPULAR MAJORS
psychology; criminal justice; English language and literature

STUDENTS SAY ". . ."

Academics
Florida State University is "a large, sports-oriented, research-intensive state school that has a niche for everybody, as long as you are willing to search." In addition to its strong academics, students tended to choose FSU for its "sports teams"—the Florida State Seminoles—the "great weather," and the fact that it's "a place with great traditions." "Florida State is a school that is so rooted in tradition it is extremely hard not to proudly call yourself a True Seminole." FSU is also "affordable" for in-state students with "excellent scholarships." "The tight vicinity of the campus [causes] the student body to be a close-unit of individuals." "FSU's reputation as a small-school feel in a big university was what drew me in," says an accounting and finance student. Reviews of the professors are mixed, as is common at many large universities. "About one-fourth of the professors are no good at teaching, about half of them are decent or good, and about one-fourth are great," one student explains. Another attests, "I have had wonderful professors that have eyes, ears, and heart to a world beyond my own, and have shown me that anything is achievable if I try hard enough." Students do wish for "smaller class sizes" and "more discussions in class." If the students have one common complaint, it's *"parking!,"* which is "always a huge hassle." Students also wish for better sustainability, recycling, and green programs. "FSU has traditionally been all about the humanities, and it's great that we're expanding into other areas, but we shouldn't forget our main focus," one student says. An English major sums up FSU: "Florida State University is a school where students are asked to uphold the garnet and gold and to live intentionally in the direction of leadership, academics, and service."

Life
"Sports is basically your whole life here," claims one student. While a university as large as FSU—the population is 40,000 plus—has students of many types, athletics and "school spirit" are what "bring everyone together" at FSU. "Everyone likes to socialize and party, usually off campus, like at bars or houses." Greek life is also "very prominent" FSU has a reputation as a party school, and "many students go out on the weekend or even sometimes during the week. The use of alcohol and marihuana is very common." "The majority of FSU students gets rowdy almost every night of the week," confirms another. However, one student claims that "FSU is a recovering party school." Since its heyday in the mid-nineties, FSU has calmed down a bit, but you can still find thriving parties and clubs any day of the week." "People go to Wakulla Springs to swim or to Bear Paw to go around the river during the weekends." Although "Tallahassee is one of the most boring cities I have ever been to," "the nightlife is…very important in Tallahassee; there are many bars and clubs to attend." "My life at Florida State is busy," one political science student explains. "I am always on the move, from class, to student government, Greek life, internships at the capital, and nightlife. I think people at FSU are constantly thinking about how they can better themselves and the university."

Student Body
Your average FSU student is a "football fan, partier, into academics and community service, [and] passionate." Students tend to be "extremely involved," whether it's in athletics, "Greek life or community service, or one of the other hundreds of groups and clubs here at FSU." "Greek [life] is a huge part of campus, but you are fine if you are not in one." Although "the majority of students are Caucasians," "students of all races and religions work together here to make FSU an enjoyable environment," and "the school continues to become more diverse each year." No matter what their background, every FSU student has "a colossal amount of school spirit and loves to go out and support the team."

FINANCIAL AID: 850-644-5716 • E-MAIL: ADMISSIONS@ADMIN.FSU.EDU • WEBSITE: WWW.FSU.EDU

THE PRINCETON REVIEW SAYS

Admissions

Very important factors considered include: GPA, rigor of secondary school record. *Important factors considered include:* Standardized test scores, state residency, talent/ability. *Other factors considered include:* Class rank, application essay, extracurricular activities, first generation, geographical residence, recommendation(s), volunteer work, work experience, alumni/ae relations, character/personal qualities. SAT or ACT required; ACT with Writing component required. TOEFL required of all international applicants. *Academic units required:* 4 English; 4 mathematics; 3 science; (2 science lab); 1 social studies; 2 foreign language; 2 history; 3 academic electives. *Academic units recommended:* 4 English; 4 mathematics; 4 science; (2 science lab); 2 social studies; 4 foreign language; 2 history; 3 academic electives.

Financial Aid

Students should submit: FAFSA. The Princeton Review suggests that all financial aid forms be submitted as soon as possible after January 1. *Need-based scholarships/grants offered:* Federal Pell, SEOG, State scholarships/grants, private scholarships, the school's own gift aid. *Loan aid offered:* Direct Subsidized Stafford Loans, Direct Unsubsidized Stafford Loans, Direct PLUS loans, Federal Perkins Loans. Federal Work-Study Program available. Institutional employment available. Off-campus job opportunities are good.

The Inside Word

With 25,000 applications to process annually, FSU must rely on a formula-driven approach to triage its applicant pool. With the exception of applicants to special programs, only borderline candidates receive a truly thorough review; all others are either clearly in or clearly out based on grades, curriculum, and test scores. Candidates for programs in fine arts, creative arts, and performing arts must undergo a more rigorous review that includes a portfolio or audition.

THE SCHOOL SAYS "..."

From the Admissions Office

"The Florida State University is an internationally recognized teaching and research institution committed to preparing our students for a life that balances knowledge, creativity, leadership, and contribution. Designated as a Carnegie Research University (very high research activity), Florida State offers more than 320 undergraduate, graduate, and professional degree programs, including medicine and law. Our students have the opportunity to conduct research alongside Nobel laureates and Pulitzer Prize winners, Guggenheim Fellows, members of the National Academy of Sciences and American Academy of Arts and Sciences, and other globally recognized teachers and researchers. Through the efforts of our Office of Undergraduate Research, students partner with faculty who share their academic interests, and who encourage them to design and conduct original research projects. Through the Office of National Fellowships, Florida State has become a leader among the state's public universities by setting records in the award of national fellowships and scholarships for our students. We offer state-of-the-art teaching techniques in our technologically enhanced classrooms and wireless networking community. Our innovative student services include a comprehensive campus-wide leadership learning program, a center for community and global-based learning through service, and an award-winning career center. World-class cultural events, championship athletics, extensive recreational facilities, and a friendly, close-knit University community enrich student life and extend learning well beyond the classroom. Our diverse student body hails from all fifty states and more than 130 countries, and our numerous international programs throughout the world include year-round programs in Florence, Italy; London, England; Panama City, Panama; and Valencia, Spain."

SELECTIVITY

Admissions Rating	91
# of applicants	29,579
% of applicants accepted	57
% of acceptees attending	36

FRESHMAN PROFILE

Range SAT Critical Reading	560–640
Range SAT Math	550–640
Range SAT Writing	560–640
Range ACT Composite	25–29
Minimum paper TOEFL	550
Average HS GPA	3.88
% graduated top 10% of class	42
% graduated top 25% of class	77
% graduated top 50% of class	97

DEADLINES

Regular	
Deadline	1/15
Nonfall registration?	Yes

FINANCIAL FACTS

Financial Aid Rating	90
Annual in-state tuition	$4,640
Annual out-of-state tuition	$19,806
Room and board	$9,912
Required fees	$1,867
Books and supplies	$1,000
% needy frosh rec. need-based scholarship or grant aid	63
% needy UG rec. need-based scholarship or grant aid	60
% needy frosh rec. non-need-based scholarship or grant aid	94
% needy UG rec. non-need-based scholarship or grant aid	79
% needy frosh rec. need-based self-help aid	67
% needy UG rec. need-based self-help aid	73
% frosh rec. any financial aid	96
% UG rec. any financial aid	87
% UG borrow to pay for school	51
Average cumulative indebtedness	$23,365
% frosh need fully met	67
% ugrads need fully met	66
Average % of frosh need met	64
Average % of ugrad need met	67

FORDHAM UNIVERSITY

441 EAST FORDHAM ROAD, NEW YORK, NY 10458 • ADMISSIONS: 718-817-4000 • FAX: 718-367-9404

CAMPUS LIFE
Quality of Life Rating	85
Fire Safety Rating	74
Green Rating	60*
Type of school	Private
Affiliation	Roman Catholic
Environment	Metropolis

STUDENTS
Total undergrad enrollment	7,451
% male/female	42/58
% from out of state	46
% frosh from public high school	47
% frosh live on campus	73
% ugrads live on campus	56
% African American	6
% Asian	7
% Caucasian	58
% Hispanic	13
% Native American	<1
% international	2
# of countries represented	58

SURVEY SAYS . . .
Internships are widely available
Students love Bronx, NY
Great off-campus food
Lots of beer drinking

ACADEMICS
Academic Rating	74
% students returning for sophomore year	90
% students graduating within 4 years	72
% students graduating within 6 years	78
Calendar	Semester
Student/faculty ratio	12:1
Profs interesting rating	79
Profs accessible rating	80

Most classes have 10–19 students.
Most lab/discussion sessions have 10–19 students.

MOST POPULAR MAJORS
communication and media studies; social sciences; business/commerce

STUDENTS SAY ". . ."

Academics

With two New York City campus locations (Rose Hill and Lincoln Center), Fordham is truly a metropolitan school, offering a great liberal arts education in a small, tight-knit community. This community of "dedicated, opinionated students" are aware of the world around them, and the university offers students "serious academic opportunities and challenges, along with amazing opportunities to become involved with urban life in NYC."

Classes are "challenging, but you leave with a new perspective on the world—I'll never see things the same way again," says a junior history major. Faculty are "so accessible beyond class and are extremely willing to help," not to mention the fact that they are "constantly researching" and at times "can ask you to help with it." Due to the location, a lot of professors currently work in their field (particularly in the business program), or did work in their field for decades, so "they truly know the material they are teaching" and "teach practical knowledge as opposed to the theoretical." "Their doors are always open and [they] will continue to let you know about things and events that might pertain to your major or might help you in your academic career," says a sophomore.

Similarly, Fordham "cares a great deal about the personal development of the students outside of the classroom," though some admit that some offices (particularly Residential Life) "aren't very helpful at times" due to red tape. Still, the administration as a whole "keeps improving," and "really does listen to the students and make the necessary changes." "In the four years that I have been here, they have added two resident halls, a new building to house the school of business, a new gym, renovated all the science labs, and are in the process of completing the new law school and residence hall at Lincoln Center," says a student. A wide network of alumni throughout New York City and the world also really "helps facilitate internship and career opportunities after college," not to mention that "recruiters from all industries are here, and Fordham has the connections."

Life

New York City is beloved by all at Fordham, and the affection spills over into the school. "Fordham is my school, New York is my campus." At the Rose Hill location in the Bronx you get "a beautiful gated campus with the city just minutes away"; at the Lincoln Center location (home to the Theatre Department) you're right in the thick of things. Either way, you "still have the college campus feel" and "truly get the best of both worlds."

Fittingly, "tons of students like to go into the city for fun and see Broadway shows, sporting events, or just walk around." There is actually also a ton of (free) stuff to do on campus ("as dictated by University law, there must be at least three activities per night every night") including "movie nights, parties for 21-plus seniors, and intramurals." "Although 'college partying' is a thing here" (note: there is no Greek life at Fordham), there are students who choose not to do so, and "they are not alone." Students tend to work hard during the week, but "day-to-day life is very easygoing and relaxed, with students always hanging out in each other's rooms." Many students (especially business and communication students) have internships.

Student Body

Fordham's population is really diverse, which is "reflective of a New York City population," but there is a fair number of "Caucasian Catholics, usually Italian or Irish," who come from "upper-middle class families" in the Northeast. The school "is not cliquey at all," and students use their freshman dorms or "a wide range of clubs and extracurriculars" in order to fit in. This "intelligent" crew is "eager to gain work experience" and explore the city, and is "very active in campus life and community service." Students here "are ambitious about their classes as well as their future careers."

FINANCIAL AID: 718-817-3800 • E-MAIL: ENROLL@FORDHAM.EDU • WEBSITE: WWW.FORDHAM.EDU

THE PRINCETON REVIEW SAYS

Admissions

Very important factors considered include: Class rank, GPA, rigor of secondary school record, standardized test scores, level of applicant's interest. *Important factors considered include:* Application essay, extracurricular activities, recommendation(s), talent/ability, character/personal qualities. *Other factors considered include:* First generation, geographical residence, racial/ethnic status, volunteer work, work experience, alumni/ae relations. SAT or ACT required; ACT with Writing component recommended. TOEFL required of all international applicants. *Academic units required:* 4 English; 3 mathematics; 3 science; 2 social studies; 2 foreign language; 2 history; 6 academic electives. *Academic units recommended:* 4 English; 4 mathematics; 4 science; 2 social studies; 3 foreign language; 2 history; 6 academic electives.

Financial Aid

Students should submit: FAFSA, CSS/Financial Aid PROFILE, Noncustodial PROFILE, Business/Farm Supplement. Regular filing deadline is 2/1. The Princeton Review suggests that all financial aid forms be submitted as soon as possible after January 1. *Need-based scholarships/grants offered:* Federal Pell, SEOG, State scholarships/grants, private scholarships, the school's own gift aid. *Loan aid offered:* Federal Perkins Loans. Applicants will be notified of awards beginning 3/31.

The Inside Word

Applicants to Fordham are required to indicate whether they are applying to the Rose Hill campus in the Bronx, the Lincoln Center campus in Manhattan, or the Gabelli School of Business at Rose Hill. Admission criteria vary by school, but all are very competitive. Graduation from a Catholic high school—particularly a prestigious one on the East Coast—is always a plus.

THE SCHOOL SAYS "..."

From the Admissions Office

"Fordham University offers a distinctive, values-centered educational experience that is rooted in the Jesuit tradition of intellectual rigor and personal attention. Located in New York City, Fordham offers to students the unparalleled educational, cultural and recreational advantages of one of the world's greatest cities. Fordham has two residential campuses in New York—the tree-lined, eighty-five-acre Rose Hill campus in the Bronx, and the cosmopolitan Lincoln Center campus in the heart of Manhattan's performing arts center. The university's state-of-the-art facilities and buildings include one of the most technologically advanced libraries in the country. Fordham offers a variety of majors, concentrations and programs that can be combined with an extensive career planning and placement program. More than 2,600 organizations in the New York metropolitan area offer students internships that provide hands-on experience and valuable networking opportunities in fields such as business, communications, medicine, law and education.

"Applicants are required to take SAT or the ACT with the writing section. SAT Subject Tests are recommended but not required."

SELECTIVITY

Admissions Rating	93
# of applicants	18,161
% of applicants accepted	47
% of acceptees attending	20
# offered a place on the wait list	3,263
% accepting a place on wait list	36
% admitted from wait list	10

FRESHMAN PROFILE

Range SAT Critical Reading	570–670
Range SAT Math	560–660
Range SAT Writing	560–660
Range ACT Composite	25–29
Minimum paper TOEFL	575
Minimum web-based TOEFL	231
Average HS GPA	3.70
% graduated top 10% of class	43
% graduated top 25% of class	73
% graduated top 50% of class	96

DEADLINES

Early action	
Deadline	11/1
Notification	12/25
Regular	
Priority	1/15
Deadline	1/15
Notification	4/1
Nonfall registration?	Yes

APPLICANTS ALSO LOOK AT
AND OFTEN PREFER
New York University; Boston College; The George Washington University

AND SOMETIMES PREFER
Georgetown University; Loyola University Maryland; College of the Holy Cross

AND RARELY PREFER
Hofstra University; Pace University; Marist College

FINANCIAL FACTS

Financial Aid Rating	76
Annual tuition	$41,000
Room and board	$15,374
Required fees	$1,057
Books and supplies	$975
% needy frosh rec. need-based scholarship or grant aid	97
% needy UG rec. need-based scholarship or grant aid	95
% needy frosh rec. non-need-based scholarship or grant aid	44
% needy UG rec. non-need-based scholarship or grant aid	46
% needy frosh rec. need-based self-help aid	73
% needy UG rec. need-based self-help aid	76
% frosh rec. any financial aid	88
% UG rec. any financial aid	83
% UG borrow to pay for school	64
Average cumulative indebtedness	$38,150
% frosh need fully met	30
% ugrads need fully met	24
Average % of frosh need met	78
Average % of ugrad need met	74

FRANKLIN & MARSHALL COLLEGE

PO Box 3003, Lancaster, PA 17604-3003 • Admissions: 717-291-3953 • Fax: 717-291-4389

CAMPUS LIFE

Quality of Life Rating	74
Fire Safety Rating	93
Green Rating	85
Type of school	Private
Affiliation	No Affiliation
Environment	Town

STUDENTS

Total undergrad enrollment	2,297
% male/female	48/52
% from out of state	71
% frosh from public high school	63
% frosh live on campus	100
% ugrads live on campus	97
# of fraternities	8
# of sororities	5
% African American	4
% Asian	4
% Caucasian	63
% Hispanic	7
% Native American	<1
% international	13
# of countries represented	44

SURVEY SAYS . . .
Lab facilities are great
Easy to get around campus
Lots of beer drinking
Hard liquor is popular

ACADEMICS

Academic Rating	92
% students returning for sophomore year	92
% students graduating within 4 years	84
% students graduating within 6 years	87
Calendar	Semester
Student/faculty ratio	9:1
Profs interesting rating	83
Profs accessible rating	95

Most classes have 20–29 students.
Most lab/discussion sessions have 10–19 students.

MOST POPULAR MAJORS
political science; business/commerce; psychology

STUDENTS SAY " . . . "

Academics

Franklin & Marshall College is "a small, focused liberal arts college dedicated to giving every student the opportunity to succeed." Known for its "extremely high academic standards" and "great faculty accessibility," the school is "about furthering academic achievement and providing superior skills and opportunities for success after graduation." Many students say, "F&M is all about good undergrad programs and tight-knit networking," and students laud the opportunity to make connections in their chosen fields. The college has "a slight emphasis on the sciences," which makes an English major grumble, "Some really fantastic humanities programs lack in administrative support whereas science programs get everything and anything they want." Nevertheless, the college's "policy of deferring major declaration until sophomore year…allows undecided students to really find a major that suits their interests." The faculty gets good marks for being available to students outside the classroom, but students acknowledge that, "as with many things, professors vary widely in style and quality." A sophomore notes, "Some are very difficult but interesting; some are very boring, etc. There are enough wonderful professors to go around, though." Many students complain about the course registration process saying it can be "competitive and difficult to get into desired classes."

Life

F&M boasts a "lush and beautiful campus" with "state-of-the-art educational and living facilities" and "a strong community feel." Students say, "Events are constantly being organized, and there's always something interesting going on if you take the time to participate." Students also point out, "If you see that there is a need for a new school group, you can definitely petition for it, and the school will back you up. F&M cares a lot about on-campus diversity." Overall, it's a, "close-knit student body," and students feel that "as an F&M student, you are not a number or a name on a class roster, you are an active contributor on campus." However, students are torn on the issue of school spirit, with some feeling it's strong and others griping that "school spirit is laughable." "There isn't enough student involvement and enthusiasm with clubs and activities." However, all students agree that "the school could stand to improve on campus dining." There are complaints about the mandatory four-year residency requirement, particularly among upperclassmen who feel it "needs to be modified" because it "makes housing far more expensive than it should be." Some feel the administration can be "hard to work with" and think the college should "streamline administrative departments" to "decrease wasteful spending."

Student Body

At F&M, the motto seems to be, "Work hard, play hard." Students say they take their academics seriously, but "because the work is so demanding, on weekends everyone gets pretty crazy." Greek life is a predominant part of the social scene, and some say, "On weekends, it's pretty much the only outlet for socializing." Many say the student body is "preppier and more Greek than you'd expect" and that "the typical student is Caucasian, upper-middle-class, from the tristate area" and looks like "a J. Crew model." However, a neuroscience major says, "While Greek life seems to dominate campus, after one or two years you come to realize that there is a lot more to do for fun," and another student adds, "It's a very laid-back lifestyle so people like to relax and enjoy time with their friends." A junior says, "In reality, everyone has their 'thing' that they're involved in," and in general "students are friendly and pleasant, but they tend to stick to themselves and their small groups of friends." However, many agree that, "For a small school, there is an enormous variety of things to do," and they say, "on any given weekend you can find people all over campus, whether it be at the artsy green room theatre, the library…in the college center, in a friend's apartment, or at a frat party."

FINANCIAL AID: 717-291-3991 • E-MAIL: ADMISSION@FANDM.EDU • WEBSITE: WWW.FANDM.EDU

THE PRINCETON REVIEW SAYS

Admissions

Very important factors considered include: Class rank, GPA, rigor of secondary school record, character/personal qualities. *Important factors considered include:* Standardized test scores, application essay, extracurricular activities, interview, recommendation(s), talent/ability, volunteer work. *Other factors considered include:* Geographical residence, racial/ethnic status, work experience, alumni/ae relations, level of applicant's interest. SAT or ACT considered if submitted; ACT with or without Writing component accepted. TOEFL required of all international applicants. *Academic units required:* 4 English; 3 mathematics; 2 science; (2 science lab); 1 social studies; 2 foreign language; 2 history; 1 visual/performing arts. *Academic units recommended:* 4 mathematics; 3 science; (3 science lab); 3 social studies; 4 foreign language; 3 history.

Financial Aid

Students should submit: FAFSA, CSS/Financial Aid PROFILE, State aid form, Noncustodial PROFILE, Business/Farm Supplement. Regular filing deadline is 2/15. The Princeton Review suggests that all financial aid forms be submitted as soon as possible after January 1. *Need-based scholarships/grants offered:* Federal Pell, SEOG, State scholarships/grants, private scholarships, the school's own gift aid. *Loan aid offered:* Direct Subsidized Stafford Loans, Direct Unsubsidized Stafford Loans, Direct PLUS loans, Federal Perkins Loans, College/university loans from institutional funds. Applicants will be notified of awards beginning 4/1. Federal Work-Study Program available.

The Inside Word

While admission at F&M is competitive, the admissions committee does show some flexibility. The college allows students who feel that standardized test scores don't reflect their true academic capacity to submit two graded writing samples to replace the test scores. Applicants are also encouraged to include nontraditional materials, such as art portfolios or recordings of musical performances, in their applications. Finally, F&M offers a "Spring Option," in which students can elect to start classes in the spring semester after spending the fall abroad, or pursuing a "challenging program in consultation with an experienced faculty advisor at F&M."

THE SCHOOL SAYS ". . ."

From the Admissions Office

"The hallmarks of a Franklin & Marshall education are individual attention and a supportive community. Our faculty members challenge you to achieve your best and engage you personally on a level you will not find at other institutions. We have one professor for every nine students, and two-thirds of our students collaborate on a research project or other directed study directly with a faculty member. Here are three more things you should know about F&M: 1) Our professors do not confine learning to classrooms and labs. They take you into the field and the local community to teach you how to *do* what students at other institutions may only read about. 2) We have College Houses, not dorms. Our five College Houses, which bring together first-year students into smaller groups, are student-governed spaces where you socialize, learn, and stretch your intellect. Based in each house are a faculty mentor and an administrative counselor to guide you. 3) No one gets lost. The depth and breadth of student activities and experiences provide everyone with a place to belong. Our students find a strong sense of self, and they find their "homes" in clubs, athletic teams, their College Houses, fraternities and sororities, the performing and musical arts, and the other strong communities they have the freedom to create for themselves."

SELECTIVITY

Admissions Rating	95
# of applicants	5,347
% of applicants accepted	36
% of acceptees attending	31
# offered a place on the wait list	1,638
# of early decision applicants	477
% accepted early decision	68

FRESHMAN PROFILE

Range SAT Critical Reading	590–690
Range SAT Math	630–720
Range ACT Composite	28–31
Minimum paper TOEFL	600
Minimum web-based TOEFL	250
Average HS GPA	3.49
% graduated top 10% of class	56
% graduated top 25% of class	86
% graduated top 50% of class	100

DEADLINES

Early decision	
Deadline	11/15
Notification	12/15
Regular	
Deadline	1/15
Notification	4/1
Nonfall registration?	Yes

APPLICANTS ALSO LOOK AT AND OFTEN PREFER

University of Pennsylvania; Cornell University; Haverford College; Hamilton College

AND SOMETIMES PREFER

Bucknell University; Colgate University; Lehigh University; Lafayette College; Dickinson College

FINANCIAL FACTS

Financial Aid Rating	96
Annual tuition	$46,185
Room and board	$12,010
Required fees	$100
Books and supplies	$1,200
% needy frosh rec. need-based scholarship or grant aid	99
% needy UG rec. need-based scholarship or grant aid	95
% needy frosh rec. non-need-based scholarship or grant aid	28
% needy UG rec. non-need-based scholarship or grant aid	23
% needy frosh rec. need-based self-help aid	95
% needy UG rec. need-based self-help aid	96
% frosh rec. any financial aid	52
% UG rec. any financial aid	49
% UG borrow to pay for school	54
Average cumulative indebtedness	$29,078
% frosh need fully met	100
% ugrads need fully met	100
Average % of frosh need met	100
Average % of ugrad need met	100

FRANKLIN W. OLIN COLLEGE OF ENGINEERING

Olin Way, Needham, MA 02492-1245 • Admissions: 781-292-2222 • Fax: 781-292-2210

CAMPUS LIFE

Quality of Life Rating	98
Fire Safety Rating	87
Green Rating	70
Type of school	Private
Affiliation	No Affiliation
Environment	Town

STUDENTS

Total undergrad enrollment	343
% male/female	50/50
% from out of state	85
% frosh live on campus	100
% ugrads live on campus	100
% African American	1
% Asian	17
% Caucasian	53
% Hispanic	4
% Native American	<1
% international	7
# of countries represented	18

SURVEY SAYS . . .

Students always studying
Students are happy
Classroom facilities are great
Lab facilities are great
Career services are great
Internships are widely available
Great financial aid
No one cheats
Students are friendly
Students get along with local community
Dorms are like palaces
Campus feels safe
Easy to get around campus
Very little drug use

ACADEMICS

Academic Rating	99
% students returning for sophomore year	96
% students graduating within 4 years	93
% students graduating within 6 years	99
Calendar	Semester
Student/faculty ratio	8:1
Profs interesting rating	99
Profs accessible rating	93
Most classes have fewer than 10 students.	

MOST POPULAR MAJORS

electrical and computer engineering, engineering, mechanical engineering

STUDENTS SAY ". . ."

Academics

If the "hands-on approach to engineering, friendly students, small and intimate setting, [and reputation as] academically one of the best schools in the nation" don't win you over, perhaps the fact that "Olin is constantly changing curriculum to try and better fit students' needs" will. New England's Olin College of Engineering takes a real-world approach to engineering education, focusing on "hands-on, project-based learning, and close relations with peers and professors. It's totally different from just about every other undergraduate institution." Olin recognizes that students don't want to become engineers because they "have a passion for learning how to solve differential equations thirty-five different ways," they become engineers "to tackle big problems and solve them effectively. But to do so," this student recognizes, "I need to be an effective communicator, an influential team member, and a capable thinker." And that is what sets Olin apart. "The professors want to make sure I actually learn the important aspects of the class. They don't grade me on when I turned things in or my spelling mistakes, they grade on my thoughts and the quality of my work." In addition, "Olin doesn't have tenure for professors, nor is it a major research institution, so the professors that are here love teaching. This shows inside and outside the classroom, as these professors care so much more about each student's learning than their own career path." But be warned, if this approach sounds easy, it's not. Olin's is a "rigorous, intense school that cranks out top-notch employable engineers that are well-rounded and able to accomplish anything thrown at them."

Life

The devotion to real-world learning at Olin means "people think a lot about self-improvement and learning." The academic focus causes some to "get overwhelmed with the amount of work," but for most this "uniquely awesome" group of students manages to find plenty of ways to keep themselves busy, even during down time. "For fun, we often go on adventures and try and get out and about … A good number of kids find odd, interesting activities to do such as river rafting or spelunking." Theater, music, the arts, Ultimate Frisbee and other activities draw plenty of interest – as does becoming a trapeze artist. That's right, "we are also a circus school. Unicycling, juggling, and fire arts are some of the biggest activities on campus." It should come as no surprise that this engineering-focused school has a rich geek culture, with video games, Doctor Who clubs, and even Pokemon proving popular among the student body. Throw in paintball, laser tag, parties and more, and there is no shortage of things to do. And if you're still having trouble? "It's also always good to keep an eye on our Carpe Diem mailing list, on which students will give notice of fun things happening around campus—from free food, to movie nights, games, dance lessons, Midnight Math, theatre, the student newspaper, paintball, art parties, and much more."

Student Body

"Olin is a vibrant community of students who are passionate about what they do and who love to get their hands dirty solving real-world problems," a whole campus made up of "awesome, smart people who are very supportive and involved and never sleep!" This student body is "not very athletic," but they are "very smart and find projects and work to be fun and often do them out of class." Typical Olin students are "usually found constantly working on various fun and interesting projects." There may be cliques here, just like at any school, but "everyone is nice to one another." Students here recognize that "everyone has quirks, but that is what makes us interesting. What makes Olin awesome is that the quirks are accepted and celebrated here instead of picked on." All in all, this "geeky" and "quirky" group "are not segregated or shunned, anyone can talk and hang out with anyone, no matter age, race, socioeconomic background, gender, orientation, what have you." As one student puts it, "It really feels like a big family here."

FRANKLIN W. OLIN COLLEGE OF ENGINEERING

FINANCIAL AID: 781-292-2343 • E-MAIL: INFO@OLIN.EDU • WEBSITE: WWW.OLIN.EDU

THE PRINCETON REVIEW SAYS

Admissions

Very important factors considered include: GPA, rigor of secondary school record, application essay, extracurricular activities, interview, recommendation(s), talent/ability, character/personal qualities, level of applicant's interest. *Important factors considered include:* Class rank, standardized test scores, racial/ethnic status, volunteer work. *Other factors considered include:* First generation, geographical residence, state residency, work experience, alumni/ae relations.. *Academic units recommended:* 4 English; 4 mathematics; 3 science; (3 science lab); 2 social studies; 2 foreign language; 2 history.

Financial Aid

Students should submit: FAFSA. Regular filing deadline is 2/15. The Princeton Review suggests that all financial aid forms be submitted as soon as possible after January 1. *Need-based scholarships/grants offered:* Federal Pell, SEOG, the school's own gift aid. *Loan aid offered:* Direct Subsidized Stafford Loans, Direct Unsubsidized Stafford Loans, Direct PLUS loans. Applicants will be notified of awards beginning 3/21. Federal Work-Study Program available. Institutional employment available. Off-campus job opportunities are good.

The Inside Word

Brains are not enough to get into Olin. Social skills, depth, and the ability to communicate are taken seriously by admissions. Olin boasts many students who have turned down offers from schools like MIT and Cal Tech for just this reason. It is a unique school that looks for passion, creativity, and a spirit of adventure in its students. If you're a reclusive genius, you will be at a disadvantage in this pool of applicants.

THE SCHOOL SAYS "..."

From the Admissions Office

"We are a vibrant community of talented, confident, energetic students and faculty and we are looking for students who are not only academically accomplished but also like adventure, thrive on creativity and have an entrepreneurial streak — and come from every kind of cultural, economic and geographic background imaginable. The Olin Tuition Scholarship, valued at more than $80,000, is awarded to every enrolled student to recognize their achievements and is complemented by our policy of meeting full demonstrated need — meaning finances should never stand in the way of an Olin education.

"Our admission process is like no other. It's done in two stages; first students apply using the Common Application; then from our exceptionally talented and academically gifted applicant pool we invite about 240 students to attend one of three Candidates' Weekends. We seek to get to know our applicants' personal qualities (like risk-taking, creativity, passion and team spirit) during these weekends of getting acquainted through group activities and interviews. Admission is then offered to candidates who possess the greatest promise of contributing to – and benefiting from – the Olin experience. Following the Candidates' Weekends admission is offered to approximately 135 students.

"We require either the SAT or ACT with Writing score, and we honor the best score combination on the SAT or best composite score achieved on the ACT."

SELECTIVITY

Admissions Rating	99
# of applicants	782
% of applicants accepted	17
% of acceptees attending	63
# offered a place on the wait list	46
% accepting a place on wait list	63
% admitted from wait list	10

FRESHMAN PROFILE

Range SAT Critical Reading	690–760
Range SAT Math	737.5–790
Range SAT Writing	670–780
Average HS GPA	3.90
Range ACT Composite	31-34

DEADLINES

Regular	
Deadline	1/1
Notification	3/21
Nonfall registration?	No

APPLICANTS ALSO LOOK AT AND OFTEN PREFER

Massachusetts Institute of Technology; Stanford University; California Institute of Technology; Princeton University; Yale University

AND SOMETIMES PREFER

Carnegie Mellon University; University of California—Berkeley; Harvey Mudd College

AND RARELY PREFER

Rose-Hulman Institute of Technology; Worcester Polytechnic Institute; Rensselaer Polytechnic Institute

FINANCIAL FACTS

Financial Aid Rating	99
Annual tuition	$43,500
Required fees	$3,181
Books and supplies	$300
% needy frosh rec. need-based scholarship or grant aid	100
% needy UG rec. need-based scholarship or grant aid	100
% needy frosh rec. non-need-based scholarship or grant aid	100
% needy UG rec. non-need-based scholarship or grant aid	100
% needy frosh rec. need-based self-help aid	40
% needy UG rec. need-based self-help aid	52
% frosh rec. any financial aid	100
% UG rec. any financial aid	100
% UG borrow to pay for school	13
Average cumulative indebtedness	$16,092
% frosh need fully met	100
% ugrads need fully met	100
Average % of frosh need met	100
Average % of ugrad need met	99

FURMAN UNIVERSITY

3300 POINSETT HIGHWAY, GREENVILLE, SC 29613 • ADMISSIONS: 864-294-2034 • FAX: 864-294-2018

CAMPUS LIFE

Quality of Life Rating	95
Fire Safety Rating	82
Green Rating	94
Type of school	Private
Affiliation	No Affiliation
Environment	City

STUDENTS

Total undergrad enrollment	2,731
% male/female	43/57
% from out of state	70
% frosh from public high school	52
% frosh live on campus	98
% ugrads live on campus	96
# of fraternities (% ugrad men join)	7 (29)
# of sororities (% ugrad women join)	7 (46)
% African American	5
% Asian	2
% Caucasian	81
% Hispanic	3
% Native American	<1
% international	4
# of countries represented	47

SURVEY SAYS . . .

Students are happy
Classroom facilities are great
Lab facilities are great
School is well run
No one cheats
Students are friendly
Students love Greenville, SC
Great off-campus food
Campus feels safe
Athletic facilities are great
Frats and sororities are popular

ACADEMICS

Academic Rating	89
% students returning for sophomore year	90
% students graduating within 4 years	79
% students graduating within 6 years	83
Calendar	Semester
Student/faculty ratio	11:1
Profs interesting rating	91
Profs accessible rating	90

Most classes have 10–19 students.

MOST POPULAR MAJORS

political science; business/commerce; health science

STUDENTS SAY ". . ."

Academics

Students can't stop talking about Furman University's "beautiful campus" and "warm, but challenging, academic community." This combination of brains and beauty is what makes Furman "an ideal choice" for four years. "Furman is about academic excellence through engaged learning," says one undergrad. Expect to hear "engaged" used "ad nauseum" on campus, but students claim that such a term "truly describes the kind of personal education available" thanks to "small class sizes," professors "who love to teach and enjoy getting to know their students," and "numerous" academic and extracurricular opportunities. Furman's science programs are "especially" challenging. Professors here are "very qualified (sometimes overqualified), passionate about what they teach, and are not easy graders." That said, they're "very willing to help their students." Students praise the administration, which is "really accessible." In the words of one undergrad, "They work with students to solve problems and genuinely care about making Furman a better school and not just a higher-ranking institution." However, some students find that the administration can be "very conservative in their thinking about student on-campus social life." Ultimately, while "Furman is not for the academically faint-of-heart," there's pride in knowing that "you're receiving a great education that will help you after you graduate."

Life

With so many students reporting that Furman's campus is "absolutely gorgeous," it's a wonder they ever leave it. However, "the surrounding city of Greenville is great," and its "thriving, small-town feel" brings in plenty of students on the weekends. Life at school is "busy, but so much fun." Students here spend "a lot of time thinking about academics, classes, and their future," but they also "invest a lot of time in their relationships with their friends." The school's "inclusive, close-knit community" is complemented with "lots of interesting things to do on campus, from music concerts to improv shows to sports games." "Weeknights are mostly spent studying," says one undergrad, which makes the library "a popular social spot." However, once the weekend rolls around, students spend their nights "out on the town." "There are tons of bars, restaurants, and clubs for people to go to" in Greenville, while those looking for a "party" can head for "fraternity houses." While the university "is not as crazy party-wise as larger schools," students "can find a party if they want to." Mostly though, students are happy to "meet up with friends for meals, coffee, or just to hang out."

Student Body

Many find that Furman is something of a "country club" when it comes to its student body, not just "because it is private and somewhat expensive," but also because the "typical" student is "wealthy, white, conservative, and preppy." Some find that "the majority of the student body is obsessed with being as 'generic' and 'normal' as possible, so that any student who does not fit the norm, be it due to a difference in religion or clothing style, will find it harder to fit in." However, others have found that there's more to the student body than first meets the eye. As one undergrad says, "The longer I stay at Furman, the more I realize that many students don't fit the stereotype." One thing that everyone seems to agree on is that everyone is "very accepting" and "very committed to their academic pursuits." That said, some wouldn't mind seeing the school "improve by attracting a more diverse student body, as well as lowering the cost of tuition."

FURMAN UNIVERSITY

FINANCIAL AID: 864-294-2204 • E-MAIL: ADMISSIONS@FURMAN.EDU • WEBSITE: WWW.FURMAN.EDU

THE PRINCETON REVIEW SAYS

Admissions

Very important factors considered include: Rigor of secondary school record. *Important factors considered include:* Class rank, GPA, application essay, extracurricular activities, character/personal qualities. *Other factors considered include:* Standardized test scores, first generation, interview, racial/ethnic status, recommendation(s), talent/ability, volunteer work, work experience, alumni/ae relations, level of applicant's interest, SAT or ACT recommended; ACT with Writing component recommended. TOEFL required of all international applicants. *Academic units required:* 4 English; 3 mathematics; 2 science; (2 science lab); 3 social studies; 2 foreign language. *Academic units recommended:* 4 English; 4 mathematics; 3 science; (2 science lab); 4 social studies; 3 foreign language.

Financial Aid

Students should submit: FAFSA, Institution's own financial aid form, CSS/Financial Aid PROFILE, State aid form. Regular filing deadline is 1/15. The Princeton Review suggests that all financial aid forms be submitted as soon as possible after January 1. *Need-based scholarships/grants offered:* Federal Pell, SEOG, State scholarships/grants, private scholarships, the school's own gift aid. *Loan aid offered:* Direct Subsidized Stafford Loans, Direct Unsubsidized Stafford Loans, Direct PLUS loans, Federal Perkins Loans, State Loans. Applicants will be notified of awards beginning 3/15. Federal Work-Study Program available. Institutional employment available. Off-campus job opportunities are excellent.

The Inside Word

Chances are, if you're applying to Furman, you already have a good idea if you can get in or not. Furman's applicant pool is highly self-selected, meaning that the university's high acceptance rate doesn't equate to easy admission; in fact, it's the direct opposite, as applicants are typically very strong. Looking for a way to stand out from the crowd? Let the admissions committee know how valuable you are through your extracurriculars—sports, community service, and artistic endeavors will go a long way in making your case.

THE SCHOOL SAYS "..."

From the Admissions Office

"Furman University is a private liberal arts university that seeks and cultivates engaged, well-rounded, and passionate students. With 2,700 undergraduates from forty-six states and forty-seven countries, Furman's academic community prepares its students for meaningful lives of service and leadership through engaged learning, a process characterized by small classes, a close-knit community, student-faculty research, internships, and faculty-led study. With emphasis on a collaborative educational experience, Furman challenges students to put into practice the theories and methods learned from a distinguished and active faculty. Furman offers eighteen NCAA Division I men's and women's athletic teams, a nationally competitive music program, and hundreds of organizations and clubs. The stunning campus is located just minutes from vibrant downtown Greenville, noted as one of America's most livable cities, and the foothills of the Blue Ridge Mountains, where hiking and other adventure sports abound. Nearby are also some of the nation's most picturesque beaches and coastal towns. The admission committee believes that a student's potential for success is not determined solely by standardized test scores. Rather, it is interested in getting to know the whole student—one who seeks leadership, service, commitment to the community, and civic engagement. Therefore, Furman does not require prospective students to submit test scores unless the student determines the scores best represent academic ability and accomplishment. If a student chooses not to submit standardized test scores, then the university recommends that the student to participate in a formal interview as part of the application."

SELECTIVITY

Admissions Rating	82
# of applicants	6,035
% of applicants accepted	64
% of acceptees attending	21
# offered a place on the wait list	319
% accepting a place on wait list	23
% admitted from wait list	3
# of early decision applicants	168
% accepted early decision	89

FRESHMAN PROFILE

Range SAT Critical Reading	550–670
Range SAT Math	580–670
Range SAT Writing	550–670
Range ACT Composite	25–30
Minimum paper TOEFL	570
Minimum web-based TOEFL	230
% graduated top 10% of class	48
% graduated top 25% of class	76
% graduated top 50% of class	93

DEADLINES

Early decision	
Deadline	11/1
Notification	12/1
Early action	
Deadline	11/15
Notification	2/1
Regular	
Deadline	1/15
Notification	4/1
Nonfall registration?	No

APPLICANTS ALSO LOOK AT AND OFTEN PREFER

Duke University; Vanderbilt University; Wake Forest University

AND SOMETIMES PREFER

Davidson College; Emory University; University of South Carolina—Columbia

FINANCIAL FACTS

Financial Aid Rating	84
Annual tuition	$44,288
Room and board	$11,204
Required fees	$380
Books and supplies	$1,200
% needy frosh rec. need-based scholarship or grant aid	100
% needy UG rec. need-based scholarship or grant aid	99
% needy frosh rec. non-need-based scholarship or grant aid	99
% needy UG rec. non-need-based scholarship or grant aid	99
% needy frosh rec. need-based self-help aid	65
% needy UG rec. need-based self-help aid	68
% frosh rec. any financial aid	85
% UG rec. any financial aid	85
% UG borrow to pay for school	45
Average cumulative indebtedness	$27,511
% frosh need fully met	32
% ugrads need fully met	29
Average % of frosh need met	60
Average % of ugrad need met	60

GEORGE MASON UNIVERSITY

4400 UNIVERSITY DRIVE, FAIRFAX, VA 22030-4444 • ADMISSIONS: 703-993-2400 • FAX: 703-993-4622

STUDENTS SAY ". . ."

Academics

When describing George Mason University, current students are quick to quote the school motto: This is a place "where innovation is tradition." One student expands on that, saying, "Mason provides a space for students to achieve academic excellence; expand their knowledge of the diverse cultures, practices, and beliefs that surround them; and be prepared to enter the real-world as a global citizen." Diversity of the student body and proximity to Washington, D.C., are major selling points at this large public university, so it's no surprise that government, global affairs, and communication are popular majors. The faculty is "extremely knowledgeable and experienced" here, and "most try to learn your name." The Robinson Professors program brings "distinguished" professors in the liberal arts and sciences to campus, and students highly recommend classes taught by these professors. "They are experts in their fields, know what they are talking about, and have real life experiences they bring into the classroom." As well, "adjunct professors can be a great strength" because many of them are practicing professionals in D.C., and they "bring stories and examples from the real-world into our classroom." "For example, my professor for my Conflict 300 course is one of the main peace facilitators in the Georgian/South Ossetian conflict…when she returned from this conference [between the two countries], she told us everything and we got to see how the material and techniques we were studying are actually applied in our field." Students are equally satisfied with the school's administration: "The school will take action immediately to fix any problems that arise."

Life

Students at GMU never seem to be bored. Campus life is "filled with classes, friends, and work." On campus activities are very popular, and there are many on offer, including the university's ambassador program and intramural sports, such as underwater hockey and even quidditch. Just a few of the regular events on campus include "movies playing in our Johnson Center Cinema that are in between theater and DVD release, there are local bands playing live in the Rathskeller, the HIV/AIDS Awareness Fashion Show, drag competitions, University dances and highlighter parties." Greek life is there for those who want it: "We're not a 'fratty' school by any means, but the Greek community is very active and they do party." The campus is "beautiful," and "there are new housing buildings going up and even new academic buildings" (which is good news, since the two things students want to see improve are parking and housing availability). Students love living close to D.C. without the "hassle of city living," but when they want to head downtown, "it's very easy to get into the city by taking the Mason-to-Metro shuttle to the Vienna Metro Station, hopping on the Orange Line and then taking the Metro into the heart of the city!" Many students have internships in the city, including those "on Capitol Hill." "The music scene and bars are fantastic as well!"

Student Body

"Diversity is off the charts" at GMU, and many students describe their school as "a melting pot." As one student puts it, "There are so many different nationalities represented, so many stories, so many languages spoken. At the same time, it didn't take me long to find a good group of friends that were interested in hanging out and just having a good time together." "The typical GMU student is always busy—between coursework and extracurricular activities we're very involved on campus and are also into other activities, such as having jobs or internships." "Mason students are also politically active and global citizens." While a majority of students come from Virginia, there are also "students from over 130 countries, so everyone adds their own personal flavor to our student body." In spite of all these different backgrounds and cultures, "There are many student organizations that successfully create programs and events to unite students."

FINANCIAL AID: 703-993-2353 • E-MAIL: ADMISSIONS@GMU.EDU • WEBSITE: WWW.GMU.EDU

THE PRINCETON REVIEW SAYS

Admissions

Very important factors considered include: GPA, rigor of secondary school record. *Important factors considered include:* Class rank, standardized test scores, talent/ ability, character/personal qualities. *Other factors considered include:* Application essay, extracurricular activities, first generation, recommendation(s), volunteer work, work experience, alumni/ae relations, level of applicant's interest. SAT or ACT required for some; SAT and SAT Subject Tests or ACT recommended; ACT with or without Writing component accepted. TOEFL required of all international applicants. *Academic units required:* 4 English; 3 mathematics; 2 science; (2 science lab); 3 social studies; 2 foreign language; 3 academic electives. *Academic units recommended:* 4 English; 4 mathematics; 3 science; (3 science lab); 4 social studies; 3 foreign language; 5 academic electives.

Financial Aid

Students should submit: FAFSA. The Princeton Review suggests that all financial aid forms be submitted as soon as possible after January 1. *Need-based scholarships/grants offered:* Federal Pell, SEOG, State scholarships/grants, private scholarships, the school's own gift aid. *Loan aid offered:* Direct Subsidized Stafford Loans, Direct Unsubsidized Stafford Loans, Direct PLUS loans, Federal Perkins Loans, Federal Nursing Loans. Applicants will be notified of awards beginning 4/1. Federal Work-Study Program available. Institutional employment available. Off-campus job opportunities are excellent.

The Inside Word

GMU is a popular college choice for two key reasons: Its proximity to Washington, D.C., and the fact that its applicant pool isn't as competitive as those of University of Virginia and The College of William & Mary, the two flagships of the Virginia state system. GMU's quality faculty and impressive facilities make it worth consideration, especially if you're looking for a school in the D.C. area and affordability is a factor.

THE SCHOOL SAYS "..."

From the Admissions Office

"George Mason University is an innovative, entrepreneurial institution with global distinction in a range of academic fields. Located just outside Washington, D.C., our beautiful residential campus boasts a student population that is one of the most diverse in the country, which gives our students the benefit of growing from a wide range of ideas and perspectives. With strong undergraduate and graduate degree programs, our students are routinely recognized with national and international scholarships and awards. Enrollment is nearly 34,000, with students studying in nearly 200 degree programs at the undergraduate, master's, doctoral, and professional levels. Our connection to the D.C. area results in faculty members who are engaged in the top research in their fields. We have professors who are regular contributors on all of the major news networks and our scholars make frequent appearances on National Public Radio. This connectivity extends to our students, who take internships and get jobs at national and international companies and organizations, ranging from National Geographic to the White House. At Mason, we pride ourselves on being among the most innovative universities in the world. Many of our degree programs are the first of their kind, including the first Ph.D. program in biodefense, the first D.C.-based undergraduate program in conflict analysis and resolution, the first engineering school based on computer related programs, and one of the most innovative performing arts management programs in the United States. Mason is at the forefront of the emerging field of biotechnology, is a leader in the performing arts, and holds a preeminent position in the fields of economics, electronic journalism, and history, just to name a few. Mason also continues to explore instructional, research, and outreach opportunities for innovative global initiatives that enhance the education of its students and increase collaborations among faculty and programs throughout the world."

SELECTIVITY

Admissions Rating	84
# of applicants	20,805
% of applicants accepted	62
% of acceptees attending	23
# offered a place on the wait list	2,228
% accepting a place on wait list	42
% admitted from wait list	27

FRESHMAN PROFILE

Range SAT Critical Reading	520–620
Range SAT Math	530–630
Range ACT Composite	24–28
Minimum paper TOEFL	570
Minimum web-based TOEFL	88
Average HS GPA	3.66
% graduated top 10% of class	20
% graduated top 25% of class	56
% graduated top 50% of class	94

DEADLINES

Early action	
Deadline	11/1
Notification	12/15
Regular	
Priority	11/1
Deadline	1/15
Notification	4/1
Nonfall registration?	Yes

APPLICANTS ALSO LOOK AT AND SOMETIMES PREFER

The George Washington University; University of Virginia; Virginia Tech; James Madison University

FINANCIAL FACTS

Financial Aid Rating	70
Annual in-state tuition	$7,220
Annual out-of-state tuition	$25,904
Room and board	$9,580
Required fees	$2,688
Books and supplies	$1,120
% needy frosh rec. need-based scholarship or grant aid	69
% needy UG rec. need-based scholarship or grant aid	73
% needy frosh rec. non-need-based scholarship or grant aid	29
% needy UG rec. non-need-based scholarship or grant aid	14
% needy frosh rec. need-based self-help aid	74
% needy UG rec. need-based self-help aid	69
% frosh rec. any financial aid	56
% UG rec. any financial aid	57
% UG borrow to pay for school	58
Average cumulative indebtedness	$26,710
% frosh need fully met	7
% ugrads need fully met	5
Average % of frosh need met	62
Average % of ugrad need met	59

THE GEORGE WASHINGTON UNIVERSITY

2121 I STREET NORTHWEST, SUITE 201, WASHINGTON, D.C. 20052 • ADMISSIONS: 202-994-6040 • FAX: 202-994-0325

CAMPUS LIFE

Quality of Life Rating	92
Fire Safety Rating	60*
Green Rating	96
Type of school	Private
Affiliation	No Affiliation
Environment	Metropolis

STUDENTS

Total undergrad enrollment	10,121
% male/female	45/55
% from out of state	98
% frosh from public high school	70
% frosh live on campus	99
% ugrads live on campus	68
# of fraternities (% ugrad men join)	12 (23)
# of sororities (% ugrad women join)	9 (23)
% African American	7
% Asian	9
% Caucasian	60
% Hispanic	7
% Native American	<1
% international	9
# of countries represented	95

SURVEY SAYS . . .

Political activism is popular
Students are happy
Internships are widely available
Students love Washington, DC
Great off-campus food
Dorms are like palaces
Easy to get around campus
Athletic facilities are great
Lots of beer drinking
Hard liquor is popular
Frats and sororities are popular
Student publications are popular

ACADEMICS

Academic Rating	84
% students returning for sophomore year	92
% students graduating within 4 years	76
% students graduating within 6 years	81
Calendar	Semester
Student/faculty ratio	13:1
Profs interesting rating	77
Profs accessible rating	79
Most classes have 20–29 students.	
Most lab/discussion sessions have 10–19 students.	

MOST POPULAR MAJORS
international relations; business administration and management; psychology

STUDENTS SAY ". . ."

Academics

Get ready for "hands-on learning in an environment unlike any other" at George Washington University, where a location "four blocks away from the White House, down the street from the State Department, and near nearly all world headquarters" means "connections and opportunity" for undergraduates. Students call it "the perfect place to study international affairs" and praise the "amazing journalism program," the excellent political communications major, the political science program ("What political science major would pass up the chance to go toe-to-toe with protestors every week at the rallies outside the White House and Congress?"), the sciences (benefiting from the region's many research operations), and other departments too numerous to name. As one student puts it, "GW is a place where everyone can find their niche. Whether you are a politically active campaign volunteer, a hip-hop dancer, or a future Broadway actor, there is a place for you at GW." The school places a premium on hiring "professors of practice," teachers who "are either currently working in their field or just retired to teach." The faculty includes "former ambassadors, governors on the Federal Reserve Board, and CNN correspondents." These instructors emphasize "a balance between theory and practice that provides a foundation of knowledge and pragmatism from which students can feel prepared to enter any sector of work after school." The resulting education "gets students prepared for post-college life through an emphasis on internships and career-focused classes," putting "a lot of emphasis on acclimation to the real world."

Life

"Life at GW is about independence," students report. "There are no real cafeterias" on campus, "you have to rely on your own feet for transportation, and there is very little regulation in dorms." As a result, "There is little school spirit, but that fact alone seems to tie everyone together." The campus isn't entirely dead; there are frat parties ("which are hard to attend for non-member males and easy to attend for women"), the "occasional dorm-room party, which is usually small," and "apartment parties off campus" for upperclassmen. Campus organizations offer all sorts of events, and the school hosts a veritable who's who of guest speakers on a regular basis. Students love the school's Midnight Monument Tour, held "during the warmer parts of the year," during which "students walk the five blocks to the National Mall at 2:00 A.M. and tour the monuments. It is an awesome experience." Still, most students prefer to spend free time exploring D.C. on their own. The city provides "so much to do…it's overwhelming: monuments, free museums, fairs, every major sports franchise, and lots of student specials on the above things." D.C.'s upscale Georgetown neighborhood is nearby for "shopping, dining, seeing movies, etc.," while culturally diverse Adams Morgan is great for shopping, ethnic dining, and live music.

Student Body

"GW students are often stereotyped as spoiled and wealthy Northeastern kids," and while quite a few students here concede that there's some basis for the stereotype, most would also add that "white, preppy, fraternity/sorority members" who "like nice labels on their clothing" neither define nor dominate the campus population. "The reality is that there's tremendous diversity here of all stripes—geographic, religious, political, racial, and intellectual," with "students from dozens of countries and all fifty states." "GW is truly a national and even international school," one student writes. "I love walking out of the library and hearing conversations happening in a half-dozen languages." The school has always been a popular destination for Jewish students. There is also "a huge LGBT group on campus, with very little discrimination." Nearly everyone here is "incredibly driven," "combining classes with an internship, maybe a sport, and usually a few extracurriculars."

FINANCIAL AID: 202-994-6620 • E-MAIL: GWADM@GWU.EDU • WEBSITE: WWW.GWU.EDU

THE PRINCETON REVIEW SAYS

Admissions

Very important factors considered include: GPA, rigor of secondary school record. *Important factors considered include:* Class rank, standardized test scores, application essay, extracurricular activities, interview, recommendation(s), talent/ ability, volunteer work. *Other factors considered include:* First generation, geographical residence, racial/ethnic status, work experience, alumni/ae relations, character/personal qualities, level of applicant's interest. SAT or ACT required; SAT and SAT Subject Tests or ACT required for some; ACT with or without Writing component accepted. TOEFL required of all international applicants. *Academic units required:* 4 English; 2 mathematics; 2 science; (1 science lab); 2 social studies; 2 foreign language. *Academic units recommended:* 4 English; 4 mathematics; 4 science; 4 social studies; 4 foreign language.

Financial Aid

Students should submit: FAFSA, CSS/Financial Aid PROFILE. Regular filing deadline is 2/1. The Princeton Review suggests that all financial aid forms be submitted as soon as possible after January 1. *Need-based scholarships/grants offered:* Federal Pell, SEOG, State scholarships/grants, the school's own gift aid. *Loan aid offered:* Direct Subsidized Stafford Loans, Direct Unsubsidized Stafford Loans, Direct PLUS loans, Federal Perkins Loans. Federal Work-Study Program available. Institutional employment available. Off-campus job opportunities are excellent.

The Inside Word

With more than 21,000 applications to process annually, GW could be forgiven if it gave student essays only a perfunctory glance. The school insists, however, that essays are carefully reviewed. Take note and proceed accordingly. Application rates have surged throughout the past decade. This school is only getting more popular, so applicants should be prepared to bring their A-game.

THE SCHOOL SAYS "..."

From the Admissions Office

"GW students are excited about putting knowledge into action so they can change the world and improve the human experience. At many universities, the edge of campus is the real world, but not at GW, where our campus and Washington, D.C., are seamless. We look for bold, bright students who are ambitious, energetic, and self-motivated. Here, where we are so close to the centers of thought and action in every field we offer, we easily integrate our outstanding academic tradition and faculty connections with the best student research, internship, service, and job opportunities of Washington, D.C. A generous scholarship and financial assistance program attracts top students from all parts of the country and the world.

"Tuition is fixed until student graduates, up to five years or ten full semesters."

SELECTIVITY

Admissions Rating	96
# of applicants	21,789
% of applicants accepted	34
% of acceptees attending	31
# offered a place on the wait list	3,770
% accepting a place on wait list	26
% admitted from wait list	11
# of early decision applicants	2,316
% accepted early decision	36

FRESHMAN PROFILE

Range SAT Critical Reading	590–690
Range SAT Math	610–700
Range SAT Writing	600–700
Range ACT Composite	27–31
Minimum paper TOEFL	550
Minimum web-based TOEFL	213
% graduated top 10% of class	50
% graduated top 25% of class	83
% graduated top 50% of class	98

DEADLINES

Early decision	
Deadline	11/1
Notification	12/15
Regular	
Priority	12/1
Deadline	1/15
Notification	4/1
Nonfall registration?	Yes

APPLICANTS ALSO LOOK AT AND OFTEN PREFER
Boston University; Emory University; Georgetown University; New York University; University of Virginia

AND SOMETIMES PREFER
Tufts University; University of Vermont; American University; The Catholic University of America; University of Maryland

FINANCIAL FACTS

Financial Aid Rating	70
Annual tuition	$48,700
Room and board	$11,000
Required fees	$60
Books and supplies	$1,275
% needy frosh rec. need-based scholarship or grant aid	93
% needy UG rec. need-based scholarship or grant aid	92
% needy frosh rec. non-need-based scholarship or grant aid	47
% needy UG rec. non-need-based scholarship or grant aid	27
% needy frosh rec. need-based self-help aid	78
% needy UG rec. need-based self-help aid	80
Average cumulative indebtedness	$30,881
% frosh need fully met	46
% ugrads need fully met	49

SEVENTH AND O STREETS, NORTHWEST, WASHINGTON, D.C. 20057 • ADMISSIONS: 202-687-3600 • FAX: 202-687-5084

CAMPUS LIFE

Quality of Life Rating	76
Fire Safety Rating	82
Green Rating	80
Type of school	Private
Affiliation	Roman Catholic
Environment	Metropolis

STUDENTS

Total undergrad enrollment	7,201
% male/female	45/55
% from out of state	97
% frosh from public high school	46
% frosh live on campus	100
% ugrads live on campus	67
% African American	6
% Asian	9
% Caucasian	62
% Hispanic	8
% Native American	<1
% international	9
# of countries represented	138

SURVEY SAYS . . .

Easy to get around campus
Students love Washington, DC
Great off-campus food
Students are happy
Frats and sororities are unpopular
or nonexistent
Student publications are popular
Political activism is popular
Lots of beer drinking

ACADEMICS

Academic Rating	91
% students returning for sophomore year	96
% students graduating within 4 years	90
% students graduating within 6 years	94
Calendar	Semester
Student/faculty ratio	11:1
Profs interesting rating	78
Profs accessible rating	71

Most classes have 10–19 students.
Most lab/discussion sessions have
10–19 students.

MOST POPULAR MAJORS

political science; international relations;
English language and literature

STUDENTS SAY ". . ."

Academics

This moderately sized elite academic establishment stays true to its Jesuit foundations by educating its students with the idea of "cura personalis," or "care for the whole person." The "well-informed" student body perpetuates upon itself, creating an atmosphere full of vibrant intellectual life, that is "also balanced with extracurricular learning and development." "Georgetown is…a place where people work very, very hard without feeling like they are in direct competition," says an international politics major. Located in Washington, D.C., there's a noted School of Foreign Service here, and the access to internships is a huge perk for those in political or government programs. In addition, the proximity to the nation's capital fetches "high-profile guest speakers," with many of the most powerful people in global politics speaking regularly, as well as a large number of adjunct professors who, either are currently working in government, or have retired from high-level positions.

Georgetown offers a "great selection of very knowledgeable professors, split with a good proportion of those who are experienced in realms outside of academia (such as former government officials) and career academics," though there are a few superstars who might be "somewhat less than totally collegial." Professors tend to be "fantastic scholars and teachers" and are "generally available to students," as well as often being "interested in getting to know you as a person (if you put forth the effort to talk to them and go to office hours)." Though Georgetown has a policy of grade deflation, meaning "A's are hard to come by," there are "a ton of interesting courses available," and TAs are used only for optional discussion sessions and help with grading. The academics "can be challenging or they can be not so much (not that they are ever really easy, just easier);" it all depends on the courses you choose and how much you actually do the work. The school administration is well-meaning and "usually willing to talk and compromise with students," but the process of planning activities can be full of headaches and bureaucracy, and the administration itself "sometimes is overstretched or has trouble transmitting its message." Nevertheless, "a motivated student can get done what he or she wants."

Life

Students are "extremely well aware of the world around them," from government to environment, social to economic, and "Georgetown is the only place where an argument over politics, history, or philosophy is preceded by a keg stand." Hoyas like to have a good time on weekends, and parties at campus and off-campus apartments and townhouses "are generally open to all comers and tend to have a somewhat networking atmosphere; meeting people you don't know is a constant theme." With such a motivated group on such a high-energy campus, "people are always headed somewhere, it seems—to rehearsal, athletic practice, a guest speaker, [or] the gym." Community service and political activism are particularly popular, as is basketball. Everything near Georgetown is in walking distance, including the world of D.C.'s museums, restaurants, and stores, and "grabbing or ordering late night food is a popular option."

Student Body

There are "a lot of wealthy students on campus," and preppy-casual is the fashion de rigueur; this is "definitely not a 'granola' school," but students from diverse backgrounds are typically welcomed by people wanting to learn about different experiences. Indeed, everyone here is well-traveled and well-educated, and there are "a ton of international students." "You better have at least some interest in politics or you will feel out-of-place," says a student. The school can also be "a bit cliquish, with athletes at the top," but there are "plenty of groups for everybody to fit into and find their niche," and "there is much crossover between groups."

FINANCIAL AID: 202-687-4547 • E-MAIL: GUADMISS@GEORGETOWN.EDU • WEBSITE: WWW.GEORGETOWN.EDU

THE PRINCETON REVIEW SAYS

Admissions

Very important factors considered include: Class rank, GPA, rigor of secondary school record, standardized test scores, application essay, first generation, recommendation(s), talent/ability, character/personal qualities. *Important factors considered include:* Extracurricular activities, interview, volunteer work. *Other factors considered include:* geographical residence, racial/ethnic status, state residency, work experience, alumni/ae relations. SAT or ACT required; ACT with or without Writing component accepted. TOEFL required of all international applicants. *Academic units required:* 4 English; 2 mathematics; 1 science; 2 social studies; 2 foreign language; 2 history.

Financial Aid

Students should submit: FAFSA, CSS/Financial Aid PROFILE, Business/Farm Supplement. Regular filing deadline is 2/1. The Princeton Review suggests that all financial aid forms be submitted as soon as possible after January 1. *Need-based scholarships/grants offered:* Federal Pell, SEOG, State scholarships/grants, private scholarships, the school's own gift aid. *Loan aid offered:* Direct Subsidized Stafford Loans, Direct Unsubsidized Stafford Loans, Direct PLUS loans, Federal Perkins Loans, Federal Nursing Loans. Applicants will be notified of awards beginning 4/1. Federal Work-Study Program available. Institutional employment available. Off-campus job opportunities are excellent.

The Inside Word

It was always tough to get admitted to Georgetown, but in the early 1980s Patrick Ewing and the Hoyas created a basketball sensation that catapulted the place into position as one of the most selective universities in the nation. There has been no turning back since. GU receives over twelve applications for every space in the entering class, and the academic strength of the pool is impressive. Virtually 80 percent of the entire student body took AP courses in high school. Candidates who are wait-listed should hold little hope for an offer of admission; over the past several years Georgetown has taken very few off their lists.

THE SCHOOL SAYS "..."

From the Admissions Office

"Georgetown was founded in 1789 by John Carroll, who concurred with his contemporaries Benjamin Franklin and Thomas Jefferson in believing that the success of the young democracy depended upon an educated and virtuous citizenry. Carroll founded the school with the dynamic Jesuit tradition of education, characterized by humanism and committed to the assumption of responsibility and action. Georgetown is a national and international university, enrolling students from all fifty states and over 100 foreign countries. Undergraduate students are enrolled in one of four undergraduate schools: the College of Arts and Sciences, School of Foreign Service, Georgetown School of Business, and Georgetown School of Nursing and Health Studies. All students share a common liberal arts core and have access to the entire university curriculum.

"Applicants must submit scores from SAT or the ACT. Three SAT Subject Tests are highly recommended."

SELECTIVITY

Admissions Rating	98
# of applicants	20,115
% of applicants accepted	17
% of acceptees attending	46
# offered a place on the wait list	2,217
% accepting a place on wait list	52
% admitted from wait list	7

FRESHMAN PROFILE

Range SAT Critical Reading	650–750
Range SAT Math	660–750
Range ACT Composite	29–33
Minimum paper TOEFL	200
Minimum web-based TOEFL	0
% graduated top 10% of class	92
% graduated top 25% of class	99
% graduated top 50% of class	100

DEADLINES

Early action	
Deadline	11/1
Notification	12/15
Regular	
Deadline	1/10
Notification	4/1
Nonfall registration?	No

APPLICANTS ALSO LOOK AT AND OFTEN PREFER

University of Pennsylvania; Duke University

AND SOMETIMES PREFER

Cornell University, University of Virginia; University of Notre Dame; Northwestern University

AND RARELY PREFER

Boston College; Tufts University; New York University; The George Washington University

FINANCIAL FACTS

Financial Aid Rating	91
Annual tuition	$42,360
Required fees	$510
Books and supplies	$1,200
% needy frosh rec. need-based scholarship or grant aid	99
% needy UG rec. need-based scholarship or grant aid	93
% needy frosh rec. non-need-based scholarship or grant aid	36
% needy UG rec. non-need-based scholarship or grant aid	27
% needy frosh rec. need-based self-help aid	95
% needy UG rec. need-based self-help aid	88
% UG borrow to pay for school	39
Average cumulative indebtedness	$28,035
% frosh need fully met	100
% ugrads need fully met	100
Average % of frosh need met	100
Average % of ugrad need met	100

GEORGIA INSTITUTE OF TECHNOLOGY

OFFICE OF UNDERGRADUATE ADMISSIONS, ATLANTA, GA 30332-0320 • ADMISSIONS: 404-894-4154 • FAX: 404-894-9511

CAMPUS LIFE

Quality of Life Rating	70
Fire Safety Rating	91
Green Rating	99
Type of school	Public
Affiliation	No Affiliation
Environment	Metropolis

STUDENTS

Total undergrad enrollment	13,975
% male/female	67/33
% from out of state	29
% frosh live on campus	98
% ugrads live on campus	52
# of fraternities (% ugrad men join)	40 (33)
# of sororities (% ugrad women join)	16 (36)
% African American	6
% Asian	17
% Caucasian	55
% Hispanic	7
% Native American	<1
% international	10
# of countries represented	83

SURVEY SAYS . . .

Athletic facilities are great
Students love Atlanta, GA
Great off-campus food
Everyone loves the Yellow Jackets
Student publications are popular

ACADEMICS

Academic Rating	72
% students returning for sophomore year	96
% students graduating within 4 years	41
% students graduating within 6 years	82
Calendar	Semester
Student/faculty ratio	18:1
Profs interesting rating	64
Profs accessible rating	65

Most classes have 10–19 students.
Most lab/discussion sessions have 20–29 students.

MOST POPULAR MAJORS

mechanical engineering; industrial engineering; bioengineering

STUDENTS SAY "..."

Academics

The Georgia Institute of Technology—Georgia Tech for short—"challenges its students academically while providing a culturally diverse environment, all culminating in preparation for life after college." Students warn that the school "is extremely challenging, academically. If you don't like learning it's probably not for you." They also point out that "since Georgia Tech is a research school, most professors are more concerned about their own research than the quality of their teaching. You're basically teaching yourself the entire subject in order to prepare for an almost impossible exam," although students also add that "while many of the professors at Georgia Tech are focused on their research, there are teachers who truly care about their students and the learning process." As one student advises, "a lot of classes seem to be more about getting the right professor: Some are bad teachers, some are inaccessible, but some are so good that their classes fill up seconds after registration opens." And while "classes are challenging," they're also "interesting" so all of that hard work is "not too bad. If you're organized and get help when you need it, you'll be okay, because we have tons of free tutoring on campus…If you need help with anything, there are countless different places that offer tutoring. The best resource is usually fellow students. Because everyone knows how tough of a school it is, there is a spirit of camaraderie here that you don't find anywhere else." Students also appreciate that Tech "is one of the only schools in the country that offers the BS distinction for liberal arts majors because we [get] such a rigorous grounding in math and science." Finally, students note that "career services are outstanding."

Life

One Georgia Tech engineer sums up the typical student itinerary this way: "Study, study, drink. Repeat." As another student puts it, "there is a saying here that between good grades, a social life, and sleep, you can only have two." That's why "basically people bust their [butts] during the week, and when the weekends arrive they're prepared to let loose a bit." Fortunately, "Georgia Tech has a little something for everyone. Salsa club on weekends, musical groups, intramural sports—even a skydiving club!" Other options include "a 'good enough' NCAA Division I sports program, a good social scene," a welcoming Greek community, "and for everyone else, there's the city of Atlanta right at your doorstep. You're just a short ride away from movies, shopping, the Fox Theatre, the High Museum of Art, Piedmont Park, and one of the best club and bar scenes in the South," centered mainly in the neighborhoods of Buckhead and Midtown. For those without cars in this driving city, transportation comes in the form of "a 'Tech Trolley' that takes a route around midtown, and a 'Stinger Shuttle' that goes to the MARTA [Atlanta's subway] station, giving students access to the airport, downtown (although that is walkable), and Lenox Square Mall." With more than "300 organizations already on campus," students seeking leadership experience can most likely find it, and they can find other students with like-minded interests.

Student Body

"The greatest strength of Georgia Tech is its diversity," undergrads report. "Students, activities, opportunities, teachers—all are diverse." One observes that the school hosts "the full range of stereotypes, from the fraternity boys with their croackies and boat shoes to the socially challenged nerds who stay in their rooms 24/7 programming computers. But no matter what, you know everyone is highly intelligent. Many times it is the students who have the best grades who are the drunkest." One student explains, "Unlike at high school, no one looks down upon you if you know the entire periodic table, if you can do differential equations, or you can speak three languages; rather, you are respected." One sore spot: Men outnumber women here by greater than a two to one ratio. The situation is most pronounced in engineering (three to one) and computer (more than four to one) disciplines. Women actually outnumber men in the liberal arts and science colleges.

FINANCIAL AID: 404-894-4160 • E-MAIL: ADMISSION@GATECH.EDU • WEBSITE: WWW.GATECH.EDU

THE PRINCETON REVIEW SAYS

Admissions

Very important factors considered include: GPA, rigor of secondary school record, extracurricular activities. *Important factors considered include:* Standardized test scores, application essay, geographical residence, state residency, talent/ability, volunteer work, work experience, character/personal qualities. *Other factors considered include:* First generation, racial/ethnic status, recommendation(s), alumni/ae relations. SAT or ACT required; SAT and SAT Subject Tests or ACT considered if submitted; ACT with Writing component required. *Academic units required:* 4 English; 4 mathematics; 4 science; (2 science lab); 3 social studies; 2 foreign language.

Financial Aid

Students should submit: FAFSA, Institution's own financial aid form. Regular filing deadline is 2/15. The Princeton Review suggests that all financial aid forms be submitted as soon as possible after January 1. *Need-based scholarships/grants offered:* Federal Pell, SEOG, State scholarships/grants, private scholarships, the school's own gift aid, United Negro College Fund. *Loan aid offered:* Direct Subsidized Stafford Loans, Direct Unsubsidized Stafford Loans, Direct PLUS loans, Federal Perkins Loans, State Loans, College/university loans from institutional funds. Applicants will be notified of awards beginning 4/15. Federal Work-Study Program available. Institutional employment available. Off-campus job opportunities are excellent.

The Inside Word

Students considering Georgia Tech shouldn't be deceived by the relatively high acceptance rate. Georgia Tech is a demanding school, and its applicant pool is largely self-selecting. While admissions counselors have begun to implement a more well-rounded approach to the admissions process, grades and test scores are still where candidates make their mark.

THE SCHOOL SAYS ". . ."

From the Admissions Office

"Georgia Tech consistently ranks among the nation's top public universities producing leaders in engineering, computing, business, architecture, and the sciences while remaining one of the best college buys in the country. The 330-acre campus is nestled in the heart of the fun, dynamic and progressive city of Atlanta. During the past decade, over $400 million invested in campus improvements has yielded new state-of-the-art academic and research buildings, apartment-style housing, phenomenal social and recreational facilities, and the most extension fiber-optic cable system on any college campus.

"Georgia Tech has a great academic reputation, and our graduates are well-prepared to meet today's challenges. A unique advantage many students find is Georgia Tech's strong emphasis on undergraduate students. Undergraduates can gain practical work experience through our co-op and internship programs and can begin doing research as early as their freshman year. Students can also gain an international perspective through study abroad, work abroad, or the international plan. In addition, Georgia Tech has added the Clough Undergraduate Center, a state-of-the-art facility that includes forty-one classrooms, two 300-plus seat auditoriums, group study rooms, presentation rehearsal studios, a rooftop garden, and a café.

"With a Division I ACC sports program and access to Atlanta's music, theater, and other cultural venues, Georgia Tech offers its diverse and passionate student body a unique combination of top academics in a thriving and vibrant setting. We encourage you to come visit campus and see why Georgia Tech continues to attract the nation's most motivated, interesting, and creative students."

SELECTIVITY

Admissions Rating	97
# of applicants	17,669
% of applicants accepted	41
% of acceptees attending	37
# offered a place on the wait list	2,612
% accepting a place on wait list	63
% admitted from wait list	16

FRESHMAN PROFILE

Range SAT Critical Reading	620–710
Range SAT Math	670–770
Range SAT Writing	630–720
Range ACT Composite	29–33
Average HS GPA	3.95
% graduated top 10% of class	81
% graduated top 25% of class	95
% graduated top 50% of class	99

DEADLINES

Early action	
Deadline	10/21
Notification	1/4
Regular	
Priority	10/21
Deadline	1/10
Notification	3/15
Nonfall registration?	Yes

APPLICANTS ALSO LOOK AT AND OFTEN PREFER

University of California-Berkeley; University of Florida; University of Georgia

AND SOMETIMES PREFER

Carnegie Mellon University; Clemson University; Purdue University

AND RARELY PREFER

Texas A&M University; UNC-Chapel Hill; Virginia Tech

FINANCIAL FACTS

Financial Aid Rating	80
Annual in-state tuition	$8,258
Annual out-of-state tuition	$27,562
Room and board	$9,814
Required fees	$2,392
Books and supplies	$1,200
% needy frosh rec. need-based scholarship or grant aid	90
% needy UG rec. need-based scholarship or grant aid	85
% needy frosh rec. non-need-based scholarship or grant aid	69
% needy UG rec. non-need-based scholarship or grant aid	61
% needy frosh rec. need-based self-help aid	57
% needy UG rec. need-based self-help aid	66
% frosh rec. any financial aid	72
% UG rec. any financial aid	74
% UG borrow to pay for school	42
Average cumulative indebtedness	$25,027
% frosh need fully met	34
% ugrads need fully met	24
Average % of frosh need met	62
Average % of ugrad need met	60

GETTYSBURG COLLEGE

ADMISSIONS OFFICE, GETTYSBURG, PA 17325-1484 • ADMISSIONS: 717-337-6100 • FAX: 717-337-6145

CAMPUS LIFE

Quality of Life Rating	94
Fire Safety Rating	92
Green Rating	80
Type of school	Private
Affiliation	Lutheran
Environment	Village

STUDENTS

Total undergrad enrollment	2,533
% male/female	48/52
% from out of state	73
% frosh from public high school	70
% frosh live on campus	100
% ugrads live on campus	93
# of fraternities	9
# of sororities	6
% African American	3
% Asian	1
% Caucasian	82
% Hispanic	4
% Native American	0
% international	2
# of countries represented	26

SURVEY SAYS . . .

Students are happy
Classroom facilities are great
Lab facilities are great
Career services are great
Internships are widely available
School is well run
Students are friendly
Great food on campus
Dorms are like palaces
Campus feels safe
Easy to get around campus
Athletic facilities are great
Lots of beer drinking
Intramural sports are popular
Frats and sororities are popular
Alumni active on campus

ACADEMICS

Academic Rating	96
% students returning for sophomore year	88
% students graduating within 4 years	81
% students graduating within 6 years	84
Calendar	Semester
Student/faculty ratio	10:1
Profs interesting rating	90
Profs accessible rating	95

Most classes have 10–19 students.

MOST POPULAR MAJORS
psychology; political science; business/
commerce

STUDENTS SAY ". . ."

Academics
Personal and intellectual growth is at the heart of the Gettysburg College experience. Students eagerly praise the school's "friendly, community-oriented atmosphere," and competent, caring professors. "The faculty takes a developed interest in the students' academics and successes, [and] the campus offers countless opportunities for leadership, self-discovery, and the like." In fact, first-year students are surprised to find that "by the first day, the professor knows each student by name and why they're taking the class." With uniformly small class sizes and an emphasis on discussion in the classroom, "Professors at Gettysburg make sure that students understand why they are learning the things that they are, and there is a lot of emphasis put on putting 'theory into practice' outside of the classroom." "Many professors go above and beyond, making themselves available to aid students." A current student shares, "My Intro to Chemistry professor would be at the Science Center until 11:00 P.M. before an exam, helping everyone study." Academic opportunities—such as the "amazing study abroad program"—are ample at Gettysburg. Plus, as an exclusively undergraduate institution, Gettysburg "allows for opportunities (i.e., research, publications) that many do not get" at larger universities. In this "nurturing environment," the "administration knows students by name" and even the "registrar, transportation services, off-campus studies, and library staff are lovely and do everything they can to help you." In particular, "President Riggs (a Gettysburg alum and former faculty member) is a phenomenal community leader and makes a sincere effort to connect with students, faculty, and staff."

Life
Enthusiastic and overcommitted, most students at Gettysburg are pursuing "a major and a minor or a double-major, and a majority are involved in at least several college organizations (whether it's a community service group, sports team, or Greek organization)." With so much on their plate, it is no surprise that "the students at Gettysburg buckle down and work hard" during the week. Socially, "Life at Gettysburg is very Greek-oriented," and, come the weekend, "frat hopping" is "popular on this campus." Not your style? No worries: Greek life may be "huge" on campus; "However, that does not mean that that is the only thing to do." For students looking for alternate activities, the school hosts "movie nights, plays, and musical performances." Many students also "love going to our theme parties and Happy Hours at the Attic, our on-campus night-club," while others "get together with friends and watch movies or go out for coffee." For a relaxing respite, "The surrounding area and town is beautiful, so one of my favorite things to do is just walk around out on the battlefields or through town." In addition, "people also like to get off campus traveling to bigger city areas like Baltimore, Harrisburg, D.C., and even Philly and New York City."

Student Body
Academics come first at Gettysburg, where "The student body is extremely intelligent and motivated and serious about their work." When they're not studying, "Gettysburg's student body is very involved" in the school and local community, and "volunteering is very popular." "Each student—in one way or another—takes part in community service during their time at Gettysburg." Demographically, "most of the student body is…middle-class, white, and from the Northeast." And, lest we forget, the Gettysburg student body is also well known for its uniform "tendency to wear preppy clothes." A current student elaborates, "Open up a J. Crew magazine and find the most attractive models in it and you have a typical Gettysburg College student." While some say the student body has a "cookie-cutter" feel to it, others remind us that "while Gettysburg has a reputation for being mostly white, upper-class students, there is diversity all around if you are willing to open up your eyes and see it."

FINANCIAL AID: 717-337-6611 • E-MAIL: ADMISS@GETTYSBURG.EDU • WEBSITE: WWW.GETTYSBURG.EDU

THE PRINCETON REVIEW SAYS

Admissions

Very important factors considered include: Class rank, GPA, rigor of secondary school record, recommendation(s). *Important factors considered include:* Standardized test scores, application essay, extracurricular activities, interview, talent/ability, volunteer work, character/personal qualities. *Other factors considered include:* First generation, geographical residence, racial/ethnic status, work experience, alumni/ae relations, level of applicant's interest. SAT or ACT required; ACT with or without Writing component accepted. TOEFL required of all international applicants. *Academic units required:* 4 English; 3 mathematics; 3 science; (3 science lab); 3 social studies; 3 foreign language; 3 history. *Academic units recommended:* 4 English; 4 mathematics; 4 science; (4 science lab); 4 social studies; 4 foreign language; 4 history.

Financial Aid

Students should submit: FAFSA, CSS/Financial Aid PROFILE. Regular filing deadline is 2/15. The Princeton Review suggests that all financial aid forms be submitted as soon as possible after January 1. *Need-based scholarships/grants offered:* Federal Pell, SEOG, State scholarships/grants, private scholarships, the school's own gift aid. *Loan aid offered:* Direct Subsidized Stafford Loans, Direct Unsubsidized Stafford Loans, Direct PLUS loans, Federal Perkins Loans, College/university loans from institutional funds. Applicants will be notified of awards beginning 3/18. Federal Work-Study Program available. Institutional employment available. Off-campus job opportunities are excellent.

The Inside Word

Prospective Gettysburg students can register for an account on the school's website to view Gettysburg events in their area or connect with students on campus. To really get a feel for Gettysburg, however, many students say a campus visit is a must. If you're lucky enough to gain admission to this competitive liberal arts school, a campus visit might be just the thing to seal the deal.

THE SCHOOL SAYS "..."

From the Admissions Office

"Four major goals of Gettysburg College to best prepare students to enter the real world, include, first, to accelerate the intellectual development of our first-year students by integrating them more quickly into the intellectual life of the campus; second, to use interdisciplinary courses combining the intellectual approaches of various fields; third, to encourage students to develop an international perspective through course work, study abroad, association with international faculty, and a variety of extracurricular activities; and fourth, to encourage students to develop (1) a capacity for independent study by ensuring that all students work closely with individual faculty members on an extensive project during their undergraduate years and (2) the ability to work with their peers by making the small group a central feature in college life.

"Gettysburg College strongly recommends that freshman applicants submit scores from the SAT. Students may also choose to submit scores from the ACT (with or without the writing component) in lieu of the SAT."

SELECTIVITY

Admissions Rating	94
# of applicants	5,453
% of applicants accepted	42
% of acceptees attending	31
# of early decision applicants	432
% accepted early decision	74

FRESHMAN PROFILE

Range SAT Critical Reading	600–690
Range SAT Math	600–680
% graduated top 10% of class	69
% graduated top 25% of class	89
% graduated top 50% of class	99

DEADLINES

Early decision	
Deadline	11/15
Notification	12/15
Regular	
Priority	2/1
Deadline	2/1
Notification	4/1
Nonfall registration?	Yes

APPLICANTS ALSO LOOK AT AND OFTEN PREFER
Colgate University

AND SOMETIMES PREFER
Bucknell University

AND RARELY PREFER
Muhlenberg College

FINANCIAL FACTS

Financial Aid Rating	93
Annual tuition	$47,480
Room and board	$11,340
Books and supplies	$500
% needy frosh rec. need-based scholarship or grant aid	95
% needy UG rec. need-based scholarship or grant aid	94
% needy frosh rec. non-need-based scholarship or grant aid	93
% needy UG rec. non-need-based scholarship or grant aid	56
% needy frosh rec. need-based self-help aid	86
% needy UG rec. need-based self-help aid	84
% frosh rec. any financial aid	53
% UG rec. any financial aid	54
% UG borrow to pay for school	59
Average cumulative indebtedness	$30,378
% frosh need fully met	91
% ugrads need fully met	92
Average % of frosh need met	91
Average % of ugrad need met	92

GONZAGA UNIVERSITY

502 EAST BOONE AVENUE, SPOKANE, WA 99258 • ADMISSIONS: 509-313-6572 • FAX: 509-313-5780

STUDENTS SAY ". . ."

Academics

Gonzaga University "has a strong Jesuit Catholic tradition and has sustained an environment of academic excellence." By far, the two most commonly cited strengths are the basketball team and the "awesome community!" Gonzaga is a "close-knit community." "At Gonzaga, we are one big family," one student says. "Everyone is incredibly friendly," and there's "a great sense of school spirit and a family-like environment." "Not to mention being able to cheer in one of the most intimidating basketball stadiums in the United States." "It is a family here, and you really get to know your professors," one student explains. "Everyone here is interconnected, and basketball is wonderful too! It's a way we all come together." Students also believe "the Jesuit mission of Gonzaga sets it apart from other schools." Gonzaga "is a socially competent, caring institution" where you'll "be constantly challenged to be your best, make lifelong relationships, and develop a critical understanding of the world around you." The professors get mixed reviews: "It is about a 50 percent chance of getting a good professor." "Professors are good in general, but adjunct faculty is typically hired at the last minute and not good," one student explains. "Many of the professors for the core requirements are very religious and not especially open to new ideas." "Gonzaga tries to get students to think about the world in a holistic way—understanding how everything is interrelated—and finding our purpose in that." Students think the "registration processes" and "cafeteria food" could "use some improvement," and "because Gonzaga is a smaller school, it is at times difficult to arrange your schedule due to limited availability of classes and time constraints."

Life

Students at Gonzaga are "devoted equally to...academics and social life." "People generally just want to socialize," one student explains. "Everyone for the most part does do their work, but there is definitely an emphasis on developing relationships." "The party scene is lively" at Gonzaga although students caution "we're not *that* big of a party school." During basketball season, Gonzaga basketball becomes "a way of life," and "basketball games and waiting in line for tickets are the largest social experience on campus." "*Everyone* goes to the basketball games. It's practically required to graduate." This leads some students to wish there was "less focus on men's basketball." Because the school is located in rainy Spokane, Washington, "the worst thing about Gonzaga is the weather, which the school can't really do anything about." Still, many students "stay active through sports" and enjoy the outdoors, "whether that's skiing, hiking, rafting, climbing, wake boarding, or just soaking up some rays." "People often snowboard at Mount Spokane, or if they are feeling adventurous, they drive the hour to Canada or hour to Montana." At Gonzaga, students "Read, Rage, Repent, Repeat. We wake up, work out, eat, and make memories."

Student Body

Although Gonzaga students stress the college's tight-knit community, many feel that while "the university claims to be accepting of all beliefs, opinions, and lifestyles," "in reality that's just not the case." "It is a community for sure, but really only if you're white and upper-middle-class, and the Jesuit Catholic mission can sometimes be troublesome for those of us with liberal and non-mainstream Catholic beliefs," explains one student. "Even feminism is kind of seen as taboo here." Others insist that "everyone here seems to blend well together," and "no matter your background, you are accepted here." Students study "hard through the week" but have "a lot of fun on weekends." Students describe themselves as "friendly, very open," "mostly preppy," "conventionally minded," "well-mannered," "religious," and tending to come "from a good family." Gonzaga has "a mostly Caucasian population," and "diversity is a huge issue, and Gonzaga could definitely improve how it treats students of diverse backgrounds." It should be no shock that "the typical student is a huge basketball fan" with "extreme school spirit."

GONZAGA UNIVERSITY

FINANCIAL AID: 509-313-6582 • E-MAIL: ADMISSIONS@GONZAGA.EDU • WEBSITE: WWW.GONZAGA.EDU

THE PRINCETON REVIEW SAYS

Admissions

Very important factors considered include: GPA, rigor of secondary school record, first generation, character/personal qualities. *Important factors considered include:* Standardized test scores, application essay, extracurricular activities, recommendation(s), talent/ability. *Other factors considered include:* Class rank, interview, racial/ethnic status, volunteer work, work experience, alumni/ae relations, level of applicant's interest. SAT or ACT required; ACT with or without Writing component accepted. TOEFL required of all international applicants. *Academic units required:* 4 English; 3 mathematics; 3 science; (3 science lab); 2 social studies; 2 foreign language; 2 history; 2 academic electives. *Academic units recommended:* 4 English; 4 mathematics; 4 science; (4 science lab); 3 social studies; 3 foreign language; 3 history; 3 academic electives.

Financial Aid

Students should submit: FAFSA. The Princeton Review suggests that all financial aid forms be submitted as soon as possible after January 1. *Need-based scholarships/grants offered:* Federal Pell, SEOG, State scholarships/grants, private scholarships, the school's own gift aid, federal nursing scholarships. *Loan aid offered:* Direct Subsidized Stafford Loans, Direct Unsubsidized Stafford Loans, Direct PLUS loans, Federal Perkins Loans, Federal Nursing Loans, College/university loans from institutional funds. Federal Work-Study Program available. Institutional employment available. Off-campus job opportunities are excellent.

The Inside Word

Gonzaga is a great example of how a high-profile athletic program can transform a competitive school into a highly competitive one. During the past decade, Gonzaga's admit rate has decreased substantially while class rank, standardized test scores, and high school GPA have all increased measurably.

THE SCHOOL SAYS "..."

From the Admissions Office

"Education at Gonzaga is not comparable to an academic 'assembly line'; rather, it is person-to-person and face-to-face. This personal quality is also true of our admission and financial aid processes. Therefore, allow us to know you beyond the boundaries of your college application. Visit campus, phone us, e-mail us—let us see the person behind the data. Good luck with your college search and your applications. Go Zags!

"All sections of the SAT will be accepted, but the written portion will not receive universal consideration. The written score will be considered in cases where more information specific to writing ability would be helpful in decision making."

SELECTIVITY

Admissions Rating	89
# of applicants	7,031
% of applicants accepted	68
% of acceptees attending	26
# offered a place on the wait list	536
% accepting a place on wait list	30
% admitted from wait list	34

FRESHMAN PROFILE

Range SAT Critical Reading	540–640
Range SAT Math	560–650
Range ACT Composite	25–29
Minimum paper TOEFL	550
Minimum web-based TOEFL	213
Average HS GPA	3.73
% graduated top 10% of class	39
% graduated top 25% of class	68
% graduated top 50% of class	95

DEADLINES

Early action	
Deadline	11/15
Notification	1/15
Regular	
Priority	11/15
Deadline	2/1
Notification	3/15
Nonfall registration?	Yes

APPLICANTS ALSO LOOK AT AND OFTEN PREFER
University of Notre Dame

AND SOMETIMES PREFER
Santa Clara University; University of Washington

AND RARELY PREFER
Washington State University; University of San Francisco

FINANCIAL FACTS

Financial Aid Rating	84
Annual tuition	$34,570
Room and board	$9,120
Required fees	$552
Books and supplies	$1,058
% needy frosh rec. need-based scholarship or grant aid	100
% needy UG rec. need-based scholarship or grant aid	99
% needy frosh rec. non-need-based scholarship or grant aid	22
% needy UG rec. non-need-based scholarship or grant aid	18
% needy frosh rec. need-based self-help aid	74
% needy UG rec. need-based self-help aid	71
% frosh rec. any financial aid	100
% UG rec. any financial aid	98
% UG borrow to pay for school	63
Average cumulative indebtedness	$32,347
% frosh need fully met	28
% ugrads need fully met	24
Average % of frosh need met	81
Average % of ugrad need met	78

GORDON COLLEGE

255 GRAPEVINE ROAD, WENHAM, MA 01984 • ADMISSIONS: 978-867-4218 • FAX: 978-867-4682

CAMPUS LIFE
Quality of Life Rating	94
Fire Safety Rating	88
Green Rating	69
Type of school	Private
Affiliation	Multidenominational
Environment	Village

STUDENTS
Total undergrad enrollment	1,707
% male/female	38/62
% from out of state	62
% frosh live on campus	98
% ugrads live on campus	89
% African American	3
% Asian	3
% Caucasian	78
% Hispanic	7
% Native American	<1
% international	5
# of countries represented	41

SURVEY SAYS . . .
Lab facilities are great
Students are friendly
Students are very religious
Students get along with local community
Students involved in community service
Great off-campus food
Campus feels safe
Very little drug use
Active minority support groups

ACADEMICS
Academic Rating	87
% students returning for sophomore year	83
% students graduating within 4 years	59
% students graduating within 6 years	72
Calendar	Semester
Student/faculty ratio	14:1
Profs interesting rating	85
Profs accessible rating	86

Most classes have 10–19 students.
Most lab/discussion sessions have
10–19 students.

MOST POPULAR MAJORS
English language and literature; psychology;
business/commerce

STUDENTS SAY ". . ."

Academics
One of the country's top Christian colleges, Gordon College is about "educating excellent leaders to work for the common good." Those who attend are taught to be "responsible and moral students in whatever field they are a part of" and are given "a holistic education that intentionally engages the intellectual, emotional and spiritual dimensions" of their lives. A generous amount of merit-based financial aid and excellent internship, research, and fellowship opportunities cap off the overwhelmingly positive experience of this tiny school that "punches above its weight."

"Top notch" professors do an excellent job of encouraging discussion and "making sure that students 'own' the material." They are "some of the best people on campus" and their level of commitment eventually means they "become mentors and friends." They "want to know what we think about the world," and "are very serious about letting us 'find our own way', rather than in indoctrinating us." "The professors care about every part of your being here," says a senior. "This personal relationship has strengthened the quality of academics, which are also of a high caliber." "I have gone on hikes with my philosophy professors, and I have been to see student bands perform at the homes of teachers," says another student.

Gordon takes "a liberal approach to Christianity that allows constructive discussion" and orients its students towards "building intimate and intentional communities" which they may grow in personally and spiritually. There is "a great integration of faith and science," and teachers excel at "showing students how the information in the class relates to their Christian faith." The rest of the staff is "very encouraging" as well; from the cafeteria to the maintenance folks, "you can count on a smile and potentially an uplifting comment." A strong alumni network "really want to help you find a job," which is fitting for a school that one student refers to as "an ideal place to make lifetime friends." "All of the alumni I had encountered were incredible people," says another.

Life
The school is located near Boston but is "more of a suburban campus," with rules limiting visitation and banning alcohol, which generally "isn't an issue [as] there is little to no party culture here." "For fun, we [go] to do laser tag at a place nearby, catch a movie, or go hang out at the mall. We also have really fun sleepovers in one another's dorms," says a student. There are usually "a good number" of intellectually stimulating events throughout the week on topics ranging from racial diversity to environmental sustainability, and people "spend a lot of time thinking about the kind of people they want to be, and exploring the deeper issues and questions of life." The campus events council also "does a great job at frequently planning fun campus events" such as dances, coffeehouses, and concerts. The student government "is great at listening to complaints from students and actually making timely changes to the school." Many say that "the buildings could use a little face lift, especially the library." For those looking to get off campus, Boston is "only a half-hour trip by commuter rail," and nearby beaches are great for day trips in warm weather. "Getting coffee with someone" is also "a very popular thing to do."

Student Body
"Christian," "middle class," "suburban," and "hard-working" sum up most of the two thousand or so students who attend Gordon. A fair number of hipsters abound; as a student says: "Every girl at Gordon has a tattoo, a nose piercing, or is vegetarian." Many admit that the student body is "perhaps a little out of touch with the 'real world'." "All groups and friends overlap somehow" in this tight knit community, where students "usually find a particular cohort or group to drift into," but "there is less of a clique culture than at many other colleges." There is "a sense of camaraderie on campus, and it spills out into the community."

FINANCIAL AID: 978-867-4246 • E-MAIL: ADMISSIONS@GORDON.EDU • WEBSITE: WWW.GORDON.EDU

THE PRINCETON REVIEW SAYS

Admissions

Very important factors considered include: GPA, rigor of secondary school record, standardized test scores, extracurricular activities, interview, recommendation(s), talent/ability, character/personal qualities, religious affiliation. *Important factors considered include:* Class rank, application essay, first generation, volunteer work, work experience, alumni/ae relations, level of applicant's interest. *Other factors considered include:* Geographical residence, racial/ethnic status. SAT or ACT required; ACT with Writing component recommended. TOEFL required of all international applicants. *Academic units required:* 4 English; 2 mathematics; 2 science; (1 science lab); 2 social studies; 2 foreign language; 5 academic electives. *Academic units recommended:* 4 English; 3 mathematics; 3 science; (1 science lab); 2 social studies; 4 foreign language; 5 academic electives.

Financial Aid

Students should submit: FAFSA. The Princeton Review suggests that all financial aid forms be submitted as soon as possible after January 1. *Need-based scholarships/grants offered:* Federal Pell, SEOG, State scholarships/grants, private scholarships, the school's own gift aid. *Loan aid offered:* Direct Subsidized Stafford Loans, Direct Unsubsidized Stafford Loans, Direct PLUS loans, Federal Perkins Loans, State Loans. Federal Work-Study Program available. Institutional employment available. Off-campus job opportunities are excellent.

The Inside Word

Interviews are required at Gordon, presumably so admissions officers can gauge candidates' readiness for the rigorous curriculum and high level of religious commitment (a Christian Faith Reference is a requirement). Students interested in studying social work must meet a second, more rigorous set of admissions requirements in addition to general requirements. Prospective music and theater majors must audition as part of their application, and prospective art majors must submit a portfolio for faculty review. The high admit rate here is somewhat misleading, as a look at the high yield percentage and the lifestyle expectations of the college should make clear.

THE SCHOOL SAYS "..."

From the Admissions Office

"There are three core distinctions that—taken together— set Gordon College apart from other academically rigorous liberal arts institutions:

"Gordon's mission. Gordon graduates men and women distinguished by intellectual maturity and Christian character, committed to lives of service, and prepared for leadership worldwide. With a liberal arts education in the tradition of New England's best colleges, our students gain the qualities most sought by employers—the ability to think critically, reason analytically, communicate persuasively and—even more importantly—to act morally. The Gordon Commission. This is the essence of our experience—to stretch the mind, deepen the faith and elevate the contribution Gordon students and graduates make to the world around us. We stretch the mind through a challenging education that is both broad and deep, and one that offers the freedom to ask and explore tough questions. We deepen the faith by integrating Christian beliefs and practice into all aspects of our educational experience. We elevate the contribution—to the common good, to our communities, to developing the next generation of thoughtful Christian leaders—through programs and outreach that emphasize service over self and that span the globe.

"Gordon's Location. Boston is the global "hub" of higher education—this is where the world comes to study. We are strategically located in the proximity of the cultural centers of education (Boston), finance (New York) and politics (Washington). Boston also has a reputation as a leader in developing talent— which means greater opportunity for students who study here."

SELECTIVITY

Admissions Rating	90
# of applicants	3,843
% of applicants accepted	43
% of acceptees attending	29
# offered a place on the wait list	62
% accepting a place on wait list	90
% admitted from wait list	63
# of early decision applicants	91
% accepted early decision	14

FRESHMAN PROFILE

Range SAT Critical Reading	516–653
Range SAT Math	499–639
Range SAT Writing	507–648
Range ACT Composite	22–29
Minimum web-based TOEFL	85
Average HS GPA	3.58
% graduated top 10% of class	34
% graduated top 25% of class	55
% graduated top 50% of class	85

DEADLINES

Early decision	
Deadline	11/1
Notification	12/1
Early action	
Deadline	11/15
Notification	12/1
Regular	
Priority	2/1
Deadline	8/1
Nonfall registration?	Yes

APPLICANTS ALSO LOOK AT AND SOMETIMES PREFER
Messiah College; Wheaton College (IL)

FINANCIAL FACTS

Financial Aid Rating	75
Annual tuition	$32,930
Room and board	$9,930
Required fees	$1,460
Books and supplies	$800
% needy frosh rec. need-based scholarship or grant aid	100
% needy UG rec. need-based scholarship or grant aid	100
% needy frosh rec. non-need-based scholarship or grant aid	12
% needy UG rec. non-need-based scholarship or grant aid	10
% needy frosh rec. need-based self-help aid	83
% needy UG rec. need-based self-help aid	87
% frosh rec. any financial aid	98
% UG rec. any financial aid	97
% UG borrow to pay for school	81
Average cumulative indebtedness	$36,942
% frosh need fully met	14
% ugrads need fully met	15
Average % of frosh need met	60
Average % of ugrad need met	68

GOUCHER COLLEGE

1021 DULANEY VALLEY ROAD, BALTIMORE, MD 21204-2794 • ADMISSIONS: 410-337-6100 • FAX: 410-337-6354

CAMPUS LIFE

Quality of Life Rating	87
Fire Safety Rating	88
Green Rating	90
Type of school	Private
Affiliation	No Affiliation
Environment	Metropolis

STUDENTS

Total undergrad enrollment	1,444
% male/female	34/66
% from out of state	74
% frosh from public high school	66
% frosh live on campus	96
% ugrads live on campus	84
% African American	9
% Asian	3
% Caucasian	68
% Hispanic	7
% Native American	<1
% international	2
# of countries represented	49

SURVEY SAYS . . .
No one cheats
Students are friendly
Students environmentally aware
Great food on campus
Easy to get around campus

ACADEMICS

Academic Rating	91
% students returning for sophomore year	86
% students graduating within 4 years	58
% students graduating within 6 years	67
Calendar	Semester
Student/faculty ratio	9:1
Profs interesting rating	90
Profs accessible rating	85

Most classes have 10–19 students.

MOST POPULAR MAJORS
biology; psychology; mass communication/
media studies

STUDENTS SAY ". . ."

Academics

Providing "a small, liberal-arts education" with a "fantastic location" just outside Baltimore, Goucher College's academic environment is one where students are encouraged to "develop close relationships with professors, and with other students." Goucher offers a "small college feel" and a "gorgeous campus" to its "tight-knit community." Goucher students "understand that exploring cultures outside your own is important" and pursue a "focused track of study within a well-rounded and rigorous liberal arts curriculum." Study abroad is not just emphasized, but mandatory, and the college offers a stipend for international study; this is highlighted by many students as a primary reason for attending and results in a "globally-minded and social justice oriented" student body. Its "attention to environmental issues" fosters green awareness in its undergraduates, who "study hard—barefoot." In the tradition of the liberal arts, Goucher "builds a foundation on critical and analytic thinking," and prides itself on small, "intimate" class sizes Students are challenged to exceed their own goals through Goucher's "immense focus on transcending boundaries to explore and grow." Goucher students offer high praise for their "knowledgeable and engaging" faculty: "Many professors serve not only as instructors but as mentors and friends to the students in their classes, guiding them as much through life as through school work." Undergraduates express high satisfaction with their academic experience—one student says "I was immediately hooked"—and enjoy the "flexibility, quantity, and quality of courses provided." The academic rigor, small campus, and close relationships all create a warm "sense of community" that makes the campus "feel like home." Goucher students name their alma mater as among those "colleges that change lives," and sum up their experience as "a rigorous education in a green environment, with a focus on community and world awareness." According to those who know best—Goucher's undergraduates—Goucher's education is a "sound choice to further any career path I choose."

Life

"You will never be bored here" because it's "really easy to get into downtown Baltimore" via Goucher's free shuttle, and because of the myriad on-campus activities: "The SGA does a wonderful job planning activities." It's definitely possible to "have too much fun" amidst the "big cuddle puddle of cynical and hyper-analytical over-achievers," but students are "hardworking" as well as social. Students have "a wide variety of interests," but "because [the school] is so small, it is common to know a lot of the people on campus." Many students report that "there is always something to do," and the on-campus "Humans vs. Zombies" game is frequently cited as a popular activity. "I get to ride horses, ballroom dance, and hunt zombies all in a single afternoon." "Quirkiness is the Goucher Normal," proclaims one student, echoing the "quirky" moniker frequently self-applied to Goucher undergrads. In the student body, "people of all colors, shapes, and styles come together to grow as students and as individuals" who are "all about helping one another and making the world a better place through persistence and innovation."

Student Body

According to students, the typical Goucher student is "very intelligent, passionate, outgoing, liberal, fun [and] quirky." One student explains Goucher's quirky moniker: "I think it fits well—I mean, I think we're the only place where students in a room would shout 'Opa!' when someone accidentally breaks a plate. No fuss—just fun and understanding." Students particularly praise the dance, equestrian, and athletic programs, as well as each other's differences: "Most students definitely dance to the beat of their own drum." Students find "friendship and support" in each other, as well as intellectual stimulation: "Our dinner conversations are about equality and then they shift to politics and to environmentalism and then finally to what we did that weekend. We're motivated, socially active students who really care about the world we live in."

FINANCIAL AID: 410-337-6141 • E-MAIL: ADMISSIONS@GOUCHER.EDU • WEBSITE: WWW.GOUCHER.EDU

THE PRINCETON REVIEW SAYS

Admissions

Very important factors considered include: GPA, rigor of secondary school record. *Important factors considered include:* Application essay, extracurricular activities, recommendation(s), talent/ability. *Other factors considered include:* Class rank, standardized test scores, first generation, geographical residence, interview, racial/ethnic status, state residency, volunteer work, work experience, alumni/ae relations, character/personal qualities, level of applicant's interest. SAT or ACT considered if submitted; ACT with Writing component required. TOEFL required of all international applicants. *Academic units required:* 4 English; 3 mathematics; 2 science; (2 science lab); 3 social studies; 2 foreign language; 2 academic electives. *Academic units recommended:* 4 English; 4 mathematics; 3 science; (3 science lab); 3 social studies; 4 foreign language; 2 academic electives.

Financial Aid

Students should submit: FAFSA, CSS/Financial Aid PROFILE, Noncustodial PROFILE. The Princeton Review suggests that all financial aid forms be submitted as soon as possible after January 1. *Need-based scholarships/grants offered:* Federal Pell, SEOG, State scholarships/grants, private scholarships, the school's own gift aid. *Loan aid offered:* Direct Subsidized Stafford Loans, Direct Unsubsidized Stafford Loans, Direct PLUS loans, Federal Perkins Loans, College/university loans from institutional funds. Applicants will be notified of awards beginning 4/1. Federal Work-Study Program available. Institutional employment available. Off-campus job opportunities are excellent.

The Inside Word

Uniquely, Goucher makes standardized test scores optional for admission, placing a high emphasis on extracurricular activities, intellectual curiosity, and personal qualities. However, if you wish to apply for merit funding—for which all admitted students are automatically considered—you must submit SAT and/or ACT scores. Goucher's admission rate is deceptively high, given the self-selection of its students, and a demonstrated record of academic achievement is necessary for admission.

THE SCHOOL SAYS ". . ."

From the Admissions Office

"Through a broad-based arts and sciences curriculum and a groundbreaking approach to study abroad, Goucher College gives students a sweeping view of the world. Goucher is an independent, coeducational institution dedicated to both the interdisciplinary traditions of the liberal arts and a truly international perspective on education. The first college in the nation to pair required study abroad with a special travel stipend for every undergraduate, Goucher believes in complementing its strong majors and rigorous curriculum with abundant opportunities for hands-on experience. In addition to participating in the college's many study abroad programs (including innovative three-week intensive courses abroad alongside traditional semester and academic year offerings), many students also complete internships and service-learning projects that further enhance their learning. The college's almost 1,500 undergraduate students live and learn on a tree-lined campus of 287 acres just north of Baltimore, Maryland. Goucher boasts a student/faculty ratio of just nine to one, and professors routinely collaborate with students on major research projects—often for publication, and sometimes as early as students' first or second years. The curriculum emphasizes international and intercultural awareness throughout, and students are encouraged to explore their academic interests from a variety of perspectives beyond their major disciplines. A Goucher College education encompasses a multitude of experiences that ultimately converge into one cohesive academic program that can truly change lives. Students grow in dramatic and surprising ways here. They graduate with a strong sense of direction and self-confidence, ready to engage the world—and succeed—as true global citizens."

SELECTIVITY

Admissions Rating	84
# of applicants	3,466
% of applicants accepted	72
% of acceptees attending	16
# offered a place on the wait list	160
% accepting a place on wait list	24
% admitted from wait list	5
# of early decision applicants	75
% accepted early decision	59

FRESHMAN PROFILE

Range SAT Critical Reading	510–660
Range SAT Math	500–620
Range SAT Writing	510–640
Range ACT Composite	23–28
Minimum paper TOEFL	550
Minimum web-based TOEFL	213
Average HS GPA	3.20
% graduated top 10% of class	31
% graduated top 25% of class	58
% graduated top 50% of class	88

DEADLINES

Early decision	
Deadline	11/15
Notification	12/15
Early action	
Deadline	12/1
Notification	2/1
Regular	
Priority	2/1
Notification	4/1
Nonfall registration?	Yes

FINANCIAL FACTS

Financial Aid Rating	76
Annual tuition	$39,808
Room and board	$11,482
Required fees	$750
Books and supplies	$800
% needy frosh rec. need-based scholarship or grant aid	100
% needy UG rec. need-based scholarship or grant aid	98
% needy frosh rec. non-need-based scholarship or grant aid	16
% needy UG rec. non-need-based scholarship or grant aid	11
% needy frosh rec. need-based self-help aid	83
% needy UG rec. need-based self-help aid	85
% frosh rec. any financial aid	97
% UG rec. any financial aid	86
% UG borrow to pay for school	64
Average cumulative indebtedness	$27,921
% frosh need fully met	21
% ugrads need fully met	16
Average % of frosh need met	78
Average % of ugrad need met	75

GREEN MOUNTAIN COLLEGE

ONE BRENNAN CIRCLE, POULTNEY, VT 05764-1199 • ADMISSIONS: 802-287-8000 • FAX: 802-287-8099

STUDENTS SAY ". . ."

Academics

Green Mountain College, located in Poultney, Vermont, is a small, private, liberal arts college near the Vermont countryside. One of the goals of Green Mountain is its active focus on sustainability and teaching all of their incoming students to live "responsibly" as global citizens. In fact, the college has a set of thirty-seven credit, core classes known as the Environmental Liberal Arts, which combines a liberal arts education with a strong focus on the environment. With most students saying that their classroom sizes "are usually around fifteen to thirty students," they really feel like they get to know their professors "not only as academic instructors, but as people," and most rave that they really bond with a majority of their teachers, saying they "haven't really met any professor that I can't connect with in some way." Since a lot of professors get to really know their students, most students say they have no problem getting personal letters from professors when they are "ready to apply for a job/ internship/graduate school, because they know…you and what you've done with your time here." The students love that the school promotes a great education with a focus on teaching students how to be themselves "while learning in dynamic and hands-on ways" ; this comes through an emphasis that an education doesn't just come from a classroom, but from real world experience as well.

Life

Being located in the Vermont country, Green Mountain College offers its students a great experience for those who love to experience nature. Its location at the foot of the Green Mountains makes it ideal for students who enjoy spending their free time "skiing, snowboarding, camping, [and] hiking." Incoming freshman and transfer students can register for one of the pre-orientation "Wilderness Challenges," where these new people bond together over a five day adventure focused on such activities as rock-climbing, canoeing, and yoga. During the school year, the student run College Programming Board does "a great job with providing concerts and other events on campus" for those wishing to stay nearby. The college isn't located right next to a big city, so many make their own fun on campus. Students also say that there are options to get away such as "a few charming…restaurants on Main Street," but in general, "There is not much to do around town." However, for those students who are willing to take a drive, the ski resort town of Killington is nearby—about forty minutes away—which students call "a huge plus."

Student Body

The student population at Green Mountain College likes to think of itself as a "very tight-knit community," with a "typical" student being "very outgoing [and] friendly." Many students here "want to make a positive impact on the world in some way or another," especially in the area of sustainability. Though many students agree that certainly a certain type of student attends Green Mountain, it's hard to nail down that typical student description. One student clarifies that there are "no [frat] bros, no sorority girls," but explains that the vast majority is happy to live "amongst other weird, happy, wonderful people while learning about sustainability," which is clear in the projects that students take on for the betterment of campus. The students worked together to help build a solar panel on the roof of the student center and a wind turbine to power the campus greenhouse.

FINANCIAL AID: 802-287-8210 • E-MAIL: ADMISS@GREENMTN.EDU • WEBSITE: WWW.GREENMTN.EDU

THE PRINCETON REVIEW SAYS

Admissions

Very important factors considered include: GPA. *Important factors considered include:* Class rank, rigor of secondary school record, standardized test scores, application essay, extracurricular activities, interview, recommendation(s), talent/ability, volunteer work, level of applicant's interest. *Other factors considered include:* Racial/ethnic status, work experience, alumni/ae relations, character/personal qualities, religious affiliation. SAT and SAT Subject Tests or ACT considered if submitted; ACT with or without Writing component accepted. TOEFL required of all international applicants. *Academic units required:* 4 English; 3 mathematics; 3 science; (2 science lab); 3 social studies; 2 foreign language; 1 history; 5 academic electives. *Academic units recommended:* 4 mathematics; 4 science; 3 foreign language; 2 history.

Financial Aid

Students should submit: FAFSA. The Princeton Review suggests that all financial aid forms be submitted as soon as possible after January 1. *Need-based scholarships/grants offered:* Federal Pell, SEOG, State scholarships/grants, private scholarships, the school's own gift aid. *Loan aid offered:* Direct Subsidized Stafford Loans, Direct Unsubsidized Stafford Loans, Direct PLUS loans. Federal Work-Study Program available. Institutional employment available. Off-campus job opportunities are fair.

The Inside Word

Green Mountain College has twenty-four majors to choose from. Because the student population sits at about 750 students, it should be known that applications are accepted throughout the year and that Green Mountain has a test-optional policy, so it is not mandatory that applicants supply their ACT or SAT scores, but if students choose not to, they have to fill out the college's Insight Portfolio and provide a graded writing sample that was written within the last two years. For those interested in financial aid, there are numerous programs that the college offers, and 94 percent of all GMC students receive financial aid and about 90 percent receive institutional support. Academic-based scholarships are awarded on a rolling basis as well.

THE SCHOOL SAYS "..."

From the Admissions Office

"Green Mountain College was named the number one 'Coolest School' by Sierra magazine. GMC is a liberal arts college that is on the forefront of sustainability education.

"While we are proud of our national recognition for sustainability, three-quarters of our students do not major in environmental studies, but rather select a liberal arts major that they are passionate about—education, business, art, psychology, biology, etc. The student body is united by a sense of social responsibility and penchant for service. Diversity thrives at Green Mountain College. The academic community is highly engaged and provides a truthful and authentic scholarly environment.

"GMC's working farm is a special attraction for students from all majors. It provides a visible model of sustainability and produces a significant quantity of food for the college community. Students can also major in sustainable agriculture and food production and/or earn twelve credits over the summer in farm life ecology, a 'field and table' intensive.

"We award scholarships for academic merit, service, leadership, creative arts, and community advancement at the time of admission, so students should submit evidence of these activities with their application for admission. The college is committed to and guarantees graduation in four years for students who meet academic requirements. An entrepreneurial spirit carries throughout the entire community resulting in a one of kind graduation."

SELECTIVITY

Admissions Rating	76
# of applicants	773
% of applicants accepted	76
% of acceptees attending	23

FRESHMAN PROFILE

Range SAT Critical Reading	480–630
Range SAT Math	440–570
Range SAT Writing	450–590
Range ACT Composite	20–27
Minimum paper TOEFL	500
Minimum web-based TOEFL	173

DEADLINES

Early action	
Deadline	11/1
Notification	12/14
Regular	
Priority	3/1
Nonfall registration?	Yes

FINANCIAL FACTS

Financial Aid Rating	64
Books and supplies	$980
% needy frosh rec. need-based scholarship or grant aid	100
% needy UG rec. need-based scholarship or grant aid	97
% needy frosh rec. non-need-based scholarship or grant aid	3
% needy UG rec. non-need-based scholarship or grant aid	5
% needy frosh rec. need-based self-help aid	94
% needy UG rec. need-based self-help aid	104
% frosh rec. any financial aid	96
% UG rec. any financial aid	93
% UG borrow to pay for school	79
Average cumulative indebtedness	$33,448
% frosh need fully met	5
% ugrads need fully met	8
Average % of frosh need met	75
Average % of ugrad need met	69

GRINNELL COLLEGE

1103 PARK STREET, GRINNELL, IA 50112-1690 • ADMISSIONS: 641-269-3600 • FAX: 641-269-4800

STUDENTS SAY ". . ."

Academics

Founded in 1846, Grinnell College is a small private liberal arts college in Iowa where innovative intellectual discourse is central to learning. Guided by a commitment to academic rigor and a "commitment to social justice," the school stresses self-governance ("Self-Gov is Love") and the "very supportive" student body has the power to make change on campus. "Grinnell operates on self-governance which means the students are held accountable for their actions by their fellow students rather than being cited by RAs or school officials," says a student.

Learning at Grinnell "can be characterized as entering into a dialogue with professors and classmates." The curriculum stresses the methodology as well as the content of a given discipline; professors "expect students to be able to evaluate scholarship critically and come to their own conclusions." Faculty here are "incredibly diverse" and "eager to teach in a small liberal arts college," and "they all are willing to meet outside of class and leave their schedule open to help you."

Grinnell is one of the few schools without required general education courses, and students here "are truly free to explore their passions without feeling obligated to study things they don't enjoy." The school encourages students "to try a bit of everything" whether or not it's related to their major, and is "wonderful about bringing in important speakers to help you learn outside of the classroom." However, the school's size means there aren't as many classes offered as larger universities, and "some classes are only offered in either the spring or fall semester." Still, the school dedicates tons of resources for students, and "individual needs, especially academics related ones, are always met." The college also heavily subsidizes "spring break volunteer trips, conference travel costs, student groups, unpaid internships, trips to job-shadow alumni, and so much more."

Life

"Fun predominates in the academic community and support systems" as well as in nonacademic ways. After being hard workers during the week, "almost everyone likes to go out on weekends and let loose a little bit," whether "in a traditional party environment with beer and drinking games on weekends, or something as goofy as a weekly Nerf gun battle in our science facility on Friday nights (yes, there's a club for that)." There are in fact many different organizations run by students, and "there's always some sort of performance going on." Popular movies are shown for free on campus, and concerts and themed dance parties are held. "Even though we are located in a small town in Iowa, most students don't feel the urge to hit a bus or car to Des Moines, Chicago or the Twin Cities every weekend," assures a student. "We make our own amusements; surprisingly little property destruction results of this boredom compared to other college towns I know." Grinnellians are "very passionate about wellness, respect and being politically correct," and this translates into a lot of talks, dialogues and activities to promote all three of these aspects. "If you have an opinion be prepared to defend it," says a student. There are of course some social divisions (notably athletes and non-athletes), but "not in a harmful way." "People love to dance here. People love to deconstruct social constructions here." It's "an amazing mix of silly times and very smart people."

Student Body

Grinnell is a school filled with an "odd bunch" of students who are "genuinely interested in developing relationships with each other and a connection with the greater world." All "have a quality about them that is a little bit awkward and silly and most people feel comfortable expressing this." "You can always find someone who really understands your brand of crazy," says a junior. This group of "socially conscious scholars" is traditionally "liberal, very intelligent," and "willing to critically think about every issue or belief mostly in constructive ways." There is no set formula for fitting in; "almost everyone finds people that they are comfortable with here." Grinnell is also home to a large international student population, hailing from more than eighty countries.

FINANCIAL AID: 641-269-3250 • E-MAIL: ADMISSION@GRINNELL.EDU • WEBSITE: WWW.GRINNELL.EDU

THE PRINCETON REVIEW SAYS

Admissions

Very important factors considered include: Class rank, GPA, rigor of secondary school record, recommendation(s). *Important factors considered include:* Standardized test scores, application essay, extracurricular activities, talent/ability. *Other factors considered include:* First generation, geographical residence, interview, racial/ethnic status, state residency, volunteer work, work experience, alumni/ae relations, character/personal qualities, level of applicant's interest. SAT or ACT required; ACT with or without Writing component accepted. TOEFL required of all international applicants. *Academic units recommended:* 4 English; 4 mathematics; 3 science; (3 science lab); 3 social studies; 3 foreign language; 3 history.

Financial Aid

Students should submit: FAFSA, CSS/Financial Aid PROFILE, Noncustodial PROFILE. Regular filing deadline is 2/1. The Princeton Review suggests that all financial aid forms be submitted as soon as possible after January 1. *Need-based scholarships/grants offered:* Federal Pell, SEOG, State scholarships/grants, private scholarships, the school's own gift aid. *Loan aid offered:* Direct Subsidized Stafford Loans, Direct Unsubsidized Stafford Loans, Direct PLUS Loans, Federal Perkins Loans, College Loans from institutional funds. Applicants will be notified of awards beginning 4/1. Federal Work-Study Program available. Institutional employment available. Off-campus job opportunities are excellent.

The Inside Word

Grinnell's admissions process is refreshingly straightforward. Students need to be able to thrive academically as well as demonstrate an ability to take an active role in their education as you'll be responsible for co-creating your curriculum with your advisor, and you'll have to find your voice in a self-governing residential community. Grinnell is extremely selective, so you'll have to give it your all. An interview isn't required here, but do it anyway.

THE SCHOOL SAYS "..."

From the Admissions Office

"Grinnell College is a place where independence of thought and social conscience are instilled. Grinnell is a college with the resources of a school ten times its size, a faculty that reads like a Who's Who of Teaching, and a learning environment where debate does not end in the classroom and often begins in the dining hall.

"Grinnellians are committed to learning, respect for themselves and others, contributing to global social good, willing collaboration, and the courage to try.

"We look for students who show strong potential, have the courage to try new things, demonstrate a willingness to speak out and share their opinions, and bring different perspectives to our international campus in the middle of Iowa. Grinnell College is filled with students who are serious about learning but are not always serious."

SELECTIVITY

Admissions Rating	96
# of applicants	3,979
% of applicants accepted	35
% of acceptees attending	30
# offered a place on the wait list	1,266
% accepting a place on wait list	41
% admitted from wait list	2
# of early decision applicants	333
% accepted early decision	48

FRESHMAN PROFILE

Range SAT Critical Reading	620–730
Range SAT Math	630–770
Range ACT Composite	28–32
% graduated top 10% of class	63
% graduated top 25% of class	88
% graduated top 50% of class	98

DEADLINES

Early decision	
Deadline	11/15
Regular	
Deadline	1/15
Nonfall registration?	No

FINANCIAL FACTS

Financial Aid Rating	98
Annual tuition	$45,217
Room and board	$9,998
Required fees	$403
Books and supplies	$900
% needy frosh rec. need-based scholarship or grant aid	99
% needy UG rec. need-based scholarship or grant aid	99
% needy frosh rec. non-need-based scholarship or grant aid	16
% needy UG rec. non-need-based scholarship or grant aid	9
% needy frosh rec. need-based self-help aid	83
% needy UG rec. need-based self-help aid	87
% frosh rec. any financial aid	89
% UG rec. any financial aid	87
% UG borrow to pay for school	57
Average cumulative indebtedness	$16,570
% frosh need fully met	100
% ugrads need fully met	100
Average % of frosh need met	100
Average % of ugrad need met	100

GROVE CITY COLLEGE

100 CAMPUS DRIVE, GROVE CITY, PA 16127-2104 • ADMISSIONS: 724-458-2100 • FAX: 724-458-3395

STUDENTS SAY ". . ."

Academics

Students avow that Grove City is "a great option for someone who wants to learn from a Christian perspective." Located near Pittsburgh, this "small, conservative, independent" college is renowned for its "great spiritual atmosphere," providing a "very high-quality and competitive education," and has "a high rate of graduate school acceptance and job placement." One student mentions, "Grove City College keeps traditional values and top-of-the-line academics at the heart of everything it does." All courses are taught by professors, seen as "tough but fair and willing to help out their students." "You probably will not do well in most classes if you just do the minimum." Grade competition is almost a pastime for some, but others effectively juggle studies and other activities. "Some people like to over-exaggerate the difficulty of the academics. It is definitely challenging, but very doable." Professors "encourage students to learn and think for themselves, rather than trying to indoctrinate them into a particular ideology." "We are typically religious and conservative in beliefs, but that doesn't mean we're not open-minded." Still, undergraduates believe instructors "are equipping them spiritually and socially to live successful, godly lives." Notes a student, "I am able to learn from people who truly love what they do and do it because they love God." "I've truly grown leaps and bounds in my spiritual life," marvels another thrilled undergraduate.

Life

"Fun outside of class is what you make it" at Grove City College. Seemingly everyone is involved in multiple organizations and extracurricular activities. Academic groups, social clubs, intramural sports...all are popular, as are opportunities "for spiritual growth through campus ministries, student-initiated small groups, and local churches." "The community is wonderful, and it is a very uplifting place to be," although many students do long for a bit more personal freedom. As one student says, "While the rules at GCC are certainly strict, they are very clearly articulated," although another asserts they "are not as strict as made out to be. Really they are quite lax compared to other conservative Christian colleges." The school's rules can lead to interaction between the sexes becoming somewhat complex. There are relatively firm "inter-visitation rules" between men and women, and students pine for "more areas to spend time coed." As for the administration, registration has reportedly become "quicker and easier" and is "pretty fair as to who gets into classes." The cafeteria does "an excellent job providing a variety of healthy food options," and the food "is amazing compared to most other college campuses." Even though Grove City is a smaller school, "the parking situation for students is very ideal" and "not far from the dorms and academic buildings." Students are effusive in their admiration for the physical surroundings. "Pretty and well-maintained." "Enchanting." "I always feel safe." "Quiet and laid-back." The town itself is small, but has "good churches, a neat old theater, nice restaurants, and a great sense of community."

Student Body

Embraced by some students, rejected by others, the moniker of a "Grover" is said to describe "a studious person, desiring to be involved in as much as possible while striving to still perform excellently in academics." Furthermore, many here describe themselves as "very type-A." "Most students are extremely conscious of their grades." At the same time, others profess to handle everything with more perspective. "Grove City can be stressful, but only if you let it!" What is universal at Grove City is this: everyone is described as "dedicated, motivated, conscientious, and responsible." Many undergrads "generally have a strong Christian faith and are excited about the opportunities to deepen that faith at college;" however, "people from all walks can further their education, grow relationships, and learn true humility and service." "The unity of the campus body is one of the greatest assets to our school," and Grove City does a "phenomenal job of integrating all freshmen or transfer students."

FINANCIAL AID: 724-458-3300 • E-MAIL: ADMISSIONS@GCC.EDU • WEBSITE: WWW.GCC.EDU

THE PRINCETON REVIEW SAYS

Admissions

Very important factors considered include: GPA, rigor of secondary school record, standardized test scores, application essay, interview, character/personal qualities, level of applicant's interest. *Important factors considered include:* Extracurricular activities, recommendation(s). *Other factors considered include:* Class rank, first generation, geographical residence, state residency, talent/ability, volunteer work, work experience, alumni/ae relations, religious affiliation. SAT or ACT required; ACT with or without Writing component accepted. TOEFL required of all international applicants. *Academic units recommended:* 4 English; 3 mathematics; 3 science; (2 science lab); 3 social studies; 3 foreign language; 2 history.

Financial Aid

Students should submit: Institution's own financial aid form. Regular filing deadline is 4/15. The Princeton Review suggests that all financial aid forms be submitted as soon as possible after January 1. *Need-based scholarships/grants offered:* State scholarships/grants, private scholarships, the school's own gift aid. *Loan aid offered:* state loans, private loans. Institutional employment available. Off-campus job opportunities are good.

The Inside Word

Gaining entrance into Grove City College is difficult and highly competitive. Students must have outstanding personal characteristics, and they need to be prepared for a strenuous but workable course load. Christian values are of utmost importance at GCC, and the school values students who seek out surroundings based on those principles. Interviews and recommendations are highly valued as components of the admission process.

THE SCHOOL SAYS "..."

From the Admissions Office

"A good college education doesn't have to cost a fortune. For decades, Grove City College has offered a quality education at costs among the lowest nationally. Since the 1990s, increased national academic acclaim has come to Grove City College. Grove City College is a place where professors teach; you will not see graduate assistants or teacher's aides in the classroom. Our professors are also active in the total life of the campus. More than 140 student organizations on campus afford opportunity for a wide variety of cocurricular activities. Outstanding scholars and leaders in education, science, and international affairs visit the campus each year. The environment at Grove City College is friendly, secure, and dedicated to high standards."

"There is a fresh spiritual vitality on campus that touches every aspect of your college life. In the classroom, we don't shy away from discussing all points of view, however we adhere to Christ's teaching as relevant guidance for living. Come visit and learn more."

SELECTIVITY

Admissions Rating	87
# of applicants	1,530
% of applicants accepted	81
% of acceptees attending	53
# offered a place on the wait list	221
% accepting a place on wait list	25
% admitted from wait list	49
# of early decision applicants	407
% accepted early decision	82

FRESHMAN PROFILE

Range SAT Critical Reading	542–669
Range SAT Math	537–665
Range ACT Composite	24–29
Minimum paper TOEFL	550
Minimum web-based TOEFL	79
Average HS GPA	3.72
% graduated top 10% of class	41
% graduated top 25% of class	65
% graduated top 50% of class	90

DEADLINES

Early decision	
Deadline	11/15
Notification	12/15
Regular	
Deadline	2/1
Notification	3/15
Nonfall registration?	Yes

APPLICANTS ALSO LOOK AT AND OFTEN PREFER
Pennsylvania State University—University Park; Wheaton College (IL); Hillsdale College

AND RARELY PREFER
Geneva College; Gordon College; Houghton College

FINANCIAL FACTS

Financial Aid Rating	69
Annual tuition	$14,880
Room and board	$8,108
Books and supplies	$1,000
% needy frosh rec. need-based scholarship or grant aid	100
% needy UG rec. need-based scholarship or grant aid	97
% needy frosh rec. non-need-based scholarship or grant aid	10
% needy UG rec. non-need-based scholarship or grant aid	9
% needy frosh rec. need-based self-help aid	53
% needy UG rec. need-based self-help aid	62
% frosh rec. any financial aid	70
% UG rec. any financial aid	71
% UG borrow to pay for school	62
Average cumulative indebtedness	$29,959
% frosh need fully met	10
% ugrads need fully met	9
Average % of frosh need met	55
Average % of ugrad need met	51

GUILFORD COLLEGE

5800 WEST FRIENDLY AVENUE, GREENSBORO, NC 27410 • ADMISSIONS: 336-316-2100 • FAX: 336-316-2954

CAMPUS LIFE
Quality of Life Rating	88
Fire Safety Rating	78
Green Rating	85
Type of school	Private
Affiliation	Quaker
Environment	City

STUDENTS
Total undergrad enrollment	2,166
% male/female	45/55
% frosh from out of state	45
% frosh from public high school	72
% frosh live on campus	95
% ugrads live on campus	77
% African American	25
% Asian	2
% Caucasian	62
% Hispanic	6
% Native American	<1
% international	1
# of countries represented	23

SURVEY SAYS . . .
Political activism is popular
Students are happy
Students are friendly
Students get along with local community

ACADEMICS
Academic Rating	85
% students returning for sophomore year	71
% students graduating within 4 years	49
% students graduating within 6 years	57
Calendar	Semester
Student/faculty ratio	15:1
Profs interesting rating	92
Profs accessible rating	87

Most classes have 10–19 students.
Most lab/discussion sessions have 10–19 students.

MOST POPULAR MAJORS
psychology; criminal justice; business administration and management

STUDENTS SAY "..."

Academics
Guilford's legendarily "accepting culture" arises through the incorporation of a number of core tenets that include "diversity, equality, community, stewardship, etc." The school is "a place where you can express yourself free from judgment," and "impacts every aspect of your life and continues to carry you as part of its family even after you graduate." Students are given the opportunity to make all of their own choices, and the school works at "providing support for those decisions," and heavily promotes the idea "that doing things the hard way is usually worth it."

The Quaker college is known for being green (to put it mildly), and the administration works to raise "student and individual awareness of the environment and everyday life through education and service learning." The level of engagement of the students is matched only by the school's willingness to listen; student involvement is in everything from policy changes to food options, and "can be one person's efforts or many." "I know someone who campaigned for getting coffee in the cafeteria's ice cream selection, and this year we had a trial run that seems to have gone over well," says a sophomore. Still, a few students do think the administration could let up on "parenting the students."

Professors are able to "create an environment that invites discussion of materials from different perspectives" that "[pushes] and [supports] you at the same time." The "intensity of academic learning" means that "your absence in a class does not go unnoticed," unsurprising at a place where teachers are called by their first name ("which is really awesome"). The small scale class sizes "really allow for individual attention and academic growth." Most classrooms are arranged with the desks in a circle and the classes are "highly interactive"; every class "is filled with questions for the class to answer, even simple questions."

Life
Fun at this "socially intriguing" comes in many forms: walking in the woods, hiking, community service, the local art and music scene. "It's always felt like more of a village than an institution," says one student. Relaxation is taken very seriously after a week of hard work (Guilford is "writing heavy" and "the library and its resources are used a great deal"), and "lying down by the lake and playing music or watching movies with friends is almost mandatory." Bars in Greensboro are also an option, but if students can't get there "the school does a good job at hosting activities around campus, which can help the slower weekends." There is admittedly "a lot of weed, but it's totally fine if you aren't into smoking or drinking."

People on this "beautiful" campus are very socially and politically aware, and "someone ...is always planning protests or creating petitions." Food options are a sore spot for Guilford students, and "there's also sometimes an athletic divide." Students are "really active" in groups and organizations, and there is "lots of talk of oppression, gender issues, and race in the social sciences and humanities."

Student Body
This is one "funky community of diverse people," all of whom "seem to share some appreciation for the outdoors and nuttier aspects of life." "Hippies or athletes" covers the majority of the student body (as does "liberal"), and there are many "refreshingly weird individuals" who've "taken their time at Guilford as an opportunity to redefine themselves." "We color outside of the lines in innovative and interesting ways," says one student. Friend groups tend to be in cliques, but are "still very friendly with other groups"; as one junior puts it, "There's a lot of varying interests but some wires tend to be the same across the board... like being culturally aware, or fighting against the oppression of minorities."

FINANCIAL AID: 336-316-2354 • E-MAIL: ADMISSION@GUILFORD.EDU • WEBSITE: WWW.GUILFORD.EDU

THE PRINCETON REVIEW SAYS

Admissions

Very important factors considered include: GPA, rigor of secondary school record, application essay, character/personal qualities. *Important factors considered include:* Class rank, standardized test scores, extracurricular activities, interview, racial/ethnic status, recommendation(s), talent/ability, volunteer work, work experience, level of applicant's interest. *Other factors considered include:* Geographical residence, state residency, alumni/ae relations, SAT or ACT recommended; ACT with or without Writing component accepted. TOEFL required of all international applicants. *Academic units recommended:* 4 English; 3 mathematics; 3 science; 3 social studies; 2 foreign language; 3 history.

Financial Aid

Students should submit: FAFSA. The Princeton Review suggests that all financial aid forms be submitted as soon as possible after January 1. *Need-based scholarships/grants offered:* Federal Pell, SEOG, State scholarships/grants, private scholarships, the school's own gift aid. *Loan aid offered:* Direct Subsidized Stafford Loans, Direct Unsubsidized Stafford Loans, Direct PLUS loans, Federal Perkins Loans. Federal Work-Study Program available. Institutional employment available. Off-campus job opportunities are fair.

The Inside Word

Getting into Guilford College goes beyond the numbers. Guilford is looking for students who demonstrate strong drive and personal motivation. Applicants to the school should have a solid high school record and good extracurricular activities (preferably of the tree-hugging and/or varsity sports variety). While a Quaker connection couldn't hurt, the school is more interested in your character and personal qualities and level of interest in the school. The admissions essay is your chance to make your case.

THE SCHOOL SAYS " . . ."

From the Admissions Office

"Guilford is proud to be included for the twenty-first consecutive year in The Princeton Review's 'Best Colleges' edition. Guilford can best be described by its academic rigor, preparation for graduate school and careers, and its commitment to service in a caring, socially aware and supportive community.

"This is a campus that celebrates all walks of life. Guilford brings together students from many different religious, socioeconomic, geographic, and ethnic backgrounds. You can be yourself here and that's a great feeling. Open-mindedness is embraced, especially in the classrooms, living spaces, and social settings on campus where you will challenge others and be challenged yourself.

"There is no stereotypical Guilford student. Our students have many passions including athletics and intramurals, community service, social justice and multiculturalism. However the bond that ties them together is the academic curriculum that prepares them for life and a career. The Guilford experience is truly a transformative one."

SELECTIVITY

Admissions Rating	72
# of applicants	3,030
% of applicants accepted	68
% of acceptees attending	19

FRESHMAN PROFILE

Range SAT Critical Reading	460–610
Range SAT Math	480–580
Range SAT Writing	450–580
Range ACT Composite	20–26
Minimum paper TOEFL	550
Minimum web-based TOEFL	213
Average HS GPA	3.16
% graduated top 10% of class	11
% graduated top 25% of class	33
% graduated top 50% of class	69

DEADLINES

Early action	
Deadline	11/15
Notification	12/15
Regular	
Priority	11/15
Deadline	2/15
Nonfall registration?	Yes

APPLICANTS ALSO LOOK AT AND OFTEN PREFER

Oberlin College; Haverford College

AND SOMETIMES PREFER

Earlham College; The University of North Carolina at Chapel Hill; Goucher College; Elon University

FINANCIAL FACTS

Financial Aid Rating	75
Annual tuition	$32,090
Room and board	$8,800
Required fees	$380
Books and supplies	$1,350
% needy frosh rec. need-based scholarship or grant aid	98
% needy UG rec. need-based scholarship or grant aid	84
% needy frosh rec. non-need-based scholarship or grant aid	88
% needy UG rec. non-need-based scholarship or grant aid	44
% needy frosh rec. need-based self-help aid	60
% needy UG rec. need-based self-help aid	65
% frosh rec. any financial aid	96
% UG rec. any financial aid	89
% UG borrow to pay for school	77
Average cumulative indebtedness	$24,255
% frosh need fully met	3
% ugrads need fully met	5
Average % of frosh need met	81
Average % of ugrad need met	83

HAMILTON COLLEGE

OFFICE OF ADMISSION, CLINTON, NY 13323 • ADMISSIONS: 315-859-4421 • FAX: 315-859-4457

CAMPUS LIFE
Quality of Life Rating	84
Fire Safety Rating	94
Green Rating	80
Type of school	Private
Affiliation	No Affiliation
Environment	Rural

STUDENTS
Total undergrad enrollment	1,926
% male/female	49/51
% from out of state	69
% frosh from public high school	56
% frosh live on campus	100
% ugrads live on campus	97
# of fraternities (% ugrad men join)	11 (27)
# of sororities (% ugrad women join)	7 (20)
% African American	4
% Asian	7
% Caucasian	62
% Hispanic	8
% Native American	0
% international	5
# of countries represented	45

SURVEY SAYS . . .
Classroom facilities are great
Lab facilities are great
No one cheats
Students are friendly
Athletic facilities are great
Lots of beer drinking
Hard liquor is popular

ACADEMICS
Academic Rating	98
% students returning for sophomore year	94
% students graduating within 4 years	90
% students graduating within 6 years	93
Calendar	Semester
Student/faculty ratio	9:1
Profs interesting rating	94
Profs accessible rating	98
Most classes have 10–19 students.	
Most lab/discussion sessions have 10–19 students.	

MOST POPULAR MAJORS
economics; political science; history

STUDENTS SAY ". . ."
Academics
Upstate New York liberal arts school Hamilton College offers fine academics and an open curriculum that give students "preparation for the future that goes far beyond exam-taking strategies." The focus on writing and speaking, the lack of core requirements, and the small class sizes put a "keen focus on students as unique individuals with different abilities and aspirations." "Hamilton allows you the freedom to be anyone, but gives you the direction to become the best person you can become," says a student. The school's "mix of old-school practices with liberal thinking" allows students to become "true intellectuals beyond the basics of academia." "Hamilton College is all about learning how to think and then conveying those ideas into writing," says a student. The professors at Hamilton are "brilliant but they do not flaunt it and instead defer to class discussions." Professors are also "always available outside of class to discuss anything further." "Their extensive office hours are when you can really connect with them," says one student. In using their "ability to bring classes to life," professors demonstrate their interest in "comprehension of the material beyond grades." The open curriculum allows for classes to be "extremely productive," because "people want to be there learning and talking about what interests them." "I know when I enroll in a class that the people I take that class with are truly interested in the class (just as I am)," says one student. "They aren't there to fulfill a requirement." Though the campus itself is large, the undergraduate population is fewer than 2,000, so class sizes are downright tiny (which is "excellent"), and if you can't get in to a class, "all you have to do is talk to the professors, and they'll usually make room for you." Research opportunities are plentiful, and facilities (such as labs) "are well-equipped." The administration "does what they can to adhere to the needs and wants of the students."

Life
The "beautiful campus" is located in the middle of relatively nowhere, but students are creative in that they "very successfully compensate for our isolated location with themed parties, clubs, and other eclectic activities." Students are "incredibly devoted" to their school work, but they are also devoted to having a good time. "A typical Hamilton student loves to learn on the weekdays, and drink…on the weekends (but gets to bed early enough to study the following afternoon!)" Still, there are plenty of people on campus that prefer to remain sober, though "whether that is a choice or due to lack of confidence in finding parties, I don't know." More often than not, "Hamiltonians aren't strictly about working themselves to death." People who have cars (a huge plus) can go downtown or into New Hartford in their free time, but "most students spend most of their time on campus." Often, students just catch the van that travels around the area and "go to the movies or the mall and just hang out with friends." Hamilton has "a very intellectually stimulating academic environment," and "it is not at all uncommon to find a whole dorm room debating about an economic theory that only one of them actually learned about in class."

Student Body
The typical student at Hamilton was "a top student at his/her high school," and is "well-rounded and involved." While most students are "white and relatively wealthy," there is "a diversity of personalities." There are "virtually no cliques," but people are often characteristically preppy, athletic "light siders," or artsy "dark siders." Everyone is "exceptionally nice," and "people here aren't afraid to be themselves." "We're all nerds in our own different ways, but that ends up being cool," says a student. Hamilton students are "extremely involved" in extracurriculars, and "everyone is passionate about their academics as well as their activities outside the classroom."

FINANCIAL AID: 800-859-4413 • E-MAIL: ADMISSION@HAMILTON.EDU • WEBSITE: WWW.HAMILTON.EDU

THE PRINCETON REVIEW SAYS

Admissions

Very important factors considered include: Class rank, GPA, rigor of secondary school record. *Important factors considered include:* Standardized test scores, application essay, extracurricular activities, interview, recommendation(s), character/personal qualities. *Other factors considered include:* First generation, geographical residence, racial/ethnic status, talent/ability, volunteer work, work experience, alumni/ae relations, level of applicant's interest. SAT and SAT Subject Tests or ACT required; ACT with or without Writing component accepted. TOEFL required of all international applicants. *Academic units recommended:* 4 English; 3 mathematics; 3 science; 3 social studies; 3 foreign language.

Financial Aid

Students should submit: FAFSA, Institution's own financial aid form, CSS/ Financial Aid PROFILE, State aid form, Noncustodial PROFILE, Business/ Farm Supplement. Regular filing deadline is 2/8. The Princeton Review suggests that all financial aid forms be submitted as soon as possible after January 1. *Need-based scholarships/grants offered:* Federal Pell, SEOG, State scholarships/ grants, private scholarships, the school's own gift aid. *Loan aid offered:* Direct Subsidized Stafford Loans, Direct Unsubsidized Stafford Loans, Direct PLUS loans, Federal Perkins Loans, College/university loans from institutional funds Applicants will be notified of awards beginning 4/1. Federal Work-Study Program available. Institutional employment available.

The Inside Word

Similar to any prestigious liberal arts schools, Hamilton takes a well-rounded, personal approach to admissions. They rely heavily on academic achievement and intellectual promise, but in a mission to create a talented and diverse incoming class, admissions officers also strive to attain a complete, accurate profile of each candidate. The admissions team at Hamilton also strongly recommends interviews either on or off campus with alumni volunteers.

THE SCHOOL SAYS " . . ."

From the Admissions Office

"As a national leader for teaching students to write effectively, learn from one another, and think for themselves, Hamilton produces graduates who have the knowledge, skills, and confidence to make their own voices heard on issues of importance to them and their communities.

"A key component of the Hamilton experience is the college's open, yet rigorous, liberal arts curriculum. In place of distribution requirements that are common at most colleges, Hamilton gives its students the freedom and responsibility to choose the courses that reflect their unique interests, plans and commitment to a broad-based education. Faculty advisors help students plan a coherent and highly individualized academic program. In fact, close student-faculty relationships at Hamilton are a distinguishing characteristic of the college, but ultimately students at Hamilton take responsibility for their own future. Part of that future includes a lifelong relationship with the college. Hamilton alumni are exceptionally loyal and passionate supporters of their alma mater. That support manifests itself through internships, speaking engagements, job-shadowing opportunities, and financial donations.

"The intellectual flexibility that distinguishes a Hamilton education extends to the application process. Students are free to choose which standardized tests to submit, based on a specified set of options, so that those who do not test well on the SAT or ACT may decide to submit the results of their AP or SAT Subject Tests. The approach allows students the freedom to decide how to present themselves best to the Committee on Admission."

SELECTIVITY

Admissions Rating	97
# of applicants	5,017
% of applicants accepted	27
% of acceptees attending	36
# offered a place on the wait list	864
% accepting a place on wait list	40
% admitted from wait list	1
# of early decision applicants	601
% accepted early decision	39

FRESHMAN PROFILE

Range SAT Critical Reading	640–730
Range SAT Math	660–740
Range SAT Writing	650–730
Range ACT Composite	29–33
% graduated top 10% of class	72
% graduated top 25% of class	97
% graduated top 50% of class	99

DEADLINES

Early decision	
Deadline	11/15
Notification	12/15
Regular	
Deadline	1/1
Notification	4/1
Nonfall registration?	Yes

APPLICANTS ALSO LOOK AT AND OFTEN PREFER

Middlebury College; Bowdoin College; Dartmouth College; Williams College; Brown University; Amherst College

AND SOMETIMES PREFER

Colgate University; Wesleyan University; Colby College

AND RARELY PREFER

Skidmore College; Union College (NY); Dickinson College

FINANCIAL FACTS

Financial Aid Rating	96
Annual tuition	$47,350
Room and board	$12,150
Required fees	$470
Books and supplies	$1,300
% needy frosh rec. need-based scholarship or grant aid	100
% needy UG rec. need-based scholarship or grant aid	100
% needy frosh rec. non-need-based scholarship or grant aid	0
% needy UG rec. non-need-based scholarship or grant aid	0
% needy frosh rec. need-based self-help aid	79
% needy UG rec. need-based self-help aid	84
% frosh rec. any financial aid	56
% UG rec. any financial aid	50
% UG borrow to pay for school	38
Average cumulative indebtedness	$19,426
% frosh need fully met	100
% ugrads need fully met	100
Average % of frosh need met	100
Average % of ugrad need met	100

HAMPDEN-SYDNEY COLLEGE

PO Box 667, HAMPDEN-SYDNEY, VA 23943-0667 • ADMISSIONS: 434-223-6120 • FAX: 434-223-6346

STUDENTS SAY ". . ."

Academics

The deep tradition of this all-male Virginia institution dates to 1775, and it is reflected in the idea that Hampden-Sydney is seen as "one of the best schools for a stepping stone to business, law and medicine careers." With that in mind, "academics are not easy at Sydney, but you will learn a lot and do well if you work hard." Those academics are provided by a group of "challenging" professors. These professors "strive to get these students on the same level as the professors, themselves, have academically achieved." And that is a high level indeed. "All classes are taught by professors who mostly hold doctorates." The idea is not simply to enforce good grades. Rather, professors teach "in a way that helps students develop" with the goal of wanting "you to succeed outside of college." These "very strict graders" do not lord over their classes—there is a "mutual respect between our outstanding professors and the students"—but "they treat you like adults and hold you to those standards." The "small, intimate setting fosters individualized learning," and also allows educators to "make an effort to know each individual student." The curriculum leans towards "class discussions instead of just listening to (lectures) the whole time," and tradition is important. Students are expected to respect the institution, their professors, but most of all themselves, because educators here "expect the best out of you and want to help you become not only a better student, but a better man."

Life

When studies are as intense as they are here, it may come as no surprise that "work hard, play hard" is a repeated motto. "People mostly think about school during school, and are able to switch over to a party mode once the week is over." Parties mean exactly what you expect. Greek life thrives here, as does tailgating for sporting events, clubs, and just plain hanging out. Some students say there is "not much to do other than party on campus" and that the "neighboring town has almost no options," but others point out "there is a club for everyone." Sports are a major draw—"the students make an effort to go to all sporting events to support our brothers and have a good time"—and so are outdoor activities such as "hunting, fishing, and backpacking." Overall, life at Hampden-Sydney boils down to weeks of intense study and weekends of intense partying and activity.

Student Body

Expect a large number of "white upper or upper-middle class [students] who are typically seen as preppy." No surprise there, as "HSC was voted preppiest college in America." The "conservative, affluent, southern" students of Hampden-Sydney embody a combination of "the characteristics of a gentleman" and the "stereotypical good ol' southern boy." Tradition and brotherhood are important at this all-male school, where those who attend tend to be "chivalrous towards women" and show "a strong sense of brotherhood." This is a party school, but when not "drinking more beer than water" students here "are committed to their studies and want to succeed upon graduation." Being "friendly" and "clean-cut" are typical, and those who don't fit the typical HSC mold "do not fit in well." Students who want to fit in must make an effort "through various activities in clubs, athletics, and classes, as well as weekend social events." And then it is time to get serious. As one student puts it, "A Hampden-Sydney man carries himself well and understands that one must work hard to enjoy things in life."

FINANCIAL AID: 434-223-6119 • E-MAIL: HSAPP@HSC.EDU • WEBSITE: WWW.HSC.EDU

THE PRINCETON REVIEW SAYS

Admissions

Very important factors considered include: GPA, rigor of secondary school record, standardized test scores, application essay, recommendation(s), character/personal qualities. *Important factors considered include:* Class rank, extracurricular activities. *Other factors considered include:* First generation, interview, talent/ability, volunteer work, work experience, level of applicant's interest. SAT or ACT required; SAT and SAT Subject Tests or ACT recommended; ACT with or without Writing component accepted. TOEFL required of all international applicants. *Academic units required:* 4 English; 3 mathematics; 2 science; (1 science lab); 1 social studies; 2 foreign language; 1 history; 3 academic electives. *Academic units recommended:* 4 mathematics; 3 science; 3 foreign language.

Financial Aid

Students should submit: FAFSA, State aid form. The Princeton Review suggests that all financial aid forms be submitted as soon as possible after January 1. *Need-based scholarships/grants offered:* Federal Pell, SEOG, State scholarships/grants, private scholarships, the school's own gift aid. *Loan aid offered:* Direct Subsidized Stafford Loans, Direct Unsubsidized Stafford Loans, Direct PLUS loans, Federal Perkins Loans, College/university loans from institutional funds. Applicants will be notified of awards beginning 3/15. Federal Work-Study Program available. Institutional employment available. Off-campus job opportunities are fair.

The Inside Word

Hampden-Sydney is a school that holds fast to its deep traditions, which in many ways makes the applicant pool largely self-selected. Since a strong percentage of those accepted ultimately choose to enroll, the admissions committee can afford to be highly selective. This means candidates must take the application process more seriously than might be necessary at other schools. That said, strong academic records and a desire to attend this school will often suffice for those attracted to Hampden-Sydney.

THE SCHOOL SAYS "..."

From the Admissions Office

"The spirit of Hampden-Sydney is its sense of community. As one of only 1,120 students, you will be in small classes and find it easy to get extra help or inspiration from professors when you want it. Many of our professors live on campus and enjoy being with students in the snack bar as well as in the classroom. They give you the best, most personal education as possible. A big bonus of small-college life is that everybody is invited to go out for everything, and you can be as much of a leader as you want to be. From athletics to debating to publications to fraternity life, this is part of the process that produces a well-rounded Hampden-Sydney graduate.

"Hampden-Sydney College requires either the SAT or ACT standardized test with essay."

SELECTIVITY

Admissions Rating	81
# of applicants	2,623
% of applicants accepted	55
% of acceptees attending	20

FRESHMAN PROFILE

Range SAT Critical Reading	495–600
Range SAT Math	510–615
Range SAT Writing	480–575
Range ACT Composite	22–27
Minimum paper TOEFL	600
Minimum web-based TOEFL	250
Average HS GPA	3.40
% graduated top 10% of class	13
% graduated top 25% of class	28
% graduated top 50% of class	85

DEADLINES

Early decision	
Deadline	11/15
Notification	12/15
Early action	
Deadline	1/15
Notification	2/15
Regular	
Deadline	3/1
Notification	4/15
Nonfall registration?	Yes

APPLICANTS ALSO LOOK AT AND OFTEN PREFER
Virginia Tech, University of Virginia

AND SOMETIMES PREFER
James Madison University; Sewanee—The University of the South; University of Georgia; University of South Carolina—Columbia; The University of North Carolina at Chapel Hill

AND RARELY PREFER
Randolph-Macon College

FINANCIAL FACTS

Financial Aid Rating	85
Annual tuition	$36,224
Room and board	$11,726
Required fees	$1,128
Books and supplies	$1,298
% needy frosh rec. need-based scholarship or grant aid	100
% needy UG rec. need-based scholarship or grant aid	100
% needy frosh rec. non-need-based scholarship or grant aid	18
% needy UG rec. non-need-based scholarship or grant aid	15
% needy frosh rec. need-based self-help aid	81
% needy UG rec. need-based self-help aid	80
% frosh rec. any financial aid	98
% UG rec. any financial aid	99
% UG borrow to pay for school	60
Average cumulative indebtedness	$28,651
% frosh need fully met	25
% ugrads need fully met	22
Average % of frosh need met	80
Average % of ugrad need met	79

HAMPTON UNIVERSITY

OFFICE OF ADMISSIONS, HAMPTON, VA 23668 • ADMISSIONS: 757-727-5328 • FAX: 757-727-5095

CAMPUS LIFE

Quality of Life Rating	69
Fire Safety Rating	65
Green Rating	60*
Type of school	Private
Affiliation	No Affiliation
Environment	City

STUDENTS

Total undergrad enrollment	3,742
% male/female	36/64
% from out of state	79
% frosh from public high school	90
% frosh live on campus	93
% ugrads live on campus	56
# of fraternities	5
# of sororities	4
% African American	90
% Asian	2
% Caucasian	7
% Hispanic	1
% Native American	<1
% international	1
# of countries represented	33

SURVEY SAYS . . .
Student publications are popular
Great library
Campus feels safe
Frats and sororities are popular

ACADEMICS

Academic Rating	75
% students returning for sophomore year	76
% students graduating within 4 years	43
% students graduating within 6 years	68
Calendar	Semester
Student/faculty ratio	10:1
Profs interesting rating	65
Profs accessible rating	66

Most classes have 20–29 students.
Most lab/discussion sessions have
10–19 students.

MOST POPULAR MAJORS
psychology; business administration; biology

STUDENTS SAY " . . ."

Academics

Virginia's Hampton University is one of the world's top historically black universities, offering students a progressive education in business, the sciences, and the liberal arts. This "school of tradition, family values, and excellent education" is well-known for its focus on STEM programs and its five-year MBA program, and proudly forces its students to be at the top of their game. "My school exudes and strives for a standard of excellence in any and every aspect," says a junior political science major of the oft-quoted motto "The Standard of Excellence".

Professors "are at the top of their field," and the majority of the faculty members provide office hours "where students can have more one-to-one assistance" on lecture topics on which they may need more clarification. "My professors have not only been teachers in the classroom, but in my personal life as well," says a student. "I have been taught how to use the communication and research skills that I have obtained outside of the classroom." In addition, the university provides "a plethora of outside resources" such as paid internships, undergraduate research, and job shadowing opportunities.

The "historically rich" institution is "supportive of its legacy being upheld by all that pass through" while at the same time making individuals aware of their own legacies and "supporting them in their professional and academic endeavors through all available resources." Alumni connections abound in such an environment, and there are plenty of "excellent career planning tools," internships, and careers available to students "during and after their tenure at Hampton." There is "an immense amount of clout and history behind Hampton University's walls." Though the campus is undoubtedly "beautiful" (and sits right on the water), many agree that some of the facilities (especially the dorms) could use renovation. In recent years, three new dorms were constructed and historic halls were modernized.

Life

Hampton does an excellent job of "blending past traditions with modern times," and Homecoming and Spring Fest are two important events for Hampton. On the "closed" campus, there is an "unlimited [number] of activities for students to participate in." During Organization Week, the student center has a two hour "12–2" period, during which "students are able to be social during the day," and many students love to "catch a Friday movie" night there as well, or hang out with friends in the new waterfront dining hall.

Hampton is small and "not a college town." and since "the University is really the only thing around," having a car is useful. Monday through Friday campus life is "mostly academic and extracurricular," with students mostly focused on class and the various clubs that they may be involved in. On the weekends students attend on and off campus parties, or go to " kickbacks," which are "a more low key version of a party." "Student life is lacking as far as dorm life," so many students "often interact with the students from NSU, ODU, and William & Mary." For the most part, "everyone on campus has the same mindset, a unanimous goal, and that's to graduate and strive for a successful life."

Student Body

The typical student here is an African-American "go-getter" who is "trying to make something of themselves." He or she is "poised, considerate, and self-sufficient" and "knows how to act and dress in the appropriate setting and time." "Hampton students have a certain attitude about themselves, you can always tell a Hamptonian. Once you have been Hamptonized, there is no going back," explains one student cryptically. This "driven," "hardworking" crowd gets along fairly well, and there are no issues of isolation "unless one chooses that lifestyle." Students are almost without fail "outgoing and involved in many organizations within the school and the community."

FINANCIAL AID: 757-727-5332 • E-MAIL: ADMIT@HAMPTONU.EDU • WEBSITE: WWW.HAMPTONU.EDU

THE PRINCETON REVIEW SAYS

Admissions

Very important factors considered include: GPA, rigor of secondary school record, application essay, first generation, character/personal qualities, level of applicant's interest. *Important factors considered include:* Class rank, standardized test scores, recommendation(s). *Other factors considered include:* Extracurricular activities, talent/ability, volunteer work, alumni/ae relations, TOEFL required of all international applicants. *Academic units required:* 4 English; 3 mathematics; 2 science; (2 science lab); 2 social studies; 6 academic electives. *Academic units recommended:* 2 foreign language.

Financial Aid

Students should submit: FAFSA. The Princeton Review suggests that all financial aid forms be submitted as soon as possible after January 1. *Need-based scholarships/grants offered:* Federal Pell, SEOG, State scholarships/grants, private scholarships, the school's own gift aid, federal nursing scholarships. *Loan aid offered:* Direct Subsidized Stafford Loans, Direct Unsubsidized Stafford Loans, Direct PLUS loans, Federal Perkins Loans, Federal Nursing Loans. Federal Work-Study Program available. Off-campus job opportunities are excellent.

The Inside Word

Hampton University allows for early action admissions, meaning that students can receive an early decision without having to commit to attending the school. Around a quarter of HU's applicant pool pursues this option. You would be wise to follow suit; the school is bound to be more lenient early in the process than later, when it has already admitted many qualified students.

THE SCHOOL SAYS " . . ."

From the Admissions Office

"Hampton attempts to provide the environment and structures most conducive to the intellectual, emotional, and aesthetic enlargement of the lives of its members. The university gives priority to effective teaching and scholarly research while placing the student at the center of its planning. Hampton will ask you to look inwardly at your own history and culture and examine your relationship to the aspirations and development of the world."

SELECTIVITY

Admissions Rating	87
# of applicants	15,337
% of applicants accepted	36
% of acceptees attending	17

FRESHMAN PROFILE

Range SAT Critical Reading	460–550
Range SAT Math	460–550
Range ACT Composite	18–23
Minimum paper TOEFL	525
Minimum web-based TOEFL	214
Average HS GPA	3.30
% graduated top 10% of class	20
% graduated top 25% of class	45
% graduated top 50% of class	89

DEADLINES

Early action	
Deadline	11/1
Notification	12/31
Regular	
Priority	3/1
Nonfall registration?	Yes

APPLICANTS ALSO LOOK AT AND OFTEN PREFER

Florida A&M University; Spelman College

AND SOMETIMES PREFER

Howard University; University of Maryland; College Park; Virginia Tech

FINANCIAL FACTS

Financial Aid Rating	76
Annual tuition	$18,618
Room and board	$9,230
Required fees	$2,106
Books and supplies	$1,100
% needy frosh rec. need-based scholarship or grant aid	91
% needy UG rec. need-based scholarship or grant aid	92
% needy frosh rec. non-need-based scholarship or grant aid	63
% needy UG rec. non-need-based scholarship or grant aid	47
% needy frosh rec. need-based self-help aid	79
% needy UG rec. need-based self-help aid	63
% frosh rec. any financial aid	63
% UG rec. any financial aid	55
% UG borrow to pay for school	98
Average cumulative indebtedness	$33,573
% frosh need fully met	51
% ugrads need fully met	51
Average % of frosh need met	50
Average % of ugrad need met	51

HANOVER COLLEGE

PO Box 108, Hanover, IN 47243-0108 • Admissions: 800-213-2178 • Fax: 812-866-7098

CAMPUS LIFE

Quality of Life Rating	79
Fire Safety Rating	90
Green Rating	77
Type of school	Private
Affiliation	Presbyterian
Environment	Rural

STUDENTS

Total undergrad enrollment	1,159
% male/female	43/57
% from out of state	31
% frosh from public high school	77
% frosh live on campus	98
% ugrads live on campus	95
# of fraternities (% ugrad men join)	4 (44)
# of sororities (% ugrad women join)	4 (29)
% African American	4
% Asian	1
% Caucasian	82
% Hispanic	2
% Native American	<1
% international	5
# of countries represented	19

SURVEY SAYS . . .

Lab facilities are great
Students are friendly
Campus feels safe
Athletic facilities are great
Lots of beer drinking
Frats and sororities are popular

ACADEMICS

Academic Rating	93
% students returning for sophomore year	81
% students graduating within 4 years	68
% students graduating within 6 years	72
Calendar	Semester
Student/faculty ratio	12:1
Profs interesting rating	93
Profs accessible rating	89
Most classes have 10–19 students.	

MOST POPULAR MAJORS
psychology; elementary education; biology

STUDENTS SAY ". . ."

Academics

Armed with a "beautiful campus [that lies] right beside the Ohio River," Hanover College helps to ease the transition to higher education by welcoming undergrads into a "close-knit community." Friendly faces abound and everyone "from the students to the professors to the maintenance workers greet you with a smile and a hello." Hanover is especially "strong in the [hard] sciences" as evidenced by the fact that "[its] students [have] a high acceptance rate into med-school." And a cheeky bio major highlights an added bonus, "[Hanover] is also one of only a few undergrad schools with a human cadaver lab." The Spanish and environmental science programs receive high marks as well. Importantly, small classes are the norm here; most "range from 8–20 students." This virtually guarantees that undergrads are never "just…a number to [their] professors." Moreover, students truly love that there are "no teaching assistants." And they are continually awed by the fact that professors, "offer to let you drop by their houses for homework help or just to chat." A communications major adds, "They don't want you to fail and they push you to reach your full potential." In short, teachers here are "amazing." Finally, a psychology major gleefully summarizes her experiences, "Since Hanover is small, there are a million and one opportunities for leadership positions, community involvement, starting student organizations, organizing a campus wide event. At Hanover, you really can do anything you set your mind to."

Life

Education takes top priority at Hanover. Therefore, "during the week students are very focused on their academic work." However, once the weekend rolls around, "students are willing to have fun." Of course, the campus is frequently buzzing with activity and there's always some event of which to take advantage. An amazed and delighted freshman shares, "We have concerts put on by the music department and by groups brought to our campus, performances like Second City (an amazing comedy group), and parties [hosted] by various clubs, sororities or fraternities. Clubs are also always meeting and [sponsoring] their own activities…I don't think anyone could be bored here." Undergrads admit that there's somewhat of a drinking culture at Hanover. Indeed, "every weekend there always seems to be a party somewhere; either at one of the Frat houses or the themed houses." Fortunately, no student is alienated if they choose not to partake. Additionally, undergrads love to participate in the "many traditions that take place on campus throughout the year like the first snowfall midnight snow ball fight and the spring term whiffle ball tournament." Lastly, "making trips to historic downtown Madison seems to be on everyone's agenda—be it catching a $5 movie at the Ohio Theatre or grabbing a world-famous hamburger from Hinkle's Sandwich Shop and Family Restaurant!"

Student Body

Hanover students think very highly of their peers. They readily assert that their classmates are "well-rounded, smart and very friendly." Moreover, they understand how to deftly "balance a healthy social life with a strong academic focus." Of course, beyond these general commonalities, many undergrads insist that there is no typical Hanover student. As one sophomore stresses, "Every student is unique. I have never seen so many different kinds of people in one place. There aren't really cliques here, but it works. Everyone gets along in one big ball of weirdness. But then again, aren't we all weird? It keeps things interesting." After reading that sentiment, it should come as no shock that students here also tend to be "open-minded," "easy-going" and "nice to everyone." A pleased elementary education major further explains, "Hanover brings out the best in us. The upperclassmen are encouraging and friendly. Most students are very outgoing by the time they reach their sophomore or junior years. Everyone who makes an effort fits in."

HANOVER COLLEGE

FINANCIAL AID: 812-866-7029 • E-MAIL: ADMISSION@HANOVER.EDU • WEBSITE: WWW.HANOVER.EDU

THE PRINCETON REVIEW SAYS
Admissions

Very important factors considered include: Class rank, GPA, rigor of secondary school record. *Important factors considered include:* Standardized test scores, recommendation(s), talent/ability. *Other factors considered include:* Application essay, extracurricular activities, first generation, geographical residence, interview, racial/ethnic status, state residency, volunteer work, work experience, alumni/ae relations, character/personal qualities, level of applicant's interest. SAT or ACT required; ACT with Writing component recommended. TOEFL required of all international applicants. *Academic units required:* 4 English; 3 mathematics; 3 science; (2 science lab); 2 social studies; 2 foreign language; 2 history; 2 academic electives. *Academic units recommended:* 4 English; 4 mathematics; 4 science; (3 science lab); 3 social studies; 4 foreign language; 3 history; 3 academic electives; 1 visual/performing arts.

Financial Aid

Students should submit: FAFSA. Regular filing deadline is 3/1. The Princeton Review suggests that all financial aid forms be submitted as soon as possible after January 1. *Need-based scholarships/grants offered:* Federal Pell, SEOG, State scholarships/grants, private scholarships, the school's own gift aid. *Loan aid offered:* Direct Subsidized Stafford Loans, Direct Unsubsidized Stafford Loans, Direct PLUS loans, College/university loans from institutional funds. Applicants will be notified of awards beginning 3/1. Institutional employment available. Off-campus job opportunities are fair.

The Inside Word

Admissions officers at Hanover take a holistic approach to the application process. Therefore, you can't cut any corners; everything from GPA to extracurricular activities will be closely evaluated. Overall, the committee is on the lookout for motivated students who will flourish at Hanover. It is recommended that interested candidates apply for (non-binding) early admission.

THE SCHOOL SAYS "..."
From the Admissions Office

"Since our founding in 1827, we have been committed to providing students with a personal, rigorous, and well-rounded liberal arts education. Part of the college search process is finding that school that proves to be a good match. For those who see the value in an education that demands engagement and who see college as a time for exploration and involvement, they will find that Hanover is all they could hope for and more.

"The admission process serves as an introduction to the personal education that students receive at Hanover College. Every application is considered individually with emphasis being placed on a student's high school curriculum and the student's academic performance in that curriculum. While we realize that not every high school has the same course offerings, we expect students to have selected a college preparatory curriculum as challenging as possible within his or her particular high school or academic setting.

"Hanover College accepts both the SAT and ACT. Students taking the ACT are required to take the optional writing section. For students who have taken one or both of the tests multiple times, we will use the highest sub scores when calculating a student's score on either test for admission and scholarship purposes."

SELECTIVITY
Admissions Rating	85
# of applicants	3,174
% of applicants accepted	67
% of acceptees attending	16

FRESHMAN PROFILE
Range SAT Critical Reading	490–600
Range SAT Math	510–600
Range SAT Writing	480–570
Range ACT Composite	23–28
Minimum paper TOEFL	550
Minimum web-based TOEFL	80
Average HS GPA	3.67
% graduated top 10% of class	32
% graduated top 25% of class	66
% graduated top 50% of class	95

DEADLINES
Early action	
Deadline	12/1
Notification	12/20
Regular	
Deadline	3/1
Nonfall registration?	Yes

APPLICANTS ALSO LOOK AT AND OFTEN PREFER
DePauw University

AND SOMETIMES PREFER
Indiana University—Bloomington; Miami University; Centre College; Wittenberg University; Wabash College

AND RARELY PREFER
Kenyon College; Earlham College

FINANCIAL FACTS
Financial Aid Rating	81
Annual tuition	$32,423
Room and board	$10,050
Required fees	$600
Books and supplies	$1,200
% needy frosh rec. need-based scholarship or grant aid	100
% needy UG rec. need-based scholarship or grant aid	100
% needy frosh rec. non-need-based scholarship or grant aid	20
% needy UG rec. non-need-based scholarship or grant aid	13
% needy frosh rec. need-based self-help aid	75
% needy UG rec. need-based self-help aid	85
% frosh rec. any financial aid	83
% UG rec. any financial aid	81
% UG borrow to pay for school	81
Average cumulative indebtedness	$27,666
% frosh need fully met	25
% ugrads need fully met	20
Average % of frosh need met	79
Average % of ugrad need met	79

THE BEST 379 COLLEGES ■ 285

HARVARD COLLEGE

86 BRATTLE STREET, CAMBRIDGE, MA 02138 • ADMISSIONS: 617-495-1551 • FAX: 617-495-8821

STUDENTS SAY ". . ."

Academics

Bully to those who get the chance to be a part of the "dynamic universe" that is Harvard College, who find themselves in an "amazing irresistible hell" that pushes them to the extremes of their intellect and ability. Unsurprisingly, the legendarily "very difficult" school attracts some of the country's most promising youth, who rise to the occasion in almost every aspect of their life on campus, not just the classroom. Harvard's recent financial aid enhancements have increased the number of applications by a landslide, but even after getting past the admissions hurdle, "people find ways to make everything (especially clubs and even partying) competitive." Happily, this streak is more of a "latent competition," as there are more than enough opportunity and resources to go around. "It is impossible to 'get the most out of Harvard' because Harvard offers so much," says one student. Much like the students, the professors at this "beautiful, fun, historic, and academically alive place" in Cambridge, Massachusetts, are among "the brightest minds in the world," and "the level of achievement is unbelievable." Some of the larger introductory classes are taught by teaching fellows (TFs), meaning "you do have to go to office hours to get to know your big lecture class professors on a personal level," but once your figurative underclass dues are paid, the access to "incredible" and "every so often, fantastic" professors is perfectly within reach. Top it off with Grade-A internship and employment opportunities, a good old alumni network, and a crimson pedigree for your résumé, and you may just end up agreeing with the Harvard student who refers to his experience as "rewarding beyond anything else I've ever done." Though the administration can be "waaaaay out of touch with students" and "reticent to change," it at least "does a good job of watching over its freshmen through extensive advising programs," and students all have faith that their best interests are being kept in mind.

Life

Cambridge and Boston are nothing if not college towns, and students never lack for options if they just want to "go see a play, a concert, hit up a party, go to the movies, or dine out." Students quickly learn when to hit the books and when to hit the streets, so "studying becomes routine." "There is a vibrant social atmosphere on campus and between students and the local community." As one student puts it, "Boredom does not exist here. There are endless opportunities and endless passionate people to do them with." "Basically, if you want to do it, Harvard either has it or has the money to give to you so you can start it." "Partying in a more traditional setting is available at Harvard, but is not a prevalent aspect of the school's social life. While there is a pub on campus that provides an excellent venue to hang out and play a game of pool or have a reasonably priced drink," and parties happen on weekends at Harvard's finals clubs, there's no real pressure for students to partake if they're not interested.

Student Body

Much as you might expect, ambition and achievement are the ties that bind at Harvard, and "Everyone is great for one reason or another," says a student. Most every student can be summed up with the same statement: "Works really hard. Doesn't sleep. Involved in a million extracurriculars." Diversity is found in all aspects of life, from ethnicities to religion to ideology, and "there is a lot of tolerance and acceptance at Harvard for individuals of all races, religions, socioeconomic backgrounds, life styles, etc."

FINANCIAL AID: 617-495-1581 • E-MAIL: COLLEGE@FAS.HARVARD.EDU • WEBSITE: WWW.COLLEGE.HARVARD.EDU

THE PRINCETON REVIEW SAYS

Admissions

Other factors considered include: GPA, rigor of secondary school record, standardized test scores, application essay, extracurricular activities, first generation, geographical residence, interview, racial/ethnic status, recommendation(s), talent/ability, volunteer work, work experience, alumni/ae relations, character/personal qualities. SAT and SAT Subject Tests or ACT required; ACT with Writing component required. *Academic units recommended:* 4 English; 4 mathematics; 4 science; 3 social studies; 4 foreign language; 2 history.

Financial Aid

Students should submit: FAFSA, CSS/Financial Aid PROFILE. Regular filing deadline is 2/1. The Princeton Review suggests that all financial aid forms be submitted as soon as possible after January 1. *Need-based scholarships/grants offered:* Federal Pell, SEOG, State scholarships/grants, private scholarships, the school's own gift aid. *Loan aid offered:* Direct Subsidized Stafford Loans, Direct Unsubsidized Stafford Loans, Direct PLUS loans, Federal Perkins Loans, College/university loans from institutional funds. Applicants will be notified of awards beginning 4/1. Federal Work-Study Program available. Institutional employment available. Off-campus job opportunities are excellent.

The Inside Word

It just doesn't get any tougher than this. Candidates to Harvard face dual obstacles—an awe-inspiring applicant pool and, as a result, admissions standards that defy explanation in quantifiable terms. Harvard denies admission to the vast majority, and virtually all of them are top students. It all boils down to splitting hairs, which is quite hard to explain and even harder for candidates to understand. Rather than being as detailed and direct as possible about the selection process and criteria, Harvard keeps things close to the vest—before, during, and after. They even refuse to admit that being from lesser populated states like South Dakota is an advantage. Thus the admissions process does more to intimidate candidates than to empower them. Moving to a common application seemed to be a small step in the right direction, but with the current explosion of early decision applicants and a super-high yield of enrollees, things aren't likely to change dramatically.

THE SCHOOL SAYS "..."

From the Admissions Office

"The admissions committee looks for energy, ambition, and the capacity to make the most of opportunities. Academic ability and preparation are important, and so is intellectual curiosity—but many of the strongest applicants have significant, non-academic interests and accomplishments, as well. There is no formula for admission, and applicants are considered carefully, with attention to future promise.

"Freshman applicants may submit the SAT. The ACT with writing component is also accepted. All students must also submit three SAT Subject Tests of their choosing."

SELECTIVITY

Admissions Rating	99
# of applicants	35,023
% of applicants accepted	6
% of acceptees attending	81

FRESHMAN PROFILE

Range SAT Critical Reading	700–800
Range SAT Math	710–800
Range SAT Writing	710–800
Range ACT Composite	32–35
Average HS GPA	4.04
% graduated top 10% of class	95
% graduated top 25% of class	99
% graduated top 50% of class	100

DEADLINES

Early action	
Deadline	11/1
Notification	12/16
Regular	
Deadline	1/1
Notification	4/1
Nonfall registration?	No

FINANCIAL FACTS

Financial Aid Rating	91
Annual tuition	$38,891
Room and board	$14,115
Required fees	$2,443
% needy frosh rec. need-based scholarship or grant aid	100
% needy UG rec. need-based scholarship or grant aid	99
% needy frosh rec. non-need-based scholarship or grant aid	0
% needy UG rec. non-need-based scholarship or grant aid	0
% needy frosh rec. need-based self-help aid	72
% needy UG rec. need-based self-help aid	84
% frosh rec. any financial aid	77
% UG rec. any financial aid	72
% UG borrow to pay for school	26
Average cumulative indebtedness	$12,560
% frosh need fully met	100
% ugrads need fully met	100
Average % of frosh need met	100
Average % of ugrad need met	100

HARVEY MUDD COLLEGE

301 PLATT BOULEVARD, CLAREMONT, CA 91711-5990 • ADMISSIONS: 909-621-8011 • FAX: 909-621-8360

CAMPUS LIFE
Quality of Life Rating	89
Fire Safety Rating	74
Green Rating	75
Type of school	Private
Affiliation	No Affiliation
Environment	Town

STUDENTS
Total undergrad enrollment	779
% male/female	56/44
% from out of state	63
% frosh from public high school	67
% frosh live on campus	100
% ugrads live on campus	98
% African American	1
% Asian	16
% Caucasian	43
% Hispanic	5
% Native American	<1
% international	6
# of countries represented	18

SURVEY SAYS . . .
Students always studying
Students are happy
Lab facilities are great
Internships are widely available
School is well run
No one cheats
Students are friendly
Easy to get around campus

ACADEMICS
Academic Rating	96
% students returning for sophomore year	98
% students graduating within 4 years	84
% students graduating within 6 years	88
Calendar	Semester
Student/faculty ratio	9:1
Profs interesting rating	98
Profs accessible rating	97

Most classes have 10–19 students.
Most lab/discussion sessions have 10–19 students.

MOST POPULAR MAJORS
engineering; computer and information science; mathematics

STUDENTS SAY ". . ."

Academics

Harvey Mudd College, one of the five Claremont Colleges in Southern California's Inland Empire, "is a small science and math school with a quirky community that is the perfect fit for those who are serious about both their technical studies and having an indefinably strange yet amazing time." With "an excellent program in the sciences and engineering," strong undergraduate research opportunities, and "a very high percentage of students [who] go to graduate school," Harvey Mudd "is unique and offers a personalized education that you can't get at a larger technical university." While the rigorous academics "can be very stressful for some," most students are quick to emphasize the support provided by professors and the student body. "The academic experience is heightened by the students…who act cooperatively rather than competitively to conquer the material rather than each other." This collaborative atmosphere is created in large part by the respected honor code, which students say "defines us and allows us to have take-home finals [and] unproctored tests." "The trust the faculty has for the students gives us a sense of responsibility, and thus everyone lives up to expectations." Students trust the faculty, as well. "I love the professors here," one student says (echoing the sentiments of many). "They are all brilliant and extremely accessible. Most of them know my name and will stop to talk any time." "Lectures and office hours are both amazing! Professors really want you to understand the material." Overall, students say their lives at Harvey Mudd are "tons of work, but really fun."

Life

Because "Harvey Mudd is a highly academic school, a lot of time is spent doing homework and studying." Students manage to find time for fun, though, even at the expense of some shut-eye: "Many people are sleep-deprived but happy in general." "Community is such a big part of Harvey Mudd, people spend a lot of time with each other," and there are many niches within the larger community. "Every dorm has a unique personality, and what people do for fun is different for each person." "Some are devoted to video games and the more classic 'nerd' activities. Some groups are devoted to drinking and partying a ton. There is a wide spectrum of unique dorm communities represented." "One can easily find groups to play sports or video games with, take on carpentry or other independent construction or engineering projects, start an afternoon game of bocce ball or croquet, compete in the fiercely competitive CMS intramural water polo league, and of course, help in the construction of the campus-wide Rube Goldberg Machine, to name a few popular activities." "CAP (Committee for Activities Planning) subsidizes concert tickets, sporting event tickets, ski trips, and other events" if at least eight Mudders plan to attend. "Dorms throw some kick-ass parties," "taking great care to make them fun for people who don't drink as well." Favorites include "Casemas," when "we import five tons of snow to celebrate winter," and "Slippery When Wet" when students "construct decks to support hundreds of dancing people" and then invite the other Claremont Colleges to test their strength over a flooded courtyard.

Student Body

"We are nerds," Mudders tell us, "and we embrace it." They also describe themselves as "outgoing, quirky, and fun but very studious." Students are united by "a brimming passion for science and a love of knowledge for its own sake." "All students are exceptionally intelligent and are able to perform their work in a professional manner." Beyond that, there's "a really diverse group of personalities" at Mudd, who are "not afraid to show their true colors" and who all have "a unique sense of humor." Students say they "are all friendly, smart, and talented, which brings us together. Upperclassmen look out for underclassmen, and students tend to bond together easily over difficult homework." In such a welcoming community, "students primarily fit in by not fitting in—wearing pink pirate hats or skateboarding while playing harmonica or practicing unicycle jousting are all good ways to fit in perfectly."

FINANCIAL AID: 909-621-8055 • E-MAIL: ADMISSION@HMC.EDU • WEBSITE: WWW.HMC.EDU

THE PRINCETON REVIEW SAYS

Admissions

Very important factors considered include: GPA, rigor of secondary school record, application essay, recommendation(s), talent/ability, character/personal qualities. *Important factors considered include:* Class rank, standardized test scores, extracurricular activities, first generation, level of applicant's interest. *Other factors considered include:* Geographical residence, interview, racial/ethnic status, state residency, volunteer work, work experience, alumni/ae relations. SAT and SAT Subject Tests or ACT required; ACT with Writing component required. TOEFL required of all international applicants. *Academic units required:* 4 English; 4 mathematics; 3 science; 1 history. *Academic units recommended:* 4 English; 4 mathematics; 4 science; (2 science lab); 2 social studies; 2 foreign language; 2 history.

Financial Aid

Students should submit: FAFSA, CSS/Financial Aid PROFILE, State aid form, Noncustodial PROFILE, Business/Farm Supplement. Regular filing deadline is 2/1. The Princeton Review suggests that all financial aid forms be submitted as soon as possible after January 1. *Need-based scholarships/grants offered:* Federal Pell, SEOG, State scholarships/grants, private scholarships, the school's own gift aid. *Loan aid offered:* Direct Subsidized Stafford Loans, Direct Unsubsidized Stafford Loans, Direct PLUS loans, Federal Perkins Loans, College/university loans from institutional funds. Applicants will be notified of awards beginning 4/1. Federal Work-Study Program available. Institutional employment available. Off-campus job opportunities are excellent.

The Inside Word

There's little mystery to the admissions process at Harvey Mudd College, but there's a lot of competition. Like most top-tier science, math, and engineering schools, Harvey Mudd considers far more qualified applicants than it can accommodate in its incoming class. Load up on science classes, don't neglect your English courses or extracurriculars, give the application everything you've got, and accept the fact that being perfectly qualified to attend this school is no guarantee of admission.

THE SCHOOL SAYS "..."

From the Admissions Office

"HMC is a wonderfully unusual combination of a liberal arts college and research institute. Our students love math and science, want to live and learn deeply in an intimate climate of cooperation and trust, thrive on innovation and discovery, and enjoy rigorous coursework in arts, humanities, and social sciences in addition to a technical curriculum. At least a year of research or our innovative clinic program is required (or guaranteed, if you prefer). The resources at HMC are astounding, and all are accessible to undergraduates: labs, shops, work areas, and most importantly, faculty. You'll find the professors and student body stimulating and supportive—they'll challenge you inside and outside the classroom, and share your love of learning and collaboration. They'll also share your love of fun and sense of humor (math jokes and all). In addition, we benefit from the unique consortium that is the Claremont Colleges.

In the final analysis, our graduates are prepared well for whatever their next steps will be. They can see relationships between disparate fields of study and investigation, are resourceful, know how to work in teams, and are able to articulate their ideas to both lay-people and specialized experts. A wide range of companies are eager to hire our seniors, and HMC sends the highest proportion of graduates to Ph.D. programs of any undergraduate college in the country."

SELECTIVITY

Admissions Rating	99
# of applicants	3,336
% of applicants accepted	19
% of acceptees attending	31
# offered a place on the wait list	501
% accepting a place on wait list	47
% admitted from wait list	10
# of early decision applicants	315
% accepted early decision	20

FRESHMAN PROFILE

Range SAT Critical Reading	680–770
Range SAT Math	740–800
Range SAT Writing	680–760
Range ACT Composite	33–35
Minimum paper TOEFL	600
Minimum web-based TOEFL	100
% graduated top 10% of class	96
% graduated top 25% of class	100
% graduated top 50% of class	100

DEADLINES

Early decision I (Early Decision II)	
Deadline	11/15 (1/1)
Notification	12/15 (2/15)
Regular	
Deadline	1/1
Notification	4/1
Nonfall registration?	No

APPLICANTS ALSO LOOK AT AND OFTEN PREFER

California Institute of Technology; Massachusetts Institute of Technology; Stanford University; Harvard College; Princeton University

AND SOMETIMES PREFER

Cornell University; University of California—Berkeley; University of California—Los Angeles

AND RARELY PREFER

University of California—San Diego

FINANCIAL FACTS

Financial Aid Rating	96
Annual tuition	$44,159
Room and board	$14,471
Required fees	$383
Books and supplies	$800
% needy frosh rec. need-based scholarship or grant aid	96
% needy UG rec. need-based scholarship or grant aid	97
% needy frosh rec. non-need-based scholarship or grant aid	41
% needy UG rec. non-need-based scholarship or grant aid	42
% needy frosh rec. need-based self-help aid	67
% needy UG rec. need-based self-help aid	77
% UG borrow to pay for school	48
Average cumulative indebtedness	$24,194
% frosh need fully met	100
% ugrads need fully met	100
Average % of frosh need met	100
Average % of ugrad need met	100

HAVERFORD COLLEGE

370 WEST LANCASTER AVENUE, HAVERFORD, PA 19041 • ADMISSIONS: 610-896-1350 • FAX: 610-896-1338

CAMPUS LIFE
Quality of Life Rating	95
Fire Safety Rating	79
Green Rating	92
Type of school	Private
Affiliation	No Affiliation
Environment	Town

STUDENTS
Total undergrad enrollment	1,187
% male/female	48/52
% from out of state	87
% frosh live on campus	100
% ugrads live on campus	98
% African American	6
% Asian	7
% Caucasian	65
% Hispanic	9
% Native American	<1
% international	6
# of countries represented	39

SURVEY SAYS . . .
Students are happy
Lab facilities are great
No one cheats
Students are friendly
Diverse student types on campus
Campus feels safe
Athletic facilities are great
Lots of beer drinking
Active student government

ACADEMICS
Academic Rating	97
% students returning for sophomore year	98
% students graduating within 4 years	91
% students graduating within 6 years	93
Calendar	Semester
Student/faculty ratio	9:1
Profs interesting rating	92
Profs accessible rating	96

Most classes have 10–19 students.
Most lab/discussion sessions have fewer than 10 students.

MOST POPULAR MAJORS
biology; English language and literature; psychology

STUDENTS SAY ". . ."

Academics

Founded in 1833, Haverford College in Pennsylvania is "small, but exceptionally vibrant and engaging," offering a "solid academic experience" under one of the country's oldest and most revered honor codes. Though founded by Quakers, the school is nonsectarian, but the community aspect of its founders remains, creating what one student calls "a challenging, interesting environment with the best people I know." The teacher education program is one of the most notable, but there is a strong emphasis on writing and a "breadth of amazing programs" for everyone else. The real love affair is with Haverford's "awesome, invested" professors, who "lead a group of idealistic students to point—but never force—us into a better way of thinking." They want to put in the time to get to know you, and the small size of the school "allows for plenty of opportunities for collaborating with faculty and staff and building a relationship." "You are more than just a face in a classroom of many; you are a unique person that has something to offer," says a student. "My 'big intro lecture course' has forty-one students," says another. "My professor still knows me by name, and we have long conversations when we pass on Founder's Green." The school's learning environment stresses "engaging in hard and honest conversations with your peers," and "students have a lot of power" through their roles in the administration of the college. "I love the amount of independence and autonomy [the school] gives to its students," says a student. Because of the kind of student this attracts, "we wind up with a really conscientious student body invested in the school." The resources available to students here are incredible, as well. You can get "credit for research" (there is plenty of research here in every department), and if you want to go off campus for research, "you can get funding for that as well."

Life

The culture of "trust, concern, and respect" created by the Honor Code carries over into the rest of this "awesome, at times idiosyncratic, place where community thrives and cliques are very loose if existent at all." "The honor code unifies everyone." "Being able to take an exam in your own room, sitting relaxed on your bed because your professor trusts you not to look at your books is one of the luxuries of being here," says a student. People study hard here, but they take a break over the weekend at a party or two "before cracking the books again. Athletics are also "really important" for much of the student body—most here are athletic, even if it's not at a varsity level—and some of the male sports teams "function like fraternities" (which do not exist at HC). Because it's a small place, "sometimes it feels like everyone knows your business," but everyone is so insanely nice that "the social scene is great" and the only thing you'll hear complaints about is the food. Students govern themselves and the happenings at the school through the "Plenaries" that happen twice a year, when the majority of the student body must be present. New York and Philadelphia are both easily accessible by train, and "Suburban Square (the local outdoor shopping center) is a great place to hang out, get coffee, or even go shopping."

Student Body

Everyone is "passionate," "people are always up for intellectual discussion," and "everyone works very hard." Students here were all motivated enough to get in and "want to succeed for themselves and not to appease others." Students describe other students as having "hearts of gold and giant brains that they put to use to change the world for the better." "It's a small school full of nice kids—not naive (well, sometimes naive), just genuinely compassionate and interested in other people, whether or not that's 'cool,'" says a student. Though all are bound by "intellectual passion and interests outside of academics," diversity otherwise on campus "lacks a little." Still, "the great thing about Haverford is that, although we have a variety of students from all different social circles, everyone is a touch awkward." This is a fact that the "nerdy and ridiculously friendly" students embrace. "I feel like I could potentially become friends with anyone on campus," says a student.

FINANCIAL AID: 610-896-1350 • E-MAIL: ADMISSION@HAVERFORD.EDU • WEBSITE: WWW.HAVERFORD.EDU

THE PRINCETON REVIEW SAYS

Admissions

Very important factors considered include: GPA, rigor of secondary school record, application essay, extracurricular activities, recommendation(s), character/personal qualities. *Important factors considered include:* Class rank, standardized test scores, talent/ability, volunteer work, work experience. *Other factors considered include:* First generation, geographical residence, interview, racial/ethnic status, alumni/ae relations, level of applicant's interest. SAT I and any 2 SAT Subject Tess or ACT with Writing component required. TOEFL or IELTS required of students whose first language is not English. *Academic units recommended:* 4 English; 3 mathematics; 3 science; 2 social studies; 3 foreign language; 3 history.

Financial Aid

Students should submit: FAFSA, CSS/Financial Aid PROFILE, Noncustodial PROFILE, Business/Farm Supplement. Regular filing deadline is 2/1. The Princeton Review suggests that all financial aid forms be submitted as soon as possible after January 1. *Need-based scholarships/grants offered:* Federal Pell, SEOG, State scholarships/grants, the school's own gift aid. *Loan aid offered:* Direct Subsidized Stafford Loans, Direct Unsubsidized Stafford Loans, Direct PLUS loans, Federal Perkins Loans. Applicants will be notified of awards beginning 4/1. Federal Work-Study Program available. Institutional employment available. Off-campus job opportunities are good.

The Inside Word

Haverford's applicant pool is an impressive and competitive lot (only about one-quarter of applicants get in). Intellectual curiosity is paramount, and applicants are expected to keep a demanding academic schedule in high school. Additionally, the college places a high value on ethics, as evidenced by its honor code. The admissions office seeks students who will reflect and promote Haverford's ideals.

THE SCHOOL SAYS ". . ."

From the Admissions Office

"Haverford strives to be a college in which integrity, honesty, and concern for others are dominant forces. The college does not have many formal rules; rather, it offers an opportunity for students to govern their affairs and conduct themselves with respect and concern for others. Each student is expected to adhere to the honor code as it is adopted each year by the Students' Association. Haverford's Quaker roots show most clearly in the relationship of faculty and students, in the emphasis on integrity, in the interaction of the individual and the community, and through the college's concern for the uses to which its students put their expanding knowledge. Haverford's 1,200 students represent a wide diversity of interests, backgrounds, and talents. They come from public, parochial, and independent schools across the United States, Puerto Rico, and thirty-nine foreign countries. Students of color are an important part of the Haverford community.

Haverford College meets 100% of the demonstrated need of all admitted students and seeks to minimize or eliminate debt for our graduates. Students with family income below $60,000 will not have any loans included in their financial aid package; students with family income above this level will have loans ranging from $1,500 to $3,000 per year. And our need-blind admission policy means that an application for financial aid has no bearing on the admission decision for U.S. citizens and eligible non-citizens.

SELECTIVITY

Admissions Rating	98
# of applicants	3,585
% of applicants accepted	23
% of acceptees attending	39
# offered a place on the wait list	769
% accepting a place on wait list	38
% admitted from wait list	3
# of early decision applicants	313
% accepted early decision	45

FRESHMAN PROFILE

Range SAT Critical Reading	660–750
Range SAT Math	650–740
Range SAT Writing	660–750
Range ACT Composite	30–33
Minimum paper TOEFL	600
Minimum web-based TOEFL	100
% graduated top 10% of class	95
% graduated top 25% of class	98
% graduated top 50% of class	100

DEADLINES

Early decision	
Deadline	11/15
Notification	12/15
Regular	
Deadline	1/15
Notification	4/15
Nonfall registration?	No

FINANCIAL FACTS

Financial Aid Rating	99
Annual tuition	$46,790
Room and board	$14,350
Required fees	$644
Books and supplies	$1,194
% needy frosh rec. need-based scholarship or grant aid	95
% needy UG rec. need-based scholarship or grant aid	96
% needy frosh rec. non-need-based scholarship or grant aid	0
% needy UG rec. non-need-based scholarship or grant aid	0
% needy frosh rec. need-based self-help aid	89
% needy UG rec. need-based self-help aid	91
% frosh rec. any financial aid	53
% UG rec. any financial aid	51
% UG borrow to pay for school	29
Average cumulative indebtedness	$15,000
% frosh need fully met	100
% ugrads need fully met	100
Average % of frosh need met	100
Average % of ugrad need met	100

HILLSDALE COLLEGE

33 East College Street, Hillsdale, MI 49242 • Admissions: 517-607-2327 • Fax: 517-607-2223

STUDENTS SAY ". . ."

Academics

Hillsdale College, "a classical liberal arts school," instills "heritage and purpose" through a curriculum that "relies heavily on primary source documents and the classics," "Socratic-style lectures," and "a very strong reputation nationally [for taking] the idea of pursuing truth and liberty seriously." Marked by "academic rigor" and the "Western tradition," "learning isn't a chore here, it's a privilege," and professors are always "accessible and are dedicated to teaching, not researching or publishing." As one student explains, "I loved the idea of going to a school where a class on the U.S. Constitution was part of the core curriculum, where the student/professor ratio was ten to one…it was small enough that would never just be another number." There also is "not any grade inflation" at Hillsdale; thus, "students spend a lot of time studying." While there has been a trend in recent years "against the economics/business/accounting department and the sciences in favor of less technical education," students find that because Hillsdale notably takes no government funding, it "remains one of two truly free institutions in the nation…uninfluenced by the whims of politicians and biased policymakers." Privately funded scholarships make it possible for "a large segment" of the student body to attend Hillsdale, and the average aid package is more than $12,000.

Life

Hillsdale College's "beautiful campus" offsets any disenchantment with the town of Hillsdale itself. While Hillsdale is "a small campus in a small town," "there are always events to attend or things to do with friends," and "you can find people whose idea of fun is across a wide spectrum." Students spend their weeks "suffering under an endless mountain of homework and papers," but on the weekends, "house parties in which students get together to sing, play games, read together, play music, and have a generally good time together are the norm." As one student states, "There are some disparate groups on campus—the kids who have intellectual discussions in the union and the kids who go out and party on the weekends. There's no animosity between different groups though." "From Greek Life to Bible Study," students "actively engage in student organizations" like intramural sports and embrace "adventures from…attempting to climb the water tower…to driving thirty minutes to an abandoned tourist trap [for] a fake woolly mammoth tusk." Hillsdale also attracts students who want to "compete in Division II athletics" and appreciate "the self-sustaining religious sincerity" on campus. Through enforcement of an honor code, the administration has been according to students "a bit draconian" lately in "cracking down on any party culture."

Student Body

While "there are different types of students at Hillsdale," most would describe the typical student as being "friendly, conservative, [and] religious." Students "come from across the country and from a variety of backgrounds. Each student finds their own niche based on their interests." The admissions process at Hillsdale is blind, therefore making "racial diversity…irrelevant." Even with a "majority [of the student body] as Christian conservatives…Hillsdale is open to any faith or belief system and accepting of anyone who has justifications for why they believe what they believe." "Some strange, narrow-minded fundamentalists still get admitted to the school," but "they choose to remain in their own circles." For the rest, Hillsdale "doesn't have cliques. Greeks, athletes, thespians, homeschoolers, etc., are often one person who falls into multiple categories." Community is shaped at Hillsdale through "a genuine love of learning…a grounding in the ideas that shaped Western society," and students on the whole "are incredibly warm to one another and enjoy the experience of close bonding through intellectual and spiritual pursuit."

HILLSDALE COLLEGE

FINANCIAL AID: 517-607-2350 • E-MAIL: ADMISSIONS@HILLSDALE.EDU • WEBSITE: WWW.HILLSDALE.EDU

THE PRINCETON REVIEW SAYS

Admissions

Very important factors considered include: GPA, rigor of secondary school record, standardized test scores, application essay, interview, character/personal qualities, level of applicant's interest. *Important factors considered include:* Class rank, extracurricular activities, recommendation(s), volunteer work, work experience. *Other factors considered include:* Geographical residence, talent/ability, alumni/ae relations. SAT or ACT required; ACT with or without Writing component accepted. TOEFL required of all international applicants. *Academic units recommended:* 4 English; 4 mathematics; 3 science; (1 science lab); 1 social studies; 2 foreign language; 2 history.

Financial Aid

Students should submit: Institution's own financial aid form. The Princeton Review suggests that all financial aid forms be submitted as soon as possible after January 1. *Need-based scholarships/grants offered:* Private scholarships, the school's own gift aid. *Loan aid offered:* College/university loans from institutional funds. Institutional employment available. Off-campus job opportunities are good.

Inside Word

Don't let Hillsdale's high acceptance rate fool you. The academic profile of incoming freshmen is tremendous and only serious, solid candidates should bother applying here. Even though you don't have to be politically conservative to get in, a passionate and well-reasoned essay singing the praises of free-market economics or defending traditional values certainly can't hurt you.

THE SCHOOL SAYS " . . ."

From the Admissions Office

"Personal attention is a hallmark at Hillsdale. Small classes are combined with teaching professors who make their students a priority. The academic environment at Hillsdale will actively engage you as a student. Extracurricular activities abound at Hillsdale with the more than 100 clubs and organizations that offer excellent leadership opportunities. From athletics and the fine arts, to Greek life and community volunteer programs, you will find it difficult not to be involved in our thriving campus community. In addition, numerous study abroad programs, a 685-acre biological station in northern Michigan, and the Washington-Hillsdale Internship Program (WHIP) are just a few of the unique off-campus opportunities available to you at Hillsdale.

"Our strength as a college is found in our mission and in our curriculum. The core curriculum at Hillsdale contains the essence of the classical liberal arts education. Through it you are introduced to the history, the philosophical and theological ideas, the works of literature, and the scientific discoveries that set Western Civilization apart. As explained in our mission statement, 'the college considers itself a trustee of modern man's intellectual and spiritual inheritance from the Judeo-Christian faith and Greco-Roman culture, a heritage finding its clearest expression in the American experiment of self-government under law.'

"We seek students who are ambitious, intellectually active and who are ready to become leaders worthy of this heritage in their personal as well as professional lives.

"Applicants can meet admissions requirements by submitting the results of the SAT, or the ACT (writing section optional). We will use the student's best composite/combined score in the evaluation process. The SAT Subject Tests in literature and U.S. history are also recommended."

SELECTIVITY

Admissions Rating	95
# of applicants	1,902
% of applicants accepted	50
% of acceptees attending	37
# offered a place on the wait list	46
% accepting a place on wait list	40
% admitted from wait list	10
# of early decision applicants	115
% accepted early decision	77

FRESHMAN PROFILE

Range SAT Critical Reading	640–730
Range SAT Math	590–680
Range SAT Writing	610–720
Range ACT Composite	27–31
Minimum paper TOEFL	580
Minimum web-based TOEFL	220
Average HS GPA	3.81
% graduated top 10% of class	56
% graduated top 25% of class	85
% graduated top 50% of class	99

DEADLINES

Early decision	
Deadline	11/15
Notification	12/1
Early action	
Deadline	12/15
Notification	2/15
Regular	
Priority	1/15
Deadline	2/15
Nonfall registration?	Yes

APPLICANTS ALSO LOOK AT AND OFTEN PREFER

Grove City College; University of Michigan—Ann Arbor; University of Notre Dame

AND SOMETIMES PREFER

Purdue University—West Lafayette

FINANCIAL FACTS

Financial Aid Rating	87
Annual tuition	$22,250
Room and board	$9,000
Required fees	$640
Books and supplies	$850
% needy frosh rec. need-based scholarship or grant aid	65
% needy UG rec. need-based scholarship or grant aid	67
% needy frosh rec. non-need-based scholarship or grant aid	88
% needy UG rec. non-need-based scholarship or grant aid	87
% needy frosh rec. need-based self-help aid	78
% needy UG rec. need-based self-help aid	74
% frosh rec. any financial aid	91
% UG rec. any financial aid	95
% UG borrow to pay for school	55
Average cumulative indebtedness	$25,502
% frosh need fully met	37
% ugrads need fully met	42
Average % of frosh need met	65
Average % of ugrad need met	70

HOBART AND WILLIAM SMITH COLLEGES

629 SOUTH MAIN STREET, GENEVA, NY 14456 • ADMISSIONS: 315-781-3622 • FAX: 315-781-3914

CAMPUS LIFE

Quality of Life Rating	71
Fire Safety Rating	87
Green Rating	93
Type of school	Private
Affiliation	No Affiliation
Environment	Village

STUDENTS

Total undergrad enrollment	2,311
% male/female	45/55
% from out of state	58
% frosh from public high school	62
% frosh live on campus	100
% ugrads live on campus	90
# of fraternities	5
% African American	4
% Asian	2
% Caucasian	69
% Hispanic	4
% Native American	1
% international	5
# of countries represented	26

SURVEY SAYS . . .

Lots of beer drinking
Hard liquor is popular
No one cheats
Career services are great

ACADEMICS

Academic Rating	90
% students returning for sophomore year	88
% students graduating within 4 years	74
% students graduating within 6 years	79
Calendar	Semester
Student/faculty ratio	11:1
Profs interesting rating	85
Profs accessible rating	87

Most classes have 10–19 students.
Most lab/discussion sessions have 10–19 students.

MOST POPULAR MAJORS

economics; political science; psychology

STUDENTS SAY ". . ."

Academics

Hobart and William Smith Colleges together are "a college that is large enough to provide a wide variety of majors, yet small enough that your professors are able to know you by your name." Students enjoy "small class sizes, [the] feel of community," a "unique liberal arts curriculum, gorgeous campus…[and] one of the country's best study abroad programs." "Everyone knows everyone" at this very small school located right on central New York's Seneca Lake. "Hobart and William Smith College has the most incredible campus community I've ever seen," one student boasts, although beware of the "cold winters!" "There are countless opportunities for involvement [at HWS] such as internships, study abroad, athletics, clubs, and student activities." Because of the small size, the "absolutely fantastic faculty" "knows, remembers, and cares about all their students." "The best thing about the professors here is that they are always accessible outside of class, either with office hours or constant e-mail communication." However, some students caution that while many professors are "amazing," others are "awful and really should not be teaching." Students did feel the school "needs to work on really trying to make environmental sustainability an actual issue on campus." In summary, HWS is "a small, liberal arts college where the professors' first priority is their students," and there's a "gorgeous lake outside [your] window!"

Life

"Life at HWS is very comfortable," and "Students fit in by being friendly and spending a lot of money on partying." "People either love HWS or they hate it," one psychology student explains. "Life here is centered almost entirely around the social aspects of the college experience, which is fine, to a point, but it doesn't allow for deeper intellectual rigor." "People think about partying a lot, and on this campus it happens a lot" especially "at frats (there are no sororities) and at on-campus houses." On the weekends, there are "wild woods parties, house parties, frats, a quiet movie night, stargazing, jazz…you can find it all on a Saturday night." Another student laments, "There isn't much to do on weekends. The Campus Activities Board is good at the occasional big event…but there should be more events throughout the year," although the "school-sponsored events are actually enjoyable" when they do occur. Although many students complain about the campus food options, luckily "there are places to [get] good off-campus food and movies in walking distance." Make sure to bring your thickest winter coats, because HWS life slows down during the "endless winter" that "sometimes starts as early as October and can yield snow as late as mid-May."

Student Body

"The males here tend to be 'bros' for the most part, and the women are referred to as 'smithies,'" which means that "they carry expensive bags and wear big sunglasses, and are usually pretty skinny (or at least dress like they think they are)." "'Ho Bros,' the typical Hobart student, will join one of the six frats, own at least one pair of pants in the color 'Nantucket Red,' and probably drive a nicer car than most faculty." However, students caution that "there are always exceptions to the rule" "who don't fit these stereotypes and actually enjoy mocking them." Most students are "WASPs" or "preppy" and "white," and students feel that HWS needs to do more to create a more diverse student body from America and bring in more international students as well. Students in different populations "hardly mingle," and students "tend to stay in separate circles." "North Face and Uggs are far more rampant among the student body now than [the traditional HWS look of] Polo, Lily Pulitzer, and Lacoste."

FINANCIAL AID: 315-781-3315 • E-MAIL: ADMISSIONS@HWS.EDU • WEBSITE: WWW.HWS.EDU

THE PRINCETON REVIEW SAYS

Admissions

Very important factors considered include: GPA, rigor of secondary school record. *Important factors considered include:* Application essay, extracurricular activities, interview, recommendation(s), volunteer work, work experience, character/ personal qualities. *Other factors considered include:* Class rank, standardized test scores, first generation, geographical residence, racial/ethnic status, state residency, talent/ability, alumni/ae relations, level of applicant's interest. SAT or ACT required for some; ACT with Writing component recommended. TOEFL required of all international applicants. *Academic units required:* 4 English; 3 mathematics; 3 science; (2 science lab); 2 social studies; 2 foreign language; 2 academic electives. *Academic units recommended:* 3 social studies; 3 foreign language; 4 academic electives.

Financial Aid

Students should submit: FAFSA, CSS/Financial Aid PROFILE, State aid form, Noncustodial PROFILE. Regular filing deadline is 2/1. The Princeton Review suggests that all financial aid forms be submitted as soon as possible after January 1. *Need-based scholarships/grants offered:* Federal Pell, SEOG, State scholarships/grants, private scholarships, the school's own gift aid. *Loan aid offered:* Direct Subsidized Stafford Loans, Direct Unsubsidized Stafford Loans, Direct PLUS loans, Federal Perkins Loans, College/university loans from institutional funds. Applicants will be notified of awards beginning 4/1. Federal Work-Study Program available. Institutional employment available. Off-campus job opportunities are good.

The Inside Word

Applicants to the academic side of Seneca Lake's scenic shores should know that HWS likes to see a student who embraces a challenge. They recommend that hopefuls prepare for a rigorous college curriculum by taking at least two years of a foreign language and a couple of AP courses for good measure.

THE SCHOOL SAYS "..."

From the Admissions Office

"Hobart and William Smith Colleges seek students with a sense of adventure and a commitment to the life of the mind. Inside the classroom, students find the academic climate to be rigorous, with a faculty that is deeply involved in teaching and working with them. Outside, they discover a supportive community that helps to cultivate a balance and hopes to foster an integration among academics, extracurricular activities, and social life. Hobart and William Smith, as coordinate colleges, have an awareness of gender differences and equality and are committed to respect and a celebration of diversity.

"Hobart and William Smith Colleges are test optional. Students may submit the SAT, ACT, or no standardized tests at all."

SELECTIVITY

Admissions Rating	90
# of applicants	4,380
% of applicants accepted	50
% of acceptees attending	29
# offered a place on the wait list	627
% accepting a place on wait list	31
% admitted from wait list	5
# of early decision applicants	425
% accepted early decision	84

FRESHMAN PROFILE

Range SAT Critical Reading	560–640
Range SAT Math	560–650
Range ACT Composite	26–29
Minimum paper TOEFL	550
Minimum web-based TOEFL	220
Average HS GPA	3.36
% graduated top 10% of class	36
% graduated top 25% of class	63
% graduated top 50% of class	87

DEADLINES

Early decision	
Deadline	11/15
Notification	12/15
Regular	
Deadline	2/1
Notification	4/1
Nonfall registration?	Yes

APPLICANTS ALSO LOOK AT AND OFTEN PREFER

Trinity College (CT), Colgate University; Connecticut College

AND SOMETIMES PREFER

St. Lawrence University; Skidmore College; Gettysburg College; Kenyon College

AND RARELY PREFER

State University of New York at Geneseo

FINANCIAL FACTS

Financial Aid Rating	91
Annual tuition	$45,180
Room and board	$11,685
Required fees	$985
Books and supplies	$1,300
% needy frosh rec. need-based scholarship or grant aid	99
% needy UG rec. need-based scholarship or grant aid	98
% needy frosh rec. non-need-based scholarship or grant aid	17
% needy UG rec. non-need-based scholarship or grant aid	15
% needy frosh rec. need-based self-help aid	80
% needy UG rec. need-based self-help aid	83
% frosh rec. any financial aid	87
% UG rec. any financial aid	82
% UG borrow to pay for school	62
Average cumulative indebtedness	$28,885
% frosh need fully met	65
% ugrads need fully met	61
Average % of frosh need met	77
Average % of ugrad need met	79

HOFSTRA UNIVERSITY

100 HOFSTRA UNIVERSITY, HEMPSTEAD, NY 11549 • ADMISSIONS: 516-463-6700 • FAX: 516-463-5100

STUDENTS SAY ". . ."

Academics

Hofstra is a school synonymous with opportunity. Located on suburban Long Island, students find Hofstra's "medium size" a great asset. Indeed, the university simultaneously "feels big, yet class sizes are small and [therefore] very conducive to a great learning environment." What's more, Hofstra's close proximity to New York City allows students to take advantage of many internship opportunities. Additionally, the School of Communications is "top-notch" and students in the sciences benefit greatly from affiliation with the university's new medical school. By and large, professors here are "excellent" and "enjoyable." As one psychology major shares, "My professors almost always seem passionate about their field of study, and even when I don't share their passion in that particular field, their enthusiasm has helped to keep me engaged and interested in the class material." Perhaps more importantly, teachers at Hofstra are "very knowledgeable…and have experience in what they are teaching." Undergrads here also call attention to the fact their professors are quite approachable. As one music education major explains, "I have also never had a teacher that won't make themselves available outside of class. All of them are extremely good about having office hours and answering any questions. They all really want us to do well." In the end, a Hofstra education is "about challenging its students and giving each one an opportunity to grow and succeed to their fullest extent."

Life

Life at this Long Island university moves at a fast and frenzied pace. As one knowledgeable senior shares, "Hofstra is one of those places where there is always something to do." A television major concurs sharing, "Everyone works really hard and takes extracurricular [activities] seriously. 'Work hard, play hard' [is] definitely [applicable]." To begin with, Hofstra offers "many music ensembles (including symphony orchestra, symphonic band, new music ensemble, wind ensemble, string orchestra, and sikh music!)" along with "free on-campus concerts and movies." Additionally, "intramural sports are also quite popular, [especially] basketball." And one pleased sophomore shares how she makes her own fun, "I play Mario Party with friends in the Game Room, watch my roommate run around our dorm lounge in a banana suit, pull all-nighter study dates with my boyfriend in the library, sit under one of the godzillian gorgeous tress on the South Side of campus, and battle to the death for an open laundry machine." Of course, with a fairly substantial commuter population, some lament that "weekends [can feel] pretty empty." However, others assure us that "there are always frats or [other] parties [to attend.]" Moreover, there's "definitely a bar scene, as there are multiple bars within walking distance that most students go out to frequently." When students are itching to get a little further off campus, they can take advantage of "nearby shopping malls, bowling alleys [and] famous landmarks (Jones Beach and Eisenhower Park)." And, of course, "New York City is only a short train ride away."

Student Body

Undergrads at Hofstra say that you'd be hard pressed to find a "typical" student roaming the campus. As one philosophy student posits, "I have friends studying all different majors and from all walks of life." And while the university definitely attracts "a lot of Long Island locals," there are also plenty of students "from the Northeast and all over the country." Of course, most of the undergrads that flock here are "serious about academics" and "well rounded." However, a music education major quickly follows up by stating, "We also know how to have fun and take advantage of our college experience." Further, to quell the doubts of even the most social skeptic, we're told that "with over 200 clubs and sports there is something for everyone." Indeed, it's "very easy to fit in here." An English major explains, "I think almost anyone can find a niche here. This is overall a very open-minded place. When students can dress in drag without anyone looking askance, I'd say you have a pretty tolerant campus."

FINANCIAL AID: 516-463-8000 • E-MAIL: ADMISSION@HOFSTRA.EDU • WEBSITE: WWW.HOFSTRA.EDU

THE PRINCETON REVIEW SAYS

Admissions

Very important factors considered include: Class rank, GPA, rigor of secondary school record, standardized test scores, application essay, recommendation(s). *Important factors considered include:* Extracurricular activities, interview, talent/ability, character/personal qualities. *Other factors considered include:* Geographical residence, racial/ethnic status, volunteer work, work experience, alumni/ae relations, level of applicant's interest. SAT or ACT required for some; ACT with Writing component required for some. TOEFL or IELTS required of all international applicants. *Academic units required:* 4 English; 3 mathematics; 3 science; (1 science lab); 3 social studies; 2 foreign language. *Academic units recommended:* 4 mathematics; 4 science; (2 science lab); 4 social studies; 3 foreign language.

Financial Aid

Students should submit: FAFSA, State aid form. The Princeton Review suggests that all financial aid forms be submitted as soon as possible after January 1. *Need-based scholarships/grants offered:* Federal Pell, SEOG, State scholarships/grants, private scholarships, the school's own gift aid. *Loan aid offered:* Direct Subsidized Stafford Loans, Direct Unsubsidized Stafford Loans, Direct PLUS loans, Federal Perkins Loans, State Loans, College/university loans from institutional funds. Federal Work-Study Program available. Institutional employment available. Off-campus job opportunities are excellent.

The Inside Word

Gaining admission to Hofstra is no easy feat. Indeed, each year competition for a coveted acceptance letter becomes tighter and tighter. Certainly, admissions officers are looking for well-rounded candidates who have pushed themselves in the classroom. It's important to note that regular admission operates on a rolling basis so the earlier you apply, the greater your chances for admission.

THE SCHOOL SAYS " . . ."

From the Admissions Office

"The value of a Hofstra degree is recognized across the country and around the globe.

"At Hofstra University, we will know your name. We provide you with the resources and advantages of a large university, but the personal attention of a small college. Hofstra offers 140 undergraduate program options in the liberal arts and sciences with schools of engineering, business, communication, education, medicine and law; a diverse undergraduate student body that comes from forty-six U.S. states and fifty countries; seventeen Division I sports; thirty-seven residence halls; eighteen eateries and cafes; a Fall Festival that has featured world-famous; and an alumni network of more than 124,000 who have been where you are now, and have become leaders in their fields.

"We're less than an hour from New York City, which means easy access to the adventure, cultural life and resources of an international metropolis, and internships at global giants in every industry.

"On-campus experiential learning includes more than 150 pre-professional, social and academic clubs, and state-of-the-art facilities. Hofstra also recognizes the value of bringing once-in-a-lifetime learning opportunities to our campus, most notably by hosting presidential debates in 2008 and 2012.

"Our faculty are scholars, artists, and scientists who are passionate about their work and dedicated to teaching and training the next generation of leaders—including you.

"Your future is full of hope and possibilities. The Hofstra experience allows you to imagine, design, and create both the journey and the destination."

SELECTIVITY

Admissions Rating	84
# of applicants	27,700
% of applicants accepted	59
% of acceptees attending	10
# offered a place on the wait list	313
% accepting a place on wait list	18
% admitted from wait list	81

FRESHMAN PROFILE

Range SAT Critical Reading	520–610
Range SAT Math	530–620
Range ACT Composite	23–27
Minimum paper TOEFL	550
Minimum web-based TOEFL	80
Average HS GPA	3.51
% graduated top 10% of class	24
% graduated top 25% of class	56
% graduated top 50% of class	88

DEADLINES

Early action	
Deadline	11/15
Notification	12/15
Nonfall registration?	Yes

APPLICANTS ALSO LOOK AT AND OFTEN PREFER

New York University; Syracuse University; Boston University

AND SOMETIMES PREFER

State University of New York—Stony Brook University; Pennsylvania State University—University Park, Fordham University; Drexel University; Northeastern University

AND RARELY PREFER

St. John's University—Queens; University of Connecticut; University of Massachusetts Amherst; Quinnipiac University

FINANCIAL FACTS

Financial Aid Rating	71
Annual tuition	$36,350
Room and board	$13,050
Required fees	$1,050
Books and supplies	$1,000
% needy frosh rec. need-based scholarship or grant aid	97
% needy UG rec. need-based scholarship or grant aid	92
% needy frosh rec. non-need-based scholarship or grant aid	19
% needy UG rec. non-need-based scholarship or grant aid	13
% needy frosh rec. need-based self-help aid	84
% needy UG rec. need-based self-help aid	80
% frosh rec. any financial aid	96
% UG rec. any financial aid	90
% UG borrow to pay for school	68
% frosh need fully met	23
% ugrads need fully met	20
Average % of frosh need met	67
Average % of ugrad need met	60

HOLLINS UNIVERSITY

PO BOX 9707, ROANOKE, VA 24020-1707 • ADMISSIONS: 540-362-6401 • FAX: 540-362-6218

STUDENTS SAY ". . ."

Academics

"Tiny," all-female Hollins University "drips in" "unique traditions" and offers "an intimate atmosphere" that "feels like a community or family, not an institution." Students assure us that "a Hollins education is inspiring and nothing short of life-changing." There are fabulous opportunities to study abroad. Double-majors are mundane. Among the thirty or so majors available here, the "strong English program" is especially notable. The creative writing program in particular is "one of the nation's best." Classes are small and extremely "interactive." "The discussions in class will start slowly," observes an English major, "but they'll suddenly be out of the teacher's control the next minute." "Don't go if you didn't do the readings," adds a physics major. "Professors pour so much time into their students," relates a studio art major. They "want to hear from their students" and "are always more than willing to help." The staff in the financial aid office, on the other hand, can sometimes be "unwilling to help."

Life

Students at Hollins "adore the school." Life on this "gorgeous" and "peaceful" campus is "a unique amalgam of individualistic zaniness and required academic hustle and bustle." "People are very concerned about homework." "Sleepless nights during weekdays" aren't uncommon. At the same time, the student community is "hugely strong." "Hollins really embodies the concept of sisterhood." "Everyone comes together for" a throng of "crazy and not-so-crazy traditions." "It isn't uncommon to put on odd costumes or break into songs or see seniors in decorated robes. It's hard to explain these things other than to say, 'it's a Hollins thing.'" In the fall, the school president cancels morning classes and declares Tinker Day. "Everyone dresses up in wacky costumes, everything from a wetsuit to a prom dress, and hikes Tinker Mountain." Ring Night ("the best weekend of your life") and faculty Christmas caroling are a couple other noteworthy traditions. Hollins is also home to "amazing extracurriculars" including "a great horseback riding program." "There is a high level of student involvement" across the board, and "there is always something happening on campus." Lectures, concerts, and recitals are abundant. The theater program "is excellent, and the shows are always worth going to." "There are several subcultures people can fit into"—everything from intercollegiate athletics to a surprisingly strong anime contingent. "If you want to attend frat parties and keggers, it is very easy with the number of coed universities nearby," but "this isn't the typical 'party school.'" "Life at Hollins is walking down the dorm hall with all the dorm doors open and girls running down the hall to each other's rooms to talk and have fun or do homework together," explains one student. "The friends we make here are still going to be our sisters long after we have gone out into the world to accomplish what our experience at Hollins gave us the courage to do." "The dorms are hospitable but old." "Every now and then, the food is great and wonderful" but, for the gourmand, meals here general have some room for improvement.

Student Body

The women of Hollins describe themselves as "empowered, enthusiastic," "worldly, aware," "strong, and confident." "There are all sorts at Hollins: horse girls, anime girls, art majors, writers, filmmakers, bio students, dancers, feminists, scientists." The gay and transgender population is "large." "The glory of Hollins is that there is seldom a stereotype," agrees another student. "There is no mold that any student must fit, regardless of what activities and groups you are involved in. It is a place to be yourself." "Odd ducks" proliferate. "You name it; you see it (minus males, that is)." "Everyone is so different, and everyone is so amazingly tolerant of everyone's differences." However, some students can be "cliquey and exclusive." "Most people are involved in several clubs and organizations so it's easy to have a very diverse group of friends," describes one student.

FINANCIAL AID: 540-362-6332 • E-MAIL: HUADM@HOLLINS.EDU • WEBSITE: WWW.HOLLINS.EDU

THE PRINCETON REVIEW SAYS

Admissions

Very important factors considered include: Class rank, GPA, rigor of secondary school record, standardized test scores, application essay, recommendation(s). *Important factors considered include:* Extracurricular activities, interview, talent/ability, character/personal qualities. *Other factors considered include:* Geographical residence, racial/ethnic status, volunteer work, work experience, alumni/ae relations, level of applicant's interest. SAT or ACT is required; ACT with Writing component is not required. TOEFL or IELTS required of all international applicants. *Academic units required:* 4 English; 3 mathematics; 3 science; (1 science lab); 3 social studies; 2 foreign language. *Academic units recommended:* 4 mathematics; 4 science; (2 science lab); 4 social studies; 3 foreign language.

Financial Aid

Students should submit: FAFSA, State aid form. The Princeton Review suggests that all financial aid forms be submitted as soon as possible after January 1. *Need-based scholarships/grants offered:* Federal Pell, SEOG, State scholarships/grants, private scholarships, the school's own gift aid. *Loan aid offered:* Direct Subsidized Stafford Loans, Direct Unsubsidized Stafford Loans, Direct PLUS loans, Federal Perkins Loans, State Loans, College/university loans from institutional funds. Federal Work-Study Program available. Institutional employment available. Off-campus job opportunities are excellent.

The Inside Word

While the overall stats at Hollins are solid, the admit rate is high, and gaining admission won't be terrifically difficult if you have decent test scores and above-average grades. Keep in mind, though, that the applicants here are a highly self-selecting group and the admissions staff is able to take a long look at everyone who applies. Consequently, your best bet is to demonstrate a sincere desire to be a part of the unique milieu on this campus.

THE SCHOOL SAYS "..."

From the Admissions Office

"Hollins University's slogan, 'Women who are going places start at Hollins,' endures because it captures what this independent liberal arts institution means to its students. Hollins has been a motivating force for women to go places creatively, intellectually, and geographically since it was founded over 170 years ago. As Hollins graduate and Pulitzer Prize–winner Annie Dillard said, Hollins is a place 'where friendships thrive, minds catch fire, careers begin, and hearts open to a world of possibility.'

"Hollins offers majors in twenty-seven fields. While perhaps best known for its creative writing discipline, the university features strong programs in the visual and performing arts and the social and physical sciences. Hollins also has an innovative general education program called Education Through Skills and Perspectives (ESP). In ESP, students acquire knowledge across the curriculum. One of the most sought-after programs at Hollins is the Batten Leadership Institute, a comprehensive curricular program designed to maximize each student's leadership style and potential and teach her skills she will use both now and in the future. It is the only program of its kind in the nation.

"Hollins was among the first colleges in the nation to offer an international study abroad program. Today, more than 40 percent of Hollins' students—many times the national average—study abroad. Internship opportunities are another of Hollins' distinctions. Thanks to an active, dedicated network of alumnae and friends of the university, 65 percent of Hollins seniors put their education to work with a diverse group of organizations.

"Hollins' slogan underscores the most important question each student is asked from the moment she arrives until the day she leaves, and it is asked by her professors, her peers, and especially by herself: 'Where do you want to go?'"

SELECTIVITY

Admissions Rating	80
# of applicants	824
% of applicants accepted	69
% of acceptees attending	26
# offered a place on the wait list	0

FRESHMAN PROFILE

Range SAT Critical Reading	500–640
Range SAT Math	470–580
Range ACT Composite	21–27
Minimum paper TOEFL	550
Minimum web-based TOEFL	80
Average HS GPA	3.5
% graduated top 10% of class	24
% graduated top 25% of class	54
% graduated top 50% of class	83

DEADLINES

Early action	
Deadline	12/1
Notification	12/15
Nonfall registration?	Yes

APPLICANTS ALSO LOOK AT

Bryn Mawr College; Randolph College; Roanoke College; Sweet Briar College; University of Mary Washington; Virginia Tech

FINANCIAL FACTS

Financial Aid Rating	79
Annual tuition	$33,660
Room and board	$11,940
Required fees	$635
Books and supplies	$1,000
% needy frosh rec. need-based scholarship or grant aid	100
% needy UG rec. need-based scholarship or grant aid	100
% needy frosh rec. non-need-based scholarship or grant aid	100
% needy UG rec. non-need-based scholarship or grant aid	100
% needy frosh rec. need-based self-help aid	91
% needy UG rec. need-based self-help aid	91
% frosh rec. any financial aid	100
% UG rec. any financial aid	98
% UG borrow to pay for school	77
Average cumulative indebtedness	$30,660
% frosh need fully met	22
% ugrads need fully met	18
Average % of frosh need met	85
Average % of ugrad need met	80

HOWARD UNIVERSITY

2400 SIXTH STREET NORTHWEST, WASHINGTON, D.C. 20059 • ADMISSIONS: 202-806-2700 • FAX: 202-806-4467

CAMPUS LIFE

Quality of Life Rating	64
Fire Safety Rating	95
Green Rating	60*
Type of school	Private
Affiliation	No Affiliation
Environment	Metropolis

STUDENTS

Total undergrad enrollment	6,974
% male/female	30/70
% from out of state	95
% frosh from public high school	80
% frosh live on campus	100
% ugrads live on campus	57
# of fraternities	10
# of sororities	8
% African American	90
% Asian	1
% Caucasian	1
% Hispanic	<1
% Native American	<1
% international	3
# of countries represented	42

SURVEY SAYS . . .
Frats and sororities are popular
Student publications are popular
Active student government

ACADEMICS

Academic Rating	73
% students returning for sophomore year	83
% students graduating within 4 years	40
% students graduating within 6 years	61
Calendar	Semester
Student/faculty ratio	8:1
Profs interesting rating	65
Profs accessible rating	66

Most classes have 10–19 students.
Most lab/discussion sessions have 10–19 students.

MOST POPULAR MAJORS
journalism; radio and television; biology

STUDENTS SAY ". . ."

Academics

Noted for "outstanding achievements as an institution as well as the accomplishments of a great majority of its alumni," Howard University takes great pride in preparing students "to compete on a local and global level." With "inspiring faculty and a perspective that cannot be found anywhere else," the school "breeds pride and excellence" and is a "formidable force in producing African American intellectuals." "Howard University is more than a place to get an education, it is a once-in-a-lifetime experience that not only strengthens your mind, but also your spirit and pride in who you are as a person and who you have the potential to become," says an appreciative student. Other undergrads add, "I wanted the experience of attending a Historically Black College," with a rich tradition and history. "Once you become a Bison" you experience "the sense of being a part of such a tremendous legacy." Students here believe that a Howard education is wonderful preparation for life in today's competitive employment environment. "Howard pushes you and teaches patience." Professors are admired for being able to "bridge the gap between the real world and the textbook;" "It is up to you to apply information outside of class through internships and supplementary experiences." They are "supportive and helpful," have "a genuine interest in their subject," and they make sure "course material is appropriate." Discussions are encouraged, which "helps to solidify understanding…I am able to have a voice in the class and share my opinion." Networking opportunities are abundant, and job placement upon graduation is high.

Life

A common theme heard throughout Howard University is how "students are very tight-knit and supportive of one another." "Dormitories are lively," and "life is fast-paced." School events are normally a "major part of the social calendar," and there is great encouragement for students "to be involved in campus organizations and student government." While there are many Greeks on campus, "the main focus of our Greek Life is community service. Any social event or gathering that is hosted by the Greeks normally has most of all of the proceeds going to a charity or community service project." There are also "student-run organizations that work in the community," providing "opportunities to be a part of something bigger than you." Students obviously love taking advantage of all of the opportunities the Washington, D.C., area provides. The Metro is a popular form of transportation, with the station "very easily accessible from the main Howard University campus." Many locations are Metro-accessible, but you must be cognizant of operating hours.

Student Body

At Howard University, there is at least one commonality everyone can agree on: Students are busy. "At any given time a student at Howard can be found taking a full course load, working, and interning." Extracurricular activities and community service are also on the plate of many Howard undergraduates. Students are often described as "friendly, outgoing, stylish, and fashionable." The campus exudes "a culture of achievement and encouragement;" "most students are very goal-oriented and driven." "A Howardite is very career-oriented and knows what he or she wants to do after graduation." Students here are also "very socially conscious." Geographic diversity is prevalent, and "Howard students are educated to think on a global scale." "Students are very accepting of each other and their backgrounds;" "We are an ever-changing, comprehensive, innovative, and supportive community." Meaningful conversation is prevalent, with many "discussions surrounding social and political issues." "Howard represents the best of the educated and progressive African American community."

FINANCIAL AID: 202-806-2840 • E-MAIL: ADMISSION@HOWARD.EDU • WEBSITE: WWW.HOWARD.EDU

THE PRINCETON REVIEW SAYS

Admissions

Very important factors considered include: Class rank, GPA, rigor of secondary school record, standardized test scores. *Important factors considered include:* Recommendation(s), character/personal qualities. *Other factors considered include:* Application essay, extracurricular activities, talent/ability, volunteer work, work experience, alumni/ae relations. SAT or ACT required; SAT and SAT Subject Tests or ACT considered if submitted; ACT with Writing component required. TOEFL required of all international applicants. *Academic units required:* 4 English; 2 mathematics; 2 science; 2 social studies; 2 foreign language; 2 history. *Academic units recommended:* 4 English; 3 mathematics; 4 science; (2 science lab); 2 social studies; 2 foreign language; 2 history.

Financial Aid

Students should submit: FAFSA. Regular filing deadline is 8/15. The Princeton Review suggests that all financial aid forms be submitted as soon as possible after January 1. *Need-based scholarships/grants offered:* Federal Pell, SEOG, State scholarships/grants, private scholarships, the school's own gift aid, federal nursing scholarships *Loan aid offered:* Direct Subsidized Stafford Loans, Direct Unsubsidized Stafford Loans, Direct PLUS loans, Federal Perkins Loans, Federal Nursing Loans. Applicants will be notified of awards beginning 4/1. Federal Work-Study Program available. Institutional employment available. Off-campus job opportunities are excellent.

The Inside Word

Howard attracts quite a significant number of applicants, and the school maintains a high rate of graduation for those who do gain admittance. While standardized testing is certainly a primary part of evaluating those looking to enroll, this does not preclude other students from seeking entrance; proven ability from high school and the capacity to handle higher learning in a diligent, responsible manner is also highly valued.

THE SCHOOL SAYS ". . ."

From the Admissions Office

"Since its founding, Howard has stood among the few institutions of higher learning where blacks and other minorities have participated freely in a truly comprehensive university experience. Thus, Howard has assumed a special responsibility in preparing its students to exercise leadership wherever their interests and commitments take them. Howard has issued approximately 111,233 degrees, diplomas, and certificates to men and women in the professions, the arts and sciences, and the humanities. The university has produced and continues to produce a high percentage of the nation's African American professionals in the fields of medicine, dentistry, pharmacy, engineering, nursing, architecture, religion, law, music, social work, education, and business. There are more than 10,036 students from across the nation and approximately eighty-five countries and territories attending the university. Their varied customs, cultures, ideas, and interests contribute to Howard's international character and vitality. More than 1,598 faculty members represent the largest concentration of black scholars in any single institution of higher education.

"All applicants who have never been to college are required to submit scores from either the SAT or the ACT (with the writing component)."

SELECTIVITY

Admissions Rating	88
# of applicants	11,599
% of applicants accepted	57
% of acceptees attending	24

FRESHMAN PROFILE

Range SAT Critical Reading	470–670
Range SAT Math	460–680
Range SAT Writing	430–670
Range ACT Composite	19–29
Minimum paper TOEFL	550
Average HS GPA	3.3
% graduated top 10% of class	23
% graduated top 25% of class	54
% graduated top 50% of class	86

DEADLINES

Early decision	
Deadline	11/1
Notification	12/24
Early action	
Deadline	11/1
Notification	12/24
Regular	
Priority	11/1
Deadline	2/15
Nonfall registration?	Yes

APPLICANTS ALSO LOOK AT AND OFTEN PREFER
Hampton University; Spelman College

AND SOMETIMES PREFER
Florida A&M University; University of Maryland; College Park; The George Washington University

AND RARELY PREFER
Morgan State University

FINANCIAL FACTS

Financial Aid Rating	66
Annual tuition	$21,450
Room and board	$13,460
Required fees	$1,233
Books and supplies	$3,000
% needy frosh rec. need-based scholarship or grant aid	49
% needy UG rec. need-based scholarship or grant aid	50
% needy frosh rec. non-need-based scholarship or grant aid	36
% needy UG rec. non-need-based scholarship or grant aid	35
% needy frosh rec. need-based self-help aid	64
% needy UG rec. need-based self-help aid	67
% frosh rec. any financial aid	84
% UG rec. any financial aid	83
% UG borrow to pay for school	91
Average cumulative indebtedness	$24,748
% frosh need fully met	11
% ugrads need fully met	10
Average % of frosh need met	71
Average % of ugrad need met	75

ILLINOIS INSTITUTE OF TECHNOLOGY

10 WEST THIRTY-THIRD STREET, CHICAGO, IL 60616 • ADMISSIONS: 312-567-3025 • FAX: 312-567-6939

STUDENTS SAY ". . ."

Academics

Those looking for an easy academic experience will want to look elsewhere, as the Illinois Institute of Technology will "challenge you beyond what you think are your limits, and settle only for excellence." Students in this Chicago-based school feel like they are "getting a better education here than what most of the country recognizes. IIT does not have the name that many other schools that I applied to do, but the education here is of a very high level." Those accepted will find themselves confronted with "a lot of hard work to learn a lot of meaningful and useful material," which contributes to this being "one of the best universities to prepare you for the workforce." Of course, "success in most courses is highly dependent on how good of a professor you have. This is because sometimes the book does not help." It's also because not all professors are created equal. "The good professors here are excellent but not all the professors are good." While most praise the "fantastic instructors and researchers who care about their students," many air complaints that "some professors seem to be more interested in research rather than teaching," saying the lower level professors are "bland" and "not instrumental in exciting the experience." But the students who have had great instructors say "they take the necessary time to cover complex topics but do not water the material down or go at too slow of a pace. Everyone has helped me tremendously, and I owe my success to them."

Life

"IIT is not a party school. Although people do drink, it is not what defines the experience. Mostly, students here are those who are concerned with their grades and graduate school outlook." That sentiment is repeated time and again by students who say, "my major requires full dedication if I want to achieve my goals." Without question students here "are focused on innovative and career-minded things." But that doesn't mean ITT students don't enjoy good times outside the classroom. Downtown Chicago is just ten minutes away, with all the music, eating, and culture one of the nation's largest cities has to offer, and thriving Greek life and student clubs provide on-campus outlets for entertainment. "The school's Greek life is really unique in that pledging in a fraternity or sorority is hugely constructive to your growth socially and academically." Others play Ultimate Frisbee, join rock-climbing clubs, or "explore a new museum, coffee shop or comic book store." A few complain that "most students leave campus to relax because they don't feel like they have the freedom to do it on campus" due to what some see as difficult hurdles put up by the school to host on-campus activities. "The school does not make having a social life easy, but that does prepare you to deal with life after college if you could figure it out." Most students, however, are not looking for major distractions. "People usually think about how they're going to pass some of their most difficult classes."

Student Body

Those who go to IIT put their coursework above all else. "The typical student here is extremely hard working. Nothing takes precedence over school work, and for the average student studying takes up a majority of their time." Indeed, "the typical student is a studious and serious nerd who wants to have a highly successful career in their field." Which isn't to say that students don't connect with one another thanks to the burden of their education. Though often "quiet and shy" and "sometimes awkward," students here are "not opposed to meeting new people or trying new things." In fact, "it's very easy for students to find a place where they can fit in, among majors, organizations and clubs, Greek life, or dorm rooms." This school is "where the nice but nerdy kids from high school go," and that's how the student body likes it. "Everyone is very friendly and helpful, and there is no shortage of students who understand the curriculum and are willing to help those who are struggling." The bottom line is, "as long as a student is willing to get a little out their comfort zone and out of their dorm room there is a place for them here."

FINANCIAL AID: 312-567-7219 • E-MAIL: ADMISSION@IIT.EDU • WEBSITE: WWW.IIT.EDU

THE PRINCETON REVIEW SAYS

Admissions

Very important factors considered include: GPA, rigor of secondary school record, standardized test scores. *Important factors considered include:* Class rank, recommendation(s). *Other factors considered include:* Application essay, extra-curricular activities, first generation, interview, talent/ability, volunteer work, work experience, alumni/ae relations, character/personal qualities, level of applicant's interest. SAT or ACT required; ACT with Writing component recommended. TOEFL required of all international applicants. *Academic units required:* 4 English; 4 mathematics; 3 science; (2 science lab); 2 social studies; 2 foreign language. *Academic units recommended:* 4 English; 4 mathematics; 3 science; (2 science lab); 2 social studies; 2 foreign language; 2 history; 1 computer science; 1 visual/performing arts.

Financial Aid

Students should submit: FAFSA. The Princeton Review suggests that all financial aid forms be submitted as soon as possible after January 1. *Need-based scholarships/grants offered:* Federal Pell, SEOG, State scholarships/grants, private scholarships, the school's own gift aid. *Loan aid offered:* Direct Subsidized Stafford Loans, Direct Unsubsidized Stafford Loans, Direct PLUS loans, Federal Perkins Loans. Federal Work-Study Program available. Institutional employment available. Off-campus job opportunities are good.

The Inside Word

Competition to get in includes students worthy of top tech schools like MIT and CalTech, so only those who feel confident they can handle the rigorous curriculum bother applying, making the admissions pools self-selecting. Those who are not exceedingly smart or exceedingly ambitious need not apply.

THE SCHOOL SAYS ". . ."

From the Admissions Office

"IIT is committed to providing students a distinctive and relevant education through hands-on learning, dedicated teachers, small class sizes, and undergraduate research opportunities. Classes are taught by senior faculty—not teaching assistants—who foster our culture of innovation with their own firsthand research experience.

"Students are immersed in our interdisciplinary approach to learning through the team-based, creative problem-solving experience of the Interprofessional Projects Program (IPROs). The Office of Undergraduate Research provides mentored collaborative research experiences for undergraduates. Our entrepreneurship program challenges students to develop start-up technology companies. University Technology Park at IIT, a business incubator located on campus, supports this challenge by providing numerous opportunities to work with companies at every stage of growth, from conception to sophistication. The Leadership Academy teaches leadership skills that advance students in their personal and professional development.

"IIT's location in the world-class city of Chicago gives students priceless access to the professional world through internships and employment. The university's own diverse student population mirrors the global work environment faced by all graduates.

"First year students applying for admission into the entering class are required to submit an SAT or ACT score. We will use the student's best scores from either test. Subject tests are accepted, but not required. It is highly recommended that transfer applicants have completed thirty credit hours and have taken calculus and/or physics. Both first-year and transfer students are evaluated for significant merit based scholarships upon admission."

SELECTIVITY

Admissions Rating	91
# of applicants	2,840
% of applicants accepted	57
% of acceptees attending	31
# of early decision applicants	121
% accepted early decision	72

FRESHMAN PROFILE

Range SAT Critical Reading	520–640
Range SAT Math	640–740
Range SAT Writing	520–640
Range ACT Composite	25–30
Minimum paper TOEFL	550
Minimum web-based TOEFL	80
Average HS GPA	3.64
% graduated top 10% of class	45
% graduated top 25% of class	74
% graduated top 50% of class	96

DEADLINES

Early action	
Deadline	12/1
Regular	
Priority	12/1
Deadline	8/1
Nonfall registration?	Yes

APPLICANTS ALSO LOOK AT AND OFTEN PREFER

Case Western Reserve University; University of Illinois at Urbana-Champaign; University of Michigan Ann Arbor

AND SOMETIMES PREFER

Purdue University—West Lafayette; University of Minnesota—Twin Cities

AND RARELY PREFER

Loyola The University of Chicago; Milwaukee School of Engineering

FINANCIAL FACTS

Financial Aid Rating	78
Annual tuition	$39,975
Room and board	$10,900
% needy frosh rec. need-based scholarship or grant aid	99
% needy UG rec. need-based scholarship or grant aid	99
% needy frosh rec. non-need-based scholarship or grant aid	15
% needy UG rec. non-need-based scholarship or grant aid	11
% needy frosh rec. need-based self-help aid	72
% needy UG rec. need-based self-help aid	79
% frosh rec. any financial aid	100
% UG rec. any financial aid	100
% UG borrow to pay for school	65
Average cumulative indebtedness	$31,073
% frosh need fully met	15
% ugrads need fully met	14
Average % of frosh need met	83
Average % of ugrad need met	78

ILLINOIS WESLEYAN UNIVERSITY

PO BOX 2900, BLOOMINGTON, IL 61702-2900 • ADMISSIONS: 309-556-3031 • FAX: 309-556-3820

CAMPUS LIFE

Quality of Life Rating	83
Fire Safety Rating	79
Green Rating	67
Type of school	Private
Affiliation	No Affiliation
Environment	City

STUDENTS

Total undergrad enrollment	2,000
% male/female	44/56
% from out of state	12
% frosh from public high school	85
% frosh live on campus	100
% ugrads live on campus	72
# of fraternities (% ugrad men join)	6 (34)
# of sororities (% ugrad women join)	5 (25)
% African American	5
% Asian	5
% Caucasian	74
% Hispanic	6
% Native American	<1
% international	5
# of countries represented	19

SURVEY SAYS . . .

Students are happy
Lab facilities are great
Internships are widely available
No one cheats
Students are friendly
Easy to get around campus
Athletic facilities are great
Frats and sororities are popular
Theater is popular

ACADEMICS

Academic Rating	90
% students returning for sophomore year	88
% students graduating within 4 years	72
% students graduating within 6 years	78
Calendar	Semester
Student/faculty ratio	11:1
Profs interesting rating	86
Profs accessible rating	87

Most classes have 10–19 students.
Most lab/discussion sessions have 10–19 students.

MOST POPULAR MAJORS

business/commerce; psychology; English language and literature

STUDENTS SAY " . . ."

Academics

Located in Bloomington, Illinois Wesleyan University is a community that "invites you to make the most of your education and is ready to bend over backwards to ensure you enjoy your experience." Though the school doesn't have that big of a reputation outside the Midwest "despite its excellent education," it is an underrated gem that is "always trying to give students opportunities that are beyond what most schools can give." It truly is "a small school that oozes big opportunities."

Professors are "brilliant and accessible" "insightful" individuals who are "the best in their field." "The exuberance they have for their subject area and their students is very evident." Many of them are involved in research and "often include students in helping them," while others are involved in other ways; for example, "the mayor of Bloomington is also a political science professor—how cool is that!" "There have been a few life-changing professors who I am so grateful to have taken their class," says a business administration major.

Facilities and the career center are excellent, there are numerous opportunities for community engagement and research, and "there are so many resources and programs that help students who are seeking any type of support, whether it be academic, moral, or health." Wesleyan also "does a great job getting students ready for graduate school," and faculty "put [a lot of] effort into the information being taught, and really try and relate it to real life."

The school has a reputation for "overinvolved students who travel abroad, are the president of three clubs, and still maintain excellent grades." "IWU pushes us to excel academically while encouraging us to pursue our passions outside of our schoolwork," says a student. Overall, IWU is "a friendly community where your professors become mentors, your classmates become lifelong friends, and you graduate prepared to make a real difference in the world."

Life

As with many colleges, there's a strong weekday-weekend divide: "There is a fair trade of work and play." Sunday through Wednesday nights, "people are studying, going to meetings for clubs, maybe going to an event or two," but come the weekend students "will go to parties at fraternity houses or off-campus houses, or go to the bars." Bloomington-Normal also has a variety of "great restaurants" and shopping venues which "are fun places to go to on the weekends," and neighboring ISU offers "some of that big college town culture can be found in the area."

The Office of Student Activities "does a great job having entertainment available for students" and almost every weekend a free event is held in the student center, "whether that be a concert, comedian, movie, or other entertainment ." There is a "plethora of study groups" ("People are very receptive to getting work done together"), "great opportunities for intellectual discussions" at the coffee shop, and "students are always in food areas discussing, reading, or doing homework." "We have a weird obsession with the Game Show network as well here," confesses a student. "Buncha dorks. We know it and we own it!"

Student Body

The typical Wesleyan student "has a major that they take great pride in studying" and "often compare workloads to bond." Students here are "very academically focused" ("it's very rare to find students who don't try") but are also aware that "having a social life is important as well." Most everyone is "very liberal and rather artistic" and "very involved with many different activities." While there are noticeable groups such as "athletes, Greek life, and theater kids" which mainly stick together, "everyone has friends in other departments and organizations." There is "lots of competition on campus for internships and research opportunities," but "everyone is very helpful when it comes to informing others of opportunities." A "large percentage" of the campus is Greek life-affiliated.

FINANCIAL AID: 309-556-3096 • E-MAIL: IWUADMIT@IWU.EDU • WEBSITE: WWW.IWU.EDU

THE PRINCETON REVIEW SAYS

Admissions

Very important factors considered include: GPA, rigor of secondary school record, interview. *Important factors considered include:* Class rank, standardized test scores, application essay, extracurricular activities, talent/ability, character/personal qualities. *Other factors considered include:* First generation, geographical residence, racial/ethnic status, recommendation(s), state residency, volunteer work, work experience, alumni/ae relations, level of applicant's interest. SAT or ACT required; ACT with or without Writing component accepted. TOEFL required of all international applicants. *Academic units recommended:* 4 English; 3 mathematics; 3 science; (2 science lab); 2 social studies; 3 foreign language.

Financial Aid

Students should submit: FAFSA, Institution's own financial aid form. The Princeton Review suggests that all financial aid forms be submitted as soon as possible after January 1. *Need-based scholarships/grants offered:* Federal Pell, SEOG, State scholarships/grants, private scholarships, the school's own gift aid. *Loan aid offered:* Direct Subsidized Stafford Loans, Direct Unsubsidized Stafford Loans, Direct PLUS loans, Federal Perkins Loans, Federal Nursing Loans, College/university loans from institutional funds. Federal Work-Study Program available. Institutional employment available. Off-campus job opportunities are good.

The Inside Word

There's no application fee at IWU, and the school accepts the Common Application, so there are few reasons not to apply to IWU if you're even slightly interested in attending. Those applying to any of the creative arts school may be required to submit additional materials such as a portfolio. Don't expect to breeze through, though. You won't get into this highly selective college without a solid academic profile or a compelling story.

THE SCHOOL SAYS "..."

From the Admissions Office

"Illinois Wesleyan University attracts a wide variety of students who are interested in pursuing diverse fields such as vocal performance, biology, psychology, German, physics, or business administration. At IWU, students are not forced into either/or choices. Rather, they are encouraged to pursue multiple interests simultaneously—a philosophy that is in keeping with the spirit and value of a liberal arts education. The distinctive 4-4-1 calendar allows students to follow their interests each school year in two semesters followed by an optional month-long class in May. May term opportunities include classes on campus; research collaboration with faculty; travel and study in such places as Australia, China, South Africa, and Europe; as well as local, national, and international internships. Study abroad is very popular, with one out of every two students enjoying a travel experience.

"The IWU mission statement reads in part: 'A liberal education at Illinois Wesleyan fosters creativity, critical thinking, effective communication, strength of character, and a spirit of inquiry; it deepens the specialized knowledge of a discipline with a comprehensive world view. It affords the greatest possibilities for realizing individual potential while preparing students for democratic citizenship and life in a global society…The university, through its policies, programs, and practices, is committed to diversity, social justice, and environmental sustainability. A tightly knit, supportive university community, together with a variety of opportunities for close interaction with excellent faculty, both challenges and supports students in their personal and intellectual development.'"

SELECTIVITY

Admissions Rating	91
# of applicants	3,556
% of applicants accepted	58
% of acceptees attending	25
# offered a place on the wait list	149
% accepting a place on wait list	19
% admitted from wait list	18

FRESHMAN PROFILE

Range SAT Critical Reading	510–620
Range SAT Math	570–740
Range ACT Composite	25–30
Minimum paper TOEFL	550
Minimum web-based TOEFL	213
Average HS GPA	3.73
% graduated top 10% of class	45
% graduated top 25% of class	77
% graduated top 50% of class	96

DEADLINES

Early action	
Deadline	11/15
Notification	1/15
Nonfall registration?	Yes

APPLICANTS ALSO LOOK AT AND OFTEN PREFER
University of Notre Dame; Northwestern University

AND SOMETIMES PREFER
University of Illinois at Urbana-Champaign; Washington University in St. Louis

AND RARELY PREFER
Augustana College (IL)

FINANCIAL FACTS

Financial Aid Rating	88
Annual tuition	$37,774
Room and board	$8,838
Required fees	$180
Books and supplies	$800
% needy frosh rec. need-based scholarship or grant aid	99
% needy UG rec. need-based scholarship or grant aid	99
% needy frosh rec. non-need-based scholarship or grant aid	12
% needy UG rec. non-need-based scholarship or grant aid	9
% needy frosh rec. need-based self-help aid	79
% needy UG rec. need-based self-help aid	86
% frosh rec. any financial aid	99
% UG rec. any financial aid	96
% UG borrow to pay for school	76
Average cumulative indebtedness	$31,343
% frosh need fully met	42
% ugrads need fully met	41
Average % of frosh need met	90
Average % of ugrad need met	86

INDIANA UNIVERSITY—BLOOMINGTON

300 NORTH JORDAN AVENUE, BLOOMINGTON, IN 47405-1106 • ADMISSIONS: 812-855-0661 • FAX: 812-855-5102

CAMPUS LIFE

Quality of Life Rating	79
Fire Safety Rating	83
Green Rating	93
Type of school	Public
Affiliation	No Affiliation
Environment	City

STUDENTS

Total undergrad enrollment	31,984
% male/female	50/50
% from out of state	29
% frosh live on campus	98
% ugrads live on campus	28
# of fraternities (% ugrad men join)	40 (21)
# of sororities (% ugrad women join)	31 (23)
% African American	4
% Asian	4
% Caucasian	73
% Hispanic	4
% Native American	<1
% international	11
# of countries represented	138

SURVEY SAYS . . .
Students are happy
Everyone loves the Hoosiers
Student publications are popular
Hard liquor is popular

ACADEMICS

Academic Rating	81
% students returning for sophomore year	90
% students graduating within 4 years	58
% students graduating within 6 years	77
Calendar	Semester
Student/faculty ratio	18:1
Profs interesting rating	73
Profs accessible rating	78

Most classes have 10–19 students.
Most lab/discussion sessions have
20–29 students.

MOST POPULAR MAJORS
exercise science; business/commerce;
biology

STUDENTS SAY ". . ."

Academics

Indiana University—Bloomington focuses on creating well-rounded students who will be successful in and after college. This large state school challenges its students academically, but it "creates a fun collegiate environment, as well." "Academics and school spirit are its specialties!" says one student. The institution offers excellent financial aid and numerous opportunities for graduate and undergraduate students across all departments to conduct research, adding to "the perfect combination of excellent undergraduate teaching, Division I athletic teams backed by a passionate sense of school spirit, and a lively social scene." The "many excellent professors" here "really care about what they do," and they really "know what they're talking about." They "clearly want what's best for their students," and "the learning environment they create is excellent." "I have been very impressed with the individual attention I have received—mostly due to the level of commitment by professors to their students," says one student. The "rigorous and competitive classroom environment" gives students "the knowledge to be successful in our futures through great faculty, facilities, and tradition." Most professors at IU have professional experiences, and therefore "can bring their subjects to life." The "world-renowned business program" and the education and journalism schools are standouts here, but students say that all of the "school systems are great and easy to access," which makes "communicating with students/professors easy." Even with 40,000 people on campus, the administration gives student groups "much freedom of planning," and this warm environment allows students to "collaborate academically and non-academically as one community." This autonomy grants students the chance to explore "anything we want, whenever, but [find] the key thing we'll love through many opportunities and great programs."

Life

This "best-kept secret of the Midwest" is located in "the vibrant city of Bloomington," where "the restaurants off campus are amazing," with "many options to choose from." During the week, people "work really hard," and the campus is very active, with "a good number of students working out or running." There is "always something going on and something to do on campus that will fit the need of any student." Weekends generally start on Thursday night and go through Saturday night, when "house parties are popular," and the Greek system, although it only encompasses roughly 20 percent of the campus, "provides a strong social scene." The legendary IU basketball team is "starting to really rebuild its legacy," and attending games is common. There are also "free movies at the Union on weekends," a college mall, and just "a very fun social scene" in general. Looking around the "beautiful" campus, you can see people jogging, and if the weather's really nice, you can find people lying outside on the grass and on benches snoozing."

Student Body

With such a large student body, "You are destined to find someone who you 'click' with." "It's unheard of that a student won't be able to fit in somewhere," says one. Typical is hard to nail down with tens of thousands of people, but many here are "very respectful of one another and ready to help out a fellow Hoosier" and "very lively and fun," and each student manages to have "an equal balance of school and social life." International students (often attracted by the business and music schools) are "accepted and encouraged to attend IU." Most students can be called "hard workers who also know how to have fun on the weekends."

FINANCIAL AID: 812-855-0321 • E-MAIL: IUADMIT@INDIANA.EDU • WEBSITE: WWW.IUB.EDU

THE PRINCETON REVIEW SAYS

Admissions

Very important factors considered include: Class rank, GPA, rigor of secondary school record, standardized test scores. *Other factors considered include:* Application essay, extracurricular activities, first generation, geographical residence, interview, racial/ethnic status, recommendation(s), state residency, talent/ability, volunteer work, work experience, alumni/ae relations, character/personal qualities, level of applicant's interest. SAT or ACT required; ACT with Writing component required. *Academic units required:* 4 English; 3 science; (2 science lab); 3 social studies; 2 foreign language; 3.5 math; 1.5 electives.

Financial Aid

Students should submit: FAFSA. The Princeton Review suggests that all financial aid forms be submitted as soon as possible after January 1 and before March 10. *Need-based scholarships/grants offered:* Federal Pell, SEOG, State scholarships/grants, private scholarships, the school's own gift aid. *Loan aid offered:* Direct Subsidized Stafford Loans, Direct Unsubsidized Stafford Loans, Direct PLUS loans, Federal Perkins Loans, Federal Nursing Loans, College/university loans from institutional funds. Federal Work-Study Program available. Institutional employment available. Off-campus job opportunities are good.

The Inside Word

Above-average high school performers (defined by both grade point average and test scores) should meet little resistance from the IU admissions office. Students will have the opportunity to meet admissions representatives at numerous recruiting events held in many locations throughout the country or during a campus visit. Rolling admissions favor those who apply early in the process. IU's music program is highly competitive, admission hinges upon a successful audition.

THE SCHOOL SAYS "..."

From the Admissions Office

"Indiana University, one of America's great teaching and research universities, extends learning and teaching beyond the traditional classroom. When visiting campus, students and parents typically describe IU as 'what college should be like.' Students bring diverse experiences, beliefs, and backgrounds from all fifty states and 137 countries to a campus often cited as one of the most beautiful in the nation. IU offers a quintessential college experience. Students enjoy the advantages, opportunities, and resources of a large school, while still receiving personal attention and support. Because of the outstanding academic and cultural resources, students have the best of both worlds.

"Indiana offers more than 5,000 courses and 183 undergraduate majors—many nationally and internationally known—including programs in the arts, sciences, humanities, and social sciences as well as highly rated Schools of Business, Music, Education, Journalism, Public and Environmental Affairs, and Public Health. Students customize academic programs with double and individualized majors, internships, and research opportunities, utilizing state-of-the-art technology. Representatives from more than 1,000 businesses, government agencies, and not-for-profit organizations come to campus yearly to recruit IU students.

"IUB requires the SAT and/or ACT with writing component. The writing sections determine possible credit, placement, or exemption from writing requirements. All application materials for admission must be submitted online or postmarked by November 1 for maximum consideration for admission and possible scholarships, based on academic achievement."

SELECTIVITY

Admissions Rating	86
# of applicants	37,826
% of applicants accepted	72
% of acceptees attending	28

FRESHMAN PROFILE

Range SAT Critical Reading	520–630
Range SAT Math	540–660
Range SAT Writing	510–620
Range ACT Composite	24–30
Minimum paper TOEFL	550
Minimum web-based TOEFL	79
Average HS GPA	3.62
% graduated top 10% of class	35
% graduated top 25% of class	70
% graduated top 50% of class	95

DEADLINES

Regular	
Priority	2/1
Deadline	Rolling
Nonfall registration?	Yes

FINANCIAL FACTS

Financial Aid Rating	82
Annual in-state tuition	$8,919
Annual out-of-state tuition	$31,060
Room and board	$9,149
Required fees	$1,290
Books and supplies	$1,500
% needy frosh rec. need-based scholarship or grant aid	77
% needy UG rec. need-based scholarship or grant aid	74
% needy frosh rec. non-need-based scholarship or grant aid	14
% needy UG rec. non-need-based scholarship or grant aid	10
% needy frosh rec. need-based self-help aid	55
% needy UG rec. need-based self-help aid	65
% UG borrow to pay for school	52
Average cumulative indebtedness	$27,619
% frosh need fully met	16
% ugrads need fully met	12
Average % of frosh need met	88
Average % of ugrad need met	88

INDIANA UNIVERSITY OF PENNSYLVANIA

1011 SOUTH DRIVE, INDIANA, PA 15705 • ADMISSIONS: 724-357-2230 • FAX: 724-357-6281

CAMPUS LIFE

Quality of Life Rating	69
Fire Safety Rating	92
Green Rating	61
Type of school	Public
Affiliation	No Affiliation
Environment	Village

STUDENTS

Total undergrad enrollment	12,108
% male/female	45/55
% from out of state	7
% frosh live on campus	80
% ugrads live on campus	32
# of fraternities (% ugrad men join)	14 (7)
# of sororities (% ugrad women join)	13 (6)
% African American	11
% Asian	1
% Caucasian	79
% Hispanic	3
% Native American	<1
% international	2
# of countries represented	66

SURVEY SAYS . . .

Political activism is unpopular or nonexistent
Lots of beer drinking
Frats and sororities are popular
Student publications are popular

ACADEMICS

Academic Rating	72
% students returning for sophomore year	73
% students graduating within 4 years	29
% students graduating within 6 years	50
Calendar	Semester
Student/faculty ratio	18:1
Profs interesting rating	68
Profs accessible rating	69

Most classes have 20–29 students.
Most lab/discussion sessions have 10–19 students.

MOST POPULAR MAJORS
health and physical education; criminology; nursing

STUDENTS SAY

Academics

Nestled in the heart of western Pennsylvania, Indiana University of Pennsylvania provides students with "a quality education at an affordable price." Across the board, undergrads here assert that their university "is the perfect size: not too small [and] not too big." Indeed, "IUP has the size of a large state school, but it has the community feeling seen in smaller, private schools." Academically, the university "prides itself on [offering] a broad range of majors," and undergrads love that there's so much opportunity to study virtually anything. Of course, it's inevitable that some departments will stand out, and students love to highlight the stellar education, nursing, criminology, and geology programs. Overall, professors at IUP get high marks from undergrads. Certainly, students really appreciate that they are pushed "to become better thinkers inside and outside of the classroom." One undergrad explains further, "I feel that my professors are passionate about the subjects that they teach and love it when students participate and/or even challenge them. They are friendly and very willing to help students with class and even with extra interest-related things." Another student concurs, stating, "The professors I have had in my business honors track are the best. Many of them have not only had real-world experience, but they are also [at the] top of their department. They are truly interested in what they are teaching their students, and they do all they can to help."

Life

Undergrads at IUP proudly proclaim, "There is always something going on here, and you'll never be bored if you take the time to look around." Certainly, "living at IUP can be very exciting...depending on [a] student's sense of drive and definition of a 'good time.'" Another undergrad agrees, sharing, "We have a ton of opportunities for campus involvement through programs, events and leadership work.... This campus is unique in that if a student is passionate about anything, they can [usually] find other students [it will] resonate with [and] they can form a club/organization if it doesn't exist." In addition, "IUP's party scene exists, but if that's not your style then you don't have to worry about it interfering with your life." And nature lovers will also be delighted to learn that there are plenty of opportunities for outdoor adventure. As one student reveals, "During the winter, people go skiing or ice skating at local places. During the warmer months, we have an awesome school park that has hiking and biking trails and fishing." To the detriment of some and to the delight of others, hometown Indiana is "very rural." Of course, when students do venture into town, they can take advantage of "an old movie theater" and "local restaurants, [which are] very good." Moreover, there's also a "very small mall...[and] a bowling alley." However, when undergrads want a little more excitement, they can head down to Pittsburgh, which provides a myriad of cultural and entertainment options.

Student Body

There seems to be a divide among the student body at IUP. Some undergrads believe you can easily categorize their peers "as the people in fraternities and sororities, and those that are not." Indeed, one student curtly states, "Those that are in the Greek life usually do not hang out with people outside of it, and vice versa." However, there are plenty of students who object to this point of view, insisting that "IUP is not cliquish" and assuring us that undergrads here "fit very nicely with each other." As one satisfied undergrad shares, "A typical student is open-minded and willing to learn." Indeed, many describe their peers as "friendly, outgoing, and eager" and perhaps most important, they "know how to have fun." As one pleased student sums up her experience, "By and large, there seems to be a place for virtually anybody to fit in here at IUP."

INDIANA UNIVERSITY OF PENNSYLVANIA

FINANCIAL AID: 724-357-2218 • E-MAIL: ADMISSIONS-INQUIRY@IUP.EDU • WEBSITE: WWW.IUP.EDU

THE PRINCETON REVIEW SAYS

Admissions

Very important factors considered include: GPA, standardized test scores. *Important factors considered include:* Rigor of secondary school record. *Other factors considered include:* Class rank, application essay, extracurricular activities, interview, recommendation(s), talent/ability, volunteer work, work experience, character/personal qualities, level of applicant's interest. SAT or ACT required; ACT with or without Writing component accepted. TOEFL required of all international applicants. *Academic units recommended:* 4 English; 3 mathematics; 3 science; (2 science lab); 3 social studies; 2 foreign language; 2 history.

Financial Aid

Students should submit: FAFSA. The Princeton Review suggests that all financial aid forms be submitted as soon as possible after January 1. *Need-based scholarships/grants offered:* Federal Pell, SEOG, state scholarships/grants, private scholarships, the school's own gift aid, United Negro College Fund. *Loan aid offered:* Federal Perkins Loans, college/university loans from institutional funds. Federal Work-Study Program available. Institutional employment available. Off-campus job opportunities are good.

The Inside Word

Admissions officers at Indiana University of Pennsylvania follow the typical protocol when making their decisions. That is to say, they look for candidates who have successfully completed a challenging, college-prep curriculum. It should be noted that certain majors such as dietetics, education, speech language pathology and audiology, nursing, and fine arts all maintain specific admissions requirements that applicants must meet.

THE SCHOOL SAYS "..."

From the Admissions Office

"At IUP, we look at each applicant as an individual, not as a number. That means we'll review your application materials very carefully. When reviewing applications, the admissions committee's primary focus is on the student's high school record and SAT scores. In addition, the committee often reviews the optional personal essay and letters of recommendations submitted by the student to aid in the decision-making process. We're always happy to speak with prospective students. Call us toll-free at 800-422-6830 or 724-357-2230, or e-mail us at admissions-inquiry@iup.edu.

"Students applying for admission are required to take the SAT or ACT."

SELECTIVITY

Admissions Rating	71
# of applicants	9,367
% of applicants accepted	90
% of acceptees attending	32

FRESHMAN PROFILE

Range SAT Critical Reading	440–530
Range SAT Math	440–540
Range SAT Writing	420–520
Minimum paper TOEFL	500
Minimum web-based TOEFL	61
% graduated top 10% of class	8
% graduated top 25% of class	23
% graduated top 50% of class	58

DEADLINES

Nonfall registration?	Yes

APPLICANTS ALSO LOOK AT AND OFTEN PREFER

Pennsylvania State University—University Park; Westminster College (PA)

AND SOMETIMES PREFER

Slippery Rock University of Pennsylvania; West Virginia University; University of Delaware; James Madison University

AND RARELY PREFER

Bloomsburg University of Pennsylvania

FINANCIAL FACTS

Financial Aid Rating	68
Annual in-state tuition	$6,622
Annual out-of-state tuition	$16,556
Room and board	$11,100
Required fees	$2,458
Books and supplies	$1,100
% needy frosh rec. need-based scholarship or grant aid	64
% needy UG rec. need-based scholarship or grant aid	63
% needy frosh rec. non-need-based scholarship or grant aid	29
% needy UG rec. non-need-based scholarship or grant aid	19
% needy frosh rec. need-based self-help aid	92
% needy UG rec. need-based self-help aid	91
% frosh rec. any financial aid	80
% UG rec. any financial aid	83
% UG borrow to pay for school	85
Average cumulative indebtedness	$37,457
% frosh need fully met	6
% ugrads need fully met	6
Average % of frosh need met	55
Average % of ugrad need met	54

Iowa State University

100 Enrollment Services, Ames, IA 50011-2011 • Admissions: 515-294-5836 • Fax: 515-294-2592

CAMPUS LIFE

Quality of Life Rating	92
Fire Safety Rating	82
Green Rating	99
Type of school	Public
Affiliation	No Affiliation
Environment	Town

STUDENTS

Total undergrad enrollment	27,112
% male/female	57/43
% from out of state	31
% frosh from public high school	92
% frosh live on campus	89
% ugrads live on campus	39
# of fraternities (% ugrad men join)	32 (13)
# of sororities (% ugrad women join)	20 (17)
% African American	3
% Asian	3
% Caucasian	77
% Hispanic	4
% Native American	<1
% international	7
# of countries represented	101

SURVEY SAYS . . .

Students are happy
Great library
Career services are great
School is well run
Students are friendly
Students get along with local community
Campus feels safe
Athletic facilities are great
Very little drug use
Everyone loves the Cyclones
Intramural sports are popular
Student publications are popular

ACADEMICS

Academic Rating	77
% students returning for sophomore year	87
% students graduating within 4 years	41
% students graduating within 6 years	75
Calendar	Semester
Student/faculty ratio	19:1
Profs interesting rating	69
Profs accessible rating	74

Most classes have 20–29 students.
Most lab/discussion sessions have 20–29 students.

MOST POPULAR MAJORS

mechanical engineering; marketing; exercise science

STUDENTS SAY ". . ."

Academics

More than 28,000 students come together in Ames to get degrees in more than 100 majors, successfully giving off "a small-school feel with a big-university atmosphere." Science and technology are the main draws at this research university, but this "welcoming and friendly environment" treats all of its students well, regardless of their academic path. Professors, academic advisors, and other staff are all "very willing to help you academically and personally," and the Cyclone Nation is all about "engaging students not only in the classroom, but in the whole college experience." Professors "do what they can" for their students, focusing on experiences outside the classroom. It's also clear to students that the professors "truly love what they teach and bring passion to their lectures," working hard "to make students truly know what they want to spend the rest of their life doing." "Iowa State is all about preparing you for an actual career through hands-on teaching," says a student. Though lecture classes in the early college years can run large, the classroom experience (both in and out) only improves as students specialize. "I've been given the opportunity to work on an independent research project with a faculty mentor, which has been a really rewarding opportunity," says one student. All of the administration, "all the way up to our president and provost," is "dedicated to making student life at Iowa State the main priority." One of the school's greatest strengths is its ability to get students involved in internships, making it "extremely easy to find a job in your area of study"; every year, there are "very large engineering, agriculture, and business/LAS career fairs [that] allow students to find internships and full-time jobs easily." Even if one of your classes isn't the greatest, there "are many computer labs, help sessions, and teacher's assistants to go to for extra help."

Life

Iowa State is all about having "a big college experience (the athletics, the clubs, the shows, the educational opportunities, the school spirit) in a small college town"; indeed, Ames' support of the university "gives it a very at home and smaller feel than it actually is." During the week, students "mostly focus on classes and schoolwork." The weekends provide more of a chance to cut loose, whether that's a free event on campus, hanging out in each others' rooms and playing video games, partying, or playing an intramural sport (basketball, flag football, broomball, and others are "very popular"). "Winning an intramural championship t-shirt is very important and highly coveted on campus," says one student. There are "hundreds of clubs and activities for any of your interests," and the campus "will host bands quite a bit, and also a lot of late-night activities such as bingo, hypnotist shows, speakers, and lots of food." If you can't find what you want on campus, go off campus into downtown Ames, which is "full of fast-food and chain restaurants, bars, movie theaters, a mall, as well as locally owned businesses, restaurants, and novelty shops." Most students live on campus for their first two years, but off campus is "still very close to campus… so it's very comfortable and relatively cheap."

Student Body

Understandably, most students here are "small-town Iowans" or from the Midwest: "corn fed and bred," as they say. There is "some diversity," but "most of the students are white, and the second largest group is Asian." These "humble," "extremely friendly" students "care about the community and get involved with as many activities as possible." "If someone gets off of the campus and city bus system without thanking the bus driver, it's practically a sin," says a student. Although enrollment is at about 30,000, "students make it feel like a small town where everyone is a member of the Cyclone family."

FINANCIAL AID: 515-294-2223 • E-MAIL: ADMISSIONS@IASTATE.EDU • WEBSITE: WWW.IASTATE.EDU

THE PRINCETON REVIEW SAYS

Admissions

Very important factors considered include: Class rank, GPA, rigor of secondary school record, standardized test scores. *Other factors considered include:* Application essay, extracurricular activities, geographical residence, interview, recommendation(s), state residency, talent/ability, volunteer work, work experience, character/personal qualities. SAT or ACT required; ACT with or without Writing component accepted. TOEFL required of all international applicants. *Academic units required:* 4 English; 3 mathematics; 3 science; (2 science lab); 2 social studies; 2 foreign language. *Academic units recommended:* 4 English; 4 mathematics; 4 science; (3 science lab); 4 social studies; 3 foreign language.

Financial Aid

Students should submit: FAFSA. The Princeton Review suggests that all financial aid forms be submitted as soon as possible after January 1. *Need-based scholarships/grants offered:* Federal Pell, SEOG, State scholarships/grants, the school's own gift aid. *Loan aid offered:* Direct Subsidized Stafford Loans, Direct Unsubsidized Stafford Loans, Direct PLUS loans, Federal Perkins Loans, College/university loans from institutional funds. Federal Work-Study Program available. Institutional employment available. Off-campus job opportunities are excellent.

The Inside Word

Admission to ISU is formula-driven and based on: ACT composite score; high school GPA; high school percentile rank; and number of high school courses completed in the core subject areas. The formula, known as the Regent Admission Index (RAI), is as follows: RAI = (2 × ACT composite score) + (1 × percentile high school rank) + (20 × high school grade point average) + (5 × number of years of high school courses completed in the core subject areas). Anyone earning an RAI score of at least 245 is automatically admitted; the admissions office reviews applicants scoring below 245 individually to determine which will also be admitted.

THE SCHOOL SAYS "..."

From the Admissions Office

"Iowa State University offers all the advantages of a major university along with the friendliness and warmth of a residential campus. There are more than 100 undergraduate programs of study in the Colleges of Agriculture and Life Sciences, Business, Design, Human Sciences, Engineering, Liberal Arts and Sciences, and Veterinary Medicine. Our 1,700 faculty members include Rhodes Scholars, Fulbright Scholars, and National Academy of Sciences and National Academy of Engineering members. Recognized for its high quality of life, Iowa State has taken practical steps to make the university a place where students feel like they belong. Iowa State has been recognized for the high quality of campus life and the exemplary out-of-class experiences offered to its students. Along with a strong academic experience, students also have opportunities for further developing their leadership skills and interpersonal relationships through any of the more than 700 student organizations, sixty intramural sports, and a multitude of arts and recreational activities."

SELECTIVITY

Admissions Rating	78
# of applicants	17,525
% of applicants accepted	85
% of acceptees attending	41

FRESHMAN PROFILE

Range SAT Critical Reading	460–620
Range SAT Math	530–680
Range ACT Composite	22–28
Minimum paper TOEFL	530
Average HS GPA	3.55
% graduated top 10% of class	25
% graduated top 25% of class	56
% graduated top 50% of class	90

DEADLINES

Regular	
Priority	
Deadline	7/1
Nonfall registration?	Yes

APPLICANTS ALSO LOOK AT AND OFTEN PREFER

University of Illinois at Urbana-Champaign; University of Minnesota—Twin Cities; University of Wisconsin-Madison; Purdue University—West Lafayette

AND RARELY PREFER

Baylor University; Western Michigan University

FINANCIAL FACTS

Financial Aid Rating	84
Annual in-state tuition	$6,648
Annual out-of-state tuition	$19,200
Room and board	$7,721
Required fees	$1,078
Books and supplies	$1,043
% needy frosh rec. need-based scholarship or grant aid	98
% needy UG rec. need-based scholarship or grant aid	98
% needy frosh rec. non-need-based scholarship or grant aid	48
% needy UG rec. non-need-based scholarship or grant aid	46
% needy frosh rec. need-based self-help aid	69
% needy UG rec. need-based self-help aid	77
% frosh rec. any financial aid	87
% UG rec. any financial aid	80
% UG borrow to pay for school	62
Average cumulative indebtedness	$29,898
% frosh need fully met	36
% ugrads need fully met	35
Average % of frosh need met	83
Average % of ugrad need met	81

ITHACA COLLEGE

ITHACA COLLEGE, OFFICE OF ADMISSION, ITHACA, NY 14850-7002 • ADMISSIONS: 607-274-3124 • FAX: 607-274-1900

STUDENTS SAY ". . ."

Academics

"Small class sizes" that afford plenty of "personal attention," "outstanding" scholarships, and cross-registration with nearby Cornell University are a few great reasons to choose Ithaca College, a smallish school in central New York that offers many of the resources you would expect to find at a much larger university. "You are able to be a part of a community and get the chance to pursue interests that are not necessarily a part of your chosen course of study," relates an English major. "We have loads of opportunities to do and try a wide variety of things." The vast multitude of academic offerings includes "one of the best communication schools in the country." Also notable are "strong" majors in music, business, and drama; a "highly competitive" six-year doctorate program in physical therapy; and the cinema and photography program. Professors are "really engaging and understand how to present the material so that it is relevant and meaningful." On the whole, faculty members are "really passionate about their fields and have a genuine interest in getting students excited about their passions." By far, the most common academic complaint about academics at Ithaca concerns registration, which can be trying. Some say, "the buildings—inside and out—are a bit outdated." Overall the campus is known for its picturesque beauty. "People aren't kidding when they say 'Ithaca is Gorges (gorgeous),'" promises one student.

Life

The number of extracurricular choices is "considerable" at Ithaca College. At the same time, "the school is small enough for anyone to get involved." There are "speakers and events offered on campus." There's also a nearly professional-quality college radio station. Many students "are part of an athletic team or participate in intramural athletics." For relaxation, students often "hang out on the quad," throwing Frisbees or "playing music on the lawns on tie-dye sheets." The social situation at Ithaca is "nothing like the party scene you'd find at a larger university," but "there are some good parties" now and then. While the campus is a little "isolated," students also frequently manage to attend frat parties at Cornell and generally "enjoy the social scene" the nearby Ivy offers. "The town of Ithaca is quaint but lively." There's "a good music scene and a lot of cool stores." When the weather is nice, "there's always some festival," or at least it seems that way. "If you're an outdoorsy person," the wooded and rocky surrounding area is a wonderland of activity. "The hiking here is unbelievable," and few other schools offer the opportunity to "go cliff jumping on a hot Saturday." On the negative side, winters are cold as a matter of course, and "the cold and rain do hinder activities." Students joke, be prepared to get your exercise walking between classes, "the hills here will kill you."

Student Body

The typical undergrad here is "genuine," "easygoing," "always busy," "well-dressed," and has a "sunny disposition despite the gray skies." Beyond those qualities, the population is "a wide mix of hipsters, jocks, theater kids, music students," and "crunchy granola hippies." "People of all kinds fit in here." "Everyone finds their niche." Cliques are often based loosely on academics. "Ithaca is not so much one community as a whole," explains one student. "Instead, each school (music, communications, business, etc.) is its own community." Ethnic diversity and other kinds of diversity are "not entirely unheard of." However, people are "usually from the Northeast," and "the population of students that fit into the typical suburban, upper-middle-class family is definitely significant." Politically, "students at Ithaca tend to be liberal." Some students tell us that you'll find "a lot of people are environmentally and socially conscious" here who want "to change the world."

FINANCIAL AID: 607-274-3131 • E-MAIL: ADMISSION@ITHACA.EDU • WEBSITE: WWW.ITHACA.EDU

THE PRINCETON REVIEW SAYS

Admissions

Very important factors considered include: GPA, rigor of secondary school record, level of applicant's interest. *Important factors considered include:* Application essay, extracurricular activities, recommendation(s), talent/ability, character/personal qualities. *Other factors considered include:* Class rank, standardized test scores, first generation, interview, volunteer work, work experience, alumni/ae relations. SAT or ACT considered if submitted; ACT with or without Writing component accepted. TOEFL required of all international applicants. *Academic units required:* 4 English; 3 mathematics; 3 science; 3 social studies; 2 foreign language; 1 academic elective. *Academic units recommended:* 4 English; 4 mathematics; 4 science; 4 social studies; 3 foreign language; 1 academic elective.

Financial Aid

Students should submit: FAFSA, CSS/Financial Aid PROFILE. The Princeton Review suggests that all financial aid forms be submitted as soon as possible after January 1. *Need-based scholarships/grants offered:* Federal Pell, SEOG, State scholarships/grants, private scholarships, the school's own gift aid. *Loan aid offered:* Direct Subsidized Stafford Loans, Direct Unsubsidized Stafford Loans, Direct PLUS loans, Federal Perkins Loans. Federal Work-Study Program available. Institutional employment available. Off-campus job opportunities are good.

The Inside Word

Ithaca's admissions profile continues to be on the rise with a good deal of highly competitive applicants. Programs requiring an audition (for example, music) or portfolio review (for example, art) are among Ithaca's most demanding for admission. If you want to pursue the six-year clinical doctorate in physical therapy, focus on completing substantial math and science coursework in high school.

THE SCHOOL SAYS "..."

From the Admissions Office

"Located in central New York's Finger Lakes region, Ithaca College offers more than 100 majors in its Schools of Business, Communications, Health Sciences and Human Performance, Humanities and Sciences, and Music.

"Whether you dream of becoming a media mogul, nonprofit hero, groundbreaking scientist, or brilliant composer—Ithaca College will make you ready. Our dedicated professors are experts in their fields and will make you an expert in yours by providing hands-on experience from day one. Experiment in a lab, light up the stage, take risks in the stock market—whatever your interests, you'll dive in right away to turn classroom theory into well-practiced skill.

"From our vibrant campus community to the world beyond, you'll find exciting opportunities to expand your mind and enhance your education. Nearly 200 student organizations provide the perfect place to create award-winning projects, volunteer, philosophize, and connect. Add more valuable skills with a fast-paced internship or enlightening study-abroad program, including our semester-long options in New York City, L.A., and London. From campus life to life experience, Ithaca College will make you ready for your career and anything that comes your way.

"To learn more, visit ithaca.edu/ready."

SELECTIVITY

Admissions Rating	86
# of applicants	15,658
% of applicants accepted	67
% of acceptees attending	17
# offered a place on the wait list	1,949
% accepting a place on wait list	21
% admitted from wait list	8
# of early decision applicants	178
% accepted early decision	90

FRESHMAN PROFILE

Range SAT Critical Reading	540–630
Range SAT Math	540–640
Range SAT Writing	540–640
Minimum paper TOEFL	550
Minimum web-based TOEFL	213
% graduated top 10% of class	27
% graduated top 25% of class	63
% graduated top 50% of class	91

DEADLINES

Early decision	
Deadline	11/1
Notification	12/15
Early action	
Deadline	12/1
Notification	2/1
Regular	
Deadline	2/1
Notification	4/15
Nonfall registration?	Yes

APPLICANTS ALSO LOOK AT AND OFTEN PREFER

Boston University; New York University

AND SOMETIMES PREFER

Pennsylvania State University—University Park; University of Vermont

AND RARELY PREFER

American University; Fordham University

FINANCIAL FACTS

Financial Aid Rating	88
Annual tuition	$38,400
Room and board	$13,900
Required fees	$0
Books and supplies	$1,458
% needy frosh rec. need-based scholarship or grant aid	96
% needy UG rec. need-based scholarship or grant aid	97
% needy frosh rec. non-need-based scholarship or grant aid	34
% needy UG rec. non-need-based scholarship or grant aid	23
% needy frosh rec. need-based self-help aid	91
% needy UG rec. need-based self-help aid	93
% frosh rec. any financial aid	95
% UG rec. any financial aid	92
% UG borrow to pay for school	
% frosh need fully met	56
% ugrads need fully met	45
Average % of frosh need met	90
Average % of ugrad need met	86

JAMES MADISON UNIVERSITY

SONNER HALL, MSC 0101, HARRISONBURG, VA 22807 • ADMISSIONS: 540-568-5681 • FAX: 540-568-3332

STUDENTS SAY ". . ."

Academics

James Madison University has a reputation as "a school that values education, respect, and integrity." The university boasts "one of the best BA programs for musical theater on the East Coast," and an "amazing" business school. A communication major says, "James Madison offered a positive, enriching, and supportive learning environment," and most students agree that JMU is an "inspiring environment filled with students striving to be productive members of society." A senior says, "I found the JMU environment to be comfortable and conducive to learning," and it seems clear that "JMU is all about taking your academics seriously." Professors get consistently high marks for being "available to help" and "interested in student achievement." Although they're often described as "challenging," students say professors are "willing to facilitate your education in any way possible" and "are very down to earth, approachable, and huge supporters of discussion based classes." Like any large university, there are "some professors you want to avoid," and students grumble that "registering for classes, if you don't have priority is a pain." It's worth noting, however, that "classrooms and facilities are always well kept and very up-to-date with all the best teaching technology."

Life

Located in Virginia's Shenandoah Valley, JMU is known for its "beautiful" campus, and students rave about the "benefits of walking in the mountains." An English major says, "The moment I walked on campus I was captured by the student spirit and how beautiful it is." School spirit is generally high and students say, "There's a huge sense of JMU pride, everyone loves the Dukes!" A senior adds, "We have so much pride for our school. There is a friendly, collaborative ambiance here that is unparalleled anywhere else." The university is known for its Southern hospitality, and one student describes the student body as "the 'door-holding freaks of America' because even when people are several feet away, we stand there to hold the door for them." There are numerous ways to get involved on campus, and the "sheer number of student activities is stellar." Students rave about the "personal involvement that JMU offer(s)," and say, "They make you feel like a part of the campus, not just another number." Food services and facilities get high marks across the board, and most agree that the "administration and faculty are always willing to talk to students and point them in the right direction," noting that one of "the greatest strengths of the school is the ability to get any sort of assistance when needed." Regardless, there are complaints about traffic on campus, and many feel, "the school could improve on parking, by a long shot."

Student Body

At JMU, "the typical student is friendly, smart, open-minded, and fun." Students describe themselves as "excellent [at] maintaining a round, balanced life," and say, "Everyone seems relaxed and knows how to have fun but keep their school work a priority." One student jokes that the typical student is "probably a girl considering our ratio seems like eighty to twenty at times," and another concurs, "more males would be nice." Students tend to be "white from the upper- to middle-class," and an International Affairs major says, "Although we do have all types here, most people consist of your typical prep wearing Uggs and a North Face." Some complain, "There is party atmosphere here that can seem dominating," and "If you do not go out and party you stand out." Others note, however, "Greek life is small," and parties "are usually open to everyone," adding that partying isn't "all students here think about. People will get together and drink for fun, but it isn't a necessity." A sophomore says, "On the weekends, students can go to downtown Harrisonburg to the various restaurants and shops," or enjoy on-campus movies at a reduced rate. Still others take advantage of the "great places to hike and spend time outdoors" and JMU's easy accessibility to nearby ski resorts.

FINANCIAL AID: 540-568-7820 • E-MAIL: ADMISSIONS@JMU.EDU • WEBSITE: WWW.JMU.EDU

THE PRINCETON REVIEW SAYS

Admissions

Very important factors considered include: GPA, rigor of secondary school record, standardized test scores. *Important factors considered include:* State residency. *Other factors considered include:* Application essay, extracurricular activities, first generation, geographical residence, racial/ethnic status, recommendation(s), talent/ability, volunteer work, work experience, alumni/ae relations, character/personal qualities, level of applicant's interest. SAT or ACT required; ACT with or without Writing component accepted. TOEFL required of all international applicants. *Academic units required:* 4 English; 4 mathematics; 3 science; (3 science lab); 2 social studies; 3 foreign language; 2 history.

Financial Aid

Students should submit: FAFSA. The Princeton Review suggests that all financial aid forms be submitted as soon as possible after January 1. *Need-based scholarships/grants offered:* Federal Pell, SEOG, State scholarships/grants, private scholarships, the school's own gift aid. *Loan aid offered:* Direct Subsidized Stafford Loans, Direct Unsubsidized Stafford Loans, Direct PLUS loans, Federal Perkins Loans. Federal Work-Study Program available. Institutional employment available. Off-campus job opportunities are good.

The Inside Word

At JMU admissions are competitive, but the admissions staff insists that they're not searching for a "magic combination" of test scores and GPA. Admissions officers review each application individually and are most interested in the quality of an applicant's secondary school education, followed by performance and test scores. The personal statement is a vehicle for conveying information an applicant deems important but that doesn't appear elsewhere in the application, as such it's optional.

THE SCHOOL SAYS "..."

From the Admissions Office

"James Madison University's philosophy of inclusiveness—known as 'all together one'—means that students become a part of a real community that nurtures its own to learn, grow, and succeed. Our professors, many of whom have a wealth of real-world experience, pride themselves on making teaching their top priority. We take seriously the responsibility to maintain an environment that fosters learning and encourages students to excel in and out of the classroom. Our rich variety of educational, social, and extracurricular activities include more than 100 innovative and traditional undergraduate majors and programs, a well-established study abroad program, a cutting-edge information security program, more than 350 student clubs and organizations, and a 147,000-square-foot, state-of-the-art recreation center. The university's picturesque, self-contained campus is located in the heart of the Shenandoah Valley, a four-season area that's easy to call home. Great food, fun times, exciting intercollegiate athletics, and rigorous academics all combine to create the unique James Madison experience. From the library to the residence halls and from our outstanding honors program to our highly successful career placement program, the university is committed to equipping our students with the tools they need to achieve their dreams."

SELECTIVITY

Admissions Rating	87
# of applicants	23,400
% of applicants accepted	60
% of acceptees attending	29

FRESHMAN PROFILE

Range SAT Critical Reading	520–620
Range SAT Math	530–620
Range SAT Writing	520–610
Range ACT Composite	23–27
Minimum paper TOEFL	550
Minimum web-based TOEFL	213
Average HS GPA	3.80
% graduated top 10% of class	26
% graduated top 25% of class	70
% graduated top 50% of class	98

DEADLINES

Early action	
Deadline	11/1
Notification	1/1
Regular	
Deadline	1/15
Notification	4/1
Nonfall registration?	No

APPLICANTS ALSO LOOK AT AND OFTEN PREFER
University of Virginia; Virginia Tech

AND SOMETIMES PREFER
University of Delaware; George Mason University

FINANCIAL FACTS

Financial Aid Rating	80
Annual in-state tuition	$9,176
Annual out-of-state tuition	$23,654
Room and board	$8,519
Required fees	$4,072
Books and supplies	$876
% needy frosh rec. need-based scholarship or grant aid	46
% needy UG rec. need-based scholarship or grant aid	43
% needy frosh rec. non-need-based scholarship or grant aid	9
% needy UG rec. non-need-based scholarship or grant aid	8
% needy frosh rec. need-based self-help aid	79
% needy UG rec. need-based self-help aid	72
% frosh rec. any financial aid	59
% UG rec. any financial aid	53
% UG borrow to pay for school	54
Average cumulative indebtedness	$22,792
% frosh need fully met	89
% ugrads need fully met	75
Average % of frosh need met	41
Average % of ugrad need met	46

JOHNS HOPKINS UNIVERSITY

3400 NORTH CHARLES STREET, BALTIMORE, MD 21218 • ADMISSIONS: 410-516-8171 • FAX: 410-516-6025

CAMPUS LIFE
Quality of Life Rating	83
Fire Safety Rating	94
Green Rating	97
Type of school	Private
Affiliation	No Affiliation
Environment	Metropolis

STUDENTS
Total undergrad enrollment	5,148
% male/female	51/49
% from out of state	87
% frosh from public high school	55
% frosh live on campus	100
% ugrads live on campus	55
# of fraternities (% ugrad men join)	14 (27)
# of sororities (% ugrad women join)	8 (32)
% African American	5
% Asian	20
% Caucasian	48
% Hispanic	11
% Native American	<1
% international	9
# of countries represented	65

SURVEY SAYS . . .
Lab facilities are great
Campus feels safe
Lots of beer drinking
Alumni active on campus

ACADEMICS
Academic Rating	81
% students returning for sophomore year	97
% students graduating within 4 years	88
% students graduating within 6 years	93
Calendar	4/1/4
Student/faculty ratio	12:1
Profs interesting rating	71
Profs accessible rating	72

Most classes have 10–19 students.
Most lab/discussion sessions have
10–19 students.

MOST POPULAR MAJORS
public health; biomedical engineering;
neuroscience

STUDENTS SAY ". . ."

Academics
Johns Hopkins University has a reputation as an academic powerhouse, one that its undergrads wholeheartedly affirm. Although the university offers "a pretty intense environment" with "really rigorous" classes, all of this is made bearable by professors who are "concerned with the individual student" and "extremely approachable, even in [an] organic chemistry class of 300 students." Indeed, "they enjoy being in the classroom and sharing what they know. Each is passionate about their area of study and eager to share it with students who are equally as enthusiastic." A satisfied senior echoes these praises, saying, "All the professors that I've encountered at Hopkins recognize that learning should be fun and thought-provoking. Their lectures or discussions engage students to think about the materials in a different way and pursue further outside study." "Engage" is the operative word here, as undergrads are "treated as though they are participants in their respective academic fields, not just 'students'." However, as one senior cautions, "There's very little grade inflation, and you work hard for the grade you get." Praise also extends to the administration, which students describe as "caring to a fault, willing to help, and generally highly interested in the undergraduate experience." As one junior sums up, "It's clear that our professors and deans genuinely care about the students, as evidenced by their attendance at student fundraisers, fraternity scholarship events, and even plays and a cappella concerts. They want students to learn about anything that interests them, but they want students to grow as people too, and it's astonishing how high their success rate is in that regard."

Life
Life at Hopkins is "certainly based around work." Indeed, most undergrads are diligent students "who put work over everything else." This is a school where "people care about what they study" and it's not uncommon to see fellow students "stay up all night debating philosophy, politics or the theory of evolution." Sound a little intense? No worries: One junior assures us that "there's never a dull moment at Johns Hopkins: You just have to step outside your room and look for five seconds." Another senior confirms, "There's always something cool going on around campus, whether it's from the world of entertainment (like Will Ferrell coming to speak) or academia." There are numerous "free on-campus movies, plays, dance, and a cappella performances" to take in along with "the *best* lacrosse team in America" and "incredibly competitive [Division III] sports like soccer and water polo." And with roughly a quarter of the student body involved in fraternities and sororities, Greek life offers a "tremendous social outlet." Fortunately, when students get bored on campus, they can always explore hometown Baltimore for entertainment options. The city offers "movie theaters, malls, shopping centers, a *ton* of restaurants, a good music scene, and proximity to D.C., clubs, and other colleges. Many undergrads can frequently be found hanging out by the Inner Harbor or the nearby Towson Mall."

Student Body
While it might be difficult to define the typical Hopkins undergrad, the vast majority are "hardworking and care about their GPAs, and will do what they can to get the grades they want." Thankfully, many are also "balance artists; they are able to balance schoolwork, extracurricular activities, jobs, and a social life without getting too bogged down or stressed." Though students "are competitive in the sense that they all want to do well," that competitiveness is never adversarial. One junior declares, "I have found that there is an incredible mutual respect that permeates the student body, one that allows engineers to discuss poetry with English majors, sees historians present at astronomy lectures, and gets linguists to help lacrosse players study for French tests, all while reserving judgment upon each other." A sophomore continues, "I've never been someplace where there are so many diverse interests. As clichéd as it may sound, there truly is a niche for everyone."

FINANCIAL AID: 410-516-8028 • E-MAIL: GOTOJHU@JHU.EDU • WEBSITE: WWW.JHU.EDU

THE PRINCETON REVIEW SAYS

Admissions

Very important factors considered include: GPA, rigor of secondary school record, recommendation(s), character/personal qualities. *Important factors considered include:* Class rank, standardized test scores, application essay, extracurricular activities, talent/ability. *Other factors considered include:* First generation, geographical residence, interview, racial/ethnic status, volunteer work, work experience, alumni/ae relations. SAT or ACT required; SAT and SAT Subject Tests or ACT recommended; ACT with Writing component required. TOEFL required of all international applicants. *Academic units recommended:* 4 English; 4 mathematics; 4 science; 2 social studies; 4 foreign language; 2 history.

Financial Aid

Students should submit: FAFSA, CSS/Financial Aid PROFILE, Noncustodial PROFILE, Business/Farm Supplement. Regular filing deadline is 3/1. The Princeton Review suggests that all financial aid forms be submitted as soon as possible after January 1. *Need-based scholarships/grants offered:* Federal Pell, SEOG, State scholarships/grants, private scholarships, the school's own gift aid. *Loan aid offered:* Direct Subsidized Stafford Loans, Direct Unsubsidized Stafford Loans, Direct PLUS loans, Federal Perkins Loans, College/university loans from institutional funds. Applicants will be notified of awards beginning 4/1. Federal Work-Study Program available. Institutional employment available. Off-campus job opportunities are good.

The Inside Word

Top schools like Hopkins receive more and more applications every year and, as a result, grow harder and harder to get into. With more than 20,000 applicants, Hopkins has to reject numerous applicants who are thoroughly qualified. Give your application everything you've got, and don't take it personally if you don't get a fat envelope in the mail.

THE SCHOOL SAYS "..."

From the Admissions Office

"Johns Hopkins University is a place where ambitious, talented, and creative students thrive. Here, students in all majors embrace a spirit of learning through exploration and discovery. We offer students the freedom to pursue their intellectual passions, the opportunity to learn from academic leaders, and the chance to make an impact right away. With no core curriculum, students are able—and encouraged—to build the academic path that is right for them, with guidance from staff and administrators to help them find their way. Our students can combine their interests—academic and otherwise—in ways that are meaningful to them, and often discover new passions while they're here. Double majoring and majoring or taking classes across disciplines are common practices; in addition, over 97% of students have at least one career-related experience as undergraduates. Studying abroad is also a common option. Outside of the classroom, students are active and engaged on a lively campus, involved in activities from dance or singing groups to international service organizations. The admissions committee approaches applications from a holistic perspective, evaluating the 'whole student.' In addition to looking at a student's academic achievement and intellectual curiosity, we seek to admit students who are excited about learning and living at Johns Hopkins. We look for students who will bring something to the campus community while taking advantage of all Johns Hopkins has to offer."

SELECTIVITY

Admissions Rating	99
# of applicants	20,614
% of applicants accepted	17
% of acceptees attending	37
# offered a place on the wait list	2,069
% accepting a place on wait list	50
% admitted from wait list	6
# of early decision applicants	1,445
% accepted early decision	37

FRESHMAN PROFILE

Range SAT Critical Reading	660–740
Range SAT Math	680–780
Range SAT Writing	660–760
Range ACT Composite	31–34
Minimum paper TOEFL	600
Average HS GPA	3.74
% graduated top 10% of class	84
% graduated top 25% of class	98
% graduated top 50% of class	99

DEADLINES

Early decision	
Deadline	11/1
Notification	12/15
Regular	
Deadline	1/1
Notification	4/1
Nonfall registration?	No

APPLICANTS ALSO LOOK AT AND OFTEN PREFER

University of Pennsylvania; Princeton University; Massachusetts Institute of Technology; Yale University; Harvard College

AND SOMETIMES PREFER

Cornell University; Northwestern University

AND RARELY PREFER

Rice University

FINANCIAL FACTS

Financial Aid Rating	94
Annual tuition	$45,470
Room and board	$13,832
Required fees	$500
Books and supplies	$1,200
% needy frosh rec. need-based scholarship or grant aid	91
% needy UG rec. need-based scholarship or grant aid	92
% needy frosh rec. non-need-based scholarship or grant aid	11
% needy UG rec. non-need-based scholarship or grant aid	8
% needy frosh rec. need-based self-help aid	86
% needy UG rec. need-based self-help aid	90
% frosh rec. any financial aid	58
% UG rec. any financial aid	55
% UG borrow to pay for school	49
Average cumulative indebtedness	$22,808
% frosh need fully met	100
% ugrads need fully met	100
Average % of frosh need met	99
Average % of ugrad need met	100

JUNIATA COLLEGE

1700 MOORE STREET, HUNTINGDON, PA 16652 • ADMISSIONS: 814-641-3420 • FAX: 814-641-3100

STUDENTS SAY "..."

Academics

Juniata College is a private liberal arts college located in Huntingdon, Pennsylvania. The college is named after the Juniata River. The school has "excellent science programs," and a few students say that there need to be "more resources [for] non-science programs." However, even students not majoring in science get access to some great facilities, with theater students exclaiming, "The theater program is unlike any other in country" and praising their new Halbritter Center for the Performing Arts. At Juniata, students can choose one of the many majors offered, or they can design their own under the Program of Emphasis. Many students do so, about 30 percent, which allows each student to work with two faculty members and choose which classes would best fit their intended area of study. The "outstanding education" is built on a bedrock of strong faculty members who offer "superior education through meaningful personal interaction." Most class sizes tend to be fairly small, and though some classes are "tough to get in to because there is only one professor for a certain subject," many agree that they love the attention that each professor gives and that the teachers "really go out of their way" to help students succeed and "value student success as much as the student does." Success, however, doesn't come without a price at Juniata, with a large amount of the students agreeing that their "good grades do not come without effort," but that the class load is "challenging, but not overwhelming."

Life

Students seem to agree that there "isn't much to do in the town" of Huntingdon, but Juniata College makes up for it by making sure there is "always something to do" on campus. There are so many activities and groups on campus that some say, "It feels like you're missing out if you go home for the weekend." There are a "lot of traditions such as Storming of the Arch, Mountain Day, and Madrigal" that have been around the campus for decades and help bring students together. For instance, during Mountain Day, classes are canceled, and students and faculty are shuttled to a state park near the school where there are lunches, nature walks, and various games being played, and neither group knows when exactly it is going to be until the morning of the event. While there might be a lot of activities to do on campus, "If you want to party you can find one." If you want to just relax with your fellow students, "Raystown Lake is only twenty minutes away," where many students like to go and relax on the beach. Back on campus, many students seem to think that the "dorms and food" need improvement, but believe that the academic experience they receive outweighs those inconveniences.

Student Body

Students tend to describe themselves as "driven" and "passionately interested in their subjects," though they also take pride in their "laid-back" attitudes, saying they "know how to balance fun and work." During the week students "tend to buckle down and get their work done." A lot of "exchange students from around the world" that come to Juniata College to pursue their education, but for the most part, "almost all the students are Caucasian." Some think "diversity is a bit lacking," but agree that "everyone fits in somewhere" at Juniata College because "people are accepted not despite their differences, but because of them."

FINANCIAL AID: 814-641-3141 • E-MAIL: ADMISSIONS@JUNIATA.EDU • WEBSITE: WWW.JUNIATA.EDU

THE PRINCETON REVIEW SAYS

Admissions

Very important factors considered include: GPA, rigor of secondary school record, standardized test scores, application essay, recommendation(s), character/personal qualities. *Important factors considered include:* Extracurricular activities, first generation, interview, talent/ability, volunteer work. *Other factors considered include:* Geographical residence, racial/ethnic status, state residency, alumni/ae relations, level of applicant's interest, SAT or ACT recommended; ACT with or without Writing component accepted. TOEFL required of all international applicants. *Academic units required:* 4 English; 3 mathematics; 3 science; (2 science lab); 1 social studies; 2 foreign language; 3 history. *Academic units recommended:* 4 English; 3 mathematics; 3 science; 1 social studies; 2 foreign language; 3 history.

Financial Aid

Students should submit: FAFSA. The Princeton Review suggests that all financial aid forms be submitted as soon as possible after January 1. *Need-based scholarships/grants offered:* Federal Pell, SEOG, State scholarships/grants, private scholarships, the school's own gift aid. *Loan aid offered:* Direct Subsidized Stafford Loans, Direct Unsubsidized Stafford Loans, Direct PLUS loans, Federal Perkins Loans, College/university loans from institutional funds. Federal Work-Study Program available. Institutional employment available. Off-campus job opportunities are good.

The Inside Word

High school seniors who are interested in Juniata must apply either by November 15 for early decision or by Feburary 1 for regular decision. Interested applicants can submit their SAT or ACT scores, or they can also submit an original, graded document of two to three pages in length and must be from either their junior or senior year in high school. This is in addition to the required essays that are part of the application process. For those looking to save some money, there is no application free for anyone who applies to Juniata via the website. They also provide incoming freshman with Inbound Retreats each August, which allows them to sign up for one of thirty-eight different retreats and get an idea of what college life is like, but without having to go to class.

THE SCHOOL SAYS "..."

From the Admissions Office

"Juniata's unique approach to learning has a flexible, student-centered focus. With the help of two advisors, more than half of Juniata's students designed their own Program of Emphasis (POE)—it's like a major but better. Those who choose a more traditional academic journey still benefit from the assistance of two faculty advisors and interdisciplinary collaboration between multiple academic departments. In addition, all students benefit from the recent, significant investments in academic facilities that help students actively learn by doing. For example, the new Halbritter Center for the Performing Arts houses an innovative theater program where theater professionals work side-by-side with students. The Sill Business Incubator provides $5,000 in seed capital to students with a desire to start their own business. The LEED-certified Raystown Environmental Studies Field Station, located on nearby Raystown Lake, gives unparalleled, hands-on study opportunities to students. And the von Liebig Center for Science provides opportunities for student/faculty research surpassing those available at even large universities. As the 2003 Middle States Accreditation Team noted, 'Juniata is truly a student-centered college. There is a remarkable cohesiveness in this commitment—faculty, students, trustees, staff, and alumni, each from their own vantage point, describe a community in which the growth of the student is central.' This cohesiveness creates a dynamic learning environment that enables students to think and grow intellectually, to evolve in their academic careers, and to graduate as active, successful participants in the global community. Freshman applicants may submit the SAT (or the ACT with or without the writing component). We will use their best scores from either test. "

SELECTIVITY

Admissions Rating	87
# of applicants	2,227
% of applicants accepted	74
% of acceptees attending	24
# offered a place on the wait list	88
# of early decision applicants	191
% accepted early decision	61

FRESHMAN PROFILE

Range SAT Critical Reading	520–630
Range SAT Math	520–630
Minimum paper TOEFL	550
Average HS GPA	3.75
% graduated top 10% of class	34
% graduated top 25% of class	73
% graduated top 50% of class	98

DEADLINES

Early decision	
Deadline	11/15
Notification	12/23
Regular	
Priority	11/15
Deadline	3/15
Nonfall registration?	Yes

APPLICANTS ALSO LOOK AT AND OFTEN PREFER
Franklin & Marshall College

AND SOMETIMES PREFER
Allegheny College; Susquehanna University; Dickinson College

AND RARELY PREFER
Pennsylvania State University—University Park; Ursinus College

FINANCIAL FACTS

Financial Aid Rating	85
Annual tuition	$37,870
Room and board	$10,710
Required fees	$760
Books and supplies	$1,000
% needy frosh rec. need-based scholarship or grant aid	100
% needy UG rec. need-based scholarship or grant aid	99
% needy frosh rec. non-need-based scholarship or grant aid	14
% needy UG rec. non-need-based scholarship or grant aid	13
% needy frosh rec. need-based self-help aid	86
% needy UG rec. need-based self-help aid	86
% frosh rec. any financial aid	100
% UG rec. any financial aid	100
% UG borrow to pay for school	81
Average cumulative indebtedness	$28,968
% frosh need fully met	20
% ugrads need fully met	22
Average % of frosh need met	86
Average % of ugrad need met	83

KALAMAZOO COLLEGE

1200 ACADEMY STREET, KALAMAZOO, MI 49006 • ADMISSIONS: 269-337-7166 • FAX: 269-337-7390

CAMPUS LIFE

Quality of Life Rating	85
Fire Safety Rating	72
Green Rating	74
Type of school	Private
Affiliation	No Affiliation
Environment	City

STUDENTS

Total undergrad enrollment	1,427
% male/female	44/56
% from out of state	30
% frosh from public high school	79
% frosh live on campus	100
% ugrads live on campus	61
% African American	4
% Asian	6
% Caucasian	63
% Hispanic	8
% Native American	<1
% international	7
# of countries represented	32

SURVEY SAYS . . .

Students are happy
Lab facilities are great
No one cheats
Students are friendly
Students environmentally aware

ACADEMICS

Academic Rating	93
% students returning for sophomore year	92
% students graduating within 4 years	72
% students graduating within 6 years	77
Calendar	Quarter
Student/faculty ratio	13:1
Profs interesting rating	96
Profs accessible rating	91

Most classes have 10–19 students.
Most lab/discussion sessions have 10–19 students.

MOST POPULAR MAJORS

English language and literature; psychology; economics

STUDENTS SAY "..."

Academics

If you are looking for a "unique" school with "close knit" community and a study abroad program that "is bar none," look no further than Kalamazoo. Founded in 1833, this Michigan school is known for its flexible "K Plan," which "allows students to design their own schedules with only a few universal requirements." "The curriculum is writing intensive and prepares students for a broad spectrum of jobs that may be available," one economics major explains. Because of its intimate size, Kalamazoo College is a place where students "feel like a name rather than a number." The school's "smart, demanding, [and] supportive" professors are "one of the best things about the school." They "take the time to get to know you" by being "really accessible" and wanting "you to come to their office hours to talk with them." The professors at Kalamazoo have real world experience in their fields and bring these "interesting experiences into the classroom to be discussed broken apart piece by piece and put back together in a meaningful and productive way." "As at any college, there are some mediocre or bad professors," one student cautions, "but I have had far more great experiences than poor ones." Kalmazoo's education goes beyond just academics. As one student explains, "We learn skills that not only prepare us for careers in the future, but also how to be better people." A psychology major sums up Kalamazoo as "a place that encompasses social justice, challenging, yet enriching academics, inside a liberal atmosphere."

Life

Kalamazoo students can't say enough about "the sense of community at this school" that students guarantee is "something that you won't be able to find at most other schools." "A welcoming spirit" abounds in this "home-like environment where everyone knows and loves everyone." Because of the school's size, "students are heavily invested in their education and engaged in campus life." Students enjoy strolling around the "Ivy League-style campus" and "club involvement is huge." Downtown Kalamazoo is right off campus, giving students access to urban amenities like "quality restaurants" and "a nice movie theater." However, another student cautions that "the downtown is basic and many shops and restaurants fall outside of a student budget." Consequently, "campus is the social hub." Kalamazoo fosters an intellectually active community and much of student life revolves around "discussing issues surrounding social justice or politics." The "work hard, play hard mentality" can be seen through the numerous parties—"more than you'd expect for such a small, academic school." However, there is something for everyone on campus as "the school puts on lots of events for those who wish to avoid partying."

Student Body

"Liberal kids dominate" at Kalamazoo, but students stress that "everyone who goes to K can find a different niche to fit in to." Although "a large percentage of students do come from Michigan or the Midwest," the student body includes many foreign students, and the majority of students study abroad. "It's no secret that everyone at K is weird," one happy student explains. "But the good thing is that we're all weird in different ways. And we're all awesome weirdos." As another student explains, "K is all about taking the smart and slightly quirky people from high school and putting them together in an environment that involves hard work and worldly experience." If there is one thing that Kalamazoo students have in common, it is creativity. Students are "creative in their schoolwork, hobbies, extracurricular activities, fashions, basically anything."

FINANCIAL AID: 269-337-7192 • E-MAIL: ADMISSION@KZOO.EDU • WEBSITE: WWW.KZOO.EDU

THE PRINCETON REVIEW SAYS

Admissions

Very important factors considered include: GPA, rigor of secondary school record, extracurricular activities. *Important factors considered include:* Standardized test scores, application essay, recommendation(s). *Other factors considered include:* First generation, geographical residence, interview, racial/ethnic status, talent/ability, volunteer work, work experience, alumni/ae relations, character/personal qualities, level of applicant's interest. SAT or ACT required; ACT with Writing component required. TOEFL required of all international applicants. *Academic units required:* 4 English; 3 mathematics; 3 science; 2 social studies; 3 foreign language; 2 history. *Academic units recommended:* 4 English; 4 mathematics; 4 science; 2 social studies; 4 foreign language; 2 history.

Financial Aid

Students should submit: FAFSA, Institution's own financial aid form. The Princeton Review suggests that all financial aid forms be submitted as soon as possible after January 1. *Need-based scholarships/grants offered:* Federal Pell, SEOG, State scholarships/grants, private scholarships, the school's own gift aid. *Loan aid offered:* Direct Subsidized Stafford Loans, Direct Unsubsidized Stafford Loans, Direct PLUS loans, Federal Perkins Loans. Federal Work-Study Program available. Institutional employment available. Off-campus job opportunities are good.

The Inside Word

The "K-Plan," which focuses on a broad liberal arts education and engagement with other cultures, is central to the Kalamazoo education. Consequently, college admissions officers are on the lookout for students that show the creativity, ambition, and motivation to thrive at Kalamazoo. Students with artistic backgrounds will want to emphasize that in their application. Admissions are competitive here, so applicants will be expected to have strong test scores and high school grades.

THE SCHOOL SAYS "..."

From the Admissions Office

"It is rare to find the purposeful integration and high participation rate of experiential education that is found at Kalamazoo College. During the past fifty years, 85 percent of our graduates have formally studied in another country while 80 percent have completed an internship or externship, and 100 percent complete a senior project. Our students often pursue international internships and senior project experiences, in addition to their planned study abroad terms. Also, Kalamazoo is one of the few selective liberal arts colleges to be found in a city—the Kalamazoo metro area has a population of approximately 225,000 with the advantage of being near a university of nearly 30,000 students. It is a diverse and vibrant community with wonderful access to the arts, athletics, service-learning, and social activism opportunities. We do more in four years so students can do more in a lifetime.

"Emphasis in Admission is placed on a student's High School experience including GPA, course selection, and co-curricular involvement."

SELECTIVITY

Admissions Rating	89
# of applicants	2,528
% of applicants accepted	67
% of acceptees attending	27
# offered a place on the wait list	294
% accepting a place on wait list	34
% admitted from wait list	0
# of early decision applicants	54
% accepted early decision	96

FRESHMAN PROFILE

Range SAT Critical Reading	550–670
Range SAT Math	540–690
Range SAT Writing	540–650
Range ACT Composite	25–30
Minimum paper TOEFL	550
Minimum web-based TOEFL	213
Average HS GPA	3.61
% graduated top 10% of class	38
% graduated top 25% of class	80
% graduated top 50% of class	98

DEADLINES

Early decision	
Deadline	11/15
Notification	12/1
Early action	
Deadline	11/15
Notification	12/20
Regular	
Priority	11/16
Deadline	2/15
Notification	4/1
Nonfall registration?	No

APPLICANTS ALSO LOOK AT AND OFTEN PREFER

University of Michigan- Ann Arbor

AND SOMETIMES PREFER

Earlham College; Denison University

FINANCIAL FACTS

Financial Aid Rating	91
Annual tuition	$39,026
Room and board	$8,475
Required fees	$325
Books and supplies	$900
% needy frosh rec. need-based scholarship or grant aid	99
% needy UG rec. need-based scholarship or grant aid	99
% needy frosh rec. non-need-based scholarship or grant aid	23
% needy UG rec. non-need-based scholarship or grant aid	17
% needy frosh rec. need-based self-help aid	77
% needy UG rec. need-based self-help aid	84
% frosh rec. any financial aid	98
% UG rec. any financial aid	97
% UG borrow to pay for school	54
Average cumulative indebtedness	$27,275
% frosh need fully met	48
% ugrads need fully met	44
Average % of frosh need met	94
Average % of ugrad need met	91

KANSAS STATE UNIVERSITY

119 ANDERSON HALL, MANHATTAN, KS 66506 • ADMISSIONS: 785-532-6250 • FAX: 785-532-6393

STUDENTS SAY "..."

Academics

Kansas State University is "all about providing a great education with tons of opportunities at an affordable cost." The low in-state tuition is the major reason many end up here, but the strong academics and plethora of resources are just as a big a draw. "Everyone wants to work together to accomplish as much as possible, which is a wonderful environment to learn in," says a student. Despite its size, K-State "still has a small-town, welcoming feeling" and "a family atmosphere that the whole university buys into," and the institution "shows each student, faculty, or staff just how appreciated and important they are to the university."

Professors are "extremely knowledgeable," "know how to relate the course information well," and make themselves available outside of class. Not only are they "welcoming and willing to help whenever you need it," they are also "doing outstanding research in their fields." "When I visited K-State, I realized as a Wildcat I would have all the opportunities of a large university without feeling like a number," says a student. In providing so many chances for students to get real-life experience, most feel that they "enter the working world well-equipped."

With such a pervasive focus on community, students say that "you'll usually be only a few degrees of separation from any other person." The long history of Kansas State University (students wear purple all the time, since "there's a lot of Wildcat pride across campus") is "something that you can't get anywhere else." Some facilities "could receive a boost," though, as "there are a lot of great buildings on campus, but there are some classrooms that need an update." At the end of the day, K-State "is all about putting students first, and they put you first as soon as you become a freshman."

Life

Manhattan, Kansas, is "the perfect college town—not too big, not too small." There are lots of student discounts, "delicious restaurants, and quirky gift shops," and on the weekends you will find most students in the beloved Aggieville, the restaurant, bar, and shopping district. "Aggieville is the place to go and shop, socialize, and party!" says one student enthusiastically. Manhattan really comes to life during football games, and "the atmosphere is at its peak during these days." "The amount of alumni who come back for the games is incredible, and the noise that fills the student section is intense," says a student.

Outside of sports, students hit up the local attractions that draw a younger crowd, as well as "the many UPC Events held on campus," such as "one dollar movies on the weekends, dances within the residence halls, and crafts at the union." The school has more than 475 student organizations to get involved in, from religious organizations to athletic clubs; "There is something for everyone here at K-State, and if we don't have it, start it." The Greek system is also "very strong," and "there is never a week when there is not an event happening around campus."

Student Body

The typical student at K-State is first and foremost friendly and "wildly passionate about being a Wildcat." "It is nearly impossible to walk clear across campus without seeing a friendly face," says a student. As most people at this "very Anglo-dominated campus" are Kansans, there is a strong Midwestern vibe amongst these "down-to-earth, family-oriented people," all of whom "consider success in college a very important aspect of their lives." Everyone is "pumped about our sports and traditions"—football is understandably big here—and most people "sport school colors/mascot on a weekly basis.

KANSAS STATE UNIVERSITY

FINANCIAL AID: 785-532-6420 • E-MAIL: K-STATE@K-STATE.EDU • WEBSITE: WWW.K-STATE.EDU

THE PRINCETON REVIEW SAYS

Admissions

Very important factors considered include: College preparatory curriculum, GPA in preparatory courses, standardized test scores (writing components not required) and class rank. *Other factors considered include:* Transferable college credit, recommendation(s) and cumulative GPA. *Academic units recommended:* 4 English; 3 natural science (to include 1 chemistry or 1 physics); 3 social studies; 3 electives; and 3 or 4 mathematics (4 mathematics units are required if a math subscore of 22 on the ACT or 560 on the SAT have not been achieved).

Financial Aid

Students should submit: FAFSA. The Princeton Review suggests that all financial aid forms be submitted as soon as possible after January 1. *Need-based scholar-ships/grants offered:* Federal Pell, SEOG, State scholarships/grants, private scholarships, the school's own gift aid. *Loan aid offered:* Direct Subsidized Stafford Loans, Direct Unsubsidized Stafford Loans, Direct PLUS loans, Federal Perkins Loans, College/university loans from institutional funds. Federal Work-Study Program available. Institutional employment available. Off-campus job opportunities are good.

The Inside Word

Though K-State is chock full of strong students, admission is refreshingly straightforward. Completion of the precollege curriculum is required, and if you're a Kansas student, you must obtain at least a 2.0 GPA on these courses. Nonresidents must obtain at least a 2.5 GPA. You will then need to get either a 21 ACT composite score, a 980 when combining the CR+M sections of the SAT, or rank in the top third of your high school class. A cumulative GPA of at least 2.0 must also be achieved on all attempted college work. These basic require ments will qualify your admission. In other words, you're in!

THE SCHOOL SAYS ". . ."

From the Admissions Office

"In addition to strong academic programs and exceptional faculty, Kansas State University is home to a one-of-a-kind family atmosphere. Take K-State Proud, a student-led, nationally recognized philanthropy that allows students to create scholarships for their peers. So far, the campaign has raised more than $700,000.

Members of the K-State family come from all 50 states and more than 100 countries. K-Staters find their footing through K-State First, a first-year experience program that helps freshmen establish a strong foundation through shared courses, learning communities, mentors and a common book program.It's easy for students to customize their college experiences to fit individual personalities and interests. Kansas State University offers more than 250 majors and options, and 475 student organizations and clubs — with the option to create your own. One prominent student organization, the Black Student Union, won the Clarence Wine Award for Outstanding Big 12 Council of the Year for the seventh time in the past nine years.

Each year, the university awards $18.8 million in scholarships and $200 million in financial aid. We're proud to offer students a multitude of ways to find success, including undergraduate research opportunities. Kansas State University undergraduates have researched everything from sustainable energy to musical lyrics. The university's numerous research facilities and centers offer invaluable resources for students to explore and discover. As the university pushes forward to become a Top 50 public research university by 2025, there has never been a better time to be a K-Stater."

SELECTIVITY	
Admissions Rating	70
# of applicants	9,839
% of applicants accepted	96
% of acceptees attending	40

FRESHMAN PROFILE	
Range ACT Composite	21–27
Average HS GPA	3.47
% graduated top 10% of class	22
% graduated top 25% of class	48
% graduated top 50% of class	77

DEADLINES	
Nonfall registration?	Yes

FINANCIAL FACTS	
Financial Aid Rating	82
Annual in-state tuition	$7,830
Annual out-of-state tuition	$20,775
Room and board	$7,710
Required fees	$755
Books and supplies	$1,100
% needy frosh rec. need-based scholarship or grant aid	60
% needy UG rec. need-based scholarship or grant aid	60
% needy frosh rec. non-need-based scholarship or grant aid	69
% needy UG rec. non-need-based scholarship or grant aid	45
% needy frosh rec. need-based self-help aid	74
% needy UG rec. need-based self-help aid	80
% UG borrow to pay for school	61
Average cumulative indebtedness	$26,725
% frosh need fully met	19
% ugrads need fully met	17
Average % of frosh need met	80
Average % of ugrad need met	79

KENYON COLLEGE

KENYON COLLEGE, ADMISSION OFFICE, GAMBIER, OH 43022-9623 • ADMISSIONS: 740-427-5776 • FAX: 740-427-5770

STUDENTS SAY ". . ."

Academics

This tiny midwestern liberal arts mainstay is Ohio's oldest private college, and is filled with "uniquely quirky and motivated" students and faculty alike. The school's "academic vigor" and intense focus on writing (it is known as "The Writers' College") are two of Kenyon's hallmarks, and the curriculum provides "a well-rounded liberal arts education in which emphasis [is] placed on critical thinking and class discussion." "Even though I don't want to be an English major, I think any college that values writing as much as Kenyon does has its priorities straight," says a student of the highly valued workforce skill.

The school "really knows how to offer a huge diversity of programs and activities to a very small campus," and "it is honestly hard to find a professor who is not thrilled by the content that they are teaching." The faculty is a deeply caring bunch who "love learning just as much as the students" and challenge them to succeed, and they make it known that "your voice is valued in class discussion." "I once met with a professor for an hour every day leading up to the final because I was so nervous about it, and he hardly batted an eye at taking that much time out of his day for only one student," says a sophomore.

"Small, individualized class sizes" make it so that classes are "terrifically interesting," and "out of class work is always meaningful." Students don't compete with each other when it comes to grades so "the cooperative learning environment makes it less stressful," and though "you will spend the vast majority of your time studying … it is also extremely rewarding." The "relatively" open curriculum allows students to take courses that they are truly interested in, and "there is a wide variety of options available in terms of classes" for students to develop new passions.

Life

People come to this "small campus with a big sense of community" because they know it will be a good fit, and it shows in the satisfaction levels here. "I stepped on campus and noticed two things: everyone was happy and the campus was gorgeous," says one of many happy students. The school is a place for "smart, forward-thinking students who study hard but also understand the necessity of taking breaks and having a good time on weekends." People at Kenyon are taught "to see, discuss, and connect the dots"; "Even though I'm not a philosophy major I feel just as at home in those conversations as I do when I discuss Mahler or the next big party," says a student.

The "utterly pastoral" campus is "absolutely lovely"; "It's like going to school in a Marlowe poem—and with all of the English majors running around, most people know who Marlowe is," says a student. The town of Gambier is "in the middle of nowhere, so campus can get to be claustrophobic at times," but it provides its fair share of entertainment. "Greeks throw great parties [and] intramurals are popular, as are activist groups for everything from gender awareness to Palestine," and the nearby Kokosing Gap Trail is oft-used. The KAC (Kenyon Athletic Center) is unparalleled for a Division III school, and the "dining hall has an amazing commitment to local food." Partying on Wednesdays and the weekends "is a typical activity to unwind after a challenging week of academics."

Student Body

The word most often used to describe Kenyon students in "quirky." There are a variety of types, but "most people have a quirk or five." There are "a lot of hipster students and then a good selection of athletes" at Kenyon, but everyone "tends to be extremely friendly, well-rounded, and smart." Everyone is seriously involved in academics and extracurriculars, and "you're either a jack of all trades here or a master of four." There aren't really many cliques; "someone on the football team could just as easily be in the community choir or quiz bowl club."

FINANCIAL AID: 740-427-5240 • E-MAIL: ADMISSIONS@KENYON.EDU • WEBSITE: WWW.KENYON.EDU

THE PRINCETON REVIEW SAYS

Admissions

Very important factors considered include: GPA, rigor of secondary school record, application essay, recommendation(s), character/personal qualities, level of applicant's interest. *Important factors considered include:* Class rank, standardized test scores, extracurricular activities, interview, talent/ability. *Other factors considered include:* First generation, geographical residence, racial/ethnic status, state residency, volunteer work, work experience, alumni/ae relations. SAT or ACT required; SAT and SAT Subject Tests or ACT considered if submitted; ACT with or without Writing component accepted. TOEFL required of all international applicants. *Academic units required:* 4 English; 4 mathematics; 3 science; (3 science lab); 3 social studies; 3 foreign language; 3 academic electives. *Academic units recommended:* 4 English; 4 mathematics; 4 science; (3 science lab); 3 social studies; 4 foreign language; 3 academic electives.

Financial Aid

Students should submit: FAFSA, CSS/Financial Aid PROFILE, Noncustodial PROFILE. Regular filing deadline is 2/15. The Princeton Review suggests that all financial aid forms be submitted as soon as possible after January 1. *Need-based scholarships/grants offered:* Federal Pell, SEOG, State scholarships/grants, private scholarships, the school's own gift aid. *Loan aid offered:* Direct Subsidized Stafford Loans, Direct Unsubsidized Stafford Loans, Direct PLUS loans, Federal Perkins Loans, College/university loans from institutional funds. Federal Work-Study Program available. Institutional employment available. Off-campus job opportunities are poor.

The Inside Word

In terms of admissions selectivity, Kenyon is of the first order of selective, small, Midwestern, liberal arts schools. Kenyon shares a lot of application and admit overlap with other schools in this niche, and the choice for many students comes down to "best fit." As Kenyon is a writing-intensive institution, applicants should expect that all written material submitted to the school in the admissions process will be scrutinized. Revise and proofread accordingly.

THE SCHOOL SAYS ". . ."

From the Admissions Office

"Students and alumni alike think of Kenyon as a place that fosters 'learning in the company of friends.' While faculty expectations are rigorous and the work challenging, the academic atmosphere is cooperative, not competitive. Indications of intellectual curiosity and passion for learning, more than just high grades and test scores, are what we look for in applications. Important as well are demonstrated interests in non-academic pursuits, whether in athletics, the arts, writing, or another passion. Life in this small college community is fueled by the talents and enthusiasm of our students, so the admission staff seeks students who have a range of talents and interests.

"The high school transcript, recommendations, and the personal statement are of primary importance in reviewing preparedness and fit. Standardized tests (SAT or ACT) are of secondary importance."

SELECTIVITY

Admissions Rating	97
# of applicants	4,051
% of applicants accepted	38
% of acceptees attending	31
# offered a place on the wait list	1,077
% accepting a place on wait list	34
% admitted from wait list	2
# of early decision applicants	353
% accepted early decision	58

FRESHMAN PROFILE

Range SAT Critical Reading	630–720
Range SAT Math	600–690
Range SAT Writing	630–730
Range ACT Composite	28–32
Minimum web-based TOEFL	100
Average HS GPA	3.90
% graduated top 10% of class	65
% graduated top 25% of class	88
% graduated top 50% of class	98

DEADLINES

Early decision	
Deadline	11/15
Notification	12/15
Regular	
Priority	1/15
Deadline	1/15
Notification	4/1
Nonfall registration?	No

APPLICANTS ALSO LOOK AT AND OFTEN PREFER

Brown University; Williams College, Amherst College

AND SOMETIMES PREFER

Bowdoin College; Middlebury College; Carleton College; Swarthmore College; Oberlin College; Grinnell College

FINANCIAL FACTS

Financial Aid Rating	93
Annual tuition	$45,500
Room and board	$11,560
Required fees	$1,830
Books and supplies	$1,900
% needy frosh rec. need-based scholarship or grant aid	95
% needy UG rec. need-based scholarship or grant aid	97
% needy frosh rec. non-need-based scholarship or grant aid	21
% needy UG rec. non-need-based scholarship or grant aid	17
% needy frosh rec. need-based self-help aid	78
% needy UG rec. need-based self-help aid	75
% frosh rec. any financial aid	48
% UG rec. any financial aid	51
% UG borrow to pay for school	50
Average cumulative indebtedness	$18,902
% frosh need fully met	65
% ugrads need fully met	67
Average % of frosh need met	96
Average % of ugrad need met	96

KNOX COLLEGE

2 East South Street, Campus Box 148, Galesburg, IL 61401 • Admissions: 309-341-7100 • Fax: 309-341-7070

CAMPUS LIFE

Quality of Life Rating	79
Fire Safety Rating	86
Green Rating	80
Type of school	Private
Affiliation	No Affiliation
Environment	Town

STUDENTS

Total undergrad enrollment	1,402
% male/female	43/57
% from out of state	42
% frosh from public high school	75
% frosh live on campus	98
% ugrads live on campus	86
# of fraternities	6
# of sororities	4
% African American	7
% Asian	5
% Caucasian	58
% Hispanic	10
% Native American	<1
% international	12
# of countries represented	37

SURVEY SAYS . . .
No one cheats
Students are friendly
Great library

ACADEMICS

Academic Rating	92
% students returning for sophomore year	88
% students graduating within 4 years	71
% students graduating within 6 years	79
Calendar	Trimester
Student/faculty ratio	11:1
Profs interesting rating	94
Profs accessible rating	92

Most classes have 10–19 students.
Most lab/discussion sessions have 10–19 students.

MOST POPULAR MAJORS
creative writing; education; economics

STUDENTS SAY ". . ."

Academics

Students say that Knox College enjoys a "great academic reputation" for its dedication to providing a "well-rounded liberal arts program" that "values independent initiative," while "staying in tune with its roots as a progressive and accessible institution." The college has a saying about students having "the freedom to flourish." The institution gives everyone "the appropriate space to grow on their own." "I knew that I would be allowed to be myself, choose the classes that I felt would have the most influence on my education and prepare me for the future." Students are highly encouraged to take classes outside of their majors. Undergraduates are "commonly studying two vastly different subjects and allowing them to merge into one interdisciplinary interest." Knox does have "one of the best creative writing programs in the country," as well as the Peace Corps Preparatory Program— offered solely through Knox. The academic trimester system, comprised of three classes each term, provides students with "a semester's worth of course work in a ten-week period." Many in the student body believe that this arrangement "promotes better study habits and more attention focused on each class," which are "tough and require a lot of time studying, reading, writing, and thinking." "You don't come to Knox if you want to shy away from class discussion," and professors "concentrate on the student having good critical thinking skills." Students are pleased to find that "you are academically challenged without fierce competition." "I've never had an easy professor, but I've always had reasonable ones." Projects and presentations are common; if tests are given, there is an honor code, and "they trust you not to cheat." The faculty and administration are spoken of highly, and they "not only encourage the students to take charge and make change, but they listen and act on the student body's opinions."

Life

Popular manners of relaxation and recreation include intramural sports, campus organizations, and "artistic expression, be it poetry, visual art, performance art, music." Students "go to parties, play games, dance, etc., just like any other college campus. The difference is, our fraternity parties are open to the entire campus and do not serve alcohol." Parties here "are places where you generally know everyone there, you have a good time and no one steals your coat or purse." Undergrads here are also very creative. "When we want to do something fun we typically organize it ourselves." A much-anticipated event is "Flunk Day, a day every spring when classes are canceled and the entire campus goes out on the lawn and plays games, eats great food and enjoys free entertainment." Union Board "brings films, entertainers, concerts, and other groups to campus, including Second City," and the Gizmo is "one of the best places to socialize and eat some late night food." Wandering off-campus a bit is also fun. Undergrads say "Galesburg is a charming town...you just have to look a little bit." "McGillacuddy's has amazing burgers, and Knox's music department hosts Jazz Nights there on Thursdays." Students enjoy the town's intimate, relaxing atmosphere. "Good coffee shops, a really nice park with a lake, and many beautiful old historic buildings," and "an annual Chocolate Festival." A twenty-four-hour diner is nearby, and "students can also drive to Peoria or take the train to Chicago."

Student Body

Knox is praised throughout the campus for its "support for first-generation college students, which really reflects Knox's history and values." "You'll meet a lot of people very fast, and by the end of your first term you'll already be good friends with a pretty big portion of the student body." Many undergrads portray themselves as "weird," with variations on a common theme: "We call it the 'Knox awkward.'" "The smart but sort of socially awkward kids in high school," what they describe as their social "Knoxwardness." "Everyone at Knox is a little eccentric, but we embrace each other's differences." "Students fit in by being themselves, no matter who they are." As one student perceptively notes, there is a "highly diverse combination of creative, intellectual minds here. It's as if every person here is some highly distinctive character from an artsy film." Another puts it a bit more succinctly: "Thank you college admission gods."

FINANCIAL AID: 309-341-7149 • E-MAIL: ADMISSION@KNOX.EDU • WEBSITE: WWW.KNOX.EDU

THE PRINCETON REVIEW SAYS

Admissions

Very important factors considered include: GPA, rigor of secondary school record, application essay. *Important factors considered include:* Class rank, interview, recommendation(s), character/personal qualities. *Other factors considered include:* Standardized test scores, extracurricular activities, first generation, geographical residence, racial/ethnic status, talent/ability, volunteer work, alumni/ae relations, level of applicant's interest. SAT and SAT Subject Tests or ACT considered if submitted; ACT with or without Writing component accepted. TOEFL required of all international applicants. *Academic units recommended:* 4 English; 4 mathematics; 4 science; (2 science lab); 2 social studies; 3 foreign language; 2 history; 1 academic elective.

Financial Aid

Students should submit: FAFSA, Institution's own financial aid form. The Princeton Review suggests that all financial aid forms be submitted as soon as possible after January 1. *Need-based scholarships/grants offered:* Federal Pell, SEOG, State scholarships/grants, private scholarships, the school's own gift aid. *Loan aid offered:* Direct Subsidized Stafford Loans, Direct Unsubsidized Stafford Loans, Direct PLUS loans, Federal Perkins Loans, College/university loans from institutional funds. Federal Work-Study Program available. Institutional employment available. Off-campus job opportunities are fair.

The Inside Word

Knox draws students from nearly fifty countries and almost fifty states—with a student body of only 1,400, diversity is hugely important here. Admission standards are high, and prospective students are viewed both qualitatively and quantitatively. Three out of every four freshman were ranked in the top quarter of their high school classes.

THE SCHOOL SAYS "..."

From the Admissions Office

"The Knox experience is one that empowers you to experience your education in the classroom, in the real world, and through an ever-expanding network of personal and professional peers. Understanding that college should be a place where you explore your academic passions and where your talents are nourished, Knox gives you the freedom to flourish. At Knox, you'll discover how to learn and think for yourself, and to discover what you want to do with the knowledge and ideas you develop. By providing you with opportunities to both explore and 'do,' a Knox education is designed to give you the agility to pursue your chosen career path—even as it changes over time. Working with your faculty advisor from your first day on campus, you'll identify educational goals and a personal educational plan to achieve them. Your plan will include a broad foundation in the liberal arts and a primary area of specialization plus a second major or minor. You'll enhance what you learn in the classroom through internships, independent research, service projects, study abroad, and other hands-on learning experiences. You'll learn by doing, which will give you perspectives that can only be found by putting your knowledge into practice. Your Knox education proceeds along a course you set for yourself. As a result, your aspirations are met and our nation and the global community gain from citizens who are able to think for themselves, understand our complex and interdependent world, and act on their principles."

SELECTIVITY

Admissions Rating	84
# of applicants	2,660
% of applicants accepted	75
% of acceptees attending	19
# offered a place on the wait list	25
% accepting a place on wait list	20
% admitted from wait list	20

FRESHMAN PROFILE

Range SAT Critical Reading	560–690
Range SAT Math	550–670
Range SAT Writing	540–650
Range ACT Composite	25–30
Minimum paper TOEFL	550
% graduated top 10% of class	26
% graduated top 25% of class	59
% graduated top 50% of class	91

DEADLINES

Early action	
Deadline	12/1
Notification	12/31
Regular	
Deadline	2/1
Notification	3/31
Nonfall registration?	No

APPLICANTS ALSO LOOK AT AND SOMETIMES PREFER

Beloit College; Lawrence University; Grinnell College

AND RARELY PREFER

Loyola The University of Chicago; Macalester College; Northwestern University; The University of Chicago; Washington University in St. Louis

FINANCIAL FACTS

Financial Aid Rating	88
Annual tuition	$39,765
Room and board	$8,724
Required fees	$732
Books and supplies	$900
% needy frosh rec. need-based scholarship or grant aid	98
% needy UG rec. need-based scholarship or grant aid	98
% needy frosh rec. non-need-based scholarship or grant aid	15
% needy UG rec. non-need-based scholarship or grant aid	14
% needy frosh rec. need-based self-help aid	88
% needy UG rec. need-based self-help aid	89
% frosh rec. any financial aid	99
% UG rec. any financial aid	95
% UG borrow to pay for school	74
Average cumulative indebtedness	$28,330
% frosh need fully met	32
% ugrads need fully met	27
Average % of frosh need met	91
Average % of ugrad need met	89

LAFAYETTE COLLEGE

118 MARKLE HALL, EASTON, PA 18042 • ADMISSIONS: 610-330-5100 • FAX: 610-330-5355

STUDENTS SAY ". . ."

Academics

Lafayette College is "a small, prestigious liberal arts school" that offers a "warm, community feel." Even before you decide to attend, "walking around campus left me with a cozy, at-home feeling," one psychology major gushes. Thanks to the "top-quality engineering education," many students say, "Lafayette is your classic liberal arts college with a twist" and point to the "vast array of research" and "study abroad opportunities" available to undergrads. The college "prides itself on student/faculty relationships." A geology major proclaims when professors are "good, they're great. Even the 'bad' professors, however, take the time to know each student and are usually available outside of class." An international affairs major says, "Whether you're an engineer, a premed student, or an art major, there is a great academic program and an embracing group of people waiting for you at Lafayette." Overall the professors get high marks because "their office doors are always open," and "are invested in seeing [students] not only graduate but also do well." The focus on undergraduate education provides "maximum opportunities and makes resumes and applications for graduate school and jobs look fierce!" Students go so far as to claim, "It's not very common to hear that someone doesn't like one of their professors at Lafayette." Generally, "classes are challenging but manageable, if you put in the time."

Life

At Lafayette, the "campus is gorgeous," and students say you feel the "close atmosphere of the school" after "immediately walking onto the campus." Overall students feel, "the campus community is very supportive," and a civil engineering major says, "The family atmosphere adds to the education and makes Lafayette feel more like home than school." With "over 200 clubs and organizations on campus," there "is something that will fit everyone's lifestyle and hobbies," and when it comes to their Division I athletics, "students radiate school pride." Lafayette boasts a "great career center due to the close ties alumni have with the college," and career services are offered to students during all four years of their undergraduate study. The administration actively requests "student forums and opinions when decisions need to be made." While some say "the facilities are first rate" and improving, others lament "the arts, while growing, are still fairly small." Lafayette has welcomed a new President and there are changes on the way. Within the last year, the food provider has been replaced and offerings have "improved tremendously."

Student Body

Lafayette students are "passionate and driven" and "tend to be athletic, very preppy, and serious about their education." A sophomore says the typical student is "white middle to upper-middle class students from the tri-state area," but another adds, "Recent years have brought in a number of different types of people." "More lower income, international, and non-white students have joined" the Lafayette community. Regardless, some students point out that it can be "a very self-segregated campus." "These cliques are not unique to Lafayette, but they are present." Just under 30 percent of the student body is "involved with Greek life," and some feel that those "not involved in Greek life or sports can be isolated"; however, many students have felt a change occurring in recent years with Lafayette "trying to add more living learning community (LLCs) to create a social living space outside the Greek system." On weekends, most students stay on campus, and Very rarely is there a weekend where something isn't going on." Organizations are always "sponsoring fun events, including Condom Bingo, which is a fan favorite. And if you're into the party scene, it isn't too hard to stumble into one."

FINANCIAL AID: 610-330-5055 • E-MAIL: ADMISSIONS@LAFAYETTE.EDU • WEBSITE: WWW.LAFAYETTE.EDU

THE PRINCETON REVIEW SAYS

Admissions

Very important factors considered include: GPA, rigor of secondary school record. *Important factors considered include:* Class rank, standardized test scores, application essay, extracurricular activities, interview, recommendation(s), talent/ability, character/personal qualities. *Other factors considered include:* First generation, geographical residence, racial/ethnic status, volunteer work, work experience, alumni/ae relations, level of applicant's interest. SAT or ACT required; ACT with Writing component required. TOEFL required of all international applicants. *Academic units recommended:* 4 English; 3 mathematics; 2 science; (2 science lab); 2 foreign language; 5 academic electives.

Financial Aid

Students should submit: FAFSA, CSS/Financial Aid PROFILE, Noncustodial PROFILE. Regular filing deadline is 3/1. The Princeton Review suggests that all financial aid forms be submitted as soon as possible after January 1. *Need-based scholarships/grants offered:* Federal Pell, SEOG, State scholarships/grants, private scholarships, the school's own gift aid. *Loan aid offered:* Direct Subsidized Stafford Loans, Direct Unsubsidized Stafford Loans, Direct PLUS loans, Federal Perkins Loans, College/university loans from institutional funds. Applicants will be notified of awards beginning 4/1. Federal Work-Study Program available. Institutional employment available. Off-campus job opportunities are good.

The Inside Word

Like all elite institutions, Lafayette College takes into account a variety of factors when evaluating prospective students. While emphasis is placed on scores, high school record, rigor of courses, and other numbers, the admissions committee also values a commitment to social awareness and potential for leadership as exhibited through extracurricular activities such as community service. In fact, service is a big part of the Lafayette community.

THE SCHOOL SAYS "..."

From the Admissions Office

"Located 70 miles from Manhattan and 60 miles from Center City Philadelphia, Lafayette provides university-size resources in an exclusively undergraduate, student-centered college.

"Our rallying cry is the Marquis de Lafayette's family motto, Cur Non ('Why not?'). It means anything is possible here—with Lafayette's muscle and energy, no dream is too wild or ambitious to make happen. All the experiences students need to create their edge are built into their four years. It's an unparalleled platform from which to find their way forward into a complex, rapidly changing world.

"There are nearly fifty majors to choose from in the humanities, social sciences, natural sciences, and engineering. The faculty are accomplished professor-mentors who are dedicated to connecting with students on both a professional and a personal level.

"While remaining dedicated to programs in which students learn to think critically, to communicate effectively, and to relate seemingly unconnected ideas, Lafayette also is dedicated to providing an education that is valuable in its relevance, in which students cross disciplinary, cultural, and international boundaries to connect in meaningful ways with faculty, with each other, and with the world. This high-impact education—with a distinctive cross-disciplinary orientation, high-level research, rigorous small-class discussion, field experiences, community-based learning projects, and global studies—attracts active, engaged learners who achieve a notable career advantage. In recent years, 95 percent or more of Lafayette's graduating classes have been employed, in graduate school, in an internship, or in service work within six months of graduation."

SELECTIVITY

Admissions Rating	96
# of applicants	6,766
% of applicants accepted	34
% of acceptees attending	27
# offered a place on the wait list	1,709
% accepting a place on wait list	27
% admitted from wait list	5
# of early decision applicants	573
% accepted early decision	53

FRESHMAN PROFILE

Range SAT Critical Reading	570–670
Range SAT Math	610–700
Range SAT Writing	580–690
Range ACT Composite	27–31
Minimum paper TOEFL	550
Average HS GPA	3.46
% graduated top 10% of class	62
% graduated top 25% of class	89
% graduated top 50% of class	97

DEADLINES

Early decision	
Deadline	11/15
Notification	12/15
Regular	
Deadline	1/15
Notification	4/1
Nonfall registration?	Yes

APPLICANTS ALSO LOOK AT AND OFTEN PREFER

Princeton University; Boston College; Tufts University; Cornell University

AND SOMETIMES PREFER

Bucknell University; Villanova University; Colgate University; Lehigh University

AND RARELY PREFER

Rensselaer Polytechnic Institute

FINANCIAL FACTS

Financial Aid Rating	94
Annual tuition	$45,230
Room and board	$13,520
Required fees	$405
Books and supplies	$1,000
% needy frosh rec. need-based scholarship or grant aid	97
% needy UG rec. need-based scholarship or grant aid	97
% needy frosh rec. non-need-based scholarship or grant aid	29
% needy UG rec. non-need-based scholarship or grant aid	22
% needy frosh rec. need-based self-help aid	92
% needy UG rec. need-based self-help aid	93
% frosh rec. any financial aid	62
% UG rec. any financial aid	61
% UG borrow to pay for school	54
Average cumulative indebtedness	$25,281
% frosh need fully met	86
% ugrads need fully met	86
Average % of frosh need met	99
Average % of ugrad need met	98

LAKE FOREST COLLEGE

555 NORTH SHERIDAN ROAD, LAKE FOREST, IL 60045 • ADMISSIONS: 847-735-5000 • FAX: 847-735-6291

STUDENTS SAY "..."

Academics

Lake Forest provides a broad-ranging general education curriculum. One student points out, "The teachers really challenge you and generally are really nice and easy to access." The academic breadth at Lake Forest College is both challenging and inspiring. Another student adds, "The small school size means administration can help you, and they actually do. The class sizes and teachers won't let anyone hide or get away with spotty work." The emphasis is giving each student an individual and well-rounded education in the liberal arts, and this cross-disciplinary education is accessible because of the attentive faculty and staff. A current student tells us, "Lake Forest is a solid college with great financial aid." Another facet of the learning experience that Lake Forest students appreciate is that the college provides and promotes numerous opportunities outside of the classroom. Studying abroad, internships, community service, and career development are all encouraged and presented across campus. Overall, the impression is that of "the world is at your fingertips and your campus experience should allow you to sample many options and explore and create in a supportive environment." Lake Forest's professors are by far its strongest asset. A sophomore tells us, "They're accessible, highly knowledgeable in their designated areas of expertise, and have very high expectations for student performance. Additionally, they encourage us as students to learn by doing as opposed to simply lecturing."

Life

When students consider Lake Forest, a word that might come to mind is 'balance.' One student explains, "The town of Lake Forest is not at all a college town, and you'd be hard-pressed to find anything more than a grocery store and a few places to eat. However, almost everything you need is on campus." The beautiful 107-acre campus is located thirty miles north of downtown Chicago, providing access to the city with the respite of a more laid-back town along the shore of Lake Michigan. "Chicago is a huge asset both socially and academically," says one student. "[It] is ever-changing and does not get dull." The school offers transit passes for a discounted price, and students visit the city often. A ten-minute walk will easily get you into the main part of town, and it is an easy train ride to Chicago, but equally attractive is that in the same ten minutes you can walk to the beach and enjoy the shores of Lake Michigan. A freshman describes, "Lake Michigan, and a beautiful beach, is only half a mile from campus, and the campus is beautiful especially in the fall and after the first snowfall." Another student sums it up nicely, saying, "At Lake Forest College, students get a world-class education and the skills they need to succeed in life while immersed in a school-spirit-rich campus lifestyle that doesn't compare to any other school."

Student Body

Student organizations are very strong at Lake Forest, and, therefore, there are always student-run events on campus that are frequented by the student body. "A typical Lake Forest student is usually pretty involved whether it is in a sport, club, theater, or music," says one sophomore. "Everyone usually finds a group that they fit into with friends with similar interests." Another student adds, "Everyone is different, and everyone fits in." Like any college, students say they can get, "Stressed out, but [are] generally upbeat. At this school it is considered normal to be in a thousand different clubs and extracurricular activities and to attend campus events and campus parties." A sophomore explains, "Life at my school can be very challenging because your classes will push you. However, there is still time for fun, and you will see a good number of your peers at social events on campus. One of the most common is the ACPs (All Campus Parties) that are held on Fridays and hosted by various student organizations." In the end, it all comes back to balance—and at Lake Forest students can cultivate the many experiences available into one productive adult life.

FINANCIAL AID: 847-735-5103 • E-MAIL: ADMISSIONS@LAKEFOREST.EDU • WEBSITE: WWW.LAKEFOREST.EDU

THE PRINCETON REVIEW SAYS

Admissions

Very important factors considered include: GPA, rigor of secondary school record, interview, recommendation(s). *Important factors considered include:* Application essay, extracurricular activities, talent/ability, character/personal qualities, level of applicant's interest. *Other factors considered include:* Class rank, standardized test scores, first generation, geographical residence, volunteer work, work experience, alumni/ae relations. SAT or ACT required for some; ACT with or without Writing component accepted. TOEFL required of all international applicants. *Academic units required:* 4 English; 3 mathematics; 3 science; (2 science lab); 3 social studies; 2 foreign language; 2 history; 3 academic electives. *Academic units recommended:* 4 English; 4 mathematics; 4 science; (2 science lab); 4 social studies; 3 foreign language; 2 history; 3 academic electives.

Financial Aid

Students should submit: FAFSA, Institution's own financial aid form. The Princeton Review suggests that all financial aid forms be submitted as soon as possible after January 1. *Need-based scholarships/grants offered:* Federal Pell, SEOG, State scholarships/grants, private scholarships, the school's own gift aid. *Loan aid offered:* Direct Subsidized Stafford Loans, Direct Unsubsidized Stafford Loans, Direct PLUS loans, Federal Perkins Loans, State Loans, College/university loans from institutional funds. Federal Work-Study Program available. Institutional employment available. Off-campus job opportunities are good.

The Inside Word

Lake Forest is small enough to give each application it receives close and careful consideration. Solid high school performers should have little difficulty gaining admission, but keep in mind that Lake Forest has a prep-school-at-the-college-level feel and likes to assess the whole candidate, not just grades and test scores. In fact, test scores are optional. Students can submit a graded essay instead.

THE SCHOOL SAYS "..."

From the Admissions Office

"Our beautiful 107-acre campus is ideally located on Chicago's North Shore near Lake Michigan. Lake Forest College gives every student direct access to superb faculty and a powerful network of alumni who help our graduates begin careers. This access provides every student with a valuable edge on a bright future.

Our flexible curriculum supports double majors and minors, and students are also offered unparalleled internships in Chicago, great lab research experiences, championship athletics, and study-abroad opportunities. Students learn in a rigorous academic environment in small class settings where professors do all of the teaching and advising. Career-building internships are plentiful in the Chicago area, and students can pursue up to three for credit. Study abroad is encouraged, and students can also spend a semester living and interning in Chicago.

The student body is comprised of students from nearly every state and eighty-one countries around the world and together they form a diverse learning community that prepares them to succeed in today's global society.

Developing career goals—and a plan of action to achieve them—is a fundamental goal of the Career Advancement Center and the College community as a whole. Students have access to programs, resources, career advisors, and a powerful network of alumni throughout their four years.

Our outcomes are hard to match: More than 90 percent of our graduates had jobs, graduate school, or other opportunities secured within six months of graduation, well above the national average."

SELECTIVITY

Admissions Rating	88
# of applicants	3,684
% of applicants accepted	57
% of acceptees attending	19
% accepting a place on wait list	80
% admitted from wait list	100
# of early decision applicants	112
% accepted early decision	41

FRESHMAN PROFILE

Range ACT Composite	23–28
Minimum paper TOEFL	550
Average HS GPA	3.63
% graduated top 10% of class	24
% graduated top 25% of class	58
% graduated top 50% of class	91

DEADLINES

Early decision	
Deadline	11/15
Notification	12/13
Early action	
Deadline	11/15
Notification	12/13
Regular	
Priority	2/15
Notification	3/10
Nonfall registration?	Yes

APPLICANTS ALSO LOOK AT AND OFTEN PREFER

University of Illinois at Urbana-Champaign

FINANCIAL FACTS

Financial Aid Rating	88
Annual tuition	$40,448
Room and board	$9,480
Required fees	$724
Books and supplies	$1,000
% needy frosh rec. need-based scholarship or grant aid	100
% needy UG rec. need-based scholarship or grant aid	100
% needy frosh rec. need-based self-help aid	78
% needy UG rec. need-based self-help aid	82
% frosh rec. any financial aid	94
% UG rec. any financial aid	95
% UG borrow to pay for school	66
Average cumulative indebtedness	$30,801
% frosh need fully met	16
% ugrads need fully met	28
Average % of frosh need met	84
Average % of ugrad need met	84

LAWRENCE UNIVERSITY

711 EAST BOLDT WAY, APPLETON, WI 54911-5699 • ADMISSIONS: 920-832-6500 • FAX: 920-832-6782

Quality of Life Rating	90
Fire Safety Rating	73
Green Rating	74
Type of school	Private
Affiliation	No Affiliation
Environment	City

STUDENTS

Total undergrad enrollment	1,517
% male/female	45/55
% from out of state	68
% frosh from public high school	70
% frosh live on campus	98
% ugrads live on campus	92
# of fraternities (% ugrad men join)	5 (20)
# of sororities (% ugrad women join)	3 (15)
% African American	3
% Asian	4
% Caucasian	74
% Hispanic	5
% Native American	1
% international	9
# of countries represented	44

SURVEY SAYS . . .
Lab facilities are great
No one cheats
Students are friendly
Campus feels safe
Easy to get around campus

ACADEMICS

Academic Rating	93
% students returning for sophomore year	88
% students graduating within 4 years	69
% students graduating within 6 years	82
Calendar	Trimester
Student/faculty ratio	9:1
Profs interesting rating	92
Profs accessible rating	94
Most classes have 10–19 students.	

MOST POPULAR MAJORS
music performance; biology; psychology

STUDENTS SAY ". . ."

Academics

The minute you step foot onto the campus of Lawrence University, you immediately sense that the school is comprised of a "beautifully warm and positive community." Soon after, you realize that it deftly manages to balance this supportive nature with a "weird, quirky vibe." And students couldn't be happier about the combination. Of course, it also doesn't hurt that Lawrence is "very helpful" when it comes to financial aid. Undoubtedly, the university really strives to make higher education "affordable." Looking beyond financials, many undergraduates are drawn to Lawrence for its "world-class" music conservatory. They also really value the fact that LU "encourages creativity and exploration." In fact, students can even "create [their] own major or design [their] own class." Another hallmark of a Lawrence education is professor "accessibility." As one extremely satisfied student states, "There is not a professor here who wouldn't at the very least get coffee or lunch upon request." After all, since LU "is an undergraduate-only school, professors really are here for their students. There's an extraordinary amount of support and academic enthusiasm [from them]."

Life

Life at Lawrence certainly moves at a hectic pace. In fact, there's usually so much activity buzzing through campus that undergrads often "argue with each other about who has a busier schedule." As one junior happily explains, "There's so much going on at any given time that [students] rarely want to leave even for a weekend. There are (free) concerts, speakers, parties, musicals/plays, movie showings, get togethers, game nights, club meetings, and a whole ton of other events." An economics major rushes to add, "Students [also] go on backpacking trips, cross-country skiing...[and] volunteer at the Boys & Girls Club." There's even "an active swing dance community!" Of course, Lawrence's stellar music program means that "conservatory concerts, shows, and recitals... account for [a large portion] of the night life." And if the aforementioned options don't excite you, a knowing senior assures us that, "Everyone [is able to have] fun in their own way—from ultimate frisbee... to raising sea urchins." Moreover, trivia nights are another extremely popular activity at Lawrence. An English major shares, "LU is home to the Great Midwestern Trivia Contest, 48 straight hours of trivia in which teams both on and off campus compete, mostly for bragging rights. It's a lot of crazy fun and sleep deprivation." Finally, if you're looking to escape the confines of the university, the "campus is surrounded by some great shops, coffee shops, and restaurants."

Student Body

When asked to reflect on their peers, one of the first words that springs to mind for many LU students is "intellectual." As one impressed freshman explains, "at any given time there will [be] plenty of conversations going on about Plato, conservation, politics, or art." However, if you're looking beyond book smarts, many LU undergrads say you'll be hard pressed to find an adjective or category that could easily encompass all of these students. A relieved freshman reports, "You'll find all sorts of people here - homebodies who like to study all the time, partygoers, musicians, athletes, scientists, gamers, you name it, we have it. There will always be someone here that you can fit in with, and it's wonderful." And a thrilled senior brags, "Talk to any student for 15 minutes and you'll learn something fascinating and unexpected - even the people you thought you would never get along with." Additionally, these "motivated" and "independent" undergrads typically maintain "a variety of interests and passions" and tend to be "openminded [and] liberal." All in all, as a linguistics and German double major confidently summarizes, "If you are at all a social person, you will have no trouble making friends within your dorm, classes, or extracurricular [activities]."

LAWRENCE UNIVERSITY

FINANCIAL AID: 920-832-6583 • E-MAIL: ADMISSIONS@LAWRENCE.EDU • WEBSITE: WWW.LAWRENCE.EDU

THE PRINCETON REVIEW SAYS

Admissions

Very important factors considered include: Class rank, GPA, rigor of secondary school record, talent/ability, character/personal qualities. *Important factors considered include:* Application essay, extracurricular activities, interview, recommendation(s). *Other factors considered include:* Standardized test scores, first generation, geographical residence, racial/ethnic status, volunteer work, work experience, alumni/ae relations, level of applicant's interest. SAT and SAT Subject Tests or ACT considered if submitted; ACT with or without Writing component accepted. TOEFL required of all international applicants. *Academic units recommended:* 4 English; 3 mathematics; 3 science; 2 social studies; 2 foreign language; 2 history.

Financial Aid

Students should submit: FAFSA, CSS/Financial Aid PROFILE, Noncustodial PROFILE. The Princeton Review suggests that all financial aid forms be submitted as soon as possible after January 1. *Need-based scholarships/grants offered:* Federal Pell, SEOG, State scholarships/grants, private scholarships, the school's own gift aid. *Loan aid offered:* Direct Subsidized Stafford Loans, Direct Unsubsidized Stafford Loans, Direct PLUS loans, Federal Perkins Loans. Federal Work-Study Program available. Institutional employment available. Off-campus job opportunities are good.

The Inside Word

Lawrence University takes a holistic approach to the admissions game. The school does its best look beyond numbers and get a full sense of each applicant. Admissions officers pay close attention to the types of classes candidates have taken and the activities pursued. They also consider a student's background. Interviews are highly important so it would behoove applicants to sit for one. Finally, those who are test averse can breathe a sigh of relief; submitting SAT and/or ACT scores is optional.

THE SCHOOL SAYS "..."

From the Admissions Office

"Lawrence believes college should not be a one-size-fits-all experience, and that you'll learn best when you're educated as a unique individual. Within our college of liberal arts and sciences and our conservatory of music—both devoted exclusively to undergraduate education—you'll have unparalleled opportunities to collaborate closely with your professors in small classes (92 percent have fewer than twenty students in them; 68 percent have total enrollments of one). Our 1,500 students come from nearly every state and about fifty countries to enjoy the distinctive benefits of this engaged—and engaging—community. It's a close-knit, residential, 24/7 campus filled with smart and talented people who are pursuing an astonishing variety of academic and extracurricular interests. Our picturesque, residential campus is nestled on the banks of the Fox River in Appleton, Wisconsin, (metro population: 220,000), one of the fastest growing metropolitan areas in the Midwest. Björklunden, our 425-acre estate on more than one mile of pristine Lake Michigan shoreline (two hours north of campus), provides educational and recreational opportunities for students to enhance their on-campus learning experiences.

"We seek students who are intellectual, imaginative, and innovative: qualities best quantified from a thorough review of your curriculum, academic performance, essay, activities, and recommendations. Accordingly, Lawrence considers—but does not require—the ACT and the SAT in our review of applications for admission and scholarship."

SELECTIVITY

Admissions Rating	91
# of applicants	2,710
% of applicants accepted	73
% of acceptees attending	20
# offered a place on the wait list	100
% accepting a place on wait list	45
% admitted from wait list	58
# of early decision applicants	31
% accepted early decision	87

FRESHMAN PROFILE

Range SAT Critical Reading	560–700
Range SAT Math	580–710
Range SAT Writing	560–690
Range ACT Composite	26–31
Minimum paper TOEFL	577
Minimum web-based TOEFL	233
Average HS GPA	3.70
% graduated top 10% of class	42
% graduated top 25% of class	76
% graduated top 50% of class	97

DEADLINES

Early decision	
Deadline	11/1
Notification	11/15
Early action	
Deadline	11/15
Notification	12/20
Regular	
Deadline	1/15
Notification	4/1
Nonfall registration?	Yes

APPLICANTS ALSO LOOK AT AND OFTEN PREFER

Beloit College; University of Wisconsin-Madison; St. Olaf College; Macalester College

AND SOMETIMES PREFER

Grinnell College; Knox College; Northwestern University; Oberlin College

FINANCIAL FACTS

Financial Aid Rating	87
Annual tuition	$42,357
Room and board	$8,808
Required fees	$300
% needy frosh rec. need-based scholarship or grant aid	100
% needy UG rec. need-based scholarship or grant aid	100
% needy frosh rec. non-need-based scholarship or grant aid	5
% needy UG rec. non-need-based scholarship or grant aid	3
% needy frosh rec. need-based self-help aid	81
% needy UG rec. need-based self-help aid	83
% frosh rec. any financial aid	95
% UG rec. any financial aid	94
% UG borrow to pay for school	67
Average cumulative indebtedness	$30,802
% frosh need fully met	31
% ugrads need fully met	25
Average % of frosh need met	89
Average % of ugrad need met	88

LE MOYNE COLLEGE

1419 SALT SPRINGS RD., SYRACUSE, NY 13214-1301 • ADMISSIONS: 315-445-4300 • FAX: 315-445-4711

Academics

Founded in 1946, Syracuse's Le Moyne College is a 3,500-student private college that "combines Jesuit teachings and traditions while engaging all students into their own development as an individual, part of the community and the world as a whole." Those who go to Le Moyne cite the "unparalleled" feeling of community and that the constant sense that the "personable and endearing administrators" "actually care about you" as the best part of their time here, and the "focus on community service" helps drive the foundational Jesuit principles home.

One of Le Moyne's greatest strengths is the amount of help available to students. "Between office hours, the Academic Support Center and friendly upperclassmen, your questions will be answered!" promises a student. "Small intimate class sizes" mean that "professors are always willing to help students," and nothing is taught by TAs so "it is easy to foster a personal connection with you professors." Classes are "intellectually challenging," the honors program is "very worthwhile," and the majority of professors really "try to bring the material to life." They "bring in outside information that connects with the material we are learning, which I find helps spark discussions with every person in the class." "I have learned so much in so little time. And I have evolved a thirst for more," says a freshman chemistry major.

Strong nursing and business programs stand out in this "active learning community," as does the desire to keep the college "a place of high moral values." Some of the facilities on school such as the science labs or library "could be renovated," but luckily nearly all the classrooms are accessible within buildings connected by tunnels and hallways, eliminating the need to travel outside from class to class (a huge benefit in the freezing, and long, Central NY winters).

Life

Life in Syracuse "offers so many opportunities," and students revel in their four years in a "perfect community—small, generous, and service oriented." Almost all students are required to live on campus all four years, which creates "a cozy campus with a homey atmosphere" (not to mention beautiful). Parking is definitely on students' wish lists, but the dining facilities receive rare high marks: "The food is great and there is a good variety."

The school keeps students pleasantly busy, and "offers a lot of activities around the campus [so] you will never get bored." Le Moyne offers "free tickets to concerts and SU basketball games" and "puts on a lot of fun events such as movie nights…comedy improv groups, and other performers." "Partying is a big factor here," and students often head up to Syracuse or to the campus bar on weekends. However, there is "a pretty sizable portion of students who don't like to go out" and there are always programs going on at night, such as "a snow tubing trip, bowling trip, and an on-campus Pinterest Live! Event…in addition to Trivia Night at the on-campus pub, of course!"

Student Body

Many students come from cities and small towns in New York State, are "family-oriented,""Catholic," and "most likely white." Everyone is "extremely friendly," though Le Moyne has a great deal of cliques, although "one can create friends easily" and said cliques "interact far more fluidly" than in high school. Most are "usually dressed nicely and seem prepared for class," and do the standard work during the week, go out on weekends routine. "A lot of students here are athletes as well," and many "bond over sports, or the performing arts." The "wide range" of people on campus means there are "many who are up all night partying non-stop from Thursday until Sunday, then there are those who still grab coloring books and sit down to watch Disney movies for fun."

FINANCIAL AID: 315-445-4400 • E-MAIL: ADMISSION@LEMOYNE.EDU • WEBSITE: WWW.LEMOYNE.EDU

THE PRINCETON REVIEW SAYS

Admissions

Other factors considered include: SAT or ACT required; ACT with or without Writing component accepted. TOEFL required of all international applicants. *Academic units required:* 4 English; 3 mathematics; 3 science; 4 social studies; 3 foreign language. *Academic units recommended:* 4 mathematics; 4 science; (3 science lab).

Financial Aid

Students should submit: FAFSA, State aid form. The Princeton Review suggests that all financial aid forms be submitted as soon as possible after January 1. *Need-based scholarships/grants offered:* Federal Pell, SEOG, State scholarships/grants, private scholarships, the school's own gift aid. *Loan aid offered:* Direct Subsidized Stafford Loans, Direct Unsubsidized Stafford Loans, Direct PLUS loans, Federal Perkins Loans. Applicants will be notified of awards beginning 3/15. Federal Work-Study Program available. Institutional employment available. Off-campus job opportunities are excellent.

The Inside Word

As a younger college, Le Moyne sees slightly lower application numbers than many other small private colleges in the Northeast. While a strong college prep record and good SAT or ACT scores are required (as well as one letter of recommendation from a guidance/college counselor or three letters of recommendation from clergy, coaches, employers, teachers, etc.), those who have decent academic record should have no trouble getting in.

THE SCHOOL SAYS "..."

From the Admissions Office

"Learning, leadership and service are the hallmarks of a Le Moyne College education. Those values are evident in the College's recently reconfigured Core Curriculum, a series of courses steeped in the Jesuit tradition and designed to develop the intellectual skills that are critical for success in the 21st century. The intent of the Core Curriculum is to do more than provide knowledge in specific disciplines, though. It was created to stretch the minds of our students, to remove barriers to their ways of thinking, and to help them discover new approaches to life's challenges. At the center of the Le Moyne experience is a commitment to social justice and to providing students with the best possible preparation for life and work.

"Le Moyne students can choose from more than 30 undergraduate majors as well as pre-professional studies and graduate programs in business administration, education, nursing and physician assistant studies. Whatever field they choose to pursue, Le Moyne graduates are prepared to lead successful lives of leadership and service to others.

"Beyond the academics, Le Moyne students have the opportunity to grow and explore on a campus with dynamic new academic, athletic and social spaces at a cost that is remarkably affordable. (More than 90 percent of undergrads receive some form of financial aid.). With over 70 clubs and organizations, students are sure to find an activity that interests them while forming life-long friendships. Our picturesque 160-acre campus in the heart of New York state enhances Le Moyne's outstanding programs."

SELECTIVITY

Admissions Rating	78
# of applicants	5,924
% of applicants accepted	62
% of acceptees attending	17
# offered a place on the wait list	93
% accepting a place on wait list	33
% admitted from wait list	61

FRESHMAN PROFILE

Range SAT Critical Reading	480–570
Range SAT Math	500–600
Range ACT Composite	21–26
Minimum paper TOEFL	550
Minimum web-based TOEFL	213
Average HS GPA	3.42
% graduated top 10% of class	21
% graduated top 25% of class	51
% graduated top 50% of class	88

DEADLINES

Early action	
Deadline	11/15
Notification	12/15
Regular	
Priority	3/1
Nonfall registration?	Yes

FINANCIAL FACTS

Financial Aid Rating	78
Annual tuition	$29,470
Room and board	$11,740
Required fees	$990
Books and supplies	$1,300
% needy frosh rec. need-based scholarship or grant aid	100
% needy UG rec. need-based scholarship or grant aid	100
% needy frosh rec. non-need-based scholarship or grant aid	14
% needy UG rec. non-need-based scholarship or grant aid	12
% needy frosh rec. need-based self-help aid	80
% needy UG rec. need-based self-help aid	84
% frosh rec. any financial aid	90
% UG rec. any financial aid	94
% UG borrow to pay for school	90
Average cumulative indebtedness	$41,117
% frosh need fully met	21
% ugrads need fully met	21
Average % of frosh need met	75
Average % of ugrad need met	73

LEHIGH UNIVERSITY

27 MEMORIAL DRIVE WEST, BETHLEHEM, PA 18015 • ADMISSIONS: 610-758-3100 • FAX: 610-758-4361

STUDENTS SAY ". . ."

Academics

Located in Pennsylvania's Lehigh Valley, this university features a "great academic and social life balance" with a campus "small enough to see familiar faces every day, but big enough to always be meeting new people." It "boasts a strong engineering program," and students say it truly "lives up to its academic reputation." Students "genuinely care about their education" and have "an incredible work ethic." A psychology major says, "People want to learn and want to do well, which creates a really good college environment." STEM majors praise the prevalence of "open-ended" projects as "bringing new dimension to our learning and understanding the concepts covered in class." Humanities majors love their "discussion-based classes" and "the variety of courses offered." A social science student confesses they sometimes have to "go out of my way to find internships and opportunities." Students are grateful for the "strong connection with alumni, which is great for prospective employment," and say, "The career opportunities post-graduation are excellent for both engineering and business students." Professors get generally high marks, with students saying "they're more often than not, fascinating people with a ton of relevant experience in their field." Academics are considered "extremely rigorous and rewarding."

Life

"Work hard, play hard" is how 80 percent of the student respondents described their life on this "beautiful, hilly campus." One senior sums up their experience succinctly as "lots of parties." Many others detail the club and school activities that "are prevalent during most of the week," as well as weekend trips to "the Promenade Shops of Saucon Valley or the Lehigh Valley Mall." While some students feel Greeks "dominate social life," many contend that all Lehigh students are "heavily involved" in some facet of extracurricular life whether they be "a Greek, athlete, or in a major club." "Uninvolved students do not exist here." It might seem overwhelming to picture yourself attending a "Lehigh-Laf[ayette] rivalry game", hitting up a few fraternity parties on "The Hill", and working to "design a chemical plant on my own!" in one weekend. Rest assured, at Lehigh "passions, parties, and work [are] balanced much in the way real life is." This balance is described as "amazing," "perfect" and "proper." What some students feel may be unbalanced are "relations between dissimilar students." But students who might not fit the traditional Lehigh student mold feel "the school is doing a lot to listen to minority concerns and address them." While the food has improved in recent years, students are looking to "pressure Sodexo [a dining service provider] for more cost efficient meal plans." A few feel "it's just not a good value for what they supply, especially for more cash strapped students."

Student Body

A few of the most popular words students use to describe their peers are "upper middle class," "hard working," "enthusiastic" and "Caucasian." Diversity is a hot topic for all students with most agreeing that the culture is moving toward "cultural awareness and acceptance," and that "people just want to be friends." "The diversity of Lehigh comes from its diversity of personalities," says one engineering student who hails from outside the United States. Belonging seems to be a big part of the social experience. Most students "end up networking with people within their classes and within the organizations that they are involved in." Those students who "struggle to find a place at Lehigh are ones who do not actively search out for the experience they want or expect opportunities to be fed to them." All in all, there is a general feeling that "Lehigh is a magical place, not unlike Hogwarts."

FINANCIAL AID: 610-758-3181 • E-MAIL: ADMISSIONS@LEHIGH.EDU • WEBSITE: WWW.LEHIGH.EDU

THE PRINCETON REVIEW SAYS

Admissions

Very important factors considered include: Rigor of secondary school record, recommendation(s). *Important factors considered include:* Standardized test scores, application essay, extracurricular activities, talent/ability, volunteer work, character/personal qualities, level of applicant's interest. *Other factors considered include:* Class rank, GPA, first generation, geographical residence, interview, racial/ethnic status, work experience, alumni/ae relations. SAT or ACT required; ACT with Writing component required. TOEFL required of all international applicants. *Academic units required:* 4 English; 3 mathematics; 2 science; (2 science lab); 2 social studies; 2 foreign language; 3 academic electives.

Financial Aid

Students should submit: FAFSA, CSS/Financial Aid PROFILE, Noncustodial PROFILE, Business/Farm Supplement. Regular filing deadline is 2/15. The Princeton Review suggests that all financial aid forms be submitted as soon as possible after January 1. *Need-based scholarships/grants offered:* Federal Pell, SEOG, State scholarships/grants, private scholarships, the school's own gift aid. *Loan aid offered:* Direct Subsidized Stafford Loans, Direct Unsubsidized Stafford Loans, Direct PLUS loans, Federal Perkins Loans, College/university loans from institutional funds. Applicants will be notified of awards beginning 3/30. Federal Work-Study Program available. Institutional employment available. Off-campus job opportunities are good.

The Inside Word

Competition for spots in Lehigh's freshmen class is perennially increasing. Students should be sure to start their applications early, be well prepared with scores and grades, as well as demonstrate their talents and passions through volunteer opportunities, work experience, or extracurricular activities. Prospective students should visit campus and make contact with the admissions staff. Interviews are recommended but not required.

THE SCHOOL SAYS ". . ."

From the Admissions Office

"Lehigh's beautifully wooded campus spans 2,358 acres, making it one of the largest private campuses in the country. More than 6,900 students call this hillside university "home." With four distinguished colleges, Lehigh strikes the perfect balance: It's an internationally recognized research university that has the atmosphere of a small college.

Lehigh is a premier private residential research university. Most of our students—undergraduate and graduate—live on campus, allowing research and discovery to happen almost anywhere. We are ranked in the top tier of national research universities each year, and have earned a reputation for an entrepreneurial and interdisciplinary approach to learning. This learning is connected to real-world applications and reinforced with cutting edge academic research and hands–on experiences. The Lehigh community shares a common set of core values: integrity, equitable community, academic freedom, intellectual curiosity and leadership.

Today, more than 75,000 alumni from around the world have earned a Lehigh diploma, and nearly 97% of last year's graduates have gone on to find career-related opportunities just six months after leaving campus.

Located in Pennsylvania's scenic Lehigh Valley, the campus is in close proximity to both New York City and Philadelphia and is in the middle of the Mid-Atlantic corridor. The Lehigh Valley region is home to about 750,000 people. Our campus is on South Mountain in Bethlehem and consists of three contiguous areas: The Asa Packer Campus (home to most academic and residential buildings), Mountaintop Campus and the Murray H. Goodman Campus (where many athletic facilities are located).

SELECTIVITY

Admissions Rating	96
# of applicants	12,589
% of applicants accepted	31
% of acceptees attending	31
# offered a place on the wait list	3,521
% accepting a place on wait list	36
% admitted from wait list	3
# of early decision applicants	936
% accepted early decision	59

FRESHMAN PROFILE

Range SAT Critical Reading	580–670
Range SAT Math	640–740
Range ACT Composite	28–32
Minimum paper TOEFL	570
% graduated top 10% of class	60
% graduated top 25% of class	88
% graduated top 50% of class	98

DEADLINES

Early decision	
Deadline	11/15
Notification	12/15
Regular	
Deadline	1/1
Notification	4/1
Nonfall registration?	Yes

APPLICANTS ALSO LOOK AT AND OFTEN PREFER

Cornell University; University of Virginia; Univeristy of Michigan–Ann Arbor; Carnegie Mellon University; Boston College

AND SOMETIMES PREFER

Villanova University; Bucknell University; Rensselaer Polytechnic Institute

AND RARELY PREFER

Boston University; Rutgers- New Brunswick; Penn State University; Drexel University

FINANCIAL FACTS

Financial Aid Rating	92
Annual tuition	$43,220
Room and board	$11,560
Required fees	$300
Books and supplies	$1,000
% needy frosh rec. need-based scholarship or grant aid	98
% needy UG rec. need-based scholarship or grant aid	98
% needy frosh rec. non-need-based scholarship or grant aid	12
% needy UG rec. non-need-based scholarship or grant aid	12
% needy frosh rec. need-based self-help aid	96
% needy UG rec. need-based self-help aid	96
% frosh rec. any financial aid	58
% UG rec. any financial aid	59
% UG borrow to pay for school	54
Average cumulative indebtedness	$33,309
% frosh need fully met	47
% ugrads need fully met	63
Average % of frosh need met	95
Average % of ugrad need met	96

Lewis & Clark College

0615 SOUTHWEST PALATINE HILL ROAD, PORTLAND, OR 97219-7899 • ADMISSIONS: 503-768-7040 • FAX: 503-768-7055

CAMPUS LIFE

Quality of Life Rating	89
Fire Safety Rating	86
Green Rating	99
Type of school	Private
Affiliation	No Affiliation
Environment	Metropolis

STUDENTS

Total undergrad enrollment	1,984
% male/female	39/61
% from out of state	82
% frosh from public high school	73
% frosh live on campus	98
% ugrads live on campus	65
% African American	2
% Asian	6
% Caucasian	65
% Hispanic	8
% Native American	1
% international	6
# of countries represented	80

SURVEY SAYS . . .

Lots of liberal students
Classroom facilities are great
Students are friendly
Students aren't religious
Students love Portland, OR
Great off-campus food

ACADEMICS

Academic Rating	91
% students returning for sophomore year	86
% students graduating within 4 years	67
% students graduating within 6 years	74
Calendar	Semester
Student/faculty ratio	12:1
Profs interesting rating	91
Profs accessible rating	88

Most classes have 10–19 students.
Most lab/discussion sessions have
20–29 students.

MOST POPULAR MAJORS
psychology; international relations; biology

STUDENTS SAY ". . ."

Academics

While living in Portland, Oregon, you may "get rained on a lot," but that doesn't stop many students from extolling about the otherwise "wonderful," "perfect," "ideal," and "exciting" location. This "suburban-hilltop liberal arts college" sits in an "absolutely beautiful" spot "next to a huge forest, [with] downtown only twenty minutes away." Besides the setting, students are lured by the school's "strong outdoors program," "great study abroad opportunities," as well as the promise of "a very green and liberal school." "Lewis & Clark is a utopia for thinkers and outdoors lovers alike. While challenging academically, the emphasis on a holistic education means that students are encouraged to explore all that Portland and the beautiful Northwest has to offer." Professors are noted for their support and "are devoted to their students in a way that wouldn't be possible in a larger school." "Lewis & Clark has professors that care so much, and if you want to put the effort into building relationships with them you will get so much from the education." Students give excellent marks for the "seasoned professors in upper-level classes." However, one student feels that "some of the temporary staff are less excellent."

Life

Life is full, and friends are plentiful at Lewis & Clark. "It's beautiful, small, and an overall friendly place with students who really take education seriously." Community supported agriculture (CSA) is taken seriously here, too. "Many are very concerned about living a healthy and sustainable life style" and are "very active gardeners and composters." The small campus is "beautiful and enjoyable to study and live in." "It feels intimate without feeling claustrophobic." When the weather is nice, "People try to find every excuse to be outside." "They generally enjoy hiking, skiing, camping, and many other activities that bring them closer to nature." Although partying exists, it is not at the forefront here. "Parties are frequent, but hardly out of control." "A lot of students are involved in student-run organizations such as a cappella, theatrical improv, open mic nights, and their own bands. Many people are advocates, and lots of students give significant amounts of their time to assist their communities." With Portland easily accessible using the school's "free shuttle that goes from campus to downtown," escaping campus is "extremely easy." "There are so many fun things to do downtown—concerts, coffee shops, restaurants, and a ton of funky antique shops that are perfect to explore on a nice day. The Pearl District, Hawthorne Boulevard, and of course the Saturday Market are all fun places to go check out." Athletics are popular at Lewis & Clark, and students speak proudly of their teams. Although some students point out of lack of fans cheering them on at games and meets, one classmate puts it into perspective. "L&C was one of the only colleges to really support me being [a part] of the athletic department as a varsity basketball player and the music department as a classical double bass player. I didn't want to go to a college that would force me to choose between my two passions. L&C has allowed me to grow as an athlete, musician, and as a student; not a lot of colleges can do that."

Student Body

To generalize, "Students are usually athletes or hippies." There seems to be some divide between the two groups, but most everyone is "very liberal, engaged in a variety of issues, and smart." One student describes the school as being "full of people that you'd actually want to make friends with." Another says classmates are "genuine" and "really independent." "Most kids are more than willing to try something adventurous, and most take advantage of the fact that our student body has students coming from all over the country and world." Students tend to value "Freedom of expression and thought, and an open environment in which to discuss differences." The fact that many students have traveled or lived in another country enriches the classroom experience. Classmates "constantly have stories about their time abroad," and "it is also very difficult to find someone who has never traveled abroad."

FINANCIAL AID: 503-768-7090 • E-MAIL: ADMISSIONS@LCLARK.EDU • WEBSITE: WWW.LCLARK.EDU

THE PRINCETON REVIEW SAYS

Admissions

Very important factors considered include: GPA, rigor of secondary school record. *Important factors considered include:* Class rank, standardized test scores, application essay, extracurricular activities, first generation, recommendation(s), talent/ability, volunteer work, work experience, alumni/ae relations, character/personal qualities. *Other factors considered include:* Geographical residence, interview, racial/ethnic status, state residency, level of applicant's interest. SAT or ACT required for some; ACT with or without Writing component accepted. TOEFL required of all international applicants. *Academic units recommended:* 4 English; 4 mathematics; 3 science; (2 science lab); 4 social studies; 2 foreign language; 1 visual/performing arts.

Financial Aid

Students should submit: FAFSA, CSS/Financial Aid PROFILE. The Princeton Review suggests that all financial aid forms be submitted as soon as possible after January 1. *Need-based scholarships/grants offered:* Federal Pell, SEOG, State scholarships/grants, private scholarships, the school's own gift aid. *Loan aid offered:* Direct Subsidized Stafford Loans, Direct Unsubsidized Stafford Loans, Direct PLUS loans, Federal Perkins Loans. Federal Work-Study Program available. Institutional employment available. Off-campus job opportunities are fair.

The Inside Word

If you have your heart set on L&C, make sure you tell that to the admissions committee. While grades and SAT scores are certainly important, L&C is also interested in students who will take advantage of the school's unique philosophy and educational environment. So make sure your application essay and interview emphasizes why L&C is the right fit for both you and the school.

THE SCHOOL SAYS "..."

From the Admissions Office

"Our record number of applicants in recent years cite a variety of reasons for choosing Lewis & Clark. Many mention the multiple educational opportunities available to our students, including a small arts and sciences college with a twelve to one student/faculty ratio; a location only six miles from dynamic downtown Portland; a setting in the heart of the Pacific Northwest, with more than eighty trips per year offered by our College Outdoors Program; and a gateway to the rest of the world—almost 62 percent of our graduates included an overseas program in their curriculum. Since 1962, more than 9,600 students and 212 faculty members have participated in 600 programs in sixty-six countries on six continents. Our curriculum has undergone a total review to better prepare graduates going into the twenty-first century and now includes a robust and fast-expanding Center for Entrepreneurship."

"At Lewis & Clark College, SAT Subject Test scores are not required."

SELECTIVITY

Admissions Rating	90
# of applicants	6,456
% of applicants accepted	63
% of acceptees attending	12
# offered a place on the wait list	509
% accepting a place on wait list	30
% admitted from wait list	37

FRESHMAN PROFILE

Range SAT Critical Reading	600–700
Range SAT Math	580–670
Range SAT Writing	580–690
Range ACT Composite	26–31
Minimum paper TOEFL	575
Minimum web-based TOEFL	213
Average HS GPA	3.70

DEADLINES

Early action	
Deadline	11/1
Notification	12/31
Early decision	
Deadline	11/1
Regular	
Priority	1/15
Deadline	3/1
Notification	4/1
Nonfall registration?	Yes

APPLICANTS ALSO LOOK AT AND OFTEN PREFER

University of California—Santa Cruz

AND SOMETIMES PREFER

University of Puget Sound; Whitman College

AND RARELY PREFER

University of Oregon; Pitzer College; University of Colorado—Boulder

FINANCIAL FACTS

Financial Aid Rating	85
% needy frosh rec. need-based scholarship or grant aid	100
% needy UG rec. need-based scholarship or grant aid	100
% needy frosh rec. non-need-based scholarship or grant aid	6
% needy UG rec. non-need-based scholarship or grant aid	4
% needy frosh rec. need-based self-help aid	93
% needy UG rec. need-based self-help aid	93
% UG rec. any financial aid	75
% UG borrow to pay for school	50
Average cumulative indebtedness	$25,134
% frosh need fully met	24
% ugrads need fully met	28
Average % of frosh need met	83
Average % of ugrad need met	86

LOUISIANA STATE UNIVERSITY

1146 PLEASANT HALL, BATON ROUGE, LA 70803 • ADMISSIONS: 225-578-1175 • FAX: 225-575-4433

CAMPUS LIFE

Quality of Life Rating	69
Fire Safety Rating	98
Green Rating	85
Type of school	Public
Affiliation	No Affiliation
Environment	City

STUDENTS

Total undergrad enrollment	23,990
% male/female	48/52
% from out of state	19
% frosh from public high school	60
% frosh live on campus	65
% ugrads live on campus	25
# of fraternities	23
# of sororities	16
% African American	11
% Asian	3
% Caucasian	76
% Hispanic	5
% Native American	<1
% international	2
# of countries represented	81

SURVEY SAYS . . .

Athletic facilities are great
Great off-campus food
Everyone loves the Tigers
Frats and sororities are popular
Student publications are popular
Lots of beer drinking
Hard liquor is popular

ACADEMICS

Academic Rating	65
% students returning for sophomore year	83
% students graduating within 4 years	40
% students graduating within 6 years	69
Calendar	Semester
Student/faculty ratio	23:1
Profs interesting rating	85
Profs accessible rating	70

Most classes have 10–19 students.
Most lab/discussion sessions have
  10–19 students.

MOST POPULAR MAJORS

biology; mass communication/media studies;
physical education

STUDENTS SAY ". . ."

Academics

At Louisiana State University's flagship campus, you'll find "outstanding academics combined with a great college life." Some students here opt for only the latter as' for many, "LSU is about football and partying." "Those who wish to apply themselves," however, "have ample opportunity and resources," and they can learn almost anything, since "the greatest strength of LSU by far is its diversity. [You] can come to LSU for sports, music…science, economics, or nearly any sort of humanities discipline you are interested in." Areas of strength include programs in premedical science, engineering, agriculture, and mass communications. The school is huge, which means "somewhere within that huge number is someone that you can get along with," but also it is easy to "get lost in the crowd," especially in intro-level classes. However, "once you get into classes that are smaller and more geared toward your chosen major, you are able to develop more of a one-on-one relationship with your professors." Fortunately "many administrative tasks" (such as "bills and registration") "can be completed online, and computers are available all across campus for students who don't have personal computers," making the bureaucracy somewhat easier to navigate. The school also offers academic lifelines such as "free tutoring all day long. The tutors are students who have already taken [the] courses."

Life

LSU is a big enough school to offer something for everyone, and undergrads here enjoy countless activities within a variety of subcultures. Most divisions, however, dissolve on game day, when tailgating is raised to the level of "an art form." A freshman reports, "On Saturdays during football season everyone is on campus before the game with friends, beer, and barbeque." Fans "come from all over and stay out all day. It's the one day when it doesn't matter who you are, as long as you're wearing purple and gold." Other entertainment options (for those of age) include Thursday nights at the bars of Tigerland, "a street with three popular college bars right next to each other," and parties wherever and whenever possible. The Greek system here is "highly influential," but students note, "This isn't the kind of school where a student doesn't have a social life if he or she isn't Greek." For the more aesthetically inclined, "LSU has an amazing art center—The Shaw Center—complete with a theater and fancy sushi bar on the top floor, which looks over the Mississippi River." Undergrads report "the beauty of our campus is amazing. The 100-plus-year-old oaks and the Italian Renaissance architecture wow any visitor to LSU's campus."

Student Body

The typical student at LSU "studies moderately—enough to get the grade he or she desires in a class"—and "frequently spends time with friends, possibly going to parties or places that serve alcohol." Mixed in is "a good number of atypical students who study more and do not go partying over the weekends. These students find fulfillment in their own interests regardless of what others think." While "conservative frat boys and sorority girls dominate the campus," the school is home to a diverse population including "many from foreign countries and other ethnic groups." There are even a few who "don't give a damn about LSU football"—hey, at a school this big, anything's possible. The student body also includes a substantial population of legacies.

FINANCIAL AID: 225-578-3103 • E-MAIL: ADMISSIONS@LSU.EDU • WEBSITE: WWW.LSU.EDU

THE PRINCETON REVIEW SAYS

Admissions

Very important factors considered include: GPA, rigor of secondary school record, standardized test scores. *Important factors considered include:* talent/ability. *Other factors considered include:* Class rank, application essay, extracurricular activities, first generation, recommendation(s), alumni/ae relations. SAT or ACT required; ACT with or without Writing component accepted. TOEFL required of all international applicants. *Academic units required:* 4 English; 4 mathematics; 4 science; 3 social studies; 2 foreign language; 1 history; 1 visual/performing arts.

Financial Aid

Students should submit: FAFSA, Institution's own financial aid form. The Princeton Review suggests that all financial aid forms be submitted as soon as possible after January 1. *Need-based scholarships/grants offered:* Federal Pell, SEOG, State scholarships/grants, private scholarships, the school's own gift aid. *Loan aid offered:* Direct Subsidized Stafford Loans, Direct Unsubsidized Stafford Loans, Direct PLUS loans, Federal Perkins Loans, College/university loans from institutional funds. Federal Work-Study Program available. Institutional employment available. Off-campus job opportunities are excellent.

The Inside Word

If you've got the right numbers, getting in to LSU is 1-2-3. Guaranteed admission requirements include completion of nineteen core units, 1030 SAT or 22 ACT, and a 3.0 academic GPA. Students who don't meet these requirements should submit supporting documentation and a letter outlining their qualifications for admission with their initial application.

THE SCHOOL SAYS "..."

From the Admissions Office

"LSU, one of only twenty-one universities nationwide designated as a land-grant, sea-grant, and space-grant institution, also holds the Carnegie Foundation's 'very high research activity' university designation.

"LSU's instructional programs include 200 undergraduate and graduate or professional degrees. Outside of the classroom, residential colleges, service-learning opportunities, and more than 350 registered student organizations contribute to an exciting and meaningful college experience.

"Louisiana State University offers the Southern hospitality of a small community while providing the benefits of a large, technologically advanced institution.

"Freshman applicants are required to take the SAT or ACT; ACT with writing component required for Honors College applicants. LSU will use the best scores from either SAT or ACT, when making admission decisions."

SELECTIVITY

Admissions Rating	78
# of applicants	16,005
% of applicants accepted	75
% of acceptees attending	46

FRESHMAN PROFILE

Range SAT Critical Reading	500–600
Range SAT Math	510–625
Range ACT Composite	23–28
Minimum paper TOEFL	550
Minimum web-based TOEFL	213
Average HS GPA	3.45
% graduated top 10% of class	25
% graduated top 25% of class	53
% graduated top 50% of class	82

DEADLINES

Regular	
Priority	11/15
Deadline	4/15
Nonfall registration?	Yes

FINANCIAL FACTS

Financial Aid Rating	75
Annual in-state tuition	$5,891
Annual out-of-state tuition	$23,808
Room and board	$10,804
Required fees	$1,982
Books and supplies	$1,500
% needy frosh rec. need-based scholarship or grant aid	94
% needy UG rec. need-based scholarship or grant aid	87
% needy frosh rec. non-need-based scholarship or grant aid	3
% needy UG rec. non-need-based scholarship or grant aid	3
% needy frosh rec. need-based self-help aid	68
% needy UG rec. need-based self-help aid	74
% frosh rec. any financial aid	93
% UG rec. any financial aid	82
% UG borrow to pay for school	39
Average cumulative indebtedness	$21,613
% frosh need fully met	25
% ugrads need fully met	23
Average % of frosh need met	70
Average % of ugrad need met	68

LOYOLA MARYMOUNT UNIVERSITY (CA)

One LMU Drive, Suite 100, Los Angeles, CA 90045-8350 • Admissions: 310-338-2750 • Fax: 310-338-2797

CAMPUS LIFE

Quality of Life Rating	97
Fire Safety Rating	78
Green Rating	95
Type of school	Private
Affiliation	Roman Catholic
Environment	Town

STUDENTS

Total undergrad enrollment	6,087
% male/female	43/57
% from out of state	22
% frosh from public high school	48
% frosh live on campus	94
% ugrads live on campus	52
# of fraternities (% ugrad men join)	8 (19)
# of sororities (% ugrad women join)	11 (34)
% African American	6
% Asian	10
% Caucasian	49
% Hispanic	22
% Native American	<1
% international	5
# of countries represented	81

SURVEY SAYS . . .

Students are happy
Classroom facilities are great
Career services are great
School is well run
Students are friendly
Students involved in community service
Students love Los Angeles, CA
Great off-campus food
Easy to get around campus
Athletic facilities are great
Active student government

ACADEMICS

Academic Rating	86
% students returning for sophomore year	91
% students graduating within 4 years	67
% students graduating within 6 years	76
Calendar	Semester
Student/faculty ratio	11:1
Profs interesting rating	84
Profs accessible rating	91

Most classes have 10–19 students.
Most lab/discussion sessions have 20–29 students.

MOST POPULAR MAJORS

communications studies; English language and literature; psychology

STUDENTS SAY ". . ."

Academics

Loyola Marymount University is a private, Jesuit liberal arts college in Los Angeles that focuses on educating every aspect of a person through learning, leadership, and service. There is "a constant presence of LMU's mission statement and if the student is willing to achieve something it can and will be achieved here." The school's Jesuit ideals "are all carried out and expressed by students, staff, and faculty" and there is an emphasis placed on social justice and each student's larger role in the world beyond the borders of the "beautiful" campus.

Classroom discussion is "apparent in all classes": even those that are lecture-based have a separate lab section devoted to intelligent conversation. The small class sizes make students "feel comfortable approaching...professors with questions and conversation." Professors "have a wealth of experience and share many stories and ethical dilemmas during class." They also "deeply care about their students… and encourage outside interaction." "Every professor I have had has been easily accessible, has known my name, and has given me a fair challenge to expand my academic prowess in the subject," says a student.

One of the greatest strengths of LMU is the networking (aided by the L.A. location and "the happiness that pervades...being in Southern California"); the school is "constantly connecting students with opportunities both on and off campus to gain experience and leadership qualities." Students are wholly committed to the ideal of "bettering yourself both personally and academically in order to give back to the greater community"; "it does not matter what cultural background you may come from, there is something at LMU for you to engage in."

Life

Loyola Marymount is "beautiful," with its "stunning views of LA, landscapes, classrooms, and people." "Happy people, beautiful campus" does seem to sum up life at LMU, which is "a melting pot of pretty people, a beautiful environment, LA culture, and education for the whole person." The school does not lack for SoCal things to do: "go to the beach, go shopping, go touristing into nearby Los Angeles, go hiking, try new food, party, [and] tan." Since the weather is "always sunny and warm," people are outside "24/7 all year round." In order to accommodate the luxury of living in LA, LMU provides buses and discounted tickets to many LA attractions. "Being at LMU is like living at a resort, but all the students work hard and earn their place," says a student.

A unique thing to LMU is that there is "both a strong Greek life presence and an even stronger service organization presence." These organizations "are well known in the LA area" and "most people join either a service organization, Greek organization, or a leadership position in housing or school administration." LMU is quite a healthy campus and the gym is frequented often, with plenty of efforts amongst students to promote healthy food choices. Life at LMU is "fulfilling," and "many opportunities for bettering your life present themselves frequently."

Student Body

The typical LMU student is "very active on campus" and engaged in many activities while balancing school, internships, and volunteering. Demographically, there is a" substantial amount of upper-class, white students" of the BMW-designer wallet sort, but "there is plenty of diversity to go around." Although Greek Life is "a large portion" of this campus, "everyone is very inclusive so finding a group of friends is not an issue of concern." People here are "genuine" and this place "will push you to do more than just attend classes, [which] is how you meet people." "I cannot imagine someone who is involved in anything in campus not fitting in," says a student.

LOYOLA MARYMOUNT UNIVERSITY (CA)

FINANCIAL AID: 310-338-2753 • E-MAIL: ADMISSIONS@LMU.EDU • WEBSITE: WWW.LMU.EDU

THE PRINCETON REVIEW SAYS

Admissions

Very important factors considered include: GPA. *Important factors considered include:* Rigor of secondary school record, standardized test scores, application essay, talent/ability, character/personal qualities. *Other factors considered include:* Class rank, extracurricular activities, first generation, recommendation(s), alumni/ae relations. SAT or ACT required; ACT with Writing component recommended. TOEFL required of all international applicants. *Academic units recommended:* 4 English; 3 mathematics; 2 science; (2 science lab); 3 social studies; 3 foreign language; 1 academic elective.

Financial Aid

Students should submit: FAFSA. The Princeton Review suggests that all financial aid forms be submitted as soon as possible after January 1. *Need-based scholarships/grants offered:* Federal Pell, SEOG, State scholarships/grants, private scholarships, the school's own gift aid. *Loan aid offered:* Direct Subsidized Stafford Loans, Direct Unsubsidized Stafford Loans, Direct PLUS loans, Federal Perkins Loans, College/university loans from institutional funds. Federal Work-Study Program available. Institutional employment available. Off-campus job opportunities are excellent.

The Inside Word

LMU's admission staff reviews each application individually. There's no minimum GPA or minimum test scores required for admission, and the school strives to consider the student's range of experiences and character. Nonetheless, the academic record is the single most important factor in an admissions decision. For interested students, the school offers an early action program, though students admitted through this program aren't required to attend.

THE SCHOOL SAYS "..."

From the Admissions Office

"Loyola Marymount University is a dynamic, student-centered university. We are medium-sized (6,000 undergraduates), and we are the only Jesuit university in the southwestern United States.

"One mile from the Pacific, our students enjoy ocean and mountain vistas as well as the moderate climate and crisp breezes characteristic of a coastal location.

"Loyola Marymount is committed to the ideals of Jesuit and Marymount education. We are a student-centered university, dedicated to the education of the whole person and to the preparation of our students for lives of service to their families, communities, and professions. Breadth and rigor are the hallmarks of the curriculum.

"Taken together, our academic program, our Jesuit and Marymount heritage, and our terrific campus environment afford our students unparalleled opportunity to prepare for life and leadership in the twenty-first century."

SELECTIVITY

Admissions Rating	91
# of applicants	11,472
% of applicants accepted	54
% of acceptees attending	22
# offered a place on the wait list	387

FRESHMAN PROFILE

Range SAT Critical Reading	540–640
Range SAT Math	550–650
Range SAT Writing	550–650
Range ACT Composite	25–29
Minimum paper TOEFL	550
Minimum web-based TOEFL	80
Average HS GPA	3.72

DEADLINES

Early action	
Deadline	11/1
Notification	12/20
Regular	
Deadline	1/15
Nonfall registration?	Yes

APPLICANTS ALSO LOOK AT AND OFTEN PREFER

University of California—Los Angeles; University of California—Berkeley; University of Southern California

AND SOMETIMES PREFER

University of California—Santa Barbara; Santa Clara University; University of California—San Diego

AND RARELY PREFER

Chapman University; Pepperdine University; University of San Diego

FINANCIAL FACTS

Financial Aid Rating	76
Annual tuition	$39,344
Required fees	$921
Books and supplies	$1,710
% needy frosh rec. need-based scholarship or grant aid	94
% needy UG rec. need-based scholarship or grant aid	92
% needy frosh rec. non-need-based scholarship or grant aid	14
% needy UG rec. non-need-based scholarship or grant aid	12
% needy frosh rec. need-based self-help aid	74
% needy UG rec. need-based self-help aid	80
% frosh rec. any financial aid	90
% UG rec. any financial aid	86
% UG borrow to pay for school	55
Average cumulative indebtedness	$32,746
% frosh need fully met	19
% ugrads need fully met	18
Average % of frosh need met	67
Average % of ugrad need met	66

LOYOLA UNIVERSITY CHICAGO

1032 WEST SHERIDAN ROAD, CHICAGO, IL 60660 • ADMISSIONS: 773-508-3075 • FAX: 773-508-8926

CAMPUS LIFE

Quality of Life Rating	81
Fire Safety Rating	82
Green Rating	95
Type of school	Private
Affiliation	Roman Catholic-Jesuit
Environment	Metropolis

STUDENTS

Total undergrad enrollment	9,931
% male/female	36/64
% from out of state	33
% frosh from public high school	63
% frosh live on campus	85
% ugrads live on campus	43
# of fraternities (% ugrad men join)	7 (9)
# of sororities (% ugrad women join)	9 (12)
% African American	4
% Asian	11
% Caucasian	61
% Hispanic	13
% Native American	<1
% international	3
# of countries represented	73

SURVEY SAYS . . .
Students love Chicago, IL
Great off-campus food
Lab facilities are great

ACADEMICS

Academic Rating	77
% students returning for sophomore year	85
% students graduating within 4 years	60
% students graduating within 6 years	71
Calendar	Semester
Student/faculty ratio	14:1
Profs interesting rating	73
Profs accessible rating	71

Most classes have 10–19 students.
Most lab/discussion sessions have
20–29 students.

MOST POPULAR MAJORS
nursing; biology; psychology

STUDENTS SAY " . . ."

Academics
Standing tall alongside the shore of Lake Michigan eight miles north of downtown Chicago, Loyola University "provides the best of both worlds: an integrated campus and a taste of the city life." The undergraduate campus is located next to Lake Michigan, and the surrounding area is "gorgeous." The academic programs are "rigorous and fascinating," and the school offers "significant financial assistance and plenty of scholarships." The school's location "allows Loyola to attract top-notch faculty while giving students of all disciplines the opportunity to find something that interests them." Built on strong Jesuit values, Loyola cares deeply about social justice ("set the world on fire" is a common credo) and "developing intellectual and socially responsible students." "My school is about preparing students for careers and being aware of problems around us," says a student.

"The majority of the professors [are] excellent." The professors "find a good balance in their teaching methods that allow students to engage the material and engage other students in the classroom." "They are the kind of teachers that one remembers for a long time," says a student. "Many bring in business professionals to relate our classroom material to the real world," and "the work is challenging, but not overbearing." "I've had several professors who I would go out of my way to take again," says a student. "The academics make everyone work hard, regardless of natural ability, but it pays off every time."

The "well-known academic integrity of the school" provides a great reputation in Chicago, and the "connections and opportunities" the school provides to students seeking jobs and internships are numerous. Since the curriculum is centered on being well-rounded, "students can build an education that will serve them well in the future." "Loyola challenges its students to be the best they can be, no matter what their major or background is."

Life
"What's great about Loyola is that it is very future-focused, but it never forgets about the present either," says a student. People at this school are quite involved, and they "find a good core group of people that they work together with in classes, clubs, organizations, and/or athletics." "Community service opportunities" abound, as do plenty of study abroad opportunities, and people "go on trips that involve doing out of the ordinary activities," including skiing and skydiving.

Many students admit that the "social atmosphere of the campus is very dull," but Chicago is "a gold mine" of clubs, bars, sports venues, shops, and sites. "Basically, the biggest hobby around here is exploring Chicago. We go out every weekend, just looking for things to do and always finding them," says a student. "Many students drink, but not all." The campus itself is "very relaxed, a sort of oasis in a bustling city," and there is even a beach right off campus on Lake Michigan, so "clearly, it does not feel much like a city most of the time."

Student Body
This group of "witty, hardworking, smart, and outgoing" people are all "studious and fairly involved but able to have fun." The typical student "comes from an upper-middle-class family, has some faith background, and balances school with social life well." Many are from local suburbs of Chicago ("being in the city, many Loyola students are fashionable and like to experiment with clothing") and care about "enjoying the city." "It is very easy to fit in because of how accepting people are," and "there is a real feel of family." Students "normally fit in the best in activities or the freshmen residence halls." Many students comment that there seems to be a lot of premed students here. Most everyone is "involved in some extracurricular or another," and many students have a job, as well.

FINANCIAL AID: 773-508-7704 • E-MAIL: ADMISSION@LUC.EDU • WEBSITE: WWW.LUC.EDU

THE PRINCETON REVIEW SAYS

Admissions

Very important factors considered include: GPA, rigor of secondary school record, standardized test scores. *Important factors considered include:* Application essay, extracurricular activities, recommendation(s), volunteer work, character/personal qualities, level of applicant's interest. *Other factors considered include:* Class rank, first generation, geographical residence, interview, state residency, talent/ability, work experience, alumni/ae relations. SAT or ACT required; ACT with or without Writing component accepted. TOEFL required of all international applicants. *Academic units required:* 4 English; 3 mathematics; 3 science; 2 social studies; 2 foreign language; 1 history. *Academic units recommended:* 4 English; 4 mathematics; 3 science; 2 social studies; 2 foreign language; 2 history; 3 academic electives.

Financial Aid

Students should submit: FAFSA. The Princeton Review suggests that all financial aid forms be submitted as soon as possible after January 1. *Need-based scholarships/grants offered:* Federal Pell, SEOG, State scholarships/grants, private scholarships, the school's own gift aid. *Loan aid offered:* Direct Subsidized Stafford Loans, Direct Unsubsidized Stafford Loans, Direct PLUS loans, Federal Perkins Loans, Federal Nursing Loans. Federal Work-Study Program available. Institutional employment available. Off-campus job opportunities are good.

The Inside Word

Loyola is fairly conventional when it comes to admissions policies. Successful candidates usually have a combination of strong grades, success in a tough college preparatory curriculum, and solid extracurricular activities. The school adheres to Jesuit teaching, so applicants with significant volunteer work should impress admissions officers.

THE SCHOOL SAYS "..."

From the Admissions Office

"Loyola University Chicago continues to open new facilities and renovate existing buildings. Loyola is in final phases of a $100 million renovation campaign, reimagine, to revolutionize the student experience. To date, Loyola has gained a new sports arena, a new student union, and two new, cutting edge residence halls, one of which, San Francisco Hall, is a green residence aimed at sustainable living. A revamped fitness center is set to open this year, followed by a new stree-facing facade on the Lake Shore Campus in 2015 and completing the transformation campaign. Loyola frequently enhances its undergraduate academic programming by modifying and adding new majors in emerging fields. In the fall of 2013, the Institute for Environmental Sustainability opened its doors. Housed in a brand new state-of-the-art and LEED certified facility featuring a greenhouse, environmental policy, and environmental science with concentrations like conservation and retoration. The Core Curriculum at Loyola solidifies student credentials by emphasizing lifelong skills and values while giving students the opportunity to complete a second major or add a minor. Between Loyoloa's two main campuses, students benefit from a traditional campus fell as well as a vibrant, urban atmosphere. For more information about undergraduate academics, housing, student life, financial aid, scholarship opportunities, and more, visit LUC.edu/undergrad."

SELECTIVITY

Admissions Rating	85
# of applicants	14,355
% of applicants accepted	91
% of acceptees attending	19

FRESHMAN PROFILE

Range SAT Critical Reading	520–630
Range SAT Math	530–630
Range SAT Writing	520–630
Range ACT Composite	24–29
Minimum paper TOEFL	550
Average HS GPA	3.65
% graduated top 10% of class	37
% graduated top 25% of class	68
% graduated top 50% of class	92

DEADLINES

Regular	
Priority	12/1
Nonfall registration?	Yes

APPLICANTS ALSO LOOK AT AND OFTEN PREFER

DePaul University; Marquette University; Northwestern University; Saint Louis University; The University of Chicago; University of Illinois at Urbana-Champaign; University of Michigan—Ann Arbor; University of Minnesota—Twin Cities; University of Wisconsin-M

AND SOMETIMES PREFER

Boston College; Boston University; Bradley University; Fordham University; Illinois State University; Miami University; Michigan State University

AND RARELY PREFER

American University; Augustana College (IL); Creighton University; Northeastern University; Vanderbilt University

FINANCIAL FACTS

Financial Aid Rating	76
Annual tuition	$37,270
Room and board	$13,110
Required fees	$1,266
Books and supplies	$1,200
% needy frosh rec. need-based scholarship or grant aid	98
% needy UG rec. need-based scholarship or grant aid	95
% needy frosh rec. non-need-based scholarship or grant aid	11
% needy UG rec. non-need-based scholarship or grant aid	8
% needy frosh rec. need-based self-help aid	83
% needy UG rec. need-based self-help aid	85
% frosh rec. any financial aid	96
% UG rec. any financial aid	86
% UG borrow to pay for school	73
Average cumulative indebtedness	$34,404
% frosh need fully met	14
% ugrads need fully met	11
Average % of frosh need met	81
Average % of ugrad need met	79

LOYOLA UNIVERSITY IN MARYLAND

4501 NORTH CHARLES STREET, BALTIMORE, MD 21210 • ADMISSIONS: 410-617-5012 • FAX: 410-617-2176

CAMPUS LIFE
Quality of Life Rating	93
Fire Safety Rating	88
Green Rating	80
Type of school	Private
Affiliation	Roman Catholic
Environment	Metropolis

STUDENTS
Total undergrad enrollment	4,004
% male/female	41/59
% from out of state	83
% frosh from public high school	51
% frosh live on campus	98
% ugrads live on campus	81
% African American	5
% Asian	3
% Caucasian	79
% Hispanic	9
% Native American	<1
% international	<1
# of countries represented	32

SURVEY SAYS . . .
Political activism is unpopular or nonexistent
Students are happy
Classroom facilities are great
Career services are great
School is well run
Students are friendly
Students involved in community service
Great off-campus food
Dorms are like palaces
Athletic facilities are great
Hard liquor is popular
Active student government

ACADEMICS
Academic Rating	92
% students returning for sophomore year	88
% students graduating within 4 years	79
% students graduating within 6 years	84
Calendar	Semester
Student/faculty ratio	12:1
Profs interesting rating	91
Profs accessible rating	90

Most classes have 20–29 students.
Most lab/discussion sessions have 20–29 students.

MOST POPULAR MAJORS
business/commerce; psychology; communications

STUDENTS SAY ". . ."

Academics

The Jesuits have a long history of excellence in higher education, and that tradition is richly reflected in the academic programs at Loyola University in Maryland. The undergraduate experience is built around Loyola's "fantastic core curriculum," which ensures "a solid foundation in the natural sciences, English, history, philosophy and theology." Through the core, students across disciplines "take some awesome classes that will completely change your perspective on the world." Jesuit values and philosophy are emphasized in the coursework, yet the school strikes the "right balance between religion, spirituality, and the everyday life of college students." No matter what field you choose to study, "the academics are outstanding and the coursework is challenging." A true teaching university, Loyola professors use "different learning techniques to cater to everyone's different learning styles." Professors "actually know each of their students by name." Serving as both personal and academic mentors, Loyola professors "get to know you personally, take time out of their office hours to have intellectual discussions, show you how to learn and how to teach, and help you out when you are having difficulties." The relationship can even extend off campus, as it's "fairly common for professors to give out their personal cell phone numbers or to even invite the class to their home for dinner." There's extensive "academic support" and tutoring for students in every discipline, and the "Career Center is open for students starting at day one." Though some would like to see a "larger variety of classes" for undergraduates, many praise the "excellent study abroad program," which offers the opportunity to spend a year in one of fourteen countries.

Life

Loyola students juggle school, service, spirituality, and social life with extraordinary flair. Monday through Friday, most undergraduates are "insanely busy doing loads of homework, projects, reading, community service, clubs, lectures, [and] sports." Of particular note, Loyola offers "amazing opportunities to get involved in the Baltimore community through service." In fact, the school uses "Baltimore city as an extension of the classroom," where students learn about real life, rather than living in a college bubble. On the weekends, things slow down around campus, though students can partake of the "numerous speakers, movies, events, or sporting events" hosted by the university. In addition, "a lot of people go out to bars on Fridays and Saturdays," because "there is no Greek life" on campus and Loyola's strict alcohol policies make it difficult to throw parties. Loyola students can be found out and about in Baltimore, "going out to eat, catching an Orioles game, attending a concert at the BSO, [or] walking around the harbor." "Most students live on campus" during the school year, enjoying a surprisingly comfortable lifestyle in Loyola's cushy dormitories. If you score a spot in one of the suites, you and your roommates will "have full kitchens in your dorm by sophomore year."

Student Body

In addition to being predominantly Catholic, "many of the students are white, from New York or New Jersey, and come from private high schools." You'll see plenty of "Uggs, North Face, pearls, and J. Crew" around campus. Although "the student body may appear homogenous," students insist that, "Everyone can fit in well if you get past the initial stereotypes and immerse yourself in the opportunities Loyola has to offer." On that note, students "try to live out the core values of the university and enjoy being a contributing member of school community." Here, students "care about their academics and do well in school, but they also try to balance that with extracurriculars and their spiritual life." On the whole, the campus "really welcoming and trustworthy," with a "great sense of community." With so many ways to get involved, most students "find their niche at Loyola very quickly."

FINANCIAL AID: 410-617-2576 • WEBSITE: WWW.LOYOLA.EDU

THE PRINCETON REVIEW SAYS

Admissions

Very important factors considered include: GPA, rigor of secondary school record, application essay, recommendation(s), character/personal qualities. *Important factors considered include:* extracurricular activities, talent/ability, volunteer work. *Other factors considered include:* Class rank, standardized test scores, first generation, geographical residence, racial/ethnic status, work experience, alumni/ae relations, level of applicant's interest. SAT and SAT Subject Tests or ACT considered if submitted; ACT with or without Writing component accepted. TOEFL required of all international applicants. *Academic units required:* 4 English; 3 mathematics; 3 science; 2 social studies; 3 foreign language; 2 history. *Academic units recommended:* 4 English; 4 mathematics; 4 science; 3 social studies; 4 foreign language; 3 history; 1 computer science; 1 visual/performing arts.

Financial Aid

Students should submit: FAFSA, CSS/Financial Aid PROFILE, Noncustodial PROFILE. Regular filing deadline is 2/15. The Princeton Review suggests that all financial aid forms be submitted as soon as possible after January 1. *Need-based scholarships/grants offered:* Federal Pell, SEOG, State scholarships/grants, private scholarships, the school's own gift aid. *Loan aid offered:* Direct Subsidized Stafford Loans, Direct Unsubsidized Stafford Loans, Direct PLUS loans, Federal Perkins Loans, College/university loans from institutional funds. Applicants will be notified of awards beginning 3/15. Federal Work-Study Program available. Institutional employment available. Off-campus job opportunities are good.

The Inside Word

Loyola University in Maryland considers a student's academic record to be among the most important factors in an admissions decision. Successful students usually rank in the top quarter of their classes. Although Loyola will consider standardized test scores if you submit them, the SAT or ACT are optional for all first-year applicants. If you decide to apply without taking the SAT, Loyola asks that you submit an additional personal essay or recommendation.

THE SCHOOL SAYS "..."

From the Admissions Office

"To make a wise choice about your college plans, you will need to find out more. We extend to you these invitations. Question-and-answer periods with an admissions counselor are helpful to prospective students. An appointment should be made in advance. Admission office hours are 9:00 A.M. to 5:00 P.M., Monday through Friday. College day programs and Saturday information programs are scheduled during the academic year. These programs include a video about Loyola, a general information session, a discussion of various majors, a campus tour, and lunch. Summer information programs can help high school juniors to get a head start on investigating colleges. These programs feature an introductory presentation about the university and a campus tour."

SELECTIVITY

Admissions Rating	87
# of applicants	13,604
% of applicants accepted	58
% of acceptees attending	14
# offered a place on the wait list	2,504
% accepting a place on wait list	23
% admitted from wait list	8

FRESHMAN PROFILE

Range SAT Critical Reading	540–630
Range SAT Math	560–640
Range ACT Composite	25–29
Minimum paper TOEFL	550
Minimum web-based TOEFL	213
Average HS GPA	3.45
% graduated top 10% of class	28
% graduated top 25% of class	67
% graduated top 50% of class	91

DEADLINES

Early action	
Deadline	11/1
Notification	1/15
Regular	
Priority	11/1
Deadline	1/15
Notification	3/15
Nonfall registration?	Yes

APPLICANTS ALSO LOOK AT AND OFTEN PREFER

Boston College; Georgetown University; University of Notre Dame

AND SOMETIMES PREFER

Villanova University; College of the Holy Cross; University of Richmond

AND RARELY PREFER

Providence College; Fordham University; Fairfield University

FINANCIAL FACTS

Financial Aid Rating	96
% needy frosh rec. need-based scholarship or grant aid	92
% needy UG rec. need-based scholarship or grant aid	92
% needy frosh rec. non-need-based scholarship or grant aid	7
% needy UG rec. non-need-based scholarship or grant aid	6
% needy frosh rec. need-based self-help aid	89
% needy UG rec. need-based self-help aid	89
% frosh rec. any financial aid	71
% UG rec. any financial aid	69
% UG borrow to pay for school	65
Average cumulative indebtedness	$34,012
% frosh need fully met	95
% ugrads need fully met	90
Average % of frosh need met	96
Average % of ugrad need met	94

LOYOLA UNIVERSITY NEW ORLEANS

6363 ST. CHARLES AVENUE, NEW ORLEANS, LA 70118-6195 • ADMISSIONS: 504-865-3240 • FAX: 504-865-3383

CAMPUS LIFE

Quality of Life Rating	98
Fire Safety Rating	99
Green Rating	73
Type of school	Private
Affiliation	Roman Catholic Jesuit
Environment	City

STUDENTS

Total undergrad enrollment	3,135
% male/female	41/59
% from out of state	58
% frosh from public high school	47
% frosh live on campus	81
% ugrads live on campus	65
# of fraternities	8
# of sororities (% ugrad women join)	7 (16)
% African American	15
% Asian	4
% Caucasian	53
% Hispanic	15
% Native American	1
% international	3
# of countries represented	57

SURVEY SAYS . . .

Students are happy
Students are friendly
Diverse student types on campus
Students get along with local community
Students love New Orleans, LA
Great off-campus food
Campus feels safe
Easy to get around campus
Student publications are popular
Active student government

ACADEMICS

Academic Rating	89
% students returning for sophomore year	74
% students graduating within 4 years	47
% students graduating within 6 years	58
Calendar	Semester
Student/faculty ratio	10:1
Profs interesting rating	90
Profs accessible rating	87

Most classes have 10–19 students.
Most lab/discussion sessions have 10–19 students.

MOST POPULAR MAJORS

psychology; mass communication/media studies; marketing

STUDENTS SAY ". . ."

Academics

A warm private school in the heart of a big, vibrant city, Loyola University New Orleans excels at "helping everyone find their niche" through a well-rounded academic program and an "emphasis on individual success." Not an ivory tower, Loyola strives "to provide students with the skills needed for a professional career." To that end, professors "know how to relate the classroom lessons to real life," in addition to promoting service learning and "hands-on experiences," both on and off campus. Furthering the Jesuit ideal of "educating the person as a whole," there is a "focus on ethics in every single class," and the coursework will "challenge you so that you are ready to think critically about the world." Students are particularly proud of the school's strong mass communications major, while others point out that Loyola's "music industry program is something that's not really available at any college unless it's a music conservatory." Described as "engaging and reliable," Loyola professors are "very passionate about their subjects, which helps them bring the class and content to life." Most important, the faculty expresses "genuine concern" for students, "always looking to help you excel" and "providing help outside of class time." A current student writes, "My professors from freshman year still remember my name and will occasionally contact me about internships, etc." This supportiveness is visible throughout the school and defines the Loyola experience: Here, "students, faculty, and staff have a great relationship, and there is a general sense of goodwill among the Loyola community."

Life

"Loyola, being so small, can make each student feel like they belong" and there is a "great sense of community" within the undergraduate college. You'll often see students "sitting out on benches talking with their friends between classes" or getting together to "hang out in the quad on nice days." For fun, "there are always events and activities" on campus. In fact, students say you never know what to expect: "Coming to the residential dorms one may find a barbecue, a Quidditch match, or even a band playing." In their downtime, Loyola students love to study or stroll in Audubon Park, located just across the street from the school, or "take walks around New Orleans," an "awesome" city to explore. On the weekends, many go out to "enjoy local cuisine" or "shop in little boutiques" along Magazine Street and St. Charles Avenue, and "because New Orleans is such a cultural hub, there is always something fun going on," especially for those who love nightlife. A student chides, "In New Orleans, people will take any opportunity they have to celebrate—holidays, birthdays, building demolitions. You name it, we'll celebrate it." Taking a cue from their upbeat surroundings, many students "head to local bars either to party or to see their friends play in bands." On that note, "art is definitely an emphasis on our campus. You can specifically notice the appreciation and commitment to music through events on campus, performances, renowned speakers, and conversations regarding music."

Students

According to their classmates, the typical Loyola undergrad is "very intelligent, open-minded, [and] politically and environmentally aware." As students, they are generally "hardworking" and committed to their major, though most are open-minded and "ready to try new things." On this "welcoming and accepting" campus, "students feel no need to 'fit in.' The diversity is so high here that it's almost impossible to stand out." In fact, "at Loyola and in New Orleans, differences are celebrated," and "Students of all religions, nationalities, races and genders interact in a friendly and respectful manner." A current student elaborates, "The student population is reflective of the city population in that no one is really afraid to be themselves." While many students are attracted to the school's religious affiliation, "one of the greatest things about my school is how welcoming it is towards other cultures, religions, and ways of life even though it is a Catholic university." Nonetheless, locals note, "Loyola could improve with the integration of on-campus students and commuters."

LOYOLA UNIVERSITY NEW ORLEANS

FINANCIAL AID: 504-865-3231 • E-MAIL: ADMIT@LOYNO.EDU • WEBSITE: WWW.LOYNO.EDU

THE PRINCETON REVIEW SAYS

Admissions

Very important factors considered include: GPA, rigor of secondary school record, standardized test scores. *Important factors considered include:* Application essay, extracurricular activities, recommendation(s), talent/ability. *Other factors considered include:* Class rank, geographical residence, interview, state residency, volunteer work, work experience, alumni/ae relations, character/personal qualities, level of applicant's interest. SAT or ACT required; ACT with or without Writing component accepted. TOEFL required of all international applicants. *Academic units required:* 4 English; 2 mathematics; 2 science; 2 social studies. *Academic units recommended:* 4 English; 3 mathematics; 3 science; (1 science lab); 2 social studies; 2 foreign language.

Financial Aid

Students should submit: FAFSA. Regular filing deadline is 6/1. The Princeton Review suggests that all financial aid forms be submitted as soon as possible after January 1. *Need-based scholarships/grants offered:* Federal Pell, SEOG, private scholarships, the school's own gift aid. *Loan aid offered:* Federal Perkins Loans. Applicants will be notified of awards beginning 3/1. Federal Work-Study Program available. Institutional employment available. Off-campus job opportunities are excellent.

The Inside Word

Admission to Loyola is competitive. In the most recent admissions cycle, the average entering student had a high school GPA of 3.66. In addition to reviewing your GPA, Loyola also evaluates students based on their standardized test scores, class rank, extracurricular activities, and personal statement. Volunteer work and community service will serve your application to any school well, but they're especially helpful at this Jesuit institution.

THE SCHOOL SAYS "..."

From the Admissions Office

"Chartered in 1912, Loyola University New Orleans is one of America's twenty-eight Jesuit institutions of higher learning. Its rich history dates back to the early eighteenth century when the Jesuits first arrived in New Orleans. As a Catholic university, Loyola has continued to emphasize the valuable Jesuit tradition of educating the whole person. Our more than 37,000 graduates have excelled in innumerable areas for ninety-seven years; their influence is felt around the world.

"Loyola's growth has increased the diversity of education available, all delivered within the educational values traditionally associated with our Jesuit heritage. This unique, nationally acclaimed institution—the crown jewel for a Jesuit education in the Southern United States—offers a welcoming and festive campus atmosphere and an emphasis on a liberal arts and sciences education, emphasizing self-discovery, exploration of values, while fostering personal initiative and critical thinking. Undergraduates enjoy individual attention in a university that strives to educate not only intellectually, but also spiritually, socially, and athletically. Undergraduate experience is broadened through special programs such as the First-Year Experience, learning communities, research, service learning, study abroad, and internships.

"Students applying for admission are required to take the SAT (or the ACT with the writing section). The highest composite scores will be used in admissions decisions."

SELECTIVITY

Admissions Rating	84
# of applicants	6,486
% of applicants accepted	66
% of acceptees attending	21

FRESHMAN PROFILE

Range SAT Critical Reading	530–650
Range SAT Math	510–620
Range ACT Composite	22–27
Minimum paper TOEFL	550
Minimum web-based TOEFL	213
Average HS GPA	3.66
% graduated top 10% of class	27
% graduated top 25% of class	47
% graduated top 50% of class	77

DEADLINES

Regular	
Priority	12/1
Nonfall registration?	Yes

APPLICANTS ALSO LOOK AT AND OFTEN PREFER

Saint Louis University; University of Miami; Boston University; Fordham University

AND SOMETIMES PREFER

Louisiana State University—Baton Rouge; Tulane University; Xavier University of Louisiana; Loyola The University of Chicago

FINANCIAL FACTS

Financial Aid Rating	78
Annual tuition	$35,504
Room and board	$12,185
Required fees	$1,106
Books and supplies	$1,200
% needy frosh rec. need-based scholarship or grant aid	100
% needy UG rec. need-based scholarship or grant aid	99
% needy frosh rec. non-need-based scholarship or grant aid	10
% needy UG rec. non-need-based scholarship or grant aid	12
% needy frosh rec. need-based self-help aid	84
% needy UG rec. need-based self-help aid	81
% frosh rec. any financial aid	92
% UG rec. any financial aid	92
% UG borrow to pay for school	66
Average cumulative indebtedness	$23,178
% frosh need fully met	15
% ugrads need fully met	16
Average % of frosh need met	79
Average % of ugrad need met	72

LYNCHBURG COLLEGE

1501 LAKESIDE DRIVE, LYNCHBURG, VA 24501 • ADMISSIONS: 434-544-8300 • FAX: 434-544-8653

CAMPUS LIFE

Quality of Life Rating	87
Fire Safety Rating	76
Green Rating	61
Type of school	Private
Affiliation	Disciples of Christ
Environment	City

STUDENTS

Total undergrad enrollment	2,140
% male/female	40/60
% from out of state	32
% frosh from public high school	85
% frosh live on campus	89
% ugrads live on campus	73
# of fraternities (% ugrad men join)	5 (11)
# of sororities (% ugrad women join)	6 (14)
% African American	11
% Asian	1
% Caucasian	77
% Hispanic	4
% Native American	<1
% international	1
# of countries represented	10

SURVEY SAYS . . .

Students are happy
Students are friendly
Everyone loves the Hornets
Intramural sports are popular

ACADEMICS

Academic Rating	82
% students returning for sophomore year	78
% students graduating within 4 years	46
% students graduating within 6 years	56
Calendar	Semester
Student/faculty ratio	11:1
Profs interesting rating	87
Profs accessible rating	88

Most classes have 10–19 students.
Most lab/discussion sessions have fewer than 10 students.

MOST POPULAR MAJORS

teacher education and professional development; speech communications and rhetoric; nursing

STUDENTS SAY "..."

Academics

Located in the foothills of the Blue Ridge Mountains, Lynchburg College "is not just a school, but a family that allows its students to learn and have fun doing it." Students describe this "small" school as having a "friendly atmosphere" and being "truly a home away from home." LC is "all about getting the job done" in "fostering and preparing the next generation of leaders." The school is especially known for its "great Nursing program." "The smaller size of the school allows for your education to be much more intimate and personal," a Biomedical Sciences student explains. "The small size of the school makes it easy to establish a relationship with your professors" and makes "it easy to get to know classmates." Professors are "very organized," "very professional," and "always willing to stop and clarify" while also trying "their best to make the class interesting and fun." At LC, you "can tell that these teachers take their job very serious and want to see their students succeed in this world." Some students say they have "mixed feelings" about the professors, as "some have been great and others not so much." The most common area of complaint is the "quality of cafeteria food," which "could be more varied" and does not do much "to accommodate vegans and vegetarians." Overall, students gave high marks to the administration. They especially praised the "communication between the Dean of Students and the actual students" and noted that the "administration truly takes the time to understand its students." One student was simply amazed at "how absolutely EVERY SINGLE PERSON who attends or works at this school is so involved." At the end of the day, LC is a college that doesn t only educate you, but "instills values and a sense of family that lasts far longer than any career you will ever have."

Life

LC is a school where "hard work is required, and fun on the weekends is encouraged." "We like to have fun, but we definitely know how to buckle down and get serious when it comes to our education," an Education major explains. "The amount of student involvement [is] astonishing" at LC. "A typical student at LC is someone who is in no less than four clubs/activities with some form of officer position in at least one or two of them," one student explains. "Life revolves around school and athletics around here" and "either Greek, clubs, or a sports team involvement is expected here at LC." Greek life is big on campus, although "Greek organizations are not the stereotypical kind you see on TV. We are all supportive of each other, play intramurals, hang out, and do community service together." Some students suggest that the student body is mainly divided between "Greeks" and "athletes," "but there is not much overlap between these groups." Off campus activities include "hiking, river rafting" as well as "many shopping options." On campus, the "very active Student Activities Board" works hard to provide students with an array of "events, concerts, and discounted opportunities throughout the city."

Student Body

Most of the students at LC are "Caucasian, upper class, prep," and from either Virginia or "the upper east coast." "Everyone is pretty laid back" and students are "not super academically inclined, but passionate about the major/career path they choose." One student sums up the typical student: "Friendly. Amazing. Smart." Although LC "is mostly White Virginians, students come from all socioeconomic statuses and walks of life." Students do wish for more "international students and diversity on campus," and say "it would be nice to have students from other areas of the States." "LC is an extremely accepting campus," an Environmental Studies major says, and "students of all kinds are able to work together." As noted above, students are "deeply involved" on campus and in student organizations. This means students are "able to connect with a lot of people on campus" and "somehow everyone seems to find their place and everyone fits in."

FINANCIAL AID: 434-544-8229 • E-MAIL: ADMISSIONS@LYNCHBURG.EDU • WEBSITE: WWW.LYNCHBURG.EDU

THE PRINCETON REVIEW SAYS

Admissions

Very important factors considered include: GPA, rigor of secondary school record, standardized test scores. *Important factors considered include:* Class rank, interview. *Other factors considered include:* Application essay, extracurricular activities, recommendation(s), talent/ability, volunteer work, work experience, character/personal qualities, level of applicant's interest. SAT or ACT required; ACT with or without Writing component accepted. TOEFL required of all international applicants. *Academic units required:* 4 English; 3 mathematics; 3 science; (2 science lab); 2 social studies; 2 foreign language; 2 history. *Academic units recommended:* 4 English; 4 mathematics; 4 science; (2 science lab); 2 social studies; 3 foreign language; 2 history; 1 academic elective.

Financial Aid

Students should submit: FAFSA, State aid form. The Princeton Review suggests that all financial aid forms be submitted as soon as possible after January 1. *Need-based scholarships/grants offered:* Federal Pell, SEOG, State scholarships/grants, private scholarships, the school's own gift aid. *Loan aid offered:* Direct Subsidized Stafford Loans, Direct Unsubsidized Stafford Loans, Direct PLUS loans, Federal Perkins Loans. Applicants will be notified of awards beginning 3/5. Federal Work-Study Program available. Institutional employment available. Off-campus job opportunities are good.

Inside Word

LC uses a rolling admission, so students can apply at any time following junior year. LC recommends applying at the start of the fall semester of senior year. Transcripts and SAT or ACT scores are required, while a college essay and a letter of recommendation are strongly recommended but not required. Applicants lucky enough to be admitted are automatically considered for academic scholarships.

THE SCHOOL SAYS "..."

From the Admissions Office

Lynchburg College is a nationally recognized private college in Virginia that offers students a challenging curriculum of liberal arts, professional, and graduate programs combined with broad-based internships, study abroad, research, leadership, community service, and athletic opportunities that prepare them to succeed in a global society. Students benefit from their engagement with faculty, staff, and alumni in a diverse community that leads to exemplary academic, social, personal, and spiritual growth.

LC freshmen participate in the First Year Engagement Program, a comprehensive and coordinated series of programs to help new students build meaningful relationships on campus and equip them with skills for success in college. Designated freshmen residence halls provide a distinctive, enriched living and learning environment that supports new students in their transition to college life.

Lynchburg College students express high satisfaction with their school. LC ranked in all five benchmarks of the National Survey of Student Engagement (NSSE), which measures how college and universities engage their students in activities related to learning and personal development. These include: student-faculty interaction, supportive campus environment, level of academic challenge, active and collaborative learning, and enriching education experiences.

From the moment prospective students step onto this beautiful campus, they begin to appreciate the Lynchburg College experience, which has been changing lives for more than 100 years. Visiting is a must! Students and families are invited to attend one of the many 'visit events' throughout the year.

SELECTIVITY

Admissions Rating	79
# of applicants	5,695
% of applicants accepted	64
% of acceptees attending	14
# of early decision applicants	226
% accepted early decision	52

FRESHMAN PROFILE

Range SAT Critical Reading	450–550
Range SAT Math	440–560
Range SAT Writing	440–540
Range ACT Composite	19–24
Minimum paper TOEFL	550
Minimum web-based TOEFL	78
Average HS GPA	3.29

DEADLINES

Early decision	
Deadline	11/15
Notification	12/1
Regular	
Notification	Rolling
Nonfall registration?	Yes

APPLICANTS ALSO LOOK AT AND OFTEN PREFER

James Madison University; Radford University; Longwood University

AND SOMETIMES PREFER

George Mason University; Roanoke College; Christopher Newport University

FINANCIAL FACTS

Financial Aid Rating	82
Annual tuition	$32,620
Room and board	$9,080
Required fees	$945
Books and supplies	$1,000
% needy frosh rec. need-based scholarship or grant aid	100
% needy UG rec. need-based scholarship or grant aid	100
% needy frosh rec. non-need-based scholarship or grant aid	15
% needy UG rec. non-need-based scholarship or grant aid	12
% needy frosh rec. need-based self-help aid	79
% needy UG rec. need-based self-help aid	82
% frosh rec. any financial aid	98
% UG rec. any financial aid	96
% UG borrow to pay for school	79
Average cumulative indebtedness	$35,330
% frosh need fully met	19
% ugrads need fully met	18
Average % of frosh need met	83
Average % of ugrad need met	76

MACALESTER COLLEGE

1600 GRAND AVENUE, ST. PAUL, MN 55105 • ADMISSIONS: 651-696-6357 • FAX: 651-696-6724

CAMPUS LIFE

Quality of Life Rating	96
Fire Safety Rating	98
Green Rating	93
Type of school	Private
Affiliation	No Affiliation
Environment	Metropolis

STUDENTS

Total undergrad enrollment	2,039
% male/female	39/61
% from out of state	84
% frosh from public high school	64
% frosh live on campus	100
% ugrads live on campus	64
% African American	3
% Asian	7
% Caucasian	67
% Hispanic	6
% Native American	<1
% international	12
# of countries represented	93

SURVEY SAYS . . .

Lots of liberal students
Political activism is popular
Students are happy
Lab facilities are great
No one cheats
Students are friendly
Students get along with local community
Students environmentally aware
Students love St. Paul, MN
Great food on campus
Great off-campus food
Easy to get around campus
Athletic facilities are great
Active minority support groups

ACADEMICS

Academic Rating	97
% students returning for sophomore year	95
% students graduating within 4 years	85
% students graduating within 6 years	87
Calendar	Semester
Student/faculty ratio	10:1
Profs interesting rating	96
Profs accessible rating	95

Most classes have 10–19 students.
Most lab/discussion sessions have fewer than 10 students.

MOST POPULAR MAJORS
economics; biology; international studies

STUDENTS SAY ". . ."

Academics

Macalester College in Minnesota is an academic powerhouse; it "opens myriad doors for students to work incredibly hard at what they love and, through research, explore avenues of interest they may not have previously considered." The school attracts a high quality of "academic-minded" students because of the generous financial aid and places an emphasis on internationalism; the college also strongly encourages students to follow their interests in developing extracurricular student organizations. "Student organizations are provided exceptional guidance and funding from the college," says a student. The atmosphere is "academically challenging without feeling competitive," and Macalester is all about "finding the balance between serious academics, service, and fun." The "genuine, resourceful, accessible, and friendly" professors "are exceptional mentors" who "share the excitement they have about their particular fields." "I have found a lot of variety both in the teaching styles of my instructors and class topics, which is something I really appreciate about my major and Macalester in general," says one student. When professors can, they "change lecture to discussion," "add various different types of course materials," and generally keep students engaged. There is also a lot of interdisciplinary work and collaborations between professors in order to "help develop new courses, research topics, and even academic majors." Personal relationships are incredibly important to the faculty here, and professors "invest their time in the success of each student." Though there's "a definite depth to courses provided," the small size of the school means that "the variety within departments could be sparse." Being in the Twin Cities, there are "a lot of opportunities for volunteering and internships," and non-achievements, whether in sports, arts, or community service, are given "equal recognition." "There is an awareness about the world, our place in it, and how our choices affect it. There is an earnest desire to learn and listen to differing perspectives," says a student.

Life

This "unique international community in the middle of a frozen metropolis" ("I wish I could pick up the entire campus and move it to a warmer climate") has an "ideal" placement in a "beautiful" residential neighborhood dotted with restaurants and shops, with quick access to two major cities. At Mac, "There is so much to do on campus that you're never bored." "So many organizations, so little time!" says a student. With more than 120 organizations, "It's hard to find the time to get involved in everything, but very easy to find something to do." For more casual fun, people "go out into St. Paul and Minneapolis, go to dances on campus, go to house parties off campus, or just hang out and watch movies or have conversations." Parties "only happen on the weekend, and they are nonexistent around midterms or finals"; "Often people end up talking about Marxism or feminist theory at parties anyway." "You know you're at Macalester when the football team had its first winning season in decades, but our poetry slam team [are] national defending champions." Deep conversations about politics, spirituality, and identity are frequent, and "class and school invade all aspects of life here."

Student Body

Macalester is full of "intelligent," "left-wing," "self-driven students who want to participate in academics, politics, and social issues." There is a "simultaneous lightheartedness and intensity" to Macalester students, and everyone here is "eager to converse and debate with peers who may have a very different background from them." "The socioeconomic range is huge, as is the geographical diversity with international students composing 19 percent of the student body." "The experience of sitting in a class of twenty with students from eight different countries discussing the cultural implications of translation is one that can only be found at Macalester," says a student. "It would be easier to define the typical kid who is not at Mac: bro / fraternity-type guys and ditsy, sorority girls," says one student. "Mainstream people without their own opinions don't make it here."

FINANCIAL AID: 651-696-6214 • E-MAIL: ADMISSIONS@MACALESTER.EDU • WEBSITE: WWW.MACALESTER.EDU

THE PRINCETON REVIEW SAYS

Admissions

Very important factors considered include: GPA, rigor of secondary school record. *Important factors considered include:* Standardized test scores, application essay, extracurricular activities, recommendation(s), character/personal qualities. *Other factors considered include:* Class rank, first generation, interview, racial/ethnic status, talent/ability, volunteer work, work experience, alumni/ae relations. SAT or ACT required; SAT and SAT Subject Tests or ACT considered if submitted; ACT with or without Writing component accepted. TOEFL required of all international applicants. *Academic units recommended:* 4 English; 3 mathematics; 3 science; (3 science lab); 3 social studies; 3 foreign language.

Financial Aid

Students should submit: FAFSA, CSS/Financial Aid PROFILE, Noncustodial PROFILE. Regular filing deadline is 2/8. The Princeton Review suggests that all financial aid forms be submitted as soon as possible after January 1. *Need-based scholarships/grants offered:* Federal Pell, SEOG, State scholarships/grants, private scholarships, the school's own gift aid. *Loan aid offered:* Direct Subsidized Stafford Loans, Direct Unsubsidized Stafford Loans, Direct PLUS loans, Federal Perkins Loans, State Loans, College/university loans from institutional funds Applicants will be notified of awards beginning 4/1. Federal Work-Study Program available. Institutional employment available. Off-campus job opportunities are excellent.

The Inside Word

To say that Macalester's star is on the rise is to put it very mildly. The number of applicants to the school continues to increase. Accordingly, it has grown substantially more difficult to gain admission here within a very short period of time. Candidates need to put their best foot forward in their applications; two thirds of the current first year class ranked in the top 10 percent of their high school classes.

THE SCHOOL SAYS "..."

From the Admissions Office

"Macalester has been preparing students for world citizenship and providing an integrated international education for over six decades. The United Nations flag has flown on campus since 1950 and 18 percent of the students are citizens of another country, with over ninety countries represented on campus. Over 60 percent of Mac students study abroad, going to nearly fifty countries all over the world each year. Graduates enter the workforce or graduate school with respected scholarship and real experience in a global community, prepared to succeed in their chosen fields. Mac students thrive in a rigorous academic environment, supported by accomplished faculty who love to teach. Located in a friendly residential neighborhood in the heart of a vibrant metropolitan area, Macalester offers unusually broad, easily accessible internship opportunities to add valuable experience, connections and practice at getting things done, often leading to job opportunities after graduation. Two out of three Mac students complete an internship at a Twin Cities business, law firm, hospital, financial institution, museum, theater, state government, research lab, environmental agency, or non-profit group (and more), all within a few miles of campus. Students rave about the food at Mac, which includes vegetarian fare, food for meat lovers, plenty of variety and entrées from around the world. A new athletic and recreation center opened in the fall of 2009, including a large fitness center, indoor track, gymnasium, natatorium, field house, gathering spaces, juice bar, atrium and more. Athletic teams frequently earn the highest cumulative GPA in the nation. Macalester meets the full demonstrated need for every admitted student, providing broad socioeconomic representation in the student body."

SELECTIVITY

Admissions Rating	96
# of applicants	6,683
% of applicants accepted	34
% of acceptees attending	24
# offered a place on the wait list	446
% accepting a place on wait list	49
% admitted from wait list	0
# of early decision applicants	247
% accepted early decision	53

FRESHMAN PROFILE

Range SAT Critical Reading	620–740
Range SAT Math	620–720
Range SAT Writing	630–720
Range ACT Composite	29–32
Minimum paper TOEFL	600
% graduated top 10% of class	64
% graduated top 25% of class	90
% graduated top 50% of class	99

DEADLINES

Early decision	
Deadline	11/15
Notification	12/15
Regular	
Deadline	1/15
Notification	3/30
Nonfall registration?	No

APPLICANTS ALSO LOOK AT AND OFTEN PREFER
Brown University; Swarthmore College

AND SOMETIMES PREFER
The University of Chicago; Wesleyan University; Pomona College; Vassar College; Middlebury College

AND RARELY PREFER
Kenyon College; Oberlin College; Colorado College

FINANCIAL FACTS

Financial Aid Rating	98
Annual tuition	$46,974
Room and board	$10,496
Required fees	$221
Books and supplies	$1,096
% needy frosh rec. need-based scholarship or grant aid	99
% needy UG rec. need-based scholarship or grant aid	99
% needy frosh rec. non-need-based scholarship or grant aid	10
% needy UG rec. non-need-based scholarship or grant aid	7
% needy frosh rec. need-based self-help aid	86
% needy UG rec. need-based self-help aid	91
% frosh rec. any financial aid	76
% UG rec. any financial aid	76
% UG borrow to pay for school	65
Average cumulative indebtedness	$21,939
% frosh need fully met	100
% ugrads need fully met	100
Average % of frosh need met	100
Average % of ugrad need met	100

MANHATTANVILLE COLLEGE

2900 PURCHASE STREET, ADMISSIONS OFFICE, PURCHASE, NY 10577 • ADMISSIONS: 914-323-5124 • FAX: 914-694-1732

CAMPUS LIFE

Quality of Life Rating	69
Fire Safety Rating	96
Green Rating	77
Type of school	Private
Affiliation	No Affiliation
Environment	Town

STUDENTS

Total undergrad enrollment	1,706
% male/female	36/64
% from out of state	38
% frosh live on campus	78
% ugrads live on campus	69
% African American	7
% Asian	2
% Caucasian	23
% Hispanic	11
% Native American	<1
% international	9
# of countries represented	49

SURVEY SAYS . . .

Frats and sororities are unpopular
or nonexistent
Great library
Great off-campus food

ACADEMICS

Academic Rating	74
% students returning for sophomore year	76
% students graduating within 4 years	54
% students graduating within 6 years	58
Calendar	Semester
Student/faculty ratio	12:1
Profs interesting rating	69
Profs accessible rating	67

Most classes have 10–19 students.

MOST POPULAR MAJORS
business/commerce; psychology;
communications

STUDENTS SAY ". . ."

Academics

Located on a "beautiful, nature-filled campus," the "small, but extremely diverse" Manhattanville College focuses on "building a community among all students." Many students agree that "Manhattanville College is very good at playing to its strengths, which are primarily its international student program and its small class size." Other students praise its "well-known and impressive writing program" and boast that the "music and theater department are very strong." They are also quick to highlight that their school is "committed to raising awareness about various global issues" and that "there is always an opportunity to go abroad for study purposes or volunteering." Students appreciate the "very favorable faculty-to-student ratio" and note that the "small classes allow the professor to create a bond with each and every student." Students also praise the high caliber of the professors who are "knowledgeable and insightful" and "brilliant and fully devoted to their work and passionate about what they're teaching." One discerning student reveals, "My professors are unbelievably versed in their field of expertise, but that does not mean it always translates to their ability to relay that information in a way that is engaging. That is, however, not the norm, but the exception." Students also recognize that their professors have their students' interests at heart and reveal that "if you reach out to a teacher when struggling, almost all will make time to assist you if they see you are putting in the same effort." Students are less enamored with their school administration, which "is in a time of transition and they don't seem to know which direction is the best to take."

Life

According to some students, Manhattanville suffers the fate of many commuter schools in the sense that "no one ever stays on campus, so it's always a ghost town." However, students who do stay on campus find plenty of ways to keep busy. Many students take part in WMVL the "killer radio station," which has "helped to strengthen communication in and around [the] community." They brag, "There are eighty-five DJs, and they broadcast outstanding music." Students report, "Most weekends our school will provide events to keep students around like comedy shows, school dances, and events like that." "When it's nice out, people are always on the quad either tanning or studying or playing Frisbee or skipping class." Students also look forward to Fall Fest and Quad Jam, which are "two huge parties out on the quad, kind of like a carnival." For more adventurous students who seek fun outside the boundaries of Manhattanville, the school offers a "free bus service that goes into White Plains every evening." Many students flock to White Plains for "tons of shops, a few malls, restaurants, and so many things to do." Students also take advantage of free transportation to nearby Manhattan on weekends "to access the museums, shows, exhibits, city life, and the food."

Student Body

As host to a "large number of international students," Manhattanville "is all about student diversity." Students agree, "The diversity is awesome but sometimes people from certain ethnic backgrounds hang out with that group." Creating even more divisions among the student population, "students seem to clump into cliques based on their socioeconomic backgrounds, sports/interests, etc." At the same time, students also note the "increased efforts at college to break down these barriers and have students from different backgrounds 'mingle' with one another." Students at this school consider themselves "very open and very friendly" and "accepting of people from all backgrounds." They also reveal that they "like to learn but don't go crazy studying." While some students agree, "Spanish-speaking students are probably the most common attendees," others feel, "there is a happy balance between all nationalities." Despite the differences in backgrounds, "students fit in just by joining clubs and attending school sponsored events." One student insightfully sums it up with the observation that "Manhattanville is a place small enough that people know who you are, but you still have the ability to figure out who you are."

FINANCIAL AID: 914-323-5357 • E-MAIL: ADMISSIONS@MVILLE.EDU • WEBSITE: WWW.MVILLE.EDU

THE PRINCETON REVIEW SAYS

Admissions

Very important factors considered include: GPA, rigor of secondary school record, level of applicant's interest. *Important factors considered include:* Application essay, extracurricular activities, interview, recommendation(s), volunteer work. *Other factors considered include:* Class rank, standardized test scores, geographical residence, talent/ability, work experience, alumni/ae relations, character/personal qualities, SAT or ACT recommended; ACT with Writing component recommended. TOEFL required of all international applicants. *Academic units required:* 4 English; 3 mathematics; 2 science; 2 social studies; 5 academic electives.

Financial Aid

Students should submit: FAFSA, State aid form. Regular filing deadline is 3/1. The Princeton Review suggests that all financial aid forms be submitted as soon as possible after January 1. *Need-based scholarships/grants offered:* Federal Pell, SEOG, State scholarships/grants, private scholarships, the school's own gift aid. *Loan aid offered:* Direct Subsidized Stafford Loans, Direct Unsubsidized Stafford Loans, Direct PLUS loans. Federal Work-Study Program available. Institutional employment available. Off-campus job opportunities are excellent.

The Inside Word

Manhattanville seeks "good fits," however and frequently attempts to assess compatibility with a candidate interview. The college still seeks to achieve greater gender balance, so male candidates enjoy a slightly higher admission rate than female candidates. In addition to meeting regular admissions requirements, students who wish to pursue a degree in fine arts or performing arts must present a portfolio or audition, respectively.

THE SCHOOL SAYS "..."

From the Admissions Office

"Manhattanville's mission—to educate ethically and socially responsible leaders for the global community—is evident throughout the college, from academics to athletics to social and extracurricular activities. With almost 1,700 undergraduates from fifty-nine nations and thirty-nine states, our diversity spans geographic, cultural, ethnic, religious, socioeconomic, and academic backgrounds. Students are free to express their views in this tight-knit community, where we value the personal as well as the global. Any six students with similar interest can start a club, and most participate in a variety of campus wide programs. Last year, students engaged in more than 23,380 hours of community service and social justice activity. Study abroad opportunities include the most desirable international locations. In the true liberal arts tradition, students are encouraged to think for themselves and develop new skills—in music, the studio arts, on stage, in the sciences, or on the playing field. With more than fifty areas of study and a popular self-designed major, there is no limit to our academic scope. Our Westchester County location, just thirty-five miles north of New York City, gives students an edge for jobs and internships. Last year, the men's and women's ice hockey teams were ranked number one in the nation for Division III."

SELECTIVITY

Admissions Rating	76

DEADLINES

Early decision	
Deadline	12/15
Notification	12/31
Regular	
Deadline	3/1
Nonfall registration?	Yes

APPLICANTS ALSO LOOK AT AND OFTEN PREFER
New York University

AND SOMETIMES PREFER
Fordham University

FINANCIAL FACTS

Financial Aid Rating	79
Annual tuition	$34,870
Room and board	$14,520
Required fees	$1,350
Books and supplies	$800
% needy frosh rec. need-based scholarship or grant aid	89
% needy UG rec. need-based scholarship or grant aid	92
% needy frosh rec. non-need-based scholarship or grant aid	97
% needy UG rec. non-need-based scholarship or grant aid	84
% needy frosh rec. need-based self-help aid	87
% needy UG rec. need-based self-help aid	87
% frosh rec. any financial aid	97
% UG rec. any financial aid	99
% UG borrow to pay for school	53
Average cumulative indebtedness	$23,138
% frosh need fully met	14
% ugrads need fully met	10
Average % of frosh need met	79
Average % of ugrad need met	83

MARIST COLLEGE

3399 NORTH ROAD, POUGHKEEPSIE, NY 12601-1387 • ADMISSIONS: 845-575-3226 • FAX: 845-575-3215

STUDENTS SAY ". . ."

Academics

While students are undoubtedly drawn to Marist College's "beautiful campus on the Hudson" and "magnificent scenery," it is the private school's abundance of academic offerings that really gets students excited. The "well-known business program," "great communications program," "five-year accelerated grad school for psychology," and "unbelievable study abroad programs, offering programs in over twenty countries," all help contribute to "Marist's continually rising prestige and national recognition." A favorite among the study abroad programs is the Freshman Florence Experience. Also of note is the school's "renowned fashion design program" where one student raves that "the job-placement rate coming out of the fashion program is amazing, especially in today's economy." Though comparatively small in size, Marist is able to hold its own against larger schools when it comes to resources. The college boasts a "connection to IBM" that promotes student internships and provides students and faculty access to advanced high performance IBM hardware and software and "an amazing library with very helpful resources and materials for research." However, when it comes to their campus, students do feel that there is one area that could use improvement—student housing. They generally agree, "Marist needs more upperclassmen housing since it is only guaranteed to freshmen and sophomores." When describing the school faculty, students gush about their professors who are "top-notch," "knowledgeable, and lively," and "often accessible and approachable outside of the classroom." One student says, "They are always inclusive in class discussions, and they have a zest and spark for what they're teaching us." A slightly more critical student reports, "Professors in lower-level courses tend to lecture too much, but the teachers in mid- and upper-level courses tend to have a real passion for their subjects and can make even accounting interesting." All in all, students generally agree, "Marist College prepares students to face the real world with knowledge and skills, rather than simply earn impressive grades."

Life

With more than "eighty clubs and organizations," as well as Division I sports at Marist College, it is clear that students aren't exaggerating when they say, "There is always something to do on campus whether it's a lecture from one of the puppeteers from Sesame Street, a hypnotist, a concert, or a live animal demonstration." The school's surrounding environment and entertainment offerings also inspire one student to wax rhapsodic: "Life is simple and beautiful. Who else gets to watch the sunset over the beautiful Hudson River? The Student Programming Council is on top of their game: Broadway trips, Yankee games, ski/snowboard trips, comedians, pop stars...we had wolves come to our school for a conservation program...what other school gets wolves?" For those students who are less exuberant about having wolves in their proximity, they can always escape off campus. "The Poughkeepsie Galleria is not too far up the road, and that poses as a good break and social outing," and "NYC is an easy train ride away."

Student Body

While it may be easy to buy into the homogenous "Marist Family" sentiment that many students express, the student population and dynamics are more nuanced than that. Some students claim that Marist is "full of bros and preppy girls," while others point out, "The average Marist student is probably white and middle-class, with a Catholic upbringing." One student chimes in, "The school could definitely work to diversify the students who go here. The majority are from New York, New Jersey, and Connecticut," though national and international enrollment is on the rise. While it seems that "students who are more free-spirited, 'hipster,' or those who do not like partying will have a much harder time fitting in," some students make the case that "if you give Marist a chance, you will definitely find people that you like to hang out with." In general, students feel warmly about their peers and describe them as "outgoing and goal-oriented" and "nice, kind, caring, and willing to talk to anyone and make them feel like they fit in."

FINANCIAL AID: 845-575-3230 • E-MAIL: ADMISSION@MARIST.EDU • WEBSITE: WWW.MARIST.EDU

THE PRINCETON REVIEW SAYS

Admissions

Very important factors considered include: GPA, rigor of secondary school record. *Important factors considered include:* Class rank, application essay, extracurricular activities, geographical residence, recommendation(s), state residency, talent/ability, volunteer work, work experience, character/personal qualities. *Other factors considered include:* Standardized test scores, racial/ethnic status, alumni/ae relations, level of applicant's interest. SAT or ACT considered if submitted; ACT with or without Writing component accepted. TOEFL required of all international applicants. *Academic units required:* 4 English; 3 mathematics; 3 science; (2 science lab); 2 social studies; 2 foreign language; 1 history; 2 academic electives. *Academic units recommended:* 4 mathematics; 4 science; (3 science lab); 3 foreign language.

Financial Aid

Students should submit: FAFSA, Institution's own financial aid form. Regular filing deadline is 5/1. The Princeton Review suggests that all financial aid forms be submitted as soon as possible after January 1. *Need-based scholarships/ grants offered:* Federal Pell, SEOG, State scholarships/grants, private scholarships, the school's own gift aid. *Loan aid offered:* Direct Subsidized Stafford Loans, Direct Unsubsidized Stafford Loans, Direct PLUS loans, Federal Perkins Loans. Federal Work-Study Program available. Institutional employment available. Off-campus job opportunities are excellent.

The Inside Word

About one-quarter of its most recent incoming class graduated outside the top 25 percent of their high school class. Those lacking academic bona fides will have to make it up in other areas, however; evidence of leadership, ability to contribute to the life of the campus (for example, artistic or athletic skill), an interesting background that will add diversity to classroom discussion, or a similar distinguishing trait will be needed to make up for a middling academic record.

THE SCHOOL SAYS "..."

From the Admissions Office

"Marist is a 'hot school' among prospective students. Applications are up over 40 percent since 2007. Meanwhile, the number of seats available for the freshman class remains at about 1,000, making for a very competitive admission process. Our recommendations: keep your grades up, participate in community service, and exercise leadership in the classroom, extracurricular endeavors, and your community. We encourage a campus visit. When prospective students see Marist—our beautiful location on the Hudson River, top-quality facilities, the close interaction between students and faculty, and the fact that everyone really enjoys their time here—they want to become a part of the Marist College community. We'll help you in the transition to college through an innovative first-year program that provides mentors for every student. You'll also learn how to use technology in whatever field you choose. Marist invests in the student experience. A new academic building for music programs and Student Center has dramatically improved performances and club space, and students call the new Grand Dining Hall "Hogwarts on the Hudson. We emphasize three aspects of a true Marist experience: excellence in education, community, and service to others. At Marist, you'll get a premium education, develop your skills, have fun and make lifelong friends, have the opportunity to gain valuable experience through our great internship and study abroad programs, including our branch campus in Florence, Italy, and be ahead of the competition for graduate school or a career."

SELECTIVITY	
Admissions Rating	91
# of applicants	10,351
% of applicants accepted	37
% of acceptees attending	30
# offered a place on the wait list	3,730
% accepting a place on wait list	24
% admitted from wait list	5
# of early decision applicants	240
% accepted early decision	90

FRESHMAN PROFILE	
Range SAT Critical Reading	540–620
Range SAT Math	550–640
Range SAT Writing	550–640
Range ACT Composite	24–28
Minimum paper TOEFL	550
Average HS GPA	3.30
% graduated top 10% of class	32
% graduated top 25% of class	64
% graduated top 50% of class	92

DEADLINES	
Early decision	
Deadline	11/1
Notification	12/15
Early action	
Deadline	11/15
Notification	1/30
Regular	
Deadline	2/1
Notification	4/1
Nonfall registration?	Yes

APPLICANTS ALSO LOOK AT AND OFTEN PREFER
Boston College; Villanova University; New York University

AND SOMETIMES PREFER
Loyola University Maryland

FINANCIAL FACTS	
Financial Aid Rating	71
Annual tuition	$30,700
Room and board	$13,100
Required fees	$590
Books and supplies	$1,800
% needy frosh rec. need-based scholarship or grant aid	79
% needy UG rec. need-based scholarship or grant aid	72
% needy frosh rec. non-need-based scholarship or grant aid	70
% needy UG rec. non-need-based scholarship or grant aid	65
% needy frosh rec. need-based self-help aid	84
% needy UG rec. need-based self-help aid	85
% frosh rec. any financial aid	84
% UG rec. any financial aid	81
% UG borrow to pay for school	69
Average cumulative indebtedness	$32,914
% frosh need fully met	16
% ugrads need fully met	14
Average % of frosh need met	62
Average % of ugrad need met	60

MARLBORO COLLEGE

PO BOX A, MARLBORO, VT 05344-0300 • ADMISSIONS: 802-258-9236 • FAX: 802-451-7555

STUDENTS SAY ". . ."

Academics

Teeny tiny Marlboro College in Vermont offers a "self-driven, free, and intimate academic climate" with a "rustic feel." With an average class size of just ten students, the school is all about creating a serious academic setting "where students are on equal footing with teachers and decide their own academic paths." "I dictate my own academics at Marlboro; I have the freedom to seriously study most anything," says one student. Marlboro's unique academic system, the Plan, is "incredibly exciting"; through this curriculum, students "can focus right in, very specifically, on the particular books or ideas that interest them most." The "incredibly sharp-witted and compassionate" faculty members at Marlboro "have strong personalities," and relationships with professors are "really intimate (in a good way)." "By the end of a class—provided you participate—they know you well, and you know them well," says a student. There's definitely "a relaxed, humorous atmosphere that manages to coexist with the intense academics, somehow." Discussions can run deep, and "there are few classes here in which the professor talks more than the students do." There are also more than 200 tutorials at Marlboro, which are typically reserved for juniors and seniors; most are one-on-one, and depend on students taking charge of a subject, preparing for and leading a weekly meeting with the faculty member and completing a piece of research or production. In addition, there is a "town-meeting-style community government" in place and "lots of energy from staff going into projects outside the classroom." Though no student lacks for attention or academic assistance, some admit that resources can be spread thin in some areas, including the "limited in number" professors; accessible as they are, some subject areas only have one professor, which means that "if you don't get along with the professor in your department you can either suck it up, or choose a different major." However, all of the "ingenious" professors are "great and really flexible. They just want to help." Grades, "while something that happen," are not considered important—instead the work students produce "is for our own pleasure and pride."

Life

With just a few hundred students enrolled, there aren't a lot of redundancies or waste. The dining hall is a central meeting place, where many students "hang out there for hours talking." People also spend a lot of time in the library, which is open 24 hours and "functions as some people's second home." In this "intellectual yet casual atmosphere," everybody "seems to be reading constantly," and students "talk about books a lot, or articles, or things people have read on the internet." "Class materials get inside people's heads, and they seem to want to share it." Parties do occur on weekends, though it's not a huge scene; "It's common to see people talk about epistemology while they're drunk and dance while they're sober." "We party a bit, play lots of video games, watch a lot of movies, and sometimes go into town," says one student. Athletics aren't really very big (other than nearby hiking), and "most of time we like *talking* to each other." People are "constantly philosophizing the state of things."

Student Body

Marlboro is "a place where 'the weird kids' from high schools all across the nation congregate and make beautiful music together (often literally)." "There is no typical student. That's the point," says one. Students here are "functionally eccentrics," "quirky," and "ready to pursue their own passions." There is a "high level of LGBTQ tolerance," and most students here are "usually politically mindful and open to challenging his or her perspectives." "It's kind of crazy, and everyone likes each other," says a student. There are people of all sorts, "from suits to rainbows, dreadlocks to comb-overs, you get the point." Essentially, "there is nothing too weird for Marlboro."

FINANCIAL AID: 802-258-9312 • E-MAIL: ADMISSIONS@MARLBORO.EDU • WEBSITE: WWW.MARLBORO.EDU

THE PRINCETON REVIEW SAYS

Admissions

Very important factors considered include: GPA, rigor of secondary school record, application essay, character/personal qualities. *Important factors considered include:* Extracurricular activities, recommendation(s). *Other factors considered include:* Class rank, standardized test scores, first generation, geographical residence, interview, racial/ethnic status, state residency, talent/ability, volunteer work, work experience, alumni/ae relations, level of applicant's interest. SAT and SAT Subject Tests or ACT considered if submitted; ACT with or without Writing component accepted. TOEFL required of all international applicants. *Academic units recommended:* 4 English; 3 mathematics; 3 science; (1 science lab); 3 social studies; 3 foreign language; 3 history; 3 academic electives.

Financial Aid

Students should submit: FAFSA. The Princeton Review suggests that all financial aid forms be submitted as soon as possible after January 1. *Need-based scholarships/grants offered:* Federal Pell, SEOG, State scholarships/grants, private scholarships, the school's own gift aid. *Loan aid offered:* Direct Subsidized Stafford Loans, Direct Unsubsidized Stafford Loans, Direct PLUS loans. Federal Work-Study Program available. Institutional employment available. Off-campus job opportunities are fair.

The Inside Word

Don't be misled by Marlboro's acceptance rate—this isn't the type of school that attracts many applications from students unsure of whether they belong at Marlboro. Most applicants are qualified both in terms of academic achievement and sincere intellectual curiosity. The school seeks candidates "with intellectual promise, a high degree of self-motivation, self-discipline, personal stability, social concern, and the ability and desire to contribute to the college community." These are the qualities you should stress on your application.

THE SCHOOL SAYS "..."

From the Admissions Office

"Marlboro College is distinguished by its curriculum, praised in higher education circles as unique; it is known for its self-governing philosophy, in which each student, faculty, and staff has an equal vote on many issues affecting the community; and it is recognized for its sixty-five year history of offering a rigorous, exciting, self-designed course of study taught in very small classes and individualized study with faculty. Marlboro's size also distinguishes it from most other schools. With 300 students and a student/faculty ratio of eight to one, it is one of the nation's smallest liberal arts colleges. Few other schools offer a program where students have such close interaction with faculty, and where community life is inseparable from academic life. The result, the self-designed, self-directed Plan of Concentration, allows students to develop their own unique academic work by defining a problem, setting clear limits on an area of inquiry, and analyzing, evaluating, and reporting on the outcome of a significant project. A Marlboro education teaches you to think for yourself, articulate your thoughts, express your ideas, believe in yourself, and do it all with the clarity, confidence, and self-reliance necessary for later success, no matter what postgraduate path you take."

SELECTIVITY

Admissions Rating	82
# of applicants	256
% of applicants accepted	79
% of acceptees attending	24
# of early decision applicants	3
% accepted early decision	100

FRESHMAN PROFILE

Range SAT Critical Reading	560–730
Range SAT Math	520–650
Range SAT Writing	530–680
Minimum paper TOEFL	577
Minimum web-based TOEFL	213
Average HS GPA	3.11

DEADLINES

Early decision	
Deadline	11/15
Notification	12/1
Early action	
Deadline	1/15
Notification	2/1
Regular	
Priority	3/1
Nonfall registration?	Yes

APPLICANTS ALSO LOOK AT AND OFTEN PREFER
Reed College

AND SOMETIMES PREFER
College of the Atlantic; Bard College; The Evergreen State College

AND RARELY PREFER
Bennington College; University of Vermont; Green Mountain College; Hampshire College

FINANCIAL FACTS

Financial Aid Rating	73
Annual tuition	$36,300
Room and board	$9,930
Required fees	$1,340
Books and supplies	$1,200
% needy frosh rec. need-based scholarship or grant aid	100
% needy UG rec. need-based scholarship or grant aid	99
% needy frosh rec. non-need-based scholarship or grant aid	85
% needy UG rec. non-need-based scholarship or grant aid	90
% needy frosh rec. need-based self-help aid	100
% needy UG rec. need-based self-help aid	97
% frosh rec. any financial aid	98
% UG rec. any financial aid	94
% UG borrow to pay for school	71
Average cumulative indebtedness	$20,051
% frosh need fully met	0
% ugrads need fully met	0
Average % of frosh need met	80
Average % of ugrad need met	75

MARQUETTE UNIVERSITY

PO Box 1881, Milwaukee, WI 53201-1881 • Admissions: 414-288-7302 • Fax: 414-288-3764

STUDENTS SAY ". . ."

Academics

As a "Jesuit university that focuses on education and service," Marquette University not only provides its students with a "commitment to academic excellence" but it also promotes "the notion of 'cura personalis'—care for the whole person." Located in downtown Milwaukee, the medium-sized Catholic institution "integrates community service, faith, faculty connections and education success in order for the whole person to succeed in their ideal future." Students appreciate Marquette's "small class sizes" and "seminar style courses" and note that "the students and faculty are genuinely friendly and help create a positive learning community." One student observes, "The courses themselves are challenging enough that I'm not bored, but not so difficult that I'm languishing." While the professors at Marquette may be "hit or miss," the majority of them are "highly educated, mostly doctorate level and very much love teaching." Students offer fair warning that "the professors here are great, but they make you work for your grade." With its "abundance of resources" and "solid alumni network," it is clear why one student raves, "Marquette focuses on the 'big picture,' and works extremely hard to better their students as people and prepare them for life after graduation."

Life

Students at Marquette enjoy "mixing the typical college experience with life experience in a major market city." They "spend a lot of time in downtown Milwaukee to go out to dinner, hit up the bars or go shopping down by the river." One student attests, "Being in the beer capital of the US, many students enjoy going to the plethora of bars on campus or downtown..." Given that "people drink beer like it's water at Marquette, and everybody pregames with liquor," it is no surprise that some students feel that the school's "new alcohol regulations feel very big-brotheresque" since they could be "slapped with huge fines for being caught." There are also plenty of options for students who would prefer not to drink. Through Late Night Marquette, "which is something Marquette created to provide alternate activities to drinking on the weekends," students can enjoy a variety of activities "such as comedy and hypnotist shows, game nights, scavenger hunts, dances, competitions, movies, and other entertainment." Chances are good that most students will end up at a game at some point since "going to Marquette Basketball games is a school ritual" and "at many of the games the student section of 4,000 is filled to the top (and with a student population of 8,000, that's a pretty big deal)."

Student Body

Students at Marquette readily admit that the student population is "comprised primarily of Wisconsin and Chicago suburb students" who "went to a private (usually Catholic high school)." They explain that "while the campus population isn't particularly diverse, as long as a student is willing to engage with others—whether it be in a study group, intramural sport, or student organization—they will fit right in" and that "there are also many organizations and groups for multicultural or diverse students." Balance seems to be a key characteristic among students and the "typical Marquette students are like acrobats; they are able to find the perfect balance between studying, socializing, and serving." When it comes to sporting the Marquette look, students often "wear a lot of North Face jackets and Ugg boots in the winter." However, one student points out that "most people here rarely go to class in pajamas, so there is a bit of a higher level of professionalism here." Students generally agree that their peers are "down to earth and easy to get along with" as well as "genuinely kind and caring in even the simple things such as holding the door for each other and smiling." Students feel a strong sense of community and highlight that "it's easy for a city campus to be divided, but at Marquette everyone is a friend, even if you don't know them yet."

FINANCIAL AID: 414-288-7390 • E-MAIL: ADMISSIONS@MARQUETTE.EDU • WEBSITE: WWW.MARQUETTE.EDU

THE PRINCETON REVIEW SAYS

Admissions

Very important factors considered include: GPA, rigor of secondary school record. *Important factors considered include:* Class rank, standardized test scores, application essay, recommendation(s). *Other factors considered include:* Extracurricular activities, first generation, geographical residence, racial/ethnic status, state residency, talent/ability, volunteer work, alumni/ae relations, character/personal qualities. SAT or ACT required; ACT with Writing component recommended. TOEFL required of all international applicants. *Academic units required:* 4 English; (2 science lab). *Academic units recommended:* 4 English; 3 science; (3 science lab); 3 social studies; 2 foreign language.

Financial Aid

Students should submit: FAFSA. The Princeton Review suggests that all financial aid forms be submitted as soon as possible after January 1. *Need-based scholarships/grants offered:* Federal Pell, SEOG, State scholarships/grants, private scholarships, the school's own gift aid. *Loan aid offered:* Direct Subsidized Stafford Loans, Direct Unsubsidized Stafford Loans, Direct PLUS loans, Federal Perkins Loans, Federal Nursing Loans, State Loans, College/university loans from institutional funds. Off-campus job opportunities are excellent.

The Inside Word

Not only do Marquette admissions counselors factor in academic performance and test scores to make their decisions, they also place a high premium on the types of courses that students took and want to see evidence that students challenged themselves. In addition to looking at upwards or downwards trends in grades, they are also looking at whether students took AP, honors or regular classes.

SELECTIVITY

Admissions Rating	89
# of applicants	23,432
% of applicants accepted	57
% of acceptees attending	15
# offered a place on the wait list	4,358
% accepting a place on wait list	39
% admitted from wait list	48

FRESHMAN PROFILE

Range SAT Critical Reading	520–630
Range SAT Math	550–650
Range SAT Writing	520–630
Range ACT Composite	25–29
Minimum paper TOEFL	530
% graduated top 10% of class	36
% graduated top 25% of class	69
% graduated top 50% of class	95

DEADLINES

Regular	
Priority	12/1
Deadline	12/1
Notification	1/31
Nonfall registration?	Yes

APPLICANTS ALSO LOOK AT AND OFTEN PREFER

University of Illinois at Urbana-Champaign; University of Notre Dame

AND SOMETIMES PREFER

Loyola The University of Chicago; Saint Louis University

AND RARELY PREFER

University of Minnesota—Twin Cities; University of Wisconsin—Madison

FINANCIAL FACTS

Financial Aid Rating	80
Annual tuition	$35,480
Required fees	$450
% needy frosh rec. need-based scholarship or grant aid	99
% needy UG rec. need-based scholarship or grant aid	98
% needy frosh rec. non-need-based scholarship or grant aid	13
% needy UG rec. non-need-based scholarship or grant aid	12
% needy frosh rec. need-based self-help aid	80
% needy UG rec. need-based self-help aid	83
% frosh rec. any financial aid	99
% UG rec. any financial aid	98
% UG borrow to pay for school	65
Average cumulative indebtedness	$33,775
% frosh need fully met	24
% ugrads need fully met	25
Average % of frosh need met	75
Average % of ugrad need met	76

MARYWOOD UNIVERSITY

OFFICE OF UNIVERSITY ADMISSIONS, SCRANTON, PA 18509 • ADMISSIONS: 570-348-6234 • FAX: 570-961-4763

CAMPUS LIFE

Quality of Life Rating	70
Fire Safety Rating	91
Green Rating	81
Type of school	Private
Affiliation	Roman Catholic
Environment	Town

STUDENTS

Total undergrad enrollment	2,034
% male/female	33/67
% from out of state	30
% frosh from public high school	89
% frosh live on campus	71
% ugrads live on campus	46
# of fraternities	1
# of sororities	2
% African American	2
% Asian	2
% Caucasian	81
% Hispanic	5
% Native American	<1
% international	1
# of countries represented	20

SURVEY SAYS . . .

Political activism is unpopular or nonexistent
Great off-campus food
Students are friendly

ACADEMICS

Academic Rating	72
% students returning for sophomore year	81
% students graduating within 4 years	54
% students graduating within 6 years	65
Calendar	Semester
Student/faculty ratio	11:1
Profs interesting rating	68
Profs accessible rating	67

Most lab/discussion sessions have
10–19 students.

MOST POPULAR MAJORS

management; nutrition & dietetics; nursing

STUDENTS SAY " . . ."

Academics

Marywood University is well-known for offering some of the most unique and outstanding pre-professional programs of study in the Pennsylvania area. Students rave about the "really fantastic" education department, and they call the art therapy program "top-notch," while the music program has a "fabulous reputation," and the strength of the speech pathology, nutrition, physician assistant, school of architecture, and interior design programs also draw students from all over the area to the university. In addition to these outstanding programs, this small Catholic university, which consists of four colleges, a school of architecture, and a school of social work also offers a wide range of traditional undergraduate majors. Students characterize Marywood as "a small community that is serious about its academics." Class sizes are "small, and it is easy to ask for help." "Professors here know your name and are always willing to help you," and according to Marywood students, "Small class sizes and attentive professors tend to favor discussion-based classroom settings." The professors at Marywood "have a good mix of personalities." Some professors "are nuns and priests, but most are not," and "many of the professors are also currently working in the field," which allows students to have a much richer, interactive learning experience.

Life

Students love "the warm and welcoming feel of the campus. Everyone is so friendly, and there is so much to do. It's more like a home than a school." There is "usually something to do during weeknights"; the student activities club "organizes events like Bingo and Trivia Night a few times each semester as well as organizing other entertainment such as comedians and movie nights. There are clubs for every interest you can imagine." There are also a "large number of recreational sports and classes available to students" on campus. On weekends, however, "campus usually turns into a ghost town." On-campus rules in regard to alcohol are "overly strict," resulting in weekend activities that often take place off campus, at "house parties and the University of Scranton." "Students also enjoy going to clubs and bars in the downtown Scranton area on weekends," and there are even clubs that allow students ages eighteen and up. First Fridays are a popular "monthly art/music/culture event that occurs downtown, providing the opportunity to meet local artists and musicians." The large population of commuter students at Marywood say, "If you dorm, it is easier to be involved on campus, but commuting life is different for most people...Clubs and events are aimed more toward people who live on campus." As for parking on campus, students say, "Finding a parking spot is as difficult as winning the lottery."

Student Body

Students describe the Marywood University community as "wholesome and welcoming." A typical Marywood student is "well-rounded, friendly, and passionate about [his or her] field of study." There tend to be subtle social divisions between various fields of study: "Students tend to gather in groups based on friendships formed through their majors." Though the campus is not very diverse ethnically or economically, there is a great deal of diversity along the lines of students' interests and personalities. Students "range from the athletic to the very religious to the extremely studious." There are many art students on campus due to the strength of the art department, and there is a "great deal of athletes" as well. There is also a significantly larger percentage of females to males on campus. Many students are local to the area, and in general, the student body is made up of equal parts commuter students and students who dorm. Because of the small size of the university, "you see many of the same faces every day" and "get to know a lot of people" in the small campus community. "Most students interact with each other and get along well."

FINANCIAL AID: 866-279-9663 • E-MAIL: YOURFUTURE@MARYWOOD.EDU • WEBSITE: WWW.MARYWOOD.EDU

THE PRINCETON REVIEW SAYS

Admissions

Very important factors considered include: Class rank, GPA, rigor of secondary school record, standardized test scores, character/personal qualities. *Important factors considered include:* Application essay, interview, recommendation(s), talent/ability. *Other factors considered include:* Extracurricular activities, volunteer work, level of applicant's interest. SAT or ACT required; ACT with or without Writing component accepted. TOEFL required of all international applicants. *Academic units required:* 4 English; 2 mathematics; 1 science; (1 science lab); 3 social studies; 6 academic electives.

Financial Aid

Students should submit: FAFSA. Regular filing deadline is 2/15. The Princeton Review suggests that all financial aid forms be submitted as soon as possible after January 1. *Need-based scholarships/grants offered:* Federal Pell, SEOG, State scholarships/grants, private scholarships, the school's own gift aid *Loan aid offered:* Direct Subsidized Stafford Loans, Direct Unsubsidized Stafford Loans, Direct PLUS loans, Federal Perkins Loans. Federal Work-Study Program available.

The Inside Word

Marywood offers applicants a chance to get an inside look at university life through their "College for a Day" program, which gives prospective students the opportunity to observe student life firsthand, from the classroom to the cafeteria. Marywood reviews applications on a rolling basis; therefore, you should apply as early as possible. Once a prospective student has submitted all of the application materials, the admissions department will usually make a decision within two or three weeks.

THE SCHOOL SAYS "..."

From the Admissions Office

"Marywood University is a comprehensive, coeducational, Catholic university of 3,300 full-time, part-time, and adult students, with over one hundred undergraduate, graduate, and doctoral degree programs. Established in 1915 by the Sisters, Servants of the Immaculate Heart of Mary, the university houses 1,100 resident students on a national award-winning campus considered one of the most beautiful in the northeast. Marywood University offered the region's first doctoral degree programs in 1996 and is the region's leading provider of graduate education with thirty-four master's degree programs and thirty-three certificate offerings. In recent years, the university made $100 million in improvements to campus, including new athletics, residence hall, and dining facilities, and one of the finest studio arts facilities in the northeast.

"Marywood operates on a rolling admissions basis. High school seniors are encouraged to submit their application for admission before March 1. Students applying for federal and state financial aid should submit the Free Application for Federal Student Aid (FAFSA) by February 15. At Marywood, you will discover that a top-notch private college experience is more affordable than you ever dreamed. In fact, 98 percent of our first-time students receive financial assistance in the form of scholarships, grants, loans, and work-study programs."

SELECTIVITY

Admissions Rating	73
# of applicants	2,059
% of applicants accepted	70
% of acceptees attending	28

FRESHMAN PROFILE

Range SAT Critical Reading	470–570
Range SAT Math	480–580
Range SAT Writing	460–570
Minimum paper TOEFL	530
Minimum web-based TOEFL	71
% graduated top 10% of class	20
% graduated top 25% of class	47
% graduated top 50% of class	84

DEADLINES

Regular	
Notification	Rolling
Nonfall registration?	Yes

APPLICANTS ALSO LOOK AT

College Misericordia; King's College(PA); University of Scranton; Wilkes University

FINANCIAL FACTS

Financial Aid Rating	69
Annual tuition	$30,700
Room and board	$13,900
Required fees	$1,625
Books and supplies	$1,000
% needy frosh rec. need-based scholarship or grant aid	100
% needy UG rec. need-based scholarship or grant aid	99
% needy frosh rec. non-need-based scholarship or grant aid	94
% needy UG rec. non-need-based scholarship or grant aid	98
% needy frosh rec. need-based self-help aid	82
% needy UG rec. need-based self-help aid	83
% frosh rec. any financial aid	99
% UG rec. any financial aid	99
% UG borrow to pay for school	84
% frosh need fully met	22
% ugrads need fully met	18
Average % of frosh need met	78
Average % of ugrad need met	72

MASSACHUSETTS INSTITUTE OF TECHNOLOGY

77 MASSACHUSETTS AVENUE, CAMBRIDGE, MA 02139 • ADMISSIONS: 617-253-3400 • FAX: 617-258-8304

CAMPUS LIFE

Quality of Life Rating	74
Fire Safety Rating	88
Green Rating	87
Type of school	Private
Affiliation	No Affiliation
Environment	City

STUDENTS

Total undergrad enrollment	4,510
% male/female	55/45
% from out of state	91
% frosh from public high school	67
% frosh live on campus	100
% ugrads live on campus	88
# of fraternities (% ugrad men join)	27 (54)
# of sororities (% ugrad women join)	6 (39)
% African American	5
% Asian	24
% Caucasian	37
% Hispanic	16
% Native American	<1
% international	10
# of countries represented	91

SURVEY SAYS . . .
Lab facilities are great
Athletic facilities are great
School is well run
Students love Cambridge, MA

ACADEMICS

Academic Rating	98
% students returning for sophomore year	98
% students graduating within 4 years	84
% students graduating within 6 years	93
Calendar	4/1/4
Student/faculty ratio	8:1
Profs interesting rating	69
Profs accessible rating	71

Most classes have fewer than 10 students.
Most lab/discussion sessions have
   10–19 students.

MOST POPULAR MAJORS
computer science; mechanical engineering;
physics

STUDENTS SAY " . . ."

Academics

Massachusetts Institute of Technology, the East Coast mecca of engineering, science, and mathematics, "is the ultimate place for information overload, endless possibilities, and expanding your horizons." The "amazing collection of creative minds" includes enough Nobel laureates to fill a jury box as well as brilliant students who are given substantial control of their educations; one explains, "The administration's attitude toward students is one of respect. As soon as you come on campus, you are bombarded with choices." Students need to be able to manage a workload that "definitely push[es you] beyond your comfort level." A chemical engineering major elaborates: "MIT is different from many schools in that its goal is not to teach you specific facts in each subject. MIT teaches you how to think, not about opinions but about problem solving. Facts and memorization are useless unless you know how to approach a tough problem." Professors here range from "excellent teachers who make lectures fun and exciting" to "dull and soporific" ones, but most "make a serious effort to make the material they teach interesting by throwing in jokes and cool demonstrations." "Access to an amazing number of resources, both academic and recreational," "research opportunities for undergrads with some of the nation's leading professors," and a rock-solid alumni network complete the picture. If you ask "MIT alumni where they went to college, most will immediately stick out their hand and show you their 'brass rat' (the MIT ring, the second most recognized ring in the world)."

Life

At MIT, "It may seem…like there's no life outside problem sets and studying for exams," but "there's always time for extracurricular activities or just relaxing" for those "with good time-management skills" or the "ability to survive on [a] lack of sleep." Options range from "building rides" (recent projects have included a motorized couch and a human-sized hamster wheel) "to partying at fraternities to enjoying the largest collection of science fiction novels in the United States at the MIT Science Fiction Library." Students occasionally find time to "pull a hack," which is an ethical prank, "like the life-size Wright brothers' plane that appeared on top of the Great Dome for the one-hundredth anniversary of flight." Undergrads tell us, "MIT has great parties—a lot of Wellesley, Harvard, and BU students come to them," but also that "there are tons of things to do other than party" here. "Movies, shopping, museums, and plays are all possible with our location near Boston. There are great restaurants only [blocks] away from campus, too…From what I can tell, MIT students have way more fun on the weekends than their Cambridge counterparts [at] Harvard."

Student Body

"There actually isn't one typical student at MIT," students here assure us, explaining that "hobbies range from building robots and hacking to getting wasted and partying every weekend. The one thing students all have in common is that they are insanely smart and love to learn. Pretty much anyone can find the perfect group of friends to hang out with at MIT." "Most students do have some form of 'nerdiness'" (like telling nerdy jokes, being an avid fan of *Star Wars*, etc.), but "Contrary to MIT's stereotype, most MIT students are not geeks who study all the time and have no social skills. The majority of the students here are actually quite 'normal.'" The "stereotypical student [who] looks techy and unkempt…only represents about 25 percent of the school." The rest include "multiple-sport standouts, political activists, fraternity and sorority members, hippies, clean-cut business types, LARPers, hackers, musicians, and artisans. There are people who look like they stepped out of an Abercrombie & Fitch catalog and people who dress in all black and carry flashlights and multi-tools. Not everyone relates to everyone else, but most people get along, and it's almost a guarantee that you'll fit in somewhere.

MASSACHUSETTS INSTITUTE OF TECHNOLOGY

FINANCIAL AID: 617-258-4917 • E-MAIL: ADMISSIONS@MIT.EDU • WEBSITE: WEB.MIT.EDU

THE PRINCETON REVIEW SAYS

Admissions

Very important factors considered include: Character/personal qualities. *Important factors considered include:* GPA, rigor of secondary school record, standardized test scores, application essay, extracurricular activities, interview, recommendation(s), talent/ability. *Other factors considered include:* Class rank, first generation, geographical residence, racial/ethnic status, volunteer work, work experience. SAT or ACT required; ACT with Writing component required. *Academic units recommended:* 4 English; 4 mathematics; 4 science; 2 social studies; 2 foreign language.

Financial Aid

Students should submit: FAFSA, CSS/Financial Aid PROFILE, Noncustodial PROFILE, Business/Farm Supplement. Regular filing deadline is 2/15. The Princeton Review suggests that all financial aid forms be submitted as soon as possible after January 1. *Need-based scholarships/grants offered:* Federal Pell, SEOG, State scholarships/grants, private scholarships, the school's own gift aid. *Loan aid offered:* Direct Subsidized Stafford Loans, Direct Unsubsidized Stafford Loans, Direct PLUS loans, Federal Perkins Loans, College/university loans from institutional funds. Applicants will be notified of awards beginning 4/1. Federal Work-Study Program available. Institutional employment available. Off-campus job opportunities are excellent.

The Inside Word

MIT has one of the nation's most competitive admissions processes. The school's applicant pool is so rich it turns away numerous qualified candidates each year. Put your best foot forward and take consolation in the fact that rejection doesn't necessarily mean that you don't belong at MIT, but only that there wasn't enough room for you the year you applied. Your best chance to get an edge: Find ways to stress your creativity, a quality that MIT's admissions director told *USA TODAY* is lacking in many prospective college students.

THE SCHOOL SAYS "..."

From the Admissions Office

"The students who come to the Massachusetts Institute of Technology are some of America's—and the world's—best and most creative. As graduates, they leave here to make real contributions—in science, technology, business, education, politics, architecture, and the arts. From any class, many will go on to do work that is historically significant. These young men and women are leaders, achievers, and producers. Helping such students make the most of their talents and dreams would challenge any educational institution. MIT gives them its best advantages: a world-class faculty, unparalleled facilities, and remarkable opportunities. In turn, these students help to make the institute the vital place it is. They bring fresh viewpoints to faculty research: More than three-quarters participate in the Undergraduate Research Opportunities Program, developing solutions for the world's problems in areas such as energy, the environment, cancer, and poverty. They play on MIT's thirty-three intercollegiate teams as well as in its fifty-plus music, theater, and dance groups. To their classes and to their out-of-class activities, they bring enthusiasm, energy, and individual style."

SELECTIVITY

Admissions Rating	99
# of applicants	18,989
% of applicants accepted	8
% of acceptees attending	72
# offered a place on the wait list	708
% accepting a place on wait list	93
% admitted from wait list	0

FRESHMAN PROFILE

Range SAT Critical Reading	680–770
Range SAT Math	750–800
Range SAT Writing	690–780
Range ACT Composite	33–35
Minimum web-based TOEFL	233
% graduated top 10% of class	99
% graduated top 25% of class	100
% graduated top 50% of class	100

DEADLINES

Early action	
Deadline	11/1
Notification	12/20
Regular	
Deadline	1/1
Notification	3/20
Nonfall registration?	No

APPLICANTS ALSO LOOK AT AND OFTEN PREFER
Harvard College

AND SOMETIMES PREFER
Princeton University; Yale University; Stanford University

AND RARELY PREFER
California Institute of Technology; Cornell University; Duke University; University of Pennsylvania; Columbia University

FINANCIAL FACTS

Financial Aid Rating	92
Books and supplies	$1,000
% needy frosh rec. need-based scholarship or grant aid	96
% needy UG rec. need-based scholarship or grant aid	96
% needy frosh rec. non-need-based scholarship or grant aid	4
% needy UG rec. non-need-based scholarship or grant aid	2
% needy frosh rec. need-based self-help aid	84
% needy UG rec. need-based self-help aid	87
% frosh rec. any financial aid	87
% UG rec. any financial aid	76
% UG borrow to pay for school	41
Average cumulative indebtedness	$17,891
% frosh need fully met	100
% ugrads need fully met	100
Average % of frosh need met	100
Average % of ugrad need met	100

McGill University

845 Sherbrooke Street West, Montreal, QC H3A 0G4, Canada • Admissions: 514-398-3910 • Fax: 514-398-4193

CAMPUS LIFE

Quality of Life Rating	78
Fire Safety Rating	71
Green Rating	76
Type of school	Public
Affiliation	No Affiliation
Environment	Metropolis

STUDENTS

Total undergrad enrollment	23,218
% male/female	42/58
% from out of state	41
% frosh live on campus	51
% ugrads live on campus	12
# of fraternities	8
# of sororities	4
% international	17
# of countries represented	140

SURVEY SAYS . . .

Class discussions are rare
Students love Montreal, Quebec
Great off-campus food
Lots of beer drinking

ACADEMICS

Academic Rating	75
% students returning for sophomore year	93
% students graduating within 4 years	67
% students graduating within 6 years	85
Calendar	Semester
Student/faculty ratio	16:1
Profs interesting rating	66
Profs accessible rating	66

Most classes have 10–19 students.
Most lab/discussion sessions have 20–29 students.

MOST POPULAR MAJORS

political science; psychology;
business/commerce

STUDENTS SAY " . . ."

Academics

A world class school in a great city (Montreal), McGill University has "a nearly unparalleled reputation" around North America and the world, and gives students "the tools [they] need, a positive environment," and the space for them to make their own opportunities. The school is known for "embracing the internationality of all the students"; those who attend pay "a fraction of the cost that a top private school in the U.S. would cost," and a McGill degree "opens the most doors for graduating students." It is "everything you want to learn and do, found in 19th century buildings and snow." The faculty is generally "high caliber" but the quality can vary slightly. "I've had drone-ish philosophy profs and some teachers whose enthusiasm, intelligence and wit made even discussing Judith Butler for the fiftieth time fascinating, some teachers who shut off after class and a few who became ersatz therapists/mothers," says one junior. Academics tend to be theoretical and "old-school," containing rigorous, structured curricula, and there is a good deal of active research going on by the faculty, which "makes lectures up-to-date and continuously changing." Professors are also "always eager to take on students for independent research projects and lab assistance, as long as students make an effort." Students do admit that the school struggles with a fair amount of "bureaucratic redundancy," but agree that the school is "a facility that works very hard in order to ensure its students' success not only within its educational system, but also in preparing them for the outside world." "McGill does not baby you, and that makes you more responsible for yourself," says a student.

Life

The size of the school means "there are many social as well as academic opportunities." Admittedly "it takes a lot of work to have time to play," but students manage just fine. "People are at the library after a night of partying," says one. Most people "take school seriously and work really hard," but also love to go out when they're through. "How many McGill students does it take to screw in a lightbulb?" asks a student. "One, just don't ask them to do it Thursday, Friday or Saturday."

Every McGill student has an abiding love for Montreal, which provides "a bilingual environment in a major metropolitan city." "McGill is very much a Montreal school… it's not uncommon for students to start renting an apartment their first year." Not to mention one other aspect: "The legal drinking age of 18 was unimportant to me when I applied, but very quickly I discovered its value," says a student. The bar and club scene in Montreal is "famous and with good reason," and Thursday is campus bar night. "The music scene and making dinners" for large groups of friends are also wildly popular activities.

The Macdonald Campus of McGill is actually "quite different" from the much larger downtown campus: the "community is smaller, in a scenic area (between the waterfront and a forest)" and there is a "different atmosphere [and a] different social life." McGill is also close to lots of good ski hills, which gives plenty of opportunities for students to leave Montreal, as well. "You have much more freedom to do what you want and there are endless places to visit, during the day and at night," says a junior finance major.

Student Body

McGill has "an incredibly diverse student body" in terms of nationalities, though "ethnicity-wise, the vast majority of the students are Caucasian." The student body "doesn't usually form cliques"; people "appreciate each other's differences" and all are "hard-working, engaged and interested in the world around them." "There's no way to not fit in with an undergrad population so large- you'll find your people," assures one student. Many American students are surprised at the "international flavor" and autonomy of the native Quebecois, but catch on by their second year. However, "it can be hard for outsiders to break into the local Quebec students' social circles, especially for non-French speakers."

FINANCIAL AID: 514-398-6013 • E-MAIL: ADMISSIONS@MCGILL.CA • WEBSITE: WWW.MCGILL.CA

THE PRINCETON REVIEW SAYS

Admissions

Very important factors considered include: GPA, rigor of secondary school record, standardized test scores. *Important factors considered include:* Class rank. *Other factors considered include:* Recommendation(s). SAT and SAT Subject Tests or ACT required for some; ACT with Writing component required. TOEFL required of all international applicants. *Academic units recommended:* 4 English; 4 mathematics; 3 science; (3 science lab); 2 social studies; 3 foreign language; 2 history.

Financial Aid

Students should submit: Institution's own financial aid form. Regular filing deadline is 6/30. The Princeton Review suggests that all financial aid forms be submitted as soon as possible after January 1. *Need-based scholarships/grants offered:* Private scholarships, the school's own gift aid. *Loan aid offered:* College/university loans from institutional funds. Institutional employment available. Off-campus job opportunities are fair.

The Inside Word

Admission to McGill is highly competitive and decisions are based on an applicant's academic record. Extracurricular activities aren't significant in the admissions decision but may pertain to entrance scholarships. Applicants from the United States are required to submit standardized test scores, and minimum test score requirements are published on the McGill website.

THE SCHOOL SAYS "..."

From the Admissions Office

"McGill processes more than 30,000 online applications a year. Very few programs are available to non-Quebec students for January admission; consult the website for details.

"Applicants may submit results from of the SAT (plus at least two appropriate SAT Subject Tests). The ACT is accepted in lieu of the SAT and SAT Subject Test combination. Please note that certain programs can require specific SAT Subject Tests."

SELECTIVITY

Admissions Rating	94
# of applicants	24,325
% of applicants accepted	53
% of acceptees attending	41

FRESHMAN PROFILE

Range SAT Critical Reading	640–740
Range SAT Math	650–720
Range SAT Writing	650–730
Range ACT Composite	29–32
Minimum paper TOEFL	577
Minimum web-based TOEFL	233
Average HS GPA	3.52

DEADLINES

Regular	
Deadline	1/15
Nonfall registration?	Yes

APPLICANTS ALSO LOOK AT AND OFTEN PREFER

University of Toronto; New York University

AND SOMETIMES PREFER

Columbia University; Harvard College; University of California—Berkeley

FINANCIAL FACTS

Financial Aid Rating	66
Annual in-state tuition	$2,168
Annual out-of-state tuition	$5,858
Room and board	$11,000
Required fees	$1,500
Books and supplies	$1,000
% needy UG rec. need-based scholarship or grant aid	63
% needy UG rec. non-need-based scholarship or grant aid	31
% needy UG rec. need-based self-help aid	89
% UG rec. any financial aid	28
% UG borrow to pay for school	24

MERCER UNIVERSITY—MACON

ADMISSIONS OFFICE, MACON, GA 31207-0001 • ADMISSIONS: 478-301-2650 • FAX: 478-301-2828

STUDENTS SAY ". . ."

Academics

Mercer University is a school that students flock to for "its reputation as a rigorous academic institution" where professors "truly want to see students succeed." Variations on that sentiment are offered repeatedly by students who say that at this "unique school" the "professors actually care about your opinion and your well-being." Attendees feel the liberal arts education they get here offers them "intense preparation as an individual and professional for my future career." Small class sizes mean students "have a personal relationship with the professor," and the faculty in general "is so supportive. They don't think your ideas are crazy and naïve; they really listen to you." Some students admit there are some "outliers" who "are a joke," but "for all their quirks they are focused on the students and trying to teach us." The overwhelming majority of students insist, "Professors really care and love to teach" and are educators who "make sure that you understand the material being taught" and who will "devote extra time if needed for those who need it." Despite being a small school, "the number of opportunities available to enhance the student's academic experience is excellent" because "Mercer is a place that respects its students and knows the enormous potential its students have." And that goes over well with the student population, since at Mercer "everyone majors in changing the world."

Life

It's hard to pin down an aspect of college life that isn't represented at Mercer. Unsurprisingly, athletics are popular. "Most people play sports such as football, soccer, and basketball," one student notes. And even those students who don't play sometimes find themselves caught up in sports, since "school spirit is very important" at Mercer. But there are options outside of athletics. There is, of course, Greek life, which "provides a number of parties to attend and good times to be had." However, most would not call Mercer a big party school. "General life at Mercer is quiet and peaceful;" so often "a lot of people end up relaxing in dorms or exploring Macon." "Junior and senior students tend to venture out into Macon more, visiting downtown bars and restaurants and exploring the city." Students can take a trolley to the downtown area, which is "currently being revitalized." Mercer "does try its best to help the poor side of Macon with lots of community service." If not engaging in formal activities, students "watch movies and go out to eat, go to church, and hang out at each other's houses." So, the school is quieter than schools known for frantic social scenes, "but if you know the right people you can do pretty much anything."

Student Body

If there is a buzzword to describe the student body at Mercer University, it is "involved." Students are involved in clubs, sports, and civic groups and "with one another." "Almost everyone aspires to be the president of this or that club and [they] are often actively involved in at least half a dozen others." That may not come as a surprise, since "there are many opportunities for students to interact with one another and become involved on campus." The student body here is "diverse," with the tie that binds being that most "take part in community service through some venue." Mercer students are "bright and intelligent," "extremely involved on campus," "opinionated but respectful," and "well-informed but open-minded." Students say, "It is small enough so I don't feel intimidated" and that the school and upperclassmen provide a strong support system. People here are "always willing to help another person with problems." This "intelligent" student body comes together from various areas of study. "English and engineering students converse frequently on all ranges of subjects from synesthesia to Doctor Who." Mercer students are achievers, but even they wouldn't claim to be overachievers. "Most students study well enough to reach their goals, whether high or moderate, but all reserve some time for fun."

FINANCIAL AID: 478-301-2670 • E-MAIL: ADMISSIONS@MERCER.EDU • WEBSITE: WWW.MERCER.EDU

THE PRINCETON REVIEW SAYS

Admissions

Very important factors considered include: GPA, rigor of secondary school record, standardized test scores, level of applicant's interest. *Important factors considered include:* Application essay, extracurricular activities, talent/ability, volunteer work, character/personal qualities. *Other factors considered include:* Class rank, interview, recommendation(s), work experience, alumni/ae relations. SAT or ACT required; SAT and SAT Subject Tests or ACT considered if submitted; ACT with or without Writing component accepted. TOEFL or IELTS required of all international applicants. *Academic units required:* 4 English; 4 mathematics; 3 science; (2 science lab); 1 social studies; 2 foreign language; 2 history.

Financial Aid

Students should submit: FAFSA, Institution's own financial aid form, State aid form. The Princeton Review suggests that all financial aid forms be submitted as soon as possible after January 1. *Need-based scholarships/grants offered:* Federal Pell, SEOG, State scholarships/grants, the school's own gift aid, federal nursing scholarships *Loan aid offered:* Direct Subsidized Stafford Loans, Direct Unsubsidized Stafford Loans, Direct PLUS loans, Federal Perkins Loans, Federal Nursing Loans, College/university loans from institutional funds. Federal Work-Study Program available.

The Inside Word

For those considering Mercer, readiness to work hard should not be taken lightly. Students report that many transfers end up dropping out after a semester, even after coming from a major university. The admissions policy is seen as lenient, yet the work certainly isn't. It may not seem difficult to get into Mercer, but graduating is another matter.

THE SCHOOL SAYS "..."

From the Admissions Office

"For many high school seniors, the college search can be a stressful process. As an admissions counseling staff, we are committed to helping each and every student that we meet to identify their best personal 'fit' for a college or university. During this process, many find that Mercer is the right place for their higher education journey. At Mercer, each student is matched with a personal admissions counselor. This counselor remains his or her primary point of contact from application through enrollment. We get to know our applicants through personal contact, high school visits, regional receptions, college fairs, and our numerous campus visitation programs. Our counselors work closely with students and their families through the application, financial aid, housing, orientation, and other enrollment processes to ensure that students make a smooth transition from high school to college. This makes for a truly enjoyable and informed admissions experience for all involved.

"Mercer University begins accepting applications for undergraduate admission on August 1. We encourage high school seniors to submit their completed applications (including official transcripts and test scores; IELTS or TOEFL for international students) before our priority application deadline of November 1 for top scholarship consideration. Our regular decision deadline is March 1. We evaluate applications on a rolling basis throughout the academic year."

SELECTIVITY

Admissions Rating	88
# of applicants	3,864
% of applicants accepted	69
% of acceptees attending	27

FRESHMAN PROFILE

Range SAT Critical Reading	540–630
Range SAT Math	540–640
Range SAT Writing	510–620
Range ACT Composite	23–28
Minimum paper TOEFL	550
Minimum web-based TOEFL	213
Average HS GPA	3.71
% graduated top 10% of class	41
% graduated top 25% of class	72
% graduated top 50% of class	92

DEADLINES

Early action	
Deadline	11/1
Notification	11/15
Regular	
Priority	3/1
Deadline	7/1
Nonfall registration?	Yes

APPLICANTS ALSO LOOK AT AND OFTEN PREFER

University of Georgia; Emory University; Georgia Institute of Technology; Samford University

AND SOMETIMES PREFER

Florida State University; Auburn University; Furman University; Vanderbilt University

AND RARELY PREFER

Clemson University

FINANCIAL FACTS

Financial Aid Rating	88
Annual tuition	$32,820
Room and board	$11,081
Required fees	$300
Books and supplies	$1,200
% needy frosh rec. need-based scholarship or grant aid	100
% needy UG rec. need-based scholarship or grant aid	99
% needy frosh rec. non-need-based scholarship or grant aid	27
% needy UG rec. non-need-based scholarship or grant aid	23
% needy frosh rec. need-based self-help aid	60
% needy UG rec. need-based self-help aid	64
% frosh rec. any financial aid	99
% UG rec. any financial aid	98
% UG borrow to pay for school	65
Average cumulative indebtedness	$29,101
% frosh need fully met	38
% ugrads need fully met	34
Average % of frosh need met	87
Average % of ugrad need met	84

MIAMI UNIVERSITY (OH)

301 SOUTH CAMPUS AVENUE, OXFORD, OH 45056 • ADMISSIONS: 513-529-2531 • FAX: 513-529-1550

STUDENTS SAY ". . ."

Academics

Attending school at Miami University may be "the iconic college experience." Located in Oxford, Ohio, "a quaint college town" with a "beautiful red brick campus," which students describe as "gorgeous" and "astoundingly beautiful," the school "has a rich tradition and history" that "is committed to its image as a premier undergraduate institution." The "prestige" of the business school affords many promising opportunities both during school and after graduation. Students agree, "Miami really prepares students for the real world after college." "A degree from Miami is worth a lot to many employers, at least in the business world." "Miami University students are recruited by companies, and that provides great leverage when looking for internships and jobs." The curriculum as a whole offers "a challenging academic workload" that truly tests a student's abilities as well as "prepares students for the workplace after graduation while also giving them the opportunity to thrive while on campus." This "devotion to excellent undergraduate instruction" is backed by "an extremely strong orientation program, a dedicated student affairs department, and an overwhelming amount of student involvement in co-curricular activities." Smaller classrooms that allow for "engaging" discussion are more highly valued than large lectures, which may be "hard to sit through." Professors are a "mixed bag." "If you get the right ones, it makes all the difference." A student in the Honors Program calls the experience "phenomenal. It offers the ability to grow as a student and person through both in and out of class experiences."

Life

Miami University offers "a vibrant social atmosphere." With 15,000 or so students on campus Miami may be "the perfect size," where you "can see everyone…but still meet many new people." With a "plethora of student activities," "Miami makes it possible to find groups or organizations that can fit any student's interest, and many tend to help in propelling graduates into jobs or programs once they leave the campus." "Greek life is everywhere you look," according to one student who posits "it often seems as though everyone is because of how visible they are on campus." On the partying front, "if you are looking to drink, you will certainly find it here if you want." "Miami students can find a wealth of great bars and clubs uptown—many of which are eighteen-plus, allowing freshmen and sophomores to enjoy the dance floors and bars that make up almost all of the nightlife." The campus also "offers a lot of alternative programs for students who wish to avoid alcohol." "Late night programming is offered through Miami, as well as athletic events and other cultural events." Among sports, "hockey is really popular." Students tend to be happy with life at Miami. "There is a ton to do on and off campus. The town is quaint, but it is mainly a college town, so it's like an extension of the school. Nightlife is pretty big here, but so are academics and activities. Students definitely are actively thinking about their futures, and they take academics seriously."

Student Body

The typical student is "very involved on campus, is concerned about his or her academics, and wants to make a good impression on others. We care about how we present ourselves, but in a good way." Another student says, "The typical student is very academically focused, challenge-driven, competitive, extraverted, and demonstrates a preference for dressing well." Several students commented that students tend to "look and dress alike." "It can be very cliquish, especially in the Greek community." Anyone can fit in though, it's "all about finding your niche on campus which is generally done through people in your major, and especially student organizations." Miami tends to attract students who are "white, upper-middle-class, and Christian. The campus lacks diversity socioeconomically, ethnically, and religiously; however, the student body is generally accepting of all students no matter the background." One student relishes the challenge "to find diversity even in people who look similar and [has] grown because of it."

FINANCIAL AID: 513-529-8734 • E-MAIL: ADMISSION@MUOHIO.EDU • WEBSITE: WWW.MIAMI.MUOHIO.EDU

THE PRINCETON REVIEW SAYS

Admissions

Very important factors considered include: Class rank, GPA, rigor of secondary school record, standardized test scores, application essay, recommendation(s), talent/ability, character/personal qualities. *Other factors considered include:* Extracurricular activities, first generation, geographical residence, state residency, volunteer work, work experience, alumni/ae relations. SAT or ACT required; ACT with or without Writing component accepted. TOEFL required of all international applicants. *Academic units recommended:* 4 English; 4 mathematics; 3 science; 2 social studies; 2 foreign language; 1 history; 1 visual/performing arts.

Financial Aid

Students should submit: FAFSA. The Princeton Review suggests that all financial aid forms be submitted by the priority date, February 15. *Need-based scholarships/grants offered:* Federal Pell, SEOG, State scholarships/grants, private scholarships, the school's own gift aid. *Loan aid offered:* Direct Subsidized Stafford Loans, Direct Unsubsidized Stafford Loans, Direct PLUS loans, Federal Perkins Loans, Federal Nursing Loans, College/university loans from institutional funds. Federal Work-Study Program available. Institutional employment available. Off-campus job opportunities are good.

The Inside Word

Getting into Miami University isn't easy. High grades and SAT scores (math and critical reading) above 1200 are a good start, and there is more you can do to better your odds. Admissions officers favor students who are active in their schools, participate in varsity sports or student organizations, and volunteer in their community.

THE SCHOOL SAYS "..."

From the Admissions Office

"At Miami, you'll find a level of involvement—in your classes, in your research, in your extracurricular activities—that you won't find at other schools. What sets Miami apart is the ability to give students a personalized small-college experience within the excitement and opportunities of a midsize university, all at a public school cost. With more than 100 majors to choose from, and a liberal arts foundation that allows students to explore different areas of interest, finding your true passion—in and out of the classroom—is at the heart of what the Miami University experience is all about. This deep level of engagement is reflected in the 90 percent freshman to sophomore retention rate and Miami's 80 percent graduation rate, which is among the top for public universities across the country. Miami's reputation for producing outstanding leaders with real-world experience makes us a target school for top national firms, and our graduates' acceptance rate into law and medical school are far above the national average. Students also benefit from small class sizes—64 percent of undergraduate classes have fewer than thirty students—and personal attention from faculty members in the classroom, through research opportunities, and through faculty mentoring programs. Full-time faculty teach 74 percent of undergraduate credit hours. Outside of the classroom, students can participate in over 450 student organizations, attend social and cultural events, or get involved with one of the most extensive intramural and club sports program in the country."

SELECTIVITY

Admissions Rating	89
# of applicants	22,520
% of applicants accepted	67
% of acceptees attending	24
# offered a place on the wait list	2,894
% accepting a place on wait list	23
% admitted from wait list	9
# of early decision applicants	939
% accepted early decision	74

FRESHMAN PROFILE

Range SAT Critical Reading	540–650
Range SAT Math	580–680
Range ACT Composite	25–30
Minimum paper TOEFL	550
Minimum web-based TOEFL	80
Average HS GPA	3.72
% graduated top 10% of class	39
% graduated top 25% of class	71
% graduated top 50% of class	96

DEADLINES

Early decision	
Deadline	11/15
Notification	12/15
Early action	
Deadline	12/1
Notification	2/1
Regular	
Deadline	2/1
Notification	3/15
Nonfall registration?	Yes

APPLICANTS ALSO LOOK AT AND OFTEN PREFER

Northwestern University; Boston College; Vanderbilt University

AND SOMETIMES PREFER

Indiana University—Bloomington; Purdue University—West Lafayette; Southern Methodist University

FINANCIAL FACTS

Financial Aid Rating	72
Annual in-state tuition	$13,266
Annual out-of-state tuition	$29,056
Room and board	$10,900
Required fees	$533
Books and supplies	$1,250
% needy frosh rec. need-based scholarship or grant aid	97
% needy UG rec. need-based scholarship or grant aid	90
% needy frosh rec. non-need-based scholarship or grant aid	11
% needy UG rec. non-need-based scholarship or grant aid	8
% needy frosh rec. need-based self-help aid	78
% needy UG rec. need-based self-help aid	81
% UG borrow to pay for school	55
Average cumulative indebtedness	$27,817
% frosh need fully met	17
% ugrads need fully met	16
Average % of frosh need met	53
Average % of ugrad need met	56

MICHIGAN STATE UNIVERSITY

250 ADMINISTRATION BUILDING, EAST LANSING, MI 48824-1046 • ADMISSIONS: 517-355-8332 • FAX: 517-353-1647

STUDENTS SAY ". . ."

Academics

The size of Michigan State University "scares some people," students tell us, but for those comfortable in crowds it's "one of the strongest advantages. Where else do you cut through the Cereal Wing of the Human Nutrition Building to get to a Navigating the Universe class (a class on the parallels between art, philosophy, and physics)?" One student sees it this way: "The size of MSU makes it like training wheels for the real world. Every type of person, value, and belief is here, so you learn just as many street smarts as academic smarts, which is what sets it apart from so many other schools." There are more than "200 majors to choose from" here, including "good engineering and science programs," an "amazing communications program," "the best political science program in Michigan," "the only agriculture school in the state," and "an absolutely amazing school of Hospitality Business." Economies of scale also allow MSU to offer "great study abroad programs," "a lot of helpful free tutoring in math and other subjects," and "great Web programs that make it very easy to download class materials and view assignments. You can also e-mail the whole class questions or just your professor, through our Angel system." As far as possible downsides to the school's size, MSU students find you have to "fend for yourself." That means potential peril for students who aren't self-motivated. One undergrad explains, "There are two roads you can follow when at MSU. You can study hard and earn a degree in a reputable, challenging setting; or you can soak your brain cells with alcohol instead of academia."

Life

"It requires a lot of studying to keep up with classes" in most disciplines at MSU, but that doesn't mean students bury their heads in the books 24/7. On the contrary, "Michigan State is great because everyone is there to learn but also to have a good time, which is important for any college to flow smoothly." When the weekend arrives, "everyone likes to go out, usually to frats, and have a good time. We do our share of partying, but we know when and how hard to hit the books. We keep our heads very level," except, perhaps, when attending sporting events. Life on campus "generally revolves around the weekend and the basketball or football game. You get through the week looking forward to one of the two." Indeed, "sports are huge, and nothing beats football Saturdays or basketball nights. Tailgating is a religion." And if neither sports appeal to you, don't sweat it. "If there's something you want to do, someone else does too. You'll be hard pressed to find an activity that doesn't have its own organization and social network." Hometown East Lansing has its own allures; a student explains, "Walking downtown on Grand River is awesome when it gets warmer out," and there are "decent stores and restaurants. Also, in the warm weather you are bound to see people sitting out on their porches. Many of them are having parties or just hanging out, and a lot of times they'll invite you to come on up!" Or you can just enjoy the "breathtaking beauty of the campus," with its "old buildings and beautiful trees and plants that make every walk to class a great one."

Student Body

MSU's size ensures that "this is a fairly diverse campus, especially considering that it is located in the northern Midwest." One student observes, "You can completely immerse yourself among different people in different situations knowing that you have the comfort of your own dorm, and somewhere there is a group just like you." Because "study abroad is emphasized at MSU," there are "a lot of foreign students, and they seem to fit right into the general population." If anything unites students—besides their love of MSU sports—it is that most "are extremely friendly. Random people in classes ask you if you need a ride home, and, even better, random people offer you a seat on the bus."

FINANCIAL AID: 517-353-5940 • E-MAIL: ADMIS@MSU.EDU • WEBSITE: WWW.MSU.EDU

THE PRINCETON REVIEW SAYS

Admissions

Very important factors considered include: GPA, standardized test scores. *Important factors considered include:* Rigor of secondary school record, application essay, extracurricular activities, first generation, level of applicant's interest. *Other factors considered include:* Class rank, geographical residence, interview, recommendation(s), talent/ability, volunteer work, work experience, character/personal qualities. SAT or ACT required; ACT with Writing component required. TOEFL required of all international applicants. *Academic units required:* 4 English; 3 mathematics; 3 science; (1 science lab); 3 social studies; 2 foreign language. *Academic units recommended:* 4 mathematics.

Financial Aid

Students should submit: FAFSA. The Princeton Review suggests that all financial aid forms be submitted as soon as possible after January 1. *Need-based scholarships/grants offered:* Federal Pell, SEOG, State scholarships/grants, private scholarships, the school's own gift aid, United Negro College Fund. *Loan aid offered:* Direct Subsidized Stafford Loans, Direct Unsubsidized Stafford Loans, Direct PLUS loans, Federal Perkins Loans, College/university loans from institutional funds. Federal Work-Study Program available. Institutional employment available. Off-campus job opportunities are excellent.

The Inside Word

Given the extraordinary volume of applications the admissions office receives, it's no wonder that Michigan State relies primarily on numbers. Decisions typically come down to grades, class rank, and test scores. Applicants who have proven to be capable students in college prep courses are relatively likely to find themselves the proud addressees of fat admissions envelopes. Applications are processed on a rolling basis, a process that typically favors early applicants.

THE SCHOOL SAYS "..."

From the Admissions Office

"Although Michigan State University is a graduate and research institution of international stature and acclaim, your undergraduate education is a high priority. More than 2,700 instructional faculty members (90 percent of whom hold a terminal degree) are dedicated to providing academic instruction, guidance, and assistance to our undergraduate students. Our 37,000 undergraduate students are a select group of academically motivated men and women. The diversity of ethnic, racial, religious, and socioeconomic heritage makes the student body a microcosm of the state, national, and international community.

"Students applying for admission to Michigan State University are required to take the new version of the SAT or the ACT exam with the Writing section. The Writing assessment will be considered in the holistic review of the application for admission. SAT Subject Tests are not required."

SELECTIVITY
Admissions Rating	82
# of applicants	31,479
% of applicants accepted	69
% of acceptees attending	37

FRESHMAN PROFILE
Range SAT Critical Reading	420–580
Range SAT Math	550–690
Range SAT Writing	460–580
Range ACT Composite	23–28
Minimum paper TOEFL	550
Minimum web-based TOEFL	213
Average HS GPA	3.62
% graduated top 10% of class	28
% graduated top 25% of class	66
% graduated top 50% of class	94

DEADLINES
Early action	
Deadline	10/16
Notification	11/15
Regular	
Priority	11/1
Nonfall registration?	Yes

APPLICANTS ALSO LOOK AT AND OFTEN PREFER
University of Michigan—Ann Arbor; Western Michigan University; Kalamazoo College

AND SOMETIMES PREFER
Indiana University—Bloomington; University of Illinois at Urbana-Champaign; University of Wisconsin-Madison

FINANCIAL FACTS
Financial Aid Rating	95
Annual in-state tuition	$12,863
Annual out-of-state tuition	$33,750
Room and board	$8,806
Books and supplies	$1,044
% needy frosh rec. need-based scholarship or grant aid	70
% needy UG rec. need-based scholarship or grant aid	72
% needy frosh rec. non-need-based scholarship or grant aid	38
% needy UG rec. non-need-based scholarship or grant aid	25
% needy frosh rec. need-based self-help aid	85
% needy UG rec. need-based self-help aid	88
% frosh rec. any financial aid	47
% UG rec. any financial aid	48
% UG borrow to pay for school	46
Average cumulative indebtedness	$25,821
% frosh need fully met	20
% ugrads need fully met	15
Average % of frosh need met	63
Average % of ugrad need met	61

MICHIGAN TECHNOLOGICAL UNIVERSITY

1400 TOWNSEND DRIVE, HOUGHTON, MI 49931 • ADMISSIONS: 906-487-2335 • FAX: 906-487-2125

CAMPUS LIFE

Quality of Life Rating	81
Fire Safety Rating	89
Green Rating	89
Type of school	Public
Affiliation	No Affiliation
Environment	Village

STUDENTS

Total undergrad enrollment	5,536
% male/female	75/25
% from out of state	24
% frosh from public high school	90
% frosh live on campus	91
% ugrads live on campus	48
# of fraternities (% ugrad men join)	13 (6)
# of sororities (% ugrad women join)	10 (3)
% African American	1
% Asian	1
% Caucasian	84
% Hispanic	2
% Native American	1
% international	6
# of countries represented	52

SURVEY SAYS . . .

Class discussions are rare
Campus feels safe
Lots of beer drinking
Students get along with local community

ACADEMICS

Academic Rating	75
% students returning for sophomore year	82
% students graduating within 4 years	24
% students graduating within 6 years	66
Calendar	Semester
Student/faculty ratio	13:1
Profs interesting rating	67
Profs accessible rating	72

Most classes have 20–29 students.
Most lab/discussion sessions have
 10–19 students.

MOST POPULAR MAJORS

mechanical engineering; civil engineering;
electrical engineering

STUDENTS SAY ". . ."

Academics

Michigan Technological University has "very high standards when it comes to education" and offers "serious study in a beautiful (often snowy) environment." It boasts a "really good reputation as an engineering school," and it's no secret that "engineering is a part of everybody's life." All agree, "Michigan Tech provides an atmosphere that nurtures learning" and "puts students first when it comes to their learning experience by providing hands-on experience." The university offers "lots of internship and co-op opportunities" and "pathways for career development and professional advancement." Students say that the courses are "challenging" and that the university "pushes students to excel academically." Professors are "generally interesting and helpful," but some can be "dull." A junior says, "Concentrated courses are great, but Gen Eds are huge, impersonal, and just plain awful," and another student adds, "The experience gets better with more time you put into your program, the professors become more interactive, and the experience becomes more meaningful."

Life

Michigan Tech "is in a small town in the middle of the deep North woods," which makes "the sense of community remarkable." Students say that campus is "incredibly safe," that "the atmosphere is very friendly," and that "there are a lot of opportunities to get involved." A physics major notes, "You start to see people you know everywhere on campus. It is really easy to find a friend and talk to someone." Enhancing the "strong student community" are "over 200 clubs" and a variety of "winter activities to be a part of." Many students take advantage of "free access to Mont Ripley," the university's own ski hill and the oldest one in Michigan. A freshman says, "We have broomball, Winter Carnival, and lots of campus-wide events!" Many students say, "The administration in every department works hard to answer questions and help out as much as possible, which is really great when you're a freshman," but some feel there's a "gap between [the] administration and students," particularly when it comes to spending. There are complaints about dorm food, leading a junior to say, "I would like to see some more selection and variation between dining halls," and students feel there's a need for "more parking spots close to campus." While "the library is a great place to study," some "of the classrooms are dated" and could use technological updating.

Student Body

At Michigan Tech, the typical student "is smart and a little more introspective than average," but still "great at balancing school and hanging out." Most students "are looking to get a good education and are fairly laid-back," and the student body consists of "down-to-earth friendly people," who "work hard during the week and look forward to relaxing and having fun on the weekends." It's no secret that "the ratio is a little guy-heavy" and that, because of this, "girls get doors opened for them across campus." Students tend to be "white and male," and a junior acknowledges, "There's little diversity ethnically, but everyone feels welcome." A chemical engineering major says, "You have to be a little bit of a nerd to fit in," and another student agrees, "I think most people think about classes first, hanging out second." It's common for students to "stay in and play video games," but there's also a large contingent of "outdoorsy people." A sophomore says, "Winters are long and cold up here," and students take advantage of the plentiful snow by "hiking, biking, four-wheeling, skiing, [and] snowmobiling." Students look forward to Winter Carnival, "a long weekend off from classes where students build giant, impressive snow sculptures, play broomball, [and] stay out all night," and for fun they enjoy "house parties and moderate drinking/merrymaking [to] warm up the cold winters."

FINANCIAL AID: 906-487-2622 • E-MAIL: MTU4U@MTU.EDU • WEBSITE: WWW.MTU.EDU

THE PRINCETON REVIEW SAYS

Admissions

Very important factors considered include: GPA, standardized test scores. *Important factors considered include:* Rigor of secondary school record. *Other factors considered include:* Class rank, application essay, extracurricular activities, recommendation(s), talent/ability, character/personal qualities. SAT or ACT required; ACT with or without Writing component accepted. TOEFL required of all international applicants. *Academic units required:* 3 English; 3 mathematics; 2 science. *Academic units recommended:* 4 English; 4 mathematics; 3 science; 3 social studies; 2 foreign language; 1 history; 2 academic electives; 1 computer science.

Financial Aid

Students should submit: FAFSA. The Princeton Review suggests that all financial aid forms be submitted as soon as possible after January 1. *Need-based scholarships/grants offered:* Federal Pell, SEOG, State scholarships/grants, private scholarships, the school's own gift aid. *Loan aid offered:* Direct Subsidized Stafford Loans, Direct Unsubsidized Stafford Loans, Direct PLUS loans, Federal Perkins Loans, College/university loans from institutional funds. Federal Work-Study Program available. Institutional employment available. Off-campus job opportunities are excellent.

The Inside Word

Michigan Tech strives to enroll bright, adventurous students. Students aren't required to submit recommendations from teachers, although they may submit a "High School Counselor Information Page" if they would like their counselor to share information regarding their high school performance. Applicants to the Visual and Performing Arts Department degree programs are required to submit supplemental materials, including an essay.

THE SCHOOL SAYS "..."

From the Admissions Office

"At Michigan Tech, our students create the future. Our unique Enterprise Program lets students work on real industry problems such as building a satellite, better alternative fuels, groundwater analysis, and video production. Through student groups like Engineers Without Borders and the campus-wide Make a Difference Day, our students impact lives in our community and around the world. Students can choose from 130 degree programs in engineering; forest resources; computing; technology; business; economics; natural, physical and environmental sciences; arts; humanities; and social sciences. We offer exciting degree programs in growing fields including biomedical engineering, wildlife ecology and management, and pre-health studies.

"Outside of the classrooms and labs, students enjoy our golf course, ski hill, trails and recreational forest, and friendly, small-town atmosphere in beautiful Upper Michigan. Located on the Keweenaw Waterway, the campus is only minutes from Lake Superior. During Winter Carnival, students build huge snow statues and play broomball, the biggest game on campus, among many other activities.

"We recommend that students applying for admission take the SAT (or the ACT)."

SELECTIVITY

Admissions Rating	83
# of applicants	4,905
% of applicants accepted	78
% of acceptees attending	33

FRESHMAN PROFILE

Range SAT Critical Reading	520–640
Range SAT Math	570–688
Range SAT Writing	493–620
Range ACT Composite	24–29
Minimum paper TOEFL	550
Minimum web-based TOEFL	79
Average HS GPA	3.66
% graduated top 10% of class	30
% graduated top 25% of class	65
% graduated top 50% of class	91

DEADLINES

Regular	
Priority	1/15
Nonfall registration?	Yes

APPLICANTS ALSO LOOK AT AND SOMETIMES PREFER

Michigan State University; Milwaukee School of Engineering; University of Michigan—Ann Arbor; University of Minnesota—Twin Cities; University of Wisconsin-Madison; Western Michigan University

AND RARELY PREFER

Grand Valley State University

FINANCIAL FACTS

Financial Aid Rating	74
Annual in-state tuition	$13,470
Annual out-of-state tuition	$28,350
Room and board	$9,175
Required fees	$258
Books and supplies	$1,200
% needy frosh rec. need-based scholarship or grant aid	86
% needy UG rec. need-based scholarship or grant aid	77
% needy frosh rec. non-need-based scholarship or grant aid	81
% needy UG rec. non-need-based scholarship or grant aid	74
% needy frosh rec. need-based self-help aid	83
% needy UG rec. need-based self-help aid	86
% frosh rec. any financial aid	93
% UG rec. any financial aid	92
% UG borrow to pay for school	73
Average cumulative indebtedness	$34,903
% frosh need fully met	19
% ugrads need fully met	18
Average % of frosh need met	79
Average % of ugrad need met	71

MIDDLEBURY COLLEGE

THE EMMA WILLARD HOUSE, MIDDLEBURY, VT 05753-6002 • ADMISSIONS: 802-443-3000 • FAX: 802-443-2056

STUDENTS SAY ". . ."

Academics

One of the most highly regarded liberal arts colleges in the United States, Middlebury College in Vermont is about "creating a person both socially and intellectually prepared for the world." The school has "a high level of global thinking and language acquisition in such a rural place," and there is an "emerging focus on creativity and entrepreneurship." When teaching students to develop communication, writing, creativity, and critical thinking skills, the school "allows you to develop these skills in whatever subject or subjects that one is most passionate about." Students' needs and choices are "of very high priority" to the administration, and there is "institutional support for whatever absurd idea might strike you." Professors are, on the whole, "truly top-notch"; not only are they "brilliant academics, but they are also adept teachers and classroom leaders." They come here because they want to teach undergraduates and research; "Middlebury expects both; most professors deliver." "Several of my professors have given out their cell phone numbers after particularly difficult lectures to make sure that students can figure things out," says one. "It's almost impossible to actually be 'invisible.'" The overall academic experience is "very intense" ("If you haven't done the reading, prepare to be called out for it"), but "students reliably enjoy their classes."

Life

Empty hours at Middlebury are in short supply; "If you've got free time in your day at Middlebury, you're doing something wrong," says a student. However, after all that reading, "at the end of the day, we all just like to get together and hit up the Snow Bowl to go skiing." "Vermont does make a difference," says one student of Middlebury's location near mountains, lakes, and ski trails, and its focus on "how important the outdoor experience is for the school." Drinking is "fairly prevalent" on Fridays and Saturdays, but "not during the week." It's a healthy culture, and "public safety does a good job of keeping things safe while not being overly intrusive." The dorms are "gorgeous," and there is even one called the Chateau, modeled after the largest chateau in Fontainebleau, France. The number of activities available are admirable, and "most people actually choose not to go into cities on weekends because they would hate to miss what's going on on-campus that weekend."

Student Body

The pervasive atmosphere at Middlebury is "super friendly and caring," and there is not only the pressure to work hard, but "also the encouragement to make sure students succeed." Students "compete with themselves, not their classmates." With a happy population, beautiful environs, and not a single student going unchallenged, the school encompasses "a perfect blend of intellectual curiosity, responsible living, and fun." As one student eloquently puts it, it's a bunch of "bright kids doing too many things—all of them good, none related to sleep." This "engaged, active," "preppy" student body "doesn't take themselves too seriously but do take serious initiative." A typical go-getter student "pursues at least one major, a minor, and is the star of at least one sports team or special interest group, but usually more." Social life can be "very centered around athletic teams," but these "well-read, outgoing," and "well-rounded students from stable backgrounds" always end up connecting with people they can relate with easily. "You will struggle to find time to spend with all the different friends you will make," says a student. Social ease is a common trait among MiddKids, and most students "know how to hold a conversation and [are] open to new experiences."

FINANCIAL AID: 802-443-5158 • E-MAIL: ADMISSIONS@MIDDLEBURY.EDU • WEBSITE: WWW.MIDDLEBURY.EDU

THE PRINCETON REVIEW SAYS

Admissions

Very important factors considered include: Class rank, GPA, rigor of secondary school record, extracurricular activities, talent/ability, character/personal qualities. *Important factors considered include:* Standardized test scores, application essay, racial/ethnic status, recommendation(s). *Other factors considered include:* First generation, geographical residence, interview, volunteer work, work experience, alumni/ae relations, level of applicant's interest. SAT, Subject tests (in three subjects), or ACT required; ACT with or without Writing component accepted. TOEFL required of all international applicants. *Academic units recommended:* 4 English; 4 mathematics; 3 science; (3 science lab); 3 social studies; 4 foreign language.

Financial Aid

Students should submit: FAFSA, CSS/Financial Aid PROFILE, Noncustodial PROFILE. Regular filing deadline is 2/1. The Princeton Review suggests that all financial aid forms be submitted as soon as possible after January 1. *Need-based scholarships/grants offered:* Federal Pell, SEOG, State scholarships/grants, private scholarships, the school's own gift aid. *Loan aid offered:* Direct Subsidized Stafford Loans, Direct Unsubsidized Stafford Loans, Direct PLUS loans, Federal Perkins Loans. Applicants will be notified of awards beginning 4/1. Federal Work-Study Program available. Institutional employment available.

The Inside Word

Middlebury gives you options in standardized testing. The school will accept either the ACT or the SAT or three SAT Subject Tests (the tests must be in three different subject areas, however). Middlebury is extremely competitive; improve your chances of admission by crafting a standardized test profile that shows you in the best possible light.

THE SCHOOL SAYS "..."

From the Admissions Office

"The successful Middlebury candidate excels in a variety of areas including academics, athletics, the arts, leadership, and service to others. These strengths and interests permit students to grow beyond their traditional 'comfort zones' and conventional limits. Our classrooms are as varied as the Green Mountains, the Metropolitan Museum of Art, or the great cities of Russia and Japan. Outside the classroom, students informally interact with professors in activities such as intramural basketball games and community service. At Middlebury, students develop critical-thinking skills, enduring bonds of friendship, and the ability to challenge themselves.

Middlebury's Commons system is the backbone of student residential life at the College. The residence halls are grouped into "living-learning communities," or Commons, which combine the academic, social, and residential components of college life. They also foster close relationships between the student residents and the faculty and staff who are part of their Commons.

Middlebury offers majors and programs in forty-six different fields, with particular strengths in languages, international studies, environmental studies, literature and creative writing, and the sciences. Opportunities for engaging in individual research with faculty abound at Middlebury."

SELECTIVITY

Admissions Rating	98
# of applicants	9,109
% of applicants accepted	18
% of acceptees attending	39
# offered a place on the wait list	1,705
% accepting a place on wait list	44
% admitted from wait list	0
# of early decision applicants	998
% accepted early decision	35

FRESHMAN PROFILE

Range SAT Critical Reading	630–750
Range SAT Math	650–740
Range SAT Writing	650–750
Range ACT Composite	29–33

DEADLINES

Early decision	
Deadline	11/1
Regular	
Deadline	1/1
Nonfall registration?	Yes

APPLICANTS ALSO LOOK AT AND OFTEN PREFER

Amherst College; Williams College; Dartmouth College; Harvard College

AND SOMETIMES PREFER

Brown University; Yale University; Stanford University; Duke University; Pomona College

AND RARELY PREFER

Bowdoin College; Colby College; Colgate University; Hamilton College

FINANCIAL FACTS

Financial Aid Rating	98
Annual tuition	$44,919
Room and board	$12,156
Required fees	$395
% needy frosh rec. need-based scholarship or grant aid	99
% needy UG rec. need-based scholarship or grant aid	99
% needy frosh rec. non-need-based scholarship or grant aid	0
% needy UG rec. non-need-based scholarship or grant aid	0
% needy frosh rec. need-based self-help aid	91
% needy UG rec. need-based self-help aid	92
% frosh rec. any financial aid	46
% UG rec. any financial aid	40
% UG borrow to pay for school	46
Average cumulative indebtedness	$17,715
% frosh need fully met	99
% ugrads need fully met	99
Average % of frosh need met	100
Average % of ugrad need met	100

MILLS COLLEGE

5000 MacArthur Boulevard, Oakland, CA 94613 • Admissions: 510-430-2135 • Fax: 510-430-3298

STUDENTS SAY ". . ."

Academics

Mills College in Oakland, California, is a small women's institution with a "rigorous academic program" defined as "the epitome of a liberal arts education." "I was drawn to the small class sizes, the beauty of the campus, and the wonderfully articulate and confident women that I came in contact with." With apporximately 1,000 undergraduates and fairly small class sizes, it is no wonder that professors "know almost all of [their students] individually." As one student attests, "Even in introductory lecture classes, you can get to know your professors." Another student concurs, "Not only am I on a first-name basis with all of my professors, I have their personal phone numbers and e-mail addresses! I feel that I matter here!" Students have high praise for the faculty. "The professors are amazing. They are extremely smart and totally accessible." "Professors are interesting and insightful and promote lively discussions in class. Standards are high and challenging. Topics are very relevant to today's issues." "Mills College is all about empowering its students and creating an environment that encourages hard work and social and political awareness." "There is great support for students with disabilities or special needs." "The library and several computer labs make it easy to find a place to get things done."

Life

"School life is pretty academically focused. Little time is spent off campus if you live on campus because social interaction usually involves study groups. There is little to no real partying on campus, though you can find it off campus if you are looking for it." "The beauty of the campus" is a significant plus for many students. Situated on 135 acres, the school has plenty of natural areas, and the atmosphere is relaxing and peaceful, which means it is very conducive to studying. "Mills exceeds expectations in creating an intimate and welcoming environment as well as in promoting student activism." Students agree that Mills is a special place. "The atmosphere at Mills is incredible! It is academic, empowering, creative, and always intellectually stimulating." Students here seem to know how to balance their schedules and how to appreciate the education they are receiving. Mills "offers a very rigorous education that is stimulating yet fun." But this enthusiasm for their school does not carry over to campus life on the weekends when "it sort of turns into a ghost town." Students also warn, "If you're looking for a party school, look elsewhere." You do not have to go very far for entertainment. "Many students love the Berkeley and San Francisco nightlife."

Student Body

Here's how some Mills students describe themselves and their peers: "The typical student is female, academically inclined, and individualistic (possesses few stereotypically mainstream qualities)." "Students are typically politically active in some way, and many have one or two causes they know really well. Students are inquisitive and very intent on doing well academically. We don't party very much. We're also very welcoming." At Mills College, "the students are really diverse; pretty much everyone is different. In order to fit in, all you have to do is be yourself." This diversity is what seems to set it apart from most other schools. "It's a unique group of people, and the school is not everyone's cup of tea." One student clarifies, "Mills is full of 'nontraditional' students from all over the world. I didn't want to be in a place where everyone was on the same track, with the same agenda. I wanted to be in a place where every other person would have their own cause, their own independent ideas." This "very open-minded environment" sets Mills apart from most other colleges in how students "embrace diversity and gender equality in hopes of creating a better world." With a wide range of ages and backgrounds, the traditional student is anything but traditional.

FINANCIAL AID: 510-430-2000 • E-MAIL: ADMISSION@MILLS.EDU • WEBSITE: WWW.MILLS.EDU

THE PRINCETON REVIEW SAYS

Admissions

Very important factors considered include: Rigor of student's academic profile. *Important factors considered include:* Class rank, GPA, standardized test scores, application essay, extracurricular activities, recommendation(s), character/personal interest. *Other factors considered include:* First generation, geographical residence, interview, racial/ethnic status, talent/ability, volunteer work, work experience, alumnae/i relations, level of applicant's interest. SAT or ACT required; ACT with or without Writing component accepted. TOEFL or IFELTS required of all international applicants. *Academic units required:* 4 English; 3 mathematics; 2 science; (2 science lab); 2 social studies; 2 foreign language; 2 history. *Academic units recommended:* 4 English; 4 mathematics; 4 science; (2 science lab); 4 social studies; 4 foreign language; 4 history; 2 visual/performing arts.

Financial Aid

Students should submit: FAFSA, Institution's own financial aid form, State aid form. Regular filing deadline is 2/15. The Princeton Review suggests that all financial aid forms be submitted as soon as possible after January 1. *Need-based scholarships/grants offered:* Federal Pell, SEOG, State scholarships/grants, private scholarships, the school's own gift aid. *Loan aid offered:* Direct Subsidized Stafford Loans, Direct Unsubsidized Stafford Loans, Direct PLUS loans, Federal Perkins Loans, College/university loans from institutional funds. Federal Work-Study Program available. Institutional employment available. Off-campus job opportunities are good.

Inside Word

Mills strives to create a diverse community of students and welcomes older, non-traditional undergraduates. In fact, 16 percent of the Mills undergraduate population is older than twenty-three. In addition to the application, test scores, and transcripts, Mills requests that all first-year applicants submit a graded writing sample. Admissions interviews, though not required, are highly encouraged.

THE SCHOOL SAYS "..."

From the Admissions Office

"For more than 160 years, Mills College has shaped women's lives. Offering a progressive liberal arts and sciences curriculum taught by nationally respected faculty, Mills gives students the personal attention that leads to extraordinary learning. Through intensive, collaborative study in a community of forward-thinking individuals, students gain the ability to make their voices heard, the strength to risk bold visions, an eagerness to experiment, and a desire to change the world.

"Situated in the heart of the San Francisco Bay Area, Mills draws energy from the college's dynamic location. Mills students connect with centers of learning, business, and technology; pursue research and internship opportunities; and explore the Bay Area's many sources of cultural, social, and recreational enrichment.

"Ranked fifth among top colleges in the West, Mills offers a renowned education for students who are seeking a challenging and rewarding college experience. With a 10:1 student to faculty ratio, you'll learn from distinguished professors who are dedicated to teaching. You'll interact with dynamic women of different backgrounds, ethnicities, cultures, ages, and mindsets in an inclusive, welcoming environment.

"With more than forty different majors to choose from at Mills, you'll have a wide variety of education options. Mills also offers seven accelerated programs that make it possible for you to earn both a bachelor's and a master's degree—increasing your career options after college. At Mills, the classroom debate will be your intellectual catalyst, but you'll find plenty of opportunities to express yourself, both inside and outside of the classroom."

SELECTIVITY

Admissions Rating	87
# of applicants	1,827
% of applicants accepted	68
% of acceptees attending	17

FRESHMAN PROFILE

Range SAT Critical Reading	540–660
Range SAT Math	500–610
Range SAT Writing	520–620
Range ACT Composite	23–28
Minimum paper TOEFL	550
Average HS GPA	3.64
% graduated top 10% of class	41
% graduated top 25% of class	71
% graduated top 50% of class	97

DEADLINES

Early action	
Deadline	11/15
Notification	12/1
Regular	
Priority	1/15
Deadline	8/1
Nonfall registration?	Yes

APPLICANTS ALSO LOOK AT AND OFTEN PREFER

Santa Clara University; University of California—Santa Barbara; University of California—Berkeley; University of California—Davis; University of California—Los Angeles

AND SOMETIMES PREFER

University of Puget Sound; Occidental College; New York University; Mount Holyoke College; Chapman University; Bryn Mawr College

AND RARELY PREFER

Pepperdine University; Scripps College; University of Southern California

FINANCIAL FACTS

Financial Aid Rating	79
Annual tuition	$40,210
Room and board	$11,850
Required fees	$1,284
Books and supplies	$1,468
% needy frosh rec. need-based scholarship or grant aid	97
% needy UG rec. need-based scholarship or grant aid	96
% needy frosh rec. non-need-based scholarship or grant aid	6
% needy UG rec. non-need-based scholarship or grant aid	3
% needy frosh rec. need-based self-help aid	89
% needy UG rec. need-based self-help aid	88
% frosh rec. any financial aid	99
% UG rec. any financial aid	95
% UG borrow to pay for school	68
Average cumulative indebtedness	$24,861
% frosh need fully met	18
% ugrads need fully met	15
Average % of frosh need met	86
Average % of ugrad need met	79

MILLSAPS COLLEGE

1701 NORTH STATE STREET, JACKSON, MS 39210 • ADMISSIONS: 601-974-1050 • FAX: 601-974-1059

STUDENTS SAY ". . ."

Academics

Millsaps is a small college, so students "get a lot of personal attention." It is a "school where everybody knows your name," as well as "a place where every student has to work hard to stay above water; excellence is the norm, not the exception." What makes Millsaps unique is how it "breaks the mold by providing superb education as well as fun, combining the two in ways so subtle that a student may not even realize they're learning!" The school "offers great courses taught by charismatic professors" who "bring the material to life...through their innovative teaching methods." "Classes are not easy but the quality of learning is top notch." "Professors always encourage students to discuss class material and voice their opinions and questions about it. They encourage you to form your own ideas." These "friendly and approachable" professors "continue to teach outside of the classroom." "They welcome one-on-one time...to further develop understanding." Students have praise for the education they are receiving saying, "coming out of Millsaps I will be fully prepared for grad school. My professors not only lecture, but they turn the material into hands-on learning opportunities," and "I seriously respect my school's standard of excellence in hiring people who are wonderful at their jobs." Besides "great professors," the school offers "a prestigious business school," "abundant study abroad programs," and "strong Southern hospitality and heritage." The school's small size provides opportunities to receive "a top-notch education, while also getting to play sports and be in clubs." Although Millsaps may not be affordable for everyone, it "strives to be generous with scholarships." One student was pleased to report, "They offered the most financial assistance by far." Although student surveys were mostly positive, like this one: "Millsaps College provides the ideal learning atmosphere for liberal arts studies where they teach us how to think and not what to think," there were complaints about "the internet and networking capabilities," and "the cafeteria is an area where great improvement is needed."

Life

"Students at Millsaps think about their classwork first and foremost. After that, we think about hanging out with friends and having fun." The campus is "so beautiful and filled with cozy spots that many students spend a lot of their time outside." "While most schools have 'the quad' where students hang out between classes, Millsaps has 'The Bowl.' It is a beautiful area of grass and trees in the center of campus." But one student notes that there is still room for improvement. "The campus is beautiful, but the insides of the buildings need a serious upgrade. Every time I walk into a building, I feel like I've been transported back to the seventies." Although "most of the upperclassmen dorms are amazing," the "freshman dorms are a little sketchy." On campus "there are concerts and fun days all throughout the semester." "There are parties at the fraternity houses, and...some really cool things to do from concerts to oxygen bars to laser tag." "I would definitely call it a 'party school,' despite the tough academics." "There is a lot of partying on the weekends but almost everyone still manages to get studying finished." Students also point out, "We don't have to drink to have fun at Millsaps, though. You can always find a friend to hang out with, go to the movies, shop, or find a new great place to eat. The Millsaps curriculum even makes study groups fun (for the most part), believe it or not." Off campus, students venture into Jackson where "there are great restaurants."

Student Body

Is there a typical Millsaps student? Some students think so: "The typical student at Millsaps was an over-involved, cool nerd in high school. We throw ourselves into sports, clubs, Greek life, and community service like it's our job. It's how we thrive." "Students fit in by being involved in Greek life and other organizations." "A typical student is involved in many activities from sports to community service clubs. Student interests are diverse, and the student body in general is very friendly and interactive." Another student disagrees, "There is no 'typical student' really—the most common thread is a desire to change the world (usually, with a stop at graduate school)."

FINANCIAL AID: 800-352-1050 • E-MAIL: ADMISSIONS@MILLSAPS.EDU • WEBSITE: WWW.MILLSAPS.EDU

THE PRINCETON REVIEW SAYS

Admissions

Very important factors considered include: GPA, rigor of secondary school record, standardized test scores, character/personal qualities. *Important factors considered include:* Class rank, application essay, extracurricular activities, recommendation(s), talent/ability. *Other factors considered include:* Interview, volunteer work, work experience. SAT or ACT required; ACT with or without Writing component accepted. TOEFL required of all international applicants. *Academic units required:* 4 English; 3 mathematics; 3 science; (2 science lab); 2 social studies; 1 foreign language; 2 history; 1 academic elective. *Academic units recommended:* 4 English; 4 mathematics; 4 science; (2 science lab); 2 social studies; 2 foreign language; 2 history; 2 academic electives.

Financial Aid

Students should submit: FAFSA. The Princeton Review suggests that all financial aid forms be submitted as soon as possible after January 1. *Need-based scholarships/grants offered:* Federal Pell, SEOG, State scholarships/grants, private scholarships, the school's own gift aid. *Loan aid offered:* Direct Subsidized Stafford Loans, Direct Unsubsidized Stafford Loans, Direct PLUS loans, Federal Perkins Loans, College/university loans from institutional funds. Federal Work-Study Program available. Institutional employment available. Off-campus job opportunities are good.

The Inside Word

Millsaps' trademark friendliness begins during the admissions process. The school encourages prospective students to get in touch with an admissions counselor to ask questions, arrange a visit, or connect you with a current student. For early action admission or scholarships, students need to apply in January. After that, the school admits students on a rolling basis.

THE SCHOOL SAYS "..."

From the Admissions Office

"Millsaps offers outstanding value in nationally ranked liberal arts education. Your academic journey begins with Critical Thinking and Academic Literacy, a comprehensive freshman experience that develops reasoning, communication, quantitative thinking, historical consciousness, aesthetic judgment, global, and multicultural awareness, and valuing and decision making. Throughout your Millsaps years you'll be encouraged to think differently; learn critical, analytical skills; embrace independence of thought; and prepare for study in your chosen major. We offer unique opportunities such as study abroad and in the field at our Yucatán Program; an exploration of your personal and professional future in relation to issues of ethics, values, faith, and the common good through our Faith and Work Initiative; highly respected pre-professional programs in law, medicine, and social work; and a five-year business track leading to an MBA or master's in accountancy with a liberal arts perspective that is accredited by the Association to Advance Collegiate Schools of Business. Our student body included Mississippi's 2003–2004 Rhodes scholar, a 2008–2009 Fulbright Scholar, and the faculty included the Carnegie Foundation's 2006, 2007, 2008, and 2009 Mississippi Professor of the Year. Our courses are taught without graduate assistants and our intimate student-faculty-community relationship is a hallmark of a Millsaps education. The emerging cultural climate in Jackson, Mississippi's capital city, provides unique artistic, athletic, and social opportunities in the modern south. We encourage you to look at Millsaps College. You'll appreciate the quality of our educational experience in comparison to the costs you'll discover at other national liberal arts institutions."

SELECTIVITY

Admissions Rating	89
# of applicants	1,901
% of applicants accepted	47
% of acceptees attending	19

FRESHMAN PROFILE

Range SAT Critical Reading	498–630
Range SAT Math	520–620
Range SAT Writing	480–610
Range ACT Composite	23–28
Minimum paper TOEFL	550
Minimum web-based TOEFL	220
Average HS GPA	3.55
% graduated top 10% of class	31
% graduated top 25% of class	59
% graduated top 50% of class	85

DEADLINES

Early action	
Deadline	11/15
Notification	1/15
Regular	
Priority	2/1
Deadline	7/1
Nonfall registration?	Yes

APPLICANTS ALSO LOOK AT AND OFTEN PREFER
Birmingham-Southern College

AND SOMETIMES PREFER
Rhodes College

AND RARELY PREFER
Texas Christian University; Furman University; Samford University

FINANCIAL FACTS

Financial Aid Rating	85
Annual tuition	$30,500
Room and board	$11,368
Required fees	$2,020
Books and supplies	$1,100
% needy frosh rec. need-based scholarship or grant aid	100
% needy UG rec. need-based scholarship or grant aid	99
% needy frosh rec. non-need-based scholarship or grant aid	32
% needy UG rec. non-need-based scholarship or grant aid	21
% needy frosh rec. need-based self-help aid	66
% needy UG rec. need-based self-help aid	74
% frosh rec. any financial aid	100
% UG rec. any financial aid	98
% UG borrow to pay for school	60
Average cumulative indebtedness	$27,926
% frosh need fully met	40
% ugrads need fully met	30
Average % of frosh need met	84
Average % of ugrad need met	78

MISSOURI UNIVERSITY OF SCIENCE AND TECHNOLOGY

300 WEST 13TH STREET; 106 PARKER HALL, ROLLA, MO 65409-1060 • ADMISSIONS: 573-341-4165 • FAX: 573-341-4082

CAMPUS LIFE

Quality of Life Rating	78
Fire Safety Rating	78
Green Rating	87
Type of school	Public
Affiliation	No Affiliation
Environment	Village

STUDENTS

Total undergrad enrollment	6,146
% male/female	77/23
% from out of state	16
% frosh from public high school	85
% ugrads live on campus	40
# of fraternities (% ugrad men join)	23 (21)
# of sororities (% ugrad women join)	5 (19)
% African American	4
% Asian	3
% Caucasian	78
% Hispanic	2
% Native American	<1
% international	6
# of countries represented	60

SURVEY SAYS . . .

Lab facilities are great
Career services are great
Class discussions are rare
School is well run
Frats and sororities are popular

ACADEMICS

Academic Rating	78
% students returning for sophomore year	83
% students graduating within 4 years	25
% students graduating within 6 years	63
Calendar	Semester
Student/faculty ratio	17:1
Profs interesting rating	77
Profs accessible rating	74

Most classes have 20–29 students.
Most lab/discussion sessions have
10–19 students.

MOST POPULAR MAJORS

civil engineering; electrical engineering;
mechanical engineering

STUDENTS SAY ". . ."

Academics

Top performers in science and technology will find a home in the school formerly known as University of Missouri—Rolla, because here "students are exposed to just about every different type of engineering," making it "one of the best universities that prepares engineers for industry." Unsurprisingly, this does not come without challenge. Classes can be "very tough and intimidating," where "it's not uncommon to have a 55 percent or less average on a test." Students ready for the rigorous academics should "not expect to be babied at all" because "the professors are there to challenge you." The aim is to "prepare students to find a job in the real world and help us to get the experience to succeed in it." Students who have run the gauntlet say "the quality of education and availability of resources here is second to none." That education comes via "hands-on learning, small class sizes, and caring professors" who are "some of the smartest professors in the world." Though they challenge their students, they don't leave them out to dry. "All of the professors have office hours, whether open or by appointment," students note. Indeed, "the accessibility of instructors and other faculty/staff" at this small school is seen as a strength. Yes, "this school definitely is willing to challenge their students," but numbers-crunching engineers will find value in their education, because S&T "comes in the top three schools in average starting salary for graduates, and won't guarantee a huge debt burden."

Life

Missouri University of Science and Technology may be "a small school in the middle of Missouri," but "our range of student organizations is mind-boggling." You name the club and it probably exists, as well as school activities ranging from "scavenger hunts, video game nights, cooking classes, viewing parties, dance lessons, and much more." Of course, in a school where "all of the students are always worrying about that next exam in calculus or dreading their lab in the afternoon," it is not surprising that studying is as big a pastime as hanging out. Here, "academics are everyone's top priority." When not studying, "drinking is pretty big on weekends," especially among the 30 percent of campus involved in Greek life. Other activities include "playing sports, video games, and working out." Downtown Rolla isn't a thriving Mecca of activity because "there's not so much to do in the town," however, "someone always has something going on." St. Louis is close enough for day trips, and there are a slew of student organizations to occupy downtime. "Virtually every student is either heavily involved in a diverse group of these student organizations or devotes much of their time to design teams or research." Generally, if you're at S&T and are not kept busy, it's probably because you don't want to be busy.

Student Body

Imagine a less stereotypical Big Bang Theory and you're close to the mark. The typical student may be "a little nerdy," "those kids that didn't fit in during high school" but who "now can be themselves." A typical S&T student "is someone who never really had to study in high school to get good grades, but they are working hard here to maintain that standard." While most S&T students are smart—"we came here primarily to learn," one attendee notes—they are not introverted or antisocial. The "very friendly" people on campus "live together in harmony." Indeed, "everyone can find a place to fit in" thanks to the "over 212 student organizations." While about half of the students here are from Missouri or nearby states, the others "are from the edges of the nation and even some foreign countries, which is astounding considering our small enrollment size." Education is the priority for those who attend, so meeting people is simple because "it is really easy just to strike up a conversation with someone." The like-minded atmosphere makes socializing easy. "We are all nerds, so we adapt to the social environment once we are introduced."

MISSOURI UNIVERSITY OF SCIENCE AND TECHNOLOGY

FINANCIAL AID: 573-341-4282 • E-MAIL: ADMISSIONS@MST.EDU • WEBSITE: WWW.MST.EDU

THE PRINCETON REVIEW SAYS

Admissions

Very important factors considered include: Class rank, GPA, rigor of secondary school record, standardized test scores. *Important factors considered include:* Recommendation(s). *Other factors considered include:* Application essay, extracurricular activities, interview, talent/ability, volunteer work, work experience, character/personal qualities. SAT or ACT required; ACT with or without Writing component accepted. TOEFL required of all international applicants. *Academic units required:* 4 English; 4 mathematics; 3 science; (1 science lab); 3 social studies; 2 foreign language; 1 visual/performing arts.

Financial Aid

Students should submit: FAFSA. The Princeton Review suggests that all financial aid forms be submitted as soon as possible after January 1. *Need-based scholarships/grants offered:* Federal Pell, SEOG, State scholarships/grants, private scholarships, the school's own gift aid. *Loan aid offered:* Federal Perkins Loans, State Loans, College/university loans from institutional funds. Federal Work-Study Program available. Institutional employment available. Off-campus job opportunities are good.

The Inside Word

Winning admission to the Missouri University of Science and Technology is largely a numbers game, as it often is with other leading public universities. Expect to have to meet class rank and standardized test cutoffs, along with distribution requirements, in order to be granted admission. And apply early if possible. The pool of applicants is competitive, and is made up of students of similar caliber. Get off to an early start and you'll have an advantage.

THE SCHOOL SAYS "..."

From the Admissions Office

"Missouri S&T is one of the nation's top technological research universities. Our students go beyond books and lectures to apply knowledge in bold new ways. With more than 8,100 students, our campus exhibits a passion and energy few universities can foster. S&T students collaborate with great researchers and other talented students to meet the global challenges of our times—in areas like energy, infrastructure, e-commerce, materials, education, and environmental sustainability.

"We're ranked among the top five public universities for highest starting salaries for graduates—averaging nearly $60,000. It's easy to see how investing in an S&T education pays off. Nearly 90 percent of grads have firm career plans (career, grad school, law/medical school, or military) even before they graduate. As a top ten "Best Value" public university, S&T is committed to small classes, quality academic advising, and personal attention. Nearly half of graduates complete a research program or study abroad. With more than 200 student organizations, you'll never run out of things to do. Enjoy the outdoors? We've got skydiving, spelunking, and more. Feeling creative? Join the student radio station, theater, orchestra, debate team, or student newspaper. Like to stay active? Join an intramural or club sports team. Want more? Start your own organization.

"Widely recognized as one of the nation's best universities for science, engineering, computing, math, and social sciences, Missouri S&T provides students an outstanding education at a price they can afford. Admissions decisions are based primarily on each applicant's academic achievement."

SELECTIVITY

Admissions Rating	86
# of applicants	3,322
% of applicants accepted	82
% of acceptees attending	47

FRESHMAN PROFILE

Range SAT Critical Reading	540–670
Range SAT Math	590–690
Range ACT Composite	25–31
Minimum paper TOEFL	550
Average HS GPA	3.60
% graduated top 10% of class	41
% graduated top 25% of class	71
% graduated top 50% of class	93

DEADLINES

Regular	
Priority	12/1
Deadline	7/1
Nonfall registration?	Yes

APPLICANTS ALSO LOOK AT AND OFTEN PREFER

Massachusetts Institute of Technology; University of Illinois at Urbana-Champaign; University of Wisconsin-Madison; Washington University in St. Louis; University of Missouri; Truman State University; Saint Louis University

AND SOMETIMES PREFER

Georgia Institute of Technology; Purdue University—West Lafayette; University of Iowa; Iowa State University

FINANCIAL FACTS

Financial Aid Rating	77
Annual in-state tuition	$8,220
Annual out-of-state tuition	$23,385
Room and board	$9,145
Required fees	$1,290
Books and supplies	$890
% needy frosh rec. need-based scholarship or grant aid	97
% needy UG rec. need-based scholarship or grant aid	88
% needy frosh rec. non-need-based scholarship or grant aid	19
% needy UG rec. non-need-based scholarship or grant aid	11
% needy frosh rec. need-based self-help aid	68
% needy UG rec. need-based self-help aid	76
% frosh rec. any financial aid	88
% UG rec. any financial aid	90
% UG borrow to pay for school	73
Average cumulative indebtedness	$21,659
% frosh need fully met	24
% ugrads need fully met	18
Average % of frosh need met	74
Average % of ugrad need met	64

MONMOUTH UNIVERSITY (NJ)

ADMISSION, MONMOUTH UNIVERSITY, WEST LONG BRANCH, NJ 07764-1898 • ADMISSIONS: 732-571-3456 • FAX: 732-263-5166

STUDENTS SAY " . . ."

Academics

Monmouth University brings to life a full array of personalized learning experiences for students through which they can grow personally and be transformed professionally. Faculty care and are connected to their students, engaging them in dynamic dialogue both in and out of the classroom. Students are also invested in their education through the many opportunities available to explore real-life experiences. Not only are Monmouth students prepared for careers, but they are prepared for life.

Monmouth University is located one mile from the beaches of the Jersey Shore and one hour from New York City, home to many prominent firms that are leaders in the technology, media, and financial industries. This allows students access to exceptional hands-on learning opportunities. Experiential education, which includes internships, study abroad, service learning projects, or cooperative learning experiences, is a required part of the curriculum.

Monmouth's student life, including cultural events, festivals, and active student clubs and organizations, reflects the school's spirit. There is a strong sense of community on campus that is supported by relevant and dedicated programs, events, and more. Monmouth's twenty-one NCAA Division I athletic teams attract lively support from students and other members of the campus and local communities.

Students at Monmouth are provided with a value-added education, personalized experience, small classes, and the foundations needed for graduates to make a difference in the marketplace and in the world. The University celebrates that Monmouth alumni are among today's employees who are valued for being creative and effective problem solvers, agile thinkers, and versatile personnel."

Life

The "small, classy campus" is "in a great location" in central New Jersey, and makes for "a very comfortable place to be." The beach is only a mile away (which one student says "reminds me paradise is only down the street"), so on a nice day "everyone will be soaking up the sun." Regardless of tanning temptations, "everyone is also really focused on school and wants to succeed." The ground maintenance here is "impeccable," and "the landscaping is always groomed and gorgeous." Students at Monmouth "are very serious about their school work and about their sport if they are an athlete, but they also want to have fun." Once the weekend hits, "everyone does their own thing." Commuters go home, "sports teams have parties, fraternities and sororities have joint parties, and "a lot of students attend games and support our athletic teams" (Monmouth is a Division I school). Campus safety is a priority for the school, and is reflected in the community. "I feel as if other students on campus are always looking out for one another in addition to our safety department, the MUPD, and the blue light system on campus," says a freshman. One common college gripe is that "the food is okay, [but] it could definitely be better." The university holds "a good number" of events on campus for students, as well, and "there are things to do in the local area that students do for entertainment."

Student Body

Most of the students here are "white, upper-middle class" and hail from nearby areas, so Monmouth can be "somewhat of a suitcase school," but there is still a close knit community where "you know just about everyone." People here are "friendly and fun-loving, but also seriously committed to their studies," and with the popularity of clubs and fraternities and sororities (Greek life "has gone 'viral' in the past few years"), all students "can fit in SOMEWHERE." It doesn't hurt that the university has a set of required general education courses that every student has to take before they graduate, so "it is easy for people from all majors to meet and socialize."

MONMOUTH UNIVERSITY (NJ)

FINANCIAL AID: 732-571-3463 • E-MAIL: ADMISSION@MONMOUTH.EDU • WEBSITE: WWW.MONMOUTH.EDU

THE PRINCETON REVIEW SAYS

Admissions

Very important factors considered include: GPA, rigor of secondary school record, standardized test scores. *Important factors considered include:* Application essay, extracurricular activities, recommendation(s), volunteer work, work experience. *Other factors considered include:* Alumni/ae relations, character/personal qualities. SAT or ACT required; ACT with Writing component required. TOEFL required of all international applicants. *Academic units required:* 4 English; 3 mathematics; 2 science; (1 science lab); 2 history; 5 academic electives. *Academic units recommended:* 2 social studies; 2 foreign language.

Financial Aid

Students should submit: FAFSA. Regular filing deadline is 6/30. The Princeton Review suggests that all financial aid forms be submitted as soon as possible after January 1. *Need-based scholarships/grants offered:* Federal Pell, SEOG, State scholarships/grants, private scholarships, the school's own gift aid, federal nursing scholarships. *Loan aid offered:* Direct Subsidized Stafford Loans, Direct Unsubsidized Stafford Loans, Direct PLUS loans, Federal Perkins Loans, State Loans, College/university loans from institutional funds. Federal Work-Study Program available. Institutional employment available. Off-campus job opportunities are good.

Inside Word

B students with slightly above-average SAT or ACT scores should find little impediment to gaining admission to Monmouth. The school's national stature is on the rise, resulting in more competitive applicant base, but Monmouth must still compete with a lot of heavy hitters for top regional students.

THE SCHOOL SAYS "..."

From the Admissions Office

"Monmouth University brings to life a full array of personalized learning experiences for students through which they can grow personally and be transformed professionally. A ratio of fourteen students to each professor ensures that learning at Monmouth is active, engaged, and powerful.

Experiential education, which includes internships, study abroad, service learning projects, or cooperative learning experiences, is a required part of the curriculum. More than 75 percent of Monmouth students complete a "real world" experience by their senior year, compared to fewer than 50 percent of graduating students at comparable institutions, according to the 2012 National Survey of Student Engagement.

Monmouth University is located one mile from the beaches of the Jersey Shore and one hour from New York City, home to many prominent firms that are leaders in the technology, media, and financial industries. This allows students access to exceptional hands-on learning opportunities.

The University is among the most affordable high-quality, comprehensive private educational institutions in New Jersey. It is found in the top tier of academic quality and in the bottom tier of costs.

Monmouth's student life, including cultural events, festivals, and active student clubs and organizations, reflects the school's spirit and community. Monmouth's twenty-one NCAA Division I athletic teams attract lively support from students and other members of the campus and local communities.

Students at Monmouth are provided with a value-added education, personalized experience, small classes, and the foundations needed for graduates to make a difference in the marketplace and in the world."

SELECTIVITY

Admissions Rating	72
# of applicants	5,537
% of applicants accepted	78
% of acceptees attending	21

FRESHMAN PROFILE

Range SAT Critical Reading	480–560
Range SAT Math	490–590
Range SAT Writing	480–570
Range ACT Composite	22–25
Minimum paper TOEFL	550
Minimum web-based TOEFL	213
Average HS GPA	3.40
% graduated top 10% of class	19
% graduated top 25% of class	49
% graduated top 50% of class	82

DEADLINES

Early action	
Deadline	12/1
Notification	1/15
Regular	
Priority	12/1
Deadline	3/1
Nonfall registration?	Yes

APPLICANTS ALSO LOOK AT AND OFTEN PREFER

AND SOMETIMES PREFER

FINANCIAL FACTS

Financial Aid Rating	75
Annual tuition	$31,682
Room and board	$11,798
Required fees	$628
Books and supplies	$1,424
% needy frosh rec. need-based scholarship or grant aid	62
% needy UG rec. need-based scholarship or grant aid	46
% needy frosh rec. non-need-based scholarship or grant aid	95
% needy UG rec. non-need-based scholarship or grant aid	93
% needy frosh rec. need-based self-help aid	80
% needy UG rec. need-based self-help aid	83
% frosh rec. any financial aid	99
% UG rec. any financial aid	96
% UG borrow to pay for school	77
Average cumulative indebtedness	$32,240
% frosh need fully met	18
% ugrads need fully met	16
Average % of frosh need met	70
Average % of ugrad need met	68

MONTANA TECH OF THE UNIVERSITY OF MONTANA

1300 WEST PARK STREET, BUTTE, MT 59701 • ADMISSIONS: 406-496-4256 • FAX: 406-496-4710

STUDENTS SAY ". . ."

Academics

Even if Montana Tech of the University of Montana weren't one of the only tech institutes in the state, its excellent science programs and reputation for developing high quality engineers to send out into the workforce would keep its classrooms filled. Located in Butte, the school "stresses the importance of knowing present technologies" and offers "hands-on experience" and "great internship opportunities" to assure great engineers after graduating (the job placement rate for many major approaches 100 percent). The "high education at lower cost school model" is well-known particularly within the mining and petroleum industries, though the (very few) students who choose a major outside of STEM typically have "limited opportunities for advancement."

For the most part, professors "have industry experience and can teach based on their personal experiences," but everyone agrees that there are "always a few bad apples" in the mix. Luckily, the size of the classrooms is small "so you have more one on one time with your instructor." The curriculum offers "ample opportunities for intellectual growth," focusing on "quantitative learning" in order to send students off with "degrees that actually accomplish things and impact the world." Students are "challenged by professors to work their hardest and to do the best that they can." "It is very easy to stand out in a very good way," says one sophomore. "If you are willing to put in the effort, the professors are more than happy to help you find internships, school jobs, and research opportunities."

The school also has "some of the most cutting edge technology at its disposal." This same equipment "can be accessed by most students no matter major or education level." Workloads "can be grueling," but interestingly (unlike many other engineering schools), the academics are "hardly competitive" as "most students attend MT Tech with the idea that they will be guaranteed a decent paying job as long as they graduate."

Life

The "historically fascinating" mining town town of Butte is "old as dirt and full of rich history," as well as "very community oriented." There are "festivals and community activities often" in the summer months; during the stretched out winter months, "temperatures are often bitter cold, and the sun shines for less than 150 days of the year." Fortunately, there are a host of rampantly popular activities in the surrounding mountains, such as "hunting, skiing, snowboarding, biking, [and] hiking."

During the school year, people generally go to class and do their homework in the evenings and then "blow off steam at bars and/or parties on the weekends." There's also a weekly movie night on campus, and campus entertainment "does its best to bring in musicians, speakers and comedians." Intramural sports are popular, as are student clubs and Frisbee golf, and there is "plenty of bar hopping nearby." Overall, MT Tech is "very calm and a great place to learn."

Student Body

The school is small enough that life borders on "knowing everyone on campus, at least [by] names," buoyed by the fact that many locals attend Montana Tech. The typical student is "a hardworking Montanan who most likely grew up on a farm/ranch and carries that hard work ethic into their studies." As expected, most students are engineers and most students "enjoy outdoor activities, as well as gaming." The gender breakdown is far from equal and not always comfortable for women; there are "a lot of guys at Tech and not so many girls." "A lot of racial diversity, but I feel like a woman in a sea of men," says one female undergraduate. The student body tends to skew a bit older, and there is also a "very large Arabic population" here due to the world-class petroleum engineering department. Despite the "bitterly cold weather" in the long winter, people are "warm and friendly."

FINANCIAL AID: 406-496-4213 • E-MAIL: ENROLLMENT@MTECH.EDU • WEBSITE: WWW.MTECH.EDU

THE PRINCETON REVIEW SAYS

Admissions

Very important factors considered include: Class rank, GPA, standardized test scores. *Other factors considered include:* SAT or ACT required; ACT with Writing component recommended. TOEFL required of all international applicants. *Academic units required:* 4 English; 3 mathematics; 2 science; (2 science lab); 3 social studies; 2 years of either foreign language, computer science, visual/performing arts or vocational education. *Academic units recommended:* 4 mathematics.

Financial Aid

Students should submit: FAFSA. The Princeton Review suggests that all financial aid forms be submitted as soon as possible after January 1. *Need-based scholarships/grants offered:* Federal Pell, SEOG, State scholarships/grants, private scholarships, the school's own gift aid. *Loan aid offered:* Direct Subsidized Stafford Loans, Direct Unsubsidized Stafford Loans, Direct PLUS loans, Federal Perkins Loans, College/university loans from institutional funds. Applicants will be notified of awards beginning 3/15. Federal Work-Study Program available. Institutional employment available. Off-campus job opportunities are good.

The Inside Word

Montana Tech is a godsend for students who are strong academically but not likely to be offered admission to nationally renowned technical institutes. In fact, because of its small size and relatively remote location, Montana Tech is a good choice for anyone leaning toward a technical career. You would be hard-pressed to find many other places as low-key and personal in the realm of academia.

THE SCHOOL SAYS "..."

From the Admissions Office

"Characterize Montana Tech by listening to what employers say. They tell us Tech graduates stand out with an incredible work ethic and top-notch technical skills. Last year, 127 companies held on-campus interviews and attended Montana Tech's career fairs competing for our students and graduates. The beneficiaries: the students! Montana Tech has had a ten-year annual average placement rate of 93 percent including acceptance into professional and graduate programs. Learning takes place in a personalized environment, in first-class academic facilities, and in the heart of the Rocky Mountains. Students at Tech work hard and play hard. Outdoor recreation provides a great balance to the rigors of the course work at Montana Tech. It's not a large, multifaceted university with lots of frills, but our students get a terrific education, and in the end, great jobs! The SAT (or the ACT with the writing section) is recommended for all students applying for admission. Students who do not take the tests with the writing component may be required to take an additional English placement test from the college before they enroll."

SELECTIVITY

Admissions Rating	76
# of applicants	877
% of applicants accepted	88
% of acceptees attending	57

FRESHMAN PROFILE

Range SAT Critical Reading	495–635
Range SAT Math	565–640
Range SAT Writing	465–600
Range ACT Composite	22–26
Minimum paper TOEFL	525
Minimum web-based TOEFL	71
Average HS GPA	3.49
% graduated top 10% of class	26
% graduated top 25% of class	57
% graduated top 50% of class	86

DEADLINES

Regular	
Deadline	No deadline
Notification	Rolling
Nonfall registration?	Yes

APPLICANTS ALSO LOOK AT

AND OFTEN PREFER Montana State University; The University of Montana

AND SOMETIMES PREFER
Colorado School of Mines

FINANCIAL FACTS

Financial Aid Rating	76
Annual in-state tuition	$6,464
Annual out-of-state tuition	$18,606
Room and board	$7,928
Books and supplies	$1,000
% needy frosh rec. need-based scholarship or grant aid	95
% needy UG rec. need-based scholarship or grant aid	88
% needy frosh rec. non-need-based scholarship or grant aid	9
% needy UG rec. non-need-based scholarship or grant aid	5
% needy frosh rec. need-based self-help aid	68
% needy UG rec. need-based self-help aid	81
% frosh rec. any financial aid	78
% UG rec. any financial aid	67
% UG borrow to pay for school	55
Average cumulative indebtedness	$26,115
% frosh need fully met	15
% ugrads need fully met	12
Average % of frosh need met	64
Average % of ugrad need met	62

MORAVIAN COLLEGE

1200 MAIN STREET, BETHLEHEM, PA 18018 • ADMISSIONS: 610-861-1320 • FAX: 610-625-7930

CAMPUS LIFE
Quality of Life Rating	78
Fire Safety Rating	92
Green Rating	84
Type of school	Private
Affiliation	Moravian
Environment	City

STUDENTS
Total undergrad enrollment	1,542
% male/female	41/59
% from out of state	32
% frosh from public high school	81
% frosh live on campus	80
% ugrads live on campus	75
# of fraternities (% ugrad men join)	3 (15)
# of sororities (% ugrad women join)	4 (25)
% African American	4
% Asian	1
% Caucasian	77
% Hispanic	5
% Native American	<1
% international	<1
# of countries represented	11

SURVEY SAYS . . .
Students are happy
Great library
Career services are great

ACADEMICS
Academic Rating	82
% students returning for sophomore year	78
% students graduating within 4 years	70
% students graduating within 6 years	74
Calendar	Semester
Student/faculty ratio	12:1
Profs interesting rating	83
Profs accessible rating	89

Most classes have 10–19 students.
Most lab/discussion sessions have
   10–19 students.

MOST POPULAR MAJORS
psychology; nursing; business administration
and management

STUDENTS SAY ". . ."

Academics

Moravian College "challenges students academically" in a "small environment," where "professors know their students on a personal level." The college is known for its "strong faculty and academic programs," and students say, "Moravian College bends over backward to accommodate its students." Students are exposed to "a good education" through "Learning in Common, which is a set of courses in multidisciplinary categories that interconnect different fields of study." Students boast about "personal attention and genuine enthusiasm from professors," and say, "Moravian College is dedicated to the education of its students as well as building a community between students and faculty." Professors are "accessible, approachable, helpful, and always willing to spend that extra time making sure you understand the material," and students attribute this to "the small student population" and the "mentoring relationship" that develops as a result. A chemistry major says, "The student-professor interactions improve the speed with which students understand course materials." However, a freshman says, "Like any school, there are the great professors and there are the not so great," adding, "You take the bad with the excellent, and it makes you a better student."

Life

Moravian College is known for being a "small school with a friendly atmosphere" that fosters a "supportive environment" for "students to learn and grow." A sophomore says, "I love the atmosphere of the campus," and another student adds, "I love the kindness and genuine concern that people have for others." Students say, "The campus itself is beautiful," and "you always run into someone you know," which creates a "sense of community and pride." A psychology major says, "Even though it's a relatively small school, there are so many things to do," and another student concurs that Moravian is "all about engaging students in real life experiences outside of the classroom using campus speakers, internships, and field study experiences." Students participate in "clubs, organizations, Greek life, and sports teams," and say, "Moravian College provides many opportunities to exceed above and beyond," noting being small allows "opportunities to get involved in different organizations and take leadership roles." Students speak highly of the staff, saying it's "a very personal experience overall" and that the "maintenance of facilities is outstanding." However, some gripe, "Communication between administration and students" could be improved in regards to "decisions [about the] use of funds." There are complaints about the requirement that students live on campus all four years, particularly because many feel "housing could be greatly improved upon."

Student Body

The typical Moravian student is "fun and hardworking," "very laid-back and sociable," and "dedicated to their education during the weekday, but able to relax and have fun on the weekends." A sophomore says, "The greatest quality is the school's diversity and acceptance of all backgrounds, religions, lifestyles," and another student adds, "You not only meet students who are like you, but students who are different in a positive way." However, others feel there's still much to be desired in terms of diversity and say most students are "middle-class [and] white," although they note, "There are [more] students of color, especially in recent years" and say generally "these individuals are not at all excluded from any aspects of campus life." When "the weekend comes, students tend to let loose and enjoy themselves while they spend time with friends," and "much of the campus population attends some sort of party over the weekend." However, because "off campus housing was taken away...it makes it easier for campus safety to bust the parties on campus during the weekends." A music education major says, "There is also a large part of the school that does not party and participates in many school events," and another student adds, "Moravian always has something to do. On weekends they offer alternatives to drinking such as movies and bingo." The small town of Bethlehem also "offers many places to eat, take a stroll, shop, or hang out."

FINANCIAL AID: 610-861-1330 • E-MAIL: ADMISSIONS@MORAVIAN.EDU • WEBSITE: WWW.MORAVIAN.EDU

THE PRINCETON REVIEW SAYS

Admissions

Very important factors considered include: GPA, rigor of secondary school record, alumni/ae relations, character/personal qualities, level of applicant's interest. *Important factors considered include:* Application essay, extracurricular activities, racial/ethnic status, recommendation(s), talent/ability, volunteer work. *Other factors considered include:* Geographical residence, work experience. TOEFL required of all international applicants. *Academic units required:* 4 English; 3 mathematics; 3 science; (2 science lab); 4 social studies. *Academic units recommended:* 4 mathematics.

Financial Aid

Students should submit: FAFSA, Institution's own financial aid form. The Princeton Review suggests that all financial aid forms be submitted as soon as possible after January 1. *Need-based scholarships/grants offered:* Federal Pell, SEOG, State scholarships/grants, private scholarships, the school's own gift aid, United Negro College Fund. *Loan aid offered:* Direct Subsidized Stafford Loans, Direct Unsubsidized Stafford Loans, Direct PLUS loans, Federal Perkins Loans. Federal Work-Study Program available. Off-campus job opportunities are good.

The Inside Word

Admissions officers at Moravian College base admissions decisions primarily on an applicant's secondary school career. Course selection and performance are crucial elements. Recommendations and community activism are also weighed heavily. The admissions staff strongly encourages a campus visit and although interviews aren't required they're recommended.

THE SCHOOL SAYS "..."

From the Admissions Office

"America's sixth-oldest college, Moravian emphasizes the deliberate integration of a broad-based liberal arts curriculum with hands-on learning experiences to effectively prepare its students, not just for jobs, but for successful careers. Moravian College excels at transforming good students into highly competent graduates that are ready to enter the workplace with confidence or shine in graduate school.

Students benefit from Moravian's strong academic majors, opportunities for internships, undergraduate research and scholarship, and programs that foster a deeper enjoyment of life. The 12:1 student-faculty ratio means students get personal attention from a scholarly and dedicated faculty who ensure their success. The proof is in the results, 97% of students who earn a bachelor's degree, do so in four years.

Moravian issues a MacBook Pro laptop and an iPad to all incoming freshmen to enhance learning and help students gain the 21st-century knowledge and skills that will be transferrable over numerous careers. The College offers 50 programs of study; business, education, health professions, social and biological sciences are among the most popular. Moravian's strong athletics, music, and art programs, and more than 80 clubs and organizations offer healthy physical and creative outlets for every student.

Located in historic Bethlehem, Pa., Moravian has long history of educating and developing leaders in many fields. Students leave Moravian College with the skills, knowledge, and support necessary to more deeply enjoy life, work, and their role in the world. More than 90% of its graduates are employed or attending graduate school within ten months of graduation."

SELECTIVITY

Admissions Rating	73
# of applicants	1,636
% of applicants accepted	80
% of acceptees attending	27

FRESHMAN PROFILE

Range SAT Critical Reading	460–580
Range SAT Math	480–590
Range SAT Writing	460–580
Range ACT Composite	20–24
Minimum paper TOEFL	500
Minimum web-based TOEFL	60
Average HS GPA	3.38
% graduated top 10% of class	19
% graduated top 25% of class	48
% graduated top 50% of class	83

DEADLINES

Regular	
Priority	3/1
Deadline	3/1
Nonfall registration?	Yes

APPLICANTS ALSO LOOK AT AND OFTEN PREFER

Bucknell University; Muhlenberg College; Lafayette College

AND SOMETIMES PREFER

Susquehanna University; Ursinus College; Gettysburg College

FINANCIAL FACTS

Financial Aid Rating	78
Annual tuition	$34,938
Room and board	$10,644
Required fees	$580
Books and supplies	$1,000
% needy frosh rec. need-based scholarship or grant aid	100
% needy UG rec. need-based scholarship or grant aid	100
% needy frosh rec. non-need-based scholarship or grant aid	0
% needy UG rec. non-need-based scholarship or grant aid	8
% needy frosh rec. need-based self-help aid	91
% needy UG rec. need-based self-help aid	92
% frosh rec. any financial aid	100
% UG rec. any financial aid	98
% UG borrow to pay for school	81
% frosh need fully met	11
% ugrads need fully met	11
Average % of frosh need met	77
Average % of ugrad need met	74

MOUNT HOLYOKE COLLEGE

NEWHALL CENTER, SOUTH HADLEY, MA 01075 • ADMISSIONS: 413-538-2023 • FAX: 413-538-2409

CAMPUS LIFE

Quality of Life Rating	95
Fire Safety Rating	78
Green Rating	88
Type of school	Private
Affiliation	No Affiliation
Environment	Town

STUDENTS

Total undergrad enrollment	2,154
% male/female	0/100
% from out of state	77
% frosh from public high school	55
% frosh live on campus	100
% ugrads live on campus	95
% African American	6
% Asian	9
% Caucasian	47
% Hispanic	8
% Native American	<1
% international	25
# of countries represented	79

SURVEY SAYS . . .
Political activism is popular
Students are happy
Classroom facilities are great
Lab facilities are great
School is well run
No one cheats
Students are friendly
Dorms are like palaces
Campus feels safe
Athletic facilities are great
Alumni active on campus
Active minority support groups

ACADEMICS

Academic Rating	98
% students returning for sophomore year	89
% students graduating within 4 years	76
% students graduating within 6 years	82
Calendar	Semester
Student/faculty ratio	10:1
Profs interesting rating	97
Profs accessible rating	95

Most classes have 10–19 students.
Most lab/discussion sessions have 10–19 students.

MOST POPULAR MAJORS
psychology; English language and literature; biology

STUDENTS SAY ". . ."

Academics

Situated in breathtaking western Massachusetts, Mount Holyoke is one of the nation's premiere colleges for women. Undergrads here quickly tout the school's ability to both foster an incredibly "collaborative and inclusive atmosphere" and embrace "student uniqueness and diversity." Indeed, from day one of freshman year, undergrads sense that Mount Holyoke "genuinely wants the best for each of its students and is willing to work for that." Undergrads also love that the college is able to pair a "rigorous liberal arts education with...career experience." And many students are quick to take advantage of the college's "great study abroad opportunities" as well. Of course, don't bother attending if you expect to slack off! After all, professors routinely "push students to go further than they expected." And these students wouldn't have it any other way. A satisfied junior expounds, "My educational experience has been characterized by small classes of passionate, intelligent students sharing in informed discussion led by inspiring professors who are leaders in their academic fields. It is this classroom experience that has kept me so invested in and excited about my coursework for the past three years." Truly, Mount Holoyoke is "a place for impassioned women to invest emotionally and intellectually in their education and emerge as capable leaders, activists, and citizens."

Life

Students here are a pretty active lot. As such, they frequently enjoy engaging in "outdoor activities like hiking and apple picking as well as a broad range of athletics." However, if you don't fancy yourself the sporty type, fear not. There "are also many clubs to fit nearly every hobby from singing to community service." Certainly, students can participate in everything "from midnight howling and fandom themed groups to the Roosevelt Institute, NARAL and equestrian clubs." And a number of students are "active in social justice [groups]." It's also quite common for these undergrads to simply sit around and engage in "very intellectual conversations...about politics, subjects in brought up in their classes, or maybe just a lively debate about a book or a movie." On the weekends, many students head "off-campus to nearby college towns such as Northampton and Amherst to socialize because...South Hadley is fairly quiet without many options." Fortunately, "bars, music venues and really good restaurants" are only "a short (free) bus ride away." And, of course, "there's always plenty going on with...the other colleges in the Five College Consortium: from lectures to theatre to concerts to exhibits to parties."

Student Body

Mount Holyoke, as a proud sophomore excitedly shares, "attracts bright, ambitious students from around the world, women who are committed both to their own success and to working for the common good." Indeed, the undergrads here are incredibly impressed with their peers. And it's completely understandable why! As a history major declares, "The typical woman is very confident and very intelligent. She's driven to do well in her courses as well as with extracurriculars. She doesn't take 'no' for an answer and stands up for what she believes in." Students also happily report "the student body is racially and ethnically diverse, internationally representative, inclusive of many sexual orientations and gender identities, and embraces this variety in student organizations and general social life." And Mt. Holyoke undergrads feel very fortunate that this affords them the opportunity to "get to meet people they might never have met otherwise." Most importantly, students here "are very friendly and loving which help creates a close and welcoming community."

FINANCIAL AID: 413-538-2291 • E-MAIL: ADMISSION@MTHOLYOKE.EDU • WEBSITE: WWW.MTHOLYOKE.EDU

THE PRINCETON REVIEW SAYS

Admissions

Very important factors considered include: Class rank, GPA, rigor of secondary school record, application essay, recommendation(s). *Important factors considered include:* Extracurricular activities, interview, talent/ability, volunteer work, work experience, character/personal qualities. *Other factors considered include:* Standardized test scores, first generation, geographical residence, racial/ethnic status, alumni/ae relations, level of applicant's interest. SAT and SAT Subject Tests or ACT considered if submitted; ACT with or without Writing component accepted. TOEFL required of all international applicants. *Academic units recommended:* 4 English; (3 science lab); 3 history; 1 academic elective.

Financial Aid

Students should submit: FAFSA, CSS/Financial Aid PROFILE, Noncustodial PROFILE. Regular filing deadline is 3/1. The Princeton Review suggests that all financial aid forms be submitted as soon as possible after January 1. *Need-based scholarships/grants offered:* Federal Pell, SEOG, State scholarships/grants, private scholarships, the school's own gift aid. *Loan aid offered:* Direct Subsidized Stafford Loans, Direct Unsubsidized Stafford Loans, Direct PLUS loans, Federal Perkins Loans, State Loans, College/university loans from institutional funds. Applicants will be notified of awards beginning 4/1. Federal Work-Study Program available. Institutional employment available. Off-campus job opportunities are fair.

The Inside Word

Competition to gain admission to Mount Holyoke is tight. Therefore, a strong academic record is a must. As such, candidates should have taken a rigorous course-load, complete with honors, AP and/or IB classes. The college also values strong writing skills so expect essays/personal statements to be closely assessed. Moreover, while interviews are not required they are strongly recommended. Therefore, it is an applicant's best interest to schedule one. Conversely, with the exception of home-schooled students, standardized tests are optional.

THE SCHOOL SAYS "..."

From the Admissions Office

"The majority of students who choose Mount Holyoke do so simply because it is an outstanding liberal arts college. After a semester or two, they start to appreciate the distinctive advantages of a women's college, even though most never thought they'd attend a women's college when they started their college search. They appreciate the remarkable array of opportunities that are available—for academic achievement, career exploration, internships, study abroad, and leadership—and the impressive, creative accomplishments of their peers. If you're looking for a college that will challenge you to be your best, most powerful self and to fulfill your potential, Mount Holyoke should be at the top of your list.

"Submission of standardized test scores is optional for most applicants to Mount Holyoke College. However, the TOEFL is required of students for whom English is not their primary language, and the SAT Subject Tests are required for homeschooled students."

SELECTIVITY

Admissions Rating	95
# of applicants	3,732
% of applicants accepted	47
% of acceptees attending	30
# offered a place on the wait list	885
% accepting a place on wait list	50
% admitted from wait list	8
# of early decision applicants	337
% accepted early decision	49

FRESHMAN PROFILE

Range SAT Critical Reading	620–710
Range SAT Math	600–720
Range SAT Writing	620–720
Range ACT Composite	27–31
Average HS GPA	3.66
% graduated top 10% of class	57
% graduated top 25% of class	84
% graduated top 50% of class	97

DEADLINES

Early decision	
Deadline	11/15
Notification	1/1
Regular	
Deadline	1/15
Notification	4/1
Nonfall registration?	Yes

APPLICANTS ALSO LOOK AT AND OFTEN PREFER

Amherst College; Dartmouth College; Swarthmore College; Wellesley College

AND SOMETIMES PREFER

Barnard College; Bates College; Boston University; Bryn Mawr College

AND RARELY PREFER

Bowdoin College; Brown College; Skidmore College

FINANCIAL FACTS

Financial Aid Rating	94
Annual tuition	$42,470
Room and board	$12,490
Required fees	$186
Books and supplies	$950
% needy frosh rec. need-based scholarship or grant aid	99
% needy UG rec. need-based scholarship or grant aid	98
% needy frosh rec. non-need-based scholarship or grant aid	11
% needy UG rec. non-need-based scholarship or grant aid	7
% needy frosh rec. need-based self-help aid	87
% needy UG rec. need-based self-help aid	90
% frosh rec. any financial aid	81
% UG rec. any financial aid	83
% UG borrow to pay for school	69
Average cumulative indebtedness	$23,291
% frosh need fully met	100
% ugrads need fully met	90
Average % of frosh need met	100
Average % of ugrad need met	100

Muhlenberg College

2400 West Chew Street, Allentown, PA 18104-5596 • Admissions: 484-664-3200 • Fax: 484-664-3032

CAMPUS LIFE

Quality of Life Rating	78
Fire Safety Rating	93
Green Rating	84
Type of school	Private
Affiliation	Lutheran
Environment	City

STUDENTS

Total undergrad enrollment	2,357
% male/female	41/59
% from out of state	78
% frosh from public high school	78
% frosh live on campus	99
% ugrads live on campus	92
# of fraternities (% ugrad men join)	4 (1)
# of sororities (% ugrad women join)	5 (2)
% African American	3
% Asian	3
% Caucasian	77
% Hispanic	5
% Native American	<1
% international	1
# of countries represented	14

SURVEY SAYS . . .

Lab facilities are great
Students are friendly
Athletic facilities are great
Theater is popular

ACADEMICS

Academic Rating	89
% students returning for sophomore year	91
% students graduating within 4 years	81
% students graduating within 6 years	86
Calendar	Semester
Student/faculty ratio	11:1
Profs interesting rating	85
Profs accessible rating	85

Most classes have 10–19 students.
Most lab/discussion sessions have 10–19 students.

MOST POPULAR MAJORS
business/commerce; psychology; theatre arts

STUDENTS SAY ". . ."

Academics

Muhlenberg College, a small "caring college" located in Allentown, Pennsylvania, is "all about a sense of community," both within the school's borders and outside of them. Add to that a rigorous academic curriculum (with a particularly good theater department) and an "extremely high" overall involvement of both the professors and students in both academic and extracurricular pursuits, and you've got a community of students, faculty, and staff committed to "delivering and receiving a quality, liberal arts education that will craft the next generation into responsible, intelligent leaders of this quickly changing world." "The brochures are not a joke; the people here really are friendly and open," says a student. Students are incredibly thankful for the school's balance of resources throughout all of the majors. "I wanted a liberal arts experience, and I appreciate how much focus Muhlenberg puts on both the arts and the sciences," says a student. The "very responsive" professors are "engaging and accommodating to students' needs," which helps to "[develop] relationships that will help you grow through your educational journey and eventually into the work force." Almost all are "easily approachable" and open to direct arguments against the topics and theories discussed in class, which "provides for an engaging classroom environment that lets students push past the direct facts of the material and learn more about what the material means for the world." The college is "very flexible" and allows students to create their own majors to reflect their interests; established majors on campus are always changing to reflect progress in the field. Students agree that the school "definitely offers a rich amount of courses that will prepare you for your future and open your mind to possibilities," and it has "many resources to help you with a variety of situations that may arise."

Life

This "friendly, tight-knit community" is "about being able to be unique yet finding a common ground with others." There are "a fair amount of clubs" on campus, and "the school works hard to make sure that there are always fun events going on so students have fun activity options." A cappella groups are popular and can be seen performing at an event almost every weekend. Come Thursday it's the weekend, as "most students don't have class Fridays." For some, this means "tame parties," as "things don't change all that often unfortunately, and you may wind up going to the same three parties each weekend." However, "there is no pressure to drink. If someone does not drink, they do not have to worry about being judged." When the weather is nice, everyone is outside, whether "playing pickup Frisbee, lacrosse, football, or just relaxing on a blanket in the sun." Generally, "people don't have an awful lot of free time between class, studying, and clubs." For those who want to get off campus, shuttles run on the weekends to the movie theater, the Lehigh Valley Mall, Target, and other local places of interest.

Student Body

The typical Muhlenberg student is "from a middle- to upper-middle-class family on the East Coast" and "driven but not type-A," with a large percentage hailing from New Jersey. There are also sizable Jewish, premed, and theater contingents. Many students "have one weird quirky talent that everyone mocked them for in high school, but here, there's a club for that." Every student here "cares about the whole community, even members of it they have not met," most "would give away a swipe meal into the dining area to a total stranger." Students come from diverse backgrounds, although not from diverse ethnic/race backgrounds ("While ethnic diversity is pretty low, our social diversity is high."), which means that "students fit in very well with all types of groups since our school is so accepting."

392 ■ THE BEST 379 COLLEGES

FINANCIAL AID: 484-664-3175 • E-MAIL: ADMISSION@MUHLENBERG.EDU • WEBSITE: WWW.MUHLENBERG.EDU

THE PRINCETON REVIEW SAYS

Admissions

Very important factors considered include: GPA, rigor of secondary school record, character/personal qualities. *Important factors considered include:* Class rank, standardized test scores, application essay, extracurricular activities, interview, recommendation(s), talent/ability, volunteer work, work experience. *Other factors considered include:* First generation, racial/ethnic status, alumni/ae relations, level of applicant's interest. SAT or ACT required for some; ACT with Writing component required. TOEFL required of all international applicants. *Academic units required:* 4 English; 3 mathematics; 2 science; (2 science lab); 2 foreign language; 2 history; 1 academic elective. *Academic units recommended:* 4 English; 4 mathematics; 3 science; (3 science lab); 2 social studies; 4 foreign language; 2 history; 1 academic elective.

Financial Aid

Students should submit: FAFSA, Institution's own financial aid form, CSS/Financial Aid PROFILE, Noncustodial PROFILE, Business/Farm Supplement. Regular filing deadline is 2/15. The Princeton Review suggests that all financial aid forms be submitted as soon as possible after January 1. *Need-based scholarships/grants offered:* Federal Pell, SEOG, State scholarships/grants, private scholarships, the school's own gift aid, United Negro College Fund. *Loan aid offered:* Direct Subsidized Stafford Loans, Direct Unsubsidized Stafford Loans, Direct PLUS loans, Federal Perkins Loans. Applicants will be notified of awards beginning 4/1. Federal Work-Study Program available. Institutional employment available. Off-campus job opportunities are excellent.

The Inside Word

Muhlenberg College accepts only the Common Application and doesn't require any supplemental essays, unless you're applying early decision. Your high school GPA and course selection are of primary importance. Muhlenberg is also part of a growing group of colleges that don't require SAT scores or other standardized tests for admission. Students who don't submit test scores are required to appear for an admissions interview and to submit an SAT-optional statement.

THE SCHOOL SAYS "..."

From the Admissions Office

"Listening to our own students, we've learned that most picked Muhlenberg mainly because it has a long-standing reputation for being academically demanding on one hand but personally supportive on the other. We expect a lot from our students, but we also expect a lot from ourselves in providing the challenge and support they need to stretch, grow, and succeed. It's not unusual for professors to put their home phone numbers on the course syllabus and encourage students to call them at home with questions. Upperclassmen are helpful to underclassmen. 'We really know about collegiality here,' says an alumna who now works at Muhlenberg. 'It's that kind of place.' The supportive atmosphere and strong work ethic produce lots of successes. The premed and pre-law programs are very strong, as are programs in theater arts, English, psychology, the sciences, business, and accounting. 'When I was a student here,' recalls Dr. Walter Loy, now a professor emeritus of physics, 'we were encouraged to live life to its fullest, to do our best, to be honest, to deal openly with others, and to treat everyone as an individual. Those are important things, and they haven't changed at Muhlenberg.'

"Students have the option of submitting SAT or ACT scores (including the writing sections) or submitting a graded paper with teacher's comments and grade on it from junior or senior year and interviewing with a member of the admissions staff."

SELECTIVITY

Admissions Rating	93
# of applicants	5,152
% of applicants accepted	46
% of acceptees attending	24
# offered a place on the wait list	1,782
% accepting a place on wait list	22
% admitted from wait list	13
# of early decision applicants	381
% accepted early decision	82

FRESHMAN PROFILE

Range SAT Critical Reading	570–670
Range SAT Math	570–670
Range SAT Writing	570–670
Range ACT Composite	25–30
Minimum paper TOEFL	550
Minimum web-based TOEFL	213
Average HS GPA	3.33
% graduated top 10% of class	45
% graduated top 25% of class	73
% graduated top 50% of class	92

DEADLINES

Early decision	
Deadline	2/15
Regular	
Priority	2/15
Deadline	2/15
Notification	3/15
Nonfall registration?	Yes

APPLICANTS ALSO LOOK AT AND OFTEN PREFER
Bucknell University; Villanova University

AND SOMETIMES PREFER
Dickinson College; Franklin & Marshall College; Gettysburg College

AND RARELY PREFER
Susquehanna University; Pennsylvania State University—University Park

FINANCIAL FACTS

Financial Aid Rating	93
Annual tuition	$42,470
Required fees	$285
Books and supplies	$1,295
% needy frosh rec. need-based scholarship or grant aid	97
% needy UG rec. need-based scholarship or grant aid	94
% needy frosh rec. non-need-based scholarship or grant aid	23
% needy UG rec. non-need-based scholarship or grant aid	17
% needy frosh rec. need-based self-help aid	68
% needy UG rec. need-based self-help aid	72
% frosh rec. any financial aid	88
% UG rec. any financial aid	85
% UG borrow to pay for school	55
Average cumulative indebtedness	$30,363
% frosh need fully met	85
% ugrads need fully met	90
Average % of frosh need met	91
Average % of ugrad need met	91

NATIONAL UNIVERSITY OF IRELAND MAYNOOTH

INTERNATIONAL OFFICE, MAYNOOTH, CO. KILDARE, IRELAND • ADMISSIONS: +353-1-7083868 • FAX: +353-1-7086113

CAMPUS LIFE

Quality of Life Rating	92
Fire Safety Rating	84
Green Rating	75
Type of school	Public
Affiliation	No Affiliation
Environment	Village

STUDENTS

Total undergrad enrollment	6,900
% frosh live on campus	40
% ugrads live on campus	8
# of countries represented	90

SURVEY SAYS . . .

Political activism is unpopular or nonexistent
Students never
Students are happy
Lab facilities are great
School is well run
Students are friendly
Lots of beer drinking

ACADEMICS

Academic Rating	70
% students returning for sophomore year	95
Calendar	Semester
Student/faculty ratio	12:1
Profs interesting rating	81
Profs accessible rating	75

STUDENTS SAY ". . ."

Academics

In emerald Ireland, just outside of Dublin, there lies the country's second-oldest and fastest growing university, the National University of Ireland Maynooth. The school's town location and its relatively small size give off a "community atmosphere," and "modern and up-to-date" facilities and a "beautiful campus" make it "a nice environment to study in" with a "great history" to back it up. "The academic standard at Maynooth is impeccable, with lecturers, lecture halls, tutors, and labs of the finest stature," says a science major. There's a wide selection of classes available at Maynooth, and course content "is generally well-explained, with tutorials and support centers available." Professors "are without exception experts in their field" and "continually encouraging us to engage in discussions, to ask questions, and to develop not only a well-informed but independent way of thinking." "Almost all my lecturers are great orators that bring their subjects to life, creating a genuine interest among their students," says a Spanish major. Add to that the fact that they're "very, very, very approachable outside of class" ("There is always someone that you can approach for help and guidance"), and students are happy to receive "the best learning experience possible." Administration is responsive to student concerns, and there's a "friendliness of everyone on campus, from the president right down to the cleaners." The services the school provides are all "brilliant," from the library to the residence services. People also all love the "great" online class system, Moodle, which allows you to upload assignments and download class notes. "You are given every little or big piece of help you require or request to ensure you can achieve your highest grades," says a student. "In my six months here, I have yet to hear a disgruntled word aimed at the campus or the staff."

Life

Maynooth is a "very vibrant town" that "has all facilities needed by third-level students (including clubs, pubs, and pizzerias)." The student body "isn't too big," and the majority "keep on top of college work, participate in a club or society or two, and enjoy a night in the pub with their friends." There's a "vast amount" of clubs and societies, which means "there's always somewhere for you to go, whether it's the Play-Doh society or the Harry Potter appreciation society—we got it all!" The student union also "hosts concerts and social events regularly," and everyone enjoys the "good mood" of their compatriots. "For fun, the nightlife is key," and "every Wednesday and Thursday [are] party nights," when people go to the nightclubs or bars, play card games, drink beers, and "hang out with…mates." The school consists of two connected campuses, which "combine the old with the new." "South campus covered in snow is like a scene from Hogwarts in Harry Potter, [and] then "the north campus is modern." For those who live on campus, "everything is just at your fingertips," including a free gym. Though there are "few facilities in the university for simply sitting and studying," there are plenty of computers for students, and a new cafeteria is under construction.

Student Body

Look around Maynooth, and for the most part you'll just see a whole bunch of "your normal average twenty-year-old Irish girl [or] boy," though there's "a great mix of both city students and those from a rural background," as well as international, traditional, and "mature" students. "Individuality is very much encouraged" here, and in the midst of this "bubbly," "friendly" group is "a good place to make new friends." "Being Irish, we all like to have the 'craic' with people, meaning have fun," says a student. This group is also very "trustworthy," and "you can leave your laptop in the library for hours, and no one would ever take it."

NATIONAL UNIVERSITY OF IRELAND MAYNOOTH

E-MAIL: INTERNATIONAL.APPLICATIONS@NUIM.IE • WEBSITE: WWW.NUIM.IE / INTERNATIONAL

THE PRINCETON REVIEW SAYS

Admissions

Very important factors considered include: GPA, rigor of secondary school record, standardized test scores. *Other factors considered include:* Class rank, application essay, recommendation(s), talent/ability, volunteer work, work experience, character/personal qualities, level of applicant's interest, TOEFL required of all international applicants. *Academic units required:* 4 English; 4 mathematics. *Academic units recommended:* 4 English; 4 mathematics; 4 science; 4 social studies; 4 foreign language; 4 history; 4 computer science.

Financial Aid

Students should submit: FAFSA. Regular filing deadline is 6/1. The Princeton Review suggests that all financial aid forms be submitted as soon as possible after January 1. *Loan aid offered:* Direct Subsidized Stafford Loans, Direct Unsubsidized Stafford Loans, Direct PLUS loans.

THE SCHOOL SAYS "..."

From the Admissions Office

"National University of Ireland Maynooth is pleased to be one of the few international universities to be included in The Princeton Review Best Colleges series. You do not require a visa to study in Ireland if you are a U.S. citizen, and the fees for National University of Ireland Maynooth are comparable to most in-state tuition fees in the United States. So, for the price of your flights, you could get an international university experience for nearly the same price as staying at home!

"Degrees awarded by Irish Universities are internationally recognized as being of high quality Irish universities do not have a general education requirement, which means that students begin studying their chosen major immediately. Due to this, degrees in the Arts and Humanities will be completed in three years, while Science and Engineering degrees will be completed in four years. Students registered on undergraduate degrees at NUIM can also apply to study abroad in their third year, in Europe, Asia, South America, or Australia. This extends your degree by one year, and you will earn a Bachelor (International) degree.

"The International Office offers full support to all international students during the application process and once you arrive on campus. National University of Ireland Maynooth is very popular with U.S. students studying in Ireland and the campus is known as one of the friendliest in Ireland, so you will receive a warm welcome. If you have questions about studying at NUIM, contact the International Office at any time."

SELECTIVITY

Admissions Rating	61

FRESHMAN PROFILE

Minimum paper TOEFL	550
Average HS GPA	3.40

DEADLINES

Regular	
Deadline	7/1
Nonfall registration?	No

FINANCIAL FACTS

Financial Aid Rating	65
Annual in-state tuition	$16,562-$20,703
Books and supplies	$83

* Fees and room rates are guidelines. Dollar amounts are subject to currency exchange rate fluctuation. To obtain an accurate quote for specific course fees, visit http://fees.nuim.ie/documents/INTERNATIONALFEES2013_14.pdf

NAZARETH COLLEGE

4245 EAST AVENUE, ROCHESTER, NY 14618-3790 • ADMISSIONS: 585-389-2860 • FAX: 585-389-2826

CAMPUS LIFE

Quality of Life Rating	91
Fire Safety Rating	62 Green Rating 60*
Type of school	Private
Affiliation	No Affiliation
Environment	Village

STUDENTS

Total undergrad enrollment	2,034
% male/female	27/73
% from out of state	7
% frosh from public high school	88
% frosh live on campus	92
% ugrads live on campus	53
% African American	5
% Asian	3
% Caucasian	72
% Hispanic	4
% Native American	<1
% international	2
# of countries represented	22

SURVEY SAYS . . .

Political activism is unpopular or nonexistent
Students are friendly
Students get along with local community
Great off-campus food

ACADEMICS

Academic Rating	85
% students returning for sophomore year	79
% students graduating within 4 years	61
% students graduating within 6 years	73
Calendar	Semester
Student/faculty ratio	10:1
Profs interesting rating	87
Profs accessible rating	81

Most classes have 10–19 students.
Most lab/discussion sessions have 10–19 students.

MOST POPULAR MAJORS

health science, nursing, communication sciences and disorders

STUDENTS SAY ". . ."

Academics

Nazareth is a small private college with a range of professional undergraduate majors not usually offered by liberal arts schools—many students note that the physical therapy program was what drew them to the college. The music education and health sciences majors receive particularly high praise, with some students calling out art, history, and psychology as well. The small class sizes—cited by many students as one of the best things about Nazareth—allow for "very close relationships with our professors" and "most professors try to make class as interactive as possible," though "of course like [at] any other school you may end up with a sub par teacher." The vast majority "take an interest in getting to know their students and are very open to helping students outside of the classroom," and "most are very easy to communicate and collaborate with, especially if [a student is] interested in research." Particularly in upper-level courses, "professors have the students' best interests in mind and always teach their classes with passion." Classes are mixed between lectures and discussions, depending on course of study, and students are strongly encouraged to pursue internships during their undergraduate studies.

Life

Nazareth offers a host of activities on campus, but students enjoy the surrounding city of Rochester as well. On weekends, many off campus head to bars and "amazing restaurants" (a good thing, since the majority of students report that they'd love to see dining hall food improve). The school also arranges for discounted tickets and transportation to concerts and sporting events. On campus, there are "mixers" (dances), Hunger Games theme nights, laser tag, bingo, and comedians. Many clubs are service-oriented, and working out is popular. Students report that the school's policies around alcohol and parties are strict and free "on-campus activities…cater to students who prefer alcohol and drug-free activities," but that plenty of parties occur off-campus for those interested. Nazareth's location makes it the rare school that keeps both residential and commuter students happy, with positive town-gown relations. Students also enjoy school-subsidized "inexpensive trips to…New York City or Montreal for the weekend."

Student Body

Nazareth has a low male-to-female ratio, and the typical student is "an upper middle class white girl," but "there are also many international students and students from the inner city. There are cliques, but most people get along from all walks of life." "They value education but also make time for social activities." While many students are from New York, there is a visible international community on campus. Male students are generally described as either athletes or theater majors. Most students are involved in "at least one club, sport, job, or activity," and anecdotally, "student athletes are almost a quarter of the student body…Every student finds their own little niche though," because "there's something for everyone here." "Students are often close with those in their major and/or those they work with." The vast majority are "friendly and easy-going," and students are very clear that "the more you get involved the better your college experience will be."

FINANCIAL AID: 585-389-2310 • E-MAIL: ADMISSIONS@NAZ.EDU • WEBSITE: WWW.NAZ.EDU

THE PRINCETON REVIEW SAYS

Admissions

Very important factors considered include: Class rank, GPA, rigor of secondary school record, application essay, recommendation(s). *Important factors considered include:* Extracurricular activities, geographical residence, interview, racial/ethnic status, state residency, talent/ability, volunteer work, work experience, character/personal qualities, level of applicant's interest. *Other factors considered include:* Standardized test scores, first generation, alumni/ae relations. SAT and SAT Subject Tests or ACT considered if submitted; ACT with or without Writing component accepted. TOEFL required of all international applicants. *Academic units required:* 4 English; 3 mathematics; 3 science; (2 science lab); 3 social studies; 3 foreign language. *Academic units recommended:* 4 English; 4 mathematics; 4 science; 4 social studies; 4 foreign language.

Financial Aid

Students should submit: FAFSA, State aid form. The Princeton Review suggests that all financial aid forms be submitted as soon as possible after January 1. *Need-based scholarships/grants offered:* Federal Pell, SEOG, State scholarships/grants, private scholarships, the school's own gift aid. *Loan aid offered:* Direct Subsidized Stafford Loans, Direct Unsubsidized Stafford Loans, Direct PLUS loans, Federal Perkins Loans, Federal Nursing Loans. Federal Work-Study Program available. Institutional employment available. Off-campus job opportunities are excellent.

The Inside Word

Nazareth has a fairly high acceptance rate, meaning solid students with good test scores shouldn't sweat over getting accepted here. Admissions officers review each applicant's Common Application, high school transcript, recommendations, and essay; SAT scores are optional. Art, music, and theatre programs require additional application materials.

THE SCHOOL SAYS "..."

From the Admissions Office

"Preparing students for a world of rapid change, and for careers yet to be defined, is the focus at Nazareth. College graduates must have relevant knowledge, exceptional critical thinking skills, a global mindset, and work experience. These four foundations of a Nazareth education prepare you for the future. Our unusually broad array of high-caliber academics for a small college includes more than 60 majors, such as education; math and sciences; business and management; visual arts, music, theatre, foreign languages, and other humanities; and a diverse mix of health programs. Expect small classes, personal attention, friendliness, and our nationally recognized community service work. Our uncommon core curriculum is student-focused and integrated with your career goals. We promote global dexterity through coursework, foreign-language houses, events, a diverse campus community, and dozens of opportunities to travel, study, intern, and experience life overseas. Our College stands out for its Fulbright scholars, selected to teach around the world, and for its commitment to developing student leaders through the 2014 Clinton Global Initiative University. Nazareth is coeducational and independent, located on 150 beautifully landscaped acres in a suburb of Rochester, which is New York's third-largest city and rich in culture and entertainment. New facilities include Peckham Hall math/science building with state-of-the-art labs and, opening in 2015, a Wellness and Rehabilitation Institute with extensive clinic and collaboration spaces. Students attend free theatre, music, dance, and international performances at the Nazareth College Arts Center. Our athletes boast one of the highest graduation rates in NCAA Division III."

SELECTIVITY

Admissions Rating	83
# of applicants	3,838
% of applicants accepted	68
% of acceptees attending	16
# offered a place on the wait list	58
% accepting a place on wait list	16
% admitted from wait list	67
# of early decision applicants	72
% accepted early decision	82

FRESHMAN PROFILE

Range SAT Critical Reading	500–570
Range SAT Math	520–610
Range SAT Writing	490–600
Range ACT Composite	23–27
Average HS GPA	89.38
% graduated top 10% of class	30
% graduated top 25% of class	65
% graduated top 50% of class	91

DEADLINES

Early decision	
Deadline	11/15
Notification	12/15
Early decision II	
Deadline	1/15
Notification	2/1
Regular	
Deadline	2/1
Notification	3/1
Nonfall registration?	Yes

FINANCIAL FACTS

Financial Aid Rating	74
Annual tuition	$28,090
Room and board	$12,166
Required fees	$1,278
Books and supplies	$1,100
% needy frosh rec. need-based scholarship or grant aid	100
% needy UG rec. need-based scholarship or grant aid	100
% needy frosh rec. non-need-based scholarship or grant aid	40
% needy UG rec. non-need-based scholarship or grant aid	32
% needy frosh rec. need-based self-help aid	94
% needy UG rec. need-based self-help aid	93
% UG borrow to pay for school	94
Average cumulative indebtedness	$28,938
% frosh need fully met	32
% ugrads need fully met	26
Average % of frosh need met	83
Average % of ugrad need met	79

NEW COLLEGE OF FLORIDA

5800 BAY SHORE ROAD, SARASOTA, FL 34243-2109 • ADMISSIONS: 941-487-5000 • FAX: 941-487-5001

CAMPUS LIFE

Quality of Life Rating	85
Fire Safety Rating	82
Green Rating	72
Type of school	Public
Affiliation	No Affiliation
Environment	Town

STUDENTS

Total undergrad enrollment	793
% male/female	43/57
% from out of state	18
% frosh from public high school	81
% frosh live on campus	99
% ugrads live on campus	80
% African American	3
% Asian	3
% Caucasian	74
% Hispanic	14
% Native American	<1
% international	1
# of countries represented	15

SURVEY SAYS . . .

Lots of liberal students
Political activism is popular
Students are happy
Class discussions encouraged
No one cheats
Students are friendly
Students environmentally aware
Campus feels safe
Easy to get around campus
Lots of beer drinking
Alumni active on campus
Active student government

ACADEMICS

Academic Rating	97
% students returning for sophomore year	81
% students graduating within 4 years	57
% students graduating within 6 years	66
Calendar	4/1/4
Student/faculty ratio	10:1
Profs interesting rating	97
Profs accessible rating	91

Most classes have 10–19 students.

MOST POPULAR MAJORS

biology; psychology; anthropology

STUDENTS SAY ". . ."

Academics

New College of Florida, a uniquely small and unconventional public institution, "provides challenging courses for highly self-motivated students who want a large amount of control over their academic choices." It's all about "self-directed learning" here (working closely with faculty advisers, "the student decides what he or she is going to learn and how she is going to learn it") that leaves undergrads "free to do what they please—with their bodies, their studies, their behavior—but while also being held to high academic standards." Those who can balance the intellectual freedom NCF offers with the academic accountability it demands, wind up with "a rounded education that enables them to critically and pragmatically examine and understand the world in which we live…and weird parties." The academics "are undeniably awesome" at NCF, while the small-school setting and the student body "encourage a love of learning, whether it be academic, political, or hobby-related." It's the sort of school where "it is very popular for groups of students to get together to talk about class readings outside of the classroom, usually at the college coffee shop, as a means of socializing." NCF undergrads receive "narrative evaluations instead of grades. These evaluations give advice and help us to become better students." Many here "love having written evaluations in which our process and progress are documented, not only the final outcome. The evaluations force students to fully participate and the professors to pay close attention." All students must write a senior thesis to graduate; reports one undergrad, "recently we had a survey…on which one of the sections dealt with the possibility of making the senior thesis optional. There was an overwhelming response that this was unacceptable. I think that says a lot about how proud we are of our academic standards."

Life

Having fun "in a glorified retirement community requires ingenuity of the New College student population," but "thankfully, most grew up in suburban Florida" and so are used to a slower pace. It helps that the campus is near Lido and Siesta Beaches, "where [students] enjoy unlimited swimming, sunning, and Frisbee playing," and that "downtown Sarasota isn't that bad either," since it's home to a number of "ethnic eateries. Thai food, in particular, seems to have a cult following on campus—with constant debate as to which restaurant is the best or most authentic and student events that advertise Thai food are bound to pull in dozens of followers." On campus, students enjoy everything "from club meetings to public speakers to 'hip' bands playing shows. There's usually something to do and usually free food to be found!" There are also "school-wide parties every Friday and Saturday night in a courtyard outside of the dorms. Different students get to decide the theme of each dance party and the music to be played. Most on-campus students never leave campus during the weekend because of these dance parties."

Student Body

New College students share "a few things in common: Most…are friendly, passionate about the things they believe in, very hard workers, liberal, and most of all, try to be open to new experiences." The students are "largely middle-class, white, and liberal. There are of course exceptions, but the school is rather small,'" there is "a fairly strong queer community here, and many transgendered people who have decided to make New College their coming-out grounds. The student body is generally aware of gender issues and respectful of queer people of all types." There are even "some Republicans on campus. Maybe four. I'm not sure. We're not the type of school that generally attracts heavy right-wingers."

FINANCIAL AID: 941-487-5000 • E-MAIL: ADMISSIONS@NCF.EDU • WEBSITE: WWW.NCF.EDU

THE PRINCETON REVIEW SAYS

Admissions

Very important factors considered include: GPA, rigor of secondary school record, application essay. *Important factors considered include:* Standardized test scores, recommendation(s), character/personal qualities. *Other factors considered include:* Class rank, extracurricular activities, first generation, geographical residence, interview, state residency, talent/ability, volunteer work, work experience, alumni/ae relations, level of applicant's interest. SAT or ACT required; SAT and SAT Subject Tests or ACT considered if submitted; ACT with Writing component required. TOEFL required of all international applicants. *Academic units required:* 4 English; 4 mathematics; 3 science; (2 science lab); 3 social studies; 2 foreign language; 2 academic electives. *Academic units recommended:* 4 English; 4 mathematics; 4 science; (2 science lab); 4 social studies; 4 foreign language; 4 academic electives.

Financial Aid

Students should submit: FAFSA. The Princeton Review suggests that all financial aid forms be submitted as soon as possible after January 1. *Need-based scholarships/grants offered:* Federal Pell, SEOG, State scholarships/grants, private scholarships, the school's own gift aid. *Loan aid offered:* Direct Subsidized Stafford Loans, Direct Unsubsidized Stafford Loans, Direct PLUS loans. Federal Work-Study Program available. Institutional employment available. Off-campus job opportunities are good.

The Inside Word

New College isn't your typical public school. The tiny student body allows admissions officers here to review each application carefully; expect a thorough going over of your essays, recommendations, and extracurricular activities. Iconoclastic students tend to thrive here, and the admissions staff knows that. Don't be afraid to let your freak flag fly; it won't get you in here if your academics aren't top flight, but it certainly won't hurt you either.

THE SCHOOL SAYS "..."

From the Admissions Office

"Inspired individualism, with a dash of quirkiness, best describes New College of Florida and its students. At New College, you participate directly in your education by collaborating with faculty to develop an individualized program of classes, seminars, independent research projects and off-campus experiences designed to meet your personal academic interests and needs. As a result, you receive the same high-quality, personalized education as a top-tier private college at the affordable cost of a public institution. New College boasts independent, open-minded students, who welcome the challenge of a rigorous academic program in a relaxed social environment. Students applying must submit scores from the SAT (or ACT) including the writing section. The best score from either test will be used for consideration."

SELECTIVITY
Admissions Rating	92
# of applicants	1,376
% of applicants accepted	61
% of acceptees attending	27
# offered a place on the wait list	111
% accepting a place on wait list	46
% admitted from wait list	18

FRESHMAN PROFILE
Range SAT Critical Reading	620–720
Range SAT Math	570–660
Range SAT Writing	590–680
Range ACT Composite	27–30
Minimum paper TOEFL	560
Minimum web-based TOEFL	220
Average HS GPA	3.92
% graduated top 10% of class	41
% graduated top 25% of class	75
% graduated top 50% of class	94

DEADLINES
Regular	
Priority	11/1
Deadline	4/15
Nonfall registration?	Yes

APPLICANTS ALSO LOOK AT AND OFTEN PREFER
University of Florida; Florida State University; University of Central Florida; University of Miami; University of South Florida; Florida Atlantic University

AND SOMETIMES PREFER
Oberlin College; Pitzer College; Reed College; The University of North Carolina at Chapel Hill; New York University; American University; Eckerd College; Rollins College

FINANCIAL FACTS
Financial Aid Rating	88
Annual in-state tuition	$5,227
Annual out-of-state tuition	$28,255
Room and board	$8,856
Required fees	$1,645
Books and supplies	$1,200
% needy frosh rec. need-based scholarship or grant aid	100
% needy UG rec. need-based scholarship or grant aid	98
% needy frosh rec. non-need-based scholarship or grant aid	23
% needy UG rec. non-need-based scholarship or grant aid	17
% needy frosh rec. need-based self-help aid	77
% needy UG rec. need-based self-help aid	78
% frosh rec. any financial aid	100
% UG rec. any financial aid	97
% UG borrow to pay for school	39
Average cumulative indebtedness	$17,927
% frosh need fully met	46
% ugrads need fully met	37
Average % of frosh need met	90
Average % of ugrad need met	87

NEW JERSEY INSTITUTE OF TECHNOLOGY

OFFICE OF UNIVERSITY ADMISSIONS, NEWARK, NJ 07102 • ADMISSIONS: 973-596-3300 • FAX: 973-596-3461

CAMPUS LIFE

Quality of Life Rating	69
Fire Safety Rating	99
Green Rating	73
Type of school	Public
Affiliation	No Affiliation
Environment	Metropolis

STUDENTS

Total undergrad enrollment	7,286
% male/female	76/24
% from out of state	5
% frosh from public high school	85
% frosh live on campus	47
% ugrads live on campus	23
# of fraternities (% ugrad men join)	19 (8)
# of sororities (% ugrad women join)	4 (5)
% African American	9
% Asian	20
% Caucasian	33
% Hispanic	20
% Native American	<1
% international	5
# of countries represented	100

SURVEY SAYS . . .

Class discussions are rare
Very little drug use
Different types of students interact

ACADEMICS

Academic Rating	71
% students returning for sophomore year	86
% students graduating within 4 years	23
% students graduating within 6 years	58
Calendar	Semester
Student/faculty ratio	17:1
Profs interesting rating	65
Profs accessible rating	66
Most classes have 20–29 students.	

MOST POPULAR MAJORS

mechanical engineering; civil engineering;
architecture

STUDENTS SAY ". . ."

Academics

NJIT is certainly a crown jewel within New Jersey's public university system. Indeed, armed with a great reputation, NJIT offers undergrads "quality academic programs" at an "affordable" price. Students here truly appreciate that they are surrounded by a "challenging, intellectual environment" that provides "plenty of advancement for high-achieving students." Fully embracing its name, NJIT is definitely a "technology-centered school," and students are quick to praise the strong engineering, math, and architecture programs. Undergrads do warn, "You must be dedicated and serious about learning, because a lot of the courses here are demanding." Moreover, students here are decidedly mixed when it comes to opinions about their professors. Some undergrads complain, "Classes are very monotonous, as they are straight lectures [with] professors adhering very strongly to the textbook." However, other students counter, "The professors hold their degrees because of their knowledge of the subject, not because of their teaching skills. Most of the learning comes from your own hard work, and the professors can be a great resource." Many also appreciate that they are able to "bring real-world experience to class projects." Further, a handful of undergrads assert, "Most professors are always willing to make time outside of classroom to talk or to explain things further"—and that's certainly the hallmark of teachers who "are very helpful and want their students to succeed."

Life

Undergrads at NJIT spend a good deal of their time hitting the books. As one student reveals (perhaps facetiously), "Fun on campus usually consists of group projects, homework, lab reports, and studying." A fellow undergrad concurs simply stating, "Most people, including myself, eat, breathe, and live for their classes because of the time commitment to the material." Of course, even these conscientious students need to kick back every now and again. Unfortunately, some undergrads grumble about the lack of options on campus: "Social events are actually nonexistent." However, another group of students assure us, "There is always some sort of activity going on every day. [For example] we have countless comedy nights and cultural nights." Additionally, while some question the safety of the surrounding area, others extol the virtues of NJIT's location. As one content student shares, "The food in the Ironbound district of Newark is fantastic. Anyone who is anyone goes there either for the food or the lounges." Moreover, "there are many bars close to the school, so they are generally a secondary option for most [students]." And, of course, NJIT undergrads love to take advantage of the school's proximity to New York City "which is only [a fifteen-minute] Path ride away!"

Student Body

Undergrads at NJIT proudly self-identify as "nerds" and assert that the main attribute unifying the student body is "a determination to learn." Perhaps even more important, undergrads are quick to call their peers "friendly" and suggest "students interact easily due to the closeness of majors and interests." For example, "video games are a popular bonding activity here." Of course, regardless of whether you are into tennis or Magic the Gathering, you can rest assured that "it's not hard to fit in." Indeed, as one pleased undergrad happily reveals, "You will find any type and every type of student here on this campus. Diversity is our forte."

FINANCIAL AID: 973-596-3479 • E-MAIL: ADMISSIONS@NJIT.EDU • WEBSITE: WWW.NJIT.EDU

THE PRINCETON REVIEW SAYS

Admissions

Very important factors considered include: Class rank, rigor of secondary school record, standardized test scores. *Important factors considered include:* GPA. *Other factors considered include:* Application essay, extracurricular activities, geographical residence, interview, racial/ethnic status, recommendation(s), state residency, talent/ability, volunteer work, work experience, alumni/ae relations, character/personal qualities, level of applicant's interest, religious affiliation. SAT or ACT required. TOEFL required of all international applicants. *Academic units required:* 4 English; 4 mathematics; 2 science; (2 science lab). *Academic units recommended:* 1 social studies; 2 foreign language; 1 history; 2 academic electives.

Financial Aid

Students should submit: FAFSA. The Princeton Review suggests that all financial aid forms be submitted as soon as possible after January 1. *Need-based scholarships/grants offered:* Federal Pell, SEOG, State scholarships/grants, private scholarships, the school's own gift aid, United Negro College Fund. *Loan aid offered:* Direct Subsidized Stafford Loans, Direct Unsubsidized Stafford Loans, Direct PLUS loans, Federal Perkins Loans, Federal Nursing Loans, State Loans, College/university loans from institutional funds. Federal Work-Study Program available. Institutional employment available. Off-campus job opportunities are good.

The Inside Word

The academics at NJIT are certainly rigorous. Therefore, admissions officers at the college are on the lookout for students whom they believe can handle the challenging workload. Successful candidates are usually in the top 30 percent of their classes with especially strong math, science, and English grades. Applicants should take heart (or heed); the committee will take note of performance trends.

THE SCHOOL SAYS "..."

From the Admissions Office

"Talented high school graduates from across the nation come to NJIT to prepare for leadership roles in architecture, business, engineering, medical, legal, science, and technological fields. Students experience a public research university conducting over $100 million in research that maintains a small-college atmosphere at a modest cost. Our attractive forty-five-acre campus is just minutes from New York City and less than an hour from the Jersey shore. Students find an outstanding faculty and a safe, diverse, and caring learning and residential community. NJIT's academic environment challenges and prepares students for rewarding careers and full-time advanced study after graduation. The campus is computing-intensive. NJIT is a *Top 50 Best Value College,* according to The Princeton Review.

"Students applying for admission to NJIT may provide scores from either the SAT or the ACT. Writing sample scores will not be used for admission purposes, but are used for placement in first-year courses. SAT Subject Test scores are not required for any major."

SELECTIVITY

Admissions Rating	85
# of applicants	4,344
% of applicants accepted	65
% of acceptees attending	36

FRESHMAN PROFILE

Range SAT Critical Reading	480–590
Range SAT Math	550–660
Range SAT Writing	470–590
Minimum paper TOEFL	550
Minimum web-based TOEFL	213
% graduated top 10% of class	27
% graduated top 25% of class	54
% graduated top 50% of class	85

DEADLINES

Regular	
Deadline	3/1
Nonfall registration?	Yes

APPLICANTS ALSO LOOK AT AND OFTEN PREFER

Drexel University; Rensselaer Polytechnic Institute; The College of New Jersey

AND SOMETIMES PREFER

Pennsylvania State University—University Park; Virginia Tech; Worcester Polytechnic Institute; Stevens Institute of Technology

FINANCIAL FACTS

Financial Aid Rating	66
Annual in-state tuition	$11,756
Annual out-of-state tuition	$23,116
Room and board	$11,566
Required fees	$2,418
Books and supplies	$3,200
% needy frosh rec. need-based scholarship or grant aid	51
% needy UG rec. need-based scholarship or grant aid	64
% needy frosh rec. non-need-based scholarship or grant aid	27
% needy UG rec. non-need-based scholarship or grant aid	17
% needy frosh rec. need-based self-help aid	77
% needy UG rec. need-based self-help aid	85
% frosh rec. any financial aid	87
% UG rec. any financial aid	72
% UG borrow to pay for school	61
Average cumulative indebtedness	$35,709
% frosh need fully met	14
% ugrads need fully met	11

NEW YORK UNIVERSITY

665 BROADWAY, NEW YORK, NY 10012 • ADMISSIONS: 212-998-4500 • FAX: 212-995-4902

STUDENTS SAY "..."

Academics

"Location, location, location" in "the most amazing city on earth," along with "great facilities" and "top-notch faculty," makes New York University an excellent choice for those seeking "an untraditional college experience" in "a paradise for the independent and motivated." With more than 20,000 students and eleven distinct schools offering more than 230 areas of study, NYU "is about diversity. Students are from all over the world; they come from different cultures, and they have different talents and interests. Similarly, NYU offers endless opportunities for students, no matter what their interests or ambitions are." The school offers voluminous opportunities to participate in research, pursue an internship, or begin a career in the arts (although "you have to be active and willing to find these opportunities"). Given the school's size, many students are "actually quite surprised by the accessibility of both the faculty and administration." Although "this is not the kind of school where students really get to know all of their teachers, as it is unlikely that a student will have a professor more than once," those who make the effort report that "it is so easy to meet with [professors] outside of class, and I still get e-mails from professors about internships, jobs, and scholarship recommendations." Many here also tout the "great study abroad programs."

Life

"Living in New York City is the biggest part of going to school at New York University," NYU students agree. The school's New York City campus is located in the heart of Greenwich Village, one of the city's major nightlife destinations, so "there is always something to do at any hour of the day," usually within walking distance of the school. One student reports, "Every weekend there are tons of things to do, both at NYU and in New York City. NYU really takes advantage of its location, so a lot of the programming provided by residence life or the student resource center is engaging you in the city that has become your new home." Living in the Big Apple means that "on any given day you can go to a museum, concert, sporting event, or theater performance…and a lot of the times, NYU will foot the bill if you go to an event in the city with your RA or with a club." The location also provides plenty of internship opportunities, which is good because "the vast majority of students at NYU are interested in interning and finding jobs through that gateway." The school has no campus per se; it surrounds Washington Square Park, a busy public square where students love to relax when the weather is accommodating.

Student Body

"There is no typical student at NYU," where an undergraduate student body of more than 20,000 and a broad range of academic interests ensure a broad demographic. "Each school at NYU attracts a different group," students tell us. "The Tisch School of the Arts attracts a very out-there group of actors and the like," while the Stern Business School "has a massive population of Asians and Indians." "Hipsters are pretty pervasive throughout all schools except Stern," although "every school has people who break those stereotypes. [Even so,] few students can find ways to not fit in because of the huge number of students" at the university. Throughout NYU, "students tend to be incredibly motivated and ambitious." Students insist that "it is also important to note that NYU students are very accepting of each other's differences," an important factor at a school that brings together "students of all different backgrounds, ethnicities, and gender identities and makes them coexist within the university."

FINANCIAL AID: 212-998-4444 • E-MAIL: ADMISSIONS@NYU.EDU • WEBSITE: WWW.NYU.EDU

THE PRINCETON REVIEW SAYS

Admissions

Very important factors considered include: Class rank, GPA, rigor of secondary school record, standardized test scores, application essay, extracurricular activities, recommendation(s), talent/ability, character/personal qualities. *Important factors considered include:* Volunteer work, work experience. *Other factors considered include:* First generation, geographical residence, interview, racial/ethnic status, state residency, alumni/ae relations, level of applicant's interest. SAT and SAT Subject Tests or ACT required; ACT with Writing component required. TOEFL required of all international applicants. *Academic units required:* 4 English; 3 mathematics; 3 science; (3 science lab); 3 social studies; 3 foreign language; 3 history. *Academic units recommended:* 4 English; 4 mathematics; 4 science; (4 science lab); 4 social studies; 4 foreign language; 4 history.

Financial Aid

Students should submit: FAFSA, CSS/Financial Aid PROFILE, Noncustodial PROFILE. Regular filing deadline is 2/15. The Princeton Review suggests that all financial aid forms be submitted as soon as possible after January 1. *Need-based scholarships/grants offered:* Federal Pell, SEOG, State scholarships/grants, private scholarships, the school's own gift aid, federal nursing scholarships *Loan aid offered:* Direct Subsidized Stafford Loans, Direct Unsubsidized Stafford Loans, Direct PLUS loans, Federal Perkins Loans, Federal Nursing Loans. Applicants will be notified of awards beginning 4/1. Federal Work-Study Program available. Institutional employment available. Off-campus job opportunities are excellent.

The Inside Word

Undergraduates must apply to one of NYU's undergraduate schools and colleges: the College of Arts and Science; the Polytechnic School of Engineering, the Liberal Studies Program; the Stern School of Business; the College of Nursing; the Gallatin School of Individualized Study; the Silver School of Social Work; the Steinhardt School of Culture, Education, and Human Development; the Tisch School of the Arts; or the School of Continuing and Professional Studies. This is different from the application process at some universities and obviously requires some forethought. Remember that this is a highly competitive university; if your application doesn't reflect a serious interest in your intended area of study, your chances of gaining admission will be diminished.

THE SCHOOL SAYS "..."

From the Admissions Office

"NYU is the largest independent research university in the United States and one of just 19 private universities in the prestigious Association of American Universities. Founded in 1831 by Albert Gallatin, it is now one the most influential universities in the world. NYU's degree-granting campuses in New York, Abu Dhabi, and Shanghai are complemented by global centers in Berlin, Buenos Aires, Florence, Ghana, London, Madrid, Paris, Prague, Sydney, Tel Aviv, and Washington, D.C. Throughout this global network, NYU students benefit from an exceptionally rich academic climate fostered by a faculty of renowned, award-winning scholars - many of whom have won Nobel Prizes and MacArthur Genius Grants, as well as Emmy, Oscar, and Grammy Awards. As a result, NYU attracts students from more students outside the United States than virtually any other American university while sending more of its own students abroad than any other American institution. With more than 4,000 course offerings and more than 230 areas of study, students can explore and develop their academic and professional interests in distinctly urban settings."

SELECTIVITY

Admissions Rating	96
# of applicants	45,779
% of applicants accepted	32
% of acceptees attending	35
# of early decision applicants	6,203
% accepted early decision	32

FRESHMAN PROFILE

Range SAT Critical Reading	630–720
Range SAT Math	630–740
Range SAT Writing	640–730
Range ACT Composite	28–32
Average HS GPA	3.58

DEADLINES

Early decision	
Deadline	11/1
Notification	12/15
Regular	
Deadline	1/1
Notification	4/1
Nonfall registration?	No

FINANCIAL FACTS

Financial Aid Rating	66
Annual tuition	$42,472
Room and board	$16,622
Required fees	$2,376
Books and supplies	$1,070
% needy frosh rec. need-based scholarship or grant aid	91
% needy UG rec. need-based scholarship or grant aid	93
% needy frosh rec. non-need-based scholarship or grant aid	9
% needy UG rec. non-need-based scholarship or grant aid	5
% needy frosh rec. need-based self-help aid	86
% needy UG rec. need-based self-help aid	86
% frosh rec. any financial aid	55
% UG rec. any financial aid	55
% UG borrow to pay for school	50
Average cumulative indebtedness	$30,688
% frosh need fully met	19
% ugrads need fully met	9
Average % of frosh need met	73
Average % of ugrad need met	60

NORTH CAROLINA STATE UNIVERSITY

Box 7103, Raleigh, NC 27695 • Admissions: 919-515-2434 • Fax: 919-515-5039

CAMPUS LIFE

Quality of Life Rating	92
Fire Safety Rating	94
Green Rating	93
Type of school	Public
Affiliation	No Affiliation
Environment	Metropolis

STUDENTS

Total undergrad enrollment	22,977
% male/female	56/44
% from out of state	10
% frosh from public high school	80
% frosh live on campus	77
% ugrads live on campus	27
# of fraternities (% ugrad men join)	33 (11)
# of sororities (% ugrad women join)	18 (15)
% African American	7
% Asian	5
% Caucasian	75
% Hispanic	4
% Native American	<1
% international	3
# of countries represented	117

SURVEY SAYS . . .

Students are happy
Lab facilities are great
Career services are great
School is well run
Students are friendly
Students get along with local community
Students love Raleigh, NC
Great off-campus food
Athletic facilities are great
Everyone loves the Wolf Pack
Alumni active on campus

ACADEMICS

Academic Rating	85
% students returning for sophomore year	93
% students graduating within 4 years	39
% students graduating within 6 years	71
Calendar	Semester
Student/faculty ratio	17:1
Profs interesting rating	75
Profs accessible rating	77

Most classes have 20–29 students.
Most lab/discussion sessions have 20–29 students.

MOST POPULAR MAJORS

mechanical engineering; biology; business administration and management

STUDENTS SAY ". . ."

Academics

The "largest and most diverse" of North Carolina's public university system, NC State provides undergrads with a "high level education" and "great value." The campus rings with a "welcoming, down-to-earth" vibe and "Wolfpack pride" is certainly infectious. Moreover, the university maintains "opportunities to fit every single type of person no matter their interest." Academically, NC State is home to a stellar engineering school that students contend is "the best engineering program in the state of North Carolina." It offers "world-renowned faculty who conduct innovative and cutting edge research in a plethora of scientific fields." Undergrads also like to emphasize the "exceptionally rigorous" design program which is "small and personal." And we'd certainly be remiss if we didn't mention the "fantastic business school" and "great entrepreneurship program" it has developed. Inside the classroom, students find their professors to be "very enthusiastic about what they teach" and appreciate that they truly "challenge you to think." As one satisfied junior adds, "My professors are extremely knowledgeable about the course material and bring in practical demonstrations to bring the lecture to life." And just as important, "professors love to discuss future professional development plans with undergraduate students." All in all, it's highly evident that "professors and TAs here love their jobs." Simply put, "they want you to succeed."

Life

Students proffer that NC State's campus is always abuzz with activity. As one excited senior quickly shares, "There's always something to do for fun—spanking the UNC Tarheels at football, painting the Free Expression Tunnel, stalking American Idol winner Scotty McCreery, and people-watching at the State Fair are just a few examples." Athletics are extremely popular here and it often feels as though "basketball games and football games are almost required [viewing]." And, naturally, these contests are accompanied by "a large tailgate culture." Additionally, the university "sponsors many different programs, ranging from concerts to a movie at the campus cinema every weekend." And there are "quite a few service and community oriented activities that go on around campus, such as Shack-A-Thon for Habitat for Humanity and the Krispey Kreme Challenge for children's hospitals." Students also love to take advantage of the surrounding area. As one freshman tells us, "Hillsborough Street has a lot of fun restaurants to go to when we want to go out and do things. Also, there [are] lots of [places] to go to the movies and shop right outside of campus." Indeed, the "Raleigh-area is full of things to do from concerts, bars, shows, restaurants, museums, malls, etc." As another freshman sums up life at NC State, "The problem isn't finding something to do, it is finding time to do it all [while] manag[ing] to stay on task and put aside time to study."

Student Body

When you first step onto the campus of NC State, "first impressions might make it seem like everyone there is a sorority girl or a frat guy who all wear cowboy boots and come from rural NC." However, "if you look closely [you'll see a] very diverse campus with lots of opportunities." Indeed, you'll find a range from "hipster to farm boy" and everything in between. Of course, no matter the easy or convenient characterization, most undergrads agree that their peers are "welcoming" and "friendly." Students tell us that "fitting in is super easy and getting involved with any of the many programs on campus help[s] with meeting new people and making friends!" And while most students are "devoted to academics," they all still manage to "go out and have fun." Additionally, undergrads say their peers "are service oriented and always think of creative ways to give back." Finally, as one junior reveals, "NCSU is huge, so every person can find a spot—and when you do, you find a family. To me, it doesn't feel like a large school. I see someone I know walking on campus every day. I don't know anyone, particularly those that began their education living on campus, that hasn't found their niche."

FINANCIAL AID: 919-515-2421 • E-MAIL: UNDERGRAD_ADMISSIONS@NCSU.EDU • WEBSITE: WWW.NCSU.EDU

THE PRINCETON REVIEW SAYS

Admissions

Very important factors considered include: Class rank, GPA, rigor of secondary school record, standardized test scores. *Other factors considered include:* Application essay, extracurricular activities, first generation, geographical residence, racial/ethnic status, recommendation(s), state residency, talent/ability, volunteer work, work experience, alumni/ae relations, character/personal qualities, level of applicant's interest, religious affiliation. SAT or ACT required; ACT with Writing component required. TOEFL required of all international applicants. *Academic units required:* 4 English; 4 mathematics; 3 science; (1 science lab); 1 social studies; 2 foreign language; 1 history; 1 academic elective. *Academic units recommended:* 4 English; 4 mathematics; 4 science; (2 science lab); 1 social studies; 2 foreign language; 1 history; 4 academic electives.

Financial Aid

Students should submit: FAFSA. The Princeton Review suggests that all financial aid forms be submitted as soon as possible after January 1. *Need-based scholarships/grants offered:* Federal Pell, SEOG, State scholarships/grants, private scholarships, the school's own gift aid, United Negro College Fund. *Loan aid offered:* Direct Subsidized Stafford Loans, Direct Unsubsidized Stafford Loans, Direct PLUS loans, Federal Perkins Loans, State Loans, College/university loans from institutional funds. Federal Work-Study Program available. Institutional employment available. Off-campus job opportunities are excellent.

The Inside Word

As one of the nation's top research universities, NC State maintains a competitive admissions process. Successful applicants take a rigorous courseload and often have a B-plus average or better. Admissions officers also closely weigh GPA, class rank and standardized test scores. Extracurricular activities are of secondary importance.

THE SCHOOL SAYS "..."

From the Admissions Office

"NC State is arguably the most popular university in the state, with more NC students seeking admission than at any other college or university. More than 20,000 students from across the nation seek one of the 4,250 available freshman spaces. Students choose NC State for its strong and varied academic programs, national reputation for excellence, low cost, location in Raleigh and the Research Triangle Park area, and very friendly atmosphere. Our students like the excitement of a large campus and the many opportunities it offers, such as Cooperative Education, Study Abroad, extensive honors programming, and theme residence halls. Each year, hundreds of NC State graduates are accepted into medical or law schools or other areas of advanced professional study. More corporate and government entities recruit graduates from NC State than from any other university in the United States.

"Freshman applicants must take either the SAT or the ACT with the writing component."

SELECTIVITY

Admissions Rating	93
# of applicants	19,863
% of applicants accepted	52
% of acceptees attending	44

FRESHMAN PROFILE

Range SAT Critical Reading	530–620
Range SAT Math	560–660
Range SAT Writing	510–610
Range ACT Composite	23–28
Minimum paper TOEFL	550
Average HS GPA	4.28
% graduated top 10% of class	43
% graduated top 25% of class	83
% graduated top 50% of class	99

DEADLINES

Early action	
Deadline	11/1
Notification	1/30
Regular	
Priority	11/1
Deadline	1/15
Nonfall registration?	Yes

APPLICANTS ALSO LOOK AT AND OFTEN PREFER

The University of North Carolina at Chapel Hill

AND SOMETIMES PREFER

Wake Forest University

AND RARELY PREFER

Auburn University; Clemson University; Georgia Institute of Technology; Virginia Tech; University of South Carolina—Columbia

FINANCIAL FACTS

Financial Aid Rating	83
Annual in-state tuition	$6,038
Annual out-of-state tuition	$19,493
Room and board	$8,434
Required fees	$2,168
Books and supplies	$1,058
% needy frosh rec. need-based scholarship or grant aid	93
% needy UG rec. need-based scholarship or grant aid	89
% needy frosh rec. non-need-based scholarship or grant aid	19
% needy UG rec. non-need-based scholarship or grant aid	11
% needy frosh rec. need-based self-help aid	72
% needy UG rec. need-based self-help aid	74
% frosh rec. any financial aid	75
% UG rec. any financial aid	69
% UG borrow to pay for school	57
Average cumulative indebtedness	$23,532
% frosh need fully met	27
% ugrads need fully met	26
Average % of frosh need met	81
Average % of ugrad need met	78

NORTHEASTERN UNIVERSITY

360 HUNTINGTON AVENUE, BOSTON, MA 02115 • ADMISSIONS: 617-373-2200 • FAX: 617-373-8780

CAMPUS LIFE

Quality of Life Rating	95
Fire Safety Rating	86
Green Rating	98
Type of school	Private
Affiliation	No Affiliation
Environment	Metropolis

STUDENTS

Total undergrad enrollment	17,107
% male/female	49/51
% from out of state	67
% frosh live on campus	98
# of fraternities (% ugrad men join)	12 (8)
# of sororities (% ugrad women join)	11(12)
% African American	3
% Asian	10
% Caucasian	51
% Hispanic	6
% Native American	<1
% international	17
# of countries represented	125

SURVEY SAYS . . .

Students are happy
Career services are great
Internships are widely available
Students love Boston, MA
Great off-campus food
Campus feels safe
Athletic facilities are great

ACADEMICS

Academic Rating	80
% students returning for sophomore year	96
% students graduating within 4 years	#VALUE!
% students graduating within 6 years	83
Calendar	Semester
Student/faculty ratio	13:1
Profs interesting rating	75
Profs accessible rating	74
Most classes have 10–19 students.	

MOST POPULAR MAJORS

engineering; health services; business/
commerce

STUDENTS SAY ". . ."

Academics

Boston's Northeastern University is all about "experiential learning, a global outlook, high standard academics and the balance of success with a happy life." The major draw is the school's signature co-op program, where students spend up to three six- month periods working full time (usually for pay) while living in the residence halls and maintaining full-time student status. "In an uncertain economy, the world-class co-op program really gives students a leg up in finding a career," says a student. A strong honors program (members of which share living quarters in a specialized Living Learning Community) adds to the list of Northeastern's benefits. From "the first day that you are on campus, the school is asking how everything you're doing affects your resume," says a student.

The professors are often actually professionals in their field, so that students can "learn from firsthand accounts and experiences." They are "very research- oriented," and proponents of "using innovation and modern technology for the students' advantage." "My professors all come from a variety of backgrounds, have fascinating research projects, and love to teach," says a student. They "always organize extra lectures, speakers, and events for students who are really interested in the course."

Aside from the co-op program, the study abroad program, the "variety of majors and classes," the "elite classroom experience.," and the "great programs available for freshman" all draw applause. However, some students do wish that there was "less red-tape," as "a lot of things get lost in the 'Northeastern shuffle'." Still, there is good advising available and "everything is well-organized.""Northeastern University encourages learning through a creative and diverse environment that allows students to broaden their view on life and helps their transition into the working world." "What other school allows you to travel abroad for internships and multiple summers and semesters but still allows you to graduate on time?" asks a student.

Life

This "urban university with a campus feeling" has the city of Boston as its backyard, which "always has something for students of all ages to do." The location is "prime" and the public transport is easy; in fact, Northeastern has two separate subway stops. "It's safe and offers a wide variety of activities from night clubs to the theater to sports"; the Museum of Fine Arts is down the street, the Red Sox are around the block and "Boston's best bars are down the corner."

"Here the focus is on academics, co-op, and student organizations." People do like to go out on occasion, but "since there aren't many parties at NU, they mostly go to BU, Harvard, and MIT." There is some Greek life at Northeastern (but no houses), and "different sororities and fraternities often interact together for various events like Homecoming." The student groups on campus put on "tons of events and programs," and people are "pretty into" the everpresent hockey and basketball games.

Student Body

Students at northeastern are smart and here to learn. With so many people taking part in different co-ops and study abroad programs, it can be hard to pin down anything as "typical" at Northeastern, and "diversity is growing every year." "At any given time, around 1/3 of students are working full time," which means that despite the very accepting student body, it can sometimes be "difficult to make friends as everyone is always coming and going." Unsurprisingly, people here are "hard-working and focused on making money as well as getting a job after graduation."

NORTHEASTERN UNIVERSITY

FINANCIAL AID: 617-373-3190 • E-MAIL: ADMISSIONS@NEU.EDU • WEBSITE: WWW.NORTHEASTERN.EDU

THE PRINCETON REVIEW SAYS

Admissions

Very important factors considered include: GPA, rigor of secondary school record, standardized test scores, application essay, recommendation(s). *Important factors considered include:* Extracurricular activities, talent/ability, volunteer work, work experience, character/personal qualities. *Other factors considered include:* Class rank, first generation, geographical residence, interview, racial/ethnic status, alumni/ae relations, level of applicant's interest. SAT or ACT required; SAT and SAT Subject Tests or ACT considered if submitted; ACT with Writing component required. TOEFL required of all international applicants. *Academic units required:* 4 English; 3 mathematics; 3 science; (2 science lab); 3 social studies; 2 foreign language; 2 history. *Academic units recommended:* 4 mathematics; 4 science.

Financial Aid

Students should submit: FAFSA, CSS/Financial Aid PROFILE, Noncustodial PROFILE. The Princeton Review suggests that all financial aid forms be submitted as soon as possible after January 1. *Need-based scholarships/grants offered:* Federal Pell, SEOG, State scholarships/grants, private scholarships, the school's own gift aid. *Loan aid offered:* Direct Subsidized Stafford Loans, Direct Unsubsidized Stafford Loans, Direct PLUS loans, Federal Perkins Loans, Federal Nursing Loans, State Loans, College/university loans from institutional funds. Applicants will be notified of awards at the time of admission. Federal Work-Study Program available. Institutional employment available. Off-campus job opportunities are excellent.

The Inside Word

Applicants to Northeastern are evaluated based on their secondary school performance, with the difficulty of courses given emphasis, and you should go beyond minimum graduation requirements for high school to show broad intellectual curiosity. The committee recommends having strong standardized test scores and does consider the writing section of the SAT in its decision.

THE SCHOOL SAYS ". . ."

From the Admissions Office

"Northeastern students take charge of their education in a way you'll find nowhere else, because a Northeastern education is like no other. Our students don't just take class: They take class further, integrating their course work with real-world experiences—professional co-op placements, research, study abroad, and community service. Northeastern's dynamic of academic excellence and experience means that our students are better prepared to succeed in the lives they choose. On top of that, they experience all of this on a beautifully landscaped, seventy-three-acre campus in the heart of Boston, where culture, commerce, civic pride, and college students from around the globe are all a part of the mix."

SELECTIVITY

Admissions Rating	97
# of applicants	47,364
% of applicants accepted	32
% of acceptees attending	19

FRESHMAN PROFILE

Range SAT Critical Reading	640–730
Range SAT Math	660–750
Range SAT Writing	640–720
Range ACT Composite	30–33
Minimum web-based TOEFL	223
% graduated top 10% of class	64
% graduated top 25% of class	91
% graduated top 50% of class	98

DEADLINES

Early decision	
Deadline	11/1
Notification	12/15
Early action	
Deadline	11/1
Notification	12/31
Regular	
Deadline	1/1
Notification	4/1
Nonfall registration?	Yes

FINANCIAL FACTS

Financial Aid Rating	83
Annual tuition	$40,780
Room and board	$14,100
Required fees	$906
Books and supplies	$1,000
% needy frosh rec. need-based scholarship or grant aid	97
% needy UG rec. need-based scholarship or grant aid	93
% needy frosh rec. non-need-based scholarship or grant aid	40
% needy UG rec. non-need-based scholarship or grant aid	34
% needy frosh rec. need-based self-help aid	80
% needy UG rec. need-based self-help aid	85
% frosh need fully met	42
% ugrads need fully met	36
Average % of frosh need met	91
Average % of ugrad need met	77

NORTHWESTERN UNIVERSITY

PO BOX 3060, EVANSTON, IL 60208-3060 • ADMISSIONS: 847-491-7271

STUDENTS SAY ". . ."

Academics

"The strength of the school is its range." Northwestern students agree, vowing their school "has everything": "Intelligent but laid-back students, excel[lence] in academic fields," "great extracurriculars and good parties," "strong [Big Ten] sports spirit," and "so many connections and opportunities during and after graduation." Undergrads here brag of "nationally acclaimed programs for almost anything anyone could be interested in, from engineering to theater to journalism to music," and report "everything is given fairly equal weight. Northwestern students and faculty do not show a considerable bias" toward specific fields. The school accomplishes all this while maintaining a manageable scale. While its relatively small size allows for good student-professor interaction, it has "all the perks" of a big school, including "many opportunities" for research and internships. Be aware, however, "Northwestern is not an easy school. It takes hard work to be average here." If you "learn from your failures quickly and love to learn for the sake of learning rather than the grade," students say it is quite possible to stay afloat and even to excel. Helping matters are numerous resources established by administrators and professors, including tutoring programs such as Northwestern's Gateway Science Workshop. Those who take advantage of these opportunities find the going much easier than those who don't.

Life

There are two distinct sections of the Northwestern campus. The North Campus is where "you can find a party every night of the week" and "the Greek scene is strong." The South Campus, about a one-mile trek from the action to the north, is "more artsy and has minimal partying on weeknights," but is closer to town so "it is easy" to "buy dinner, see a show at the movies, and go shopping. People who live on North Campus have a harder time getting motivated to go into Evanston and tap into all that is offered." As one South Campus resident puts it, "South Campus is nice and quiet in its own way. I enjoy reading and watching movies here, and the quietude is appreciated when study time rolls around. But for more exciting fun, a trip north is a must." Regardless of where students live, extracurriculars are "incredible here. There is a group for every interest, and the groups are amazingly well-managed by students alone. This goes hand-in-hand with how passionate students at Northwestern are about what they love." Many students "are involved in plays, a cappella groups, comedy troupes, and other organizations geared toward the performing arts. Activism is also very popular, with many involved in political groups, human-rights activism, and volunteering." In addition, Northwestern's membership in the Big Ten means students "attend some of the best sporting events in the country." Chicago, of course, "is a wonderful resource. People go into the city for a wide variety of things—daily excursions, jobs, internships, nights out, parties, etc."

Student Body

The typical Northwestern student "was high school class president with a 4.0, swim team captain, and on the chess team." So it makes sense everyone here "is an excellent student who works hard" and "has a leadership position in at least two clubs, plus an on-campus job." Students also tell us "there's [a] great separation between North Campus (think: fraternities, engineering, state school mentality) and South Campus (think: closer to Chicago and its culture, arts and letters, liberal arts school mentality). Students segregate themselves depending on background and interests, and it's rare for these two groups to interact beyond a superficial level." The student body here includes sizeable Jewish, Indian, and East-Asian populations.

FINANCIAL AID: 847-491-7400 • E-MAIL: UG-ADMISSION@NORTHWESTERN.EDU • WEBSITE: WWW.NORTHWESTERN.EDU

THE PRINCETON REVIEW SAYS

Admissions

Very important factors considered include: Class rank, GPA, rigor of secondary school record, standardized test scores, application essay. *Important factors considered include:* Extracurricular activities, recommendation(s), talent/ability, character/personal qualities. *Other factors considered include:* First generation, interview, racial/ethnic status, volunteer work, work experience, alumni/ae relations, level of applicant's interest. SAT or ACT required; ACT with Writing component required. TOEFL required of all international applicants. *Academic units recommended:* 4 English; 3 mathematics; 2 science; (2 science lab); 2 social studies; 2 foreign language; 1 academic elective.

Financial Aid

Students should submit: FAFSA, CSS/Financial Aid PROFILE, Noncustodial PROFILE, Business/Farm Supplement. Regular filing deadline is 2/15. The Princeton Review suggests that all financial aid forms be submitted as soon as possible after January 1. *Need-based scholarships/grants offered:* Federal Pell, SEOG, State scholarships/grants, the school's own gift aid. *Loan aid offered:* Direct Subsidized Stafford Loans, Direct Unsubsidized Stafford Loans, Direct PLUS loans, Federal Perkins Loans, College/university loans from institutional funds. Applicants will be notified of awards beginning 4/15. Federal Work-Study Program available. Institutional employment available. Off-campus job opportunities are excellent.

The Inside Word

Northwestern is among the nation's most expensive undergraduate institutions, a fact that dissuades some qualified students from applying. The school is working to attract more low-income applicants by increasing the number of full scholarships available for students whose family income is less than $45,000. Low-income students who score well on the ACT may receive a letter from the school encouraging them to apply. Even if you don't receive this letter, you should consider applying if you've got the goods—you may be pleasantly surprised by the offer you receive from the financial aid office.

THE SCHOOL SAYS "..."

From the Admissions Office

"Consistent with its dedication to excellence, Northwestern provides both an educational and an extracurricular environment that enables its undergraduate students to become accomplished individuals and informed and responsible citizens. To the students in all its undergraduate schools, Northwestern offers liberal learning and professional education to help them gain the depth of knowledge that will empower them to become leaders in their professions and communities. Furthermore, Northwestern fosters in its students a broad understanding of the world in which we live as well as excellence in the competencies that transcend any particular field of study: writing and oral communication, analytical and creative thinking and expression, and quantitative and qualitative methods of thinking.

"Applicants are required to take the SAT or the ACT with the writing section."

SELECTIVITY

Admissions Rating	98
# of applicants	25,369
% of applicants accepted	27
% of acceptees attending	31
# offered a place on the wait list	2,850
% accepting a place on wait list	49
% admitted from wait list	3
# of early decision applicants	1,498
% accepted early decision	39

FRESHMAN PROFILE

Range SAT Critical Reading	670–750
Range SAT Math	690–780
Range SAT Writing	670–760
Range ACT Composite	31–33
Minimum paper TOEFL	600
Minimum web-based TOEFL	250
% graduated top 10% of class	90
% graduated top 25% of class	99
% graduated top 50% of class	100

DEADLINES

Early decision	
Deadline	11/1
Notification	12/15
Regular	
Deadline	1/1
Notification	4/15
Nonfall registration?	Yes

APPLICANTS ALSO LOOK AT AND OFTEN PREFER

Yale University; Harvard College

AND SOMETIMES PREFER

Princeton University; Stanford University; The University of Chicago

AND RARELY PREFER

DePaul University; Purdue University—West Lafayette; Marquette University

FINANCIAL FACTS

Financial Aid Rating	90
Annual tuition	$45,120
Room and board	$13,862
Required fees	$407
Books and supplies	$1,878
% needy frosh rec. need-based scholarship or grant aid	94
% needy UG rec. need-based scholarship or grant aid	94
% needy frosh rec. non-need-based scholarship or grant aid	0
% needy UG rec. non-need-based scholarship or grant aid	0
% needy frosh rec. need-based self-help aid	86
% needy UG rec. need-based self-help aid	87
% frosh rec. any financial aid	60
% UG rec. any financial aid	60
% UG borrow to pay for school	48
Average cumulative indebtedness	$20,802
% frosh need fully met	100
% ugrads need fully met	100
Average % of frosh need met	100
Average % of ugrad need met	100

OBERLIN COLLEGE

101 NORTH PROFESSOR STREET, OBERLIN, OH 44074 • ADMISSIONS: 440-775-8411 • FAX: 440-775-6905

STUDENTS SAY " . . ."

Academics

Oberlin College, a school "for laid-back people who enjoy learning and expanding social norms, allows each and every student to have the undergrad experience for which he or she is looking, all the while challenging the students to change themselves and the world for the better." Oberlin is a place where students "focus on learning for learning's sake rather than making money in a career." As one student explains, "I didn't plan on becoming a scholar when I entered Oberlin....As fate would have it, I ended up loving my college classes and professors. Now I hope to be a professor of religion." At Oberlin, "academics are very highly valued, but balanced with a strong interest in the arts and a commitment to society." Some might suggest Oberlin puts the "liberal" in "liberal arts," and the school's staunchest supporters agree, stressing the school's emphasis on open-mindedness and the belief that "one person can change the world." Among the school's offerings, "the sciences, English, politics, religion, music, environmental studies, and East-Asian studies are particularly noteworthy." The presence of a prestigious music school imbues the entire campus community. One undergrad writes, "Oberlin's greatest strength is the combination of the college and the conservatory. They are not separated, so students mix with each other all the time." Professors here—the "heart and soul of the school"—are dedicated teachers who "treat you more like collaborators and realize that even with their Ph.D.s, they can learn and grow from you, as well as you from them." They are "excellent instructors and fantastic people" who are "focused on learning instead of deadlines." Undergrads also appreciate "a cooperative learning environment" in which "students bond over studying together for difficult exams."

Life

Life during the week at Oberlin can be "pretty bland," as "almost everyone has to crack the books and study it up." It's not always bland, though. Some here manage to find time for the many "events [going on] each weekend—operas, plays, organ pumps, etc.," or "rally to stage to help the oppressed." Thursday afternoons at Oberlin means "Classical Thursdays," an event during which "you get free beer from the college if you bring a professor to the on-campus pub." Another feature of campus life is "the musical scene, which has its heart in the conservatory. All of the other arts—performing, studio, whatever—are intertwined with the talent in the conservatory." On weekends, "people let loose and drink beer. Not everyone does this every weekend. Some don't do it at all," and "there is absolutely no pressure on those who don't." There are also "tons of student-produced social events like parties, fundraisers, concerts, dances, etc.," keeping students "very connected to each other and to what's going on in the community." Hometown Oberlin "is a small town, and about all there is to do there is go out for pizza or Chinese, see a movie for two or three dollars at the Apollo, or go to the Feve, the bar in town."

Student Body

"If you're a liberal, artsy, indie loner who likes to throw around the phrase 'heteronormative white privilege,'" then Oberlin might be the place for you. "We're like the Island of Misfit Toys, but together we make a great toy chest." "We're all different and unusual, which creates a common bond between students." "Musicians, jocks, science geeks, creative writing majors, straight, bi, questioning, queer, and trans [students]," all have their place here, alongside "straight-edge, international, local, and joker students." Oberlin has a reputation for a left-leaning and active student body. One undergrad observes, "They are less active politically than they would like to think, but still more active than most people elsewhere." Another adds, "Most students are very liberal, but the moderates and (few) Republicans have a fine time of it. Every student has different interests and isn't afraid to talk about them." Some here worry "Oberlin's student body is becoming more and more mainstream each year."

FINANCIAL AID: 440-775-8142 • E-MAIL: COLLEGE.ADMISSIONS@OBERLIN.EDU • WEBSITE: WWW.OBERLIN.EDU

THE PRINCETON REVIEW SAYS
Admissions
Very important factors considered include: Class rank, GPA, rigor of secondary school record, standardized test scores. *Important factors considered include:* Application essay, extracurricular activities, first generation, recommendation(s), talent/ability, character/personal qualities. *Other factors considered include:* Interview, racial/ethnic status, volunteer work, work experience, alumni/ae relations, level of applicant's interest. SAT or ACT required; ACT with Writing component recommended. TOEFL required of all international applicants. *Academic units required:* 4 English; 3 mathematics; 3 science; 3 social studies; 3 foreign language. *Academic units recommended:* 4 mathematics; 4 science.

Financial Aid
Students should submit: FAFSA, Institution's own financial aid form, CSS/Financial Aid PROFILE, State aid form, Noncustodial PROFILE, Business/Farm Supplement. Regular filing deadline is 2/1. The Princeton Review suggests that all financial aid forms be submitted as soon as possible after January 1. *Need-based scholarships/grants offered:* Federal Pell, SEOG, State scholarships/grants, private scholarships, the school's own gift aid. *Loan aid offered:* Direct Subsidized Stafford Loans, Direct Unsubsidized Stafford Loans, Federal Perkins Loans, College/university loans from institutional funds.

The Inside Word
Oberlin's music conservatory is one of the most elite programs in the nation. Aspiring music students should expect stiff competition for one of the 600 available slots. Other applicants won't have a much easier time of it. Oberlin is a highly selective institution that attracts a highly competitive applicant pool. Your personal statement could be the make-or-break factor here.

THE SCHOOL SAYS "..."
From the Admissions Office
"Oberlin College is an independent, coeducational, liberal arts college. It comprises two divisions, the College of Arts and Sciences, with roughly 2,300 students enrolled, and the Conservatory of Music, with about 600 students. Students in both divisions share one campus; they also share residence and dining halls as part of one academic community. Many students take courses in both divisions. Oberlin awards the Bachelor of Arts and the Bachelor of Music degrees; a five-year program leads to both degrees. Selected master's degrees are offered in the conservatory. Oberlin is located thirty-five miles southwest of Cleveland. Founded in 1833, Oberlin College is highly selective and dedicated to recruiting students from diverse backgrounds. Oberlin was the first coeducational college in the United States, as well as a historic leader in educating African Americans. Oberlin's 440-acre campus provides outstanding facilities, modern scientific laboratories, a large computing center, a library unexcelled by other college libraries for the depth and range of its resources, and one of the top-five college- or university-based art museums in the country.

"Freshman applicants must take the SAT or the ACT with writing component."

SELECTIVITY
Admissions Rating	97
# of applicants	7,395
% of applicants accepted	30
% of acceptees attending	34
# offered a place on the wait list	1,223
% accepting a place on wait list	37
% admitted from wait list	31
# of early decision applicants	431
% accepted early decision	57

FRESHMAN PROFILE
Minimum paper TOEFL	600
Minimum web-based TOEFL	200
Average HS GPA	3.61
% graduated top 10% of class	68
% graduated top 25% of class	90
% graduated top 50% of class	100

DEADLINES
Early decision	
Deadline	11/15
Notification	12/20
Regular	
Priority	1/15
Deadline	1/15
Nonfall registration?	No

APPLICANTS ALSO LOOK AT AND OFTEN PREFER
Swarthmore College; Brown University; Wesleyan University; Yale University; Stanford University

AND SOMETIMES PREFER
Vassar College; Williams College; Grinnell College; Carleton College; Macalester College; Northwestern University

AND RARELY PREFER
Connecticut College

FINANCIAL FACTS
Financial Aid Rating	93
Annual tuition	$44,512
Room and board	$12,120
Required fees	$393
Books and supplies	$830
% needy frosh rec. need-based scholarship or grant aid	73
% needy UG rec. need-based scholarship or grant aid	78
% needy frosh rec. non-need-based scholarship or grant aid	54
% needy UG rec. non-need-based scholarship or grant aid	56
% needy frosh rec. need-based self-help aid	80
% needy UG rec. need-based self-help aid	84
% frosh rec. any financial aid	61
% UG rec. any financial aid	60
% frosh need fully met	100
% ugrads need fully met	100
Average % of frosh need met	100
Average % of ugrad need met	100

OCCIDENTAL COLLEGE

1600 CAMPUS ROAD, LOS ANGELES, CA 90041-3314 • ADMISSIONS: 323-259-2700 • FAX: 323-341-4875

STUDENTS SAY "..."

Academics

An "intellectual, accepting, beautiful" liberal arts college in northeast Los Angeles, Occidental is "perfect for hard-working and involved students who not only want to be challenged academically, but also want to be pushed to learn more about the world around them." At this small school, classes are "intellectually stimulating," spearheaded by professors who "encourage critical analysis, ask interesting questions, and allow students to create informed opinions about the subject." The faculty and staff "really encourage students to take a proactive role in their education," giving them the freedom to "experiment with a wide range of courses." A current undergrad enthuses, "I love the interdisciplinary aspect of academics. I can really tailor my coursework to what I am interested in." In the classroom, Oxy professors "find ways to connect the lectures to the real world," and many are "very willing to have students help them with their research," providing valuable hands-on experience to undergraduates. Students further augment their coursework through numerous extracurricular and off-campus opportunities, including study abroad, academic conferences, and the school's popular "UN internship program." "Courses are challenging," but Oxy "professors want to see you succeed," and the favorably low student-to-faculty ratio means "there are plenty of opportunities to get extra help on the tough material." In fact, most professors "go the extra mile to make themselves available" and "are invested in cultivating real relationships with students."

Life

"People are really passionate about their extracurricular activities and internships" at Occidental, where most students are "busy from dawn to dusk, and loving it." Clubs and intramural sports, "from quidditch to women's rugby," are popular across campus, and "Greek life is getting bigger and bigger every year." On campus, "there are frequently guest speakers, dialogues, and workshops," and on the weekends, the school organizes "dances, trivia nights, movie screenings, fashion shows, concerts, food tastings, beer gardens, and many other events." When it comes to parties, the alcohol policy is "strict" (even students of legal age are "forbidden from drinking in their dorms"), so most campus get-togethers are small and subdued. Off campus, "house parties are a huge source of fun on the weekends," as are "music shows, bars, and clubs" in surrounding L.A. When they don't have anything planned, students "listen to and make music, watch movies, have impromptu dance parties, and do wacky things." You can't beat having the "intimacy of a small college with Los Angeles as your backyard," and students love the fact that Oxy is "not isolated from the surrounding community like many other college campuses." In their free time, many take advantage of the Southern California setting to "go to the beach, go shopping in L.A., go out to eat in Eagle Rock, [and] go hiking." "Having a car definitely helps" if you want to explore the surrounding city, though "the school has a 'Bengal Bus' system that provides free rides to areas close to campus."

Students

Oxy students are "well rounded," "socially and politically conscious," and "excited to be at Occidental." Though they take academics seriously, "people at Oxy are concerned with much, much more than their education. They are focused on academically succeeding, sure, but they are also concerned with social issues, identity, meeting new people, having fun, and gathering a variety of other skills to help them succeed in life outside of Oxy." Many note the "overwhelmingly left-wing atmosphere" on campus, admitting that the people and their viewpoints can feel a little "homogeneous" at times. However, "every student at Oxy treats all persons equally, regardless of sexual orientation, gender identity, or religious views," and most are readily "accepting of different opinions." With such a tiny enrollment, it's easy to find "a good niche of close friends at Oxy," and "if you're involved on campus, expect your friend group to continually grow." Despite the rigors of the academic program, "there is a communal desire to help each other succeed."

OCCIDENTAL COLLEGE

FINANCIAL AID: 323-259-2548 • E-MAIL: ADMISSION@OXY.EDU • WEBSITE: WWW.OXY.EDU

THE PRINCETON REVIEW SAYS

Admissions

Very important factors considered include: Rigor of secondary school record, extra-curricular activities, volunteer work, work experience. *Important factors considered include:* Class rank, GPA, standardized test scores, application essay, recommendation(s), character/personal qualities. *Other factors considered include:* First generation, geographical residence, interview, racial/ethnic status, talent/ability, alumni/ae relations, level of applicant's interest. SAT or ACT required; ACT with Writing component required. TOEFL required of all international applicants. *Academic units recommended:* 4 English; 4 mathematics; 3 science; (2 science lab); 2 social studies; 3 foreign language; 2 history; 2 academic electives.

Financial Aid

Students should submit: FAFSA, CSS/Financial Aid PROFILE, State aid form, Noncustodial PROFILE. Regular filing deadline is 2/1. The Princeton Review suggests that all financial aid forms be submitted as soon as possible after January 1. *Need-based scholarships/grants offered:* Federal Pell, SEOG, State scholarships/grants, private scholarships, the school's own gift aid. *Loan aid offered:* Direct Subsidized Stafford Loans, Direct Unsubsidized Stafford Loans, Direct PLUS loans, Federal Perkins Loans, College/university loans from institutional funds. Applicants will be notified of awards beginning 4/1. Federal Work-Study Program available. Institutional employment available. Off-campus job opportunities are good.

The Inside Word

The admissions team at Occidental does not use any minimums or formulas when evaluating an applicant's eligibility for the incoming class. In addition to academic achievement, they place a lot of weight on essays and recommendations in their mission to create a diverse incoming class. A demanding course load in high school is essential for competitive candidates, but successful applicants will also show what makes them unique, from volunteer experiences to artistic talent.

THE SCHOOL SAYS "..."

From the Admissions Office

"Here's what our students tell us:

'The professors have all been just amazing. They're all very willing to coordinate times to meet and discuss how you feel about a class and what you want to get out of it.'

'I realize the caliber of discussion that occurs at Oxy is not easily matched. I've developed very strong relationships with many professors, and that's something I believe is unique to Oxy.'

'The program has been awesome. Whether you want to go to med school or grad school, it's a great experience. The professors really want you to succeed.'

'I've been working with postdoctoral researchers as an undergraduate. It's very rewarding. Oxy challenges me both inside and outside the classroom.'

'Occidental opened my eyes to different beliefs, values, and ideas. Discussions in class are much more interesting, because you consider things you might not have thought about before.'

'Oxy's close-knit community and its size make me feel this is a place I can call home.'

'Oxy instills curiosity and makes students want to go out and learn a subject on their own. I've gotten a broader sense of self and have been able to fulfill my learning goals.'

'Occidental requires all applicants (including international students) to take either the SAT or ACT with the writing component. SAT Subject Tests are recommended but not required.'"

SELECTIVITY

Admissions Rating	95
# of applicants	6,072
% of applicants accepted	42
% of acceptees attending	21
# offered a place on the wait list	874
% accepting a place on wait list	39
% admitted from wait list	6
# of early decision applicants	251
% accepted early decision	49

FRESHMAN PROFILE

Range SAT Critical Reading	600–700
Range SAT Math	610–700
Range SAT Writing	610–700
Range ACT Composite	27–31
Minimum paper TOEFL	600
Minimum web-based TOEFL	250
Average HS GPA	3.60
% graduated top 10% of class	60
% graduated top 25% of class	91
% graduated top 50% of class	100

DEADLINES

Early decision	
Deadline	11/15
Notification	12/15
Regular	
Deadline	1/10
Notification	4/1
Nonfall registration?	No

APPLICANTS ALSO LOOK AT AND OFTEN PREFER

Stanford University; University of California—Berkeley; University of California—Los Angeles; University of Southern California; Pomona College

AND SOMETIMES PREFER

Claremont McKenna College; Macalester College

FINANCIAL FACTS

Financial Aid Rating	96
Annual tuition	$45,190
Room and board	$12,940
Required fees	$1,462
Books and supplies	$1,244
% needy frosh rec. need-based scholarship or grant aid	100
% needy UG rec. need-based scholarship or grant aid	99
% needy frosh rec. non-need-based scholarship or grant aid	0
% needy UG rec. non-need-based scholarship or grant aid	0
% needy frosh rec. need-based self-help aid	90
% needy UG rec. need-based self-help aid	92
% frosh rec. any financial aid	73
% UG rec. any financial aid	77
% UG borrow to pay for school	62
Average cumulative indebtedness	$32,254
% frosh need fully met	100
% ugrads need fully met	100
Average % of frosh need met	100
Average % of ugrad need met	100

OHIO NORTHERN UNIVERSITY

525 SOUTH MAIN STREET, ADA, OH 45810 • ADMISSIONS: 419-772-2260 • FAX: 419-772-2821

STUDENTS SAY ". . ."

Academics

The fairly remote location of Ohio Northern University has done little to prevent the school from developing "a great academic reputation, especially in the Midwest." This "great all-around school…really places an emphasis on life after college," especially in "teaching students to think critically and out of the box." Students admit the academics are "tough," and that toughness "challenges us to do our best," but they say the small class sizes and "personal attention from teachers" make the challenge one that "allows students the opportunity to be successful." The cozy school size means "it is much easier to get to know your professors on a more personal level." This benefits students since educators at Ohio Northern "are so willing to help you succeed in whatever way they can." Indeed, the "extraordinarily friendly" staff "are always willing to help," and "every professor has office hours and encourages you to utilize them." The goal of the teaching staff, students say, is "preparing their students to be contributing members of society" and giving them "the knowledge, skills, and abilities to be successful throughout life." The result is that the typical ONU student is "a hardworking individual who strives to do well in the classroom and gives back to the community."

Life

The "cozy village" of Ada, Ohio, "provides all the essentials, from groceries to a movie theater to bowling lanes to bars." However, it doesn't provide the kind of vibrant nightlife of an urban setting, so students often have to make their own entertainment. And they do. "There are tons of on-campus activities provided by the student planning committee," such as open music nights, music, "a ghost hunt around Halloween, a comedy show, or a foam party." Relaxing and studying consumes plenty of free time. "Education comes first," one student notes, while another says, "School is my number one priority, and I spend quite a bit of time in the library." Many students take to leaving town for things to do. Nearby Lima, for instance, has "a shopping mall, movie theater, and tons of restaurants and grocery stores." Ada itself provides "a small bowling alley, movie theater that plays one movie a week at discounted prices, a ferocious pizza parlor, and a Mexican restaurant." And, of course, there are parties. "If students are looking to find parties," students note, "they will." That said, "people who never drink have plenty of options for having fun, and ONU often brings entertainment to campus, too." Dorm luxuries increase as students climb through the grades, and Ada's small town feel means that "the campus is also very safe."

Student Body

Ohio Northern is not a campus teeming with diversity. Its students are "typically middle- to upper-class white students," though students are noticing efforts to address this in recent years. ONU students share other common traits. They are "intelligent and outgoing," a "very friendly and easy to talk to" group who tend to have "strong leadership skills and is outgoing, compassionate, intelligent, and very involved on campus." Though it is true that "students often tend to hang out with other students similar to them," this is not a sign of divisions on campus. "There is definitely no tension between any groups of people." The school's size means "you don't go anywhere without seeing someone you know," a direct result of the "close-knit feel of the campus." Those attending recognize that "being a student at Northern requires dedication to academics," but they also acknowledge, "it helps to have a balanced social life on campus." Overall, "students interact well with one another and work well together."

FINANCIAL AID: 419-772-2272 • E-MAIL: ADMISSIONS-UG@ONU.EDU • WEBSITE: WWW.ONU.EDU

THE PRINCETON REVIEW SAYS

Admissions

Very important factors considered include: GPA, rigor of secondary school record, standardized test scores. *Important factors considered include:* Class rank, application essay, extracurricular activities, interview, recommendation(s). *Other factors considered include:* First generation, talent/ability, volunteer work, alumni/ae relations, character/personal qualities, level of applicant's interest. SAT or ACT required; ACT with or without Writing component accepted. TOEFL required of all international applicants. *Academic units required:* 4 English; 2 mathematics; 2 science; (2 science lab); 2 social studies; 2 history; 4 academic electives. *Academic units recommended:* 4 English; 4 mathematics; 3 science; (2 science lab); 3 social studies; 2 foreign language; 2 history; 4 academic electives; 1 computer science; 1 visual/performing arts.

Financial Aid

Students should submit: FAFSA. The Princeton Review suggests that all financial aid forms be submitted as soon as possible after January 1. *Need-based scholarships/grants offered:* Federal Pell, SEOG, State scholarships/grants, private scholarships, the school's own gift aid. *Loan aid offered:* Direct Subsidized Stafford Loans, Direct Unsubsidized Stafford Loans, Direct PLUS loans, Federal Perkins Loans, State Loans, College/university loans from institutional funds. Federal Work-Study Program available. Institutional employment available. Off-campus job opportunities are good.

The Inside Word

Ohio Northern is a school focused on high academic achievement, so the best way to get your foot in the door is with good high school grades and strong standardized test scores. Those test scores and high school grades could help applicants qualify for generous merit-based scholarships. The school's website provides details. Take note that the highly acclaimed pharmacy school demands much higher standards.

THE SCHOOL SAYS "..."

From the Admissions Office

"The purpose of Ohio Northern is to help students develop into self-reliant, mature men and women capable of clear and logical thinking and sensitive to the higher values of truth, beauty, and goodness. ONU selects its student body from among those students possessing characteristics congruent with the institution's objectives. Generally, a student must be prepared to use the resources of the institution to achieve personal and educational goals.

"Students applying for admission are urged to submit scores for the SAT or the ACT with the writing section. The student's best composite scores will be used for scholarship purposes.

"The Office of Admissions highly encourages a campus visit. To schedule a visit, please visit www.onu.edu/admissions/visit_us or call 888-408-4668."

SELECTIVITY
Admissions Rating	83
# of applicants	2,922
% of applicants accepted	81
% of acceptees attending	27

FRESHMAN PROFILE
Range SAT Critical Reading	510–620
Range SAT Math	540–660
Range SAT Writing	505–630
Range ACT Composite	23–28
Minimum paper TOEFL	480
Minimum web-based TOEFL	157
Average HS GPA	3.70
% graduated top 10% of class	35
% graduated top 25% of class	65
% graduated top 50% of class	87

DEADLINES
Regular	
Priority	12/1
Nonfall registration?	Yes

APPLICANTS ALSO LOOK AT AND SOMETIMES PREFER
Miami University; Wittenberg University; The Ohio State University—Columbus

FINANCIAL FACTS
Financial Aid Rating	71
Annual tuition	$36,470
Room and board	$10,520
Required fees	$250
Books and supplies	$1,800

THE OHIO STATE UNIVERSITY—COLUMBUS

STUDENT ACADEMIC SVCS. BLDG. 281 WEST LANE AVE., COLUMBUS, OH 43210 • ADMISSIONS: 614-292-3980 • FAX: 614-292-4818

CAMPUS LIFE

Quality of Life Rating	82
Fire Safety Rating	78
Green Rating	93
Type of school	Public
Affiliation	No Affiliation
Environment	Metropolis

STUDENTS

Total undergrad enrollment	43,139
% male/female	53/47
% from out of state	14
% frosh from public high school	85
% frosh live on campus	93
% ugrads live on campus	26
# of fraternities (% ugrad men join)	42 (6)
# of sororities (% ugrad women join)	25 (6)
% African American	6
% Asian	5
% Caucasian	72
% Hispanic	3
% Native American	<1
% international	7
# of countries represented	109

SURVEY SAYS . . .

Students are happy
Athletic facilities are great
Great off-campus food
Everyone loves the Buckeyes
Student publications are popular

ACADEMICS

Academic Rating	79
% students returning for sophomore year	92
% students graduating within 4 years	58
% students graduating within 6 years	83
Calendar	Semester
Student/faculty ratio	19:1
Profs interesting rating	66
Profs accessible rating	66

Most classes have 20–29 students.
Most lab/discussion sessions have
20–29 students.

MOST POPULAR MAJORS

psychology; biology; finance

STUDENTS SAY ". . ."

Academics

Opportunities abound at The Ohio State University in Columbus, Ohio. Located "in a growing city," OSU has the distinction of being one of the largest schools in the United States. The "amazing opportunities" that come from such a large campus extend beyond the classrooms, "both academically and socially." "Everywhere you turn, there are always new and exciting things to be doing and learning." But the school's above-average size should not intimidate students. "OSU has a great way of breaking down the large school into much smaller communities." Established in 1870, "Ohio State has traditions like [nowhere] else. The feeling you get by being a Buckeye is truly one of a kind." What makes OSU special is how it "combines the love of tradition with the excellence of modern facilities and technology." "Ohio State really wants to offer students the most it can, including providing some state-of-the-art facilities and unique opportunities on campus to engage in the community. The school is very committed to bringing Ohio State students into the world as educated individuals." Students have many decisions to make when choosing from all the "very prestigious majors and classes" available. Student opinions about professors vary. One student says, "Some are better than others." Another is more enthusiastic about the faculty: "My academic experience has been great! I have admired and become very close to many professors, and I feel as though I have taken something away from every class I have taken." Overall, most students feel they "can learn a great deal here and take away an abundance of knowledge." Although "some of the big lectures are hard to keep up with…there is always free tutoring to help students get caught up."

Life

"Ohio State is a sports fan's paradise. [The] campus is bursting with Buckeye spirit, and it's infectious." "There may not be another school in the country that is as excited, spirited, and proud of literally everything they do like Ohio State is." "Not only do students love attending games, but we also have so many intramural sports that students get involved in for fun. You really never need to leave campus because there is always something fun happening." Plus, "there is a large city to explore as well. People who love sports, theater, and the arts will never run out of activities." Taking advantage of these options is easy because "students ride the city bus for free." Still, students feel the need to be careful and are concerned about "on and off campus safety." For some, the sheer number of choices can be overwhelming. "There are so many opportunities that it is easy to get lost in everything you feel you should be doing." Another student wonders if the school is doing its best to get messages out to everyone. "There have been occasions where things are not communicated to the entire student body as a whole, most likely due to the large student population. Sometimes I feel like I miss out on interesting and exciting things because I just wasn't made aware it was available." One student strongly recommends a visit to the school before you apply: "You will know as soon as you step on campus if it's the perfect fit for you!"

Student Body

Many students had good things to say about how the large amount of diversity positively affects life on campus. "Students here are open to different types of people—there is little or no discrimination. Diversity is valued here." "We have people from all different backgrounds, all different ethnicities. Students embrace the diversity and learn about new cultures and meet new people!" Somehow, Ohio State manages to bring everyone together. "The one common thing that seems to unite [us] is the love for our institution. Not everyone is a sports fan, but everyone bleeds scarlet and gray about something on this campus, whether it be sports, their research, or their classes." While at Ohio State, many students take advantage of the vast opportunity to travel to further broaden their world knowledge. "Studying abroad is something a lot of students do to learn more about other types of people, but there are also students here from so many places that a student can learn a lot by just making friends from different geographical areas."

FINANCIAL AID: 614-292-0300 • E-MAIL: ASKABUCKEYE@OSU.EDU • WEBSITE: WWW.OSU.EDU

THE PRINCETON REVIEW SAYS

Admissions

Very important factors considered include: Class rank, GPA, rigor of secondary school record, standardized test scores. *Important factors considered include:* Application essay, extracurricular activities, first generation, talent/ability, volunteer work, work experience. *Other factors considered include:* Geographical residence, racial/ethnic status, recommendation(s), state residency, character/personal qualities. SAT or ACT required; ACT with Writing component required. TOEFL required of all international applicants. *Academic units required:* 4 English; 3 mathematics; 3 science; (3 science lab); 2 social studies; 2 foreign language; 1 academic elective; 1 visual/performing arts. *Academic units recommended:* 4 English; 4 mathematics; 3 science; (3 science lab); 3 social studies; 3 foreign language; 1 academic elective; 1 visual/performing arts.

Financial Aid

Students should submit: FAFSA. The Princeton Review suggests that all financial aid forms be submitted as soon as possible after January 1. *Need-based scholarships/grants offered:* Federal Pell, SEOG, State scholarships/grants, private scholarships, the school's own gift aid. *Loan aid offered:* Direct Subsidized Stafford Loans, Direct Unsubsidized Stafford Loans, Direct PLUS loans, Federal Perkins Loans, Federal Nursing Loans, College/university loans from institutional funds. Applicants will be notified of awards beginning 4/1. Federal Work-Study Program available. Institutional employment available. Off-campus job opportunities are good.

The Inside Word

Standards are high at OSU, which attracts a huge number of applicants. But OSU is still worth a shot for the average student. Applications are reviewed with an eye for more than just grades and class rank, and the university's great reputation and affordable cost make it a good choice for anyone looking at large schools.

THE SCHOOL SAYS "..."

From the Admissions Office

"The Ohio State University has changed dramatically in the last decade, and, as a result, has seen its academic reputation thrive. A strong focus on helping first-year students make a successful transition to the university, competitive admissions, and a physical transformation (amazing new and renovated facilities across campus) are changes that have increased Ohio State's ability to draw students and faculty of exceptional scholarly talent."

"Once you're on campus, "big school" translates to depth, diversity, and opportunity. Ohio State prides itself on offering just about any academic or extracurricular opportunity a student could dream of: 175-plus majors; 100 study abroad programs; internship, research, and service-learning opportunities in every college; multiple Honors and Scholars programs; and a wide range of learning communities. Professional and faculty advisors help identify the opportunities that meet the student's interests and goals.

"Ohio State consistently boasts an impressive first-year retention rate over 90 percent. Ohio State's focus on the first year is campus-wide, including strong orientation and first-year programs.

"A tremendous bonus for Buckeyes is the city of Columbus. Consistently ranked as a top city for new grads and job growth, Columbus provides a wide range of opportunities for student internships, research, and service (and fun!)."

SELECTIVITY

Admissions Rating	92
# of applicants	31,359
% of applicants accepted	56
% of acceptees attending	41
# offered a place on the wait list	1,010
% accepting a place on wait list	24
% admitted from wait list	0

FRESHMAN PROFILE

Range SAT Critical Reading	540–660
Range SAT Math	610–720
Range SAT Writing	550–660
Range ACT Composite	27–31
Minimum paper TOEFL	550
Minimum web-based TOEFL	79
% graduated top 10% of class	58
% graduated top 25% of class	92
% graduated top 50% of class	99

DEADLINES

Early action	
Deadline	11/1
Notification	12/15
Regular	
Deadline	2/1
Nonfall registration?	Yes

APPLICANTS ALSO LOOK AT AND SOMETIMES PREFER

University of Cincinnati; Case Western Reserve University

FINANCIAL FACTS

Financial Aid Rating	68
Annual in-state tuition	$9,615
Annual out-of-state tuition	$25,335
Room and board	$9,850
Required fees	$422
Books and supplies	$1,248
% needy frosh rec. need-based scholarship or grant aid	90
% needy UG rec. need-based scholarship or grant aid	78
% needy frosh rec. non-need-based scholarship or grant aid	7
% needy UG rec. non-need-based scholarship or grant aid	3
% needy frosh rec. need-based self-help aid	78
% needy UG rec. need-based self-help aid	88
% frosh rec. any financial aid	90
% UG rec. any financial aid	79
% UG borrow to pay for school	56
Average cumulative indebtedness	$26,472
% frosh need fully met	24
% ugrads need fully met	16
Average % of frosh need met	71
Average % of ugrad need met	64

OHIO UNIVERSITY—ATHENS

CHUBB HALL 120, 1 OHIO UNIVERSITY, ATHENS, OH 45701 • ADMISSIONS: 740-593-4100 • FAX: 740-593-0560

CAMPUS LIFE

Quality of Life Rating	74
Fire Safety Rating	73
Green Rating	91
Type of school	Public
Affiliation	No Affiliation
Environment	Town

STUDENTS

Total undergrad enrollment	23,332
% male/female	40/60
% from out of state	14
% frosh from public high school	82
% frosh live on campus	99
% ugrads live on campus	44
# of fraternities (% ugrad men join)	19 (8)
# of sororities (% ugrad women join)	12 (8)
% African American	5
% Asian	1
% Caucasian	83
% Hispanic	2
% Native American	<1
% international	4
# of countries represented	113

SURVEY SAYS . . .
Athletic facilities are great
Students are friendly
Students are happy
Student publications are popular
Lots of beer drinking
Hard liquor is popular

ACADEMICS

Academic Rating	71
% students returning for sophomore year	79
% students graduating within 4 years	48
% students graduating within 6 years	67
Calendar	Semester
Student/faculty ratio	18:1
Profs interesting rating	71
Profs accessible rating	70

Most classes have 20–29 students.
Most lab/discussion sessions have
10–19 students.

MOST POPULAR MAJORS
biology; journalism; psychology

STUDENTS SAY ". . ."

Academics
"Academically, OHIO has something for everyone, from astrophysics to the history of rock and roll," students at this large state-run university boast. And students have an equally wide range of choices when it comes to committing themselves to academics; "You can take advantage of the vast amount of knowledge and resources directly available, or you can forget studies and party," students tell us. Those seeking a challenge will have no trouble finding it here, however; OHIO boasts "a strong engineering faculty," a noteworthy aviation program offered within the university's demanding college of engineering and technology, an "excellent and very selective early childhood education program," and "one of the best journalism schools in the country"—the E.W. Scripps School of Journalism—which offers "frequent opportunities to learn and grow outside the classroom with guest speakers and special events." The Scripps College houses "a great communications school" offering great hands-on experience; one student informs us that "Southeast Ohio depends on our college television and radio station for their news, weather, and high school sports." As at any large university, unassertive students are in danger of getting lost in the crowd, but those who make the effort to seek out faculty and administrators assure us that "the school is very supportive of the students. I have close relationships with multiple professors, and I think that they generally take a strong interest in the students."

Life
"Ohio University has a beautiful campus with lots of character, both in academia and nightlife," students here report. Greek organizations play a major role in the life of the campus, providing service to the community and serving as a social catalyst. Some undergraduates assure us that the school "truly lives up to its reputation as a party school. It is never hard to find a party on any given night, whether in the dorms or off campus." One undergrad writes, "A nationwide reputation as a party school is not something I'm proud of," but most accept things as they are, noting that "Ohio University is a school where everyone can find a group of people doing whatever they're particularly interested in," which is to say that partying is hardly the only option here. College athletics are a big draw (especially football, men's basketball, and women's volleyball), as are such annual events as Homecoming and the school is host to literally hundreds of student clubs and organizations serving interests of every variety. Hometown Athens is a typical small college town with access to a wide variety of outdoor activities. The closest cities of note—Columbus, Ohio, and Charleston, West Virginia—are each about a ninety-minute drive from the OHIO campus.

Student Body
The OHIO student body "is pretty homogenous," with a large contingent of undergrads who are "white, middle- to upper-class, and from Ohio." "We have a small minority population, especially in the undergraduate programs," one student concedes, "but it's easy to interact with other cultures if you seek them out." Students here "try to get involved in community service, especially those involved in Greek life," and they are "generally friendly." Most work hard enough to get by but rarely harder; one student observes that "students totally devoted to their schoolwork are atypical here." Yet, it should be noted that OHIO students have succeeded in claiming a number of nationally competitive academic awards in recent years, with The Chronicle of Higher Education having recognized Ohio University as being among the nation's top producers of U.S. Fulbright Students.

FINANCIAL AID: 740-593-4141 • E-MAIL: ADMISSIONS@OHIO.EDU • WEBSITE: WWW.OHIO.EDU

THE PRINCETON REVIEW SAYS

Admissions

Very important factors considered include: GPA, rigor of secondary school record, standardized test scores. *Important factors considered include:* Class rank, application essay, first generation. *Other factors considered include:* Extracurricular activities, geographical residence, recommendation(s), state residency, talent/ability, volunteer work, work experience, character/personal qualities. SAT or ACT required; ACT with Writing component recommended. *Academic units required:* 4 English; 4 mathematics; 3 science; 3 social studies; 2 foreign language; 4 academic electives. *Academic units recommended:* 4 English; 4 mathematics; 3 science; 3 social studies; 2 foreign language; 4 academic electives; 1 visual/performing arts.

Financial Aid

Students should submit: FAFSA. Regular filing deadline is 3/15. The Princeton Review suggests that all financial aid forms be submitted as soon as possible after January 1. *Need-based scholarships/grants offered:* Federal Pell, SEOG, State scholarships/grants, private scholarships, the school's own gift aid. *Loan aid offered:* Direct Subsidized Stafford Loans, Direct Unsubsidized Stafford Loans, Direct PLUS loans, Federal Perkins Loans. Applicants will be notified of awards beginning in late March. Federal Work-Study Program available. Institutional employment available.

The Inside Word

Admissions requirements vary from school to school at Ohio University. The Honors Tutorial College is most selective (you should be in the top 10 percent of your graduating class and earn at least a 30/1300 on your ACT/SAT for consideration), followed by the journalism school (top 15 percent, 25/1140), the business school (top 20 percent, 24/1100), media arts and studies, engineering, and visual communication. Admissions decisions are made through holistic review; those on the cusp should get in if they've demonstrated academic improvement during their junior and senior years and show evidence of academic preparation.

THE SCHOOL SAYS "..."

From the Admissions Office

"Ohio University offers a welcoming campus and more than 250 outstanding academic programs that make a degree from OHIO an instant advantage. Our dedicated professors do more than just teach—they serve as mentors and advisors who prepare students for success. Our students also are building a tradition of winning highly competitive academic awards, consistently placing us among the top universities in the state and in elite company nationally. In addition, Ohio University is home to an Honors Tutorial College that offers high-ability students distinctive, tutorial-based learning opportunities that mirror the instructional model used for centuries at British universities such as Cambridge and Oxford.

"Students can enhance their educational experiences with adventures beyond the classroom. Education abroad opportunities can range from studying the plays of Shakespeare in London to retail merchandising in China. Students also can participate in meaningful research and internships, community service, and more than 400 student organizations. OHIO's picturesque campus—among the most beautiful in the nation—residential learning communities that create a welcoming environment for first-year students. Friendships are forged as students with diverse backgrounds study, learn, and socialize together.

"Many students proudly cheer on Ohio University's athletics teams. The Bobcats have garnered increasing national attention in recent years, with the football team winning back-to-back bowl games and the men's basketball team reaching the Sweet 16 round of the NCAA Tournament. Swimming and diving, volleyball, and other sports round out the athletic program. Many students participate in club and intramural sports or learn to rappel, kayak, or canoe through OHIO's Outdoor Pursuits Program."

SELECTIVITY

Admissions Rating	73
# of applicants	20,765
% of applicants accepted	73
% of acceptees attending	28

FRESHMAN PROFILE

Range SAT Critical Reading	480–600
Range SAT Math	490–600
Range SAT Writing	470–580
Range ACT Composite	22–26
Average HS GPA	3.42
% graduated top 10% of class	17
% graduated top 25% of class	42
% graduated top 50% of class	82

DEADLINES

Regular	
Priority	2/1
Nonfall registration?	Yes

APPLICANTS ALSO LOOK AT AND OFTEN PREFER

Miami University; The Ohio State University—Columbus; Bowling Green State University; Kent State University

FINANCIAL FACTS

Financial Aid Rating	65
Annual in-state tuition	$10,446
Annual out-of-state tuition	$19,410
Room and board	$10,230
Books and supplies	$902
% needy frosh rec. need-based scholarship or grant aid	81
% needy UG rec. need-based scholarship or grant aid	70
% needy frosh rec. non-need-based scholarship or grant aid	8
% needy UG rec. non-need-based scholarship or grant aid	5
% needy frosh rec. need-based self-help aid	95
% needy UG rec. need-based self-help aid	87
% frosh rec. any financial aid	90
% UG rec. any financial aid	72
% UG borrow to pay for school	66
Average cumulative indebtedness	$26,928
% frosh need fully met	35
% ugrads need fully met	29
Average % of frosh need met	53
Average % of ugrad need met	52

OHIO WESLEYAN UNIVERSITY

61 SOUTH SANDUSKY STREET, DELAWARE, OH 43015 • ADMISSIONS: 740-368-3020 • FAX: 740-368-3314

STUDENTS SAY ". . ."

Academics

Ohio Wesleyan University is "an outstanding, small, liberal arts college" that manages to cultivate a "welcoming and diverse" community. With "fantastic scholarships," a "beautiful" campus, and academic "flexibility" that allows undergrads to pursue multiple passions, it's no wonder students love it here. Undergrads truly appreciate the school's "emphasis on having an international experience," which is fostered "through our large percentage of international students, OWU's travel learning courses, and studying abroad." And while the university is bursting with academic options and opportunities, students especially like to tout the premed, zoology and English programs. Of course, no matter the major, OWU undergrads value that their "educational experience is marked by close relationships with professors." Indeed, these "incredibly supportive [and] knowledgeable" teachers manage to create a "wonderful" classroom environment. Moreover, as one pleased student adds, "Professors are enthusiastic and genuinely enjoy teaching the material. They are eager to help you outside of the classroom and strive to form personal bonds with their students." And a fellow student supports this sentiment, sharing, "Professors have amazing dedication to their students. They have office hours daily, respond to e-mails frequently, answer questions whenever available, and are active in all aspects of their students' lives." All in all, "OWU is a place where students can experience the opportunities of a larger school with the personality and personal attention of a smaller school."

Life

Ohio Wesleyan students are typically always on the go, as most undergrads are "active in politics, school government, sports, and other special interest clubs." What's more, undergrads excitedly tell us that "there [is] almost always some sort of event going on [be it] performing arts [shows], parties…or free food on the JAYwalk." Additionally, fraternities and sororities are popular hangouts on the weekend for "relaxing, drinking, dancing, and having fun. But if you're not into that, there are constantly fun nonalcoholic parties thrown by the school. There are plenty of mixers so that everyone gets to know each other." When students are itching to get off campus for a bit, they'll head into downtown Delaware, which is "easily in walking distance" and offers "cute little shops and restaurants." Indeed, "it's pretty common to find people studying in the [local] bookstore or coffee shop." And should students be feeling slightly more adventurous, Columbus is only about a thirty-minute ride away. In short, "if you are bored at this school, it's because you are trying to be."

Student Body

While undergrads at OWU admit, "there are several groups of typical students (sorority girls, lax bros, athletes, fraternity boys, eccentric kids, etc.)," they assert just as fervently that "no single stereotype is predominant on campus; there's pretty much an equal distribution among the groups." In turn, this makes for an "outgoing [and] involved" student body that's "willing to try new things and meet new people." Of course, if pressed to find additional common ground, undergrads would also likely say their fellow students are also "fairly politically aware, passionate about something, tolerant of diversity, involved on campus, like to learn inside and outside of the classroom, and care about academics." Moreover, they "are very driven and motivated to do well and succeed." Most important, we're told that "any kind of person can feel pretty comfortable at Ohio Wesleyan, as long as they can be friendly and accepting in a small, tight-knit community." Perhaps this happy student sums up his peers best, "Everyone has their own unique style, and they're not afraid to be who they are. It's interesting to watch students walk up and down the JAYwalk. There's this buzz on campus that just keeps the community going."

FINANCIAL AID: 740-368-3050 • E-MAIL: OWUADMIT@OWU.EDU • WEBSITE: WWW.OWU.EDU

THE PRINCETON REVIEW SAYS

Admissions

Very important factors considered include: GPA, rigor of secondary school record, application essay, interview, recommendation(s), character/personal qualities. *Important factors considered include:* Class rank, standardized test scores, extracurricular activities, talent/ability. *Other factors considered include:* First generation, geographical residence, racial/ethnic status, volunteer work, work experience, alumni/ae relations, level of applicant's interest. SAT or ACT required; ACT with or without Writing component accepted. TOEFL required of all international applicants. *Academic units required:* 4 English; 3 mathematics; 3 science; 3 social studies; 2 foreign language. *Academic units recommended:* 4 mathematics; 4 science; 4 social studies; 3 foreign language.

Financial Aid

Students should submit: FAFSA. The Princeton Review suggests that all financial aid forms be submitted as soon as possible after January 1. *Need-based scholarships/grants offered:* Federal Pell, SEOG, State scholarships/grants, private scholarships, the school's own gift aid. *Loan aid offered:* Direct Subsidized Stafford Loans, Direct Unsubsidized Stafford Loans, Direct PLUS loans, Federal Perkins Loans, College/university loans from institutional funds. Federal Work-Study Program available. Institutional employment available. Off-campus job opportunities are excellent.

The Inside Word

Ohio Wesleyan takes a well-rounded approach to the admissions game. The school is looking for students who will actively contribute to and thrive within OWU. To that end, all application components, from transcript to teacher evaluations, matter. Make sure you don't slack on any facet.

THE SCHOOL SAYS "..."

From the Admissions Office

"Ohio Wesleyan University, a national liberal arts university with a major international presence, is remarkable for the broad range of its academic and pre-professional programs, the international dimensions of its curriculum, an emphasis on community through leadership and service, and its unwavering commitment to focus on linking theory and practice in every field of study. The university is located in Delaware, Ohio, just north of Columbus, the capital city.

"OWU's Theory-to-Practice initiative includes competitive university-funded grants that allow students to propose and conduct original research, serve meaningful internships, and participate in service opportunities and cultural immersion throughout the world. Travel-Learning Courses augment classroom theory with international travel and study in multiple fields in countries throughout the world. The university offers ninety-three majors, sequences, and courses of study, far more than most institutions of its size.

"For the past five consecutive years, the university has been honored with the President's Honor Roll Award for Community Service, with Distinction; in 2010, OWU was one of three colleges nationwide to win the 2009 President's Award for Excellence in General Community Service.

"Ohio Wesleyan has twenty-three varsity athletic teams: eleven men's and twelve women's. OWU boasts more team championships and Academic All-America® scholar-athletes than any other school in the North Coast Athletic Conference and has won Division III national championships in men's soccer (two), women's soccer (two), and men's basketball, with individual national titles in several other sports.

"Applicants may submit the SAT or the ACT. Best scores from either test will considered in the application review."

SELECTIVITY
Admissions Rating	84
# of applicants	3,835
% of applicants accepted	74
% of acceptees attending	19
# offered a place on the wait list	182

FRESHMAN PROFILE
Range SAT Critical Reading	510–620
Range SAT Math	520–640
Range SAT Writing	500–620
Range ACT Composite	23–28
Minimum paper TOEFL	550
Minimum web-based TOEFL	213
Average HS GPA	3.49
% graduated top 10% of class	32
% graduated top 25% of class	63
% graduated top 50% of class	89

DEADLINES
Early decision	
Deadline	11/15
Notification	11/30
Early action	
Deadline	1/15
Regular	
Priority	3/1
Notification	3/1
Nonfall registration?	Yes

APPLICANTS ALSO LOOK AT AND OFTEN PREFER
Denison University; Miami University; The College of Wooster; The Ohio State University—Columbus; Wittenberg University

AND SOMETIMES PREFER
Kenyon College; University of Dayton

AND RARELY PREFER
Oberlin College

FINANCIAL FACTS
Financial Aid Rating	86
Annual tuition	$40,250
Room and board	$10,670
Required fees	$260
Books and supplies	$1,300
% needy frosh rec. need-based scholarship or grant aid	100
% needy UG rec. need-based scholarship or grant aid	99
% needy frosh rec. non-need-based scholarship or grant aid	28
% needy UG rec. non-need-based scholarship or grant aid	25
% needy frosh rec. need-based self-help aid	77
% needy UG rec. need-based self-help aid	80
% frosh rec. any financial aid	97
% UG rec. any financial aid	97
% UG borrow to pay for school	65
Average cumulative indebtedness	$30,900
% frosh need fully met	31
% ugrads need fully met	28
Average % of frosh need met	84
Average % of ugrad need met	80

Pennsylvania State University—University Park

201 Shields Building, Box 3000, University Park, PA 16802-3000 • Admissions: 814-865-5471 • Fax: 814-863-7590

CAMPUS LIFE

Quality of Life Rating	96
Fire Safety Rating	98
Green Rating	97
Type of school	Public
Affiliation	No Affiliation
Environment	Town

STUDENTS

Total undergrad enrollment	39,460
% male/female	54/46
% from out of state	31
% ugrads live on campus	37
# of fraternities(% ugrad men join)	59(19)
# of sororities(% ugrad women join)	30(16)
% African American	4
% Asian	5
% Caucasian	72
% Hispanic	5
% Native American	<1
% international	9
# of countries represented	129

SURVEY SAYS . . .

Students are happy
Classroom facilities are great
Lab facilities are great
Career services are great
School is well run
Students are friendly
Students get along with local community
Great off-campus food
Campus feels safe
Athletic facilities are great
Lots of beer drinking
Hard liquor is popular
Everyone loves the Nittany Lions
Intramural sports are popular
Student publications are popular
Alumni active on campus

ACADEMICS

Academic Rating	81
% students returning for sophomore year	92
% students graduating within 4 years	65
% students graduating within 6 years	85
Calendar	Semester
Student/faculty ratio	17:1
Profs interesting rating	76
Profs accessible rating	77

Most classes have 20–29 students.
Most lab/discussion sessions have 20–29 students.

STUDENTS SAY ". . ."

Academics

Immense "pride and a sense of community" pervade every aspect of life at Penn State. Students love the remarkable "school spirit" and "strong family feel" on this vibrant campus, and they are equally proud of the "quality education" they receive. An affordable public institution, PSU offers "highly regarded programs across a wide range of academic colleges," including a "prestigious undergrad business school," top engineering and education majors, and the competitive Schreyer Honors College, which participants describe as "the finest honors program in the nation." "Classes freshman year are mostly lectures," which can be "intimidating" for new students. Fortunately, "even in lectures with hundreds of students, many professors still make an effort to get to know their class and have plenty of office hours to make themselves more accessible." Plus, the academic experience becomes more individualized as you move through the system. A current student shares, "As I have gotten into my majors, my classes are down to about 15–40 people and there are a lot more discussions. I know all of my professors personally now." Academics are often described as "rigorous" and "competitive," but most students are able to stay afloat; here, "professors will challenge you, but it's nothing that a hard-working student can't handle." Job-seeking seniors praise the career center, as well as the school's fantastic alumni connections, saying "The Penn State networking web is incredible!" Not to mention, the school's enviable "location within driving distance to Philadelphia, Washington, and New York" makes it easier to score a job at graduation.

Life

If you are looking for the "full college experience," you'll find "the perfect mix of great academics, social life, and sports" at Penn State. While "the library is usually filled with students" during the week, "everyone counts down the days till the weekend, then its party, party, party." Throughout fall semester, football is a campus-wide obsession; "game days are super exciting and unifying for the student population," which turns out in large numbers to tailgate and cheer at Beaver Stadium. In addition to sports, "Greek Life dominates the social scene," though students also flock to the many bars in downtown State College. A current student jokes, "Nothing brings the Penn State community together like stumbling around downtown with 3,000 other drunken students." Those looking for a mellower night out will find "on-campus concerts, stand up comedians, craft nights, sporting events, and other ways of having fun without drugs or alcohol." Others like to "go out to the local avenue and try new eateries, and walk around campus and enjoy the scenery." In addition to the "killer social life," there are hundreds of clubs and student groups; of particular note, many students "fit in by joining THON, the largest student-run philanthropy in the world, that raises money for children with pediatric cancer." No matter what your interests, "between football games, Late Nights at the HUB, festivities downtown, movies, shows at Eisenhower Auditorium or the Penn State Theatre, concerts at the BJC…there is something for everyone."

Students

With a total enrollment of more than 40,000, "Penn State is the passion and pride of a large and diverse student body." Demographically, the school draws heavily from the Northeast; in particular, there are "lots of kids from the tri-state area," and most could be described as "athletic, suburban, and friendly middle-class." While some note that, "the percentage of minorities and foreign students is low," they also say, "pretty much every student will find somewhere to fit in." Especially during the first year, "there are many opportunities to meet new people," and "mostly everyone is friendly," making it easy to form bonds and build relationships. The best way to make friends is to "try different clubs and find your niche"; from Greek organizations to sports, most Penn Staters have "a great enthusiasm for extracurricular and philanthropic involvement." On that note, most undergrads "take their education seriously," but achieve a "good balance of school and social life."

PENNSYLVANIA STATE UNIVERSITY—UNIVERSITY PARK

FINANCIAL AID: 814-865-6301 • E-MAIL: ADMISSIONS@PSU.EDU • WEBSITE: WWW.PSU.EDU

THE PRINCETON REVIEW SAYS

Admissions

Very important factors considered include: GPA, standardized test scores. *Important factors considered include:* Rigor of secondary school record. *Other factors considered include:* Class rank, application essay, extracurricular activities, talent/ability, volunteer work, work experience, alumni/ae relations, character/personal qualities. SAT or ACT required; ACT with Writing component required. TOEFL required of all international applicants. *Academic units required:* 4 English; 3 mathematics; 3 science; 3 social studies; 2 foreign language. *Academic units recommended:* 3 foreign language.

Financial Aid

Students should submit: FAFSA. The Princeton Review suggests that all financial aid forms be submitted as soon as possible after January 1. *Need-based scholarships/grants offered:* Federal Pell, SEOG, State scholarships/grants, private scholarships, the school's own gift aid. *Loan aid offered:* Direct Subsidized Stafford Loans, Direct Unsubsidized Stafford Loans, Direct PLUS loans, Federal Perkins Loans, College/university loans from institutional funds. Federal Work-Study Program available. Institutional employment available. Off-campus job opportunities are good.

The Inside Word

Though the school does not have any minimum requirements for an incoming student's GPA or standardized test scores, high school GPA is by far the most important factor in PSU admissions. According to the school's website, high school grades account for two-thirds of the final admissions decision. Other factors, like standardized test scores, make up the remaining third. PSU is a popular choice for Pennsylvania residents and admits on a rolling basis; prospective students should submit their applications as early as possible.

THE SCHOOL SAYS "..."

From the Admissions Office

"Unique among large public universities, Penn State combines the more than 40,000 student setting of its University Park campus with twenty academically and administratively integrated undergraduate locations across Pennsylvania.

Ranging in size from 600 to 4,000 students, most of Penn State's residential and commuter locations offer the first two years of baccalaureate instruction as well as a limited number of two- and four-year degree programs. These small-college settings focus on the needs of new students by offering smaller classes and close interaction with faculty. More than half of the undergraduates who complete their studies at University Park start at another Penn State campus.

Applicants are qualified for review for any of Penn State's campuses, with preferences considered in the order requested. Choice of location and entrance difficulty are based, in part, on demand. Due to its popularity, the University Park campus is the most competitive for admission. Freshman applicants may submit the results from the SAT or the ACT with the writing component."

SELECTIVITY

Admissions Rating	90
# of applicants	42,570
% of applicants accepted	55
% of acceptees attending	34

FRESHMAN PROFILE

Range SAT Critical Reading	520–620
Range SAT Math	550–660
Range SAT Writing	530–630
Range ACT Composite	24–29
Minimum paper TOEFL	550
Minimum web-based TOEFL	80
Average HS GPA	3.57
% graduated top 10% of class	36
% graduated top 25% of class	78
% graduated top 50% of class	98

DEADLINES

Regular	
Priority	11/30
Nonfall registration?	Yes

FINANCIAL FACTS

Financial Aid Rating	68
Annual in-state tuition	$16,090
Annual out-of-state tuition	$28,664
Room and board	$10,090
Required fees	$902
Books and supplies	$1,696
% needy frosh rec. need-based scholarship or grant aid	43
% needy UG rec. need-based scholarship or grant aid	52
% needy frosh rec. non-need-based scholarship or grant aid	42
% needy UG rec. non-need-based scholarship or grant aid	33
% needy frosh rec. need-based self-help aid	75
% needy UG rec. need-based self-help aid	84
% frosh rec. any financial aid	68
% UG rec. any financial aid	69
% UG borrow to pay for school	66
Average cumulative indebtedness	$35,430
% frosh need fully met	8
% ugrads need fully met	8
Average % of frosh need met	58
Average % of ugrad need met	60

PEPPERDINE UNIVERSITY

24255 PACIFIC COAST HIGHWAY, MALIBU, CA 90263 • ADMISSIONS: 310-456-4392 • FAX: 310-506-4861

CAMPUS LIFE

Quality of Life Rating	93
Fire Safety Rating	74
Green Rating	85
Type of school	Private
Affiliation	Church of Christ
Environment	City

STUDENTS

Total undergrad enrollment	3,516
% male/female	41/59
% from out of state	15
% frosh live on campus	98
% ugrads live on campus	58
# of fraternities (% ugrad men join)	5 (16)
# of sororities (% ugrad women join)	7 (27)
% African American	7
% Asian	14
% Caucasian	42
% Hispanic	16
% Native American	<1
% international	9
# of countries represented	64

SURVEY SAYS . . .
Students are happy
Classroom facilities are great
Students are friendly
Students involved in community service
Campus feels safe

ACADEMICS

Academic Rating	85
% students returning for sophomore year	92
% students graduating within 4 years	70
% students graduating within 6 years	80
Calendar	Semester
Student/faculty ratio	13:1
Profs interesting rating	85
Profs accessible rating	88

Most classes have 10–19 students.
Most lab/discussion sessions have 10–19 students.

MOST POPULAR MAJORS
business administration and management; psychology; political science

STUDENTS SAY "..."

Academics

A small private college overlooking the Pacific Ocean, Pepperdine is an "amazingly beautiful" place to get an education. With about 3,500 undergraduates and an excellent teacher/student ratio, Pepperdine and its "smaller class sizes make it beyond easy to form personal yet academic relationships with your professors." Although "academics are quite challenging," professors "take their role as a mentor seriously. They invite classes over for meals, meet students for coffee, and are eager to help you move in the direction of your dreams." While universally supportive, professors get mixed reviews regarding the ability to keep your attention: Some professors "are very lively and exciting, while some are boring and you would rather take a nap." Career and internship opportunities naturally grow out of the school's prime location, strong alumni network, and regional ties. "Professors are well-connected with both corporations and the surrounding community," and there are "endless internship and volunteer opportunities" in the region. Plus, "Pepperdine's International Program is consistently ranked as one of the best," offering "programs in Florence, London, Shanghai, Buenos Aires…the list goes on! Anyone who is looking forward to studying abroad should definitely look into our programs." Pepperdine is affiliated with the Church of Christ, and Christian values are "prevalent but not overwhelming" in academic curriculum; all students, regardless of their background, are required to attend the "mandatory Convocation program"—a series of chapels, Bible studies, and speakers, designed to promote spirituality. While there's a conservative slant among the higher-ups, Pepperdine's administration is "much more moderate than what you would find at other small, Christian schools."

Life

Pepperdine students gloat about their school's perfect location in Malibu, California, where "there is a 360-degree view of the Pacific Ocean, and students can walk to the beach." The "campus is surrounded by national parks and beach," so nature lovers enjoy "countless opportunities for hiking, swimming, running, waterfall jumping, camping, [and] rock-climbing." "The close proximity to LA, Santa Monica, Hollywood, and the Pacific Coast Highway make it easy for students to find things to do." Students say that a car is a necessity. Fortunately, "there are enough students with cars to hitch a ride," if you don't have your own set of wheels. Alcohol is prohibited at Pepperdine, and "the dry campus policy is strictly enforced." Therefore, "people have to go off campus to drink and party." "The people who party can do so without it affecting the people who don't at all." While the campus is undeniably dreamy, students would like to see the school "improve is the student health facilities and workout facilities"—as well as provide more student parking.

Student Body

"Academics, service, athletics, and social events are all a big part of the life of a typical student." During college, "the typical Pepperdine student is involved in two service projects, spends their spring break building homes in Central America, has huge career goals, is involved in a performing arts group, looks forward to new student orientation all year, and studies abroad as a sophomore." Pepperdine students are also good about "being healthy and eating well and exercising right." It can feel "as if all the popular kids across all the different high schools across America convened in Malibu." However, students tell us "there is a lot more diversity" at Pepperdine today. You get a nice mix of "art majors to the science kids to the surfers to the hardcore studiers to the philosophy majors." Most students come from "a Christian background whether or not they are religious now," and some students are strongly religious and conservative. "Finding alternative viewpoints may be tough," but most students are "fairly open-minded" and "extremely nice."

FINANCIAL AID: 310-506-4301 • E-MAIL: ADMISSION-SEAVER@PEPPERDINE.EDU • WEBSITE: WWW.PEPPERDINE.EDU

THE PRINCETON REVIEW SAYS

Admissions

Very important factors considered include: GPA, rigor of secondary school record, application essay, extracurricular activities, talent/ability, character/personal qualities, religious affiliation. *Important factors considered include:* Standardized test scores, recommendation(s), volunteer work. *Other factors considered include:* first generation, racial/ethnic status, work experience, alumni/ae relations. SAT or ACT required; ACT with Writing component recommended. TOEFL required of all international applicants. *Academic units required:*

Financial Aid

Students should submit: FAFSA. The Princeton Review suggests that all financial aid forms be submitted as soon as possible after January 1. *Need-based scholarships/grants offered:* Federal Pell, SEOG, State scholarships/grants, private scholarships, the school's own gift aid, United Negro College Fund. *Loan aid offered:* Direct Subsidized Stafford Loans, Direct Unsubsidized Stafford Loans, Direct PLUS loans, Federal Perkins Loans, College/university loans from institutional funds. Applicants will be notified of awards beginning 4/15. Federal Work-Study Program available. Institutional employment available. Off-campus job opportunities are good.

The Inside Word

Admission to Pepperdine is highly selective. The school generally receives almost 8,600 applications for the incoming class of fewer than 1,000 students. Decisions are made based on a student's academic record, standardized test scores, and two letters of recommendation—one personal and the other academic. Students affiliated with the Church of Christ are eligible for special Church of Christ scholarships; to be considered, applicants must submit a letter of recommendation from a church leader.

THE SCHOOL SAYS ". . ."

From the Admissions Office

"As a selective university, Pepperdine seeks students who show promise of academic achievement at the collegiate level. However, we also seek students who are committed to serving the university community, as well as others with whom they come into contact. We look for community-service activities, volunteer efforts, and strong leadership qualities, as well as a demonstrated commitment to academic studies and an interest in the liberal arts.

"Seaver College of Pepperdine University requires freshman applicants to submit scores from either the SAT Reasoning Test (including the writing portion) or the ACT (including the writing test). The scores are evaluated in conjunction with the grade point average in specific courses completed."

SELECTIVITY

Admissions Rating	94
# of applicants	9,721
% of applicants accepted	37
% of acceptees attending	22
# offered a place on the wait list	1,289
% accepting a place on wait list	42
% admitted from wait list	0

FRESHMAN PROFILE

Range SAT Critical Reading	560–660
Range SAT Math	570–680
Range SAT Writing	570–670
Range ACT Composite	26–31
Minimum paper TOEFL	550
Minimum web-based TOEFL	220
Average HS GPA	3.59
% graduated top 10% of class	47
% graduated top 25% of class	83
% graduated top 50% of class	96

DEADLINES

Regular	
Deadline	1/5
Notification	4/1
Nonfall registration?	Yes

APPLICANTS ALSO LOOK AT AND OFTEN PREFER

University of Southern California; University of California—Los Angeles; University of San Diego; University of California—San Diego; Loyola Marymount University

AND SOMETIMES PREFER

Vanderbilt University; New York University

AND RARELY PREFER

Occidental College

FINANCIAL FACTS

Financial Aid Rating	84
% needy frosh rec. need-based scholarship or grant aid	95
% needy UG rec. need-based scholarship or grant aid	95
% needy frosh rec. non-need-based scholarship or grant aid	0
% needy UG rec. non-need-based scholarship or grant aid	0
% needy frosh rec. need-based self-help aid	84
% needy UG rec. need-based self-help aid	84
% UG borrow to pay for school	60
Average cumulative indebtedness	$30,311
% frosh need fully met	28
% ugrads need fully met	23
Average % of frosh need met	82
Average % of ugrad need met	80

PITZER COLLEGE

1050 NORTH MILLS AVENUE, CLAREMONT, CA 91711-6101 • ADMISSIONS: 909-621-8129 • FAX: 909-621-8770

CAMPUS LIFE

Quality of Life Rating	94
Fire Safety Rating	79
Green Rating	86
Type of school	Private
Affiliation	No Affiliation
Environment	Town

STUDENTS

Total undergrad enrollment	1,099
% male/female	38/62
% from out of state	50
% frosh live on campus	100
% ugrads live on campus	74
% African American	6
% Asian	8
% Caucasian	46
% Hispanic	16
% Native American	1
% international	3
# of countries represented	15

SURVEY SAYS . . .
Lots of liberal students
Political activism is popular
Students are happy
Lab facilities are great
Students are friendly
Students aren't religious
Students involved in community service
Students environmentally aware
Great food on campus
Campus feels safe
Active minority support groups

ACADEMICS

Academic Rating	95
% students returning for sophomore year	93
% students graduating within 4 years	75
% students graduating within 6 years	81
Calendar	Semester
Student/faculty ratio	12:1
Profs interesting rating	92
Profs accessible rating	93

Most classes have 10–19 students.

MOST POPULAR MAJORS
psychology; film studies; sociology

STUDENTS SAY "..."

Academics

Pitzer College is "small, personal, and unique," but because students have access to the classes and "excellent resources" at four other local colleges through the Claremont Consortium, "you can choose to make your college experience as large or as small as you want!" Pitzer doesn't have a lot of requirements, so there's a high degree of academic freedom and flexibility, including the opportunity to create your own major. Students gush about the level of "student autonomy," calling Pitzer "a challenging school that allows students to become effective leaders." Emphasis is on "social responsibility" and "intercultural understanding," and classes "are constantly being connected to present society and how you can pursue social issues through your field of study." "Professors are as zesty and zany as they are brilliant and intriguing" and they "encourage respectful dialogue inside and outside the classroom." Generally, "emphasis [is] on discussion; besides intro courses you won't find many lecture classes." "Pitzer is all about analytical thinking and learning to think beyond the material in front of you. Professors won't settle for summary; be prepared to form and argue your own opinions." Students are very positive about their professors, calling them "life changing" and "dedicated and enthusiastic." A history major says professors "demand a lot from their students," and a political science major adds that "they want to know each of their students individually and help them out as much as they can."

Life

Pitzer's location means great weather, which means "year-round outdoor activities." "Everyday walking through campus you'll see classes being held outside on the grass, students lying in hammocks reading, students studying while laying out by the pool, or students fixing old bikes at the Green Bike Program (a student-run club, promoting green transportation by providing bikes for the community)." Pitzer students love the "very laid-back and easy-going environment," but find the school is still able to enforce "a serious education." The College Consortium means there's always something going on, whether it's a "speaker series, dances, parties, or concerts," and there's "no shortage of things to do." Students report an "average" amount of drinking and drug use, and a few noted that though there's "a lot of pot smoking" they "never felt pressured" to take part. The five colleges "sponsor parties...with kegs, deejays, etc.," though the big parties usually take place at the other colleges, or off campus. Pitzer is "close enough to Los Angeles to head in for concerts, museums, shopping, etc., [and] many students do camping trips in Southern California [or] head to the beach." There's also a campus organization, Pitzer Outdoor Adventures (POA), that "funds students each week to basically go out on epic adventures. Want gas money for surfing? Okay! Want some funds for a back packing trip? Done!" A leader of POA admits with the school funding adventures, it "doesn't get much better."

Student Body

"The one thing all Pitzer students do have in common is awareness and community involvement. Every student on this campus has a strong voice." Pitzer students are hard workers and "passionate thinkers," "intelligent, chill, accepting, and friendly." Though Pitzer is small, "there is such a wide variety of people [that] you'll find a place where you fit in," and a sociology student adds that, "You only really don't fit in if you're unfriendly and mean." "At Pitzer, there are countless ways to meet people...and if you can't find something at Pitzer you can definitely find it at one of the other Claremont Colleges." Pitzer has a reputation as a "hippie" (and sometimes "hipster") school, but students say the "diversity among personalities is growing rapidly." One student says that Pitzer students "are a collection of creative people who, in their different ways, like to think outside of the box."

FINANCIAL AID: 909-621-8208 • E-MAIL: ADMISSION@PITZER.EDU • WEBSITE: WWW.PITZER.EDU

THE PRINCETON REVIEW SAYS

Admissions

Very important factors considered include: Class rank, GPA, rigor of secondary school record, application essay, extracurricular activities, racial/ethnic status, recommendation(s), character/personal qualities. *Important factors considered include:* First generation, geographical residence, interview, talent/ability, volunteer work, level of applicant's interest. *Other factors considered include:* Standardized test scores, work experience, alumni/ae relations. SAT and SAT Subject Tests or ACT considered if submitted; ACT with Writing component recommended. TOEFL required of all international applicants. *Academic units required:* 4 English; 3 mathematics; 3 science; (3 science lab); 3 social studies; 3 foreign language; 1 history; 1 visual/performing arts.

Financial Aid

Students should submit: FAFSA, CSS/Financial Aid PROFILE, State aid form, Noncustodial PROFILE. Regular filing deadline is 2/1. The Princeton Review suggests that all financial aid forms be submitted as soon as possible after January 1. *Need-based scholarships/grants offered:* Federal Pell, SEOG, State scholarships/grants, private scholarships, the school's own gift aid, *Loan aid offered:* Direct Subsidized Stafford Loans, Direct Unsubsidized Stafford Loans, Direct PLUS loans, Federal Perkins Loans, College/university loans from institutional funds. Applicants will be notified of awards beginning 4/1. Federal Work-Study Program available. Institutional employment available. Off-campus job opportunities are good.

The Inside Word

This is a place where applicants can feel confident in letting their thoughts flow freely on admissions essays. Not only does the committee read them (a circumstance more rare in college admissions that one is led to believe), but they've also set up the process to emphasize them! Thus, what you have to say for yourself will go much further than numbers in determining your suitability for Pitzer.

THE SCHOOL SAYS "..."

From the Admissions Office

"Pitzer is about opportunities. It's about possibilities. The students who come here are looking for something different from the usual 'take two courses from column A, two courses from column B, and two courses from column C.' That kind of arbitrary selection doesn't make a satisfying education at Pitzer. So we look for students who want to have an impact on their own education, who want the chief responsibility—with help from their faculty advisors—in designing their own futures.

"Pitzer's admission policy uses a test-optional policy. Students in the top 10 percent of their class or those who have an unweighted academic GPA of 3.5 or higher are not required to submit test scores. Others are allowed to choose from a variety of choices, including standardized tests (i.e., the SAT and ACT with the writing component)."

SELECTIVITY

Admissions Rating	96
# of applicants	3,743
% of applicants accepted	24
% of acceptees attending	30

FRESHMAN PROFILE

Range SAT Critical Reading	605–710
Range SAT Math	590–690
Minimum paper TOEFL	520
Average HS GPA	3.88
% graduated top 10% of class	55
% graduated top 25% of class	89
% graduated top 50% of class	100

DEADLINES

Early decision	
Deadline	11/15
Notification	1/1
Regular	
Deadline	1/1
Notification	4/1
Nonfall registration?	No

APPLICANTS ALSO LOOK AT AND OFTEN PREFER

Claremont McKenna College; Scripps College; University of California—Berkeley; University of California—Los Angeles; Occidental College; University of Southern California; Pomona College

AND SOMETIMES PREFER

Boston University; Colorado College; Whitman College; Lewis & Clark College; New York University

FINANCIAL FACTS

Financial Aid Rating	98
Annual tuition	$43,136
Room and board	$13,864
Required fees	$266
Books and supplies	$1,000
% needy frosh rec. need-based scholarship or grant aid	95
% needy UG rec. need-based scholarship or grant aid	98
% needy frosh rec. non-need-based scholarship or grant aid	0
% needy UG rec. non-need-based scholarship or grant aid	0
% needy frosh rec. need-based self-help aid	89
% needy UG rec. need-based self-help aid	95
% frosh rec. any financial aid	34
% UG rec. any financial aid	40
% UG borrow to pay for school	35
Average cumulative indebtedness	$22,568
% frosh need fully met	100
% ugrads need fully met	98
Average % of frosh need met	100
Average % of ugrad need met	100

POMONA COLLEGE

333 NORTH COLLEGE WAY, CLAREMONT, CA 91711-6312 • ADMISSIONS: 909-621-8134 • FAX: 909-621-8952

STUDENTS SAY "..."

Academics

At Pomona College in Claremont, you can get "an academically rigorous education" in a "low-stress California atmosphere." At this prestigious liberal arts school, "The professors are, for the most part, fantastic—engaging, creative, and sharp," and "all classes are taught by professors, not grad students or TAs." With small class sizes in every department, "there is an emphasis on collaborative learning," and "many professors are great discussion leaders and really motivate students to get involved in class." Students have the advantage of "getting to know professors outside the classroom, in any setting, from office hours, to Thanksgiving dinner at their homes." Illustrating how personal the experience can be, a student tells us, "Today, I had a class with seven people in it, then lunch with a physics professor, and then a personal tutorial with a philosophy professor." Another student adds, "Between department barbecues, parties, and weekend retreats, by the time you're an upperclassman, you will know most of the professors in your major department quite well." In complement to the intimate academic atmosphere, Pomona "offers the resources of a large university" through the Claremont College consortium, which offers joint events and cross-registration with four adjoining colleges. Among other programs, "Pomona pays for students to take otherwise unpaid internship positions." Students praise Pomona's "efficiency in taking care of administrative tasks such as financial aid and registration," adding that the administration "is very good at responding to what students want."

Life

Pomona students are "ridiculously happy" about their lot in life, and why shouldn't they be? They're living in a "perfect world full of intelligent, engaging, and open individuals, amazing academics, brilliant opportunities to get involved in, and enough sunshine to make anyone happy to be alive." The weather is a key aspect of the experience, and "on a nice day, everyone heads outside in shorts and t-shirts to do their class work." On any given day, "you'll see people setting up telescopes outside the dorms at night to try to get a glimpse of the stars, you'll find people practicing ukulele on our quad, you'll see students filming for a project in the dining halls, [or] you'll see someone riding around campus on a bamboo bike." "Many people are involved in intramural sports," and students love "hiking, skiing, and going to the beach year round." There are many beautiful beaches in the area, and "Joshua Tree is only an hour and a half away, so there are camping trips there just about every weekend." Though the school is small, there are four other undergraduate colleges in the Claremont Consortium, and Pomona students can "take their classes, eat at their dining halls, go to their parties, swim in their pools, and generally share in a great experience." When its time to blow off steam, "there are large 5C-sponsored parties that people go to and enjoy."

Student Body

At Pomona, "only a third or so of students are from California," yet the California attitude reigns supreme. Here, you'll find a number of "tree-hugging, rock-climbing, Tom's shoes–wearing" undergraduates, with most students generally falling within the "liberal, upper-middle-class, hipster-athlete" continuum. Students report a "decent level of diversity and a strong international community." Studious and talented, Pomona undergraduates "excel in the classroom and usually have some sort of passion that they pursue outside of the classroom." "Underneath our sundresses and rainbow flip-flops, we're all closet nerds—everybody is really passionate about something or other." At Pomona, "you will meet the football player who got a perfect score on his SAT or the dreadlocked hippie who took multivariable calculus when he was sixteen." Dress code is uniformly casual, and "flip-flops, polo, or tank tops and shorts" are the unofficial uniform.

FINANCIAL AID: 909-621-8205 • E-MAIL: ADMISSIONS@POMONA.EDU • WEBSITE: WWW.POMONA.EDU

THE PRINCETON REVIEW SAYS

Admissions

Very important factors considered include: Class rank, GPA, rigor of secondary school record, standardized test scores, application essay, extracurricular activities, recommendation(s), talent/ability, character/personal qualities. *Important factors considered include:* Interview. *Other factors considered include:* First generation, racial/ethnic status, volunteer work, work experience, alumni/ae relations. SAT and SAT Subject Tests or ACT required; ACT with Writing component recommended. TOEFL required of all international applicants. *Academic units required:* 4 English; 4 mathematics; 2 science; (2 science lab); 2 social studies; 3 foreign language. *Academic units recommended:* 4 English; 4 mathematics; 4 science; (3 science lab); 4 social studies; 4 foreign language.

Financial Aid

Students should submit: FAFSA, CSS/Financial Aid PROFILE, Noncustodial PROFILE, Business/Farm Supplement. Regular filing deadline is 2/15. The Princeton Review suggests that all financial aid forms be submitted as soon as possible after January 1. *Need-based scholarships/grants offered:* Federal Pell, SEOG, State scholarships/grants, private scholarships, the school's own gift aid. *Loan aid offered:* Direct Subsidized Stafford Loans, Direct Unsubsidized Stafford Loans, Direct PLUS loans, College/university loans from institutional funds. Applicants will be notified of awards beginning 4/1. Federal Work-Study Program available. Institutional employment available. Off-campus job opportunities are good.

The Inside Word

For first-year applicants, Pomona College offers regular decision admissions, as well as two binding early decision programs. Admissions officials evaluate a student's academic record carefully, examining the rigor of high school coursework, class rank, and grade point average. Ninety-one percent of Pomona admits rank in the top 10 percent of their class. If you live in Southern California, Pomona expects you to interview on campus; students in other regions are strongly encouraged to visit campus and meet with admissions staff, though it's not required.

THE SCHOOL SAYS ". . ."

From the Admissions Office

"Pomona College is a place for adventurous, creative students, who have talent and passion and are prepared to dream big and work hard in order to make a difference in the world.

Pomona students enjoy both the advantages of a small college, where professors teach every class, and the opportunities and resources of a larger university, with more than 7,000 students.

The founding member of the Claremont Colleges, Pomona is one of five adjacent undergraduate colleges and two graduate institutions that make up this unique, Oxford-style consortium. Students may supplement Pomona's extensive curricular offerings with classes at any of the other Claremont Colleges, each no more than a few minutes' walk away.

Pomona's Southern California location provides its students with rich educational resources, exciting opportunities for both scientific and community-based research, and geographic and cultural diversity."

SELECTIVITY

Admissions Rating	99
# of applicants	7,153
% of applicants accepted	14
% of acceptees attending	40
# offered a place on the wait list	602
% accepting a place on wait list	42
% admitted from wait list	29
# of early decision applicants	769
% accepted early decision	20

FRESHMAN PROFILE

Range SAT Critical Reading	690–760
Range SAT Math	690–780
Range SAT Writing	690–780
Range ACT Composite	31–34
Minimum paper TOEFL	600
Minimum web-based TOEFL	250
% graduated top 10% of class	92
% graduated top 25% of class	99
% graduated top 50% of class	100

DEADLINES

Early decision	
Deadline	11/1
Notification	12/15
Regular	
Deadline	1/1
Notification	4/1
Nonfall registration?	No

APPLICANTS ALSO LOOK AT AND OFTEN PREFER

Stanford University; Yale University; Brown University; Harvard University; University of Chicago

FINANCIAL FACTS

Financial Aid Rating	99
Annual tuition	$43,255
Room and board	$14,100
Required fees	$325
Books and supplies	$1,150
% needy frosh rec. need-based scholarship or grant aid	100
% needy UG rec. need-based scholarship or grant aid	100
% needy frosh rec. non-need-based scholarship or grant aid	0
% needy UG rec. non-need-based scholarship or grant aid	0
% needy frosh rec. need-based self-help aid	100
% needy UG rec. need-based self-help aid	100
% frosh rec. any financial aid	58
% UG rec. any financial aid	54
% UG borrow to pay for school	33
Average cumulative indebtedness	$13,441
% frosh need fully met	100
% ugrads need fully met	100
Average % of frosh need met	100
Average % of ugrad need met	100

PORTLAND STATE UNIVERSITY

OFFICE OF ADMISSIONS AND RECORDS, PORTLAND, OR 97207-0751 • ADMISSIONS: 503-725-3511 • FAX: 503-725-5525

CAMPUS LIFE

Quality of Life Rating	77
Fire Safety Rating	66
Green Rating	99
Type of school	Public
Affiliation	No Affiliation
Environment	Metropolis

STUDENTS

Total undergrad enrollment	23,489
% male/female	48/52
% from out of state	17
% frosh from public high school	85
# of fraternities	3
# of sororities	3
% African American	3
% Asian	8
% Caucasian	61
% Hispanic	9
% Native American	1
% international	7
# of countries represented	68

SURVEY SAYS . . .

Students love Portland, OR
Great off-campus food
Athletic facilities are great

ACADEMICS

Academic Rating	70
% students returning for sophomore year	73
Calendar	Semester
Profs interesting rating	73
Profs accessible rating	66

Most classes have 20–29 students.
Most lab/discussion sessions have 10–19 students.

MOST POPULAR MAJORS

psychology; business/commerce; social sciences

STUDENTS SAY ". . ."

Academics

Portland State University's motto is "let knowledge serve the city," and students echo this philosophy, saying their school "has a strong focus on civic engagement and sustainability." "PSU is a great learning environment in the heart of the city" and a "good value" for your tuition dollars. It's also "a green-minded urban school" that's "training students to be good community members." "There is a wealth of courses" on offer here, with degrees in social work, a range of business majors, and the hard sciences all receiving praise. "Classes are usually pretty small," and professors "promote lots of in-class discussion and are readily available to meet outside of class as well." "They really care about the student's success, and they really help broaden our scope of learning [and] thinking critically." Adjunct professors are "very connected to the community and their particular areas of expertise." Overall, students are happy with their instructors, saying, "Most professors are engaging and truly want to challenge you and help you succeed." They "are well-educated [and] well-versed in current issues and research." There's "the occasional dud thrown into the mix," though. Generally, "they are prepared and are passionate about the classes they teach. They have a wealth of experiences to bring to classroom," and they're "easily accessible for questions or further assistance, students just need to reach out."

Life

The city of Portland is a big draw for PSU students. "The campus is extraordinarily beautiful and ideally located." Outdoor activities are big here: "There's skiing, hiking, camping, [and] fishing." "The downtown area has plenty of microbrew pubs, nightlife, eateries, and theaters." "The people are friendly, and the city is gorgeous and easy to navigate. You can go to the beach or to the mountain in about two hours, and there are many things to do outdoors. There are great parks throughout the city." "The public transportation is outstanding." It's bike- and vegan-friendly. "There are lots of activist and awareness-raising events going on all the time, and lots of students are involved in volunteering (on and off campus)." Because PSU has a large nontraditional undergraduate population and the majority of students live off campus, the sense of community extends beyond the school and into the city. "There are a lot of things to do on campus, and there are different groups on campus that promote going out into the community at large and helping out." "Because the student body is so big and really diverse, PSU has tons of programs/clubs/groups that help make you feel more involved with your school. PSU is also committed to sustainability: Any new buildings are made with the latest green technology, and recycling is a big deal."

Student Body

"It is difficult to define the typical PSU student, because there are so many of us from so many different backgrounds," one student says, and diversity does indeed seem to be the name of the game at PSU. Students describe themselves as "environmentally aware, hip," and "very liberal." Overall, people at PSU are "invested in their education and are friendly." There's a large population of nontraditional undergraduates, so students are "either typical college-age...or people in their thirties and forties with kids and full-time job trying to juggle everything." Even within this large, diverse student body, "everyone finds a niche pretty quickly." "It's easy to find people you get along with, but it's also easy to find people who are completely different from you, which makes school a lot more interesting."

PORTLAND STATE UNIVERSITY

FINANCIAL AID: 800-547-8887 • E-MAIL: ADMISSIONS@PDX.EDU • WEBSITE: WWW.PDX.EDU

THE PRINCETON REVIEW SAYS

Admissions

Very important factors considered include: GPA, rigor of secondary school record. *Other factors considered include:* Standardized test scores, application essay. SAT or ACT required; ACT with Writing component required. TOEFL required of all international applicants. *Academic units required:* 4 English; 3 mathematics; 2 science; 2 social studies; 2 foreign language; 1 history. *Academic units recommended:* (1 science lab).

Financial Aid

Students should submit: FAFSA. The Princeton Review suggests that all financial aid forms be submitted as soon as possible after January 1. *Need-based scholarships/grants offered:* Federal Pell, SEOG, State scholarships/grants, private scholarships, the school's own gift aid, United Negro College Fund. *Loan aid offered:* Direct Subsidized Stafford Loans, Direct Unsubsidized Stafford Loans, Direct PLUS loans, Federal Perkins Loans, State Loans. Federal Work-Study Program available. Institutional employment available. Off-campus job opportunities are excellent.

The Inside Word

PSU offers a range of admission options for new freshmen, transfers, students enrolled at local community colleges, continuing students, and those with nontraditional high school backgrounds. Regardless of an applicant's status, admissions officers look for a secondary school GPA of at least 3.0, though high test scores can make up for a lower average.

THE SCHOOL SAYS "..."

From the Admissions Office

"Portland State University is Oregon's largest and most diverse public university located in the heart of one of America's most progressive cities. It offers more than sixty undergraduate and forty graduate programs in fine and performing arts, liberal arts and sciences, business administration, education, urban and public affairs, social work, engineering, and computer science. PSU offers more than 120 bachelor's, master's, and doctoral degrees.

"The forty-nine-acre downtown campus—whose motto is 'Let Knowledge Serve the City'—places students in a vibrant center of culture, business, and technology. Portland State's urban mission offers opportunities for every student to participate in internships and community-based projects in business, education, social services, government, technology, and the arts and sciences.

"The award-winning University Studies curriculum provides small class sizes and mentoring for undergraduates and culminates in Senior Capstone, which takes students out of the classroom and into the field, where they utilize their knowledge and skills to develop community projects.

"Portland State has taken aggressive steps to enhance the student experience and campus life, with new student housing and a comprehensive recreation complex and remodeled science and performing arts facilities. The university also has hired more academic and career advisers and created new programs to support students. Sustainability—initiatives that balance environmental, economic, and social concerns—is incorporated throughout the curriculum and across the campus."

SELECTIVITY	
Admissions Rating	68

FRESHMAN PROFILE	
Minimum paper TOEFL	527
Minimum web-based TOEFL	197

DEADLINES	
Regular	
Priority	6/1
Nonfall registration?	Yes

FINANCIAL FACTS	
Financial Aid Rating	71
Annual in-state tuition	$6,525
Annual out-of-state tuition	$21,825
Room and board	$11,349
Required fees	$1,263
% frosh rec. any financial aid	75
% UG rec. any financial aid	56

PRESCOTT COLLEGE

220 GROVE AVENUE, PRESCOTT, AZ 86301 • ADMISSIONS: 877-350-2100 • FAX: 928-776-5242

STUDENTS SAY "..."

Academics

Prescott College, a small, progressive school, "encourages critical and forward thinking around issues of social justice and sustainability." The school shines in interdisciplinary fields, such as environmental studies, human development and psychology, outdoor adventure education, and arts-based fields such as photography and creative writing. Prescott "is about taking learning out of the classroom," and true to its word, classes, according to the university, "take place in field sites throughout the Southwest, in art galleries, wilderness areas, along the U.S./Mexico border and in local schools, to name a few." Students see their education as "experiential, hands-on, real-world, and self-directed," and consider it to be a "journey, not a destination." Prescott's academic calendar is a unique "block and quarter system," which is "very effective at immersing students in their studies." Students take only one course for three four-week blocks before entering a ten-week semester. The quality of teaching "really varies. Some teachers are excellent and experienced and work well with the majority of the student body," and are "engaging and committed to their students." However, many students feel that "visiting" and "adjunct" professors "tend to be not so good." All the freedom at Prescott means that "academics are what you make them," and while some students find Prescott to be "academically stimulating but not very challenging," others think "there are plenty of opportunities for a rigorous academic experience."

Life

Prescott's emphasis on outdoor education and its ideal location near 1.4 million acres of National Forest mean that most students "live and play outside." One student says, "The majority of students rock climb, mountain bike, ski, snowboard, surf, raft, kayak, skydive, or ice climb." "If you want to go on an adventure, have no fear, you'll have an accomplice in less than an hour." The laid-back, artsy town of Prescott has a few bars that host "some good live music," which lots of students see whenever possible, though "sometimes you have to go to a larger city for that." Most students at Prescott are community-minded individuals, so it makes sense that one of the most popular social activities is to go to, or host, a potluck. As one student enthuses, "students also love potlucks; cooking is huge here." Others confirm that "potlucks are a huge part of student life," and that "much revolves around food." These gatherings can be "really fun and sometimes is crazy and sometimes really low-key." At potlucks and other gatherings, students "really enjoy each other's company." Generally, students do "not drink to get drunk, but drink as a part of a great evening out with friends," and most students seem to think people at Prescott "have good heads on their shoulders" and don't indulge in out-of-control partying.

Student Body

Prescott's emphasis on individual education, the environment, and sustainability means students are "environmentally and politically conscious" and "committed to their learning and creating a better community." Students are there because "they want to better themselves and have a positive impact on the world at large," and they're "motivated, empowered, and feisty." Additionally, students are very invested in social activism. Prescott's location means it attracts "athletic nerds" and "typical students love spending time outdoors." Yes, you'll probably see a lot of "hippies, hippies, hippies," but many students "wouldn't identify themselves that way." Though the school is predominantly white, students feel the community is "from a wide variety of cultural backgrounds" and that there's "a colorful array of people." As one student put it, the school "is made up of hundreds of different individuals who all bring their unique aspects to classes and social settings." Though students at Prescott tend to lean left, they say "any student fits in here. Everyone talks to everyone."

FINANCIAL AID: 928-350-1112 • E-MAIL: ADMISSIONS@PRESCOTT.EDU • WEBSITE: WWW.PRESCOTT.EDU

THE PRINCETON REVIEW SAYS

Admissions

Very important factors considered include: Rigor of secondary school record, application essay, recommendation(s). *Important factors considered include:* GPA, standardized test scores, extracurricular activities, interview, talent/ability, volunteer work, work experience, level of applicant's interest. *Other factors considered include:* Character/personal qualities. SAT or ACT required; SAT and SAT Subject Tests or ACT considered if submitted; ACT with or without Writing component accepted. TOEFL required of all international applicants. *Academic units recommended:* 4 English; 3 mathematics; 2 science; 3 social studies; 1 foreign language; 1 visual/performing arts.

Financial Aid

Students should submit: FAFSA. The Princeton Review suggests that all financial aid forms be submitted as soon as possible after January 1. *Need-based scholarships/grants offered:* Federal Pell, SEOG, State scholarships/grants, private scholarships, the school's own gift aid. *Loan aid offered:* Direct Subsidized Stafford Loans, Direct Unsubsidized Stafford Loans, Direct PLUS loans. Federal Work-Study Program available. Institutional employment available. Off-campus job opportunities are good.

The Inside Word

The acceptance rate at Prescott is high, but the applicant pool is very self-selecting, and Prescott is the kind of place where you have to want to be. For example, while many colleges have fun-filled, low-pressure orientation programs for incoming students, Prescott students spend their first four weeks engaged in an immersion orientation experience in the Arizona wilderness that builds student's experiential education skills and integrates them into the Prescott academic community.

THE SCHOOL SAYS " . . ."

From the Admissions Office

"Prescott College highlights the dramatic educational return on investment when experience is at the center of learning. Tucked into a corner of the town in central Arizona of the same name, Prescott College is based in collaboration and teamwork as the cornerstone of learning. This is an educational institution that puts students at the center in everything it does and is. Narrative Evaluations are an essential part of grading. No barriers. Limited bureaucracy. No summa or magna or 'best in show' ribbons. Just a peripatetic community of lively intellects and fearless explorers whose connecting threads are a passion for social responsibility, practical application of theory and the environment, and a keen sense of adventure.

"At Prescott College, our goal is to fuel your passion and give you a deeper understanding of the world around you through collaborative learning and personal experience. We don't settle for the mundane college experience. Instead, we take learning outside the classroom and into the real world through experiential and field-based learning. From field studies, internships, and independent studies to community service and study abroad opportunities (about 50 percent of PC students study abroad!), our students are challenged to think critically, explore the world up close, and form solutions through collaborative efforts.

"If you're looking for a college experience unlike any other—the kind that enables you to take control of your education , have practical impact and truly make a positive impact in your community and in the world—then Prescott College is the ideal college for you."

SELECTIVITY

Admissions Rating	78
# of applicants	399
% of applicants accepted	73
% of acceptees attending	17
# of early decision applicants	8
% accepted early decision	63

FRESHMAN PROFILE

Range SAT Critical Reading	480–650
Range SAT Math	430–610
Range SAT Writing	490–580
Range ACT Composite	20–26
Minimum paper TOEFL	550
Minimum web-based TOEFL	213
Average HS GPA	3.11
% graduated top 10% of class	0
% graduated top 50% of class	0

DEADLINES

Early decision	
Deadline	12/1
Notification	12/15
Regular	
Priority	3/1
Deadline	8/15
Nonfall registration?	Yes

APPLICANTS ALSO LOOK AT AND OFTEN PREFER
College of the Atlantic; Mills College

AND SOMETIMES PREFER
Whitman College

AND RARELY PREFER
Sarah Lawrence College; The Evergreen State College; University of Arizona; Reed College; Hendrix College

FINANCIAL FACTS

Financial Aid Rating	72
Annual tuition	$24,960
Room and board	$8,000
Required fees	$605
Books and supplies	$720
% needy frosh rec. need-based scholarship or grant aid	93
% needy UG rec. need-based scholarship or grant aid	95
% needy frosh rec. non-need-based scholarship or grant aid	3
% needy UG rec. non-need-based scholarship or grant aid	3
% needy frosh rec. need-based self-help aid	93
% needy UG rec. need-based self-help aid	95
% frosh rec. any financial aid	93
% UG rec. any financial aid	88
% UG borrow to pay for school	93
Average cumulative indebtedness	$27,213
% frosh need fully met	14
% ugrads need fully met	6
Average % of frosh need met	69
Average % of ugrad need met	60

PRINCETON UNIVERSITY

PO Box 430, Admission Office, Princeton, NJ 08542-0430 • Admissions: 609-258-3060 • Fax: 609-258-6743

CAMPUS LIFE

Quality of Life Rating	91
Fire Safety Rating	89
Green Rating	92
Type of school	Private
Affiliation	No Affiliation
Environment	Town

STUDENTS

Total undergrad enrollment	5,244
% male/female	51/49
% from out of state	82
% frosh from public high school	59
% frosh live on campus	100
% ugrads live on campus	97
% African American	8
% Asian	20
% Caucasian	47
% Hispanic	8
% Native American	<1
% international	11
# of countries represented	107

SURVEY SAYS . . .

Classroom facilities are great
Lab facilities are great
School is well run
Great financial aid
Campus feels safe
Athletic facilities are great
Lots of beer drinking
Alumni active on campus
Active student government

ACADEMICS

Academic Rating	93
% students returning for sophomore year	98
% students graduating within 4 years	88
% students graduating within 6 years	97
Calendar	Semester
Student/faculty ratio	6:1
Profs interesting rating	83
Profs accessible rating	76

Most classes have 10–19 students.
Most lab/discussion sessions have
10–19 students.

MOST POPULAR MAJORS

economics; political science; mechanical
engineering

STUDENTS SAY ". . ."

Academics

As a member of the grand old Ivy League, Princeton University has long maintained a "sterling reputation" for quality academics; however, students say Princeton's "unique focus on the undergraduate experience" is what makes their school stand out among institutions. It attracts "really experienced and big-name professors, who actually want to teach undergraduates." Introductory lecture classes can be rather large, but "once you take upper-level courses, you'll have a lot of chances to work closely with professors and study what you are most interested in." A current undergrad enthuses, "The discussions I have in seminar are the reason I get out of bed in the morning; after a great class, I feel incredibly invigorated." Though all Princeton professors are "leading scholars in their field," students admit that some classes can be "dry." Fortunately, "the overwhelming majority of professors are wonderful, captivating lecturers" who are "dedicated to their students." While you may be taking a class from a Nobel laureate, "The humility and accessibility of world-famous researchers and public figures is always remarkable." At Princeton, "there are so many chances to meet writers, performers, and professionals you admire." A student details, "The two years I've been here, I've been in discussions with Frank Gehry, David Sedaris, Peter Hessler, John McPhee, Jeff Koons, Chang-rae Lee, Joyce Carol Oates, W.S. Merwin, and on and on." No matter what you study, Princeton is an "intellectually challenging place," and the student experience is "intense in almost every way." Hard work pays off, though "the academic caliber of the school is unparalleled," and a Princeton education is "magnificently rewarding."

Life

Princeton students "tend to participate in a lot of different activities, from varsity sports (recruits), intramural sports (high school athletes), and more academically restricted activities like autonomous vehicle design club, Engineers Without Borders, and the literary magazine." In and out of the classroom, there are a "billion opportunities to do what you know you love" on the Princeton campus, from performance to sports to research. "Princeton offers a lot of different opportunities to relax and de-stress," including "sporting events, concerts, recreational facilities," "a movie theater that frequently screens current films for free," and "arts and crafts at the student center." For some, social life is centered along Prospect Avenue, where "Princeton's eating clubs are lined up like ten booze-soaked ducklings in a row." These eating clubs—private houses that serve as social clubs and cafeterias for upperclassmen—"play a large role in the social scene at the university." On the weekends, "the eating clubs are extremely popular for partying, chatting, drinking, and dancing"—not to mention, "free beer." "The campus is gorgeous year-round;" however, when students need a break from the college atmosphere, "there's NJ Transit if you want to go to New York, Philly, or even just the local mall."

Student Body

It's not surprising that most undergraduates are "driven, competitive, and obsessed with perfection." "Academics come first," and Princeton students are typified by dedication to their studies and "a tendency to overwork." "Almost everyone at Princeton is involved with something other than school about which they are extremely passionate," and most have "at least one distinct, remarkable talent." "It's fairly easy for most people to find a good group of friends with whom they have something in common," and many students get involved in one of the "infinite number of clubs" on campus. Superficially, "the preppy Ivy League stereotype" is reflected in the student population, and many students are "well-spoken," "dress nicely," and stay in shape. A student jokes, "Going to Princeton is like being in a contest to see who can be the biggest nerd while simultaneously appearing least nerdy."

FINANCIAL AID: 609-258-3330 • E-MAIL: UAOFFICE@PRINCETON.EDU • WEBSITE: WWW.PRINCETON.EDU

THE PRINCETON REVIEW SAYS

Admissions

Very important factors considered include: Class rank, GPA, rigor of secondary school record, standardized test scores, application essay, recommendation(s), talent/ability, character/personal qualities. *Important factors considered include:* Extracurricular activities. *Other factors considered include:* First generation, geographical residence, interview, racial/ethnic status, volunteer work, work experience, alumni/ae relations, level of applicant's interest. SAT or ACT required; ACT with Writing component required. TOEFL required of all international applicants. *Academic units recommended:* 4 English; 4 mathematics; 4 science; (2 science lab); 2 social studies; 4 foreign language; 2 history; 1 visual/performing arts.

Financial Aid

Students should submit: FAFSA, Institution's own financial aid form. The Princeton Review suggests that all financial aid forms be submitted as soon as possible after January 1. *Need-based scholarships/grants offered:* Federal Pell, SEOG, State scholarships/grants, private scholarships, the school's own gift aid. *Loan aid offered:* Direct Subsidized Stafford Loans, Direct Unsubsidized Stafford Loans, Direct PLUS loans, Federal Perkins Loans. Applicants will be notified of awards beginning 4/1. Federal Work-Study Program available. Institutional employment available. Off-campus job opportunities are good.

The Inside Word

Not surprisingly, admission to Princeton is highly selective. Only about 9 percent of applicants are accepted, and these students usually rank at the top of their high school class. Prospective students should prepare for Princeton by excelling in honors, AP, and upper level course work during high school. The application materials and personal essays are carefully read and evaluated, so students should also allocate time to prepare their applications. Admission to Princeton comes with a great deal of prestige, and to make the deal even sweeter, Princeton's remarkable no-loan financial aid program means that every student has 100 percent of their financial need met, without student loans.

THE SCHOOL SAYS "..."

From the Admissions Office

"Methods of instruction [at Princeton] vary widely, but common to all areas is a strong emphasis on individual responsibility and the free interchange of ideas. This is displayed most notably in the wide use of preceptorials and seminars, in the provision of independent study for all upperclass students and qualified underclass students, and in the availability of a series of special programs to meet a range of individual interests. The undergraduate college encourages the student to be an independent seeker of information and to assume responsibility for gaining both knowledge and judgment that will strengthen later contributions to society. Two hallmarks of the academic experience are the junior paper and senior thesis, which allow students the opportunity to pursue original research and scholarship in a field of their choosing.

"Princeton offers a distinctive financial aid program that provides grants, which do not have to be repaid, rather than loans. Princeton meets the full demonstrated financial need of all students—domestic and international—offered admission. About 60 percent of Princeton's undergraduates receive financial aid.

"All applicants must submit results for both the SAT as well as SAT Subject Tests in two different subject areas."

SELECTIVITY

Admissions Rating	99
# of applicants	26,664
% of applicants accepted	8
% of acceptees attending	65
# offered a place on the wait list	1,472
% accepting a place on wait list	67
% admitted from wait list	0

FRESHMAN PROFILE

Range SAT Critical Reading	700–800
Range SAT Math	710–800
Range SAT Writing	710–790
Range ACT Composite	31–35
Minimum paper TOEFL	600
Average HS GPA	3.9
% graduated top 10% of class	95
% graduated top 25% of class	98
% graduated top 50% of class	100

DEADLINES

Early action	
Deadline	11/1
Notification	12/15
Regular	
Deadline	1/1
Notification	3/31
Nonfall registration?	No

APPLICANTS ALSO LOOK AT AND SOMETIMES PREFER

Massachusetts Institute of Technology; Yale University; Stanford University; Harvard College

AND RARELY PREFER

University of Pennsylvania; Brown University

FINANCIAL FACTS

Financial Aid Rating	99
Annual tuition	$40,170
Required fees	$545
Books and supplies	$2,600
% needy frosh rec. need-based scholarship or grant aid	100
% needy UG rec. need-based scholarship or grant aid	100
% needy frosh rec. non-need-based scholarship or grant aid	0
% needy UG rec. non-need-based scholarship or grant aid	0
% needy frosh rec. need-based self-help aid	100
% needy UG rec. need-based self-help aid	100
% frosh rec. any financial aid	59
% UG rec. any financial aid	59
% UG borrow to pay for school	24
Average cumulative indebtedness	$5,096
% frosh need fully met	100
% ugrads need fully met	100
Average % of frosh need met	100
Average % of ugrad need met	100

PROVIDENCE COLLEGE

HARKINS 222, PROVIDENCE, RI 02918 • ADMISSIONS: 401-865-2535 • FAX: 401-865-2826

CAMPUS LIFE
Quality of Life Rating	81
Fire Safety Rating	98
Green Rating	66
Type of school	Private
Affiliation	Roman Catholic
Environment	City

STUDENTS
Total undergrad enrollment	3,866
% male/female	43/57
% from out of state	91
% frosh from public high school	58
% frosh live on campus	98
% ugrads live on campus	77
% African American	4
% Asian	1
% Caucasian	77
% Hispanic	7
% Native American	<1
% international	2
# of countries represented	28

SURVEY SAYS . . .
Students are happy
Students are friendly
Great off-campus food
Athletic facilities are great
Lots of beer drinking
Hard liquor is popular
Intramural sports are popular
Alumni active on campus

ACADEMICS
Academic Rating	84
% students returning for sophomore year	91
% students graduating within 4 years	83
% students graduating within 6 years	85
Calendar	Semester
Student/faculty ratio	12:1
Profs interesting rating	75
Profs accessible rating	79

Most classes have 20–29 students.
Most lab/discussion sessions have 20–29 students.

MOST POPULAR MAJORS
marketing; biology; finance

■ THE BEST 379 COLLEGES

STUDENTS SAY ". . ."

Academics

Providence College is committed to maintaining small class sizes and facilities in order to provide its students with a strong liberal arts education and traditional campus life. With fewer than 5,000 undergrads, it is "uncommon for a student to not know or have interacted with the school president, dean of student affairs, dean of undergraduate studies, etc."

The universally small classes lead to "more discussion and less lecture," and professors "encourage student participation to not only learn concepts but apply them as well." They are "truly invested in student understanding/success," making themselves available through multiple channels, and "their passion for teaching can be felt within the classroom." Most teachers "provide plenty of opportunities to meet outside of class for help with school, talk about of life, or possibilities for careers after graduation." The classes "are no cake walk, but will give you the knowledge and experience for the real world," and "even the toughest graders have been reasonable with their explanations," says a junior English major.

The "strong liberal core curriculum" (using the Development of Western Civilization program as its centerpiece) and Catholic values of the school helps to prepare students "to serve as responsible and engaged world citizens." PC is "fantastic" at setting up students with internships that lead to future jobs, and professors place "a high value in experiential learning: getting involved with the community and taking advantage of opportunities to work and serve in the greater Providence Community." PC also has an incredible alumni base; alumni "are dedicated to the school, and dedicated to PC graduates."

Life

The school's location and the city of Providence offers the perfect balance for living: with "a beautiful, friendly campus as well as a vibrant city life just three minutes away from campus, students get the best of both worlds." It's the smallest 'big' school and the biggest small school," sums up a student. With Division I athletics (there are also "many opportunities to play through intramurals") but a small class size, students "can easily say that there is so much to do and so many opportunities that it's easy to get involved and not be bored." "Club involvement is huge," and just about everyone is on some type of club or in a student leadership position.

The "welcoming, upbeat, friendly environment" created on campus is due in part to the fact that "all the students live in one giant community." For fun, students like to explore the city of Providence, which "has a lot to offer", or go to on-campus events, such as "movie showings, bingo nights," and hockey and basketball games. There is "a large drinking culture" at PC, and though "students love to party and go out…come Sunday night, the library is packed and everyone has their nose in the books." The city and campus are quite secure: "I have never felt unsafe on campus, even if I am walking across it by myself at 3:00 A.M.," says a student. "Diversity and dining" are the two Ds that many students agree could use improvement; others also complain about the parietal rules, which impose curfews for the opposite sex to be in one another's dorms.

Student Body

"The Catholic Dominican tradition has a strong presence here," and the majority of the student body "is from New England and proud of it." Most students "look like they stepped out of a J. Crew advertisement," though there is a hipster contingent; everyone "is friendly and generally hangs out together," possibly because "the homogeneity and common experience creates strong bonds among the student body." Social groups "do not revolve around your class background at all," and students fit in through joining clubs or attending a lot of the big social events on campus. "We all bond over our Western Civ experience in our freshmen and sophomore years, so if you have gone through that then you fit in here," adds one junior.

FINANCIAL AID: 401-865-2286 • E-MAIL: PCADMISS@PROVIDENCE.EDU • WEBSITE: WWW.PROVIDENCE.EDU

THE PRINCETON REVIEW SAYS

Admissions

Very important factors considered include: GPA, rigor of secondary school record, application essay. *Important factors considered include:* Extracurricular activities, recommendation(s), character/personal qualities. *Other factors considered include:* Class rank, standardized test scores, first generation, geographical residence, racial/ethnic status, talent/ability, volunteer work, work experience, alumni/ae relations, level of applicant's interest. SAT or ACT considered if submitted; ACT with or without Writing component accepted. TOEFL required of all international applicants. *Academic units required:* 4 English; 4 mathematics; 3 science; (2 science lab); 2 social studies; 3 foreign language; 2 history. *Academic units recommended:* 4 English; 4 mathematics; 4 science; (2 science lab); 2 social studies; 3 foreign language; 2 history.

Financial Aid

Students should submit: FAFSA, CSS/Financial Aid PROFILE. Regular filing deadline is 2/1. The Princeton Review suggests that all financial aid forms be submitted as soon as possible after January 1. *Need-based scholarships/grants offered:* Federal Pell, SEOG, State scholarships/grants, private scholarships, the school's own gift aid. *Loan aid offered:* Direct Subsidized Stafford Loans, Direct Unsubsidized Stafford Loans, Direct PLUS loans, Federal Perkins Loans, State Loans. Applicants will be notified of awards beginning 3/15. Federal Work-Study Program available. Institutional employment available. Off-campus job opportunities are good.

The Inside Word

Few schools can claim a more transparent admissions process than Providence College. The admissions section of the school's website includes a voluminous blog authored by the assistant dean of admissions. Surf on over to the PC website and learn everything you could possibly want to know about the how, what, when, and why of Providence admissions. Providence has a test-optional policy, meaning applicants aren't required to submit standardized test scores.

THE SCHOOL SAYS "..."

From the Admissions Office

"A Providence College education challenges students to find commonality among topics that seem, on the surface, to be opposites. "Or" often becomes "and." There are shared academic experiences such as the Core Curriculum and the distinctive Development of Western Civilization sequence, but the college also encourages students to explore differences of opinion and unfamiliar lines of thought. PC's Catholic and Dominican identity fuels intellectual, spiritual, and emotional growth by encouraging students to view subjects through the complementary lenses of faith and reason. It also fosters a respectful, supportive community that feels like home.

"Submission of standardized test scores is optional for students applying for admission. This policy change allows each student to decide whether they wish to have their standardized test results considered as part of their application for admission. Students who choose not to submit SAT or ACT test scores will not be penalized in the review for admission. Additional details about the test-optional policy can be found on our website at www.providence.edu/admission/Pages/test-optional-policy.aspx."

SELECTIVITY

Admissions Rating	90
# of applicants	9,660
% of applicants accepted	60
% of acceptees attending	18
# offered a place on the wait list	2,469
% accepting a place on wait list	26
% admitted from wait list	56

FRESHMAN PROFILE

Range SAT Critical Reading	520–620
Range SAT Math	530–640
Range SAT Writing	530–640
Range ACT Composite	23–28
Minimum paper TOEFL	550
Minimum web-based TOEFL	80
Average HS GPA	3.37
% graduated top 10% of class	37
% graduated top 25% of class	67
% graduated top 50% of class	92

DEADLINES

Early decision	
Deadline	12/1
Notification	1/1
Early action	
Deadline	11/1
Notification	1/1
Regular	
Priority	1/15
Deadline	1/15
Notification	4/1
Nonfall registration?	Yes

APPLICANTS ALSO LOOK AT AND OFTEN PREFER
Boston College; College of the Holy Cross

AND SOMETIMES PREFER
Boston University; Villanova University

AND RARELY PREFER
Fairfield Universtiy; Loyola University Maryland

FINANCIAL FACTS

Financial Aid Rating	86
Annual tuition	$42,385
Room and board	$12,750
Required fees	$860
Books and supplies	$900
% needy frosh rec. need-based scholarship or grant aid	99.5
% needy UG rec. need-based scholarship or grant aid	99.9
% needy frosh rec. non-need-based scholarship or grant aid	8
% needy UG rec. non-need-based scholarship or grant aid	8
% needy frosh rec. need-based self-help aid	81
% needy UG rec. need-based self-help aid	87
% frosh rec. any financial aid	84
% UG rec. any financial aid	79
% UG borrow to pay for school	87
Average cumulative indebtedness	$31,070
% frosh need fully met	26
% ugrads need fully met	35
Average % of frosh need met	88
Average % of ugrad need met	84

PURDUE UNIVERSITY—WEST LAFAYETTE

1080 SCHLEMAN HALL, WEST LAFAYETTE, IN 47907-2050 • ADMISSIONS: 765-494-1776 • FAX: 765-494-0544

CAMPUS LIFE

Quality of Life Rating	91
Fire Safety Rating	87
Green Rating	90
Type of school	Public
Affiliation	No Affiliation
Environment	Town

STUDENTS

Total undergrad enrollment	29,216
% male/female	57/43
% from out of state	32
% ugrads live on campus	36
# of fraternities (% ugrad men join)	50 (10)
# of sororities (% ugrad women join)	31 (8)
% African American	3
% Asian	5
% Caucasian	67
% Hispanic	4
% Native American	<1
% international	17
# of countries represented	126

SURVEY SAYS . . .

Students are happy
Lab facilities are great
Career services are great
Students are friendly
Great food on campus
Everyone loves the Boilermakers
Student publications are popular
Alumni active on campus

ACADEMICS

Academic Rating	79
% students returning for sophomore year	91
% students graduating within 4 years	47
% students graduating within 6 years	71
Calendar	Semester
Student/faculty ratio	13:1
Profs interesting rating	69
Profs accessible rating	77

Most classes have 10–19 students.
Most lab/discussion sessions have
10–19 students.

MOST POPULAR MAJORS
mechanical engineering, computer science,
management

STUDENTS SAY ". . ."

Academics
Purdue is a Big Ten school that provides "a world class education" with a name "that is known all over the world and not just the state of Indiana." The university is especially "known for being a great engineering school," but has a bevy of amazing programs including "a great nursing program," "a great Pharmacy program" and a "speech pathology program [that] is one of the best." "I knew that I would receive an unparalleled education here," an Aeronautical and Astronautical Engineering major says. Purdue, "cradle of engineers and quarterbacks alike," is known for its athletics as well its academics. There is "great school spirit exhibited in student organizations and athletic events." Yet despite the "big campus atmosphere," the school still maintains "small-school feel within its individual colleges." The "knowledgeable and helpful" professors are "very excited about their topic of teaching" and "the classes are excellent and stimulating." "Many of my professors have at least 10 years under their belts with Ph. D's," one student boasts. Students are not going to find easy classes here. Purdue has teachers that "expect the most out of you." However, "the difficult and rigorous curriculum" is a bonding experience that "increases out of the classroom skills such as communication and collaboration." Some students did worry that "many things (such as Industrial Roundtable) are focused almost exclusively on engineers, which leaves some other majors out in the cold." "The dining services are immaculate" at Purdue, and students love how the school "promotes green technology." One Biology major explains the Purdue appeal: "It has everything a college kid could want: sports, academics, clubs, and delicious food." Purdue provides an educational experience that students will remember the rest of their lives. As one student puts it: "Once a Boilermaker, always a Boilermaker."

Life
Life at Purdue involves a lot of "time management" and "a typical student has a hard time completing all three S's (sleep, study, socialize) but has fun trying." As a Big Ten university, athletics make up a large part of campus life. "We have Ross-Ade Brigade and Paint Crew, student clubs for cheering on the athletic teams, and they're fairly large," one Biology major explains. "Partying and hard alcohol [are] common," but seem to divide the student body. Some wish the administration put "more control on partying and drinking" while others wish it was "less strict on alcohol/drug policies." "Sometimes there isn't a lot to do in West Lafayette besides drink," and "students typically spend their time partying hard on Thursday nights at the Cactus and cramming on Sunday nights." "Greek life is huge at Purdue" although "not essential." West Lafayette is "close to Chicago and Indy" for weekend trips, and "students stay on campus most of the time, so it's not a huge deal that the town around us sucks." There is "always something fun to do on campus" too, such as "a club meeting, a social event/recreational event, or just plain studying." "Most people unwind and have fun by joining a club or organization" and everyone seems to find a place to fit in. Even quiet students blossom at Purdue as "the atmosphere on campus coaxes most out of their shell sooner or later."

Student Body
Located in Indiana, Purdue has a student body that is largely "white and from the Midwest" with "conservative political views." That said, one student points out that "West Lafayette is a pretty progressive town and usually ends up going Democratic if you check election records." A fair number of students say the school needs to work to bring "better diversity." "Most students are really down to earth" and "students can all find their niche here and get along well." Students tend to bond "within their majors" which "helps create a small-school feel within a huge university," although "it is not unheard of for people involved in different things to be with different people." There is a fair amount of animosity between majors since "science and engineering majors DO look down on other majors" and tend to think that non-technical majors "are a 'joke' to the point that people are arrogant, obnoxious, and rude." Still, most students "fit in well" and at the end of the day "we take all kinds here and turn everyone into Boilermakers."

FINANCIAL AID: 765-494-0998 • E-MAIL: ADMISSIONS@PURDUE.EDU • WEBSITE: WWW.PURDUE.EDU

THE PRINCETON REVIEW SAYS

Admissions

Very important factors considered include: Core academic GPA, rigor of secondary school record, standardized test scores. *Important factors considered include:* Application essay, first generation, recommendation(s), character/personal qualities. *Other factors considered include:* Class rank, extracurricular activities, geographical residence, racial/ethnic status, state residency, talent/ability, volunteer work, work experience, alumni/ae relations, level of applicant's interest. SAT or ACT required; ACT with Writing component required. TOEFL required of all international applicants. *Academic units required:* 4 English; 4 mathematics; 3 science; (3 science lab); 3 social studies; 2 foreign language.

Financial Aid

Students should submit: FAFSA. The Princeton Review suggests that all financial aid forms be submitted as soon as possible after January 1. *Need-based scholarships/grants offered:* Federal Pell, SEOG, State scholarships/grants, private scholarships, the school's own gift aid. *Loan aid offered:* Direct Subsidized Stafford Loans, Direct Unsubsidized Stafford Loans, Direct PLUS loans, Federal Perkins Loans, College/university loans from institutional funds. Applicants will be notified of awards beginning 4/15. Federal Work-Study Program available. Institutional employment available. Off-campus job opportunities are good.

The Inside Word

Purdue looks at student applications holistically, considering everything together without letting a single component—such as class rank or SAT/ACT score—override the others. Having said that, Purdue does have minimum high school course requirements, so make sure you have met all of those requirements before applying.

THE SCHOOL SAYS "..."

From the Admissions Office

"Although it is one of America's largest universities, Purdue does not 'feel' big to its students. The campus is very compact when compared to universities with similar enrollment. Purdue is a comprehensive university with an international reputation in a wide range of academic fields. A strong work ethic prevails at Purdue. As a member of the Big Ten, Purdue has a strong and diverse athletic program. Purdue offers more than 900 clubs and organizations. The residence halls and Greek community offer many participatory activities for students. Numerous convocations and lectures are presented each year. Purdue is all about people, and allowing students to grow academically as well as socially, preparing them for the real world.

"Applicants seeking admission are required to have their SAT or ACT test score sent from the testing agency. Purdue accepts either test, will use the best score, and requires a writing score.

"To be considered for the full range of merit-based scholarships, students must apply by November 1."

SELECTIVITY

Admissions Rating	92
# of applicants	30,955
% of applicants accepted	60
% of acceptees attending	34
# offered a place on the wait list	342
% accepting a place on wait list	98
% admitted from wait list	9

FRESHMAN PROFILE

Range SAT Critical Reading	520–630
Range SAT Math	560–690
Range SAT Writing	520–630
Range ACT Composite	24–30
Minimum paper TOEFL	550
Minimum web-based TOEFL	79
Average HS GPA	3.70
% graduated top 10% of class	47
% graduated top 25% of class	80
% graduated top 50% of class	98

DEADLINES

Early action	
Deadline	11/1
Notification	December
Regular	
Priority	2/1
Notification	Rolling
Nonfall registration?	Yes

APPLICANTS ALSO LOOK AT AND SOMETIMES PREFER

Indiana University—Bloomington; Rose-Hulman Institute of Technology; University of Illinois at Urbana-Champaign; Valparaiso University

FINANCIAL FACTS

Financial Aid Rating	88
Annual in-state tuition	$9,208
Annual out-of-state tuition	$28,010
Room and board	$10,030
Required fees	$794
Books and supplies	$1,210
% needy frosh rec. need-based scholarship or grant aid	69
% needy UG rec. need-based scholarship or grant aid	69
% needy frosh rec. non-need-based scholarship or grant aid	45
% needy UG rec. non-need-based scholarship or grant aid	33
% needy frosh rec. need-based self-help aid	82
% needy UG rec. need-based self-help aid	88
% frosh rec. any financial aid	74
% UG rec. any financial aid	77
% UG borrow to pay for school	51
Average cumulative indebtedness	$29,121
% frosh need fully met	46
% ugrads need fully met	35
Average % of frosh need met	87
Average % of ugrad need met	86

QUINNIPIAC UNIVERSITY

275 MOUNT CARMEL AVENUE, HAMDEN, CT 06518 • ADMISSIONS: 203-582-8600 • FAX: 203-582-8906

CAMPUS LIFE

Quality of Life Rating	77
Fire Safety Rating	96
Green Rating	73
Type of school	Private
Affiliation	No Affiliation
Environment	Town

STUDENTS

Total undergrad enrollment	6,486
% male/female	38/62
% from out of state	75
% frosh from public high school	70
% frosh live on campus	96
% ugrads live on campus	78
# of fraternities (% ugrad men join)	5 (15)
# of sororities (% ugrad women join)	6 (14)
% African American	4
% Asian	2
% Caucasian	78
% Hispanic	8
% Native American	<1
% international	2
# of countries represented	23

SURVEY SAYS . . .

Political activism is unpopular or nonexistent
Classroom facilities are great
Lab facilities are great
Hard liquor is popular

ACADEMICS

Academic Rating	82
% students returning for sophomore year	87
% students graduating within 4 years	72
% students graduating within 6 years	76
Calendar	Semester
Student/faculty ratio	11:1
Profs interesting rating	78
Profs accessible rating	79

Most classes have 10–19 students.
Most lab/discussion sessions have
10–19 students.

MOST POPULAR MAJORS
psychology; physical therapy; business/
commerce

STUDENTS SAY ". . ."

Academics

Located on a "beautiful" campus near New Haven, Connecticut, Quinnipiac University is a liberal arts school that "wants every student to graduate with a well-rounded education." The school "is about educating students in both their major and in general knowledge so they are prepared for life after college." Though health science, business, and communications are the school's most notable programs, the entire university "takes pride in its academics" and is "invested in preparing students for their potential career in the best way possible." No matter your major, the school stresses that "the most important aspect is the student's undergraduate experience on the journey of finding themselves."

Since class sizes are so small, teachers "are able to engage with each student individually." The professors at Quinnipiac "really look out for the students and want them to achieve." Like at any college, "there are amazing professors and terrible professors," but "looking up the reviews and trusting students' opinions" will help you know which ones to pick. Professors all "encourage discussion and bring in real-life stories," and "they are always enthusiastic to share their knowledge. They implement hands-on learning, too." Students cite "the accessibility to meet with professors during their office hours" as a huge plus. "It is very easy to get in contact with them when needed," says a student. "I have close bonds with several, and my academic experience has been nothing but enjoyable," says another. As one student sums up, "Quinnipiac University is extremely dedicated to helping students make their college experience not only beneficial, but enjoyable as well."

Life

Students at the school "value the closeness of our community and bringing everyone together," according to a student. The campus is "just plain gorgeous" ("When I came to this school I got the 'wedding dress feeling,'" says a student.), and there's a lot going on there, too. "Campus life is awesome!" There are "so many ways" of getting involved: "numerous clubs and activities, supporting the athletic teams, intramural sports, and much more." The student body is "heavily devoted" to the subjects they are involved in, and everywhere you look "friendly faces" are taking advantage of the "very programmed schedule" of events. A "good majority of the students here like to party hard Thursday through Saturday night," but if you don't like to drink or go out, the programming board "does an excellent job providing events on campus such as casino night, drive-in movies, stand-up comics, games, etc."

Despite the Quinnipiac love, there are some gripes. The living facilities "could stand to be updated," "more onsite parking" is definitely needed, and everyone pretty much universally agrees that the "food could always be better." However, people do love the duality of a "college-town feel with a city nearby," and the shuttles that run into nearby New Haven are extremely popular. The "great sports teams" also help bring together the student body, and "on Friday nights, hockey and basketball are big."

Student Body

The typical student here is a "middle- to upper-class Caucasian from the tristate area" and "a little preppy, but casual at the same time." "Students are easy to make friends with," so "it's easy to find a niche here." "Students all seem to have a place, there are so many different groups that it's hard not to find someplace for everyone," says one. "I feel like it's a good place to go if you want a balance between social life and school work," says a student. This "studious" and "well-motivated" group is usually "involved in at least one program outside of academics," but also "likes to enjoy themselves on weekends." Though Quinnipiac "is not very diverse", it "is becoming more diverse." Many students are "very interested in fashion and culture."

FINANCIAL AID: 203-582-8750 • E-MAIL: ADMISSIONS@QUINNIPIAC.EDU • WEBSITE: WWW.QUINNIPIAC.EDU

THE PRINCETON REVIEW SAYS

Admissions

Very important factors considered include: GPA, rigor of secondary school record. *Important factors considered include:* Class rank, standardized test scores, application essay, recommendation(s). *Other factors considered include:* Extracurricular activities, first generation, interview, racial/ethnic status, talent/ability, volunteer work, work experience, alumni/ae relations, character/personal qualities, level of applicant's interest. SAT or ACT required; ACT with Writing component recommended. TOEFL required of all international applicants. *Academic units required:* 4 English; 3 mathematics; 3 science; (2 science lab); 2 social studies; 2 foreign language. *Academic units recommended:* 4 English; 4 mathematics; 4 science; (3 science lab); 3 social studies; 2 foreign language.

Financial Aid

Students should submit: FAFSA, CSS/Financial Aid PROFILE. The Princeton Review suggests that all financial aid forms be submitted as soon as possible after January 1. *Need-based scholarships/grants offered:* Federal Pell, SEOG, State scholarships/grants, private scholarships, the school's own gift aid. *Loan aid offered:* Direct Subsidized Stafford Loans, Direct Unsubsidized Stafford Loans, Direct PLUS loans, Federal Perkins Loans, Federal Nursing Loans, State Loans. Federal Work-Study Program available. Institutional employment available. Off-campus job opportunities are excellent.

The Inside Word

Quinnipiac offers early decision (deadline November 1) and also admits students on a rolling basis, a process that favors those who get their applications in early. Programs in physical therapy, nursing, and physician assistant are quite competitive. The school strongly recommends that those seeking spots in these programs apply no later than November 15.

THE SCHOOL SAYS "..."

From the Admissions Office

"Quinnipiac today is 'three settings, one university,' with an undergraduate population growing to 6,500, many of whom remain at QU for the ever expanding graduate programs, and a continuing focus on our core values: academic excellence, a student oriented environment and a strong sense of community.

"The Mount Carmel campus, the academic home to all undergraduates with traditional, suite and apartment housing for freshmen and sophomores, is 250-acres in a stunning setting adjacent to Sleeping Giant state park. The nearby 250-acre York Hill campus is home to juniors and seniors in apartments with breathtaking views, a lodge style student center, covered parking, and the TD Bank sports center with twin arenas for hockey and basketball. The 100-acre North Haven campus, just four miles distant, is the home to graduate programs in Health Sciences, and Education, and the Frank H. Netter, MD School of Medicine.

"Academic initiatives such as the honors program, 'writing across the curriculum', QU seminar series, extensive internship experiences, study abroad opportunities and a highly regarded emerging leaders student-life program form the foundation for excellence in business, communication, health sciences, nursing, engineering, education, liberal arts, and law.

"State of the art facilities include the Financial Technology Center, HD fully digital production studio, extensive health science labs, recreation and sports fields and arenas. More than 100 student organizations, twenty-one Division I teams, community service, student publications, and a strong student government offer a variety of outside-of-class experiences."

SELECTIVITY

Admissions Rating	85
# of applicants	20,696
% of applicants accepted	67
% of acceptees attending	13
# offered a place on the wait list	1,800
% accepting a place on wait list	51
% admitted from wait list	21
# of early decision applicants	347
% accepted early decision	70

FRESHMAN PROFILE

Range SAT Critical Reading	490–580
Range SAT Math	510–610
Range SAT Writing	500–590
Range ACT Composite	22–27
Minimum paper TOEFL	550
Minimum web-based TOEFL	81
Average HS GPA	3.40
% graduated top 10% of class	25
% graduated top 25% of class	66
% graduated top 50% of class	93

DEADLINES

Early decision	
Deadline	11/1
Notification	12/1
Regular	
Priority	2/1
Nonfall registration?	Yes

APPLICANTS ALSO LOOK AT AND OFTEN PREFER

Boston University; Villanova University; University of Connecticut

AND SOMETIMES PREFER

Fairfield University; Northeastern University; University of Delaware; University of Massachusetts Amherst; Marist College

AND RARELY PREFER

Sacred Heart University; Ithaca College

FINANCIAL FACTS

Financial Aid Rating	71
Annual tuition	$39,170
Room and board	$14,250
Required fees	$1,500
Books and supplies	$800
% needy frosh rec. need-based scholarship or grant aid	98
% needy UG rec. need-based scholarship or grant aid	97
% needy frosh rec. non-need-based scholarship or grant aid	67
% needy UG rec. non-need-based scholarship or grant aid	54
% needy frosh rec. need-based self-help aid	80
% needy UG rec. need-based self-help aid	83
% frosh rec. any financial aid	85
% UG rec. any financial aid	80
% UG borrow to pay for school	71
Average cumulative indebtedness	$44,552
% frosh need fully met	15
% ugrads need fully met	13
Average % of frosh need met	67
Average % of ugrad need met	64

RANDOLPH COLLEGE

2500 RIVERMONT AVENUE, LYNCHBURG, VA 24503-1555 • ADMISSIONS: 434-947-8100 • FAX: 434-947-8996

CAMPUS LIFE
Quality of Life Rating	88
Fire Safety Rating	89
Green Rating	97
Type of school	Private
Affiliation	Methodist
Environment	City

STUDENTS
Total undergrad enrollment	665
% male/female	36/64
% from out of state	40
% frosh from public high school	82
% frosh live on campus	95
% ugrads live on campus	86
% African American	9
% Asian	2
% Caucasian	69
% Hispanic	6
% Native American	1
% international	11
# of countries represented	19

SURVEY SAYS . . .
Students are happy
Lab facilities are great
No one cheats
Students are friendly
Diverse student types on campus
Students get along with local community
Campus feels safe
Active student government

ACADEMICS
Academic Rating	89
% students returning for sophomore year	75
% students graduating within 4 years	46
% students graduating within 6 years	52
Calendar	Semester
Student/faculty ratio	9:1
Profs interesting rating	97
Profs accessible rating	96
Most classes have fewer than 10 students.	

MOST POPULAR MAJORS
psychology; biology; English language
and literature

STUDENTS SAY "..."

Academics
Rest assured, at Randolph College, "You're not just a number; you matter as an individual." Indeed, this "small, tight-knit community" instantly "makes you feel welcome." Additionally, students at Randolph are grateful they attend a college that "promotes self discovery, personal growth, and individuality." Further, "small class sizes" allow for an "emphasis on student-professor relationships," a hallmark of a Randolph education. One undergrad happily confirms, "My academic experience has been challenging, there's no doubt, but the professor support has made that challenge enjoyable and exciting." A fellow student agrees, sharing, "My professors are excellent. Everyone I have had here has been supremely knowledgeable, understanding and helpful to students. The number one goal is always to make students better thinkers." Finally, as this student gushes, "My professors are amazing! Their passion for the subject matter and course content is infectious. I look forward to each class each day and feel confident in my education. Learning is interesting and fun here, and professors are eager to answer questions and provide resources to supplement lectures and experiments. Often professors list their home phone numbers on syllabi to allow students to contact them outside of office hours. Every professor replies to e-mail quickly, and professors are all very easy to communicate with in the classroom and one-on-one."

Life
According to many undergrads, "life at Randolph is always busy and exciting." As one ecstatic student quickly asserts, "I don't think I have [been] bored [since] the day I stepped foot on this campus." And why would you be? Indeed, there are "a wide variety of clubs and organizations [in which] to become involved." Moreover, there are "many sports teams and exciting competitions to watch" as well as intramurals, which "offer a chance for non-athletes to" participate. In addition, there are a myriad of "parties and dances...sponsored by various organizations." These events are typically well-attended by students, as "they never disappoint." And for those undergrads looking for an activity a little more out of the box, there's "even a game called Humans vs Zombies where students dress up and try to 'turn people into zombies' with Nerf guns. It's a lot of fun." Randolph is also home to many proud traditions and students love to partake. An insider reveals, "The even-odd class rivalry is definitely one popular school tradition. Skeller Sings are one of the events where the even spirit society (ETAs) and odd spirit society (Gammas) will sing (read: shout) songs at each other and try to create distractions while the other group sings." Finally, when students want to look beyond the campus for fun, they can "go hiking, swimming, and boating at all the lakes, rivers, and trails. [Indeed] there is a lot of nature and history surrounding the Lynchburg area."

Student Body
Undergrads at Randolph emphatically state that there's no typical student to be found wandering around campus. As one knowing undergrad shares, "Students vary widely in background and personality, preferences, [and] habits." Additionally, a "considerable percentage of the student body is comprised of international students," which certainly adds to the diversity of the school. Of course, if pressed to throw out some adjectives, Randolph undergrads will likely say that their peers are "hardworking, artistic, and caring." They are also "intelligent," "unafraid to speak their minds," and "committed to doing excellent work." Fortunately, "being such a small campus, it is hard not [to] develop lots of friends from several different social groups," and certainly, "campus traditions help form a very strong sense of community here." Or, as one content undergrad simply states, "Everyone gets along fairly well and it's not too hard to fit in when there aren't really any labels for people."

FINANCIAL AID: 434-947-8128 • E-MAIL: ADMISSIONS@RANDOLPHCOLLEGE.EDU • WEBSITE: WWW.RANDOLPHCOLLEGE.EDU

THE PRINCETON REVIEW SAYS

Admissions

Very important factors considered include: GPA, standardized test scores, application essay, interview, recommendation(s). *Important factors considered include:* Class rank, rigor of secondary school record, extracurricular activities, alumni/ae relations, level of applicant's interest. *Other factors considered include:* First generation, talent/ability, volunteer work, work experience, character/personal qualities. SAT or ACT required; SAT and SAT Subject Tests or ACT considered if submitted; ACT with or without Writing component accepted. *Academic units required:* 4 English; 3 mathematics; 3 science; (2 science lab); 2 history; 1 academic elective. *Academic units recommended:* 4 mathematics; 3 foreign language; 3 academic electives.

Financial Aid

Students should submit: The Princeton Review suggests that all financial aid forms be submitted as soon as possible after January 1. *Need-based scholarships/grants offered:* Federal Pell, SEOG, State scholarships/grants, private scholarships, the school's own gift aid, United Negro College Fund. *Loan aid offered:* Direct Subsidized Stafford Loans, Direct Unsubsidized Stafford Loans, Direct PLUS loans, Federal Perkins Loans, State Loans, College/university loans from institutional funds. Applicants will be notified of awards beginning 10/1. Federal Work-Study Program available. Institutional employment available. Off-campus job opportunities are good.

The Inside Word

Officers at Randolph College take a fairly traditional approach to their admissions decisions. Certainly your transcript and test scores hold the most weight. However, recommendations, personal essays, and extracurricular activities are also taken into consideration, so it's best not to slack off any facet of your application. The School Says "..."

THE SCHOOL SAYS "..."

From the Admissions Office

"Students who thrive in a close-knit community that values original thinking and research will enjoy the educational and cultural environment at Randolph College where they may earn a B.A., B.S., or B.F.A. degree.

"Nationally ranked for both its academic programs and affordability, Randolph College offers students the best features of an honors education with a wide range of majors and an emphasis on developing intercultural competence. Embedded within the strong, liberal arts foundation are ample opportunities for study abroad, leadership roles, working closely with faculty on research, and real-world experience through internships and service learning. All students are encouraged to pursue and achieve goals with personal meaning.

"A graduate of Randolph College understands the intellectual foundations of the arts, sciences, and humanities and has developed critical skills to learn, adapt, and succeed in a rapidly changing global environment. The college's strong emphasis on writing enables students to communicate clearly and persuasively, and the diverse student population and study abroad programs enable students to see and live through the eyes of another culture. The long-standing and distinctive honor system is a central part of daily life at Randolph and adds to the already close-knit community feel.

"A member of the Old Dominion Athletic Conference and IHSA (Randolph has a 100-acre riding center), Randolph enables scholar-athletes to excel and participate in a variety of sports while focusing on academics. Located in the heart of Virginia near the Blue Ridge Mountains, Randolph College's campus is part of the growing college town of Lynchburg with its abundant cultural, entertainment, and recreational opportunities."

SELECTIVITY

Admissions Rating	76
# of applicants	1,056
% of applicants accepted	83
% of acceptees attending	25

FRESHMAN PROFILE

Range SAT Critical Reading	490–610
Range SAT Math	480–590
Range SAT Writing	480–590
Range ACT Composite	21–28
Average HS GPA	3.61
% graduated top 10% of class	17
% graduated top 25% of class	54
% graduated top 50% of class	91

DEADLINES

Early action	
Deadline	12/1
Notification	1/1
Regular	
Priority	12/1
Deadline	3/1
Nonfall registration?	Yes

APPLICANTS ALSO LOOK AT AND OFTEN PREFER

Christopher Newport University; James Madison University

AND SOMETIMES PREFER

Randolph-Macon College; Virginia Commonwealth University

AND RARELY PREFER

George Mason University; University of Virginia; College of William and Mary

FINANCIAL FACTS

Financial Aid Rating	71
Annual tuition	$32,240
Room and board	$11,210
Required fees	610
Books and supplies	$1,000
% needy frosh rec. need-based scholarship or grant aid	97
% needy UG rec. need-based scholarship or grant aid	74
% needy frosh rec. non-need-based scholarship or grant aid	98
% needy UG rec. non-need-based scholarship or grant aid	62
% needy frosh rec. need-based self-help aid	99
% needy UG rec. need-based self-help aid	91
% frosh rec. any financial aid	99
% UG rec. any financial aid	97
% UG borrow to pay for school	68
Average cumulative indebtedness	$12,454
% frosh need fully met	3
% ugrads need fully met	2
Average % of frosh need met	34
Average % of ugrad need met	33

RANDOLPH-MACON COLLEGE

P. O. BOX 5005, ASHLAND, VA 23005-5505 • ADMISSIONS: 804-752-7305 • FAX: 804-752-4707

CAMPUS LIFE
Quality of Life Rating	86
Fire Safety Rating	85
Green Rating	71
Type of school	Private
Affiliation	Methodist
Environment	Village

STUDENTS
Total undergrad enrollment	1,294
% male/female	48/52
% from out of state	26
% frosh from public high school	77
% frosh live on campus	92
% ugrads live on campus	78
# of fraternities (% ugrad men join)	7 (20)
# of sororities (% ugrad women join)	4 (24)
% African American	10
% Asian	2
% Caucasian	76
% Hispanic	4
% Native American	<1
% international	3
# of countries represented	23

SURVEY SAYS . . .
Students are happy
Career services are great
Internships are widely available
Students are friendly
Campus feels safe
Easy to get around campus
Athletic facilities are great
Alumni active on campus

ACADEMICS
Academic Rating	83
% students returning for sophomore year	77
% students graduating within 4 years	58
% students graduating within 6 years	61
Calendar	4/1/4
Student/faculty ratio	12:1
Profs interesting rating	81
Profs accessible rating	91

Most classes have 10–19 students.

MOST POPULAR MAJORS
biology; psychology; economics

STUDENTS SAY "..."

Academics

Randolph-Macon College in Virginia is a small liberal arts school that "puts the needs of the student first, creates equal opportunity," and "provides as much as the student wishes to garner from the experience." The school places a focus on student development both inside and outside of the classroom, and offers "a lot of free resources and support for every student" that wishes to take advantage, including generous financial aid and study abroad included in tuition.

The majority of students here cite the possibility of "personal connections" as the main reason for coming to Randolph-Macon, which "is all about the one-on-one interactions between the entire community." Lectures are relatively infrequent and most of the academic classes are interactive and discussion-based so as to "maximize learning," and students also "get a lot of opportunities to write throughout your classes." "I love the small class sizes here; my largest class has eighteen students in it which makes it easy to get extra help and ask questions," says a freshman. To top it off, the "very personable" professors are "extremely helpful and are willing to meet with you if you want to go over material." They "bring their dogs to class, have class outside, invite students over for dinner and supply us with the resources to succeed."

There are "many different opportunities to get involved and strengthen your leadership skills" outside of the classroom, such as study abroad, "the J-Term, working on campus, and career services/internship offices." The "challenging but rewarding academic environment" also allows for undergrads to conduct and publish research quite easily. The "accessible" alumni network and staff are also "wonderful." They are "truly interested in your success and are more than helpful when it comes to resumes, cover letters, internships, and anything related to the business professional world."

Life

Students at Randolph-Macon fit in by being a part of something bigger than themselves, whether it's "greek life, athletics, intramurals, choir, orientation leaders, or Resident Assistants," and "virtually EVERYONE is involved." In addition, "many of the clubs are given a grant, so all of the events and trips you go on are free." "It is impossible to not be involved in something here," says a student. "If you are bored here, it is your own fault." There is a college-sponsored activity going on every weekend, such as "ice cream socials, crafting, performances, comedians, etc,"; occasionally students travel off-campus for parties or other activities (Richmond is nearby for students who want a little urban action), but "life is generally centered on campus." Some students do wish they could be kept a little more abreast of happenings around campus: "There isn't a lot of advertisement for campus events, even though most of them are pretty fun."

Dining options are universally panned by students, who frequently grab bites to eat elsewhere, and though "there is a party scene" it's not the only option by a long shot. "There are so many subgroups that you might have to try to NOT find someone with similar interests," assures a junior.

Student Body

Though most students here are "white," "preppy," and "southern," the common thread is that this is "a small community of intelligent minded students that enjoy their weekends." There is "fantastic student involvement and diversity of interests" at R-MC, and the typical "knows that academics are the most important, but never forgets that extracurriculars are a must!" People here are "driven and passionate about their success here while at college and in their futures." By "going to parties on the weekend and saying hi to people you have classes with" students have no problem making friends, as "the campus is too small to not find a group to fit in with."

FINANCIAL AID: (804) 752-7259 • E-MAIL: ADMISSIONS@RMC.EDU • WEBSITE: WWW.RMC.EDU

THE PRINCETON REVIEW SAYS

Admissions

Very important factors considered include: GPA, rigor of secondary school record. *Important factors considered include:* Class rank, standardized test scores, application essay, recommendation(s). *Other factors considered include:* Extracurricular activities, first generation, interview, racial/ethnic status, talent/ability, volunteer work, work experience, alumni/ae relations, character/personal qualities, level of applicant's interest. SAT or ACT required; ACT with Writing component recommended. TOEFL required of all international applicants. *Academic units required:* 4 English; 3 mathematics; 3 science; (2 science lab); 2 social studies; 1 history; 1 academic elective. *Academic units recommended:* 4 English; 4 mathematics; 4 science; (4 science lab); 3 social studies; 4 foreign language; 3 history; 2 academic electives.

Financial Aid

Students should submit: FAFSA, State aid form. Regular filing deadline is 3/1. The Princeton Review suggests that all financial aid forms be submitted as soon as possible after January 1. *Need-based scholarships/grants offered:* Federal Pell, SEOG, State scholarships/grants, private scholarships, the school's own gift aid. *Loan aid offered:* Direct Subsidized Stafford Loans, Direct Unsubsidized Stafford Loans, Direct PLUS loans, Federal Perkins Loans. Applicants will be notified of awards beginning 3/15. Federal Work-Study Program available. Institutional employment available. Off-campus job opportunities are good.

The Inside Word

Randolph-Macon is a solid liberal arts college, but it must contend with a wealth of Virginia schools for applicants. Students who are academically competitive should easily gain acceptance. Admissions Officers ascribe the most weight to objective data, primarily grades and test scores. Recommendations, special skills and talents, and personal attributes also figure into the decision.

THE SCHOOL SAYS "..."

From the Admissions Office

"At Randolph-Macon College, education begins with the future in mind. The college's unique approach integrates an extraordinary education with a personalized, four-year career preparation program, The EDGE, to give students a distinct, competitive advantage after graduation. Starting in the freshman year, students begin honing skills they'll need to excel in any career or graduate school. Our dedicated, collaborative team of faculty, staff, coaches and alumni provides a campus-wide support system to help you make the most of your Randolph-Macon experience.

"This distinctive, hands-on immersion prepares students for post-graduate success. Self-assessment programs, workshops to develop strong communication and life skills, and opportunities to network with and be mentored by business leaders and well-connected alumni, culminate in confident students developing their own "brand." Along the way, Randolph-Macon's challenging curriculum and practical opportunities on national and global levels through internships, field studies, and study-abroad adventures, make students competitive for any career or continued academic pursuits. The college's location just outside of Richmond, Virginia, offers a wide range of educational and career possibilities. Graduate school preparation and testing strategies are available, along with medical school and health career forums and partnerships with prestigious medical institutions that guarantee admission to qualified students to medical or nursing school. Our Four-Year-Degree Guarantee program promises in writing that freshmen who meet the requirements will graduate within four calendar years. 95 percent of Randolph-Macon graduates earn their degree in four years or fewer. Randolph-Macon helps you navigate your path to success, gives you a competitive advantage and helps you build an extraordinary future."

SELECTIVITY

Admissions Rating	81
# of applicants	2,996
% of applicants accepted	64
% of acceptees attending	20
# offered a place on the wait list	224
% accepting a place on wait list	17
% admitted from wait list	162

FRESHMAN PROFILE

Range SAT Critical Reading	490–590
Range SAT Math	490–590
Range SAT Writing	480–580
Range ACT Composite	21–26
Minimum paper TOEFL	550
Minimum web-based TOEFL	213
Average HS GPA	3.57
% graduated top 10% of class	14
% graduated top 25% of class	48
% graduated top 50% of class	83

DEADLINES

Early action	
Deadline	11/15
Notification	1/1
Regular	
Priority	2/1
Deadline	3/1
Notification	4/1
Nonfall registration?	Yes

APPLICANTS ALSO LOOK AT AND OFTEN PREFER
James Madison University; University of Virginia

AND SOMETIMES PREFER
Lynchburg College

AND RARELY PREFER
Christopher Newport University; Hampden-Sydney College; Roanoke College; University of Mary Washington; Virginia Tech

FINANCIAL FACTS

Financial Aid Rating	85
Annual tuition	$33,900
Room and board	$10,390
Required fees	$950
Books and supplies	$1,100
% needy frosh rec. need-based scholarship or grant aid	100
% needy UG rec. need-based scholarship or grant aid	100
% needy frosh rec. non-need-based scholarship or grant aid	20
% needy UG rec. non-need-based scholarship or grant aid	18
% needy frosh rec. need-based self-help aid	79
% needy UG rec. need-based self-help aid	81
% frosh rec. any financial aid	99
% UG rec. any financial aid	99
% UG borrow to pay for school	74
Average cumulative indebtedness	$32,020
% frosh need fully met	24
% ugrads need fully met	24
Average % of frosh need met	79
Average % of ugrad need met	78

REED COLLEGE

3203 SOUTHEAST WOODSTOCK BOULEVARD, PORTLAND, OR 97202-8199 • ADMISSIONS: 503-777-7511 • FAX: 503-777-7553

STUDENTS SAY ". . ."

Academics

Reed is a college synonymous with academic rigor and a "passion for learning" certainly permeates this campus. A political science major steadfastly agrees stating, "Reed's commitment to academic excellence blew me away. The students here work like demons and love it!" In fact, "Reedies are proud that the most popular location on campus is the library, regardless of the night of the week." Fortunately, "there is a collective humor on campus and no one takes themselves too seriously." Undergrads also closely adhere to an "Honor Principle" which ensures that "cheating, peer-pressure or antagonism of any kind [is] extremely rare." This also helps to foster a culture where "people would rather help each other learn than be the best." Additionally, small classes are integral to the academic experience here. The "10:1 student to faculty ratio assures that the professors have the time to devote to their students, and students have plenty of opportunities to use that time, be it in thesis meetings, regular office hours, or just to bug the professor about a question they had about that day's conference or lab." And these undergrads are eager to lap up conversation with their "brilliant" professors who "love teaching" and "will not allow you to settle for mediocrity." All in all, the college "breeds free thought, pushes students to their intellectual limits, and strengthens each student's character all in the context of the liberal, free-spirited, and welcoming environment that is the Reed campus and the surrounding city of Portland, Oregon."

Life

Intellectual discussions and debates are most definitely woven into the fabric of life here. As a physics major reveals, "One of my favorite things about Reed is how often people will strike up engaged discussions about anything. Be it conversations about the axiom of choice, the existence of free will, or the various merits of 1990s television shows, every conversation is fascinating. Best, you'll hear these conversations everywhere you go: dining hall, dorms, academic buildings, even just people walking around campus." Of course, this isn't wholly surprising given that life at Reed "revolves around academics." But fear not; even Reedies cannot survive by books alone. And, "while work and fun are, in many cases, synonymous, the need to break free from the library manifests on the weekends by campus dances and other forms of spontaneous creativity." A psychology major quickly adds, "I'm never bored because there's always something going on and it's never the same. Glittery dance parties in the Student Union? Check. Movie night in one of the Language Houses? Check. Debate-watching in Vollum? Check. Visiting lecturers? Check. Pool hall tournament? Check. RPG gaming night? Check." We are also told that "a lot of students partake in various substances." However, an understanding junior qualifies this statement, "If you are straightedge or the like, like me, your boundaries will be pushed, but almost always by people who are respectful and who genuinely desire to keep the dorms a safe space for you." Finally, despite grumblings that public transport "can be annoying," undergrads may take advantage of anything downtown Portland has to offer. Transportation woes will be alleviated when a new TriMet MAX Light Rail station opens near campus come September 2015

Student Body

As you probably already gleaned, the typical Reedie has "an overwhelming curiosity and desire to question everything." "Socially liberal" and a tad "socially awkward," these undergrads also define their peers as "smart," "quirky," "witty and talented." A content sophomore explains, "Everyone brings their own unique spin to everything—everyone has a hidden talent or skill that they would love to teach you about, or a wealth of knowledge in some obscure subject you've probably never heard of. Everyone is passionate about something, and it creates a dynamic and wonderful atmosphere." Additionally, "fitting in isn't hard, because student interests are so diverse that there's almost always a number of other people who like the same things you like and want to do the same things you want to do." Finally, a succinct sophomore sums up, "At Reed I found the kind of student body I craved in high school."

FINANCIAL AID: 503-777-7223 • E-MAIL: ADMISSION@REED.EDU • WEBSITE: WWW.REED.EDU

THE PRINCETON REVIEW SAYS

Admissions

Very important factors considered include: GPA, rigor of secondary school record, application essay. *Important factors considered include:* Class rank, standardized test scores, interview, recommendation(s), level of applicant's interest. *Other factors considered include:* Extracurricular activities, first generation, geographical residence, racial/ethnic status, talent/ability, volunteer work, work experience, alumni/ae relations, character/personal qualities. SAT or ACT required; ACT with or without Writing component accepted. TOEFL required of all international applicants. *Academic units recommended:* 4 English; 4 mathematics; 3 science; 1 social studies; 3 foreign language; 3 history.

Financial Aid

Students should submit: FAFSA, CSS/Financial Aid PROFILE, Noncustodial PROFILE. Regular filing deadline is 2/1. The Princeton Review suggests that all financial aid forms be submitted as soon as possible after January 1. *Need-based scholarships/grants offered:* Federal Pell, SEOG, State scholarships/grants, private scholarships, the school's own gift aid. *Loan aid offered:* Direct Subsidized Stafford Loans, Direct Unsubsidized Stafford Loans, Direct PLUS loans, Federal Perkins Loans, College/university loans from institutional funds. Applicants will be notified of awards beginning 4/1. Federal Work-Study Program available. Institutional employment available.

The Inside Word

While there are no fixed requirements or "cut-off" points for applicants, Reed College is definitely on the lookout for students who maintain a thirst for knowledge and take their academics seriously. A rigorous curriculum is a must, so if possible load up on honors and advanced placement classes. Candidates who demonstrate social consciousness, a desire to join an intellectual community and who appear to be independent thinkers might have a leg up.

THE SCHOOL SAYS "..."

From the Admissions Office

"Reed is animated and energized by its seemingly paradoxical features. Reed has, for example: (1) a traditional, classical, highly structured curriculum—yet, at the same time, a progressive, free-thinking, decidedly unstructured community culture; (2) a powerful emphasis on intellectuality, serious study, and the very highest standards of academic achievement—yet, at the same time, a rich and rewarding program of recreational and extracurricular activity, including a ski cabin on Mt. Hood, a P.E. requirement, and over 100 clubs and organizations;; (3) a refusal to overemphasize grades—yet, third in the nation in the production of future Ph.D.s; (4) a faculty culture absolutely dedicated to superb undergraduate teaching—yet, at the same time, a faculty culture that supports and celebrates high-level research and scholarship at the cutting edge of each academic discipline.

"Reed is not a simple place. It's a complex amalgam of diverse elements. But those elements have been chosen and developed over the years with great care. The result is an intricate—even ornate—but utterly coherent and clearly articulated architecture that has been called by at least one outside observer 'exquisite' and by another 'the most intellectual college in the country.' For students who are interested in both exploring great ideas and developing personal autonomy, it makes very good sense.

"Reed accepts either the ACT or SAT and does not require SAT Subject Tests or the ACT writing exam."

SELECTIVITY

Admissions Rating	97
# of applicants	3,075
% of applicants accepted	43
% of acceptees attending	28
# offered a place on the wait list	620
% accepting a place on wait list	99
% admitted from wait list	1
# of early decision applicants	179
% accepted early decision	53

FRESHMAN PROFILE

Range SAT Critical Reading	670–750
Range SAT Math	640–710
Range SAT Writing	660–730
Range ACT Composite	30–33
Minimum paper TOEFL	600
Average HS GPA	3.90
% graduated top 10% of class	63
% graduated top 25% of class	90
% graduated top 50% of class	99

DEADLINES

Early decision	
Deadline	11/15
Notification	12/15
Regular	
Deadline	1/15
Notification	4/1
Nonfall registration?	No

APPLICANTS ALSO LOOK AT AND OFTEN PREFER

University of California—Berkeley; The University of Chicago

AND SOMETIMES PREFER

Oberlin College; Swarthmore College

AND RARELY PREFER

Lewis & Clark College

FINANCIAL FACTS

Financial Aid Rating	99
Annual tuition	$45,750
Room and board	$11,770
Required fees	$260
Books and supplies	$950
% needy frosh rec. need-based scholarship or grant aid	87
% needy UG rec. need-based scholarship or grant aid	89
% needy frosh rec. non-need-based scholarship or grant aid	0
% needy UG rec. non-need-based scholarship or grant aid	0
% needy frosh rec. need-based self-help aid	92
% needy UG rec. need-based self-help aid	93
% frosh rec. any financial aid	53
% UG rec. any financial aid	54
% UG borrow to pay for school	53
Average cumulative indebtedness	$16,910
% frosh need fully met	100
% ugrads need fully met	99
Average % of frosh need met	100
Average % of ugrad need met	100

RENSSELAER POLYTECHNIC INSTITUTE

110 EIGHTH STREET, TROY, NY 12180-3590 • ADMISSIONS: 518-276-6216 • FAX: 518-276-4072

CAMPUS LIFE

Quality of Life Rating	77
Fire Safety Rating	87
Green Rating	75
Type of school	Private
Affiliation	No Affiliation
Environment	City

STUDENTS

Total undergrad enrollment	5,379
% male/female	70/30
% from out of state	66
% frosh from public high school	71
% frosh live on campus	100
% ugrads live on campus	57
# of fraternities (% ugrad men join)	32 (23)
# of sororities (% ugrad women join)	5 (15)
% African American	2
% Asian	10
% Caucasian	65
% Hispanic	7
% Native American	<1
% international	7
# of countries represented	63

SURVEY SAYS . . .

Political activism is unpopular or nonexistent
Career services are great
Athletic facilities are great
Intramural sports are popular

ACADEMICS

Academic Rating	86
% students returning for sophomore year	93
% students graduating within 4 years	65
% students graduating within 6 years	85
Calendar	Semester
Student/faculty ratio	15:1
Profs interesting rating	73
Profs accessible rating	90
Most classes have 10–19 students.	

MOST POPULAR MAJORS

computer engineering; electrical engineering;
business/commerce

STUDENTS SAY ". . ."

Academics

As the nation's oldest technological university, Rensselaer Polytechnic Institute in upstate New York has a rightfully deserved reputation in the science and engineering world, having led tens of thousands of bright minds to look at "innovation and the future." "Research opportunities" and facilities are everywhere, and students are encouraged to work in interdisciplinary programs that allow them to combine scholarly work from several departments or schools. When their four years are complete, students are encouraged to take what they learn and use it for the greater good. "Why not change the world?" asks a student.

The professors at RPI are "passionate about teaching," "very accessible, and really there for the students." Though there are certainly some "dull" professors ("I've seen the good, the bad, and the ugly!" says one student), most find that the faculty is praiseworthy and "serve as great mentors for students." "My professors in my direct major are extremely hands-on and discussion-based," says a student. Thanks to the "focus on problem-solving," professors are always looking to get students involved in projects, and one of "the greatest strengths of [the] school is the resources that they offer." On top of that, the "welcoming overall community" fosters success, as "students are not extremely competitive and everyone tends to help each other out."

The school is "rigorous," but the students "do find time to enjoy the downtime when we get it." RPI "is a place where nerds can get both an excellent education and an enjoyable four years," according to one student. The student union is entirely student-run, giving students "a lot of freedom to control our educational experience." Many of the student clubs both "suit your interests and work toward your professional career after college." All in all, "community and knowledge drive this school to push students to excel in school and after graduation."

Life

Everyone agrees that RPI is just the right size: "The kind of size where you don't know everybody but you see ten people you know as you walk across campus (and it only takes ten minutes to walk across campus)." People at RPI "don't care how weird or different you are, they let you be." "You can be anyone you want—the kid sword-fighting with his friends in quad or an avid musician who has a 4.0," says a student. Most students do have a "nerdy" side to them, and they inherently love math/science—"Even the humanities at RPI are laced with the sweet smell of science," and "Physics equation graffiti" can be found on some walls.

Academics are definitely an important priority here, but "extracurricular activities are balanced alongside the classes, labs, homework, and studying." There are hundreds of clubs on campus (such as Engineers for a Sustainable World and the Model Railroad Society, which does model railroading of upstate New York and Vermont all circa the early- to mid-1950s), and "most people are involved in several." There are always campus events that students can attend, which range from "athletic events and cultural programs to student ensemble concerts and open mic shows." Downtown Troy has some "quaint cafes and places to explore," Albany has shopping malls, parks, and movie theaters, and a ski trip to Lake Placid is easily accomplished. "There is so much to do around here—you'll never be bored if you take the time to explore." Men's hockey games are a large part of student life here, and "Greek life accounts for about one-fourth of the undergraduate student body and is a great leadership experience and a large contributor to the social scene."

Student Body

Everyone here is pretty much without a doubt "a little bit nerdy, but friendly and helpful." This tinge of nerdiness in everyone "brings the students together and makes it a fun environment with little to no discrimination." "The typical student at my school is studious, but also social in their own way," explains a student. There is a whole spectrum of social students, which ranges "from socializing with a select few to the person that is a social butterfly," but no matter which path you choose, "people don't judge at RPI."

RENSSELAER POLYTECHNIC INSTITUTE

FINANCIAL AID: 518-276-6813 • E-MAIL: ADMISSIONS@RPI.EDU • WEBSITE: WWW.RPI.EDU

THE PRINCETON REVIEW SAYS

Admissions

Very important factors considered include: Class rank, GPA, rigor of secondary school record, standardized test scores. *Important factors considered include:* Application essay, extracurricular activities, recommendation(s), character/personal qualities, level of applicant's interest. *Other factors considered include:* Geographical residence, racial/ethnic status, talent/ability, volunteer work, work experience, alumni/ae relations. SAT or ACT required; SAT and SAT Subject Tests or ACT required for some; ACT with Writing component required. TOEFL required of all international applicants. *Academic units required:* 4 English; 4 mathematics; 3 science; 2 social studies. *Academic units recommended:* 4 science; 3 social studies.

Financial Aid

Students should submit: FAFSA, CSS/Financial Aid PROFILE. The Princeton Review suggests that all financial aid forms be submitted as soon as possible after January 1. *Need-based scholarships/grants offered:* Federal Pell, SEOG, State scholarships/grants, private scholarships, the school's own gift aid. *Loan aid offered:* Direct Subsidized Stafford Loans, Direct Unsubsidized Stafford Loans, Direct PLUS loans, Federal Perkins Loans, State Loans. Applicants will be notified of awards beginning 3/15. Federal Work-Study Program available. Institutional employment available. Off-campus job opportunities are good.

The Inside Word

Outstanding test scores and grades are pretty much a must for any applicant hopeful of impressing the RPI admissions committee. Underrepresented minorities and women—two demographics the school would like to augment—will get a little more leeway than others, but in all cases, the school is unlikely to admit anyone who lacks the skills and background to survive here.

THE SCHOOL SAYS "..."

From the Admissions Office

"The oldest degree-granting technological research university in North America, Rensselaer was founded in 1824 to instruct students to apply 'science to the common purposes of life.' A Rensselaer education is challenging, interactive, and highly relevant. Students immerse themselves in course work that combines theory with learning by experience in unparalleled facilities, using advanced technology. Rensselaer offers more than 100 programs and 1,000 courses leading to bachelor's, master's, and doctoral degrees. Undergraduates pursue studies in architecture, engineering, humanities, arts, and social sciences, management, science, and information technology (IT). A pioneer in interactive learning, Rensselaer provides real-world, hands-on educational opportunities that cut across academic disciplines. Students have ready access to laboratories and classes involving lively discussion, problem solving, and faculty mentoring. The First-Year Experience office provides programs for students and their families that begin even before students arrive on campus. Students are able to take full advantage of Rensselaer's unique research platforms: the $80 million Center for Biotechnology and Interdisciplinary Studies; one of the world's most powerful academic supercomputers, the Center for Computational Innovations; and the Experimental Media and Performing Arts Center, which encourages students to explore the intersection of science, technology, and the arts. Newly renovated residence halls, wireless computing network, and studio classrooms create a fertile environment for study and learning. Rensselaer offers recreational and fitness facilities plus numerous student-run organizations and activities, including fraternities and sororities, newspaper and radio station, drama and musical groups, and more than 200 clubs. In addition to intramural sports, NCAA varsity sports include Division I men's and women's ice hockey teams and 21 Division III men's and women's teams in 13 sports. The East Campus Athletic Village, opened in 2009, raises the bar for student athletic facilities for varsity and non-varsity athletes alike, and includes a new football arena, basketball stadium, and sports medicine complex."

SELECTIVITY

Admissions Rating	96
# of applicants	16,150
% of applicants accepted	41
% of acceptees attending	21
# offered a place on the wait list	3,787
% accepting a place on wait list	65
% admitted from wait list	0
# of early decision applicants	649
% accepted early decision	52

FRESHMAN PROFILE

Range SAT Critical Reading	620–720
Range SAT Math	670–768
Range ACT Composite	27–31
Minimum paper TOEFL	570
Minimum web-based TOEFL	230
% graduated top 10% of class	72
% graduated top 25% of class	95
% graduated top 50% of class	98

DEADLINES

Early decision	
Deadline	11/1
Notification	12/14
Regular	
Deadline	1/15
Notification	3/8
Nonfall registration?	Yes

APPLICANTS ALSO LOOK AT AND OFTEN PREFER
Massachusetts Institute of Technology; Cornell University

AND SOMETIMES PREFER
University of Rochester; Boston University

AND RARELY PREFER
State University of New York at Binghamton; Rochester Institute of Technology

FINANCIAL FACTS

Financial Aid Rating	79
Annual tuition	$46,700
Room and board	$13,620
Required fees	$1,208
Books and supplies	$2,670
% needy frosh rec. need-based scholarship or grant aid	100
% needy UG rec. need-based scholarship or grant aid	100
% needy frosh rec. non-need-based scholarship or grant aid	21
% needy UG rec. non-need-based scholarship or grant aid	13
% needy frosh rec. need-based self-help aid	99
% needy UG rec. need-based self-help aid	97
% frosh rec. any financial aid	92
% UG rec. any financial aid	93
% UG borrow to pay for school	67
Average cumulative indebtedness	$32,000
% frosh need fully met	27
% ugrads need fully met	19
Average % of frosh need met	85
Average % of ugrad need met	77

RHODES COLLEGE

2000 NORTH PARKWAY, MEMPHIS, TN 38112 • ADMISSIONS: 901-843-3700 • FAX: 901-843-3631

STUDENTS SAY " . . ."

Academics

A "beautiful" campus located in the heart of Memphis, Tennessee, the "tight-knit community" of Rhodes College offers "individual study in a liberal arts mold," which involves exposing students to "as many different disciplines as possible in order to gain a broader understanding of the world." Academics here are extremely challenging, "but nothing that hard work and study time can't handle." "I have been pushed (in a good way) to the outer limits of my academic capabilities," says a sophomore. Professors are undoubtedly "one of Rhodes' best assets"—invitations to faculty members' houses for dinner are par for the course—and "truly care about our achievement, grasping the right concepts, and progressing in our education." "Professors don't just care about passing the tests, they want students to be able to take what they have learned and apply it to real life," beams a student. The "small classes" and "comprehensive honor code" only help to further students' love of the Rhodes' classroom experience. The concerned individuals making up the Rhodes administration are "not just doing a job," they are "dedicated to the mission of this college and committed to the students they serve." Though some students have had some bad experiences with administrators, most are content, and it doesn't hurt that the school "took all of the different offices that were spread throughout campus and consolidated them into one newly-renovated building that makes any form or process/meeting much simpler."

Life

With "gothic architecture [that] will make you feel like you live in a fantasy world," the Rhodes campus is "easy on the eyes," while the food used to be "tough on the gut," Rhodes opened a new best-in-class dining facility in the fall of 2012. There is a huge Greek contingent here—"frat parties on campus are always fun and wild"—and all students are sure to find their niche since "each fraternity is different." Generally speaking, the typical student schedule breaks down like this: "weekdays and nights in the library (which is beautiful, so it's not as bad as it could be), and starting Thursdays, partying." Don't be fooled, though: "Most people here work hard and see it academically pay off." "Students focus on getting their school work done before going out and hold their friends accountable so not many get behind," says another student. The school itself offers tons of service activities, cultural events, speakers, and intramurals, and people like to get off campus and have fun in Memphis, which is "surrounded by fun sports teams" to which the school provides cheap tickets. The library can also be a social place, especially during exams, "because so many people spend their time there."

Student Body

Rhodes has its fair share of "white, upper-middle-class" students, but "no one is elitist," and the overall student body itself is diverse on many fronts. Many students here are from the South and "preppy," and you can spot many "polos and khakis around campus." "Everyone is well accepted regardless of socioeconomic status," and the few atypical student groups "mix freely" and "interact with few problems." The school is full of hard workers ("academic but not full of nerds") and the school's honor code is taken very seriously. "People rarely ever cheat or steal"—most students live on campus and "a large percentage don't ever lock their doom rooms." One thing is for certain, though—students here are "busy" in all areas of their life: studying, taking advantage of the "countless service opportunities," arts/athletics, and Greek life. The typical student is generally an "overachiever" while still "[liking] to have fun and enjoy him or herself." "Rhodes is filled with the types of students that are any high school counselor's…dream," sums up a student.

FINANCIAL AID: 901-843-3810 • E-MAIL: ADMINFO@RHODES.EDU • WEBSITE: WWW.RHODES.EDU

THE PRINCETON REVIEW SAYS

Admissions

Very important factors considered include: Class rank, GPA, rigor of secondary school record. *Important factors considered include:* Standardized test scores, application essay, racial/ethnic status, recommendation(s), alumni/ae relations, character/personal qualities. *Other factors considered include:* Extracurricular activities, first generation, geographical residence, interview, state residency, talent/ability, volunteer work, work experience, level of applicant's interest, TOEFL required of all international applicants. *Academic units required:* 4 English; 3 mathematics; 2 science; (2 science lab); 2 social studies; 2 foreign language; 3 academic electives.

Financial Aid

Students should submit: FAFSA, CSS/Financial Aid PROFILE, Noncustodial PROFILE. Regular filing deadline is 3/1. The Princeton Review suggests that all financial aid forms be submitted as soon as possible after January 1. *Need-based scholarships/grants offered:* Federal Pell, SEOG, State scholarships/grants, private scholarships, the school's own gift aid. *Loan aid offered:* Direct Subsidized Stafford Loans, Direct Unsubsidized Stafford Loans, Direct PLUS loans, Federal Perkins Loans. Federal Work-Study Program available. Institutional employment available. Off-campus job opportunities are good.

The Inside Word

Rhodes' national profile is growing. Even though the majority of students come from Tennessee and nearby states, students from farther-flung points of origin will enjoy a leg up because they add to the geographic diversity. As with all small, selective schools, applicants are advised to schedule a campus visit and to interview to demonstrate their interest in attending.

THE SCHOOL SAYS "..."

From the Admissions Office

"Rhodes is a residential college committed to liberal arts and sciences. Our highest priorities are intellectual engagement, service to others, and honor among ourselves. We live this life on one of the country's most beautiful campuses in the heart of Memphis, Tennessee, an economic, political, and cultural center, making Rhodes one of a handful of top-tier, liberal arts colleges in a major metropolitan area.

"Rhodes has the soul of a liberal arts college coupled with a real-world mindset. Our students put their liberal arts knowledge to work in the world starting their first year. You'll be encouraged to engage in research, leadership and service opportunities—and to take responsibility for shaping your educational experience to meet your personal interests and goals. Memphis is a thriving city right on Rhodes' doorstep, with spectacular resources for students, and the college has pioneered the establishment of programs with world-class institutions and companies, including St. Jude Children's Research Hospital, FedEx and the Memphis Zoo, which take advantage of the college's metropolitan location and provide students with real-world opportunities for academic and personal growth."

SELECTIVITY

Admissions Rating	94
# of applicants	3,555
% of applicants accepted	58
% of acceptees attending	27
# offered a place on the wait list	828
% accepting a place on wait list	17
% admitted from wait list	16
# of early decision applicants	98
% accepted early decision	86

FRESHMAN PROFILE

Range SAT Critical Reading	590–690
Range SAT Math	580–680
Range SAT Writing	590–690
Minimum paper TOEFL	550
Average HS GPA	3.78
% graduated top 10% of class	50
% graduated top 25% of class	82
% graduated top 50% of class	95

DEADLINES

Early decision	
Deadline	11/1
Notification	12/1
Early action	
Deadline	11/15
Notification	1/15
Regular	
Priority	1/15
Notification	4/1
Nonfall registration?	Yes

APPLICANTS ALSO LOOK AT AND OFTEN PREFER
Washington University in St. Louis

AND SOMETIMES PREFER
Emory University; Tulane University

AND RARELY PREFER
Millsaps College; Elon University

FINANCIAL FACTS

Financial Aid Rating	85
Annual tuition	$39,484
Room and board	$9,884
Required fees	$310
Books and supplies	$1,125
% needy frosh rec. need-based scholarship or grant aid	100
% needy UG rec. need-based scholarship or grant aid	99
% needy frosh rec. non-need-based scholarship or grant aid	44
% needy UG rec. non-need-based scholarship or grant aid	25
% needy frosh rec. need-based self-help aid	63
% needy UG rec. need-based self-help aid	71
% frosh rec. any financial aid	92
% UG rec. any financial aid	93
% UG borrow to pay for school	44
Average cumulative indebtedness	$26,581
% frosh need fully met	52
% ugrads need fully met	36
Average % of frosh need met	92
Average % of ugrad need met	81

RICE UNIVERSITY

MS 17, PO Box 1892, Houston, TX 77251-1892 • Admissions: 713-348-7423 • Fax: 713-348-5952

CAMPUS LIFE
Quality of Life Rating	99
Fire Safety Rating	91
Green Rating	72
Type of school	Private
Affiliation	No Affiliation
Environment	Metropolis

STUDENTS
Total undergrad enrollment	3,920
% male/female	51/49
% from out of state	49
% frosh live on campus	98
% ugrads live on campus	71
% African American	6
% Asian	21
% Caucasian	39
% Hispanic	15
% Native American	<1
% international	11
# of countries represented	51

SURVEY SAYS . . .
Students are happy
Classroom facilities are great
Lab facilities are great
School is well run
Students are friendly
Diverse student types on campus
Students get along with local community
Great off-campus food
Campus feels safe
Athletic facilities are great
Lots of beer drinking
Active minority support groups

ACADEMICS
Academic Rating	93
% students returning for sophomore year	98
% students graduating within 4 years	79
% students graduating within 6 years	91
Calendar	Semester
Student/faculty ratio	6:1
Profs interesting rating	84
Profs accessible rating	86

MOST POPULAR MAJORS
biology; psychology; economics

STUDENTS SAY ". . ."

Academics
Students at Rice are generous with their praise for professors, who "are very accessible and happy to talk about the material and give help outside of class," and make "their course material relevant, being sure to include modern-day and industry applications." Students caution that some faculty members are "more focused on their research," but others "learn every student's name in their 200-person lecture" and "everyone certainly knows their stuff very well." While "a lot is expected of you, so be prepared to have to do a lot of work on your own," professors "are there if you are struggling," the academic "emphasis is more on collaboration than competition," and that work will contribute to "meaningful discussion during class." Professors serve as "masters" within the residential colleges, "which provides a wonderful opportunity [for students] to get to know the faculty and staff on a more personal level." Students are assigned to one of eleven colleges for all four years and about 75 percent of undergrads live at their colleges, which creates smaller, close-knit communities within the university. All of this crossover between personal and academic areas helps make life at Rice well-balanced: "Overall the academic experience is rigorous, but not particularly stressful."

Life
Continuing with the theme of balance, "students at Rice work hard and accomplish great things in academics and extracurriculars. But this is complemented and supported by a thriving social life." Students report a wide range of activities and interests outside the classroom. What they all have in common is their satisfaction with life at Rice. "The environment is very inclusive. People are free to do whatever they want with whoever they want." "On any given Friday night you might find various religious organizations meeting, a group of friends playing board games in the commons space, a crowd of people heading to a party, and a carload of students heading off-campus to see a movie." School-sponsored activities often include "lecture series, recruiting sessions, movie nights, sporting events, parties, board game nights, etc, usually…with free food."

Intramural sports and campus traditions are popular, and "the typical student seems to be involved in at least three or four activities." Rice undergrads also seem to have a healthy perspective on partying: "This is a wet campus, after all…that said, Rice's alcohol policy fosters a culture of care in which students… help each other stay safe and make good decisions." "You can be a drinker or not a drinker and you will find others who choose the same as you." Finally, some students report that they don't get off campus much, but others praise Houston's music and restaurant scenes, and everyone loves the warm, sunny weather!

Student Body
Most students are quick to claim they can't be typified, and many use the term "quirky" to describe themselves and each other. Rather than quirky in the hipster sense, they seem to mean that "everyone is…interesting in some way" and "people have such a far-reaching range of interests." One student shares their "impression that Rice admits people who excel in [a] particular area or who have specialized interests rather than…a cookie-cutter class of people." "There is no racial majority here on campus, and I've met students of varied political affiliations, religions, socio-economic status, and sexual orientations." Commonalities across this "wide array of people" include dedication to rigorous academic courses and "a leadership position in one or two campus clubs or organizations." "The student body is extremely collaborative, friendly, accepting, and social—it's not cliquey," though "there are some rifts…but these are not very pronounced." "Most students respect others students and enjoy learning more about people who have different backgrounds and beliefs than their own…there is most likely someone with whom to share a common interest, be it something like LARPing, rock-climbing, or fashion."

FINANCIAL AID: 713-348-4958 • E-MAIL: ADMI@RICE.EDU • WEBSITE: WWW.RICE.EDU

THE PRINCETON REVIEW SAYS

Admissions

Very important factors considered include: Class rank, GPA, rigor of secondary school record, standardized test scores, application essay, extracurricular activities, recommendation(s), talent/ability, character/personal qualities. *Other factors considered include:* First generation, geographical residence, interview, racial/ethnic status, state residency, volunteer work, work experience, alumni/ae relations, level of applicant's interest. SAT and SAT Subject Tests or ACT required; ACT with Writing component required. TOEFL required of all international applicants. *Academic units required:* 4 English; 3 mathematics; 2 science; (2 science lab); 2 social studies; 2 foreign language; 3 academic electives. *Academic units recommended:* 4 English; 4 mathematics; 4 science; (3 science lab); 2 social studies; 4 foreign language; 3 academic electives.

Financial Aid

Students should submit: FAFSA, CSS/Financial Aid PROFILE, Noncustodial PROFILE, Business/Farm Supplement. The Princeton Review suggests that all financial aid forms be submitted as soon as possible after January 1. *Need-based scholarships/grants offered:* Federal Pell, SEOG, State scholarships/grants, private scholarships, the school's own gift aid. *Loan aid offered:* Direct Subsidized Stafford Loans, Direct Unsubsidized Stafford Loans, Direct PLUS loans, Federal Perkins Loans, State Loans. Applicants will be notified of awards beginning 4/1. Federal Work-Study Program available. Institutional employment available. Off-campus job opportunities are excellent.

The Inside Word

With students who are so vocal about their happiness, it's no surprise that Rice has a large applicant pool and a low acceptance rate. In addition to strong transcripts and test scores, prospective students should demonstrate their unique passions through electives and extracurricular activities: admissions officers look for applicants who are motivated and creative. Interviews are optional, but recommended.

THE SCHOOL SAYS "..."

From the Admissions Office

"We seek students of keen intellect and diverse backgrounds who show potential to succeed at Rice and will also contribute to the educational environment of those around them.

"Student applications are reviewed within the context of the division to which they apply. Admission committee decisions are based not only on high school grades and test scores but also on such qualities as leadership, participation in extracurricular activities, and personal creativity. Admission is extremely competitive. Rice attempts to seek out and identify those students who have demonstrated exceptional ability and the potential for personal and intellectual growth.

"Our individualized, holistic evaluation process employs many different means to identify these qualities in applicants.

"Required admission testing includes the SAT and two Subject Tests, or ACT with writing. All test scores must be sent to Rice directly from the official testing agency."

SELECTIVITY

Admissions Rating	99
# of applicants	15,415
% of applicants accepted	17
% of acceptees attending	38
# offered a place on the wait list	2,552
% accepting a place on wait list	59
% admitted from wait list	0
# of early decision applicants	1,298
% accepted early decision	25

FRESHMAN PROFILE

Range SAT Critical Reading	670–760
Range SAT Math	700–790
Range SAT Writing	670–770
Range ACT Composite	31–34
Minimum paper TOEFL	600
Minimum web-based TOEFL	250
% graduated top 10% of class	87
% graduated top 25% of class	97
% graduated top 50% of class	100

DEADLINES

Early decision	
Deadline	11/1
Notification	12/15
Regular	
Deadline	1/1
Notification	4/1
Nonfall registration?	No

APPLICANTS ALSO LOOK AT AND OFTEN PREFER

Yale University; Stanford University; Harvard College

AND SOMETIMES PREFER

University of Pennsylvania; Cornell University; Duke University

AND RARELY PREFER

The University of Texas at Austin

FINANCIAL FACTS

Financial Aid Rating	98
Annual tuition	$38,260
Room and board	$13,000
Required fees	$681
Books and supplies	$800
% needy frosh rec. need-based scholarship or grant aid	100
% needy UG rec. need-based scholarship or grant aid	100
% needy frosh rec. non-need-based scholarship or grant aid	5
% needy UG rec. non-need-based scholarship or grant aid	5
% needy frosh rec. need-based self-help aid	61
% needy UG rec. need-based self-help aid	57
% frosh rec. any financial aid	
% UG rec. any financial aid	
% UG borrow to pay for school	30
Average cumulative indebtedness	$17,856
% frosh need fully met	100
% ugrads need fully met	100
Average % of frosh need met	100
Average % of ugrad need met	100

RIDER UNIVERSITY

2083 LAWRENCEVILLE ROAD, LAWRENCEVILLE, NJ 08648-3099 • ADMISSIONS: 609-896-5042 • FAX: 609-895-6645

STUDENTS SAY "..."

Academics

A private coed institution in Lawrenceville, New Jersey, Rider University offers a friendly and intimate college experience to a largely local crowd. In addition to dozens of majors in the liberal arts and sciences, Rider operates a "highly respected business school" and an accounting program that's "the best in the state of New Jersey." Rider "prepares you for all facets of life after college," fostering "interpersonal relationships between successful alumni and under- graduates" and offering great services like "tutoring for every class, writing labs, career services, internships, and co-ops." A current student attests, "The science professors have been really helpful with helping me achieve my goals by introducing me to opportunities for grants, internships, and other experien- tial learning." While course work can be challenging, "the professors present the material in a way in which you can do well if you work hard." Teaching is emphasized, and there are "some phenomenal professors at Rider University who go out of their way to give their students a great education." At the same time, students admit, "While many professors are highly accessible, there are surely a few—mostly adjunct-professors—who are inadequate," both as men- tors and as teachers. On the whole, Rider is "very student-oriented," and the administration "goes the extra mile in making sure all students are treated equally." Even so, things don't always run smoothly, and "dealing with finan- cial aid, administrative offices such as residence life, and career services is the hardest part about going to Rider University." While Rider is a private college, it helps students finance their education through "generous financial aid pack- age," loans, and "lots of opportunities for work study."

Life

Whether they live on campus or commute to school, students enjoy a friendly and social atmosphere at Rider. On campus, "basketball games are always a big draw," and the university hosts "major comedians, musicians, [and] film nights" in the evenings. Even though the university's alcohol rules are rather strict, "most students drink for fun, either on campus or off." For mellower times, the "residence advisors set up a lot events in their respective dorm," or students get together to "play video games, go to Zumba classes, hold hallway-parties (no alcohol), or movie nights." In addition, the "Student Rec Center is a great place to hang out because it's got basketball courts, a pool table, ping pong table, all the video game systems, a gym, a track, and a pool." When they want to pop off campus, "there are coffee shops, frozen yogurt places, [and] a house of cupcakes" in the nearby town of Princeton, and "New York City and Philly are only a train ride away." "On the weekends, the school empties out pretty quickly," as most students go home. While some complain that Rider is a "suitcase school," others insist, "the lifestyle on campus is what people make of it." For those who want a more traditional college experience, "Greek life is a great way to meet new people and get involved in campus."

Student Body

Many Rider students come from a "middle-class background," and most are East Coasters "from the Lawrenceville area" or greater New Jersey. However, "the student body is very diverse politically, socially, and academically," reflect- ing the "vastly varied demographics of the state of New Jersey: all races, all religions, and all levels of mental and physical abilities." "There is a good mix of jocks, brainy people who are committed to studying, and artsy hipster types," so most "students can usually find at least one group to fit in with." While some students "love to party," others "really care about how well they do in school and are involved in so many different organizations on campus." Rider also operates an evening program, which attracts "older, working, returning stu- dents," who are often very serious about their studies.

FINANCIAL AID: 609-896-5360 • E-MAIL: ADMISSIONS@RIDER.EDU • WEBSITE: WWW.RIDER.EDU

THE PRINCETON REVIEW SAYS

Admissions

Very important factors considered include: GPA, rigor of secondary school record, standardized test scores, application essay, recommendation(s). *Important factors considered include:* Level of applicant's interest. *Other factors considered include:* Class rank, extracurricular activities, geographical residence, interview, state residency, talent/ability, volunteer work, work experience, alumni/ae relations, character/personal qualities. SAT or ACT required; ACT with Writing component required. TOEFL required of all international applicants. *Academic units required:* 4 English; 3 mathematics. *Academic units recommended:* 4 mathematics; 4 science; (2 science lab); 2 social studies; 2 foreign language; 2 history.

Financial Aid

Students should submit: FAFSA. The Princeton Review suggests that all financial aid forms be submitted as soon as possible after January 1. *Need-based scholarships/grants offered:* Federal Pell, SEOG, State scholarships/grants, private scholarships, the school's own gift aid. *Loan aid offered:* Direct Subsidized Stafford Loans, Direct Unsubsidized Stafford Loans, Direct PLUS loans, Federal Perkins Loans. Federal Work-Study Program available. Institutional employment available. Off-campus job opportunities are good.

The Inside Word

To prepare for college, Rider University suggests that high school students follow a rigorous curriculum of college prep courses, including AP and honors classes. Students need at least four years of high school English and three years of math to be considered for admission to Rider. The most recent incoming class had an average high school GPA of 3.35 and a SAT score of 1610. Although most students major in the liberal arts and sciences, more than a quarter of undergraduates are enrolled in the business school.

THE SCHOOL SAYS "..."

From the Admissions Office

"Rider students are driven by their dreams of a fulfilling career and a desire to have an impact on the world around them. Rider is a place to apply your imagination, talents and aspirations in ways that will make a difference. A Rider education will prepare you as a leader and as a member of a team. When you graduate from Rider, you'll be a different person, confidently ready for your life's challenges and opportunities.

"We invite you to visit and experience Rider firsthand. Open houses are offered in the fall. Tours are available daily and Information Sessions are offered most weekends throughout the academic year and weekdays in the summer.

"Freshmen applicants are required to submit the results of either the SAT or ACT exam. The highest scores from either test will be considered for admission."

SELECTIVITY

Admissions Rating	72
# of applicants	8,076
% of applicants accepted	69
% of acceptees attending	16
# offered a place on the wait list	94
% accepting a place on wait list	100
% admitted from wait list	50

FRESHMAN PROFILE

Range SAT Critical Reading	460–570
Range SAT Math	470–580
Range SAT Writing	460–570
Range ACT Composite	19–25
Minimum paper TOEFL	550
Minimum web-based TOEFL	213
Average HS GPA	3.32
% graduated top 10% of class	14
% graduated top 25% of class	38
% graduated top 50% of class	68

DEADLINES

Early action	
Deadline	11/15
Notification	12/15
Nonfall registration?	Yes

APPLICANTS ALSO LOOK AT AND OFTEN PREFER
Rutgers University

AND SOMETIMES PREFER
Montclair State; Monmouth University; Seton Hall University;

AND RARELY PREFER
University of Scranton; LaSalle University

FINANCIAL FACTS

Financial Aid Rating	75
Annual tuition	$36,120
Room and board	$13,300
Required fees	$710
Books and supplies	$1,500
% needy UG rec. need-based scholarship or grant aid	98
% needy frosh rec. non-need-based scholarship or grant aid	24
% needy UG rec. non-need-based scholarship or grant aid	13
% needy UG rec. need-based self-help aid	84
% UG borrow to pay for school	82
Average cumulative indebtedness	$34,837
% frosh need fully met	16
% ugrads need fully met	14
Average % of frosh need met	74
Average % of ugrad need met	70

RIPON COLLEGE

PO BOX 248, RIPON, WI 54971 • ADMISSIONS: 920-748-8337 • FAX: 920-748-8335

STUDENTS SAY ". . ."

Academics

Described as a "close-knit community," "Ripon is a place where a student's best interest matters; all other agendas are secondary." One student chose Ripon because, "I was looking for a liberal arts school that allowed me to do the things I like, namely, be involved in multiple student groups, study abroad, and take classes in different fields, all of which I have been able to do at Ripon." The "quiet beauty," "welcoming nature of the campus," along with "small class sizes and a lot of personal attention from professors" create a "friendly, home-away-from-home atmosphere." Students appreciate the education they are receiving and how it prepares them for a productive life after college. The school's motto, "more together" "is exactly what our school is all about; becoming something more with the help of those here to guide us." "Ripon College prepares students to be productive, service-minded leaders who are ready and willing to influence the direction of our nation's future." "Ripon College is not all about sitting in a classroom listening to lectures and taking notes; it's about teaching us to become more educated in the world around us and helping us to develop the skills needed to succeed." "The hands-on, experiential, service-learning projects have been particularly valuable for my own personal growth and for preparing me for life after college." Another student agrees, saying, "Ripon is a prime example of a college with a positive and supportive living and learning community." "Ripon professors provide an interesting and intellectually challenging environment for students to discuss and to learn." Students say, Ripon is an "amazing community of learners and educators who support one another" and a "unique institution that helps ordinary people uncover their extraordinary potential to do great things." Professors "are not just teachers, but mentors!" Scholarships make a Ripon College education possible for some that otherwise could not attend. One student says, "They offered me a great scholarship and were really willing to work with me to make my college education affordable."

Life

With its "tight-knit and welcoming community," Ripon conveys "a friendly environment conducive to learning, fun, and overall personal growth." It is "not uncommon to sit down to lunch with a professor, or even go over to their house for tea." Life at Ripon has proven blissful for one student who now says, "I cannot remember a time when I wanted to be anywhere else." Besides a "strong academic core," Ripon College has "many successful sports teams," and Greek life "is abundant." Greeks host events and are a big part of many students' life. Partying "is evident but not huge by any respect." "Since Ripon College is in a small town, the college sets up a lot of events on weekends for us to take part in!" "The small-town feel of Ripon forces you sometimes to create your own fun, which usually makes for the best memories." "Being close to several metropolitan areas (Chicago, Milwaukee, Madison, and the Twin Cities), there is rarely a weekend when people are not getting off campus to go explore." But if you are looking for snow days to figure into your schedule, then Ripon may not be for you "because most professors will keep classes going even in negative temperatures with two feet of snow."

Student Body

A typical Ripon student is described as "laid-back and friendly." One student cautions, "You have to plan extra time in between classes because you're guaranteed to be stopped by someone you know along the way to talk for a few minutes." Students are "outgoing, personable, and motivated," "involved in multiple clubs," and may "hold more than one internship at a time. From Student Senate to Ultimate Frisbee to volunteering in the community, there is never a lack of activities in which one can participate." Students are "always looking for something new and exciting to do, and [are] ready to volunteer their time and energy to someone in need."

FINANCIAL AID: 920-748-8301 • E-MAIL: ADMINFO@RIPON.EDU • WEBSITE: WWW.RIPON.EDU

THE PRINCETON REVIEW SAYS

Admissions

Very important factors considered include: Rigor of secondary school record, interview. *Important factors considered include:* Class rank, GPA, standardized test scores, extracurricular activities, recommendation(s), character/personal qualities. *Other factors considered include:* Application essay, talent/ability, volunteer work. SAT or ACT required; ACT with or without Writing component accepted. TOEFL required of all international applicants. *Academic units required:* 4 English; 2 mathematics; 2 science; 2 social studies. *Academic units recommended:* 4 mathematics; 4 science; 4 social studies; 2 foreign language.

Financial Aid

Students should submit: FAFSA. The Princeton Review suggests that all financial aid forms be submitted as soon as possible after January 1. *Need-based scholarships/grants offered:* Federal Pell, SEOG, State scholarships/grants, private scholarships, the school's own gift aid. *Loan aid offered:* Direct Subsidized Stafford Loans, Direct Unsubsidized Stafford Loans, Direct PLUS loans, Federal Perkins Loans. Federal Work-Study Program available. Institutional employment available. Off-campus job opportunities are good.

The Inside Word

Ripon seeks accomplished high school students who have challenged themselves in and out of the classroom. Solid performers—those earning a B-plus average in a college-prep curriculum and exceeding 1100 SAT/22 ACT—should find a clear path awaiting them, although the school does also consider such peripherals as potential contribution to extracurricular life and the likelihood a candidate will flourish in a small-school environment.

THE SCHOOL SAYS "..."

From the Admissions Office

"Since its founding in 1851, Ripon College has adhered to the philosophy that the liberal arts offer the richest foundation for intellectual, cultural, social, and spiritual growth. Academic strength is a 150-year tradition at Ripon. We attract excellent professors who are dedicated to their disciplines; they in turn attract bright, committed students. Together with the other members of our tightly knit learning community, students at Ripon learn more deeply, live more fully, and achieve more success. Students are surprised to discover that here there are more opportunities—to be involved, to lead, to speak out, to make a difference, to explore new interests—than at a college ten times our size. Through collaborative learning, group living, teamwork, and networking, students tap into the power of a community where we all work together to ensure success—at Ripon and beyond.

"All of the best residential liberal arts colleges strive to be true learning communities like Ripon. We succeed better than most because our enrollment of about 1,000 students is perfect for fostering connections inside and outside the classroom. Our students flourish in this environment of mutual respect, where shared values are elevated and diverse ideas are valued. If you are seeking academic challenge and want to benefit from an environment of personal attention and support—then you should take a closer look at Ripon.

"Applicants to Ripon College must submit scores from either the ACT (writing section not required) or the SAT."

SELECTIVITY

Admissions Rating	78
# of applicants	1,320
% of applicants accepted	75
% of acceptees attending	24

FRESHMAN PROFILE

Range SAT Critical Reading	490–630
Range SAT Math	510–680
Range ACT Composite	21–28
Minimum paper TOEFL	550
Minimum web-based TOEFL	213
Average HS GPA	3.43
% graduated top 10% of class	23
% graduated top 25% of class	53
% graduated top 50% of class	84

DEADLINES

Regular	
Priority	3/15
Nonfall registration?	Yes

APPLICANTS ALSO LOOK AT AND OFTEN PREFER
St. Norbert College; Carroll College (WI)

AND SOMETIMES PREFER
University of Wisconsin–Madison

AND RARELY PREFER
Lawrence University; Beloit College

FINANCIAL FACTS

Financial Aid Rating	86
Annual tuition	$33,207
Room and board	$9,085
Required fees	$275
Books and supplies	$750
% needy frosh rec. need-based scholarship or grant aid	100
% needy UG rec. need-based scholarship or grant aid	99
% needy frosh rec. non-need-based scholarship or grant aid	18
% needy UG rec. non-need-based scholarship or grant aid	12
% needy frosh rec. need-based self-help aid	83
% needy UG rec. need-based self-help aid	86
% frosh rec. any financial aid	95
% UG rec. any financial aid	96
% UG borrow to pay for school	87
Average cumulative indebtedness	$33,119
% frosh need fully met	25
% ugrads need fully met	19
Average % of frosh need met	89
Average % of ugrad need met	84

ROANOKE COLLEGE

221 COLLEGE LANE, SALEM, VA 24153-3794 • ADMISSIONS: 540-375-2270 • FAX: 540-375-2267

STUDENTS SAY ". . ."

Academics

Located in the mountains in the heart of historic Salem, Virginia, Roanoke College is a small Lutheran-affiliated liberal arts college that is dedicated to making sure all students have the opportunities and resources necessary to succeed after graduation. This school of about 2,000 "guides students in exploring relevant studies and teaches them how to carefully evaluate important issues in society"; excellent scholarships, good work-study opportunities, and "a high commitment to achieving academically" among students round out the package.

The "always available" professors are "very engaging and invite a warm personal relationship" and desire "to not only act as a teacher, but as a mentor to their students." They are "excited about what they are teaching" and "really convey a sense of wonder about their respective subjects." Roanoke "does not just hand A's out like candy"; the course load is "challenging, with an abundant amount of work inside and outside of the classroom" but "getting an A is… worth all the more for the effort." The required core classes are set up "in a unique and exciting way" and incredibly small classes mean "there is a lot of opportunity to make relationships with professors, counselors, and even dining service [staff.]"

This "community-based school with southern values" is most definitely "student-centered," and "the ability to conduct meaningful research as an undergraduate is a major benefit." The curriculum places an emphasis on "broad exposure to the liberal arts," and the tutoring and writing centers are "fabulous and free" for those who need help. "Both my professors and my peers have given me opportunities to succeed in ways I never dreamed I would want, let alone have," says a junior.

Life

Life at Roanoke is filled with "the perfect balance of comfort and challenge." The Roanoke campus "thrives on students that want to get involved" and therefore provides plenty of chances to do so. Clubs and organizations "are always being advertised all across campus" and the Campus Activities Board is always creating "wonderful events for the students, such as Bingo and concerts." "Social interaction is a must": Greek life "takes over the social scene," and "Greek-like" off-campus organizations and athletics help fill in the void. "On the weekends, there are always lots of parties, but it isn't a big deal to not participate," says a student. The mountains near the "gorgeous campus" also provide plenty of relaxation options (the Blue Ridge Parkway and the Appalachian Trail are close), and "kayaking, hiking, mountain biking, and geocaching are all easy things to do nearby." However, students know that working hard "is a good thing" at Roanoke and "the library is always full of students on Sundays."

"Hanging out in the cafeteria is really popular" for the social aspect (you are required to buy a meal plan if you live on campus), but the food options are limited. Older individuals can go to downtown Roanoke or the Main street of Salem "to have drinks with friends," while underage students "go there for a great dinner." Many say that "it is very difficult to live off-campus, which results in chaos during housing selection," and that "dorm maintenance" should be made a priority.

Student Body

Almost everyone here is "studious" but "knows how to have fun." Typically, you'll find a Roanoke student to be "an overachiever who has at least one minor or concentration, is involved in at least one organization, and [has] a social life." People come from all over the country, and "it's impossible to not notice the 'Ivy League' feel of Roanoke (incorporating both 'southern-Preppy' and 'northern-preppy')." Greek life is quite popular on campus, and the stereotype of "Lacoste, Lily Pulitzer," and lacrosse is pervasive. There "is not a lot of diversity, but it is celebrated when it is present." "It would be surprising to me for someone to struggle to fit in," says a freshman.

FINANCIAL AID: 540-375-2235 • E-MAIL: ADMISSIONS@ROANOKE.EDU • WEBSITE: WWW.ROANOKE.EDU

THE PRINCETON REVIEW SAYS

Admissions

Very important factors considered include: GPA, rigor of secondary school record, standardized test scores, character/personal qualities. *Important factors considered include:* Class rank, extracurricular activities, interview, level of applicant's interest. *Other factors considered include:* Application essay, racial/ethnic status, recommendation(s), talent/ability, volunteer work, work experience, alumni/ae relations. SAT or ACT required; SAT and SAT Subject Tests or ACT considered if submitted; ACT with or without Writing component accepted. TOEFL required of all international applicants. *Academic units required:* 4 English; 3 mathematics; 2 science; (2 science lab); 2 social studies; 5 academic electives. *Academic units recommended:* 4 foreign language.

Financial Aid

Students should submit: FAFSA, State aid form. The Princeton Review suggests that all financial aid forms be submitted as soon as possible after January 1. *Need-based scholarships/grants offered:* Federal Pell, SEOG, the school's own gift aid. *Loan aid offered:* Direct Subsidized Stafford Loans, Direct Unsubsidized Stafford Loans, Direct PLUS loans, Federal Perkins Loans, College/university loans from institutional funds. Federal Work-Study Program available. Institutional employment available. Off-campus job opportunities are good.

The Inside Word

Roanoke takes a holistic approach to the admissions process, so the story your whole application tells is important. While the average grades and test scores of accepted students are high, there are no formulas here, and applicants should show they're well-rounded, emphasizing their passions and extracurriculars. The optional personal statement is highly recommended; use it as an opportunity to both show off your achievements and speak to the specific reasons Roanoke appeals to you.

THE SCHOOL SAYS "..."

From the Admissions Office

"Roanoke College prepares students for their futures by providing a classic undergraduate liberal arts experience that is applied to modern issues. Roanoke is one of only 10 percent of colleges in the U.S. that qualify academically to house a chapter of the prestigious Phi Beta Kappa honor society. Over 91 percent of surveyed alumni received job offers or continued to graduate school within six months of graduation, and approximately 49 percent of Roanoke graduates attend or complete graduate school within six years.

"Roanoke is nationally recognized for its core curriculum. Unlike most colleges that require a series of introductory courses in various disciplines, all of Roanoke's core courses are topic based, and students see firsthand how fundamental concepts are applied to important issues. For example, instead of taking a generic Introduction to Chemistry course, students might choose Chemistry and Crime, where they use forensic chemistry to solve crimes. Or, instead of Statistics 101, students might choose Statistics and the Weather and discover how statistical analysis is used in weather forecasting.

"Roanoke provides a residential experience with most students living on campus, making it easy to engage in the life of the college through extracurricular and out-of-classroom activities. With more than 100 clubs, it's easy for students to meet others with common interests and build friendships. Residence halls include a mix of traditional double rooms, singles, suites and apartment-style living. All halls have air conditioning, free laundry and wi-fi access. Nine residence halls either have been constructed or renovated in the past ten years."

SELECTIVITY

Admissions Rating	76
# of applicants	4,167
% of applicants accepted	73
% of acceptees attending	18
# offered a place on the wait list	112
# of early decision applicants	164
% accepted early decision	68

FRESHMAN PROFILE

Range SAT Critical Reading	490–600
Range SAT Math	490–590
Range SAT Writing	490–580
Range ACT Composite	21–26
Minimum paper TOEFL	520
Minimum web-based TOEFL	190
Average HS GPA	3.44
% graduated top 10% of class	18
% graduated top 25% of class	42
% graduated top 50% of class	76

DEADLINES

Early decision	
Deadline	11/1
Notification	12/1
Regular	
Deadline	3/15
Nonfall registration?	Yes

APPLICANTS ALSO LOOK AT AND OFTEN PREFER

University of Virginia; James Madison University

AND SOMETIMES PREFER

Christopher Newport University; Lynchburg College; University of Mary Washington; Virginia Tech; Elon University

FINANCIAL FACTS

Financial Aid Rating	82
Annual tuition	$36,688
Room and board	$11,924
Required fees	$1,489
Books and supplies	$1,000
% needy frosh rec. need-based scholarship or grant aid	100
% needy UG rec. need-based scholarship or grant aid	99
% needy frosh rec. non-need-based scholarship or grant aid	98
% needy UG rec. non-need-based scholarship or grant aid	97
% needy frosh rec. need-based self-help aid	80
% needy UG rec. need-based self-help aid	81
% frosh rec. any financial aid	99
% UG rec. any financial aid	98
% UG borrow to pay for school	78
Average cumulative indebtedness	$32,311
% frosh need fully met	19
% ugrads need fully met	20
Average % of frosh need met	79
Average % of ugrad need met	77

ROCHESTER INSTITUTE OF TECHNOLOGY

60 LOMB MEMORIAL DRIVE, ROCHESTER, NY 14623-5604 • ADMISSIONS: 585-475-5502 • FAX: 585-475-7424

CAMPUS LIFE

Quality of Life Rating	79
Fire Safety Rating	84
Green Rating	96
Type of school	Private
Affiliation	No Affiliation
Environment	City

STUDENTS

Total undergrad enrollment	12,587
% male/female	67/33
% from out of state	48
% frosh from public high school	85
% frosh live on campus	95
% ugrads live on campus	55
# of fraternities (% ugrad men join)	19 (5)
# of sororities (% ugrad women join)	10 (5)
% African American	5
% Asian	6
% Caucasian	61
% Hispanic	6
% Native American	<1
% international	5
# of countries represented	107

SURVEY SAYS . . .

Lab facilities are great
Career services are great
Internships are widely available
Athletic facilities are great

ACADEMICS

Academic Rating	80
% students returning for sophomore year	87
% students graduating within 4 years	28
% students graduating within 6 years	66
Calendar	Semester
Student/faculty ratio	13:1
Profs interesting rating	76
Profs accessible rating	74
Most classes have 10–19 students.	
Most lab/discussion sessions have 10–19 students.	

MOST POPULAR MAJORS

photography; mechanical engineering; information technology

STUDENTS SAY " . . ."

Academics

Rochester Institute of Technology is bursting at the seams with a myriad of fantastic academic opportunities. Students here greatly value the fact that the university maintains a strong "focus on innovation" and heavily encourages "collaboration [between] business and technology." Moreover, an RIT education isn't merely theoretical. Indeed, undergrads have many chances to participate in "[all] manner of labs and workshops," applying what they study and partaking in a number of "hands-on" experiences. Perhaps this is best illustrated by RIT's fabulous co-op program which allows students to "get real world experience while still in school." And with amazing departments ranging from game design and animation to computer science and biotechnology, your academic needs and interests are guaranteed to be met. While some students caution that "the workload is difficult," a self-assured freshman tells us that "you feel accomplished after you've completed it." By and large, undergrads here find that the "majority of professors are engaging" and "very knowledgeable." Undoubtedly, they "know [their] material inside and out and do a great job of explaining it to the students." Undergrads also brag that their teachers "are all active in their field and/or conduct some sort of research." Overall, an RIT education encourages students "to think in new ways and challenge what seem impossible."

Life

Dull moments are a rare occurrence at RIT. Although undergrads here must slog through "hours upon hours of homework," they also to manage to carve out time to kick back and have fun. And fortunately, "there is a large enough pool of students to find any interest, from a powerlifting team and on-campus rock climbing club to various intramural sports." Additionally, "CAB, the College Activities Board, always provides some source of entertainment." For example, as one freshman delights in sharing that, "Just a few weeks ago my friends and I saw the band Fun." Moreover, "there are tons of societies and clubs on campus that are always hosting game nights or dances or off campus parties." And a mechanical engineering happily chimes in, "There have been free Zumba lessons and yoga parties in random classrooms or in the quads and we have 2 giant festivals every year: Spring Fest and Freeze Fest."

Student Body

Undergrads at RIT wholeheartedly embrace the fact that their peers definitely have a "nerdy" and "quirky" side to their personality. However, they readily assert that even those who likely "play Minecraft everyday" are "a lot of fun." An industrial and systems engineering major further explains, "RIT students are nerdy science people, but we know how to have a good time and socialize. The same people you see at a gaming party one night will be at the RIT hockey game the next, having just as much fun." Of course, there is certainly far more to these students than a few dorky or intellectual interests. As an animation major shares, "There are all kinds of people here. Making friends is stupidly easy. Most everyone is genuinely friendly and I have friends of all kinds. It's hard to not fit in… because RIT accepts everyone." Undergrads also tend to be "dedicated" to their studies as well as "very willing to work together and help each other out." Finally, a software engineering major sums up his peers by stating, "Weird and unique is the normal at RIT. Walk across campus and you'll see couples of all sexual orientations, people riding unicycles, wearing trench coats, riding something of their own creation. Sometimes all at the same time. Basically as long as someone is friendly and open, they'll fit in."

FINANCIAL AID: 585-475-5502 • E-MAIL: ADMISSIONS@RIT.EDU • WEBSITE: WWW.RIT.EDU

THE PRINCETON REVIEW SAYS

Admissions

Very important factors considered include: GPA, rigor of secondary school record. *Important factors considered include:* Class rank, standardized test scores. *Other factors considered include:* Application essay, extracurricular activities, first generation, geographical residence, interview, recommendation(s), talent/ability, volunteer work, work experience, alumni/ae relations, character/personal qualities, level of applicant's interest. SAT or ACT required; ACT with or without Writing component accepted. TOEFL required of all international applicants. *Academic units required:* 4 English; 2 mathematics; 2 science; (1 science lab); 4 social studies; 1 academic elective. *Academic units recommended:* 4 English; 3 mathematics; 3 science; (2 science lab); 4 social studies; 3 foreign language; 5 academic electives.

Financial Aid

Students should submit: FAFSA, Institution's own financial aid form, State aid form. The Princeton Review suggests that all financial aid forms be submitted as soon as possible after January 1. *Need-based scholarships/grants offered:* Federal Pell, SEOG, State scholarships/grants, private scholarships, the school's own gift aid, *Loan aid offered:* Direct Subsidized Stafford Loans, Direct Unsubsidized Stafford Loans, Direct PLUS loans, Federal Perkins Loans. Federal Work-Study Program available. Institutional employment available. Off-campus job opportunities are excellent.

The Inside Word

Competition to gain admission into Rochester Institute of Technology is tight. The admissions committee is on the lookout for bright, highly motivated students who will make the most out of the university's experiential learning opportunities. Moreover, you'll need to have successfully completed a rigorous high school curriculum (we're talking APs and honors classes) if you hope to crack this admission's nut.

THE SCHOOL SAYS "..."

From the Admissions Office

"RIT is a place where brilliant minds pool together their individual talents across disciplines in service of big projects and big ideas. It is a vibrant community of students collaborating with experts and specialists: a hub of innovation and creativity. As one of the world's leading technological universities, RIT offers undergraduate and graduate programs in areas such as engineering, computing, engineering technology, business, hospitality, science, visual arts, biomedical sciences, game design and development, psychology, advertising, public relations, and public policy. Students may choose from more than eighty different minors to develop personal and professional interests. RIT attracts students from every state and over 2,000 international students from more than 100 countries. Embodying our commitment to diversity, more than 2,700 students of color have elected to study at RIT. Adding a social and educational dynamic not found at any other university are more than 1,200 deaf and hard-of-hearing students supported by RIT's National Technical Institute for the Deaf. Experiential learning has been a hallmark of an RIT education since 1912. Every academic program offers some form of experiential education opportunity, which may include cooperative education, internships, study abroad, and undergraduate research. Students work hard, but learning is complemented with plenty of organized and spontaneous events and activities. RIT is a unique blend of rigor and fun, creativity and specialization, intellect and practice. It is a launching pad for a brilliant career, and a highly unique state of mind. It is a perfect environment in which to pursue your passion."

SELECTIVITY

Admissions Rating	88
# of applicants	16,354
% of applicants accepted	60
% of acceptees attending	28
# offered a place on the wait list	376
% accepting a place on wait list	98
% admitted from wait list	22
# of early decision applicants	1,461
% accepted early decision	66

FRESHMAN PROFILE

Range SAT Critical Reading	540–640
Range SAT Math	570–680
Range SAT Writing	520–630
Range ACT Composite	25–31
Minimum paper TOEFL	550
Minimum web-based TOEFL	215
Average HS GPA	3.60
% graduated top 10% of class	31
% graduated top 25% of class	64
% graduated top 50% of class	94

DEADLINES

Early decision	
Deadline	12/1
Notification	1/15
Regular	
Priority	2/1
Deadline	2/1
Nonfall registration?	Yes

APPLICANTS ALSO LOOK AT AND OFTEN PREFER

Cornell University; Carnegie Mellon University

AND SOMETIMES PREFER

Worcester Polytechnic Institute; University of Rochester; Rensselaer Polytechnic Institute

AND RARELY PREFER

State University of New York—University at Buffalo; Drexel University

FINANCIAL FACTS

Financial Aid Rating	92
Annual tuition	$33,932
Room and board	$11,178
Required fees	$492
Books and supplies	$1,050
% needy frosh rec. need-based scholarship or grant aid	95
% needy UG rec. need-based scholarship or grant aid	93
% needy frosh rec. non-need-based scholarship or grant aid	28
% needy UG rec. non-need-based scholarship or grant aid	30
% needy frosh rec. need-based self-help aid	90
% needy UG rec. need-based self-help aid	91
% frosh rec. any financial aid	87
% UG rec. any financial aid	77
% UG borrow to pay for school	68
Average cumulative indebtedness	$26,000
% frosh need fully met	81
% ugrads need fully met	82
Average % of frosh need met	87
Average % of ugrad need met	87

ROLLINS COLLEGE

1000 HOLT AVENUE, WINTER PARK, FL 32789-4499 • ADMISSIONS: 407-646-2161 • FAX: 407-646-1502

STUDENTS SAY "..."

Academics

Located in sunny central Florida, Rollins College is "small enough to help the individual but is fortunate enough to have a large endowment capable of providing each student with necessary academic means." The generous academic merit scholarships bring in a smart crowd, and the small class sizes, dedicated faculty, and numerous "student leadership opportunities, internships, academic presentations, [and] conference opportunities" sweeten the pot.

Rollins is "all about individual growth personally and educationally," but it also stresses "responsible community leadership both on and off campus." Students have a great deal of freedom to study what they choose, and many large projects are individualized toward the student, meaning a student "can tailor my topic to my interests." In addition to the autonomy this approach grants students, it "reinforces the idea of a holistic education," which helps to "make [students] competitive in an ever-changing job market." Working at this speed, students are able to "discover purpose and identify goals." Many services are also available to students, such as free tutoring and counseling.

Professors "perform very well" and create an "open and invigorating classroom environment" that is "open to diverse ideas and perspectives." Teachers "know every student's name, and they will remember you throughout your college experience." "My first year, one called my cell phone when I missed class," says a student. "The interactions that I have with the professors are second to none," says another. The small class sizes (even introductory courses are tiny) make it "very easy to learn and share your opinion," and since professors are "very engaging and willing to hear all points of view," "no one is left feeling like they don't matter."

Life

The "very beautiful and relaxing" campus can often feel sort of like a "country club" in both appearance and attitude. With "so many attractions in the Orlando area, the accessibility of the lake and the beach it is hard not to bring your books outside." Some people like "to go out to nearby downtown Orlando" (which is fifteen minutes away from school), some "live for Disney World," and some just stay in and hang out. A favorite activity among students is "walking up Park Avenue and exploring the delicious culinary endeavors there," and Lake Virginia is a great spot for perching, wakeboarding, or sailing. Students here tend "to travel a lot and explore other towns in Florida during the school year."

There are "always events on campus that are fun," like "a student who is a DJ [who] had a concert on the lawn one night," and almost one-third of the school is involved in Greek life. Community service is also "a pretty big part of the campus," and there is "always something service-related going on either from student groups or from the community engagement office."

Student Body

Rollins is such a small school that "everyone knows everyone." It's a true split at Rollins between in-staters and out-of-staters (and the international contingent) and among socioeconomic classes. "There are extremely wealthy spoiled kids driving Mercedes and smoking, [and] then there are true nerds who busted their butts to get in," says a student. Since the two groups mix constantly, "it is often hard to differentiate between the students who are set to inherit their parent's company after they graduate and those here on scholarship." Luckily, the "family environment and the closeness of all of the campus bring all the students together as scholars." Everyone may have small groups to which they belong, but "there is intermingling going on all the time."

FINANCIAL AID: 407-646-2395 • E-MAIL: ADMISSION@ROLLINS.EDU • WEBSITE: WWW.ROLLINS.EDU

THE PRINCETON REVIEW SAYS

Admissions

Very important factors considered include: GPA, rigor of secondary school record. *Important factors considered include:* Standardized test scores, application essay, extracurricular activities, recommendation(s), talent/ability. *Other factors considered include:* Class rank, first generation, volunteer work, work experience, alumni/ae relations, character/personal qualities, level of applicant's interest. SAT or ACT required. Test Score Waived Option available. TOEFL required of all international applicants. *Academic units required:* 4 English; 3 mathematics; 2 science; 2 social studies; 2 foreign language; 2 history; 2 academic electives. *Academic units recommended:* 4 English; 4 mathematics; 4 science.

Financial Aid

Students should submit: FAFSA. The Princeton Review suggests that all financial aid forms be submitted as soon as possible after January 1. *Need-based scholarships/grants offered:* Federal Pell, SEOG, State scholarships/grants, private scholarships, the school's own gift aid. *Loan aid offered:* Direct Subsidized Stafford Loans, Direct Unsubsidized Stafford Loans, Direct PLUS loans, Federal Perkins Loans. Federal Work-Study Program available. Institutional employment available.

The Inside Word

Applicants to Rollins who don't seek academic merit scholarships have the option of submitting a personal representation of their strengths, talents, or interests (YouTube video or PowerPoint presentation) in place of SAT or ACT scores. in place of SAT or ACT scores. It's the school's way of creating another opportunity for students who test poorly but otherwise excel in academics, and it's characteristic of the individualized approach taken here (about 10 percent of applicants opt for this method). Each applicant is assigned an admissions officer who acts as his or her liaison, ensuring a personalized admissions experience. Early decision applicants are given priority in admissions as well as in considerations for merit-based scholarships and need-based financial aid.

THE SCHOOL SAYS " . . ."

From the Admissions Office

"As you begin the college selection process, remember that you are in control of your destiny. Your academic record—course load, grades earned, test scores—are the most important part of your application credentials. But Rollins also pays close attention to your personal dimension—interests, strengths, values, and potential to contribute to college life. Don't sell yourself short in the application process. Be proud of what you've accomplished and who you are, and be honest when you describe yourself. Finally, the admission committee always likes to see candidates who express interest in the college. If we're your first choice, apply early decision. Each year we admit approximately one-third of the entering class through the early decision process. Are you unsure about your choice? If you can, schedule some visits, meet with an admission counselor, tour campus, and spend time in a class so you can see for yourself what Rollins and other colleges are all about. Take control of your destiny, and enjoy the process along the way.

SELECTIVITY

Admissions Rating	88
# of applicants	4,729
% of applicants accepted	59
% of acceptees attending	17
# offered a place on the wait list	84
% accepting a place on wait list	25
% admitted from wait list	43

FRESHMAN PROFILE

Range SAT Critical Reading	550–650
Range SAT Math	540–650
Range SAT Writing	540–640
Range ACT Composite	24–29
Minimum paper TOEFL	550
Minimum web-based TOEFL	213
Average HS GPA	3.26
% graduated top 10% of class	34
% graduated top 25% of class	67
% graduated top 50% of class	90

DEADLINES

Early decision	
Deadline	11/15
Notification	12/15
Regular	
Deadline	2/15
Notification	4/1
Nonfall registration?	Yes

APPLICANTS ALSO LOOK AT AND OFTEN PREFER

Florida State University; University of Florida

AND SOMETIMES PREFER

University of Miami; College of Charleston; Furman University; Southern Methodist University

AND RARELY PREFER

University of Tampa; University of Central Florida; Elon University; Eckerd College

FINANCIAL FACTS

Financial Aid Rating	87
Annual tuition	$41,460
Books and supplies	$818
% needy frosh rec. need-based scholarship or grant aid	96
% needy UG rec. need-based scholarship or grant aid	96
% needy frosh rec. non-need-based scholarship or grant aid	18
% needy UG rec. non-need-based scholarship or grant aid	14
% needy frosh rec. need-based self-help aid	66
% needy UG rec. need-based self-help aid	73
% frosh rec. any financial aid	86
% UG rec. any financial aid	83
% UG borrow to pay for school	53
Average cumulative indebtedness	$30,634
% frosh need fully met	29
% ugrads need fully met	25
Average % of frosh need met	79
Average % of ugrad need met	79

RUTGERS, THE STATE UNIVERSITY OF NEW JERSEY—NEW BRUNSWICK

65 DAVIDSON ROAD, PISCATAWAY, NJ 08854-8097 • ADMISSIONS: 732-445-4636 • FAX: 732-445-0237

STUDENTS SAY "..."

Academics

Rutgers is "a big school with many different types of people," a "diverse university in all aspects of the word—academically, culturally, politically, ethnically, linguistically, and socially," which offers "opportunities around every corner." No matter what students seek from their educations, they're likely to find it here, from engineering to business to pharmacy programs and more. That kind of all-encompassing diversity means the school "offers everyone the opportunity to pursue anything they're interested in." It also means, however, that your instructors will run the gamut "from vivacious to narcoleptic"; students will have their "fair share of great professors, average professors, and bad professors." However, for every professor who is "rude when dealing with students," there are ten who are "intelligent people who have a lot of information to share and a lot of experience that allows them to elaborate on many topics." The best of these professors are "experienced, intelligent, and helpful," as well as "diverse, accessible, proactive, involved in research, and interested in students who take initiative." These educators know how to make learning "enjoyable and informative." Most classes employ a traditional lecture format, but many elective classes "are much smaller and thus much more open to discussion and student presentation." Even more attractive for many, Rutgers' status as a research university means there are ample opportunities for undergraduates "to conduct research and work with professors in any number of fields."

Life

A big campus, "awesome" public transportation, and activities of every type mean staying active at Rutgers is easy. There is certainly no lack of things to do. "There is always something going on," students boast, with sports, "movie screenings, arcade games at the RutgersZone, performing arts, local theaters, university-sponsored concerts, free food events, community service days, Greek life," and more filling whatever down time students might have. Local restaurants abound. School clubs and organizations exist by the dozens, including those dedicated to theater, music, dance, and community service. "The party scene is definitely present, more so in the warmer months," and there are plenty of bars popular with students. The on-campus party scene tends to be safe, since the school "sends out (campus) police to patrol around the campus twenty-four hours to ensure student safety." Maybe most popular of all is rooting for the scarlet. "During football season...everyone can be found cheering in the student section at the games." For those who need to get off campus, New York City and Philadelphia are both a modest bus drive away. With so many opportunities, "Rutgers allows students to do well in school, be a part of an organization, have relationships with friends, and even have a job." Here, "there's rarely a dull moment."

Student Body

Typical student? Not here. The universal refrain from Rutgers students is there is no such thing. "The one common thread most students have is that they are from New Jersey, since it is a state school." Other than that, "Rutgers is truly a melting pot of people from all over the world of all different backgrounds with different interests." Rather than making it more difficult to fit in, students say this melting pot makes it easier because "no matter what you're interested in, there is a group of students here who share the same exact interests. It's really easy to find your own niche." Most students are "dedicated to academics and community service and also to having fun," students who, no matter which group they fall in with, are "very friendly, funny, and nice." Notice the combination of strong academics and a dedication to fun? That, too, is a frequently cited trait common at Rutgers. Even though "there is not one typical student," at the very least most are "serious about their work and studying but know how to party and have fun." With a large, diverse campus of 30,000, it doesn't matter the kind of person you are. "It is not uncommon to meet someone new weekly... With so many students here, everyone is able to find someone to befriend and interact with."

Rutgers, The State University of New Jersey—New Brunswick

Financial Aid: 848-932-7305 • E-mail: admissions@ugadm.rutgers.edu • Website: www.rutgers.edu

THE PRINCETON REVIEW SAYS

Admissions

Very important factors considered include: GPA, rigor of secondary school record, standardized test scores. *Other factors considered include:* Application essay, extracurricular activities, talent/ability, volunteer work, work experience. SAT or ACT required. TOEFL required of all international applicants. *Academic units required:* 4 English; 3 mathematics; 2 science; 2 foreign language; 5 academic electives. *Academic units recommended:* 4 mathematics; 2 foreign language.

Financial Aid

Students should submit: FAFSA. The Princeton Review suggests that all financial aid forms be submitted as soon as possible after January 1. *Need-based scholarships/grants offered:* Federal Pell, SEOG, State scholarships/grants, private scholarships, the school's own gift aid. *Loan aid offered:* Direct Subsidized Stafford Loans, Direct Unsubsidized Stafford Loans, Direct PLUS loans, Federal Perkins Loans, State Loans, College/university loans from institutional funds.

The Inside Word

One does not need to jump through hoops to get into Rutgers. Because of the vast number of applications the university gets each year, applicants will be reviewed based on the standard criteria—grades, the quality of your high school curriculum, standardized test scores, and your student essay—without much beyond that. Solid students should find acceptance into Rutgers a relatively painless process.

THE SCHOOL SAYS "..."

From the Admissions Office

"Rutgers, The State University of New Jersey, one of only sixty-two members of the Association of American Universities, is a research university that attracts students from across the nation and around the world. What does it take to be accepted for admission to Rutgers University? Our primary emphasis is on your past academic performance as indicated by your high school grades (particularly in required academic subjects), your class rank or cumulative average, the strength of your academic program, your standardized test scores on the SAT or ACT, any special talents you may have, and your participation in school and community activities. We seek students with a broad diversity of talents, interests, and backgrounds. Above all else, we're looking for students who will get the most out of a Rutgers education—students with the intellect, initiative, and motivation to make full use of the opportunities we have to offer.

First-year applicants should take the SAT or the ACT (with writing component). Test scores are not required for students who graduated high school more than two years ago or have completed more than twelve college credits since graduating.

Rutgers' absorption of the University of Medicine and Dentistry of New Jersey (UMDNJ) in July 2013 has added two medical schools, a dental school, and a host of health professions programs that have dramatically enhanced already robust undergraduate academic and research opportunities."

SELECTIVITY

Admissions Rating	89
# of applicants	30,631
% of applicants accepted	60
% of acceptees attending	35

FRESHMAN PROFILE

Range SAT Critical Reading	520–640
Range SAT Math	570–690
Range SAT Writing	540–650
Minimum paper TOEFL	550
% graduated top 10% of class	22
% graduated top 25% of class	52
% graduated top 50% of class	88

DEADLINES

Regular	
Priority	12/1
Notification	3/1
Nonfall registration?	Yes

APPLICANTS ALSO LOOK AT AND OFTEN PREFER

University of Pennsylvania; Cornell University; University of Virginia

AND SOMETIMES PREFER

Pennsylvania State University—University Park; Boston College

AND RARELY PREFER

The George Washington University

FINANCIAL FACTS

Financial Aid Rating	71
Annual in-state tuition	$10,718
Annual out-of-state tuition	$24,742
Room and board	$11,578
Required fees	$2,781
Books and supplies	$1,550
% needy frosh rec. need-based scholarship or grant aid	63
% needy UG rec. need-based scholarship or grant aid	64
% needy frosh rec. non-need-based scholarship or grant aid	26
% needy UG rec. non-need-based scholarship or grant aid	20
% needy frosh rec. need-based self-help aid	87
% needy UG rec. need-based self-help aid	86
% frosh rec. any financial aid	67
% UG rec. any financial aid	69
% UG borrow to pay for school	57
Average cumulative indebtedness	$23,320
% frosh need fully met	11
% ugrads need fully met	13
Average % of frosh need met	52
Average % of ugrad need met	52

SACRED HEART UNIVERSITY

5151 PARK AVENUE, FAIRFIELD, CT 06825 • ADMISSIONS: 203-371-7880 • FAX: 203-365-7607

STUDENTS SAY ". . ."

Academics

Sacred Heart University in Connecticut provides students with everything: "above average academics, numerous student events, and opportunities for students not found many other places." The "Catholic intellectual tradition" here is all about "educating the entire individual, be it academically, spiritually or through important experiences" such as studying abroad and exclusive internship opportunities. The focus on tying the tight-knit community and religion into education is a main reason that students seek SHU out, not to mention the benefits of more than thirty Division I programs, country-leading volunteer programs, and a gorgeous campus. "When I toured there I fell in love right away," says a junior Criminal Justice major.

Professors "engage the class on a regular basis" and "provide useful examples that relate to the subject matter." They are "for the most part very enthusiastic, approachable, smart and cool" and "usually willing to give extra help or guidance." There are no huge lecture halls at SHU, which "makes every class have so much more opportunity for actual education." All students must complete the multidisciplinary Common Core curriculum, which is a series of four classes that incorporate the humanities, social sciences and natural sciences. Some say that classes could stand to be a bit more rigorous, but "if you look for lively academic discussion, you will find it (eventually)."

The school is "great with communing messages to students" and the "very e-mail driven school" makes assistance and answers easy to come by. Everyone is more than satisfied with SHU's overall appearance, and "the constant renovations…help make the school more up to date and modern."

Life

The campus ministry outreach is "extremely strong" (as are the volunteer programs, which are "top in the country"), and this "really provides a sense of community." "Everything is just happy and everyone is so supportive of one another," says a student. Students "care a lot about their studies" so "the library is always packed." There is a lot to do on campus that is "free and really fun": every couple of weeks there is a bingo night, which "is popular because you can win some really good prizes," and the Student Events Team throws annual Fall and Spring Fests. "I am never disappointed by the options I have when it comes to events outside of class," says a student. Fairfield's proximity to New Haven and New York City also provides a welcome dose of culture.

The "public safety that patrol our school are on duty 24 hours a day," and the classrooms "are up to date" (all have been redone within the past two years), but "the food on campus definitely needs improving," as does the parking situation. Unsurprisingly for "a huge jock school," the "kids here like sports" and the typical SHU student "is involved in multiple activities across the spectrum." "Between sports, clubs, Greek life, and community service it is very easy to find people you click with," says a student. Most students at SHU "have a lot of school spirit," and "people enjoy going to games and being active." "A lot of people like to go to parties or clubs" on weekends when work is done, but it "is definitely not something that is forced upon other students."

Student Body

Sacred Heart is a "door holding" school; "it may seem silly but it is nice to know that someone is always willing to help you out," says a student. Diversity is definitely lacking, as most everyone is "white," "preppy and usually from middle to upper class," "Catholic," and "from New England, New York, or New Jersey." Playing sports and taking part in Greek life are popular pursuits among the SHU population. Name brands abound, so "don't be surprised when you pull into campus and the girls (and guys) are getting out of their Range Rovers with Starbucks in their hand and a Michael Kors bag."

FINANCIAL AID: 203-371-7980 • E-MAIL: ENROLL@SACREDHEART.EDU • WEBSITE: WWW.SACREDHEART.EDU

THE PRINCETON REVIEW SAYS

Admissions

Very important factors considered include: GPA, rigor of secondary school record, volunteer work, work experience. *Important factors considered include:* Class rank, application essay, extracurricular activities, recommendation(s), talent/ability, character/personal qualities, level of applicant's interest. *Other factors considered include:* Standardized test scores, first generation, geographical residence, interview, racial/ethnic status, state residency, alumni/ae relations, religious affiliation. SAT or ACT considered if submitted; ACT with or without Writing component accepted. TOEFL required of all international applicants. *Academic units required:* 4 English; 3 mathematics; 3 science; (1 science lab); 3 social studies; 2 foreign language; 3 history; 3 academic electives. *Academic units recommended:* 4 English; 4 mathematics; 4 science; (2 science lab); 4 social studies; 4 foreign language; 4 history; 4 academic electives.

Financial Aid

Students should submit: FAFSA, CSS/Financial Aid PROFILE, Noncustodial PROFILE. The Princeton Review suggests that all financial aid forms be submitted as soon as possible after January 1. *Need-based scholarships/grants offered:* Federal Pell, SEOG, State scholarships/grants, private scholarships, the school's own gift aid. *Loan aid offered:* Direct Subsidized Stafford Loans, Direct Unsubsidized Stafford Loans, Direct PLUS loans, Federal Perkins Loans, State Loans. Federal Work-Study Program available. Institutional employment available. Off-campus job opportunities are excellent.

The Inside Word

Admissions officers at Sacred Heart take the time to consider each applicant on his or her own merits. There's no formula-crunching here; applicants have ample opportunity to make the case why they belong here on their applications. A campus visit is strongly recommended as a way of expressing your interest in the school and setting yourself apart from the crowd. SHU accepts the Common Application.

THE SCHOOL SAYS "..."

From the Admissions Office

"Sacred Heart University, recognized for blending excellence in the Liberal Arts with career-focused academic and student development programs, is the second-largest Catholic university in New England. Sacred Heart continues its exceptional growth in enrollment; academic programs including a variety of accelerated Bachelor's-Master's degree programs; and the physical campus where a new Welch College of Business and Department of Communication & Media Studies are currently under construction and will be followed by a new College of Health Professions building and a new freshman residence hall. With an ideal New England location 55 miles from New York City in Fairfield County, Connecticut, plentiful undergraduate research or internship experiences are in place for all majors, and the Career Center works with students as soon as they arrive as freshmen. Students also gain real-world experience taking a wide variety of courses at SHU's two international campuses in Europe, including pre-fall programs for incoming freshmen as well as short-term winter break and late May programs. These experiential learning opportunities are complemented by a rich student life program offering more than eighty student organizations including strong performing arts programs, media clubs, Greek life and an array of community service organizations, as well as 31 Division I varsity sports and 24 club sports teams."

SELECTIVITY

Admissions Rating	78
# of applicants	7,908
% of applicants accepted	61
% of acceptees attending	26
# of early decision applicants	228
% accepted early decision	86

FRESHMAN PROFILE

Range SAT Critical Reading	500–570
Range SAT Math	520–600
Range ACT Composite	22–26
Minimum paper TOEFL	550
Average HS GPA	3.30
% graduated top 10% of class	14
% graduated top 25% of class	39
% graduated top 50% of class	80

DEADLINES

Early decision	
Deadline	12/1
Notification	12/15
Regular	
Priority	2/1
Nonfall registration?	Yes

APPLICANTS ALSO LOOK AT AND OFTEN PREFER

University of Connecticut; Villanova University

AND SOMETIMES PREFER

Fordham University; Providence College; Loyola University Maryland; Fairfield University

AND RARELY PREFER

Hofstra University; St. John's University—Queens

FINANCIAL FACTS

Financial Aid Rating	70
Annual tuition	$34,800
Room and board	$35,050
Required fees	$250
Books and supplies	$1,200
% needy frosh rec. need-based scholarship or grant aid	100
% needy UG rec. need-based scholarship or grant aid	97
% needy frosh rec. non-need-based scholarship or grant aid	13
% needy UG rec. non-need-based scholarship or grant aid	11
% needy frosh rec. need-based self-help aid	82
% needy UG rec. need-based self-help aid	82
% frosh rec. any financial aid	73
% UG rec. any financial aid	72
% UG borrow to pay for school	84
Average cumulative indebtedness	$40,975
% frosh need fully met	15
% ugrads need fully met	15
Average % of frosh need met	59
Average % of ugrad need met	58

SAINT ANSELM COLLEGE

100 SAINT ANSELM DRIVE, MANCHESTER, NH 03102-1310 • ADMISSIONS: 603-641-7500 • FAX: 603-641-7550

STUDENTS SAY ". . ."

Academics

Saint Anselm College offers a well-rounded, high-standard curriculum, as well as a close-knit community, all while upholding a liberal arts education with an emphasis on the Benedictine values of hospitality and service. In addition to having a well-regarded nursing program, the school gives students "a solid foundation academically, politically, socially, and in sports," which means students emerge, "in one word, well-rounded." "Saint Anselm works very hard to produce intellectual students with good morals," says a student. Saint Anselm also has a legendarily strict attendance policy, which has its detractors, but its fans as well: "I love the attendance policy. You will not hear many students say that, but the extra motivation gets you out of bed at eight!" says a student. The professors in this "intimate college community" are "enthusiastic about what they do," and that's what makes the classes more motivating and interesting." Depending on the major and classes the student has enrolled in, "class discussion and participation are crucial." In the liberal arts majors, such as philosophy and great books, "there is much more discussion than in most nursing and science courses." However, "the amount of discussion and participation is proper and proportional to its importance in one's major." Regardless, the faculty is "always there to answer questions," and the small classroom setting "makes the learning environment a lot easier." In accordance with the school's Benedictine Catholic tradition, there are plenty of "opportunities for service involvement," and there is a monastic community to help students keep the faith. The school is also "one of the centers of politics in New England," and students are all required to take two courses in theology and philosophy. "Saint Anselm College is all about creating an educational, fun, respectful, and peaceful environment that is open to all faculty and students."

Life

The scenic campus in New Hampshire has plenty going for it (though certainly not "Internet speed"), but one particular affirmation isn't heard all that often on college campuses: "The food rules!" Many who go here speak of the feeling of acceptance from before they matriculated: "When I first toured the campus, it instantly felt like home. Everyone was very welcoming, and the beauty of the campus really lured me in." "Saint A's always has some sort of event going on, and the gym, Carr Center, coffee shop, and pub are always great places to hang out and have some fun," says a student. Since the school is right in the Manchester area, off campus is also fruitful in its options; "You can always get to restaurants, the mall, clubs, and stores pretty easily." Many students party over the weekend, "but it's not crazy at all," and "if you don't want to drink you don't have to." Service in general is also a popular extracurricular, and "a good portion of the students are involved in one way or another through course-based experiences, service societies, or Campus Ministry or participation in volunteering through the Meelia Center for Community Engagement." There are also "a lot of club sports and intramurals that are fun and easy to join," including the popular flag football and club hockey teams. If you aren't into athletics, you can "definitely find people who like video games and board games as well." The overwhelming majority of students do live on campus, so a lot of people "hang out in the common rooms on each floor and interact with their floor mates."

Student Body

"Academics are the number one priority for all the students here," so it shouldn't be surprising that "people work hard for the most part and are smart about their studies." Many students describe the typical student as white, Catholic ("mass is always crowded with students"), and from the Boston area (or New England at least), and there is a "large percentage of preppy, Red Sox–loving students." All students are quick to point out that the student body as a whole is "very friendly" and "extremely polite to anyone they meet or just pass by." Students "create a very comfortable and friendly environment for everyone on campus," says a student. It "can be sort of cliquey, but if you find the right group of people you will meet some of your greatest friends." By following your interests, "you will meet a lot of people who share your interest and find a lot of new friends that way."

FINANCIAL AID: 603-641-7110 • E-MAIL: ADMISSION@ANSELM.EDU • WEBSITE: WWW.ANSELM.EDU

THE PRINCETON REVIEW SAYS

Admissions

Very important factors considered include: GPA, rigor of secondary school record, standardized test scores, interview. *Important factors considered include:* Application essay, extracurricular activities, recommendation(s). *Other factors considered include:* Class rank, first generation, geographical residence, racial/ethnic status, state residency, talent/ability, volunteer work, work experience, alumni/ae relations, character/personal qualities. SAT and SAT Subject Tests or ACT considered if submitted; ACT with or without Writing component accepted. TOEFL required of all international applicants. *Academic units required:* 4 English; 3 mathematics; 3 science; (2 science lab); 2 social studies; 2 foreign language. *Academic units recommended:* 4 mathematics; 4 science; (2 science lab); 4 social studies; 4 foreign language.

Financial Aid

Students should submit: FAFSA, CSS/Financial Aid PROFILE, Noncustodial PROFILE, Business/Farm Supplement. Regular filing deadline is 3/15. The Princeton Review suggests that all financial aid forms be submitted as soon as possible after January 1. *Need-based scholarships/grants offered:* Federal Pell, SEOG, State scholarships/grants, private scholarships, the school's own gift aid. *Loan aid offered:* Direct Subsidized Stafford Loans, Direct Unsubsidized Stafford Loans, Direct PLUS loans, Federal Perkins Loans. Federal Work-Study Program available. Institutional employment available. Off-campus job opportunities are excellent.

The Inside Word

Admission to St. Anselm isn't too hard to come by if you have strong grades and some service-based extracurriculars. The school exclusively uses the Common Application, and SAT and ACT scores are optional (except for those applying to the nursing school). Still, as with most schools that provide this as an option, most students (about 70 percent) do provide scores.

THE SCHOOL SAYS "..."

From the Admissions Office

"Saint Anselm is New England's only Benedictine College, a place where a 1,500 year tradition that values a love of learning and a balanced life is coupled with a very contemporary liberal arts education with strong professional preparation on a beautiful 400-acre campus. The college offers over eighty academic programs, but is particularly well-known for nursing, criminal justice, business, politics and psychology. Located in the first in the nation primary state, Saint Anselm is the home of the New Hampshire Institute of Politics which hosts national debates and provides countless opportunities for students of any major to engage with candidates, journalists, elected officials and scholars. A student who wants to meet the next President of the United States has a reasonably good chance of doing so here. Saint Anselm has been named a 'college with a conscience' by the Princeton Review, hailed by the Carnegie Foundation with Classification in both Curricular Engagement and Outreach and Partnerships, and has won federal grants to support its work in public advocacy and engagement with social problems. Faculty from many departments teach in the seminar-based program where students contemplate the fundamental question of what it means to be great. The college's Dana Center for the Arts and Humanities, used by both students and the public, hosts a broad and eclectic range of theater programming including contemporary dance and music. Saint Anselm's Chapel Arts Center provides an extraordinary array of art exhibitions from classic to contemporary with recent acquisitions focused on the human form in art. Eighty-five percent of the college's students participates in athletics, intramurals and club sports. New academic majors have been added over the past two years. Saint Anselm College offers more than eighty academic programs."

SELECTIVITY

Admissions Rating	82
# of applicants	3,829
% of applicants accepted	74
% of acceptees attending	18
# offered a place on the wait list	437
% accepting a place on wait list	45
% admitted from wait list	19

FRESHMAN PROFILE

Range SAT Critical Reading	540–610
Range SAT Math	520–620
Range SAT Writing	520–620
Range ACT Composite	23–27
Minimum paper TOEFL	550
Minimum web-based TOEFL	213
Average HS GPA	3.21
% graduated top 10% of class	22
% graduated top 25% of class	58
% graduated top 50% of class	90

DEADLINES

Early action	
Deadline	11/15
Notification	1/15
Regular	
Deadline	2/1
Notification	3/15
Nonfall registration?	Yes

APPLICANTS ALSO LOOK AT AND OFTEN PREFER

Stonehill College; Providence College; Boston College; College of the Holy Cross; Fairfield University

AND SOMETIMES PREFER

University of Massachusetts Amherst; University of New Hampshire

FINANCIAL FACTS

Financial Aid Rating	83
Annual tuition	$34,084
Room and board	$12,690
Required fees	$1,550
Books and supplies	$1,000
% needy frosh rec. need-based scholarship or grant aid	100
% needy UG rec. need-based scholarship or grant aid	99
% needy frosh rec. non-need-based scholarship or grant aid	18
% needy UG rec. non-need-based scholarship or grant aid	13
% needy frosh rec. need-based self-help aid	81
% needy UG rec. need-based self-help aid	85
% frosh rec. any financial aid	97
% UG rec. any financial aid	98
% UG borrow to pay for school	80
Average cumulative indebtedness	$42,196
% frosh need fully met	24
% ugrads need fully met	21
Average % of frosh need met	81
Average % of ugrad need met	81

SAINT LOUIS UNIVERSITY

ONE NORTH GRAND BOULEVARD, SAINT LOUIS, MO 63103 • ADMISSIONS: 314-977-2500 • FAX: 314-977-7136

CAMPUS LIFE

Quality of Life Rating	66
Fire Safety Rating	82
Green Rating	87
Type of school	Private
Affiliation	Roman Catholic
Environment	Metropolis

STUDENTS

Total undergrad enrollment	8,687
% male/female	41/59
% from out of state	61
% frosh live on campus	90
% ugrads live on campus	50
# of fraternities (% ugrad men join)	8 (12)
# of sororities (% ugrad women join)	6 (16)
% African American	6
% Asian	8
% Caucasian	64
% Hispanic	4
% Native American	<1
% international	8
# of countries represented	75

SURVEY SAYS . . .
Students are friendly
Lots of beer drinking
Very little drug use
Hard liquor is popular

ACADEMICS

Academic Rating	67
% students returning for sophomore year	87
% students graduating within 4 years	62
% students graduating within 6 years	71
Calendar	Semester
Student/faculty ratio	12:1
Profs interesting rating	65
Profs accessible rating	64

Most classes have 10–19 students.
Most lab/discussion sessions have
20–29 students.

MOST POPULAR MAJORS
biology; business administration and
management; nursing

STUDENTS SAY ". . ."

Academics

"The Jesuit tradition really resonates in everything that happens at SLU," a place where "service, social justice, and political awareness are stressed at every level of your education." This "medium-sized Jesuit school with solid academic programs and a campus that feels close-knit" is best known for its "great premedical programs," which include "a great direct-entry physical therapy program" and "a well-respected accelerated nursing program" as well as the school's premed tracks. Students also speak highly of SLU's offerings in business and pre-law, as well as its unique programs in aviation and "the one-of-a-kind nutrition program with a culinary emphasis." Students praise the way this curriculum "forces you to examine your worldview from the moment you step on campus and helps you discover what your beliefs really are." Academics, especially in the high-profile departments, can be rigorous. In this regard, SLU is "perfect for high achievers and scholars who strive for the best. The professors are nice and professional but are very stern about assignments being turned in on time." One student says, "When it comes to natural sciences, particularly chemistry, biology, etc., I think SLU can be very hard. I guess it works, though. A nursing degree or physical therapy degree from SLU is very highly respected in the health care profession."

Life

"SLU manages to provide everything your parents wish for your college experience and still everything you wouldn't want them to know about," undergrads here confide. Campus life includes "a lot of fun activities the student government puts on…such as outdoor movies, balls, and dances." "Dorm life is very strict and not much fun." The party scene "is decent," because "there are a lot of off-campus living opportunities that are close by and great places to live. The Lofts and Coronado are two great off-campus apartments that are extremely close by." College sports are in the mix. "With the new arena, basketball games are becoming the thing to do." Greek life "is great at SLU." The fraternities and sororities "provide many parties and events for the students and activities such as laser tag and barbecue" to help the students "become involved" and "get to know each other." Being in St. Louis means "great city life around, but most of it is for students that are twenty-one and above," and "off-campus eateries that are close by and range from Drunken Fish Sushi to Rally's Burgers." Students tell us "safety is a huge importance in SLU since we are so close to the city, [and fortunately] there is usually a DPS officer that is always close by to help students in need." "SLU's Jesuit influence encourages the student body to become active in the community. SLU's efforts to encourage community service give many students their first taste of the real world and better prepare them to venture out into it after graduation."

Student Body

SLU "has a pretty homogeneous student population of white, upper-middle-class students coming from a private high school (usually Jesuit, and single-sex) or from the suburbs of bigger Midwestern cities. The girls wear Uggs and North Face fleeces and dye their hair, while the boys live in their…American Eagle jeans." Many "have been in the Catholic school system their entire lives," although there are also "quite a few kids who went to public school." Students are generally committed to the concept of service, and they "put forth a lot of community service hours into the surrounding area, from Habitat for Humanity to the Big Brothers/Big Sisters programs. There are plenty of clubs students use to help raise money for their organizations."

FINANCIAL AID: 314-977-2350 • E-MAIL: ADMISSION@SLU.EDU • WEBSITE: WWW.SLU.EDU

THE PRINCETON REVIEW SAYS

Admissions

Very important factors considered include: GPA, standardized test scores, application essay. *Important factors considered include:* Rigor of secondary school record, extracurricular activities, interview, talent/ability, volunteer work, character/personal qualities. *Other factors considered include:* First generation, recommendation(s), work experience, alumni/ae relations, level of applicant's interest. SAT or ACT required; ACT with or without Writing component accepted. TOEFL required of all international applicants. *Academic units required:* 4 English; 4 mathematics; 3 science; 3 social studies; 3 foreign language; 3 academic electives. *Academic units recommended:* 4 English; 4 mathematics; 3 science; 3 social studies; 3 foreign language; 3 academic electives.

Financial Aid

Students should submit: FAFSA. The Princeton Review suggests that all financial aid forms be submitted as soon as possible after January 1. *Need-based scholarships/grants offered:* Federal Pell, SEOG, State scholarships/grants, private scholarships, the school's own gift aid, federal nursing scholarships *Loan aid offered:* Direct Subsidized Stafford Loans, Direct Unsubsidized Stafford Loans, Direct PLUS loans, Federal Perkins Loans, Federal Nursing Loans, State Loans, College/university loans from institutional funds. Applicants will be notified of awards beginning 3/15. Federal Work-Study Program available. Institutional employment available. Off-campus job opportunities are excellent.

The Inside Word

Saint Louis University's student body is primarily regional, but it continually expands its draw so that today nearly 61 percent of all undergrads arrive from out of state. This increase in geographic diversity has brought with it elevated admissions standards. The grades and test scores that got your older brother or sister in here may not be good enough for you (although family ties to the school are a plus). Admissions officers look for students who display a commitment to both scholarship and Jesuit principles. Applicants must demonstrate success in college preparatory classes and a desire to be active participants in the community.

THE SCHOOL SAYS "..."

From the Admissions Office

"A hot Midwestern university with a growing national and international reputation, Saint Louis University gives students the knowledge, skills, and values to build a successful career and make a difference in the lives of those around them. Students live and learn in a safe and attractive campus environment. The beautiful urban, residential campus offers loads of internship, outreach, and recreational opportunities. Ranked as one of the best educational values in the country, the university welcomes students from all fifty states and seventy-five foreign countries who pursue rigorous majors that invite individualization. Accessible faculty, study abroad opportunities, and many small, interactive classes make SLU a great place to learn.

"A leading Jesuit, Catholic university, SLU's goal is to graduate men and women of competence and conscience—individuals who are not only capable of making wise decisions but who also understand why they made them. Since 1818, Saint Louis University has been dedicated to academic excellence, service to others, and preparing students to be leaders in society. Saint Louis University truly is the place where knowledge touches lives.

"For admission, Saint Louis University will accept either the SAT or the ACT with or without the writing component."

SELECTIVITY

Admissions Rating	91
# of applicants	13,091
% of applicants accepted	64
% of acceptees attending	19
# offered a place on the wait list	131

FRESHMAN PROFILE

Range SAT Critical Reading	530–640
Range SAT Math	550–680
Range ACT Composite	25–30
Minimum paper TOEFL	550
Minimum web-based TOEFL	80
Average HS GPA	3.82
% graduated top 10% of class	41
% graduated top 25% of class	74
% graduated top 50% of class	91

DEADLINES

Regular	
Priority	12/1
Deadline	8/20
Notification	8/20
Nonfall registration?	Yes

APPLICANTS ALSO LOOK AT AND OFTEN PREFER

Fordham University; Notre Dame University; Washington University in St. Louis

AND SOMETIMES PREFER

Marquette University; University of Illinois at Urbana/Champaign; University of Missouri; Xavier University of Louisiana; Loyola University of Chicago

AND RARELY PREFER

University of Dayton

FINANCIAL FACTS

Financial Aid Rating	65
Annual tuition	$36,090
Room and board	$9,868
Required fees	$636
Books and supplies	$1,500
% needy frosh rec. need-based scholarship or grant aid	98
% needy UG rec. need-based scholarship or grant aid	95
% needy frosh rec. non-need-based scholarship or grant aid	11
% needy UG rec. non-need-based scholarship or grant aid	9
% needy frosh rec. need-based self-help aid	71
% needy UG rec. need-based self-help aid	76
% frosh rec. any financial aid	93
% UG rec. any financial aid	87
% UG borrow to pay for school	63
Average cumulative indebtedness	$36,808
% frosh need fully met	18
% ugrads need fully met	16
Average % of frosh need met	69
Average % of ugrad need met	67

SAINT MARY'S COLLEGE OF CALIFORNIA

PO BOX 4800, MORAGA, CA 94575-4800 • ADMISSIONS: 925-631-4224 • FAX: 925-376-7193

CAMPUS LIFE

Quality of Life Rating	80
Fire Safety Rating	83
Green Rating	77
Type of school	Private
Affiliation	Roman Catholic
Environment	Village

STUDENTS

Total undergrad enrollment	3,055
% male/female	41/59
% from out of state	9
% frosh from public high school	58
% frosh live on campus	99
% ugrads live on campus	55
% African American	4
% Asian	11
% Caucasian	46
% Hispanic	25
% Native American	<1
% international	2
# of countries represented	26

SURVEY SAYS . . .
Students are friendly
Everyone loves the Gaels
Frats and sororities are unpopular
or nonexistent
Lab facilities are great
Lots of beer drinking
Hard liquor is popular
Frats and sororities are unpopular
or nonexistent

ACADEMICS

Academic Rating	86
% students returning for sophomore year	89
% students graduating within 4 years	50
% students graduating within 6 years	60
Calendar	4/1/4
Student/faculty ratio	12:1
Profs interesting rating	84
Profs accessible rating	84
Most classes have 20–29 students.	

MOST POPULAR MAJORS
business administration; psychology;
communications and media studies

STUDENTS SAY ". . ."

Academics
Intimacy rules the day at Saint Mary's, a Catholic college where "small class sizes" and professors who you "get to know personally" are the rule rather than the exception. "They make time for me outside of class," one student boasts, "I even have some of their phone numbers." This intimacy offers "unlimited opportunities for students and very direct interaction with staff and faculty," and makes it feel as if "the professors are learning at the same time from the students." These teachers are "are very optimistic and love what they teach, so it's great to be taught by them because they're so passionate about their subject. It helps make learning about the subject fun and interesting." Indeed, as one student points out, "It's usually very difficult for a math or physics professor to inject their personality into their classes, but the faculty that Saint Mary's employs somehow manage to do it." Some do complain that "when they teach they go really fast and it makes it hard to keep up with them," but that may be a result of the attitude that "lectures are overrated." Instead, "professors help students learn by engaging one another in meaningful dialogue and debate." The idea is to help you to "learn how to talk more in public settings and (give) you life skills that you can rely on and use the rest of your life." The bottom line is, "Saint Mary's offers students an unparalleled education with small class sizes, seminars, high accessibility to professors, and a strong alumni and network association."

Life
Don't expect non-stop parties at Saint Mary's. This is a "distinguished, calm campus" with students focused on their studies. When it comes time to wind down, sports, clubs, and mellow socializing are far more prevalent than rowdy keggers. Saint Mary's "is what you make it, it takes time to adjust," but "there are vast opportunities provided by the school to get involved with others inside and outside of the community." There is "a grove that is a secluded area where everyone goes to just leave the urban world for a bit and just relax," while others "go on great hiking and outdoor adventure trips the rec sports provides the students with." The school is six miles off the freeway, so access to other communities isn't as easy as at other schools, but nearby Orinda has beautiful theaters and restaurants, and all that San Francisco has to offer is accessible to students willing to make the journey. The biggest draw is sports and athletic recreation. Students here are "very active. Everyone wears some sort of active clothes because everyone is basically a regularly active individual. Sports are a big focus at my school, whether it be intercollegiate or just for fun."

Student Body
The "smart, humble, dedicated, and compassionate" students of Saint Mary's make up a group with a "wide range of students from a large spectrum of life and socioeconomic status. Students mix easily and the college climate promotes equality and understanding." At this "very welcoming" school you'll find "few cliques among students," only "normal people who are looking to go on and succeed at life." The "hard-working" students of Saint Mary's have a reputation for being friendly. "You walk through the halls and say hi to almost everyone even if you have never seen them before." Indeed, "students always smile and say have a good day. Students fit in by taking the time to meet others. A simple smile can make a day for a lot of people." Typical students are "involved in sports or some type of club on campus. They are a big part of the community, and are avid NCAA college basketball fans." That, or they are engaged in their studies. Saint Mary's is filled with people serious about their educations—but not at the expense of social interaction. "Students can engage in complex discussion and easily switch to witty banter at any given moment."

SAINT MARY'S COLLEGE OF CALIFORNIA

FINANCIAL AID: 925-631-4522 • E-MAIL: SMCADMIT@STMARYS-CA.EDU • WEBSITE: WWW.STMARYS-CA.EDU

THE PRINCETON REVIEW SAYS

Admissions

Very important factors considered include: GPA, rigor of secondary school record. *Important factors considered include:* Standardized test scores, application essay, first generation, racial/ethnic status, recommendation(s). *Other factors considered include:* Extracurricular activities, geographical residence, interview, talent/ability, volunteer work, work experience, alumni/ae relations, character/personal qualities, level of applicant's interest, religious affiliation. SAT or ACT required; ACT with or without Writing component accepted. TOEFL required of all international applicants. *Academic units required:* 4 English; 3 mathematics; 2 science; (1 science lab); 1 social studies; 2 foreign language; 1 history; 2 academic electives. *Academic units recommended:* 4 English; 4 mathematics; 3 science; (1 science lab); 1 social studies; 3 foreign language; 1 history; 2 academic electives.

Financial Aid

Students should submit: FAFSA, State aid form. The Princeton Review suggests that all financial aid forms be submitted as soon as possible after January 1. *Need-based scholarships/grants offered:* Federal Pell, SEOG, State scholarships/grants, private scholarships, the school's own gift aid. *Loan aid offered:* Direct Subsidized Stafford Loans, Direct Unsubsidized Stafford Loans, Direct PLUS loans, Federal Perkins Loans. Federal Work-Study Program available. Institutional employment available. Off-campus job opportunities are good.

The Inside Word

Saint Mary's has a deep commitment to serving underprivileged students and offering opportunities for low-income students with strong academic potential, which is why the school sets aside 25 percent of its undergraduate population for low economic status students. That core philosophy of the school won't be changing anytime soon, so students with economic difficulties should not hesitate to apply if their academics are strong.

THE SCHOOL SAYS "..."

From the Admissions Office

"Today, Saint Mary's College continues to offer a value-oriented education by providing a classical liberal arts background second to none. The emphasis is on teaching an individual how to think independently and responsibly, how to analyze information in all situations, and how to make choices based on logical thinking and rational examination. Such a program develops students' ability to ask the right questions and to formulate meaningful answers, not only within their professional careers but also for the rest of their lives. Saint Mary's College is committed to preparing young men and women for the challenge of an ever-changing world, while remaining faithful to an enduring academic and spiritual heritage. We believe the purpose of a college experience is to prepare men and women for an unlimited number of opportunities, and that this is best accomplished by educating the whole person, both intellectually and ethically. We strive to recruit, admit, enroll, and graduate students who are generous, faith-filled, and human, and we believe this is reaffirmed in our community of brothers, in our faculty, and in our personal concern for each student.

"For freshman applicants, we will accept the SAT, and the ACT is also accepted. The ACT writing assessment is optional. The highest critical reading and the highest math scores attained on the SAT will be used. SAT Subject Tests are not required."

SELECTIVITY

Admissions Rating	80
# of applicants	4,864
% of applicants accepted	69
% of acceptees attending	18
# offered a place on the wait list	680
% accepting a place on wait list	33
% admitted from wait list	19

FRESHMAN PROFILE

Range SAT Critical Reading	500–600
Range SAT Math	510–610
Range ACT Composite	22–27
Minimum paper TOEFL	550
Minimum web-based TOEFL	197
Average HS GPA	3.61
% graduated top 10% of class	31
% graduated top 25% of class	64
% graduated top 50% of class	92

DEADLINES

Early action	
Deadline	11/15
Notification	1/15
Regular	
Priority	11/15
Deadline	2/1
Notification	3/15
Nonfall registration?	Yes

APPLICANTS ALSO LOOK AT AND OFTEN PREFER

Santa Clara University, University of California—Davis; Gonzaga University; Loyola Marymount University

AND SOMETIMES PREFER

University of San Francisco

AND RARELY PREFER

Sonoma State University; University of the Pacific; University of California—Santa Cruz

FINANCIAL FACTS

Financial Aid Rating	71
Annual tuition	$41,230
Room and board	$14,400
Required fees	$150
Books and supplies	$1,107
% needy frosh rec. need-based scholarship or grant aid	98
% needy UG rec. need-based scholarship or grant aid	95
% needy frosh rec. non-need-based scholarship or grant aid	50
% needy UG rec. non-need-based scholarship or grant aid	39
% needy frosh rec. need-based self-help aid	82
% needy UG rec. need-based self-help aid	90
% frosh rec. any financial aid	77
% UG rec. any financial aid	74
% UG borrow to pay for school	75
Average cumulative indebtedness	$33,000
% frosh need fully met	7
% ugrads need fully met	7
Average % of frosh need met	67
Average % of ugrad need met	61

SAINT MICHAEL'S COLLEGE

ONE WINOOSKI PARK, BOX 7, COLCHESTER, VT 05439 • ADMISSIONS: 802-654-3000 • FAX: 802-654-2906

STUDENTS SAY "..."

Academics

Tucked away in "the heart of Vermont ski country," Saint Michael's College offers a "close-knit and familial atmosphere" where everyone "will always value and support you." "Small classes" help to ensure that "you are not just another number in a lecture hall." Indeed, the college "really wants to help its students realize their full potential." Many tout the "strong academics" and highlight the education, biology, and religion departments in particular. Classes are often "discussion-based" and "require a conscientious student who will actively participate in discussion." Moreover, undergrads here speak effusively about their professors. As one English and theater double-major shares, "the professors strongly encourage you to visit them during office hours and are always working hard to engage students and keep them interested in learning. It is clear that the majority of the professors at St. Mike's care about what they are teaching and seem genuinely interested in the subject matter." A history major succinctly adds, "Whether you like it or not, your professor will know your name." Another satisfied undergrad concludes that the professors "bring real life experience to the material, apply it to current events and to our lives, and are always available to talk about a paper, grade, or class in general. I've been able to push the limits of my mind and branch out during classes, exploring [in ways] that traditional textbook approaches don't [afford]."

Life

Though undergrads at St. Mike's take their academics seriously, they also love to take advantage of life beyond the library. While "partying is popular at Saint Mike's" it's certainly "not a requirement." Fortunately, "the college is great at providing alternative activities on weekends for those who choose to abstain." Indeed, "whether it's a benefit concert, a dance, or a pie-eating contest organized by residential life," one content student promises us that "there is always something to do on campus." A psych major adds to the list, exclaiming, "There are always socials to [attend], bowling, athletic events, concerts, plays, [and] guest speakers." Volunteering is also extremely popular. When students are itching to get off campus, they frequently head to nearby Burlington. "Church Street is crowded with unique shops, fantastic restaurants, and interesting people." Many also love to take advantage of Vermont's outdoor recreational options and the school counts many avid skiers, snowboarders, and hikers among it ranks. In fact, "Saint Michael's provides amazing ski pass deals and transportation to amazing ski resorts in the area." All these options help ensure that life at St. Mike's is "never boring."

Student Body

At first glance, the typical St. Mike's student appears to be a "white, middle-class New Englander" who quickly dons "North Faces and UGGs during the cold Vermont winters." However, once you look past the surface you'll find a vibrant undergrad community where "everyone is unique and different" and even "a little quirky." Though the college is Catholic, undergrads assure us that "there are students of other [faiths and students] who do not practice [a] religion and they are not treated any differently." Undergrads define their peers as "intelligent, outgoing, and active" and quickly assert that "they're friendly and open to new perspectives and new types of people." Indeed, it's even commonplace to "hold doors open for people who are ridiculously far away." Many students are active in "social justice movements, green movements, [and] community service" and also frequently participate in "the school's wilderness program." And don't be fooled: While the average St. Mike's undergrad is "laid-back," students here are "committed to their studies" and "focused on getting all they can out of their college experience." As this math and econ double-major sums up, "Every student here is passionate about something, and it shows in their education and in their actions."

SAINT MICHAEL'S COLLEGE

FINANCIAL AID: 802-654-3243 • E-MAIL: ADMISSION@SMCVT.EDU • WEBSITE: WWW.SMCVT.EDU

THE PRINCETON REVIEW SAYS

Admissions

Very important factors considered include: Class rank, GPA, rigor of secondary school record. *Important factors considered include:* Standardized test scores, application essay, recommendation(s), talent/ability, character/personal qualities. *Other factors considered include:* Extracurricular activities, first generation, geographical residence, interview, racial/ethnic status, state residency, volunteer work, work experience, alumni/ae relations, level of applicant's interest. SAT or ACT considered if submitted; ACT with Writing component required. TOEFL required of all international applicants. *Academic units required:* 4 English; 4 mathematics; 3 science; (2 science lab); 3 social studies; 2 foreign language. *Academic units recommended:* 4 English; 4 mathematics; 4 science; (3 science lab); 4 social studies; 4 foreign language.

Financial Aid

Students should submit: FAFSA. Regular filing deadline is 2/15. The Princeton Review suggests that all financial aid forms be submitted as soon as possible after January 1. *Need-based scholarships/grants offered:* Federal Pell, SEOG, State scholarships/grants, private scholarships, the school's own gift aid. *Loan aid offered:* Direct Subsidized Stafford Loans, Direct Unsubsidized Stafford Loans, Direct PLUS loans, Federal Perkins Loans. Federal Work-Study Program available. Institutional employment available. Off-campus job opportunities are excellent.

Inside Word

Applicants to St. Mike's are more than just a number, and admissions officers do their utmost to consider candidates in their entirety. Officers consider everything from essays to extracurricular activities, though most weight is given to academic record. The college has recently made standardized tests optional, and applicants won't be penalized if they choose not to submit their scores.

THE SCHOOL SAYS "..."

From the Admissions Office

"A residential Catholic college, Saint Michael's is steeped in the social justice spirit of its founding priests, the Edmundites. Students are challenged to do their best, find their niche, take on opportunities to grow, and immerse themselves in academic pursuits. Intellectual rigor, compassion, teamwork, caring—these characterize a Saint Michael's experience.

"The Saint Michael's academic world is collaborative. Students join scholars on a learning continuum as interested rookies apprenticed to expert guides. Professors model engagement in the academic life, informed by the heart, as the path to make a difference in the world. Students are individually nurtured, and collectively applauded. Professors care. Students care about each other. The supportive ethos at Saint Michael's empowers success, and leads to leadership.

"Leadership opportunities abound, and underscore the transformation of Saint Michael's students. Academically, students are guided to engage in research projects, present results at conferences, study abroad, do service-learning activities. High-impact experiential practices are embedded throughout the Saint Michael's curriculum. Real-world experiences and deeper academic know-how are the result.

"Outside the classroom, Saint Michael's students grow into impressive leaders through their engagement with the challenging Wilderness Leadership Program, the skilled Fire & Rescue Squads, the intensity of MOVE service work, varsity and club athletics, a uniquely active student government, radio DJ gigs, editorial positions in student media, and numerous other opportunities.

"Located three minutes from Burlington, Vermont, Saint Michael's enjoys the energy and fun of that top-ten college town, as well as the best skiing in the East and the beauty of Lake Champlain."

SELECTIVITY

Admissions Rating	83
# of applicants	4,431
% of applicants accepted	75
% of acceptees attending	15
# offered a place on the wait list	55
% accepting a place on wait list	29
% admitted from wait list	13

FRESHMAN PROFILE

Range SAT Critical Reading	530–650
Range SAT Math	530–640
Range SAT Writing	530–630
Range ACT Composite	23–28
Minimum paper TOEFL	550
Average HS GPA	3.43
% graduated top 10% of class	25
% graduated top 25% of class	54
% graduated top 50% of class	81

DEADLINES

Early action	
Deadline	12/1
Notification	2/1
Regular	
Priority	11/1
Deadline	2/1
Notification	4/1
Nonfall registration?	Yes

APPLICANTS ALSO LOOK AT AND OFTEN PREFER
Boston College; College of the Holy Cross

AND SOMETIMES PREFER
Stonehill College; University of Vermont; Fairfield University

AND RARELY PREFER
St. Anselm College

FINANCIAL FACTS

Financial Aid Rating	83
Annual tuition	$39,050
Room and board	$10,600
Required fees	$326
Books and supplies	$1,280
% needy frosh rec. need-based scholarship or grant aid	97
% needy UG rec. need-based scholarship or grant aid	100
% needy frosh rec. non-need-based scholarship or grant aid	31
% needy UG rec. non-need-based scholarship or grant aid	18
% needy frosh rec. need-based self-help aid	68
% needy UG rec. need-based self-help aid	78
% frosh rec. any financial aid	99
% UG rec. any financial aid	98
% UG borrow to pay for school	73
Average cumulative indebtedness	$33,743
% frosh need fully met	42
% ugrads need fully met	27
Average % of frosh need met	83
Average % of ugrad need met	75

SALISBURY UNIVERSITY

ADMISSIONS OFFICE, SALISBURY, MD 21801 • ADMISSIONS: 410-543-6161 • FAX: 410-546-6016

CAMPUS LIFE

Quality of Life Rating	76
Fire Safety Rating	88
Green Rating	94
Type of school	Public
Affiliation	No Affiliation
Environment	Town

STUDENTS

Total undergrad enrollment	7,767
% male/female	43/57
% from out of state	14
% frosh from public high school	80
% frosh live on campus	99
% ugrads live on campus	28
# of fraternities (% ugrad men join)	10 (6)
# of sororities (% ugrad women join)	5 (5)
% African American	11
% Asian	2
% Caucasian	74
% Hispanic	4
% Native American	<1
% international	1
# of countries represented	68

SURVEY SAYS . . .

Lots of beer drinking
Lab facilities are great
Great food on campus
Intramural sports are popular
Hard liquor is popular

ACADEMICS

Academic Rating	80
% students returning for sophomore year	81
% students graduating within 4 years	47
% students graduating within 6 years	67
Calendar	4/1/4
Student/faculty ratio	16:1
Profs interesting rating	81
Profs accessible rating	78

Most classes have 20–29 students.
Most lab/discussion sessions have 20–29 students.

MOST POPULAR MAJORS

biology; nursing; elementary education

STUDENTS SAY " . . . "

Academics

A member of Maryland's university system, Salisbury University provides undergraduates with a variety of majors and small class sizes coupled with the benefit of a state school price tag. A "good medium size[d]" University, Salisbury is "big enough where [you] can meet new people all the time" and yet not so big "that you become invisible and unheard." The school really works to foster a "comfortable and personalized environment in which students focus on learning and achievement." The university is an especially good option for those students interested in pursuing a major in education, exercise science, nursing, or environmental studies. Students describe classes as "small, which gives the professors an opportunity to help students individually and reach their potential." For the most part, undergrads at Salisbury speak very highly of their professors. As one elementary education major shares, "The professors here are down-to-earth, friendly, and just passionate about what they are teaching." Those relatively small classes also mean "every professor gets to know your name. A biology major sums up their academic experience as teaching "you lessons that you will be able to take far beyond the classroom. They don't just teach so that you will pass a test, they teach for life. They're awesome."

Life

Undergrads at Salisbury are experts at balancing work and play. Though plenty of students "party every weekend," one biology major says that "there [are] definitely other options." Indeed, "it's not uncommon for friends to just hang out on weekends, play board games, watch movies, or have a bonfire." While some people grumble that "there's not much going on," others maintain that "Salisbury has lots of different clubs and organizations for people who want to join one." Students also get creative and make their own fun, as this happy undergrad shares: "One time we put bubble wrap down in the hall while no one was watching and then a bunch of us jumped on it and danced around." A handful of undergrads are less than enamored with hometown Salisbury and proclaim some neighborhoods a little "rough." Others enjoy taking advantage of the "mall, movies, skating, bowling, Wal-Mart runs in the middle of the night....job opportunities" that the surrounding area offers. However, students are nearly unanimous in agreeing that "when the weather is warm, everyone tries to find time to go to Ocean City (only thirty minutes away!)" to escape academic stress and relax on the beach.

Student Body

Salisbury University appears to attract "all types of people," and most undergrads describe their peers as generally "welcoming and friendly." One student expands further, exclaiming, "Finding a group of people you agree with or get along with is rather easy and the diversity of people and things to do seem limitless at times. We each fit into the campus in our own way." A significant portion of students hail "from Maryland, New Jersey, or New York." Salisbury students are also highly active individuals and many are "involved outside of the classroom with a sports team, a club, or a student organization." A number of undergrads also keep "part-time jobs to help pay for tuition." Despite all the activity, we're told that the typical student is "fairly laid-back." Of course, he or she "will put a lot of effort into their field of study." There is a "party culture in the off campus community" for those students interested in those pursuits. Perhaps the one thing that truly unites these kids is the pride they feel in their school. As an earth science major coyly reveals, "The typical student...never passes up the opportunity to squawk proudly when told [to] by the president as a Salisbury Sea Gull."

SALISBURY UNIVERSITY

FINANCIAL AID: 410-543-6165 • E-MAIL: ADMISSIONS@SALISBURY.EDU • WEBSITE: WWW.SALISBURY.EDU

THE PRINCETON REVIEW SAYS

Admissions

Very important factors considered include: GPA, rigor of secondary school record. *Important factors considered include:* Class rank, standardized test scores. *Other factors considered include:* Application essay, extracurricular activities, first generation, geographical residence, racial/ethnic status, recommendation(s), state residency, talent/ability, volunteer work, work experience, alumni/ae relations, character/personal qualities, level of applicant's interest. SAT and SAT Subject Tests or ACT considered if submitted; ACT with or without Writing component accepted. TOEFL required of all international applicants. *Academic units required:* 4 English; 3 mathematics; 3 science; (2 science lab); 3 social studies; 2 foreign language. *Academic units recommended:* 4 English; 4 mathematics; 4 science; (3 science lab); 3 social studies; 3 foreign language; 3 academic electives.

Financial Aid

Students should submit: FAFSA. Regular filing deadline is 3/1. The Princeton Review suggests that all financial aid forms be submitted as soon as possible after January 1. *Need-based scholarships/grants offered:* Federal Pell, SEOG, State scholarships/grants, private scholarships, the school's own gift aid. *Loan aid offered:* Direct Subsidized Stafford Loans, Direct Unsubsidized Stafford Loans, Direct PLUS Loans, Federal Perkins Loans. Applicants will be notified of awards beginning 3/15. Federal Work-Study Program available. Institutional employment available. Off-campus job opportunities are fair.

The Inside Word

Admission to this increasingly popular Maryland university is competitive and aspiring Sea Gulls need to prove that they are capable of thriving and contributing to the campus culture. While academic records are given the most weight, admissions officers are also looking for attributes such as leadership qualities, artistic and athletic talent, and diversity. Those with a weighted cumulative HS GPA of 3.5 or higher (on a 4.0 scale) may be considered standardized test optional. However, those students should provide evidence of other types of achievement and all scholarship applicants are required to submit standardized test scores.

THE SCHOOL SAYS " . . ."

From the Admissions Office

"Friendly, convenient, safe, and beautiful are just a few of the words used to describe the campus of Salisbury University. The campus is a compact, self-contained community that offers the full range of student services. New facilities, traditional-style architecture and landscaped grounds combine to create an atmosphere that inspires learning and fosters student pride. Located just thirty minutes from the beaches of Assateague and Ocean City, Maryland, SU students enjoy year-round recreational areas as well as an inside track on summer jobs. Situated some two hours from the urban excitement of Baltimore and Washington, D.C., greater Salisbury makes up for its lack of size—its population is about 80,000—by being strategically located. Within easy driving distance of a number of other major cities, including New York City, Philadelphia, and Norfolk, Salisbury is the hub of the Delmarva Peninsula, a mostly rural region flavored by the salty air of the Chesapeake Bay and Atlantic Ocean.

"Submission of SAT and/or ACT scores when applying would be optional to freshman applicants who present a weighted high school grade point average (GPA) of 3.5 or higher on a 4.0 scale. Any student applying with less than a 3.5 would still need to submit a standardized test score to supplement the official high school transcript. Additionally, an applicant may wish to submit a standardized test score subsequent to admission for full scholarship consideration as the majority of the university's scholarships include test scores as a requirement."

SELECTIVITY

Admissions Rating	85
# of applicants	8,905
% of applicants accepted	55
% of acceptees attending	25

FRESHMAN PROFILE

Range SAT Critical Reading	540–610
Range SAT Math	540–620
Range SAT Writing	530–610
Range ACT Composite	22–26
Minimum paper TOEFL	550
Minimum web-based TOEFL	79
Average HS GPA	3.71
% graduated top 10% of class	23
% graduated top 25% of class	59
% graduated top 50% of class	93

DEADLINES

Early decision	
Deadline	11/15
Notification	12/15
Early action	
Deadline	12/1
Notification	1/15
Regular	
Deadline	1/15
Notification	3/15
Nonfall registration?	Yes

APPLICANTS ALSO LOOK AT AND SOMETIMES PREFER

Towson University; University of Maryland; Baltimore County; University of Maryland; College Park

FINANCIAL FACTS

Financial Aid Rating	69
Annual in-state tuition	$5,912
Annual out-of-state tuition	$14,258
Room and board	$10,240
Required fees	$2,216
Books and supplies	$1,300
% needy frosh rec. need-based scholarship or grant aid	89
% needy UG rec. need-based scholarship or grant aid	72
% needy frosh rec. non-need-based scholarship or grant aid	0
% needy UG rec. non-need-based scholarship or grant aid	0
% needy frosh rec. need-based self-help aid	75
% needy UG rec. need-based self-help aid	82
% frosh rec. any financial aid	88
% UG rec. any financial aid	75
% UG borrow to pay for school	62
Average cumulative indebtedness	$23,545
% frosh need fully met	14
% ugrads need fully met	12
Average % of frosh need met	53
Average % of ugrad need met	50

SANTA CLARA UNIVERSITY

500 El Camino Real, Santa Clara, CA 95053 • Admissions: 408-554-4700 • Fax: 408-554-5255

STUDENTS SAY ". . ."

Academics

Santa Clara University is a medium sized Jesuit school, distinctly influenced by its unique location in California's Silicon Valley. SCU is known for its strong programs in the liberal arts; however, the school also operates a "nationally ranked business school" and "fabulous engineering degree." No matter what your field, SCU is "exceptionally good at preparing students for the real world," and, within all academic programs, the "focus of the course work is very application-based." In the Jesuit tradition, the school "encourages us to apply our education to our surrounding communities." As such, many "courses are based on social justice, so they think about the global application. Even math classes." Serious students recommend the university honors program, with "its small seminar styled classes led by the school's top professors." While there are "a handful of teachers that just don't make the cut," most SCU professors are "highly qualified" and "very enthusiastic about the material they teach." With a student to teacher ratio of twelve to one, "classes are discussion-based, with an emphasis on learning from each other instead of only from the professor." Professors consistently "take the time necessary to ensure that students understand the material discussed in class," and outside of class, "they are always available for office hours for extra help." For anyone looking to get into the software or Internet industry, you can't beat SCU's "great location in the heart of the Silicon Valley." "Santa Clara has a fantastic career center that provides numerous resources to students in their internship and job searches," and participating in a local internship can "enrich what we've learned through classroom curriculum with on-the-job experience." Though some students feel the campus could be even greener, they're happy to report that "the school is huge on sustainability and having a green mindset."

Life

For campus residents, life at SCU is largely defined by the school's system of Residential Learning Communities (RLCs), which group students in housing according to their interests. From your first day on campus, "RLC is a place where you meet most of your friends and are able to hang out and have a great time." With more than 150 student groups on campus, "most people are involved in numerous clubs, whether that is community service or athletics." There's also a prevailing interest in current events, social responsibility, and service: "Volunteering and community service is a cool thing to do at SCU." In their free time, "students work out together, volunteer together, get involved with clubs, go shopping, go clubbing, go out to dinner, hang out in San Francisco, hang out in Santa Cruz, and party." With "only two or three bars conveniently close by" and strict campus policies against alcohol, "SCU is mainly a house party school." In student residences near campus, "parties are big on the weekends, and students get to let loose and have fun." Things get particularly upbeat when the sun comes out, and "you will never see more people outside boozing and partying in the sun than spring quarter at Santa Clara." Though surrounding town of SCU can be rather quiet, the campus is located "across the street from the Caltrain and bus stop, making it easy to get to Santa Cruz or San Francisco for the weekend."

Student Body

Embodying the laid-back California lifestyle, SCU "students are the flip-flop and tank-top-wearing type" and are generally "social and sun loving." "Students are concerned with sustainability, politics, and improving our nation," and "many students spend time volunteering in support of the local community." "The typical student is middle-class," yet, "there are students of all races, shapes, and sizes." Philosophically, "The Jesuits encourage acceptance of all races, religions, and sexual orientations," and there's "a lot of support for minority groups and cultural awareness on campus." A sizable percentage of "students come from a Catholic background," and the prevailing personality is "amiable, culturally understanding, and welcoming of all people." "A lot of the campus population is committed to remaining fit, so you'll see a lot of people at the gym."

FINANCIAL AID: 408-554-4505 • E-MAIL: ADMISSION@SCU.EDU • WEBSITE: WWW.SCU.EDU

THE PRINCETON REVIEW SAYS

Admissions

Very important factors considered include: GPA, rigor of secondary school record, application essay. *Important factors considered include:* Class rank, standardized test scores, extracurricular activities, racial/ethnic status, recommendation(s), talent/ability, volunteer work, alumni/ae relations, character/personal qualities. *Other factors considered include:* First generation, geographical residence, state residency, work experience, level of applicant's interest, religious affiliation. SAT or ACT required; ACT with or without Writing component accepted. TOEFL required of all international applicants. *Academic units required:* 4 English; 3 mathematics; 2 science; (2 science lab); 3 social studies; 2 foreign language; 1 academic elective. *Academic units recommended:* 4 English; 4 mathematics; (3 science lab); 3 social studies; 1 academic elective; 1 visual/performing arts; 3 to 4 foreign language.

Financial Aid

Students should submit: FAFSA, CSS/Financial Aid PROFILE. The Princeton Review suggests that all financial aid forms be submitted as soon as possible after January 1. *Need-based scholarships/grants offered:* Federal Pell, SEOG, State scholarships/grants, private scholarships, the school's own gift aid. *Loan aid offered:* Direct Subsidized Stafford Loans, Direct Unsubsidized Stafford Loans, Direct PLUS loans, Federal Perkins Loans. Applicants will be notified of awards beginning 4/1. Federal Work-Study Program available. Institutional employment available. Off-campus job opportunities are good.

The Inside Word

SCU carefully evaluates each applicant's file, considering a student's academic record and test scores in addition to his or her personal qualities and family background. Extracurricular activities, letters of recommendation, and personal statements are all carefully reviewed. Accepted students had an average GPA of 3.69 on a 4.0 scale. Students can apply regular decision, through the nonbinding early action program, or the binding early decision program.

THE SCHOOL SAYS "..."

From the Admissions Office

"Santa Clara University is a comprehensive Jesuit, Catholic university located 40 miles south of San Francisco in Silicon Valley. SCU offers its undergraduates an opportunity to be educated within a challenging, dynamic, and caring community, with more than 50 majors, numerous interdisciplinary programs, and some 2,000 courses from which to choose. Undergraduates find many opportunities to conduct important research alongside professors in a way that is usually reserved for graduate students. Study abroad programs are offered in 55 countries. The University blends a sense of tradition and history—as the oldest college in California—with a vision that values innovation and a deep commitment to social justice. Santa Clara's faculty members are talented scholars who are demanding, supportive, and accessible. The students are serious about academics, are ethnically diverse, and enjoy a full range of social, community service, religious, and cultural activities—both on campus and through the many options presented by our northern California location. SCU competes in 19 Division I athletic teams and offers several varsity, club, and intramural sports. Distinguished nationally by one of the highest graduation rates among all U.S. master's universities, SCU provides rigorous undergraduate curricula in the arts and sciences, business, and engineering. It has nationally

SELECTIVITY	
Admissions Rating	93
# of applicants	14,980
% of applicants accepted	50
% of acceptees attending	17
# offered a place on the wait list	2,436
% accepting a place on wait list	49
% admitted from wait list	12
# of early decision applicants	193
% accepted early decision	54

FRESHMAN PROFILE	
Range SAT Critical Reading	580–680
Range SAT Math	610–700
Range ACT Composite	27–31
Minimum paper TOEFL	575
Minimum web-based TOEFL	90
Average HS GPA	3.66
% graduated top 10% of class	50
% graduated top 25% of class	80
% graduated top 50% of class	97

DEADLINES	
Early decision	
Deadline	11/1
Early action	
Deadline	11/1
Regular	
Deadline	1/7
Nonfall registration?	No

APPLICANTS ALSO LOOK AT AND OFTEN PREFER
Stanford University; University of Southern California

AND SOMETIMES PREFER
Loyola Marymount University; University of San Diego; University of California—Davis

AND RARELY PREFER
University of San Francisco

FINANCIAL FACTS	
Financial Aid Rating	75
Annual tuition	$42,156
Room and board	$12,546
% needy frosh rec. need-based scholarship or grant aid	81
% needy UG rec. need-based scholarship or grant aid	68
% needy frosh rec. non-need-based scholarship or grant aid	39
% needy UG rec. non-need-based scholarship or grant aid	35
% needy frosh rec. need-based self-help aid	56
% needy UG rec. need-based self-help aid	53
% frosh rec. any financial aid	75
% UG rec. any financial aid	89
% UG borrow to pay for school	46
Average cumulative indebtedness	$29,026
% frosh need fully met	36
% ugrads need fully met	35
Average % of frosh need met	74
Average % of ugrad need met	69

SARAH LAWRENCE COLLEGE

ONE MEAD WAY, BRONXVILLE, NY 10708-5999 • ADMISSIONS: 914-395-2510 • FAX: 914-395-2515

CAMPUS LIFE
Quality of Life Rating	71
Fire Safety Rating	82
Green Rating	71
Type of school	Private
Affiliation	No Affiliation
Environment	Metropolis

STUDENTS
Total undergrad enrollment	1,471
% male/female	28/72
% from out of state	79
% frosh live on campus	99
% ugrads live on campus	82
% African American	4
% Asian	4
% Caucasian	58
% Hispanic	10
% international	11
# of countries represented	50

SURVEY SAYS . . .
Lots of liberal students
Political activism is popular
Class discussions encouraged
No one cheats
Students aren't religious
Theater is popular

ACADEMICS
Academic Rating	97
% students returning for sophomore year	83
% students graduating within 4 years	62
% students graduating within 6 years	69
Calendar	Semester
Student/faculty ratio	10:1
Profs interesting rating	98
Profs accessible rating	96

Most classes have 10–19 students.
Most lab/discussion sessions have 10-19

MOST POPULAR MAJORS
liberal arts and sciences; liberal studies

STUDENTS SAY ". . ."

Academics
Nestled in a picturesque suburb of New York City, Sarah Lawrence College is a breath of fresh air for intellectually curious students who would chafe within the confines of a more traditional academic setting. The college prides itself on offering "a personal education" that's "tailored to [each] student's interests and needs." Indeed, "self-directed" is the key phrase here, and students really value "the flexibility and openness" that SLC provides. There are no majors or grades at SLC, only concentrations and evaluations (grades are given by professors and recorded by the Registrar). Undergrads are unanimous in their praise for the "conference system," which allows students to conduct "one-on-one" research with professors in topics of their choosing. Students also greatly appreciate "the strong focus on truly learning versus simply preparing…for [a] career." Importantly, "small" class sizes allow for lots of "discussion" and "close teacher relations." When it comes to describing their professors, undergrads are full of superlatives. One content student describes them as "passionate, engaging, and extremely intelligent." She goes on to explain, "they take an interest in you personally to understand your goals, and then they cater their teaching to that." Further, they "are also readily available for any questions outside of class." Another student simply concludes, "I couldn't ask for more."

Life
While undergrads at SLC are very academically oriented, they also fortunately "engage in a wide variety of social activities." The arts are huge here, and attendance is always high for "theatrical productions, burlesque shows, [and] the annual *Rocky Horror Picture Show* shadowcast on Halloween." Additionally, "concerts by local and campus bands are pretty popular, as are dances." Moreover, "student art shows, film screenings, political lectures, guest speakers, and workshops take place on campus throughout the year." Though a "party scene exists and thrives," it's more common to attend smaller get-togethers or gather with close friends. A "typical Friday night involves an overcrowded room, several bottles of wine, a variety of poets and musicians jamming, and often home-cooked food." Students also love to take advantage of SLC's proximity to New York City (roughly twenty minutes away by train). Many people "go into the city on the weekends" and take in "a Broadway show, check out the farmers market in Union Square, or have a picnic in Central Park."

Student Body
Though undergrads at SLC would debate vociferously as to whether a typical student exists, many define their peers as "artistically and musically inclined, intelligent, voraciously well-read, [and] outspoken with a biting wit." While some might assert you could roam the campus playing a game of spot the "hipster," others insist that "you can find any type of person at Sarah Lawrence." One student goes further, saying, "We're all different, and we all love that. We fit in by not fitting in." Although undergrads are "friendly," some caution that they can also be "aloof" and "reclusive." Fortunately, everyone "can find their niche" and make a "close-knit" group of friends. Additionally, "lots of students here are also in the process of figuring out their sexual orientation and/or gender identity, so most people (even those who aren't figuring that out) are pretty open-minded." Indeed, students at SLC "take risks with style and identity." Perhaps this satisfied undergrad sums his fellow students up best: "Everyone is passionate about something and often several things, be they academic subjects, creative outlets, sports, or political causes, but you will never find two of us who are exactly alike in our interests. I think that makes us the most interesting student body there is, and there's no better place to find an engaging conversation about something completely unexpected."

FINANCIAL AID: 914-395-2570 • E-MAIL: SLCADMIT@SLC.EDU • WEBSITE: WWW.SARAHLAWRENCE.EDU

THE PRINCETON REVIEW SAYS

Admissions

Very important factors considered include: Rigor of secondary school record, application essay, recommendation(s). *Important factors considered include:* GPA, extracurricular activities, talent/ability, character/personal qualities. *Other factors considered include:* Class rank, standardized test scores, first generation, geographical residence, interview, racial/ethnic status, volunteer work, work experience, alumni/ae relations, level of applicant's interest. SAT or ACT considered if submitted; ACT with or without Writing component accepted. TOEFL required of all international applicants. *Academic units required:* 4 English; 2 mathematics; 2 science; 2 foreign language; 2 history. *Academic units recommended:* 4 mathematics; 4 science; 4 social studies; 4 foreign language; 4 history.

Financial Aid

Students should submit: FAFSA, CSS/Financial Aid PROFILE, State aid form, Noncustodial PROFILE. Regular filing deadline is 2/1. The Princeton Review suggests that all financial aid forms be submitted as soon as possible after January 1. *Need-based scholarships/grants offered:* Federal Pell, SEOG, State scholarships/grants, private scholarships, the school's own gift aid. *Loan aid offered:* Direct Subsidized Stafford Loans, Direct Unsubsidized Stafford Loans, Direct PLUS loans, Federal Perkins Loans. Applicants will be notified of awards beginning 4/1. Federal Work-Study Program available. Institutional employment available. Off-campus job opportunities are good.

The Inside Word

Admissions officers at SLC really take the time to try and understand who each applicant is, not only as a student but also as an individual. Candidates should display an inquisitive nature, a passion for learning, and the ability to be an independent thinker. Writing skills are considered critical at SLC and heavy consideration is given to each applicant's essays and short-answer questions. To the relief of some, standardized tests are optional.

THE SCHOOL SAYS " . . ."

From the Admissions Office

"Students who come to Sarah Lawrence are curious about the world, and they have an ardent desire to satisfy that curiosity. Sarah Lawrence offers such students two innovative academic structures: the seminar/conference system and the arts components. Courses in the humanities, social sciences, natural sciences, and mathematics are taught in the seminar/conference style. The seminars enroll an average of eleven students and consist of lecture, discussion, readings, and assigned papers. For each seminar, students also meet one-on-one in biweekly conferences, for which they conceive of individualized projects and shape them under the direction of professors. Arts components let students combine history and theory with practice. Painters, printmakers, photographers, sculptors, filmmakers, composers, musicians, choreographers, dancers, actors, and directors work in readily available studios, editing facilities, and darkrooms, guided by accomplished professionals. The secure, wooded campus is thirty minutes from midtown Manhattan, and the diversity of people and ideas at Sarah Lawrence make it an extraordinary educational environment.

"Sarah Lawrence College is 'test optional,' accepting and reviewing standardized test scores if they are submitted; however, they are not required as part of the admission application."

SELECTIVITY

Admissions Rating	90
# of applicants	2,236
% of applicants accepted	77
% of acceptees attending	25
# of early decision applicants	190
% accepted early decision	51

FRESHMAN PROFILE

Range SAT Critical Reading	600-700
Range SAT Math	550-650
Range SAT Writing	590-680
Minimum paper TOEFL	600
Minimum web-based TOEFL	100
Average HS GPA	3.60
% graduated top 10% of class	35
% graduated top 25% of class	66
% graduated top 50% of class	96

DEADLINES

Early decision	
Deadline	11/1
Notification	12/15
Regular	
Deadline	1/15
Notification	4/1
Nonfall registration?	No

APPLICANTS ALSO LOOK AT

Bard College; Barnard College; Boston University; Brown University; Columbia University; Emerson College; Fordham University; Hampshire College, New York University; Oberlin College; Skidmore College; University of Chicago; Vassar College; Wesleyan Universit

FINANCIAL FACTS

Financial Aid Rating	91
Annual tuition	$47,640
Room and board	$13,936
Required fees	$1,056
Books and supplies	$600
% needy frosh rec. need-based scholarship or grant aid	80
% needy UG rec. need-based scholarship or grant aid	82
% needy frosh rec. non-need-based scholarship or grant aid	9
% needy UG rec. non-need-based scholarship or grant aid	13
% needy frosh rec. need-based self-help aid	58
% needy UG rec. need-based self-help aid	71
% frosh rec. any financial aid	79
% UG rec. any financial aid	68
% UG borrow to pay for school	36
Average cumulative indebtedness	$20,613
% frosh need fully met	1
% ugrads need fully met	2
Average % of frosh need met	86
Average % of ugrad need met	86

SCRIPPS COLLEGE

1030 COLUMBIA AVENUE, CLAREMONT, CA 91711 • ADMISSIONS: 909-621-8149 • FAX: 909-607-7508

CAMPUS LIFE

Quality of Life Rating	98
Fire Safety Rating	71
Green Rating	83
Type of school	Private
Affiliation	No Affiliation
Environment	Town

STUDENTS

Total undergrad enrollment	980
% male/female	0/100
% from out of state	49
% frosh live on campus	100
% ugrads live on campus	96
% African American	3
% Asian	17
% Caucasian	51
% Hispanic	8
% Native American	0
% international	4
# of countries represented	21

SURVEY SAYS . . .

Students are happy
Classroom facilities are great
Lab facilities are great
Career services are great
School is well run
No one cheats
Students are friendly
Great food on campus
Great off-campus food
Dorms are like palaces
Campus feels safe
Easy to get around campus
Athletic facilities are great
Active student government
Active minority support groups

ACADEMICS

Academic Rating	98
% students returning for sophomore year	93
% students graduating within 4 years	80
% students graduating within 6 years	84
Calendar	Semester
Student/faculty ratio	10:1
Profs interesting rating	95
Profs accessible rating	98
Most classes have 10–19 students.	

MOST POPULAR MAJORS

political science; psychology; biology

STUDENTS SAY "..."

Academics

Academically focused women seeking "a more personalized education" will find it at Claremont, California's Scripps College. Small class sizes, "extremely approachable, personable" professors who are "ready to sit down to help you one on one," and strong academics are the rule of the day here. Because the school is part of the five-school Claremont College Consortium, students can have their cake and eat it, too, enjoying the benefits of a small- to mid-sized school while also having access to the resources of a large university. The school's focus on "challenging the whole person" means women attending Scripps will engage with educators who work toward "fostering and strengthening the voice of its students by piquing our curiosity, honing our critical thinking skills, and developing our confidence." The workload can be "challenging...rigorous, and sometimes daunting," but professors are "always willing to meet with you and help you" because they "want you to succeed more than anything else." Students find that the "beautiful campus" and "fun living environment" help reduce the stress of the workload. Others feel that going to an all-female school provides "an educational environment where I could be free to be myself, something I didn't feel I could do in classes that were male-dominated." Those seeking "the personal attention and relationships with professors of a liberal arts college with the resources of a mid-size university" will find it at Scripps.

Life

"The most common group activity is studying in groups." Most students find they are "completely absorbed in class time and homework during the week" because "Scripps students are here to be in school and are very engaged in their school work." These "very smart" students "know the difference between study time and party time." The lack of males on campus does not mean there is a lack of partying at Scripps. "If you wanted to, you could go to a big party any day of the week." Those inclined toward big get-togethers will find that "the party scene is mostly off campus, at the other Claremont colleges." Movies, dancing, and other activities help provide distractions during the down time students get from their studies, as well as "participating in volunteer clubs and working with the local community." Indeed, "Scripps has a ton of extracurricular options," including options available via the Consortium. One student summed it up like this: "I'm on the mock trial team, my best friend is on the track team, and my co-RA is in the Latina students group. There really is a hobby for everyone."

Student Body

As an acclaimed women's college, it should come as no surprise that Scripps boasts "assertive women who do not fear taking on the world." These "friendly yet strong women...welcome all types of people with open arms." Demographically, Scripps skews white and upper-middle class, but when it comes to personality "students range from girly daddy's girls to LGBT to work-oriented introverts." Unsurprisingly, many students at Scripps are politically minded, women who are "very critical of the world around them and love to use the knowledge they gain in class to examine society in new ways." Even those students who don't enter Scripps with strong political views sometimes find it "impossible to go through Core without learning to see social constructs in everything." Most say that despite the eclectic student body "everyone treats each other kindly and respectfully, and there's a lot of crossing over between social groups," though some complain that "students can be very cliquey," making it "difficult to survive socially and to make friends if you are not a clique person." By and large, however, there is usually somewhere for students to fit in. The women of Scripps "pride themselves on being unique and independent, so there is not really a culture to fit in to, but there is any number of subcultures."

FINANCIAL AID: 909-621-8275 • E-MAIL: ADMISSION@SCRIPPSCOLLEGE.EDU • WEBSITE: WWW.SCRIPPSCOLLEGE.EDU

THE PRINCETON REVIEW SAYS

Admissions

Very important factors considered include: Class rank, GPA, rigor of secondary school record, standardized test scores, application essay, extracurricular activities, recommendation(s), talent/ability, character/personal qualities. *Other factors considered include:* First generation, geographical residence, interview, racial/ethnic status, volunteer work, work experience, alumni/ae relations, level of applicant's interest. SAT or ACT required; SAT and SAT Subject Tests or ACT considered if submitted; ACT with Writing component required. TOEFL required of all international applicants. *Academic units required:* 4 English; 3 mathematics; 3 science; 3 social studies; 3 foreign language.

Financial Aid

Students should submit: FAFSA, CSS/Financial Aid PROFILE, State aid form, Noncustodial PROFILE, Business/Farm Supplement. Regular filing deadline is 2/1. The Princeton Review suggests that all financial aid forms be submitted as soon as possible after January 1. *Need-based scholarships/grants offered:* Federal Pell, SEOG, State scholarships/grants, private scholarships, the school's own gift aid. *Loan aid offered:* Direct Subsidized Stafford Loans, Direct Unsubsidized Stafford Loans, Direct PLUS loans, Federal Perkins Loans, College/university loans from institutional funds. Applicants will be notified of awards beginning 4/1. Federal Work-Study Program available. Institutional employment available. Off-campus job opportunities are good.

The Inside Word

Strong academics are important, yes, but women hoping to be accepted to Scripps should be ready to showcase more than academic excellence. A strong and unique personal statement, powerful writing skills, and intellectual curiosity are all vital to being accepted here. Successful applicants will show strengths in all aspects of their application, with a focus on what sets them apart from the average college student.

THE SCHOOL SAYS "..."

From the Admissions Office

"What distinguishes Scripps College from other liberal arts colleges is our interdisciplinary Core Curriculum, which emphasizes critical thinking and intellectual innovation. We believe that learning involves much more than amassing information. A truly educated person can think analytically, communicate effectively, question confidently, and create change in the world. Our curriculum balances breadth requirements in all areas of the liberal arts; a multicultural and a gender studies requirement; and major course work in sixty different fields. With an average class size of fifteen, students are comfortable participating, challenging old assumptions, and testing new ideas. More than a quarter of all Scripps College students dual or double major, and all complete a senior thesis or performance/project. Almost half study abroad, and, on campus, they can choose from a vast range of clubs, organizations, and activities to participate in through the Claremont Colleges Consortium."

SELECTIVITY

Admissions Rating	97
# of applicants	2,378
% of applicants accepted	36
% of acceptees attending	32
# offered a place on the wait list	489
% accepting a place on wait list	43
% admitted from wait list	0
# of early decision applicants	179
% accepted early decision	53

FRESHMAN PROFILE

Range SAT Critical Reading	640–733
Range SAT Math	640–720
Range SAT Writing	660–750
Range ACT Composite	29–32
Minimum paper TOEFL	600
Minimum web-based TOEFL	100
Average HS GPA	4.13
% graduated top 10% of class	75
% graduated top 25% of class	99
% graduated top 50% of class	100

DEADLINES

Early decision	
Deadline	11/15
Notification	12/15
Regular	
Deadline	1/1
Notification	4/1
Nonfall registration?	No

APPLICANTS ALSO LOOK AT AND OFTEN PREFER

Barnard College; Pitzer College; Pomona College; University of California—Berkeley; University of California—Los Angeles; University of Southern California; Wellesley College; Claremont McKenna College; Princeton University; Whitman College

FINANCIAL FACTS

Financial Aid Rating	98
Annual tuition	$45,350
Room and board	$14,006
Required fees	$214
Books and supplies	$800
% needy frosh rec. need-based scholarship or grant aid	100
% needy UG rec. need-based scholarship or grant aid	99
% needy frosh rec. non-need-based scholarship or grant aid	7
% needy UG rec. non-need-based scholarship or grant aid	8
% needy frosh rec. need-based self-help aid	86
% needy UG rec. need-based self-help aid	89
% frosh rec. any financial aid	61
% UG rec. any financial aid	60
% UG borrow to pay for school	48
Average cumulative indebtedness	$20,125
% frosh need fully met	100
% ugrads need fully met	100
Average % of frosh need met	100
Average % of ugrad need met	100

SEATTLE UNIVERSITY

ADMISSIONS OFFICE, SEATTLE, WA 98122-1090 • ADMISSIONS: 206-296-2000 • FAX: 206-296-5656

CAMPUS LIFE

Quality of Life Rating	93
Fire Safety Rating	96
Green Rating	90
Type of school	Private
Affiliation	Roman Catholic-Jesuit
Environment	Metropolis

STUDENTS

Total undergrad enrollment	4,621
% male/female	42/58
% from out of state	55
% frosh from public high school	66
% frosh live on campus	92
% ugrads live on campus	45
% African American	3
% Asian	12
% Caucasian	38
% Hispanic	7
% Native American	<1
% international	9
# of countries represented	56

SURVEY SAYS . . .

Students get along with local community
Students love Seattle, WA
Great food on campus
Great off-campus food
Athletic facilities are great

ACADEMICS

Academic Rating	88
% students returning for sophomore year	86
% students graduating within 4 years	59
% students graduating within 6 years	77
Calendar	Semester
Student/faculty ratio	12:1
Profs interesting rating	87
Profs accessible rating	86

Most classes have 10–19 students.
Most lab/discussion sessions have
10–19 students.

MOST POPULAR MAJORS

liberal arts and sciences; nursing; business/
commerce

STUDENTS SAY ". . ."

Academics

Though Seattle University is renowned for its excellent academics, particularly a "sensational" nursing program, it is its Jesuit philosophy of holistic education that is its main claim to fame. The university requires students to take a collection of core classes that are more than "just a random collection of math, writing, and social science classes. There's a lot more philosophy, theology, psychology, ethics, and actual service-learning" involved, and students say that "often times the core classes that I was required to take ended up being the most memorable classes." The university's commitment to social justice issues is "more than just rhetoric—there are classes structured *around* specific kinds of service learning." Professors "encourage discussion and active participation" by students, and in turn, students receive a lot of "personal attention from faculty" in "intimate and inviting classroom environments." They can also be counted on to be "helpful in finding internships and networking." It is significant to note, that while Seattle University is steeped in a strong Jesuit tradition, it is "not an extremely religious school." Overall, students here are very happy with the "wonderful academic atmosphere."

Life

Students love Seattle University because it "provides a small campus experience in the middle of an exciting big city." "Seattle is our playground," say the students of the university. "As soon as you step off campus, you are in the hustle and bustle of Capitol Hill, a booming, youthful neighborhood that is LGBT friendly. There are coffee shops…concert venues, and parks within a two-block radius." Getting to downtown Seattle is "easy by bus or foot." It's even easier when "the university loans out bus passes free of charge. It's a quick bus ride to downtown and Pike's Place Market or a nice half-hour walk. Chinatown is nearby, too." On weekends, "being in the heart of Seattle…means that you can never run out of fun things to do: walk to Pike's Place Market, shop at the stores downtown, see plays, go to the Seattle Arts museum, eat all sorts of different types of food, hang out in the international district, attend film festivals; you name it, Seattle has it!" Live music is a popular attraction here too and is "at the top of most people's lists for a good time." The party scene is "present but not crazy." As for life on campus, students couldn't be happier in this "small, homey, and very welcoming" environment. The campus is "super green," providing students with "composting and recycling options in every location possible." The food is not only "delicious," but is also "locally grown, organic, [and] well-prepared." The recent switch to Division I athletics has added a new emphasis on athletics on campus, much to the chagrin of some students, who think that more money "should be more directed to class resources and the arts" rather than sports.

Student Body

As "one of the most liberal Catholic schools," Seattle University is a place where "all faiths are not only accepted, but they are welcomed and encouraged." The "majority of students are liberal," and "everyone is aware of social issues." Because people are so "politically and socially aware, you can always find a good debate if you're looking for it." The "typical student is committed to academics, involved on campus outside of school, friendly, loves the city of Seattle, and [is] environmentally conscious." There is a "very large LGBTQ community" on campus, as well as "lots of international students" and "hipsters galore." In short, "there are many different types of people here, and they all try to be inclusive." "Every student who graduates from Seattle University will have become a well-rounded individual, recognizing the importance of diversity, sustainability, justice, academic excellence, and leadership on creating a better world for the future."

FINANCIAL AID: 206-296-2000 • E-MAIL: ADMISSIONS@SEATTLEU.EDU • WEBSITE: WWW.SEATTLEU.EDU

THE PRINCETON REVIEW SAYS

Admissions

Very important factors considered include: GPA, rigor of secondary school record, standardized test scores, character/personal qualities. *Important factors considered include:* Application essay, extracurricular activities, recommendation(s), level of applicant's interest. *Other factors considered include:* Class rank, first generation, geographical residence, interview, racial/ethnic status, state residency, talent/ability, volunteer work, work experience, alumni/ae relations, religious affiliation. SAT or ACT required; ACT with or without Writing component accepted. TOEFL required of all international applicants. *Academic units required:* 4 English; 3 mathematics; 2 science; (2 science lab); 3 social studies; 2 foreign language; 1 history; 2 academic electives. *Academic units recommended:* 4 English; 3 mathematics; 2 science; (2 science lab); 3 social studies; 2 foreign language; 1 history; 2 academic electives.

Financial Aid

Students should submit: FAFSA. The Princeton Review suggests that all financial aid forms be submitted as soon as possible after January 1. *Need-based scholarships/grants offered:* Federal Pell, SEOG, State scholarships/grants, private scholarships, the school's own gift aid, federal nursing scholarships. *Loan aid offered:* Direct Subsidized Stafford Loans, Direct Unsubsidized Stafford Loans, Direct PLUS loans, Federal Perkins Loans, Federal Nursing Loans. Federal Work-Study Program available. Institutional employment available. Off-campus job opportunities are excellent.

The Inside Word

Because this is a Jesuit school, admissions officers tend to value community service. Those who demonstrate a significant commitment to volunteering will find themselves at an advantage, as will those who convey a clear sense of their academic and career goals. Applicants should keep in mind that Seattle University has more stringent test score and course work requirements for certain majors.

THE SCHOOL SAYS "..."

From the Admissions Office

"Students who are adventurous, forward-thinking, creative and have an interest in social justice are drawn to Seattle University, located in the heart of a city with unparalleled access to innovation and culture.

Personalized learning provides opportunities for research alongside accomplished faculty. Internships and community involvement give students relevant experience for their resumes and the chance to be noticed by some of the world's most influential nonprofits and companies that call the Seattle area home, such as Microsoft, the Gates Foundation, Starbucks, Amazon and Costco.

Seattle U is a school of action with an ever-growing impact on the city, the region and throughout the world. In Washington state, where dozens of different languages are spoken and every race, religion and perspective is represented, Seattle U's 4,600 undergraduate students from 53 states and territories and 89 nations fit right in.

Service is a cornerstone of the Seattle U experience. That spirit is especially visible in the Seattle University Youth Initiative—recognized by the White House in 2012 with its highest recognition for community service. As the university's largest-ever community engagement project, the Youth Initiative is transforming lives of Seattle's underserved children while becoming a model of service. An increasing number of new students say the Youth Initiative is a key reason they selected SU.

Discover Seattle University's sustainable campus, which is pesticide-free and wins top awards for its environmental leadership and energy conservation. The urban campus is woven into Seattle's thriving Capitol Hill neighborhood, which pulsates with culture and entertainment options."

SELECTIVITY

Admissions Rating	84
# of applicants	7,159
% of applicants accepted	73
% of acceptees attending	18
# offered a place on the wait list	746
% accepting a place on wait list	56
% admitted from wait list	5

FRESHMAN PROFILE

Range SAT Critical Reading	530–630
Range SAT Math	530–630
Range SAT Writing	530–640
Range ACT Composite	24–29
Minimum paper TOEFL	520
Minimum web-based TOEFL	68
Average HS GPA	3.58
% graduated top 10% of class	23
% graduated top 25% of class	62
% graduated top 50% of class	90

DEADLINES

Early action	
Deadline	11/15
Notification	12/23
Regular	
Priority	1/15
Nonfall registration?	Yes

APPLICANTS ALSO LOOK AT AND OFTEN PREFER

University of Washington; Gonzaga University; University of Portland

AND SOMETIMES PREFER

Santa Clara University; Washington State University

FINANCIAL FACTS

Financial Aid Rating	77
Annual tuition	$37,485
Room and board	$10,830
% needy frosh rec. need-based scholarship or grant aid	100
% needy UG rec. need-based scholarship or grant aid	98
% needy frosh rec. non-need-based scholarship or grant aid	87
% needy UG rec. non-need-based scholarship or grant aid	85
% needy frosh rec. need-based self-help aid	78
% needy UG rec. need-based self-help aid	8
% frosh rec. any financial aid	94
% UG rec. any financial aid	83
% UG borrow to pay for school	73
Average cumulative indebtedness	$29,424
% frosh need fully met	10
% ugrads need fully met	10
Average % of frosh need met	76
Average % of ugrad need met	75

SETON HALL UNIVERSITY

ENROLLMENT SERVICES, SOUTH ORANGE, NJ 07079 • ADMISSIONS: 973-761-9332 • FAX: 973-275-2040

CAMPUS LIFE

Quality of Life Rating	67
Fire Safety Rating	85
Green Rating	60*
Type of school	Private
Affiliation	Roman Catholic
Environment	Village

STUDENTS

Total undergrad enrollment	5,295
% male/female	41/59
% from out of state	22
% frosh from public high school	70
% frosh live on campus	74
% ugrads live on campus	41
# of fraternities	11
# of sororities	11
% African American	13
% Asian	8
% Caucasian	51
% Hispanic	16
% Native American	<1
% international	2
# of countries represented	71

SURVEY SAYS . . .

Political activism is popular
Student publications are popular
College radio is popular

ACADEMICS

Academic Rating	69
% students returning for sophomore year	85
% students graduating within 4 years	52
% students graduating within 6 years	66
Calendar	Semester
Profs interesting rating	70
Profs accessible rating	72

STUDENTS SAY ". . ."

Academics

With its South Orange, New Jersey location "fourteen miles from New York City," students at Seton Hall, many of whom are Jersey natives, enjoy prime bridge-and-tunnel access to the world's capital. The university's academic programs are "renowned in many subjects," but the Whitehead School of Diplomacy and International relations is "practically unparalleled," affording students direct "connections to the U.N." Seton Hall's Stillman School of Business, offering concentrations in finance, accounting, sport management, and marketing, among others, also attracts a number of students, who find numerous "internship opportunities" and "connections" in New York and New Jersey. While "professors are for the most part very engaging and work hard to encourage students to learn," students find mixed results when it comes to personal attention, concurring that "the level of involvement really depends on the professor." The "technologically connected" campus "completely dedicates itself to its undergrads," who appreciate the administrative "connectivity of students to staff" and find that Seton Hall achieves "cohesiveness as one unit to give us the best possible education." Financially, even though many students choose Seton Hall because "it's affordable" or because "I got a fantastic scholarship," once they get to campus they're pleased to discover that "the school offers all the great things that come with a private education." Whether students know what they want to study upon their entrance or not, Seton Hall's academic experience offers plenty of choices to "fuel my own desire to educate myself in fields that both pertain and have little to do with my major."

Life

On one hand, because "a lot of students are from the NY or NJ area," it's perceptible that "life at Seton Hall revolves around the hours 9:00 A.M.–5:00 P.M.," and "campus is a ghost town on weekends." On the other hand, "New York City is only twenty minutes away and is frequented by many students during the weekends." Residents who do stick around "develop close bonds, heading to the nearby city or taking a day trip to one of the small towns near by." Students enjoy Hoboken's close proximity, and around campus in South Orange there are "plenty of parties to attend but none of them last very long. South Orange PD is always out to shut them down." South Orange is "not very safe but we are well informed to stay safe." In terms of housing, "quality of facilities" doesn't rank highly on things to love about Seton Hall, and upperclassmen confide that "student life improves dramatically as you move through the years, and you move off campus." However, others say that the school does succeed in "creating a sense of community," that there "are a plethora of clubs and organizations that students can get involved in and those groups are always hosting events," and that spending "free time doing activities with clubs or with friends" is common.

Student Body

According to Seton Hall's undergrads, the "typical student is from New Jersey, goes home on the weekends, and out to off campus parties on Thursday and Friday nights," but "there is still a considerable amount of students who attend SHU from all over the country." As at many schools, "there are certain patterns within students in certain majors." Students in business and diplomacy are known as the most studious: "Diplomacy students focus on academics and are often very intelligent. Business students give 100 percent to their programs." "Students fit in very easily" at the university "by being themselves and getting involved." Seton Hall is a Catholic university with enduring values of "servant leadership," but "diversity is at the heart of the university": "The Seton Hall community consists of good-hearted, friendly people." Overall, students reflect that the university surrounds them with a "strong and loving community that fosters emotional, educational, and social growth."

FINANCIAL AID: 973-761-9332 • E-MAIL: THEHALL@SHU.EDU • WEBSITE: WWW.SHU.EDU

THE PRINCETON REVIEW SAYS

Admissions

Other factors considered include: TOEFL required of all international applicants. *Academic units required:* 4 English; 3 mathematics; 1 science; (1 science lab); 2 social studies; 2 foreign language; 4 academic electives.

Financial Aid

Students should submit: FAFSA. The Princeton Review suggests that all financial aid forms be submitted as soon as possible after January 1. Federal Work-Study Program available. Institutional employment available. Off-campus job opportunities are good.

The Inside Word

Seton Hall accepts both its online application and the Common Application. The university publicizes that its students' median test scores are 1070 for the SAT and 24 for the ACT, and it is generally acknowledged that students with reasonably solid high school transcripts, strong recommendations, and test scores within the median range won't have trouble getting in, and Seton Hall makes an effort to sweeten the deal financially for standout students.

THE SCHOOL SAYS " . . ."

From the Admissions Office

"For more than 150 years, Seton Hall University has been a catalyst for leadership, developing the whole student—mind, heart and spirit. As a Catholic university that embraces students of all races and religions, Seton Hall combines the resources of a large university with the personal attention of a small liberal arts college. The university's attractive suburban campus is only fourteen miles by train, bus or car to New York City, with the wealth of employment, internship, cultural, and entertainment opportunities the city offers. Outstanding faculty, a technologically advanced campus, and a values-centered curriculum challenge Seton Hall students. Students are exposed to a world of ideas from great scholars, opening their minds to the perspectives, history and achievements of many cultures. Our new core curriculum focuses on the need for our students to have common experiences and encourages them to become thinking, caring, communicative and ethically responsible leaders while emphasizing practical proficiencies and intellectual development. Our commitment to our students goes beyond textbooks and homework assignments, though. At Seton Hall, developing servant leaders who will make a difference in the world is a priority. That's why all students take classes in ethics and learn in a community informed by Catholic ideals and universal values. While Seton Hall certainly enjoys a big reputation, our campus community is close-knit and inclusive. Students, faculty and staff come from around the world, bringing with them a kaleidoscope of experiences and perspectives to create a diverse yet unified campus environment."

SELECTIVITY

Admissions Rating	79
# of applicants	10,180
% of applicants accepted	84
% of acceptees attending	17

FRESHMAN PROFILE

Range SAT Critical Reading	490–590
Range SAT Math	510–610
Range SAT Writing	490–600
Minimum paper TOEFL	550
Minimum web-based TOEFL	213
Average HS GPA	3.47
% graduated top 10% of class	37
% graduated top 25% of class	61
% graduated top 50% of class	86

DEADLINES

Early action	
Deadline	12/15
Notification	1/1
Regular	
Priority	3/1
Nonfall registration?	Yes

APPLICANTS ALSO LOOK AT AND OFTEN PREFER

Pennsylvania State University—University Park; New York University

AND SOMETIMES PREFER

Rider University; Fordham University; University of Connecticut; Fairfield University

AND RARELY PREFER

St. Bonaventure University; Monmouth University (NJ); Hofstra University

FINANCIAL FACTS

Financial Aid Rating	64
% frosh rec. any financial aid	97
% UG rec. any financial aid	97

SEWANEE—THE UNIVERSITY OF THE SOUTH

735 UNIVERSITY AVENUE, SEWANEE, TN 37383-1000 • ADMISSIONS: 931-598-1238 • FAX: 931-538-3248

CAMPUS LIFE

Quality of Life Rating	74
Fire Safety Rating	87
Green Rating	89
Type of school	Private
Affiliation	Episcopal
Environment	Rural

STUDENTS

Total undergrad enrollment	1,599
% male/female	49/51
% from out of state	76
% frosh from public high school	42
% frosh live on campus	100
% ugrads live on campus	96
# of fraternities (% ugrad men join)	12 (67)
# of sororities (% ugrad women join)	9 (72)
% African American	5
% Asian	2
% Caucasian	83
% Hispanic	4
% Native American	0
% international	3
# of countries represented	23

SURVEY SAYS . . .
No one cheats
Students are friendly
Campus feels safe
Students are happy
Frats and sororities are popular
Lots of beer drinking
Hard liquor is popular

ACADEMICS

Academic Rating	89
% students returning for sophomore year	91
% students graduating within 4 years	76
% students graduating within 6 years	78
Calendar	Semester
Student/faculty ratio	11:1
Profs interesting rating	87
Profs accessible rating	89

Most classes have 10–19 students.
Most lab/discussion sessions have 10–19 students.

MOST POPULAR MAJORS
English language and literature; economics; environmental studies

STUDENTS SAY " . . ."

Academics

The University of the South is a small, "very demanding" school "in the middle of rural Tennessee." Students describe it as "an oasis of perfection" "dripping with both Southern and academic tradition." "Sewanee embodies what a liberal arts education should," beams a history major. Classes are "small" and there's a "well-rounded curriculum." "The volume of work can make you want to pull your hair out," warns an economics major. "Sewanee does not inflate grades," either. "You must work hard to earn an A." "Occasionally a professor or two takes the absent-minded professor stereotype to a ridiculous level," but "it is hard to find a truly bad teacher among the whole lot." Professors here "care about their students." "Their passion for their fields and students is unparalleled." Profs are also very approachable. "We have incredible access to the faculty," gushes a religion major. "Many professors invite students to their homes for social and educational activities somewhat regularly," adds a music major. Students also love the "extremely reachable" administration. The only complaint we hear about academic life concerns the lack of course availability.

Life

A few dorms at Sewanee "really need some work." "Give me air conditioning," demands a sweaty sophomore. The "secluded" town that surrounds the school is "void of any good restaurants, bars, and general distractions a city provides." The campus is "absolutely gorgeous," though. It's a "serene haven" in "an idyllic setting" atop a mountain. Also, the school owns an "incredible amount of land." "Hiking the beautiful perimeter trail" is a favorite pastime, and students can bike, kayak, and "play in the woods" to their hearts' content. Socially, "Sewanee is unique in its quirks." There's a revered honor code. Faculty members wear academic gowns when they teach, and "most Sewanee students follow the tradition of dressing up for class." You'll see men in bow ties and seersucker suits and women in "pointy heels and pearls." There's also an "ever-present" sense of community. "You can't compartmentalize your life here," and for good or ill, "everyone knows what everyone else did last night." During the week, studying is paramount. "We spend a lot of time in the library," notes a sophomore. However, alcohol policies here are "lenient" and "Sewanee is a pretty big party school." Booze is "by no means forced upon you," but "students here drink often and heavily." The frat scene is absolutely massive. "Almost everyone becomes involved in a fraternity or a sorority." "The administration requires all Greek events to be open to the entire campus," but "there is no other social network except the Greek organizations."

Student Body

Even though the administration here is "pushing the diversity card to the nth degree," Sewanee is "strikingly homogenous." "A lot more students here are liberal than you would guess," and Yankees are "not viewed as aliens," but "Sewanee is a Southern and conservative school in every sense of the word." Students are typically "laid-back," "rich, conservative, and fun" "children of the Southern aristocracy" who like to "get drunk on the weekends." Some are "heavily spoiled and coddled." "We have lots of cookie-cutter, preppy, extreme social drinkers, but then again you can also find people who wear only organic hemp, sleep outside, and have dreadlocks," explains a junior. "There are a lot of outdoorsy styles mixed in as well." While "social arrangements are very cliquish," students tell us they are "relatively peacefully coexisting." "It really is one of the friendliest communities that I have ever seen," declares a sophomore.

FINANCIAL AID: 800-522-2234 • E-MAIL: ADMISS@SEWANEE.EDU • WEBSITE: WWW.SEWANEE.EDU

THE PRINCETON REVIEW SAYS

Admissions

Very important factors considered include: GPA, rigor of secondary school record, recommendation(s). *Important factors considered include:* Standardized test scores, application essay, extracurricular activities, volunteer work, work experience, character/personal qualities. *Other factors considered include:* Class rank, first generation, geographical residence, interview, racial/ethnic status, talent/ability, alumni/ae relations, level of applicant's interest. SAT and SAT Subject Tests or ACT considered if submitted; ACT with or without Writing component accepted. TOEFL required of all international applicants. *Academic units required:* 4 English; 3 mathematics; 2 science; (2 science lab); 1 social studies; 2 foreign language; 1 history. *Academic units recommended:* 4 English; 4 mathematics; 4 science; (3 science lab); 2 social studies; 4 foreign language; 2 history.

Financial Aid

Students should submit: FAFSA, Institution's own financial aid form. Regular filing deadline is 3/1. The Princeton Review suggests that all financial aid forms be submitted as soon as possible after January 1. *Need-based scholarships/grants offered:* Federal Pell, SEOG, State scholarships/grants, private scholarships, the school's own gift aid. *Loan aid offered:* Direct Subsidized Stafford Loans, Direct Unsubsidized Stafford Loans, Direct PLUS loans, Federal Perkins Loans, State Loans, College/university loans from institutional funds. Applicants will be notified of awards beginning 2/25. Federal Work-Study Program available. Institutional employment available. Off-campus job opportunities are fair.

The Inside Word

The admissions office at Sewanee is very personable and accessible to students. Its staff includes some of the most well-respected admissions professionals in the South, and it shows in the way they work with students. Despite a fairly high acceptance rate, candidates who take the admissions process here lightly may find themselves disappointed. Applicant evaluation is too personal for a lackadaisical approach to succeed.

THE SCHOOL SAYS "..."

From the Admissions Office

"Sewanee is consistently ranked among the top tier of national liberal arts universities. Sewanee is committed to a rigorous academic curriculum that focuses on the liberal arts as the most enlightening and valuable form of undergraduate education. It offers thirty-six majors, thirty-two minors, and pre-professional programs including business, medicine, and education. Founded by leaders of the Episcopal Church in 1857, Sewanee continues to be owned by twenty-eight Episcopal dioceses in twelve states. The university is located on a 13,000-acre campus atop Tennessee's Cumberland Plateau between Chattanooga and Nashville. Largely forested, rich in biodiversity, this land is a distinctive asset offering an unparalleled outdoor laboratory and boundless recreational opportunities.

"The university has an impressive record of academic achievement—thirty Rhodes Scholars and twenty-seven NCAA postgraduate scholarship recipients have graduated from Sewanee. Four of the last ten Tennessee Professors of the Year have been members of Sewanee's faculty. Professors are leading scholars and researchers with a commitment to teaching, and in Sewanee's close community they develop rich and enduring relationships with their students.

"Beginning in 2009, prospective students may choose not to submit standardized test scores. Those who make that choice must instead submit a graded academic paper and complete an evaluative interview with a Sewanee representative. Other critical factors long considered in the Sewanee admission process remain, including strength of the high school curriculum, high school academic performance, extracurricular activities, and evidence of character and talent."

SELECTIVITY

Admissions Rating	92
# of applicants	3,285
% of applicants accepted	60
% of acceptees attending	25
# offered a place on the wait list	486
% accepting a place on wait list	25
% admitted from wait list	6
# of early decision applicants	167
% accepted early decision	74

FRESHMAN PROFILE

Range SAT Critical Reading	580–670
Range SAT Math	560–650
Range SAT Writing	570–670
Range ACT Composite	26–30
Minimum paper TOEFL	550
Minimum web-based TOEFL	213
Average HS GPA	3.62
% graduated top 10% of class	42
% graduated top 25% of class	72
% graduated top 50% of class	96

DEADLINES

Early decision	
Deadline	11/15
Notification	12/15
Early action	
Deadline	12/1
Notification	1/25
Regular	
Deadline	2/1
Notification	3/17
Nonfall registration?	No

APPLICANTS ALSO LOOK AT AND OFTEN PREFER

University of Georgia; Washington and Lee University; Rhodes College; University of Tennessee; University of Virginia; Furman University; Vanderbilt University; University of Alabama—Tuscaloosa; Auburn University

FINANCIAL FACTS

Financial Aid Rating	87
Annual tuition	$36,828
Room and board	$10,600
Required fees	$272
Books and supplies	$900
% needy frosh rec. need-based scholarship or grant aid	99
% needy UG rec. need-based scholarship or grant aid	99
% needy frosh rec. non-need-based scholarship or grant aid	58
% needy UG rec. non-need-based scholarship or grant aid	57
% needy frosh rec. need-based self-help aid	75
% needy UG rec. need-based self-help aid	72
% frosh rec. any financial aid	80
% UG rec. any financial aid	80
% UG borrow to pay for school	40
Average cumulative indebtedness	$23,721
% frosh need fully met	44
% ugrads need fully met	47
Average % of frosh need met	92
Average % of ugrad need met	91

SIENA COLLEGE

515 LOUDON ROAD, LOUDONVILLE, NY 12211-1462 • ADMISSIONS: 518-783-2423 • FAX: 518-783-2436

STUDENTS SAY ". . ."

Academics

The Franciscan tradition "is all about community," and, at Siena College, a small school with "a strong Franciscan atmosphere," students benefit from a friendly community in which "there is always someone to lend a helping hand." That someone may be a professor, a tutor, or, on occasion, a friar driving through campus in his golf cart. "My school is probably has the best sense of community and tradition in America" one finance major raves. Biology and other premedical disciplines are highly regarded, and students especially love the Siena College–Albany Medical College Program, a joint acceptance program that focuses on humanities and community service. In addition, the school's many business undergrads feel their program, which is enhanced by a loyal alumni base that helps newly minted grads quickly find jobs, is the school's "greatest strength." Students also sing the praises on the social work program with the availability of "internships in downtown Albany." Regardless of discipline, Siena professors are "incredibly approachable and want you to succeed; but they are challenging, want you to learn, not skirt by."

Student Life

For many students, recreation time at Siena means it's time for a beer or two, and lately that's become a point of contention with the administration. Despite this "people do party but it is not over the top here." Siena is "definitely a college campus, but a very safe one where no one feels pressured to drink." The campus still bustles during the week, however, because "most people are involved in clubs" and at least "one sport, whether intramural or intercollegiate." Other diversions include a school-sponsored bus that takes students to the Crossgates Mall, which "is pretty large and houses a bunch of amazing stores," and "a whole strip of dining-out places." Still, an English major admits, "If you don't drink, I can see where weekends would be boring, especially in the winter." The school does sponsor activities on campus designed "to draw students away from the drinking scene." Overall, students are quite busy but while those "activities keep me busy throughout the week, I still manage to make time for myself and have fun." One complaint echoed among students is that "dining options could be inproved." Siena also provides its students with free access to public buses so that students can travel safely to jobs, internships and the Capital Region's many attractions

Student Body

There "isn't much diversity" on the Siena campus, where it seems just about everyone "is from an upper-middle-class Catholic family from Long Island" or "upstate New York." There are some who don't fit the mold, but not many; students speculate that they're mostly nontraditional or international students. Minority students tend to "stick together, but all seem well-liked." Many students "are involved either in D1 athletics, intramural teams, or clubs and Student Senate activities"; students in these groups tend to party together on the weekends "and generally create a strong group of friends easily." While there's a solid contingent of folks at Siena who "drink, party, and hardly ever study," there are also students, particularly in the sciences, who work hard but "don't socialize much outside of their departments, due to the nature of their programs." But most are "super friendly" and students "just have to find your niche."

FINANCIAL AID: 888-AT-SIENA • E-MAIL: ADMIT@SIENA.EDU • WEBSITE: WWW.SIENA.EDU

THE PRINCETON REVIEW SAYS

Admissions

Very important factors considered include: GPA, rigor of secondary school record, *Important factors considered include:* Interview, standardized test scores, recommendation(s). *Other factors considered include:* Class rank, application essay, extracurricular activities, first generation, geographical residence, racial/ethnic status, talent/ability, volunteer work, work experience, alumni/ae relations, character/personal qualities, level of applicant's interest, SAT or ACT required; ACT with Writing component required. TOEFL required of all international applicants. *Academic units required:* 4 English; 3 mathematics; 3 science; (3 science lab); 3 social studies/history; 2 foreign language. *Academic units recommended:* 4 English; 4 mathematics; 4 science; (4 science lab); 4 social studies/history; 3 foreign language.

Financial Aid

Students should submit: FAFSA, NYS TAP form. Suggested filing deadline is 2/15. *Need-based scholarships/grants offered:* Federal Pell, SEOG, State scholarships/grants, Private scholarships, the school's own gift aid. *Loan aid offered:* Direct Subsidized Stafford Loans, Direct Unsubsidized Stafford Loans, Direct PLUS loans, Federal Perkins Loans. Applicants will be notified of awards beginning in early March. Federal Work-Study Program available. Institutional employment available.

The Inside Word

Siena's draw is still primarily regional, with 78 percent of freshmen originating from the Empire State. The relatively high acceptance rate coupled with the all-star programs offered has led to more competition but the standards are still very manageable. Expect to meet higher standards if you indicate an interest in the School of Science, as it is the gateway to the school's desirable premedical programs. The school does applicants a favor here—substandard students stand little chance of surviving the school's science regimen.

THE SCHOOL SAYS "..."

From the Admissions Office

"Siena College is a welcoming community that encourages its students to pursue their academic passions, get involved and develop skills and connections that will prepare them for a lifetime of career success and achievement. Siena is a private, Franciscan and Catholic college located in the heart of New York's Capital Region and Tech Valley. Students enjoy life on a park-like suburban campus yet they are minutes away from high-tech companies, city hotspots, entertainment options and historic sites. The College boasts a four-year graduation rate of 74%, which is well above the national average. There are no teaching assistants at Siena which means all classes are taught by faculty members. Siena students are able to customize their curriculum to match their career interests through internships, study abroad and travel courses, undergraduate research with faculty and more than 1,200 program combinations. Popular programs include the liberal arts, accounting, marketing, biology, pre-law and the Siena College/Albany Medical College joint acceptance program. The College also offers a master's in accounting program to meet New York State requirements to sit for the CPA exam. Siena is also the only college in New York State to offer the Bonner Service Leaders scholarship program."

SELECTIVITY

Admissions Rating	87
# of applicants	9,438
% of applicants accepted	58
% of acceptees attending	14
# offered a place on the wait list	835
% accepting a place on wait list	19
% admitted from wait list	18
# of early decision applicants	660
% accepted early decision	12

FRESHMAN PROFILE

@stats:Range SAT Critical Reading	490–590
Range SAT Math	510–610
Range SAT Writing	480–590
Range ACT Composite	22–27
Minimum paper TOEFL	550
Minimum web-based TOEFL	213
Average HS GPA	89.70
% graduated top 10% of class	24
% graduated top 25% of class	58
% graduated top 50% of class	90

DEADLINES

Early decision	
Deadline	12/1
Notification	12/15
Early action	
Deadline	12/1
Notification	1/1
Regular	
Priority	2/15
Deadline	2/15
Notification	3/15
Nonfall registration?	Yes

APPLICANTS ALSO LOOK AT AND OFTEN PREFER
Massachusetts College of Pharmacy and HealthSciences; Boston University

AND SOMETIMES PREFER
Northeastern University

FINANCIAL FACTS

Financial Aid Rating	72
Annual tuition	$32,043
Room and board	$13,060
Required fees	$750
Books and supplies	$1,291
% needy frosh rec. need-based scholarship or grant aid	100
% needy UG rec. need-based scholarship or grant aid	100
% needy frosh rec. non-need-based scholarship or grant aid	95
% needy UG rec. non-need-based scholarship or grant aid	91
% needy frosh rec. need-based self-help aid	80
% needy UG rec. need-based self-help aid	82
% frosh rec. any financial aid	98
% UG rec. any financial aid	97
% UG borrow to pay for school	79
Average cumulative indebtedness	$35,569
% frosh need fully met	24
% ugrads need fully met	22
Average % of frosh need met	71
Average % of ugrad need met	71

SIMMONS COLLEGE

300 The Fenway, Boston, MA 02115 • Admissions: 617-521-2051 • Fax: 617-521-3190

CAMPUS LIFE

Quality of Life Rating	84
Fire Safety Rating	93
Green Rating	76
Type of school	Private
Affiliation	Roman Catholic
Environment	Town

STUDENTS

Total undergrad enrollment	1,732
% male/female	0/100
% from out of state	37
% frosh live on campus	95
% ugrads live on campus	58
% African American	5
% Asian	9
% Caucasian	68
% Hispanic	6
% Native American	<1
% international	3
# of countries represented	25

SURVEY SAYS . . .

Classroom facilities are great
Students get along with local community
Students love Boston, MA
Great off-campus food

ACADEMICS

Academic Rating	85
% students returning for sophomore year	86
% students graduating within 4 years	66
% students graduating within 6 years	71
Calendar	Semester
Student/faculty ratio	10:1
Profs interesting rating	88
Profs accessible rating	80

Most classes have 20–29 students.
Most lab/discussion sessions have
10–19 students.

STUDENTS SAY ". . ."

Academics

A women's college "rich in history and achievement," Simmons College equips its undergraduates with the tools and confidence they need to succeed in the real-world. With a student population of about "2,000 very driven, smart, active, and hard working women," Simmons offers a surprisingly wide range of undergraduate majors, while also running a "nursing program that is second to none." Across academic programs, there's a "particular focus on experiential learning and leadership," and the curriculum excels at "educating women for positions of powerful and principled leadership." Simmons professors "are very dedicated to the classes they teach as well as their students." A chemistry major remembers, "My college has many research opportunities and connections. I have been able to do scientific research every semester since my first year at Simmons." Small discussion-based classes "really challenge you to do your best and to actually put some thought into your work," and Simmons professors are described as "the greatest strengths of Simmons College." The Simmons School of Management also offers "many other networking opportunities." Students have mixed opinions when it comes to the administrative offices of the college. Some majors "with hard-to-come-by internships have ALOT of red tape" and others "do not communicate well all the time" with both professors and students. The college does "take advantage of its Boston location through class trips, job placement, and internship opportunities." However, when it comes to the all-important problem of paying for school, students admit that the "financial aid counselors make you want to rip out your hair out."

Life

Location, location, location is a sentiment echoed far and wide by Simmons undergraduates. "We are in Boston," raves one sophomore. "We can do anything the city has to offer." Packed with culture and entertainment, "the city offers many great places to hang out like bowling places, karaoke bars, college parties at other colleges, and great scenery." In addition, Simmons is part of the Colleges of the Fenway association, so "students get discounts at art museums and cultural events around the city such as plays or dances." Simmons is a "dry campus so the bar scene is where to go, and where else is better than right in the heart of Boston?" Other students prefer mellower activities, like "sitting in the common room and talking or watching a show together." Since so much social life takes place off campus, "the dorms are quiet and a great place to concentrate on school work." The peacefulness of campus is a plus for many students, who "spend a lot of time studying and preparing for labs and lecture." Housing has become more of an issue as the "dorms are beginning to get overcrowded" as each year brings a "large influx of first-year students" and some "freshman now live in forced triples."

Student Body

Putting aside the fact that they're all female, Simmons students say there's a lot of diversity on their small campus. "Students attempt to be aware of cultural diversity," and "the community here is very accepting, regardless of race, ethnicity, economic status, religion, sexual orientation, gender expression, or disability." Politically, you'll meet students who are "very conservative to very liberal," though "most students are very supportive of the LGBTQ community and women's rights in general." When it comes to academics, "all of the people here have their lives together and have an idea of what they want to do with their lives." Socially, "birds of a feather flock together," and students admit, "There are different cliques within the student body." However, "everyone is generally accepted" on this friendly and community-oriented campus. A general sentiment that "people here work very hard at everything they do," pervades the student responses.

FINANCIAL AID: 617-521-2001 • E-MAIL: UGADM@SIMMONS.EDU • WEBSITE: WWW.SIMMONS.EDU

THE PRINCETON REVIEW SAYS

Admissions

Very important factors considered include: GPA, rigor of secondary school record. *Important factors considered include:* Standardized test scores, interview, recommendation(s). *Other factors considered include:* Class rank, application essay, extracurricular activities, first generation, geographical residence, racial/ethnic status, talent/ability, volunteer work, work experience, alumni/ae relations, character/personal qualities, level of applicant's interest. SAT or ACT required; ACT with Writing component required. TOEFL required of all international applicants. *Academic units required:* 4 English; 3 mathematics; 3 science; (3 science lab); 3 social studies; 2 foreign language; 3 history. *Academic units recommended:* 4 English; 4 mathematics; 4 science; (4 science lab); 4 social studies; 3 foreign language; 4 history.

Financial Aid

Students should submit: FAFSA, State aid form. Regular filing deadline is 5/1. The Princeton Review suggests that all financial aid forms be submitted as soon as possible after January 1. *Need-based scholarships/grants offered:* Federal Pell, SEOG, State scholarships/grants, private scholarships, the school's own gift aid. *Loan aid offered:* Direct Subsidized Stafford Loans, Direct Unsubsidized Stafford Loans, Direct PLUS loans, Federal Perkins Loans. Applicants will be notified of awards beginning 4/1. Federal Work-Study Program available. Institutional employment available.

The Inside Word

Simmons evaluates prospective students for both academic strength and personal qualities, like community involvement or leadership. Applicants to Simmons should use their personal essays, letters of recommendation, and applications to show the admissions committee who they are as a person. Although a personal interview isn't required, it can be a great way to augment your application, as well as a chance to experience Simmons unique environment. A current student tells us, "It felt like a I belonged here when I visited."

THE SCHOOL SAYS ". . ."

From the Admissions Office

"Founded in 1899, Simmons was the first college in the nation to offer women a liberal arts education integrated with professional preparation. Today, Simmons is known for providing transformative learning that links passion with lifelong purpose. The college is committed to preparing students for their careers, while also helping them discover who they are and what they can contribute to society over the course of their lifetimes.

"As a student-focused institution, Simmons offers a learning experience that is highly collaborative and much more personal than that of large universities. Simmons professors include distinguished researchers, published authors, Fulbright scholars, health professionals, and community leaders. More than three-quarters are women, and nearly 100 percent hold doctorate or other terminal degrees in their field. They advise numerous government, nonprofit, and corporate organizations in the United States and around the world—yet passionately uphold their primary obligation to teach.

"To help students succeed, career support starts as soon as students step on campus and continues as an ongoing, lifelong service. Ninety-seven percent of the class of 2010 were employed or in graduate school within one year of graduation (either full or part time). Of this population, more than 89 percent are employed at jobs in a field related, or closely related, to their major while at Simmons. At Simmons, we are committed to preparing women to be well-informed, open-minded, intellectually curious, and lifelong learners."

SELECTIVITY

Admissions Rating	81
# of applicants	4,239
% of applicants accepted	49
% of acceptees attending	16

FRESHMAN PROFILE

Range SAT Critical Reading	490–590
Range SAT Math	520–620
Range SAT Writing	530–640
Range ACT Composite	23–28
Minimum paper TOEFL	550
Minimum web-based TOEFL	83
Average HS GPA	3.4
% graduated top 10% of class	26
% graduated top 25% of class	61
% graduated top 50% of class	90

DEADLINES

Early action	
Deadline	11/1
Notification	12/15
Regular	
Priority	11/1
Deadline	2/15
Notification	3/15
Nonfall registration?	Yes

APPLICANTS ALSO LOOK AT AND OFTEN PREFER

Massachusetts College of Pharmacy and HealthSciences; Boston University

AND SOMETIMES PREFER

Northeastern University

FINANCIAL FACTS

Financial Aid Rating	70
Annual tuition	$35,200
Room and board	$13,376
Required fees	$1,030
Books and supplies	$1,280
% needy frosh rec. need-based scholarship or grant aid	99
% needy UG rec. need-based scholarship or grant aid	99
% needy frosh rec. non-need-based scholarship or grant aid	8
% needy UG rec. non-need-based scholarship or grant aid	3
% needy frosh rec. need-based self-help aid	89
% needy UG rec. need-based self-help aid	93
% frosh rec. any financial aid	96
% UG rec. any financial aid	90
% frosh need fully met	13
% ugrads need fully met	8
Average % of frosh need met	78
Average % of ugrad need met	69

SKIDMORE COLLEGE

815 NORTH BROADWAY, SARATOGA SPRINGS, NY 12866-1632 • ADMISSIONS: 518-580-5570 • FAX: 518-580-5584

STUDENTS SAY ". . ."

Academics

"Creative Thought Matters": this is the motto of upstate New York's Skidmore College, which can be found all over campus and in every student's mind. The small school looks to turn out "well-rounded, open-minded, [and] interested" students, and to that end stresses "the doing of interesting things outside of, or in complement to, academics." Students, faculty, and staff alike embrace the tenets of Skidmore life, and make sure that the college "represents the meeting point between a phenomenal social atmosphere and an interdisciplinary take on academics."

Professors "actively engage students in friendships, or at the very least, senior colleague to junior colleague camaraderie." This "enriches the experience of learning" and "makes 'doing work' an inspired, meaningful, and highly consequential practice." Faculty expects a lot from their students in regards to papers and class participation: "Reading is almost always a must." "I love that the professors hold me accountable," says a junior. They "present the material in the context of Skidmore's community and general student body's political and social values" and "show a true interest in their field which they attempt to stir within their students." "Even the classes I have taken to fulfill requirements have been some of my favorite classes," says a student.

Some of Skidmore's greatest strengths are the academic support resources available to all students and the variety of majors available; there are also "many opportunities to study abroad or do internships." The school has "a great balance of arts and sciences"; the crossing point between the two areas is a pleasant surprise for those who study here. Within the science departments, Skidmore "melds a small college atmosphere with equipment and resources expected at a large university." Students also "have a good amount of freedom to explore within their academic field of interest beyond the standard curriculum."

Life

Located in "the city in the country" in upstate Saratoga Springs, New York (a "horse town" due to the famed racetracks), Skidmore is "very close to the Adirondacks and beautiful hiking." The city itself is just a 15-minute walk from campus, and people often make a quick trip to nearby Lake George or to the mall. Aside from all the events going on, it's also great "to just sit on the main lawn with a group of friends, pretend to do work or actually do work, chat about nothing in particular, people watch, play Frisbee, enjoy the live music and the beautiful weather."

The excellent first-year experience kicks off the Skidmore love-fest; it helps that the school is "just the right size" so that "you still meet new people, but it's small enough to make you feel comfortable." The "diverse and abundant club opportunities" offer many outlets for creativity, as "we have a capella groups (five), comedy groups (three), writing clubs (two), and dance troupes (two)." During the week people don't typically party, it's "more a time for extracurriculars and school work"; however on the weekends, "the bar scene is very popular as well as apartment parties" and "everyone smokes weed." The arts are also a huge draw if substances aren't your thing, and "there's always plays and shows to go to."

Student Body

Some people stereotype Skidmore as a "hipster" school ("you see a lot of people chain-smoking cigarettes, drinking coffee out of mason jars, and wearing torn-up 'vintage' clothing), though there is also an athlete contingent in the mix. Generally, "everyone gets along pretty well." Students are "very open-minded," and everyone can find a niche here. "We love people who think creatively and critically while accepting any weirdness that comes with those traits," says a student. Many agree that "while there is a lot of intellectual diversity, Skidmore could definitely make more of an effort to include more diverse backgrounds."

FINANCIAL AID: 518-580-5750 • E-MAIL: ADMISSIONS@SKIDMORE.EDU • WEBSITE: WWW.SKIDMORE.EDU

THE PRINCETON REVIEW SAYS

Admissions

Very important factors considered include: Rigor of secondary school record. *Important factors considered include:* Class rank, GPA, application essay, extracurricular activities, recommendation(s), talent/ability, volunteer work, work experience, character/personal qualities. *Other factors considered include:* Standardized test scores, first generation, geographical residence, interview, racial/ethnic status, alumni/ae relations, level of applicant's interest. SAT or ACT required; ACT with Writing component required. TOEFL required of all international applicants. *Academic units recommended:* 4 English; 4 mathematics; 4 science; (3 science lab); 4 social studies; 4 foreign language.

Financial Aid

Students should submit: FAFSA, CSS/Financial Aid PROFILE, Noncustodial PROFILE. Regular filing deadline is 2/1. The Princeton Review suggests that all financial aid forms be submitted as soon as possible after January 1. *Need-based scholarships/grants offered:* Federal Pell, SEOG, State scholarships/grants, private scholarships, the school's own gift aid. *Loan aid offered:* Direct Subsidized Stafford Loans, Direct Unsubsidized Stafford Loans, Direct PLUS loans, Federal Perkins Loans, State Loans. Applicants will be notified of awards beginning 4/1. Federal Work-Study Program available. Institutional employment available. Off-campus job opportunities are fair.

The Inside Word

Admission to Skidmore is highly competitive, and the admissions staff carefully considers each applicant's academic background and standardized test scores. However, consistent with their motto—"Creative Thought Matters" Skidmore carefully reviews a student's extracurricular talents, achievements, and passions when making an admissions decision. While admissions interviews aren't a requirement for a Skidmore applicant, students may request a personal interview on campus or with an alumnus in their area.

THE SCHOOL SAYS "..."

From the Admissions Office

"At Skidmore, we believe a great education is about putting academic theory and creative expression into practice; hence, our belief that creative thought matters. It's a place where faculty and students work together, then figure out how to use what they've learned to make a difference. This often leads to multidisciplinary approaches, where students carry more than one major, student-faculty research is common, most students study abroad, and internships and community service are standard. Skidmore students develop into independent, creative problem-solvers who aren't restricted to looking at things in traditional ways.

"This personal journey starts with the First-Year Experience—fifty seminars from which to choose, faculty and peer mentors, and living in close proximity to seminar classmates in residence halls. It's meant to ensure that first-year students hit the ground running on day one, connected and involved. When it comes to your major, you can choose from nearly 50 offerings in the sciences, social sciences, and humanities, as well as pre-professional fields like management and business.

"Since we have no fraternities or sororities, student life centers on the nearly 100 student clubs and organizations, which range from the Environmental Action Club to a capella groups to snowboarding. Add to this the prominence of the arts, which has long set Skidmore apart. Science classes collaborate on exhibits at the Tang Museum. Hundreds of students perform, often in the new Zankel Music Center. Enroll in dance courses. Do theater performances. Most are not even arts majors. At Skidmore, the arts don't dominate, they permeate.

"As for location, who wouldn't want to go to college in Saratoga Springs? A downtown brimming with shops, galleries, coffeehouses, and great restaurants. Boston, New York City, and Montreal are a 3-hour car ride from campus. The Adirondacks, Berkshires, and Green Mountains provide opportunities for skiing, mountain biking, hiking, rock-climbing, and kayaking."

SELECTIVITY

Admissions Rating	95
# of applicants	8,285
% of applicants accepted	35
% of acceptees attending	23
# offered a place on the wait list	1,843
% accepting a place on wait list	23
% admitted from wait list	5
# of early decision applicants	429
% accepted early decision	68

FRESHMAN PROFILE

Range SAT Critical Reading	560–680
Range SAT Math	570–670
Range SAT Writing	570–690
Range ACT Composite	26–30
Minimum paper TOEFL	590
Minimum web-based TOEFL	96
% graduated top 10% of class	45
% graduated top 25% of class	81
% graduated top 50% of class	97

DEADLINES

Early decision	
Deadline	11/15
Notification	12/15
Regular	
Deadline	1/15
Notification	4/1
Nonfall registration?	No

APPLICANTS ALSO LOOK AT AND OFTEN PREFER

Vassar College; Wesleyan University; Tufts University

AND SOMETIMES PREFER

Boston University; Connecticut College; New York University; Sarah Lawrence College

FINANCIAL FACTS

Financial Aid Rating	94
Annual tuition	$44,820
Room and board	$12,202
Required fees	$1,054
Books and supplies	$1,300
% needy frosh rec. need-based scholarship or grant aid	100
% needy UG rec. need-based scholarship or grant aid	99
% needy frosh rec. non-need-based scholarship or grant aid	4
% needy UG rec. non-need-based scholarship or grant aid	3
% needy frosh rec. need-based self-help aid	86
% needy UG rec. need-based self-help aid	81
% frosh rec. any financial aid	55
% UG rec. any financial aid	52
% UG borrow to pay for school	39
Average cumulative indebtedness	$24,371
% frosh need fully met	100
% ugrads need fully met	91
Average % of frosh need met	100
Average % of ugrad need met	93

SMITH COLLEGE

SEVEN COLLEGE LANE, NORTHAMPTON, MA 01063 • ADMISSIONS: 413-585-2500 • FAX: 413-585-2527

STUDENTS SAY ". . ."

Academics

Smith College is "an incredibly prestigious, diverse, academically rigorous, socially liberal, and well-respected institution," located in the consummate college town of Northampton, Massachusetts. A Smith education is all about "finding and pursuing your passions." Offering "academic freedom," "Smith doesn't have course requirements" beyond the major, and "self-scheduled finals" allow students to take exam week at their own pace. "One of the most prominent women's colleges in the country," Smith "builds the self-confidence of smart women," and "most classes, even in math and sciences, are very interdisciplinary and often have a feminist bias." Classes are "engaging and promote critical thought," and professors are "inspiring, dynamic, accessible, and brilliant." Smith professors "care deeply about students" and "take the time to get to know you on a first-name basis." Smith also offers fabulous academic facilities and "countless resources" to augment your education, including a "wonderful study abroad department" and ample opportunities for research. There's "a large number of undergrads doing serious scientific research" in addition to course work. If they can't find what they need amid Smith's ample course selection, students "can take classes at the other four schools nearby (UMass Amherst, Amherst College, Hampshire College, and Mount Holyoke College)" through the Five College Consortium. When graduation approaches, Smith students benefit from the school's "excellent alumnae network." "The Career Development Office will do everything in its power to help you get a job."

Life

Smith attracts hardworking and idealistic students, who are "striving to succeed in our classes, as well as make a difference in the Smith College community and the outside community." There's a decided "focus on academics" at Smith, and most students "study, write papers, rehearse, or practice the majority of the time." Students augment course work with "lectures and symposium on campus," as well as "involvement in community service and activism for global issues, women's rights, LGBTQ rights, the environment, and pretty much anything that fights oppression." When they want to relax, Smithies can attend "free movies and concerts, plays, speakers, sports events, and dances," as well as "school-sponsored house parties almost every weekend." When they want to branch out or rub elbows with the opposite sex, students "go to other college parties at surrounding campuses," or head out in Northampton, which is "always bustling" with "concerts, restaurants, and cute shops." The "quality of life is outstanding" on campus, where "the dorms are not dorms but beautiful houses," and cafeteria food is a cut above the average.

Student Body

"Smithies are passionate about everything they do," especially academics. Throughout the semester, undergraduates are known to "study hard" and get "ridiculously stressed" about course work. "It's the nature of Smithies to be driven, but we all want to see our friends and housemates succeed as well." Smith's unique environment attracts "a great mix of nerdy, edgy, [and] traditional" students, including "hipsters, WASPs, crazy partiers, international students, and the average New Englander." Fortunately, there's a "strong sense of community," and "students fit in easily, even if they have different interests." Despite diversity, "one thing all students have in common here is the will for women's empowerment and acceptance of any gender or sexual preference." On that note, many students "love the queer life on campus," where some students are either gay or have "a fluid perception of sexuality." Though there's some political diversity on campus, most Smithies hold "very liberal views," and many are "very conscious and aware, not only of their community but the world in general."

FINANCIAL AID: 413-585-2530 • E-MAIL: ADMISSION@SMITH.EDU • WEBSITE: WWW.SMITH.EDU

THE PRINCETON REVIEW SAYS

Admissions

Very important factors considered include: GPA, rigor of secondary school record, application essay, recommendation(s), character/personal qualities. *Important factors considered include:* Class rank, extracurricular activities, interview, talent/ability. *Other factors considered include:* Standardized test scores, first generation, racial/ethnic status, volunteer work, work experience, alumni/ae relations. SAT or ACT considered if submitted; ACT with or without Writing component accepted. Testing required of all international applicants. *Academic units recommended:* 4 English; 3 mathematics; 3 science; (3 science lab); 3 foreign language; 2 history; 1 academic elective.

Financial Aid

Students should submit: FAFSA, Institution's own financial aid form, CSS/Financial Aid PROFILE, Noncustodial PROFILE. Regular filing deadline is 2/15. The Princeton Review suggests that all financial aid forms be submitted as soon as possible after January 1. *Need-based scholarships/grants offered:* Federal Pell, SEOG, State scholarships/grants, private scholarships, the school's own gift aid. *Loan aid offered:* Direct Subsidized Stafford Loans, Direct Unsubsidized Stafford Loans, Direct PLUS loans, Federal Perkins Loans, College/university loans from institutional funds. Applicants will be notified of awards beginning 4/1. Federal Work-Study Program available. Institutional employment available. Off-campus job opportunities are excellent.

The Inside Word

Every prospective Smithie is carefully evaluated by at least two members of the admissions staff. No hard numbers guarantee admission. Smith is looking for students who will succeed academically and socially in college, evaluating each applicant for both personal and intellectual qualities. To best prepare for admission, Smith recommends that students follow a rigorous college prep curriculum in high school. If you're feeling particularly enthused about your future at Smith, you can become a fan of the admissions department on Facebook, take the online tour, or read student blogs on the admission page.

THE SCHOOL SAYS "..."

From the Admissions Office

"Smith students choose from 1,000 courses in more than fifty areas of study. There are no specific course requirements outside the major; students meet individually with faculty advisers to plan a balanced curriculum. Smith programs offer unique opportunities, including interdisciplinary concentrations, the chance to study abroad, or at another college in the United States, and a semester in Washington, D.C. The Ada Comstock Scholars Program encourages women beyond the traditional age to return to college and complete their undergraduate studies. Smith is located in the scenic Connecticut River valley of western Massachusetts near a number of other outstanding educational institutions. Through the Five College Consortium, Smith, Amherst, Hampshire, and Mount Holyoke colleges, and the University of Massachusetts enrich their academic, social, and cultural offerings by means of joint faculty appointments, joint courses, student and faculty exchanges, shared facilities, and other cooperative arrangements. Smith is the only women's college to offer an accredited major in engineering; it's also the only college in the country that offers a guaranteed paid internship program ('Praxis')."

SELECTIVITY

Admissions Rating	96
# of applicants	4,403
% of applicants accepted	43
% of acceptees attending	34
# offered a place on the wait list	522
% accepting a place on wait list	55
% admitted from wait list	15
# of early decision applicants	379
% accepted early decision	47

FRESHMAN PROFILE

Range SAT Critical Reading	610–720
Range SAT Math	610–730
Range SAT Writing	630–730
Range ACT Composite	28–31
Minimum paper TOEFL	600
Minimum web-based TOEFL	250
Average HS GPA	3.90
% graduated top 10% of class	62
% graduated top 25% of class	89
% graduated top 50% of class	99

DEADLINES

Early decision	
Deadline	11/15
Notification	12/15
Regular	
Deadline	1/15
Nonfall registration?	No

APPLICANTS ALSO LOOK AT AND OFTEN PREFER

Harvard College; Princeton University; Yale University

AND SOMETIMES PREFER

Stanford University; Columbia University; Massachusetts Institute of Technology

AND RARELY PREFER

Cornell University; Georgetown University; Duke University; The University of Chicago

FINANCIAL FACTS

Financial Aid Rating	96
Annual tuition	$44,450
Room and board	$14,950
Required fees	$274
Books and supplies	$800
% needy frosh rec. need-based scholarship or grant aid	97
% needy UG rec. need-based scholarship or grant aid	95
% needy frosh rec. non-need-based scholarship or grant aid	1
% needy UG rec. non-need-based scholarship or grant aid	1
% needy frosh rec. need-based self-help aid	94
% needy UG rec. need-based self-help aid	96
% frosh rec. any financial aid	67
% UG rec. any financial aid	69
% UG borrow to pay for school	68
Average cumulative indebtedness	$22,699
% frosh need fully met	100
% ugrads need fully met	100
Average % of frosh need met	100
Average % of ugrad need met	100

SONOMA STATE UNIVERSITY

1801 East Cotati Avenue, Rohnert Park, CA 94928 • Admissions: 707-664-2778 • Fax: 707-664-2060

STUDENTS SAY ". . ."

Academics

A member of the reputable California state university system, Sonoma State University distinguishes itself from similar institutions through its low-key atmosphere and strong "focus on undergraduates." Employing "teachers who are willing to take the time to make a difference in students' lives," SSU limits most classes to fewer than fifty, giving students the opportunity to "develop close and meaningful relationships with professors and classmates that will continue even after graduation." During class time, professors often "allow open discussions and emphasize a comfortable, safe environment to express oneself." After class, they "are always available through e-mail or in person during their office hours." Most SSU instructors are excellent in the classroom, but the school is big enough that you'll find "a wide variety of professors, ranging from spectacular to pretty poor." Fortunately, professors are generally "experts in their field" and "stay up to date on current events that affect our field of study." While students benefit from a very low in-state tuition, SSU has been affected by California budget cuts, and the resulting unit cap "makes it almost impossible to graduate in four years." The school could also improve some of its bureaucratic processes; for example, the class "registration process is notoriously buggy." For those hoping to stay in California after graduation, "Sonoma County and the city of San Francisco are two places very rich in career opportunities for Sonoma State students."

Life

SSU boasts a "gorgeous campus" and "impressive" facilities, including "incredible" dormitories and "a new rec center with [a] climbing wall and indoor courts, as well as outside fields." A current student enthuses, "Just come look at the housing and you realize that Sonoma is trying to make everyone as comfortable as possible." With its "beautiful setting in the heart of wine country," "the pace here seems to be a slower one, which creates a peaceful and calm environment to take classes and study in; the stress level here is relatively low." After class, students might "hang out by the pools" or study in the "many little redwood groves" around campus. "There are hundreds of clubs" on campus, including many popular Greek organizations, and, for those with a little initiative, "the leadership opportunities are endless." Off campus, surrounding Rohnert Park is a "more suburban" environment, so "it is difficult to go anywhere unless you have a car." With a set of wheels, students love to take day trips to San Francisco, or go miniature golfing, hiking, and bowling nearby. "Outdoor activities are abundant year-round" and, for those of legal drinking age, "there are also a lot of wineries and vineyards to go wine tasting!" Come the weekend, "a lot of students like to party," while others "enjoy on-campus activities like midnight improv and free movies."

Students

"Many students pick Sonoma because it is close to home," whether they live on campus or commute. Southern Californians and other in-staters round out the largely "Bay Area" crowd, and there are a number of older students mixed in with traditional undergrads. In broad strokes, "Most students here come from middle- to upper-class backgrounds, and they are all fairly down-to-earth and really very nice and socially aware." More superficially, you'll notice "a lot of white girls wearing yoga pants, Nike shocks, and drinking Starbucks coffee." That said, "everyone has their own thing" at SSU. Though the school is "not really racially diverse" there is an "eclectic group of students," making it easy to fit in. A wise junior advises, "The important thing is to find your passions, your niche, and pursue it. In the process, you'll come upon like-minded students who share the same interests." "Most of the students here are part of the Greek life," telling us that fraternities and sororities are the best way to make friends and have fun (though others complain that "Greeks feel like they run the school," to the detriment of non-affiliated students). Even if you don't pledge, "the residential community helps build great friendships" for those who live on campus, and "because everyone is friendly most people find it easy to make friends."

FINANCIAL AID: 707-664-2389 • E-MAIL: STUDENT.OUTREACH@SONOMA.EDU • WEBSITE: WWW.SONOMA.EDU

THE PRINCETON REVIEW SAYS

Admissions

Very important factors considered include: GPA, rigor of secondary school record, standardized test scores. *Other factors considered include:* First generation, geographical residence, state residency. SAT or ACT required; ACT with or without Writing component accepted. TOEFL required of all international applicants. *Academic units required:* 4 English; 3 mathematics; 2 science; (1 science lab); 2 foreign language; 2 history; 1 academic elective; 1 visual/performing arts.

Financial Aid

Students should submit: FAFSA. The Princeton Review suggests that all financial aid forms be submitted as soon as possible after January 1. *Need-based scholarships/grants offered:* Federal Pell, SEOG, State scholarships/grants, private scholarships, *Loan aid offered:* Direct Subsidized Stafford Loans, Direct Unsubsidized Stafford Loans, Direct PLUS loans, Federal Perkins Loans. Federal Work-Study Program available. Institutional employment available. Off-campus job opportunities are good.

The Inside Word

SSU makes admissions decisions based on an "eligibility index" number, which is calculated using a student's standardized test scores and GPA; note that honors and advanced placement course work is weighted more heavily than regular courses in calculating a grade point average. Because of the school's budget problems, students applying for admission to impacted majors must meet a higher index number. Currently, impacted majors include communication studies, biology, kinesiology, liberal studies, pre-nursing, and psychology.

THE SCHOOL SAYS "..."

From the Admissions Office

"Sonoma State University occupies 269 acres in the beautiful wine country of Sonoma county, in northern California. Located at the foot of the Sonoma hills, the campus is an hour's drive north of San Francisco and centrally located between the Pacific Ocean to the west and the wine country to the north and east. SSU is deeply committed to the teaching of the liberal arts and sciences with selected professional programs. Within its thirty-four academic departments, SSU awards bachelor's degrees in forty-six areas of specialization and master's degrees in fifteen areas. In addition, the university offers a joint master's degree in mathematics with San Francisco State University and a joint Ed.D. with UC Davis.

"All freshmen applicants are required to provide SAT or ACT scores."

SELECTIVITY

Admissions Rating	66
# of applicants	14,272
% of applicants accepted	90
% of acceptees attending	14

FRESHMAN PROFILE

Range SAT Critical Reading	440–540
Range SAT Math	440–540
Range ACT Composite	18–23
Minimum paper TOEFL	500
Minimum web-based TOEFL	173
Average HS GPA	3.20

DEADLINES

Regular	
Priority	11/30
Deadline	11/30
Notification	3/1
Nonfall registration?	Yes

FINANCIAL FACTS

Financial Aid Rating	74
Annual in-state tuition	
Annual out-of-state tuition	$17,824
Room and board	$11,545
Required fees	$8,996
Books and supplies	$1,788
% needy frosh rec. need-based scholarship or grant aid	54
% needy UG rec. need-based scholarship or grant aid	63
% needy frosh rec. non-need-based scholarship or grant aid	17
% needy UG rec. non-need-based scholarship or grant aid	14
% needy frosh rec. need-based self-help aid	65
% needy UG rec. need-based self-help aid	66
% frosh rec. any financial aid	59
% UG rec. any financial aid	51
% UG borrow to pay for school	62
Average cumulative indebtedness	$20,461
% frosh need fully met	14
% ugrads need fully met	5
Average % of frosh need met	48
Average % of ugrad need met	27

SOUTHERN METHODIST UNIVERSITY

PO Box 750181, Dallas, TX 75275-0181 • Admissions: 214-768-3147 • Fax: 214-768-1083

CAMPUS LIFE

Quality of Life Rating	99
Fire Safety Rating	95
Green Rating	77
Type of school	Private
Affiliation	Methodist
Environment	Metropolis

STUDENTS

Total undergrad enrollment	6,295
% male/female	49/51
% from out of state	50
% frosh from public high school	52
% frosh live on campus	97
% ugrads live on campus	38
# of fraternities (% ugrad men join)	15 (32)
# of sororities (% ugrad women join)	13 (48)
% African American	5
% Asian	7
% Caucasian	66
% Hispanic	12
% Native American	<1
% international	7
# of countries represented	101

SURVEY SAYS . . .

Lots of conservative students
Students are happy
Classroom facilities are great
Lab facilities are great
Career services are great
Internships are widely available
School is well run
Students are friendly
Students get along with local community
Students love Dallas, TX
Great off-campus food
Dorms are like palaces
Campus feels safe
Athletic facilities are great
Lots of beer drinking
Frats and sororities are popular
Alumni active on campus

ACADEMICS

Academic Rating	77
% students returning for sophomore year	89
% students graduating within 4 years	67
% students graduating within 6 years	79
Calendar	Semester
Student/faculty ratio	11:1
Profs interesting rating	89
Profs accessible rating	91

Most classes have 10–19 students.
Most lab/discussion sessions have
30–39 students.

MOST POPULAR MAJORS
accounting; economics; finance

STUDENTS SAY "..."

Academics

Located on a tree-lined, "beautiful campus" in the heart of Dallas, Southern Methodist University is a mid-size private university with a lot going on. The school has a "unique culture" that relies on "top academics" and a "long-standing history of strong traditions" to build "incredible alumni support," which in turn brings students excellent internship and job opportunities. SMU offers everything "from a great social life and extracurricular activities to fun and interesting classes," including a "phenomenal business school" and "amazing" facilities. The school prides itself on being "a close-knit community of the intellectually elite," and this translates into "a wealth of academic resources [with which] to be successful, a flood of opportunities for those who want them, and thus a community of intellectuals who happen to genuinely care about each other." Professors are "incredibly gifted in their fields and exceptional communicators." They "love interacting with students" and "are willing to put in extra time to convey the material accurately to students." "If their office hours don't match yours, they will change their schedule to accommodate people," says a student. Most have worked in the industry that they teach in, and therefore they "can offer real-life connections to the material we learn." The syllabus is also modeled "to what you'll face in the real world." The legion of SMU alumni provides excellent connections into the business world (among others), and a "dedicated career services center" only sweetens the employment pot. Since many attend SMU for the Cox School of Business, it helps that the school is in the ideal location "to secure great jobs with Fortune 500 companies right here in Dallas." The school's administration also "understands that studying abroad, internships, extracurriculars, etc., also play a crucial role in developing students into the adults and professionals they want to become." "SMU puts the 'classy' back in classical education," says a student.

Life

Despite the fact it is located in the heart of Dallas, "the atmosphere is very calm and relaxing." SMU students frequently head to uptown Dallas "for fine dining and dancing" and often see movies, shop, and attend concerts and sports games. Everyone is always on campus for the football games for "boulevarding" ("basically tailgating but on steroids"), and "we love to have alums come visit us for the tailgate," says a student. Students generally fit in with this "a vibrant social life" best once they have found an extracurricular organization that is right for them, and oftentimes "sororities and fraternities tend to be this venue." However, some wish there was "less emphasis on Greek Life," since "if you're not Greek, you can sometimes feel left out or looked down on." Students devote a large portion of their time to their studies, but "there is always a social event every weekend night to blow off steam." This heavy concentration on future careers means that most here are "definitely wanting to become leaders in their field or profession," so "fraternity parties and formals are popular, but at the same time so are speeches from prominent members of the community and theatrical performances."

Student Body

This student body is "happy and leads a balanced life" at a school that it loves. Most students at SMU "tend to be a bit preppy," "polite," and tend to come from "influential backgrounds." Many "work a lot for pay or do internships," take a lot of class hours, "are involved...and have fun a lot." "They are very busy people, and they prefer it that way," says one student. All of these "motivated, outgoing," people "thrive on leadership" and are "dedicated to academics and involvement, both at SMU and in the greater community." Fashion "is a big part of SMU culture." This group is "very social" and frequently interacts with the Dallas community and "amazing arts and restaurant scene around campus."

SOUTHERN METHODIST UNIVERSITY

FINANCIAL AID: 214-768-3147 • E-MAIL: UGADMISSION@SMU.EDU • WEBSITE: WWW.SMU.EDU

THE PRINCETON REVIEW SAYS

Admissions

Very important factors considered include: Class rank, GPA, rigor of secondary school record, standardized test scores, application essay, recommendation(s). *Important factors considered include:* Extracurricular activities, talent/ability, character/personal qualities. *Other factors considered include:* First generation, racial/ethnic status, volunteer work, work experience, alumni/ae relations, level of applicant's interest. SAT or ACT required; ACT with or without Writing component accepted. TOEFL required of all international applicants. *Academic units required:* 4 English; 3 mathematics; 3 science; (2 science lab); 3 social studies; 2 foreign language. *Academic units recommended:* 4 English; 4 mathematics; 3 science; (2 science lab); 3 foreign language; 3 history; 3 academic electives.

Financial Aid

Students should submit: FAFSA, CSS/Financial Aid PROFILE, Noncustodial PROFILE. The Princeton Review suggests that all financial aid forms be submitted as soon as possible after January 1. *Need-based scholarships/grants offered:* Federal Pell, SEOG, State scholarships/grants, private scholarships, the school's own gift aid. *Loan aid offered:* Direct Subsidized Stafford Loans, Direct Unsubsidized Stafford Loans, Direct PLUS loans, Federal Perkins Loans, State Loans, College/university loans from institutional funds. Off-campus job opportunities are good.

The Inside Word

SMU boasts a potent combination: high-caliber academics, a desirable location, and a beautiful campus. No surprise then that gaining admission is challenging, and growing more so all the time. Solid high school grades and a compelling list of extracurricular activities will usually do the trick. "Special talent" students—aesthetes and athletes in particular—can make up for academic deficiencies; those in the arts must undergo an audition/portfolio review, while promising athletes are scouted. Except for those in the performing arts, all admitted students enter as "pre-majors" in the Dedman College of Humanities and Sciences.

THE SCHOOL SAYS ". . ."

From the Admissions Office

"SMU students are ambitious and motivated, balancing rigorous academics with a vibrant campus experience in the booming city of Dallas. Professors who are as dedicated to teaching as they are to their research give personal attention in small classes. With a diverse student body representing every state and more than 100 countries, students thrive in a community built on a convergence of ideas and backgrounds. Opportunities outside the classroom abound in the form of undergraduate research, internships, community service and study abroad programs. Unique to SMU is the campus in Taos, New Mexico, which offers credit-bearing experiential learning courses on the site of a 13th-century pueblo. On the main campus, the George W. Bush Presidential Center and renowned Tate Lecture Series offer students access to dignitaries ranging from former presidents to Nobel Laureates in a non-partisan context. Students can attend the more than 400 arts and cultural events on campus each year, or take in one of thousands more events in the nation's largest urban arts district, located in downtown Dallas. The more than 180 student organizations and Board of Trustees, which includes a voting student member, gives them the chance to hone their leadership skills. Generous merit scholarship programs enhance the financial aid offered to more than 70 percent of undergraduates. Top-rated career services and close ties with the global city of Dallas ensure students have access to some of the best graduate and professional schools in the nation and careers with firms recognized around the world."

SELECTIVITY

Admissions Rating	94
# of applicants	12,080
% of applicants accepted	51
% of acceptees attending	23
# offered a place on the wait list	1,496
% accepting a place on wait list	37
% admitted from wait list	33

FRESHMAN PROFILE

Range SAT Critical Reading	600–690
Range SAT Math	620–700
Range SAT Writing	590–680
Range ACT Composite	27–31
Minimum paper TOEFL	550
Minimum web-based TOEFL	80
Average HS GPA	3.65
% graduated top 10% of class	48
% graduated top 25% of class	80
% graduated top 50% of class	95

DEADLINES

Early decision	
Deadline	11/1
Notification	12/31
Early action	
Deadline	11/1
Notification	12/31
Regular	
Priority	1/16
Deadline	1/15
Nonfall registration?	Yes

APPLICANTS ALSO LOOK AT AND OFTEN PREFER
University of Southern California; Duke University; New York University

AND SOMETIMES PREFER
Vanderbilt University; Boston University

AND RARELY PREFER
Texas Christian University; Tulane University

FINANCIAL FACTS

Financial Aid Rating	89
Annual tuition	$40,770
Room and board	$14,645
Required fees	$5,170
Books and supplies	$800
% needy frosh rec. need-based scholarship or grant aid	65
% needy UG rec. need-based scholarship or grant aid	75
% needy frosh rec. non-need-based scholarship or grant aid	73
% needy UG rec. non-need-based scholarship or grant aid	65
% needy frosh rec. need-based self-help aid	75
% needy UG rec. need-based self-help aid	83
% frosh rec. any financial aid	75
% UG rec. any financial aid	73
% UG borrow to pay for school	39
Average cumulative indebtedness	$29,829
% frosh need fully met	38
% ugrads need fully met	31
Average % of frosh need met	87
Average % of ugrad need met	86

SOUTHWESTERN UNIVERSITY

ADMISSIONS OFFICE, GEORGETOWN, TX 78627-0770 • ADMISSIONS: 512-863-1200 • FAX: 512-863-9601

CAMPUS LIFE

Quality of Life Rating	88
Fire Safety Rating	93
Green Rating	93
Type of school	Private
Affiliation	Methodist
Environment	Town

STUDENTS

Total undergrad enrollment	1,535
% male/female	43/57
% from out of state	12
% frosh from public school	81
% frosh live on campus	100
% ugrads live on campus	77
# of fraternities	4
# of sororities	4
% African American	5
% Asian	4
% Caucasian	67
% Hispanic	19
% Native American	1
% international	1
# of countries represented	9

SURVEY SAYS . . .

Students are happy
Career services are great
No one cheats
Students are friendly
Campus feels safe
Easy to get around campus

ACADEMICS

Academic Rating	90
% students returning for sophomore year	87
% students graduating within 4 years	67
% students graduating within 6 years	74
Calendar	Semester
Student/faculty ratio	11:1
Profs interesting rating	94
Profs accessible rating	90

Most classes have 10–19 students.
Most lab/discussion sessions have fewer
  than 10 students.

MOST POPULAR MAJORS

business/commerce; biology; English
language and literature

STUDENTS SAY ". . ."

Academics

One of Texas' top-ranked universities, Southwestern offers students a "welcoming environment" and invites them to become part of a "close community" of scholars. "Small and rigorous," undergrads here truly appreciate that Southwestern "focuses heavily on student development and improvement." Though at times they might complain about the "huge work load," many value the fact that they're really learning "to think critically" and gaining "leadership skills." Impressively, a number of students feels that the university really imbues them with "the love for knowledge." Undergrads are quick to praise their professors, noting that they "sincerely care about their students' education" and are always "willing to help students in any way they can." For the most part, they encourage "participation, whether it is a class discussion or in the middle of a lecture, which allows you to get a feel for the real core of whatever topic you're studying." One history major does caution, "Don't expect to just show up and succeed—you're going to have to work." Fortunately, though the academics might be "challenging," professors are always ready to "meet with you whenever you need guidance or clarification on an assignment." Overall, the university provides a "very engaging learning experience" and allows undergrads to reach their "full potential." And as this supremely satisfied student shares, Southwestern is "the best liberal arts school you've never heard of."

Life

Though students at Southwestern are "very focused on their studies," many also try and take advantage of the myriad activities happening around campus. Fraternities and sororities are fairly popular here, and "Greek life provides the main entertainment for students if they're into the partying scene." However, don't fret if you fear that frat life isn't for you; they're not the only game in town. As one math and music double-major tells us, "There are plenty of opportunities to see shows put on by the theater department, concerts of all types, or recitals. The school also brings in music groups like Cake or Spoon or comedians like Eric O'Shea for Friday Night Live every week." Additionally, campus sponsored events like "movie nights" and "casino nights" are usually well-attended. Undergrads also appreciate leisure time outdoors and students can frequently be found "lounging on the academic mall or riding their bikes to the local park." Though some students find that the surrounding Georgetown area offers "little to do," others enjoy taking advantage of the local "movie theater or bowling alley." As when undergrads are anxious for a little more action, they often head to nearby Austin.

Student Body

Southwestern attracts "intelligent," academically inclined students who fortunately don't "obsess over their grades." They manage to be both "studious" and "fun-loving" and are typically "swamped with a million activities." Though it's a small school, undergrads assure us that "everybody finds their niche somewhere." Indeed, people at Southwestern are "warm," "friendly," and "pretty approachable." An English major adds, "Students are willing to make friends with just about anyone." While the majority are "white, middle- or upper-middle-class, [and] Christian" there are students "from every race, religion, and background," and many people are "open-minded." A large number of students are "in sororities/fraternities," and "liberals outnumber conservatives." Further, most "people dress fairly conservatively, but it is not unheard of to see colored hair, Disturbed t-shirts, or a random guy in a skirt." Perhaps this English and business double-major says it best: "It doesn't take long to find some people you fit in with at school, because you find so many types of people here that it is hard to feel like an outcast."

SOUTHWESTERN UNIVERSITY

FINANCIAL AID: 512-863-1259 • E-MAIL: ADMISSION@SOUTHWESTERN.EDU • WEBSITE: WWW.SOUTHWESTERN.EDU

THE PRINCETON REVIEW SAYS

Admissions

Very important factors considered include: Class rank, GPA, rigor of secondary school record, standardized test scores, application essay, recommendation(s). *Important factors considered include:* Extracurricular activities, first generation, geographical residence, interview, racial/ethnic status, talent/ability, volunteer work, work experience, alumni/ae relations, character/personal qualities, level of applicant's interest. TOEFL required of all international applicants. *Academic units required:* 4 English; 4 mathematics; 3 science; (2 science lab); 2 social studies; 2 foreign language; 1 history; 1 academic elective. *Academic units recommended:* 4 English; 4 mathematics; 4 science; (3 science lab); 3 social studies; 3 foreign language; 2 history.

Financial Aid

Students should submit: FAFSA. Regular filing deadline is 3/1. The Princeton Review suggests that all financial aid forms be submitted as soon as possible after January 1. *Need-based scholarships/grants offered:* Federal Pell, SEOG, State scholarships/grants, private scholarships, the school's own gift aid. *Loan aid offered:* Direct Subsidized Stafford Loans, Direct Unsubsidized Stafford Loans, Direct PLUS loans, Federal Perkins Loans, State Loans, College/university loans from institutional funds. Federal Work-Study Program available. Institutional employment available. Off-campus job opportunities are good.

The Inside Word

Successful applicants to Southwestern demonstrate intellectual curiosity and a strong desire to participate in an active collegiate community. Students need to be well-rounded and highly motivated. The vast majority of those who receive that coveted thick envelope are in the top quarter of their class and have above-average SAT scores.

THE SCHOOL SAYS "..."

From the Admissions Office

"Southwestern is the leading liberal arts institution in Texas. As Texas's first institution of higher learning, Southwestern has been providing students with a distinctive, values-centered education since 1840. Our tree-lined residential campus is everything you imagine when you dream about going to college, and then some. Grand, century-old limestone buildings accent the heart of campus, offering spacious sports and recreational facilities, multiple research laboratories, two live-performance theaters, roomy residence halls, and so much more. Our community Pirate Bike program is unlike anything in Texas. These bright yellow bikes scattered across campus are ready to ride anytime, day or night.The Paideia (pī•dā•ə) experience introduces students to intentional connections. Through collaboration, participation in civic engagement activities, intercultural learning experiences and undergraduate research, students think across the disciplines to form new solutions, ultimately integrating their knowledge, high-level problem solving skills and deep learning as they apply their scholarship to essential questions of the world around them. The results are impressive, Post Graduate Survey data for 2012 reports that 91% of students are either employed, attending medical, law and other professional schools or pursuing advanced studies.Georgetown has much to offer, but if at the end of the day you are in the mood for a quick drive, grab your friends and help 'Keep Austin Weird!' Experience SXSW Music, Film and Interactive, ACL Music Festival, or face your fears at Bat Fest. What's more, with the year-round sunshine and a wealth of recreational activities within your reach, the outdoors becomes a popular playground."

SELECTIVITY

Admissions Rating	88
# of applicants	2,456
% of applicants accepted	52
% of acceptees attending	27
# offered a place on the wait list	42
% accepting a place on wait list	17
% admitted from wait list	0

FRESHMAN PROFILE

Range SAT Critical Reading	520–640
Range SAT Math	353–640
Range ACT Composite	22–29
Minimum paper TOEFL	550
Minimum web-based TOEFL	88
% graduated top 10% of class	37
% graduated top 25% of class	72
% graduated top 50% of class	95

DEADLINES

Early action	
Deadline	11/15
Notification	2/15
Regular	
Priority	2/1
Notification	4/1
Nonfall registration?	Yes

APPLICANTS ALSO LOOK AT AND OFTEN PREFER
Trinity University

AND SOMETIMES PREFER
Texas A&M University—College Station; The University of Texas at Austin; Austin College; Rhodes College

AND RARELY PREFER
Texas Christian University; Baylor University; Rice University; Hendrix University

FINANCIAL FACTS

Financial Aid Rating	89
Annual tuition	$36,120
Room and board	$11,760
Books and supplies	$1,200
% needy frosh rec. need-based scholarship or grant aid	100
% needy UG rec. need-based scholarship or grant aid	99
% needy frosh rec. non-need-based scholarship or grant aid	99
% needy UG rec. non-need-based scholarship or grant aid	95
% needy frosh rec. need-based self-help aid	81
% needy UG rec. need-based self-help aid	84
% frosh rec. any financial aid	99
% UG rec. any financial aid	95
% UG borrow to pay for school	51
Average cumulative indebtedness	$34.997 %
frosh need fully mot	25
% ugrads need fully met	30
Average % of frosh need met	87
Average % of ugrad need met	88

SPELMAN COLLEGE

350 SPELMAN LANE, SOUTHWEST, ATLANTA, GA 30314-4399 • ADMISSIONS: 404-270-5193 • FAX: 404-270-5201

CAMPUS LIFE

Quality of Life Rating	79
Fire Safety Rating	92
Green Rating	88
Type of school	Private
Affiliation	No Affiliation
Environment	Metropolis

STUDENTS

Total undergrad enrollment	2,129
% male/female	0/100
% from out of state	73
% frosh from public high school	84
% frosh live on campus	92
% ugrads live on campus	69
# of sororities	6
% African American	85
% Asian	<1
% Caucasian	0
% Hispanic	<1
% Native American	<1
% international	1
# of countries represented	11

SURVEY SAYS . . .
Students are happy
Lab facilities are great
Career services are great
Campus feels safe
Frats and sororities are popular
Active student government

ACADEMICS

Academic Rating	82
% students returning for sophomore year	88
% students graduating within 4 years	64
% students graduating within 6 years	73
Calendar	Semester
Student/faculty ratio	10:1
Profs interesting rating	77
Profs accessible rating	73

Most classes have 10–19 students.
Most lab/discussion sessions have 10–19 students.

MOST POPULAR MAJORS
psychology; political science; English
language and literature

STUDENTS SAY ". . ."

Academics

A historically black women's institution, Spelman College has built a strong reputation for "molding intelligent, goal-oriented young ladies into determined, successful, free-thinking women." Many prospective students are attracted to the school's "powerful history," including the "long list of successful, educated, strong, black women who have attended Spelman College" during the century since its founding. Once on campus, students are happy to report that Spelman's "professors are committed to the mission of the school," and they really "bring out the best" in their students. In the classroom, students are "encouraged to state our opinions," and professors "allow room for us to challenge and discuss what they present." You'll definitely work hard to stay afloat in this "challenging academic environment," because professors "do not allow for even a minute amount of slacking when it comes to completing assignments and being on time for class." Fortunately, there are "many academic resources available to help us, such as tutoring services and a writing center." Plus, the majority of Spelman professors "take additional time outside of instructional time to assist their students" with course work. Of particular note, Spelman is "very focused on the sciences and improving the number of African American women in this field, and they offer many facilities, faculty, and opportunities" for advanced study. As graduation approaches, the "Career Counseling Center is extremely strong and has helped numerous students find employment and graduate school placements." While the future looks bright for Spelman grads, many say this private institution could better serve its students by freeing up "more money for scholarships and financial aid."

Life

There's a "strong sense of tradition and loyalty" on the Spelman campus, and most students are deeply involved in the community. From service groups to sororities, "there are so many organizations and clubs that you're bound to find one that fits you." There are tons of "opportunities to obtain leadership positions" outside the classroom, and many students are "very involved in campus life." A first-year student details, "In my freshman year already, I've walked in a fashion show, I was crowned Miss Glee Club, I write for the campus newspaper, and I play on the softball team." There's a constant buzz of activity on campus, and "informational forums, career fairs, college fairs, performances, and sporting events are at the forefront of everyone's campus life." Socially, "Greek Life is quite important at Spelman College, but isn't a must." Even if you don't join a sorority, "there are a lot of social events on campus," and two other historically black colleges, Clark Atlanta and Morehouse, "are only inches away." Spelman undergrads say, "The camaraderie between the schools is great," and "joint homecoming with Morehouse is the highlight of the entire year." Off campus, students "go skating, bowling, and to Six Flags Over Georgia, as well as to Atlanta Falcons, Hawks, and Braves." Nearby, Atlantic Station is home to "a major movie theater, shopping, restaurants, and a bowling alley."

Student Body

Spelman College is "full of warm, welcoming, sisterly, and highly educated African American women." A unique environment, "Spelman College offers a chance for African American women to be the majority," and students appreciate being "surrounded and empowered by other young, intelligent, and goal-oriented women like myself." At the same time, "the institution promotes diversity within the student body," and Spelman women "come in all shapes and sizes and from all walks of life, though linked by our African descent. Anyone can find their place here." Confidence and individuality are prized at Spelman, and the typical undergraduate "speaks her mind, wears what she wants, [and] is comfortable in her own skin, yet she has empathy and a strong sense of social justice." Many students "love to do service for the community" and are involved in philanthropic projects around Atlanta. Spelman women are "hardworking and focused on academics." However, most are "excellent at balancing a full course load and an active social life."

FINANCIAL AID: 404-270-5222 • E-MAIL: ADMISS@SPELMAN.EDU • WEBSITE: WWW.SPELMAN.EDU

THE PRINCETON REVIEW SAYS

Admissions

Very important factors considered include: GPA, rigor of secondary school record, standardized test scores, recommendation(s), character/personal qualities. *Important factors considered include:* Application essay, extracurricular activities. *Other factors considered include:* Class rank, first generation, geographical residence, talent/ability, volunteer work, work experience, alumni/ae relations, level of applicant's interest. SAT or ACT required; ACT with or without Writing component accepted. TOEFL required of all international applicants. *Academic units required:* 4 English; 3 mathematics; 3 science; (2 science lab); 3 social studies; 3 foreign language; 2 history; 2 academic electives. *Academic units recommended:* 4 English; 4 mathematics; 4 science; (3 science lab); 4 social studies; 4 foreign language; 3 history.

Financial Aid

Students should submit: FAFSA, State aid form. The Princeton Review suggests that all financial aid forms be submitted as soon as possible after January 1. *Need-based scholarships/grants offered:* Federal Pell, SEOG, State scholarships/grants, private scholarships, the school's own gift aid, United Negro College Fund. *Loan aid offered:* Direct Subsidized Stafford Loans, Direct Unsubsidized Stafford Loans, Direct PLUS loans, Federal Perkins Loans, State Loans. Applicants will be notified of awards beginning 2/15. Federal Work-Study Program available. Institutional employment available. Off-campus job opportunities are good.

The Inside Word

The best way to prepare for admission to Spelman is to pursue a strong, precollege academic curriculum during high school. In 2010, admitted students had an average GPA of 3.65. Students who are particularly interested in Spelman have two early application options: early decision, which is binding, and early notification, which is nonbinding, but allows students to receive a response more quickly.

THE SCHOOL SAYS "..."

From the Admissions Office

"As an outstanding Historically Black College for women, Spelman strives for academic excellence in liberal arts education. This predominantly residential private college provides students with an academic climate conducive to the full development of their intellectual and leadership potential. The college is a member of the Atlanta University Center consortium, and Spelman students enjoy the benefits of a small college while having access to the resources of the other three participating institutions. The purpose extends beyond intellectual development and professional career preparation of students. It seeks to develop the total person. The college provides an academic and social environment that strengthens those qualities that enable women to be self-confident as well as culturally and spiritually enriched. This environment attempts to instill in students both an appreciation for the multicultural communities of the world and a sense of responsibility for bringing about positive change in those communities.

"Applicants for are required to submit standardized test scores from an appropriate venue (i.e., ACT, TOEFL, SAT). The highest composite score will be used in admissions decisions. Writing scores from either the SAT or ACT will not be taken into consideration in the admission process."

SELECTIVITY

Admissions Rating	88
# of applicants	5,123
% of applicants accepted	41
% of acceptees attending	24

FRESHMAN PROFILE

Range SAT Critical Reading	470–570
Range SAT Math	460–550
Range ACT Composite	20–24
Minimum paper TOEFL	559
Minimum web-based TOEFL	250
Average HS GPA	3.55
% graduated top 10% of class	35
% graduated top 25% of class	38
% graduated top 50% of class	52

DEADLINES

Early decision	
Deadline	11/1
Notification	12/15
Early action	
Deadline	11/15
Notification	12/31
Regular	
Deadline	2/1
Notification	4/1
Nonfall registration?	No

APPLICANTS ALSO LOOK AT AND OFTEN PREFER

Georgia Institute of Technology

AND SOMETIMES PREFER

Howard University; Hampton University; Florida A&M University; Tuskegee University

AND RARELY PREFER

University of Georgia; Emory University; University of Maryland; College Park

FINANCIAL FACTS

Financial Aid Rating	67
Annual tuition	$21,309
Room and board	$11,945
Required fees	$3,325
Books and supplies	$2,000
% needy frosh rec. need-based scholarship or grant aid	84
% needy UG rec. need-based scholarship or grant aid	85
% needy frosh rec. non-need-based scholarship or grant aid	0
% needy UG rec. non-need-based scholarship or grant aid	0
% needy frosh rec. need-based self-help aid	75
% needy UG rec. need-based self-help aid	80
% frosh rec. any financial aid	94
% UG rec. any financial aid	93
% UG borrow to pay for school	72
Average cumulative indebtedness	$35,168
% frosh need fully met	7
% ugrads need fully met	6
Average % of frosh need met	37
Average % of ugrad need met	40

ST. BONAVENTURE UNIVERSITY

3261 WEST STATE ROAD, BONAVENTURE, NY 14778 • ADMISSIONS: 716-375-2400 • FAX: 716-375-4005

STUDENTS SAY " . . . "

Academics

Uniting a liberal arts education with "Franciscan values," St. Bonaventure University is a small Catholic school that succeeds in "shaping its students into well-rounded, intelligent, and good people." Many students choose St. Bonaventure for its "nationally recognized journalism program" or for one of several prestigious "dual-admissions programs with medical, dental, physical therapy, and pharmacy schools" in the region. No matter what their major, undergrads must complete the Clare College curriculum, which provides an "overall liberal arts education" mixed with religion and philosophy. While students are encouraged to "become extraordinary" and ethics are woven into the curriculum, "religion is by no means forced on you," despite the college's Catholic heritage. Within major departments, "classes are no larger than thirty students per classroom" and "professors are always available if you need help." Talented instructors "make class both fun and informative," and most "do a good job at engaging the class and promoting discussion" between students. "The school is very focused on making successful graduates, and not just in the classroom"; therefore, the curriculum "puts a huge emphasis on real-world experience in a student's field, whether it is journalism, business, or education." Students are further benefited by the school's "amazing alumni network" in and around New York State. While engaging and worthwhile, "academics are serious, no matter your major." However, "a steady effort will get you good grades" in most Bonaventure classes, and students appreciate the fact that "the school isn't super-competitive like the Ivy League schools. Students are willing to help each other out, and there's no cutthroat competition for internships or job interviews."

Life

Outgoing and social, students enjoy a classic college lifestyle in the "Bona bubble." "November to March is Bonnies' basketball season," and attending games is a universally popular pastime. There's also an active intramural sports program, and many students "love going to the fitness center on campus" to work out or take classes. "Student involvement in the radio station is huge," and many claim, "WSBU is the best college radio station in the country." Because the school is located in upstate New York, "it is ridiculously snowy" in the winter months and there's little to do in surrounding Olean, a "very, very small town." "People drink, snowboard, or leave for Buffalo." On campus, "nearly everyone parties every Friday and Saturday." A student elaborates, "Occasionally people will go to the movies or order in and have a quiet night in the dorm, but parties are definitely the big plans on the weekend." At the same time, "there are options for people who do not want to party and drink." In particular, "The Campus Activities Board always has something going on." By the time they graduate, most Bonas share "a lifetime bond forged over beer, basketball, and the worst weather ever."

Student Body

St. Bonaventure students describe their classmates as "hardworking, religious, fun-loving, outgoing, involved in many activities, friendly, and accepting." "Everyone loves sports, as evidenced by the huge intramural program," and "nearly all students love to party." Demographically similar, most undergraduates are "white and from the tristate area." However, the "student body is becoming increasingly diverse" and currently includes students "from all different age groups and backgrounds." Despite the school's religious affiliation, "not everyone is Catholic," and politically speaking, "there are some diehard conservatives, but most people are pretty open-minded." When it comes to social groups, you'll meet plenty of East Coast preppies, but also "edgy kids who work at the campus radio station and listen to underground music." With extracurricular activities catering to a wide range of interests, "it's easy to make friends and find a good fit" at St. Bonaventure. There are some cliques; however, most "people tend to branch out of their comfort zone" to make friends.

FINANCIAL AID: 800-462-5050 • E-MAIL: ADMISSIONS@SBU.EDU • WEBSITE: WWW.SBU.EDU

THE PRINCETON REVIEW SAYS

Admissions

Very important factors considered include: GPA, rigor of secondary school record, recommendation(s), character/personal qualities. *Important factors considered include:* Standardized test scores, application essay, extracurricular activities, talent/ability, volunteer work. *Other factors considered include:* Class rank, first generation, geographical residence, interview, state residency, work experience, alumni/ae relations, level of applicant's interest. SAT or ACT required; SAT and SAT Subject Tests or ACT required for some; ACT with or without Writing component accepted. TOEFL required of all international applicants. *Academic units recommended:* 4 English; 3 mathematics; 3 science; (3 science lab); 4 social studies; 2 foreign language.

Financial Aid

Students should submit: FAFSA, State aid form. The Princeton Review suggests that all financial aid forms be submitted as soon as possible after January 1. *Need-based scholarships/grants offered:* Federal Pell, SEOG, State scholarships/grants, private scholarships, the school's own gift aid. *Loan aid offered:* Direct Subsidized Stafford Loans, Direct Unsubsidized Stafford Loans, Direct PLUS loans, Federal Perkins Loans. Applicants will be notified of awards beginning 3/1. Federal Work-Study Program available. Institutional employment available. Off-campus job opportunities are fair.

The Inside Word

There's no admissions formula at St. Bonaventure. Here, prospective students are evaluated individually and accepted based on their capacity for success in college. Though St. Bonaventure recommends that applicants submit academic transcripts, standardized test scores, recommendations, and a personal essay, the admissions committee will consider any other supporting materials that prove a student's overall eligibility for admission. St. Bonaventure has a rolling admissions program, so applications are reviewed as soon as they arrive at the admissions office.

THE SCHOOL SAYS "..."

From the Admissions Office

"The St. Bonaventure University family has been imparting an extraordinary Franciscan tradition to men and women of a rich diversity of backgrounds for more than 150 years. This tradition encourages all who become a part of it to face the world confidently, respect the earthly environment, and work for productive change in the world. Every student participates in community service, and many make it their primary co-curricular activity. The charm of our campus and the inspirational beauty of the surrounding hills provide a special place where growth in learning and living is abundantly realized. St. Bonaventure establishes pathways to internships, graduate schools and careers through its innovate Career and Professional Readiness Center, which engages students from the time they step onto campus. The Richter Recreation Center provides all students with state-of-the-art facilities for athletics and wellness. As a student at one of the smallest Division I schools in the country, you get the benefits of big-time sports along with those of a small, student-centered university. St. Bonaventure is a member of the Atlantic 10.

"Academics at St. Bonaventure are challenging. Small classes and personalized attention encourage individual growth and development. St. Bonaventure's nationally known schools of Arts and Sciences, Business, Journalism & Mass Communication, and Education offers more than forty-five majors. The School of Graduate Studies also offers several programs leading to the master's degree.

"Applicants can submit SAT or ACT scores. The biology Subject Test is required only for students applying to one of our many dual-degree medical programs."

SELECTIVITY

Admissions Rating	69
# of applicants	2,754
% of applicants accepted	80
% of acceptees attending	20

FRESHMAN PROFILE

Range SAT Critical Reading	460–580
Range SAT Math	470–600
Range SAT Writing	450–570
Range ACT Composite	21–27
Minimum paper TOEFL	550
Minimum web-based TOEFL	213
Average HS GPA	3.30
% graduated top 10% of class	14
% graduated top 25% of class	35
% graduated top 50% of class	68

DEADLINES

Regular	
Priority	2/15
Deadline	7/1
Nonfall registration?	Yes

APPLICANTS ALSO LOOK AT AND RARELY PREFER
Syracuse University

FINANCIAL FACTS

Financial Aid Rating	81
Annual tuition	$28,624
Room and board	$10,715
Required fees	$1,380
Books and supplies	$800
% needy frosh rec. need-based scholarship or grant aid	100
% needy UG rec. need-based scholarship or grant aid	100
% needy frosh rec. non-need-based scholarship or grant aid	94
% needy UG rec. non-need-based scholarship or grant aid	94
% needy frosh rec. need-based self-help aid	74
% needy UG rec. need-based self-help aid	78
% frosh rec. any financial aid	99
% UG rec. any financial aid	99
% UG borrow to pay for school	78
Average cumulative indebtedness	$36,208
% frosh need fully met	20
% ugrads need fully met	20
Average % of frosh need met	72
Average % of ugrad need met	75

ST. JOHN'S COLLEGE (MD)

60 COLLEGE AVE., ANNAPOLIS, MD 21401 • ADMISSIONS: 410-626-2522 • FAX: 410-269-7916

CAMPUS LIFE

Quality of Life Rating	78
Fire Safety Rating	94
Green Rating	66
Type of school	Private
Affiliation	No Affiliation
Environment	Small city

STUDENTS

Total undergrad enrollment	443
% male/female	55/45
% from out of state	72
% frosh from public high school	60
% frosh live on campus	94
% ugrads live on campus	78
% African American	2
% Asian	2
% Caucasian	70
% Hispanic	6
% Native American	<1
% international	11
# of countries represented	28

SURVEY SAYS . . .

Class discussions are encouraged
No one cheats
Frats and sororities are unpopular
or nonexistent

ACADEMICS

Academic Rating	93
% students returning for sophomore year	90
% students graduating within 4 years	52
% students graduating within 6 years	61
Calendar	Semester
Student/faculty ratio	8:1
Profs interesting rating	94
Profs accessible rating	94
Most classes have 10–19 students.	

MOST POPULAR MAJORS
liberal arts

STUDENTS SAY ". . ."

Academics

St. John's College is a "one of a kind" institution, which "teaches its students how to think for themselves" through a series of rigorous, discussion-based seminars. Here, every student follows the same academic curriculum, which consists entirely of "reading and discussing the great books of Western civilization." Students study "math, science, philosophy, language, history, and literature," and then, through in-class debate, are "encouraged to question everything, develop their own logical conclusions, and understand Western thought starting at the basics." The school's "brilliant" professors (known as tutors in St. John's parlance) gently oversee class discussions, though they're "more like moderators" in that they "do not lecture or 'teach' in the traditional sense." Tutors always "treat the students as equals," and "outside of class, they are available and friendly." A current undergrad relates, "The fact that tutors are always available (for lunch, coffee, or just to chat with a student) is wonderful. I have had many delightful discussions with tutors outside of class on topics ranging from Baudelaire to quantum mechanics." With tons of assigned reading and provoking in-class debates, the curriculum is "difficult and taxing, yet supremely rewarding." Tutors "don't cut you slack if you don't deserve it," and most "have high expectations" for their students throughout the semester. "Grades are sometimes based on a tutor's subjective opinion of the student's personality," which can be frustrating for those accustomed to receiving top marks. "Work is sometimes stressful, and the material is often difficult," but students reassure us that "there is always someone to work through it with you, and you can always ask for help."

Life

There's no strict division between study and social life at St. John's. "Discussions from in class spill out into the quad." While most Johnnies say their school is sublime, they also warn that, "If you don't like endlessly talking about books, you'll feel oppressed by the social scene at St. John's." While "school is intense and exhausting," students "rarely differentiate between schoolwork and lives outside of class." On this quirky campus, "fun can be translating Greek or it can be taking a nap; it can be playing intramurals or drinking a beer and watching 'les sportifs' run around; it can be making music or researching Appalachian folk songs." For a lighter evening, students attend "school-run dance parties" or get together for "hard liquor, film noir, classical books, cigarettes, and being off on an adventure." "Impromptu trips off campus are frequent," and students head to Annapolis for "sailing, watching tourists, bowling, [or] ice skating." In addition, "many students participate in the excellent intramural sports program," which includes "soccer, football, Ultimate Frisbee, basketball, croquet, crew, fencing, aikido, boxing, and more." Social dance is also remarkably popular, and there are "swing dancing parties on a regular basis."

Student Body

The unusual St. John's curriculum tends to attract students who are "intellectual, very thoughtful, and inclined to discuss Aristotle, Hobbes, or Tolstoy at the dinner table." Talkative and analytical, St. John's students are "always down for a good conversation, whether one-on-one or in a group, whether the topic is personal or impersonal." "Students come from across the country and around the world, from all religious, political, and economic backgrounds," though there's a noticeable "proliferation of East Coast preppies and hipsters." "The diversity of personalities is astounding," and, exclusivity is minimized on this "friendly" campus. "Because the school is so small, and because of the universal curriculum, by your senior year you have a pretty strong bond with your entire class." Activists and pop culture junkies take note: "If you're interested in current events, or pretty much anything that happened after, say, 1925, it can sometimes be hard to find people who know what you're talking about."

FINANCIAL AID: 410-626-2502 • E-MAIL: ANNAPOLIS.ADMISSIONS@SJC.EDU • WEBSITE: WWW.STJOHNSCOLLEGE.EDU

THE PRINCETON REVIEW SAYS

Admissions

Very important factors considered include: Rigor of secondary school record, application essay, recommendation(s), level of applicant's interest. *Important factors considered include:* Interview, character/personal qualities. *Other factors considered include:* Class rank, academic GPA, standardized test scores, extra-curricular activities, talent/ability, volunteer work, work experience. SAT and SAT Subject Tests or ACT considered if submitted; ACT with or without Writing component accepted. TOEFL required of all international applicants. *Academic units required:* 3 mathematics; 2 foreign language. *Academic units recommended:* 4 English, 3-4 mathematics, 3 science, 2-3 foreign language, 3 social studies.

Financial Aid

Students should submit: FAFSA, State aid form, Noncustodial PROFILE. The Princeton Review suggests that all financial aid forms be submitted as soon as possible after January 1. *Need-based scholarships/grants offered:* Federal Pell, SEOG, State scholarships/grants, private scholarships, the school's own gift aid. *Loan aid offered:* Direct Subsidized Stafford Loans, Direct Unsubsidized Stafford Loans, Direct PLUS loans, Federal Perkins Loans, College/university loans from institutional funds. Federal Work-Study Program available. Institutional employment available. Off-campus job opportunities are good.

The Inside Word

St. John's is a unique environment, best suited to students of a quirky yet serious intellectual predilection. To test the waters before you jump in, consider taking a campus tour or even sitting in on an active tutorial session with students. You can also send your questions about the school to a current student through the St. John's website. Each applicant is evaluated individually for potential success in the program. Among application materials, SAT/ACT scores are an optional component.

THE SCHOOL SAYS " . . ."

From the Admissions Office

"St. John's College offers a unique and transformative education for the intellectually adventurous. Across a wide-ranging, interdisciplinary curriculum, students read and discuss foundational works of Western philosophy, literature, history, political science, theology, economics, music, mathematics, and the laboratory sciences. Classes are small (14-20 students) and conducted as conversational seminars in which students assume a leadership role. The college's coeducational community, without religious affiliation, takes an open-minded approach to ideas of all kinds. St. John's students are asked to reach their own conclusions about questions that have been the subject of human inquiry from prehistory yet still have great relevance to contemporary problems.

All students at St. John's College earn a B.A. in Liberal Arts. There are no majors and no departments; the four-year curriculum is a unified, all-required whole. Each year's work lays the foundation for the next. The Program's structure, rather than making distinctions between "sciences" and "humanities," encourages students to see the interrelatedness of modes of human thought.

In 1964, a second campus was opened in historic Santa Fe, a cultural center and the capital of New Mexico. With a shared curriculum, students can alternate their studies between Annapolis and Santa Fe without sacrificing any time toward graduation, quality of instruction, or benefit of the curriculum. More than a third of students spend at least a year on both campuses. The college also offers a Summer Academy for rising high school juniors and seniors, a great way to try this remarkable academic experience on for size."

SELECTIVITY

Admissions Rating	84
# of applicants	342
% of applicants accepted	81
% of acceptees attending	45

FRESHMAN PROFILE

Range SAT Critical Reading	600–720
Range SAT Math	550–690
Range ACT Composite	27–30
Minimum paper TOEFL	600
Minimum web-based TOEFL	100
% graduated top 10% of class	19
% graduated top 25% of class	37
% graduated top 50% of class	77

DEADLINES

Early Action	
Deadline	11/15
Notification	12/15
Regular	
Priority	3/1
Nonfall registration?	No

APPLICANTS ALSO LOOK AT AND OFTEN PREFER

The University of Chicago; Williams College; Oberlin College; Emory University; Sarah Lawrence College

AND SOMETIMES PREFER

Wellesley College; Kenyon College; Smith College; Bard College; Carleton College

AND RARELY PREFER

Moravian College; Middlebury College; Antioch College

FINANCIAL FACTS

Financial Aid Rating	75
Annual tuition	$45,846
Room and board	$10,954
Required fees	$450
Books and supplies	$630
% needy frosh rec. need-based scholarship or grant aid	100
% needy UG rec. need-based scholarship or grant aid	97
% needy frosh rec. non-need-based scholarship or grant aid	23
% needy UG rec. non-need-based scholarship or grant aid	9
% needy frosh rec. need-based self-help aid	99
% needy UG rec. need-based self-help aid	98
% frosh rec. any financial aid	100
% UG rec. any financial aid	84
% UG borrow to pay for school	78
Average cumulative indebtedness	$25,510
% frosh need fully met	31
% ugrads need fully met	10

St. John's College (NM)

1160 Camino Cruz Blanca, Santa Fe, NM 87505 • Admissions: 505-984-6060 • Fax: 505-984-6162

STUDENTS SAY "..."

Academics

St. John's College in Santa Fe operates on a similar program as the Annapolis campus: Students read and explore a common body of "great books"—including many of the most important books in history—in close partnership with their classmates and teachers. Every professor "must teach (learn) Euclid, Plato, and Darwin, whether he or she has a Ph.D. in mathematics, classics, or biology." This common curriculum and dedication to the liberal arts means that "students are respected for what they can bring, and need never feel self-conscious about whether they're 'smart enough.'" Everywhere you look, there is a "commitment, sincerity, and passion for learning of the community and the faculty." This truly is an academic community that sincerely loves "the journey in its pursuit of knowledge, not simply the destination." The "liberation of the mind" at SJC comes primarily by means of the Socratic Method. SJC does not have professors, but tutors, who are there not to lecture, but to "help lead the class through the curriculum." The tutors are "very different in personality," but also "very knowledgeable and excitable about what we do." As experienced academics, they are "skillful when it comes to managing the classroom discussions and helping students articulate their thoughts" and are "truly open-minded and give everyone a chance to give participate." "They really care about their students and treat us as peers in the classroom since they consider themselves also to be constantly learning." "Everyone shares fundamental values of how to treat others in the classroom," says a student. The greatest asset of SJC is the community; with everyone on board this nontraditional learning train, it's hard not to be at your best. "You're thinking nonstop at SJC," says a student. Though the self-selecting student body pretty much ensures success, students can choose how connected they wish to be to the rest of the school. "You can go four years without having an interaction with the president of the college, or you can see him every Tuesday at the Foreign Relations study group," says a student.

Life

At St. John's, "you have to work intensely and relax intensely. Life is more distilled, here." "Is it hard work?" asks a student. "Yes and no. Does staying up until 1:00 A.M. reading Shakespeare or Darwin sound like work?" Santa Fe is "stunning," and the proximity of the mountains (for hiking and skiing) is more than welcome. Though each week is "epic" in its schoolwork, there are dozens of clubs and activities to take part in, from "dance (beginners always welcome) to search and rescue to astronomy to rock-climbing." If you're artsy, there are many galleries in Santa Fe, or "you can stay on campus, join a study group or sports team, or go to the gym." The student government is also responsible for dispersing several thousand dollars to support student clubs annually, so "if you can get signatures to show support, you can probably get funding for snacks or supplies." Many say that food services could have better hours and prices. There are "frequent" field trips to some of the extraordinary places in New Mexico.

Student Body

Most of the 450 undergrads at St. John's are "friendly," "big readers," and "interested in discussions." It's easy to find commonalities, since "you're always able to discuss the program as long as they're the same year or lower." All are here "because we have a genuine interest in the larger questions that are posed in life through academia," and "that's enough for most of us to feel like we're 'fitting in,' however that may be defined." Johnnies are "fascinated with learning in a way different from most schools" and "thrive on epiphanies through the 'great books,' especially ones shared with others."

St. John's College (NM)

FINANCIAL AID: 505-984-6058 • E-MAIL: ADMISSIONS@MAIL.SJCSF.EDU • WEBSITE: WWW.SJCSF.EDU

THE PRINCETON REVIEW SAYS

Admissions

Very important factors considered include: Application essay. *Important factors considered include:* Rigor of secondary school record, recommendation(s), character/personal qualities, level of applicant's interest. *Other factors considered include:* Class rank, GPA, standardized test scores, extracurricular activities, first generation, interview, racial/ethnic status, talent/ability, volunteer work, work experience, alumni/ae relations. SAT or ACT considered if submitted; ACT with or without Writing component accepted. TOEFL required of all international applicants. *Academic units required:* 3 mathematics; 2 foreign language. *Academic units recommended:* 4 English; 4 mathematics; 3 science; (3 science lab); 4 foreign language; 2 history.

Financial Aid

Students should submit: FAFSA, CSS/Financial Aid PROFILE, Noncustodial PROFILE, Business/Farm Supplement. The Princeton Review suggests that all financial aid forms be submitted as soon as possible after January 1. *Need-based scholarships/grants offered:* Federal Pell, SEOG, State scholarships/grants, private scholarships, the school's own gift aid. *Loan aid offered:* Direct Subsidized Stafford Loans, Direct Unsubsidized Stafford Loans, Direct PLUS loans, Federal Perkins Loans, College/university loans from institutional funds. Federal Work-Study Program available. Institutional employment available. Off-campus job opportunities are excellent.

The Inside Word

Self-selection drives this admissions process—more than one-half of the entire applicant pool each year indicates that St. John's is their first choice, and half of those admitted send in tuition deposits. Even so, no one in admissions takes things for granted, and neither should any student considering an application. The admissions process is highly personal on both sides of the coin. Only the intellectually curious and highly motivated need apply.

THE SCHOOL SAYS "..."

From the Admissions Office

"St. John's appeals to students who value good books, love to read, and are passionate about discourse and debate. There are no lectures and virtually no tests or electives. Instead, classes of sixteen to twenty students occur around conference tables where professors are as likely to be asked to defend their points of view as are students. Great books provide the direction, context, and stimulus for conversation. The entire student body adheres to the same, all-required arts and science curriculum. Someone once said, 'A classic is a house we still live in,' and at St. John's, students and professors alike approach each reading on the list as if the ideas it holds were being expressed for the first time—questioning the logic behind a geometrical proof, challenging the premise of a scientific development, or dissecting the progression of modern political theory as it unfolds."

SELECTIVITY

Admissions Rating	75
# of applicants	251
% of applicants accepted	124
% of acceptees attending	32
# of early decision applicants	0

FRESHMAN PROFILE

Range SAT Critical Reading	580–740
Range SAT Math	550–680
Range SAT Writing	560–670
Range ACT Composite	25–29
Minimum paper TOEFL	550
Minimum web-based TOEFL	213
% graduated top 10% of class	16
% graduated top 25% of class	41
% graduated top 50% of class	70

DEADLINES

Early decision	
Deadline	11/15
Notification	12/15
Early action	
Deadline	11/15
Notification	12/15
Regular	
Priority	11/15
Nonfall registration?	Yes

APPLICANTS ALSO LOOK AT AND OFTEN PREFER

Stanford University; Deep Springs College

AND SOMETIMES PREFER

Bard College; Rice University; The University of Chicago; Reed College

AND RARELY PREFER

Whitman College; Grinnell College; Oberlin College

FINANCIAL FACTS

Financial Aid Rating	95
Annual tuition	$44,554
Room and board	$9,994
Required fees	$450
Books and supplies	$630
% needy frosh rec. need-based scholarship or grant aid	100
% needy UG rec. need-based scholarship or grant aid	96
% needy frosh rec. non-need-based scholarship or grant aid	0
% needy UG rec. non-need-based scholarship or grant aid	0
% needy frosh rec. need-based self-help aid	100
% needy UG rec. need-based self-help aid	100
% frosh rec. any financial aid	81
% UG rec. any financial aid	75
% UG borrow to pay for school	77
Average cumulative indebtedness	$20,750
% frosh need fully met	90
% ugrads need fully met	94
Average % of frosh need met	97
Average % of ugrad need met	97

ST. JOHN'S UNIVERSITY

8000 UTOPIA PARKWAY, QUEENS, NY 11439 • ADMISSIONS: 718-990-2000 • FAX: 718-990-2096

STUDENTS SAY ". . ."

Academics

Located in Queens, New York, St. John's University is a Catholic university that provides its students with "events and other great opportunities for them to more easily reach the goals they have set for themselves." The school has many strong professional programs, and a "good selection of majors and course offerings." These features combined with an "amazing" honors program, a plethora of study abroad opportunities, and "significant" scholarship and financial aid packages forms "a thriving metropolitan university, diverse in students, programs, and activities."

Professors are "strict enough for us to know we are responsible for our own actions, but also lenient enough for us students to know that they are understanding people who can be helpful and approached." "Each one of my professors brings the classroom to life through teaching about the things that would interest us," says a freshman. Sure, there are "some iffy professors," but "with the resources they give you, any student can choose the cream of the crop as a teacher!" The location in New York City "offers a lot of internships" and helps students form "good connections to jobs."

St. John's administration is "very aware of its students and has always made the college experience enjoyable and comfortable," while still fostering "an enriching learning environment." On a day-to-day basis, "everything is run pretty efficiently." The school revels in the diversity of its student base and "stresses theses cultural backgrounds in class." "The lecture series are wonderful," and the business and pharmacy programs in particular stand out. Simply put," St. John's is the real deal."

Life

The university does an excellent job of making sure everything is personalized, and "there is abundance of resources all over the campus that help all students (especially the freshmen) to become involved in a college life." St. John's "gives importance to being social along with studying," and students here are generally "very outgoing and involved in activities" and "generally very tolerant and accepting of others." The "beautiful campus" has a large number of commuters as well as residents, and there is "transportation to other events" provided by the school. School spirit definitely hits its peak "during basketball season."

People have the resources of "literally the world through the proximity to New York City," all while keeping the "safety of the students…a strength." "I get to experience campus life but still get to live in NYC," says a senior biology and English major. "The perk of going to school at St John's you have the typical small town college campus feel, but a quick subway ride away is the best city in the world!"

There are over 180 student organizations ("I'm never bored," says a freshman), and they "get a lot of support from administration and faculty." As a Catholic school, there is a real "sense of community and service" throughout the campus, and most here "are particularly committed to community service and to helping those in deprived socioeconomic backgrounds."

Student Body

Much like its surrounding city, the student body at this "global school" is a mix of "diversity blended into school pride." Though many are commuters, there is a "strong sense of community in the residence villages" and the "welcoming" school is home to "one of the most diverse universities in the United States." "Because everyone is so different and there are so many minorities, people treat others the way they would like to be treated," says a senior. A typical student "will focus on his or her school work first, then elaborate their college experience with multiple school events and activities."

FINANCIAL AID: 718-990-2000 • E-MAIL: ADMHELP@STJOHNS.EDU • WEBSITE: WWW.STJOHNS.EDU

THE PRINCETON REVIEW SAYS

Admissions

Very important factors considered include: GPA, standardized test scores. *Important factors considered include:* Rigor of secondary school record. *Other factors considered include:* Class rank, application essay, extracurricular activities, first generation, geographical residence, recommendation(s), state residency, talent/ability, volunteer work, work experience, alumni/ae relations, character/personal qualities. SAT or ACT required; ACT with or without Writing component accepted. TOEFL required of all international applicants. *Academic units required:* 4 English; 2 mathematics; 1 science; 1 history; 5 academic electives. *Academic units recommended:* 4 English; 3 mathematics; 1 science; 2 foreign language; 1 history; 8 academic electives.

Financial Aid

Students should submit: FAFSA. The Princeton Review suggests that all financial aid forms be submitted as soon as possible after January 1. *Need-based scholarships/grants offered:* Federal Pell, SEOG, State scholarships/grants, private scholarships, the school's own gift aid. *Loan aid offered:* Direct Subsidized Stafford Loans, Direct Unsubsidized Stafford Loans, Direct PLUS loans, Federal Perkins Loans Applicants will be notified of awards beginning 3/15. Federal Work-Study Program available. Institutional employment available. Off-campus job opportunities are good.

The Inside Word

The admissions process at St. John's doesn't include many surprises. High school grades and standardized test scores are undoubtedly the most important factors though volunteer work and extracurricular activities are also highly regarded. What is surprising is that this Catholic university doesn't consider religious affiliation at all when making admissions decisions; there are students of every religious stripe here.

THE SCHOOL SAYS "..."

From the Admissions Office

"Founded in 1870, St. John's is a Catholic and Vincentian university that emphasizes academic excellence without bounds, providing talented students with an outstanding education that builds upon their abilities and aspirations. This past year, 10 students won Fulbright Awards. Undergraduates also received prestigious awards including a Marshall Fellowship to pursue advanced study at the University of London. On the playing courts and fields, St. John's is New York City's team—with 17 men's and women's athletic teams.

Faith, service, and success are central to a St. John's education. This year, students logged 96,833 service hours in 125 city agencies and at 11 sites on four continents. St. John's is among the few universities admitted with distinction to the President's Higher Education Community Service Honor Roll.

St. John's offers more than 100 associate, bachelor's, master's, and doctoral degrees in the arts, business, education, law, pharmacy, and the natural and applied sciences. More than 90 percent of our professors hold a Ph.D. or comparable terminal degree in their field. Our 17-to-one student/faculty ratio ensures personal attention.

Our students enjoy a global experience that starts at our three residential New York City campuses—in Queens, Staten Island, and Manhattan; an international campus in Rome, Italy; and study abroad locations in Paris, France, and Seville, Spain, and around the world. Enhancing the University's cosmopolitan character, students come from nearly 50 states and close to 120 foreign countries—all of them benefiting from the University's network of 160,000 alumni."

SELECTIVITY
Admissions Rating	82
# of applicants	51,207
% of applicants accepted	53
% of acceptees attending	10

FRESHMAN PROFILE
Range SAT Critical Reading	490–590
Range SAT Math	500–620
Range ACT Composite	21–27
Minimum paper TOEFL	600
Average HS GPA	3.40
% graduated top 10% of class	17
% graduated top 25% of class	42
% graduated top 50% of class	73

DEADLINES
Nonfall registration?	Yes

APPLICANTS ALSO LOOK AT AND OFTEN PREFER
Baruch College-City University of New York; State University of New York-Stony Brook University

AND SOMETIMES PREFER
Fordham University; Rutgers, The State University of New Jersey-New Brunswick

FINANCIAL FACTS
Financial Aid Rating	73
Annual tuition	$36,450
Room and board	$15,880
Required fees	$810
Books and supplies	$1,045
% needy frosh rec. need-based scholarship or grant aid	85
% needy UG rec. need-based scholarship or grant aid	86
% needy frosh rec. non-need-based scholarship or grant aid	90
% needy UG rec. non-need-based scholarship or grant aid	76
% needy frosh rec. need-based self-help aid	79
% needy UG rec. need-based self-help aid	80
% frosh rec. any financial aid	98
% UG rec. any financial aid	96
% UG borrow to pay for school	75
Average cumulative indebtedness	$33,533
% frosh need fully met	12
% ugrads need fully met	10
Average % of frosh need met	74
Average % of ugrad need met	71

ST. LAWRENCE UNIVERSITY

PAYSON HALL, CANTON, NY 13617 • ADMISSIONS: 315-229-5261 • FAX: 315-229-5818

CAMPUS LIFE

Quality of Life Rating	81
Fire Safety Rating	76
Green Rating	93
Type of school	Private
Affiliation	No Affiliation
Environment	Village

STUDENTS

Total undergrad enrollment	2,414
% male/female	45/55
% from out of state	60
% frosh from public high school	68
% frosh live on campus	100
% ugrads live on campus	98
# of fraternities(% ugrad men join)	2(8)
# of sororities(% ugrad women join	4(18)
% African American	3
% Asian	2
% Caucasian	80
% Hispanic	4
% Native American	<1
% international	8
# of countries represented	47

SURVEY SAYS . . .

Political activism is popular
Classroom facilities are great
Lab facilities are great
Career services are great
Students are friendly
Athletic facilities are great
Lots of beer drinking
Hard liquor is popular
Everyone loves the Saints
Alumni active on campus
Active student government

ACADEMICS

Academic Rating	92
% students returning for sophomore year	90
% students graduating within 4 years	77
% students graduating within 6 years	80
Calendar	Semester
Student/faculty ratio	12:1
Profs interesting rating	92
Profs accessible rating	86

Most classes have 10–19 students.
Most lab/discussion sessions have 10–19 students.

MOST POPULAR MAJORS
economics; biology; conservation biology

STUDENTS SAY ". . ."

Academics

"The best-kept secret in the Northeast," St. Lawrence University provides an "excellent well-rounded liberal arts education" that is "intellectually stimulating, personally enriching, and culturally engaging." "The high quality of professors and facilities" attract "individuals who are serious about their education" and build "an oasis of learning, separated from distractions, but preparing you for the real world." Boasting a science program that "is one of the strongest" among liberal arts schools, "well-developed study abroad programs," and "admissions and financial aid offices [that] seek to offer many scholarship opportunities," St. Lawrence offers a wide array of academic prospects. Although some students feel that the university may be "understaffed," small class sizes and a "faculty who desire achievement" play a critical role in the St. Lawrence experience. Professors are "approachable, funny, and extremely able" and they "have flexible hours." As one student says, "The professors here are truly exceptional…they put so much time into ensuring you grow as a scholar and as a person." "Very rarely will a professor lecture for the full amount of class time," which encourages discussion and "experiential learning." Students are encouraged to "make a sustainable and meaningful impact in communities on both local and global scales" and cite that "alumni are extremely successful."

Life

Canton is "a quaint town that has a lot of farms" located "in the beautiful Adirondacks." Perhaps this is why much of campus life is centered on the outdoors. Aside from the typical Canton "haunts" like Hoot Owl and Tick Tock, students at St. Lawrence go "canoeing on campus, rock-climbing, hiking, and even cross-country skiing" or participate in the school's "excellent outdoor program" and outing club. Every year, Peak Weekend takes place and assigns adventurers to "every high peak in the Adirondacks." "A large portion of the student body are varsity athletes" who were drawn to the school for its "strong athletic tradition," while others are "passionate, active students who work hard and play hard." One student proudly described her weekly routine: "Monday [through] Thursday: school, homework, and campus involvement in clubs and organization. Thursday: pre-game and ticker. Friday: Chill out in the dorms, casual drinking. Saturday: pre-game and ticker. Sunday: Dana Brunch and library all day." "Theme houses" provide an "alternative party-hangout spot for the students not involved with the 'Greek life' system," and while some say drinking is prevalent, it is "not forced" on campus life. In terms of the "huge" music scene, "people like to go to Java, the music venue on campus, which books small bands every weekend," and students "also go to Ottawa or Montreal and Burlington fairly often for concerts." Life here may be nature-focused, but students do criticize the administration for not "following through with the green initiatives they pride themselves on" and providing more public transportation resources. Still, the "unique environment" of St. Lawrence leaves students here "genuinely happy."

Student Body

Though "Bean boots, Patagonia, and J. Crew" describe the "homogeneous" dominant atmosphere at St. Lawrence, the school "seamlessly fuses the three major social categories of preps, jocks, and hippies" and "blends future activists, executives, and business professionals…to foster a mixed culture of preppiness and crunchiness." Extracurricular activities are vehicles for fitting in on campus, and students characterize the student body as "made up of overachievers" who are "easy to get along with and a lot of fun." Students are "motivated to be successful and are genuinely interested in their classes" while also being "engaging and thoughtful, seeking to take advantage of campus activities and to make a difference." Despite the fact that "many members of the student body are definitely rich, there is a lot of economic diversity that goes unnoticed." More than anything, it's the "strong sense of community" and the feeling that "everybody loves everybody" that make this "a wonderful place for just about anyone who can stand the cold."

FINANCIAL AID: 315-229-5265 • E-MAIL: ADMISSIONS@STLAWU.EDU • WEBSITE: WWW.STLAWU.EDU

THE PRINCETON REVIEW SAYS

Admissions

Very important factors considered include: GPA, rigor of secondary school record, application essay, recommendation(s), character/personal qualities. *Important factors considered include:* Class rank, extracurricular activities, interview, racial/ethnic status. *Other factors considered include:* Standardized test scores, first generation, geographical residence, talent/ability, volunteer work, work experience, alumni/ae relations, level of applicant's interest. SAT and SAT Subject Tests or ACT considered if submitted; ACT with or without Writing component accepted. TOEFL required of all international applicants. *Academic units recommended:* 4 English; 4 mathematics; 4 science; 2 social studies; 4 foreign language; 2 history.

Financial Aid

Students should submit: FAFSA, CSS/Financial Aid PROFILE, Noncustodial PROFILE. Regular filing deadline is 2/1. The Princeton Review suggests that all financial aid forms be submitted as soon as possible after January 1. *Need-based scholarships/grants offered:* Federal Pell, SEOG, State scholarships/grants, private scholarships, the school's own gift aid. *Loan aid offered:* Direct Subsidized Stafford Loans, Direct Unsubsidized Stafford Loans, Direct PLUS loans, Federal Perkins Loans, College/university loans from institutional funds. Applicants will be notified of awards beginning 3/30. Federal Work-Study Program available. Institutional employment available. Off-campus job opportunities are poor.

The Inside Word

At St. Lawrence, you're not required to submit scores from the SAT or the ACT—it is "test-optional"— but that means your high school transcript and teacher recommendations better be stellar. If you're a homeschooled student or an international student seeking financial aid, it's probably a good idea to submit some standardized test scores. Good scores help since scholarship selection is based on overall academic profile.

THE SCHOOL SAYS "..."

From the Admissions Office

"Situated in an ideal location, St. Lawrence University is a diverse liberal arts learning community of talented students and inspiring faculty, guided by tradition and focused on the future. We are a vibrant, collaborative community of learners who value thought and action. Students tap into their full potential, as they embrace the nature environment, engage with global challenges, and experience the relevance and adventure of a liberal arts education in a complex and changing world.

"Our faculty chosen St. Lawrence intentionally because they know there is institutional commitment to support great teaching. They are dedicated to making each student's experience challenging and rewarding. Our graduates make up one of the strongest networks of support among any alumni body and are ready, willing, and able to connect with students and help them succeed.

"Every student has diverse opportunities to connect classroom theory to hands-on, real-world experience through internships, international study, and community projects. Faculty know their students and act as their mentors, guides, and colleagues on their journeys. Creative degree paths allow students to discover new dimensions of themselves and prepare for lives of personal fulfillment and career success.

"Our location on the edge of the Adirondack Mountains gives us easy access to enviable outdoor spaces to learn and to practice environmental sustainability and to participate year-round in all things outdoors. You must visit and meet our students to get a sense of the energy on campus to begin to understand just what makes St. Lawrence University different!"

SELECTIVITY

Admissions Rating	93
# of applicants	4,424
% of applicants accepted	46
% of acceptees attending	31
# offered a place on the wait list	148
% accepting a place on wait list	7
% admitted from wait list	5
# of early decision applicants	258
% accepted early decision	90

FRESHMAN PROFILE

Range SAT Critical Reading	550–650
Range SAT Math	570–660
Range SAT Writing	550–650
Range ACT Composite	25–30
Average HS GPA	3.5
% graduated top 10% of class	34
% graduated top 25% of class	71
% graduated top 50% of class	95

DEADLINES

Early decision	
Deadline	11/1
Regular	
Deadline	2/1
Nonfall registration?	Yes

APPLICANTS ALSO LOOK AT AND OFTEN PREFER
Middlebury College; Williams College; Dartmouth College

AND SOMETIMES PREFER
Bowdoin College; Colby College; Colgate University

AND RARELY PREFER
Ithaca College

FINANCIAL FACTS

Financial Aid Rating	89
Annual tuition	$47,350
Room and board	$12,286
Required fees	$346
Books and supplies	$750
% needy frosh rec. need-based scholarship or grant aid	98
% needy UG rec. need-based scholarship or grant aid	97
% needy frosh rec. non-need-based scholarship or grant aid	16
% needy UG rec. non-need-based scholarship or grant aid	13
% needy frosh rec. need-based self-help aid	74
% needy UG rec. need-based self-help aid	76
% frosh rec. any financial aid	97
% UG rec. any financial aid	93
% UG borrow to pay for school	67
Average cumulative indebtedness	$26,832
% frosh need fully met	40
% ugrads need fully met	38
Average % of frosh need met	89
Average % of ugrad need met	88

St. Mary's College of Maryland

Admissions Office, 18952 East Fisher Road, St. Mary's City, MD 20686-3001 • Admissions: 240-895-5000 • Fax: 240-895-5001

CAMPUS LIFE

Quality of Life Rating	92
Fire Safety Rating	79
Green Rating	91
Type of school	Public
Affiliation	No Affiliation
Environment	Rural

STUDENTS

Total undergrad enrollment	1,794
% male/female	41/59
% from out of state	10
% frosh from public high school	75
% frosh live on campus	96
% ugrads live on campus	87
% African American	8
% Asian	3
% Caucasian	75
% Hispanic	6
% Native American	<1
% international	1
# of countries represented	23

SURVEY SAYS . . .

Students are happy
Lab facilities are great
Students are friendly
Diverse student types on campus
Students environmentally aware
Campus feels safe
Athletic facilities are great
Lots of beer drinking
Intramural sports are popular
Active student government

ACADEMICS

Academic Rating	90
% students returning for sophomore year	90
% students graduating within 4 years	71
% students graduating within 6 years	86
Calendar	Semester
Student/faculty ratio	11:1
Profs interesting rating	93
Profs accessible rating	92

Most classes have 10–19 students.
Most lab/discussion sessions have
10–19 students.

MOST POPULAR MAJORS

English language and literature; biology

STUDENTS SAY ". . ."

Academics

Undergrads at St. Mary's College of Maryland proudly boast that from the moment you step onto campus your freshman year, "you are instantly part of a family." Indeed there's an "immense sense of community" here, and it's no surprise that a "friendly atmosphere" reverberates throughout the school. Importantly, as "a public honors college," St. Mary's is able to provide "a rigorous academic curriculum" at an affordable price. It also offers a "small and intimate learning environment" with "classes where the professors actually care about teaching and your success." Classes tend to have "a great combination of lecture, discussion, and experiential learning," which translates into "a stimulating, challenging and altogether high-quality academic experience." Additionally, students are quick to brag about their "passionate" and "approachable" professors who are "always available for discussion and clarification." As one public policy major further explains, "Most [teachers] are willing to meet outside their office hours for as long as needed to help a student and many professors are known to give out their cell phone numbers…in case a student needs to reach them at night." They truly want "students to succeed" and work hard to ensure you'll "enjoy even the hardest of classes." A content senior sums up, "At St. Mary's, you are not just a number in the classroom, but an essential part of the classroom experience."

Life

Similar to many college kids, undergrads at St. Mary's have a "work hard, play hard mentality." While they're "definitely focused on their studies," students here also make the most of their time outside of the library. One psych major shares, "There are many opportunities to get involved on campus whether by participating in club activities or taking a student position in campus affairs, or just becoming a student tutor." The school also sponsors a number of events. For example, "every Thursday we have coffeehouse where artists perform at our local coffee shop, we have comedians Friday nights, and we also have movies showing Fridays, Saturdays, and Sundays." Further, "there are intramural events that take place every semester for almost every sport." Though St. Mary's is a "non-Greek" campus, "themed and house parties are always a hit." Fortunately, "nobody's looked down upon if they choose not to drink." St. Mary's students also love to take advantage of their location on the water. An anthropology majors explains, "When it's nice out, *everyone* is outside, and on the weekends, the docks are crowded by 11:00 A.M. People throw Frisbees [and] footballs, run around barefoot, grill, and chill." As an added bonus, "students can take out sail boats or kayaks whenever they want for free." With all these options, it's no wonder why one bio student exclaims that undergrads here "will never be bored."

Student Body

"Friendliness" is the hallmark of the typical St. Mary's undergrad, and many are quick to assert that there's "a very welcoming student body." Indeed, as this junior gushes, "you could sit down and have dinner with someone you have never seen before, and be completely comfortable." The average "Seahawk" is also "focused on their studies" and "involved in all sorts of activities." Students here tend to be "politically aware and left-leaning, and very concerned with the environment." While many St. Mary's undergrads do often share these attributes, another junior assures us, "there are many different types of students [here]: some preppy kids, jocks, the artsy kids, bookworms, hippies, country kids, city kids. Everyone finds their niche, but then mixes up with other people." An excited sophomore interjects, "Quirkiness is more than tolerated here; it is often the norm." A knowledgeable senior concludes, "With every new class there is an opportunity to make new friends, which makes every semester here exciting."

FINANCIAL AID: 240-895-3000 • E-MAIL: ADMISSIONS@SMCM.EDU • WEBSITE: WWW.SMCM.EDU

THE PRINCETON REVIEW SAYS

Admissions

Very important factors considered include: GPA, rigor of secondary school record, application essay. *Important factors considered include:* Class rank, standardized test scores, extracurricular activities, recommendation(s), talent/ability, volunteer work, character/personal qualities. *Other factors considered include:* First generation, geographical residence, interview, racial/ethnic status, state residency, work experience, alumni/ae relations, level of applicant's interest. SAT or ACT required; ACT with or without Writing component accepted. TOEFL required of all international applicants. *Academic units required:* 4 English; 3 mathematics; 3 science; (2 science lab); 2 social studies; 1 history. *Academic units recommended:* 4 mathematics; 3 social studies; 4 foreign language.

Financial Aid

Students should submit: FAFSA. Regular filing deadline is 2/28. The Princeton Review suggests that all financial aid forms be submitted as soon as possible after January 1. *Need-based scholarships/grants offered:* Federal Pell, SEOG, State scholarships/grants, private scholarships, the school's own gift aid. *Loan aid offered:* Direct Subsidized Stafford Loans, Direct Unsubsidized Stafford Loans, Direct PLUS loans, Federal Perkins Loans. Applicants will be notified of awards beginning 4/1. Federal Work-Study Program available. Institutional employment available. Off-campus job opportunities are good.

The Inside Word

As Maryland's public honors college, gaining admissions to St. Mary's is competitive. Admissions officers here really strive to get to know the applicant as an individual, not just a set of numbers on a paper. While academic rigor definitely holds the most weight, admissions officers thoroughly evaluate your essays, recommendations, and extracurricular activities as well.

THE SCHOOL SAYS "..."

From the Admissions Office

"St. Mary's College of Maryland occupies a distinctive niche and represents a real value in American higher education. It is a public college, dedicated to the ideal of affordable, accessible education and committed to quality teaching and excellent programs for undergraduate students. St. Mary's is designated by law the state of Maryland's 'public honors college,' one of only two public colleges in the nation to hold that distinction. It is this mix of honors and affordability that makes St. Mary's an education for the twenty-first century."

SELECTIVITY

Admissions Rating	85
# of applicants	2,321
% of applicants accepted	73
% of acceptees attending	22
# offered a place on the wait list	246
% accepting a place on wait list	18
% admitted from wait list	98
# of early decision applicants	130
% accepted early decision	87

FRESHMAN PROFILE

Range SAT Critical Reading	540–670
Range SAT Math	530–640
Range SAT Writing	530–650
Range ACT Composite	23–28
Minimum paper TOEFL	550
Minimum web-based TOEFL	250
Average HS GPA	0.00
% graduated top 10% of class	28
% graduated top 25% of class	64
% graduated top 50% of class	87

DEADLINES

Early decision	
Deadline	11/1
Notification	12/15
Regular	
Priority	11/1
Deadline	1/1
Notification	1/1
Nonfall registration?	Yes

FINANCIAL FACTS

Financial Aid Rating	70
Annual in-state tuition	$12,245
Annual out-of-state tuition	$26,045
Room and board	$11,635
Required fees	$2,619
Books and supplies	$1,000
% needy frosh rec. need-based scholarship or grant aid	83
% needy UG rec. need-based scholarship or grant aid	78
% needy frosh rec. non-need-based scholarship or grant aid	48
% needy UG rec. non-need-based scholarship or grant aid	49
% needy frosh rec. need-based self-help aid	68
% needy UG rec. need-based self-help aid	73
% frosh rec. any financial aid	72
% UG rec. any financial aid	74
% UG borrow to pay for school	53
Average cumulative indebtedness	$24,624
% frosh need fully met	5
% ugrads need fully met	5
Average % of frosh need met	70
Average % of ugrad need met	65

ST. OLAF COLLEGE

1520 St. Olaf Avenue, Northfield, MN 55057 • Admissions: 507-786-3025 • Fax: 507-786-3832

CAMPUS LIFE

Quality of Life Rating	97
Fire Safety Rating	70
Green Rating	77
Type of school	Private
Affiliation	Lutheran
Environment	Village

STUDENTS

Total undergrad enrollment	3,079
% male/female	44/56
% from out of state	50
% frosh from public high school	76
% frosh live on campus	100
% ugrads live on campus	92
% African American	1
% Asian	5
% Caucasian	78
% Hispanic	4
% Native American	<1
% international	6
# of countries represented	67

SURVEY SAYS . . .

Students are happy
Classroom facilities are great
Lab facilities are great
Career services are great
School is well run
No one cheats
Students are friendly
Students get along with local community
Great food on campus
Campus feels safe
Athletic facilities are great
Very little drug use
Active student government

ACADEMICS

Academic Rating	95
% students returning for sophomore year	94
% students graduating within 4 years	83
% students graduating within 6 years	87
Calendar	4/1/4
Student/faculty ratio	12:1
Profs interesting rating	91
Profs accessible rating	92

Most classes have 10–19 students.
Most lab/discussion sessions have 20–29 students.

MOST POPULAR MAJORS
biology; economics; psychology

STUDENTS SAY ". . ."

Academics

Tucked away in quaint Northfield, Minnesota, St. Olaf College provides undergraduates with a "great academic program" and a "great community." Though technically a Christian school, St. Olaf does a good "job of emphasizing the Lutheran tradition without making students feel pressured to have similar religious beliefs." While the college is home to many solid departments, undergrads are quick to highlight St. Olaf's strong "reputation for the natural sciences" and "excellent music program." Further, students also love to call attention to the school's "incredible study abroad program." Additionally, undergrads are prone to gushing about their "very knowledgeable" professors, especially given that availability and accessibility are hallmarks at St. Olaf. As one senior brags, "Professors are more than willing to talk academics. They literally sit in their office waiting for students to come." Importantly, they "also know how to get students excited about a subject." Although "classes are hard" and professors "have high expectations," they also "genuinely want to see you grow as a student in their class." Finally, as this supremely content junior summarizes, "Saint Olaf is a place where you will not only be pushed as an academic but you will be pushed and forced to examine your political beliefs, spiritual beliefs [and] moral beliefs." The college "allows you to grow as a global citizen and not just a student."

Life

At St. Olaf, students can readily participate in a vibrant campus life. As one eager freshman regales us, "Life here at Olaf is always busy; whether it's going to a concert or playing Quidditch in the courtyard, there's always something to do…For fun, we can play club sports, watch the Limestones perform, attend an improv comedy performance, get our groove on at school dances, zip line in the athlete center parking lot, learn swing dancing and anything else you could possibly imagine! It's remarkable!" Although St. Olaf maintains a "dry campus," a neuroscience major admits that "a lot of students still use alcohol on a regular basis, so it's not that hard to find a party." However, he then goes on to assure us that "Oles know how to have good, clean fun." A chemistry/econ double-major agrees adding, "There is no pressure to drink." There's a lot for students to take advantage of off-campus as well. For example, "skiing, hiking, and biking are pretty popular pursuits on weekends depending on the season, and Oles are always down for a trip into Northfield to visit apple orchards, music venues, restaurants and bars." Additionally, the "proximity of the Twin Cities also enables students to take a weekend to catch some sports games, fabulous theater, or travelling national musical acts, as well." Perhaps this sophomore best sums up life here, "[There's] hardly a dull moment!"

Student Body

If one were to superficially assess St. Olaf's student body, he/she would easily conclude that the "typical student is white, blonde, and Norwegian." However, these undergrads are far more than their exteriors. Certainly, no one understands that better than St. Olaf students themselves. Speaking very highly of their peers, undergrads describe their friends as "well-rounded" individuals who maintain a "wide range of interests." Though at times that might make students here appear to be "over-committed overachievers," many assure us that it's simply because 'Oles' are just "so excited about so many things." Of course, given St. Olaf's renown for its music program, it's no wonder that a sophomore quickly adds, "A typical student at St. Olaf is usually involved with one of the five choirs the school offers, or is in the orchestra or band." Fortunately, though the vast majority of undergrads are indeed "hard-working," you won't find any cutthroat behavior here. As one freshman proudly reports, "The students on campus are like one big family [with] everyone look[ing] out for one another. For example, people trust one another enough to leave computers and other valuables unattended for long periods of time." Moreover, undergrads are "very friendly and open to new ideas." A senior biology major concurs sharing, "It is easy to get to know people, regardless of religious beliefs or sexual orientation. People are very welcoming and understanding."

FINANCIAL AID: 507-786-3019 • E-MAIL: ADMISSIONS@STOLAF.EDU • WEBSITE: WWW.STOLAF.EDU

THE PRINCETON REVIEW SAYS

Admissions

Very important factors considered include: GPA, rigor of secondary school record, application essay. *Important factors considered include:* Class rank, standardized test scores, extracurricular activities, interview, recommendation(s), talent/ability, character/personal qualities. *Other factors considered include:* First generation, geographical residence, racial/ethnic status, state residency, volunteer work, work experience, alumni/ae relations, level of applicant's interest, religious affiliation. SAT or ACT required; SAT and SAT Subject Tests or ACT considered if submitted; ACT with or without Writing component accepted. TOEFL required of all international applicants. *Academic units recommended:* 4 English; 4 mathematics; 4 science; (2 science lab); 4 social studies; 4 foreign language.

Financial Aid

Students should submit: FAFSA, CSS/Financial Aid PROFILE, Noncustodial PROFILE, Business/Farm Supplement. Regular filing deadline is 3/1. The Princeton Review suggests that all financial aid forms be submitted as soon as possible after January 1. *Need-based scholarships/grants offered:* Federal Pell, SEOG, State scholarships/grants, private scholarships, the school's own gift aid. *Loan aid offered:* Direct Subsidized Stafford Loans, Direct Unsubsidized Stafford Loans, Direct PLUS loans, Federal Perkins Loans, Federal Nursing Loans, State Loans, College/university loans from institutional funds. Applicants will be notified of awards beginning 4/1. Federal Work-Study Program available. Off-campus job opportunities are fair.

The Inside Word

As St. Olaf's academic reputation steadily rises, so too does competition to gain admission. First and foremost, admissions officers here assess the rigor of each applicant's course load (and subsequent success in the classroom). Of course, as a tight-knit community, the college also looks to admit students who will complement St. Olaf's ethos. To that end, admissions officers also closely analyze personal essays, recommendations and participation in extracurricular activities.

THE SCHOOL SAYS "..."

From the Admissions Office

"One of the nation's leading liberal arts colleges, St. Olaf College offers a distinctive education grounded in academic rigor, residential learning, global engagement, and a vibrant Lutheran faith tradition.

Many excellent colleges provide one, two, or even three elements of the St. Olaf experience. What makes St. Olaf unique is the combination of so many distinguishing features working together at the highest level: an intense academic program that sharpens minds and an emphasis on a global perspective that broadens them; the vitality of a residential community that engages thoughtful people across the full range of human experiences; and a faith tradition that encourages reflection and honors different perspectives.

By cultivating the habits of mind and heart that enable graduates to lead lives of financial independence, professional accomplishment, and personal fulfillment, St. Olaf College provides an uncommon educational experience that fully prepares students to make a meaningful difference in our changing.

SELECTIVITY

Admissions Rating	93
# of applicants	4,011
% of applicants accepted	59
% of acceptees attending	32
# offered a place on the wait list	694
% accepting a place on wait list	85
% admitted from wait list	11
# of early decision applicants	295
% accepted early decision	63

FRESHMAN PROFILE

Range SAT Critical Reading	590–710
Range SAT Math	590–710
Range SAT Writing	580–690
Range ACT Composite	26–31
Average HS GPA	3.63
% graduated top 10% of class	54
% graduated top 25% of class	76
% graduated top 50% of class	98

DEADLINES

Early decision	
Deadline	11/15
Notification	12/7
Regular	
Deadline	1/15
Notification	3/20
Nonfall registration?	Yes

APPLICANTS ALSO LOOK AT AND SOMETIMES PREFER

Carleton College; Gustavus Adolphus College; University of Minnesota—Twin Cities; University of Wisconsin-Madison; Grinnell College; Lawrence University; Macalester College; Northwestern University

FINANCIAL FACTS

Financial Aid Rating	93
% needy frosh rec. need-based scholarship or grant aid	100
% needy UG rec. need-based scholarship or grant aid	100
% needy frosh rec. non-need-based scholarship or grant aid	25
% needy UG rec. non-need-based scholarship or grant aid	20
% needy frosh rec. need-based self-help aid	100
% needy UG rec. need-based self-help aid	100
% frosh rec. any financial aid	93
% UG rec. any financial aid	92
% UG borrow to pay for school	66
Average cumulative indebtedness	$27,483
% frosh need fully met	78
% ugrads need fully met	78
Average % of frosh need met	99
Average % of ugrad need met	96

STANFORD UNIVERSITY

UNDERGRADUATE ADMISSION, STANFORD, CA 94305-6106 • ADMISSIONS: 650-723-2091 • FAX: 650-725-2846

CAMPUS LIFE

Quality of Life Rating	98
Fire Safety Rating	79
Green Rating	99
Type of school	Private
Affiliation	No Affiliation
Environment	City

STUDENTS

Total undergrad enrollment	6,980
% male/female	53/47
% from out of state	53
% frosh from public high school	58
% frosh live on campus	100
% ugrads live on campus	91
# of fraternities (% ugrad men join)	16 (24)
# of sororities (% ugrad women join)	14 (28)
% African American	8
% Asian	22
% Caucasian	41
% Hispanic	14
% Native American	3
% international	8
# of countries represented	90

SURVEY SAYS . . .

Students are happy
Classroom facilities are great
Lab facilities are great
Career services are great
Internships are widely available
School is well run
Great financial aid
Students are friendly
Diverse student types on campus
Great off-campus food
Campus feels safe
Athletic facilities are great
Lots of beer drinking
Everyone loves the Cardinal
Alumni active on campus
Active minority support groups

ACADEMICS

Academic Rating	94
% students returning for sophomore year	99
% students graduating within 4 years	76
% students graduating within 6 years	96
Calendar	Quarter
Student/faculty ratio	5:1
Profs interesting rating	84
Profs accessible rating	81

Most classes have fewer than 10 students.
Most lab/discussion sessions have fewer than 10 students.

MOST POPULAR MAJORS
computer science; human biology; engineering

STUDENTS SAY ". . ."

Academics
There are few universities that can match the prestige and caliber of Stanford University. At "the forefront of [nearly] every field of study," it's easy to understand why so many students are attracted to the school. Of course, far more than simply offering access to highly rated departments, Stanford strives to "expand your creativity, challenge and deepen your world view, and make you a passionate and informed citizen of the world." Moreover, the opportunities for research "are incredible" and "the support for students (residential, emotional, academic) is unrivaled." And while the university is certainly "academically rigorous," it is "without the competitive edge that many top-tier institutions are known for." Inside the classroom, undergrads are privy to "dynamic" professors who easily "draw [students] into the material because they are so excited to share their passion for the subject." Though instructors are "at the top of their respective fields," most are also "engaging and approachable." A mechanical engineering major supports this sentiment sharing, "I play basketball on Friday mornings with my major adviser and will often bring my homework with me in order to talk to him about problems I'm stuck on afterward." Ultimately, as this senior boasts, "At Stanford, anything is possible; I've lived on a schooner with faculty studying sharks, snorkeled on the Great Barrier Reef, hiked in the Australian rainforest, studied Antarctic phytoplankton with world-class scientists, and spent countless nights discussing philosophy, politics, film, and art until sunrise."

Life
Undergrads agree that "it's pretty much impossible to be bored" at Stanford. Though students "work insanely hard during the week," they "also make it a priority to have a great time." And with so much to take advantage of, having fun is pretty easy. For example, the university sponsors "Cardinal Nights," a program that hosts a number of events including "trips to Great America, a local amusement park, The Great Gatsby movie pre-screening, and Stanford's Got Talent. All of the events are either free or extremely cheap for students." Undergrads also look forward to "special dinners...a common event in upper class housing." These are "nice on-campus dinners that are catered by house chefs. The meals usually have themes, such as Saturday Night Live or Moulin Rouge." Moreover, while there is certainly a drinking scene, it's pretty laid back. A sophomore explains, "You can find as much or as little of a party culture here as you're looking for. There's always a frat party to attend on the weekends, and there's always people to just hang out with at the dorm." Finally, students love the fact that hometown Palo Alto leaves them in close proximity to San Francisco. "A trip to the city is a short train-ride or car-ride away, so going to concerts and events in the city is always a fun option. Same goes for the nearby beaches." However, "there's always so much going on on campus that sometimes it's hard to leave!"

Student Body
Stanford undergrads speak glowingly of their peers: "Everyone here is smart and has some story that will blow you out of the water if you ask, but are very humble and really just looking to have a good time." They also steadfastly assert, "There really is no typical Stanford student." And, thankfully, that "makes it easy to be an integrated and diverse student body." That being said, most Stanford undergrads are "very driven, independently motivated and willing to seek out opportunities." One senior elaborates by sharing, "Everyone fits in because we're united by a fire that drives us all to be excited about what we do. The trends you'll see will be along the lines of leadership and crazy intellect." Ultimately, students at Stanford are "ridiculously friendly and you can meet new people all over campus at almost every type of event."

FINANCIAL AID: 650-723-3058 • E-MAIL: ADMISSION@STANFORD.EDU • WEBSITE: WWW.STANFORD.EDU

THE PRINCETON REVIEW SAYS

Admissions

Very important factors considered include: Class rank, GPA, rigor of secondary school record, standardized test scores, application essay, extracurricular activities, recommendation(s), talent/ability, character/personal qualities. *Other factors considered include:* First generation, geographical residence, interview, racial/ethnic status, volunteer work, work experience, alumni/ae relations. SAT or ACT required; ACT with Writing component required. *Academic units recommended:* 4 English; 4 mathematics; 3 science; 3 social studies or history; 3 foreign language.

Financial Aid

Students should submit: FAFSA, CSS/Financial Aid PROFILE. The Princeton Review suggests that all financial aid forms be submitted as soon as possible after January 1. *Need-based scholarships/grants offered:* Federal Pell, SEOG, State scholarships/grants, private scholarships, the school's own gift aid. *Loan aid offered:* Direct Subsidized Stafford Loans, Direct Unsubsidized Stafford Loans, Direct PLUS loans, Federal Perkins Loans, College/university loans from institutional funds. Federal Work-Study Program available. Institutional employment available. Off-campus job opportunities are good.

The Inside Word

Receiving a highly coveted acceptance letter from Stanford is no easy feat! Indeed, competition to gain admission is fierce. And, unfortunately, there is no magic formula. Clearly, a stellar academic record is a must. Beyond strong transcripts and test scores, successful applicants readily display intellectual curiosity and vigor, commitment to the topics and activities they are passionate about and initiative in seeking out opportunity.

THE SCHOOL SAYS "..."

From the Admissions Office

"Stanford looks for distinctive students who exhibit energy, personality, a sense of intellectual vitality and extraordinary impact outside the classroom. While there is no minimum grade point average, class rank, or test score one needs to be admitted to Stanford, the vast majority of successful applicants will be among the strongest students (academically) in their secondary schools. The most compelling applicants for admission will be those who have thus far achieved state, regional, national, and international recognition in their academic and extracurricular areas of interest."

"The Common Application and Stanford Writing Supplement are both required and must be submitted online. In the Stanford Writing Supplement, accessed at www.commonapp.org, candidates write about an idea or experience important to their intellectual development, as well as a note to their future roommate. In the final essay, candidates are asked to write about what matters to them and why."

"While the SAT or ACT is required for admission, SAT subject tests are not required (and only recommended). AP scores are also not required but can be used for placement/credit purposes if an admitted student decides to enroll."

SELECTIVITY

Admissions Rating	99
# of applicants	38,828
% of applicants accepted	6
% of acceptees attending	76
# offered a place on the wait list	814
% accepting a place on wait list	71
% admitted from wait list	0

FRESHMAN PROFILE

Range SAT Critical Reading	680–780
Range SAT Math	700–790
Range SAT Writing	690–780
Range ACT Composite	31–34
Average HS GPA	4.18
% graduated top 10% of class	96
% graduated top 25% of class	100
% graduated top 50% of class	100

DEADLINES

Early action	
Deadline	11/1
Notification	12/15
Regular	
Deadline	1/3
Notification	4/1
Nonfall registration?	No

APPLICANTS ALSO LOOK AT AND OFTEN PREFER
Harvard College

AND SOMETIMES PREFER
Massachusetts Institute of Technology; Yale University; Princeton University

FINANCIAL FACTS

Financial Aid Rating	96
Annual tuition	$44,184
Room and board	$13,631
Required fees	$573
Books and supplies	$1,425
% needy frosh rec. need-based scholarship or grant aid	96
% needy UG rec. need-based scholarship or grant aid	97
% needy frosh rec. non-need-based scholarship or grant aid	1
% needy UG rec. non-need-based scholarship or grant aid	2
% needy frosh rec. need-based self-help aid	66
% needy UG rec. need-based self-help aid	76
% UG rec. any financial aid	83
% UG borrow to pay for school	23
Average cumulative indebtedness	$16,640
% frosh need fully met	91
% ugrads need fully met	86
Average % of frosh need met	100
Average % of ugrad need met	100

STATE UNIVERSITY OF NEW YORK AT BINGHAMTON

PO Box 6001, Binghamton, NY 13902-6001 • Admissions: 607-777-2171 • Fax: 607-777-4445

CAMPUS LIFE

Quality of Life Rating	70
Fire Safety Rating	85
Green Rating	97
Type of school	Public
Affiliation	No Affiliation
Environment	City

STUDENTS

Total undergrad enrollment	12,940
% male/female	53/47
% from out of state	11
% frosh from public high school	88
% frosh live on campus	98
% ugrads live on campus	59
# of fraternities	34
# of sororities	18
% African American	5
% Asian	14
% Caucasian	54
% Hispanic	10
% Native American	<1
% international	11
# of countries represented	116

SURVEY SAYS . . .

Diverse student types on campus
Campus feels safe
Student publications are popular
Lots of beer drinking

ACADEMICS

Academic Rating	76
% students returning for sophomore year	91
% students graduating within 4 years	69
% students graduating within 6 years	81
Calendar	Semester
Student/faculty ratio	20:1
Profs interesting rating	67
Profs accessible rating	69

Most classes have 20–29 students.
Most lab/discussion sessions have
20–29 students.

MOST POPULAR MAJORS

business administration and management;
engineering; psychology

STUDENTS SAY ". . ."

Academics

SUNY Binghamton provides "the best bang for your buck" to "hard-working, high-achieving kids" who want an "Ivy League workload at a SUNY school price." The school provides "students the ability to receive a top notch education at an affordable price" while maintaining "high standards" and a "commitment to excellence." Like many SUNY schools, Binghamton has "a diverse and active student body" that "take responsibility and pursue what is interesting" to them. Its "great reputation," "value" and "positive, respectful environment" make for "the archetype of an overall college experience." A key part of a great college experience is challenging professors, and Binghamton boasts "approachable, understanding," "very knowledgeable and experienced professors who care about their students." While some students say "professors are very hit or miss," they agree that the faculty is generally "available outside of class" and "eager to help students." "My academic experience is truly amazing, I can honestly say I'm learning from the best of the bests," a Political Science major proclaims. One student wished the school would "improve on getting more diverse faculty/staff," while another says "there is diversity in the student body, faculty, and courses taught." "There is a wide range of majors to choose from and a lot of interesting course options" making for "a great value for the quality of the education." The school's location is "close enough to a number of really fun and interesting cities" to be a selling point. Some of "the buildings and classrooms" need improvement, but "the school has been under constant construction for years and seems to be addressing this issue." One undecided student says SUNY Binghamton "is about finding the right path for you with challenging academics and a lot of fun along the way."

Life

"The motto" at Binghamton is "work hard, play hard." Students here "have a pretty rigorous workload but we also have fun on the weekends whether it be at a party or hanging out with friends." Since SUNY Binghamton does "not have a lot going on in the immediate towns surrounding it," student life revolves around campus. "Binghamton offers a wide array of student-run organizations and school-run activities to participate in during the year," a Bioengineering major explains. "There are a number of different clubs and groups for people to join" and many students participate in them. Still, "school spirit could be improved." "The bus system runs efficiently overall and gives transportation around the city" although students are divided on the value of venturing off campus. Some say the city of Binghamton is "very rundown and somewhat terrifying," but others caution that "the surrounding town, although not fantastic, does have things to do" such as "shopping centers, restaurants, cafes, bars, galleries and museums." Things are improving off campus as "the town of Binghamton is growing because of the University's influence and it has so much potential." Other students use the weekends "to travel because the relative distance to large cities isn't too far." The heavy workload means that a casual air pervades campus, and students "don't care how they look. Sweatpants or pajama pants and a sweatshirt are a must!" That said, there is a sizable contingent who "take[s] the time to look nice here." When the weekend rolls around, it is "button downs, polos, cocktail dresses, tights, heels, leather jackets."

Student Body

"Diversity" is a real plus at Binghamton. As a SUNY state school, "there's about every type of person you can imagine making it easy to make friends expand what you're used to." If you have to generalize, "most students are from New York City" and often "Jewish & from Long Island or Asian & from NYC." Most people "were serious student in high school with many AP classes" and now are "really driven," "really smart," "liberal" and "willing to be friends with everyone." The typical student is active on campus, being "involved with [a] school organization, committed to their studies, but also goes out on the weekends." The school's "rich, diverse atmosphere…challenges its students while providing an enjoyable experience." Overall, students at SUNY Binghamton "seem to have a very optimistic and happy attitude of just about everything."

STATE UNIVERSITY OF NEW YORK AT BINGHAMTON

FINANCIAL AID: 607-777-2428 • E-MAIL: ADMIT@BINGHAMTON.EDU • WEBSITE: WWW.BINGHAMTON.EDU

THE PRINCETON REVIEW SAYS

Admissions

Very important factors considered include: GPA, rigor of secondary school record, standardized test scores. *Important factors considered include:* Class rank, application essay, extracurricular activities, recommendation(s). *Other factors considered include:* First generation, geographical residence, racial/ethnic status, state residency, talent/ability, volunteer work, work experience, alumni/ae relations, character/personal qualities, level of applicant's interest. SAT or ACT required; ACT with Writing component required. TOEFL required of all international applicants. *Academic units required:* 4 English; 3 mathematics; 2 science; 2 social studies; 3 foreign language. *Academic units recommended:* 4 mathematics; 4 science; 4 social studies; 4 history.

Financial Aid

Students should submit: FAFSA, State aid form. The Princeton Review suggests that all financial aid forms be submitted as soon as possible after January 1. *Need-based scholarships/grants offered:* Federal Pell, SEOG, State scholarships/grants, private scholarships, the school's own gift aid. *Loan aid offered:* Direct Subsidized Stafford Loans, Direct Unsubsidized Stafford Loans, Direct PLUS loans, Federal Perkins Loans, Federal Nursing Loans, College/university loans from institutional funds. Federal Work-Study Program available. Institutional employment available. Off-campus job opportunities are excellent.

The Inside Word

Like the vast majority of New York state schools, Binghamton accepts the single applySUNY application. Binghamton also accepts the Common Application, making it easy to apply to SUNY Binghamton and other schools at the same time. Binghamton is one of the top public universities in the country, so expect competition to be stiff.

THE SCHOOL SAYS "..."

From the Admissions Office

"Binghamton has established itself as the premier public university in the Northeast, because of our outstanding undergraduate programs, vibrant campus culture, and committed faculty. Students are academically motivated, but there is a great deal of mutual help as they compete against the standard of a class rather than each other. Faculty and students work side by side in research labs or on artistic pursuits. Achievement, exploration, and leadership are hallmarks of a Binghamton education. Add to that a campus wide commitment to internationalization that includes a robust study abroad program, cultural offerings, languages and international studies, and you have a place where graduates leave prepared for success. Binghamton University graduates lead the nation in top starting salaries among public universities, demonstrating that our students are recognized by employers and recruiters for having strong abilities to be leaders, critical thinkers, decision makers, analysts, and researchers in many fields and industries."

SELECTIVITY

Admissions Rating	94
# of applicants	29,067
% of applicants accepted	42
% of acceptees attending	22
# offered a place on the wait list	2,474

FRESHMAN PROFILE

Range SAT Critical Reading	583–675
Range SAT Math	620–710
Range SAT Writing	570–670
Range ACT Composite	27–30
Minimum paper TOEFL	560
Minimum web-based TOEFL	80
Average HS GPA	3.60
% graduated top 10% of class	52
% graduated top 25% of class	84
% graduated top 50% of class	96

DEADLINES

Early action	
Deadline	11/15
Notification	1/15
Regular	
Priority	1/15
Nonfall registration?	Yes

FINANCIAL FACTS

Financial Aid Rating	72
Annual in-state tuition	$6,170
Annual out-of-state tuition	$17,810
Room and board	$11,264
Required fees	$2,309
Books and supplies	$1,000
% needy frosh rec. need-based scholarship or grant aid	77
% needy UG rec. need-based scholarship or grant aid	81
% needy frosh rec. non-need-based scholarship or grant aid	17
% needy UG rec. non-need-based scholarship or grant aid	10
% needy frosh rec. need-based self-help aid	98
% needy UG rec. need-based self-help aid	98
% frosh rec. any financial aid	81
% UG rec. any financial aid	70
% UG borrow to pay for school	51
Average cumulative indebtedness	$23,912
% frosh need fully met	10
% ugrads need fully met	16
Average % of frosh need met	63
Average % of ugrad need met	72

STATE UNIVERSITY OF NEW YORK AT GENESEO

ONE COLLEGE CIRCLE, GENESEO, NY 14454-1401 • ADMISSIONS: 585-245-5571 • FAX: 585-245-5550

CAMPUS LIFE

Quality of Life Rating	82
Fire Safety Rating	94
Green Rating	92
Type of school	Public
Affiliation	No Affiliation
Environment	Village

STUDENTS

Total undergrad enrollment	5,463
% male/female	42/58
% from out of state	2
% frosh from public high school	82
% frosh live on campus	99
% ugrads live on campus	55
# of fraternities (% ugrad men join)	11 (15)
# of sororities (% ugrad women join)	15 (24)
% African American	3
% Asian	7
% Caucasian	75
% Hispanic	6
% Native American	<1
% international	2
# of countries represented	42

SURVEY SAYS . . .

Lab facilities are great
Students are friendly
Campus feels safe
Lots of beer drinking

ACADEMICS

Academic Rating	82
% students returning for sophomore year	90
% students graduating within 4 years	67
% students graduating within 6 years	78
Calendar	Semester
Student/faculty ratio	19:1
Profs interesting rating	78
Profs accessible rating	82

Most classes have 20–29 students.
Most lab/discussion sessions have
10–19 students.

STUDENTS SAY "..."

Academics

Undergrads at SUNY Geneseo laud their university for offering "an outstanding education [at] an affordable price." With the combined "top-notch" academics and "small-town feel," it's no wonder so many students "feel at home" the minute they set foot on the campus. Indeed, Geneseo provides a "close-knit community," which in turn creates "a family environment." While the university has a number of great programs, students are especially quick to highlight the stellar education, business, and science departments. Importantly, "small classes" translates into highly "accessible" professors. Moreover, they're "truly dedicated to helping students succeed" and "are always open to talk...even during non-office hours." Undergrads do caution that you can't slack off here. Professors "seek to challenge" their students, and the "course load is tough" especially given that Geneseo is "doing a lot to combat grade inflation." Luckily, for the most part, students find their teachers "very engaging" and appreciate that they're able "to make classes very interesting" in large part through "personal stories that are relevant to the material." Perhaps this knowing senior says it best: "Geneseo has a great atmosphere, challenging classes, a wonderful student population, and the best price!"

Life

By and large, undergrads proclaim that "life is great" at SUNY Geneseo. Students "study hard and play hard" and are quite adept at striking a balance between the two. Fortunately, "weekends are very lively, both on campus and off." An active lot, undergrads like to take advantage of Geneseo's "good" athletic facilities, which include "an ice rink, a swimming pool, a cardio room, and a weight room, as well as lots of intramural and club sports." Additionally, "Varsity sports competitions are extremely popular, especially hockey." There are also "many on-campus activities for students to get involved in throughout the week and especially late at night on the weekends." Indeed, there's "everything from laser tag to crafts to midnight bowling." Of course, "there are also outstanding clubs that [offer] a variety of services and activities such as Colleges Against Cancer, Figure Skating Club, Sports Medicine Club, Outing Club, Ski and Snowboard Club, and so many more." Though "many people do party on the weekend," students assure us, "You don't have to go to parties or join a Greek organization to have a good time." For those with an itch to explore, a content sophomore shares, "The surrounding country is beautiful and provides lots of fun outdoorsy activities. Rochester and Buffalo are within reach, and Livingston County provides bus service to Rochester."

Student Body

What is one thing that unites Geneseo undergrads? Students here agree that their peers are "very good at time management." Indeed, "they know how to study, but they also know how to have a good time." Having multitasking down to an art form, "They are able to get their work done and excel in classes while still participating in social events and hanging out with their friends." Fortunately, Geneseo is "not a pressure cooker school," and most students are "pretty relaxed." While some assert that the school is "very diverse," others say that the "typical student is a white, middle-class, well-rounded, high school overachiever." Regardless of stereotype, students are very "open to meeting new people," and "making friends [is] really easy here." As one content freshman elaborates, "The students are very accepting. They come together frequently and support each other, causes, and the community." A fellow classmate adds, "It's really hard to find anyone who doesn't fit in with at least one group on campus because there are so many with so many different interests."

FINANCIAL AID: 585-245-5731 • E-MAIL: ADMISSIONS@GENESEO.EDU • WEBSITE: WWW.GENESEO.EDU

THE PRINCETON REVIEW SAYS

Admissions

Very important factors considered include: Rigor of secondary school record, standardized test scores. *Important factors considered include:* Class rank, GPA, application essay, extracurricular activities, racial/ethnic status, recommendation(s), talent/ability. *Other factors considered include:* First generation, volunteer work, work experience, alumni/ae relations, character/personal qualities, level of applicant's interest. SAT or ACT required; SAT and SAT Subject Tests or ACT considered if submitted; ACT with or without Writing component accepted. TOEFL required of all international applicants. *Academic units recommended:* 4 English; 4 mathematics; 4 science; 4 social studies; 4 foreign language.

Financial Aid

Students should submit: FAFSA, State aid form. Regular filing deadline is 2/15. The Princeton Review suggests that all financial aid forms be submitted as soon as possible after January 1. *Need-based scholarships/grants offered:* Federal Pell, SEOG, State scholarships/grants. *Loan aid offered:* Direct Subsidized Stafford Loans, Direct Unsubsidized Stafford Loans, Direct PLUS loans, Federal Perkins Loans. Federal Work-Study Program available. Institutional employment available. Off-campus job opportunities are poor.

The Inside Word

SUNY Geneseo increasingly receives applications from a strong candidate pool, and gaining admission is no easy feat. First and foremost, the admissions committee reviews your high school transcript and college entrance exam scores. Applicants who have excelled in honors, IB, or advanced placement courses will have a leg up. Additionally, those reviewing prospective students attempt to take a holistic approach so be sure to submit a well-crafted essay and to demonstrate extracurricular commitment.

THE SCHOOL SAYS "..."

From the Admissions Office

"Geneseo has carved a distinctive niche among the nation's premier public liberal arts colleges. Geneseo is the only undergraduate college in the state of New York system to be granted a chapter of Phi Beta Kappa. The college now competes for students with some of the nation's most selective private colleges, including Colgate, Vassar, Hamilton, and Boston College. Founded in 1871, the college occupies a 220-acre hillside campus in the historic Village of Geneseo, overlooking the scenic Genesee Valley. As a residential campus—with nearly two-thirds of the students living in college residence halls—it provides a rich and varied program of social, cultural, recreational, and scholarly activities as well as numerous volunteer service opportunities. Geneseo is noted for its distinctive core curriculum and the extraordinary opportunities it offers undergraduates to pursue independent study and research with faculty who value close working relationships with talented students. Equally impressive is the remarkable success of its graduates, 35 percent of whom study at leading graduate and professional schools immediately following graduation. Geneseo is in the top five among all the country's Master's colleges in the number of alumni who earn doctorates in STEM fields and in the top ten in the number who earn doctorates in all disciplines.

"SUNY Geneseo will use either SAT or ACT test results in the admission selection process. The SAT writing test result will not be used. SAT Subject Test results are not required but will be considered if the applicant submits the test results."

SELECTIVITY

Admissions Rating	93
# of applicants	9,069
% of applicants accepted	53
% of acceptees attending	24
# offered a place on the wait list	900
% accepting a place on wait list	58
% admitted from wait list	4
# of early decision applicants	292
% accepted early decision	44

FRESHMAN PROFILE

Range SAT Critical Reading	580–680
Range SAT Math	597.5–680
Range ACT Composite	26–29
Minimum paper TOEFL	525
Average HS GPA	3.69
% graduated top 10% of class	48
% graduated top 25% of class	84
% graduated top 50% of class	99

DEADLINES

Early decision	
Deadline	11/15
Notification	12/15
Regular	
Deadline	1/1
Notification	3/1
Nonfall registration?	Yes

APPLICANTS ALSO LOOK AT AND OFTEN PREFER

Colgate University; Cornell University; Hamilton College; New York University

AND SOMETIMES PREFER

Skidmore College; State University of New York at Binghamton; University of Rochester; Vassar College; Boston College

AND RARELY PREFER

State University of New York—Stony Brook University; Syracuse University; Nazareth College

FINANCIAL FACTS

Financial Aid Rating	73
Annual in-state tuition	$5,870
Annual out-of-state tuition	$15,320
Room and board	$11,242
Required fees	$1,560
% needy frosh rec. need-based scholarship or grant aid	83
% needy UG rec. need-based scholarship or grant aid	79
% needy frosh rec. non-need-based scholarship or grant aid	19
% needy UG rec. non-need-based scholarship or grant aid	25
% needy frosh rec. need-based self-help aid	83
% needy UG rec. need-based self-help aid	78
% frosh rec. any financial aid	50
% UG rec. any financial aid	49
% UG borrow to pay for school	65
Average cumulative indebtedness	$20,790

1 Forestry Drive, Syracuse, NY 13210-2779 • Admissions: 315-470-6600 • Fax: 315-470-6933

CAMPUS LIFE

Quality of Life Rating	87
Fire Safety Rating	96
Green Rating	94
Type of school	Public
Affiliation	No Affiliation
Environment	City

STUDENTS

Total undergrad enrollment	1,713
% male/female	60/40
% from out of state	20
% frosh from public high school	90
% frosh live on campus	90
% ugrads live on campus	33
# of fraternities	26
# of sororities	21
% African American	1
% Asian	3
% Caucasian	87
% Hispanic	3
% Native American	<1
% international	2
# of countries represented	39

SURVEY SAYS . . .
Students are happy
Lab facilities are great
Students are friendly
Students get along with local community
Students environmentally aware
Great off-campus food
Dorms are like palaces

ACADEMICS

Academic Rating	81
% students returning for sophomore year	87
% students graduating within 4 years	51
% students graduating within 6 years	72
Calendar	Semester
Student/faculty ratio	13:1
Profs interesting rating	87
Profs accessible rating	76

Most classes have 10–19 students.
Most lab/discussion sessions have 20–29 students.

MOST POPULAR MAJORS
environmental science; environmental biology; landscape architecture

STUDENTS SAY " . . ."

Academics
SUNY's College of Environmental Science and Forestry is "dedicated to its mission of sustainability." It is "a great school for those interested in research and theory." The school's "unique class offerings" include using its "thousands of acres of forest" for "education, research, and forestry." Students are "out in the field learning how to do what they want to do in life." With Syracuse University right next-door, SUNY ESF "has a great small school atmosphere," with "all of the perks of a big university." This "great partnership" between the two schools gives SUNY ESF students "the option to take their classes" and "enjoy the amenities and even the social life of a larger, private school." For in-state students, SUNY ESF is "very affordable." One transfer student says, "ESF is definitely the best 'bang for your buck.' I attended a private university prior, and I have paid for four years what one year costs there. And the courses are just as well taught." Professors "have diverse teaching styles, and different students prefer different teachers. Some seem over-committed between their research and teaching duties, and this can make them difficult to reach or rely on." "Professors are committed to their beliefs and are mostly all in active research." Don't expect to breeze through classes at ESF. "If you plan on coasting through college, ESF is not for you!" Professors "set the bar high for expectations and keep it there. I'm consistently challenged and encouraged." There are "well maintained chemistry and computing lab facilities," and the "newer lab buildings are first class." "SUNY ESF is a great school whether you love plants, animals, or the environment, and offers great opportunities for real world experience related to your field of study."

Life
Students at SUNY ESF have access to Syracuse University's "food services, gyms, and health center." ESF "doesn't have many sports (but we can play club sports over at SU)" which are "formed with students of both colleges." "The dorms are fantastic; the building was built in 2011 and all the rooms have private baths." "ESF offers lots of activities including monthly free movies, breakfasts, presentations, ski trips, ice-skating, craft fairs, etc. We get weekly emails letting us know about all the events, and there's always something to do." In nice weather, students make good use of the quad. "It's fairly large, so people hang out there between classes with friends." Because of the "outdoorsy" nature of many students also enjoy, "running, biking, hiking, scuba, rock climbing, travel, you name it!" "Armory Square is a short bus ride away and offers some great off campus lunch and dinner options." There are "fun house parties and the downtown scene is great in my opinion. There are also several ski resorts and lakes nearby for fun in every season." According to one student, "drug use is more prevalent than it should be," but there is a sober crowd, like this student who says, "I spend my Friday nights at Insomniac Events, which is for people who don't want to go out and party. Each event is themed and they are really fun."

Student Body
"There's extremes here at ESF... It's likely that you'll see someone with bare feet, dreadlocks and a tie-dye t-shirt walking around campus, and there's people who dress in slacks everyday. The typical student is usually happily between the two extremes, and spends a lot of time in the library and/or the computer labs!" "Attending SUNY ESF means being surrounded by people who are passionate about the earth and science in general, while all having unique perspectives and interests to share."

STATE UNIVERSITY OF NEW YORK—COLLEGE OF ENVIRONMENTAL SCIENCE AND FORESTRY

FINANCIAL AID: 315-470-6706 • E-MAIL: ESFINFO@ESF.EDU • WEBSITE: WWW.ESF.EDU

THE PRINCETON REVIEW SAYS

Admissions

Very important factors considered include: GPA, rigor of secondary school record, standardized test scores, application essay, level of applicant's interest. *Important factors considered include:* Class rank, extracurricular activities, interview, recommendation(s), talent/ability, volunteer work, work experience, character/personal qualities. *Other factors considered include:* First generation, geographical residence, racial/ethnic status, state residency, alumni/ae relations. SAT or ACT required; SAT and SAT Subject Tests or ACT considered if submitted; ACT with or without Writing component accepted. TOEFL required of all international applicants. *Academic units required:* 4 English; 3 mathematics; 3 science; (3 science lab); 3 social studies. *Academic units recommended:* 4 mathematics; 4 science; 3 social studies; 2 foreign language; 1 history.

Financial Aid

Students should submit: FAFSA, State aid form. The Princeton Review suggests that all financial aid forms be submitted as soon as possible after January 1. *Need-based scholarships/grants offered:* Federal Pell, SEOG, State scholarships/grants, private scholarships, the school's own gift aid. *Loan aid offered:* Direct Subsidized Stafford Loans, Direct Unsubsidized Stafford Loans, Direct PLUS loans, Federal Perkins Loans, College/university loans from institutional funds. Federal Work-Study Program available. Institutional employment available. Off-campus job opportunities are excellent.

The Inside Word

SUNY ESF is an excellent value even for those students hailing from outside the Empire State. While there are many specialized Bachelor of Science degrees, there are also coordinated programs between the university and the Upstate Medical School as well as a host of pre-professional programs. Stats are an important aspect in the calculus of admission but level of demonstrated interest is considered equal to SAT scores. Aspiring Mighty Oaks should make their interest known early and often.

SELECTIVITY

Admissions Rating	88
# of applicants	1,538
% of applicants accepted	50
% of acceptees attending	38
# offered a place on the wait list	151
% accepting a place on wait list	28
% admitted from wait list	40
# of early decision applicants	128
% accepted early decision	66

FRESHMAN PROFILE

Range SAT Critical Reading	530–630
Range SAT Math	550–630
Range ACT Composite	22–26
Minimum paper TOEFL	550
Minimum web-based TOEFL	213
Average HS GPA	3.65
% graduated top 10% of class	27
% graduated top 25% of class	66
% graduated top 50% of class	95

DEADLINES

Early decision	
Deadline	12/1
Notification	1/15
Regular	
Priority	2/1
Nonfall registration?	Yes

APPLICANTS ALSO LOOK AT AND OFTEN PREFER
Cornell University; State University of New York—Stony Brook

AND SOMETIMES PREFER
Penn State—University Park; Rochester Institute of Technology; State University of New York at Binghamton

AND RARELY PREFER
Clarkson University; Syracuse University

FINANCIAL FACTS

Financial Aid Rating	92
Annual in-state tuition	$5,870
Annual out-of-state tuition	$15,320
Room and board	$14,630
Required fees	$1,065
Books and supplies	$1,200
% needy frosh rec. need-based scholarship or grant aid	91
% needy UG rec. need-based scholarship or grant aid	96
% needy frosh rec. non-need-based scholarship or grant aid	60
% needy UG rec. non-need-based scholarship or grant aid	50
% needy frosh rec. need-based self-help aid	100
% needy UG rec. need-based self-help aid	91
% frosh rec. any financial aid	91
% UG rec. any financial aid	93
% UG borrow to pay for school	80
Average cumulative indebtedness	$15,335
% frosh need fully met	80
% ugrads need fully met	80
Average % of frosh need met	88
Average % of ugrad need met	88

STATE UNIVERSITY OF NEW YORK—PURCHASE COLLEGE

735 ANDERSON HILL ROAD, PURCHASE, NY 10577 • ADMISSIONS: 914-251-6300 • FAX: 914-251-6314

CAMPUS LIFE

Quality of Life Rating	70
Fire Safety Rating	60*
Green Rating	91
Type of school	Public
Affiliation	No Affiliation
Environment	Town

STUDENTS

Total undergrad enrollment	3,900
% male/female	44/56
% from out of state	17
% frosh live on campus	91
% ugrads live on campus	66
% African American	7
% Asian	2
% Caucasian	52
% Hispanic	16
% Native American	<1
% international	2
# of countries represented	39

SURVEY SAYS . . .
Theater is popular
Students aren't religious
Frats and sororities are unpopular
or nonexistent

ACADEMICS

Academic Rating	84
% students returning for sophomore year	83
% students graduating within 4 years	52
% students graduating within 6 years	63
Calendar	Semester
Student/faculty ratio	16:1
Profs interesting rating	84
Profs accessible rating	71

Most classes have fewer than 10 students.
Most lab/discussion sessions have
10–19 students.

MOST POPULAR MAJORS
visual and performing arts; liberal arts

STUDENTS SAY " . . ."

Academics

In urging its students to "Think Wide Open," SUNY Purchase features "unique and artistic minds" within in its "wonderfully diverse community of people." Boasting both great value and close proximity to New York City, SUNY Purchase is consequently well known for its outstanding curricula in the arts, and its "very creative, often artistic" students cite its film, music, creative writing, graphic design, and generally "artsy atmosphere" as major draws: "The School of the Arts is very rigorous and has a reputation of being one of the best in the country." While Purchase's arts programs are very frequently named by students as their reason for attending, the school offers a "wide variety of majors," and students report being "in love" with their diverse courses of study. Students, particularly locals who benefit from in-state tuition, also appreciate their education's "affordability," and say that Purchase leaders don't sacrifice personal attention for cost value, creating an "efficient, helpful and...very welcoming community." Many students choose the "very academically sound" SUNY Purchase over private options for this reason, affirming that their education offers the "same likeliness of obtaining a suitable and successful job/career as a private school" with "the affordability [of] a state school." Students attribute much of this "overall fantastic academic experience" to "highly motivated, engaged, and knowledgeable" professors, who are "dedicated" and "willing to do anything to ensure the success of their students." "I have learned more in college than I have in my entire life," one student encapsulates her academic experience. "That alone should sum up how fantastic Purchase College has been to me."

Life

Both resident and commuter students attend lots of arts-oriented performances on campus, especially at The Stood student center, which is "home to frequent excellent musical performances." One undergraduate echoes the common themes: "My life at school revolves around several things. The arts, my studies, seeing my friends and trying to attend as many campus events as possible." Student clubs and activities, arts programs, and "house parties" populate the "very social atmosphere" on campus, and off campus, further entertainment can be enjoyed through the "easy access" to New York City and also neighboring White Plains. Drugs seem to make an appearance in social life without dominating it, while drinking is more prominent in students' depictions of Purchase's party culture. "Athletic" teams and games are less ubiquitously attended than artsier fare, but are present nonetheless. Purchase students enjoy themselves, but not at the expense of their studies: "people are focused on their work" because "everyone is constantly working towards bettering their talent."

Student Body

The "creative, vibrant, eclectic, and diverse" Purchase student body "want[s] to do something great, often something odd, but great." They're "arty," "opinionated and smart," "liberal" and "open minded." They express pride in how "very bohemian" and inclusive they perceive their campus to be: "It's a haven and a safe space for those of us who have spent life being misfits or outcasts, and it harbors a creative community like no other." It's "okay to be weird" at Purchase, and the collective weirdness engenders a "free-thinking," "non-judgmental," "non-conforming" social zeitgeist. "Purchase is full of bright students who flourish, work hard, and study hard, but who don't always fit into standard avenues to 'success'," one summarizes. At least for "eclectic" "hipsters," it's easy to fit in at Purchase because "being unique is seen as a value." "Think wide open" is the near-unanimous summary of the Purchase student experience, both academically and socially.

FINANCIAL AID: 914-251-6350 • E-MAIL: ADMISSIONS@PURCHASE.EDU • WEBSITE: WWW.PURCHASE.EDU

THE PRINCETON REVIEW SAYS

Admissions

Very important factors considered include: GPA, application essay, talent/ability. *Important factors considered include:* Standardized test scores. *Other factors considered include:* Class rank, rigor of secondary school record, extracurricular activities, interview, recommendation(s), character/personal qualities. SAT or ACT required; ACT with or without Writing component accepted. TOEFL required of all international applicants. *Academic units recommended:* 4 English; 4 mathematics; 3 science; 4 social studies; 3 foreign language; 2 academic electives.

Financial Aid

Students should submit: FAFSA, State aid form. The Princeton Review suggests that all financial aid forms be submitted as soon as possible after January 1. *Need-based scholarships/grants offered:* Federal Pell, SEOG, State scholarships/grants, private scholarships, the school's own gift aid. *Loan aid offered:* Direct Subsidized Stafford Loans, Direct Unsubsidized Stafford Loans, Direct PLUS loans, Federal Perkins Loans. Federal Work-Study Program available. Institutional employment available. Off-campus job opportunities are excellent.

The Inside Word

Almost 40 percent of Purchase students are enrolled in the highly selective School of the Arts, making it a popular choice for prospective students who prefer a world-class arts education at a state school price. Arts applicants should know that to apply to the Conservatories—Dance, Theatre Arts, Music, School of Art +Design and School of Film and Media Studies—the audition, portfolio, or other applicable work samples are of paramount importance, and criteria such as standardized test scores and high school transcripts are weighted less than demonstrated artistic excellence. However, to apply to Purchase's Liberal Arts and Sciences programs, traditional academic criteria are the primary considerations for admission.

THE SCHOOL SAYS "..."

From the Admissions Office

"At Purchase College, 'Think Wide Open' is not just a slogan—it's our way of teaching, learning, and being. Our academic community integrates the spirit of discovery in the liberal arts and sciences with the excitement of the arts that encourages exploration beyond expected boundaries. At Purchase you will find an unparalleled environment of creativity and innovation, amid an atmosphere of respect for individuality and diversity.

"Purchase offers rich disciplinary and interdisciplinary programs in the liberal arts and sciences, art and design, film and media studies, dance, music, and theatre arts. Our engaging and dynamic faculty are among the most accomplished in their fields, and work hard to ensure students succeed in their fields of study.

"Although it's tempting to characterize the Purchase College student as simply creative, passionate, and inquisitive, our students are each unique and not easily categorized. Purchase students represent a broad spectrum of familial, social, ethnic, economic, and geographical backgrounds. Highly talented, motivated, and entrepreneurial, they strive to impact our society through civic and cultural engagement.

"Still a relatively young college, Purchase offers students an opportunity to build upon established campus traditions and create new ones. Our proximity to NYC provides students pursue to outstanding cultural and career-related opportunities. On campus, students can see world-class performances at the PAC and notable exhibitions at the Neuberger Museum.

"We seek to enroll highly motivated, hard-working and academically strong students with a consistent record of achievement in a challenging high school curriculum. Admission criteria vary amongst programs."

SELECTIVITY

Admissions Rating	88
# of applicants	8,907
% of applicants accepted	33
% of acceptees attending	23

FRESHMAN PROFILE

Range SAT Critical Reading	500–610
Range SAT Math	480–570
Range SAT Writing	480–600
Range ACT Composite	21–27
Minimum paper TOEFL	550
Minimum web-based TOEFL	213
Average HS GPA	3.20
% graduated top 10% of class	10
% graduated top 25% of class	39
% graduated top 50% of class	71

DEADLINES

Early action	
Deadline	11/15
Notification	12/15
Regular	
Priority	3/1
Deadline	7/15
Nonfall registration?	Yes

APPLICANTS ALSO LOOK AT AND OFTEN PREFER

New York University

FINANCIAL FACTS

Financial Aid Rating	68
Annual in-state tuition	$5,570
Annual out-of-state tuition	$14,820
Room and board	$11,566
Required fees	$1,660
Books and supplies	$1,168
% needy frosh rec. need-based scholarship or grant aid	83
% needy UG rec. need-based scholarship or grant aid	83
% needy frosh rec. non-need-based scholarship or grant aid	1
% needy UG rec. non-need-based scholarship or grant aid	1
% needy frosh rec. need-based self-help aid	97
% needy UG rec. need-based self-help aid	97
% UG borrow to pay for school	60
Average cumulative indebtedness	$26,684
% frosh need fully met	3
% ugrads need fully met	4
Average % of frosh need met	50
Average % of ugrad need met	53

STATE UNIVERSITY OF NEW YORK—STONY BROOK UNIVERSITY

OFFICE OF ADMISSIONS, STONY BROOK, NY 11794-1901 • ADMISSIONS: 631-632-6868 • FAX: 631-632-9898

CAMPUS LIFE

Quality of Life Rating	73
Fire Safety Rating	72
Green Rating	99
Type of school	Public
Affiliation	No Affiliation
Environment	Town

STUDENTS

Total undergrad enrollment	15,786
% male/female	54/46
% from out of state	9
% frosh from public high school	90
% frosh live on campus	84
% ugrads live on campus	60
# of fraternities	18
# of sororities	15
% African American	6
% Asian	24
% Caucasian	38
% Hispanic	10
% Native American	<1
% international	10
# of countries represented	110

SURVEY SAYS . . .

Class discussions are rare
Lots of beer drinking
Great library

ACADEMICS

Academic Rating	74
% students returning for sophomore year	90
% students graduating within 4 years	45
% students graduating within 6 years	66
Calendar	Semester
Student/faculty ratio	18:1
Profs interesting rating	65
Profs accessible rating	67

Most classes have 10–19 students.
Most lab/discussion sessions have 20–29 students.

MOST POPULAR MAJORS
biology; psychology; health services

STUDENTS SAY " . . . "

Academics

Students at Stony Brook University get all the advantages of a "premiere science and research university," while also benefiting from the diverse atmosphere and low tuition costs of a large public institution. The school has a "great reputation in science and engineering," as well as strong pre-med and pre-health programs; however, it's the "access to hands-on, real-world experiences" that truly distinguishes a Stony Brook education. Motivated undergrads find "the opportunities to do research are phenomenal"; in addition to the school's proximity to the myriad opportunities in New York City, "there is a hospital right across the street, shuttles to Brookhaven National Lab, and hundreds of professors that look for undergrads to work in the lab." That said, "you must be proactive in order to succeed" at Stony Brook. "The professors are challenging and expect a lot from you," and the "vast, sometimes overwhelming size" means classes are sometimes "packed to the brim with 500-some students." Fortunately, Stony Brook has found ways to make the experience more personal. For one thing, first-year students are all "broken down into smaller colleges," learning communities of "like minded individuals" who live in the same dorms and take freshman seminars together. On top of that, "all classes in large lecture styles attempt to make the learning experience more personal through section meetings with TAs, online interactive discussion boards and/or professors that are very willing to discuss the material with you." Once you get through the first few years, "Upperclassmen have excellent classes," which are often smaller and lead by "very entertaining, interactive and challenging" professors.

Life

Academics at Stony Brook University are no walk in the park, and many students say their life consists of little more than "studying all the time and staying up very late and just stressing" to stay on top of course work. Others have an easier time finding the "balance between getting work done and socializing with friends," and the majority of students are "involved in at least one or two clubs on campus." When they want to blow off steam, students "hang out and drink and listen to music," or partake of the "brand new, state-of-the-art recreational facility, indoor swimming pool, and bike trails all around campus through woods." Come Friday, a lot of students leave campus for home, so "social life dies down on weekends." In response, the school is working hard to make student life at Stony Brook more exciting. Currently, "The Weekend Life council has partnered up with organizations to make weekend events commonplace, and larger groups like the Undergraduate Student Government have done amazing things, like reviving the Stony Brook Concert Series." A testament to the changing culture, a student points out that, "This past year we set an attendance record at our stadium for homecoming (which is a Saturday!)." Even if life on campus can be a bit subdued, students reassure us, "As long as you make a solid group of friends you'll always have something to do."

Students

"Students from around the world and all different socio-economic backgrounds" come to Stony Brook, and the school excels at "bringing a large population of diverse backgrounds, identities and cultures together for the common purpose of learning." In addition to the "many international students," there are "a lot of commuters" from the Stony Brook area, as well as "Long Island locals" who live on campus but spend weekends at home. In terms of personality, you'll meet people of every ilk, including "gamers that never leave their rooms and social butterflies that are very involved and generally know what's going on everywhere on campus." No matter what your style, "There are so many different social circles that it would be more impossible to not find somewhere to fit in." While social life is important to many Stony Brook undergrads, academics come first for the majority of this "very bright" and "studious" student body. Always keeping an eye on their future, "students are committed to their academics so that they can get a solid job soon after they graduate."

STATE UNIVERSITY OF NEW YORK—STONY BROOK UNIVERSITY

FINANCIAL AID: 631-632-6840 • E-MAIL: ENROLL@STONYBROOK.EDU • WEBSITE: WWW.STONYBROOK.EDU

THE PRINCETON REVIEW SAYS

Admissions

Very important factors considered include: GPA, rigor of secondary school record, standardized test scores. *Important factors considered include:* Application essay, recommendation(s). *Other factors considered include:* Class rank, extracurricular activities, first generation, geographical residence, talent/ability, volunteer work, work experience, alumni/ae relations, character/personal qualities, level of applicant's interest. SAT or ACT required; ACT with Writing component required. TOEFL required of all international applicants. *Academic units required:* 4 English; 3 mathematics; 3 science; 4 social studies; 2 foreign language. *Academic units recommended:* 4 mathematics; 4 science; 3 foreign language.

Financial Aid

Students should submit: FAFSA. The Princeton Review suggests that all financial aid forms be submitted as soon as possible after January 1. *Need-based scholarships/grants offered:* Federal Pell, SEOG, State scholarships/grants, private scholarships, the school's own gift aid. *Loan aid offered:* Direct Subsidized Stafford Loans, Direct Unsubsidized Stafford Loans, Direct PLUS loans, Federal Perkins Loans. Federal Work-Study Program available. Institutional employment available. Off-campus job opportunities are excellent.

The Inside Word

Admission to Stony Brook University is competitive. Successful applicants for the freshman class will have typically followed a rigorous college-prep curriculum in high school and have strong standardized test scores, though the university will also give special consideration to students with leadership experience or talents demonstrated through extracurricular activities or volunteer work. Students with a particularly strong academic record may be considered for the university's special programs, including the Honors Program, the University Scholars program, and the Scholars in Medicine program.

THE SCHOOL SAYS "..."

From the Admissions Office

"Our graduates include Carolyn Porco, the leader of the Imaging Team for the Cassini mission to Saturn; John Hennessy, the president of Stanford University; and Scott Higham, a Pulitzer Prize–winning investigative journalist for the Washington Post who has come to speak to students at our new School of Journalism. Situated on 1,040 wooded acres on the North Shore of Long Island, Stony Brook offers more than 200 majors, minors, and combined-degree programs for undergraduates, including our Fast Track MBA program, a thriving research environment, and a dynamic first-year experience in one of six small undergraduate communities. Faculty include four members of our School of Marine and Atmospheric Sciences who are co-winners of the Nobel Peace Prize. Students enjoy comfortable campus housing, outstanding recreational facilities that include an 8,300 seat stadium, modern student activities center, indoor sports complex, and a new 85,000-square foot campus recreation center. In addition, the Staller Center for the Arts offers spectacular theatrical and musical performances throughout the year. We invite students who possess both intellectual curiosity and academic ability to explore the countless exciting opportunities available at Stony Brook. Freshmen applying for admission to the university are required to take the SAT (or the ACT with the writing section)."

SELECTIVITY

Admissions Rating	93
# of applicants	30,300
% of applicants accepted	39
% of acceptees attending	23
# offered a place on the wait list	2,176
% accepting a place on wait list	42
% admitted from wait list	20

FRESHMAN PROFILE

Range SAT Critical Reading	550–650
Range SAT Math	600–700
Range SAT Writing	540–650
Range ACT Composite	26–30
Minimum paper TOEFL	550
Minimum web-based TOEFL	213
Average HS GPA	3.76
% graduated top 10% of class	45
% graduated top 25% of class	74
% graduated top 50% of class	93

DEADLINES

Regular	
Priority	1/15
Notification	4/1
Nonfall registration?	Yes

APPLICANTS ALSO LOOK AT AND OFTEN PREFER

State University of New York at Binghamton; New York University; Rensselaer Polytechnic Institute; Cornell University

AND SOMETIMES PREFER

Pennsylvania State University—University Park; Rutgers The State University of New Jersey—New Brunswick; State University of New York at Geneseo; University of Connecticut

AND RARELY PREFER

Pace University; Hofstra University

FINANCIAL FACTS

Financial Aid Rating	71
Annual in-state tuition	$5,870
Annual out-of-state tuition	$17,810
Room and board	$11,364
Required fees	$2,131
Books and supplies	$900
% needy frosh rec. need-based scholarship or grant aid	89
% needy UG rec. need-based scholarship or grant aid	86
% needy frosh rec. non-need-based scholarship or grant aid	7
% needy UG rec. non-need-based scholarship or grant aid	4
% needy frosh rec. need-based self-help aid	95
% needy UG rec. need-based self-help aid	95
% frosh rec. any financial aid	78
% UG rec. any financial aid	68
% UG borrow to pay for school	60
Average cumulative indebtedness	$22,920
% frosh need fully met	16
% ugrads need fully met	13
Average % of frosh need met	68
Average % of ugrad need met	64

STATE UNIVERSITY OF NEW YORK—UNIVERSITY AT ALBANY

OFFICE OF UNDERGRADUATE ADMISSIONS, ALBANY, NY 12222 • ADMISSIONS: 518-442-5435 • FAX: 518-442-5383

CAMPUS LIFE

Quality of Life Rating	65
Fire Safety Rating	78
Green Rating	95
Type of school	Public
Affiliation	No Affiliation
Environment	City

STUDENTS

Total undergrad enrollment	12,542
% male/female	52/48
% from out of state	6
% frosh live on campus	92
% ugrads live on campus	59
# of fraternities	18
# of sororities	19
% African American	14
% Asian	8
% Caucasian	53
% Hispanic	13
% Native American	<1
% international	5
# of countries represented	84

SURVEY SAYS . . .

Class discussions are rare
Diverse student types on campus
Lots of beer drinking
Hard liquor is popular

ACADEMICS

Academic Rating	70
% students returning for sophomore year	82
% students graduating within 4 years	56
% students graduating within 6 years	66
Calendar	Semester
Student/faculty ratio	20:1
Profs interesting rating	66
Profs accessible rating	64

Most classes have 20–29 students.
Most lab/discussion sessions have
10–19 students.

MOST POPULAR MAJORS

English language and literature; psychology;
business administration and management

STUDENTS SAY ". . ."

Academics

Is SUNY Albany (UAlbany to those in the know) the perfect-sized school? Many here think so. Students describe it as "a big school numbers-wise that feels small." Notes one student, "It has a very broad range of quality academic programs, which is very important for an undecided senior in high school." Another adds, "If you know what you want and are motivated, the sky is the limit." The school exploits its location in the state capital to bolster programs in political science, criminal justice, and business, and it "offers internship opportunities to college students that very few schools can." Other standout departments include psychology, Japanese studies, mathematics, and many of the hard sciences. Professors here vary widely in quality, but a surprising number "are receptive, active, and engaging"—in other words, "a lot more accessible than I would have thought for a school this big." Teachers are especially willing to "go out of their way to help students who are interested in learning, come to class regularly, and care about their academic work." The administration, as at most state-run schools, "is basically an over-bloated bureaucracy. Students are sent from department to department in each of their endeavors. It is advisable to avoid [the] administration if at all possible."

Life

There are three distinct social orbits on the Albany campus. Some students take the initiative "by joining one of the many clubs or groups or getting involved with the student government." Others "party for a good time," telling us that "any night of the week you can find people to go out to the bars and clubs with you" and that "the average night ends between 2:30 A.M. and 4:00 A.M." Both of these groups are likely to tell you that "there is a lot to do in Albany and the surrounding area," including "a great arts district, tons of awesome restaurants, museums, [and] a state park." A third, sizable group primarily complains about the cold weather and asserts that "there's nothing to do in Albany." The school works to excite these students with "fun programs and entertainers who come to the campus. We have had a series of comedians, rappers/singers, guests from MTV and VH1, authors, political figures, musical performances, sporting events, spirit events, and many other things around campus." School spirit is on the rise among all groups, we're told. The reason? "A few years ago, the basketball team began winning, and everyone came out of the woodwork to support them—it was really a great thing to see."

Student Body

Undergrads here believe that the student body is very diverse in terms of ethnicity and also in terms of personality type; one student observes, "You have your motivated students [who] get good grades, are involved, and get amazing jobs in NYC after college. Then you have your unmotivated kids [who] complain, don't go to class, and blame a bad grade on the professor (when really it is because they crammed the night before and didn't go to class)." Geographically, the school is less diverse. Nearly everyone is a New York State resident, with many coming from "downstate New York"—Long Island, New York City, and Westchester County. There's a fair amount of upstate kids as well, and "a lot of people have certain stereotypes in their heads when they first come to Albany. The Long Islander has his idea about the upstater and vice versa. After a few weeks, though, people see that these aren't always true. I think people from anywhere get along pretty well." The international students, who form a small but noticeable contingent, "tend to keep to themselves," perhaps "due to a culture or language barrier." About one-quarter of the campus population is Jewish.

STATE UNIVERSITY OF NEW YORK—UNIVERSITY AT ALBANY

FINANCIAL AID: 518-442-3202 • E-MAIL: UGADMISSIONS@ALBANY.EDU • WEBSITE: WWW.ALBANY.EDU

THE PRINCETON REVIEW SAYS

Admissions

Very important factors considered include: Class rank, GPA, rigor of secondary school record, standardized test scores, racial/ethnic status, recommendation(s), character/personal qualities, level of applicant's interest. *Important factors considered include:* Application essay. *Other factors considered include:* Extracurricular activities, first generation, geographical residence, talent/ability, volunteer work, work experience, alumni/ae relations. SAT or ACT required; ACT with Writing component required. TOEFL required of all international applicants. *Academic units required:* 4 English; 2 mathematics; 2 science; (2 science lab); 3 social studies; 1 foreign language; 2 history; 4 academic electives. *Academic units recommended:* 4 mathematics; 3 science; (3 science lab); 3 foreign language.

Financial Aid

Students should submit: FAFSA. The Princeton Review suggests that all financial aid forms be submitted as soon as possible after January 1. *Need-based scholarships/grants offered:* Federal Pell, SEOG, State scholarships/grants, private scholarships, the school's own gift aid. *Loan aid offered:* Direct Subsidized Stafford Loans, Direct Unsubsidized Stafford Loans, Direct PLUS loans, Federal Perkins Loans. Federal Work-Study Program available. Institutional employment available. Off-campus job opportunities are good.

The Inside Word

The Wall Street Journal has noted a growing trend among students who, in the past, had limited their postsecondary options to high-end private schools: More such students, the paper reported, have broadened their vision to include prestigious state schools such as SUNY Albany. The driving force, unsurprisingly, is economic. Unless there is an unlikely decline in the cost of private education, expect admissions at schools like UAlbany to grow more competitive in coming years.

THE SCHOOL SAYS "..."

From the Admissions Office

"Increasing numbers of well-prepared students are discovering the benefits of study in UAlbany's nationally ranked programs and are taking advantage of outstanding internship and employment opportunities in upstate New York's 'Tech Valley.' The already strong undergraduate program is further enhanced by The Honors College, a university-wide program for ambitious students, offering enhanced honors courses and co-curricular options including honors housing. Living-Learning Communities provide additional opportunities for incoming freshmen to live and take classes with others who share their interests. Study Abroad programs offer global access to nearly 500 programs worldwide.

"Eight schools and colleges offer bachelor's, master's, and doctoral programs to nearly 13,000 undergraduates and 4,500 graduate students. An award-winning advisement program helps students take advantage of all these options by customizing the undergraduate experiences. More than two-thirds of UAlbany graduates go on for advanced degrees, and acceptance to law and medical school is above the national average.

"Student life on campus includes 200 clubs, honor societies, and other groups, and nineteen Division I varsity teams. Over 7,200 UAlbany students engage in community service activities. With twenty other colleges in the region, Albany is a great college town, adjacent to the spectacular natural and recreational centers of New York and New England.

"Freshmen are awarded more than 1.7 million dollars in merit scholarships each year and nearly two-thirds of our students receive financial aid."

SELECTIVITY

Admissions Rating	83
# of applicants	21,591
% of applicants accepted	56
% of acceptees attending	21

FRESHMAN PROFILE

Range SAT Critical Reading	500–570
Range SAT Math	510–610
Range ACT Composite	22–26
Minimum paper TOEFL	550
Minimum web-based TOEFL	213
Average HS GPA	3.50
% graduated top 10% of class	19
% graduated top 25% of class	53
% graduated top 50% of class	88

DEADLINES

Early action	
Deadline	11/15
Notification	1/15
Regular	
Priority	3/1
Deadline	3/1
Nonfall registration?	Yes

FINANCIAL FACTS

Financial Aid Rating	68
Annual in-state tuition	$5,870
Annual out-of-state tuition	$16,190
Room and board	$11,634
Required fees	$2,170
Books and supplies	$1,200
% needy frosh rec. need-based scholarship or grant aid	86
% needy UG rec. need-based scholarship or grant aid	84
% needy frosh rec. non-need-based scholarship or grant aid	3
% needy UG rec. non-need-based scholarship or grant aid	2
% needy frosh rec. need-based self-help aid	80
% needy UG rec. need-based self-help aid	81
% frosh rec. any financial aid	64
% UG rec. any financial aid	57
% UG borrow to pay for school	69
Average cumulative indebtedness	$24,209
% frosh need fully met	7
% ugrads need fully met	7
Average % of frosh need met	62
Average % of ugrad need met	62

STEPHENS COLLEGE

1200 EAST BROADWAY, COLUMBIA, MO 65215 • ADMISSIONS: 573-876-7207 • FAX: 573-876-7237

STUDENTS SAY ". . ."

Academics

A student-oriented liberal arts school with an "amazing family atmosphere," "Stephens empowers women to take on leadership roles in the workplace and the world." This historic women's college offers "strong programs in performing arts, dance, and fashion," as well as a unique equestrian studies department, among other "uncommon fields" of study. In and out of the classroom, "Stephens gives its students everything they could possibly need to pursue their dreams," encouraging them to "think independently" while offering "a plethora of opportunities to build a résumé and gain connections" in their field. For example, "in the dance department we have an amazing world dance program, that brings in famous teachers and choreographers from around the world to teach us for eight weeks!" Career-oriented instructors are "all very qualified in their fields. They love teaching here and are excited to work with students." Plus, "all of them go by their first name, which is pretty awesome." Thanks to the limited undergraduate enrollment, "class sizes are small and the education is very personal; you can achieve to the highest level you want." Students are always treated with respect, and "Instructors give their full attention to the students that speak during discussion." Likewise, when dealing with the higher-ups, "the answer is never no. If a student wants something to happen the faculty, especially the president, will make sure it happens." Among other recent improvements, Stephens just completed "some amazing renovations to our classrooms, our academic offerings, and our campus."

Life

Students "love the atmosphere" at Stephens College, where a "tremendous community feel" unites students academically and socially. One student describes life at Stephens as "a giant sleep-over all the time, just with classes during the day." There is a nice mix of extracurricular clubs and activities, including "two national sororities on campus, various academic associations, a student government, and numerous athletic groups." Students also support their classmates by attending campus events, including many "excellent theater productions and musicals," "exhibits and shows put on by fashion and graphic design majors," and "various social activities such as TV-watch parties, game nights, guest speakers, and seasonal festivities." Located "right next to Mizzou and Columbia College" in the fantastic "college town" of Columbia, Missouri, there are a multitude of student-friendly bars, shops, and restaurants within walking distance of Stephens. On the weekends, "some girls go out swing dancing or to frat parties" at neighboring Mizzou, while others "hang out and watch movies and drink" with their friends. Students note that the "dorm rooms need to be updated," but they love the fact that the school "allows pets of all kinds on campus," which means you might share a dorm with dogs, cats, rabbits, or other furry friends.

Students

Stephens students dole out praise for their "strong, independent, friendly, funny, [and] intelligent" classmates, describing the typical undergrad as a "professional, driven woman who strives to do everything to the best of her ability." A current student details, "We all have a plan for what we want to do in life, and we know that we will achieve it by being here." With robust programs in visual and performing arts, a lot of students are "a bit on the artistic side," while others are "into fashion and boys." On campus, you'll hear "conversations about social interaction, the meaning of friendships, our class discussions, our paper topics, books and magazines we read, crafting and creation." Although they "all come from different backgrounds," "students here are very accepting" and "generally very friendly." In particular, students say you can expect to "spend a lot of time with the people you are in classes with"; many forge their closest friendships with other students in their major program. However, given the small size, students "tend to fit in very well," no matter what their academic or personal interests. At Stephens, "you get to know practically everybody in your graduating class which makes you become really close with those women."

FINANCIAL AID: 573-876-7106 • E-MAIL: APPLY@STEPHENS.EDU • WEBSITE: WWW.STEPHENS.EDU/

THE PRINCETON REVIEW SAYS

Admissions

Very important factors considered include: GPA, rigor of secondary school record, standardized test scores, application essay. *Important factors considered include:* Extracurricular activities, recommendation(s). *Other factors considered include:* Class rank, interview, talent/ability, volunteer work, work experience, character/personal qualities, level of applicant's interest. SAT or ACT required; ACT with or without Writing component accepted. TOEFL required of all international applicants. *Academic units required:* 4 English; 3 mathematics; 2 science; 1 social studies; 2 foreign language.

Financial Aid

Students should submit: FAFSA. The Princeton Review suggests that all financial aid forms be submitted as soon as possible after January 1. *Need-based scholarships/grants offered:* Federal Pell, SEOG, State scholarships/grants, private scholarships, the school's own gift aid. *Loan aid offered:* Federal Perkins Loans. Federal Work-Study Program available. Institutional employment available. Off-campus job opportunities are good.

The Inside Word

Stephens accepts students on a rolling basis, so those who apply early in the year may receive priority in admission. All applicants must submit a signed and completed application form, standardized test scores, an official transcript, and a counselor recommendation; once you have submitted all application materials, you will receive a response from the admissions department within two weeks. All applicants are automatically evaluated for merit scholarships and grants.

SELECTIVITY

Admissions Rating	75
# of applicants	783
% of applicants accepted	68
% of acceptees attending	32

FRESHMAN PROFILE

Range SAT Critical Reading	440–630
Range SAT Math	410–580
Range SAT Writing	440–590
Range ACT Composite	19–26
Minimum paper TOEFL	550
Minimum web-based TOEFL	213
Average HS GPA	3.30
% graduated top 10% of class	17
% graduated top 25% of class	39
% graduated top 50% of class	73

DEADLINES

Early decision	
Deadline	11/15
Notification	12/1
Early action	
Deadline	1/1
Notification	1/15
Regular	
Priority	1/1
Nonfall registration?	Yes

APPLICANTS ALSO LOOK AT AND OFTEN PREFER
University of Missouri—Columbia

AND RARELY PREFER
William Woods University

FINANCIAL FACTS

Financial Aid Rating	79
% needy frosh rec. need-based scholarship or grant aid	93
% needy UG rec. need-based scholarship or grant aid	98
% needy frosh rec. non-need-based scholarship or grant aid	77
% needy UG rec. non-need-based scholarship or grant aid	95
% needy frosh rec. need-based self-help aid	84
% needy UG rec. need-based self-help aid	91
% frosh rec. any financial aid	100
% UG rec. any financial aid	97
% UG borrow to pay for school	84
Average cumulative indebtedness	$22,974
% frosh need fully met	30
% ugrads need fully met	30
Average % of frosh need met	73
Average % of ugrad need met	76

STEVENS INSTITUTE OF TECHNOLOGY

CASTLE POINT ON HUDSON, HOBOKEN, NJ 07030 • ADMISSIONS: 201-216-5194 • FAX: 201-216-8348

STUDENTS SAY " . . ."

Academics

Distinguished by its "prestigious engineering history and its proximity to NYC," Stevens is a "technical school" that has a "reputation with employers." Students at the prestigious research university get "the opportunity to get to know professors and career development personnel," and Stevens' "engineering program is unique in the design core in that you start general engineering labs first semester," providing a hands-on engineering experience right from the start. In addition to location, reputation, and "close-knit community," Stevens "has great facilities for tech students," its "smaller student body allows for a more student centered curriculum in all fields of study, and academic success is awarded with generous scholarships." "Many professors are there to help you" outside of class, if you need it, though the prevalence of international lecturers may "require a strong background in understanding accents." Particularly in engineering, where "the course load is hard" and "great research opportunities" are within reach, faculty members have "an impressive amount" of "real world experience and know how to cater classes to that." "Stevens has a heavy workload but a high reward if you survive" in that "students choose Stevens to graduate with a job waiting for them." The administration, which students praise as "innovative and inventive," is "always approaching its students on how to improve its facilities and its academic curriculum." The paradigmatic Stevens academic experience is "about working harder than you ever have before in class, experiencing the city during the weekends, and building great networking relationships with professors, fellow students, and companies."

Life

"Class time is nerdy but nightlife is great," Stevens undergrads report, with equal regard for the many "things to do in Hoboken and New York City." "Because we work so hard with our classes, we also play hard on the weekends or other nights when we finally have a break." A visible but not overwhelming Greek presence facilitates consistent "frat parties," and other social events crop up "to relax during the week and over the weekend," but at least on campus, "people generally study and work during the week," and "many of these are low-key events as opposed to your typical college parties." Lots of students prefer to socialize off campus, taking in the "fabulously exciting island of Manhattan" or frequenting the many "bars, boutiques, or eateries" in up-and-coming "Hoboken, one if the best college towns in the nation." Nerds will find plenty of opportunities for "video games with friends" who would "never miss an 'Epic LAN' party," but while "this isn't Rutgers," "someone who thinks of Stevens as nothing more than a nerdy tech school would be surprised." One student sums it up thus: "People think of me as career oriented during the week and relaxed during the weekend."

Student Body

Stevens undergrads "are nerds at heart, but they can still interact very will with others" and "students usually find their place." Lest one perceive that the school is comprised entirely of engineering geeks, many students are quick to point out that this is hardly the case: "There's a range of different type of students ranging from athletes to hardcore gamers." Some say that participation in Greek life signifies how social you intend to be: "There are two main groups of people on campus who don't mingle much: those students who are in Greek Life and those who are not." Undergrads see themselves as "very polite, hard working and approachable," as well as "devoted to academic success" and "intelligent and eager to learn." Despite the prevalence of "stereotypical nerds, dorks, geeks, and brainiacs," and the fact that "students expect to work hard here," "we all get along well despite our obvious social shortcomings."

FINANCIAL AID: 201-216-5555 • E-MAIL: ADMISSIONS@STEVENS.EDU • WEBSITE: WWW.STEVENS.EDU

THE PRINCETON REVIEW SAYS

Admissions

Very important factors considered include: GPA, rigor of secondary school record, standardized test scores, application essay, extracurricular activities, interview, recommendation(s), volunteer work, work experience, character/personal qualities. *Important factors considered include:* Class rank, talent/ability. *Other factors considered include:* Alumni/ae relations. SAT or ACT required; ACT with or without Writing component accepted. TOEFL required of all international applicants. *Academic units required:* 4 English; 4 mathematics; 3 science; (3 science lab). *Academic units recommended:* 4 science; (4 science lab); 2 social studies; 2 foreign language; 2 history; 4 academic electives; 1 computer science.

Financial Aid

Students should submit: FAFSA. The Princeton Review suggests that all financial aid forms be submitted as soon as possible after January 1. *Need-based scholarships/grants offered:* Federal Pell, SEOG, State scholarships/grants, private scholarships, the school's own gift aid. *Loan aid offered:* Direct Subsidized Stafford Loans, Direct Unsubsidized Stafford Loans, Direct PLUS loans, Federal Perkins Loans, State Loans. Federal Work-Study Program available. Institutional employment available. Off-campus job opportunities are excellent.

The Inside Word

Often preferred by students who can't (or don't want to) get into MIT or Caltech, Stevens is among the best of the second-tier programs in engineering, math, science, and technology, and its visibility to employers in New York and New Jersey makes it a great choice for students who dream of jobs in the tri-state area. As well as grades, test scores, and recommendations, the school encourages all applicants to interview with them, and requires an interview for international applicants and students applying to its accelerated programs.

THE SCHOOL SAYS ". . ."

From the Admissions Office

"A strong commitment to discovery, collaboration and mentorship drive the Stevens academic culture, which has been built on a legacy of technological innovation since 1870. Students and faculty collaborate in an interdisciplinary, student-centric, entrepreneurial environment to leverage technology to confront global challenges. From Habitat to Humanity projects to the Solar Decathlon team advancing energy efficient housing, Stevens continues to contribute to the community on our campus, in our hometown of Hoboken, NJ, and to the global community at large.

"Stevens is known as The Innovation University® and is consistently ranked among the nation's elite for ROI for students, career services, and mid-career salaries of alumni. Stevens' proximity to New York City and the surrounding metro area cultivates unmatchable internships, cooperative education placements, and other project-based learning opportunities for Stevens students.

"Choose from more than thirty undergraduate majors in business, humanities, arts, computer science, engineering and sciences; double major or pursue both a bachelor's and a master's degrees. Students participate in a capstone project often undertaken in collaboration with students from other disciplines, mentored by faculty, and sponsored by industry partners. Graduates are highly skilled in creating solutions at the intersections of disciplines and can lead in today's complex, cross-functional and highly technical environments. A strong career development program and excellent preparation pay off: graduates fare exceptionally well in career and graduate school placement. A robust student life, an exciting college town, and more than 100 student organizations and twenty-six NCAA Division III athletics teams add to an enriching student experience."

SELECTIVITY

Admissions Rating	95
# of applicants	3,239
% of applicants accepted	47
% of acceptees attending	36
# offered a place on the wait list	692
# of early decision applicants	493
% accepted early decision	63

FRESHMAN PROFILE

Range SAT Critical Reading	560–640
Range SAT Math	620–700
Range SAT Writing	550–650
Range ACT Composite	25–30
Minimum paper TOEFL	550
Minimum web-based TOEFL	213
Average HS GPA	3.83
% graduated top 10% of class	58
% graduated top 25% of class	88
% graduated top 50% of class	98

DEADLINES

Early decision	
Deadline	11/15
Notification	12/15
Regular	
Priority	11/15
Deadline	2/1
Notification	3/15
Nonfall registration?	Yes

APPLICANTS ALSO LOOK AT AND OFTEN PREFER
Princeton University; Massachusetts Institute of Technology; Carnegie Mellon University

AND SOMETIMES PREFER
Lehigh University; New York University; Johns Hopkins University

AND RARELY PREFER
Rensselaer Polytechnic Institute; Worcester Polytechnic Institute; Drexel University

FINANCIAL FACTS

Financial Aid Rating	73
Annual tuition	$42,920
Room and board	$14,214
Required fees	$1,746
Books and supplies	$950
% needy frosh rec. need-based scholarship or grant aid	83
% needy UG rec. need-based scholarship or grant aid	67
% needy frosh rec. non-need-based scholarship or grant aid	78
% needy UG rec. non-need-based scholarship or grant aid	68
% needy frosh rec. need-based self-help aid	82
% needy UG rec. need-based self-help aid	71
% frosh rec. any financial aid	82
% UG rec. any financial aid	75
% UG borrow to pay for school	66
Average cumulative indebtedness	$35,319
% frosh need fully met	21
% ugrads need fully met	18
Average % of frosh need met	82
Average % of ugrad need met	75

STONEHILL COLLEGE

320 WASHINGTON STREET, EASTON, MA 02357-5610 • ADMISSION: 508-565-1373 • FAX: 508-565-1545

CAMPUS LIFE
Quality of Life Rating	83
Fire Safety Rating	92
Green Rating	89
Type of school	Private
Affiliation	Roman Catholic
Environment	Village

STUDENTS
Total undergrad enrollment	2,473
% male/female	38/62
% from out of state	45
% frosh from public high school	69
% frosh live on campus	95
% ugrads live on campus	91
% African American	3
% Asian	2
% Caucasian	85
% Hispanic	4
% Native American	0
% international	1
# of countries represented	8

SURVEY SAYS . . .
Lab facilities are great
Career services are great
Students are friendly
Hard liquor is popular

ACADEMICS
Academic Rating	86
% students returning for sophomore year	87
% students graduating within 4 years	82
% students graduating within 6 years	85
Calendar	Semester
Student/faculty ratio	12:1
Profs interesting rating	84
Profs accessible rating	86

Most classes have 10–19 students.
Most lab/discussion sessions have 10–19 students.

MOST POPULAR MAJORS
psychology; accounting; communications

STUDENTS SAY ". . ."

Academics

This small liberal arts college located between Boston and Providence "creates an inclusive environment and presents its students with countless opportunities for internships and other pre-grad networking opportunities," opportunities pushed by educators who are "very engaging and passionate about their material." The professors here "have all worked in the field they teach," meaning "the academics are incredibly relevant to the real world." The school's modest size carries over to the classroom, where "class sizes are small enough to engage in meaningful discussions" with professors who "provide plenty of opportunities to meet with them outside of class and form lasting relationships with students." These discussion-based classes "involve the students and engage them in the learning process," while the "extremely helpful" educators "make students aware that they consider students real people and are always available both to discuss class material or personal matters if they can help." The idea is to help students "work toward nurturing the whole person through a comprehensive education." Some see the lack of graduate students as a plus, too, since "no graduate students means more opportunities for undergraduates, especially research positions." With "small classes so students get to know their professors more intimately than at a larger university" and opportunities to study abroad and for internships, students say Stonehill is "worth the money."

Life

For many at Stonehill, life is "mainly centered around academics." Even downtime is spent doing things other than partying. Students are "provided with opportunities that abound, especially in the form of internships and community service," so most "get pretty involved in clubs, sports, and community service." These organizations allow students to "form very strong, long lasting relationships." The "great atmosphere" includes a strong focus on sports— "even if someone isn't involved in varsity sports, the campus is very active in Rec sports, intramurals, and just general fitness and use of the athletic facility"—along with the expected "watching movies, taking hikes around campus, playing video games with friends and taking the school shuttle to the mall." Trivia, bingo, campus coffeehouse gatherings, and going out to "sweat all over each other on a dance floor" provide other distractions. If this sounds far removed from keggers and drunken binges, it is. The idea that partying is not the be-all and end-all of weekend life "is present among a strong population of Stonehill College students." One student sums it up: "I never thought my weekends would be full of volunteering until I came here and now I truly wouldn't have it any other way."

Student Body

"Stonehill is always described as a place where people hold the door open for you," a campus full of "relatively normal and sociable" "middle class white kids." Expect a student body that is "very New England—lots of plaid, jeans, Stonehill sweatshirts." There may be "some diversity," but not much in the way of ethnic minorities. Instead, "students stand out like they would in high school; there's the jocks, nerds, school activists, party animals, and so on." For the most part, "everyone is pretty laid back." The "friendly and helpful" students here are "academically driven and community focused," making it "feel like family even after being here for only a couple months." There are cliques, but they "tend to be predicated on what type of activities you do or your major" rather than who you are, because no matter what, "everyone is still friendly to everyone else." Though "there is a place for everyone at Stonehill," those "who are less community-focused have a harder time clicking with the student body but will undoubtedly find friends if they try." This openness and willingness to embrace one another "is what has led us to become such a strong community."

FINANCIAL AID: 508-565-1088 • E-MAIL: ADMISSION@STONEHILL.EDU • WEBSITE: WWW.STONEHILL.EDU

THE PRINCETON REVIEW SAYS

Admissions

Very important factors considered include: Class rank, GPA, rigor of secondary school record, talent/ability, character/personal qualities. *Important factors considered include:* Application essay, extracurricular activities, recommendation(s), volunteer work, work experience, level of applicant's interest. *Other factors considered include:* Standardized test scores, first generation, geographical residence, interview, racial/ethnic status, alumni/ae relations, religious affiliation. SAT or ACT considered if submitted; ACT with Writing component required. TOEFL required of all international applicants. *Academic units required:* 4 English; 3 mathematics; 1 science; (1 science lab); 2 foreign language; 3 history; 3 academic electives. *Academic units recommended:* 4 English; 4 mathematics; 3 science; (2 science lab); 3 foreign language; 3 history; 3 academic electives.

Financial Aid

Students should submit: FAFSA, CSS/Financial Aid PROFILE, Noncustodial PROFILE. Regular filing deadline is February 1. The Princeton Review suggests that all financial aid forms be submitted as soon as possible after January 1. *Need-based scholarships/grants offered:* Federal Pell, SEOG, State scholarships/grants, private scholarships, the school's own gift aid. *Loan aid offered:* Direct Subsidized Stafford Loans, Direct Unsubsidized Stafford Loans, Direct PLUS loans, Federal Perkins Loans, State Loans. Applicants will be notified of awards beginning April 1. Federal Work-Study Program available. Institutional employment available. Off-campus job opportunities are good.

The Inside Word

Stonehill may not be as selective as the elite colleges of the Boston area, but students here are still expected to be top students. Half were in the top 10 percent of their high school classes, so if you want to compete, ensure your grades and test scores are strong.

THE SCHOOL SAYS "..."

From the Admissions Office

"Founded by the Congregation of Holy Cross, Stonehill is a selective Catholic college that values integrity, tradition and the rewards that come when you pair rigorous academics with world-class faculty committed to student success. Our approach to liberal arts education is distinctive because it melds challenging courses, nationally recognized experiential learning and life-changing service opportunities to shape graduates into compassionate leaders and global thinkers.

"Stonehill is on a beautiful 384-acre campus with architecture ranging from traditional brick-and-ivy academic buildings to a state-of-the-art science center. With its ideal location between Boston and Providence, two of New England's most vibrant cities, Stonehill is perfectly situated for internships, professional networking, cultural experiences, pro sports and countless entertainment and dining options.

"More than 80 percent of our students study abroad, complete an internship or perform field research before graduation. Such experiences along with 39 majors and 45 minors in the liberal arts, sciences and business prepare them for productive careers or lives of service. Our students are also active outside of class. Whether its Ultimate Disc, dance or one of our Division II varsity teams, most participate in some form of athletics. With a student/faculty ratio of 13:1 and an average class size of 19, individual attention is a Stonehill hallmark. Whether collaborating on research or mentoring students on careers and graduate school, our faculty puts students first. The result shows in our students' successes: 97 percent of Stonehill graduates over the last five years were employed, volunteering or in graduate school within one year of graduation."

SELECTIVITY

Admissions Rating	84
# of applicants	6,547
% of applicants accepted	71
% of acceptees attending	13
# offered a place on the wait list	979
% accepting a place on wait list	30
% admitted from wait list	52
# of early decision applicants	62
% accepted early decision	87

FRESHMAN PROFILE

Range SAT Critical Reading	510–610
Range SAT Math	520–620
Range SAT Writing	510–620
Range ACT Composite	23–28
Minimum paper TOEFL	550
Minimum web-based TOEFL	213
Average HS GPA	3.34
% graduated top 10% of class	31
% graduated top 25% of class	69
% graduated top 50% of class	95

DEADLINES

Early decision	
Deadline	12/1
Notification	12/31
Early action	
Deadline	11/1
Notification	1/15
Regular	
Deadline	1/15
Notification	3/15
Nonfall registration?	Yes

APPLICANTS ALSO LOOK AT AND OFTEN PREFER

Providence College; Northeastern University; College of the Holy Cross; Boston College; Bentley University

AND SOMETIMES PREFER

University of Massachusetts Amherst; University of Connecticut

FINANCIAL FACTS

Financial Aid Rating	90
Annual tuition	$36,160
Room and board	$13,710
Books and supplies	$893
% needy frosh rec. need-based scholarship or grant aid	82
% needy UG rec. need-based scholarship or grant aid	83
% needy frosh rec. non-need-based scholarship or grant aid	20
% needy UG rec. non-need-based scholarship or grant aid	17
% needy frosh rec. need-based self-help aid	52
% needy UG rec. need-based self-help aid	61
% frosh rec. any financial aid	92
% UG rec. any financial aid	93
% UG borrow to pay for school	76
Average cumulative indebtedness	$32,248
% frosh need fully met	53
% ugrads need fully met	50
Average % of frosh need met	92
Average % of ugrad need met	91

SUFFOLK UNIVERSITY

Eight Ashburton Place, Boston, MA 02108 • Admissions: 617-573-8460 • Fax: 617-573-1574

CAMPUS LIFE
Quality of Life Rating	86
Fire Safety Rating	97
Green Rating	91
Type of school	Private
Affiliation	No Affiliation
Environment	Metropolis

STUDENTS
Total undergrad enrollment	5,627
% male/female	45/55
% from out of state	31
% frosh from public high school	66
% frosh live on campus	63
% ugrads live on campus	21
# of fraternities	1
# of sororities	2
% African American	5
% Asian	7
% Caucasian	41
% Hispanic	11
% Native American	<1
% international	19
# of countries represented	107

SURVEY SAYS . . .
Diverse student types on campus
Students love Boston, MA
Theater is popular

ACADEMICS
Academic Rating	76
% students returning for sophomore year	75
% students graduating within 4 years	41
% students graduating within 6 years	55
Calendar	Semester
Student/faculty ratio	11:1
Profs interesting rating	78
Profs accessible rating	72

Most classes have 20–29 students.
Most lab/discussion sessions have 10–19 students.

MOST POPULAR MAJORS
business/corporate communications

STUDENTS SAY ". . ."

Academics

Located in "the heart of downtown Boston," Suffolk University offers a "happy environment" for "anyone who wants to be at a school and still be directly in the city." The university offers "a wide selection of interesting majors" and small class sizes throughout its College of Arts and Sciences and business school, giving this "united, diverse mass of students" a "global perspective in a real-world, urban setting." Students observe that depending on "[which] professor you have…you will like the class or not." Across the board, the teachers come across as being "very friendly" and genuine, and they "speak to you like an adult with respect." Some professors are "a bit dry;" however, "when you find [a great professor], they will be there for you through anything." Many here "wish the classes were more challenging," saying that course work is "not as challenging as the school implies, but it is not easy." The school "offers students the resources they need should they want to put more effort into classes, job searching, and anything else, really;" students simply need to be self-motivated to take advantage of it. "Class participation comes naturally because class size is so small and the professor knows your name," says a freshman. "The administration is a little ridiculous sometimes with [its] rules," but overall it has "good relationships with the students."

Life

With the city as its "campus and playground," there is an "endless array of things to do" at Suffolk University, including shopping, museums, restaurants, and culture. "The students become part of the city," says a sophomore. "Suffolk doesn't really have a campus," though no one really seems to mind, as most students knew what they had signed on for when they enrolled. Due to space constraints, not all upperclassmen can live on campus, and many happily choose to live in Boston apartments. "My classes require me to walk through the Common everyday," says one student. For those who do live on campus, the university offers freshman orientation activities that "students can participate [in] to ease the tensions of moving into a dorm and being on your own." Most students take their social lives off campus, choosing to hang out at other colleges and in the city itself. Suffolk's campus is dry, so "students have to find other places in which to party" on the weekends (weeknights are typically dedicated to homework). As for the commuters, most "don't interact directly with [resident] students as much." Unsurprisingly, "there's a lot of Boston pride among Suffolk students." "Everyone loves the Red Sox, the Celtics, and the Bruins."

Student Body

Most of the kids here come out of "a medium to high income family" and are from "some town in Massachusetts," though Suffolk has a lot of international students. "It is very easy for a student to blend in due to Suffolk being a very diverse campus." Cultures and beliefs do indeed vary greatly—"that is definitely a part of what makes Suffolk so unique"—but "most students are friendly and interact with one another regardless of where they are from." However, there is a slight—though not tense—divide between two other classifications of Suffolk students: the large commuter populations and those who live in on-campus housing. "Suffolk is not very successful at integrating the two, but everyone seems to get along okay," says a student. Luckily, classes also require several group projects, "forcing students to work together." Preppy seems to be what the Suffolk student body preaches, and button downs, polo shirts, and Uggs abound—"most would *never* wear pajamas or sweatpants to class."

FINANCIAL AID: 617-573-8470 • E-MAIL: ADMISSION@SUFFOLK.EDU • WEBSITE: WWW.SUFFOLK.EDU

THE PRINCETON REVIEW SAYS

Admissions

Very important factors considered include: Rigor of secondary school record. *Important factors considered include:* Class rank, GPA, application essay, recommendation(s), character/personal qualities. *Other factors considered include:* Standardized test scores, extracurricular activities, first generation, interview, talent/ability, volunteer work, work experience, alumni/ae relations, level of applicant's interest. SAT or ACT required; ACT with Writing component required. TOEFL required of all international applicants. *Academic units required:* 4 English; 3 mathematics; 2 science; (1 science lab); 2 foreign language; 1 history; 4 academic electives. *Academic units recommended:* 4 English; 4 mathematics; 4 science; 3 foreign language; 4 history; 4 academic electives.

Financial Aid

Students should submit: FAFSA. Regular filing deadline is 3/1. The Princeton Review suggests that all financial aid forms be submitted as soon as possible after January 1. *Need-based scholarships/grants offered:* Federal Pell, SEOG, State scholarships/grants, private scholarships, the school's own gift aid. *Loan aid offered:* Direct Subsidized Stafford Loans, Direct Unsubsidized Stafford Loans, Direct PLUS loans, Federal Perkins Loans, College/university loans from institutional funds. Federal Work-Study Program available. Institutional employment available. Off-campus job opportunities are excellent.

The Inside Word

Suffolk is unapologetic about its mission to provide access and opportunity to college-bound students. That said, test scores and high school GPA requirements are average. Applicants whose numbers are above-average have a good chance of gaining admission.

THE SCHOOL SAYS "..."

From the Admissions Office

"Located in "the heart of downtown Boston," Suffolk University offers an "engaging environment" for "anyone who wants to be at school and still be directly in the city." The University offers "a wide selection of interesting majors" throughout its College of Arts and Sciences and Sawyer Business School, giving a "diverse mass of students" a "global perspective in an urban setting." Professors are "as diverse as the students," "always willing to help you," and "bring real-world experience right into the classroom." Because of that, they are "able to tell you what's expected academically but also what's expected in the real world." "Class participation comes naturally because the professor knows your name," says a freshman. Many say "you get out of a class what you put into it," meaning "some students just coast" but "if you challenge yourself, you'll really get a lot out of a course." The school "offers students the resources they need should they want to put more effort into classes, job searching, and anything else."

SELECTIVITY

Admissions Rating	68
# of applicants	9,275
% of applicants accepted	83
% of acceptees attending	16
# offered a place on the wait list	710
% accepting a place on wait list	37
% admitted from wait list	68

FRESHMAN PROFILE

Range SAT Critical Reading	440–560
Range SAT Math	450–570
Range SAT Writing	440–560
Range ACT Composite	20–25
Minimum paper TOEFL	550
Minimum web-based TOEFL	197
Average HS GPA	3.14
% graduated top 10% of class	13
% graduated top 25% of class	42
% graduated top 50% of class	79

DEADLINES

Early action	
Deadline	11/15
Notification	12/20
Regular	
Deadline	2/15
Nonfall registration?	Yes

FINANCIAL FACTS

Financial Aid Rating	69
Annual tuition	$32,530
Room and board	$14,638
% needy frosh rec. need-based scholarship or grant aid	95
% needy UG rec. need-based scholarship or grant aid	92
% needy frosh rec. non-need-based scholarship or grant aid	33
% needy UG rec. non-need-based scholarship or grant aid	36
% needy frosh rec. need-based self-help aid	92
% needy UG rec. need-based self-help aid	90
% frosh rec. any financial aid	81
% UG rec. any financial aid	73
% UG borrow to pay for school	76
Average cumulative indebtedness	$33,812
% frosh need fully met	5
% ugrads need fully met	9
Average % of frosh need met	65
Average % of ugrad need met	66

SUSQUEHANNA UNIVERSITY

514 UNIVERSITY AVENUE, SELINSGROVE, PA 17870 • ADMISSIONS: 570-372-4260 • FAX: 570-372-2722

CAMPUS LIFE

Quality of Life Rating	79
Fire Safety Rating	99
Green Rating	73
Type of school	Private
Affiliation	Lutheran
Environment	Village

STUDENTS

Total undergrad enrollment	2,138
% male/female	45/55
% from out of state	51
% frosh from public high school	79
% frosh live on campus	96
% ugrads live on campus	86
# of fraternities	6
# of sororities	5
% African American	5
% Asian	1
% Caucasian	84
% Hispanic	5
% Native American	<1
% international	1
# of countries represented	21

SURVEY SAYS . . .

Political activism is unpopular or nonexistent
Lab facilities are great
Athletic facilities are great
Dorms are like palaces
Campus feels safe

ACADEMICS

Academic Rating	80
% students returning for sophomore year	84
% students graduating within 4 years	71
% students graduating within 6 years	75
Calendar	Semester
Student/faculty ratio	12:1
Profs interesting rating	76
Profs accessible rating	80

Most classes have 10–19 students.
Most lab/discussion sessions have
10–19 students.

MOST POPULAR MAJORS
business administration and management;
speech communications and rhetoric;
psychology

STUDENTS SAY ". . ."

Academics

Susquehanna University is an institution that "thrives on building strong leaders and independent thinkers." The school's "small" size means undergrads are joining a "close-knit community" replete with a "strong alumni network." Perhaps more importantly, it's evident that the school "is invested...in the success of their students." While Susquehanna offers a variety of great majors, students are prone to highlight the "top-notch creative writing program," "outstanding music education program" and "strong" science departments. Undergrads also praise a more unique aspect of a Susquehanna education—mandatory study abroad. One senior elated about this requirement shares, "I believe that every young adult should have access to a cross-cultural experience and I value Susquehanna for making such an experience a priority for its students." Thankfully, for the most part, undergrads enjoy their on-campus education as well. By and large, this can be attributed to "fantastic" professors who "take a personal interest in their students." Indeed, the "friendly" teachers here really strive to make themselves "accessible." And, as one impressed creative writing major adds, a handful "often invite [students] up to their houses for dinner and discussion." However, one neuroscience major does caution that "you usually have to fight to get into a class with a 'good' professor and the registration process is always a hassle."

Life

There is always something exciting to seek out at Susquehanna! To begin with, "there are over 100 clubs and organizations (academic, cultural, religious, arts, service, special interest, etc.)" in which students can participate. Additionally, "the Student Activities Committee [sponsors] a lot of free events—including the occasional trapeze and gyroscope!" Many undergrads also enjoy the "on-campus nightclub [which] hosts free dances on the weekends." Moreover, Susquehanna is a fairly athletic school. Indeed, "varsity sports are huge on campus; we have a large number of athletic teams for such a small school. Students love "tailgating [at] sporting events" as well. Undergrads also flock to "Charlie's coffee house to watch movies or hang out with friends during the week." And, for students looking to unwind, "every Wednesday, Friday and Saturday night there is usually off campus partying happening." If students are itching to escape for a bit, they can take advantage of several "recreational places off campus (Bounce Plex, bowling alley, racetrack, rock climbing, hiking, etc.)" And though Selinsgrove "is a small town, it's got everything you need." A senior confidently proclaims that "there are plenty of places to eat and shop!"

Student Body

It can easily feel as though most Susquehanna students hail from "upper-middle class" homes located in either the "Mid-Atlantic [region or] New England." Fortunately, to the delight of many students, the "campus has been steadily diversifying over the years." And besides, these "outgoing" undergrads are able to forge bonds that go well beyond geography. After all, this is the type of student body that "will hold the door for you, even if you are 100 feet away." However, there are a handful of students who feel that, to fully fit in, you have to be "part of either Greek life or a sport." Naturally, other undergrads vehemently disagree, emphatically stating that "students find their niche quickly and make friends easily." A history major helps clarify by relaying that "roughly 25 percent of students are athletes and 17 percent are involved in Greek life. However for the most part students from every range of the spectrum interact and support each other." And one immensely proud and satisfied speech communication major triumphantly sums up, "We are all awesome. There's no other way to describe it besides awesomeness."

SUSQUEHANNA UNIVERSITY

FINANCIAL AID: 570-372-4450 • E-MAIL: SUADMISS@SUSQU.EDU • WEBSITE: WWW.SUSQU.EDU

THE PRINCETON REVIEW SAYS

Admissions

Very important factors considered include: GPA, rigor of secondary school record. *Important factors considered include:* Class rank, standardized test scores, application essay, extracurricular activities, interview, racial/ethnic status, recommendation(s), talent/ability, volunteer work, work experience, alumni/ae relations, character/personal qualities, level of applicant's interest. *Other factors considered include:* First generation, geographical residence, state residency. SAT and SAT Subject Tests or ACT considered if submitted; ACT with or without Writing component accepted. TOEFL required of all international applicants. *Academic units required:* 4 English; 3 mathematics; 2 science; (2 science lab); 2 social studies; 2 foreign language; 2 history; 2 academic electives. *Academic units recommended:* 4 English; 4 mathematics; 3 science; (3 science lab); 4 social studies; 4 foreign language; 2 history; 3 academic electives.

Financial Aid

Students should submit: FAFSA, CSS/Financial Aid PROFILE, Business/Farm Supplement. Regular filing deadline is 5/1. The Princeton Review suggests that all financial aid forms be submitted as soon as possible after January 1. *Need-based scholarships/grants offered:* Federal Pell, SEOG, State scholarships/grants, private scholarships, the school's own gift aid. *Loan aid offered:* Direct Subsidized Stafford Loans, Direct Unsubsidized Stafford Loans, Direct PLUS loans, Federal Perkins Loans, College/university loans from institutional funds. Applicants will be notified of awards beginning 3/15. Federal Work-Study Program available. Institutional employment available. Off-campus job opportunities are good.

The Inside Word

Admissions officers at Susquehanna aim to understand the candidate behind the numbers. They want students who demonstrate intellect, creativity and leadership. The university also realizes that standardized test scores aren't always representative of a student's abilities. Therefore, applicants may choose between submitting scores or two graded, academic papers (from either junior or senior year). Finally, Susquehanna operates on a rolling admissions policy. Hence, the earlier you apply the better.

THE SCHOOL SAYS "..."

From the Admissions Office

"Susquehanna University prepares its graduates to achieve, lead, and serve in a diverse and interconnected world. Graduates consistently say their Susquehanna experiences give them a competitive edge over other recent graduates entering the workplace. Susquehanna's central curriculum features the GO (Global Opportunities) program, the only one of its kind in the nation. GO requires every student to prepare, complete, and reflect on an immersion experience in a culture different from one's own, either in the United States or abroad. A cross-cultural experience is designed to take students out of their everyday environment. It might be a traditional semester study abroad program (GO Long), a short-term faculty/staff-led program (GO Short), a self-designed experience proposed and accepted in advance, or service in a cross-cultural setting.

With more than fifty majors and minors, students find a fine balance of liberal arts and professional studies, and state-of-the-art facilities to support intellectual and personal growth. The Sigmund Weis School of Business is accredited by the prestigious Association to Advance Collegiate Schools of Business (AACSB). A new 'green' science facility opened in 2010. As the largest academic building on campus, it includes nineteen teaching and research labs, thirty prep and support spaces, and a rooftop greenhouse. Susquehanna's success is demonstrated by its placement rate. Typically 94 percent of Susquehanna's graduates have a job or are attending graduate school within six months of graduation. About 94 percent of our graduates report they would likely choose Susquehanna again, and 97 percent would recommend Susquehanna University to a high school senior."

SELECTIVITY

Admissions Rating	80
# of applicants	3,217
% of applicants accepted	72
% of acceptees attending	25
# offered a place on the wait list	188
% accepting a place on wait list	12
% admitted from wait list	27
# of early decision applicants	135
% accepted early decision	79

FRESHMAN PROFILE

Range SAT Critical Reading	510–620
Range SAT Math	510–610
Range SAT Writing	490–610
Range ACT Composite	23–27
Minimum paper TOEFL	550
Minimum web-based TOEFL	213
Average HS GPA	3.28
% graduated top 10% of class	26
% graduated top 25% of class	52
% graduated top 50% of class	80

DEADLINES

Early decision	
Deadline	11/1
Notification	11/15
Early action	
Deadline	11/1
Notification	11/15
Regular	
Priority	1/1
Deadline	2/1
Nonfall registration?	Yes

APPLICANTS ALSO LOOK AT AND OFTEN PREFER
Bucknell University; Villanova University; Gettysburg College

AND SOMETIMES PREFER
Quinnipiac University; Ithaca College

FINANCIAL FACTS

Financial Aid Rating	82
Annual tuition	$38,280
Room and board	$10,390
Required fees	$500
Books and supplies	$900
% needy frosh rec. need-based scholarship or grant aid	100
% needy UG rec. need-based scholarship or grant aid	99
% needy frosh rec. non-need-based scholarship or grant aid	16
% needy UG rec. non-need-based scholarship or grant aid	13
% needy frosh rec. need-based self-help aid	82
% needy UG rec. need-based self-help aid	84
% frosh rec. any financial aid	99
% UG rec. any financial aid	96
% UG borrow to pay for school	72
Average cumulative indebtedness	$31,829
% frosh need fully met	21
% ugrads need fully met	18
Average % of frosh need met	83
Average % of ugrad need met	81

SWARTHMORE COLLEGE

500 COLLEGE AVENUE, SWARTHMORE, PA 19081 • ADMISSIONS: 610-328-8300 • FAX: 610-328-8580

STUDENTS SAY ". . ."

Academics

Swarthmore College "has a lovely campus, the people are almost unbelievably friendly, it's a safe environment, and it's really, really challenging academically," and "although it's not one of the most well-known schools, those who do know of it also know of its wonderful reputation. It's where to go for a real education—for learning for the sake of truly learning, rather than just for grades." Students warn that "academics here are definitely stressful, especially when you sign up for extracurricular activities that take up some more time—and almost everyone here is involved in something outside of classes, because you don't want to just go to class, study, and sleep every day." As a result, "Swarthmore is truly challenging. It teaches its students tough lessons not only about classes but about life, and though it may be extremely, almost unbearably difficult sometimes, it's totally worth it." Undergrads also note that "there are tons of resources to help you—professors, academic mentors, writing associates (who are really helpful to talk to when you have major papers), residential assistants, psychological counseling, multicultural support groups, queer/trans support groups—basically, whenever you need help with something, there's someone you can talk to." Swatties also love how "Swarthmore is amazingly flexible. The requirements are very limited, allowing you to explore whatever you are interested in and change your mind millions of times about your major and career path. If they don't offer a major you want, you can design your own with ease."

Life

The Swarthmore community is "a family of students who are engaged in academics, learning, politics, activism, and civic responsibility, with a work hard, play hard, intense mentality, who don't get enough sleep because they're too busy doing all they want to do in their time here, and who (this is kind of cheesy, but true) when you really think about it are really just smart students who care about the world and want to make it better." There "is a misconception that Swarthmore students do nothing but study, [but] while we certainly do a lot of it, we still find many ways to have fun." Not so much in hometown Swarthmore—"there isn't a lot to do right in the area"—but "with a train station on campus, Philly is very accessible." Additionally, "there are so many organizations and clubs on campus that you'd be pressed to find none of the activities interesting. Even then, you can start your own club, so that takes care of it." The small size of the school means that "opportunities to participate in many different programs" are usually available. On-campus activities "are varied, and there is almost always something to do on the weekend. There are student musical performances, drama performances, movies, speakers, and comedy shows," as well as "several parties every weekend, with and without alcohol, and a lot of pre-partying with friends." One student sums up, "While it is tough to generalize on the life of a Swarthmore student, one word definitely applies to us all: busy. All of us are either working on extracurriculars, studying, or fighting sleep to do more work."

Student Body

Students are "not sure if there is a typical Swattie" but suspect that "the defining feature among us is that each person is brilliant at something: maybe dance, maybe quantum physics, maybe philosophy. Each person here has at least one thing that [he or she does] extraordinarily well." A Swattie "is [typically] liberal, involved in some kind of activism group or multicultural group, talks about classes all the time, was labeled a nerd by people in high school, and is really smart—one of those people where you just have to wonder, how do they get all their homework done and manage their extracurriculars and still have time for parties?" The campus "is very diverse racially but not in terms of thought—in other words, pretty much everyone's liberal, you don't get many different points of view. Multicultural and queer issues are big here, but you don't have to be involved in that to enjoy Swarthmore. You just have to accept it."

FINANCIAL AID: 610-328-8358 • E-MAIL: ADMISSIONS@SWARTHMORE.EDU • WEBSITE: WWW.SWARTHMORE.EDU

THE PRINCETON REVIEW SAYS

Admissions

Very important factors considered include: Class rank, GPA, rigor of secondary school record, application essay, recommendation(s), character/personal qualities. *Important factors considered include:* Standardized test scores, extracurricular activities. *Other factors considered include:* First generation, geographical residence, interview, racial/ethnic status, state residency, talent/ability, volunteer work, work experience, alumni/ae relations, level of applicant's interest, religious affiliation. SAT and SAT Subject Tests or ACT required; ACT with Writing component required. *Academic units recommended:* 4 English; 3 mathematics; 3 science; 3 social studies; 3 foreign language; 3 history.

Financial Aid

Students should submit: FAFSA, Institution's own financial aid form, CSS/Financial Aid PROFILE, State aid form, Noncustodial PROFILE, Business/Farm Supplement. Regular filing deadline is 2/15. The Princeton Review suggests that all financial aid forms be submitted as soon as possible after January 1. *Need-based scholarships/grants offered:* Federal Pell, SEOG, State scholarships/grants, private scholarships, the school's own gift aid. *Loan aid offered:* Direct Subsidized Stafford Loans, Direct Unsubsidized Stafford Loans, Direct PLUS loans, Federal Perkins Loans, State Loans, College/university loans from institutional funds. Applicants will be notified of awards beginning 4/1. Federal Work-Study Program available. Institutional employment available. Off-campus job opportunities are good.

The Inside Word

Competition for admission to Swarthmore remains fierce, as the school consistently receives applications from top students across the country. Applicants should understand that Swarthmore receives more than enough applications from well-qualified students to fill its classrooms. At some point, perfectly good candidates get rejected simply because there's no more room. Admissions officers comb applications carefully for evidence of intellectually curious, highly motivated, and creative-minded candidates.

THE SCHOOL SAYS ". . ."

From the Admissions Office

"Swarthmore College is a highly selective college of liberal arts and engineering. Since 1864, it has lifted students to their full intellectual and personal potential. With a global outlook and 8:1 student/faculty ratio, Swarthmore gives students the knowledge, insight, skills, and experience to become leaders of industries and agents of change. The collaborative Honors program brims with intellectual exploration, and the innovative externship program matches students with alums from Wall Street to Silicon Valley. When you step onto the Swarthmore campus, you engage the world. A world of intellect and action, collaboration and connection. One where idyllic lawns and hills mark your journey to a class on robotics or international cinema. One with a dynamic array of arts spaces to enjoy — or stage — a performance. Think intellectual exploration with no limits, whether it's sharing perspectives with a classmate from another continent or listening to a Rhodes Scholar. A place replete with avenues of exploration, where you can immerse yourself in the Language Resource Center's offerings, get lost in the stars from the observatory, or relish the rich cultural tapestry of nearby center city Philadelphia. When you become a Swarthmore student, you forge connections with alumni around the world — cutting-edge professionals as invested in the success of their alma mater and its graduates as they are in making a difference.

Swarthmore makes admissions and financial aid decisions separately for U.S. citizens and permanent residents, meeting the full demonstrated need of admitted students without loans and offering aid to international students."

SELECTIVITY

Admissions Rating	99
# of applicants	6,615
% of applicants accepted	14
% of acceptees attending	41
# of early decision applicants	538
% accepted early decision	33

FRESHMAN PROFILE

Range SAT Critical Reading	680–760
Range SAT Math	670–770
Range SAT Writing	680–770
Range ACT Composite	31–34
% graduated top 10% of class	89
% graduated top 25% of class	99
% graduated top 50% of class	100

DEADLINES

Early decision	
Deadline	11/15
Notification	12/15
Regular	
Deadline	1/1
Notification	4/1
Nonfall registration?	No

FINANCIAL FACTS

Financial Aid Rating	96
Annual tuition	$44,368
Required fees	$350
Books and supplies	$1,210
% needy frosh rec. need-based scholarship or grant aid	100
% needy UG rec. need-based scholarship or grant aid	100
% needy frosh rec. non-need-based scholarship or grant aid	0
% needy UG rec. non-need-based scholarship or grant aid	0
% needy frosh rec. need-based self-help aid	99
% needy UG rec. need-based self-help aid	98
% frosh rec. any financial aid	52
% UG rec. any financial aid	50
% UG borrow to pay for school	36
Average cumulative indebtedness	$19,338
% frosh need fully met	100
% ugrads need fully met	100
Average % of frosh need met	100
Average % of ugrad need met	100

SWEET BRIAR COLLEGE

PO Box 1052, Sweet Briar, VA 24595 • Admissions: 434-381-6142 • Fax: 434-381-6152

STUDENTS SAY ". . ."

Academics

"A place where students want to be a part of something bigger than themselves," Sweet Briar College is a small, all-female, liberal arts college set in rural Virginia. Known as "a sisterhood" that fosters "leadership in and out of the classroom," this college attracts women interested in a personalized academic environment where "my professors know me by name, and [the] administration has immense respect for me." "Small class sizes" and "professors [that] become like family" are the school's biggest draws. The professors provide "so many opportunities for students to do undergraduate research, hands-on projects…fieldtrips, networking, jobs, and internships," but they are engaged enough with the student body that "they will join you for lunch in the cafeteria or joke around with you in class." This type of care and attention, so characteristic of Sweet Briar, begins even before students are admitted to the school through "truly special" hand-written recruitment letters sent from the admissions office. As one student explains, "Sweet Briar creates a whole person, one capable of taking on the world's problems with creativity, enthusiasm, and class." In addition to "an incredible study abroad program" and career services center, Sweet Briar boasts "100 percent job-placement rate post-graduation" in particular programs like education and a dedicated network of alumnae that "have time to sit down and talk with you, let you stay with them if you are visiting the area, or even help you find a job, and take you to happy hour."

Life

Set in the foothills of the beautiful Blue Ridge Mountains of the rural South, the school offers access to the outdoors, and that is a big draw for many here. With more than "3,000 acres to explore," students at Sweet Briar are involved in many outdoors activities "like hiking, camping, and rock-climbing, with kayaking thrown in as well" in an environment that makes this campus "one of the most beautiful in the country." In addition to its "wonderful horse riding program," athletics like lacrosse and Division III field hockey are also popular. Sweet Briar strikes a balance between being "a suitcase school" where the campus "becomes a ghost town" on weekends and being a bustling campus full of student involvement. The weeks are spent "focusing on school work Monday through Friday," while on the weekends, students "jet off to Hampden-Sydney, VMI, W&L, or UVA" for a more "raging nightlife." Nightlife at Sweet Briar itself—marked by "boathouse" parties held on campus every Thursday—is more of a "'girls' night' with a box of wine and good girlfriends" rather than debaucherous partying. In addition, students have a wide range of activities to choose from, such as movie nights, laser tag, "clubs, Campus Christian Fellowship, music, [and] theater." Traditions such as "freshmen versus sophomore paint wars, junior week, secret sophomores and seniors" continue to foster "an extremely close and tightly knit community."

Student Body

"Students come to Sweet Briar to discover who they are [and] to learn to challenge themselves." It is overwhelmingly felt that their "goals of achieving in life" is what bonds the student body together. While there's still a want of diversity and marketing, for the school seems "to aim for a certain demographic" of the "preppy, white girl who…comes from a middle- to upper-middle-class family," the typical Sweet Briar woman "isn't always in pearls and talking about the latest stuff from Lilly Pulitzer…[She] is clever, independent, and adaptable." Sweet Briar women also "tend to fill their plates completely," and it "is not unusual for a student to be involved in four or more clubs or leadership opportunities on campus." The most important facet of the student body, however, is the friendship developed between its students. "Every student is able to find a niche," and through shared values and the many available campus activities, women here create "lasting memories" and "friends that will last a lifetime."

FINANCIAL AID: 434-381-6156 • E-MAIL: ADMISSIONS@SBC.EDU • WEBSITE: WWW.SBC.EDU

THE PRINCETON REVIEW SAYS

Admissions

Very important factors considered include: GPA, rigor of secondary school record. *Important factors considered include:* Standardized test scores, application essay, interview, recommendation(s). *Other factors considered include:* Class rank, extracurricular activities, first generation, racial/ethnic status, talent/ability, volunteer work, work experience, alumni/ae relations, character/personal qualities. SAT or ACT required; ACT with or without Writing component accepted. TOEFL required of all international applicants. *Academic units required:* 4 English; 3 mathematics; 3 science; (2 science lab); 3 social studies; 2 foreign language; 3 history. *Academic units recommended:* 4 English; 4 mathematics; 4 science; (3 science lab); 4 social studies; 4 foreign language; 4 history.

Financial Aid

Students should submit: FAFSA, Noncustodial PROFILE. The Princeton Review suggests that all financial aid forms be submitted as soon as possible after January 1. *Need-based scholarships/grants offered:* Federal Pell, SEOG, State scholarships/grants, private scholarships, the school's own gift aid. *Loan aid offered:* Direct Subsidized Stafford Loans, Direct Unsubsidized Stafford Loans, Direct PLUS loans, Federal Perkins Loans, College/university loans from institutional funds. Federal Work-Study Program available. Institutional employment available. Off-campus job opportunities are fair.

The Inside Word

Due to its fairly self-selecting applicant pool, Sweet Briar is able to consider each application closely. The school looks for "fit" with the school as much as it looks for evidence of academic achievement and ability. The question then is, how well will you meld with the Sweet Briar community? Can the school deliver quality academics in your areas of interest? (After all, a school this small can't provide in-depth instruction in every discipline.) Especially if your test scores and/or high school grades are less than stellar, these are the questions that will determine your admission to Sweet Briar.

THE SCHOOL SAYS "..."

From the Admissions Office

"The woman who applies to Sweet Briar is mature and far-sighted enough to know what she wants from her college experience. She is intellectually adventuresome, more willing to explore new fields, and more open to challenging her boundaries. Sweet Briar attracts the ambitious, confident woman who enjoys being immersed not only in a first-rate academic program, but in a variety of meaningful activities outside the classroom. Our students take charge and revel in their accomplishments. This attitude follows graduates, enabling them to compete confidently in the corporate world and in graduate school.

"The faculty and staff do not simply give students individual attention; rather they pay attention to individuals. As an institution, we commit to every student, and our mission is to provide a learning community that prepares her to be successful in whatever she chooses to do after college."

SELECTIVITY

Admissions Rating	78
# of applicants	905
% of applicants accepted	84
% of acceptees attending	26

FRESHMAN PROFILE

Range SAT Critical Reading	480–620
Range SAT Math	458–590
Range SAT Writing	460–580
Range ACT Composite	21–27
Minimum paper TOEFL	550
Minimum web-based TOEFL	213
Average HS GPA	3.51
% graduated top 10% of class	30
% graduated top 25% of class	58
% graduated top 50% of class	82

DEADLINES

Regular	
Priority	2/1
Deadline	2/1
Nonfall registration?	Yes

FINANCIAL FACTS

Financial Aid Rating	80
Annual tuition	$34,460
Room and board	$12,160
Required fees	$475
Books and supplies	$1,250
% needy frosh rec. need-based scholarship or grant aid	100
% needy UG rec. need-based scholarship or grant aid	98
% needy frosh rec. non-need-based scholarship or grant aid	18
% needy UG rec. non-need-based scholarship or grant aid	16
% needy frosh rec. need-based self-help aid	77
% needy UG rec. need-based self-help aid	75
% frosh rec. any financial aid	100
% UG rec. any financial aid	96
% UG borrow to pay for school	56
Average cumulative indebtedness	$23,265
% frosh need fully met	17
% ugrads need fully met	18
Average % of frosh need met	75
Average % of ugrad need met	76

SYRACUSE UNIVERSITY

100 CROUSE-HINDS HALL, SYRACUSE, NY 13244-2130 • ADMISSIONS: 315-443-3611 • FAX: 315-443-4226

STUDENTS SAY ". . ."

Academics

The school spirit is definitely palpable the minute you set foot onto Syracuse's campus. Indeed, it's highly evident that "everyone here bleeds orange." Frankly, it's no surprise that 'Cuse undergrads truly love their school. The university provides students with the triple threat of "a great reputation," "incredible academic programs" and a "great social scene." Many also highlight the "excellent study abroad program" and boast about "the quality of career services." Additionally, known for its fabulous arts and media departments, undergrads especially tout the S. I. Newhouse School of Public Communications. At Newhouse, students benefit from "prestige and connections" as well as "hands-on, interactive learning environments." Of course, not to be outdone, undergrads also praise (among others) the "reputable business school," "great architecture school" and "top ranked sports management program." Further, students value that professors have a lot of real world experience. As one pleased senior shares, "Our professors are all accomplished in their respective industries and bring that to life in classes." Importantly, for the most part, they "truly care about their students and have your best interests at heart." However, a sophomore does caution, "Classes can be hard if you don't stay on top of things." Finally, as an impressed nutrition major brags, "The opportunities are endless and when I say endless I mean endless! This school has so many connections and great opportunities for every single student on campus."

Life

Life at Syracuse moves at a frenzied pace and the busy undergrads here wouldn't have it any other way. To begin with, the university nets a fairly athletic student body and participation in club sports is quite high. A bioengineering major chimes in adding, "All of the sports here are huge events, especially basketball. Every team is worth going to see at least once." Many undergrads are also civic minded. Indeed, "volunteering is also a big part of life at Syracuse—there is a large effort to get students off 'the hill' that is our campus and into the larger Syracuse community." Students do cop to the fact that they maintain a lively party culture. For starters, "fraternities and sororities are huge." As a freshman reveals, "We're a pretty big party school…On the weekends, most people go to house parties, frat parties or apartment parties on South Campus. Many people also go to the bars that are short walks from all the dorms." However, she also assures that "not everyone parties like you would think . . . and there are plenty of things to do for all social groups." When students are itching to get off campus, downtown Syracuse offers "great shops and food." A pleased senior elaborates, "The newly expanded shopping and entertainment center—Destiny USA—is also a huge draw. You can literally see a movie, ride Go-Karts, and shop all in one place. It makes for a pretty great Saturday."

Student Body

At first glance, it can seem as though the typical Syracuse student is "wealthy," "from the Northeast," and "[involved with] Greek life." However, others insist that the campus "is a melting pot of different cultures and ethnicities" and that "there is something to fit everyone." As a proud junior exclaims, "Our international student population is huge and we attract students not only from across the country but across the world." By and large, undergrads at Syracuse are the types who excel at maintaining a work/life balance. Certainly, they "care deeply…about academic pursuits" but also realize that there is more to college than studying. Indeed, a public relations major tells us that "many students spend just as much time in extracurricular activities and internships, as well as managing a fruitful social life." Perhaps this content junior best explains his peers by stating, "It's a mix of people out to have a great time and people focused on learning. As well as everything in between. It's easy to find a spot to fit in."

FINANCIAL AID: 315-443-1513 • E-MAIL: ORANGE@SYR.EDU • WEBSITE: WWW.SYR.EDU

THE PRINCETON REVIEW SAYS

Admissions

Very important factors considered include: Class rank, GPA, rigor of secondary school record, standardized test scores, application essay, extracurricular activities, interview, recommendation(s), talent/ability, volunteer work, character/personal qualities, level of applicant's interest. *Important factors considered include:* First generation. *Other factors considered include:* Geographical residence, racial/ethnic status, work experience, alumni/ae relations. SAT or ACT required; ACT with Writing component required. TOEFL required of all international applicants. *Academic units required:* 4 English; 4 mathematics; 4 science; 3 social studies. *Academic units recommended:* 4 social studies; 3 foreign language.

Financial Aid

Students should submit: FAFSA, CSS/Financial Aid PROFILE, Noncustodial PROFILE. Regular filing deadline is 2/1. The Princeton Review suggests that all financial aid forms be submitted as soon as possible after January 1. *Need-based scholarships/grants offered:* Federal Pell, SEOG, State scholarships/grants, private scholarships, the school's own gift aid. *Loan aid offered:* Direct Subsidized Stafford Loans, Direct Unsubsidized Stafford Loans, Direct PLUS loans, Federal Perkins Loans. Applicants will be notified of awards beginning 3/15. Federal Work-Study Program available. Institutional employment available. Off-campus job opportunities are good.

The Inside Word

Syracuse's admissions process is certainly competitive. Successful candidates often have strong GPAs and solid test scores. It's also important to note that students interested in applying to any fine or performing arts or architecture programs will need to audition and/or submit a portfolio. Finally, applicants who strongly feel that Syracuse is their first choice are highly encouraged to apply early decision.

THE SCHOOL SAYS "..."

From the Admissions Office

"Syracuse University students prepare for the world in the world. You'll customize your education through interdisciplinary study across a collection of prominent schools and colleges; and connect classroom learning and hands-on experience through internships, research, start-up ventures, and professional immersion experiences in the City of Syracuse and via University centers in New York City, Washington D.C., and Los Angeles. SU experiential learning also spans the globe, and nearly half of undergraduates study abroad. The university operates centers in Beijing, Florence, Hong Kong, Istanbul, London, Madrid, Santiago, and Strasbourg, and offers short-term, summer, and semester options in these and many other cities.

"An SU education is also defined by breadth of opportunity combined with individualized attention. You'll choose from more than 200 majors and 100 minors, and work closely with top scholars who are professionals in their fields that share their research/writing to further the classroom experience. You can pursue multiple majors and/or minors, and round out your experience with participation in one or more of 300 extracurricular groups. Upon graduation, you'll join one of the proudest, most supportive alumni networks in the world with alum that include founding principal of Fox & Fowle Architects Bruce Fowle (1960), Joe Biden, Law (1968), space shuttle commander Eileen Collins (1978), screenwriter Aaron Sorkin (1983), actor Taye Diggs (1993), Arielle Tepper Madover (1994), and Foursquare cofounder Dennis Crowley (1998)."

SELECTIVITY

Admissions Rating	92
# of applicants	28,269
% of applicants accepted	49
% of acceptees attending	25
# offered a place on the wait list	5,145
% accepting a place on wait list	34
% admitted from wait list	39
# of early decision applicants	1,276
% accepted early decision	75

FRESHMAN PROFILE

Range SAT Critical Reading	500–620
Range SAT Math	540–650
Range SAT Writing	520–630
Range ACT Composite	23–28
Minimum paper TOEFL	550
Minimum web-based TOEFL	85
Average HS GPA	3.60
% graduated top 10% of class	39
% graduated top 25% of class	71
% graduated top 50% of class	94

DEADLINES

Early decision	
Deadline	11/15
Regular	
Priority	1/1
Nonfall registration?	Yes

FINANCIAL FACTS

Financial Aid Rating	87
Annual tuition	$38,970
Room and board	$14,054
% needy frosh rec. need-based scholarship or grant aid	91
% needy UG rec. need-based scholarship or grant aid	91
% needy frosh rec. non-need-based scholarship or grant aid	7
% needy UG rec. non-need-based scholarship or grant aid	6
% needy frosh rec. need-based self-help aid	93
% needy UG rec. need-based self-help aid	93
% frosh rec. any financial aid	73
% UG rec. any financial aid	74
% UG borrow to pay for school	67
Average cumulative indebtedness	$33,455
% frosh need fully met	46
% ugrads need fully met	39
Average % of frosh need met	95
Average % of ugrad need met	89

TEMPLE UNIVERSITY

1801 NORTH BROAD STREET (041-09), PHILADELPHIA, PA 19122-6096 • ADMISSIONS: 215-204-7200 • FAX: 215-204-5694

STUDENTS SAY ". . ."

Academics

Temple University is "a large school" that "makes you feel at home in the city of Philadelphia" and offers "rigorous academic classes and many outside activities." This "wonderful" school is "located right in the city," and students praise the campus as being "one of the most diverse in the country." "Temple University is a place where everyone fits in and walks away with a little more knowledge than they had the day before," says one undergrad. This diversity also extends to classes. There's a "wide variety of classes" and "lots of awesome majors," all of which are supported by a "helpful and passionate set of professors who learn right along with students." There's also the "top-notch" honors program, which is a "favorite part of Temple by far," explains one student. "It's an outstanding program, and I feel very fortunate to be a part of it." Most here agree their academic experience has been "amazing." In the words of one undergrad, "Temple's standard of access and excellence is evident in its students' success." The "knowledgeable" professors "really want to see students succeed." While some feel that the administration "doesn't always run so smoothly," noting that "Temple is pretty much a small city, and it often runs like a bureaucracy," overall, students agree that administrators are "accessible at any time" and are "helpful when you need them."

Life

As you'd expect from a big school in a big city, "Temple has something for everyone." Whether you're looking for "city life," "friendly people," or "a million and one clubs or groups to join," you'll find it here at Temple. "There are tons of things to do," says one student. "If students get bored on campus, they were probably boring to begin with." Life on campus is "very interconnected," and "there's usually always something going on" thanks to "student organizations that appeal to every interest and social group." Most students keep busy by "studying, going to the gym, [and] playing intramural sports," but even if nothing is happening on campus, "there's much to do in the city." Not surprisingly, Philadelphia plays a substantial part in students' social lives. "There are amazing bars in the city," says one undergrad. "The only nights that students do not go out for drinks are Sunday and Monday." That said, if imbibing isn't your cup of tea, not to worry—there's plenty more on offer than watering holes. "You can have tons of fun on campus without drinking," explains a student. "There are lots of fun things to do because of our close proximity to Center City Philadelphia." Some examples are "great clubs, shopping, hookah bars, and restaurants." Also, if you get tired of Temple's campus you can always check out another—"Drexel, LaSalle, and UPenn's campuses are close by."

Student Body

Diversity isn't just a word at Temple; it's a fact. "At Temple, the atypical students are the typical students," explains an undergrad. "The majority population is made up of ethnic minorities." The student body here is made up of "many different kinds of ethnicities, sexual orientations, and economic and political stances," all of whom "contribute to the overall sense of school spirit and pride." Students agree that everyone here is "unique," and that makes for a place where "everyone becomes comfortable with each other's differences." "Every student brings their own light to Temple, which is what makes the school shine so bright," says one student. Despite this "huge mixture of types," students here do share similarities, particularly in their "motivation" to do well. Students here fill their time with "studying" and "extracurricular activities," all while also "experiencing life in the city of Philadelphia." One thing that all students agree on is that "The typical student at Temple University is approachable and greatly accepts diversity." As one undergrad says, "Everyone just kind of fits in, which is why the students like Temple so much."

FINANCIAL AID: 215-204-8760 • E-MAIL: ASKANOWL@TEMPLE.EDU • WEBSITE: WWW.TEMPLE.EDU

THE PRINCETON REVIEW SAYS

Admissions

Very important factors considered include: GPA, rigor of secondary school record. *Important factors considered include:* Class rank, standardized test scores. *Other factors considered include:* Application essay, extracurricular activities, geographical residence, racial/ethnic status, recommendation(s), state residency, talent/ability, volunteer work, work experience, alumni/ae relations, character/personal qualities. SAT or ACT required; ACT with Writing component required. TOEFL required of all international applicants. *Academic units required:* 4 English; 3 mathematics; 2 science; (1 science lab); 2 social studies; 2 foreign language; 1 history; 1 academic elective. *Academic units recommended:* 4 English; 4 mathematics; 3 science; (2 science lab); 2 social studies; 2 foreign language; 2 history; 3 academic electives.

Financial Aid

Students should submit: FAFSA. The Princeton Review suggests that all financial aid forms be submitted as soon as possible after January 1. *Need-based scholarships/grants offered:* Federal Pell, SEOG, State scholarships/grants, private scholarships, the school's own gift aid, federal nursing scholarships. *Loan aid offered:* Direct Subsidized Stafford Loans, Direct Unsubsidized Stafford Loans, Direct PLUS loans, Federal Perkins Loans, Federal Nursing Loans, State Loans, College/university loans from institutional funds. Federal Work-Study Program available. Institutional employment available. Off-campus job opportunities are excellent.

The Inside Word

Temple is a well-recognized name in higher education, and its location is one of the nation's most popular cities. Competition can be steep when it comes to admissions, particularly if you aren't a resident of Pennsylvania. Admissions officers are fairly objective about their approach to application assessment in that they focus primarily on the solid numbers: class rank, GPA, and standardized test scores. That said, keep in mind that there are no minimum requirements, so if you have skills and talents that can't be mathematically calculated, it would behoove you to point them out in your application.

THE SCHOOL SAYS "..."

From the Admissions Office

"Temple combines the academic resources and intellectual stimulation of a large research university with the intimacy of a small college. The university experienced record growth in attracting new students from all 50 states and more than 125 countries. Students choose from 122 undergraduate majors. Special academic programs include the Honors Program, Diamond Research Scholars, learning communities for first-year undergraduates, co-op education, and study abroad. Temple has seven regional campuses, including Main Campus and the Health Sciences Center in historic Philadelphia, suburban Temple University, Ambler, and overseas campuses in Tokyo and Rome. Main Campus is home to Alter Hall for the Fox School of Business, the Tyler School of Art, and a new Architecture building, all state-of-the-art facilities that have opened since 2009. A new residence hall as well as a new Science and Research Center will open in 2013 and 2014, respectively. Our TECH Center has more than 600 computer workstations, 100 laptops, and a Starbucks. The Liacouras Center is a modern entertainment, recreation, and sports complex that hosts concerts, plays, trade shows, and college and professional athletics. It also includes the Independence Blue Cross Student Recreation Center, a major fitness facility for students now and in the future. Students can also take advantage of the new Temple University Fitness (TUF) Center.

"Applicants are required to take the SAT (or the ACT with Writing) and will be considered using the 2400 scale. The best Critical Reading, Math and Writing scores from either test will be considered."

SELECTIVITY	
Admissions Rating	79
# of applicants	18,813
% of applicants accepted	64
% of acceptees attending	37
# offered a place on the wait list	1,479
% accepting a place on wait list	46
% admitted from wait list	39

FRESHMAN PROFILE	
Range SAT Critical Reading	500–610
Range SAT Math	510–620
Range SAT Writing	500–610
Range ACT Composite	22–27
Minimum paper TOEFL	550
Minimum web-based TOEFL	213
Average HS GPA	3.44
% graduated top 10% of class	20
% graduated top 25% of class	52
% graduated top 50% of class	88

DEADLINES	
Regular	
Deadline	3/1
Nonfall registration?	Yes

APPLICANTS ALSO LOOK AT AND OFTEN PREFER
Pennsylvania State University—University Park; Drexel University; Rutgers- The State University of New Jersey—New Brunswick; University of Pittsburgh—Pittsburgh Campus

AND SOMETIMES PREFER
University of Maryland; College Park; Syracuse University; University of Massachusetts Amherst

FINANCIAL FACTS	
Financial Aid Rating	78
Annual in-state tuition	$13,406
Annual out-of-state tuition	$23,432
Room and board	$10,296
Required fees	$690
Books and supplies	$1,000
% needy frosh rec. need-based scholarship or grant aid	87
% needy UG rec. need-based scholarship or grant aid	85
% needy frosh rec. non-need-based scholarship or grant aid	49
% needy UG rec. non-need-based scholarship or grant aid	35
% needy frosh rec. need-based self-help aid	83
% needy UG rec. need-based self-help aid	87
% frosh rec. any financial aid	88
% UG rec. any financial aid	82
% UG borrow to pay for school	76
Average cumulative indebtedness	$34,382
% frosh need fully met	31
% ugrads need fully met	26
Average % of frosh need met	70
Average % of ugrad need met	68

TEXAS A&M UNIVERSITY—COLLEGE STATION

PO BOX 30014, COLLEGE STATION, TX 77843-3014 • ADMISSIONS: 979-845-3741 • FAX: 979-847-8737

CAMPUS LIFE

Quality of Life Rating	84
Fire Safety Rating	85
Green Rating	93
Type of school	Public
Affiliation	No Affiliation
Environment	City

STUDENTS

Total undergrad enrollment	43,930
% male/female	52/48
% from out of state	4
% frosh live on campus	62
% ugrads live on campus	25
# of fraternities	20
# of sororities	36
% African American	3
% Asian	5
% Caucasian	68
% Hispanic	20
% Native American	<1
% international	1
# of countries represented	127

SURVEY SAYS . . .

Lots of conservative students
Students are happy
Career services are great
Class discussions are rare
Students are friendly
Students are very religious
Students get along with local community
Students involved in community service
Great off-campus food
Campus feels safe
Athletic facilities are great
Everyone loves the Aggies
Alumni active on campus

ACADEMICS

Academic Rating	73
% students returning for sophomore year	91
% students graduating within 4 years	49
% students graduating within 6 years	78
Calendar	Semester
Student/faculty ratio	22:1
Profs interesting rating	74
Profs accessible rating	75

Most classes have 20–29 students.
Most lab/discussion sessions have
20–29 students.

MOST POPULAR MAJORS
psychology; accounting

STUDENTS SAY ". . ."

Academics

The "untold spirit at Texas A&M" lies in its tradition, which is "the underlying pulse of Aggieland." This large research school has "deep-rooted values" and "runs as a tight-knit family despite the numerous population." This strong family dynamic makes the school an "open, friendly place to learn and grow," and the incredibly strong engineering and life science programs certainly don't hurt. The academics can be "difficult," but "the goal is to set [students] apart from the rest, so [they] can excel." The "wonderful" professors "do their best to bring the topics from pages to the real world." They "all have life experiences working with the topics that they teach making them the perfect resource for information." These "top-notch" professors (well, aside from a very few who are "extremely dry") come back to A&M after working in powerful industry positions "because they love the atmosphere and the students." "I have never skipped a class because I thoroughly enjoy going," says one student. Particularly with the sciences, professors offer students the opportunity to participate in "world-changing research," and all such experiences "have had something useful to add to the material," which helps students when they go out into the real world. The "Aggie network" is something to behold; it reaches far across the nation ("Aggie alumni are loyal to their school forever") and "is good for getting jobs after graduation." The sense of pride here motivates students to do well "because they're part of something bigger than themselves." There is "great support" from both the faculty and staff together. "The mindset they have is to effectively prepare students for world-class challenges," says one student. "At Texas A&M, you learn to be a well-rounded, moral, and ethical person."

Life

Student organizations positively abound at Texas A&M (there are more than 800), and they are a huge social outlet for students looking to find those with similar interests. "Get involved in something you're passionate about; there is a club for just about *everything*," says a student. Off-campus, there are "four-dollar movies, many dancehalls, endless restaurants to eat at, and a large mall," as well as "an ice-skating rink, bowling alley, and miniature golf place." Students at Texas A&M are "loyal to one another and are always willing to support their fellow Aggies." "Tradition and chivalry run the school," and students all "work hard during the week so we can party hard on the weekends," usually at Northgate, the "bar street." "Texas A&M is kind of like a cult—a really happy cult," explains a student. The "immense school spirit" is derived from the many "time-honored traditions," including the Big Event, which is the largest one-day, student-run service project in the nation. That's not even to mention the football: "Saturdays in the fall are owned by football." "Although the school is very large, whenever the…Aggies at Kyle Field are belting the war hymn and linking arms, I feel like I am part of a huge family." As one student cryptically sums up his school's mythology, "From the outside looking in, you can't understand it. From the inside looking out you can't explain it."

Student Body

A typical student is "white," "conservative," "involved in at least one club, spends a fair amount of time studying, and learns to two-step for Thursday nights." This being Texas, "some wear cowboy boots, a flannel shirt, a cowboy hat/baseball cap, and jeans." There is also a strong faction of members of the Corps of Cadets, as well as religious folk (the school has "the largest Bible study in the world"). Though lacking cultural diversity, interests and hobbies run the gamut, and "students from other races and classes fit in just fine and are able to make friends just like anybody else." While it's a big school, "a lot of classes are pretty small, so it's easy to make friends in class." There are "no pretenses" among Aggies, and "everyone shows who they are." "Most of the people I have met here are truly genuine individuals," says a student.

FINANCIAL AID: 979-845-3236 • E-MAIL: ADMISSIONS@TAMU.EDU • WEBSITE: WWW.TAMU.EDU

THE PRINCETON REVIEW SAYS

Admissions

Very important factors considered include: Class rank, GPA, rigor of secondary school record, standardized test scores, extracurricular activities, talent/ability, alumni/ae relations. *Important factors considered include:* Application essay, first generation, geographical residence, state residency, volunteer work, work experience. *Other factors considered include:* Recommendation(s), character/personal qualities. SAT or ACT required; ACT with Writing component required. TOEFL required of all international applicants. *Academic units required:* 4 English; 3 science; (2 science lab); 2 social studies; 2 foreign language; 1 history. *Academic units recommended:* 4 English; 3 science; (2 science lab); 2 social studies; 2 foreign language; 1 history; 1 computer science.

Financial Aid

Students should submit: FAFSA. The Princeton Review suggests that all financial aid forms be submitted as soon as possible after January 1. *Need-based scholarships/grants offered:* Federal Pell, SEOG, State scholarships/grants, private scholarships, the school's own gift aid. *Loan aid offered:* Direct Subsidized Stafford Loans, Direct Unsubsidized Stafford Loans, Direct PLUS loans, Federal Perkins Loans, State Loans, College/university loans from institutional funds. Applicants will be notified of awards beginning 3/15. Federal Work-Study Program available. Institutional employment available. Off-campus job opportunities are excellent.

The Inside Word

Texas A&M uses some cut-and-dried admissions criteria: Students graduating in the top 10 percent of a recognized public or private high school in the state of Texas are automatically in, all they have to do is get their applications in on time. Applicants in the top quarter of their graduating class who have a combined SAT math/critical reading score of 1300 (minimum score of 600 in each component) are also automatically in, as are such students who earn a composite ACT score of 30 (minimum 27 on the math and English sections). Students must also take the writing component of the SAT and/or ACT for the test score to be considered. All other applications are deemed "Review Admits" to be sorted through by the admissions committee.

THE SCHOOL SAYS "..."

From the Admissions Office

"Established in 1876 as the first public college in the state, Texas A&M University has become a world leader in teaching, research, and public service. Located in College Station in the heart of Texas, it is centrally situated among three of the country's ten largest cities: Dallas, Houston, and San Antonio. Texas A&M is ranked nationally in these four areas: enrollment, enrollment of top students, value of research, and endowment.

"Freshman applicants are required to take the SAT or the ACT. We will use the applicant's best single testing date score in decision making."

SELECTIVITY

Admissions Rating	84
# of applicants	31,388
% of applicants accepted	69
% of acceptees attending	47

FRESHMAN PROFILE

Range SAT Critical Reading	520–630
Range SAT Math	550–660
Range SAT Writing	490–610
Range ACT Composite	23–29
Minimum paper TOEFL	550
Minimum web-based TOEFL	0
% graduated top 10% of class	53
% graduated top 25% of class	78
% graduated top 50% of class	85

DEADLINES

Regular	
Priority	12/1
Deadline	1/15
Nonfall registration?	Yes

APPLICANTS ALSO LOOK AT AND OFTEN PREFER
Rice University

AND SOMETIMES PREFER
The University of Texas at Austin; Baylor University; Louisiana State University—Baton Rouge

AND RARELY PREFER
Southern Methodist University

FINANCIAL FACTS

Financial Aid Rating	81
Annual in-state tuition	$5,297
Annual out-of-state tuition	$21,917
Room and board	$8,450
Required fees	$3,209
Books and supplies	$1,246
% needy frosh rec. need-based scholarship or grant aid	97
% needy UG rec. need-based scholarship or grant aid	86
% needy frosh rec. non-need-based scholarship or grant aid	16
% needy UG rec. non-need-based scholarship or grant aid	10
% needy frosh rec. need-based self-help aid	45
% needy UG rec. need-based self-help aid	62
% frosh rec. any financial aid	77
% UG rec. any financial aid	65
% UG borrow to pay for school	49
Average cumulative indebtedness	$25,223
% frosh need fully met	50
% ugrads need fully met	42
Average % of frosh need met	77
Average % of ugrad need met	70

TEXAS CHRISTIAN UNIVERSITY

OFFICE OF ADMISSIONS, FORT WORTH, TX 76129 • ADMISSIONS: 817-257-7490 • FAX: 817-257-7268

STUDENTS SAY ". . ."

Academics

The popular conception of Texas is that everything there is big, big, big, but Texas Christian University is one Lone Star institution that bucks this trend, insisting on "smaller classroom sizes" that allows professors to be "very interested in [students] personally." One undergrad explains: "If I have a problem and need to talk with the profs, they go out of their way to meet with me, especially when it comes to career options and what my best options are in terms of what I want to do. They are very helpful." While "there are some programs with more students than others, overall the academic experience at TCU is very personal and rewarding. Many students are easily able to latch onto a professor's lab research…Getting involved in the academic programs at TCU will really pay off." Students enjoy a strong support network; the school "offers many resources such as the library, writing center, career center, student support services, and other educational and personal resources," and alumni "are really involved and give a lot back to the school." Business, education, and physical therapy are among the standout offerings here. Access to the Fort Worth–Dallas business community means plenty of good internship and networking opportunities.

Life

"Greek life is one of the most popular activities" at TCU; some say "the Greeks rule the social scene at the school," while others see slightly more diverse options. The school "puts a lot of its money to good use, such as new residence halls, a nice recreational facility, funding for numerous clubs and organizations, and great activities to bring the campus community together," creating "a focus on the student community" that extends beyond the Greek houses. TCU football is another pillar of campus life, and students "have a lot of pride" in both the program and the school itself. Beyond these choices, life at TCU "is what you make it. If you want to make grades your top priority, it's very easy to do so. If you want to go out and party a lot, it's very easy to do [that] as well. Lots of people drink on campus, but not everyone makes that their life. It's all about what your priorities are because it is easy to go either way." Off-campus opportunities are plentiful thanks to access to Fort Worth–Dallas, a major metropolis.

Student Body

Undergrads tend to be "middle- to upper-class…in good physical shape, and like to have a good time." Many, "but not all, dress extremely well…First impressions mean a lot here, so do not mess up." "The student body is very Greek" at TCU. Students differ on how this impacts social dynamics; some insist that "if you aren't in a fraternity or sorority, it is very hard to fit in," while others point out that "there are other types of people on campus", and "if you are open-minded and have a good personality overall you won't find it hard to make friends inside and outside of Greek life and find yourself belonging at TCU." While "the student population is mostly made up of Caucasian students," there is "a growing minority student population," the largest segment of which is Latina. Some complain about the pervasive materialism, but others think the issue is overblown; one tells us, "Some may find the money an issue, but that's only because they make it an issue. I've never been ashamed that I can't buy the latest Prada handbag, and no one has ever looked down on me because of that. If you don't bring it up, nobody cares. A lack of character may make these people feel left out."

FINANCIAL AID: 817-257-7858 • E-MAIL: FROGMAIL@TCU.EDU • WEBSITE: WWW.TCU.EDU

THE PRINCETON REVIEW SAYS

Admissions

Very important factors considered include: Class rank, GPA, rigor of secondary school record, standardized test scores, application essay, recommendation(s), character/personal qualities. *Important factors considered include:* Extracurricular activities, first generation, geographical residence, racial/ethnic status, talent/ability, volunteer work, work experience, religious affiliation. *Other factors considered include:* interview, alumni/ae relations, level of applicant's interest. SAT or ACT required; ACT with or without Writing component accepted. TOEFL required of all international applicants. *Academic units required:* 4 English; 3 mathematics; 3 science; 3 social studies; 2 foreign language; 2 academic electives. *Academic units recommended:* 4 English; 4 mathematics; 4 science; 4 social studies; 4 foreign language.

Financial Aid

Students should submit: FAFSA, CSS/Financial Aid PROFILE, Noncustodial PROFILE. Regular filing deadline is 3/15. The Princeton Review suggests that all financial aid forms be submitted as soon as possible after January 1. *Need-based scholarships/grants offered:* Federal Pell, SEOG, State scholarships/grants, private scholarships, the school's own gift aid. *Loan aid offered:* Direct Subsidized Stafford Loans, Direct Unsubsidized Stafford Loans, Direct PLUS loans, Federal Perkins Loans, Federal Nursing Loans, State Loans. Federal Work-Study Program available. Institutional employment available. Off-campus job opportunities are excellent.

The Inside Word

The sheer volume of applications sent to TCU—the school receives more than 18,000 each year—requires the school to apply some baseline criteria for winnowing out unlikely candidates. That said, the school works hard to consider applications holistically and to find mitigating evidence to offset sub-par performance in any one category (for example, standardized test scores).

THE SCHOOL SAYS "..."

From the Admissions Office

"TCU is a major teaching and research university with the feel of a small college. The TCU academic experience includes small classes with top faculty; cutting-edge technology; a liberal arts and sciences core curriculum; and real-life application though faculty-directed research, group projects, and internships. While TCU faculty members are recognized for research, their main focus is on teaching and mentoring students. The friendly campus community welcomes new students at Frog Camp before classes begin, where students find three days of fun meeting new friends, learning campus traditions, and serving the community. Campus life includes 200 clubs and organizations, a spirited NCAA Division I athletics program in the Big 12 Conference, and numerous productions from professional schools of the arts. More than half of the students participate in a wide array of intramural sports, and about 40 percent are involved in Greek organizations, including ones emphasizing ethnic diversity as well as the Christian faith. The historic relationship to the Christian Church (Disciples of Christ) means that instead of teaching a particular viewpoint, TCU encourages students to consider and follow their own beliefs. The university's mission—to educate individuals to think and act as ethical leaders and responsible citizens in a global community—influences everything from course work to study abroad to the way Horned Frogs act and interact. From National Merit Scholars to those just now realizing their academic potential, TCU attracts and serves students who are learning to change the world.

"TCU will accept either the SAT or the ACT (with or without the writing component) in admission and scholarship processes. The writing sections will be considered alongside the TCU application essay."

SELECTIVITY

Admissions Rating	92
# of applicants	18,551
% of applicants accepted	47
% of acceptees attending	22
# offered a place on the wait list	1,680
% accepting a place on wait list	30
% admitted from wait list	13

FRESHMAN PROFILE

Range SAT Critical Reading	540–620
Range SAT Math	550–650
Range SAT Writing	540–640
Range ACT Composite	25–29
Minimum paper TOEFL	550
% graduated top 10% of class	42
% graduated top 25% of class	75
% graduated top 50% of class	96

DEADLINES

Early decision	
Deadline	11/1
Notification	1/1
Early action	
Deadline	11/1
Notification	1/1
Regular	
Priority	2/15
Deadline	2/15
Notification	4/1
Nonfall registration?	Yes

FINANCIAL FACTS

Financial Aid Rating	69
Annual tuition	$36,500
Room and board	$10,980
Required fees	$90
Books and supplies	$1,050
% needy frosh rec. need-based scholarship or grant aid	96
% needy UG rec. need-based scholarship or grant aid	93
% needy frosh rec. non-need-based scholarship or grant aid	62
% needy UG rec. non-need-based scholarship or grant aid	57
% needy frosh rec. need-based self-help aid	69
% needy UG rec. need-based self-help aid	76
% frosh rec. any financial aid	72
% UG rec. any financial aid	73
% UG borrow to pay for school	43
Average cumulative indebtedness	$38,317
% frosh need fully met	28
% ugrads need fully met	23
Average % of frosh need met	68
Average % of ugrad need met	62

THOMAS AQUINAS COLLEGE

10000 OJAI ROAD, SANTA PAULA, CA 93060 • ADMISSION: 805-525-4417 • FAX: 805-421-5905

STUDENTS SAY " . . ."

Academics

Students at Thomas Aquinas College relish attending a school that "takes learning seriously for its own sake, not just as preparation for a job." With a "strong Catholic identity" and "rigorous curriculum," TAC offers a "holistic education" that's "demanding on every level." The college promotes a "Great Books education," which really forces its undergrads to "read and think critically." All classes are seminar-based, a method many students here feel "better facilitates learning." Importantly, the "Catholic/small-college setting creates an atmosphere of trust and faith that makes it easier to study, to live, and to grow at school." Unlike other colleges, "there aren't any majors at Thomas Aquinas." Students simply graduate with a bachelor's degree in liberal arts. Class time is solely "devoted to discussion of the [reading] material assigned" with professors (or tutors as they are known) facilitating said discussion. Undergrads happily report that professors are "more than happy to continue the discussion outside class and are always ready to help their students." Moreover, they're "welcoming" and "easy to talk to," and all seem to "have a passion for intellectual formation." As one content senior succinctly states, "The professors are great and lead you to truth without forcing it on you."

Life

TAC inspires and encourages a contemplative life, and students spend a large portion of their time in "an intellectual discussion." That being said, even TAC undergrads need to kick back every now and again. On this active campus, intramural sports are quite popular, and "running, hiking, basketball, soccer, and football are major pastimes on campus." Further, "four times a year there is a formal dance hosted by one of the classes." As one enthusiastic sophomore explains, "I waltz, swing, lindy hop, tango, salsa, rumba, contra dance, polka, Virginia reel, and do other dances. People on this campus actually learn and know how to dance well." Students here also know how to make their own fun. As one freshman shares, there are "spontaneous student pranks, such as the day the freshmen men all wore blue while the freshmen women wore pink (officially titled 'Trip Out the Tutors Tuesday')." Additionally, "once or twice a semester, the school arranges field trips to the Getty Center, Villa, operas, art galleries, science museums, and other points of interest in the wider LA area." It's also quite common for students to "leave campus for the weekend for fun activities either to Ventura Beach (thirty minutes), Santa Barbara (one hour), or Ojai (twenty minutes)."

Student Body

Undergrads at TAC might, in some respects, appear "homogenous." Indeed, the vast majority of students "are Catholic," "devoted to learning and their faith," and politically "conservative." That being said, a senior assures us, "Any student with any interest can usually find a group that shares his or her passion." Importantly, many agree that their peers are "very kind and inclusive" as well as "joyful and inviting." One junior elaborates saying, "You walk down the hallways and sidewalks and are personally greeted by freshmen and seniors alike." An overwhelming number of undergrads here declare their fellow students "intellectually curious" and "somewhat obsessed with philosophy." Indeed, the typical student "is a thinker [who] will never hesitate to get in[to] a philosophical argument." Naturally, people here are "committed to the academic life," and most students study "very hard." They're "focused [and] mature" and make a point of "coming prepared to class." As one honest and insightful senior admits, "Most [students] would probably be considered a bit geeky elsewhere." But perhaps this student sums up his TAC peers the best, "You get all different kinds of people here—but one thing they have in common is a desire to search for the truth."

FINANCIAL AID: 800-634-9797 • E-MAIL: ADMISSIONS@THOMASAQUINAS.EDU • WEBSITE: WWW.THOMASAQUINAS.EDU

THE PRINCETON REVIEW SAYS

Admissions

Very important factors considered include: Rigor of secondary school record, standardized test scores, application essay, recommendation(s), character/personal qualities, level of applicant's interest. *Important factors considered include:* GPA. *Other factors considered include:* Class rank, extracurricular activities, interview, talent/ability, volunteer work, work experience, religious affiliation. SAT or ACT required; ACT with or without Writing component accepted. TOEFL required of all international applicants. *Academic units required:* 4 English; 3 mathematics; 2 science; 2 foreign language; 2 history. *Academic units recommended:* 4 English; 4 mathematics; 3 science; (2 science lab); 2 history; 3 academic electives.

Financial Aid

Students should submit: FAFSA, Institution's own financial aid form, State aid form. Regular filing deadline is 3/2. The Princeton Review suggests that all financial aid forms be submitted as soon as possible after January 1. *Need-based scholarships/grants offered:* Federal Pell, State scholarships/grants, private scholarships, the school's own gift aid. *Loan aid offered:* Direct Subsidized Stafford Loans, Direct Unsubsidized Stafford Loans, Direct PLUS loans, College/university loans from institutional funds. Off-campus job opportunities are fair.

The Inside Word

A unique academic institution, TAC thoroughly analyzes their applicants to ensure their accepted students will be a good fit. Academic prowess is a must, and candidates should also demonstrate intellectual curiosity. Because of their holistic approach, admissions officers pay close attention to the application essays. The college operates on a rolling admissions schedule and, if interested, you should apply as early as possible.

THE SCHOOL SAYS "..."

From the Admissions Office

"Thomas Aquinas College holds with confidence that the human mind is capable of knowing the truth about reality, that living according to the truth is necessary for human happiness, and that truth is best comprehended through the harmonious work of faith and reason. The intellectual virtues are understood to be essential, and the college considers the cultivation of those virtues the primary work of Catholic liberal education.

"The academic program designed to achieve this goal is comprehensive and unified—and it includes no textbooks or lecture classes. In every subject—from philosophy, theology, mathematics, and science to language, music, literature, and history—students read the greatest written works in those disciplines, both ancient and modern: Homer, Plato, Aristotle, Augustine, Aquinas, Newton, Maxwell, Einstein, the Founding Fathers of the American Republic, Shakespeare, and T. S. Eliot, to name just a few. Instead of attending lecture classes, students gather in small tutorials, seminars, and laboratories for Socratic-style discussions.

"One mark of the program's success is the variety of professions and careers that graduates enter. Many attend graduate and professional schools in a wide array of disciplines; among them, philosophy, theology, law, literature, and the sciences are most often chosen.

"SAT or ACT scores are required, and the writing component on each test is encouraged. However, scores in critical reading and math (SAT), or English and mathematics (ACT) are more central in the consideration of that aspect of a student's application."

SELECTIVITY

Admissions Rating	84
# of applicants	189
% of applicants accepted	81
% of acceptees attending	57
# offered a place on the wait list	38
% accepting a place on wait list	100
% admitted from wait list	61

FRESHMAN PROFILE

Range SAT Critical Reading	590–700
Range SAT Math	570–640
Range SAT Writing	570–690
Range ACT Composite	23–31
Minimum paper TOEFL	570
Minimum web-based TOEFL	230
Average HS GPA	3.78
% graduated top 10% of class	29
% graduated top 25% of class	50
% graduated top 50% of class	93

DEADLINES

Regular	
Nonfall registration?	No

APPLICANTS ALSO LOOK AT AND OFTEN PREFER
University of Notre Dame

AND SOMETIMES PREFER
The Catholic University of America; University of Dallas

FINANCIAL FACTS

Financial Aid Rating	99
Annual tuition	$24,500
Room and board	$7,950
Required fees	$0
Books and supplies	$50
% needy frosh rec. need-based scholarship or grant aid	98
% needy UG rec. need-based scholarship or grant aid	95
% needy frosh rec. non-need-based scholarship or grant aid	0
% needy UG rec. non-need-based scholarship or grant aid	0
% needy frosh rec. need-based self-help aid	98
% needy UG rec. need-based self-help aid	99
% frosh rec. any financial aid	81
% UG rec. any financial aid	79
% UG borrow to pay for school	89
Average cumulative indebtedness	$15,521
% frosh need fully met	100
% ugrads need fully met	100
Average % of frosh need met	100
Average % of ugrad need met	100

TRANSYLVANIA UNIVERSITY

300 NORTH BROADWAY, LEXINGTON, KY 40508-1797 • ADMISSIONS: 859-233-8242 • FAX: 859-281-3649

STUDENTS SAY ". . ."

Academics

Tucked away in the heart of Lexington, Kentucky, Transylvania University is able to marry a "small-school atmosphere" with "big-city" living. An "extremely close-knit campus," one truly feels a "strong sense of community" while strolling around the grounds. Undergrads here greatly appreciate that the school "values community, education for the sake of education, and producing students with the skills to tackle any career the job market has to offer." Moreover, Transy strives to provide "a holistic educational experience where one can grow intellectually and academically while participating in a vibrant social community." Students are quick to heap praise on their professors who "are both very knowledgeable and fun to be around." They're all "accomplished within their fields" and seem to "love teaching here at Transylvania." As one pleased Spanish and English double-major confidently declares, "It doesn't matter whether a class is lecture- or discussion-based, because either way you're guaranteed to learn something." One junior does warn that most professors "require students [to] participate in classroom discussion," which can be "intimidating" for some. Perhaps most important, their accessibility is "amazing," and they "are almost always willing to let you stop by during their office hours and discuss just about anything." As this anthropology major simply and smartly quips, "I am never bored."

Life

During the week, life at Transylvania University can be fairly harried and "stressful," and most students have their noses "to the grindstone." In turn, because of working "ridiculously hard," students are pumped to "have some fun when [the week] is over." The vast majority of undergrads "are involved in Greek life," and "parties in the fraternity dorms are very popular." Fortunately, we have been assured that neither the fraternities nor sororities are "exclusive." Moreover, "every social event is practically open invitation." Of course, there's plenty to do aside from simply attending frat parties. For example, the "Student Activities Board [sponsors] a lot of activities that are pretty fun and have a relatively good turn out." There's always something to do as one freshman indicates, "This weekend I'll be going to a huge musical/talent show, then tomorrow I'll be volunteering to raise money for a local church, then after that I'll be going ice skating with some friends." Athletics are also fairly big, and "Transylvania has several perennially successful sports programs, some of which include men's and women's basketball, men's and women's soccer, and softball." Undergrads also love to take advantage of hometown Lexington, and you'll often find students "walking downtown to theaters, art exhibits, or other downtown events" as well as "the shopping district."

Student Body

Transylvania manages to attract students who "seem to be genuinely concerned with their education." Indeed, undergrads are quick to define their peers as "studious," "intellectually motivated," and full of "ambitious goals." As a result, "the average Transylvania student is extremely adept at balancing his or her academics with the many extracurricular activities available." Additionally, "Greek life is very prominent on campus." However, one student insists that overall, the "Transy campus has very diverse individuals." Of course, a handful of students begrudge the "lack of…geographic diversity," asserting that "most students come from the region around Lexington" and are "upper-middle-class." Others take issue with this sentiment, quickly stating, "We also have a huge population of individuals from different backgrounds including differences in sexual orientation, class, religion, region, and political orientation." Fortunately, undergrads do find their fellow students "approachable and friendly," and "most students will find themselves right at home on campus."

FINANCIAL AID: 859-233-8239 • E-MAIL: ADMISSIONS@TRANSY.EDU • WEBSITE: WWW.TRANSY.EDU

THE PRINCETON REVIEW SAYS

Admissions

Very important factors considered include: GPA, rigor of secondary school record, standardized test scores. *Important factors considered include:* Application essay, extracurricular activities, recommendation(s), work experience. *Other factors considered include:* First generation, geographical residence, interview, racial/ethnic status, talent/ability, volunteer work, alumni/ae relations, character/personal qualities. SAT or ACT required; ACT with or without Writing component accepted. TOEFL required of all international applicants. *Academic units required:* 4 English; 3 mathematics; 3 science; (2 science lab); 2 social studies; 2 foreign language; 2 academic electives. *Academic units recommended:* 4 English; 4 mathematics; 4 science; (3 science lab); 2 social studies; 3 foreign language; 1 history; 2 academic electives; 1 visual/performing arts.

Financial Aid

Students should submit: FAFSA. The Princeton Review suggests that all financial aid forms be submitted as soon as possible after January 1. *Need-based scholarships/grants offered:* Federal Pell, SEOG, State scholarships/grants, private scholarships, the school's own gift aid. *Loan aid offered:* Direct Subsidized Stafford Loans, Direct Unsubsidized Stafford Loans, Direct PLUS loans, Federal Perkins Loans, College/university loans from institutional funds. Federal Work-Study Program available. Institutional employment available. Off-campus job opportunities are excellent.

Inside Word

The admissions committee at Transylvania University is tasked with finding a freshman class that will mesh well with the existing Transy community. That being the case, they do their utmost to consider the entire applicant. Of course, academic rigor is the most important factor. However, don't shirk on your essays, recommendations, or extracurricular involvement.

THE SCHOOL SAYS " . . ."

From the Admissions Office

"Bright, highly motivated students choose Transylvania for our personal approach to learning and our record of success in preparing them for rewarding careers and fulfilling lives. They attend small classes (many have fewer than ten students) with highly qualified professors (no teaching assistants) and tackle faculty-directed student research projects in intriguing subjects like neurotransmitters and receptors, computer animation, and local Hispanic culture. Transylvania graduates have won prestigious scholarships and distinguished themselves at highly selective graduate and professional schools.

"Transylvania students consider the world their classroom. They enjoy May term travel courses studying the ancient polis in Greece, language and culture in France, and tropical ecology in Hawaii. Study abroad takes them to Germany, England, Japan, Mexico, and other destinations for a summer, a semester, or a year.

"You'll find Transylvania, a small college, nestled in a big city. Transylvania students soak up the advantages of Lexington, Kentucky, with its population of 300,000, numerous internships and job opportunities, and lots of entertainment. On campus, we have more than sixty co-curricular activities, and twenty-three varsity teams competing in NCAA Division III.

"While Transylvania is the nation's sixteenth oldest college and proud of its rich history, its commitments to the exploration of a variety of disciplines, to intellectual inquiry, and to critical thinking have never been more relevant than in today's rapidly changing twenty-first-century world.

"Applicants are not required to submit writing scores from the ACT or the SAT."

SELECTIVITY

Admissions Rating	85
# of applicants	1,539
% of applicants accepted	83
% of acceptees attending	23

FRESHMAN PROFILE

Range SAT Critical Reading	520–660
Range SAT Math	520–620
Range ACT Composite	24–30
Minimum paper TOEFL	550
Minimum web-based TOEFL	213
Average HS GPA	3.70
% graduated top 10% of class	39
% graduated top 25% of class	75
% graduated top 50% of class	95

DEADLINES

Early action	
Deadline	12/1
Notification	1/15
Regular	
Priority	12/1
Deadline	2/1
Notification	3/15
Nonfall registration?	Yes

APPLICANTS ALSO LOOK AT AND OFTEN PREFER

AND SOMETIMES PREFER
Centre College, University of Kentucky

FINANCIAL FACTS

Financial Aid Rating	84
Annual tuition	$30,280
Room and board	$8,975
Required fees	$1,280
Books and supplies	$1,000
% needy frosh rec. need-based scholarship or grant aid	100
% needy UG rec. need-based scholarship or grant aid	100
% needy frosh rec. non-need-based scholarship or grant aid	20
% needy UG rec. non-need-based scholarship or grant aid	13
% needy frosh rec. need-based self-help aid	76
% needy UG rec. need-based self-help aid	79
% frosh rec. any financial aid	99
% UG rec. any financial aid	98
% UG borrow to pay for school	60
Average cumulative indebtedness	$28,026
% frosh need fully met	27
% ugrads need fully met	21
Average % of frosh need met	85
Average % of ugrad need met	82

TRINITY COLLEGE (CT)

300 SUMMIT STREET, HARTFORD, CT 06016 • ADMISSIONS: 860-297-2180 • FAX: 860-297-2287

CAMPUS LIFE

Quality of Life Rating	70
Fire Safety Rating	93
Green Rating	82
Type of school	Private
Affiliation	No Affiliation
Environment	Metropolis

STUDENTS

Total undergrad enrollment	2,331
% male/female	52/48
% from out of state	83
% frosh from public high school	44
% frosh live on campus	100
% ugrads live on campus	89
# of fraternities (% ugrad men join)	7 (20)
# of sororities (% ugrad women join)	3 (16)
% African American	6
% Asian	5
% Caucasian	65
% Hispanic	7
% Native American	<1
% international	8
# of countries represented	57

SURVEY SAYS . . .

Political activism is popular
Great financial aid
Great off-campus food
Lots of beer drinking
Hard liquor is popular
Everyone loves the Bantams
Alumni active on campus

ACADEMICS

Academic Rating	94
% students returning for sophomore year	91
% students graduating within 4 years	81
% students graduating within 6 years	86
Calendar	Semester
Student/faculty ratio	9:1
Profs interesting rating	82
Profs accessible rating	77

Most classes have 10–19 students.
Most lab/discussion sessions have
10–19 students.

MOST POPULAR MAJORS

economics; political science; English
language and literature

STUDENTS SAY ". . ."

Academics

"[It's all] about getting a top-notch education in small classes with professors who know you and being able to also have a good time outside of class" at Trinity College, a small and prestigious liberal arts school located in Connecticut's state capital. A "great political science department" exploits TC's location "about two blocks away from the state capitol, which is great for internships." Other social sciences, including economics and history, earn students' praises, as do offerings in engineering and education. Strength across the liberal arts bolsters the school's Guided Studies Program, in which students undertake a fixed curriculum of interdisciplinary study to survey the entirety of Western civilization from the classical age to the present. In all disciplines, "small classes, very involved professors, and a very conscious student body" combine to provide "an excellent liberal arts education that will provide [students] with the skills to be thoughtful, independent adults." Professors "are always available to talk and offer help to students. They often invite students out to lunch." Likewise, administrators are easy to access. "Even the president of the school, James F. Jones, is accessible. He goes on the Quest Orientation hiking trip for first-year students and regularly attends various student events on campus." Students also appreciate that "the career services office is amazing" here.

Life

"The fraternity scene is the draw for the majority of campus" at Trinity College, where "on a typical weekend night, people go out to dinner, go back to their room and nap, get ready for the evening, and go meet up with a friend or two where they chill out and then go to someone's room for pregaming…Then when it's about 1:00 A.M. they go out and do some frat hopping. It's great for people who like their life to be predictable." The frats are hardly the only option, though; in fact, "there are a ton of underappreciated options on or near campus. Hartford has amazing restaurants, there are movie theaters and bowling alleys nearby, the Cinestudio is a ninety-second walk from the main dining hall, and there are two dorms on campus devoted specifically to alcohol-free activities. Plus, plenty of student groups hold events" in such places as "the arts and cultural houses." Trinity's theater and dance department offer regular performances. Hometown Hartford "may be [an economically] depressed city, but it is still a city, and it affords benefits that tiny college towns just can't match."

Student Body

The stereotype about Trinity undergrads is that "most…are from the tristate area and appear to have just stepped off a yacht or out of a country club," and students confirm that while "there are a lot of students who are not" in this crowd, the preppy contingent is "the main group" and "socially dominant" here. "There are definitely some very preppy girls and boys—blond hair, sunglasses, Chanel flats, a polo," one student concedes before adding that "sometimes people identify these students as typical Trinity students; however there are many students who are not like that at all." All students tend to be "well-rounded" and "very passionate," "intelligent but also social," with "good verbal skills." They "care deeply about their work and really like to have fun when they can," and while many gravitate to the Greek community for their fun, "there are [also] communities here for those who do not enjoy the frat scene, for people who are passionate about music and acting, and [for] those who want to spend their weekends giving back to the community."

FINANCIAL AID: 860-297-2047 • E-MAIL: ADMISSIONS.OFFICE@TRINCOLL.EDU • WEBSITE: WWW.TRINCOLL.EDU

THE PRINCETON REVIEW SAYS

Admissions

Very important factors considered include: Rigor of secondary school record. *Important factors considered include:* Class rank, GPA, standardized test scores, application essay, extracurricular activities, interview, racial/ethnic status, recommendation(s), talent/ability, character/personal qualities. *Other factors considered include:* First generation, geographical residence, volunteer work, work experience, alumni/ae relations, level of applicant's interest. SAT or ACT required; ACT with Writing component recommended. *Academic units required:* 4 English; 3 mathematics; 2 science; (2 science lab); 3 foreign language; 2 history.

Financial Aid

Students should submit: FAFSA, CSS/Financial Aid PROFILE, Noncustodial PROFILE, Business/Farm Supplement. Regular filing deadline is 3/1. The Princeton Review suggests that all financial aid forms be submitted as soon as possible after January 1. *Need-based scholarships/grants offered:* Federal Pell, SEOG, State scholarships/grants, private scholarships, the school's own gift aid. *Loan aid offered:* Direct Subsidized Stafford Loans, Direct Unsubsidized Stafford Loans, Direct PLUS loans, Federal Perkins Loans, College/university loans from institutional funds. Applicants will be notified of awards beginning 4/1. Federal Work-Study Program available. Institutional employment available. Off-campus job opportunities are good.

The Inside Word

Students describe Trinity as "the home of Yale rejects," an appraisal that accurately, if somewhat hyperbolically, characterizes the school's reputation as an Ivy safety. The hefty tuition and fees here ensure that a large percentage of the student body is made up of wealthy, preppy types, but the school does offer generous financial aid packages to top candidates who can't afford the considerable price of attending. The school would love to broaden its demographic, so competitive minority students should receive a very welcome reception here.

THE SCHOOL SAYS "..."

From the Admissions Office

"An array of distinctive curricular options—including an interdisciplinary neuroscience major and a professionally accredited engineering degree program, a unique Human Rights Program, a Health Fellows Program, and interdisciplinary programs such as the Cities Program, Interdisciplinary Science Program, and InterArts—is one reason record numbers of students are applying to Trinity. In fact, applications are up 80 percent over the past five years. In addition, the college has been recognized for its commitment to diversity; students of color have represented approximately 20 percent of the freshman class for the past four years, setting Trinity apart from many of its peers. Trinity's capital city location offers students unparalleled 'real-world' learning experiences to complement classroom learning. Students take advantage of extensive opportunities for internships for academic credit and community service, and these opportunities extend to Trinity's global learning sites in cities around the world. Trinity's faculty is a devoted and accomplished group of exceptional teacher-scholars; our 100-acre campus is beautiful; Hartford is an educational asset that differentiates Trinity from other liberal arts colleges; our global connections and foreign study opportunities prepare students to be good citizens of the world; and our graduates go on to excel in virtually every field. We invite you to learn more about why Trinity might be the best choice for you.

"Students applying for admission may submit the following testing options: SAT or ACT with writing."

SELECTIVITY

Admissions Rating	95
# of applicants	7,652
% of applicants accepted	32
% of acceptees attending	25
# offered a place on the wait list	2,032
% accepting a place on wait list	34
% admitted from wait list	6
# of early decision applicants	497
% accepted early decision	63

FRESHMAN PROFILE

Range SAT Critical Reading	570–660
Range SAT Math	580–670
Range SAT Writing	590–670
Range ACT Composite	25–29
% graduated top 10% of class	23
% graduated top 25% of class	59
% graduated top 50% of class	99

DEADLINES

Early decision	
Deadline	11/15
Notification	12/15
Regular	
Deadline	1/1
Notification	4/1
Nonfall registration?	No

APPLICANTS ALSO LOOK AT AND SOMETIMES PREFER

Middlebury College; Wesleyan University; Boston College

AND RARELY PREFER

Boston University

FINANCIAL FACTS

Financial Aid Rating	99
Annual tuition	$46,796
Room and board	$12,700
Required fees	$2,260
Books and supplies	$1,000
% needy frosh rec. need-based scholarship or grant aid	96
% needy UG rec. need-based scholarship or grant aid	95
% needy frosh rec. non-need-based scholarship or grant aid	6
% needy UG rec. non-need-based scholarship or grant aid	2
% needy frosh rec. need-based self-help aid	70
% needy UG rec. need-based self-help aid	76
% frosh rec. any financial aid	42
% UG rec. any financial aid	42
% UG borrow to pay for school	45
Average cumulative indebtedness	$24,148
% frosh need fully met	100
% ugrads need fully met	100
Average % of frosh need met	100
Average % of ugrad need met	100

TRINITY COLLEGE DUBLIN

WEST THEATRE, DUBLIN, DUBLIN 2, IRELAND • INTERNATIONAL ADMISSIONS: +353-1-896-3150/2011/2872

STUDENTS SAY ". . ."

Academics

Perhaps Ireland's most famous university, Trinity College Dublin is an idyllic, world famous institution that has carried on a 400-year-old tradition of scholarship on the Emerald Isle. This "beautiful and prestigious university" boasts a lot on offer, both academically and socially, and the degree graduates receive is highly respected internationally. "Personal development is available for those who pursue it," says a student. "You grow up to be an adult here, one that has diverse life experience and a broad exposure to classical and modern study."

Professors in general are "pleasant and fluid," "bring their passion and enthusiasm for their subject to every lecture." "A professor of mine has cried during a lecture when explaining why Kant's attempt at revising metaphysics was so important," says a sophomore. The school "really holds you to a higher standard" so self-motivation is key, and "the teachers don't baby [students]. You are expected to be responsible for your own study." "Your job is to be a university student and to do it well," says another student. However, if help is needed then teachers are "extremely good at helping you outside class hours. Just email them and they will arrange a time to meet."

The scene here is "more like a master's program in the states, but with [student] societies that are given millions of euros to make sure you have fun and opportunities." There is always room for discussion in lectures, and "classes tend to be really interactive so students aren't just sitting there passively learning." Many do feel that there could "be a slicker process administratively," particularly with regard to registration and exams. The libraries "own an incredibly broad selection of works between them," and is "absolutely incredible both in selection of books, and space to study." On top of the very active clubs and societies, a great strength is the "small tutorials that correspond with lectures," as well the "great speakers giving talks on a weekly basis."

Life

It's "a self-contained university world, bang-smack in Dublin's city centre," acting as "an island all to itself." The legendary front entrance "looks damn good" to all ye who enter here, and passing through the gothic arches "[is] like [entering] a calm academic hub within a busy city." In fact, those who live on campus "practically have their own world if they so desire, as it is so self-contained."

In general, people are "fairly studious and interested in their course, [but] they make room in their schedule for partying though as well." Students have great choice for meeting people and fitting in with a large number of societies, which "are inclusive and social, [and] all are catered for in the vast smorgasbord of college life." The annual Trinity ball is "an amazing event, Europe's largest private party." Alcohol plays a big part in college life (there is even a college bar, the Pav, "overlooking the cricket pitch"), and "outside of society events it is by far the most common social activity." However, by the time exams roll around in May, everyone is "all about cramming into the library and getting to work."

Student Body

This "self-motivated, tightly knit intellectual community of a huge variety of students" is composed of "bright inquisitive minds" who tend to be "trendy and intelligent and well-travelled and somewhat well-off." The vast majority come from Ireland, and since "there's literally a niche or society for everyone to fit in, all varieties of personality interact agreeably." "There are a lot sociable societies which are easy to join and they generally welcome you with open arms," says a biochemistry major. Ireland is a small country, so "often students know each other from school before coming to Trinity."

FINANCIAL AID: • E-MAIL: ADMISSIONS@TCD.IE • WEBSITE: WWW.TCD.IE / INTERNATIONAL@TCD.IE

THE PRINCETON REVIEW SAYS

Admissions

Very important factors considered include: GPA, rigor of secondary school record, standardized test scores. *Important factors considered include:* Application essay, recommendation(s). *Other factors considered include:* Extracurricular activities, volunteer work, work experience, character / personal qualities, level of applicant's interest, TOEFL required of all international applicants. SAT/ACT is required.

Financial Aid

Students should submit: The Princeton Review suggests that all financial aid forms be submitted as soon as possible after January 1.

The Inside Word

The cost of attendance at Trinity is still less for most Irish students than the cost of a private university in the United States, so the school tends to draw Ireland's best students; only around 4 percent of students come from North or Central America, and only around 11 percent from the EU. Non-EU students from the United States must have completed all of the necessary high school curriculum (with a GPA of at least 3.3) and have minimum SAT score of 1300 on any two of the Critical Reading, Math and Writing sections (and no score less than 500); or, an ACT composite score of 29.

SELECTIVITY	
Admissions Rating	61
# of applicants	18,995
% of applicants accepted	16
% of acceptees attending	93
# offered a place on the wait list	388
% accepting a place on wait list	52
% admitted from wait list	100

DEADLINES	
Regular	
Deadline	2/1
Notification	Rolling
Nonfall registration?	No

FINANCIAL FACTS	
Financial Aid Rating	65

TRINITY UNIVERSITY (TX)

ONE TRINITY PLACE, SAN ANTONIO, TX 78212-7200 • ADMISSIONS: 210-999-7207 • FAX: 210-999-8164

CAMPUS LIFE

Quality of Life Rating	92
Fire Safety Rating	86
Green Rating	70
Type of school	Private
Affiliation	Presbyterian
Environment	Metropolis

STUDENTS

Total undergrad enrollment	2,211
% male/female	47/53
% from out of state	26
% frosh from public high school	65
% frosh live on campus	100
% ugrads live on campus	74
# of fraternities	7
# of sororities	6
% African American	4
% Asian	7
% Caucasian	58
% Hispanic	17
% Native American	<1
% international	7
# of countries represented	69

SURVEY SAYS . . .
Classroom facilities are great
Students are friendly
Great off-campus food
Dorms are like palaces

ACADEMICS

Academic Rating	88
% students returning for sophomore year	88
% students graduating within 4 years	70
% students graduating within 6 years	82
Calendar	Semester
Student/faculty ratio	9:1
Profs interesting rating	88
Profs accessible rating	92

Most classes have 10–19 students.
Most lab/discussion sessions have 10–19 students.

MOST POPULAR MAJORS
business administration; English language
and literature; foreign languages
and literature

STUDENTS SAY " . . ."

Academics

"Trinity University is a place where one can be focused and diligent with studies—while also being in a great place to have fun on the side." In other words, this school is ideal for those seeking a well-rounded college experience and an "outstanding liberal arts education." Pre-med, accounting, and education are all popular majors, and the school offers "excellent science departments," and "the arts are amazing." Students praise the small class sizes and say they have access to "Ivy League smarts without the attitude." "The lectures are interesting, and class activities are unique and engaging." "The professors here, on the whole, are brilliant and helpful and are willing to work with you." "Professors are *always* accessible (some even give out home/cell phone numbers). They generally seem to enjoy students who stop by [during] office hours for help [or] just to chat." Slackers beware: While "the professors are usually very dedicated and excited to teach their subjects…that also means they expect each of their classes to be the most important class at Trinity." "Trinity professors assign a ridiculous amount of course work, but most will go to any length to help the students understand and complete the assignments." There are some complaints about the challenges of the current registration process, but overall, Trinity students are very happy with their classes, their extracurriculars, and their "gorgeous" campus.

Life

"Just about everybody at Trinity is involved in extracurricular activities," making the campus "fairly lively on its own, and it's easy to almost never leave it," though hometown San Antonio "is a great location: lots to do, lots to see, and it's right in the middle of everything exciting. Austin is only an hour away, and Padre Island is only a two-hour drive." Students have free admission to local art museums, too. But back to campus (students are required to live there for three years, after all): "There are plenty of clubs and organizations to get involved with, and Greek life at Trinity is great." Greek life and athletics are popular activities, but Trinity offers "something for everyone." Students tell us they're "always blown away by the stage productions on campus," and they enjoy working at the radio station, "which is an enormously respected jazz station by day and [broadcasts] quirky college indie radio by night." A typical week includes "a lecture one night, a cultural taste test the night after, and a concert over the weekend. There is always something to do." "There is always a party going on" at Trinity, "but they hardly dominate the social landscape." Plenty of students "watch movies or bake" for fun, and "it's not unusual to spend an afternoon with friends talking about a lecture from earlier in the day."

Student Body

"The typical student is pretty easygoing but hardworking. They want to embrace the college experience while still getting an education." Pretty much what you would expect at a university that offers such a well-balanced experience. Most students come from an "upper-middle-class upbringing…and likely came to Trinity to be a 'big fish in a small pond.'" Students do say "the school can be a bit cliquey at times," and "because [it] is so small, there is certainly a high school–like feel," but "there are many organizations and groups that anyone can join," and most students make friends easily in the dorms or via extracurricular activities. "The student body is very active in different organizations and athletics," and students note that "people who are happy at Trinity generally don't take advantage of all the different activities it has to offer." Lastly, "even though it's in Texas, it's a fairly liberal and tolerant school."

TRINITY UNIVERSITY (TX)

FINANCIAL AID: 210-999-8315 • E-MAIL: ADMISSIONS@TRINITY.EDU • WEBSITE: WWW.TRINITY.EDU

THE PRINCETON REVIEW SAYS

Admissions

Very important factors considered include: Class rank, GPA, rigor of secondary school record. *Important factors considered include:* Standardized test scores, application essay, extracurricular activities, interview, recommendation(s), talent/ability, character/personal qualities. *Other factors considered include:* First generation, geographical residence, racial/ethnic status, volunteer work, work experience, alumni/ae relations, level of applicant's interest. SAT or ACT required; ACT with or without Writing component accepted. TOEFL required of all international applicants. *Academic units required:* 4 English; 3 mathematics; 3 science; (2 science lab); 3 social studies; 2 foreign language. *Academic units recommended:* 4 English; 3 mathematics; 3 science; (3 science lab); 3 social studies; 3 foreign language; 3 academic electives.

Financial Aid

Students should submit: FAFSA. Regular filing deadline is 4/1. The Princeton Review suggests that all financial aid forms be submitted as soon as possible after January 1. *Need-based scholarships/grants offered:* Federal Pell, SEOG, State scholarships/grants, private scholarships, the school's own gift aid. *Loan aid offered:* Direct Subsidized Stafford Loans, Direct Unsubsidized Stafford Loans, Direct PLUS loans, Federal Perkins Loans, State Loans, College/university loans from institutional funds. Applicants will be notified of awards beginning 4/1. Federal Work-Study Program available. Institutional employment available. Off-campus job opportunities are good.

The Inside Word

As Trinity embraces a small, close-knit community of students, admissions officers are looking for the complete package: bright, capable, motivated students who are ready to take advantage of all the school has to offer. While academic performance is the factor considered most heavily on each application, recommendations, extracurricular activities, and standardized test scores should all be very strong as well.

THE SCHOOL SAYS "..."

From the Admissions Office

"Three qualities separate Trinity University from other selective, academically challenging institutions around the country. First, Trinity is unusual in the quality and quantity of resources devoted almost exclusively to its undergraduate students. Those resources give rise to a second distinctive aspect of Trinity—its emphasis on undergraduate research. Our students prefer being involved over observing. With superior laboratory facilities and strong, dedicated faculty, our undergraduates fill many of the roles formerly reserved for graduate students, and our professors often go to their undergraduates for help with their research. Other hands-on learning experiences including internships, study abroad, and service projects are also available to students. Finally, Trinity stands apart for the attitude of its students. In an atmosphere of academic camaraderie and fellowship, our students work together to stretch their minds and broaden their horizons across academic disciplines. For quality of resources, for dedication to undergraduate research, and for the disposition of its student body, Trinity University holds a unique position in American higher education.

"Students applying for admission must submit either the SAT or the ACT. The highest composite test scores from one or multiple dates are evaluated. The SAT writing section and ACT writing component are not required."

SELECTIVITY

Admissions Rating	90
# of applicants	4,505
% of applicants accepted	64
% of acceptees attending	19
# offered a place on the wait list	177
% accepting a place on wait list	51
% admitted from wait list	55
# of early decision applicants	68
% accepted early decision	57

FRESHMAN PROFILE

Range SAT Critical Reading	560–690
Range SAT Math	590–680
Range SAT Writing	550–660
Range ACT Composite	26–31
Minimum paper TOEFL	600
Minimum web-based TOEFL	250
Average HS GPA	3.50
% graduated top 10% of class	47
% graduated top 25% of class	73
% graduated top 50% of class	93

DEADLINES

Early decision	
Deadline	11/1
Notification	12/15
Early action	
Deadline	11/1
Notification	12/15
Regular	
Deadline	2/1
Notification	4/1
Nonfall registration?	No

APPLICANTS ALSO LOOK AT AND OFTEN PREFER
Rice University

AND SOMETIMES PREFER
Texas Christian University; Texas A&M University—College Station

FINANCIAL FACTS

Financial Aid Rating	91
Annual tuition	$34,152
Room and board	$10,968
Required fees	$1,110
Books and supplies	$1,000
% needy frosh rec. need-based scholarship or grant aid	100
% needy UG rec. need-based scholarship or grant aid	99
% needy frosh rec. non-need-based scholarship or grant aid	18
% needy UG rec. non-need-based scholarship or grant aid	12
% needy frosh rec. need-based self-help aid	70
% needy UG rec. need-based self-help aid	74
% frosh rec. any financial aid	94
% UG rec. any financial aid	86
% UG borrow to pay for school	44
Average cumulative indebtedness	$38,540
% frosh need fully met	52
% ugrads need fully met	46
Average % of frosh need met	93
Average % of ugrad need met	91

TRUMAN STATE UNIVERSITY

100 EAST NORMAL AVENUE, KIRKSVILLE, MO 63501 • ADMISSIONS: 660-785-4114 • FAX: 660-785-7456

CAMPUS LIFE

Quality of Life Rating	82
Fire Safety Rating	89
Green Rating	63
Type of school	Public
Affiliation	No Affiliation
Environment	Village

STUDENTS

Total undergrad enrollment	5,898
% male/female	40/60
% from out of state	17
% frosh from public high school	83
% frosh live on campus	98
% ugrads live on campus	42
# of fraternities (% ugrad men join)	12 (21)
# of sororities (% ugrad women join)	11 (18)
% African American	3
% Asian	2
% Caucasian	82
% Hispanic	3
% Native American	<1
% international	6
# of countries represented	50

SURVEY SAYS . . .

Students are happy
Lab facilities are great
Great financial aid
Students are friendly
Campus feels safe
Easy to get around campus

ACADEMICS

Academic Rating	81
% students returning for sophomore year	87
% students graduating within 4 years	54
% students graduating within 6 years	72
Calendar	Semester
Student/faculty ratio	17:1
Profs interesting rating	84
Profs accessible rating	89

Most classes have 20-29 students.
Most lab/discussion sessions have fewer than 10 students.

MOST POPULAR MAJORS
biology; business administration; psychology

STUDENTS SAY " . . ."

Academics

If you are looking for "value," check out Truman State University. "Few schools can provide a similar undergraduate experience at a comparable price." Most current students were hard-pressed to find a better deal than they got at this "highly regarded," "very affordable" school located in Kirksville, Missouri. A high percentage of students receive financial aid and/or scholarships making Truman "far more affordable than other institutions." One out-of-state student who experienced this firsthand says, "It was far cheaper for me to go to Truman than to any of the schools in my own state or to any private school to which I applied. Between Truman scholarships and private scholarships, I'm basically being paid to go here. My friends from high school are already panicking about how they're going to pay off their loans, and knowing I'm graduating debt-free is the best feeling in the world." Students do not appear to be sacrificing quality for a cheaper education. They say professors "really push you to work hard." They are all "very qualified," and students say, "Grades actually reflect the student's qualifications." Small class sizes enable "fantastic one-on-one experience between professors and students." "The faculty care way more about teaching than about their own research or interests." Classes are "small and engaging," and "Nearly all [professors] are available beyond their scheduled office hours and do their best to make sure we understand material." Students did also mention that there seems to be a lack of funding recently and that "some majors seem short-staffed." "Truman could improve by offering more classes and hiring more professors in order to decrease the congestion in classrooms for the more popular courses." One student sums up why this school was a good choice: "I wanted a college where I could be academically challenged as well as actively involved in [extracurricular] activities. I wanted to be surrounded by intellectually stimulating peers and professors in order to gain a comprehensive liberal arts education. I found all of this at Truman and saved a significant amount of money in the process." Another student is concerned that "Truman is a small school and is not easily recognized on a national scale. In the post-graduation job search, this fact could become very frustrating."

Life

"College life is hectic and amazing all at the same time." "Truman is an academically challenging school, so separating your school time and social life is an important task that we need to learn." The school's "very pretty" campus might be "in the middle of nowhere," but Truman brings "tons of really great activities, shows, bands, etc., to campus to keep us entertained." "Kirksville is not a big town," and homework consumes much of a student's day. Still, "there is always time to have a social life though. Hanging out with friends and just watching a movie or going out to [see] a comedian or performance on campus are viable options on any given weekend. A social life is just something that you have to plan for rather than something that is just given to you." "On the weekends, students usually go out to parties. The students who do not party will go to events on campus or hang out with friends in the dorms." Students are pleased with facilities, including "newly renovated" dorms, and the "library is excellent." "Also, the atmosphere on campus is very safe and welcoming." However, administrative services sometimes make life difficult. "A lot of the offices (financial aid, study abroad, registrar, etc.) are extremely disorganized."

Student Body

Students coined the "term T.T.S. (Typical Truman Student)…to describe academically focused, very studious students." This is reflected in classrooms where "teachers barely ever take attendance because people go to class." That term seems to fit most, but definitely not everyone on campus. Students point out, "People definitely party, somewhat during the week, and a lot on the weekends, especially if they're involved in a sorority/fraternity." Truman is not an overly diverse campus, but classmates are "accepting of others." A student says, "It is not hard to fit in at this school. Every single person I have met brings something unique to this institution."

FINANCIAL AID: 660-785-4130 • E-MAIL: ADMISSIONS@TRUMAN.EDU • WEBSITE: WWW.TRUMAN.EDU

THE PRINCETON REVIEW SAYS

Admissions

Very important factors considered include: Class rank, GPA, rigor of secondary school record, standardized test scores. *Important factors considered include:* Application essay. *Other factors considered include:* Extracurricular activities, first generation, geographical residence, racial/ethnic status, recommendation(s), state residency, talent/ability, volunteer work, work experience, alumni/ac relations, character/personal qualities, level of applicant's interest. SAT or ACT required; ACT with or without Writing component accepted. English proficiency exam required of all international applicants. *Academic units required:* 4 English; 3 mathematics; 3 science; (2 science lab); 2 social studies; 2 foreign language; 1 history; 5 academic electives; 1 visual/performing arts. *Academic units recommended:* 4 English; 4 mathematics; 3 science; (2 science lab); 2 social studies; 2 foreign language; 1 history; 5 academic electives; 1 visual/performing arts.

Financial Aid

Students should submit: FAFSA, Institution's own financial aid form. The Princeton Review suggests that all financial aid forms be submitted as soon as possible after January 1. *Need-based scholarships/grants offered:* Federal Pell, SEOG, State scholarships/grants, private scholarships, the school's own gift aid. *Loan aid offered:* Direct Subsidized Stafford Loans, Direct Unsubsidized Stafford Loans, Direct PLUS loans, Federal Perkins Loans, Federal Nursing Loans, College/university loans from institutional funds. Federal Work-Study Program available. Institutional employment available. Off-campus job opportunities are good.

The Inside Word

Those interested in studying at Truman had better get to work; the school places a large emphasis on GPA, class rank, and academic rigor. The selectivity and quality of education numbers are high, but annual tuition is low for all students. Although early application has no bearing on admission, greatest scholarship consideration is given to those who apply before December 1st.

THE SCHOOL SAYS "..."

From the Admissions Office

"Truman's talented student body enjoys small classes where undergraduate research and personal interaction with professors are the norm. Our outstanding internship and study abroad opportunities allow students to attend top graduate schools and have great job prospects.

"Truman is recognized consistently as one of the nation's 'Best Values' in higher education. The university offers a variety of competitive scholarships, and there is no separate scholarship application. Students wishing to be considered for all scholarship programs are strongly encouraged to apply for admission by December 1st.

"Students applying to Truman State University can submit scores from both the ACT and the SAT. The best composite score from either test will be considered in admission and scholarship selection. The writing section is not required. Admission requirements are selective and there is no application fee.

"At Truman, we believe a quality college experience does not stop at the classroom door. It should permeate the entire campus, offering opportunities that entertain, pique students' interest, and invite them to fully embrace this extraordinary journey. It is about making great friends, getting involved in one of over 200 student organizations, exploring the amazing world that surrounds them and creating memories that will last a lifetime. This is a university that transforms lives. Truman's success as one of the nation's premier public liberal arts and sciences institutions can be traced to one guiding principle: an unwavering devotion to the pursuit of knowledge, wherever your journey leads you."

SELECTIVITY

Admissions Rating	90
# of applicants	4,462
% of applicants accepted	72
% of acceptees attending	41

FRESHMAN PROFILE

Range SAT Critical Reading	540–680
Range SAT Math	540–680
Range ACT Composite	25–30
Minimum paper TOEFL	550
Minimum web-based TOEFL	213
Average HS GPA	3.77
% graduated top 10% of class	47
% graduated top 25% of class	80
% graduated top 50% of class	98

DEADLINES

Regular	
Priority	12/1
Nonfall registration?	Yes

APPLICANTS ALSO LOOK AT AND OFTEN PREFER

University of Missouri; Saint Louis University; Missouri State University

AND SOMETIMES PREFER

Washington University in St. Louis

AND RARELY PREFER

Illinois State University; Illinois Wesleyan University; University of Iowa

FINANCIAL FACTS

Financial Aid Rating	89
Annual in-state tuition	$7,096
Annual out-of-state tuition	$12,968
Room and board	$7,720
Required fees	$272
Books and supplies	$1,000
% needy frosh rec. need-based scholarship or grant aid	100
% needy UG rec. need-based scholarship or grant aid	93
% needy frosh rec. non-need-based scholarship or grant aid	97
% needy UG rec. non-need-based scholarship or grant aid	78
% needy frosh rec. need-based self-help aid	74
% needy UG rec. need-based self-help aid	82
% frosh rec. any financial aid	99
% UG rec. any financial aid	88
% UG borrow to pay for school	55
Average cumulative indebtedness	$23,761
% frosh need fully met	37
% ugrads need fully met	33
Average % of frosh need met	86
Average % of ugrad need met	80

ꓔUFTS UNIVERSITY

ꓓETSON HALL, MEDFORD, MA 02155 • ADMISSIONS: 617-627-3170 • FAX: 617-627-3860

CAMPUS LIFE

Quality of Life Rating	96
Fire Safety Rating	87
Green Rating	94
Type of school	Private
Affiliation	No Affiliation
Environment	Town

STUDENTS

Total undergrad enrollment	5,146
% male/female	49/51
% from out of state	77
% frosh from public high school	56
% frosh live on campus	100
% ugrads live on campus	63
# of fraternities(% ugrad men join)	10 (14)
# of sororities(% ugrad women join)	3 (19)
% African American	4
% Asian	11
% Caucasian	56
% Hispanic	6
% international	8
# of countries represented	71

SURVEY SAYS . . .

Students are happy
No one cheats
Students are friendly
Students environmentally aware
Students love Medford, MA
Great food on campus
Great off-campus food
Lots of beer drinking
Hard liquor is popular
Student publications are popular

ACADEMICS

Academic Rating	94
% students returning for sophomore year	96
% students graduating within 4 years	87
% students graduating within 6 years	92
Calendar	Semester
Student/faculty ratio	9:1
Profs interesting rating	88
Profs accessible rating	83

Most classes have 10–19 students.
Most lab/discussion sessions have
10–19 students.

MOST POPULAR MAJORS
economics; international relations; biology

STUDENTS SAY ". . ."

Academics

The campus culture at Tufts University in Massachusetts is "thriving and alive," and as such it really encourages students to merge their academic and social interests and "pursue both in a passionate way." This is a place where, through active discussion and a student body with a zest for life, "passion meets reality." The academic experience here is marked by "small classes with knowledgeable and interesting professors." "I have had the opportunity to explore a huge amount of academic subjects and really challenge myself," says a student. If students actively seek out their "highly accessible and prompt" professors, they will be rewarded with "a better learning experience and with incomparable relationships with brilliant (yet down to earth) professors." "Whenever I ask them a question that they might not know the answer to, they do research on it immediately and return quickly with a detailed response." The academic curriculum is a "perfect mix of liberal arts and university," and the professors are actively concerned with making sure that students leave with a true understanding of the course material, "not just a book list under their arms." These "global minded, ambitious" students rise to the challenge and beyond, as "most every student focuses on life beyond their education" and seeks out a well-rounded life. "It is far easier to succeed here than to fail, as long as you are committed to getting as strong an education as possible," advises a student. "I've literally been offered a research position by asking questions multiple times," says another. The international relations program at this globally-aware school is particularly strong (as are study abroad options), but activism spills over into the entirety of the student body. "Change is easily made here," and "if you have a problem with something, you can easily address it." A lot of effort is put into ensuring that every student transitions well into college and success. A strong alumni network and excellent internship opportunities also "open up a world of opportunities after graduation."

Life

Though the campus itself is gorgeous, "the true beauty of the school is in the unique and quirky nature of its student body." Generally, there are "always a lot of events going on around campus that attract students every weekend" and the variety of clubs and activities available is "amazing." "Almost everything here is run by clubs and student organizations," and the Tufts Dance Collective and Quidditch clubs are some of the most popular and fun options, as is a capella. The "T makes everything accessible," and on the weekends, students often go into Boston or Davis Square and spend the day shopping and "eating non-dining hall food," and at night "there are usually good parties to go to." "There is more to do in this city than anyone can possibly do in four years," says a student.

People here are "always thinking about politics" and all have a lot of spirit for Tufts and "it's really nice to walk around campus knowing that you're in a place where almost everyone is excited to be there." "This is a great place to share knowledge you have, because everyone wants to hear it and share their own experiences and thoughts," says a student.

Student Body

This is a group of go-getters, so here "everyone has the same passion for excellence" and "is engaged in so many activities on campus." Tufts is "a quirky (yet normal) compilation of a bunch of young adults with not only big dreams for the world, but with dedication and motivation to complete them." "It's like a competition to be the "most interesting man/woman in the world," says a senior. Even better, "being nerdy is cool!" "We here embrace weirdness. If talking to new people in daily life is awkward, we know it and we revel in it," says a sophomore. There is "no discrimination whatsoever," though "it can actually get frustrating how politically correct everyone is." From "dancing and singing to teaching and tutoring to international community service," students here are "stunningly busy, and happy to be so."

FINANCIAL AID: 617-627-2000 • E-MAIL: ADMISSIONS.INQUIRY@ASE.TUFTS.EDU • WEBSITE: WWW.TUFTS.EDU

THE PRINCETON REVIEW SAYS

Admissions

Very important factors considered include: Class rank, GPA, rigor of secondary school record, standardized test scores, application essay, recommendation(s), character/personal qualities. *Important factors considered include:* Extracurricular activities, talent/ability, volunteer work, work experience. *Other factors considered include:* First generation, geographical residence, interview, racial/ethnic status, alumni/ae relations. SAT and SAT Subject Tests or ACT required; ACT with Writing component required. TOEFL required of all international applicants. *Academic units recommended:* 4 English; 4 mathematics; 4 science; 4 social studies; 4 foreign language.

Financial Aid

Students should submit: FAFSA, CSS/Financial Aid PROFILE, Noncustodial PROFILE. Regular filing deadline is 2/15. The Princeton Review suggests that all financial aid forms be submitted as soon as possible after January 1. *Need-based scholarships/grants offered:* Federal Pell, SEOG, State scholarships/grants, private scholarships, the school's own gift aid. *Loan aid offered:* Direct Subsidized Stafford Loans, Direct Unsubsidized Stafford Loans, Direct PLUS loans, Federal Perkins Loans, College/university loans from institutional funds. Applicants will be notified of awards beginning 4/1. Federal Work-Study Program available. Institutional employment available. Off-campus job opportunities are good.

The Inside Word

The admissions process is rigorous. Tufts rejects more than 75 percent of its applicants. You'll need to demonstrate fairly exceptional academic accomplishments and submit a thorough and well-prepared application to get admitted. On the bright side, Tufts is still a little bit of a safety school for aspiring Ivy Leaguers. Since many applicants will also get into an Ivy League school and will likely pass on Tufts, it has spots for "mere mortals" at the end of the day.

THE SCHOOL SAYS "..."

From the Admissions Office

"The world we live in is not easily segmented by academic disciplines. Problems in the world will not fit into neatly labeled categories and solutions will not come from a single point of view. Global challenges like the European debt crisis or climate change are intertwined across economic, political, technological, linguistic, and cultural lines. Tufts' educational philosophy recognizes this and adapts to it with requirements that push students towards interdisciplinary thought. Students are asked to understand world culture and languages, and to see the importance of context beyond any singular discipline. Tufts believes in using intellect to impact the world and in understanding how the world impacts our intellectual pursuits. It is not uncommon to find a computer scientist partnering with faculty in mechanical engineering and drama to program robots that can tell a good story or a religion major studying to become a doctor who understands of how faith, ethics, and health are linked. Tufts' cross-disciplinary strength is possible because of its intimate size contrasted against a world-class research focus. Tufts' mission to impact the world benefits from Boston, the premier higher education destination in the United States as well as the constellation of schools that defines the university: the School of Arts & Sciences, the School of Engineering, the Fletcher School of Law and Diplomacy, the Graduate School of Arts & Sciences, the Cummings School of Veterinary Medicine, the Friedman School of Nutrition Science and Policy, the Sackler School of Graduate Biomedical Sciences, and the School of Medicine."

SELECTIVITY

Admissions Rating	98
# of applicants	18,419
% of applicants accepted	19
% of acceptees attending	38

FRESHMAN PROFILE

Range SAT Critical Reading	680–750
Range SAT Math	690–770
Range SAT Writing	680–770
Range ACT Composite	30–33
Minimum paper TOEFL	600
Minimum web-based TOEFL	100
% graduated top 10% of class	91
% graduated top 25% of class	99
% graduated top 50% of class	100

DEADLINES

Early decision	
Deadline	11/1
Notification	12/15
Regular	
Deadline	1/1
Notification	4/1
Nonfall registration?	No

FINANCIAL FACTS

Financial Aid Rating	95
Annual tuition	$45,590
Room and board	$12,182
Required fees	$1,008
Books and supplies	$800
% needy frosh rec. need-based scholarship or grant aid	93
% needy UG rec. need-based scholarship or grant aid	93
% needy frosh rec. non-need-based scholarship or grant aid	7
% needy UG rec. non-need-based scholarship or grant aid	4
% needy frosh rec. need-based self-help aid	88
% needy UG rec. need-based self-help aid	92
% frosh rec. any financial aid	41
% UG rec. any financial aid	40
% UG borrow to pay for school	41
Average cumulative indebtedness	$24,266
% frosh need fully met	100
% ugrads need fully met	100
Average % of frosh need met	100
Average % of ugrad need met	100

TULANE UNIVERSITY

6823 St. Charles Avenue, New Orleans, LA 70118 • Admissions: 504-865-5260 • Fax: 504-862-8715

STUDENTS SAY ". . ."

Academics

Since Hurricane Katrina in 2005, Tulane has risen with New Orleans as a phoenix from the ashes, and the way students value their academic experience's connection to the city continues unabated: "Tulane has made a commitment to the city of New Orleans that defines the ideal relationship between a city and a university." Students describe their learning environment as "vibrant and culturally diverse," and one which fosters "a culture of collaborative academic success." Many of Tulane's "profoundly knowledgable" faculty members "are not only incredible instructors, but are interesting and insightful people," and students say "our classes are small and engaging, encouraging us to develop personal relationships with professors." Looking toward the future, students say that professors have helped them "so many important connections" for jobs. Students maximize their location in New Orleans, "one of the greatest strengths of Tulane," too: "There are so many opportunities available outside the classroom—from student organizations, to community service projects, internships, events happening in New Orleans." Indeed, the Tulane and New Orleans experiences are inseparable, and this ethos motivates the fact that Tulane is "the only major research institution in the nation with a public service requirement for graduation." Students love Tulane's combination of "high level academics, and a wonderful culture to pair with it," and take seriously not just the task of "applying what you learn to better the community around us." In terms of value, many students choose Tulane because it "not only provides the largest academic scholarship, but also has the largest variety of experiences and opportunities available." While Tulane students are fun-loving, they can be just as serious: "Tulane is a work hard, play hard school, but the work part comes first."

Life

Embracing the school's slogan of "Only at Tulane, only in New Orleans," students are eager to take advantage of "one of the most culturally stimulating cities in the world" and "can't express how much I love" living "in a city that loves to celebrate—no reason required." New Orleans' unique energy pervades the campus, too: "There is a Mardi Gras tree in the middle of our Academic Quad. We are Tulane. We are New Orleans. We are smart. We are fun." Students are crazy about "the beautiful year-round weather," "the local festivals such as Jazz Fest and Po'boy Fest," and the city's "unbelievable food and tons of outdoor attractions." "There is always something to do in the city, whether it's going downtown to listen to live music, going to a festival or just staying around the Uptown New Orleans bar scene." On campus, "there's a club and society for nearly everything," and Greek life exists, but "even though Tulane is in the South, Greek life is nothing like typical SEC schools." While "fun at Tulane is UNLIMITED," and some students claim "life at Tulane revolves around drinking and having fun," lots of students also say that Tulane's is "the perfect balance between academic difficulty and fun."

Student Body

Tulane's student body comes from origins near and far: "Tulane is the most geographically diverse school in the country—something like 80 percent of our students come from over 300-plus miles away and the average distance traveled is like 800 miles." Its undergraduates are proud of this diversity, saying that "no matter your race, religion, gender, or background, you will have many like-minded friends that accept you," and calling Tulane's "a fascinating student body with an eclectic group of characters, from your native south Louisianans to Long Islanders to hipsters to future civic and community leaders committed to public service." On campus, they find plenty in common, and "we all love meeting people from new and interesting places." Apart from the partying, students extol their peers, saying "I've never been so surrounded by intelligent, focused people, which just isn't highly enough advertised." All of Tulane's undergrads have "a passion, whether it be academic or extra-curricular, and they actively pursue it."

FINANCIAL AID: 504-865-5723 • E-MAIL: UNDERGRAD.ADMISSION@TULANE.EDU • WEBSITE: WWW.TULANE.EDU

THE PRINCETON REVIEW SAYS

Admissions

Very important factors considered include: Class rank, GPA, rigor of secondary school record, standardized test scores. *Important factors considered include:* Application essay, recommendation(s), character/personal qualities. *Other factors considered include:* Extracurricular activities, first generation, interview, talent/ability, volunteer work, work experience, alumni/ae relations, level of applicant's interest. SAT or ACT required; ACT with Writing component recommended. TOEFL required of all international applicants. *Academic units recommended:* 4 English; 4 mathematics; 4 science; (4 science lab); 3 social studies; 3 foreign language; 3 academic electives.

Financial Aid

Students should submit: FAFSA, CSS/Financial Aid PROFILE, Noncustodial PROFILE, Business/Farm Supplement. The Princeton Review suggests that all financial aid forms be submitted as soon as possible after January 1. *Need-based scholarships/grants offered:* Federal Pell, SEOG, State scholarships/grants, private scholarships, the school's own gift aid. *Loan aid offered:* Direct Subsidized Stafford Loans, Direct Unsubsidized Stafford Loans, Direct PLUS loans, Federal Perkins Loans. Federal Work-Study Program available. Institutional employment available. Off-campus job opportunities are good.

The Inside Word

With an admissions rate that hovers consistently around one-quarter of applicants, Tulane is extremely competitive, and only those with seriously great scores and high school transcripts should expect to get the fat envelope from Tulane in the spring. However, Tulane often loses exceptional students to bigger-name universities, so if you've got an outstanding record but can't afford to attend a school that doesn't award merit-based scholarships, Tulane may make you an offer too good to refuse.

THE SCHOOL SAYS "..."

From the Admissions Office

"With more than 6,700 full-time undergraduate students in five schools, Tulane University offers the personal attention and teaching excellence traditionally associated with small colleges together with the facilities and interdisciplinary resources found only at major research universities. As the only major research University in America with a Public Service requirement for graduation, Tulane students are wholly committed to giving back to their communities. The opportunities for students to be involved in the rebirth of New Orleans offer an experience unavailable at any other place, at any other time.

"Tulane is committed to undergraduate education. Senior faculty members teach most introductory and lower-level courses, and most classes have twenty-five or fewer students. The close student-teacher relationship pays off. Tulane graduates are among the most likely to be selected for several prestigious fellowships that support graduate study abroad. Founded in 1834 and reorganized as Tulane University in 1884, Tulane is one of the major private research universities in the South.

"The Tulane campus offers a traditional collegiate setting in an attractive residential neighborhood, four miles from downtown New Orleans."

SELECTIVITY

Admissions Rating	96
# of applicants	30,122
% of applicants accepted	26
% of acceptees attending	20
# offered a place on the wait list	2,774
% accepting a place on wait list	25
% admitted from wait list	-46

FRESHMAN PROFILE

Range SAT Critical Reading	620–700
Range SAT Math	620–700
Range SAT Writing	630–720
Range ACT Composite	29–32
Minimum paper TOEFL	550
Minimum web-based TOEFL	213
Average HS GPA	3.49
% graduated top 10% of class	58
% graduated top 25% of class	83
% graduated top 50% of class	95

DEADLINES

Early action	
Deadline	11/15
Notification	12/15
Regular	
Deadline	1/15
Notification	4/1
Nonfall registration?	Yes

APPLICANTS ALSO LOOK AT AND RARELY PREFER

Skidmore College; Southern Methodist University; University of Richmond

FINANCIAL FACTS

Financial Aid Rating	93
Annual tuition	$43,150
Room and board	$12,012
Required fees	$3,780
Books and supplies	$1,200
% needy frosh rec. need-based scholarship or grant aid	99
% needy UG rec. need-based scholarship or grant aid	97
% needy frosh rec. non-need-based scholarship or grant aid	37
% needy UG rec. non-need-based scholarship or grant aid	25
% needy frosh rec. need-based self-help aid	62
% needy UG rec. need-based self-help aid	73
% UG borrow to pay for school	43
Average cumulative indebtedness	$29,122
% frosh need fully met	72
% ugrads need fully met	69
Average % of frosh need met	96
Average % of ugrad need met	94

TUSKEGEE UNIVERSITY

OLD ADMINISTRATION BUILDING, TUSKEGEE, AL 36088 • ADMISSIONS: 334-727-8500 • FAX: 334-727-5750

STUDENTS SAY ". . ."

Academics

For the past 132 years, Tuskegee University has strived to continue the legacy of higher learning created by Booker T. Washington and upheld by its other notable presidents and benefactors. The "rich history" of the school has always been about "achieving the...highest level of performance" in all areas of service, leadership, and academics, and everyone in the community works to ensure that "the Tuskegee Experience is like none other." The veterinary and engineering schools are standouts here, but the school can transform any individual into a leader. "Tuskegee, figuratively speaking, is often given coal, and it *always* produces diamonds," says one student. Academics are "a top priority" for Tuskegee, and the classes and structure are designed to "effectively nurture students' academic, social, and professional potentials and produce great leaders in society." "School is about gaining independence and responsibility so that you will be able to grow and compete in the real world." Small classes and personal interaction with professors help further this process along, and the school aims for "excellence within every aspect of education offered at the institution." "My professors don't teach because it's their job, they do it because they care and want you to learn and succeed. It's very obvious," says one student. Though the alumni network is positively rock solid, and fundraising isn't a problem, some students question the allocation of funds. Many agree that "the development of new facilities/buildings around the campus" is a sore spot, and though the administration is in the process of updating some, "there is a lot of work to be done," particularly in the student housing arena.

Life

The heritage of Tuskegee is felt in every step; "We literally walk on historic grounds," says a student of going to school on the only college or university campus in the nation to be designated a National Historic Site by Congress. The traditional festivities the school usually hosts are "quite enjoyable," and the school is in a "very quaint" town, which "allows for constant interaction among students on campus to occur." When there is nothing to do in Tuskegee, students usually go to Auburn, Montgomery, or even Atlanta. TU is for "academically inclined individuals," but when the books do shut, most people "go to the local clubs (The Soul Inn or Club Extreme)," or hangout at houses off campus. "Home football and basketball games are usually really fun," as well. "Even though people are serious about their work and classes, we all know how to have fun," says one student. "We're a school of weekend warriors." "It can be raining cats and dogs...and you will still see people going to class, or if it's the weekend you will see students going to a party."

Student Body

At this go-getter university, the typical student here is "someone who is driven to becoming successful in the future through studious methods." Though this HBCU is naturally predominantly black, there is much diversity in that "people from all across the country come to school in this small city in Alabama." Most students here are "very outspoken and easy to work with" and "open to meeting and interacting with new people"; with students from all over the world, "the diverse environment helps keep the campus from getting too dull."

FINANCIAL AID: 334-727-8500 • E-MAIL: ADMISSIONS@TUSKEGEE.EDU • WEBSITE: WWW.TUSKEGEE.EDU

THE PRINCETON REVIEW SAYS

Admissions

Very important factors considered include: Class rank, GPA, rigor of secondary school record, standardized test scores, racial/ethnic status, recommendation(s), talent/ability, level of applicant's interest. *Important factors considered include:* Alumni/ae relations, character/personal qualities. *Other factors considered include:* Application essay, extracurricular activities, first generation, geographical residence, interview, state residency, volunteer work, work experience. SAT or ACT required; ACT with or without Writing component accepted. TOEFL required of all international applicants. *Academic units required:* 4 English; 3 mathematics; 2 science; 3 social studies; 4 academic electives.

Financial Aid

Students should submit: FAFSA, Institution's own financial aid form, CSS/Financial Aid PROFILE. The Princeton Review suggests that all financial aid forms be submitted as soon as possible after January 1. *Need-based scholarships/grants offered:* Federal Pell, SEOG, State scholarships/grants, private scholarships, the school's own gift aid, United Negro College Fund, federal nursing scholarships. *Loan aid offered:* Direct Subsidized Stafford Loans, Direct Unsubsidized Stafford Loans, Direct PLUS loans, Federal Perkins Loans, Federal Nursing Loans, State Loans, College/university loans from institutional funds. Federal Work-Study Program available. Institutional employment available. Off-campus job opportunities are good.

The Inside Word

Tuskegee presents its students with a myriad of opportunities for discovery and research. Therefore, Tuskegee seeks applicants who have proven themselves successful in the classroom. Admissions counselors consider each application holistically and individually. What they really like to see, though, is a GPA of at least 3.0 and a composite ACT score of 21 or better. Note also that requirements for the nursing and engineering programs are more stringent. For example, you'll probably need four years of high school math if you want to major in engineering here. Prospective students interested in either field should investigate the specific criteria.

THE SCHOOL SAYS "..."

From the Admissions Office

"Tuskegee University, located in south central Alabama, was founded in 1881 under the dynamic and creative leadership of Booker T. Washington. As a state-related, independent institution, Tuskegee offers undergraduate and graduate degrees through five colleges and two schools: the College of Agriculture, Environment and Nutrition Sciences; the Brimmer College of Business and Information Sciences; the College of Engineering; the College of Veterinary Medicine, Nursing and Allied Health; the Taylor School of Architecture and Construction Science; and the School of Education. Substantial research and service programs make Tuskegee University an effective comprehensive institution geared toward preparing tomorrow's leaders today."

"First-year applicants must take the SAT or ACT; the SAT is preferred. International applicants must complete the TOEFL. Nursing applicants must complete the National Nursing exam."

SELECTIVITY

Admissions Rating	86
# of applicants	10,022
% of applicants accepted	35
% of acceptees attending	18

FRESHMAN PROFILE

Range SAT Critical Reading	400–510
Range SAT Math	400–520
Range ACT Composite	18–22
Minimum paper TOEFL	500
Minimum web-based TOEFL	62
Average HS GPA	3.24
% graduated top 10% of class	20
% graduated top 25% of class	60
% graduated top 50% of class	100

DEADLINES

Early action	
Deadline	8/31
Notification	10/1
Regular	
Priority	3/31
Deadline	7/15
Notification	3/15
Nonfall registration?	Yes

APPLICANTS ALSO LOOK AT AND RARELY PREFER

University of Alabama—Tuscaloosa; Auburn University

FINANCIAL FACTS

Financial Aid Rating	85
Annual tuition	$18,100
Room and board	$8,510
Required fees	$1,425
Books and supplies	$1,282
% needy frosh rec. need-based scholarship or grant aid	84
% needy UG rec. need-based scholarship or grant aid	86
% needy frosh rec. non-need-based scholarship or grant aid	47
% needy UG rec. non-need-based scholarship or grant aid	41
% needy frosh rec. need-based self-help aid	49
% needy UG rec. need-based self-help aid	53
% frosh rec. any financial aid	80
% UG rec. any financial aid	92
% UG borrow to pay for school	91
Average cumulative indebtedness	$23,000
% frosh need fully met	57
% ugrads need fully met	71
Average % of frosh need met	75
Average % of ugrad need met	75

UNION COLLEGE (NY)

GRANT HALL, SCHENECTADY, NY 12308 • ADMISSIONS: 518-388-6112 • FAX: 518-388-6986

CAMPUS LIFE

Quality of Life Rating	76
Fire Safety Rating	90
Green Rating	95
Type of school	Private
Affiliation	No Affiliation
Environment	Town

STUDENTS

Total undergrad enrollment	2,206
% male/female	54/46
% from out of state	62
% frosh from public high school	66
% frosh live on campus	99
% ugrads live on campus	86
# of fraternities(%ugrad men join)	14 (39)
# of sororities(% ugrad women join)	6 (39)
% African American	4
% Asian	6
% Caucasian	75
% Hispanic	7
% Native American	<1
% international	6
# of countries represented	29

SURVEY SAYS . . .

Students are happy
Lab facilities are great
Athletic facilities are great
Lots of beer drinking
Hard liquor is popular
Everyone loves the Dutchmen
Frats and sororities are popular
Alumni active on campus

ACADEMICS

Academic Rating	94
% students returning for sophomore year	92
% students graduating within 4 years	82
% students graduating within 6 years	88
Calendar	Trimester
Student/faculty ratio	10:1
Profs interesting rating	93
Profs accessible rating	93

Most classes have 10–19 students.
Most lab/discussion sessions have
10–19 students.

MOST POPULAR MAJORS

psychology; economics; biology

STUDENTS SAY ". . ."

Academics

Founded in 1795, Union College in upstate New York is a small, independent liberal arts college that provides a wide "breadth of education" that allows students to learn across the curriculum and graduate with a respected degree and a true liberal arts education. The "great historical roots" are apparent all around the "beautiful campus full of school-spirited students," but the school keeps a firm eye on the future as well, and "encourages students to develop and be prepared for graduation."

The professors are "interested in the lives of their students" and "work to make sure the student gets the academic support needed to succeed," and best of all, "you will never EVER have a teaching assistant instead of a professor at Union." Professors have an open door policy to always allow students right on in—"students are their main priority." Research opportunities are plentiful—"any professor with a lab is always looking for new recruits"—and a small but strong engineering department ensures that the sciences get a fair shake at a traditionally liberal arts school. The school also strives "to create interesting interdisciplinary classes that combine science and humanities in innovative ways."

Union is small, so "the sense of community is very important to the overall experience." The administration "wants you to enjoy your four years of college not just by studying but get to know other people and do things you never did before." A senior neuroscience major agrees: "Union is all about finding the best mix of the challenging courses and millions of activities happening each night." The trimester schedule is "fantastic," and the school "melds academic, social, and cultural life together seamlessly." "Union is also a prestigious institution that is small enough to allow every student a presence on campus," says one.

Life

The unique Minerva House system blends academic, social and residential interests. All students and faculty are assigned to one of the seven houses, which host hundreds of events each year (some professors even teach preceptorials there). There are also "Theme Houses," which are on-campus housing where people who have similar interests can live, such as the Ozone House for environmentally-oriented people.

Between Greek and Minerva life, there is "a vibrant social life" for all students, though quite a few admit that the emphasis on the "huge" Greek life "could certainly be reduced." "Most of the campus attends parties on weekends," which is "a great way to relieve the stress caused by being at such an academically rigorous schools and also meet new people." In class, however, "we're all nerds at heart, and we can talk books and numbers all day long." Everyone also goes to free campus movies and other events like "concerts, magicians, comedians, roller skating, and others."

The Capital Region is "all around us, so if you're bored you're just not trying hard enough," says a student. There is a bounty of events and organizations, so "one has to try to NOT be involved." "I never feel like the campus runs out of things for me to do," says a senior. Dating is "thin" at Union: "it is not a couples' school," however it IS a hockey school.

Student Body

Most come to Union from "some part of the northeast," are "from middle/upper-middle class families," and are "very active, career-oriented, [and] serious about academics." One student tells us, "I'm not going to lie, it's a pretty white campus," says a student. "Everyone fits in because everyone seems to love Union." These "intellectuals" tend to dress "very preppy" ("wearing Patagonia jackets, Lily Pulitzer handbags, and Ugg boots is basically the uniform") and are "a great group of people"; "there don't seem to be any barriers between them."

FINANCIAL AID: 518-388-6123 • E-MAIL: ADMISSIONS@UNION.EDU • WEBSITE: WWW.UNION.EDU

THE PRINCETON REVIEW SAYS
Admissions
Very important factors considered include: Class rank, GPA, rigor of secondary school record. *Important factors considered include:* Standardized test scores, application essay, extracurricular activities, recommendation(s), talent/ability, volunteer work, work experience, character/personal qualities. *Other factors considered include:* First generation, geographical residence, interview, racial/ethnic status, state residency, alumni/ae relations, level of applicant's interest. SAT or ACT required for some; SAT and SAT Subject Tests or ACT required for some; ACT with or without Writing component accepted. TOEFL required of all international applicants. *Academic units required:* 4 English; 3 mathematics; 2 science; (2 science lab); 1 social studies; 2 foreign language; 1 history. *Academic units recommended:* 4 English; 4 mathematics; 4 science; (4 science lab); 2 social studies; 4 foreign language; 2 history.

Financial Aid
Students should submit: FAFSA, CSS/Financial Aid PROFILE, State aid form, Noncustodial PROFILE. Regular filing deadline is 2/1. The Princeton Review suggests that all financial aid forms be submitted as soon as possible after January 1. *Need-based scholarships/grants offered:* Federal Pell, SEOG, State scholarships/grants, private scholarships, the school's own gift aid. *Loan aid offered:* Direct Subsidized Stafford Loans, Direct Unsubsidized Stafford Loans, Direct PLUS loans, Federal Perkins Loans, College/university loans from institutional funds. Applicants will be notified of awards beginning 3/25. Federal Work-Study Program available. Institutional employment available. Off-campus job opportunities are good.

The Inside Word
Union College is an SAT-optional college. Students may simply indicate on their application if they would like the admissions committee to consider their test scores or not. However, applicants to the Leadership in Medicine Program (an eight-year M.D./M.B.A. program with Albany Medical College) and to the Law and Public Policy program (a combined B.A. and J.D.) must submit test scores for consideration. For students who know that Union is their first choice, the school offers two early decision deadlines.

THE SCHOOL SAYS ". . ."
From the Admissions Office
"The Union academic program is characterized by breadth and flexibility across a range of disciplines and interdisciplinary programs in the liberal arts, sciences, and engineering. With nearly 1,000 courses to choose from, Union students may major in a single field, combine work in two or more departments or create their own organizing-theme major. Opportunities for undergraduate research are robust and give students a chance to work closely with professors year-round, take part in professional-level conferences and use sophisticated scientific equipment. More than half of Union's students take advantage of the college's extensive international study program, with new opportunities created regularly. A rich array of service learning programs and strong athletic, cultural, and social activities also enhance the overall Union experience. Union's seven student-run Minerva Houses are lively hubs for intellectual and social activities. They bring together students, faculty and staff for hundreds of events, from dinners with invited speakers, lectures, and live bands, to trips to local attractions.

"The Union community welcomes talented and diverse students, and we work closely with each one to help identify and cultivate their passions. Admission to the college is based on excellent academic credentials as reflected in the high school transcript, quality of courses selected, teacher and counselor recommendations, personal essays, and writing samples. Personal interviews are strongly recommended. All candidates who apply to Union receive a thorough and thoughtful review of their application. Submission of SAT and ACT scores is optional except for the law and medicine programs."

SELECTIVITY
Admissions Rating	95
# of applicants	5,725
% of applicants accepted	37
% of acceptees attending	26
# offered a place on the wait list	1,059
% accepting a place on wait list	49
% admitted from wait list	12
# of early decision applicants	374
% accepted early decision	67

FRESHMAN PROFILE
Range SAT Critical Reading	590–680
Range SAT Math	630–720
Range SAT Writing	590–690
Range ACT Composite	28–31
Minimum paper TOEFL	600
Minimum web-based TOEFL	250
Average HS GPA	3.41
% graduated top 10% of class	64
% graduated top 25% of class	84
% graduated top 50% of class	97

DEADLINES
Early decision	
Deadline	11/15
Notification	12/15
Regular	
Deadline	1/15
Notification	4/1
Nonfall registration?	Yes

APPLICANTS ALSO LOOK AT AND OFTEN PREFER
Colgate University; Cornell University; Tufts University

AND SOMETIMES PREFER
Hamilton College; Lafayette College; University of Rochester

AND RARELY PREFER
Boston University; Hobart and William Smith Colleges; University of Vermont

FINANCIAL FACTS
Financial Aid Rating	95
Annual tuition	$46,314
Room and board	$11,463
Required fees	$471
Books and supplies	$1,500
% needy frosh rec. need-based scholarship or grant aid	98
% needy UG rec. need-based scholarship or grant aid	96
% needy frosh rec. non-need-based scholarship or grant aid	17
% needy UG rec. non-need-based scholarship or grant aid	15
% needy frosh rec. need-based self-help aid	96
% needy UG rec. need-based self-help aid	93
% frosh rec. any financial aid	76
% UG rec. any financial aid	77
% UG borrow to pay for school	70
Average cumulative indebtedness	$27,911
% frosh need fully met	100
% ugrads need fully met	98
Average % of frosh need met	100
Average % of ugrad need met	98

UNITED STATES AIR FORCE ACADEMY

HQ USAFA / RRS, USAF ACADEMY, CO 80840-5025 • ADMISSIONS: 719-333-2520 • FAX: 719-333-3012

CAMPUS LIFE

Quality of Life Rating	76
Fire Safety Rating	87
Green Rating	70
Type of school	Public
Affiliation	No Affiliation
Environment	Metropolis

STUDENTS

Total undergrad enrollment	3,993
% male/female	78/22
% from out of state	92
% frosh live on campus	100
% ugrads live on campus	100
% African American	6
% Asian	5
% Caucasian	67
% Hispanic	9
% Native American	<1
% international	1
# of countries represented	35

SURVEY SAYS . . .

Internships are widely available
No one cheats
Lab facilities are great
Athletic facilities are great
Career services are great
Campus feels safe
Very little drug use
Frats and sororities are unpopular
or nonexistent

ACADEMICS

Academic Rating	94
% students returning for sophomore year	90
% students graduating within 4 years	83
% students graduating within 6 years	85
Calendar	Semester
Student/faculty ratio	8:1
Profs interesting rating	84
Profs accessible rating	91

Most classes have 10–19 students.
Most lab/discussion sessions have
10–19 students.

MOST POPULAR MAJORS
business/commerce; social sciences;
aerospace and space engineering

STUDENTS SAY ". . ."

Academics

"Honor, Discipline, and hard work" are three characteristics that summarize what the U.S. Air Force Academy in Colorado is about. The chosen few that make it through the gauntlet of getting admitted to USAFA are rewarded with a free education, "tremendous opportunities after graduation," as the "rigorous" institution is designed to "[create] officers of good character, ready to lead in the Air Force."

The academy has "a very difficult academic environment with a high focus on engineering classes," and the core curriculum includes basic engineering, engineering mechanics, electrical engineering, aeronautical engineering, and astronautical engineering. Fortunately, professors are "very accessible," "present a challenging classroom experience that promotes critical thought," and "make class a discussion." There is "also extra instruction from teachers and the resources available for research," and students help each other out when another is struggling, as well. Faculty is a mix of civilian and military professors, which "gives a great insight into the jobs we can expect in the military after graduation as well as potential civilian career fields after service," according to one cadet.

Students can expect "absolutely no lecture hall classes," as every section is held in a classroom with anywhere from five to thirty students. Given the future careers of the cadets, plenty of learning takes place experientially, and airmanship programs (such as "powered flight, soaring (flying gliders), the aerobatic demonstration team, and our skydiving teams") are a huge part of the school and are "an extremely fun and unique part of our lives." If there is one downside to such thorough training, it is that cadets universally clamor for more freedom and free time.

Life

"Everyone here is pretty accepting to other cultures and backgrounds and it is easy to make friends," says a cadet of the many organizations to fit into, including "your squad, your team, your club, your academic major, and failing all that your friends." Regardless of what social group you find yourself in, "you end up knowing everyone eventually." There are plenty of USAFA-specific traditions; most interaction occurs within the squadron, and "most cadets really enjoy the squadron activities and leadership opportunities."

Life is "very controlled" here, and as it is a military academy students "have to follow military laws in addition to civilian laws." Therefore, most students "do not drink underage and would not ever do any sort of drug." In order to leave, one must sign out on a "pass" which is limited for each class (freshman have six passes per semester), and in the "likely" event that students are restricted to campus for a random weekend, they can always "find creative ways to have fun, such as tying bedsheets to chairs and sailing across the terrazzo (main campus area) at high speed." For fun, cadets do "normal things," such as "[skiing] in the winter, pickup basketball, video games, go watch a movie, [and] go to Denver and walk around the city."

Student Body

Unsurprisingly, cadets here are all "highly motivated, A-type personalities that give 100 percent in everything they do." This group of "super smart," "driven" individuals are also "respectable" and "athletic," which explains what one junior refers to as "the smartest offensive line in the NCAA." The majority of the "patriotic" student body is a "fairly conservative white male," and everyone is in a uniform from 7 A.M. to 4 P.M. so there is a commonality from the start. Basic Cadet Training (BCT) "makes people work together," and "with going through the same experience, allows lifetime bonds to start growing." This experience is unique, and "each class year has a specific sense of pride and unity as a team." "We are all going into the same Air Force after we graduate so we need to learn to work together," says a junior.

E-MAIL: RR_WEBMAIL@USAFA.EDU • WEBSITE: WWW.ACADEMYADMISSIONS.COM

THE PRINCETON REVIEW SAYS

Admissions

Very important factors considered include: Class rank, GPA, rigor of secondary school record, standardized test scores, application essay, extracurricular activities, interview, recommendation(s), character/personal qualities, level of applicant's interest. *Important factors considered include:* Talent/ability, volunteer work, work experience. *Other factors considered include:* First generation, geographical residence, racial/ethnic status, alumni/ae relations. SAT or ACT required; ACT with or without Writing component accepted. *Academic units recommended:* 4 English; 4 mathematics; 4 science; (4 science lab); 3 social studies; 2 foreign language; 3 history; 1 computer science.

Financial Aid

The Princeton Review suggests that all financial aid forms be submitted as soon as possible after January 1.

The Inside Word

The Air Force Academy promises a demanding four years, and the fainthearted need not apply. Due to the arduous nature of the school, it's no wonder that applicants face stringent requirements right at the outset. Aside from an excellent academic record, successful candidates need to be physically fit. They also must typically win a nomination from their congressperson. Honor is a valued quality at the academy, and admissions officers will accept only those with the strength of character and determination necessary to succeed at one of the country's most elite institutions.

THE SCHOOL SAYS "..."

From the Admissions Office

"The United States Air Force Academy offers one of the most prestigious and respected undergraduate programs available. With more than 30 majors and 3 minors offered at the Academy, there are programs of study for every interest. The academic challenges and expectations are high — but so are the rewards. You will emerge from the Academy with a well-rounded knowledge in many fields, an intimate knowledge in your major area of study, and the ability to serve our nation as a Second Lieutenant in the world's greatest air, space, and cyberspace force.

At the United States Air Force Academy, every cadet is an athlete. Our extensive athletic program includes 27 men's and women's NCAA Division I intercollegiate teams, intramural sports, physical education courses, and physical fitness tests tailored to prepare you for Air Force leadership by building confidence, physical courage, and the ability to perform under pressure.

The Academy experience requires cadets to become active participants in leadership roles and opportunities that give a sense of honor and duty. The Air Force Academy's mission is to educate, train, and inspire men and women to become officers of character motivated to lead the United States Air Force in service to our nation. If you choose to accept the challenges, you will be rewarded with unique experiences and opportunities incomparable to any other college experience and the honor of serving your country in the United States Air Force."

SELECTIVITY

Admissions Rating	97
# of applicants	9,634
% of applicants accepted	15
% of acceptees attending	78

FRESHMAN PROFILE

Range SAT Critical Reading	590–690
Range SAT Math	620–710
Range ACT Composite	29–32
Average HS GPA	3.83
% graduated top 10% of class	55
% graduated top 25% of class	85
% graduated top 50% of class	97

DEADLINES

Early action	
Deadline	11/1
Notification	1/15
Regular	
Deadline	12/31
Nonfall registration?	No

APPLICANTS ALSO LOOK AT AND SOMETIMES PREFER

United States Military Academy; United States Naval Academy; United States Coast Guard Academy; United States Merchant Marine Academy

FINANCIAL FACTS

Financial Aid Rating	60*
Annual in-state tuition	$0
Annual out-of-state tuition	$0
Room and board	$0
Required fees	$0

UNITED STATES COAST GUARD ACADEMY

31 MOHEGAN AVENUE, NEW LONDON, CT 06320-8103 • ADMISSIONS: 860-444-8503 • FAX: 860-701-6700

CAMPUS LIFE
Quality of Life Rating	73
Fire Safety Rating	86
Green Rating	63
Type of school	Public
Affiliation	No Affiliation
Environment	City

STUDENTS
Total undergrad enrollment	902
% male/female	66/34
% from out of state	94
% frosh from public high school	76
% frosh live on campus	100
% ugrads live on campus	100
% African American	2
% Asian	5
% Caucasian	68
% Hispanic	13
% Native American	1
% international	3
# of countries represented	15

SURVEY SAYS . . .
Lots of conservative students
Career services are great
School is well run
Great financial aid
No one cheats
Students are friendly
Diverse student types on campus
Students involved in community service
Campus feels safe
Very little drug use
Everyone loves the Bears
Intramural sports are popular
Alumni active on campus

ACADEMICS
Academic Rating	88
% students returning for sophomore year	94
% students graduating within 4 years	88
% students graduating within 6 years	91
Calendar	Semester
Student/faculty ratio	7:1
Profs interesting rating	78
Profs accessible rating	97

Most classes have 10–19 students.
Most lab/discussion sessions have fewer than 10 students.

MOST POPULAR MAJORS
oceanography; political science; business administration and management

STUDENTS SAY ". . ."

Academics
Students at the United States Coast Guard Academy recommend their school as "highly demanding, immensely rewarding, professionally oriented and the best choice to make the best friends you are ever going to have." Many appreciate the "regimented environment," which, according to one management major, "Gives me a standard to live up to and hold myself to, even when I am away from here." Cadets are "pushed to [the] limits" "academically, emotionally, and physically," and they wouldn't have it any other way. Importantly, "the academy fosters camaraderie amongst the Corps of Cadets that can't be found anywhere else. With a student body numbering a little over 1,000, the Coast Guard Academy is truly unique in its ability to provide an environment where classmates become shipmates, friends, and eventually family." Though there are a number of excellent programs, cadets call the most attention to the strong engineering department. The academics are "challenging but rewarding." Professors challenge cadets "to reach farther, expand their horizons, and to develop outside the classroom as much as inside of it." An electrical engineering major expounds "the most surprising and excellent trait that all teachers have is that they are always willing to help outside of the class rooms. Always." Some students contend "the best part about my school is the summer training programs." Students have traveled "across the Atlantic Ocean" stopping "in London, Iceland, and Nova Scotia." Others have been to "Bermuda, St. Pierre France, Guantanamo Bay, and St. Petersburg Florida since coming to the Academy which is absolutely amazing."

Life
"Life at USCGA is unique. Only way to put it," says one junior. Day-to-day life at the Coast Guard Academy is "orderly and predictable." During the week, it's difficult for people to do anything "outside of their military, athletic, and academic obligations." As one honest marine and environmental science major reveals, "Every moment of every day is planned out." Required sports credits "keep people active and involved either intercollegiate or intramurals." Of course, life at the Academy isn't 100 percent work and stress. Free time is at a premium on weekdays but "Weekends are the time to explore New England, New York City, and the downtown New London area." A senior shares, cadets "go to the beach, head up to Vermont for some hiking or skiing... there is a lot to do if you look for it." While "students aren't allowed off campus during the week," unless participating in an academy sanctioned activity, "most try and get away for the weekend." Another senior elaborates, "Underage students tend to go to the movies or the local mall. Of-age students usually spend their time off drinking at the bars downtown." Life at USCGA can be "very challenging and demanding at times, but the goal of becoming an officer makes it worth it." A "guaranteed job upon graduation" is pretty persuasive as well.

Student Body
While in past, USGCA has been described as homogeneous; "the academy has been stressing diversity in its admissions and has had a good deal of success." Luckily, a civil engineering major assures us, "Those students of different backgrounds easily fit in with everyone else." In fact, one cadet goes so far to say "sometimes, I don't think that cadets recognize diversity because we all wear the same uniforms, take the same classes, and are going through the same experiences." Not surprisingly, the academy seems to attract "highly motivated [people] with a strong desire to serve in the Coast Guard." Certainly, another hallmark of Coast Guard cadets is that they're "hard working, smart, motivated, and in great shape." A naval architecture and marine engineering major adds, "Type-A personalities are most common among the Corps." A senior describes student as "very close with each other and for the most part, everyone has a group of friends that they fit in quite well with." This sophomore cheekily sums up his peers, "A typical student here is just like a typical student anywhere else but works harder, follows stricter rules, is in better shape, and is owned by the federal government."

UNITED STATES COAST GUARD ACADEMY

FINANCIAL AID: 860-444-8309 • E-MAIL: ADMISSIONS@USCGA.EDU • WEBSITE: WWW.USCGA.EDU

THE PRINCETON REVIEW SAYS

Admissions

Very important factors considered include: Class rank, GPA, rigor of secondary school record, standardized test scores, extracurricular activities, character/personal qualities. *Important factors considered include:* Application essay, recommendation(s), talent/ability. *Other factors considered include:* First generation, geographical residence, interview, racial/ethnic status, state residency, volunteer work, work experience, alumni/ae relations, level of applicant's interest, religious affiliation. SAT or ACT required; ACT with Writing component required. TOEFL required of all international applicants. *Academic units required:* 4 English; 4 mathematics; 3 science; (3 science lab). *Academic units recommended:* 4 English; 4 mathematics; 4 science; (3 science lab).

Financial Aid

The Princeton Review suggests that all financial aid forms be submitted as soon as possible after January 1.

The Inside Word

Gaining acceptance into the Coast Guard Academy is a highly competitive process. The admissions committee is looking not only for outstanding academic achievement but also for applicants who demonstrate leadership ability and strong moral character. In addition, unlike other colleges, you'll also need a physical fitness examination and evaluation.

THE SCHOOL SAYS "..."

From the Admissions Office

"Founded in 1876, the United States Coast Guard Academy enjoys a proud tradition of graduating leaders of character. The academy experience melds academic rigor, leadership development, and athletic participation to prepare you to graduate as a commissioned officer. Character development of cadets is founded on the core values of honor, respect, and devotion to duty. You build friendships that last a lifetime, study with inspiring professors in small classes, and train during the summer aboard America's tall ship Eagle, as well as the service's ships and aircraft. Top performers spend their senior summer traveling on exciting internships around the nation and overseas. Graduates serve for five years and have unmatched opportunities to attend flight school and graduate school, all funded by the Coast Guard.

"Appointments to the academy are based on a selective admissions process; Congressional nominations are not required. Your leadership potential and desire to serve your country are what counts. Our student body reflects the best America has to offer—with all its potential and diversity!

"Applicants are required to take the SAT (or the ACT with the writing section).

"The Coast Guard Academy boasts a prolific honor's program that has produces three consecutive Truman Scholars and several Fulbright Scholars over the last three years. The academy is ranked nationally among the top ten for women in STEM fields. The academy embraces a diversity of race and gender. Women comprise approximately 30 percent of the student body and approximately 20 percent of the student body are underrepresented minorities."

SELECTIVITY

Admissions Rating	96
# of applicants	1,992
% of applicants accepted	16
% of acceptees attending	66
# offered a place on the wait list	112
% accepting a place on wait list	80
% admitted from wait list	48

FRESHMAN PROFILE

Range SAT Critical Reading	570–670
Range SAT Math	620–690
Range SAT Writing	560–650
Range ACT Composite	25–30
Minimum paper TOEFL	560
Minimum web-based TOEFL	220
Average HS GPA	3.92
% graduated top 10% of class	47
% graduated top 25% of class	80
% graduated top 50% of class	94

DEADLINES

Early action	
Deadline	11/15
Notification	2/1
Regular	
Priority	11/15
Deadline	2/1
Notification	4/15
Nonfall registration?	No

FINANCIAL FACTS

Financial Aid Rating	60*
Annual in-state tuition	$0
Annual out-of-state tuition	$0
Room and board	$0
Required fees	$0
% frosh rec. any financial aid	0
% UG rec. any financial aid	0

UNITED STATES MERCHANT MARINE ACADEMY

OFFICE OF ADMISSIONS, KINGS POINT, NY 11024-1699 • ADMISSIONS: 516-773-5391 • FAX: 516-773-5390

CAMPUS LIFE

Quality of Life Rating	69
Fire Safety Rating	60*
Green Rating	60*
Type of school	Public
Affiliation	No Affiliation
Environment	Town

STUDENTS

Total undergrad enrollment	1,058
% male/female	87/13
% from out of state	87
% frosh from public high school	75
% frosh live on campus	100
% ugrads live on campus	100
# of countries represented	4

SURVEY SAYS . . .
Lots of conservative students
Class discussions are rare
Great financial aid
Very little drug use
Alumni active on campus

ACADEMICS

Academic Rating	69
% students returning for sophomore year	92
Calendar	Trimester
Profs interesting rating	65
Profs accessible rating	66

Most classes have 20–29 students.

MOST POPULAR MAJORS
engineering; naval architecture and marine engineering; transportation and materials moving

STUDENTS SAY ". . ."

Academics
Tucked away on Long Island, the United States Merchant Marine Academy offers students the chance to pursue a prestigious though rigorous and regimented education. Further, it allows undergrads to join "a group of elite students who work hard and [are] honest and patriotic." Students here caution that the academics are "extremely difficult," especially given the "fast-paced classroom environment." Additionally, when asked about their professors, students dole out mixed reviews. Though most assert that their teachers are "very intelligent," some bemoan a "lack of enthusiasm." While some professors are described as "fair, approachable, and extremely helpful," other professors come across as "heartless and condescending." Regardless of which classes you enroll in, the Merchant Marine Academy is "a school that requires plenty of effort on behalf of the student." As one midshipman proudly sums up, "The opportunities afforded by this Academy are unparalleled by any other college I have come across. Despite the immense sacrifices and hardships of this school, it is completely worth it for the right person."

Life
Undergrads at the Merchant Marine Academy don't mince words about life at their school. Indeed, the majority seem to be in agreement that because "it is a military academy, fun is generally limited." As one straightforward student explains, "We are restricted to the campus grounds during the week until senior year. Life is pretty drab, dull, and boring [with] most time spent either in class, studying, or working out." Moreover, undergrads are "restricted by the regiment and disciplinary system." Of course, even these hardworking midshipmen get to kick back every now and again. Another undergrad cheerfully shares, "When the spring comes, everyone gets out to play rec sports (Ultimate Frisbee, tag football, soccer, swim, or bike ride) and goes to the park to BBQ." A fellow student chimes in, "We have a good time, and usually, it is the little things that make us happy. We enjoy hanging out on weekends and doing things that normal college students would do. Recently a few friends and I had a Nerf gun battle, which was pretty fun." When they are allowed, midshipmen rush to get off campus. Indeed, students here love to take advantage of the fact that they are "only twenty minutes from downtown NYC." As this wise midshipman concludes, "New York City in uniform boils down to cheap food, movies, plays, concerts, easy way to meet girls, you name it...we work hard all week, but when it comes time, we get to play hard as well."

Student Body
At first glance, the average Merchant Marine Academy midshipman could be described as "a white, conservative male." Of course, there's definitely more to these students than race, gender, and political views. Certainly, undergrads can also be depicted as "respectful," "athletic," and "outgoing." They can also be categorized as "those that want to work in the maritime industry and those that want to join the military." Moreover, many are "hardworking and serious." As one undergrad explains, "If you aren't willing to work, you won't be here long." Another student continues, "The typical student has tons on his plate, whether it's regimental duties or academic ones. [However], no matter what, if you need help with something, somebody will be there for you." A fellow midshipman concurs, summing up, "The students here are all a family. Each one of us here at the Merchant Marine Academy [has] experienced the same rigorous training and tough treatment plebe year. We all work together in everything we do, and without one another it is almost impossible to succeed at the Academy." Actually, the U.S. Merchant Marine Academy is increasing the diversity of its student body every year. The number of women in this year's graduating class is 10 percent, while the class of 2016 is at 15 percent. Ethnic minorities comprise 20 percent of the class of 2016.

FINANCIAL AID: 516-773-5295 • E-MAIL: ADMISSIONS@USMMA.EDU • WEBSITE: WWW.USMMA.EDU

THE PRINCETON REVIEW SAYS

Admissions

Very important factors considered include: Rigor of secondary school record, standardized test scores, character/personal qualities. *Important factors considered include:* Class rank, GPA, application essay, extracurricular activities, recommendation(s), talent/ability, level of applicant's interest. *Other factors considered include:* Geographical residence, interview, racial/ethnic status, state residency, volunteer work, work experience. SAT or ACT required; ACT with or without Writing component accepted. TOEFL required of all international applicants. *Academic units required:* 4 English; 3 mathematics; 3 science; (2 science lab); 8 academic electives. *Academic units recommended:* 4 mathematics; 4 science; (3 science lab); 4 social studies; 2 foreign language.

Financial Aid

Students should submit: FAFSA, Institution's own financial aid form. Regular filing deadline is 5/1. The Princeton Review suggests that all financial aid forms be submitted as soon as possible after January 1. *Need-based scholarships/grants offered:* Federal Pell, private scholarships. *Loan aid offered:* Direct Subsidized Stafford Loans, Direct Unsubsidized Stafford Loans, Direct PLUS loans. Off-campus job opportunities are poor.

The Inside Word

Securing admittance to the Merchant Marine Academy is no easy feat. The admissions committee is looking for stellar candidates who have the intelligence, fortitude, and leadership capabilities to survive (and thrive) at this institution. In addition to your transcripts and test scores, the admissions crew will closely assess your letters of recommendation. Moreover, unlike traditional colleges, you'll also have to pass a fitness requirement and secure a nomination from a U.S. representative or senator.

THE SCHOOL SAYS "..."

From the Admissions Office

"What makes the U.S. Merchant Marine Academy different from the other federal service academies? The difference can be summarized in two phrases that appear in our publications. The first: 'The World Is Your Campus.' You will spend a year at sea—a third of your sophomore year and two-thirds of your junior year—teamed with a classmate aboard a U.S. merchant ship. You will visit an average of eighteen foreign nations while you work and learn in a mariner's true environment. You will graduate with seataring experience and as a citizen of the world. The second phrase is 'Options and Opportunities.' Unlike students at the other federal academies, who are required to enter the service connected to their academy, you have the option of working in the seagoing merchant marine and transportation industry or applying for active duty in the Navy, Coast Guard, Marine Corps, Air Force, or Army. Nearly 25 percent of our most recent graduating class entered various branches of the armed forces with an officer rank. As a graduate of the U.S. Merchant Marine Academy, you will receive a Bachelor of Science degree, a government-issued merchant marine officer's license, and a Naval Reserve commission (unless you have been accepted for active military duty). No other service academy offers so attractive a package. The academy is in the midst of a multi-year capital improvement program valued at over $60 million that will achieve the strategic plan goal of a first-class infrastructure. The dormitories have undergone complete renovations and the dining hall has been redesigned and modernized. The main pier is being replaced in 2013-14. The next phase of the program includes plans to renovate and upgrade the Academy's academic facilities.

"Applicants must take the SAT or the ACT with the writing component. For homeschooled students, we recommend they also submit scores from SAT Subject Tests in chemistry and/or physics."

SELECTIVITY

Admissions Rating	94
# of applicants	2,076
% of applicants accepted	20
% of acceptees attending	69
# offered a place on the wait list	197
% accepting a place on wait list	100
% admitted from wait list	0

FRESHMAN PROFILE

Range SAT Critical Reading	555–635
Range SAT Math	600–680
Range ACT Composite	25–29
Minimum paper TOEFL	533
Minimum web-based TOEFL	200
Average HS GPA	3.60
% graduated top 10% of class	24
% graduated top 25% of class	62
% graduated top 50% of class	92

DEADLINES

Regular Deadline	3/1
Nonfall registration?	No

APPLICANTS ALSO LOOK AT AND OFTEN PREFER
United States Naval Academy

AND SOMETIMES PREFER
United States Military Academy; United States Coast Guard Academy; United States Air Force Academy

AND RARELY PREFER

FINANCIAL FACTS

Financial Aid Rating	67
Annual in-state tuition	$0
Annual out-of-state tuition	$0
Room and board	$0
Required fees	$2,718
Books and supplies	$767
Average % of frosh need met	100
Average % of ugrad need met	100

UNITED STATES MILITARY ACADEMY (WEST POINT)

646 SWIFT ROAD, WEST POINT, NY 10996-1905 • ADMISSIONS: 845-938-4041 • FAX: 845-938-3021

CAMPUS LIFE

Quality of Life Rating	74
Fire Safety Rating	84
Green Rating	70
Type of school	Public
Affiliation	No Affiliation
Environment	Village

STUDENTS

Total undergrad enrollment	4,591
% male/female	83/17
% from out of state	93
% frosh from public high school	73
% frosh live on campus	100
% ugrads live on campus	100
% African American	8
% Asian	6
% Caucasian	69
% Hispanic	10
% Native American	1
% international	1
# of countries represented	31

SURVEY SAYS . . .

Lots of conservative students
Political activism is popular
Classroom facilities are great
Lab facilities are great
Career services are great
Internships are widely available
School is well run
Great financial aid
No one cheats
Campus feels safe
Athletic facilities are great
Very little drug use
Everyone loves the Moose
Intramural sports are popular
Alumni active on campus

ACADEMICS

Academic Rating	99
% students returning for sophomore year	95
% students graduating within 4 years	80
% students graduating within 6 years	84
Calendar	Semester
Student/faculty ratio	7:1
Profs interesting rating	94
Profs accessible rating	99

Most classes have 10–19 students.
Most lab/discussion sessions have
10–19 students.

MOST POPULAR MAJORS

economics; business administration and
management; engineering/industrial
management

STUDENTS SAY ". . ."

Academics

Duty. Honor. Country. Having produced two U.S. presidents, numerous generals, and 74 Medal of Honor recipients in its 210 years in existence, an institution such as West Point doesn't need to hear outside praise. The rigorous admission process (you must be nominated by your Congressional representative just to apply) is just the start of the character building process on the way to "working hard to develop yourself into the best student, leader and officer you can be." "It's a lot of work, you don't have a lot of free time, but the education you receive will pay dividends in the long run," says a sophomore.

"Leadership is what West Point is all about," and cadets are held to "high standards" of ""selfless service to the U.S. people and Constitution" from the second they set foot on campus. The heavy academic load is "rigorous and very challenging," but the professors (both civilian and officers) are "very personable" and "truly strive to stimulate our minds with the material they are teaching." "They provide relevant and exciting application to material covered in class" and are "role models for the cadets to look at and emulate" (almost all professors live on campus). "I have never had a teacher here that doesn't love their job. They really are here for our assistance," says a cadet.

The classroom system "forces students to take responsibility for their own education" and "countless opportunities" are presented to cadets, "whether they be academic, athletic, or a hobby." Classes are rarely bigger than eighteen cadets thereby setting the conditions for one-on-one with the professor, and are "100 percent discussion based," so…are always interesting." As one physics and nuclear engineering major sums up: "West Point is not just an institution of higher learning. The academy is a culture that immerses me in academics, discipline, and physical rigors."

Life

To put it artfully, there "is not a better place on the planet to learn time management skills." "There is a lot of hard work to be done preparing for officership," says a cadet. Everyone is busy "from when they wake up until they go to bed," and "people generally think about getting by their classes and making it to the weekend," when cadets love "to play sports and watch Netflix." As cadets get older, they gain more privileges to leave for weekends, but some do wish that the school administration were into "giving the students more freedoms," particularly the freshmen, whose lives mainly consist of "observing the upperclassmen's leadership styles, going to classes, and working out." However, above everything else "cadets have a strong love of traveling America and the world during their breaks."

Since all activities and meals are based off a daily schedule, "everything is run like a clock, and we are expected at certain places at certain times." "Food in the mess hall is free to cadets, but very low in quality," and gets worked off quickly in the many trips to the gym. All students are athletes and "must play a sport at some level." There is "a strong culture of athleticism, national service, and freedom to pursue whatever you are interested [in]," but for the four years you are at West Point, "life doesn't include parties" and "it doesn't includ[e] drinking or drugs."

Student Body

Those who choose to go to West Point "are like machines": "smart, focused, physically fit, and disciplined." Students are naturally very close with members of their company, and all "clean cut, in shape" students "have a place and fit in increasingly you progress through the classes." "You go through hardships and tough challenges that bring you closer than I imagine any other interstudent relations could ever attain," says one cadet. There are plenty of "strong willed" "alpha males/females" to be found in this "very cohesive unit," as "people work tirelessly to succeed" and "are committed to service in the military."

United States Military Academy (West Point)

Financial Aid: 845-938-4041 • E-mail: admissions@usma.edu • Website: www.westpoint.edu

THE PRINCETON REVIEW SAYS

Admissions

Very important factors considered include: Class rank, GPA, rigor of secondary school record, standardized test scores, extracurricular activities, character/personal qualities. *Important factors considered include:* Application essay, recommendation(s), talent/ability, level of applicant's interest. *Other factors considered include:* First generation, interview, racial/ethnic status, volunteer work, work experience. SAT or ACT required; ACT with Writing component recommended. TOEFL required of all international applicants. *Academic units recommended:* 4 English; 4 mathematics; 4 science; (2 science lab); 3 social studies; 2 foreign language; 1 history; 3 academic electives.

Financial Aid

The Princeton Review suggests that all financial aid forms be submitted as soon as possible after January 1.

The Inside Word

The fact that you must be nominated by your Congressional representative in order to apply to West Point tells you all you need to know about the school's selectivity. Contact your district's Congressional representative to learn the deadline for nomination requests; typically these are made in the spring of your junior year. Successful candidates must demonstrate excellence in academics, physical conditioning, extracurricular involvement, and leadership. They must also be willing to commit to five years of active duty and three years of reserve duty upon graduation. The rigorous requirements and demanding commitments of a West Point education hardly dissuade applicants. More than 15,000 applied for the 1,150 available slots.

THE SCHOOL SAYS "..."

From the Admissions Office

"West Point is searching for applicants who possess the leadership skills, cultural sensibilities, and the moral fiber to handle the volatile, uncertain, complex, and ambiguous contemporary operating environment of today's world as a future U.S. Army Officer. As a crucible for leadership, we are looking for critical thinkers that have who have the judgment and experience to become a leader of character upon graduation.

"To assess your ability and preparation, admissions looks at more than your GPA or standardized test scores. The applications of almost 15,000 students are evaluated based on academic, physical, and leadership potential to find approximately 1,150 candidates who are ready to be offered the challenge of admission into the Corps of Cadets. With an amazingly high offer-acceptance rate, only the most dedicated, enthusiastic applicants make it to the finish line for the report date each June.

"If you accept the challenge, you will be immersed in a military training program that ranges from marksmanship to orienteering, an academic program that offers over forty majors ranging from electrical engineering to philosophy, and a physical program that finds every cadet participating in an intercollegiate, club, or intramural-level sport. The fully funded, four-year college education includes tuition, room, board, and full medical and dental care. In return, you will graduate with a Bachelor of Science degree and be commissioned as a U.S. Army Officer with an active duty service obligation of five years active and three years reserve. Complete admissions guidance found online."

SELECTIVITY

Admissions Rating	98
# of applicants	15,408
% of applicants accepted	9
% of acceptees attending	85

FRESHMAN PROFILE

Range SAT Critical Reading	580–695
Range SAT Math	600–690
Range SAT Writing	550–665
Range ACT Composite	27–32
Minimum paper TOEFL	500
% graduated top 10% of class	71
% graduated top 25% of class	19
% graduated top 50% of class	8

DEADLINES

Regular	
Deadline	2/28
Nonfall registration?	No

APPLICANTS ALSO LOOK AT AND SOMETIMES PREFER

United States Naval Academy; United States Air Force Academy

FINANCIAL FACTS

Financial Aid Rating	60*
Annual in-state tuition	$0
Annual out-of-state tuition	$0
Room and board	$0
Required fees	$0
% UG borrow to pay for school	0
Average cumulative indebtedness	$0

UNITED STATES NAVAL ACADEMY

117 DECATUR ROAD, ANNAPOLIS, MD 21402 • ADMISSIONS: 410-293-4361 • FAX: 410-295-1815

STUDENTS SAY ". . ."

Academics

One of the nation's most prestigious institutions, the United States Naval Academy provides undergraduates with the opportunity "to be among America's next generation of leaders, and to represent the best this country has to offer." Certainly, these midshipmen are drawn to the promise of serving their country and "receiving an Ivy League-equivalent education" all while "push[ing themselves] further than [they] ever thought possible." Indeed, students greatly value the fact that, "[t]he curriculum is designed around training and developing leaders, and takes a whole-person aspect into view." As one senior explains, "character is a must, and ethical-leadership is the standard. We are encouraged and enabled to perform academically, physically, and morally." Additionally, undergrads speak highly of their overall classroom experience as well as their "excellent" professors. Many students are pleased to discover that their teachers focus on "how course material can be applied in the real world." They also feel that, by and large, professors here are "extremely knowledgeable in their field." Perhaps even more importantly, these midshipmen brag that instructors "are willing to devote a lot of extra time to help students outside of class." And a grateful sophomore emphasizes, "Professors will go out of their way to help students at practically every hour of the day." Surely, there's no doubt that the Naval Academy provides students "with the tools to succeed."

Life

"I call the Naval Academy the world's most beautiful prison...we work to defend freedom, not enjoy it." Yes, as this midshipman colorfully alludes, life at the Naval Academy is quite regimented and rules here are "strictly enforced." Students are quick to note that, with the exception of a few seniors, "no one is allowed to leave campus during the week." Nevertheless, the "lifestyle is very busy" despite the ban. An aerospace engineering major explains, "There is constantly something to be done between formations, room inspections, mandatory parades and evening lectures." Thankfully, even with these highly regulated schedules, students can participate in "a wide variety of extracurricular activities." Indeed, "from salsa dancing to marathon club to combat arms team, there is something for everyone to get involved with." When precious free time is available, many students enjoy engaging in outdoor activities such as "rock climbing, sailing, fishing, hiking, and camping." Additionally, a lot of midshipmen can be found "running and biking when the weather is good." The Academy itself has virtually no party scene since "it's a completely dry campus." And a sophomore warns that "if you are found with alcohol you are kicked out." However, during the weekends, midshipmen who are of age love sampling the bars around Annapolis. And all undergrads appreciate the school's proximity to both Baltimore and Washington, D.C. Finally, many midshipmen conclude by stressing that life at the Academy "gets better as you progress."

Student Body

Without a doubt, many midshipmen would define their peers as "hard charging," "motivated," "type A personalities." They could also easily be seen as "goal-oriented, physically fit" and occasionally "cynical about academy life." Of course, wandering around campus, it might appear as though the typical student is "a Caucasian male...very conservative, religious [and] very morally upright." However, a junior happily points out, "Our school is required to have students from all over the country, and people from very different backgrounds all meld together." And one sophomore explains that ultimately, "Because we all go through such rigorous evolutions every week, we have this unspoken understanding/respect for each other that acts as a great ice breaker when making friends."

E-MAIL: WEBMAIL@USNA.EDU • WEBSITE: WWW.USNA.EDU

THE PRINCETON REVIEW SAYS

Admissions

Very important factors considered include: Class rank, GPA, rigor of secondary school record, application essay, extracurricular activities, interview, recommendation(s), character/personal qualities, level of applicant's interest. *Important factors considered include:* Standardized test scores, talent/ability. *Other factors considered include:* First generation, geographical residence, racial/ethnic status, state residency, volunteer work, work experience, alumni/ae relations. SAT or ACT required. TOEFL required of all international applicants. *Academic units recommended:* 4 English; 4 mathematics; 2 science; (1 science lab); 2 foreign language; 2 history.

Financial Aid

The Navy pays for the tuition, room, and board, medical, and dental care of Naval Academy Midshipmen. Midshipmen also earn a monthly salary while at the academy.

The Inside Word

Securing admission to the Naval Academy is no easy feat. To begin with, a top-notch academic record is a must. In addition to strong GPA and test scores, applicants also have to secure an official nomination (typically granted by a U.S. representative, U.S. senator, or the Vice President). Further, candidates need to prove physical fitness, be an unmarried U.S. citizen between the ages of 17 and 23 and have no dependents. And, perhaps most importantly, applicants should also demonstrate strong moral character. Finally, the earlier you apply the better.

THE SCHOOL SAYS "..."

From the Admissions Office

"The finest young men and women in the country come to the Naval Academy to develop into leaders to serve the nation; USNA is the school of admirals, presidents, Nobel Prize winners, astronauts, jet pilots and CEOs. At USNA, you will have the opportunity to pursue a four-year degree program that develops you mentally, morally, and physically as no civilian college can. As you might expect, this program is demanding, but the opportunities are limitless and more than worth the effort.

"Upon throwing the iconic Midshipmen hat into the air at graduation, you will serve your country in one of dozens of professional fields—primarily aviation, submarines, ships, or the Marine Corps, but with additional limited options for the SEALs, medical, and other communities."

SELECTIVITY

Admissions Rating	98
# of applicants	19,146
% of applicants accepted	7
% of acceptees attending	85
# offered a place on the wait list	182
% accepting a place on wait list	73
% admitted from wait list	30

FRESHMAN PROFILE

Range SAT Critical Reading	570–680
Range SAT Math	610–700
% graduated top 10% of class	54
% graduated top 25% of class	81
% graduated top 50% of class	95

DEADLINES

Regular	
Deadline	1/31
Notification	4/15
Nonfall registration?	No

APPLICANTS ALSO LOOK AT AND OFTEN PREFER

Duke University; Harvard College; University of Virginia; United States Air Force Academy

AND SOMETIMES PREFER

Pennsylvania State University—University Park; Massachusetts Institute of Technology; Georgia Institute of Technology; United States Military Academy

AND RARELY PREFER

Boston University; St. John's College (MD); Purdue University—West Lafayette

FINANCIAL FACTS

Financial Aid Rating	60*
Annual in-state tuition	$0
Annual out-of-state tuition	$0
Room and board	$0
Required fees	$0

THE UNIVERSITY OF ALABAMA AT BIRMINGHAM

OFFICE OF UNDERGRADUATE ADMISSIONS, BIRMINGHAM, AL 35294-1150 • ADMISSIONS: 205-934-8221 • FAX: 205-975-7114

CAMPUS LIFE

Quality of Life Rating	91
Fire Safety Rating	86
Green Rating	69
Type of school	Public
Affiliation	No Affiliation
Environment	Metropolis

STUDENTS

Total undergrad enrollment	11,014
% male/female	42/58
% from out of state	8
% frosh live on campus	69
% ugrads live on campus	22
# of fraternities (% ugrad men join)	12 (4)
# of sororities (% ugrad women join)	10 (7)
% African American	27
% Asian	5
% Caucasian	59
% Hispanic	2
% Native American	<1
% international	2
# of countries represented	87

SURVEY SAYS . . .
Students are happy
Lab facilities are great
Students are friendly
Diverse student types on campus
Students get along with local community
Students involved in community service
Great off-campus food
Athletic facilities are great
Alumni active on campus
Active student government

ACADEMICS

Academic Rating	76
% students returning for sophomore year	80
% students graduating within 4 years	29
% students graduating within 6 years	47
Calendar	Semester
Student/faculty ratio	18:1
Profs interesting rating	81
Profs accessible rating	78
Most classes have 20–29 students.	
Most lab/discussion sessions have 20–29 students.	

MOST POPULAR MAJORS
biology; psychology; accounting

STUDENTS SAY "..."

Academics

At the University of Alabama at Birmingham, professors and administrators "care about you." "For many of the professors, it's not just about a grade in a class that you are taking. Rather it's an experience and preparation for any of our further endeavors." The professors here are "experts in their fields," they're "accessible and exciting," and "they're down-to-earth enough to give students a real view of what it's like to enter the world of academia." Despite the fact that this is a large university, there are "small class sizes in even the 100-level classes," and "many professors are available for help outside the classroom and care about teaching their subjects to the students." Of particular note, students say professors in the science departments "are great. They do a great job with interactive learning, and they really put forth every effort to make sure that those who want help get it." Academically, students feel that the workload is rigorous, but "certainly worth the challenge." As one student notes, a graduate tends to feel like "a better person for having experienced the challenge of UAB as well as the diversity." With an annual student forum, "the faculty and administration are very close with students and actively look to pursuing perfection and improving the collegiate experience."

Life

"Campus life is vibrant and exciting," boasts the student body. With UAB being "in the city of Birmingham, right outside of the school is something for everyone. There are malls, many restaurants, museums, and live music." UAB "strongly encourages their students to get involved on campus in some shape or form," presenting the student body with such opportunities as "the widely used Campus Recreation Center where students can take free U-Fit Classes (kickboxing, krunk/hip-hop class, yoga, spin, etc.), swim in the wave pool, climb the rock wall, or play intramurals (flag football, dodgeball, soccer, volleyball, slow pitch softball, etc.)." In addition, the surrounding city of Birmingham offers many venues for arts and entertainment; "students can dine or shop at the many malls located throughout the city. There are also many museums, art shows, concerts, dance clubs, [and] movie theaters to choose from." Students say that the list of attractions in Birmingham "goes on and on." "Students have the problem of having to narrow down their opportunities, rather than having to find something to do." Students "love the size of the school," finding it "like a small town in a big city." The impression is that "the campus is large enough that [you] meet and see new faces daily, but small enough to where [you] have personal relationships with teachers and the administration." Additionally, "there is a genuine interest among students in learning about the other cultures and religions represented on campus and in other cultures around the world."

Student Body

"Everyone is so diverse that there is literally something for everyone to get involved in." With more than 250 campus organizations, students say "you literally have to choose to not become involved." Many students love "how no one looks down on anyone," and how "everyone is so down-to-earth!" Most feel that they all come "from modest households." Regarding potential changes that could be made, "the meal plan situation could use some serious help." At UAB students feel, "it is easy to find a place where you fit in." Although the student body will insist that "there is no typical student!" In general, students are "hardworking and serious," while doing their best to always "enjoy weekend fun with friends."

586 ■ THE BEST 379 COLLEGES

THE UNIVERSITY OF ALABAMA AT BIRMINGHAM

FINANCIAL AID: 205-934-8223 • E-MAIL: UNDERGRADADMIT@UAB.EDU • WEBSITE: WWW.UAB.EDU

THE PRINCETON REVIEW SAYS

Admissions

Very important factors considered include: GPA, rigor of secondary school record, standardized test scores. *Other factors considered include:* SAT or ACT required; ACT with or without Writing component accepted. TOEFL required of all international applicants. *Academic units required:* 4 English; 3 mathematics; 3 science; (2 science lab); 3 social studies; 1 foreign language; 3 academic electives.

Financial Aid

Students should submit: FAFSA. The Princeton Review suggests that all financial aid forms be submitted as soon as possible after January 1. *Need-based scholarships/grants offered:* Federal Pell, SEOG, State scholarships/grants, private scholarships, the school's own gift aid, United Negro College Fund. *Loan aid offered:* Direct Subsidized Stafford Loans, Direct Unsubsidized Stafford Loans, Direct PLUS loans, Federal Perkins Loans, State Loans, College/university loans from institutional funds. Federal Work-Study Program available. Institutional employment available. Off-campus job opportunities are excellent.

The Inside Word

UAB's incoming class tends to have an average GPA of 3.5. The most important factors for admission are GPA and test scores. At the minimum, students need a GPA of 2.25 and a 950 SAT score. Administrators here are looking to admit a student body that's friendly, diverse, and intelligent with students who strive to be active in the community.

THE SCHOOL SAYS "..."

From the Admissions Office

"The University of Alabama at Birmingham (UAB) is a young, dynamic teaching and research university that has- in just four decades- won international renown for our collaborative and interdisciplinary culture. Our academic programs afford students unrivaled, hands-on experience in research and scholarship as UAB is first in the nation among public universities of federal research dollars per freshman. With over 110 areas of study, UAB attracts the best and brightest students from Alabama, the nation, and 109 countries around the globe.

"UAB students learn from- and work alongside- some of the world's top researchers, scholars, performers, and experts. Programs from the sciences and engineering to the arts and humanities give students the benefit of globally recognized faculty, exciting academic challenges, and experiences that will prepare them for a future in the job market.

"At UAB, we understand that having a fulfilling student life experience is as important as having a fulfilling academic experience. UAB has a rich mix of academic organizations, honor clubs, social fraternities and sororities, volunteer groups, and activities ranging from intramural sports and SGA to supporting Blazer sports. With more than 200 campus organizations to keep students involved, UAB offers the chance to make lifelong friendships while assisting in the development of skills essential to leadership and teamwork."

SELECTIVITY

Admissions Rating	77
# of applicants	5,689
% of applicants accepted	87
% of acceptees attending	36

FRESHMAN PROFILE

Range ACT Composite	22–28
Minimum paper TOEFL	500
Minimum web-based TOEFL	173
Average HS GPA	3.62
% graduated top 10% of class	30
% graduated top 25% of class	56
% graduated top 50% of class	83

DEADLINES

Regular	
Priority	6/1
Nonfall registration?	Yes

FINANCIAL FACTS

Financial Aid Rating	68
Annual in-state tuition	$8,904
Annual out-of-state tuition	$20,394
Required fees	$0
Books and supplies	$1,000
% needy frosh rec. need-based scholarship or grant aid	57
% needy UG rec. need-based scholarship or grant aid	64
% needy frosh rec. non-need-based scholarship or grant aid	63
% needy UG rec. non-need-based scholarship or grant aid	34
% needy frosh rec. need-based self-help aid	71
% needy UG rec. need-based self-help aid	78
% UG borrow to pay for school	59
Average cumulative indebtedness	$28,430
% frosh need fully met	18
% ugrads need fully met	11
Average % of frosh need met	42
Average % of ugrad need met	41

THE UNIVERSITY OF ALABAMA AT TUSCALOOSA

Box 870132, Tuscaloosa, AL 35487-0132 • Admissions: 205-348-5666 • Fax: 205-348-9046

CAMPUS LIFE

Quality of Life Rating	**69**
Fire Safety Rating	**70**
Green Rating	**79**
Type of school	Public
Affiliation	No Affiliation
Environment	City

STUDENTS

Total undergrad enrollment	28,692
% male/female	46/54
% from out of state	45
% frosh live on campus	91
% ugrads live on campus	26
# of fraternities (% ugrad men join)	32 (25)
# of sororities (% ugrad women join)	23 (35)
% African American	11
% Asian	1
% Caucasian	79
% Hispanic	3
% Native American	<1
% international	3
# of countries represented	77

SURVEY SAYS . . .
Athletic facilities are great
Everyone loves the Crimson Tide
Frats and sororities are popular
Student publications are popular

ACADEMICS

Academic Rating	**67**
% students returning for sophomore year	87
% students graduating within 4 years	43
% students graduating within 6 years	67
Calendar	Semester
Student/faculty ratio	21:1
Profs interesting rating	72
Profs accessible rating	74

Most classes have 10–19 students.
Most lab/discussion sessions have
20–29 students.

MOST POPULAR MAJORS
marketing; nursing; business administration
and management

STUDENTS SAY ". . ."

Academics
The University of Alabama is a ridiculously affordable, "technologically advanced," "student-centered" institution that enjoys an outrageous degree of alumni support. "Course offerings are pretty diverse," and there are "tons of majors." Highlights include a "great" engineering college and three honors programs. Other standout programs include business, communication studies, and nursing. Some students say that the "bold and visionary" top brass runs the school "fairly well." Others gripe that the administration is "very bogged down in red tape." "Working with the administration is really terrible sometimes," undergrads say. Professors here are "top researchers or writers in their fields," and some are "very enthusiastic about having undergraduate students helping them with research." The faculty as a whole is also "approachable" and "generally very easy to get in touch with for outside assistance." Teaching ability is "hit-or-miss," though. While many professors are "very animated and interesting to listen to," "others do not have the same talent." "Being a great researcher does not necessarily make a person a good teacher," notes one student.

Life
"An atmosphere of almost antebellum charm" permeates this "pretty" campus. "On sunny days in the fall and spring, students enjoy studying and playing on the quad." Recreational facilities are "excellent." "Life during football season revolves around football." So does morale. Win or lose, though, UA boasts "one of the best college football atmospheres in the country. On Saturdays when the Crimson Tide plays at home, the campus is "a sea of tents for tailgating," "and Alabama fans are singing the fight song." Otherwise, "the Greek organizations rule this campus." They wield "an inordinate amount of power" in student government as well. Whether you pledge or not, though, students promise "an outstanding social atmosphere." "While not everyone participates in the party scene on campus, it is very popular." In addition to the house parties and the festivities at the frat houses, "people enjoying going to the bars on the strip." "Comfort" abounds in surrounding Tuscaloosa, and it is "definitely a college town." People are "very open and courteous" to the students, and virtually everything you need is within "walking distance." When students at UA hanker for more urban environs, "Birmingham is only an hour away, and there is plenty to do there."

Student Body
Students here are "extremely friendly" and "usually well-dressed and well-mannered." "People tend to be a bit conservative," and "a lot are religious." "The typical student is active in a few organizations, makes decent grades, and finds time to relax, too." African American students are the largest minority group. They represent more than 10 percent of the student body. Some students maintain that UA is "not diverse socially, ideologically, and culturally." "The different ethnic groups stick together," they say. They look around campus and see "frat boys or sorority girls for the most part"—"same hair, same sunglasses with a string on the back, and stupid visors." Other students vigorously disagree. "We truly aren't a university filled with cookie-cutter people," asserts one student. "There are many diverse groups of students who all have their own roles on campus." "It is easy for someone to come from up north and say this campus is full of close-minded Southern Baptist Republicans, just like it is easy for someone to come from a small town…and think this campus is full of liberal heathens," points out another student. "Few people are really atypical, because no matter where you fall in any category, there are people around you who you can connect with."

FINANCIAL AID: 205-348-6756 • E-MAIL: ADMISSIONS@UA.EDU • WEBSITE: WWW.UA.EDU

THE PRINCETON REVIEW SAYS

Admissions

Very important factors considered include: GPA, rigor of secondary school record, standardized test scores. *Important factors considered include:* Class rank. *Other factors considered include:* Application essay, extracurricular activities, first generation, interview, recommendation(s), talent/ability, volunteer work, work experience, alumni/ae relations, character/personal qualities. SAT or ACT required; ACT with Writing component required. TOEFL required of all international applicants. *Academic units required:* 4 English; 3 mathematics; 3 science; (2 science lab); 4 social studies; 1 foreign language; 5 academic electives. *Academic units recommended:* 4 English; 3 mathematics; 3 science; (2 science lab); 4 social studies; 1 foreign language; 5 academic electives.

Financial Aid

Students should submit: FAFSA. The Princeton Review suggests that all financial aid forms be submitted as soon as possible after January 1. *Need-based scholarships/grants offered:* Federal Pell, SEOG, State scholarships/grants, private scholarships, the school's own gift aid, federal nursing scholarships. *Loan aid offered:* Direct Subsidized Stafford Loans, Direct Unsubsidized Stafford Loans, Direct PLUS loans, Federal Perkins Loans, College/university loans from institutional funds. Federal Work-Study Program available. Institutional employment available. Off-campus job opportunities are good.

The Inside Word

The University of Alabama relies heavily on objective data in the application process. Admission is not highly competitive, and applicants with satisfactory grades and modest test scores are likely to be accepted.

THE SCHOOL SAYS "..."

From the Admissions Office

"Since its founding in 1831 as the first public university in the state, the University of Alabama has been committed to providing the best, most complete education possible for its students. Our commitment to that goal means that as times change, we sharpen our focus and methods to keep our graduates competitive in their fields. By offering outstanding teaching in a solid core curriculum enhanced by multimedia classrooms and campus-wide computer labs, the University of Alabama keeps its focus on the future while maintaining a traditional college atmosphere. Extensive international study opportunities, internship programs, and cooperative education placements help our students prepare for successful futures. Consisting of eleven colleges and schools offering 220 degrees in more than 100 fields of study, the university gives its students a wide range of choices and offers courses of study at the bachelor's, master's, specialist, and doctoral levels. The university emphasizes quality and breadth of academic opportunities and challenging programs for well-prepared students through its Honors College, including the University Honors Program, International Honors Program, and Computer-Based Honors Programs and Blount Undergraduate Initiative (liberal arts program). Thirty-one percent of undergraduates are from out of state, providing an enriching social and cultural environment.

"Applicants may submit either the SAT or the ACT. The writing component is required for admission."

SELECTIVITY

Admissions Rating	88
# of applicants	30,975
% of applicants accepted	57
% of acceptees attending	37

FRESHMAN PROFILE

Range SAT Critical Reading	490–620
Range SAT Math	500–640
Range SAT Writing	480–600
Range ACT Composite	22–30
Minimum paper TOEFL	527
Minimum web-based TOFFL	71
Average HS GPA	3.60
% graduated top 10% of class	41
% graduated top 25% of class	60
% graduated top 50% of class	83

DEADLINES

Regular	
Priority	2/1
Nonfall registration?	Yes

APPLICANTS ALSO LOOK AT AND OFTEN PREFER

Florida State University; University of Georgia; Duke University; University of Tennessee; Vanderbilt University

AND SOMETIMES PREFER

Auburn University; Tulane University; Samford University; Louisiana State University—Baton Rouge

FINANCIAL FACTS

Financial Aid Rating	64
Annual in-state tuition	$9,450
Annual out-of-state tuition	$23,950
Room and board	$8,756
Required fees	$0
Books and supplies	$1,200
% needy frosh rec. need-based scholarship or grant aid	75
% needy UG rec. need-based scholarship or grant aid	72
% needy frosh rec. non-need-based scholarship or grant aid	58
% needy UG rec. non-need-based scholarship or grant aid	44
% needy frosh rec. need-based self-help aid	71
% needy UG rec. need-based self-help aid	82
% frosh rec. any financial aid	76
% UG rec. any financial aid	71
% UG borrow to pay for school	46
Average cumulative indebtedness	$28,508
% frosh need fully met	22
% ugrads need fully met	14
Average % of frosh need met	53
Average % of ugrad need met	49

UNIVERSITY OF ARIZONA

PO Box 210073, Tucson, AZ 85721-0073 • Admissions: 520-621-3237 • Fax: 520-621-9799

CAMPUS LIFE

Quality of Life Rating	84
Fire Safety Rating	87
Green Rating	96
Type of school	Public
Affiliation	No Affiliation
Environment	Metropolis

STUDENTS

Total undergrad enrollment	31,399
% male/female	48/52
% from out of state	26
% frosh from public high school	90
% frosh live on campus	72
% ugrads live on campus	20
# of fraternities	22
# of sororities	25
% African American	3
% Asian	6
% Caucasian	55
% Hispanic	24
% Native American	1
% international	6
# of countries represented	108

SURVEY SAYS . . .
Students are happy
Lab facilities are great
Career services are great
Great off-campus food
Athletic facilities are great
Lots of beer drinking
Everyone loves the Wildcats
Frats and sororities are popular
Active student government

ACADEMICS

Academic Rating	75
% students returning for sophomore year	82
% students graduating within 4 years	40
% students graduating within 6 years	61
Calendar	Semester
Student/faculty ratio	22:1
Profs interesting rating	68
Profs accessible rating	70

Most classes have 20–29 students.
Most lab/discussion sessions have 20–29 students.

MOST POPULAR MAJORS
psychology; political science; cell and molecular biology

STUDENTS SAY ". . ."

Academics

In the simplest terms, University of Arizona is all about providing its students with "endless opportunities." Located on a "gorgeous" campus in vibrant Tucson, UA offers a "great education" in a "relaxed community." Students here truly appreciate the university's "strong commitment to undergraduate research." Moreover, Arizona really "helps make the cost of education manageable," even "offering many scholarships to out-of-state students who qualify." While undergrads are impressed by a myriad of disciplines, they call special attention to the "excellent" agriculture department and the "great" engineering program. Students also highlight the physiology program and note that UA is "the only university that offers an undergraduate major through its medical school." Undergrads do admit that professors can range from "very boring" to "extremely fun and interesting." One sophomore does assure us, by and large, "Professors are enthusiastic and genuinely care about students." A knowledgeable junior adds, "As I get into the higher level classes or the classes that are more focused on my major, I find that the teachers are more enthusiastic and dedicated to their students to see that they succeed." Fortunately, "one thing that is consistent about all of them (and the TAs as well) is their availability through office hours for one-on-one instruction." As this public health major concludes, "The University of Arizona is an institution that provides a well-rounded education and numerous opportunities that prepare students for their future ambitions, whatever they may be."

Life

Students at the UA are "motivated academically" and devote a decent percentage of their weekdays to hitting the books. Of course, undergrads here are also "very social," and as a sophomore enthusiastically shares, "There is always something to do on campus, and there are a variety of clubs to get involved in." Indeed, there are a number of activities available, ranging "from swing dance to intramural volleyball," which "help alleviate stress." Additionally, "people are really into the athletics. It builds school spirit for everyone involved, [and] tailgates are common on the weekends." Greek life is also extremely popular, and "on the weekends, frats have huge [theme] parties including ZBTahiti, AEPirates, Heaven and Hell, Swampwater, Pajama Jam, and many more." Undergrads also enjoy hometown Tucson, which has "great live music, art, and cinema." The city also "generally has a lot of community activities like Day of the Dead, which is extremely popular." Lastly, students also like to take advantage of the numerous outdoor recreation options available, and many often go "hiking or biking at the nearby mountain ranges."

Student Body

Undergrads at UA report that the "relaxed" nature of their peers contributes to a "laid-back" atmosphere, which permeates the campus. While some students are most assuredly "in school to learn," others seem "to party their way through." However, an optical engineering major confidently states, "There is a place for you to fit in no matter what you want to get out of your college education." A fellow engineering student adds, "Most students are very friendly and will greet each other around campus." UA is quite "diverse," and you can easily find students of/from all different "socio-economic statuses, states, countries, races, ethnicities, ages, etc." A junior tells us that people often make friends by simply getting "involved with something they are interested in and meeting like-minded individuals." One thing that unites these undergrads? Nearly all these "Wildcats" are "full of pride for their school." Perhaps this content freshman says it best, "In a school of 30,000, there is really no typical student, but with such a great number of students, people find their niche."

FINANCIAL AID: 520-621-1858 • E-MAIL: ADMISSIONS@ARIZONA.EDU • WEBSITE: WWW.ARIZONA.EDU

THE PRINCETON REVIEW SAYS

Admissions

Very important factors considered include: GPA, rigor of secondary school record, standardized test scores, application essay. *Important factors considered include:* Extracurricular activities, talent/ability, character/personal qualities, level of applicant's interest. *Other factors considered include:* Class rank, first generation, recommendation(s), volunteer work, work experience. SAT and SAT Subject Tests or ACT considered if submitted; ACT with or without Writing component accepted. TOEFL required of all international applicants. *Academic units required:* 4 English; 4 mathematics; 3 science; (3 science lab); 1 social studies; 2 foreign language; 1 history. *Academic units recommended:* 4 English; 4 mathematics; 3 science; (3 science lab); 1 social studies; 2 foreign language; 1 history.

Financial Aid

Students should submit: FAFSA. The Princeton Review suggests that all financial aid forms be submitted as soon as possible after January 1. *Need-based scholarships/grants offered:* Federal Pell, SEOG, State scholarships/grants, private scholarships, the school's own gift aid, federal nursing scholarships. *Loan aid offered:* Direct Subsidized Stafford Loans, Direct Unsubsidized Stafford Loans, Direct PLUS loans, Federal Perkins Loans, Federal Nursing Loans, College/university loans from institutional funds. Federal Work-Study Program available. Institutional employment available. Off-campus job opportunities are good.

The Inside Word

Admission to the UA is competitive, and you'll need to demonstrate achievement in college prep courses. Arizona resident should take note: Candidates applying from within the state who graduate in the top 25 percent of their class and meet all course requirements gain automatic acceptance through the assured admission program. Applicants should also recognize that some programs, such as the College of Engineering and College of Fine Arts, mandate additional materials and requirements.

THE SCHOOL SAYS "..."

From the Admissions Office

"The University of Arizona offers endless opportunities for its students to make an impact on campus and beyond. From day one students are part of Arizona's mission to provide every undergrad with gain real-world experience in the form of internships, research, study abroad, or community service by the time they graduate. Arizona boasts many of the nation's best programs in fields as diverse as astronomy, business, nursing, management information systems, computer and aerospace engineering, anthropology, sociology, and creative writing. The UA fills its world-class research curriculum with a faculty that includes Nobel and Pulitzer Prize winners and offers more than 100 majors, as well as minors and many concentration options. Our students also enjoy an active, cheerful, and inviting campus atmosphere that includes more than 500 student clubs and organizations, conference-winning and national title–winning basketball, baseball, swimming, softball, and football teams; and countless recreational opportunities."

SELECTIVITY

Admissions Rating	79
# of applicants	26,481
% of applicants accepted	78
% of acceptees attending	33

FRESHMAN PROFILE

Range SAT Critical Reading	480–600
Range SAT Math	490–620
Range SAT Writing	470–590
Range ACT Composite	21–27
Minimum web-based TOEFL	173
Average HS GPA	3.40
% graduated top 10% of class	31
% graduated top 25% of class	60
% graduated top 50% of class	88

DEADLINES

Regular	
Priority	5/1
Deadline	5/1
Nonfall registration?	Yes

APPLICANTS ALSO LOOK AT AND OFTEN PREFER
University of Washington

AND RARELY PREFER
Baylor University; Arizona State University

FINANCIAL FACTS

Financial Aid Rating	70
Annual in-state tuition	$9,388
Annual out-of-state tuition	$20,070
Room and board	$9,714
Required fees	$1,003
Books and supplies	$1,000
% needy frosh rec. need-based scholarship or grant aid	91
% needy UG rec. need-based scholarship or grant aid	88
% needy frosh rec. non-need-based scholarship or grant aid	13
% needy UG rec. non-need-based scholarship or grant aid	8
% needy frosh rec. need-based self-help aid	53
% needy UG rec. need-based self-help aid	62
% UG borrow to pay for school	49
Average cumulative indebtedness	$22,497
% frosh need fully met	15
% ugrads need fully met	11
Average % of frosh need met	65
Average % of ugrad need met	62

UNIVERSITY OF ARKANSAS—FAYETTEVILLE

232 SILAS HUNT HALL, FAYETTEVILLE, AR 72701 • ADMISSIONS: 479-575-5346 • FAX: 479-575-7515

CAMPUS LIFE

Quality of Life Rating	83
Fire Safety Rating	83
Green Rating	87
Type of school	Public
Affiliation	No Affiliation
Environment	Town

STUDENTS

Total undergrad enrollment	20,776
% male/female	49/51
% from out of state	37
% frosh from public high school	83
% frosh live on campus	86
% ugrads live on campus	29
# of fraternities (% ugrad men join)	16 (25)
# of sororities (% ugrad women join)	11 (41)
% African American	5
% Asian	2
% Caucasian	79
% Hispanic	6
% Native American	1
% international	3
# of countries represented	122

SURVEY SAYS . . .
Athletic facilities are great
Students love Fayetteville, AR
Everyone loves the Razorbacks
Frats and sororities are popular

ACADEMICS

Academic Rating	73
% students returning for sophomore year	82
% students graduating within 4 years	37
% students graduating within 6 years	60
Calendar	Semester
Student/faculty ratio	19:1
Profs interesting rating	67
Profs accessible rating	68

Most classes have 10–19 students.
Most lab/discussion sessions have 20–29 students.

MOST POPULAR MAJORS
finance; marketing; journalism

STUDENTS SAY ". . ."

Academics

The University of Arkansas is affordable, "student-centered," and large but not gargantuan. Though you'll see some sizeable lectures during your first year, most classes are "relatively small." "The facilities are exceptional" and otherwise "state-of-the-art." More than 100 undergraduate majors and programs are available. The Sam Walton College of Business is awash in cash and "one of the strongest assets." Engineering majors can participate in cutting-edge research. Agricultural programs are strong and diverse. The honors college is "wonderful." Also, some 25 percent of all Arkansas students study abroad. There are summer programs available in China and Egypt, just to a name two examples. Programs during the academic year take place in every nook and cranny of the globe. Student opinion is split with regard to the administration. Some students call the management "very friendly." "Things run pretty smoothly," they say. Others contend that UA is "overly bureaucratic." "The odds of being sent to three different buildings, none of which is right, are pretty much even," wagers one malcontent. Despite "a few really atrocious instructors," students generally praise Arkansas's "dynamic faculty." "The professors are almost always good teachers," and they "know their material." Outside of class, professors tend to be "accessible" and "willing to do anything it takes for the success of their students."

Life

"Parking is horrible," but UA boasts a "beautiful," "well-defined campus with lots of green space." The rolling hills provide plenty of "great exercise," too. Students here reportedly enjoy a "vibrant extracurricular and social scene." "There are lots of things to do that don't involve booze." With more than 300 clubs and groups to choose from "the vast majority of students participate in at least a few campus organizations." "Greek life is prevalent," according to some students. "Intramural sports are popular." Razorback football "is the big highlight of the fall," and the campus has "a lot of spirit" for the beloved Hogs. There are ample activities that do involve booze as well. "Parties are everywhere." "A lot of people will go to the fraternity houses" for revelry. There's also "great nightlife" and "a very enthusiastic bar scene" off campus. "Funky," "charming," and "not-too-expensive," Fayetteville is, by all accounts, a "pretty neat town." Eclectic restaurants and live music venues are ample. "The always-enticing Dickson Street," "located a couple blocks away," is the hub of it all. "On the weekends, it borders on insanity." For outdoorsy types, wilderness activities abound throughout northwestern Arkansas. "The nearby mountains" provide numerous opportunities for climbing, biking, and hiking.

Student Body

They typical student here is "overly friendly," "fun-loving," "at least somewhat religious, and has a southern accent." Most students come "from either Arkansas or Texas." There are "a lot of international students," but "there is little ethnic diversity." Like at virtually every other flagship state university, you'll find "all kinds of students" on this campus. Fayetteville is called "the melting pot of Arkansas." Politics range from "conservative" to "incredibly liberal." "Students come from all walks of life and have many different experiences to share with others." "Party-frat kids abound," as do "southern sorority girls who walk to class in pearls and heels." However, you'll also find "hicks," "artists, musicians, nerds," and "NPR listening, sandal-wearing, health-food-shopping people," as well as the occasional "middle-aged boomer returning to school to start a whole new career." "There is always someone just as weird as you to run with," and students generally "mesh well" even if "groups don't often commingle."

UNIVERSITY OF ARKANSAS—FAYETTEVILLE

FINANCIAL AID: 479-575-3806 • E-MAIL: UOFA@UARK.EDU • WEBSITE: WWW.UARK.EDU

THE PRINCETON REVIEW SAYS

Admissions

Very important factors considered include: Class rank, GPA, rigor of secondary school record, standardized test scores. *Important factors considered include:* State residency. *Other factors considered include:* Application essay, extracurricular activities, geographical residence, recommendation(s), talent/ability, volunteer work, work experience, character/personal qualities. SAT or ACT required; ACT with or without Writing component accepted. TOEFL required of all international applicants. *Academic units required:* 4 English; 4 mathematics; 3 science; (2 science lab); 3 social studies; 2 academic electives. *Academic units recommended:* 4 English; 4 mathematics; 3 science; (2 science lab); 3 social studies; 2 foreign language.

Financial Aid

Students should submit: FAFSA. The Princeton Review suggests that all financial aid forms be submitted as soon as possible after January 1. *Need-based scholarships/grants offered:* Federal Pell, SEOG, State scholarships/grants, private scholarships, the school's own gift aid. *Loan aid offered:* Direct Subsidized Stafford Loans, Direct Unsubsidized Stafford Loans, Direct PLUS loans, Federal Perkins Loans, State Loans, College/university loans from institutional funds. Applicants will be notified of awards beginning 4/1. Federal Work-Study Program available. Institutional employment available.

The Inside Word

The admissions policy at the University of Arkansas is very straightforward. You need a 3.0 grade-point average (on a 4.0 scale) in your serious academic course work and at least a 20 on the ACT. The SAT is fine, too, as long as get a comparable minimum score. If you fail to meet these requirements, you still may gain admission based on a case-by-case review process. Also, UA has a rolling admissions policy. As such, candidates will find it in their best interest to apply early.

THE SCHOOL SAYS "..."

From the Admissions Office

"The University of Arkansas, the flagship campus of the University of Arkansas System, is located in Fayetteville and overlooks the beautiful Ozark Mountains. The university is both the major land-grant university for Arkansas and the state university, encompassing more than 130 buildings on 345 acres and providing more than 200 graduate and undergraduate academic programs—more than some universities twice its size. At the same time, the University of Arkansas maintains a low student-to-faculty ratio—currently nineteen to one—that makes personal attention possible. The university aggressively promotes undergraduate research in virtually every discipline and makes higher education affordable with competitively priced tuition and generous financial aid. In the last decade, university undergraduates have earned many honors: forty-eight received Goldwater Scholarships; thirteen have been recognized by the USA Today All-USA College Academic Team. There have been ninety-two National Science Foundation graduate fellows; fifty Fulbright scholars; three British Marshall scholars and five Truman scholars. Seven undergraduates have received Udall scholarships; five earned Madison scholarships; three have received Tylenol scholarships; and ten named Rhodes scholars. Quality programs, affordable tuition and the level of student achievement all contribute to the University of Arkansas consistently being ranked in the top tier of national universities. The city of Fayetteville is home to more than 76,000 people and is growing every day. Northwest Arkansas is the headquarters to several major international corporations that have close ties to the university: Tyson Foods, the world's largest protein producer; J.B. Hunt Transport Services Inc., a major transportation and logistics company; and Wal-Mart Stores Inc., the world's largest corporation. Fayetteville has been named 'One of America's Most Livable Cities,' 'One of America's 'Hottest' Cities,' one of the nation's 'least stressful' metro areas, and among the 'Best Places to Live in America' by publications such as Forbes, Frommer's Guide, and Money magazine. The university enjoys academic partnerships with the world-class Crystal Bridges Museum of American Art, located in nearby Bentonville, Ark.'"

SELECTIVITY

Admissions Rating	86
# of applicants	18,908
% of applicants accepted	59
% of acceptees attending	39

FRESHMAN PROFILE

Range SAT Critical Reading	500–600
Range SAT Math	520–630
Range ACT Composite	23–28
Minimum paper TOEFL	550
Minimum web-based TOEFL	213
Average HS GPA	3.62
% graduated top 10% of class	28
% graduated top 25% of class	57
% graduated top 50% of class	88

DEADLINES

Early action	
Deadline	11/1
Notification	12/15
Regular	
Priority	11/1
Deadline	8/1
Nonfall registration?	Yes

FINANCIAL FACTS

Financial Aid Rating	71
Annual in-state tuition	$6,354
Annual out-of-state tuition	$17,610
Room and board	$9,042
Required fees	$1,464
Books and supplies	$1,380
% needy frosh rec. need-based scholarship or grant aid	83
% needy UG rec. need-based scholarship or grant aid	79
% needy frosh rec. non-need-based scholarship or grant aid	17
% needy UG rec. non-need-based scholarship or grant aid	11
% needy frosh rec. need-based self-help aid	67
% needy UG rec. need-based self-help aid	74
% UG borrow to pay for school	45
Average cumulative indebtedness	$24,647
% frosh need fully met	24
% ugrads need fully met	18
Average % of frosh need met	68
Average % of ugrad need met	60

UNIVERSITY OF CALIFORNIA—BERKELEY

110 Sproul Hall, Berkeley, CA 94720-5800 • Admissions: 510-642-3175 • Fax: 510-642-7333

STUDENTS SAY "..."

Academics

The flagship campus of the University of California school system with a "highly respectable name," UC Berkeley "has great faculty, great research, great classes, and everyone knows it." The school "really encourages us to go out and learn, both inside and outside the classroom," and there is a real commitment to "a well- rounded, diverse education" that permeates the curriculum. "Berkeley is defined by its open, liberal education and culture for independent and collaborative thinking across all fields," sums up a senior molecular toxicology major.

Professors here are "fantastic," "the best in their fields," and each "offers a diverse perspective" toward the academic experience. There are some complaints that larger freshman courses can be "somewhat terrible" and "experience from professors can range widely" (though graduate student instructors "are very accessible and helpful"), but it is universally agreed that "after getting through lower division prerequisite classes, [the] academic experience has significantly improved." All faculty "have full command of their subjects and are determined to find an answer to anything they don't know, within their discipline."

UC Berkeley is known for having "some of the best engineering programs across the board among colleges," and it doesn't hurt that the school's Silicon Valley home is the "best location in the country for entrepreneurship and innovation." "Top-notch" research abounds, and there are "plenty of opportunities for undergrads to engage in it." "Berkeley will offer you all the opportunity you can handle, it's up to you to take hold of I," says a student.

Life

There's "a constant buzz of student activity that drives everyday life" at Cal, where "academics are a priority" and "every single person has something that they are very passionate about and talking to them for five minutes about it makes you wonder if you should change your major." Students also really appreciate all of the tradition present at Cal. "It's a great choice for students who want the feeling of a big state school but want to also be pushed to their limits," says one.

Berkeley is "very hard so free time isn't like it is at other places," but an "amazing community" of student run organizations and "clubs, sports, student-run classes, seminars, [and] research opportunities" are among the "many different venues for people to find their passion." There's a lot to do off-campus in the downtown Berkeley area, and using the BART is "really convenient and time-saving to go to San Francisco." On campus, there is everything "from frat houses to coffee shop discussions, hiking the fire trails to studying for finals." In those moments that studying abates (a particular rarity for engineers), a lot of students enjoy going to football games, restaurant hopping, or (especially during welcome week) party hopping. Many people here do like to party and drink, but "if that's not your style there are plenty of other to spend time with."

Student Body

Berkeley is a large school, so clusters naturally form along lines such as major or dorm, but all "mix among each other easily." "From clubs to DeCal courses, there is no way a student will not make a group of friends while here at Cal," says a junior. Most Berkeley students are generally "politically liberal, nonreligious, and pretty independent," and there is a large Asian student contingent here. One of the defining characteristics of a Cal student is "the ability to hold high level conversation about basically anything." Everyone is accepted in here, "regardless of their sexual orientation, religion or political beliefs."

FINANCIAL AID: 510-642-6442 • WEBSITE: WWW.BERKELEY.EDU

THE PRINCETON REVIEW SAYS

Admissions

Very important factors considered include: GPA, rigor of secondary school record, standardized test scores, application essay, talent/ability. *Important factors considered include:* Extracurricular activities, volunteer work, work experience, character/personal qualities. *Other factors considered include:* First generation, state residency. SAT or ACT required; ACT with Writing component required. TOEFL required of all international applicants. *Academic units required:* 4 English; 3 mathematics; 2 science; (2 science lab); 2 foreign language; 2 history; 1 academic elective; 1 visual/performing arts. *Academic units recommended:* 4 English; 4 mathematics; 3 science; (3 science lab); 3 foreign language; 2 history; 1 academic elective; 1 visual/performing arts.

Financial Aid

Students should submit: FAFSA, State aid form. Regular filing deadline is 3/2. The Princeton Review suggests that all financial aid forms be submitted as soon as possible after January 1. *Need-based scholarships/grants offered:* Federal Pell, SEOG, State scholarships/grants, private scholarships, the school's own gift aid. *Loan aid offered:* Direct Subsidized Stafford Loans, Direct Unsubsidized Stafford Loans, Direct PLUS loans, Federal Perkins Loans. Applicants will be notified of awards beginning 3/31. Federal Work-Study Program available. Institutional employment available. Off-campus job opportunities are excellent.

The Inside Word

UC Berkeley is a top-notch public university with a well-regarded English and Literature department. Importance is placed on the totality of a student's application with a joint focus on the personal essay and academic excellence as noted by a student's GPA. Class rank isn't considered. The school is home to an incredible amount of students with as wide a range of interests. Successful applicants here are generally stellar both academically and personally. Applications, especially the essay, should create a picture of a unique candidate with a diversity of skills to offer this active community.

THE SCHOOL SAYS "..."

From the Admissions Office

"One of the top public universities in the nation and the world, the University of California—Berkeley offers a vast range of courses and a full menu of extracurricular activities. Berkeley's academic programs are internationally recognized for their excellence. Undergraduates can choose one of 100 majors. Thirty-five departments are top ranked, more than any other college or university in the country. Access to one of the foremost university libraries enriches studies. There are twenty-three specialized libraries on campus and distinguished museums of anthropology, paleontology, and science.

"All applicants must take the ACT plus writing or the SAT Reasoning Test. UC admissions requirements are found at http://www.universityofcalifornia.edu/admissions/freshman/requirements/index.html."

SELECTIVITY

Admissions Rating	98
# of applicants	67,717
% of applicants accepted	18
% of acceptees attending	0

FRESHMAN PROFILE

Range SAT Critical Reading	600–730
Range SAT Math	650–770
Range SAT Writing	620–740
Range ACT Composite	27–33
Minimum paper TOEFL	550
Average HS GPA	3.86
% graduated top 10% of class	98
% graduated top 25% of class	100
% graduated top 50% of class	100

DEADLINES

Regular	
Deadline	11/30
Nonfall registration?	Yes

APPLICANTS ALSO LOOK AT AND OFTEN PREFER
Stanford University

AND SOMETIMES PREFER
University of California—Los Angeles

AND RARELY PREFER
University of California—Santa Barbara; University of California—Davis; University of California—Santa Cruz; University of California—San Diego

FINANCIAL FACTS

Financial Aid Rating	70
Annual in-state tuition	$11,220
Annual out-of-state tuition	$34,098
Room and board	$15,180
Required fees	$1,644
Books and supplies	$1,226

UNIVERSITY OF CALIFORNIA—DAVIS

UC DAVIS WELCOME CENTER 550 ALUMNI LANE DAVIS, CA 95616 • ADMISSIONS: 530-752-2971 • FAX: 530-752-1280

STUDENTS SAY ". . ."

Academics

Backed by "strong science programs," "cutting-edge research," and "the incredible amount of internships available," UC Davis is many students' idea of great academia. It's not every university where you can "touch a pig, pet a baby goat, and milk a cow if you'd like." But what else would you expect from "one of the top agriculture and animal science schools in the United States?" For those who don't handle stress all that well, "UC Davis is the perfect combination of a top-rated institution and a calm and non-competitive student body." This "prestigious" school is located in northern California and is well-known for its "agricultural sustainability and awareness." "The campus is very green and embraces biking to the maximum." "If you can't bike, you probably shouldn't go here." Opinions on professors vary but most students agree that they "are all experts in their field." Some students report that UC Davis professors "are driven by their research" and "tend to take teaching as a secondary position to [it]. However, when they integrate their research and knowledge of the subject in their classes, it can make for a very interesting and enlightening education." Students also point out that UC Davis offers "a lot of majors to choose from and a variety of interesting classes that most schools don't offer." Not everyone is comfortable with classes divided by the quarter system because "learning material and exams go by kind of fast." For some, "the quarter system is a drastic change from the pace, but not necessarily the demands, of the semester system. In what most schools cover in about fifteen weeks, UC Davis covers in ten weeks."

Life

Known for its "good weather," UC Davis is located about "an hour out of the Bay Area [where] every outdoor option [is] possible." Davis is "a quaint little college town "with a great personality," and "the campus is beautiful." It is a "beautiful farmland university" that is "very safe and clean." One student comments, "I love how there are places where you can take a break and a nap without worrying about your safety." Although there are your typical "parties at frat houses," there are tons of other forms of entertainment to be had. "There's more than just partying. The student clubs open you up to anything from rock climbing and water skiing to badminton and pool." There is also a bowling alley on campus. The school is proactive in promoting both "sustainable living" and a "healthy lifestyle." There is a "good variety of healthy meals/food to choose from (and local products)," and students are encouraged to exercise and make use of the numerous bike paths (albeit "bumpy" ones). According to one student, "The gym is the best of any campus I have seen." There is also a "giant library" that gets rave reviews from many students. When venturing off campus, "The Davis Farmer's Market is legendary and a requirement at least once while you're here. There are also a great many small businesses and fantastic restaurants downtown that offer students great experiences at fairly reasonable prices." The "small" town of Davis has a "community feel" as well as a "college town atmosphere." As one student eloquently explains, "Although it smells like cows, you'll miss it after you graduate."

Student Body

"The student body here is very diverse." They range from "athletes to engineers. But they all have one thing in common. They are here to have a serious college education." The vibe from students at UC Davis is "liberal, challenging, and accepting," while also "very friendly, easygoing," and "environmentally aware." Although students are "very studious," they "know how to manage their priorities and still find ways to enjoy themselves." Even though "everyone is so different; you have the agriculture people, the political science people, and the premed people all mixed together," problems are minimal. "everyone is so accepting of everyone else and fitting in just comes naturally because everyone gets along very well." "There is such a huge variety of clubs, fraternities/sororities, societies and groups on campus, it is almost impossible to not have friends."

FINANCIAL AID: 530-752-2390 • E-MAIL: ADMISSIONS.UCDAVIS.EDU/CONTACT • WEBSITE: WWW.UCDAVIS.EDU

THE PRINCETON REVIEW SAYS

Admissions

Very important factors considered include: GPA, rigor of secondary school record, standardized test scores, application essay. *Important factors considered include:* Extracurricular activities, talent/ability, volunteer work, character/personal qualities. *Other factors considered include:* First generation, work experience. SAT or ACT required; ACT with Writing component required. TOEFL required of all international applicants. *Academic units required:* 4 English; 3 mathematics; 2 science; (2 science lab); 1 social studies; 2 foreign language; 1 history; 1 visual/performing arts. *Academic units recommended:* 4 English; 4 mathematics; 3 science; (3 science lab); 1 social studies; 3 foreign language; 1 history; 1 academic elective; 1 visual/performing arts.

Financial Aid

Students should submit: FAFSA, State aid form. The Princeton Review suggests that all financial aid forms be submitted as soon as possible after January 1. *Need-based scholarships/grants offered:* Federal Pell, SEOG, scholarships/grants, private scholarships, the school's own gift aid. *Loan aid offered:* Direct Subsidized Stafford Loans, Direct Unsubsidized Stafford Loans, Direct PLUS loans, Federal Perkins Loans, College/university loans from institutional funds. Applicants will be notified of awards with their admissions decision.

The Inside Word

Admission to UC Davis is not as competitive as, say, admission to Berkeley. Nevertheless, every school in the UC system is world-class, and the UC system in general is geared toward the best and brightest of not only California's high school students but the nation and the globe.

THE SCHOOL SAYS "..."

From the Admissions Office

"UC Davis is characterized by a distinguished faculty of scholars, scientists, and artists; a treasured sense of community; and a dedication to innovative teaching, research and public service. Student involvement in academics, leadership and honors programs, as well as internships, study abroad and research, exemplify the undergraduate experience. These experiences enhance the quality of faculty-student interactions at a premier research university addressing the critical issues facing our world today. Students can choose from more than 100 majors, work alongside professional researchers, get real-world experience through programs like our student-run community clinics and receive pre-graduate advising in nearly any field imaginable."

"The friendly, supportive nature of the campus and Davis community also defines the undergraduate experience. More than 500 student-run clubs and organizations, themed residence hall programs, NCAA Division I sports and cultural celebrations provide opportunities for students to learn about themselves and their peers from around the world. UC Davis students are active and enjoy year-round events and activities at cultural, academic, and recreational facilities such as the Mondavi Center for the Performing Arts, Aggie Stadium, the Equestrian Center, and the Activities and Recreation Center. UC Davis also provides many resources to help undergraduates build social and career networks before they graduate, so that students are well connected by the time they don their cap and gown."

"The UC application is available in August. Freshman applicants are required to take the ACT Assessment plus Writing or the SAT Reasoning Test no later than December—SAT Subject Tests are not required."

SELECTIVITY
Admissions Rating	93
# of applicants	55,833
% of applicants accepted	41
% of acceptees attending	22
# offered a place on the wait list	6,604
% accepting a place on wait list	32
% admitted from wait list	51

FRESHMAN PROFILE
Range SAT Critical Reading	510–640
Range SAT Math	570–700
Range SAT Writing	540–650
Range ACT Composite	24–30
Minimum paper TOEFL	550
Minimum web-based TOEFL	80
Average HS GPA	3.99

DEADLINES
Regular	
Deadline	11/30
Notification	3/31
Nonfall registration?	No

APPLICANTS ALSO LOOK AT AND OFTEN PREFER
University of California—Berkeley; University of California—San Diego; University of California—Los Angeles

AND SOMETIMES PREFER
University of California—Santa Barbara

AND RARELY PREFER
University of California—Riverside

FINANCIAL FACTS
Financial Aid Rating	78
Annual in-state tuition	$11,220
Annual out-of-state tuition	$34,098
Room and board	$13,961
Required fees	$2,676
Books and supplies	$1,620
% needy frosh rec. need-based scholarship or grant aid	97
% needy UG rec. need-based scholarship or grant aid	97
% needy frosh rec. non-need-based scholarship or grant aid	1
% needy UG rec. non-need-based scholarship or grant aid	1
% needy frosh rec. need-based self-help aid	69
% needy UG rec. need-based self-help aid	67
% UG rec. any financial aid	55
% UG borrow to pay for school	52
Average cumulative indebtedness	$18,386
% frosh need fully met	16
% ugrads need fully met	17
Average % of frosh need met	83
Average % of ugrad need met	82

UNIVERSITY OF CALIFORNIA—LOS ANGELES

1147 MURPHY HALL, LOS ANGELES, CA 90095-1436 • ADMISSIONS: 310-825-3101 • FAX: 310-206-1206

CAMPUS LIFE

Quality of Life Rating	82
Fire Safety Rating	97
Green Rating	97
Type of school	Public
Affiliation	No Affiliation
Environment	Metropolis

STUDENTS

Total undergrad enrollment	28,661
% male/female	45/55
% from out of state	8
% frosh from public high school	74
% frosh live on campus	95
% ugrads live on campus	39
# of fraternities (% ugrad men join)	29 (15)
# of sororities (% ugrad women join)	32 (15)
% African American	4
% Asian	35
% Caucasian	28
% Hispanic	18
% Native American	1
% international	12
# of countries represented	111

SURVEY SAYS . . .

Students love Los Angeles, CA
Athletic facilities are great
Everyone loves the Bruins
Student publications are popular

ACADEMICS

Academic Rating	79
% students returning for sophomore year	96
% students graduating within 4 years	73
% students graduating within 6 years	90
Calendar	Quarter
Student/faculty ratio	17:1
Profs interesting rating	66
Profs accessible rating	67

Most classes have 10–19 students.
Most lab/discussion sessions have 20–29 students.

MOST POPULAR MAJORS

biology; psychology; business/managerial economics

STUDENTS SAY ". . ."

Academics

Undergrads at this esteemed university don't mince words when boasting about all that UCLA has to offer. As a geography and environmental science double-major proudly declares, "There's nothing that can't be accomplished at UCLA. The possibilities are endless, and the resources are unparalleled." Moreover, students appreciate the "ideal" location as well as the "pride of going to a Division I school with more NCAA championships than any other college/university." Perhaps more notable, "UCLA is the kind of school that pushes you to work hard academically but reminds you that interaction with people outside of the classroom is just as important." Students are continually impressed by their professors who are "leaders in their field." Indeed, most consider it "a privilege to study under them." While some undergrads caution that you might encounter some teachers simply "in it for the research," others insist, "Most professors care about their students." A political science major interjects, saying that professors "Are willing to work extra hours with students and help us with anything we need." An English major concurs, sharing, "I have never had a professor that I did not feel comfortable approaching, which has made my academic experience incredibly more beneficial." As this grateful junior succinctly explains, "UCLA is the campus. The people, the weather, the academics, the sports; it has absolutely everything I could ever want."

Life

There's so much "hustle and bustle" at UCLA that it would be virtually "impossible to [be] bored." While nearly everyone's "main focus is on school," most students also know how to "play hard." Indeed, "whether it be in Greek life, a club or organization, everybody has somewhere they can go to relax and have some fun. The apartments are close to campus, so nearly everybody lives in a small area with close proximity." Sports "are extremely popular here, and conversations about the Bruins are common." There are also "tons of movie showings on campus, recreation centers, pools, activities, [and] events." Additionally, students love being located in Los Angeles. A happy senior reveals, "You can take a five-minute drive and you'll be soaking in the Pacific Ocean, or take an hour drive where you can be hitting the slopes in Big Bear. You can walk down to the theater and run into Jennifer Lopez or head to the UCLA gym and watch…Kobe Bryant practicing. The possibilities are endless here, with or without money."

Student Body

UCLA "is the mold that fits you." Indeed, "26,000 students and more than 950 student groups," virtually assures that "there is no 'typical' student" to be found at UCLA. This wide range of individuals and activities guarantees that "everyone has their niche." Certainly, the Bruin community is a "vibrant" one, and "the unmatched diversity broadens students' horizons culturally and socially." Of course, undergrads here do tread some common ground. Many define their peers as "very hardworking and ambitious," and they typically "strive for success and to do their absolute best." They "know how to have a good time, but they also know when it is time to study." Further, it's an active student body, and it often "seems like everyone is in at least one club or organization." Friendliness is another trademark of UCLA undergrads as a physiology major assures us, "It is very easy to talk to and meet new people and make new friends." Fortunately, most people are "laid-back" and while "academically invested…[they're] not outright competitive with other students." This bio major sums up his peers easily by saying, "Everyone comes from different backgrounds with varied interests. The only common denominator is truly an appetite for excellence."

UNIVERSITY OF CALIFORNIA—LOS ANGELES

FINANCIAL AID: 310-206-0400 • E-MAIL: UGADM@SAONET.UCLA.EDU • WEBSITE: WWW.UCLA.EDU

THE PRINCETON REVIEW SAYS

Admissions

Very important factors considered include: GPA, rigor of secondary school record, standardized test scores, application essay. *Important factors considered include:* Extracurricular activities, talent/ability, volunteer work, work experience, character/personal qualities. *Other factors considered include:* First generation, geographical residence. SAT or ACT required; ACT with Writing component required. TOEFL required of all international applicants. *Academic units required:* 4 English; 3 mathematics; 2 science; (2 science lab); 2 foreign language; 2 history; 1 academic elective; 1 visual/performing arts. *Academic units recommended:* 4 English; 4 mathematics; 3 science; (3 science lab); 3 foreign language; 2 history; 1 academic elective; 1 visual/performing arts.

Financial Aid

Students should submit: FAFSA. The Princeton Review suggests that all financial aid forms be submitted as soon as possible after January 1. *Need-based scholarships/grants offered:* Federal Pell, SEOG, State scholarships/grants, private scholarships, the school's own gift aid, United Negro College Fund. *Loan aid offered:* Direct Subsidized Stafford Loans, Direct Unsubsidized Stafford Loans, Direct PLUS loans, Federal Perkins Loans, Federal Nursing Loans, College/university loans from institutional funds. Federal Work-Study Program available. Institutional employment available. Off-campus job opportunities are good.

The Inside Word

Competition is fierce to secure admittance to one of the nation's top public universities. Academic success is paramount, and your GPA and standardized test scores factor heavily into admissions decisions. You'll want to load up on challenging courses in high school. Indeed, taking advanced placement, IB, or honors classes is a must. Of course, UCLA also wants students who will actively contribute to their community, and it's also important to demonstrate commitment to extracurricular activities.

THE SCHOOL SAYS "..."

From the Admissions Office

"Undergraduates arrive at UCLA from throughout California and around the world with exceptional levels of academic preparation. They are attracted by our acclaimed degree programs, distinguished faculty, and the beauty of a park-like campus set amid the dynamism of the nation's second-largest city. UCLA's highly ranked undergraduate programs incorporate cutting-edge technology and teaching techniques that hone the critical-thinking skills and the global perspectives necessary for success in our rapidly changing world. The diversity of these programs draws strength from a student body that mirrors the cultural and ethnic vibrancy of Los Angeles. Generally ranked among the nation's top half-dozen universities, UCLA is at once distinguished and dynamic, academically rigorous and responsive.

"All applicants must take the ACT plus writing or the SAT Reasoning Test. Be sure to complete these tests by December. Engineering applicants are strongly urged to take the SAT Subject Test in math level 2, to demonstrate the proficiency in mathematics needed for success in Engineering courses."

SELECTIVITY

Admissions Rating	98
# of applicants	80,522
% of applicants accepted	20
% of acceptees attending	35

FRESHMAN PROFILE

Range SAT Critical Reading	570–690
Range SAT Math	600–750
Range SAT Writing	580–720
Range ACT Composite	25–32
Minimum paper TOEFL	550
Minimum web-based TOEFL	83
Average HS GPA	4.29
% graduated top 10% of class	97
% graduated top 25% of class	100
% graduated top 50% of class	100

DEADLINES

Regular	
Deadline	11/30
Nonfall registration?	No

FINANCIAL FACTS

Financial Aid Rating	83
Annual in-state tuition	$12,895
Annual out-of-state tuition	$31,477
Room and board	$12,675
Required fees	$1,642
Books and supplies	$1,536
% needy frosh rec. need-based scholarship or grant aid	06
% needy UG rec. need-based scholarship or grant aid	95
% needy frosh rec. non-need-based scholarship or grant aid	1
% needy UG rec. non-need-based scholarship or grant aid	1
% needy frosh rec. need-based self-help aid	63
% needy UG rec. need-based self-help aid	65
% frosh rec. any financial aid	54
% UG rec. any financial aid	55
% UG borrow to pay for school	40
Average cumulative indebtedness	$20,409
% frosh need fully met	25
% ugrads need fully met	25
Average % of frosh need met	84
Average % of ugrad need met	83

UNIVERSITY OF CALIFORNIA—RIVERSIDE

3106 STUDENT SERVICES BUILDING, RIVERSIDE, CA 92521 • ADMISSIONS: 951-827-3411 • FAX: 951-827-6344

CAMPUS LIFE

Quality of Life Rating	71
Fire Safety Rating	88
Green Rating	94
Type of school	Public
Affiliation	No Affiliation
Environment	City

STUDENTS

Total undergrad enrollment	18,612
% male/female	49/51
% from out of state	0
% frosh from public high school	90
% frosh live on campus	74
% ugrads live on campus	31
# of fraternities	20
# of sororities	20
% African American	5
% Asian	36
% Caucasian	14
% Hispanic	36
% Native American	<1
% international	3
# of countries represented	100

SURVEY SAYS . . .

Political activism is unpopular or nonexistent
Great library
Athletic facilities are great
Different types of students interact
Frats and sororities are popular
Student publications are popular

ACADEMICS

Academic Rating	78
% students returning for sophomore year	89
% students graduating within 4 years	41
% students graduating within 6 years	69
Calendar	Quarter
Student/faculty ratio	19:1
Profs interesting rating	68
Profs accessible rating	70

Most classes have 20–29 students.
Most lab/discussion sessions have 20–29 students.

MOST POPULAR MAJORS
psychology; business administration and management; biomedical science

STUDENTS SAY ". . ."

Academics
Students at the University of California—Riverside are in love with many things—the "small class size" and "beautiful campus" come up often—but the educators here receive the lion's share of the praise. Professors here are "very skilled in teaching" and "have passion to teach and help their students." Teachers "don't just read from a book and teach you the stuff, they also bring the material to life and make class really enjoyable." This is because they "really know the material they are teaching and are very passionate about it," resulting in "lively discussions" and an "open and diverse campus." This is a school that is devoted to "helping students achieve their academic goals while at the same time connecting them to their community." Some students admit their "overall academic experience has had its ups and downs," saying, "Some classes were interesting and structured well, while others were not," but by and large, educators are "willing to dedicate an enormous amount of time to interact with and help students in order for us to succeed." Career-minded students will find that counselors here are "more than willing to help you with your career path," and the school also "has great connections and support, which is vital for creating a network that helps with internships and future jobs in your major." Graduates of UCR "have integrity, accountability, excellence, and respect."

Life
It's not hard to make friends at UCR, "but I know it would've been easier if I tried joining a club or organization," one student comments, which comes as no surprise, since "many students are involved in campus clubs and organizations." It's easy to find activities for the student who looks, since "there is always an event going on such as athletic games, plays, and musical shows." Students here "aren't under extreme pressure," so they manage to "find the time to explore our own interests and ideas with others." School-based clubs and organizations may be the option of choice, however, since "Riverside city isn't the prettiest, and it gets ridiculously hot during the summer." That said, some students think that "downtown Riverside is beautiful," and UCR students like going there to "go ice skating or shopping at the various malls." Outdoorsy types will be glad to know that the "weather is awesome," and "the beaches are an hour away, and so are the mountains and desert in opposite directions." Active students say, "It's always nice to travel, hike, camp, and just have fun with friends."

Student Body
The active, community-focused students of UCR are "usually part of at least one extracurricular group," the result of "a diverse student body anxious to learn about the world and what they can do to make the world a better place." Though UCR's campus can't be called cozy, it is small enough that "everyone knows everyone through at least one connection." The typical student is "friendly, engaging, outgoing, and eager to learn." Those attending almost universally report that making friends here is easy "because the acceptance level at UCR [among students] is 100 percent." The school "is like a giant melting pot; every student is different but we all fit together perfectly." Getting involved in social causes is not unusual among the student body, though "a typical student is always more worried about their outfits than politics and social issues," which isn't to say many aren't driven by such causes. One student reports, "I like to organize forums and participate in social justice rallies on and off campus." Overall, though, laid-back and inviting is the rule of the day. "Students fit in by being who they are because everyone is friendly," and they "always attend classes, go to org meetings, and campus events, and make it home in time to do four to five hours of studying."

FINANCIAL AID: 951-827-3878 • E-MAIL: ADMIT@UCR.EDU • WEBSITE: WWW.UCR.EDU

THE PRINCETON REVIEW SAYS

Admissions

Very important factors considered include: GPA, rigor of secondary school record, standardized test scores, application essay. *Other factors considered include:* Extracurricular activities, first generation, state residency, talent/ability, volunteer work, work experience, character/personal qualities. SAT or ACT required; ACT with Writing component required. TOEFL required of all international applicants. *Academic units required:* 4 English; 3 mathematics; 2 science; (2 science lab); 2 foreign language; 2 history; 1 academic elective; 1 visual/performing arts. *Academic units recommended:* 4 mathematics; 3 science; (3 science lab); 3 foreign language.

Financial Aid

Students should submit: FAFSA, State aid form. Regular filing deadline is 5/1. The Princeton Review suggests that all financial aid forms be submitted as soon as possible after January 1. *Need-based scholarships/grants offered:* Federal Pell, SEOG, State scholarships/grants, private scholarships, the school's own gift aid. *Loan aid offered:* Direct Subsidized Stafford Loans, Direct Unsubsidized Stafford Loans, Direct PLUS loans, Federal Perkins Loans, College/university loans from institutional funds. Applicants will be notified of awards beginning 3/1. Federal Work-Study Program available. Institutional employment available. Off-campus job opportunities are excellent.

The Inside Word

The UC—Riverside admissions process is based heavily on quantitative factors. Applicants who have strong GPAs and standardized test scores should have no problem gaining acceptance. There is a priority filing period, so students should apply as early as possible.

THE SCHOOL SAYS " . . ."

From the Admissions Office

"The University of California—Riverside offers the quality, rigor, and facilities of a major research institution, while assuring its undergraduates personal attention and a sense of community. Academic programs, teaching, advising, and student services all reflect the supportive attitudes that characterize the campus. Among the exceptional opportunities are the Thomas Haider Program in Biomedical Sciences, which provides an exclusive path to medical school: the University Honors Program, an extensive undergraduate research program, UC's largest undergraduate program is psychology, and UC's only bachelor's degree in creative writing. Additionally, the opening of UCR's School of Medicine is anticipated for August 2013. More than 300 student clubs and organizations and a variety of athletic and arts events give students a myriad of ways to get involved and have fun.

"Effective fall 2012, all applicants must take the ACT plus writing or the SAT Reasoning Test. The SAT Subject Tests will no longer be required for admission; however, students interested in admission to any major in the College of Natural and Agricultural Sciences or the Bourns College of Engineering are strongly recommended to take the SAT Subject Test math level 2 and the SAT Subject Test in chemistry or physics."

SELECTIVITY

Admissions Rating	94
# of applicants	34,816
% of applicants accepted	60
% of acceptees attending	20
# offered a place on the wait list	3,678
% accepting a place on wait list	49
% admitted from wait list	76

FRESHMAN PROFILE

Range SAT Critical Reading	480–580
Range SAT Math	510–630
Range SAT Writing	480–590
Range ACT Composite	20–26
Minimum paper TOEFL	550
Average HS GPA	3.60
% graduated top 10% of class	94
% graduated top 25% of class	100
% graduated top 50% of class	100

DEADLINES

Regular	
Deadline	11/30
Notification	3/31
Nonfall registration?	No

APPLICANTS ALSO LOOK AT AND OFTEN PREFER

University of California—Los Angeles; University of California—Berkeley; University of California—San Diego

AND SOMETIMES PREFER

University of California—Santa Barbara; University of California—Davis

AND RARELY PREFER

University of California—Santa Cruz

FINANCIAL FACTS

Financial Aid Rating	81
Annual in-state tuition	$11,220
Annual out-of-state tuition	$34,098
Room and board	$13,500
Required fees	$1,752
Books and supplies	$1,800
% needy frosh rec. need-based scholarship or grant aid	94
% needy UG rec. need-based scholarship or grant aid	94
% needy frosh rec. non-need-based scholarship or grant aid	1
% needy UG rec. non-need-based scholarship or grant aid	1
% needy frosh rec. need-based self-help aid	79
% needy UG rec. need-based self-help aid	72
% frosh rec. any financial aid	89
% UG rec. any financial aid	85
% UG borrow to pay for school	70
Average cumulative indebtedness	$21,300
% frosh need fully met	25
% ugrads need fully met	25
Average % of frosh need met	87
Average % of ugrad need met	83

UNIVERSITY OF CALIFORNIA—SAN DIEGO

9500 GILMAN DRIVE, LA JOLLA, CA 92093-0021 • ADMISSIONS: 858-534-4831 • FAX: 858-534-5723

STUDENTS SAY ". . ."

Academics

UCSD is widely regarded by students as "one of the top science universities in the United States." As a result, the school attracts bright students who benefit from "access to cutting edge technology and theories" and "great opportunities for undergraduates to do research." Professors "are incredibly knowledgeable about their material, and many of them are actively doing research in their field." Research opportunities are widely available to undergraduate science majors. However, sciences are not the only attraction at UCSD. The university is home to six separate colleges, a system that students say is "a great way to not feel like a small fish in a huge ocean." Whereas it might seem like some science professors "are more interested in research than teaching," students say, "Humanities professors tend to be more accessible and more interested in their students as well as what they are teaching." Overall, however, "Professors are very helpful and willing to take extra time to help students understand material." Given the fact that UCSD is a large public university, students say, "Professors are extremely willing to help and mentor students if you seek them out." Another major benefit to attending a large university is that "there are a lot of resources, and there is always a faculty member or organization that will help you achieve what you want." Students say they are excited about "where UCSD is going; this university will undoubtedly set the new standard of what it means to be an elite public university in the years to come."

Life

Students love to take advantage of UCSD's "unbeatable location," ten minutes from the beach and a quick ride away from downtown San Diego. It is easy to enjoy "all the nature around the campus by hiking, biking, [and] camping," or taking surf lessons, which "are offered on campus for a modest fee." It is also "super easy to get to San Diego proper for a fun night out." There is a perception that social life is somewhat lacking on the campus itself, which may be the result of UCSD being such a large, academically intensive school. While some students have trouble fitting a social life into their busy study schedules, others say that, in fact, there are "tons of resources and ways to get involved" on campus; students "just have to actively seek them." Plenty of people "play sports or participate in clubs." "Lots of people enjoy kickbacks and small parties but the party scene isn't too big here." In the spring, the Sun God Festival is "always a popular event" that brings the entire campus together. There "is not really a huge emphasis on the athletics department," much to the annoyance of some students. However, students who make the most of their experience here maintain, "There is always an event going on and so many clubs to be involved in. From the Greek life, to the intramural sports, to the variety of clubs, there is literally a place for everyone."

Student Body

The typical student at UCSD "is a little nerdy and studies a lot." "Doing well academically at UCSD is an extreme priority, even to students who are not good students. Most of the students are geared toward extended education or professional school." However, "there are plenty of students who balance academics with other things, like sports or clubs." The student body "has such a diverse range of personalities" that most anyone "can fit in here because it's such a big school, and there are so many different organizations and places where you can find people that enjoy the same things as you." Students say that the population of students in the humanities has been growing "rapidly" in recent years, but some still see room for improvement among the diversity of the student body. There are those who would love "to see more students become socially conscious" to enhance the overall student body experience on campus.

FINANCIAL AID: 858-534-4480 • E-MAIL: ADMISSIONSINFO@UCSD.EDU • WEBSITE: WWW.UCSD.EDU

THE PRINCETON REVIEW SAYS

Admissions

Very important factors considered include: GPA, rigor of secondary school record, standardized test scores, application essay. *Important factors considered include:* Extracurricular activities, state residency, talent/ability, volunteer work, character/personal qualities. *Other factors considered include:* First generation, geographical residence, work experience. SAT or ACT required; ACT with Writing component required. TOEFL required of all international applicants. *Academic units required:* 4 English; 3 mathematics; 2 science; (2 science lab); 2 foreign language; 2 history; 1 visual/performing arts. *Academic units recommended:* 4 English; 4 mathematics; 3 science; (3 science lab); 3 foreign language; 2 history; 1 academic elective; 1 visual/performing arts.

Financial Aid

Students should submit: FAFSA, State aid form. The Princeton Review suggests that all financial aid forms be submitted as soon as possible after January 1. *Need-based scholarships/grants offered:* Federal Pell, SEOG, State scholarships/grants, private scholarships, the school's own gift aid. *Loan aid offered:* Direct Subsidized Stafford Loans, Direct Unsubsidized Stafford Loans, Direct PLUS loans, Federal Perkins Loans, College/university loans from institutional funds. Federal Work-Study Program available. Institutional employment available. Off-campus job opportunities are good.

The Inside Word

While not as lauded as Berkeley or UCLA, UCSD is rapidly earning its place as one of the gems of the UC system. It distinguishes itself in a number of ways, including its individualized approach to admissions. Although admissions officers do implement a formula, they factor in extracurricular pursuits and personal experiences. Applicants will need to be strong in all areas if they hope to attend UCSD.

THE SCHOOL SAYS "..."

From the Admissions Office

"UCSD is recognized for the exceptional quality of its academic programs. UCSD ranks fifth in the nation and first in the University of California system for the amount of federal research dollars spent on research and development; and the university ranks tenth in the nation in the excellence of its graduate programs and the quality of its faculty, according to the most recent National Research Council college rankings.

"About 40 percent of UCSD's undergraduates participate in research, developing critical thinking and effective communication skills as well as greater cultural understanding. Their faculty mentors are in the divisions and schools of arts and humanities, biology, engineering, medicine, pharmacy, physical sciences, social sciences, and UCSD's Scripps Institution of Oceanography, California Institute for Telecommunications and Information Technology and the San Diego Supercomputer Center. Undergraduates also participate in research at the Salk Institute for Biological Studies and other nearby research institutes and biotechnology companies.

"All applicants must take the ACT plus writing or the SAT Reasoning Test. In addition, all applicants must take two SAT Subject Tests in two different subject areas. (If a math SAT Subject Test is chosen by the applicant, he/she must take the math level 2 exam.)"

SELECTIVITY
Admissions Rating	97
# of applicants	67,400
% of applicants accepted	37
% of acceptees attending	21

FRESHMAN PROFILE
Range SAT Critical Reading	560–660
Range SAT Math	620–740
Range SAT Writing	570–680
Range ACT Composite	26–31
Minimum paper TOEFL	550
Average HS GPA	4.00
% graduated top 10% of class	100
% graduated top 25% of class	100
% graduated top 50% of class	100

DEADLINES
Regular	
Deadline	11/30
Notification	3/31
Nonfall registration?	Yes

APPLICANTS ALSO LOOK AT AND OFTEN PREFER
University of Southern California; University of California—Los Angeles; University of California—Davis; University of California—Berkeley; Stanford University

AND SOMETIMES PREFER
Stanford University; University of California—Davis; University of California—Santa Barbara

FINANCIAL FACTS
Financial Aid Rating	86
Annual in-state tuition	$12,192
Annual out-of-state tuition	$35,070
Room and board	$11,978
Required fees	$1,042
Books and supplies	$1,489
% needy frosh rec. need-based scholarship or grant aid	92
% needy UG rec. need-based scholarship or grant aid	94
% needy frosh rec. non-need-based scholarship or grant aid	1
% needy UG rec. non-need-based scholarship or grant aid	0
% needy frosh rec. need-based self-help aid	82
% needy UG rec. need-based self-help aid	83
% frosh rec. any financial aid	77
% UG rec. any financial aid	63
% UG borrow to pay for school	56
Average cumulative indebtedness	$20,474
% frosh need fully met	41
% ugrads need fully met	36
Average % of frosh need met	87
Average % of ugrad need met	87

UNIVERSITY OF CALIFORNIA—SANTA BARBARA

OFFICE OF ADMISSIONS, SANTA BARBARA, CA 93106-2014 • ADMISSIONS: 805-893-2881 • FAX: 805-893-2676

CAMPUS LIFE

Quality of Life Rating	95
Fire Safety Rating	92
Green Rating	99
Type of school	Public
Affiliation	No Affiliation
Environment	City

STUDENTS

Total undergrad enrollment	18,974
% male/female	47/53
% from out of state	3
% frosh from public high school	87
% frosh live on campus	92
% ugrads live on campus	37
# of fraternities (% ugrad men join)	17 (5)
# of sororities (% ugrad women join)	18 (12)
% African American	4
% Asian	23
% Caucasian	42
% Hispanic	24
% Native American	1
% international	3
# of countries represented	72

SURVEY SAYS . . .
Students are happy
Lab facilities are great
Class discussions are rare
Students are friendly
Students love Santa Barbara, CA
Athletic facilities are great
Lots of beer drinking
Hard liquor is popular

ACADEMICS

Academic Rating	84
% students returning for sophomore year	91
% students graduating within 4 years	67
% students graduating within 6 years	80
Calendar	Quarter
Student/faculty ratio	17:1
Profs interesting rating	82
Profs accessible rating	80

Most classes have fewer than 10 students.
Most lab/discussion sessions have
20–29 students.

MOST POPULAR MAJORS
biology; economics; psychology; sociology

STUDENTS SAY ". . ."

Academics
It's easy to be dazzled by this University of California's "incredible location" in stunning Santa Barbara, but UCSB is much more than a "safe and beautiful campus." "It has one of the top chemical engineering departments in the country," a "highly ranked" mechanical engineering program, and is generally "strong in the sciences." Outstanding students can enroll in the College of Creative Studies, which acts as the university's Honors program and requires a supplemental application: CCS students report that it "allows me to pursue my academic interests with maximum freedom." While they love the "laid-back" atmosphere, students regard their course work in any school as both "academically challenging" and "down to earth": "Every other college on my list seemed locked in an ivory tower. UCSB was the exception with both the warm, sun-kissed charm of a beach town and excellent academics." "I would challenge any Ivy school to match" the quality of professors at UCSB, asserts one student, and another says the "outstanding professors" "are definitely an important source of inspiration for me." Some students comment on the "wide range of professors," and point out that "many of [the] professors are Nobel Prize winners or well-known in their field; however, these individuals are not necessarily the best teachers." Overall, though, UBSB undergrads name the "accessibility and knowledge of the professors" as one of the university's strengths. If you're seeking a dynamic college experience with choices within and outside the classroom, UCSB could be for you: "UCSB is the perfect blend of academics and social life. I get to study at a renowned research university and work closely with professors, while living on the beach and making lifelong friendships."

Life
No matter the activity, UCSB students love to be involved: "85 percent of our student body is in at least one extracurricular activity—and I've met the smartest people of my life here." Outdoor pastimes like "rock climbing, beach volleyball," "surfing and hiking," "bik[ing], skateboard[ing]," figure prominently in students' favorite ways to spend free time wholesomely. After the sun goes down, "A lot of people party at UCSB. What do you expect, we live on a beach? But don't be fooled. I've met some of the smartest, most hard-working people at UCSB." Social life at UCSB is as "varied" as you want it to be: "People think of UCSB exclusively as a party school but it's what you make of it." The party scene "is totally avoidable if you want," but "UCSB is famous for its party life" for a reason. Students looking to avoid drinking and drug culture entirely might be best advised to look elsewhere, and insiders say that "substance abuse is somewhat common off campus and not as much on campus; campus alcohol and drug policies are typically enforced strictly." At the end of the day, "everything is give and take here. You spend your week busting your butt in your internship and churning out research papers, and finish everything up in time to go indulge in some of the debauchery that is DP on a Friday night."

Student Body
To find your place at a big school, get ready to get out and do something: "The typical student is active and involved. Whether it be with sports, or in a community service or environmental club, rock climbing, politics, the list goes on. Students fit in by finding a good group of friends in the dorms and by getting involved in extracurricular activities." Because the university is accessible to so many different types of students, "there is a great sense of community among the students, and those with all sorts of socio-economic backgrounds feel at home here." UCSB undergrads care about more than partying, and are "intelligent, sociable, engaging" as well as "very motivated and driven to succeed academically." People are "laid-back but hard-working," at least partially because "the sunny weather keeps people happy." UCSB is "extremely diverse personality wise": "We've got the hippies, the sorority girls, the surfer dudes, the Jesus-lovers, the anarchists, the school-oriented folk and everything in between. Everyone finds their niche here."

UNIVERSITY OF CALIFORNIA—SANTA BARBARA

FINANCIAL AID: 805-893-2118 • E-MAIL: ADMISSIONS@SA.UCSB.EDU • WEBSITE: WWW.UCSB.EDU

THE PRINCETON REVIEW SAYS

Admissions

Very important factors considered include: GPA, rigor of secondary school record, standardized test scores, application essay. *Other factors considered include:* Class rank, extracurricular activities, first generation, state residency, talent/ability, volunteer work, work experience, character/personal qualities. SAT or ACT required; ACT with Writing component required. TOEFL required of all international applicants. *Academic units required:* 4 English; 3 mathematics; (2 science lab); 2 foreign language; 2 history; 1 academic elective; 1 visual/performing arts. *Academic units recommended:* 4 mathematics; (3 science lab); 3 foreign language.

Financial Aid

Students should submit: FAFSA. Regular filing deadline is 5/31. The Princeton Review suggests that all financial aid forms be submitted as soon as possible after January 1. *Need-based scholarships/grants offered:* Federal Pell, SEOG, State scholarships/grants, private scholarships, the school's own gift aid. *Loan aid offered:* Direct Subsidized Stafford Loans, Direct Unsubsidized Stafford Loans, Direct PLUS loans, Federal Perkins Loans. Federal Work-Study Program available. Institutional employment available. Off-campus job opportunities are good.

The Inside Word

UCSB uses a "minimum eligibility" index as a formula to calculate a student's viability for admission; other standards in high school courseload and standardized tests are synthesized with a 3.0 minimum GPA for California students and a 3.4 for out-of-state applicants. Weakness in one area may be balanced out by strength in another, but don't be fooled by the fact that it's a state school: UCSB is competitive.

The School Says ". . ."
From the Admissions Office

"The University of California—Santa Barbara is a major research institution offering undergraduate and graduate education in the arts, humanities, sciences and technology, and social sciences. Large enough to have excellent facilities for study, research, and other creative activities, the campus is also small enough to foster close relationships among faculty and students. The faculty numbers more than 1,000. A member of the most distinguished system of public higher education in the nation, UC—Santa Barbara is committed equally to excellence in scholarship and instruction. Through the general education program, students acquire good grounding in the skills, perceptions, and methods of a variety of disciplines. In addition, because they study with a research faculty, they not only acquire basic skills and broad knowledge but also are exposed to the imagination, inventiveness, and intense concentration that scholars bring to their work. UCSB is one of sixty-one members of the prestigous Association of American Universities.

"All applicants must take the ACT plus writing or the SAT Reasoning Test. SAT Subject Tests are no longer required by the University of California. Students applying to engineering majors are encouraged to take SAT Subject Tests in math (level 2) and a science exam of their choice."

SELECTIVITY

Admissions Rating	97
# of applicants	54,762
% of applicants accepted	44
% of acceptees attending	20
# offered a place on the wait list	3,262
% accepting a place on wait list	70
% admitted from wait list	15

FRESHMAN PROFILE

Range SAT Critical Reading	540–660
Range SAT Math	570–690
Range SAT Writing	560–670
Range ACT Composite	24–29 Minimum paper
TOEFL	550
Minimum web-based TOEFL	213
Average HS GPA	3.91
% graduated top 10% of class	100
% graduated top 25% of class	100
% graduated top 50% of class	100

DEADLINES

Regular	
Deadline	11/30
Notification	3/1
Nonfall registration?	No

APPLICANTS ALSO LOOK AT AND OFTEN PREFER

University of California—Davis; University of California—Berkeley

AND SOMETIMES PREFER

University of California—Los Angeles

AND RARELY PREFER

University of California—Santa Cruz

FINANCIAL FACTS

Financial Aid Rating	78
Annual in-state tuition	$12,192
Annual out-of-state tuition	$35,070
Room and board	$13,805
Required fees	$1,554
Books and supplies	$1,444
% needy frosh rec. need-based scholarship or grant aid	88
% needy UG rec. need-based scholarship or grant aid	88
% needy frosh rec. non-need-based scholarship or grant aid	1
% needy UG rec. non-need-based scholarship or grant aid	1
% needy frosh rec. need-based self-help aid	82
% needy UG rec. need-based self-help aid	83
% frosh rec. any financial aid	
% UG rec. any financial aid	
% UG borrow to pay for school	53
Average cumulative indebtedness	$19,325
% frosh need fully met	23
% ugrads need fully met	23
Average % of frosh need met	85
Average % of ugrad need met	85

UNIVERSITY OF CALIFORNIA—SANTA CRUZ

OFFICE OF ADMISSIONS, COOK HOUSE, SANTA CRUZ, CA 95064 • ADMISSIONS: 831-459-4008 • FAX: 831-459-4452

CAMPUS LIFE

Quality of Life Rating	67
Fire Safety Rating	76
Green Rating	97
Type of school	Public
Affiliation	No Affiliation
Environment	City

STUDENTS

Total undergrad enrollment	15,695
% male/female	47/53
% from out of state	4
% frosh from public high school	87
% frosh live on campus	99
% ugrads live on campus	48
# of fraternities	6
# of sororities	11
% African American	4
% Asian	25
% Caucasian	37
% Hispanic	30
% Native American	1
% international	1
# of countries represented	82

SURVEY SAYS . . .

Students environmentally aware
Political activism is popular
Students are happy
Students are friendly

ACADEMICS

Academic Rating	76
% students returning for sophomore year	89
% students graduating within 4 years	55
% students graduating within 6 years	72
Calendar	Quarter
Student/faculty ratio	19:1
Profs interesting rating	65
Profs accessible rating	68

Most classes have 10–19 students.
Most lab/discussion sessions have
10–19 students.

MOST POPULAR MAJORS
business/commerce; art studies; ecology

STUDENTS SAY ". . ."

Academics

The University of California—Santa Cruz offers one of the nation's best combinations of "focus on scholastic endeavors in a beautiful forest setting" and is, by all accounts "a great place to live and study!" Students attribute their enthusiasm to "intelligent, eloquent, and easily accessible professors," academics that are "impressive and challenging," and fellow students who are "happy, open-minded, and a little bit crazy." This school is best suited to those who can motivate themselves in a "chill" environment and the sort of student whose motto might be, "There's no point in learning if you're too stressed to enjoy it." The sciences are "world-class" at UCSC, and the school also boasts "one of the finest engineering programs in the UCs" as well as "a great marine biology program." While the "professors all do research," what sets them apart from those at the typical research-driven university is that "they are very passionate about their subject even when teaching undergrads," and they "also tend to be quite approachable despite having large class sizes and allow students to attend their office hours for extra help." The school also offers undergrads "a lot of opportunities in terms of internships, research opportunities, job opportunities, and networking." "There's a focus on undergraduate study" here, one student contentedly reports.

Life

Undergrads rave about the "take-your-breath-away beauty" of the heavily wooded UCSC campus; one says it's like "taking paths through the forest that resemble Endor only to find a lecture hall at the end." Another adds, "Almost every time my friends and I walk around outside, someone comments on how lucky we are to be surrounded by such beauty. Whether the silvery ocean, the fog in the trees, the wind in the fields of green, the wildlife such as deer, raccoons, squirrels, newts, etc., it all comes together like a painting." The school's setting means "there is much to do recreationally, such as hiking, biking, swimming, trail running, tree climbing, or rock-climbing. You can walk in any direction and find some hiking trail that leads to some other part of the forest." Students note that, "It is also nice to get off campus from time to time and enjoy the city of Santa Cruz. Downtown is lively and usually has something fun going on such as local farmer's markets and cultural festivals." Ambitious students "may head to San Jose or San Francisco on the weekend for a more rowdy bar or club scene." Both cities are "readily accessible via public transportation." The party scene on and off campus consists of "mostly decentralized, smaller parties, due to the near-absence of fraternities and sororities." It also includes "a lot of drug use" that is limited to "specific locations" and "easy to avoid" for abstaining students.

Student Body

"The 'stereotypical' Santa Cruz student is a hippie," and the school certainly has its fair share of those. "The typical student is very hardworking until about 9:00 P.M., when hikes to the forest are common practice and returning to your room smelling like reefer is acceptable," one undergrad explains—but "there are many different types who attend UCSC." "It seems that almost every student here has a personal passion, whether it be an activism or cause of some sort, etc.," one student writes. "Everyone is so…alive." "Most are liberal," and there's a definite propensity for earnestness; it's the sort of place where students declare without irony that they "not only possess a great respect for one another but the world and life in general. The world to an average UCSC student is a sacred and beautiful place to be shared and enjoyed by all its inhabitants."

606 ■ THE BEST 379 COLLEGES

UNIVERSITY OF CALIFORNIA—SANTA CRUZ

FINANCIAL AID: 831-459-2963 • E-MAIL: ADMISSIONS@UCSC.EDU • WEBSITE: WWW.UCSC.EDU

THE PRINCETON REVIEW SAYS

Admissions

Very important factors considered include: GPA, rigor of secondary school record, standardized test scores, application essay. *Important factors considered include:* Class rank, extracurricular activities, first generation, geographical residence, state residency, talent/ability, character/personal qualities. *Other factors considered include:* Volunteer work, work experience. SAT or ACT required; ACT with Writing component required. TOEFL required of all international applicants. *Academic units required:* 4 English; 3 mathematics; 2 science; (2 science lab); 1 social studies; 2 foreign language; 1 history; 1 academic elective; 1 visual/performing arts. *Academic units recommended:* 4 English; 4 mathematics; 3 science; (3 science lab); 3 foreign language.

Financial Aid

Students should submit: FAFSA, State aid form. Regular filing deadline is 3/2. The Princeton Review suggests that all financial aid forms be submitted as soon as possible after January 1. *Need-based scholarships/grants offered:* Federal Pell, SEOG, State scholarships/grants, private scholarships, the school's own gift aid. *Loan aid offered:* Direct Subsidized Stafford Loans, Direct Unsubsidized Stafford Loans, Direct PLUS loans, Federal Perkins Loans. Federal Work-Study Program available. Institutional employment available. Off-campus job opportunities are excellent.

The Inside Word

Professionally-trained Admissions readers conduct an in-depth review of your academic and personal achievements in light of the opportunities available to you and your demonstrated capacity to contribute to the intellectual and cultural life at UCSC. UCSC's acceptance rate belies the high caliber of applicants it regularly receives. UCSC's acceptance rate belies the high caliber of applicants it regularly receives.

THE SCHOOL SAYS "..."

From the Admissions Office

"UC—Santa Cruz students, faculty, and researchers are working together to make a world of difference. Within our extraordinary educational community, students participate in the creation of new knowledge, new technologies, and new forms of expressing and understanding cultures. From helping teachers improve their skills to building more efficient solar cells and working to save endangered sea turtles, our focus is on improving our planet and the lives of all its inhabitants. The academic programs at UCSC are challenging and rigorous, and many of them are in newer fields that focus on interdisciplinary thinking. At UCSC, undergraduates conduct and publish research, working closely with faculty on leading-edge projects. Taking advantage of the campus' proximity to centers of industry and innovation such as the Monterey Bay National Marine Sanctuary and Silicon Valley, many students at UC—Santa Cruz take part in fieldwork and internships that complement their studies and provide practical experience in their fields.

"All frosh applicants must take the ACT assessment plus the ACT writing test or the SAT Reasoning Test."

SELECTIVITY

Admissions Rating	94
# of applicants	38,640
% of applicants accepted	52
% of acceptees attending	17
# offered a place on the wait list	2,573
% accepting a place on wait list	47

FRESHMAN PROFILE

Range SAT Critical Reading	490–630
Range SAT Math	510–650
Range SAT Writing	490–630
Range ACT Composite	20–27
Minimum paper TOEFL	550
Minimum web-based TOEFL	220
Average HS GPA	3.66
% graduated top 10% of class	96
% graduated top 25% of class	100
% graduated top 50% of class	100

DEADLINES

Regular	
Deadline	11/30
Notification	3/31
Nonfall registration?	Yes

APPLICANTS ALSO LOOK AT AND OFTEN PREFER
Stanford University; University of California—Berkeley; University of California—Los Angeles

AND SOMETIMES PREFER
University of California—Santa Barbara; University of California—Davis; University of California—San Diego

AND RARELY PREFER
University of California—Riverside

FINANCIAL FACTS

Financial Aid Rating	71
Annual in-state tuition	$12,192
Annual out-of-state tuition	$35,070
Room and board	$14,856
Required food	$1,224
Books and supplies	$1,407
% needy frosh rec. need-based scholarship or grant aid	87
% needy UG rec. need-based scholarship or grant aid	88
% needy frosh rec. non-need-based scholarship or grant aid	1
% needy UG rec. non-need-based scholarship or grant aid	1
% needy frosh rec. need-based self-help aid	86
% needy UG rec. need-based self-help aid	86
% frosh rec. any financial aid	59
% UG rec. any financial aid	56
% UG borrow to pay for school	53
Average cumulative indebtedness	$16,024
% frosh need fully met	51
% ugrads need fully met	49
Average % of frosh need met	89
Average % of ugrad need met	89

UNIVERSITY OF CENTRAL FLORIDA

PO Box 160111, Orlando, FL 32816-0111 • Admissions: 407-823-3000 • Fax: 407-823-5625

CAMPUS LIFE

Quality of Life Rating	84
Fire Safety Rating	84
Green Rating	80
Type of school	Public
Affiliation	No Affiliation
Environment	City

STUDENTS

Total undergrad enrollment	51,269
% male/female	45/55
% from out of state	5
% frosh live on campus	72
% ugrads live on campus	18
# of fraternities (% ugrad men join)	24 (8)
# of sororities (% ugrad women join)	23 (9)
% African American	11
% Asian	6
% Caucasian	57
% Hispanic	22
% Native American	<1
% international	1
# of countries represented	147

SURVEY SAYS . . .
Great off-campus food
Athletic facilities are great
Active student government

ACADEMICS

Academic Rating	74
% students returning for sophomore year	87
% students graduating within 4 years	36
% students graduating within 6 years	67
Calendar	Semester
Student/faculty ratio	31:1
Profs interesting rating	71
Profs accessible rating	69

Most classes have 10–19 students.
Most lab/discussion sessions have 30–39 students.

MOST POPULAR MAJORS
marketing; psychology; health services

STUDENTS SAY ". . ."

Academics
One of Florida's premiere institutions, University of Central Florida is rapidly gaining a strong national reputation. Impressively, despite being one of the largest universities in the country, UCF manages to feel "like one big family." Indeed, undergrads here stress that the administration truly "cares about the success of each student." While UCF offers many great academic options, students are quick to emphasize the phenomenal nursing, engineering, sports medicine, psychology, speech disorder, and communication programs. Though some undergrads gripe that professors can be "hit and miss," most students are full of praise for their teachers. As one appreciative undergrad relays, "My professors always [make] sure we [are] involved and engaged [with] material and that the material covered in class [is] relevant to the degree we [are] earning." A fellow student agrees, stating, "Professors are very creative when it comes to teaching and make learning fun and interesting." Moreover, they are "always willing to help and available for contact outside of classroom hours." They truly "want to make sure we make the most of our educational opportunities." As this truly satisfied undergrad gratefully sums up his experience, "UCF is an amazing college, and deciding to attend is one of the best decisions I have ever made in my life."

Life
University of Central Florida is always abuzz with activity. Indeed, "Between classes, sporting events, our top of the line two-story gym, canoeing Lake Claire, concerts and shows, or even Light Up UCF (a holiday carnival on campus for the general public as well as students), one never has a reason to be bored." Further, there are "so many different clubs [for students to join] from recreational [and] religious [groups to] food [organizations and] volunteering." Moreover, "UCF is big on school spirit, especially when it comes to football." Tailgating is definitely a popular pastime during the season. Students also love to take advantage of hometown Orlando, which offers a myriad of cultural and entertainment options. Shares one undergrad, "People around here love going clubbing and bar-hopping. It's totally normal for the typical student to have a Disney pass or Universal pass and carloads of students can be seen at either of these parks." Additionally, "there are some fun college bars right across from campus that are very popular, and Orlando has an amazing downtown that is great for once students turn twenty-one and want something new." When undergrads are itching to get a little farther away, it's common to "go to either coast to visit the awesome beaches."

Student Body
Though undergrads assert that with a population this large, this is "no typical student" at UCF, they're still able to make a few generalizations regarding their peers. If pressed to define their fellow students, undergrads are likely to suggest that they're "generally laid-back" and "fit into the Florida [stereotype]: flip-flops, very down-to-earth, not uptight, [and] like to have fun." They are also "very kind, intelligent, and hardworking." Most students "are welcoming [and] if you want to find people with like-[minded] interests, there are tons of clubs and organizations." Impressively, many undergrads here confidently declare that students just seem to "fit in." "Whether its clubs or study groups or coming into class late and having to take the seat furthest in the row and closest to the wall, conversations brew naturally." One student concurs succinctly, stating, "I feel like you'd have to go out of your way to not make friends." Simply put, "there's a little bit of everything [and everyone] at UCF."

UNIVERSITY OF CENTRAL FLORIDA

FINANCIAL AID: 407-823-2827 • E-MAIL: ADMISSION@UCF.EDU • WEBSITE: WWW.UCF.EDU

THE PRINCETON REVIEW SAYS

Admissions

Very important factors considered include: GPA, rigor of secondary school record, standardized test scores. *Important factors considered include:* Application essay, recommendation(s). *Other factors considered include:* Class rank, extracurricular activities, first generation, geographical residence, state residency, talent/ability, volunteer work, work experience, alumni/ae relations, character/personal qualities, level of applicant's interest. SAT or ACT required; ACT with Writing component required. TOEFL or IELTS may be required for students whose first language is not English. *Academic units required:* 4 English; 4 mathematics; 3 science; (2 science lab); 3 social studies; 2 foreign language; 2 academic electives.

Financial Aid

Students should submit: FAFSA. Regular filing deadline is 6/30. The Princeton Review suggests that all financial aid forms be submitted as soon as possible after January 1. *Need-based scholarships/grants offered:* Federal Pell, SEOG, State scholarships/grants, private scholarships, the school's own gift aid. *Loan aid offered:* Direct Subsidized Stafford Loans, Direct Unsubsidized Stafford Loans, Direct PLUS loans, Federal Perkins Loans. Federal Work-Study Program available. Institutional employment available.

Inside Word

Not surprising for a school of its size, University of Central Florida takes a quantitative approach to its admissions game. Therefore, your cumulative high school GPA and standardized test scores will likely hold the most weight when it comes to deciding factors.

THE SCHOOL SAYS " . . ."

From the Admissions Office

"The University of Central Florida offers competitive advantages to its student body. We're committed to teaching, providing advisement, and academic support services for all students. Our undergraduates have access to state-of-the-art wireless buildings, high-tech classrooms, research labs, web-based classes, and an undergraduate research and mentoring program.

"Our Career Services professionals help students gain practical experiences at NASA, schools, hospitals, high-tech companies, local municipalities, and the entertainment industry. With an international focus to our curricula and research programs, we enroll international students from 126 nations. Our study abroad programs and other study and research opportunities include agreements with ninety-eight institutions and thirty-six countries.

"UCF's 1,415-acre campus provides a safe and serene setting for learning, with natural lakes and woodlands. The bustle of Orlando lies a short distance away: the pro sport teams, the Kennedy Space Center, film studios, Walt Disney World, Universal Orlando, Sea World, and sandy beaches are all nearby.

"Applicants are required to take the SAT or the ACT (with writing). We will use a student's best scores from either test."

SELECTIVITY

Admissions Rating	89
# of applicants	31,820
% of applicants accepted	49
% of acceptees attending	39
# offered a place on the wait list	1,895
% accepting a place on wait list	48
% admitted from wait list	61

FRESHMAN PROFILE

Range SAT Critical Reading	540–630
Range SAT Math	550–640
Range SAT Writing	510–610
Range ACT Composite	23–28
Minimum paper TOEFL	550
Minimum web-based TOEFL	213
Average HS GPA	3.81
% graduated top 10% of class	30
% graduated top 25% of class	71
% graduated top 50% of class	97

DEADLINES

Regular	
Deadline	5/1
Nonfall registration?	Yes

FINANCIAL FACTS

Financial Aid Rating	70
Annual in tuition	$6,317
Annual out-of-state tuition	$22,415
Room and board	$9,394
Required fees	$0
Books and supplies	$1,146
% needy frosh rec. need-based scholarship or grant aid	66
% needy UG rec. need-based scholarship or grant aid	72
% needy frosh rec. non-need-based scholarship or grant aid	91
% needy UG rec. non-need-based scholarship or grant aid	59
% needy frosh rec. need-based self-help aid	48
% needy UG rec. need-based self-help aid	58
% frosh rec. any financial aid	89
% UG rec. any financial aid	81
% UG borrow to pay for school	48
Average cumulative indebtedness	$23,186
% frosh need fully met	10
% ugrads need fully met	8
Average % of frosh need met	57
Average % of ugrad need met	58

THE UNIVERSITY OF CHICAGO

1101 EAST FIFTY-EIGHTH STREET, CHICAGO, IL 60637 • ADMISSIONS: 773-702-8650 • FAX: 773-702-4199

CAMPUS LIFE

Quality of Life Rating	92
Fire Safety Rating	93
Green Rating	92
Type of school	Private
Affiliation	No Affiliation
Environment	Metropolis

STUDENTS

Total undergrad enrollment	5,587
% male/female	53/47
% from out of state	81
% frosh from public high school	62
% frosh live on campus	100
% ugrads live on campus	55
% African American	5
% Asian	18
% Caucasian	46
% Hispanic	8
% Native American	<1
% international	9
# of countries represented	103

SURVEY SAYS . . .
Political activism is popular
Students are happy
Classroom facilities are great
Lab facilities are great
Career services are great
Internships are widely available
School is well run
Students love Chicago, IL
Dorms are like palaces
Athletic facilities are great
Active minority support groups

ACADEMICS

Academic Rating	98
% students returning for sophomore year	99
% students graduating within 4 years	86
% students graduating within 6 years	92
Calendar	Quarter
Student/faculty ratio	6:1
Profs interesting rating	86
Profs accessible rating	84

Most classes have 10–19 students.
Most lab/discussion sessions have
10–19 students.

MOST POPULAR MAJORS
economics; biology; political science

STUDENTS SAY ". . ."

Academics

Described as "an academic paradise near an awesome city," the University of Chicago is a place where students "aren't embarrassed by the fact that they're smart." Students say, UChicago "is a rigorous institution," and they celebrate the fact that "you can't just stick up your hand and not expect to be challenged by your professors and your peers." Classrooms are small and foster a "collaborative learning environment." "It's a place that pushes smart people to make new discoveries, challenge their limits, and find new ways of understanding the world." The "wide array of strong academic programs" offered at UChicago are set on the quarter system, which can be "a bit intensive." "The sheer amount of material one covers in any given quarter is simply massive." If you are up for it, you can "learn a ton" in this fast-paced system. The "rigorous" core curriculum leads "you to learn about things that you never thought you would enjoy." "The school is at the forefront of research in most subjects, and the core really helps develop students into thinkers." There is "lots of focus on discussion, analyzing original texts, and critical thinking." Professors are a main reason students love this school. "Professors are celebrities in their field—it's extremely common to begin doing research on a topic and realize that the world's expert is two buildings down." Remarkably, even "first-year students are often exposed to the best professors the school has to offer." "This school is challenging, but it's not anything you can't handle. Everyone gets to pick the classes they take and how many they take at any time. You can make it as easy or hard as you want."

Life

The "College Houses" are a very important aspect of student life and gets rave reviews for being a "supportive, fun, community environment" with a "family atmosphere." "Your house becomes your family and the center of your social life on campus. You go to parties with your house, your best friends come from the house, and you will likely move off campus with members of your house. The house system is truly one of the great aspects of the University of Chicago." Although the "harsh Chicago winter" may not appeal to everyone, the city of Chicago clearly does. "Chicago offers anything that you want," from "the great nightlife," to "concerts, restaurants, movies, [and] plays," to "operas at the Lyric." "The most difficult part of finding fun is deciding which of your many options you want to pursue that day!" Staying on school grounds is also a popular option. "There's a healthy party scene on campus during the weekends, with frats and apartments throwing events." There are other happenings, "like cultural shows, food festivals, and movie screenings that you can enjoy on a day-to-day basis." The library is a popular place "when it comes to crunch-time studying."

Student Body

Students at UChicago are an "engaged" lot, "attracted to living and learning among really smart, interesting people." Students find it difficult to describe a typical student except as someone "you wouldn't expect. Football players are computer programmers, sorority girls are poets, [and] nerds are hip-hop dance prodigies." "It runs the gamut from complete nerd to complete jock. It even includes people who are both!" What students do "have in common is a genuine interest in ideas and a profound investment in the life of the mind." They take pride in "a commitment to a certain kind of excellence here, one that values intellectualism both inside and outside the classroom, [and one] that places a premium on the ability to think critically, and integrate and apply these skills in ways not traditionally used." One student advises that UChicago is "an incredibly intense place, academically speaking, and students should be prepared to live what they learn because studies surround every aspect of campus life here. This doesn't mean that people are constantly in the library, though. It means that people bring with them wherever they go a certain spirit of adventurous inquiry that makes every conversation an interesting one."

FINANCIAL AID: 773-702-8655 • E-MAIL: COLLEGEADMISSIONS@UCHICAGO.EDU • WEBSITE: WWW.UCHICAGO.EDU

THE PRINCETON REVIEW SAYS

Admissions

Very important factors considered include: Rigor of secondary school record, application essay, recommendation(s). *Important factors considered include:* Talent/ability, character/personal qualities, extracurricular activities, volunteer work, level of applicant's interest. *Other factors considered include:* Standardized test scores, class rank, GPA, first generation, interview, racial/ethnic status, work experience, alumni/ae relations. SAT or ACT required; ACT with or without Writing component accepted. TOEFL, IELTS or PTE required of all international applicants. *Academic units recommended:* 4 English; 4 mathematics; 4 science; 2 social studies; 3 foreign language; 2 history.

Financial Aid

Students should submit: FAFSA, CSS/Financial Aid PROFILE, Noncustodial PROFILE. Regular filing deadline is 2/1. *Need-based scholarships/grants offered:* Federal Pell, SEOG, State scholarships/grants, private scholarships, the school's own gift aid. *Loan aid offered:* Direct Subsidized Stafford Loans, Direct Unsubsidized Stafford Loans, Direct PLUS loans, Federal Perkins Loans. Applicants will be notified of awards beginning 4/16. Federal Work-Study Program available. Institutional employment available. Off-campus job opportunities are excellent.

The Inside Word

People at the University of Chicago dwell on deep thoughts and big ideas. In your application, you'll need to demonstrate outstanding grades in the tough courses and that you will fit in with a bunch of thinkers. Although the University of Chicago uses the common application, essay topics remain "uncommon" and thought-provoking. Interviews are recommended but not required.

THE SCHOOL SAYS "..."

From the Admissions Office

"The University of Chicago is universally recognized for its devotion to open and rigorous inquiry. The strength of our intellectual traditions—intense critical analysis, lively debate, and creative solutions to complex problems—rests on the scholars who continue to engage them. Graduates of the college have made discoveries in every field of academic study; they are ambitious thinkers who are unafraid to take on the most pressing questions of our time. Their accomplishments have helped establish the university's legacy as one of the world's finest academic institutions. The University of Chicago has been home to eighty-nine Nobel Prize winners, thirty-two MacArthur "Genius" Fellows, and twenty Pulitzer Prize winners. With over 150 research centers and institutes, numerous cultural opportunities, and three of the nation's top professional schools in law, business, and medicine—all within blocks of one another on our campus—UChicago is known for the unparalleled resources it provides its undergraduate students.

"UChicago maintains a student-faculty ratio of six to one, ensuring that every classroom experience exemplifies our commitment to a student's ability to interact closely with our faculty. Our Core Curriculum provides students with a common vocabulary and a well-balanced academic experience, while allowing the flexibility to explore their own particular interests in small discussion-style seminars. Students also enjoy a successful Division III sports program, small but active Greek life, over thirty student theatrical productions a year, a rich music scene, celebrations of culture and community—and the extraordinary opportunities in politics, music, theater, commerce, architecture, and neighborhood life in the city of Chicago."

SELECTIVITY

Admissions Rating	99
# of applicants	25,273
% of applicants accepted	13
% of acceptees attending	46

FRESHMAN PROFILE

Range SAT Critical Reading	710–780
Range SAT Math	710–790
Range SAT Writing	700–780
Range ACT Composite	31–34
Minimum paper TOEFL	600
Minimum web-based TOEFL	104
% graduated top 10% of class	97
% graduated top 25% of class	99
% graduated top 50% of class	100

DEADLINES

Early action	
Deadline	11/1
Notification	12/17
Regular	
Deadline	1/2
Notification	4/1
Nonfall registration?	No

FINANCIAL FACTS

Financial Aid Rating	96
Annual tuition	$43,581
Room and board	$13,137
Required fees	$2,028
Books and supplies	$3,679
% needy frosh rec. need-based scholarship or grant aid	100
% needy UG rec. need-based scholarship or grant aid	99
% needy frosh rec. need-based self-help aid	64
% needy UG rec. need-based self-help aid	79
% frosh rec. any financial aid	64
% UG rec. any financial aid	58
% UG borrow to pay for school	43
Average cumulative indebtedness	$23,930
% frosh need fully met	100
% ugrads need fully met	100
Average % of frosh need met	100
Average % of ugrad need met	100

UNIVERSITY OF CINCINNATI

PO Box 210091, Cincinnati, OH 45221-0091 • Admissions: 513-556-1100 • Fax: 513-556-1105

CAMPUS LIFE

Quality of Life Rating	75
Fire Safety Rating	92
Green Rating	94
Type of school	Public
Affiliation	No Affiliation
Environment	Metropolis

STUDENTS

Total undergrad enrollment	23,360
% male/female	50/50
% from out of state	11
% frosh live on campus	77
% ugrads live on campus	21
# of fraternities (% ugrad men join)	23(11)
# of sororities (% ugrad women join)	15(11)
% African American	8
% Asian	3
% Caucasian	76
% Hispanic	3
% Native American	<1
% international	4
# of countries represented	127

SURVEY SAYS . . .
Great off-campus food
Athletic facilities are great
Everyone loves the Bearcats

ACADEMICS

Academic Rating	75
% students returning for sophomore year	85
% students graduating within 4 years	25
% students graduating within 6 years	64
Calendar	Semester
Student/faculty ratio	18:1
Profs interesting rating	71
Profs accessible rating	71
Most classes have 20–29 students.	

MOST POPULAR MAJORS
marketing; speech communications and rhetoric

STUDENTS SAY ". . ."

Academics

The University of Cincinnati "offers students a balance of educational excellence and real-world experience" on an expansive campus comprised of twelve separate colleges. Students agree it's "a large school with many great programs and infinite opportunities that still retains the feeling of a small university." Many have praise for the "cooperative education program that gives students a real edge in the job market" by allowing them the opportunity to pursue competitive internships while enrolled. Students also feel confident that "UC provides excellent opportunities outside of the classroom to make me successful post-graduation." As one student puts it, "The University of Cincinnati is not only known for its great academics, but for all of the incredible opportunities students have including cooperative education, on-campus activities and clubs, along with athletics and one of the most beautiful campuses in the world." The university's size assures that there are "a wide variety of majors to choose from," and students name the Conservatory of Music, the School of Architecture and Interior Design, and the engineering programs as stand outs. Nevertheless, many carp, "the school could be a little bit better at communicating" and say the "registration process is terrible." Overall, students feel that "the professors here have so much life experience in what they are teaching. It makes me trust and respect them more," and "Advisors have been helpful." However, they note, "The professors are as diverse as the classes offered here," which means that, "like anything else, there is variation. Some are horrible, and some are fantastic."

Life

It's common for students to remark on the "ample green spaces, [and] innovative architectural designs" that make up the "beautiful campus" at UC. One student explains, "The University of Cincinnati has rewarding educational programs and a beautiful urban campus with many opportunities to stay involved. What more can I ask for?" Although most feel that "campus is very safe," some note, "As soon as you step off of campus, it's a different story." However, many acknowledge, "The school does work hard on maintaining a safe environment for us to live and work in." The majority of students describe campus as having a "fun atmosphere" that makes "UC great" but are divided on the topic of university-sponsored activities. Some think the administration should provide "more afterschool activities," while others believe "UC offers a million and one activities for students to partake in during school and on the weekend. Friday Night Live is an extremely popular program offering awesome activities that don't involve alcohol or drugs." A significant portion of undergraduates are from Cincinnati and point out that UC "is a huge commuter school, so many of the students do things all over the city." However, all agree, "People are very passionate about sports here and have great school spirit." A common campus exclamation is "go Bearcats!!"

Student Body

The most common sentiment from UC students is that "there really isn't a typical student." Although "many students are from Cincinnati," most agree, "UC has students from all walks of life, which makes it extremely diverse and very interesting." While many say, "Students can find their niche, be it in LGBTQ groups, ethnic groups, or academic intercollegiate groups," some reveal that although "students fit in well…racial cliques are obvious around campus." However, all concur that the student body is "outgoing and expressive" and proclaim that "students come together to work on issues they care about such as sustainability." Most UC students can be found in a "sweatshirt, [and] jeans…[with a] coffee in hand," and students like to point out that "many students work as well so they seem to be more 'grounded' and well-rounded." Speaking about the student body, one UC student declares, "The majority are young sports fans that like to party, but being a research school there are some academic heavyweights as well." The consensus seems to be that "students at UC are open-minded, and everyone can find a place to fit in."

FINANCIAL AID: 513-556-6982 • E-MAIL: ADMISSIONS@UC.EDU • WEBSITE: WWW.UC.EDU

THE PRINCETON REVIEW SAYS

Admissions

Very important factors considered include: Class rank, GPA, rigor of secondary school record, standardized test scores. *Important factors considered include:* Application essay, extracurricular activities, talent/ability. *Other factors considered include:* SAT or ACT required; ACT with Writing component required. TOEFL required of all international applicants. *Academic units required:* 4 English; 4 mathematics; 2 science; 2 social studies; 2 foreign language; 2 academic electives; 1 visual/performing arts. *Academic units recommended:* 4 mathematics.

Financial Aid

Students should submit: FAFSA. The Princeton Review suggests that all financial aid forms be submitted as soon as possible after January 1. *Need-based scholarships/grants offered:* Federal Pell, SEOG, State scholarships/grants, private scholarships, the school's own gift aid, United Negro College Fund, federal nursing scholarships. *Loan aid offered:* Direct Subsidized Stafford Loans, Direct Unsubsidized Stafford Loans, Direct PLUS loans, Federal Perkins Loans, Federal Nursing Loans, State Loans, College/university loans from institutional funds. Federal Work-Study Program available. Institutional employment available. Off-campus job opportunities are excellent.

The Inside Word

The UC offers hundreds of undergraduate majors and stresses the importance of exploring the specific admission criteria for your program of choice. Prospective students are reminded to work hard while still in high school, with admissions representative saying to hone your GPA from ninth grade on because "it counts!" UC seeks a student who shows evidence of self-reflection. Ideal candidates will exhibit this self-awareness through participation in extra-curricular activities that speak to who they are, not to what they think an admissions board wants. Campus visits are strongly suggested.

THE SCHOOL SAYS ". . ."

From the Admissions Office

"Remarkable architecture, park-like open spaces, engaging student tour guides, and a welcoming admissions staff make the University of Cincinnati a must-visit destination. UC's campus has been transformed over the past ten years and is drawing national and international attention for blending student life, learning, research, and recreation in a unique urban environment.

"UC is a member of The Common Application. Freshman Freshman application materials include high school transcripts, test scores, a personal statement, and a list of co-curricular activities. Some academic programs require additional materials.

"Sign up for a visit, become a Bearcat VIP, and apply online via the Common Application. Information about all UC majors is linked from the website. We also have Tuesday-night online chat sessions for students and parents. Nothing beats a visit, however, for assessing how well you'll fit in here.

"Either the SAT or ACT is required for students applying to bachelor's degree programs; the ACT writing component is required. SAT Subject Tests are not required."

SELECTIVITY

Admissions Rating	77
# of applicants	16,069
% of applicants accepted	73
% of acceptees attending	38

FRESHMAN PROFILE

Range SAT Critical Reading	490–620
Range SAT Math	510–640
Range SAT Writing	490–600
Range ACT Composite	22–28
Minimum paper TOEFL	515
Average HS GPA	3.44
% graduated top 10% of class	22
% graduated top 25% of class	50
% graduated top 50% of class	81

DEADLINES

Regular	
Priority	12/1
Deadline	3/1
Nonfall registration?	Yes

FINANCIAL FACTS

Financial Aid Rating	67
Annual in tuition	$9,124
Annual out-of-state tuition	$24,156
Room and board	$10,290
Required fees	$1,660
Books and supplies	$1,566
% needy frosh rec. need-based scholarship or grant aid	39
% needy UG rec. need-based scholarship or grant aid	43
% needy frosh rec. non-need-based scholarship or grant aid	52
% needy UG rec. non-need-based scholarship or grant aid	41
% needy frosh rec. need-based self-help aid	78
% needy UG rec. need-based self-help aid	77
% frosh rec. any financial aid	84
% UG rec. any financial aid	83
% UG borrow to pay for school	68
Average cumulative indebtedness	$28,333
% frosh need fully met	5
% ugrads need fully met	4
Average % of frosh need met	47
Average % of ugrad need met	42

UNIVERSITY OF COLORADO BOULDER

552 UCB, BOULDER, CO 80309-0552 • ADMISSIONS: 303-492-6301 • FAX: 303-492-6301

CAMPUS LIFE

Quality of Life Rating	87
Fire Safety Rating	88
Green Rating	94
Type of school	Public
Affiliation	No Affiliation
Environment	City

STUDENTS

Total undergrad enrollment	25,461
% male/female	55/45
% from out of state	37
% frosh from public high school	91
% frosh live on campus	94
% ugrads live on campus	28
# of fraternities (% ugrad men join)	21 (11)
# of sororities (% ugrad women join)	16 (17)
% African American	2
% Asian	5
% Caucasian	74
% Hispanic	10
% Native American	<1
% international	4
# of countries represented	114

SURVEY SAYS . . .

Students are happy
Students environmentally aware
Students love Boulder, CO
Great off-campus food
Intramural sports are popular

ACADEMICS

Academic Rating	79
% students returning for sophomore year	85
% students graduating within 4 years	44
% students graduating within 6 years	70
Calendar	Semester
Student/faculty ratio	18:1
Profs interesting rating	78
Profs accessible rating	72

Most classes have 10–19 students.
Most lab/discussion sessions have 20–29 students.

MOST POPULAR MAJORS
physiology; psychology; speech communications and rhetoric

STUDENTS SAY "..."

Academics

Strong academics paired with many opportunities to get involved with research and obtain work experience make UC—Boulder appealing. One sophomore tells us, "UC does a fantastic job of keeping students up-to-date on the goings-on and important news around school, town, and the world." Another current student sums it up perfectly, explaining that UC—Boulder has "a sense of vitality and curiosity that fills the campus, and yet it's comfortable and relaxed." Students repeatedly tell us, "UC is an amazing place because you can find an array of challenges and opportunities whether your drive is research, the arts, sports, a job, or tough class work. However, at the same time, you can find a great social life outside of school in an amazing place like Boulder." Another student shares, "I am being taught not only about class material, but also about finding who I am as a student, individual, and community member, [as well as] how to efficiently apply that to today's world."

UC—Boulder offers an excellent liberal arts education, and the social life is diverse enough so that everyone is able to find a niche that suits their interests. Students point out, "UC has some of the best research facilities in the world." When asked about staff, students say, "Most professors are here for research but that isn't necessarily a bad thing because many incorporate and relate their fascinating work experience with lecture." Another student tells us, "My professors represent a wide range of ages, nationalities, and genders. Professors are helpful and entertaining, and they have real-world experience." Students seem satisfied with the academics overall. A member of the junior class tells us, "I have very involved professors who have helped me better my overall academic experience by providing me the possibilities to learn beyond the classroom." Another junior adds, "Professors are usually knowledgeable, and a few are exceptional. Academic experience has transferred very well to internships that I found while attending a university sponsored career fair."

Life

The city of Boulder is a place of beauty and academic prominence at the foot of the Rocky Mountains. It is full of coffee shops and quaint shopping areas, in addition to being the home to UC—Boulder. Students say, "The campus at UC—Boulder is gorgeous, and there is always something to do, much of it outdoors." Another student adds, "People are very active in Boulder. Hiking, kayaking, mountain biking, skiing, and snowboarding are all popular weekend (or weekday) activities." One student reflects, "People think about having fun and making the most of their time while at the same time figuring out what their purposes and life goals are." A junior observes, "There are many smart conversations going on around campus; walking from class to class you hear people debating anything from the newest engineering or physics discovery, to philosophy, to politics, to the state of contemporary education." Learning is not an experience isolated to the classroom, as this student points out, "You can learn so much—it's great talking to students studying different things."

Student Body

Students choose UC—Boulder because of the many opportunities available academically, socially, and financially. We hear, "My school is all about progress, inclusion, and sustainability." In-state tuition benefits are a large draw, as well as the prolific research facilities. One student tells us, "I received a full-ride scholarship, and I felt comfortable going to a school with a diversity of majors and opportunities." In addition, one in four graduates has studied abroad. One student shares her experience, saying, "The students and staff are friendly and open-minded, and the academics are excellent." "I wanted a large public university that would allow me access to a diverse selection of student groups, research labs, fellow peers, faculty, and life experiences, and I found it here at UC—Boulder." Another student sums it up, "I think there are many different types of students, but they all interact smoothly and efficiently. Most students enjoy the outdoors and being outside." "UC—Boulder offers an excellent liberal arts education, and the social life is diverse enough so that everyone is able to find a niche that suits his or her interests."

FINANCIAL AID: 303-492-5091 • E-MAIL: APPLY@COLORADO.EDU • WEBSITE: WWW.COLORADO.EDU

THE PRINCETON REVIEW SAYS

Admissions

Very important factors considered include: Class rank, GPA, rigor of secondary school record, standardized test scores. *Important factors considered include:* Application essay, extracurricular activities, first generation, recommendation(s), talent/ability, character/personal qualities. *Other factors considered include:* Geographical residence, racial/ethnic status, state residency, volunteer work, work experience, alumni/ae relations, level of applicant's interest. SAT or ACT required; ACT with or without Writing component accepted. TOEFL required of all international applicants. *Academic units required:* 4 English; 4 mathematics; 3 science; (2 science lab); 3 social studies; 3 foreign language; 1 history.

Financial Aid

Students should submit: FAFSA. The Princeton Review suggests that all financial aid forms be submitted as soon as possible after January 1. *Need-based scholarships/grants offered:* Federal Pell, SEOG, State scholarships/grants, private scholarships, the school's own gift aid. *Loan aid offered:* Direct Subsidized Stafford Loans, Direct Unsubsidized Stafford Loans, Direct PLUS loans, Federal Perkins Loans, College/university loans from institutional funds. Federal Work-Study Program available. Institutional employment available. Off-campus job opportunities are excellent.

The Inside Word

Applicants must indicate the school within CU to which they wish to be admitted. Engineering and Applied Science is most competitive, followed by the College of Music, the Leeds School of Business, and the College of Architecture and Planning. The College of Arts and Sciences is the least competitive; those applying to and not selected by the more competitive schools are automatically entered into consideration for admission to the College of Arts and Sciences. With nearly one-third of the student body from out of state, CU boasts far more geographic diversity than most state schools.

THE SCHOOL SAYS "..."

From the Admissions Office

"The University of Colorado—Boulder is a place of beauty and academic prominence at the foot of the Rocky Mountains. A sense of vitality and curiosity fills the campus, and yet it's comfortable and relaxed. It's a place you can be yourself and let your imagination soar. We have programs for you if you seek leadership training, research experience, academic honors, international experience (one in four graduates has studied abroad), community involvement, and more. There are a number of enrichment programs that give exceptionally talented and intellectually committed students the opportunity to expand their education outside the classroom, build a sense of community, and help prepare for post-graduate opportunities. Residential Academic Programs (RAPs) and Living and Learning Communities (LLCs) in several residence halls provide undergraduates with shared learning and living experiences.

"Getting involved is easy at CU—Boulder. If you are interested in student government, clubs, athletics, recreation, Greek life, volunteer work, theater, dance, film, exhibits, planetarium shows, or concerts, you will find them here.

"To find out if CU—Boulder is the place for you, we encourage you to visit. Contact the office of admissions, or take a virtual tour online. The University of Colorado at Boulder requires either SAT or ACT scores for admissions; the writing tests are currently not used in making decisions. SAT Subject Test scores are not required."

SELECTIVITY

Admissions Rating	78
# of applicants	22,473
% of applicants accepted	88
% of acceptees attending	30
# offered a place on the wait list	469
% accepting a place on wait list	24
% admitted from wait list	0

FRESHMAN PROFILE

Range SAT Critical Reading	520–630
Range SAT Math	540–650
Range ACT Composite	24–29
Minimum paper TOEFL	75
Average HS GPA	3.56
% graduated top 10% of class	27
% graduated top 25% of class	56
% graduated top 50% of class	88

DEADLINES

Early action	
Deadline	11/15
Notification	2/1
Regular	
Priority	11/15
Deadline	1/15
Notification	4/1
Nonfall registration?	Yes

APPLICANTS ALSO LOOK AT AND RARELY PREFER

University of Utah; University of Wyoming

FINANCIAL FACTS

Financial Aid Rating	89
Annual in-state tuition	$8,760
Annual out-of-state tuition	$30,528
Room and board	$12,258
Required fees	$1,587
Books and supplies	$1,800
% needy frosh rec. need-based scholarship or grant aid	72
% needy UG rec. need-based scholarship or grant aid	72
% needy frosh rec. non-need-based scholarship or grant aid	5
% needy UG rec. non-need-based scholarship or grant aid	4
% needy frosh rec. need-based self-help aid	88
% needy UG rec. need-based self-help aid	89
% frosh rec. any financial aid	72
% UG rec. any financial aid	61
% UG borrow to pay for school	46
Average cumulative indebtedness	$24,880
% frosh need fully met	54
% ugrads need fully met	48
Average % of frosh need met	81
Average % of ugrad need met	81

UNIVERSITY OF CONNECTICUT

2131 HILLSIDE ROAD, STORRS, CT 06268-3088 • ADMISSIONS: 860-486-3137 • FAX: 860-486-1476

CAMPUS LIFE

Quality of Life Rating	75
Fire Safety Rating	82
Green Rating	97
Type of school	Public
Affiliation	No Affiliation
Environment	Town

STUDENTS

Total undergrad enrollment	17,684
% male/female	51/49
% from out of state	21
% frosh from public high school	88
% frosh live on campus	96
% ugrads live on campus	72
# of fraternities (% ugrad men join)	18 (5)
# of sororities (% ugrad women join)	15 (11)
% African American	5
% Asian	9
% Caucasian	63
% Hispanic	8
% Native American	<1
% international	3
# of countries represented	99

SURVEY SAYS . . .

Lots of beer drinking
Hard liquor is popular
Everyone loves the Huskies

ACADEMICS

Academic Rating	75
% students returning for sophomore year	94
% students graduating within 4 years	68
% students graduating within 6 years	83
Calendar	Semester
Student/faculty ratio	16:1
Profs interesting rating	66
Profs accessible rating	68

Most classes have 10–19 students.
Most lab/discussion sessions have 10–19 students.

MOST POPULAR MAJORS

Psychology; Biology/Biological Sciences; Economics

STUDENTS SAY ". . ."

Academics

The University of Connecticut is an "academically strong, athletically powerful [and] environmentally aware" school that fosters "a strong sense of school pride." The school "has big-time sports and activities in a large campus" while maintaining "a strong sense of school pride and community." This "public ivy" is especially attractive to in-state students, providing them with "low," "affordable" tuition and an "excellent return on investment." UConn "instills direction and passion in each of [its] students" while "providing a well-rounded educational." This is a campus where everyone walks around with the hashtag "#BleedBlue" trending in their hearts. Academically, UConn is all about "Opportunities!!!" UConn "offers nearly any degree that one could possibly want," a Chemistry major explains. "There are so many opportunities offered here at UConn that anyone could find their niche," says a Mathematics and Statistics double major. The quality of professors seems to vary widely. The top level professors are "extremely knowledgeable," "open to discussion" and "really want students to do their best." However, "introductory professors don't care as much as upper-level ones do" and many of the courses are taught by graduate students who are often "not native English speakers." As a Division I sports school, "basketball is king" at UConn. This can sometimes be problematic. "It seems that athletics (mostly basketball) are a higher priority than academics," one student says. Another bemoans the fact that the school is "cutting funding to the humanities" while "wasting money on huge sports stadiums!" Many other students love the "great social atmosphere" provided by "Huskies basketball!" "The campus itself is beautiful" and "has everything you need" including "great buildings and classrooms, and great student services." At the end of the day, UConn is "a big, loud and extremely proud mess of blue."

Life

"The mantra around campus is definitely 'Work Hard, Play Hard'," meaning that "students at UConn love to party, but most take their studies seriously as well." Your average student works "all week and then gets plastered on Friday" before rounding off the weekend "with a regret day Saturday and a work day Sunday." "Parties are popular, but other UConn run activities are popular too," one student argues. Student clubs and organizations are big on campus, with your average student being "involved in one to three clubs." As one freshman explains: "There is a saying on campus that takes a spin on 'there's an app for that'; it goes, 'there's a club for that' in reference to the fact that there is literally a club for any interest." There are also "guest lectures almost every day on a wide array of topics" and "movies are also shown at the Student Union [on] Friday, Saturday, and Sunday night." The Jorgensen Theater puts on "tons of shows" in "a diverse range of acts, such as African tribal dancers, classical musicians…and a variety of plays, musicals, and ballets." "UConn Pride runs deep throughout the campus community" and often manifests itself around Huskies sporting events, especially "football games, men's and women's basketball games, and men's soccer games." If students feel the itch to get off campus, the school is "located between New York, Boston, and Providence (and very close to Hartford) so there is no lack of places to take day trips."

Student Body

UConn students "are typically friendly, inclusive, and studious." Demographically, they tend to be "middle class or upper-middle class" "Caucasian" and "most often from Connecticut." While "they skew on the preppy side of the spectrum" and tend to wear "Sperry's, Polo, Vera Bradley, etc." this isn't always the case. The university is large enough that "you have people in Greek life, hipsters who live in EcoHouse, theatre kids, you name it." "As with all schools, there are cliques," but "there is a 'home' or place for every student to fit in or belong to." The safest way to dress on campus is in full "UConn attire" as "everyone is always wearing it." "One of the things I like most is that there isn't a typical student here," a Mathematics major says. "We have so many majors and organizations on campus that I don't think you can perfectly pinpoint the average UConn student."

FINANCIAL AID: 860-486-2819 • E-MAIL: BEAHUSKY@UCONN.EDU • WEBSITE: WWW.UCONN.EDU

THE PRINCETON REVIEW SAYS

Admissions

Very important factors considered include: Class rank, GPA, rigor of secondary school record, standardized test scores. *Important factors considered include:* Application essay, extracurricular activities, first generation, racial/ethnic status, recommendation(s), talent/ability, volunteer work, character/personal qualities. *Other factors considered include:* Geographical residence, state residency, work experience, alumni/ae relations, level of applicant's interest. SAT or ACT required; ACT with Writing component required. TOEFL required of all international applicants. *Academic units required:* 4 English; 3 mathematics; 2 science; (2 science lab); 2 social studies; 2 foreign language; 3 academic electives. *Academic units recommended:* 3 foreign language.

Financial Aid

Students should submit: FAFSA. The Princeton Review suggests that all financial aid forms be submitted as soon as possible after January 1. *Need-based scholarships/grants offered:* Federal Pell, SEOG, State scholarships/grants, private scholarships, the school's own gift aid, federal nursing scholarships. *Loan aid offered:* Direct Subsidized Stafford Loans, Direct Unsubsidized Stafford Loans, Direct PLUS loans, Federal Perkins Loans, Federal Nursing Loans. Federal Work-Study Program available. Institutional employment available. Off-campus job opportunities are good.

The Inside Word

The UConn admissions committee takes a holistic approach to evaluating applicants. Everything from GPA and class rank to extracurricular activates and letters of recommendation is taken into consideration. UConn is a very selective school, so students will want to make sure each and every part of their application is up to snuff.

THE SCHOOL SAYS "..."

From the Admissions Office

"Founded in 1881, the University of Connecticut is ranked as one of the best public universities in the United States. With a combination of dynamic faculty, strong athletic pride and an extraordinary sense of community, UConn is a university like no other. Offering over 100 majors and the ability to create a major of your own, a broad range of academic choices is provided. Faculty members are top experts in their fields, and serve as mentors and advisors to students. Distinctive research opportunities pair undergraduate students with faculty in every academic discipline offered. The main campus in Storrs is located in a safe, rural New England town midway between New York City and Boston. With the highest percentage of students living on campus of any public university in the United States, UConn is its own community within a thriving small town. With on-campus museums and performances, and newly-released movies right inside the Student Union's theater, UConn students work hard and play hard. Almost 600 student clubs and organizations allow students to pursue their passions outside the classroom. Face paint, chants, and school spirit permeate throughout the campus. Students can cheer on one of our 24 Division I teams, or join one of our intramural or club sports teams. No matter how students are involved, they exemplify the Husky Spirit.

Interested in learning more about what UConn can offer you? For details on the admissions process or to schedule a campus tour, visit admissions.uconn.edu.

"

SELECTIVITY

Admissions Rating	92
# of applicants	27,479
% of applicants accepted	54
% of acceptees attending	25
# offered a place on the wait list	2,601
% accepting a place on wait list	49
% admitted from wait list	2

FRESHMAN PROFILE

Range SAT Critical Reading	550–650
Range SAT Math	580–680
Range SAT Writing	560–660
Range ACT Composite	25–30
Minimum paper TOEFL	550
Minimum web-based TOEFL	213
% graduated top 10% of class	45
% graduated top 25% of class	82
% graduated top 50% of class	97

DEADLINES

Regular	
Deadline	1/15
Nonfall registration?	Yes

APPLICANTS ALSO LOOK AT AND OFTEN PREFER

University of Maryland; College Park; University of Delaware; Boston College

AND SOMETIMES PREFER

Boston University; Northeastern University; Pennsylvania State University—University Park

AND RARELY PREFER

University of Massachusetts Amherst; University of New Hampshire; University of Rhode Island; Rutgers- The State University of New Jersey—New Brunswick; University of Vermont

FINANCIAL FACTS

Financial Aid Rating	72
Annual in-state tuition	$9,256
Annual out-of-state tuition	$20,204
Room and board	$12,074
Required fees	$2,872
Books and supplies	$850
% needy frosh rec. need-based scholarship or grant aid	66
% needy UG rec. need-based scholarship or grant aid	72
% needy frosh rec. non-need-based scholarship or grant aid	49
% needy UG rec. non-need-based scholarship or grant aid	34
% needy frosh rec. need-based self-help aid	68
% needy UG rec. need-based self-help aid	72
% frosh rec. any financial aid	49
% UG rec. any financial aid	48
% UG borrow to pay for school	62
Average cumulative indebtedness	$24,600
% frosh need fully met	14
% ugrads need fully met	14
Average % of frosh need met	59
Average % of ugrad need met	62

UNIVERSITY OF DALLAS

1845 EAST NORTHGATE DRIVE, IRVING, TX 75062 • ADMISSIONS: 972-721-5266 • FAX: 972-721-5017

CAMPUS LIFE

Quality of Life Rating	83
Fire Safety Rating	80
Green Rating	61
Type of school	Private
Affiliation	Roman Catholic
Environment	City

STUDENTS

Total undergrad enrollment	1,353
% male/female	48/52
% from out of state	52
% frosh from public high school	43
% frosh live on campus	87
% ugrads live on campus	65
% African American	1
% Asian	4
% Caucasian	69
% Hispanic	17
% Native American	<1
% international	3
# of countries represented	53

SURVEY SAYS . . .

Lots of conservative students
Students are happy
Students are friendly
Students are very religious
Students get along with local community
Very little drug use

ACADEMICS

Academic Rating	88
% students returning for sophomore year	80
% students graduating within 4 years	60
% students graduating within 6 years	69
Calendar	Semester
Student/faculty ratio	10:1
Profs interesting rating	93
Profs accessible rating	90

Most classes have 10–19 students.
Most lab/discussion sessions have
10–19 students.

MOST POPULAR MAJORS

English language and literature; business
administration and management; biology

STUDENTS SAY ". . ."

Academics

At the University of Dallas, a Catholic school in Irving, Texas, "the core curriculum provides an amazing foundation for any major," a broad, sweeping curriculum that "really pushes students to use the greatest amount of brain power." Push you this school will. The "rigorous core curriculum" has an "emphasis on independent thought and the intelligence of the student population," and students are expected to keep up. Academics here are "extremely challenging so that when you graduate, no one has the same degree as you unless they are well-educated." The "really passionate" educators here "motivate students to complete the work load whatever the size and take genuine interest even if the class is different from a student's major." These "intelligent and sophisticated teachers" strive to "understand their students and try to make the most of theirs and their students' time, both inside the class and out." Another comments, "I would say you would be hard-pressed to find more accessible professors in the nation." One student who had a "somewhat bumpy" academic experience even admitted that it was "mainly due to my own shortcomings." What truly sets the school's curriculum apart, however, is not the challenge, but rather the scope and diversity of it. As one student enthused, "I never thought I'd have so many different takes on all the subjects I've studied."

Life

If students are hitting the books hard during the week, many are also hitting the bottle hard on weekends. "It is rare to find someone at this school who does not drink." Another breaks it down this way: "The students here fall under two categories, drinkers and non-drinkers. The percentage of each is about fifty-fifty." But that may paint too simplistic picture of life at UD. Yes, "you could probably find a group to drink with any night of the week," but you can just as easily find yourself lost in a wealth of other things to do. With the Dallas Metro area so easily accessible, entertainment abounds. Some students "go two-stepping or play basketball," others play volleyball or soccer. "Watching movies is another favorite occupation," and "there are many restaurants in the area, and the Arts District is always a treat." Arlington is an easy drive away, offering all its history, pubs, and of course, the Six Flags theme park. A new DART station "allows easy access to the entire Dallas area," and "the Student Activities Committee also charters busses to take students to events around the DFW area such as the State Fair, Billy Bob's, and Oktoberfest in Addison." No matter what, UD students feel "the weekend is the weekend, and students give it due respect," drinkers and non-drinkers alike.

Student Body

The largely Catholic and conservative students of UD are "highly motivated and religious," a group for whom "the topic of faith is a regular part of conversation." While there are deep philosophical divides—"my Protestant friends do find themselves defending their faith often," one student notes—these divides aren't "a battle as much as an intellectual conversation." Indeed, "everyone is treated with equal dignity." If there is a true divide, it is in personalities. One group of students are "extremely conservative, nerdy, philosophy major types who can sometimes be socially inept." Contrasting them are "business and Econ major types who play sports and party." Despite these divides, many students insist that "we all treat each other with respect and can be friendly to one another." Perhaps that comes with having a relatively small campus. "With an intimate student body, everyone is friends with everyone else." The common themes of faith certainly do not hurt. On campus, most are "upbeat and friendly" young people who come from a "background of big families and regular church attendees." No matter your specific background or beliefs, "almost all students can find someone with similar values with themselves."

FINANCIAL AID: 972-721-5266 • E-MAIL: UGADMIS@UDALLAS.EDU • WEBSITE: WWW.UDALLAS.EDU

THE PRINCETON REVIEW SAYS

Admissions

Very important factors considered include: GPA, rigor of secondary school record, standardized test scores, application essay, recommendation(s), character/personal qualities. *Important factors considered include:* Class rank, talent/ability. *Other factors considered include:* Extracurricular activities, first generation, interview, volunteer work, work experience, alumni/ae relations, level of applicant's interest. SAT or ACT required; ACT with Writing component required. TOEFL required of all international applicants. *Academic units required:* 4 English; 3 mathematics; 3 science; 3 social studies; 2 foreign language; 3 history; 4 academic electives; 2 visual/performing arts. *Academic units recommended:* 4 English; 4 mathematics; 3 science; (3 science lab); 4 social studies; 3 foreign language; 4 history; 4 academic electives; 2 visual/performing arts.

Financial Aid

Students should submit: FAFSA. Regular filing deadline is 3/1. The Princeton Review suggests that all financial aid forms be submitted as soon as possible after January 1. *Need-based scholarships/grants offered:* Federal Pell, SEOG, State scholarships/grants, private scholarships, the school's own gift aid. *Loan aid offered:* Direct Subsidized Stafford Loans, Direct Unsubsidized Stafford Loans, Direct PLUS loans, Federal Perkins Loans, State Loans. Federal Work-Study Program available. Institutional employment available. Off-campus job opportunities are fair.

The Inside Word

While having a solid academic background is important, UD admissions officers are looking for something more than grades. A dedication to serious academic inquiry is near vital, and the university's conservative nature means the admissions office places significant emphasis on the "fit" part of the admissions process.

THE SCHOOL SAYS "..."

From the Admissions Office

"Quite unabashedly, the curriculum at the University of Dallas is based on the supposition that truth and virtue exist and are the proper objects of search in an education. The curriculum further supposes that this search is best pursued through an acquisition of philosophical and theological principles on the part of a student and has for its analogical field a vast body of great literature—perhaps more extensive than is likely to be encountered elsewhere—supplemented by a survey of the sweep of history and an introduction to the political and economic principles of society. An understanding of these subjects, along with an introduction to the quantitative and scientific worldview and a mastery of a language, is expected to form a comprehensive and coherent experience, which, in effect, governs the intellect of a student in a manner that develops independence of thought in its most effective mode.

"Students applying for admission are required to take the SAT Reasoning Test or the ACT with writing assessment."

SELECTIVITY

Admissions Rating	88
# of applicants	1,178
% of applicants accepted	88
% of acceptees attending	34

FRESHMAN PROFILE

Range SAT Critical Reading	550–670
Range SAT Math	530–640
Range SAT Writing	530–660
Range ACT Composite	23–29
Minimum paper TOEFL	550
Minimum web-based TOEFL	213
Average HS GPA	3.65
% graduated top 10% of class	53
% graduated top 25% of class	72
% graduated top 50% of class	85

DEADLINES

Early action	
Deadline	12/1
Notification	1/15
Regular	
Priority	12/1
Deadline	3/1
Nonfall registration?	No

APPLICANTS ALSO LOOK AT AND OFTEN PREFER

Southern Methodist University; University of Notre Dame

AND SOMETIMES PREFER

Austin College; Texas Christian University; Trinity University

AND RARELY PREFER

Texas A&M University—College Station; The University of Texas at Austin; Loyola University New Orleans; Saint Louis University

FINANCIAL FACTS

Financial Aid Rating	67
Annual tuition	$30,850
Room and board	$10,500
Required fees	$2,160
Books and supplies	$1,200
% needy frosh rec. need-based scholarship or grant aid	99
% needy UG rec. need-based scholarship or grant aid	98
% needy frosh rec. non-need-based scholarship or grant aid	55
% needy UG rec. non-need-based scholarship or grant aid	50
% needy frosh rec. need-based self-help aid	76
% needy UG rec. need-based self-help aid	78
% frosh rec. any financial aid	96
% UG rec. any financial aid	93
% UG borrow to pay for school	58
Average cumulative indebtedness	$31,466
% frosh need fully met	18
% ugrads need fully met	16

UNIVERSITY OF DAYTON

300 COLLEGE PARK, DAYTON, OH 45469-1300 • ADMISSIONS: 937-229-4411 • FAX: 937-229-4729

STUDENTS SAY " . . ."

Academics
The University of Dayton not only prepares students for the real world, but it also "challenges them to better that world." This institution takes the Marianist values of "intense education, strong community, and deep faithfulness, and wraps it into a place that is a fun place to be"; there is also a palpable connection among all levels of the university. The school is "large enough to have all of the necessary resources and opportunities, but it is small enough to have a feeling of intimacy," and students have the "opportunity to meet with the president and administration and bring ideas up to them" on a regular basis. "No one likes UD—everyone loves it," says one of many happy students. Professors at UD are "always willing to help their students and do their part to make our course work academically challenging." "My professors are extremely intelligent; they provide optimal learning experiences," says a student. They bring their real-life experiences to the classroom, and the courses have "taught me not only to think on a more global scale, but they have armed me to make more conscious decisions in my day-to-day life," according to one student. "I have never had a professor here that I did not enjoy, and I have had many that I sincerely admire," says another. Under the university's requirements, fieldwork abounds, and students are "not just sitting in a classroom for four years, we actually go out and see our learning in action." Students also note that the university "has a promising vision for the future of the school." There is always change occurring on campus, whether it's "new residential halls, cafeterias, or new student programs and clubs," and "faculty and administration respect and listen to the advice of students." The focus on giving back means that numerous resources are devoted to making it easy "for students to get involved here in Dayton or in another country."

Life
"Open doors in dorms and an inviting campus" make UD an inviting and friendly place to be. With so many organizations, clubs, and (extremely popular) intramural sports "there are always new things to do and new people to meet." The vast majority of students live on campus all four years, which "helps keep a very strong community." "The focus on community cannot be described in words; I instantly felt something different when I stepped on the campus," says one student. Service orientation is prevalent in UD life: "UD has opened up so many doors for me to explore service, while having fun and connecting with fellow UD students," says a student. Weekdays, there are "all kinds of club meetings and practices that keep people busy into the evening," but on weekends, most people venture out to the "ghetto," (the jokingly named student neighborhood), where "upperclassman open up their houses for other students." This neighborhood rests next to campus and consists of more than 400 homes, which "provides a student with a quintessential college experience." Campus clubs and organizations also plan bigger events on campus and off campus on weekends, including "art programs and performances," "Cincinnati Reds Baseball games, shopping trips to Columbus, and whitewater rafting trips to West Virginia."

Student Body
Though many admit that diversity is lacking (but growing) at UD, it is generally agreed that every single student here is "friendly, outgoing, involved, and service-oriented." "[Students are] the most welcoming people I have ever known," says one. Most here are from the Midwest, and sweat/yoga pants and UD gear are the standard uniform. Students are so friendly at this close-knit campus of around 7,500 or so that there are "two to three degrees of separation" between everyone. Most people "love UD basketball," participate in "multiple intramural sports, do a lot of service in the community," and "go out both Friday and Saturday night (and most Thursdays)."

FINANCIAL AID: 800-427-5029 • E-MAIL: ADMISSION@UDAYTON.EDU • WEBSITE: WWW.UDAYTON.EDU

THE PRINCETON REVIEW SAYS

Admissions

Very important factors considered include: GPA, rigor of secondary school record, standardized test scores, application essay. *Important factors considered include:* Extracurricular activities, recommendation(s), alumni/ae relations, character/personal qualities, level of applicant's interest. *Other factors considered include:* Class rank, first generation, racial/ethnic status, talent/ability, volunteer work, work experience. SAT or ACT required; SAT and SAT Subject Tests or ACT considered if submitted; ACT with or without Writing component accepted. TOEFL required of all international applicants. *Academic units recommended:* 4 English; 4 mathematics; 4 science; (1 science lab); 4 social studies; 2 foreign language; 4 history; 4 computer science; 4 visual/performing arts.

Financial Aid

Students should submit: FAFSA. Regular filing deadline is 3/1. The Princeton Review suggests that all financial aid forms be submitted as soon as possible after January 1. *Need-based scholarships/grants offered:* Federal Pell, SEOG, State scholarships/grants, private scholarships, the school's own gift aid. *Loan aid offered:* Direct Subsidized Stafford Loans, Direct Unsubsidized Stafford Loans, Direct PLUS loans, Federal Perkins Loans. Federal Work-Study Program available. Institutional employment available. Off-campus job opportunities are good.

The Inside Word

University of Dayton is an excellent option for students who want to attend a Catholic university but don't meet the stringent criteria of Georgetown or Notre Dame. UD gives "balanced consideration" to all academic factors—for example, class rank, GPA—on the application. Candidates who demonstrate a modicum of success in the classroom and intellectual promise will most likely be accepted. Applicants must apply to one of the university's four divisions; admissions criteria vary slightly among the different divisions.

THE SCHOOL SAYS "..."

From the Admissions Office

"The University of Dayton founded in 1850 by the Society of Mary, is a top ten Catholic research university. The university seeks outstanding diverse faculty, staff, and students who value its mission and share its commitment to academic excellence in teaching, study, research and creativity, the development of the whole person, and leadership and service in the local and global community. More than seventy challenging academic programs are offered in the College of Arts and Sciences and the Schools of Business Administration, Education and Allied Professions, Engineering, and Law. Classes are small—twenty-six students on average. Our more than 1,000 full-time and part-time faculty are committed to teaching undergraduate students and involving them in their research projects. The University of Dayton Research Institute ranks second in the nation in the amount of materials research performed annually. Technology-enhanced learning ensures students gain expertise in the tools that will prepare them for the future. All areas of campus and surrounding neighborhoods have access to our high speed wireless network. Recent campus construction provides a modern home for the university's cutting-edge academic programs. A new fitness and recreation complex, the RecPlex, provides 130,000 square feet of space for classrooms, courts, a natatorium, offices, and other recreational facilities. A strong sense of community is a hallmark feature of the university; a dual emphasis on leadership and service contributes to students' participation in more than 180 clubs and organizations. Division I intercollegiate athletics and club and intramural sports are also popular.

"Students applying for admission may provide scores from either the SAT or the ACT. The highest composite scores from either test will be used in admission and merit-based aid decisions."

SELECTIVITY

Admissions Rating	86
# of applicants	16,279
% of applicants accepted	52
% of acceptees attending	21

FRESHMAN PROFILE

Range SAT Critical Reading	500–600
Range SAT Math	530–640
Range ACT Composite	24–29
Minimum paper TOEFL	523
Minimum web-based TOEFL	193
Average HS GPA	3.59
% graduated top 10% of class	24
% graduated top 25% of class	54
% graduated top 50% of class	87

DEADLINES

Early action	
Deadline	12/15
Notification	2/1
Regular	
Priority	12/15
Deadline	3/1
Nonfall registration?	Yes

APPLICANTS ALSO LOOK AT AND OFTEN PREFER

The Ohio State University—Columbus; Miami University

AND SOMETIMES PREFER

Indiana University—Bloomington; Xavier University (OH); University of Cincinnati; Saint Louis University; Purdue University—West Lafayette

AND RARELY PREFER

Marquette University; Loyola The University of Chicago

FINANCIAL FACTS

Financial Aid Rating	87
Annual tuition	$35,800
Books and supplies	$1,000
% needy frosh rec. need-based scholarship or grant aid	100
% needy UG rec. need-based scholarship or grant aid	100
% needy frosh rec. non-need-based scholarship or grant aid	23
% needy UG rec. non-need-based scholarship or grant aid	22
% needy frosh rec. need-based self-help aid	80
% needy UG rec. need-based self-help aid	83
% frosh rec. any financial aid	98
% UG rec. any financial aid	94
% UG borrow to pay for school	63
Average cumulative indebtedness	$37,551
% frosh need fully met	34
% ugrads need fully met	34
Average % of frosh need met	80
Average % of ugrad need met	78

UNIVERSITY OF DELAWARE

210 SOUTH COLLEGE AVENUE, NEWARK, DE 19716-6210 • ADMISSIONS: 302-831-8123 • FAX: 302-831-6905

CAMPUS LIFE

Quality of Life Rating	85
Fire Safety Rating	96
Green Rating	73
Type of school	Public
Affiliation	No Affiliation
Environment	Town

STUDENTS

Total undergrad enrollment	16,871
% male/female	42/58
% from out of state	60
% frosh from public high school	80
% frosh live on campus	94
% ugrads live on campus	44
# of fraternities	24
# of sororities	19
% African American	5
% Asian	4
% Caucasian	76
% Hispanic	7
% Native American	<1
% international	4
# of countries represented	55

SURVEY SAYS . . .
Students are happy
Class discussions are rare
Students are friendly
Great off-campus food
Lots of beer drinking
Hard liquor is popular

ACADEMICS

Academic Rating	79
% students returning for sophomore year	92
% students graduating within 4 years	69
% students graduating within 6 years	82
Calendar	4/1/4
Student/faculty ratio	13:1
Profs interesting rating	72
Profs accessible rating	77

Most classes have 20–29 students.
Most lab/discussion sessions have
10–19 students.

MOST POPULAR MAJORS
finance; nursing; biological sciences

STUDENTS SAY ". . ."

Academics

If you're looking for a "well-rounded" college experience, University of Delaware delivers on every front. According to the school's satisfied undergraduates, "the University of Delaware is everything college should be," from its "gorgeous campus" and "amazing school spirit," to "top notch" academics and "vibrant campus life." At UD, as at many public schools, "college is what you make it: If you take easy classes, college is a breeze; if you challenge yourself, classes will be more difficult." First-year courses are often large and impersonal; fortunately, major classes are usually smaller and "electives are interesting and engaging." Highly qualified students may also apply to the school's "excellent" honors program, which provides access to "challenging, interesting classes taught by distinguished yet friendly professors." Through the touted undergraduate research program, students have access to "diverse research opportunities," and the school's extensive study abroad program is "one of the best in the nation." Overall, faculty get good reviews, though students warn it's a mixed bag: "Some professors shouldn't be allowed within ten miles of a classroom; others will change your life. It's up to you to weed out the bad ones." While you won't have your hand held, professors are responsive to student needs: "If you ever need any help, a quick e-mail or a phone call usually solves your problem." On a similar note, "the administration is extremely approachable and talks to students on the same level."

Life

Work and play come together at the University of Delaware, an institution that offers "the perfect balance of academic intensity and excellent social life." Come the weekend (or even during the week), "UD kids like to have their share of fun," and "there is always a party happening." For an alternative to the party scene, students go to "movies in the student center or to ice skating on Fridays," and "there are a lot of great guest speakers, bands, and cultural events on campus." In addition, "there are social groups for almost anything you can think of from the adventure club to organic cooking to ultimate Frisbee." While fraternities and sororities do exist, they do not dominate the social scene; still Greeks are "very spirited, have a ton of fun, and are widely supported by our campus community." Intramural and varsity sports are wildly popular, both for athletes and their raucous fans. In fact, "Homecoming is a university holiday where people wake up as early as 5:00 A.M. to start tailgating." What's more, the campus location can't be beat. Main Street, which runs right through campus, "is packed with great restaurants and shopping." For a fun day trip, "Philly is cheap and easy to get to by Septa train," and "the Chinatown bus costs thirty-five dollars round trip into NYC."

Student Body

It's a largely East Coast crowd at University of Delaware, drawing the vast majority of its undergraduates from "around NYC, Philly, or Baltimore." Within that demographic, "preppy sorority kids are probably the most common, but no matter who you are or what your into, the school population is big enough [that] you're bound to find a group that shares your interest." At UD, "you'll have your jocks and frat boys, but you'll also find skaters, rockers, artsy types, and everything else in between." However, most UD students share an incredible enthusiasm for their school community, and "a typical student is engaged in coursework and a multitude of various extracurricular [activities]." Despite its long-standing repute as a party school, "students here have become more focused on academics. Most students here really do have a passion for learning and study really hard in order to get those grades and graduate." Even so, UD's reputation for revelry isn't lost on undergraduates: "The typical UD student cares about their school work but loves to have fun on the weekends."

FINANCIAL AID: 302-831-8761 • E-MAIL: ADMISSIONS@UDEL.EDU • WEBSITE: WWW.UDEL.EDU

THE PRINCETON REVIEW SAYS

Admissions

Very important factors considered include: GPA, rigor of secondary school record, state residency. *Important factors considered include:* Standardized test scores, application essay, extracurricular activities, recommendation(s), talent/ability, volunteer work, work experience, character/personal qualities. *Other factors considered include:* Class rank, first generation, geographical residence, interview, racial/ethnic status, alumni/ae relations, level of applicant's interest. SAT or ACT required; ACT with Writing component required. TOEFL required of all international applicants. *Academic units required:* 4 English; 3 mathematics; 3 science; (2 science lab); 2 social studies; 2 foreign language; 2 history; 2 academic electives. *Academic units recommended:* 4 English; 4 mathematics; 4 science; (3 science lab); 2 social studies; 4 foreign language; 2 history.

Financial Aid

Students should submit: FAFSA. Regular filing deadline is 3/15. The Princeton Review suggests that all financial aid forms be submitted as soon as possible after January 1. *Need-based scholarships/grants offered:* Federal Pell, SEOG, State scholarships/grants, private scholarships, the school's own gift aid. *Loan aid offered:* Direct Subsidized Stafford Loans, Direct Unsubsidized Stafford Loans, Direct PLUS loans, Federal Perkins Loans, Federal Nursing Loans. Applicants will be notified of awards beginning 3/15. Federal Work-Study Program available. Institutional employment available. Off-campus job opportunities are excellent.

Inside Word

Although UD is run by the state of Delaware, out-of-state students also benefit from the school's excellent academic and social offerings at a reasonable tuition. Even so, the school is expressly committed to supporting Delawarean students, who comprise about 40 percent of the student body. More details and samples of qualifying high school curricula are available on the admissions department website. In all admissions decisions, UD considers the entirety of a student's application; there are no minimum test scores or grades.

THE SCHOOL SAYS "..."

From the Admissions Office

"An East Coast classic, the University of Delaware is a rich, historic campus in Newark, Delaware, midway between New York City and Washington, D.C. UD is known for its problem-based, hands-on learning in every college and a relatively small enrollment that engages students with interested, accessible faculty. Over 90 percent of our students land jobs within six months of graduation and continue their educations at the top graduate and professional schools in the world. Three signers of the Declaration of Independence were among our first class and recent alumni include the vice president of the United States, the governor of New Jersey, and the top campaign strategist for the president of the United States. UD is also a talent magnet, attracting top scholars and innovators, including a recent Nobel Prize winner and a Rhodes Scholar. The University of Delaware is working on the most compelling social, civic, artistic, and scientific challenges of our age. As the flagship university in the first state of the union, we dare to be first in ways that matter—first in new energy technologies, first in global study, first in political leadership, first in interdisciplinary engineering, first in educating teachers, first in design innovation, first in championship athletics, first in translational medicine. We challenge our students to be first in what matters most to them."

SELECTIVITY	
Admissions Rating	92
# of applicants	25,423
% of applicants accepted	62
% of acceptees attending	24
# offered a place on the wait list	2,634
% accepting a place on wait list	45
% admitted from wait list	64

FRESHMAN PROFILE	
Range SAT Critical Reading	540–640
Range SAT Math	550–660
Range SAT Writing	540–640
Range ACT Composite	24–29
Minimum paper TOEFL	570
Minimum web-based TOEFL	213
Average HS GPA	3.78
% graduated top 10% of class	40
% graduated top 25% of class	76
% graduated top 50% of class	97

DEADLINES	
Regular	
Priority	12/1
Deadline	1/15
Notification	3/15
Nonfall registration?	Yes

APPLICANTS ALSO LOOK AT AND OFTEN PREFER
University of Pennsylvania; Princeton University; The College of William & Mary

AND SOMETIMES PREFER
Cornell University; University of Virginia; New York University; Brandeis University; University of Michigan—Ann Arbor

AND RARELY PREFER
Northeastern University; Rutgers—The State University of New Jersey—New Brunswick

FINANCIAL FACTS	
Financial Aid Rating	79
Annual in-state tuition	$10,580
Annual out-of-state tuition	$28,400
Room and board	$11,500
Required fees	$1,532
Books and supplies	$800
% needy frosh rec. need-based scholarship or grant aid	91
% needy UG rec. need-based scholarship or grant aid	77
% needy frosh rec. non-need-based scholarship or grant aid	42
% needy UG rec. non-need-based scholarship or grant aid	28
% needy frosh rec. need-based self-help aid	75
% needy UG rec. need-based self-help aid	80
% frosh rec. any financial aid	59
% UG rec. any financial aid	50
% UG borrow to pay for school	62
Average cumulative indebtedness	$32,571
% frosh need fully met	44
% ugrads need fully met	44
Average % of frosh need met	76
Average % of ugrad need met	74

UNIVERSITY OF DENVER

OFFICE OF ADMISSION, DENVER, CO 80208 • ADMISSIONS: 303-871-2036 • FAX: 303-871-3301

STUDENTS SAY ". . ."

Academics
From the moment you set foot on campus, it's evident that the University of Denver is truly "committed to its students." Undoubtedly, the school offers "academic rigor," a "beautiful campus" and an unbeatable location. Moreover, with a student population hovering at nearly 5,500, DU is "big enough to meet new people constantly" yet small enough to maintain an "intimate" feel. Undergrads here also value that the university operates on a quarter system, providing "a great alternative to the [traditional] semester." Academically, Denver has "a wide array of very unique majors" and especially strong programs in international studies, music, and business. Students really appreciate their experiences in the classroom. One content undergrad shares, "The professors engage the students; the students engage with the material. We dig deeply into each subject. It's the most amazing learning environment I've ever experienced." Further, professors are "very knowledgeable and passionate. The majority are very willing to help and are accessible out of class. They treat students as unique individuals, not just a 'number.'" As this wholly satisfied student encapsulates her school, "DU is about providing opportunities both socially and academically that go above and beyond students' wildest dreams!"

Life
Undergrads at DU are "very dedicated to school" but also "like to kick back and have a good time on weekends." Fortunately, there's no shortage of opportunity for fun and amusement around campus. To begin with, "like all schools, there is partying going on, but the pressure to go out and party is nonexistent." Additionally, the "majority of the student body goes to many [weekly] sporting events, and if you are a Pioneer you try to attend as many hockey games as possible." Further, the "DU programs board hosts a free movie every Thursday night, and it's a great way to relax after a long day of classes." Of course, "there are [also] endless events, seminars, and other opportunities [for] student [participation]." Outdoor activities are also all the rage here. Indeed, "skiing and spending time in the mountains is huge—hiking, biking, and climbing as well." After all, "some of the world's best alpine areas [are] just an hour or two away." Music is also pretty popular, and "lots of people go to concerts downtown or at Red Rocks in the fall and spring." Just as important, "Downtown Denver is easily accessible by light rail, [with] a stop located right next to the campus." Students love to take advantage of everything from the great restaurant scene to a Rockies baseball game. Simply put, "if you can't find something to do, you're doing something wrong."

Student Body
On the surface, University of Denver's student population tends to skew "white" and "affluent." Thankfully, while acknowledging this truth, undergrads quickly stress that "most students fit in quite well, regardless of background or ethnicity." They are also quick to point out, "We have every type of person from the foreign exchange students to the engineers to the band geeks and theater majors to the athletes." Indeed, "if you look for it, you will meet interesting people from all around the country and the world." Undergrads at DU generally find their peers to be "outgoing and welcoming" and confidently assert, "Everyone seems to have a group that they can easily belong in." Moreover, the vast majority are "very athletic or like to participate in outdoor activities." Perhaps more important, "most students care about their education and are motivated to complete their degree and even more." Of course, regardless of adjectives or categorizations, DU is "a great community no matter what your interests are, [and] you will find some way to fit in."

FINANCIAL AID: 303-871-4020 • E-MAIL: ADMISSION@DU.EDU • WEBSITE: WWW.DU.EDU

THE PRINCETON REVIEW SAYS

Admissions

Very important factors considered include: GPA, rigor of secondary school record, standardized test scores. *Important factors considered include:* Application essay, extracurricular activities, recommendation(s), talent/ability, character/personal qualities. *Other factors considered include:* First generation, geographical residence, racial/ethnic status, volunteer work, work experience, alumni/ae relations, level of applicant's interest. SAT or ACT required; ACT with or without Writing component accepted. TOEFL required of all international applicants. *Academic units recommended:* 3-4 in Mathematics, 3-4 in Science (of these, 2 lab units), 2-4 foreign language, & 3-4 Social Studies.

Financial Aid

Students should submit: FAFSA, CSS/Financial Aid PROFILE, Noncustodial PROFILE. Priority filing deadline is 2/15. The Princeton Review suggests that all financial aid forms be submitted as soon as possible after January 1. *Need-based scholarships/grants offered:* Federal Pell, SEOG, State scholarships/grants, private scholarships, the school's own gift aid. *Loan aid offered:* Direct Subsidized Stafford Loans, Direct Unsubsidized Stafford Loans, Direct PLUS loans, Federal Perkins Loans, College/university loans from institutional funds. Applicants will be notified of awards beginning in late March. Off-campus job opportunities are excellent.

The Inside Word

Admissions officers at University of Denver take a holistic approach to the application process. Therefore, they strive to look beyond quantitative factors and will heavily review your essay, recommendations, and extracurricular activities.

THE SCHOOL SAYS "..."

From the Admissions Office

"At the University of Denver—in our setting of great natural beauty, cultural richness, and intellectual energy—you'll experience meaningful interaction with professors who set you on paths toward personal discovery, paths that can change the course of your future. Our diverse student body, engaged faculty, and prime location provide a culture of opportunity that is unique and unrivaled. DU is continually developing educational initiatives that help students prepare for an ever-changing world. Our Living and Learning Communities provide extracurricular and co-curricular programming in specialized areas; the Partners in Scholarship (PinS) program funds undergraduate research for students wishing to pursue a topic of personal interest in greater depth; and 65 to 70 percent of our students are taking advantage of invaluable internship opportunities in laboratories, corporate offices, government agencies, and cultural settings. One of the university's signature offerings is the Cherrington Global Scholars program, which allows students to study abroad at the same cost of a quarter spent on campus at DU. Nearly 70 percent of our students study abroad, which ranks DU fourth in the nation among doctoral and research institutions for percentage of students participating. Outside the classroom, DU students put ideas and ideals into action. They are active members of our community and they take advantage of the numerous recreational opportunities available to them, including club, intramural, and seventeen Division I sports. Whatever their majors and interests, DU students are inspired by Denver's Rocky Mountain spirit of exploration and openness, and are encouraged to engage in and personalize their educational journey."

SELECTIVITY

Admissions Rating	89
# of applicants	13,735
% of applicants accepted	75
% of acceptees attending	13
# offered a place on the wait list	1,509
% accepting a place on wait list	33
% admitted from wait list	20

FRESHMAN PROFILE

Range SAT Critical Reading	540–660
Range SAT Math	560–660
Range SAT Writing	520–630
Range ACT Composite	25–30
Minimum paper TOEFL	550
Minimum web-based TOEFL	80
Average HS GPA	3.67
% graduated top 10% of class	45
% graduated top 25% of class	76
% graduated top 50% of class	95

DEADLINES

Early action	
Deadline	11/1
Notification	1/15
Regular	
Deadline	1/15
Notification	3/15
Nonfall registration?	Yes

APPLICANTS ALSO LOOK AT AND OFTEN PREFER

Colorado College; Colorado State University; University of Colorado—Boulder

AND SOMETIMES PREFER

Boston University; University of Vermont; University of Puget Sound

FINANCIAL FACTS

Financial Aid Rating	86
Annual tuition	$41,112
Room and board	$11,307
Required fees	$978
Books and supplies	$1,800
% needy frosh rec. need-based scholarship or grant aid	99
% needy UG rec. need-based scholarship or grant aid	98
% needy frosh rec. non-need-based scholarship or grant aid	24
% needy UG rec. non-need-based scholarship or grant aid	21
% needy frosh rec. need-based self-help aid	71
% needy UG rec. need-based self-help aid	76
% frosh rec. any financial aid	85
% UG rec. any financial aid	83
% UG borrow to pay for school	49
Average cumulative indebtedness	$31,501
% frosh need fully met	32
% ugrads need fully met	35
Average % of frosh need met	84
Average % of ugrad need met	84

UNIVERSITY OF FLORIDA

201 Criser Hall, Gainesville, FL 32611-4000 • Admissions: 352-392-1365 • Fax: 352-392-3987

CAMPUS LIFE

Quality of Life Rating	76
Fire Safety Rating	60*
Green Rating	94
Type of school	Public
Affiliation	No Affiliation
Environment	City

STUDENTS

Total undergrad enrollment	32,346
% male/female	45/55
% from out of state	3
% frosh from public high school	75
% frosh live on campus	85
% ugrads live on campus	23
# of fraternities (% ugrad men join)	35 (20)
# of sororities (% ugrad women join)	26 (21)
% African American	7
% Asian	8
% Caucasian	58
% Hispanic	19
% Native American	<1
% international	1
# of countries represented	153

SURVEY SAYS . . .

Career services are great
Great off-campus food
Athletic facilities are great
Lots of beer drinking
Everyone loves the Gators
Intramural sports are popular
Frats and sororities are popular
Alumni active on campus

ACADEMICS

Academic Rating	75
% students returning for sophomore year	96
% students graduating within 4 years	64
% students graduating within 6 years	85
Calendar	Semester
Student/faculty ratio	21:1
Profs interesting rating	68
Profs accessible rating	71
Most classes have 10–19 students.	
Most lab/discussion sessions have 10–19 students.	

MOST POPULAR MAJORS

psychology; biology; mechanical engineering

STUDENTS SAY ". . ."

Academics

Located in the heart of "Gator Nation," Gainesville, Florida, the University of Florida offers "a hell of a deal" on "one of the best educations in the nation." Students are proud that UF is "the best state school in Florida" and "one of the top public universities in the nation"; they also love that it's "a great school with a large alumni network," that there's plenty of "intellectual stimulation" to be found there, and that UF's "research opportunities are abundant." Though the school has "strong academic standards" across the board, programs in Business and Journalism are particularly "highly ranked." "Access to alumni" pays off when students seek "opportunities for networking and research," and they find that "as a large school, [UF] has a lot of funding and a large number of opportunities for student involvement." Students say that the university's size doesn't sacrifice individuals' ability to focus on their course of study: "Classes for your major are hard, but they prepare you for more than easier classes would. They better prepare you for your career." Moreover, "as a research university with nearly every graduate program imaginable, the opportunities are endless." Students praise the "truly incredible faculty and staff" and appreciate that "one of the greatest strengths of UF is the fact there is always someone to turn to for help." Class structure is still impacted by the school's size in that "lectures are 80–90 percent of class activities," but conversely, students love "having experts in my field teaching all of my classes for my major." If "breadth of opportunities" for a value price is a priority for you, "the Gator Nation is one where anyone can build a future for themselves."

Life

"The University of Florida is in Gainesville. The Gator Nation is everywhere." In terms of town-gown relations, "Gainesville revolves around UF, most everything is catered to the students and student life." "Bars are the big scene," and students "love going out with friends on the weekends to Midtown. It is a UF staple to party at Grog, Balls, and Salty Dog once you turn 21." "Tons of school spirit" ranks high on the list of things students love about UF, as "A lot of UF culture is based around sports." "Greek life…is a big deal in both the social and extracurricular scene" and "When you are in the Greek community, there are many things to do." For other students, "I find myself working or studying in a computer lab most of the time" and "There is a really intense night-life but when it comes to exams, papers and finals week it is pretty quiet everywhere." Extracurricular life can also be as forward-looking as you want it to be: "In addition to classes, I research in a lab with the College of Medicine and volunteer at the hospital located on campus." Students "play sports," and "For fun, there are several places to go such as Paynes Prairie, Devil's Millhopper, or other outdoor activities." If you want to get involved, join one of the "850 clubs": "There is literally a club for everyone at UF" and "You make it what you want. You can party every day or you can study every day. I keep it pretty balanced."

Student Body

While "everyone is different," "fraternity and sorority participation….dominates the student culture." Students are "hard working and interested in getting ahead," and "even though UF is considered a party school, it is full of people who put their future careers first." "Students fit in by taking part in and participating in the various things our campus offers" and are often "busy and focused usually on one subject matter or area of interest to be involved in through extracurricular activities." Even though it's a large campus, one student remarks on the sense of community: "We're students? I thought we were all part of one big family!" They find each other "mostly accepting and friendly," but as a whole "hard to define. Gators are religious and non religious, Greek and non Greek, obsessed with athletics and some couldn't care less." Overall, the typical UF student "knows how to balance their school work and still have a good time."

FINANCIAL AID: 352-392-6684 • WEBSITE: WWW.UFL.EDU

THE PRINCETON REVIEW SAYS

Admissions

Very important factors considered include: GPA, rigor of secondary school record, application essay, extracurricular activities, talent/ability, volunteer work, character/personal qualities. *Important factors considered include:* Standardized test scores, first generation, geographical residence, work experience. *Other factors considered include:* Class rank, state residency, alumni/ae relations, level of applicant's interest. SAT or ACT required; ACT with Writing component required. *Academic units required:* 4 English; 4 mathematics; 3 science; (2 science lab); 3 social studies; 2 foreign language; 2 academic electives.

Financial Aid

Students should submit: FAFSA. The Princeton Review suggests that all financial aid forms be submitted as soon as possible after January 1. *Need-based scholarships/grants offered:* Federal Pell, SEOG, State scholarships/grants, private scholarships, the school's own gift aid. *Loan aid offered:* Direct Subsidized Stafford Loans, Direct Unsubsidized Stafford Loans, Direct PLUS loans, Federal Perkins Loans, College/university loans from institutional funds. Federal Work-Study Program available. Institutional employment available. Off-campus job opportunities are fair.

The Inside Word

Unlike many state universities, UF doesn't publish an admissions formula, saying rather that they use a "holistic review" process to determine candidates' eligibility. Their application's short-answer and essay questions are emphasized in factors considered, and first-generation college students from low-income backgrounds should take note of the Florida Opportunity Scholars program, which covers four years of tuition in full.

THE SCHOOL SAYS "..."

From the Admissions Office

"University of Florida students come from more than 100 countries, all fifty states, and every one of the sixty-seven counties in Florida. Twenty-four percent of the student body is comprised of graduate students. Approximately 3,300 African American students, 7,850 Hispanic students, and 3,450 Asian American students attend UF. Ninety percent of the entering freshmen rank above the national mean of scores on standard entrance exams. UF consistently ranks near the top among public universities in the number of new National Merit and Achievement scholars in attendance."

"Students must submit the SAT or ACT with the writing section. UF considers your highest section scores across all SAT test dates."

SELECTIVITY	
Admissions Rating	96
# of applicants	27,107
% of applicants accepted	47
% of acceptees attending	51

FRESHMAN PROFILE	
Range SAT Critical Reading	580–670
Range SAT Math	590–690
Range SAT Writing	570–680
Range ACT Composite	26–31
% graduated top 10% of class	77
% graduated top 25% of class	97
% graduated top 50% of class	100

DEADLINES	
Regular	
Deadline	11/1
Nonfall registration?	Yes

FINANCIAL FACTS	
Financial Aid Rating	77
Annual in-state tuition	$6,263
Annual out-of-state tuition	$28,540
Room and board	$9,520
Books and supplies	$1,080
% needy frosh rec. need-based scholarship or grant aid	58
% needy UG rec. need-based scholarship or grant aid	60
% needy frosh rec. non-need-based scholarship or grant aid	95
% needy UG rec. non-need-based scholarship or grant aid	81
% needy frosh rec. need-based self-help aid	41
% needy UG rec. need-based self-help aid	48
% frosh rec. any financial aid	98
% UG rec. any financial aid	90
% UG borrow to pay for school	43
Average cumulative indebtedness	$20,708
% frosh need fully met	21
% ugrads need fully met	20
Average % of frosh need met	71
Average % of ugrad need met	70

UNIVERSITY OF GEORGIA

TERRELL HALL, ATHENS, GA 30602 • ADMISSIONS: 706-542-8776 • FAX: 706-542-1466

STUDENTS SAY " . . . "

Academics

As at many large universities, UGA has a "mixed bag of professors," but there are "more good teachers" than bad. Though students don't love the core curriculum classes due to their large size and the prevalence of TAs, "once [you're] in your particular program, the teachers are outstanding and easy to reach." "The professors really do want to see you at office hours if you have questions," and they "want to share their love of learning with you." "My major-related classes are very small, and each student receives individual attention." The honors program also receives raves: "Many of my best classes and favorite teachers have come from the honors program, but non-honors classes are generally good as well." "The study spaces are well-equipped and quiet," but "the school of social work is still housed in an old dorm." "Administration is a pain (not the people, only the requirements), but I think that describes academia in general." In general students "feel that the administration can be very accommodating at times, but at other times it can seem like it is full of red tape." Registration technology "needs to be brought out of the 1980s and into the twenty-first century." "The administration [can] seem like a bunch of penny-pinchers, but they must be to run a major research facility."

Life

Life at UGA seems to be a good mix of the two different worlds of sports and arts: football, frats, and tailgating on campus come together nicely with the coffee shops and music scene in downtown Athens. "On Saturday afternoons in the fall, nearly everyone on campus is at the football game. It's a way of life here." "Everybody really gets behind the team, and Saturdays in Athens feel like mini vacations." Fraternities and sororities dominate the party scene, but "there is definitely plenty to do, even if you don't go Greek." Students love to brag about the high number of bars per capita in Athens, but there's plenty more to boast about. "The Athens music and art scene is very inspiring, and there are tons of opportunities for creativity here." "Downtown Athens is fabulous! Whether you drink or don't drink, all are welcome and all congregate there." Campus life offers plenty of activity, too. "Fun is a part of daily life…with a dozen intramural sports each semester…and many community activities (multiple movie theaters, bowling allies, golf course)." "Ultimate Frisbee, walks around the multiple parks, days lounging on North Campus, and spending *lots* of time downtown are a couple ways I like to have fun at school." "There are so many organizations that everyone can find a place that will feel like home or find a place to meet new people." "It's no secret that UGA knows how to party. However, most of the students know how to manage social and academic time."

Student Body

"Students are generally white, upper-middle-class, smart, [and] involved, and [they] have a good time," "seem to be predominantly conservative," and "are usually involved in at least one organization whether it be Greek, a club, or sports." "The typical student at UGA is one who knows how and when to study but allows himself or herself to have a very active social life." The majority are Southerners, with many students from within Georgia. "The stereotype is Southern, Republican, football-loving, and beer-drinking. While many, many of UGA's students do not fit this description, there is no lack of the above," and "there is a social scene for everyone in Athens." "There are a great number of atypical students in the liberal arts," which "creates a unique and exciting student body with greatly contrasting opinions."

FINANCIAL AID: 706-542-6147 • E-MAIL: ADMPROC@UGA.EDU • WEBSITE: WWW.UGA.EDU

THE PRINCETON REVIEW SAYS

Admissions

Very important factors considered include: GPA, rigor of secondary school record. *Important factors considered include:* Standardized test scores. *Other factors considered include:* Application essay, extracurricular activities, first generation, recommendation(s), talent/ability, volunteer work, work experience, character/personal qualities. SAT or ACT required; ACT with Writing component required. TOEFL required of all international applicants. *Academic units required:* 4 English; 4 mathematics; 4 science; (2 science lab); 3 social studies; 2 foreign language. *Academic units recommended:* 4 English; 4 mathematics; 4 science; (2 science lab); 1 social studies; 3 foreign language; 2 history; 1 academic elective.

Financial Aid

Students should submit: FAFSA. The Princeton Review suggests that all financial aid forms be submitted as soon as possible after January 1. *Need-based scholarships/grants offered:* Federal Pell, SEOG, State scholarships/grants, private scholarships, the school's own gift aid. *Loan aid offered:* Direct Subsidized Stafford Loans, Direct Unsubsidized Stafford Loans, Direct PLUS loans, Federal Perkins Loans, State Loans, College/university loans from institutional funds. Federal Work-Study Program available. Institutional employment available. Off-campus job opportunities are good.

The Inside Word

A school as large as UGA must start winnowing applicants by the numbers. If you fail to meet certain baseline curricular, GPA, and standardized-test-score floors, only exceptional talent elsewhere (a gift for the arts or, better still, throwing a football) will get you past the first cut. Some students here are Georgia residents reaping the benefits of the state's HOPE/Zell Miller scholarship programs, which pays tuition and most school-related fees for state residents who earn at least a 3.7 GPA in high school, a 1200 SAT or 26 ACT score, and maintain a 3.3 in college. Georgia state residents who earn at least a 3.0 in high school will also have a large portion of their tuition paid.

THE SCHOOL SAYS ". . ."

From the Admissions Office

"The University of Georgia offers students the advantages and resources of a top public research university, including a wide range of majors and exceptional academic facilities such as the 260,000 square-foot Miller Learning Center. At the same time, UGA provides opportunities more common to smaller, private schools, such as first-year seminars led by distinguished faculty and learning communities that connect students with similar academic interests. The university is committed to challenging its academically superior students in the classroom and beyond, with increased emphasis on undergraduate research, service-learning, and study abroad. UGA students taking advantage of such offerings find themselves well positioned to compete with the best undergraduates in the country, as evidenced by their recent string of successes in winning Rhodes, Marshall, Truman, and other major scholarships. The UGA campus, considered one of the most beautiful in the nation, adjoins vibrant downtown Athens. While Athens is renowned for its local music scene, UGA also houses the Performing Arts Center, the Hugh Hodgson School of Music, the Lamar Dodd School of Art, and the Georgia Museum of Art. Sports—from football to gymnastics—are also a major attraction, with UGA teams perennially ranked among the best in the country. To experience the excitement of UGA, most prospective students visit campus, a ninety-minute drive northeast of the Atlanta airport. See the admissions website to sign up for a tour with the Visitors Center, view the weekday schedule of admissions information sessions, and find application details. Applicants for first-year admission will be required to submit either the SAT or ACT. Students submitting only the ACT must also submit the optional ACT writing test."

SELECTIVITY

Admissions Rating	93
# of applicants	20,045
% of applicants accepted	55
% of acceptees attending	48
# offered a place on the wait list	1,206
% accepting a place on wait list	61
% admitted from wait list	1

FRESHMAN PROFILE

Range SAT Critical Reading	570–660
Range SAT Math	580–670
Range SAT Writing	560–670
Range ACT Composite	26–30
Minimum paper TOEFL	550
Minimum web-based TOEFL	213
Average HS GPA	3.86
% graduated top 10% of class	53
% graduated top 25% of class	91
% graduated top 50% of class	99

DEADLINES

Early action	
Deadline	10/15
Notification	12/1
Regular	
Priority	10/15
Deadline	1/15
Nonfall registration?	Yes

FINANCIAL FACTS

Financial Aid Rating	78
Annual out-of-state tuition	$26,238
Room and board	$9,246
Required fees	$2,234
Books and supplies	$916
% needy frosh rec. need-based scholarship or grant aid	98
% needy UG rec. need-based scholarship or grant aid	91
% needy frosh rec. non-need-based scholarship or grant aid	16
% needy UG rec. non-need-based scholarship or grant aid	11
% needy frosh rec. need-based self-help aid	62
% needy UG rec. need-based self-help aid	70
% frosh rec. any financial aid	45
% UG rec. any financial aid	46
% UG borrow to pay for school	48
Average cumulative indebtedness	$20,254
% frosh need fully met	24
% ugrads need fully met	20
Average % of frosh need met	72
Average % of ugrad need met	66

UNIVERSITY OF HAWAII—MANOA

2600 CAMPUS ROAD, HONOLULU, HI 96822 • ADMISSIONS: 808-956-8975 • FAX: 808-956-4148

STUDENTS SAY ". . ."

Academics

The University of Hawaii—Manoa, the flagship school of the University of Hawaii system, offers a solid education and university experience at a competitive price. Students appreciate the diversity of the school—"not only of the students and staff, but of what is offered"—and the "great feeling of collaboration and integration across all levels—amongst colleges, students, faculty, and the community." Even those who are not from Hawaii are treated with "the aloha spirit" in which the school goes out of its way to "include those who are not from Hawaii into the UH Ohana" (a Hawaiian term that refers to a family).

Professors are "knowledgeable in their field, share their knowledge easily, and seem to be enthusiastic in making sure that I understand the subject matter." The majority of the faculty gets top marks, and most "care more about the actual education of the students...others are just there to teach." "My professors are incredibly helpful and always willing to lend an ear if I need it," says a student. "A lot of them are laid-back, reflecting the Hawaiian lifestyle." While some admit that "the absolute academic standards are not high," the school is "always encouraging interested students to push themselves and think outside the box. There is just enough competition between students to maintain quality." Notably, the Hawaiian program is strong here. "We have a lo'i, which is a taro patch where students plant and learn sustainability through the old Hawaiian irrigation system," says a student. As a large state school, UH "has a lot of research going on," but students admit, "The administrative organization leaves much to be desired." The school "is big on improvements for students," and it does "a very good job when it comes to presenting students with all types of internship and job opportunities."

Life

As expected, the campus is located in a "paradise with an urban center," though some of the buildings are "rundown." Almost everyone, from students to staff, lead a "laid-back lifestyle," including—of course—surfing. For the most part, "Students think about going to the beach, surfing, and many of the activities you can do here in Hawaii." There are many other student organizations and extracurricular activities to choose from, and "the different clubs are always hosting events that everyone is invited to enjoy, which makes a great way to wind down for the weekend." The commuting students do tend to empty out the campus and school spirit a little, but the beach certainly helps to fill that void. Many of the out-of-state students "feel great living in an environment with so much beauty and cultural influences."

Student Body

This large school represents an "amalgamation of many different cultures," and students fit in "by doing the usual college biz—joining clubs, mingling with classmates, and not being a wallflower." Everyone gets along just fine, as "there are too many students to form any sort of social hierarchy." There are a decent number of nontraditional aged students, and many students are from one of the islands of Hawaii, "so most go home on holidays or even for weekends." Though a lot of students like to go to the beach and have fun on their days off, "a lot of people here work really hard and have jobs in addition to being full-time students, because the cost of living out here is pretty high." All in all, "It's a very easygoing place. You can stop and talk to any random student and they will chat with you."

FINANCIAL AID: 808-956-7251 • E-MAIL: UHMANOA.ADMISSIONS@HAWAII.EDU • WEBSITE: MANOA.HAWAII.EDU

THE PRINCETON REVIEW SAYS

Admissions

Very important factors considered include: GPA, rigor of secondary school record, standardized test scores. *Important factors considered include:* Class rank, state residency. *Other factors considered include:* Application essay, extracurricular activities, geographical residence, interview, recommendation(s), talent/ability. SAT or ACT required; ACT with Writing component required. TOEFL required of all international applicants. *Academic units required:* 4 English; 3 mathematics; 3 science; 3 social studies; 5 academic electives.

Financial Aid

Students should submit: FAFSA. The Princeton Review suggests that all financial aid forms be submitted as soon as possible after January 1. *Need-based scholarships/grants offered:* Federal Pell, SEOG, State scholarships/grants, private scholarships, the school's own gift aid. *Loan aid offered:* Direct Subsidized Stafford Loans, Direct Unsubsidized Stafford Loans, Direct PLUS loans, Federal Perkins Loans, State Loans. Federal Work-Study Program available. Institutional employment available. Off-campus job opportunities are good.

The Inside Word

All students must have a minimum GPA of 2.8 and must take either the SAT or the ACT. All applicants are encouraged to apply by the priority consideration deadline of January 5, as this deadline increases your chance of receiving financial aid and student housing. Certain programs (nursing, social work, education, and others) may have earlier admission deadlines.

THE SCHOOL SAYS "..."

From the Admissions Office

"Aloha and welcome to UH Manoa, the largest campus in the University of Hawaii System. We are located on the island of O'ahu, in Honolulu's lush Manoa valley. With almost 90 undergraduate majors, over 200 student organizations, and a variety of Division I and intramural sports to choose from, we think you'll agree that UH Manoa is a great place for you to realize your academic, professional, and personal dreams.

"UH Manoa is one of only thirteen institutions to hold the distinction of being a land-, sea-, and space-grant research institution. Classified by the Carnegie Foundation as having 'very high research activity,' UH Manoa is known for its pioneering research in such fields as oceanography, astronomy, Pacific Islands and Asian area studies, linguistics, cancer research, and genetics.

"Applicants to UH Manoa are expected to have a minimum score of 510 on all three sections of the SAT (or a 22 on all four sections of the ACT), and have completed a college preparatory high school curriculum. All applicants are encouraged to apply for priority consideration. Applying by this deadline (January 5 for fall admission, September 1 for spring) increases your chance of receiving financial aid and student housing."

SELECTIVITY

Admissions Rating	77
# of applicants	7,361
% of applicants accepted	80
% of acceptees attending	34

FRESHMAN PROFILE

Range SAT Critical Reading	470–580
Range SAT Math	500–620
Range SAT Writing	470–570
Range ACT Composite	20–26
Minimum paper TOEFL	500
Minimum web-based TOEFL	173
Average HS GPA	3.46
% graduated top 10% of class	27
% graduated top 25% of class	58
% graduated top 50% of class	89

DEADLINES

Regular	
Priority	1/5
Deadline	3/1
Nonfall registration?	Yes

FINANCIAL FACTS

Financial Aid Rating	74
Annual in-state tuition	$9,840
Annual out-of-state tuition	$28,632
Room and board	$10,218
Required fees	$740
Books and supplies	$1,246
% needy frosh rec. need-based scholarship or grant aid	97
% needy UG rec. need-based scholarship or grant aid	92
% needy frosh rec. non-need-based scholarship or grant aid	26
% needy UG rec. non-need-based scholarship or grant aid	16
% needy frosh rec. need-based self-help aid	55
% needy UG rec. need-based self-help aid	63
% frosh rec. any financial aid	62
% UG rec. any financial aid	59
% UG borrow to pay for school	43
Average cumulative indebtedness	$21,512
% frosh need fully met	32
% ugrads need fully met	24
Average % of frosh need met	73
Average % of ugrad need met	68

UNIVERSITY OF HOUSTON

OFFICE OF ADMISSIONS, HOUSTON, TX 77204-2023 • ADMISSIONS: 713-743-1010

CAMPUS LIFE

Quality of Life Rating	77
Fire Safety Rating	93
Green Rating	85
Type of school	Public
Affiliation	No Affiliation
Environment	Metropolis

STUDENTS

Total undergrad enrollment	30,400
% male/female	50/50
% from out of state	2
% frosh from public high school	93
% frosh live on campus	48
% ugrads live on campus	18
# of fraternities (% ugrad men join)	23 (3)
# of sororities (% ugrad women join)	19 (4)
% African American	12
% Asian	21
% Caucasian	28
% Hispanic	30
% Native American	<1
% international	5
# of countries represented	101

SURVEY SAYS . . .

Athletic facilities are great
Great library
Career services are great
Students are friendly
Different types of students interact
Great off-campus food

ACADEMICS

Academic Rating	77
% students returning for sophomore year	85
% students graduating within 4 years	16
% students graduating within 6 years	48
Calendar	Semester
Student/faculty ratio	22:1
Profs interesting rating	73
Profs accessible rating	69

Most classes have 20–29 students.
Most lab/discussion sessions have 20–29 students.

MOST POPULAR MAJORS
business administration and management; biology; psychology

STUDENTS SAY ". . ."

Academics

With more than 120 undergraduate majors and minors, a 667-acre campus, and 39,000 students, the University of Houston is a world-class research institution and fixture in Texas education. The school "provides some of the greatest opportunities in the world" at an affordable price and urges its students to achieve as much as they can "while living in a real-world environment." The school has been on the rise in recent years and "is attracting many more bright students to the university" as it begins to toughen up admission standards.

Professors here are "always prepared and make lecture interesting" through "effective teaching strategies" that "provide eye opening real-life information" to what can be "a motley group of students coming together to pursue higher education." Though there are a few who receive low marks, most "take into consideration the needs of students and many post lectures and notes online." Even in the larger classes, professors make and keep their office hours, so "if you are willing to work hard, you do have the tools available to learn the material." TAs are especially helpful, and "the tutoring services are very accessible and widely used."

Careers are a main focus of Cougars, and there is a wide range of majors and many interdisciplinary systems for students looking to specify their education, and there are also "many ties to local business and industry," including the chemical and space industries, and the medical center. "The flexibility of my degree plan cannot be found in any other school," says a student. Red tape is the main grumble for UH students, with the financial aid office drawing the most ire, and many students also "have difficulty fixing problems regarding registration and enrollment for classes."

Life

A very large percentage of the student body lives at home, so "the campus grows much more quiet in the evenings and on weekends," and stores and restaurants close earlier than normal. However, UH "is in the middle of a transition from being a commuter campus to a residential campus" and has announced plans to build two more dorms in the next few years and to require freshmen to live on campus. Even for those who travel home at night, "the recreational facility and other organizations are a way to meet friendly people." Flyers for events "can be found everywhere on campus," which is "great for networking purposes or if you just need a break from studying."

Football is understandably huge, but be warned: "If you don't come early enough to the football game, forget about it." Basically, "unless you are supremely shy, there are countless opportunities to make friends and fit in." "We also can't leave out the tiny fact that we are in Houston," says a proud local. There are plenty of fun places "to eat, party, hang out, and exercise, and it's all within a fifteen-minute radius." As one student sums up, "If you feel there's nothing you could do here…you, my friend, are wrong."

Student Body

University of Houston "is the epitome of the grand melting pot." This remarkably "ethnically and culturally diverse" student body loves the variety that the university offers and the ensuing "acceptance on all levels." "One can come and grow socially, politically, and intellectually," says a student. One commonality is the "dedicated spirit" of all Cougars, helped in part of their devotion to UH sports, and "a typical student supports our athletic teams by wearing our red." Many take part in some sort of extracurricular club, but mostly, "everyone is trying to pass their classes and set themselves on the best track to get a job after school."

UNIVERSITY OF HOUSTON

FINANCIAL AID: 713-743-1010 • E-MAIL: ADMISSIONS@UH.EDU • WEBSITE: WWW.UH.EDU

THE PRINCETON REVIEW SAYS

Admissions

Very important factors considered include: Class rank, rigor of secondary school record, standardized test scores. *Important factors considered include:* GPA. *Other factors considered include:* Application essay, extracurricular activities, first generation, recommendation(s), talent/ability, volunteer work, work experience, level of applicant's interest. SAT or ACT required; ACT with or without Writing component accepted. TOEFL required of all international applicants. *Academic units required:* 4 English; 4 mathematics; 4 science; 4 social studies. *Academic units recommended:* (2 science lab); 2 foreign language; 1 computer science; 1 visual/performing arts.

Financial Aid

Students should submit: FAFSA. The Princeton Review suggests that all financial aid forms be submitted as soon as possible after January 1. *Need-based scholarships/grants offered:* Federal Pell, SEOG, State scholarships/grants, private scholarships, the school's own gift aid. *Loan aid offered:* Direct Subsidized Stafford Loans, Direct Unsubsidized Stafford Loans, Direct PLUS loans, Federal Perkins Loans, State Loans. Federal Work-Study Program available. Institutional employment available. Off-campus job opportunities are good.

Inside Word

The school's large size means that acceptance is easier to achieve than at some smaller schools. Students who meet the State of Texas Uniform Admissions Policy and satisfy a certain scale of requirements for class ranking and/or SAT or ACT scores are assured admission. But even if your grades aren't seemingly up to par, the admissions committee will consider students individually based on a holistic review of certain aspects, such as first-generation, socioeconomic background, rigor of high school curriculum, family responsibilities, special talents, public service, and strong letters of recommendation or a persuasive statement explaining your special circumstances.

THE SCHOOL SAYS "..."

From the Admissions Office

"The University of Houston is a Carnegie-designated Tier-One public research university that is recognized throughout the world as a leader in energy research, which is centered in a visionary Energy Research Park, law, business, and environmental education. Located in America's fourth-largest city, the University of Houston is the most ethnically diverse metropolitan research university in the United States. Its 39,540 students hail from 101 countries.

"In addition to preparing its students to succeed in today's global economy, the University of Houston also is a catalyst within its own community—changing lives through health, education, and outreach projects that help build a future for children in Houston, in Texas, and in the world.

"Other distinctive merits of the University of Houston include a strong student experience, a historic Division I athletic programs, top-level arts programs, and an internationally recognized faculty including a Nobel Laureate; winners of the National Medal of Science, Pulitzer, and Tony awards; and members of prestigious National Academies. The Princeton Review has chosen the University of Houston for inclusion in its guidebook of the nation's best colleges.

"Discover the greatness of the University of Houston's dynamic tree-lined campus of more than 650 acres—nestled just minutes from Houston's bustling theater and museum districts—where world-class teaching, revolutionary research, and nationally recognized students work together to create a globally competitive educational environment."

SELECTIVITY
Admissions Rating	88
# of applicants	17,407
% of applicants accepted	58
% of acceptees attending	34

FRESHMAN PROFILE
Range SAT Critical Reading	490–610
Range SAT Math	540–640
Range ACT Composite	22–27
Minimum paper TOEFL	550
Minimum web-based TOEFL	213
% graduated top 10% of class	34
% graduated top 25% of class	69
% graduated top 50% of class	92

DEADLINES
Regular	
Priority	12/1
Deadline	4/1
Notification	4/15
Nonfall registration?	Yes

FINANCIAL FACTS
Financial Aid Rating	73
Annual in-state tuition	$8,760
Annual out-of-state tuition	$19,380
Room and board	$8,912
Required fees	$918
Books and supplies	$1,200
% needy frosh rec. need-based scholarship or grant aid	88
% needy UG rec. need-based scholarship or grant aid	83
% needy frosh rec. non-need-based scholarship or grant aid	9
% needy UG rec. non-need-based scholarship or grant aid	4
% needy frosh rec. need-based self-help aid	62
% needy UG rec. need-based self-help aid	76
% frosh rec. any financial aid	85
% UG rec. any financial aid	76
% UG borrow to pay for school	49
Average cumulative indebtedness	$18,244
% frosh need fully met	20
% ugrads need fully met	16
Average % of frosh need met	72
Average % of ugrad need met	68

UNIVERSITY OF IDAHO

UI ADMISSIONS OFFICE, MOSCOW, ID 83844-4264 • ADMISSIONS: 208-885-6326 • FAX: 208-885-9119

CAMPUS LIFE
Quality of Life Rating	73
Fire Safety Rating	80
Green Rating	80
Type of school	Public
Affiliation	No Affiliation
Environment	Town

STUDENTS
Total undergrad enrollment	8,455
% male/female	54/46
% from out of state	26
% frosh from public high school	90
% frosh live on campus	87
% ugrads live on campus	19
# of fraternities (% ugrad men join)	17 (25)
# of sororities (% ugrad women join)	15 (30)
% African American	1
% Asian	1
% Caucasian	80
% Hispanic	8
% Native American	1
% international	3
# of countries represented	77

SURVEY SAYS . . .
Athletic facilities are great
Lots of beer drinking
Frats and sororities are popular

ACADEMICS
Academic Rating	74
% students returning for sophomore year	79
% students graduating within 4 years	25
% students graduating within 6 years	54
Calendar	Semester
Student/faculty ratio	18:1
Profs interesting rating	72
Profs accessible rating	72

Most classes have 20–29 students.
Most lab/discussion sessions have
10–19 students.

MOST POPULAR MAJORS
psychology; mechanical engineering; biology

STUDENTS SAY ". . ."

Academics
With its annual tuition for Idaho residents hovering around just $6,000, numerous students name "in-state tuition" and "bang for the buck" among their top reasons for attending the University of Idaho. There's much more to love about the university, though, whether it's "one of the best agricultural programs in the northwest," "a great college of engineering," "an excellent natural resources program" or "a great art program." U of I takes a "progressive and modern attitude towards education" and fosters "tight-knit connections between the faculty [and] students." Undergraduates are rewarded when they reach out: "UI has a lot to offer to those who seek help, resources, or advice." While professors are "experts in their field," and often "some of the most interesting and enlightening people I've ever met," students offered them mixed reviews, saying their quality "varies substantially; some professors are dedicated to giving their students a engaging and hands-on experience while other professors seem to be stuck in the world of academia and care very little for the input of students in discussions." Despite this, students feel loyal to U of I's "holistic approach to education," where "academics are only part of the focus." They appreciate the university's emphasis on "giving you experiences to prepare you for the real world with a balance of classroom instruction and hands on learning." One student offers the ultimate endorsement: "If knowledge was a drug, we would be high all the time."

Life
"There isn't a lot to do in little Moscow," and "life is pretty slow during the weekdays," but on the weekends, students find "activities in the town and people blowing off steam at the bars or 18-and-up clubs" off campus. Because "there are a lot of Greek students"—indeed, "nearly half of campus is or has been affiliated to a fraternity or sorority"—"partying is undeniably one of the most widespread activities" and "Greek life is at the center of the campus social scene." Whether you decide to rush or not may determine your social life entirely: "Unfortunately, non-Greeks and Greeks don't always interact a whole lot." Drinking and partying are hardly the only things to do, though: "There's really strong volunteer programs all over campus and a ton of involvement opportunities through a host of clubs and organizations…student government provides weekly entertainment in the form of movies, concerts, speakers, and comedians." Students also "enjoy the outdoors," and "Hunting, fishing, and skiing are especially popular," as well as "biking, hiking, running, mountain biking, ice skating and rock climbing." They recommend ways to find your tribe: "Living in the dorms was a great way to meet new people that you could later move off campus with." As with anywhere, the quality of your social life depends on who you spend it with: "Students usually find their group of friends early and keep them."

Student Body
In order to find their place, the typical U of I student "is very involved in campus life." Students' interests run the gamut, from "a lot of Greek students and outdoorsy students" to "a math oriented student looking for a technical degree." Many students "are laid back and enjoy the outdoors," and "party but know where to draw the line and get to work." Students don't take their education for granted: "The typical student is someone who knows they are paying for their education, and takes pride" in that fact. They bring hometown values to the campus, and are often "religious and from some type of country background, [as] not very many students [come] from bigger cities like Portland or Seattle." "They are down-to-earth, friendly, kind, motivated, and many view family, friends, and social awareness [as] important." For these reasons, U of I students are "really into community and the small town atmosphere."

UNIVERSITY OF IDAHO

FINANCIAL AID: 208-885-6312 • E-MAIL: ADMISSIONS@UIDAHO.EDU • WEBSITE: WWW.UIDAHO.EDU

THE PRINCETON REVIEW SAYS

Admissions

Very important factors considered include: GPA, standardized test scores. *Other factors considered include:* SAT or ACT required; ACT with or without Writing component accepted. TOEFL required of all international applicants. *Academic units required:* 4 English; 3 mathematics; 3 science; (1 science lab).

Financial Aid

Students should submit: FAFSA. The Princeton Review suggests that all financial aid forms be submitted as soon as possible after January 1. *Need-based scholarships/grants offered:* Federal Pell, SEOG, State scholarships/grants, private scholarships, the school's own gift aid. *Loan aid offered:* Direct Subsidized Stafford Loans, Direct Unsubsidized Stafford Loans, Direct PLUS loans, Federal Perkins Loans, College/university loans from institutional funds. Applicants will be notified of awards beginning 3/30. Federal Work-Study Program available. Institutional employment available. Off-campus job opportunities are good.

The Inside Word

The U of I doesn't put a whole lot of bells and whistles on the application process: If you meet their requirements for high school GPA and standardized test scores, which they publish on their website, you'll probably get in. As with many schools' formulas, a weaker test score can be balanced out by a stronger GPA, and vice versa.

THE SCHOOL SAYS "..."

From the Admissions Office

"A leading public research university in the West, the University of Idaho offers a traditional residential campus experience in a spectacular natural setting. It provides more than 130 undergraduate degree options and graduate degrees in forty-seven discipline areas, which helps provide unprecedented undergraduate research opportunities. Idaho has become known for its academic excellence, student-centered, experiential learning, and an exceptional student living environment that coupled with dedicated faculty, world-class facilities, and renowned research has produced a proven track record of high-achieving graduates. The student population of 12,000 includes first-generation college students and ethnically diverse scholars, who select from hands-on learning experiences in the colleges of Agricultural and Life Sciences; Art and Architecture; Business and Economics; Education; Engineering; Law; Letters, Arts, and Social Sciences; Natural Resources; and Science. The university also provides medical education for the state through the WWAMI program. Increasingly its interdisciplinary teams involved in environmental, sustainability, engagement, and resource management have gained national recognition. Idaho combines the strength of a large, land grant university with the intimacy of a small learning community to help students succeed and become leaders. It is home to the Vandals and competes in the Western Athletic Conference.

"Students applying for admission are required to take either the SAT or the ACT. The writing component is not required from the ACT. SAT Subject Test scores are not used for admission purposes."

SELECTIVITY

Admissions Rating	75
# of applicants	7,994
% of applicants accepted	65
% of acceptees attending	32

FRESHMAN PROFILE

Range SAT Critical Reading	450–580
Range SAT Math	460–590
Range SAT Writing	440–590
Range ACT Composite	20–26
Minimum paper TOEFL	525
Minimum web-based TOEFL	193
Average HS GPA	3.39
% graduated top 10% of class	16
% graduated top 25% of class	42
% graduated top 50% of class	73

DEADLINES

Regular	
Priority	2/15
Deadline	8/1
Nonfall registration?	Yes

APPLICANTS ALSO LOOK AT AND SOMETIMES PREFER
Boise State University; Utah State University

AND RARELY PREFER
Idaho State University

FINANCIAL FACTS

Financial Aid Rating	79
Annual in-state tuition	$4,534
Annual out-of-state tuition	$17,610
Room and board	$8,034
Required fees	$1,982
Books and supplies	$1,232
% needy frosh rec. need-based scholarship or grant aid	80
% needy UG rec. need-based scholarship or grant aid	74
% needy frosh rec. non-need-based scholarship or grant aid	77
% needy UG rec. non-need-based scholarship or grant aid	51
% needy frosh rec. need-based self-help aid	71
% needy UG rec. need-based self-help aid	79
% frosh rec. any financial aid	88
% UG rec. any financial aid	81
% UG borrow to pay for school	68
Average cumulative indebtedness	$25,961
% frosh need fully met	31
% ugrads need fully met	26
Average % of frosh need met	79
Average % of ugrad need met	74

UNIVERSITY OF ILLINOIS AT URBANA-CHAMPAIGN

901 WEST ILLINOIS STREET, URBANA, IL 61801 • ADMISSIONS: 217-333-0302 • FAX: 217-244-0903

CAMPUS LIFE

Quality of Life Rating	72
Fire Safety Rating	72
Green Rating	99
Type of school	Public
Affiliation	No Affiliation
Environment	City

STUDENTS

Total undergrad enrollment	31,260
% male/female	55/45
% from out of state	9
% frosh from public high school	75
% frosh live on campus	99
% ugrads live on campus	50
# of fraternities (% ugrad men join)	60 (21)
# of sororities (% ugrad women join)	36 (21)
% African American	6
% Asian	14
% Caucasian	56
% Hispanic	8
% Native American	<1
% international	13
# of countries represented	123

SURVEY SAYS . . .

Students are happy
Career services are great
Athletic facilities are great
Lots of beer drinking
Hard liquor is popular
Everyone loves the Illini
Frats and sororities are popular

ACADEMICS

Academic Rating	78
% students returning for sophomore year	94
% students graduating within 4 years	69
% students graduating within 6 years	84
Calendar	Semester
Student/faculty ratio	19:1
Profs interesting rating	69
Profs accessible rating	73

Most classes have 10–19 students.
Most lab/discussion sessions have 20–29 students.

MOST POPULAR MAJORS
cell and molecular biology; psychology; political science

STUDENTS SAY "..."

Academics

The University of Illinois' massive size means "opportunities, lots of classes, lots of student groups," and "an incredibly lively campus." "The research support is phenomenal on campus" and "there are a lot of resources to supplement your studies." Students find the university's "fantastic library system" and "phenomenal advisors" to be "such a benefit for research projects," and "countless on-campus resources such as the Career Center, Writers Workshop, Office of Minority Student Affairs, free tutoring services, and the Study Abroad Office" also support students' academic experiences. They praise their professors as "wonderful," "not just good at research but also instructing and mentoring," and "very approachable," and students thrive on the emphasis on experiences outside the classroom: "The field work (tons of field work) that they make us do really helped in getting used to the field." "Most professors here are devoted to teaching, not researching." Classes can be big—"As an underclassman, many classes I've taken have been with very large classes"— but "the professors are engaging and know how to keep a class of 700-plus entertained." U of I's programs in business and engineering have long been recognized as among the best, and one student says, "I liked the breadth of the engineering program and the opportunities associated with it." Even if you're not sure what you want to study yet, its undergrads feel that the university has "an amazing reputation and strong programs in many different majors, and that if I needed to change majors (which I ended up doing) I would still be getting a great degree."

Life

In terms of location, "campus is located perfectly between Chicago, Indianapolis, and St. Louis, providing a unique atmosphere in town but close access to other urban areas for a change of pace." Students call social life "very exciting," and say, "The bars in downtown Champaign are great and super relaxed, plus there is an awesome music scene that most people don't expect from a college town." "People here like to party, but there are a lot of other fun things to do," whether it's "going to the Krannert Center to see plays or concerts" or the "movie theater and mall...on Saturday afternoons. Champaign-Urbana seems small to city kids, but to me it's the land of opportunity." Students relish the "nineteen-year-old bar age," and U of I also has "one of the largest Greek communities in the country." The combination of these facts does mean that "drinking culture is huge here" but "there's also tons to do beyond the bars." The range of social opportunities is nearly limitless: "There are 40,000 students, thousands of clubs, two gyms and several sport facilities, and array of establishments to explore on Green Street." As a whole, students report happily that "life is busy, but rewarding."

Student Body

"The diversity of the students here is astounding. Race, religion, major, you've got it all." Because in-state tuition is a major draw, "a majority of the students that you meet here will be from the Chicago suburbs," but the school also attracts "a wide variety of students from all across the world." "University of Illinois houses so many different types of students that the only way we are alike is our dedication to getting an education and our loyalty to UIUC." Undergrads feel that their peers "really know how to be academically successful," and shed state-school stereotypes like so many dirty socks: "It obviously takes a lot to get into this school so students aren't ready to throw it all away to sleep in every day." Social life changes as you find your "niche": "The typical student starts out going to a school of 40,000 students and are lucky if they know a handful of people. Within one week, life as that freshman student grows. There are so many opportunities to get involved on the floor of your residence hall, in organizations, in your classes, that it's hard not to make friends and close relationships."

FINANCIAL AID: 217-333-0100 • E-MAIL: UGRADADMISSIONS@ILLINOIS.EDU • WEBSITE: WWW.ILLINOIS.EDU

THE PRINCETON REVIEW SAYS

Admissions

Very important factors considered include: GPA, rigor of secondary school record. *Important factors considered include:* Standardized test scores, application essay, extracurricular activities, talent/ability. *Other factors considered include:* Class rank, first generation, geographical residence, racial/ethnic status, state residency, volunteer work, work experience, character/personal qualities. SAT or ACT required; ACT with or without Writing component accepted. TOEFL required of all international applicants. *Academic units required:* 4 English; (2 science lab); 2 social studies; 2 foreign language; 2 academic electives. *Academic units recommended:* 4 English; 4 mathematics; (4 science lab); 4 social studies; 4 foreign language; 4 academic electives.

Financial Aid

Students should submit: FAFSA. The Princeton Review suggests that all financial aid forms be submitted as soon as possible after January 1. *Need-based scholarships/grants offered:* Federal Pell, SEOG, State scholarships/grants, private scholarships, the school's own gift aid, United Negro College Fund. *Loan aid offered:* Direct Subsidized Stafford Loans, Direct Unsubsidized Stafford Loans, Direct PLUS loans, Federal Perkins Loans, College/university loans from institutional funds. Federal Work-Study Program available. Institutional employment available. Off-campus job opportunities are excellent.

The Inside Word

The University of Illinois' application review process distinguishes itself from that of many state schools in that every application is considered individually—no small feat for a campus of about 30,000 students. Don't be fooled by the university's high acceptance rate: U of I's applicant pool tends to be self-selective, and those without sufficient qualifications won't make the cut.

THE SCHOOL SAYS "..."

From the Admissions Office

"The campus has been aptly described as a collection of neighborhoods constituting a diverse and vibrant city. The neighborhoods are of many types: students and faculty within a department; people sharing a room or house; the members of a professional organization, a service club, or an intramural team; or simply people who, starting out as strangers sharing a class or a study lounge or a fondness for a weekly film series, have become friends. The city of this description is the university itself—a rich cosmopolitan environment constructed by students and faculty to meet their educational and personal goals. The quality of intellectual life parallels that of other great universities, and many faculty and students who have their choice of top institutions select Illinois over its peers. While such choices are based often on the quality of individual programs of study, another crucial factor is the 'tone' of the campus life that is linked with the virtues of Midwestern culture. There is an informality and a near-absence of pretension, which, coupled with a tradition of commitment to excellence, creates an atmosphere that is unique among the finest institutions.

"Applicants are required to take the SAT or the ACT with the writing section."

SELECTIVITY

Admissions Rating	92
# of applicants	31,432
% of applicants accepted	63
% of acceptees attending	35
# offered a place on the wait list	2,138
% accepting a place on wait list	61
% admitted from wait list	34

FRESHMAN PROFILE

Range SAT Critical Reading	550–680
Range SAT Math	680–790
Range SAT Writing	570–680
Range ACT Composite	26–31
Minimum paper TOEFL	550
Minimum web-based TOEFL	213
% graduated top 10% of class	54
% graduated top 25% of class	88
% graduated top 50% of class	99

DEADLINES

Regular	
Priority	11/1
Deadline	1/2
Notification	2/17
Nonfall registration?	No

APPLICANTS ALSO LOOK AT AND OFTEN PREFER
University of Michigan—Ann Arbor; Northwestern University

AND SOMETIMES PREFER
Indiana University—Bloomington; University of Wisconsin-Madison; Washington University in St. Louis; University of Iowa

AND RARELY PREFER
Illinois State University; Purdue University—West Lafayette

FINANCIAL FACTS

Financial Aid Rating	72
Annual in-state tuition	$11,636
Annual out-of-state tuition	$25,778
Room and board	$10,332
Required fees	$3,324
Books and supplies	$1,200
% needy frosh rec. need-based scholarship or grant aid	77
% needy UG rec. need-based scholarship or grant aid	76
% needy frosh rec. non-need-based scholarship or grant aid	16
% needy UG rec. non-need-based scholarship or grant aid	9
% needy frosh rec. need-based self-help aid	81
% needy UG rec. need-based self-help aid	84
% frosh rec. any financial aid	69
% UG rec. any financial aid	72
% UG borrow to pay for school	52
Average cumulative indebtedness	$24,657
% frosh need fully met	33
% ugrads need fully met	27
Average % of frosh need met	66
Average % of ugrad need met	63

THE UNIVERSITY OF IOWA

107 CALVIN HALL, IOWA CITY, IA 52242 • ADMISSIONS: 319-335-3847 • FAX: 319-333-1535

CAMPUS LIFE

Quality of Life Rating	83
Fire Safety Rating	82
Green Rating	98
Type of school	Public
Affiliation	No Affiliation
Environment	City

STUDENTS

Total undergrad enrollment	21,974
% male/female	48/52
% from out of state	34
% frosh from public high school	90
% frosh live on campus	93
% ugrads live on campus	25
# of fraternities (% ugrad men join)	23 (12)
# of sororities (% ugrad women join)	21 (17)
% African American	3
% Asian	3
% Caucasian	71
% Hispanic	6
% Native American	<1
% international	10
# of countries represented	114

SURVEY SAYS . . .

Students love Iowa City, IA
Great off-campus food
Athletic facilities are great
Lots of beer drinking
Hard liquor is popular
Everyone loves the Hawkeyes

ACADEMICS

Academic Rating	76
% students returning for sophomore year	86
% students graduating within 4 years	47
% students graduating within 6 years	70
Calendar	Semester
Student/faculty ratio	16:1
Profs interesting rating	69
Profs accessible rating	73

Most classes have 10–19 students.
Most lab/discussion sessions have 20–29 students.

MOST POPULAR MAJORS

business/commerce; engineering; psychology

STUDENTS SAY ". . ."

Academics

The University of Iowa manages to pull off an amazing feat: It's a "Big Ten university full of exciting opportunities," yet it's still able to maintain "a small-college feel." Moreover, as the state's flagship school, Iowa provides a "great education" at a "reasonable price." Additionally, students here welcome the fact that "requirements are minimal." In turn, this truly encourages undergrads to "make [their] education [their] own." While there are certainly a "[wide] range of degree programs" from which to choose, students here are especially impressed with Iowa's journalism, premed, writing, nursing, and engineering departments. Though professors certainly run the gamut from "amazing" to "boring," the majority of them are "very engaged with students and are always helpful to any student looking to push their learning beyond the classroom." A fellow student concurs adding that her professors are "passionate, encouraging, and invested in the success of their students both inside and outside of academia." Undergrads at Iowa also appreciate that their teachers really "do a nice job of balancing lectures with real-world applications of the material." Finally, as this pleased undergrad summarizes her school, "The University of Iowa is a platform to launch yourself to the top of your field at an affordable price."

Life

If there's one thing that undergrads tend to agree on, it's that "life is pretty fun at the University of Iowa." To begin with, sports culture is definitely big here. As one student relays, "During football season, Saturdays get crazy. There is just a sea of black and gold swarming toward the stadium. Nothing can really compare to 70,000 Hawkeye fans in one place." Additionally, students love the new rec center, which frequently runs trips "to go rock-climbing, camping, hiking, or kayaking." Of course, the university also sponsors a number of other events outside of athletics. For example, "there are always concerts and comedians on campus, [and] many [of these shows] are even free to students. There are also free movies shown at the Iowa Memorial Union." Students also stress that the university has a lively drinking scene. Indeed, "there is always a party going on here at Iowa." Lastly, undergrads also love hometown Iowa City, which offers a "vibrant downtown" that's "literally across the street from campus." Students happily take advantage of the city's "unique places to eat, shop, or go out." As this undergrad poetically concludes, "When a man is tired of Iowa City, he is tired of life."

Student Body

With such a large student body, undergrads here all posit that there is no "typical" student. One pleased undergrad elaborates, "Everyone is unique and has a different story, but that's one thing that makes life here so great. You have the ability to meet people from around the country and around the world, and we all get to share the experience of college together." Indeed, students feel very fortunate to be surrounded by such diversity. "We have a strong LGBTQA presence on campus, [along with] different religious places near campus. [In addition,] there are many different organizations for minorities, religions, and everything else here on campus. I couldn't imagine someone coming here and not being able to find a student organization that is for them." Of course, if pressed to generalize, students will describe their fellow Hawkeyes as "friendly, hardworking, and studious" but also "laid-back" and "very social." However, what ultimately unites this student body is the fact that most undergrads have "their season football tickets by June."

FINANCIAL AID: 319-335-1450 • E-MAIL: ADMISSIONS@UIOWA.EDU • WEBSITE: WWW.UIOWA.EDU

THE PRINCETON REVIEW SAYS

Admissions

Very important factors considered include: Class rank, GPA, rigor of secondary school record, standardized test scores. *Other factors considered include:* Recommendation(s), state residency, talent/ability, character/personal qualities. SAT or ACT required; ACT with Writing component recommended. TOEFL required of all international applicants. *Academic units required:* 4 English; 3 mathematics; 3 science; 3 social studies; 2 foreign language. *Academic units recommended:* 4 mathematics; 4 foreign language.

Financial Aid

Students should submit: FAFSA, Institution's own financial aid form. The Princeton Review suggests that all financial aid forms be submitted as soon as possible after January 1. *Need-based scholarships/grants offered:* Federal Pell, SEOG, State scholarships/grants, private scholarships, the school's own gift aid. *Loan aid offered:* Direct Subsidized Stafford Loans, Direct Unsubsidized Stafford Loans, Direct PLUS loans, Federal Perkins Loans, Federal Nursing Loans, College/university loans from institutional funds. Federal Work-Study Program available. Institutional employment available. Off-campus job opportunities are good.

The Inside Word

Like many large public universities, admissions officers at the University of Iowa rely heavily on quantitative factors when determining an applicant's status. Therefore, GPA and standardized test scores will likely hold the most weight. It should also be noted that the majority of applicants are admitted to the College of Liberal Arts & Sciences or the College of Engineering. Students interested in other programs (say within the College of Business or Nursing) often apply after they have enrolled in the university.

THE SCHOOL SAYS "..."

From the Admissions Office

"The University of Iowa offers all of the opportunities and resources of a large, research university, while putting a strong emphasis on the undergraduate student experience. As the first public university to enroll men and women on an equal basis, Iowa is proud of its history in providing a world-class education to students from all backgrounds. Today, the University of Iowa offers nationally ranked academic programs, strong pre-professional programs in the health sciences and law, and access to world-renowned faculty. With an emphasis on small class sizes, students interact with faculty both inside and outside the classroom. Located in one of the top college towns in American, Iowa's campus is undergoing a historic physical makeover with construction underway on a new residence hall, school of music, school of art and art history, and Hancher Auditorium, the UI's world-renowned performing arts venue."

SELECTIVITY

Admissions Rating	79
# of applicants	21,644
% of applicants accepted	83
% of acceptees attending	26

FRESHMAN PROFILE

Range SAT Critical Reading	460–620
Range SAT Math	540–680
Range SAT Writing	480–610
Range ACT Composite	23–28
Minimum paper TOEFL	530
Average HS GPA	3.61
% graduated top 10% of class	24
% graduated top 25% of class	57
% graduated top 50% of class	90

DEADLINES

Regular	
Deadline	4/1
Nonfall registration?	Yes

APPLICANTS ALSO LOOK AT AND OFTEN PREFER

University of Illinois at Urbana-Champaign; Northwestern University

AND SOMETIMES PREFER

Indiana University—Bloomington; Iowa State University

AND RARELY PREFER

Illinois State University; Missouri University of Science and Technology (formerly University of Missouri—Rolla); Cornell College

FINANCIAL FACTS

Financial Aid Rating	72
Annual in-state tuition	$6,678
Annual out-of-state tuition	$26,008
Room and board	$9,614
Required fees	$1,401
Books and supplies	$1,040
% needy frosh rec. need-based scholarship or grant aid	70
% needy UG rec. need-based scholarship or grant aid	64
% needy frosh rec. non-need-based scholarship or grant aid	66
% needy UG rec. non-need-based scholarship or grant aid	44
% needy frosh rec. need-based self-help aid	78
% needy UG rec. need-based self-help aid	83
% frosh rec. any financial aid	79
% UG rec. any financial aid	72
% UG borrow to pay for school	61
Average cumulative indebtedness	$28,131
% frosh need fully met	25
% ugrads need fully met	21
Average % of frosh need met	63
Average % of ugrad need met	60

UNIVERSITY OF KANSAS

OFFICE OF ADMISSIONS, LAWRENCE, KS 66045-7576 • ADMISSIONS: 785-864-3911 • FAX: 785-864-5017

CAMPUS LIFE

Quality of Life Rating	97
Fire Safety Rating	87
Green Rating	88
Type of school	Public
Affiliation	No Affiliation
Environment	City

STUDENTS

Total undergrad enrollment	18,731
% male/female	50/50
% from out of state	23
% frosh live on campus	62
% ugrads live on campus	25
# of fraternities (% ugrad men join)	29 (16)
# of sororities (% ugrad women join)	16 (21)
% African American	4
% Asian	4
% Caucasian	75
% Hispanic	6
% Native American	1
% international	5
# of countries represented	107

SURVEY SAYS . . .

Students are happy
School is well run
Students are friendly
Students get along with local community
Students love Lawrence, KS
Great off-campus food
Athletic facilities are great
Lots of beer drinking
Hard liquor is popular
Everyone loves the Jayhawks
Frats and sororities are popular
Student publications are popular
Alumni active on campus

ACADEMICS

Academic Rating	76
% students returning for sophomore year	80
% students graduating within 4 years	36
% students graduating within 6 years	62
Calendar	Semester
Student/faculty ratio	18:1
Profs interesting rating	75
Profs accessible rating	79

Most classes have 10–19 students.
Most lab/discussion sessions have 10–19 students.

MOST POPULAR MAJORS
biology; business/commerce; psychology; psychology

STUDENTS SAY " . . ."

Academics

Located in the heartland's quintessential college town, University of Kansas's flagship campus is a "place of tradition" as well as opportunity, combining "stimulating academics with a community that is passionate about the school." Most of KU's 2,600 faculty members are "actively engaged in research in their particular field," but there is nonetheless a real emphasis on undergraduate teaching. Here, "the faculty is obviously willing to do what it takes to help," and "teachers are always urging students to contact them with questions or visit their office hours." An undergrad details, "The personalities and teaching styles of KU's professors vary widely, but all of the instructors I have had are fully engaged in teaching and truly enjoy helping students learn." That said, "there are a lot of giant lecture halls your freshmen and sophomore year," which some students find "overwhelming." Others complain that general education requirements are "too strict and unnecessary." On the flip side, the big-school setting proffers "abundant resources," including "research opportunities" for undergraduates and "one of the best study abroad programs in the nation." In fact, many say, "The experience outside of the classroom is what sets you up for success after college." Speaking of life after graduation, KU's "career center is committed to getting students hired," and "there are many job opportunities" in nearby Topeka and Kansas City. To make the deal sweeter, KU graduates aren't strapped with insurmountable debt: "In-state tuition is very affordable."

Life

In the pursuit of an "incredible college experience," KU undergrads definitely keep busy: "The typical student probably volunteers in the community, has a part time job, [and] has some special hobby (from rock climbing to tightrope walking)." Incoming freshman will find "over 600 student groups to participate in," ranging from "Quidditch to chess club to the arts," and "there is never a dull night" on campus, where "Student Union Activities brings in comedians, authors, and movies on a regular basis." During the winter months, "KU basketball is our religion, and Allen Fieldhouse is our church." An undergrad admits, "I schedule everything in my life around the KU men's basketball schedule, as does much of the student population." Described as "the perfect college town," "Lawrence has a great live music scene, cool coffee shops, and eclectic stores," as well as bars and nightclubs popular with students. "People in Lawrence are also very outdoorsy," and, when the weather is nice, "you can rent camping equipment from the rec for a weekend out at the lake" or "go rock climbing" nearby. For a more cosmopolitan outing, "being close to Kansas City provides a lot of entertainment from museums and art shows to music and dining."

Students

Students say you'd be surprised by the diversity on this friendly Midwestern campus, lauding the KU's "ability to unite 30,000 people of different values and backgrounds." There are "students from every county in Kansas, every state, and over 100 countries," with noticeable representations from out-of-state cities like St. Louis and Denver mixing into the large in-state crowd. "KU students find a great balance in work and play," with some undergrads tipping the scales in one direction or the other: "You have your 'here for a good time' types, absolutely rock-star scholars, and dedicated students who balance their GPA and their social calendar." In terms of making friends and fitting in, getting involved is the best way to mitigate the campus's size: "There are so many opportunities at KU that it can seem a bit overwhelming, but students really find their niche and run with it." Of particular note, "there is definitely a big Greek life presence" on campus, which some say causes a "schism" in the undergraduate community. In counterpoint, a student reassures us, "The Greek community does intermingle frequently with non-Greeks. I'm not Greek, but I see it a lot and have a lot of Greek friends."

FINANCIAL AID: 785-864-4700 • E-MAIL: ADM@KU.EDU • WEBSITE: WWW.KU.EDU

THE PRINCETON REVIEW SAYS

Admissions

Very important factors considered include: Class rank, GPA, standardized test scores. *Other factors considered include:* SAT or ACT required; ACT with or without Writing component accepted. TOEFL required of all international applicants. *Academic units required:* 4 English; 3 mathematics; 3 science; (1 science lab); 3 social studies. *Academic units recommended:* 4 English; 4 mathematics; 3 science; 3 social studies; 2 foreign language.

Financial Aid

Students should submit: FAFSA. The Princeton Review suggests that all financial aid forms be submitted as soon as possible after January 1. *Need-based scholarships/grants offered:* Federal Pell, SEOG, State scholarships/grants, private scholarships, the school's own gift aid. *Loan aid offered:* Direct Subsidized Stafford Loans, Direct Unsubsidized Stafford Loans, Direct PLUS loans, Federal Perkins Loans, Federal Nursing Loans, College/university loans from institutional funds. Federal Work-Study Program available. Institutional employment available. Off-campus job opportunities are excellent.

The Inside Word

To be admitted to KU, Kansans graduating high school in 2015 need a 2.0+ GPA in the Kansas Qualified Admission curriculum and either a 21+ ACT (980+ SAT) or rank in the top third of their high school class. Nonresident 2015 high school graduates must have a 2.5+ GPA in the Kansas Qualified Admission curriculum and either a 24+ ACT (1090+ SAT) or rank in the top third of their high school class. Note that professional schools, such as architecture, health professors, and engineering, have more rigorous admissions standards; check the school's web page for details.

Admission requirements for 2016 high school graduates will be different. Consult the website for updates.

THE SCHOOL SAYS "..."

From the Admissions Office

"The University of Kansas has a long and distinguished tradition for academic excellence. Outstanding students from across the nation are attracted to KU's top-ranked academics, four-year-renewable scholarships and four-year fixed tuition for first-time freshmen, beautiful campus, and contagious school spirit. KU provides students extraordinary opportunities in honors programs, service learning, undergraduate research, internships, and study abroad. The university is located in Lawrence (forty minutes from Kansas City), a vibrant community of 90,000 consistently recognized as one of the nation's top ten college towns.

"Students applying for admissions may submit an ACT or SAT score, and KU will only look at math and critical reading (verbal) section of SAT for admissions purposes."

SELECTIVITY
Admissions Rating	76
# of applicants	13,256
% of applicants accepted	88
% of acceptees attending	34

FRESHMAN PROFILE
Range ACT Composite	22–28
Average HS GPA	3.50
% graduated top 10% of class	26
% graduated top 25% of class	59
% graduated top 50% of class	90

DEADLINES
Regular	
Priority	11/1
Nonfall registration?	Yes

FINANCIAL FACTS
Financial Aid Rating	70
Annual in-state tuition	$9,225
Annual out-of-state tuition	$23,991
Room and board	$7,702
Required fees	$882
Books and supplies	$900
% needy frosh rec. need-based scholarship or grant aid	49
% needy UG rec. need-based scholarship or grant aid	60
% needy frosh rec. non-need-based scholarship or grant aid	46
% needy UG rec. non-need-based scholarship or grant aid	30
% needy frosh rec. need-based self-help aid	68
% needy UG rec. need-based self-help aid	76
% frosh rec. any financial aid	69
% UG rec. any financial aid	57
% UG borrow to pay for school	54
Average cumulative indebtedness	$27,219
% frosh need fully met	15
% ugrads need fully met	11
Average % of frosh need met	53
Average % of ugrad need met	52

University of Kentucky

100 Funkhouser Building, Lexington, KY 40506 • Admissions: 859-257-2000 • Fax: 859-257-3823

CAMPUS LIFE
Quality of Life Rating	73
Fire Safety Rating	91
Green Rating	60*
Type of school	Public
Affiliation	No Affiliation
Environment	City

STUDENTS
Total undergrad enrollment	20,436
% male/female	49/51
% from out of state	21
% frosh live on campus	92
% ugrads live on campus	26
# of fraternities (% ugrad men join)	19 (10)
# of sororities (% ugrad women join)	16 (33)
% African American	8
% Asian	2
% Caucasian	80
% Hispanic	3
% Native American	<1
% international	2
# of countries represented	117

SURVEY SAYS . . .
Great library
Everyone loves the Wildcats
Student publications are popular

ACADEMICS
Academic Rating	69
% students returning for sophomore year	81
% students graduating within 4 years	34
% students graduating within 6 years	59
Calendar	Semester
Student/faculty ratio	18:1
Profs interesting rating	64
Profs accessible rating	64

Most classes have 20–29 students.
Most lab/discussion sessions have 20–29 students.

STUDENTS SAY ". . ."

Academics

The University of Kentucky in Lexington is "all about making a name for yourself by preparing for and getting involved in future career goals while having fun and enjoying what college is all about." "Making a name for yourself" here requires distinguishing yourself in a crowd of almost 19,000 undergraduates; daunting as that sounds, students tell us it can be done. "Getting involved in future career goals" is easy enough, given the "great selection of courses and majors" available. Kentucky offers undergraduate degrees in twelve of its nineteen divisions. Choices include the College of Agriculture (with popular majors in animal science, agricultural economics, and hospitality management), the College of Business and Management, the College of Education, the College of Engineering, the College of Communications and Information Studies (advertising, journalism, and library science), and the College of Arts and Sciences (biology, history, and political science). Students here laud the "impressive teaching staff, dedicated to enhancing student knowledge and teaching students about the future." UK's brand-new library "is also quite amazing. It is the perfect place to go study because usually the dorms can be a bit too distracting." All told, go-getters willing to take initiative will find UK offers "a safe and fun atmosphere where you have unlimited opportunities to get involved at a reasonable price."

Life

"Everyone is a Wildcat" at UK, because "UK has tremendous sports programs and big fans all around the United States." Men's basketball fans "are among the craziest in the nation," and students "would be football fanatics if our team would win a game every now and then." "Because UK is dry, most parties are held off campus." Social life for many revolves around the off-campus Greek houses where "there is always a party going on, but you have to be a part of a fraternity or sorority to really know about it and attend." Some students report, "There are a lot of nonalcoholic parties in the dorms that might be crazier than the alcoholic parties," although others advise, "It's better to live off campus because the residence halls are pretty bad (except for the new ones), the meal plan is awful, and everything off campus is a lot cheaper." Hometown Lexington "is a great city with much to do and lots of opportunities. It offers many different clubs, bars, and restaurants that college students can go to as well as horse racing. All of these venues have a 'College Day' where students get discounts." One sophomore warns, however, "Small-town students can become distracted by the lights of the city."

Student Body

"The typical UK student has a Southern accent, likes to party, and often shops at J. Crew," but, "as the undergraduate population is about 19,000, there are a lot of people who do not fit that description." True, one of the most common "types"—or at least the most conspicuous one—are the "beautiful people, the hot girls and guys who roam the campus and dress up to go to class." But for every "collar-popping, stuck-up frat boy" there's also "your typical country Kentucky boy, boots and all." What you won't find many of at UK are "liberals—they are few and far between—and the type of atypical student with wild hair colors or other style extremes." Most "lean right politically, but generally the student body is apathetic." School spirit is rampant, so much so that "on an average day, one in three students will have some sort of UK clothing on."

FINANCIAL AID: 859-257-3172 • E-MAIL: ADMISSION@UKY.EDU • WEBSITE: WWW.UKY.EDU

THE PRINCETON REVIEW SAYS

Admissions

Very important factors considered include: GPA, rigor of secondary school record, standardized test scores. *Other factors considered include:* Class rank, application essay, extracurricular activities, geographical residence, interview, racial/ethnic status, recommendation(s), talent/ability, volunteer work, alumni/ae relations, character/personal qualities. SAT or ACT required; ACT with or without Writing component accepted. TOEFL required of all international applicants. *Academic units required:* 4 English; 3 mathematics; 3 science; 3 social studies; 2 foreign language; 5 academic electives. *Academic units recommended:* 4 English; 4 mathematics; 4 science; 3 social studies; 2 foreign language; 3 academic electives.

Financial Aid

Students should submit: FAFSA. Regular filing deadline is 2/15. The Princeton Review suggests that all financial aid forms be submitted as soon as possible after January 1. *Need-based scholarships/grants offered:* Federal Pell, SEOG, State scholarships/grants, private scholarships, the school's own gift aid. *Loan aid offered:* Direct Subsidized Stafford Loans, Direct Unsubsidized Stafford Loans, Direct PLUS loans, Federal Perkins Loans, State Loans, College/university loans from institutional funds. Applicants will be notified of awards beginning 4/1. Federal Work-Study Program available.

The Inside Word

The University of Kentucky's admissions team is about as objective as they come. If you have the GPA, class rank, and test scores, you'll in all likelihood be welcomed into the Wildcat community. The university is continually looking to improve its selectivity, so hitting the books is a must if you want to be a serious contender.

THE SCHOOL SAYS "..."

From the Admissions Office

"The University of Kentucky offers you an outstanding learning environment and quality instruction through its excellent faculty. Of the 1,892 full-time faculty, 98 percent hold the doctorate degree or the highest degree in their field of study. Many are nationally and internationally known for their research, distinguished teaching, and scholarly service to Kentucky, the nation, and the world. UK's scholars (students, faculty, and alumni) have been honored by Nobel, Pulitzer, Rhodes, Fulbright, Guggenheim, and Grammy awards, and most recently the Metropolitan Opera and the Marshall Foundation. Yet, with a student to teacher ratio of only seventeen to one, UK faculty are accessible and willing to answer your questions and discuss your interests.

"UK will accept the SAT. The writing sections of the ACT and SAT will not be used in the admission process."

SELECTIVITY

Admissions Rating	83
# of applicants	18,802
% of applicants accepted	67
% of acceptees attending	37

FRESHMAN PROFILE

Range SAT Critical Reading	500–620
Range SAT Math	510–630
Range SAT Writing	480–600
Range ACT Composite	23–28
Minimum paper TOEFL	527
Minimum web-based TOEFL	197
Average HS GPA	3.46
% graduated top 10% of class	32
% graduated top 25% of class	61
% graduated top 50% of class	88

DEADLINES

Regular	
Priority	2/15
Deadline	2/15
Nonfall registration?	Yes

APPLICANTS ALSO LOOK AT AND OFTEN PREFER

Indiana University—Bloomington; Miami University; Centre College; Transylvania University

AND SOMETIMES PREFER

University of Louisville; Bellarmine University; University of Tennessee

AND RARELY PREFER

Florida State University; University of Florida; University of Illinois at Urbana-Champaign; Purdue University—West Lafayette; The Ohio State University—Columbus

FINANCIAL FACTS

Financial Aid Rating	73
Annual in-state tuition	$8,610
Annual out-of-state tuition	$18,798
Room and board	$10,192
Required fees	$1,066
Books and supplies	$800
% needy frosh rec. need-based scholarship or grant aid	46
% needy UG rec. need-based scholarship or grant aid	49
% needy frosh rec. non-need-based scholarship or grant aid	89
% needy UG rec. non-need-based scholarship or grant aid	71
% needy frosh rec. need-based self-help aid	59
% needy UG rec. need-based self-help aid	68
% frosh rec. any financial aid	40
% UG rec. any financial aid	38
% UG borrow to pay for school	40
Average cumulative indebtedness	$21,774
% frosh need fully met	22
% ugrads need fully met	19
Average % of frosh need met	67
Average % of ugrad need met	63

University of Louisiana at Lafayette

PO Drawer 41210, Lafayette, LA 70504 • Admissions: 337-482-6553 • Fax: 337-482-1112

CAMPUS LIFE

Quality of Life Rating	83
Fire Safety Rating	88
Green Rating	60*
Type of school	Public
Affiliation	No Affiliation
Environment	City

STUDENTS

Total undergrad enrollment	15,053
% male/female	45/55
% from out of state	5
% frosh live on campus	51
% ugrads live on campus	18
# of fraternities (% ugrad men join)	12 (9)
# of sororities (% ugrad women join)	6 (10
% African American	21
% Asian	2
% Caucasian	69
% Hispanic	3
% Native American	<1
% international	2
# of countries represented	101

SURVEY SAYS . . .

Students are friendly
Diverse student types on campus
Students get along with local community
Students love Lafayette, LA
Great off-campus food
Student publications are popular

ACADEMICS

Academic Rating	67
% students returning for sophomore year	74
% students graduating within 4 years	13
% students graduating within 6 years	45
Calendar	Semester
Student/faculty ratio	22:1
Profs interesting rating	66
Profs accessible rating	66
Most classes have 20–29 students.	

MOST POPULAR MAJORS
nursing; biology; management

STUDENTS SAY "..."

Academics

At the "medium-sized" University of Louisiana at Lafayette—in "the heart of Cajun country"—many students feel "under the shadow" of their mammoth cousin, LSU. We really don't know why. UL Lafayette offers "serious bang for your buck;" tremendously generous grant and scholarship programs and out-of-state fee waivers make UL Lafayette one of the best bargains in the country. Programs in "education, computer science, and engineering" are "ranked as some of the best in the nation." The nursing program is the "third largest" in the country and "one of the best" anywhere. "Seasoned" and "overwhelmingly helpful" professors are "friendly, fun," and "honestly interested in having you learn." "The experience has been absolutely wonderful academically," gushes a senior. "In more than 120 hours of course study, I cannot remember having one bad professor." Other students disagree; they remember a "couple of bad apples." A perennial complaint among students at UL Lafayette is that many professors from other countries "cannot be understood by the students." The administration is generally unpopular. "The bureaucracy is ridiculous," reports a general studies major. "The university is run like an out-of-date chicken farm," adds a finance major. "No one knows the answer to anything" and "getting financial aid in a timely manner is a real problem." Students are generally very satisfied, though. "My overall college experience at University of Louisiana at Lafayette has been terrific," asserts a junior. "I would recommend this college to anyone."

Life

UL Lafayette's "beautiful campus" is "full of big trees and handsome Southern architecture." Unfortunately, "it always floods when it rains," some "lousy buildings" "need updating," and the parking situation is just "painful." Nevertheless, "school spirit is really high." "Football games are huge events," and Lafayette is, by all accounts, a "great" college town. "Believe me," swears a wide-eyed first-year student, "it is an experience." The Strip "is right by campus" and "lined with numerous bars and clubs." "Most people," however, "congregate downtown," where it's "almost like Bourbon Street in New Orleans." The local music scene is hopping, and festivals are frequent, including a very large International Music Festival and a gigantic Mardi Gras celebration. If partying isn't your bag, or if you get sick of it, Lafayette also offers an "abundance of coffee shops" and "numerous art venues." "There is so much history and culture in Louisiana" that, frankly, it's hard to "ever be bored or without something fun to do on any day of the week," and you can find "great food anywhere." "If you're looking for a good, inexpensive college education that is packed with good food, cold beer, and excitement, look no further than UL Lafayette."

Student Body

Students at UL Lafayette are "friendly and fun" and "always seem to be in a good mood." They have "Southern flair with a little bit of our Cajun cayenne," a marketing major quips. They're also "very strongly rooted in their religions;" in that regard, "Catholic conservatives" seem to dominate. Many "are from the surrounding area of Acadiana," are "lower- to upper-middle-class," and "receive some financial support from [their] parents." Many also "have part-time job[s]." Beyond that, "there are many different types of people," and "everyone seems to get along together." One undergrad reports, "Our campus includes a very diverse group of students from various religious and racial backgrounds." There are also "a few oddballs" who "try to get themselves noticed by the way they dress and their eccentric hair." For the most part, however, "everyone blends in." "No one really points out or harasses other students here at UL Lafayette, unless that student happens to be wearing LSU paraphernalia."

FINANCIAL AID: 337-482-6506 • E-MAIL: ENROLL@LOUISIANA.EDU • WEBSITE: WWW.LOUISIANA.EDU

THE PRINCETON REVIEW SAYS

Admissions

Very important factors considered include: Class rank, GPA, rigor of secondary school record, standardized test scores, level of applicant's interest. *Other factors considered include:* State residency. SAT or ACT required; ACT with or without Writing component accepted. TOEFL required of all international applicants. *Academic units required:* 4 English; 4 mathematics; 3 science; 1 social studies; 2 foreign language; 2 history; 1 visual/performing arts.

Financial Aid

Students should submit: FAFSA. The Princeton Review suggests that all financial aid forms be submitted as soon as possible after January 1. *Need-based scholarships/grants offered:* Federal Pell, SEOG, State scholarships/grants, private scholarships, the school's own gift aid, federal nursing scholarships. *Loan aid offered:* Federal Perkins Loans, Federal Nursing Loans. Federal Work-Study Program available. Institutional employment available. Off-campus job opportunities are good.

The Inside Word

UL Lafayette is still a fallback school for many applicants. You are pretty much guaranteed admission if you carry an ACT score of at least 20 and complete a basic college-prep high school curriculum with a GPA of 2.5 or better. If your numbers are a little lower, you can submit an essay and some other credentials for possible admission through UL Lafayette's admission by committee. It should be noted, however, that admission by committee is limited to 6 percent of each incoming class.

THE SCHOOL SAYS "..."

From the Admissions Office

"The University of Louisiana at Lafayette offers students from throughout the United States and more than ninety countries strong academic training and personal enrichment opportunities in a friendly, comfortable, student-centered environment. UL Lafayette students are taught, mentored, and advised by some of the brightest and most accomplished faculty members in the United States. Although UL Lafayette offers more than 100 programs of study and the research opportunities, internship possibilities, and facilities of a major research-intensive university, average class size is approximately the same as that at many high schools and smaller higher education institutions. "UL students receive a good deal of individual attention and support—both personal and academic—from faculty and staff.

"A wide range of cultural, recreational, and social activities are available on and off campus, including more than 150 campus organizations and clubs, NCAA Division I and intramural athletics, a state-of-the-art recreation and aquatic center, a thriving arts scene, a wide range of live music venues, shopping, a great variety of excellent restaurants, theaters, the second largest Mardi Gras in the nation, and an international music festival. In fact, *Utne Reader* magazine selected the city of Lafayette as Louisiana's 'Most Enlightened Town.' Recently, Lafayette was also listed as one of America's most optimistic cities.

"Our generous financial aid and scholarship programs, including an out-of-state tuition waiver for qualified students, make UL Lafayette one of the most affordable universities in the nation. "Students who have completed the required college preparatory core curriculum in high school may qualify for admission on the basis of a combination of their high school cumulative grade point average and ACT or SAT scores."

SELECTIVITY

Admissions Rating	75
# of applicants	8,506
% of applicants accepted	59
% of acceptees attending	53

FRESHMAN PROFILE

Range ACT Composite	21–25
Minimum paper TOEFL	525
Average HS GPA	3.3
% graduated top 10% of class	17
% graduated top 25% of class	43
% graduated top 50% of class	75

DEADLINES

Regular	
Priority	7/20
Nonfall registration?	Yes

FINANCIAL FACTS

Financial Aid Rating	67
Annual in-state tuition	$4,469
Annual out-of-state tuition	$14,019
Room and board	$8,594
Required fees	$1,723
Books and supplies	$1,200
% needy frosh rec. need-based scholarship or grant aid	95
% needy UG rec. need-based scholarship or grant aid	89
% needy frosh rec. non-need-based scholarship or grant aid	13
% needy UG rec. non-need-based scholarship or grant aid	8
% needy frosh rec. need-based self-help aid	48
% needy UG rec. need-based self-help aid	59
% frosh rec. any financial aid	93
% UG rec. any financial aid	84
% frosh need fully met	13
% ugrads need fully met	8
Average % of frosh need met	60
Average % of ugrad need met	53

UNIVERSITY OF LOUISVILLE

2301 SOUTH THIRD STREET, LOUISVILLE, KY 40292-0001 • ADMISSIONS: 502-852-6531 • FAX: 502-852-4776

STUDENTS SAY ". . ."
Academics
University of Louisville is an institution that affords undergraduates "endless opportunities." Certainly, as one of Kentucky's premiere public universities, a Louisville education means students are getting a "great value" and an affordable price tag. And when you combine those attributes with a "beautiful" campus that's "easy to navigate," well it's understandable why students eagerly exclaim that Louisville "feels...like home." With regards to academics, undergrads truly appreciate the university's "[emphasis on] critical thinking" as well as the "personalized" attention they receive. Therefore, it's no surprise to hear that Louisville professors "generally [seem to] care about student success [both] in[side] and outside the classroom." As one satisfied biology student further explains, "They are willing to go above and beyond to help you gain a better understanding of course material and obtain supplementary experience outside of the classroom using their own collaborations and affiliations in the field." However, some students do find cause to mention that professors in "higher up courses...are better than professors who teach gen-ed courses." Fortunately, students are pleased to discover that, for the most part, "U of L is about immersing yourself in a diverse community where you have the chance to grow academically, socially, spiritually, and in whatever other ways you choose."

Life
As one excited junior quickly exclaims, life at University of Louisville is "always lively." Indeed, "there is always something going on both on and off campus and numerous ways to get involved and have a great time." To begin with, Greek life is "fairly prominent." And, naturally, there's a small party scene to go with it. Fortunately, we're assured that "things never get out of hand; it's just students trying to wind down and have a good time." Sporting events are extremely popular as well and these undergrads generate a lot of Cardinal pride. As one music education major boasts, "We have several conference championships already this year and our basketball team looks to repeat as national champions." Additionally, Louisville students like to give back and community service is a common activity here. An impressed junior reveals, "People are pretty conscientious. They volunteer a lot and there are a million and one volunteer groups throughout the city. Same goes for environmental groups." Of course Louisville itself is a vibrant city and one which undergrads love to take advantage. For example, students flock to "4th Street Live!, a popular hangout." And they also "enjoy Churchill Downs and going to horse races as well as the eclectic Highlands area of Bardstown Road."

Student Body
Undergrads at University of Louisville really value the amount of diversity found among their student body. As a highly content nursing student immediately chimes in, "We have so many people with different backgrounds, religions, and interests that no matter where you come from or what you are interested in you will fit in." This sentiment is bolstered by a peer who states, "We have a little bit of everyone, from sorority girls to hippies to those who study all the time. You will not have trouble finding friends here." Certainly, there are also plenty of similarities to be found across the student body as well. After all, many undergrads hail from "the Louisville area" and hold "moderate political views." Students also say that "the majority of [individuals] are extremely nice and easy to get along with." And they are more than "willing to help" their peers whenever they're in need. Then again that's not terribly surprising given that, as this music education major eloquently states, "We are all Cardinals."

FINANCIAL AID: 502-852-5511 • E-MAIL: ADMITME@LOUISVILLE.EDU • WEBSITE: WWW.LOUISVILLE.EDU

THE PRINCETON REVIEW SAYS

Admissions

Very important factors considered include: GPA, rigor of secondary school record, standardized test scores. *Other factors considered include:* Class rank, extracurricular activities, racial/ethnic status, recommendation(s), state residency, talent/ability, volunteer work, work experience. SAT or ACT required; ACT with or without Writing component accepted. TOEFL required of all international applicants. *Academic units required:* 4 English; 3 mathematics; 3 science; (1 science lab); 3 social studies; 2 foreign language; 5 academic electives; 1 visual/performing arts. *Academic units recommended:* 4 mathematics; 4 science; 3 foreign language.

Financial Aid

Students should submit: FAFSA. The Princeton Review suggests that all financial aid forms be submitted as soon as possible after January 1. *Need-based scholarships/grants offered:* Federal Pell, SEOG, State scholarships/grants, private scholarships, the school's own gift aid. *Loan aid offered:* Direct Subsidized Stafford Loans, Direct Unsubsidized Stafford Loans, Direct PLUS loans, Federal Perkins Loans, Federal Nursing Loans. Federal Work-Study Program available. Institutional employment available.

The Inside Word

By and large, admissions decisions at University of Louisville are highly dependent on quantitative data. This means that each applicant's class rank, GPA and standardized test scores will be of utmost importance. Attention will also be paid to course selection; a strong college prep curriculum should be a given. Requirements will vary depending on the specific school to which a candidate is applying. For example, applicants interested in the School of Music must also pass an audition. And nursing students face a two-part process; applying for the lower-level division in freshman year and then applying for the upper-level division in junior year.

THE SCHOOL SAYS "..."

From the Admissions Office

"The University of Louisville (UofL) has transformed into a premier metropolitan university – and it keeps getting better. It is a tight knit community with the feel of a small college where you can walk anywhere on campus in only 10 minutes. Over the past 10 years it has dramatically improved its on-campus environment with the addition of new residence halls, new apartments near campus, a new state-of-the-art student recreation center and restaurants and shopping near campus with the right mix of local flavor. Located in a vibrant city that is known worldwide for the Kentucky Derby, students quickly learn to navigate its great parks, discover local restaurants and explore a revitalized downtown and neighborhoods with an eclectic environment.

With over 50 percent of our entering freshmen beginning their studies with college credit, U of L is a strong academic environment with opportunities inside and outside the classroom to prepare you for professional school or your first job. The city and UofL are closely linked, providing opportunities for internships, coops, part-time jobs and service learning experiences. Our commitment to diversity has created a culture with support for LGBT students and students of all socioeconomic and ethnic backgrounds.

Although widely known for our engineering, business and medical programs, we offer over 200 academic programs and in recent years have added undergraduate programs in Public Health, Social Work, Asian Studies and Latin American and Latino Studies, demonstrating a desire to prepare students for the 21st Century needs of our city, region and beyond."

SELECTIVITY	
Admissions Rating	82
# of applicants	9,142
% of applicants accepted	71
% of acceptees attending	44
% admitted from wait list FRESHMAN PROFILE	
Range SAT Critical Reading	500–620
Range SAT Math	510–640
Range ACT Composite	22–28
Minimum paper TOEFL	550
Minimum web-based TOEFL	213
Average HS GPA	3.53

DEADLINES	
Regular	
Priority	2/15
Deadline	8/25
Nonfall registration?	Yes

FINANCIAL FACTS	
Financial Aid Rating	74
Annual in-state tuition	$9,750
Annual out-of-state tuition	$23,638
Room and board	$7,710
Books and supplies	$1,000
% needy frosh rec. need-based scholarship or grant aid	96
% needy UG rec. need-based scholarship or grant aid	88
% needy frosh rec. non-need-based scholarship or grant aid	18
% needy UG rec. non-need-based scholarship or grant aid	11
% needy frosh rec. need-based self-help aid	55
% needy UG rec. need-based self-help aid	64
% frosh rec. any financial aid	97
% UG rec. any financial aid	79
% UG borrow to pay for school	47
Average cumulative indebtedness	$19,864
% frosh need fully met	25
% ugrads need fully met	20
Average % of frosh need met	63
Average % of ugrad need met	61

UNIVERSITY OF MAINE

5713 CHADBOURNE HALL, ORONO, ME 04469-5713 • ADMISSIONS: 207-581-1561 • FAX: 207-581-1213

CAMPUS LIFE

Quality of Life Rating	72
Fire Safety Rating	92
Green Rating	98
Type of school	Public
Affiliation	No Affiliation
Environment	Village

STUDENTS

Total undergrad enrollment	8,619
% male/female	53/47
% from out of state	20
% frosh live on campus	89
% ugrads live on campus	40
# of fraternities	17
# of sororities	8
% African American	2
% Asian	1
% Caucasian	81
% Hispanic	2
% Native American	1
% international	3
# of countries represented	65

SURVEY SAYS . . .
Athletic facilities are great
Lots of beer drinking
Student publications are popular
Hard liquor is popular

ACADEMICS

Academic Rating	72
% students returning for sophomore year	81
% students graduating within 4 years	36
% students graduating within 6 years	56
Calendar	Semester
Student/faculty ratio	16:1
Profs interesting rating	68
Profs accessible rating	68
Most classes have 10–19 students.	
Most lab/discussion sessions have 10–19 students.	

MOST POPULAR MAJORS
education; engineering; business/commerce

STUDENTS SAY ". . ."

Academics

The University of Maine is proud to have "one of the top engineering schools in the Northeast!" Students describe the atmosphere as "engineering with a dash of liberal arts," and also praise the forestry and business programs. However, some point out, "As with many schools focused on funding their science departments, the arts programs tend to suffer and feel like the neglected, malnourished stepchildren." Yet, the overall consensus is that "UMaine has challenging courses that push students to reach their potential." Many students say they chose UMaine for its balance of "the friendly, small feeling while still at a state university," and Maine residents cite the "financially feasible" in-state tuition combined with the fact that "it's close to home but far enough away and large enough to feel different and exciting" as big selling points. Most agree, "The faculty and administrators take an active interest in the students" and say, "Education is top priority." Professor reviews offer a mixed bag, with some students saying, "The professors here are open-minded and teach with enthusiasm," and others finding, "There is the occasional dud professor." One zoology major sums up the disparity this way: "Professors in the lower-level courses tend to be more focused on lecturing than anything else. As you move up in the course levels, and classes get smaller, the professors tend to pay more attention to class discussion and the opinions of individual students."

Life

Despite the fact that "it can get rather gloomy with the long winters" and "winters are pretty harsh," UMaine students agree, "The administration, in conjunction with the student government, does whatever they can to make it better." One business administration major says, "We have a saying: If you're bored, you're doing something wrong. There is stuff going on six nights a week, and there is lots to do in the Bangor area. Hiking, dining, arts, sports, anything you need, really." Most students point to the overall "outdoorsyness" of campus life, saying, "The only thing more plentiful than the friendly people are the deer and the squirrels." UMaine students "love to use the recreation facilities and explore the great outdoors," and they're proud to add, "Our school has a really strong campus culture." A common sentiment is that "UMaine is a great place to work and play." One sophomore says, "Hockey is life; the rest is just classes." The Division I hockey team at UMaine has many shouting, "Go Black Bears!" and all agree that "UMaine Hockey is a huge event for any Maine student." While some rave about the recently upgraded gym complex, others grumble that some "facilities are old and falling apart," and some students believe the university should focus on "upgrading outdated classroom buildings in some majors." The most common complaint about the administration: "They could start by backing off with the parking tickets…It's crazy."

Student Body

The majority of students here hail from Maine and the Northeast. However, despite a lack of external diversity, students say, "There is a wide range of diversity in thought and belief," and students say that although "diversity is rare because of the school's location…it is encouraged and accepted." Most students agree, "One of the best aspects of UMaine is the camaraderie that everyone has for each other," and agree, "Students have many opportunities to meet people in and out of class." In fact, one theater major proclaims, "The majority of the students who attend the University of Maine are either athletes or soon-to-be scientists…however, both groups tend to mix fairly well with each other." Another student concurs, "I've seen former high school jocks socializing with brilliant engineers." UMaine has a reputation for its lively social life; "there is no denying that most everybody drinks for fun," students are careful to point out, "The campus is huge, so if partying isn't your scene it's easy to find another one."

FINANCIAL AID: 207-581-1324 • E-MAIL: UM-ADMIT@MAINE.EDU • WEBSITE: WWW.UMAINE.EDU

THE PRINCETON REVIEW SAYS

Admissions

Very important factors considered include: Class rank, GPA, rigor of secondary school record, standardized test scores. *Important factors considered include:* Application essay, recommendation(s). *Other factors considered include:* Extracurricular activities, geographical residence, interview, state residency, talent/ability, volunteer work, work experience, character/personal qualities. SAT or ACT required; ACT with or without Writing component accepted. TOEFL required of all international applicants. *Academic units required:* 4 English; 3 mathematics; 2 science; (2 science lab); 2 social studies; 2 foreign language; 4 academic electives. *Academic units recommended:* 4 English; 4 mathematics; 4 science; (3 science lab); 2 social studies; 2 foreign language; 1 history; 4 academic electives.

Financial Aid

Students should submit: FAFSA. Regular filing deadline is 5/15. The Princeton Review suggests that all financial aid forms be submitted as soon as possible after January 1. *Need-based scholarships/grants offered:* Federal Pell, SEOG, State scholarships/grants, private scholarships, the school's own gift aid. *Loan aid offered:* Direct Subsidized Stafford Loans, Direct Unsubsidized Stafford Loans, Direct PLUS loans, Federal Perkins Loans, State Loans, College/university loans from institutional funds. Federal Work-Study Program available. Institutional employment available. Off-campus job opportunities are good.

The Inside Word

UMaine has rolling admissions but cautions that deadlines are still important, particularly for early action students who want to be considered for merit scholarships. The university recommends campus visits; tours are available at the Buchanan Alumni House. While interviews aren't required, they're considered mutually beneficial and informative for prospective students and admissions representatives.

THE SCHOOL SAYS "..."

From the Admissions Office

"The University of Maine offers the lauded academics, major research and close-knit community that go beyond your expectations. As Maine's flagship university, UMaine offers more than ninety undergraduate majors and academic programs, seventy-five master's programs and thirty doctoral programs. Top students are invited to join UMaine's Honors College, one of the country's oldest and most prestigious.

"Ranked 105 in the National Science Foundation's top research universities, UMaine is also included in the top 8 percent of colleges and universities nationwide to be classified by the Carnegie Foundation for the Advancement of Teaching as a "Research University-High Research Activity" institution. The Laboratory for Surface Science and Technology is a hub for cutting-edge sensor and nanotechnology research, and our Advanced Structures and Composites Center is a global leader in deepwater offshore wind energy development.

"At UMaine, undergraduate classes are taught by professors—and here, faculty members are known for having an open-door policy. Our students work alongside some of the most renowned scholars and scientists in the world—whether they're talking civil engineering over lunch in the Bear's Den or traversing an Antarctic ice sheet with climate researchers.

"UMaine students garner real-world experience that exceeds their expectations. SPIFFY, our student investment club, manages a $2 million real-money portfolio. Wildlife ecology majors learn about bear behavior by going out and tagging cubs. Engineering majors take advantage of co-ops and internships that often lead to employment after graduation. Marine science undergrads spend a semester by the sea at our internationally renowned Darling Marine Center."

SELECTIVITY

Admissions Rating	71
# of applicants	9,336
% of applicants accepted	83
% of acceptees attending	28

FRESHMAN PROFILE

Range SAT Critical Reading	470–590
Range SAT Math	480–600
Range SAT Writing	460–570
Range ACT Composite	21–27
Minimum paper TOEFL	530
Minimum web-based TOEFL	197
Average HS GPA	3.22
% graduated top 10% of class	19
% graduated top 25% of class	46
% graduated top 50% of class	78

DEADLINES

Early action	
Deadline	12/15
Notification	1/31
Regular	
Priority	2/1
Nonfall registration?	Yes

APPLICANTS ALSO LOOK AT AND OFTEN PREFER

University of Vermont; University of New Hampshire

AND SOMETIMES PREFER

University of Rhode Island, University of Massachusetts Amherst; University of Connecticut

FINANCIAL FACTS

Financial Aid Rating	75
Annual in-state tuition	$8,370
Annual out-of-state tuition	$25,740
Room and board	$9,112
Required fees	$2,230
Books and supplies	$1,000
% needy frosh rec. need-based scholarship or grant aid	92
% needy UG rec. need-based scholarship or grant aid	82
% needy frosh rec. non-need-based scholarship or grant aid	6
% needy UG rec. non-need-based scholarship or grant aid	4
% needy frosh rec. need-based self-help aid	85
% needy UG rec. need-based self-help aid	86
% frosh rec. any financial aid	80
% UG rec. any financial aid	78
% UG borrow to pay for school	78
Average cumulative indebtedness	$34,389
% frosh need fully met	14
% ugrads need fully met	14
Average % of frosh need met	80
Average % of ugrad need met	78

UNIVERSITY OF MARY WASHINGTON

1301 COLLEGE AVENUE, FREDERICKSBURG, VA 22401 • ADMISSIONS: 540-654-2000 • FAX: 540-654-1857

CAMPUS LIFE

Quality of Life Rating	76
Fire Safety Rating	92
Green Rating	95
Type of school	Public
Affiliation	No Affiliation
Environment	City

STUDENTS

Total undergrad enrollment	4,303
% male/female	36/64
% from out of state	11
% frosh from public high school	87
% frosh live on campus	92
% ugrads live on campus	61
% African American	6
% Asian	4
% Caucasian	66
% Hispanic	7
% Native American	<1
% international	1
# of countries represented	24

SURVEY SAYS . . .

No one cheats
Athletic facilities are great
Students are friendly
Great off-campus food
Students are happy
Frats and sororities are unpopular
or nonexistent
Student publications are popular
Political activism is popular

ACADEMICS

Academic Rating	76
% students returning for sophomore year	80
% students graduating within 4 years	66
% students graduating within 6 years	74
Calendar	Semester
Student/faculty ratio	14:1
Profs interesting rating	84
Profs accessible rating	81

Most classes have 20–29 students.
Most lab/discussion sessions have
20–29 students.

MOST POPULAR MAJORS

psychology; English language and literature;
business administration and management

STUDENTS SAY " . . ."

Academics

University of Mary Washington "lives up to its reputation" while providing "rigorous education in a fun and engaging atmosphere." As an art history major explains, "it is one of (possibly the only) public choice in Virginia for someone who wants to attend a small liberal arts college." Students rave about the "small, beautiful campus" and "strong sense of community." This is a school where "everyone is so friendly" and you are "able to walk somewhere and always see someone" that you know. This "small and quaint school" is filled with "amazing" professors who "are committed to providing outside of the classroom help." "All of my professors know me by name and make classes interesting," one student says. The professors are "passionate about the material they teach" and UMW "does not have TA's so the professors are always the ones teaching the classes." Like the faculty at any school, "some are good; some are bad." However, the "small class sizes" mean "you can get one-on-one attention if you need it." UMW is about "finding what you're passionate about and studying it through multiple disciplines & perspectives while building strong relationships with faculty and peers." There is a "strongly supported honor code" and in general UMW "puts the responsibility in the hands of the students to act respectful and to prove themselves as students who are committed to their education." Some students feel the school "has a bit of a Napoleon complex" and think it should accept that it is "AMAZING at being" a "small liberal arts school." All in all, the school has "an amazing sense of community" that unlike many schools is "not so much featured around sports as it's about the students." "I've never felt so loved, accepted, and academically challenged in my life," one student says. Another sums up UMW as simply the "best school that no one has ever heard of."

Life

UMW is "fun but not [a] crazy party school." There is no "football team or Greek life," which is either a benefit or a drawback depending on your temperament. Some students "think it would be beneficial to have one or the other" to help "improve on social events" on campus. "A lot of people who transfer do so because they crave the excitement of big parties and social drama of Greek life," one student says, but explains that the remaining students "are serious about their studies which makes classes more fun." "Students fit in by finding a club on campus that suits their interests" and "sporting events are popular." Without a football team, students watch "rugby, soccer, lacrosse, or baseball." The campus has "a very inviting atmosphere" and there is "a huge amount of school spirit, but it is not the 'in your face' type of school spirit that plagues most large universities." Events on campus include "bingo Tuesday, trivia Thursday, 1 dollar movies on the weekend, acoustic night Wednesdays, club carnival, be a kid night, etc." On weekends, "there are parties but you have to know the right people to go to them." The town of Fredericksburg itself is "not a fantastic town due to the lack of entertainment" outside of some "not too shabby" bars. However, many students are "very active and outdoorsy" and find fun off campus in nature. The school is "five minutes away from the river which has awesome kayaking opportunities" and close to "mountains where a lot of students go hiking on the weekends."

Student Body

Most students are "laid back, fun, yet also studious." Several students noted there is "very little diversity" and "the school is not racially balanced AT ALL." With a student population that is over 60 percent female, the student body is "mostly girls but everyone is treated equally" as students are "pretty non-judgmental and open to differences." Others say the school is "very clique like" with "very little intermingling of different student groups." Still, "everyone has a place to fit in" among their "friendly, down to earth" peers. While many students fit "the liberal arts stereotype" of "liberal-leaning or moderate, environmentally conscious, supports social progress...there's a large number of conservative Catholic students as well." Without the giant Greek life other universities have, students "don't get 'distracted' as easily" leading to a student body that is "goal-driven and ready to succeed."

UNIVERSITY OF MARY WASHINGTON

FINANCIAL AID: 800-468-5614 • E-MAIL: ADMIT@UMW.EDU • WEBSITE: WWW.UMW.EDU

THE PRINCETON REVIEW SAYS

Admissions

Very important factors considered include: GPA, rigor of secondary school record. *Important factors considered include:* Class rank, standardized test scores, application essay, extracurricular activities, recommendation(s). *Other factors considered include:* First generation, geographical residence, racial/ethnic status, state residency, talent/ability, volunteer work, work experience, alumni/ae relations, character/personal qualities. SAT or ACT required; ACT with or without Writing component accepted. TOEFL required of all international applicants. *Academic units required:* 4 English; 3 mathematics; 3 science; (3 science lab); 2 social studies; 2 foreign language; 1 history. *Academic units recommended:* 4 English; 4 mathematics; 4 science; (4 science lab); 2 social studies; 4 foreign language; 2 history.

Financial Aid

Students should submit: FAFSA. Regular filing deadline is 5/15. The Princeton Review suggests that all financial aid forms be submitted as soon as possible after January 1. *Need-based scholarships/grants offered:* Federal Pell, SEOG, State scholarships/grants, private scholarships, the school's own gift aid. *Loan aid offered:* Direct Subsidized Stafford Loans, Direct Unsubsidized Stafford Loans, Direct PLUS loans, Federal Perkins Loans. Applicants will be notified of awards beginning 3/15. Federal Work-Study Program available. Institutional employment available. Off-campus job opportunities are good.

The Inside Word

There is no special secret to getting into the University of Mary Washington. The school is selective and looks only for quality students. Great SAT/ACT scores and honors and AP class credits are a definite plus. The school uses the Common Application exclusively, and applying online is easy.

THE SCHOOL SAYS ". . ."

From the Admissions Office

"The University of Mary Washington is one of the nation's premier public, liberal arts and sciences institutions. Highly respected for its commitment to academic excellence, the University boasts three colleges—business, education and arts and sciences and three campuses, conveniently located between Richmond, VA, and Washington, D.C. These two capitals provide a rich resource for undergraduate student internships, as well as a promising job market for graduates. Mary Washington's talented and intellectually curious students work collaboratively in small, interactive classes with innovative and accessible master teachers, including a Fulbright scholars, who motivate them to think critically, engage meaningfully and communicate effectively.

"In addition to rigorous academics, the UMW experience is based on a culture of honor as well as community and global service, exemplified in the 2014 Peace Corps ranking of Mary Washington as one of the nation's top volunteer producers among small colleges. With multiple opportunities for student research and service learning, UMW graduates thrive in our fast-changing society.

"Distinctive to UMW is one of the nation's leading historic preservation programs, as well as strong creative writing and debate programs. Other top majors include political science and international affairs, English, biology, psychology, earth and environmental science, history, visual and performing arts, economics and business. With its classic Jeffersonian architecture, and beautifully manicured grounds, UMW offers an unparallelled American college experience. More than 100 student organizations and clubs provide opportunities for leadership. UMW Eagles varsity teams compete at the championship level in NCAA Division III."

SELECTIVITY

Admissions Rating	73
# of applicants	4,501
% of applicants accepted	81
% of acceptees attending	26
# offered a place on the wait list	225
% accepting a place on wait list	36
% admitted from wait list	68

FRESHMAN PROFILE

Range SAT Critical Reading	510–620
Range SAT Math	500–590
Range SAT Writing	490–600
Range ACT Composite	22–26
Minimum paper TOEFL	570
Minimum web-based TOEFL	230
Average HS GPA	3.51
% graduated top 10% of class	16
% graduated top 25% of class	50
% graduated top 50% of class	86

DEADLINES

Early action	
Deadline	11/15
Notification	1/31
Regular	
Priority	11/15
Deadline	2/1
Notification	4/1
Nonfall registration?	Yes

APPLICANTS ALSO LOOK AT AND OFTEN PREFER
The College of William & Mary; University of Virginia

AND SOMETIMES PREFER
James Madison University; University of Richmond; Virginia Tech

AND RARELY PREFER
George Mason University

FINANCIAL FACTS

Financial Aid Rating	68
Annual in-state tuition	$6,758
Annual out-of-state tuition	$19,628
Room and board	$9,122
Required fees	$2,902
Books and supplies	$1,100
% needy frosh rec. need-based scholarship or grant aid	40
% needy UG rec. need-based scholarship or grant aid	46
% needy frosh rec. non-need-based scholarship or grant aid	33
% needy UG rec. non-need-based scholarship or grant aid	21
% needy frosh rec. need-based self-help aid	73
% needy UG rec. need-based self-help aid	79
% frosh rec. any financial aid	58
% UG rec. any financial aid	61
% UG borrow to pay for school	57
Average cumulative indebtedness	$23,700
% frosh need fully met	12
% ugrads need fully met	11
Average % of frosh need met	46
Average % of ugrad need met	48

UNIVERSITY OF MARYLAND—BALTIMORE COUNTY

1000 HILLTOP CIRCLE, BALTIMORE, MD 21250 • ADMISSIONS: 410-455-2291 • FAX: 410-455-1094

CAMPUS LIFE

Quality of Life Rating	76
Fire Safety Rating	95
Green Rating	78
Type of school	Public
Affiliation	No Affiliation
Environment	Metropolis

STUDENTS

Total undergrad enrollment	10,838
% male/female	55/45
% from out of state	6
% frosh from public high school	NA
% frosh live on campus	75
% ugrads live on campus	34
# of fraternities	11
# of sororities	12
% African American	16
% Asian	20
% Caucasian	47
% Hispanic	5
% Native American	<1
% international	4
# of countries represented	96

SURVEY SAYS . . .
Great library
Diverse student types on campus
Campus feels safe

ACADEMICS

Academic Rating	79
% students returning for sophomore year	85
% students graduating within 4 years	33
% students graduating within 6 years	79
Calendar	Semester
Student/faculty ratio	20:1
Profs interesting rating	79
Profs accessible rating	72

Most classes have 10–19 students.
Most lab/discussion sessions have
20–29 students.

MOST POPULAR MAJORS
computer and information science; biology;
mechanical engineering

STUDENTS SAY ". . ."

Academics

The University of Maryland, Baltimore County has a "great regional reputation" as a "quiet academic school" where "students take education seriously." Undergraduates are enthusiastic about the "academic opportunities and scholarship programs available," and say, "UMBC wants to see every student succeed—they provide you with the tools, people, and resources to make sure you get where you want to go in life." The university is particularly known for its "strong" science and mathematics programs and a commitment to the performing arts. Some students grumble, "The school needs to serve those with different majors apart from the sciences," but others are quick to point out that "UMBC is changing a bit to offer more to the fine arts students," including construction of a new technologically advanced fine arts building. Most agree the university has "extremely intelligent professors that have a knack for inspiring the students," and say, "UMBC is a place where professors aren't just talking heads." Although some complain about dull lectures, a common consensus is that "this is a university where teaching comes first, followed by research, and it shows," and that "most of the professors are so helpful, you can find most of them sitting in their office and they don't mind if you come and ask them questions."

Life

UMBC has a large contingent of commuters and one ancient studies major says, "There are a lot of activities held by student organizations on campus during the week and on the weekends, but many students live close to campus and choose to go home for the weekend." While some may see this as a downside others say, "The location of UMBC is true brilliance—so close to Baltimore. We hop over there on the weekdays even to go shopping or go out to eat." Most lament the absence of a football team and say, "The only real issue with UMBC is the lack of visible school spirit…People have made efforts to try and pump up the school, but nothing's come to fruition yet." In fact, students give the administration poor marks, saying, "Students are not given adequate attention on the matters of housing, financial aid, and advising," and there are complaints about the parking facilities, as well as a desire for "better buildings and food options." Despite these criticisms, a sociology major says, "Everyone on campus is nice and helpful to other students. People will always hold a door for you, help you pick up a dropped folder, or offer to share their notes with a student who missed class."

Student Body

More than one student says, "UMBC is a place where it is cool to be smart, and everything about the campus, including the students, exudes 'nerd-chic.'" In fact, an English major says that even "our president likes to say that it's cool to be smart at UMBC." This mentality is captured by a student who remarks, "Life at UMBC, aside from special events, revolves around classes and learning," and most undergrads agree: "The typical student at UMBC is interested in doing well academically and not just here to party until graduation." However, despite their dedication to hard work, UMBC students call themselves "enthusiastic and bright" and say "that almost every student at UMBC is involved with at least a couple of extracurricular activities, which connect them to the campus." The school has a strong reputation for diversity and students feel "it enriches our school and everyone gets to know everyone despite culture or ethnicity." A mechanical engineering student says, "This is even reflected in the high number of interracial couples I see on campus." Overall, it seems, "People fit in by being intellectually creative and finding a community with which to discuss important issues."

FINANCIAL AID: 410-455-2387 • E-MAIL: ADMISSIONS@UMBC.EDU • WEBSITE: WWW.UMBC.EDU

THE PRINCETON REVIEW SAYS

Admissions

Very important factors considered include: GPA, rigor of secondary school record, standardized test scores. *Important factors considered include:* Application essay, recommendation(s). *Other factors considered include:* Class rank, extracurricular activities, talent/ability, volunteer work, work experience, character/personal qualities. SAT or ACT required; ACT with or without Writing component accepted. TOEFL required of all international applicants. *Academic units required:* 4 English; 4 mathematics; 3 science; 2 foreign language. *Academic units recommended:* 4 English; 4 mathematics; 3 science; 2 foreign language.

Financial Aid

Students should submit: FAFSA. The Princeton Review suggests that all financial aid forms be submitted as soon as possible after January 1. *Need-based scholarships/grants offered:* Federal Pell, SEOG, State scholarships/grants, private scholarships, the school's own gift aid, United Negro College Fund. *Loan aid offered:* Direct Subsidized Stafford Loans, Direct Unsubsidized Stafford Loans, Direct PLUS loans, Federal Perkins Loans. Applicants will be notified of awards beginning 3/26. Federal Work-Study Program available. Institutional employment available. Off-campus job opportunities are excellent.

The Inside Word

UMBC maintains an Admissions Counselor Blog where prospective students can connect with current members of the admissions team to questions during the application process. The admissions committee considers the strength of your secondary school curriculum and class rank in combination with traditional factors, such as GPA, test scores, and essay when making an acceptance decision. Additionally, it's suggested that at least one letter of recommendation be written by a teacher.

THE SCHOOL SAYS "..."

From the Admissions Office

"When it comes to universities, a mid-sized school can be just right. Some students want the resources of a large community. Others are looking for the attention found at a smaller one. With an undergraduate population of over 9,000, UMBC can offer the best of both. There are always new people to meet and things to do—from Division I sports to more than 170 student clubs. As a research university, we offer an abundance of programs, technology, and opportunities for hands-on experiences. Yet we are small enough that students don't get lost in the shuffle. More than 80 percent of our classes have fewer than forty students. Among public research universities, UMBC is recognized for its success in placing students in the most competitive graduate programs and careers. Of course, much of the success of UMBC has to do with the students themselves—highly motivated students who get involved in their education."

"Freshman applicants are required to take the SAT or ACT."

SELECTIVITY

Admissions Rating	86
# of applicants	8,514
% of applicants accepted	60
% of acceptees attending	30
# offered a place on the wait list	393
% accepting a place on wait list	100
% admitted from wait list	41

FRESHMAN PROFILE

Range SAT Critical Reading	550–650
Range SAT Math	580–670
Range SAT Writing	530–640
Range ACT Composite	24–29
Minimum paper TOEFL	460
Minimum web-based TOEFL	140
Average HS GPA	3.71
% graduated top 10% of class	29
% graduated top 25% of class	56
% graduated top 50% of class	85

DEADLINES

Early action	
Deadline	11/1
Notification	12/15
Regular	
Priority	11/1
Deadline	2/1
Nonfall registration?	Yes

APPLICANTS ALSO LOOK AT AND OFTEN PREFER
Johns Hopkins University; Virginia Tech

AND SOMETIMES PREFER
Pennsylvania State University—University Park; University of Maryland; College Park

AND RARELY PREFER
Salisbury University; St. Mary's College of Maryland

FINANCIAL FACTS

Financial Aid Rating	71
Annual in-state tuition	$9,764
Annual out-of-state tuition	$20,825
Room and board	$10,866
Books and supplies	$1,200
% needy frosh rec. need-based scholarship or grant aid	72
% needy UG rec. need-based scholarship or grant aid	75
% needy frosh rec. non-need-based scholarship or grant aid	22
% needy UG rec. non-need-based scholarship or grant aid	9
% needy frosh rec. need-based self-help aid	56
% needy UG rec. need-based self-help aid	69
% frosh rec. any financial aid	70
% UG rec. any financial aid	64
% UG borrow to pay for school	53
Average cumulative indebtedness	$22,600
% frosh need fully met	20
% ugrads need fully met	12
Average % of frosh need met	59
Average % of ugrad need met	56

UNIVERSITY OF MARYLAND—COLLEGE PARK

MITCHELL BUILDING, COLLEGE PARK, MD 20742-5235 • ADMISSIONS: 301-314-8385 • FAX: 301-314-9693

STUDENTS SAY " . . ."

Academics

The University of Maryland—College Park is a grand mix of "twenty-minute walks to class across one of the country's most beautiful campuses, [an introduction] to high-level courses taught by the nation's top researchers, [and] a motivated 'green' campus" as well as "crowded, smelly frat parties, [and] living-learning communities that can make the gigantic campus much smaller." Students are quick to boast about sports, too, especially the school's titles as "the 2008 national champions in men's soccer and women's field hockey." In short: It's a quintessential large university, offering "a great experience with a variety of opportunities that are what you make of them." Students crow about Maryland's "nationally recognized business program," a "top-ranked criminology program," a solid engineering school, a great political science department that capitalizes on the school's proximity to Washington, D.C., and the "top-notch honors program." Most of all, they love the "great price. This school gives you a great education for a really cheap price." Low cost doesn't translate to budget accommodations. On the contrary, "the administration shows a desire to always upgrade facilities, as can be witnessed by the tremendous business school and the brand new engineering building." In conclusion, students applaud "the widely diverse opportunities available at UMD. You can never get bored because there is always something to do."

Life

"Life at UMD is awesome," with "a good mix of fun activities" including "school-sponsored parties, games," a "campus recreation center that has virtually everything you could wish for, including pools, an extensive gym, a rock wall, squash courts, an indoor track," and a student union "loaded with fun places like the arcade area, bowling alley," and "tons of places to eat as well." In addition, "there are always open games of soccer, football, or ultimate Frisbee being played on the mall and elsewhere." There are bars close to campus, and "students are always having parties," especially along College Park's raucous Frat Row. Terrapin sports are a passion for many. If all that isn't enough, "the proximity to D.C. makes clubbing, nights out on the town, and general visits to D.C. frequent." With all this going on, no wonder students say that "the social life at UMD is unsurpassed." Some warn the surrounding area is dicey; "It's pretty annoying and scary to get crime alerts from the police informing us of incidents close to campus," one student explains. Undergrads also warn that parking regulations are brutal. "Bus transportation around campus provided by the university is great, but for students and visitors with cars, it's a huge hassle. Permits are expensive, and free parking for visitors is impossible to find. School officials are strict with violations, and tickets are seventy-five dollars. They are hard to refute and very costly."

Student Body

"The University of Maryland is a very large school," so "there is no 'typical' student here. Everyone will find that they can fit in somewhere." Better still, "different groups are very accepting of other groups. Students in Greek life are just as accepting of students in non-Greek life. Athletes blend in with non-athletes. UMD provides a great environment for students to meet people they would normally not know and helps to provide great connections with these people." UMD is "an especially diverse school," and this makes people "more tolerant and accepting of people from different backgrounds and cultures." A student from New Jersey explains it this way: "Coming from a very diverse area, I thought it was going to be hard to find a school that had that same representation of minority and atypical students until I found Maryland. I don't think I have ever learned so much about different religions, cultures, orientations, or lifestyles. All of them are accepted and even celebrated" at UMD.

FINANCIAL AID: 301-314-9000 • E-MAIL: UM-ADMIT@UMD.EDU • WEBSITE: WWW.MARYLAND.EDU

THE PRINCETON REVIEW SAYS

Admissions

Very important factors considered include: GPA, rigor of secondary school record, standardized test scores. *Important factors considered include:* Class rank, application essay, first generation, recommendation(s), state residency, talent/ability. *Other factors considered include:* Extracurricular activities, geographical residence, racial/ethnic status, volunteer work, work experience, alumni/ae relations, character/personal qualities. SAT or ACT required; ACT with Writing component required. TOEFL required of all international applicants. *Academic units required:* 4 English; 4 mathematics; 3 science; (2 science lab); 3 social studies; 2 foreign language; 3 history. *Academic units recommended:* 4 English; 4 mathematics; 3 science; (2 science lab); 3 social studies; 2 foreign language; 3 history.

Financial Aid

Students should submit: FAFSA. The Princeton Review suggests that all financial aid forms be submitted as soon as possible after January 1. *Need-based scholarships/grants offered:* Federal Pell, SEOG, State scholarships/grants, private scholarships, the school's own gift aid. *Loan aid offered:* Direct Subsidized Stafford Loans, Direct Unsubsidized Stafford Loans, Direct PLUS loans, Federal Perkins Loans. Federal Work-Study Program available. Institutional employment available. Off-campus job opportunities are good.

The Inside Word

Maryland admissions officers don't simply crunch numbers and apply a formula. The school considers no fewer than twenty-five factors when determining who's in and who's out. Essays, recommendations, extracurricular activities, talents and skills, and demographic factors all figure into the mix along with high school transcript and standardized test scores. Give all aspects of your application your utmost attention; admissions is very competitive.

THE SCHOOL SAYS "..."

From the Admissions Office

"The University of Maryland is one of the nation's top-ranked universities, offering students unique opportunities to learn, explore and discover in the D.C. region and around the world. It attracts outstanding faculty—including Nobel, Pulitzer, Emmy and Tony winners—and some of the most accomplished students in the nation. The beautiful 1,250-acre campus is located just outside Washington, D.C., making it easy for students to extend their education beyond the classroom, whether in the College Park community or through internships in federal agencies, labs and think tanks; the media; or some of the country's most successful companies. The university strongly encourages innovation, entrepreneurship and creativity, whether helping students and state residents launch startups or serving as a model of cultural excellence through its arts programming. The campus also thrives on diversity and engagement, celebrating similarities and differences and preparing graduates to become leaders in their communities and careers."

SELECTIVITY

Admissions Rating	94
# of applicants	26,205
% of applicants accepted	47
% of acceptees attending	33

FRESHMAN PROFILE

Range SAT Critical Reading	580–690
Range SAT Math	620–730
Average HS GPA	4.11
% graduated top 10% of class	71
% graduated top 25% of class	88
% graduated top 50% of class	98

DEADLINES

Early decision	
Notification	Early action
Deadline	11/1
Notification	1/31
Regular	
Priority	11/1
Deadline	1/20
Notification	4/1
Nonfall registration?	Yes

FINANCIAL FACTS

Financial Aid Rating	72
Annual in-state tuition	$7,390
Annual out-of-state tuition	$26,576
Room and board	$10,280
Required fees	$1,772
Books and supplies	$1,130
% needy frosh rec. need-based scholarship or grant aid	56
% needy UG rec. need-based scholarship or grant aid	59
% needy frosh rec. non-need-based scholarship or grant aid	54
% needy UG rec. non-need-based scholarship or grant aid	40
% needy frosh rec. need-based self-help aid	84
% needy UG rec. need-based self-help aid	89
% frosh rec. any financial aid	86
% UG rec. any financial aid	71
% UG borrow to pay for school	45
Average cumulative indebtedness	$25,254
% frosh need fully met	30
% ugrads need fully met	24
Average % of frosh need met	76
Average % of ugrad need met	71

UNIVERSITY OF MASSACHUSETTS AMHERST

UNIVERSITY ADMISSIONS CENTER, AMHERST, MA 01003-9291 • ADMISSIONS: 413-545-0222 • FAX: 413-545-4312

CAMPUS LIFE

Quality of Life Rating	84
Fire Safety Rating	84
Green Rating	99
Type of school	Public
Affiliation	No Affiliation
Environment	Town

STUDENTS

Total undergrad enrollment	21,672
% male/female	51/49
% from out of state	22
% frosh live on campus	100
% ugrads live on campus	64
# of fraternities (% ugrad men join)	22 (5)
# of sororities (% ugrad women join)	18 (7)
% African American	4
% Asian	8
% Caucasian	67
% Hispanic	5
% Native American	<1
% international	2
# of countries represented	115

SURVEY SAYS . . .
Political activism is unpopular or nonexistent
Great food on campus
Great off-campus food
Athletic facilities are great
Hard liquor is popular

ACADEMICS

Academic Rating	77
% students returning for sophomore year	89
% students graduating within 4 years	59
% students graduating within 6 years	73
Calendar	Semester
Student/faculty ratio	18:1
Profs interesting rating	68
Profs accessible rating	67

Most classes have 10–19 students.
Most lab/discussion sessions have 20–29 students.

MOST POPULAR MAJORS
psychology; communications; political science

STUDENTS SAY ". . ."

Academics

The University of Massachusetts Amherst "offers an incredible education at a relatively-affordable price." As the "best state university in Massachusetts," UMass is "a very well rounded school" that provides "top notch academics." "UMass is a large, well rounded, diverse group of intellectual students and there is something here for every one of us that suits us perfectly," one happy student claims. With "over one hundred undergraduate majors to choose from," UMass has "a large variety of different majors and opportunities" and "certain degree programs that are outstanding." As a national research university, "the greatest strengths are our science and math programs." UMass has a "great track record with faculty involving students in research." Some students do wish UMass cared "more about the humanities!" You can't have a great education without great professors, and students rave about the "amazing!!" faculty. Professors here are "educated and interested in their subjects" and "have eye opening perspectives on the classes they teach." They "will often encourage discussion within the class to make sure that students are all on the same page." As with any school, the quality of instruction varies but "the good outweigh the bad." That said, students do wish for "smaller class rooms" and say you might "feel like just a number for the teacher" in a giant UMass lecture class. Unlike students at many universities, UMass students rave about the "delicious food" in the dinning commons. "The quantity, quality and diversity for food options are awesome," one student says. Green conscious students will love how "eco friendly" UMass is. The university and the surrounding "town of Amherst sufficiently try and protect the environment." Students also praise the "school spirit" that abounds on campus. "UMass is a multicultural environment that strives to promote community awareness, academics, and teamwork through the many programs offered," a Hospitality and Tourism Management major explains. Another student sums the school up as "a liberal, progressive school with an accepting atmosphere and great dining."

Life

At UMass, "a world class education" combines "with a very lively student life." There are "many clubs on campus" and students frequently find their friend groups by participating in campus life. Nighttime means "heavy drinking" at "parties," earning the school the nickname "Zoomass." Some students say "the pressure to go along with the party lifestyle is high if you aren't part of a social group devoted to a niche interest." Others point out that "if you want to party, you seek out the party. The party does not knock down your dorm room wall and suck you in." The school works hard to provide "many fun activities for students to attend, such as free ice skating" and "concerts on campus." Students enjoy going "on trips to nearby mountains with the ski and snowboard club" or staying closer to campus and "going out to the cinemas or restaurants…when there's time to spare." "There are SO many things to do for fun," an Art History major says, including "the Outing Club, swimming at Totman" "and check[ing] out student art at the Student Union Art Gallery." Another student explains that "College is a cushion before being thrown into the real world, so we all want to enjoy it and get involved in some fun shenanigans before we have to leave."

Student Body

"The typical UMass student is very accepting of all people and as progressive as the state itself" one student boasts. The typical student here is "cool, relaxed, funny," and "very academically focused" yet "super chill." The school does not have a lot of diversity "race-wise" and "the typical student is usually a white American." Still, "there is a broad range of students here" and "there's a place for everyone." Most people are "open to meeting new people" and "never [turn] down the opportunity to make more friends." "Minuteman pride" brings everyone together on campus. Students "fit in by joining cultural student run associations and other extra-curricular activities." "I feel so lucky to go to a school that I feel absolutely no need to change who I am to fit in," a happy Studio Arts major says.

FINANCIAL AID: 413-545-0801 • E-MAIL: MAIL@ADMISSIONS.UMASS.EDU • WEBSITE: WWW.UMASS.EDU

THE PRINCETON REVIEW SAYS

Admissions

Very important factors considered include: GPA, rigor of secondary school record, standardized test scores. *Important factors considered include:* Class rank, application essay, recommendation(s), talent/ability. *Other factors considered include:* Extracurricular activities, first generation, geographical residence, racial/ethnic status, state residency, volunteer work, work experience, character/personal qualities, level of applicant's interest. SAT or ACT required; ACT with Writing component recommended. TOEFL required of all international applicants. *Academic units required:* 4 English; 3 mathematics; 3 science; (2 science lab); 2 social studies; 2 foreign language; 2 academic electives.

Financial Aid

Students should submit: FAFSA. The Princeton Review suggests that all financial aid forms be submitted as soon as possible after January 1. *Need-based scholarships/grants offered:* Federal Pell, SEOG, State scholarships/grants, private scholarships, the school's own gift aid. *Loan aid offered:* Direct Subsidized Stafford Loans, Direct Unsubsidized Stafford Loans, Direct PLUS loans, Federal Perkins Loans. Federal Work-Study Program available. Institutional employment available. Off-campus job opportunities are good.

The Inside Word

UMass has a unique application that requires applicants to declare both a first and second choice major (although selecting "undeclared" is allowed). You will need to ensure that your academic background matches the major(s) you pick, or else the school may put you in the undeclared pool. Accepted undeclared majors will have to apply to majors later on. UMass is a very selective state school in general and even more selective in its standout majors like business, economics, and engineering.

THE SCHOOL SAYS ". . ."

From the Admissions Office

"The University of Massachusetts Amherst is the flagship campus of the Commonwealth and the largest public university in New England,New England, offering its students an almost limitless variety of academic programs and activities. Over one-hundred majors are offered, including a unique program called Bachelor's Degree with Individual Concentration (BDIC) in which students create their own program of study. The outstanding full-time faculty of over 1,200 is the best in their fields and they take teaching seriously. he Commonwealth Honors College Residential Complex is a national model and welcomes students who seek additional academic challenge and meet the requirements for acceptance. Through the Five College Interchange, students enroll in classes at nearby Amherst, Hampshire, Mount Holyoke, and Smith Colleges at no extra charge. A free bus system connects these five campuses, allowing students to participate in a wide array of social and cultural events. First-year students participate in the Residential First-Year Year Experience with opportunities to explore every possible interest through residential life. The extensive library system is the largest at any public institution in the Northeast. The Center for Student Development brings together more than 300 clubs and organizations, fraternities and sororities, multicultural and religious centers. The campus completes in NCAA Division I sports for men and women, with teams winning national recognition. About 5,000 students a year participate in the intramural sports program. SAT or ACT scores are required for admission to the university. The town of Amherst is consistently ranked one of the top college towns in the country. The school takes a holistic view of the student's application package and considers these scores as only part of the evaluation criteria. Additionally, any Advanced Placement, Honors, and SAT Subject Test scores are considered when reviewing each applicant. Increased applications in recent years have made admission more selective. "

SELECTIVITY

Admissions Rating	88
# of applicants	35,868
% of applicants accepted	63
% of acceptees attending	20
# offered a place on the wait list	4,902
% accepting a place on wait list	25
% admitted from wait list	9

FRESHMAN PROFILE

Range SAT Critical Reading	540–640
Range SAT Math	570–670
Range ACT Composite	24–29
Minimum web-based TOEFL	80
Average HS GPA	3.73
% graduated top 10% of class	28
% graduated top 25% of class	69
% graduated top 50% of class	97

DEADLINES

Early action	
Deadline	11/1
Regular	
Deadline	1/15
Nonfall registration?	Yes

APPLICANTS ALSO LOOK AT AND OFTEN PREFER

Boston University; Boston College; Syracuse University; University of Delaware; Tufts University

AND SOMETIMES PREFER

University of Connecticut; Northeastern University

AND RARELY PREFER

University of New Hampshire; University of Vermont; University of Rhode Island

FINANCIAL FACTS

Financial Aid Rating	75
Annual in-state tuition	$13,443
Annual out-of-state tuition	$28,159
Room and board	$11,166
Books and supplies	$1,000
% needy frosh rec. need-based scholarship or grant aid	86
% needy UG rec. need-based scholarship or grant aid	82
% needy frosh rec. non-need-based scholarship or grant aid	6
% needy UG rec. non-need-based scholarship or grant aid	4
% needy frosh rec. need-based self-help aid	77
% needy UG rec. need-based self-help aid	82
% frosh rec. any financial aid	87
% UG rec. any financial aid	83
% UG borrow to pay for school	70
Average cumulative indebtedness	$28,999
% frosh need fully met	10
% ugrads need fully met	13
Average % of frosh need met	79
Average % of ugrad need met	82

UNIVERSITY OF MIAMI

PO Box 248025, Coral Gables, FL 33124-4616 • Admissions: 305-284-4323 • Fax: 305-284-6605

STUDENTS SAY ". . ."

Academics

Located in Coral Gables, the University of Miami offers "the best balance between social life and academics." The school boasts a "beautiful campus, many research opportunities, [and] helpful resources throughout campus available to students," and the curriculum mirrors the diversity of the school's location by "catering to the students with a multitude of student-oriented classes and organizations." Tons of extracurricular activities, events happening "constantly," and the "ability to bring in amazing world-class guests" help flesh out the experience at UM. "Miami is the type of school where you can go to the beach in the morning, class in the afternoon, a club meeting in the evening, and then still hit the gym and the library before you ever think about going to bed," says a student.

The "caring and renowned faculty" at UM are "insightful and have years of professional experience in the fields they teach." They are "very willing to meet during office hours and exceptionally helpful during that time," are "engaging and force students to think critically when learning," and "get very involved in helping the students with advising and internships/job opportunities." The networking opportunities also happen to be "second-to-none." "You are more than confident that you are going to get a job in your desired field when you graduate," says a senior broadcast journalism major.

The marine science and pre-med programs are standouts at University of Miami, but a "strong undergraduate focus" means that no matter the major, "career development is great" and has "amazing opportunities that are not available anywhere else." While the atmosphere at the school is "very positive" overall, some admit that the infrastructure could use some updates ("some buildings seem old and need work"); red tape can also be a problem for those who experience the "Miami shuffle," where "you'll ask one person for something who will send you somewhere else who will send you somewhere else and so on."

Life

Students are pretty blunt about their love of the University of Miami: "It quite literally is a paradise." Palm trees surrounding a vast lake at the heart of campus, an amazing wellness center, and a brand new student activities center are just a few of the school's beloved attributes, and "students proudly wear green and orange and participate in many school events." Greek life doesn't run the campus, but "it's apparent," and most students head to the beach during the day and clubs (South Beach, Brickell and Coconut Grove) at night. If you're not interested in partying constantly—and there are "quite a few"—relaxing around campus or near campus is "still really enjoyable." Concerts are also very popular, and "involvement in club and intramural sports is significant."

Though the temptations are plentiful, when it comes down to it ("the location is conducive to limitless activities"), "students at University of Miami get their work done." "Going to school in one of Miami's most affluent neighborhoods certainly makes you think about success and your career goals," says a junior electronic media major. Students "are generally happy all the time because the warm weather positively influences their lives."

Student Body

The typical UM student is "relatively wealthy," "takes pride in their appearance," and is "very hardworking but also extremely involved in social activities." While there are a good deal of international students and students on scholarship, the availability of organizations and activities help unite the population into "a big friendly family who always has your back." Miami being Miami, many students are "Greek life types," and there is "a lot of importance placed on dress and material possessions." One student jokes, "The gym is mandatory for full-time students." Thanks to the location in "a tropical paradise with a million things to do," people "are really easy to get along with."

FINANCIAL AID: 305-284-5212 • E-MAIL: ADMISSION@MIAMI.EDU • WEBSITE: WWW.MIAMI.EDU

THE PRINCETON REVIEW SAYS

Admissions

Very important factors considered include: Class rank, GPA, rigor of secondary school record, standardized test scores, application essay, extracurricular activities, recommendation(s), character/personal qualities. *Other factors considered include:* First generation, geographical residence, interview, racial/ethnic status, talent/ability, volunteer work, work experience, alumni/ae relations, level of applicant's interest. SAT or ACT required; SAT and SAT Subject Tests or ACT required for some; ACT with or without Writing component accepted. TOEFL required of all international applicants. *Academic units recommended:* 4 English; 4 mathematics; 3 science; (2 science lab); 3 social studies; 2 foreign language; 2 history; 1 computer science; 1 visual/performing arts.

Financial Aid

Students should submit: FAFSA, CSS/Financial Aid PROFILE, Noncustodial PROFILE. The Princeton Review suggests that all financial aid forms be submitted as soon as possible after January 1. *Need-based scholarships/grants offered:* Federal Pell, SEOG, State scholarships/grants, private scholarships, the school's own gift aid. *Loan aid offered:* Direct Subsidized Stafford Loans, Direct Unsubsidized Stafford Loans, Direct PLUS loans, Federal Perkins Loans, Federal Nursing Loans, College/university loans from institutional funds, Private Alternative Education Loan Programs. Federal Work-Study Program available. Institutional employment available. Off-campus job opportunities are excellent.

The Inside Word

The University of Miami's campaign to overcome its reputation as a "football school" is an unqualified success. Each recent academic year has seen an increase in applications, and UM's selectivity is on the rise. The school partially attributes this accomplishment to its alumni and gladly repays them by giving legacies a boost during the admissions process. Of course, having a Cane for a parent isn't enough; students must demonstrate achievement in arduous classes, intellectual promise, and strong moral character.

THE SCHOOL SAYS "..."

From the Admissions Office

"The University of Miami in Coral Gables, is an innovative private research university in a location unlike any other in the country. Located ten miles from the vibrant international city of Miami, UM's approximately 10,000 undergraduates come from every state and 100 nations, allowing people of many cultures to challenge and champion each other. Faculty work closely with students, and internships and research experiences are integral to academic life. Students work hard as community volunteers and exert leadership in a range of lively clubs and organizations, including the student-managed TV station, radio station, and newspaper.

"The University of Miami will accept the critical reading and math scores from the SAT, as well as the ACT with or without the writing component."

SELECTIVITY

Admissions Rating	97
# of applicants	28,902
% of applicants accepted	40
% of acceptees attending	18
# of early decision applicants	616
% accepted early decision	25

FRESHMAN PROFILE

Range SAT Critical Reading	600–700
Range SAT Math	630–720
Range SAT Writing	590–690
Range ACT Composite	28–32
Minimum paper TOEFL	550
Minimum web-based TOEFL	80
Average HS GPA	4.20
% graduated top 10% of class	72
% graduated top 25% of class	92
% graduated top 50% of class	98

DEADLINES

Early decision	
Deadline	11/1
Notification	12/20
Early action	
Deadline	11/1
Notification	2/1
Regular	
Deadline	1/1
Notification	4/15
Nonfall registration?	Yes

FINANCIAL FACTS

Financial Aid Rating	81
Annual tuition	$43,040
Room and board	$12,684
% needy frosh rec. need-based scholarship or grant aid	99
% needy UG rec. need-based scholarship or grant aid	95
% needy frosh rec. non-need-based scholarship or grant aid	23
% needy UG rec. non-need-based scholarship or grant aid	26
% needy frosh rec. need-based self-help aid	70
% needy UG rec. need-based self-help aid	80
% frosh rec. any financial aid	77
% UG rec. any financial aid	76
% UG borrow to pay for school	44
Average cumulative indebtedness	$27,827
% frosh need fully met	25
% ugrads need fully met	28
Average % of frosh need met	76
Average % of ugrad need met	75

UNIVERSITY OF MICHIGAN—ANN ARBOR

1220 STUDENT ACTIVITIES BUILDING, ANN ARBOR, MI 48109-1316 • ADMISSIONS: 734-764-7433 • FAX: 734-936-0740

CAMPUS LIFE

Quality of Life Rating	89
Fire Safety Rating	96
Green Rating	98
Type of school	Public
Affiliation	No Affiliation
Environment	City

STUDENTS

Total undergrad enrollment	28,077
% male/female	51/49
% from out of state	36
% frosh live on campus	97
% ugrads live on campus	33
# of fraternities(% ugrad men join)	40(18)
# of sororities(% ugrad women join)	24(23)
% African American	4
% Asian	12
% Caucasian	63
% Hispanic	4
% Native American	<1
% international	7
# of countries represented	114

SURVEY SAYS . . .

Students love Ann Arbor, MI
Great off-campus food
Everyone loves the Wolverines
Student publications are popular
Political activism is popular

ACADEMICS

Academic Rating	83
% students returning for sophomore year	97
% students graduating within 4 years	76
% students graduating within 6 years	90
Calendar	Trimester
Student/faculty ratio	16:1
Profs interesting rating	71
Profs accessible rating	67

Most classes have 10–19 students.
Most lab/discussion sessions have 20–29 students.

MOST POPULAR MAJORS

experimental psychology; economics; business administration and management

STUDENTS SAY "..."

Academics

Among the many allures of the University of Michigan—Ann Arbor is that the school offers "a great environment both academically and socially." One student explains, "It has the social, fun atmosphere of any Big Ten university, but most people are still incredibly focused on their studies. It's great to be at a place where there is always something to do, but your friends completely understand when you have to stay in and get work done." With "an amazing honors program," a "wide range of travel-abroad opportunities," and "research strength" all available "at a low cost," it's no wonder students tell us that UM "provides every kind of opportunity at all times to all people." Academically, Michigan "is very competitive, and the professors have high academic standards for all the students." In fact, some here insist that "Michigan is as good as Ivy League schools in many disciplines." Standout offerings include business ("We have access to some of the brightest leaders" in the business world, students report), a "great engineering program," and "a good undergraduate program for medical school preparation." Those seeking add-on academic experiences here will find "a vast amount of resources. Internships, career opportunities, tutoring, community service projects, a plethora of student organizations, and a wealth of other resources" are all available, but "you need to make the first move" because no one "will seek you out."

Life

Michigan is a huge university, meaning that students have endless extracurricular options here. One explains: "If you seek it out, you can find organizations for *any* interest. There are always people out there who share your interests. That's part of the benefit of 40,000-plus students!" There is a robust party scene. Students tell us that "most students go to house parties [or] hit the bars." There's also a vigorous social scene for the non-drinking crowd, with "great programs like UMix...phenomenal cultural opportunities in Ann Arbor especially music and movies," and "the hugely popular football Saturdays. The sense of school spirit here is impressive." Michigan students tend to be both academically serious and socially outgoing, which "is great because you can have a stimulating conversation with someone one day, and, the next day, be watching a silly movie or playing video games with this person."

Student Body

The Michigan student body "is hugely diverse," which "is one of the things Michigan prides itself on." "If you participate in extracurricular activities and make an effort to get to know other students in class and elsewhere, you'll definitely end up with a pretty diverse group of friends," undergrads assure us. Although varied, students tend to be similar in that they "are social but very academically driven." A number of students "are on the cutting edge of both research and progressive thinking," and there is a decided liberal tilt to campus politics. Even so, there's a place for everyone here, because "there are hundreds of mini-communities within the campus, made of everything from service fraternities to political organizations to dance groups. If you have an interest, you can find a group of people who enjoy the same thing."

FINANCIAL AID: 734-763-6600 • WEBSITE: WWW.UMICH.EDU

THE PRINCETON REVIEW SAYS

Admissions

Very important factors considered include: GPA, rigor of secondary school record. *Important factors considered include:* Standardized test scores, application essay, first generation, recommendation(s), character/personal qualities. *Other factors considered include:* Extracurricular activities, geographical residence, state residency, talent/ability, volunteer work, work experience, alumni/ae relations, level of applicant's interest. SAT or ACT required; SAT and SAT Subject Tests or ACT considered if submitted; ACT with Writing component required. TOEFL required of all international applicants. *Academic units required:* 4 English; 3 mathematics; 3 science (1 science lab); 3 social studies. *Academic units recommended:* 4 English; 4 mathematics; 4 science; (1 science lab); 4 social studies; 4 foreign language; 4 history; 1 computer science; 2 visual/performing arts.

Financial Aid

Students should submit: FAFSA, CSS/Financial Aid PROFILE. Regular filing deadline is 4/30. The Princeton Review suggests that all financial aid forms be submitted as soon as possible after January 1. *Need-based scholarships/grants offered:* Federal Pell, SEOG, State scholarships/grants, private scholarships, the school's own gift aid. *Loan aid offered:* Direct Subsidized Stafford Loans, Direct Unsubsidized Stafford Loans, Direct PLUS loans, Federal Perkins Loans, Federal Nursing Loans, College/university loans from institutional funds. Federal Work-Study Program available. Institutional employment available. Off-campus job opportunities are excellent.

The Inside Word

Michigan admissions are extremely competitive. Generally, about a quarter of the incoming freshman class graduates in the top 1 percent of their high school class. The volume of applications—Michigan receives over 46,000 applications—means the admissions office must rely heavily on numbers to make its decision, so do what you can to get those test scores and GPA as high as you can. Michigan admits on a rolling basis, a process that favors those who apply early.

THE SCHOOL SAYS "..."

From the Admissions Office

"Michigan is a place of incredible possibility. Students shape that possibility according to their diverse interests, goals, energy, and initiative. Undergraduate education is in the academic spotlight at Michigan, offering more than 220 fields of study in twelve schools and colleges; more than 150 first-year seminars with twenty or fewer students taught by senior faculty; composition classes of twenty or fewer students; more than 1,200 first- and second-year students in undergraduate research partnerships with faculty; and numerous service learning programs linking academics with volunteerism. Some introductory courses have large lectures, but these are combined with labs or small group discussions where students get plenty of individualized attention. A Michigan degree is one of distinction and promise; graduates are successful in medical, law, and graduate schools all over the nation and world. A year after graduation, more than 95 percent of UM alumni report that they are in the 'next step' of their career—whether that is graduate or professional school, working, or volunteering."

SELECTIVITY

Admissions Rating	97
# of applicants	46,813
% of applicants accepted	33
% of acceptees attending	40
# offered a place on the wait list	10,709
% accepting a place on wait list	33
% admitted from wait list	3

FRESHMAN PROFILE

Range SAT Critical Reading	620–720
Range SAT Math	660–760
Range SAT Writing	630–730
Range ACT Composite	28–32
Minimum paper TOEFL	570
Average HS GPA	3.82

DEADLINES

Early action	
Deadline	11/1
Notification	12/24
Regular	
Priority	11/1
Deadline	2/1
Nonfall registration?	Yes

APPLICANTS ALSO LOOK AT AND OFTEN PREFER

Cornell University; Northwestern University; UC-Berkeley; Washington University

AND SOMETIMES PREFER

New York University; Purdue University; UCLA; University of Illinois at Champaign- Urbana

AND RARELY PREFER

Boston University; Indiana University; Michigan State University; Pennsylvania State University

FINANCIAL FACTS

Financial Aid Rating	88
Annual in-state tuition	$12,948
Annual out-of-state tuition	$40,198
Room and board	$9,996
Required fees	$194
Books and supplies	$1,048
% needy frosh rec. need-based scholarship or grant aid	72
% needy UG rec. need-based scholarship or grant aid	77
% needy frosh rec. non-need-based scholarship or grant aid	71
% needy UG rec. non-need-based scholarship or grant aid	66
% needy frosh rec. need-based self-help aid	81
% needy UG rec. need-based self-help aid	85
% frosh rec. any financial aid	61
% UG rec. any financial aid	62
% UG borrow to pay for school	47
Average cumulative indebtedness	$27,163
% frosh need fully met	79
% ugrads need fully met	80
Average % of frosh need met	84
Average % of ugrad need met	85

UNIVERSITY OF MINNESOTA—TWIN CITIES

240 WILLIAMSON HALL, MINNEAPOLIS, MN 55455-0213 • ADMISSIONS: 612-625-2008

CAMPUS LIFE
Quality of Life Rating	81
Fire Safety Rating	82
Green Rating	98
Type of school	Public
Affiliation	No Affiliation
Environment	Metropolis

STUDENTS
Total undergrad enrollment	30,271
% male/female	49/51 % from out of state 26
% frosh live on campus	89
% ugrads live on campus	23
# of fraternities	22
# of sororities	12
% African American	4
% Asian	9
% Caucasian	71
% Hispanic	3
% Native American	<1
% international	9
# of countries represented	132

SURVEY SAYS . . .
Students love Minneapolis, MN
Great off-campus food
Athletic facilities are great
Student publications are popular

ACADEMICS
Academic Rating	73
% students returning for sophomore year	90
% students graduating within 4 years	54
% students graduating within 6 years	75
Calendar	Semester
Profs interesting rating	69
Profs accessible rating	68

Most classes have 20–29 students.
Most lab/discussion sessions have
10–19 students.

MOST POPULAR MAJORS
psychology; journalism; rhetoric
and composition

STUDENTS SAY "..."

Academics

The University of Minnesota is a massive, well-run, public research university located in the Twin Cities. The science departments here are "across the board...superb," and the prestigious Carlson School of Management is "one of the best business schools in the Midwest, with a reasonable tuition" to boot. Students say that the university boasts "just about every major you can think of," and students appreciate the "never-ending resources available to them" within the university and the city. Research is of paramount importance at the university, which means that "there are incredible opportunities [for undergraduates] to work in ANY field of research." Given the size of the university, students have to contend with some "introductory level classes with 300-plus students, but as you get into the higher level classes, there are fewer students and the professors make lots of effort to connect personally." Many professors are "professionals working in the field; therefore, they have practical working knowledge of the subject material," which improves students' academic experience. Additionally, "the school does a good job of connecting with the outside community to set up internships and service learning opportunities" for students. The fact that the university is so "close to the city [makes] it easy to make connections with professionals" and provides ample "opportunities to intern in your field of study." Students of the University of Minnesota's Honors Program give it rave reviews and add that it is a "very valuable part of the university, and it sets Minnesota apart."

Life

Life on the University of Minnesota's "beautiful" and "environmentally friendly" campus is filled with "unlimited opportunities" for fun and recreation. Students say they "love how easy it is to get involved" on campus, whether it is in the popular Greek life on campus or the multitudes of clubs and sports readily available to them. On the weekends, "drinking is very wide-spread but is by no means the only source of fun." Many students say that their "favorite part of living at the U of M is that there is plenty to do on and near campus, but you are also in the heart of a vibrant, exciting city." Due to its location in an "incredible city" with a flourishing music and arts scene, students often "venture into the heart of Minneapolis to clubs, music shows, sporting events, and more." Outdoor activities are also "popular year-round—we have famous biking and walking trails, parks, and wide open spaces for students to take advantage of...to ski, skate, run, unicycle, and leapfrog around to their hearts' content." The campus in general is "pretty active, which has led to our recreation center being expanded. It's nice to live in an encouraging, athletic environment like that because it makes it easier to make healthy choices." Though the University of Minnesota is a huge school, students say they feel a sense of pride in their community: "I love the atmosphere, I love the city, and I love the size. It isn't a school incredibly focused on a high octane 'school spirit,' but I do feel incredibly united with the rest of the student body."

Student Body

The university is filled with a diverse body of students that runs the gamut from "typical Midwesterners" to "pockets of people from all over the world, most notably from China and India," as well as a good deal of hipsters and a large LGBT community. Students "respect the differences in each other," and students are, overall, "very welcoming and friendly." "It's not difficult to find friends or people to talk to in any class. The students are one of the university's high points." Though the campus "tends to lean liberal," students say that "political activeness/awareness is lacking." "Students have strong affiliation with their individual colleges and student groups that they are involved in." Students find their different niches "by joining different clubs and activities outside of the classroom." The general consensus is that the typical University of Minnesota student "has no trouble fitting in here. We have such a large, diverse community that it is almost impossible not to find people you get along with and share the same values with."

Fax: 612-626-1693 • Financial Aid: 612-624-1111 • Website: www.umn.edu

THE PRINCETON REVIEW SAYS

Admissions

Very important factors considered include: Class rank, GPA, rigor of secondary school record, standardized test scores. *Other factors considered include:* Extracurricular activities, first generation, geographical residence, racial/ethnic status, talent/ability, volunteer work, alumni/ae relations, character/personal qualities. SAT or ACT required; ACT with Writing component required. TOEFL required of all international applicants. *Academic units required:* 4 English; 3 mathematics; 3 science; 3 social studies; 2 foreign language; 1 history; 1 visual/performing arts. *Academic units recommended:* 4 English; 4 mathematics; 4 science; (1 science lab); 3 social studies; 2 foreign language; 1 history; 1 visual/performing arts.

Financial Aid

Students should submit: FAFSA, Institution's own financial aid form. The Princeton Review suggests that all financial aid forms be submitted as soon as possible after January 1. *Need-based scholarships/grants offered:* Federal Pell, SEOG, State scholarships/grants, private scholarships, the school's own gift aid, federal nursing scholarships. *Loan aid offered:* Direct Subsidized Stafford Loans, Direct Unsubsidized Stafford Loans, Direct PLUS loans, Federal Perkins Loans, Federal Nursing Loans, State Loans, College/university loans from institutional funds. Federal Work-Study Program available. Institutional employment available.

The Inside Word

The University of Minnesota receives an enormous volume of applications every year, creating what looks like a fairly selective admissions rate. Make sure your grades, extracurriculars, and test scores are competitive.

THE SCHOOL SAYS "..."

From the Admissions Office

"The University of Minnesota is one of the nation's top public research universities. That means your college experience will be enhanced by world-renowned faculty, state-of-the-art learning facilities, and an unprecedented variety of options (such as 135 majors). Eighty-one percent of our classes have fewer than fifty students, and our caring advisers will help you find opportunities that are right for you.

"Hands-on courses, volunteer opportunities, internships, study abroad, and undergraduate research are part of the U of M experience. Students benefit from programs and traditions designed to support their success, like Welcome Week, where freshmen explore campus, meet their classmates, and connect with faculty and staff before the school year begins. Our classic Big Ten campus is located in the heart of the vibrant Twin Cities. Just minutes away, intern at a Fortune 500 company, volunteer at a major hospital, or relax at the beautiful Chain of Lakes. With a wealth of cultural, career, and recreational opportunities, there's no better place to earn your degree.

"Last year, we awarded over $12 million in four-year scholarship packages. Residents of Minnesota benefit from in-state tuition. Minnesota residents may also qualify for the University of Minnesota Promise Scholarship, which guarantees tuition aid to eligible students with a family income up to $100,000. Residents of North Dakota, South Dakota, Wisconsin, or Manitoba qualify for special reciprocity tuition rates.

"The University of Minnesota has been named a 'Best Value in Public Colleges' by multiple ranking organizations. As a U of M student, you will experience this value first-hand: you will step into a thriving academic community with some of the world's most renowned researchers. In fact, you'll often find that your professors are leading discoveries in their fields and developing curricula used across the country. With direct access to these incredible resources, you will get a great education and a prestigious degree that helps you achieve your dreams."

SELECTIVITY

Admissions Rating	94
# of applicants	43,048
% of applicants accepted	44
% of acceptees attending	29

FRESHMAN PROFILE

Range SAT Critical Reading	550–690
Range SAT Math	620–740
Range SAT Writing	570–670
Range ACT Composite	26–30
Minimum paper TOEFL	550
Minimum web-based TOEFL	213
% graduated top 10% of class	45
% graduated top 25% of class	82
% graduated top 50% of class	100

DEADLINES

Regular	
Priority	12/15
Nonfall registration?	Yes

APPLICANTS ALSO LOOK AT AND OFTEN PREFER

University of Michigan—Ann Arbor;
Northwestern University

FINANCIAL FACTS

Financial Aid Rating	77
% needy frosh rec. need-based scholarship or grant aid	86
% needy UG rec. need-based scholarship or grant aid	86
% needy frosh rec. non-need-based scholarship or grant aid	15
% needy UG rec. non-need-based scholarship or grant aid	11
% needy frosh rec. need-based self-help aid	85
% needy UG rec. need-based self-help aid	85
% UG borrow to pay for school	61
Average cumulative indebtedness	$28,384
% frosh need fully met	32
% ugrads need fully met	27
Average % of frosh need met	75
Average % of ugrad need met	71

UNIVERSITY OF MISSISSIPPI

145 MARTINDALE, UNIVERSITY, MS 38677 • ADMISSIONS: 662-915-7226 • FAX: 662-915-5869

CAMPUS LIFE
Quality of Life Rating	96
Fire Safety Rating	60*
Green Rating	81
Type of school	Public
Affiliation	No Affiliation
Environment	Village

STUDENTS
Total undergrad enrollment	16,677
% male/female	45/55
% from out of state	41
% ugrads live on campus	31
# of fraternities (% ugrad men join)	17 (29)
# of sororities (% ugrad women join)	14 (36)
% African American	15
% Asian	2
% Caucasian	76
% Hispanic	3
% Native American	<1
% international	2
# of countries represented	72

SURVEY SAYS . . .
Students are happy
Students are friendly
Students get along with local community
Students love University, MS
Great off-campus food
Campus feels safe
Lots of beer drinking
Hard liquor is popular
Everyone loves the Rebels
Frats and sororities are popular
Student publications are popular
Alumni active on campus
Active student government

ACADEMICS
Academic Rating	75
% students returning for sophomore year	86
% students graduating within 4 years	36
% students graduating within 6 years	58
Calendar	Semester
Student/faculty ratio	19:1
Profs interesting rating	79
Profs accessible rating	81

Most classes have 20–29 students.
Most lab/discussion sessions have 20–29 students.

MOST POPULAR MAJORS
elementary education; accounting; journalism

STUDENTS SAY ". . ."

Academics

Ole Miss is a prime example of Southern hospitality combined with the opportunity for greatness. Founded in 1848, the legendary university offers "'big-time' SEC athletics in the safe, quaint, and picturesque town of Oxford." Many of the school's services "are cheap if not free," and the school "puts on many programs that bring together lots of different people of different backgrounds." "It has a togetherness about it…there is something for a person with any interest here," says a student. There is also "a highly academic side to Ole Miss that many outsiders do not see." Business and international studies are programs of note, and the Honors College is a particular standout here, as it provides "unparalleled academic opportunities, such as beginning research as a freshman."

Most of the professors "hit the ball out of the park" when it comes to teaching, being available, and helping students acquire internships. Professors constantly organize discussion groups, dinner events, and other gatherings in order to "develop our ability to speak academically in a non-academic setting." Going to class is "critical"; professors "add much more than the textbook has to offer." Classes are designed to be "informative but also engaging and dynamic," and there is a deep understanding that individuals have an effect on the whole. "The teachers care, the university cares, [and] the students all care about the school and what it stands for."

It can be said again and again, but even beyond the "world-class programs and faculty," the thing that students at Ole Miss value the most is the traditions and legacy of this school. People "are proud to have graduated from Ole Miss," and the tremendous amount of alumni support "gives Ole Miss a lot of confidence."

Life

An Ole Miss existence is "always super busy." There is "a lot of work to be done" as "school and grades are a very important aspect of life," but there are also "a lot of opportunities for fun." "During football season, the Grove consumes our weekends. It's an amazing experience!" says a student. As a school that most admit is "known for its Greek life, beautiful women, and great parties," it's a common misconception that "most people's minds revolve around drinking, college football, and church on Sunday." If you take a closer look, you'll find that there is a huge literary scene "with Thacker Mountain Radio on Thursdays and poetry readings monthly at Proud Larry's," and students here also "really want to be active in making changes in the world."

The closeness of the community makes it easy to feel part of the University. "You'll hear the term the 'Ole Miss family,' and it won't seem forced or strange," explains a student. Oxford is also very appealing due to its "small, hometown feel," and the rich history you see everywhere you go (the Square is the center of town life, and most students can be found there at some point in a week). Basically, "there is never a dull moment, especially on the weekends."

Student Body

Ole Miss is a fairly diverse campus, with most students possessing "decent grades and an extravagant social life." One third of the student body "belongs to either a fraternity or sorority, fancying the appropriate attire of a Polo shirt and loafers or baggy t-shirts and Nike shorts." The divide between Greek and non-Greek is stark here, though the two groups are not necessarily always adverse towards each other; this is a group of "open minds" in "a small-town" setting, with "a blend of Southern charm and laid-back manners" thrown in, after all. "Studying for your next exam over a glass of sweet tea is a common practice." As there are a lot of different groups on campus, "you can find a group of friends without much effort."

FINANCIAL AID: 800-891-4596 • E-MAIL: ADMISSIONS@OLEMISS.EDU • WEBSITE: WWW.OLEMISS.EDU

THE PRINCETON REVIEW SAYS

Admissions

Important factors considered include: GPA, standardized test scores. *Other factors considered include:* Class rank, rigor of secondary school record. SAT or ACT required for some; ACT with or without Writing component accepted. TOEFL required of all international applicants. *Academic units required:* 4 English; 3 mathematics; 3 science; (2 science lab); 3 social studies; 1 academic elective. *Academic units recommended:* 4 English; 4 mathematics; 4 science; (2 science lab); 4 social studies; 2 foreign language.

Financial Aid

Students should submit: FAFSA. The Princeton Review suggests that all financial aid forms be submitted as soon as possible after January 1. *Need-based scholarships/grants offered:* Federal Pell, SEOG, State scholarships/grants, private scholarships, the school's own gift aid. *Loan aid offered:* Direct Subsidized Stafford Loans, Direct Unsubsidized Stafford Loans, Direct PLUS loans, Federal Perkins Loans, College/university loans from institutional funds. Applicants will be notified of awards beginning 4/1. Federal Work-Study Program available. Institutional employment available. Off-campus job opportunities are fair.

The Inside Word

While Ole Miss offers students tremendous educational opportunities, the university's admissions policies are less than strenuous. Applicants who demonstrate moderate success (a 3.2 GPA or greater, or a 2.5 GPA and a 16 on the ACT) in college prep curricula will most likely secure admittance.

THE SCHOOL SAYS "..."

From the Admissions Office

"The flagship university of the state, The University of Mississippi, widely known as Ole Miss, offers extraordinary opportunities through more than 100 areas of study, including programs such as the Sally McDonnell Barksdale Honors College and the Croft Institute for International Studies. UM students are the only public university students in the state who have the opportunity to be tapped by the nation's oldest and most prestigious honor society, Phi Beta Kappa. Strong academic programs and a rich and varied campus life have helped Ole Miss graduate twenty-five Rhodes Scholars, and fourteen Truman Scholars. Since 1998 alone, UM has produced 10 Goldwater Scholars, a Marshall Scholar, and 12 Fulbright Scholars.

"The campus is diverse; 41 percent come from other states and countries and 15 percent are black Americans. Recent significant campus improvements include the two state-of-the-art Residential Colleges, a Center for Manufacturing Excellence and the 155,000-square-foot Robert C. Khayat Law Center. UM ranks thirty-third in the nation among public universities for endowment per student. Ole Miss is home to twenty research centers, including the National Center for Justice and the Rule of Law, which provides training on investigating and prosecuting cybercrime; the William Winter Institute for Racial Reconciliation; and the National Center for Natural Products Research.

"The university is located in Oxford, consistently recognized as a great college town and as a center for writers and other artists. Like Ole Miss, Oxford is modest in size and large in the opportunities it provides residents, offering many of the advantages of a larger place in a friendly and open environment.

"Students applying will be allowed to take the SAT or the ACT but are not required to take the ACT writing section. The university will not consider the writing section of either exam when evaluating students for admission, but certain specialty programs may request these scores."

SELECTIVITY
Admissions Rating	81
# of applicants	14,258
% of applicants accepted	59
% of acceptees attending	42

FRESHMAN PROFILE
Range SAT Critical Reading	490–590
Range SAT Math	490–600
Range ACT Composite	21–27
Minimum paper TOEFL	550
Minimum web-based TOEFL	213
Average HS GPA	3.46
% graduated top 10% of class	24
% graduated top 25% of class	48
% graduated top 50% of class	77

DEADLINES
Regular	
Priority	4/1
Deadline	9/1
Nonfall registration?	Yes

FINANCIAL FACTS
Financial Aid Rating	77
Annual in-state tuition	$6,600
Annual out-of-state tuition	$17,628
Room and board	$9,566
% needy frosh rec. need-based scholarship or grant aid	85
% needy UG rec. need-based scholarship or grant aid	85
% needy frosh rec. non-need-based scholarship or grant aid	14
% needy UG rec. non-need-based scholarship or grant aid	8
% needy frosh rec. need-based self-help aid	69
% needy UG rec. need-based self-help aid	74
% frosh rec. any financial aid	83
% UG rec. any financial aid	78
% UG borrow to pay for school	46
Average cumulative indebtedness	$23,986
% frosh need fully met	14
% ugrads need fully met	11
Average % of frosh need met	77
Average % of ugrad need met	74

UNIVERSITY OF MISSOURI

230 JESSE HALL, COLUMBIA, MO 65211 • ADMISSIONS: 573-882-7786 • FAX: 573-882-7887

CAMPUS LIFE

Quality of Life Rating	91
Fire Safety Rating	91
Green Rating	91
Type of school	Public
Affiliation	No Affiliation
Environment	City

STUDENTS

Total undergrad enrollment	26,585
% male/female	48/52
% from out of state	23
% frosh live on campus	85
% ugrads live on campus	25
# of fraternities (% ugrad men join)	31 (28)
# of sororities (% ugrad women join)	23 (39)
% African American	8
% Asian	2
% Caucasian	80
% Hispanic	3
% Native American	<1
% international	3
# of countries represented	120

SURVEY SAYS . . .

Students are happy
Students get along with local community
Students love Columbia, MO
Great off-campus food
Athletic facilities are great
Lots of beer drinking
Hard liquor is popular
Everyone loves the Tigers
Frats and sororities are popular
Alumni active on campus

ACADEMICS

Academic Rating	74
% students returning for sophomore year	84
% students graduating within 4 years	47
% students graduating within 6 years	70
Calendar	Semester
Student/faculty ratio	20:1
Profs interesting rating	68
Profs accessible rating	71

Most classes have 10–19 students.
Most lab/discussion sessions have
20–29 students.

MOST POPULAR MAJORS

business/commerce; biomedical science;
journalism

STUDENTS SAY ". . ."

Academics

The "gorgeous campus" at the University of Missouri is filled with "a diverse group of students who are eager to learn and a staff that is eager to teach them." The school is all about "learning while networking," and the administration always has an ear to the students. "When we say there is a problem, it gets fixed," one student says. Mizzou takes pride in tradition, which is to be found "in all aspects that involve the University name," which makes for "a campus full of pride and spirit." There is a "constant focus on beautification, which makes for a great campus," and "top-of-the-line facilities" are available to all. One of the university's greatest strengths is its dependability: "From mass e-mails to mass texts, if there is an issue anywhere on campus you will know about it."

Professors teach "comprehensive courses" and "are always available to answer a question"; "even with large classes they are very attentive to individuals." "I've always had professors who have had a million ways to explain any given theory, problem, or question," says a student. The school boasts one of the country's best and most "intense" journalism schools (nursing is also a strong suit), and there are tons of "participation opportunities" for whatever area you choose to study. Classes may be hard, but "good grades are attainable." In addition to the "quality" academics, the advising system is "great," and Mizzou sets itself as a real model for its students: "It is always striving to achieve better, and not in just one specific category or area, but all around." "I came into college undecided and wanted to have plenty of options and opportunities to decide on a major," says a student of her reasoning for choosing Mizzou.

Life

"There is never a dull moment to be had" at the University of Missouri. All athletic events are "heavily attended," especially football and basketball. Everyone walks or bikes everywhere in Columbia "because it's such a pedestrian friendly place," and "there are plenty of opportunities to chill out downtown." It is "the perfect mixture of small town and big city," and local attractions include a mall, small shops, micro-breweries, and tons of parks and hiking trails. If you're used to bigger cities, then it also happens to be located between Kansas City and St. Louis. "Best of both worlds!" says a student. The school has "a huge Greek Life," and "it's a pretty close community." "Students enjoy going to off-campus parties or the bars downtown." "A lot of students spend their time in class, but every night of the week there is a party to go to," explains a student. Many agree that both the residential life system and the dorms "could use some work," and "having a car is the key to living off campus."

Student Body

The school has a giant spectrum of diversity, meaning "everyone is different. Anyone could fit in and find a group here." If a typical student has to be defined, most here are "friendly, outgoing, social, [and] very involved." Most of all, they are "proud to be Tiger[s]." "We all fit in because we have this in common," says a student. "It's pretty great company." "Classes have always felt like big families," and the majority of students find friends "by joining one of our million organizations," which is a common pastime among this "on-the-go" group. As everyone is "pretty easygoing and easy to get along with," "fitting in is easy; you just act like yourself!"

FINANCIAL AID: 573-882-7506 • E-MAIL: MU4U@MISSOURI.EDU • WEBSITE: WWW.MISSOURI.EDU

THE PRINCETON REVIEW SAYS

Admissions

Very important factors considered include: GPA, standardized test scores. *Important factors considered include:* Class rank, rigor of secondary school record. *Other factors considered include:* Application essay, first generation, racial/ethnic status, recommendation(s), talent/ability, volunteer work, work experience, level of applicant's interest. SAT or ACT required; ACT with or without Writing component accepted. TOEFL required of all international applicants. *Academic units required:* 4 English; 4 mathematics; 3 science; (1 science lab); 3 social studies; 2 foreign language.

Financial Aid

Students should submit: FAFSA. The Princeton Review suggests that all financial aid forms be submitted as soon as possible after January 1. *Need-based scholarships/grants offered:* Federal Pell, SEOG, State scholarships/grants, private scholarships, the school's own gift aid, federal nursing scholarships. *Loan aid offered:* Direct Subsidized Stafford Loans, Direct Unsubsidized Stafford Loans, Direct PLUS loans, Federal Perkins Loans, Federal Nursing Loans, State Loans, College/university loans from institutional funds. Federal Work-Study Program available. Institutional employment available. Off-campus job opportunities are excellent.

The Inside Word

If your application suggests that you can handle the workload here, the school will find a place for you. Average test scores in conjunction with a college-prep high school curriculum should be all it takes. Even those who don't meet these criteria have a chance; admissions officers consider essays, recommendations, and special talents in the cases of borderline candidates.

THE SCHOOL SAYS "..."

From the Admissions Office

"Founded in 1839 as the first public university west of the Mississippi River, MU is a member of the nation's most prestigious group of sixty-two public and private teaching/research institutions: the Association of American Universities. The National Science Foundation has recognized MU as one of the top ten universities in the country for integrating research into undergraduate education; Missou offers 12 major undergraduate research programs, some with freshmen participants.

"Service learning is important at Mizzou. The Service Learning Office at MU formally integrates community service into 250 courses. Last year 4,400 undergraduates earned academic credit while volunteering 190,000 hours for 290 community and government partners.

"More than 38 percent of the fall 2013 freshman class came from another state or another country, and a strong international community thrives in Columbia. t the same time, MU's Study Abroad program is Missouri's largest with 300 programs in 50 countries.

"Mizzou offers many strong, unique programs. Some in the sciences are taught in collaboration with MU's medical school, and humanities classes include such areas as music composition and creative writing where students frequently win national awards.

"Students can find admissions requirements at missouri.edu. As students apply online, it is clear whether they are admissible or not. That may partially explain Missouri's high acceptance rate."

SELECTIVITY	
Admissions Rating	79
# of applicants	20,956
% of applicants accepted	79
% of acceptees attending	37

FRESHMAN PROFILE	
Range SAT Critical Reading	520–640
Range SAT Math	520–650
Range ACT Composite	23–28
Minimum paper TOEFL	500
% graduated top 10% of class	27
% graduated top 25% of class	58
% graduated top 50% of class	88

DEADLINES	
Regular	
Priority	5/1
Nonfall registration?	Yes

FINANCIAL FACTS	
Financial Aid Rating	74
Annual in-state tuition	$8,082
Annual out-of-state tuition	$22,191
Room and board	$8,944
Required fees	$1,175
Books and supplies	$930
% needy frosh rec. need-based scholarship or grant aid	87
% needy UG rec. need-based scholarship or grant aid	81
% needy frosh rec. non-need-based scholarship or grant aid	6
% needy UG rec. non-need based scholarship or grant aid	4
% needy frosh rec. need-based self-help aid	75
% needy UG rec. need-based self-help aid	78
% UG borrow to pay for school	59
Average cumulative indebtedness	$23,588
% frosh need fully met	14
% ugrads need fully met	15
Average % of frosh need met	80
Average % of ugrad need met	80

THE UNIVERSITY OF MONTANA—MISSOULA

LOMMASSON CENTER 103, MISSOULA, MT 59812 • ADMISSIONS: 406-243-6266 • FAX: 406-243-5711

CAMPUS LIFE
Quality of Life Rating	82
Fire Safety Rating	84
Green Rating	96
Type of school	Public
Affiliation	No Affiliation
Environment	City

STUDENTS
Total undergrad enrollment	12,443
% male/female	46/54
% from out of state	25
% frosh live on campus	80
% ugrads live on campus	25
# of fraternities	6
# of sororities	4
% African American	1
% Asian	1
% Caucasian	81
% Hispanic	3
% Native American	3
% international	1
# of countries represented	71

SURVEY SAYS . . .
Political activism is unpopular or nonexistent
Students get along with local community
Students love Missoula, MT
Athletic facilities are great
Everyone loves the Grizzlies

ACADEMICS
Academic Rating	73
% students returning for sophomore year	74
% students graduating within 4 years	22
% students graduating within 6 years	48
Calendar	Semester
Student/faculty ratio	18:1
Profs interesting rating	75
Profs accessible rating	70

Most classes have 10–19 students.
Most lab/discussion sessions have 20–29 students.

MOST POPULAR MAJORS
psychology; business administration and management; natural resources conservation and research

STUDENTS SAY " . . ."

Academics

Nestled in beautiful Missoula, The University of Montana is "a great place to live, work, and study." Indeed, Montana's awesome location and solid reputation coupled with low in-state tuition make it "hard to beat." Moreover, while it has a substantial number of students, we're assured that you're never "just a number" here. Undergrads also appreciate the university's focus on "environmental sustainability…and social justice" along with the fact that the University of Montana strives to develop "creative thinkers and engaged citizens." While the university maintains a fantastic liberal arts program, students especially laud the wildlife biology, forestry, physical therapy, and forensic anthropology departments. Moreover, undergrads at Montana are highly complementary of their teachers who are generally "helpful, engaging, and accessible." One thrilled student claims that the professors are "amazing! Math and science has never come easy for me, and my professors have taught in a way I completely understand the material." Another enthusiastic student summarizes her experience by stating, "The professors here are very knowledgeable and passionate about what they are teaching, because of this, the learning experience is always interesting and inviting. I truly appreciate all the effort that is put forward to help students succeed and prepare for the next steps in their life."

Life

Undergrads seem to truly enjoy life at U of M. Indeed, the campus is often buzzing with activity. As one student happily shares, "When it's not snowing in the fall or spring you can find people playing Frisbee, walking their dogs, catching footballs, and even playing with lightsabers." Additionally, there are "many music concerts and dance parties" one can attend. "Football is [also] really big here," and games are often packed with students. Beyond the campus, Montana offers a myriad of options for the outdoor enthusiast. As one ecstatic undergrad tells us, "Western Montana is a divine place for hiking, hunting, fishing, camping, snowshoeing, swimming, huckleberry picking, going to hot springs, mushroom picking, antler collecting, and just being immersed in nature. Near where I live there is access to the Rattlesnake Wilderness, mountains surround the valley, and the Clark Fork River runs right through town." Those with a more adventurous spirit can delight in "skiing and skydiving, hand gliding and parasailing, mountain climbing and repelling, caving and biking." As this pleased undergrad summarizes, "There is always something to do no matter what your interest are and great people to do them with."

Student Body

The University of Montana attracts a student body that's "pretty laid-back and easygoing." Many are "outdoorsy" and self-described as "hippies." Indeed, there are "quite a few granola kids" and "Carhartt-sporting, plaid-proud, future biologists" types. Though many students hail from within the state, one undergrad assures us that "increasing diversity efforts have begun to show in the past three years." Fortunately, for the most part, everyone is "accepting, friendly, and very involved in college and community life." Another student expands on this idea, stating, "People here do not seem to judge others or hold stereotypes against each other. If you're lost or need to ask a question you can ask anyone, and they're willing to give you the best answer they know in order to help you out even if they don't know you." A fellow undergrad agrees softly, sharing, "I feel like I've stepped into a melting pot of all beliefs and ideals. You can be yourself, and never be looked down on for that at this school."

THE UNIVERSITY OF MONTANA—MISSOULA

FINANCIAL AID: 406-243-5373 • E-MAIL: ADMISS@UMONTANA.EDU • WEBSITE: WWW.UMONTANA.EDU

THE PRINCETON REVIEW SAYS

Admissions

Very important factors considered include: Class rank, GPA, rigor of secondary school record, standardized test scores, first generation, level of applicant's interest. *Important factors considered include:* Extracurricular activities, talent/ability. *Other factors considered include:* Application essay, recommendation(s). SAT or ACT required; ACT with Writing component recommended. TOEFL required of all international applicants. *Academic units required:* 4 English; 3 mathematics; 2 science; (2 science lab); 3 social studies; 2 history. *Academic units recommended:* 2 foreign language; 2 computer science; 2 visual/performing arts.

Financial Aid

Students should submit: FAFSA. The Princeton Review suggests that all financial aid forms be submitted as soon as possible after January 1. *Need-based scholarships/grants offered:* Federal Pell, SEOG, State scholarships/grants, private scholarships, the school's own gift aid. *Loan aid offered:* Direct Subsidized Stafford Loans, Direct Unsubsidized Stafford Loans, Direct PLUS loans, Federal Perkins Loans. Federal Work-Study Program available. Institutional employment available. Off-campus job opportunities are good.

The Inside Word

The admissions game at the University of Montana is fairly straightforward. Officers here rely heavily on quantitative data. Applicants who meet standardized test and GPA minimums and are in the top half of their graduating class generally receive an acceptance letter. Those who did not meet the minimum requirements can often enroll on a conditional basis.

THE SCHOOL SAYS "..."

From the Admissions Office

"There's something special about this place. It's something different for each person. For some, it's the blend of academic quality and outdoor recreation. The University of Montana ranks fifth in the nation among public institutions for producing Rhodes scholars, and Outside Magazine lists Missoula in its 'Top Ten Amazing Places for Outdoor Recreation.' For others, it's size—not too big, not too small. The University of Montana is a midsized university in the heart of the Rocky Mountains—accessible in both admission and tuition bills—that produces graduates considered among the best and brightest in the world. It is located in a community that could pass for a cozy college town or a bustling big city, depending on your point of view. There's a lot happening, but you won't get lost. People are friendly and diverse. They come from all over the world to study and learn and to live a good life. They come to a place to be inspired, a place where they feel comfortable yet challenged. Some never leave. Most never want to."

SELECTIVITY

Admissions Rating	71
# of applicants	5,327
% of applicants accepted	94
% of acceptees attending	40

FRESHMAN PROFILE

Range SAT Critical Reading	480–600
Range SAT Math	470–600
Range SAT Writing	460–580
Range ACT Composite	21–26
Minimum paper TOEFL	500
Minimum web-based TOEFL	173
Average HS GPA	3.30
% graduated top 10% of class	17
% graduated top 25% of class	41
% graduated top 50% of class	72

DEADLINES

Regular	
Priority	3/1
Nonfall registration?	Yes

FINANCIAL FACTS

Financial Aid Rating	68
Annual in-state tuition	$4,373
Annual out-of-state tuition	$20,047
Room and board	$8,109
Required fees	$1,972
Books and supplies	$950
% needy frosh rec. need-based scholarship or grant aid	63
% needy UG rec. need-based scholarship or grant aid	69
% needy frosh rec. non-need-based scholarship or grant aid	68
% needy UG rec. non-need-based scholarship or grant aid	27
% needy frosh rec. need-based self-help aid	77
% needy UG rec. need-based self-help aid	86
% frosh rec. any financial aid	50
% UG rec. any financial aid	57
% UG borrow to pay for school	56
Average cumulative indebtedness	$29,126
% frosh need fully met	12
% ugrads need fully met	8
Average % of frosh need met	60
Average % of ugrad need met	52

UNIVERSITY OF NEBRASKA—LINCOLN

1410 Q STREET, LINCOLN, NE 68588-0417 • ADMISSIONS: 402-472-2023

STUDENTS SAY ". . ."

Academics

Students love the University of Nebraska–Lincoln for its "great community atmosphere" within what is actually a large, "major research institution." The school offers a "wide range of majors" and "opportunities to be involved in research" for those who seek them. Students say that, "Although UNL is a large college, most professors here are very approachable and willing to help students, as long as they are willing to ask for it." According to one student, "If I ever have an issue come up, most professors are willing to work with me to get things resolved; however, some departments (usually the larger ones) are not as "student-friendly" as others." Another student says that "UNL professors have pushed me to be a better, well-rounded student who looks at situations from every angle." Academic resources abound at UNL. "With many of our professors performing research, there is such a great opportunity to get experience." Also, "we have so many resources such as the Career Center, Student Involvement, Writing Resource Center, etc." Students are "particularly pleased with the honors program at the University of Nebraska–Lincoln...The opportunities for unique academic projects are endless and strongly supported by the faculty." Because of the university's location "right next to downtown Lincoln... there are infinite opportunities for socializing or jobs and internships within walking distance." Students are very happy with "the endless opportunities available" at UNL, which "extends to majors, extracurricular activities, research, internships, study abroad, volunteering, jobs, and so on."

Life

"The sense of community on our campus is second to none," according to students. They are proud to be members of the University of Nebraska–Lincoln and think that the sense of "tradition here is amazing, and the support from the alumni and the community is awesome." "There is a real sense of unity around the athletics here," as students rally around Husker football games with "so much school spirit and pride." Life around campus is "lively," and it is "really easy to get involved on campus." "UNL offers many activities throughout the week. Whether it is the performing arts with the dance, choir, or theater performances, or the athletics with collegiate, club, or intramural sports, UNL has something going on for everyone." Lincoln is a beautiful, small-sized city and "a good college town, so there are lots of things to go do-concert halls, restaurants, sports teams, theaters, bars, coffee shops, shops and boutiques, two malls, etc." UNL helps students access to all that Lincoln has to offer by "offering a program called Arts-For-All, which allows students to go to shows at the Lied Performing Arts Center for free." These cultural activities are supplemented by "great nightlife" off campus and in downtown Lincoln. Some students think that the school "could certainly improve on our sustainability efforts and awareness," but "this issue is beginning to be addressed," with the help of some passionate students and a progressive administration.

Student Body

Students say that some of UNL's greatest strengths are "the unity among the student body and the acceptance of everyone." Though they admit that their university does "lack the multiculturalism...of other schools," they say, "There is no typical student here." "There are so many different types of people with different interests. Everyone can find a place to fit in." One thing most students have in common is that they are "friendly, fun, and laid-back," as well as "hardworking and involved." It is "easy to make friends in classes or the residence halls because everyone wants to meet people." Students love to get involved in extracurricular activities and campus-wide events, which is usually how "everyone can find a niche that suits them." "Even though it's a big school," says one student, "I never feel lost in the crowd."

Fax: 402-472-0670 • Financial Aid: 402-472-2030 • E-mail: ADMISSIONS@UNL.EDU • Website: WWW.UNL.EDU

THE PRINCETON REVIEW SAYS

Admissions

Very important factors considered include: Class rank, standardized test scores, first generation, recommendation(s), talent/ability. *Important factors considered include:* Rigor of secondary school record. *Other factors considered include:* GPA. SAT or ACT required; ACT with or without Writing component accepted. TOEFL required of all international applicants. *Academic units required:* 4 English; 4 mathematics; 3 science; (1 science lab); 2 social studies; 2 foreign language; 1 history.

Financial Aid

Students should submit: FAFSA. The Princeton Review suggests that all financial aid forms be submitted as soon as possible after January 1. *Need-based scholarships/grants offered:* Federal Pell, SEOG, State scholarships/grants, private scholarships, the school's own gift aid. *Loan aid offered:* Direct Subsidized Stafford Loans, Direct Unsubsidized Stafford Loans, Direct PLUS loans, Federal Perkins Loans. Federal Work-Study Program available. Institutional employment available. Off-campus job opportunities are excellent.

The Inside Word

UNL offers more than 150 majors. All applications will be weighed on the combined strength of course work, GPAs, and test scores. Applicants interested in applying to a specific school at UNL should take into account those school's specialized requirements as they may include additional high school course work than what is required by UNL's general studies program.

THE SCHOOL SAYS "..."

From the Admissions Office

"The University of Nebraska–Lincoln offers one of today's most dynamic college experiences. The university has developed a national reputation for its substantial out-of-state scholarship program, and now for its participation in the Big Ten Conference. As a result, more students nationwide are finding that the university, with all its strength in undergraduate research and education, its tradition of student engagement, its lively campus atmosphere, and its connection to downtown Lincoln, is uniquely suited to provide an enriching student experience. It is an exciting time on the University of Nebraska—Lincoln campus. As a Big Ten institution, students are able to take advantage of all the Big Ten Conference has to offer including more academic opportunities, collaboration, student discovery and value.

"Established in 1869, the University of Nebraska–Lincoln has a rich tradition of excellence. Students join more than 200,000 alumni who have made their mark as industry leaders in business, engineering, the arts, journalism, education, and the sciences. Employers and grad schools have always held UNL degrees in high regard, and the added value of Big Ten affiliation gives UNL alumni an even bigger advantage in the U.S. and around the world.

"Freshman students seeking admission should either be ranked in the upper one-half of their high school class, or have received an ACT composite score of 20 or higher or an SAT total score of 950 or higher (critical reading and math only; writing portion not considered)."

SELECTIVITY

Admissions Rating	87
# of applicants	10,929
% of applicants accepted	64
% of acceptees attending	63

FRESHMAN PROFILE

Range SAT Critical Reading	490–660
Range SAT Math	520–670
Range ACT Composite	22–28
Minimum paper TOEFL	523
Minimum web-based TOEFL	70
% graduated top 10% of class	26
% graduated top 25% of class	52
% graduated top 50% of class	83

DEADLINES

Regular	
Priority	1/15
Deadline	5/1
Notification	Rolling
Nonfall registration?	Yes

FINANCIAL FACTS

Financial Aid Rating	77
Annual in-state tuition	$6,480
Annual out-of-state tuition	$19,807
Room and board	$9,122
Required fees	$1,495
Books and supplies	$1,050
% needy frosh rec. need-based scholarship or grant aid	80
% needy UG rec. need-based scholarship or grant aid	76
% needy frosh rec. non-need-based scholarship or grant aid	7
% needy UG rec. non-need-based scholarship or grant aid	6
% needy frosh rec. need-based self-help aid	70
% needy UG rec. need-based self-help aid	73
% frosh rec. any financial aid	88
% UG rec. any financial aid	67
% UG borrow to pay for school	59
Average cumulative indebtedness	$23,951
% frosh need fully met	18
% ugrads need fully met	15
Average % of frosh need met	83
Average % of ugrad need met	80

UNIVERSITY OF NEW HAMPSHIRE

UNH Office of Admissions, Durham, NH 03824 • Admissions: 603-862-1360 • Fax: 603-862-0077

CAMPUS LIFE
Quality of Life Rating	68
Fire Safety Rating	93
Green Rating	99
Type of school	Public
Environment	Village

STUDENTS
Total undergrad enrollment	12,288
% male/female	46/54
% from out of state	46
% frosh from public high school	81
% frosh live on campus	89
% ugrads live on campus	58
# of fraternities (% ugrad men join)	11 (9)
# of sororities (% ugrad women join)	7 (11)
% African American	1
% Asian	2
% Caucasian	80
% Hispanic	3
% Native American	<1
% international	1
# of countries represented	57

SURVEY SAYS . . .
Great library
Athletic facilities are great
Frats and sororities are popular
Lots of beer drinking
Hard liquor is popular

ACADEMICS
Academic Rating	69
% students returning for sophomore year	86
% students graduating within 4 years	69
% students graduating within 6 years	80
Calendar	Semester
Student/faculty ratio	19:1
Profs interesting rating	68
Profs accessible rating	64

Most classes have 10–19 students.
Most lab/discussion sessions have 20–29 students.

MOST POPULAR MAJORS
business administration and management; psychology; speech communications and rhetoric

STUDENTS SAY ". . ."

Academics

The benefits of going to a large, well-established state school, such as the University of New Hampshire, are exactly what one expects—its low in-state tuition, firmly established reputation, and place in the system allow it to offer "many resources to help students out in life." Located in tiny, beautiful Durham, the school "emphasizes research in every field, including non-science fields," and a lot of importance is placed "on the outdoors and the environment." The small town really fosters "lots of school spirit," and the laid-back denizens of UNH make it known that "having a good time" is a priority in their lives: "Weekends are for the Warriors." Most professors "truly care" about the students' learning so that "you never feel like a number at the school but rather a respected student," and professors "will get down and dirty when it comes to experiencing what they're teaching firsthand." Though there are definitely complaints that some can be "sub-par," a student "just needs to posses the initiative to go to their office hours" and they will get all the help they need. Some of the general education classes "are *huge*," and TAs can be difficult to understand, but for the most part, students report that they've had a "good experience" and that their academic careers has been "very successful." The Honors program is particularly challenging (in a very positive way) and offers "great seminar/inquiry classes that have about fifteen students." Students universally pan the administration, claiming it "is a massive bureaucracy that gets little done," partially due to poor communication, or one student puts it that "the left hand has no idea what the right hand is doing." "The school is way more challenging than I thought it would be because the administration makes things harder than they need to be," says a sophomore.

Life

The school is just "fifteen minutes to the beach, one hour to the mountains, and one hour to Boston," making the world a Wildcat's oyster. Partying is big here, and the weekends are crazy; "Everyone goes out pretty much every Thursday, Friday, and Saturday night." The small number of bars in town "makes the age limit pretty well enforced." After a hard night out, "there are many late night convenience stores and food places to go to." In fact, it can be "difficult to find activities to do on the weekend that don't involve drinking," though UNH does a good job of bringing in "popular comedians, musicians, bands, political figures, etc.," and the school has tons of "amazing" a capella groups, so there is "almost always something to go see." Sports are also big here: "We love our hockey and football," says a student. Though there's a pretty big housing crunch, the oft-used athletic and recreational facilities here are both convenient and excellent, and since everything on this "beautiful" campus is only about ten minutes away, "you walk pretty much everywhere," though public transportation and school-provided buses run often. Students do a lot of socializing over meals at the "eight cafés or in any of the three dining halls."

Student Body

This being New Hampshire, people are "very politically and socially aware." Students here are mostly middle-class and hail from New England (especially from New Hampshire, naturally), and a main point of contention among students is that there "is not a lot of ethnic/racial diversity," though the school is working on it. The size of UNH means that "even the most unique individual will find a group of friends," and even the most atypical students "fit in perfectly well." Most of these "laid-back" and "easy-to-get-along-with" Wildcats party, and it can be "hard to find one that doesn't." "*Everyone* skis or snowboards," and in the cold weather "Uggs and North Face fleece jackets abound."

FINANCIAL AID: 603-862-3600 • E-MAIL: ADMISSIONS@UNH.EDU • WEBSITE: WWW.UNH.EDU

THE PRINCETON REVIEW SAYS

Admissions

Very important factors considered include: Class rank, GPA, rigor of secondary school record. *Important factors considered include:* Recommendation(s). *Other factors considered include:* Standardized test scores, application essay, extracurricular activities, first generation, geographical residence, racial/ethnic status, state residency, talent/ability, volunteer work, work experience, alumni/ae relations, character/personal qualities. SAT or ACT required; ACT with Writing component required. TOEFL required of all international applicants. *Academic units required:* 4 English; 3 mathematics; 3 science; (2 science lab); 3 social studies; 2 foreign language. *Academic units recommended:* 4 English; 4 mathematics; 4 science; (3 science lab); 3 social studies; 3 foreign language; 1 visual/performing arts.

Financial Aid

Students should submit: FAFSA. Regular filing deadline is 3/1. The Princeton Review suggests that all financial aid forms be submitted as soon as possible after January 1. *Need-based scholarships/grants offered:* Federal Pell, SEOG, State scholarships/grants, private scholarships, the school's own gift aid. *Loan aid offered:* Direct Subsidized Stafford Loans, Direct Unsubsidized Stafford Loans, Direct PLUS loans, Federal Perkins Loans. Federal Work-Study Program available. Institutional employment available. Off-campus job opportunities are excellent.

The Inside Word

New Hampshire's emphasis on academic accomplishment in the admissions process makes it clear that the admissions committee is looking for students who have taken high school seriously. Standardized tests take as much of a backseat here as is possible at a large, public university.

THE SCHOOL SAYS "..."

From the Admissions Office

"The University of New Hampshire is an institution best defined by the students who take advantage of its opportunities. Enrolled students who are willing to engage in a high-quality academic community in some meaningful way, who have a genuine interest in discovering or developing new ideas, and who believe in each person's obligation to improve the community they live in typify the most successful students at UNH. Undergraduate students practice these three basic values in a variety of ways: by undertaking their own, independent research projects; by collaborating in faculty research; and by participating in study abroad, residential communities, community service, and other cultural programs.

"University of New Hampshire will require all high school graduates to submit results from the new SAT or the ACT (with the writing component). Students graduating from high school prior to 2006 can submit results from the old SAT or ACT. The UNH admissions process does not require SAT Subject tests."

SELECTIVITY

Admissions Rating	77
# of applicants	17,938
% of applicants accepted	78
% of acceptees attending	21

FRESHMAN PROFILE

Range SAT Critical Reading	490–600
Range SAT Math	510–610
Range SAT Writing	490–600
Range ACT Composite	22–27
Minimum paper TOEFL	550
Minimum web-based TOEFL	80
% graduated top 10% of class	20
% graduated top 25% of class	50
% graduated top 50% of class	89

DEADLINES

Early action	
Deadline	11/15
Notification	1/15
Regular	
Deadline	2/1
Nonfall registration?	Yes

APPLICANTS ALSO LOOK AT AND OFTEN PREFER
University of Vermont; University of Massachusetts Amherst; University of Connecticut

AND SOMETIMES PREFER
University of Rhode Island; Providence College; Boston University; Northeastern University

AND RARELY PREFER
University of Maine; Syracuse University; Boston College

FINANCIAL FACTS

Financial Aid Rating	70
Annual in-state tuition	$13,670
Annual out-of-state tuition	$26,390
Room and board	$10,056
Required fees	$2,826
Books and supplies	$1,200
% needy frosh rec. need-based scholarship or grant aid	74
% needy UG rec. need-based scholarship or grant aid	67
% needy frosh rec. non-need-based scholarship or grant aid	4
% needy UG rec. non-need-based scholarship or grant aid	4
% needy frosh rec. need-based self-help aid	95
% needy UG rec. need-based self-help aid	95
% frosh rec. any financial aid	86
% UG rec. any financial aid	81
% UG borrow to pay for school	77
Average cumulative indebtedness	$36,064
% frosh need fully met	18
% ugrads need fully met	16
Average % of frosh need met	79
Average % of ugrad need met	76

UNIVERSITY OF NEW MEXICO

OFFICE OF ADMISSIONS, ALBUQUERQUE, NM 87196-4895 • ADMISSIONS: 505-277-8900 • FAX: 505-277-6686

CAMPUS LIFE

Quality of Life Rating	65
Fire Safety Rating	72
Green Rating	84
Type of school	Public
Affiliation	No Affiliation
Environment	Urban

STUDENTS

Total undergrad enrollment	21,138
% male/female	44/56
% from out of state	10
% ugrads live on campus	45
# of fraternities(% ugrad med join)	14(5)
# of sororities(% ugrad women join)	10(6)
% African American	3
% Asian	3
%Caucasian	40
% Hispanic	42
% Native American	7
% international	2
# of countries represented	92

SURVEY SAYS . . .
Diverse student types on campus
Students get along with local community
Great off-campus food
Students are happy
Student publications are popular

ACADEMICS

Academic Rating	66
% students returning for sophomore year	78
% students graduating within 4 years	15
% students graduating within 6 years	48
Calendar	Semester
Student/faculty ratio	20:1
Profs interesting rating	67
Profs accessible rating	64

Most classes have 20–29 students.
Most lab/discussion sessions have
20–29 students.

MOST POPULAR MAJORS
biology; psychology; business administration

STUDENTS SAY "..."

Academics

Offering a "solid education" in a beautiful setting, the University of New Mexico offers "academic excellence...through some of the best teachers and tough classes." Students also cited affordability and excellent scholarships awarded to both in-state and out-of-state applicants as a decisive factor in attending UNM. The affordability also extends to "amazing opportunities to travel abroad." At UNM, "there is something here for everyone." The education program and variety of science programs—including Earth and planetary sciences, biology, and the premed and nursing programs—also attract students. Some students express frustration with it at times being "difficult to work your way around the student services system," but the "very knowledgeable" teaching faculty are roundly praised as "teachers who care." UNM students also agree that "professors are helpful [and] genuinely interested in your personal success." Professors are approachable both in class and out and "talk to and with you and not just at you." "It's very easy to come to instructors outside of class with questions," and "most professors are willing to meet with you at your convenience." As for UNM's greatest strengths, students cite both the "research-oriented staff" and "the research opportunities available. Oftentimes the research can be done with top-of-the-line equipment" nearby at Sandia National Labs, Los Alamos National Labs, and other well-known research institutes. In UNM's collaborative environment, students also often work together and "are eager to form study groups." Also, students who need additional help can rely on academic support with "tutoring, study groups and, supplemental instruction for most courses."

Life

With "ways for everyone to get involved," UNM offers "hundreds of great student organizations" providing "opportunities for fun events." There is a student group "that will fit everyone," and at UNM, "everyone seems to find their niche." Offering another opportunity to become more involved on campus, the Greek community "makes up a lot of the senate and other extracurricular activities" and "with them, any activity has fun attached." UNM students are divided in their support of the school's athletics program. With some thinking "this school should concentrate less on sports and more on academics," other students feel "attending games is a must." Students enjoy spending time at the Student Union Building (SUB), because "there is always something going on." Even with a dry campus, "a lot of people drink, just like at any college." Students often leave campus for Albuquerque and its "excellent nightlife." UNM students also mention attending concerts and art shows for fun. Students also go to the weekly free movies at The Cellar, and to stay active, students frequent the Johnson Gym. Students say that "hanging out at the duck pond is a great way to pass time between classes in warmer months," and "during the winter season, there are numerous ski resorts and places to go snowboarding that are not far away."

Student Body

Time and time again, students select UNM's "diversity" as its greatest strength, and one student even stated "no one will ever feel ethnically alone since there are so many different kinds of people." This also means at UNM, "people never get boring," and "you meet someone different every day." In addition to the diversity, the prevailing atmosphere is a friendly one where "people get along regardless of origin," but "like any school there are cliques...but that does not mean they do not interact with each other." One student reserved special praise for the university, "UNM is sensitive and very engaged with its diverse population of students...concerned with facilitating in-depth inquiry and learning," and more than one student observed that at UNM, "everyone brings something to the table."

FINANCIAL AID: 505-277-8900 • E-MAIL: APPLY@UNM.EDU • WEBSITE: WWW.UNM.EDU

THE PRINCETON REVIEW SAYS

Admissions

Factors considered include: Rigor of secondary school record, Academic GPA, Standardized Test Scores. SAT or ACT required; ACT with or without Writing component accepted. TOEFL required of all international applicants. *Academic units required:* 16 credits.

Financial Aid

Students should submit: FAFSA. The Princeton Review suggests that all financial aid forms be submitted as soon as possible after January 1. *Need-based scholarships/grants offered:* Federal Pell, SEOG, State scholarships/grants, private scholarships, the school's own gift aid, United Negro College Fund, federal nursing scholarships. *Loan aid offered:* Direct Subsidized Stafford Loans, Direct Unsubsidized Stafford Loans, Direct PLUS loans, Federal Perkins Loans, Federal Nursing Loans, State Loans, College/university loans from institutional funds. Federal Work-Study Program available.

The Inside Word

UNM offers online applications through its website, and you will also find specific scholastic standards for traditional and nontraditional students interested in applying to UNM. Traditional applicants should have completed core coursework, taken the ACT or SAT exam and have an average or above-average GPA if they would like to be considered for admission at UNM.

THE SCHOOL SAYS "..."

From the Admissions Office

"The University of New Mexico is a major research institution nestled in the heart of multicultural Albuquerque on one of the nation's most beautiful and unique campuses. Students learn in an environment graced by distinctive Southwestern architecture, beautiful plazas and fountains, spectacular art and a national arboretum...all within view of the 10,000-foot Sandia Mountains. At UNM, diversity is a way of learning with education enriched by a lively mix of students being taught by a world-class research faculty that includes a Nobel laureate, a MacArthur Fellow, and members of several national academies. UNM offers more than 200 degree programs and majors and has earned national recognition in dozens of disciplines, ranging from primary care medicine and clinical law to engineering, photography, Latin American history, and intercultural communications. Research and the quest for new knowledge fuels the university's commitment to an undergraduate education where students work side-by-side with many of the finest scholars in their fields.

"The university will continue to accept SAT or ACT scores, but the University of New Mexico does not require the writing component at this time. The SAT critical reading portion will be used with the SAT math to be considered in any admission decision based on formula. The use of ACT composite remains unchanged. These requirements are subject to change."

SELECTIVITY	
Admissions Rating	82
# of applicants	11,995
% of applicants accepted	57
% of acceptees attending	52

FRESHMAN PROFILE	
Range SAT Critical Reading	470–610
Range SAT Math	470–610
Range ACT Composite	19–25
Minimum paper TOEFL	520
Minimum web-based TOEFL	68
Average HS GPA	3.3

DEADLINES	
Regular	
Priority	6/15
Deadline	5/01
Notification	Rolling
Nonfall registration?	Yes

FINANCIAL FACTS	
Financial Aid Rating	65
Annual in-state tuition	$6,447
Annual out-of-state tuition	$25,860
Room and board	$8,454
Books and supplies	$1,048

UNIVERSITY OF NEW ORLEANS

UNIVERSITY OF NEW ORLEANS ADMISSIONS, NEW ORLEANS, LA 70148 • ADMISSIONS: 504-280-6595 • FAX: 504-280-5522

STUDENTS SAY ". . ."

Academics

The University of New Orleans is a public research university in one of the world's most fascinating and unique cities. This "not too big, not too small" school is a "diverse environment that makes it a welcoming area to be" and provides "lots of opportunities to develop our personality, leadership skills, and career skills." The diversity is a huge draw to students from all over the world (international students can even receive financial aid), and UNO "opens doors to students who come from different social and economic backgrounds," giving them "the opportunity to get an education that helps students to get a better future."

Professors at this "inclusive" school "push students to do excellence." You "can always find them in their office during office hours," and they "really connect with students." The engineering, film, and accounting programs are all "programs of distinction" at UNO (accounting is one of the few accredited by AACSB International), and classes stress real-world applicability. "There has never been a moment at UNO that I wasn't able to leave the classroom and go apply what I learned to my job immediately," says one part-time student. "My professors are generous with their time and knowledge," says another. Class sizes are small, and many classes focus on discussion, which "allows for increased learning and understanding." The school is "blessed" with having a large traditional student body matched with an equal percentage of nontraditional students (adult education), which "allows great mentorship between students and also pushed both sides to be aware of how they can positively affect the other generation's education."

Life

Obviously, the fact that the school is located in New Orleans "is a big plus," and "there is never a dull moment." "Eating and nightlife in New Orleans is a big part of our lives," says a student. "There is so much to do on campus and around the city, students often have to make efforts to keep their social calendars in check so that they have time to study," says a student. The campus is large enough to offer "many diverse academic, extracurricular, and social activities," yet small enough to easily access all classes. However, "upgrading facilities" (and cleaning them) is on the wish list of pretty much everyone here.

UNO offers "plenty of on campus activities" for students "to meet and work with other students of all backgrounds," including sports, movies, and "a lot of free entertainment." There are also "always political discussions happening on campus, as well as debates." "You can feel at home here but not get bored," says a student. The older students feel similarly comfortable in their environment. "I am unusual in that I am a much older student living on campus. Yet, the younger students have accepted me warmly and I have many friends," says one.

Student Body

More so than most schools, there really is no typical at this "very eclectic university," other than "determined, hardworking, and considerate." The school's large number of international students, adult learners, commuters, and locals "tend to get along rather well," with "those who live right on or near campus probably being more close-knit." Many students live off campus and work full time, which "creates in an environment where the people in your classes are there for a purpose." People here are "very colorful and outgoing" and "have no problem expressing themselves whether it's through clothing, lifestyles, or speech." "It is very easy to make friends here," says a student.

FINANCIAL AID: 504-280-6603 • E-MAIL: ADMISSIONS@UNO.EDU • WEBSITE: WWW.UNO.EDU

THE PRINCETON REVIEW SAYS

Admissions

Very important factors considered include: Class rank, GPA, rigor of secondary school record, standardized test scores. *Other factors considered include:* Geographical residence, state residency. SAT or ACT required; ACT with or without Writing component accepted. TOEFL required of all international applicants. *Academic units required:* 4 English; 4 mathematics; 4 science; 4 social studies; 2 foreign language; 1 visual/performing arts.

Financial Aid

Students should submit: FAFSA. The Princeton Review suggests that all financial aid forms be submitted as soon as possible after January 1. *Need-based scholarships/grants offered:* Federal Pell, SEOG, State scholarships/grants, private scholarships, the school's own gift aid. *Loan aid offered:* Direct Subsidized Stafford Loans, Direct Unsubsidized Stafford Loans, Direct PLUS loans, Federal Perkins Loans. Federal Work-Study Program available. Institutional employment available.

The Inside Word

Admission is straightforward here. Complete a basic college-bound high school curriculum with a GPA of at least 2.5 (with no remedial course work) and get at least an 23 on your ACT (SAT 1060), including a minimum score at or above 19 Math (460 SAT), 18 English (450 SAT). Nontraditional students who don't want to pay the exorbitant prices of the more well-known private universities in New Orleans can find their niche at UNO; if you're twenty-five or older, the only requirement for admission is a legitimate high school diploma or a GED.

THE SCHOOL SAYS "..."

From the Admissions Office

"The University of New Orleans has a wide array of academic programs. Quality student life programs include a campus bar, first-run movies, and a host of exciting student activities.

"UNO embraces its mission by providing the best educational opportunities for undergraduate and graduate students, conducting world-class research, and serving a diverse and cultured community in critical areas. UNO's most outstanding offerings include planning and urban studies; hotel, restaurant and tourism administration; educational leadership; earth and environmental studies; one of the nation's few programs in naval architecture and marine engineering; a leading jazz studies program; one of the top film programs in the region; and the only graduate arts administration program in the Gulf South."

"UNO will use the total score from the critical reading/verbal and math sub sections of the SAT or the composite score for the ACT. The writing components of the ACT and SAT will be used for placement purposes, but not for admission purposes, at the time."

SELECTIVITY

Admissions Rating	79
# of applicants	3,197
% of applicants accepted	50
% of acceptees attending	52

FRESHMAN PROFILE

Range SAT Critical Reading	470–590
Range SAT Math	490–620
Range ACT Composite	21–25
Minimum paper TOEFL	525
Average HS GPA	3.21
% graduated top 10% of class	16
% graduated top 25% of class	41
% graduated top 50% of class	66

DEADLINES

Regular	
Priority	1/15
Deadline	7/25
Notification	Rolling
Nonfall registration?	Yes

FINANCIAL FACTS

Financial Aid Rating	68
Annual in-state tuition	$5,164
Annual out-of-state tuition	$17,176
Room and board	$8,504
Required fees	$758
Books and supplies	$1,300
% needy frosh rec. need-based scholarship or grant aid	75
% needy UG rec. need-based scholarship or grant aid	65
% needy frosh rec. non-need-based scholarship or grant aid	73
% needy UG rec. non-need-based scholarship or grant aid	40
% needy frosh rec. need-based self-help aid	35
% needy UG rec. need-based self-help aid	49
% frosh rec. any financial aid	74
% UG rec. any financial aid	66
% UG borrow to pay for school	19
Average cumulative indebtedness	$19,957
% frosh need fully met	11
% ugrads need fully met	5
Average % of frosh need met	55
Average % of ugrad need met	46

THE UNIVERSITY OF NORTH CAROLINA AT ASHEVILLE

CPO #1320, ASHEVILLE, NC 28804-8502 • ADMISSIONS: 828-251-6481 • FAX: 828-251-6482

CAMPUS LIFE

Quality of Life Rating	96
Fire Safety Rating	95
Green Rating	74
Type of school	Public
Affiliation	No Affiliation
Environment	Town

STUDENTS

Total undergrad enrollment	3,323
% male/female	43/57
% from out of state	12
% frosh from public high school	87
% frosh live on campus	95
% ugrads live on campus	40
# of fraternities (% ugrad men join)	2 (3)
# of sororities (% ugrad women join)	2 (3)
% African American	3
% Asian	1
% Caucasian	83
% Hispanic	4
% Native American	<1
% international	<1
# of countries represented	32

SURVEY SAYS . . .

Political activism is popular
Students are happy
Lab facilities are great
Students are friendly
Students get along with local community
Students environmentally aware
Students love Asheville, NC
Great off-campus food
Campus feels safe
Athletic facilities are great

ACADEMICS

Academic Rating	87
% students returning for sophomore year	80
% students graduating within 4 years	37
% students graduating within 6 years	60
Calendar	Semester
Student/faculty ratio	14:1
Profs interesting rating	96
Profs accessible rating	83

Most classes have 20–29 students.
Most lab/discussion sessions have 20–29 students.

MOST POPULAR MAJORS

English language and literature; psychology; environmental studies

STUDENTS SAY ". . ."

Academics

Undergrads at UNC—Asheville rave about their top-notch academic experience. Professors are "devoted and passionate [about] their fields of study, and it shows in the classroom." Importantly, "even though you may not be totally fascinated by the subject initially, the professors' enthusiasm for each course is contagious." Students also appreciate Asheville's "liberal arts approach." As one senior English lit major says, "It's wonderful when every semester, at least two seemingly unrelated classes end up teaching the same lessons through different means and subjects." Though "course material is challenging," students take solace in knowing that "an A is totally achievable." This is due in part to the fact that "professors are available and more than willing to assist students outside of class." One environmental studies major adds, "The classes are small enough that the professors know you by name and seem to care if you do well." Furthermore, "tutoring sessions…are free and plentiful" for those undergrads who feel that they require more assistance. There are some undergrads who feel that the administration is "relatively detached from school life" and "out of touch with the students," others tout the deans as being "unusually accessible."

Life

With roughly "two-thirds of [the] student [body] living off-campus," some undergrads warn that life "can be slow on the weekends." Fortunately, one senior confidently declares that campus life "has started to pick up in the last few years." Freshman are required to live on campus their first year. Indeed, "students enjoy a wide range of activities" from playing "Frisbee golf on the quad" to attending one of many "lectures" or "basketball games" held on campus. While there is a Greek system, "partying does not define the school." Many students are "environmentally conscious" and spend a lot of energy helping shape "campus policies, including [instituting] new, reusable take-out boxes from the school cafeteria." Undergrads love the fact that they are nestled "in the Blue Ridge Mountains." The university offers a fantastic "outdoors program that [hosts] popular rock-climbing, caving, hiking, and kayaking [trips]." Students also give hometown Asheville high marks. One student says, "You can't take three steps downtown without tripping over some kind of festival or street performance." A favorite Asheville activity for many students is "the drum circle" where "people gather every Friday evening (in warm weather), circulating, dancing, thrumming, and drumming. Drummers, amateur to experienced, bring their own instruments to bang upon. People without personal beat abilities twist through the crowds to dance or simply watch from the sidelines."

Student Body

UNC—Asheville seems to hold appeal for self-described "hippies." One sophomore says, "This school attracts the sort of people who get excited about local, organic, dairy-free muffins and sandals made from recycled flax." Indeed many undergrads "care about the environment, [are] liberal-leaning, enjoy the outdoors, [and are] pretty sociable." Happily, the university "fosters the idea that individuality is essential," and students assure us that everyone "is easily accepted here" regardless of political affiliation. Perhaps this acceptance stems from the fact that the campus welcomes students from a variety of "economic backgrounds, religious backgrounds and sexual orientations." Asheville does manage to attract both a large number of "commuter students" as well as "a lot of nontraditional students."

THE UNIVERSITY OF NORTH CAROLINA AT ASHEVILLE

FINANCIAL AID: 828-251-6535 • E-MAIL: ADMISSIONS@UNCA.EDU • WEBSITE: WWW.UNCA.EDU

THE PRINCETON REVIEW SAYS

Admissions

Very important factors considered include: GPA, rigor of secondary school record. *Important factors considered include:* Class rank, standardized test scores, application essay, recommendation(s). *Other factors considered include:* Extracurricular activities, first generation, geographical residence, interview, racial/ethnic status, state residency, talent/ability, volunteer work, work experience, alumni/ae relations, level of applicant's interest. SAT or ACT required; ACT with Writing component required. TOEFL required of all international applicants. *Academic units required:* 4 English; 4 mathematics; 3 science; (1 science lab); 1 social studies; 2 foreign language; 1 history. *Academic units recommended:* 4 academic electives.

Financial Aid

Students should submit: FAFSA. The Princeton Review suggests that all financial aid forms be submitted as soon as possible after January 1. *Need-based scholarships/grants offered:* Federal Pell, SEOG, State scholarships/grants, private scholarships, the school's own gift aid. *Loan aid offered:* Direct Subsidized Stafford Loans, Direct Unsubsidized Stafford Loans, Direct PLUS loans, Federal Perkins Loans, State Loans, College/university loans from institutional funds. Federal Work-Study Program available. Institutional employment available. Off-campus job opportunities are good.

The Inside Word

UNC at Asheville provides a sound public education in a small campus atmosphere, and an increasing number of students are setting their sights on it each year. In kind, the school works diligently to create a diverse student body and thoroughly analyzes each application it receives. Although selectivity is rising, candidates who demonstrate reasonable academic success and involvement in a variety of extracurricular activities should be able to secure admittance.

THE SCHOOL SAYS "..."

From the Admissions Office

"If you want to learn how to think, how to analyze and solve problems on your own, and how to become your own best teacher then, a broad-based liberal arts education is the key. UNC Asheville focuses on undergraduates, with a core curriculum covering natural science, math, social sciences, humanities, language and culture, arts and ideas, and health and fitness. Students thrive in small classes, with a faculty dedicated first of all to teaching. The liberal arts emphasis develops discriminating thinkers, expert and creative communicators with a passion for learning. These are qualities you need for today's challenges and the changes of tomorrow.

"The University of North Carolina at Asheville requires the SAT or for students submitting an ACT score, the ACT with the writing component."

SELECTIVITY

Admissions Rating	85
# of applicants	3,173
% of applicants accepted	69
% of acceptees attending	27

FRESHMAN PROFILE

Range SAT Critical Reading	560–660
Range SAT Math	540–630
Range SAT Writing	530–630
Range ACT Composite	24–27
Minimum paper TOEFL	550
Minimum web-based TOEFL	79
Average HS GPA	3.98
% graduated top 10% of class	22
% graduated top 25% of class	54
% graduated top 50% of class	90

DEADLINES

Early action	
Deadline	11/15
Notification	12/15
Regular	
Priority	11/15
Deadline	2/15
Notification	Rolling
Nonfall registration?	Yes

FINANCIAL FACTS

Financial Aid Rating	87
Annual in tuition	$3,666
Annual out-of-state tuition	$17,488
Room and board	$7,904
Required fees	$2,575
Books and supplies	$950
% needy frosh rec. need-based scholarship or grant aid	96
% needy UG rec. need-based scholarship or grant aid	90
% needy frosh rec. non-need-based scholarship or grant aid	11
% needy UG rec. non-need-based scholarship or grant aid	12
% needy frosh rec. need-based self-help aid	65
% needy UG rec. need-based self-help aid	73
% frosh rec. any financial aid	71
% UG rec. any financial aid	72
% UG borrow to pay for school	58
Average cumulative indebtedness	$17,696
% frosh need fully met	27
% ugrads need fully met	29
Average % of frosh need met	76
Average % of ugrad need met	77

THE UNIVERSITY OF NORTH CAROLINA AT CHAPEL HILL

CAMPUS BOX #2200, CHAPEL HILL, NC 27599-2200 • ADMISSIONS: 919-966-3621 • FAX: 919-962-3045

CAMPUS LIFE

Quality of Life Rating	90
Fire Safety Rating	89
Green Rating	97
Type of school	Public
Affiliation	No Affiliation
Environment	Town

STUDENTS

Total undergrad enrollment	17,882
% male/female	42/58
% from out of state	18
% frosh from public high school	79
% frosh live on campus	100
% ugrads live on campus	53
# of fraternities (% ugrad men join)	32 (17)
# of sororities (% ugrad women join)	23(18)
% African American	8
% Asian	9
% Caucasian	66
% Hispanic	7
% Native American	<1
% international	2
# of countries represented	106

SURVEY SAYS . . .

Everyone loves the Tar Heels
Student publications are popular
Students are happy
Great library
Students love Chapel Hill, NC
Great off-campus food
Athletic facilities are great
Intramural sports are popular

ACADEMICS

Academic Rating	77
% students returning for sophomore year	96
% students graduating within 4 years	81
% students graduating within 6 years	90
Calendar	Semester
Student/faculty ratio	13:1
Profs interesting rating	75
Profs accessible rating	71

Most classes have 10–19 students.
Most lab/discussion sessions have 10–19 students.

MOST POPULAR MAJORS
biology; psychology; economics

STUDENTS SAY ". . ."

Academics

It's quite an understatement to say students at UNC—Chapel Hill are proud of their school. One calls it his "dream school," while another calls it the "perfect mixture of academics, sports, and social life." Although its relative low cost makes UNC a great bargain in higher education, academic rigor doesn't take a back seat, and the vast majority of students say it's one of the main reasons they chose the school. The journalism, business, public health, and nursing programs are ranked among the best in the country, but the students hail the overall liberal arts curriculum because it creates well-rounded adults who "can handle any intellectual obstacle." In describing the instructors, students use words like "world-class," "brilliant," and "incredible," while also noting that they're "warm," "welcoming," and "passionate" about their work and their students. "Most of my professors have been great, and some have been phenomenal." Faculty members are generous with their time outside of class, patiently explaining "even the most difficult material" and using e-mail to announce changes. Some complain about large classes and warn incoming students that they will have to take the initiative and "speak up," because they won't be "coddled." The school's academic-advising system still comes in for sharp criticism. "Students are on their own there," one student says.

Life

With nearly 18,000 undergrads, UNC is large enough that students rarely are lacking for something to do. Tar Heel men's basketball probably is at the top of the list; indeed, for many rabid fans, the Dean Smith Center is the center of the universe, especially when Duke is the opponent. One student sums up the school's essence this way: "It's the feeling of running through the beautiful old quad by Davie Poplar on the way to Franklin Street after a big win." The consensus is maintaining grades requires such an effort, letting off steam on weekends is a reward. "Life at UNC is full throttle. People work hard and play hard." Many flock to the bars, restaurants and coffee shops of Franklin Street, but others prefer the music scene in nearby Carrboro or staying on campus to participate in a function sponsored by one of the hundreds of student groups. The campus itself is gorgeous and filled with history. Although only 17 percent of students belong to a fraternity or sorority, the Greek organizations are a big part of the social scene. "When you're writing thirty-page papers on twentieth-century German philosophy and working two jobs, a night where you get to dress up as a biker chick and listen to AC/DC all night at the bar is a welcome reprieve," one sorority member says.

Student Body

One student after another comments about the feeling of generosity that pervades UNC—"the epitome of Southern hospitality"—and how it extends beyond mere school spirit and the wearing of Carolina blue and white on game days. "Carolina is family," one student says. "Most of us here are crazy about sports, but most will do anything at all to help a fellow UNC student." "Although the student body is very diverse, a commonality among students is the desire to serve others and work for humanitarian efforts." One reason for the closeness is that the vast majority of students hail from the Tar Heel state. So there are "lots of down-home, North Carolina types who excelled in their rural high schools." Students and faculty are viewed as leaning liberal politically, which makes for some interesting exchanges. "Political activism is huge here," a student says. But even though it's a vast school, "it has a place for everyone." "There are really only two common denominators: commitment to some kind of excellence (academic, extracurricular, etc.) and rooting against Duke."

THE UNIVERSITY OF NORTH CAROLINA AT CHAPEL HILL

FINANCIAL AID: 919-962-8396 • E-MAIL: UNCHELP@ADMISSIONS.UNC.EDU • WEBSITE: WWW.UNC.EDU

THE PRINCETON REVIEW SAYS

Admissions

Very important factors considered include: GPA, rigor of secondary school record, standardized test scores, application essay, extracurricular activities, recommendation, state residency, talent/ability, character/personal qualities. *Important factors considered include:* Class rank, volunteer work, work experience. *Other factors considered include:* First generation, racial/ethnic status, alumni/ae relations. SAT or ACT required; ACT with Writing component required. TOEFL or IELTS required of all international applicants for whom English is not a first language. *Academic units required:* 4 English; 4 mathematics; 3 science; (1 science lab); 1 social studies; 2 foreign language; 1 history; 1 academic elective.

Financial Aid

Students should submit: FAFSA, CSS/Financial Aid PROFILE. The Princeton Review suggests that all financial aid forms be submitted as soon as possible after January 1. *Need-based scholarships/grants offered:* Federal Pell, SEOG, State scholarships/grants, private scholarships, the school's own gift aid. *Loan aid offered:* Direct Subsidized Stafford Loans, Direct Unsubsidized Stafford Loans, Direct PLUS loans, Federal Perkins Loans, State Loans, College/university loans from institutional funds. Applicants will be notified of awards beginning 3/15. Federal Work-Study Program available. Institutional employment available. Off-campus job opportunities are good.

The Inside Word

UNC's admissions process is highly selective. North Carolina students compete against other students from across the state for 82 percent of all spaces available in the freshman class; out-of-state students compete for the remaining 18 percent of the spaces. State residents will find the admissions standards high, and out-of-state applicants will find that it's one of the hardest offers of admission to come by in the country.

THE SCHOOL SAYS "..."

From the Admissions Office

"One of the leading research and teaching institutions in the world, UNC Chapel Hill offers first-rate faculty, innovative academic programs, and students who are smart, friendly, and committed to public service. Students take full advantage of extensive undergraduate research opportunities, a study abroad program with programs on every continent except Antarctica, and 600-plus clubs and organizations. We offer all this in Chapel Hill, one of the greatest and most welcoming college towns anywhere.

"Carolina's commitment to excellence, access, and affordability is reflected in premier scholarships, such as the prestigious Morehead-Cain and Robertson Scholarships, as well the Carolina Covenant, a national model that enables students from low-income families to graduate from Carolina debt-free. We invite you to visit—talk with our professors, attend a class, spend time with our students, and stroll across our beautiful residential campus, where friendly people and exciting events are within easy walking distance.

"All first-year applicants are required to submit an SAT or an ACT with the writing component. While test scores are important, our holistic review includes other important factors such course work, grades, and extracurricular activities.

"Just by applying for admission, applicants are considered for a variety of special programs open only to first-year students including assured admission into business, education and journalism or summer study abroad immersion and research programs. We offer two admission deadlines, neither of which are binding."

SELECTIVITY

Admissions Rating	97
# of applicants	30,835
% of applicants accepted	27
% of acceptees attending	48
# offered a place on the wait list	2,445
% accepting a place on wait list	49
% admitted from wait list	32

FRESHMAN PROFILE

Range SAT Critical Reading	590–700
Range SAT Math	610–710
Range SAT Writing	590–690
Range ACT Composite	26–31
Minimum paper TOEFL	600
Minimum web-based TOEFL	100
Average HS GPA	4.56
% graduated top 10% of class	78
% graduated top 25% of class	96
% graduated top 50% of class	99

DEADLINES

Early action	
Deadline	10/15
Notification	1/31
Regular	
Deadline	1/10
Nonfall registration?	No

APPLICANTS ALSO LOOK AT AND SOMETIMES PREFER

Duke University; University of Virginia; Vanderbilt University; Harvard University; Yale University; Princeton University

AND RARELY PREFER

Wake Forest University; North Carolina State University

FINANCIAL FACTS

Financial Aid Rating	90
Annual in-state tuition	$6,423
Annual out-of-state tuition	$28,205
Room and board	$10,008
Required fees	$1,917
Books and supplies	$1,328
% needy frosh rec. need-based scholarship or grant aid	95
% needy UG rec. need-based scholarship or grant aid	96
% needy frosh rec. non-need-based scholarship or grant aid	9
% needy UG rec. non-need-based scholarship or grant aid	6
% needy frosh rec. need-based self-help aid	65
% needy UG rec. need-based self-help aid	71
% frosh rec. any financial aid	70
% UG rec. any financial aid	64
% UG borrow to pay for school	39
Average cumulative indebtedness	$17,602
% frosh need fully met	68
% ugrads need fully met	82
Average % of frosh need met	100
Average % of ugrad need met	100

THE UNIVERSITY OF NORTH CAROLINA AT GREENSBORO

1400 SPRING GARDEN STREET, GREENSBORO, NC 27402-6170 • ADMISSIONS: 336-334-5243 • FAX: 336-334-4180

CAMPUS LIFE

Quality of Life Rating	77
Fire Safety Rating	77
Green Rating	95
Type of school	Public
Affiliation	No Affiliation
Environment	City

STUDENTS

Total undergrad enrollment	14,138
% male/female	35/65
% from out of state	6
% frosh from public high school	95
% frosh live on campus	81
% ugrads live on campus	32
# of fraternities	10(4)
# of sororities	9(4)
% African American	25
% Asian	4
% Caucasian	58
% Hispanic	6
% Native American	<1
% international	2
# of countries represented	45

SURVEY SAYS . . .

Diverse student types on campus
Students get along with local community
Students are happy

ACADEMICS

Academic Rating	75
% students returning for sophomore year	74
% students graduating within 4 years	30
% students graduating within 6 years	55
Calendar	Semester
Student/faculty ratio	17:1
Profs interesting rating	71
Profs accessible rating	70

Most classes have 20–29 students.
Most lab/discussion sessions have
20–29 students.

MOST POPULAR MAJORS

business administration and management;
biology

STUDENTS SAY " . . ."

Academics

Students describe the University of North Carolina at Greensboro as "about a half-and-half commuter school with great specialized programs and schools such as nursing, education, dance, and music." Undergrads here praise the "high quality of education at a significantly reduced rate, while having the smaller classes allowing closer bonds between faculty and students" than one could reasonably expect for the tuition charged. The key here is the faculty, because according to one student, "UNCG places a big emphasis on having great teachers. There are some duds, but overall, more of them are fantastic than anything else." The school excels in some off-the-beaten-path areas like programs in kinesiology, deaf education, and human development and family studies, which all receive enthusiastic praise from students. Undergrads also love the "opportunities that are given to network with businesses and people outside of campus" and the "great internships" the school helps them find. Nontraditional students appreciate the "great support system for adult students." As the school's reputation continues to improve, some worry this "historically moderate-sized university where student well-being was the first priority…will change into a large research university where the focus is raising more and more money." One undeniable upside of the school's increased stature is that "you feel like you are respected in the community when you tell someone that you are a student at UNCG."

Life

UNCG is conveniently located "a mile from downtown and close to surrounding schools: Guilford College, NC A&T, Greensboro College, Elon, UNC, and NC State." One student observes, "With six colleges around UNCG, a metropolis of 270,000-plus (1.1 million in the metro area), and access within a three-hour drive to both beaches and mountains, there is always something to do." On campus "UNCG makes it easy for anyone and everyone to fit in and feel included. Through clubs, students have the ability to offer ideas and have them implemented. There's also intramural sports and free events." The high-profile arts programs on campus yield some wonderful cultural opportunities. "The Weatherspoon Museum of Art is amazing at showcasing the most modern American art and keeps this provincial little town on its toes," writes one artist. A performing arts student adds, "There are wonderful concerts and plays and lectures here. It's a great cultural center and you can always have something to do as long as you look for it." Intercollegiate athletics, students tell us, "are not as popular as they could be, even though they are often ranked nationally, or at least ranked in the conference." Many here feel the addition of a football team (the school has none) would change that. "It would really bring the school spirit up," opines one undergrad. The school's many commuters warn that "parking is horrendous."

Student Body

UNCG is a big school with "many people from all walks of life, social/cultural backgrounds, etc. The university promotes cultural diversity and acceptance and tolerance of people of different backgrounds." One student reports, "One minute you see a bunch of music majors talking about how much Bach has affected their life, and the next minute, you see a bunch of sorority girls discussing the Gap. Mainly, I have observed that sorority girls stick together, jocks stick together, etc." As at many state schools, "about half of the students at UNCG came here to party. The other half consists of hardworking students who are generally frustrated with the slacker mentality in a lot of our classes. This is less of a problem once you get past the intro-level lectures."

FINANCIAL AID: 336-334-5702 • E-MAIL: ADMISSIONS@UNCG.EDU • WEBSITE: WWW.UNCG.EDU

THE PRINCETON REVIEW SAYS

Admissions

Very important factors considered include: GPA, rigor of secondary school record. *Important factors considered include:* Standardized test scores. *Other factors considered include:* Application essay, recommendation(s). SAT or ACT required; ACT with Writing component required. TOEFL required of all international applicants. *Academic units required:* 4 English; 4 mathematics; 3 science; (1 science lab); 2 social studies; 2 foreign language.

Financial Aid

Students should submit: FAFSA. The Princeton Review suggests that all financial aid forms be submitted as soon as possible after January 1. *Need-based scholarships/grants offered:* Federal Pell, SEOG, State scholarships/grants, private scholarships, the school's own gift aid. *Loan aid offered:* Direct Subsidized Stafford Loans, Direct Unsubsidized Stafford Loans, Direct PLUS loans, Federal Perkins Loans, State Loans, College/university loans from institutional funds. Federal Work-Study Program available. Institutional employment available. Off-campus job opportunities are good.

The Inside Word

UNCG has yet to gain much attention outside of regional circles so, at least for the moment, gaining admission is not particularly difficult. The usual public university considerations apply; expect the admissions office to focus primarily on grades and test scores, but the required essay and other items submitted by the student are considered as well. Out-of-staters will find a much smoother path to admission here than at Chapel Hill and will still be within reasonable reach of internship and career possibilities in the Research Triangle.

THE SCHOOL SAYS "..."

From the Admissions Office

"UNCG is committed to student success. Challenging academic programs and exceptional teaching provide a solid learning foundation in a supportive environment. Hands-on experiences in internships, undergraduate research, and service-learning programs bring learning to life. An ambitious expansion of on-campus housing and learning communities (now open to more than half of our freshman class) creates a close-knit campus atmosphere and an engaged community.

"In addition to excellence in our academic programs, we are looking for students with outstanding records who will benefit from these challenging programs. As admission to UNCG becomes more competitive, our goal is to assess students' entire academic record, beginning with a combination of their overall cumulative grade point average (GPA) and SAT or ACT scores. Freshman applicants must submit at least one SAT or ACT score (including the writing component). We also will review other factors such as students' entire high school record, course selection, senior class schedule, and an essay.

"UNCG takes pride in its global focus and offers an extensive (but affordable) study abroad exchange program. The Lloyd International Honors College offers a unique opportunity for talented students in any major to benefit from a rich intellectual life with a global perspective. UNCG's ideal size enables students to excel as individuals and get connected through more than 200 student organizations, intramural, club and intercollegiate sports, Greeks, outdoor adventures, a vibrant arts community, and a friendly Southern city that quickly starts to feel like home."

SELECTIVITY

Admissions Rating	78
# of applicants	10,154
% of applicants accepted	58
% of acceptees attending	42

FRESHMAN PROFILE

Range SAT Critical Reading	470–560
Range SAT Math	480–560
Range SAT Writing	450–540
Range ACT Composite	21–25
Minimum paper TOEFL	550
Minimum web-based TOEFL	213
Average HS GPA	3.64
% graduated top 10% of class	22
% graduated top 25% of class	48
% graduated top 50% of class	84

DEADLINES

Regular	
Priority	11/1
Deadline	3/1
Nonfall registration?	Yes

FINANCIAL FACTS

Financial Aid Rating	72
Annual in-state tuition	$3,932
Annual out-of-state tuition	$18,794
Required fees	$2,507
Books and supplies	$916
% needy frosh rec. need-based scholarship or grant aid	62
% needy UG rec. need-based scholarship or grant aid	64
% needy frosh rec. non-need-based scholarship or grant aid	78
% needy UG rec. non-need-based scholarship or grant aid	71
% needy frosh rec. need-based self-help aid	66
% needy UG rec. need-based self-help aid	68
% frosh rec. any financial aid	77
% UG rec. any financial aid	71
% UG borrow to pay for school	73
Average cumulative indebtedness	$24,595
% frosh need fully met	21
% ugrads need fully met	18
Average % of frosh need met	52
Average % of ugrad need met	56

THE UNIVERSITY OF NORTH DAKOTA

GORECKI CENTER, 3501 UNIVERSITY AVE., GRAND FORKS, ND 58202-8357 • ADMISSIONS: 701-777-3000 • FAX: 701-777-2721

CAMPUS LIFE

Quality of Life Rating	72
Fire Safety Rating	75
Green Rating	80
Type of school	Public
Affiliation	No Affiliation
Environment	Town

STUDENTS

Total undergrad enrollment	11,724
% male/female	57/43
% from out of state	59
% frosh from public high school	92
% frosh live on campus	87
% ugrads live on campus	27
# of fraternities (% ugrad men join)	12 (13)
# of sororities (% ugrad women join)	6 (15)
% African American	2
% Asian	2
% Caucasian	81
% Hispanic	3
% Native American	2
% International	6
# of countries represented	65

SURVEY SAYS . . .
Athletic facilities are great
Lots of beer drinking
Hard liquor is popular

ACADEMICS

Academic Rating	72
% students returning for sophomore year	75
% students graduating within 4 years	24
% students graduating within 6 years	55
Calendar	Semester
Student/faculty ratio	19:1
Profs interesting rating	67
Profs accessible rating	68

Most classes have 20–29 students.
Most lab/discussion sessions have
  10–19 students.

MOST POPULAR MAJORS
nursing; psychology; biology

STUDENTS SAY ". . ."

Academics
The University of North Dakota, located in the town of Grand Forks, is a public university that is "incredibly proud of its aviation department," and many students agree that the pride shows through. While the professors early in a student's career may be a little bit of "a mixed bag," everyone agrees that almost every professor is "willing to help…outside of class at any time." Once students get beyond the general education classes and into their majors, most professors are "absolutely great and inspiring," "specifically in [the] School of Aerospace Sciences." Many of the professors in the School of Aerospace Sciences, and other colleges in the university, such as the College of Nursing and Professional Disciplines, have "worked in [their respective] industry," before coming to UND to teach. It's a sincere desire of the professors that each student learns the material and real-world applications and doesn't just "pass the class," that probably leads to the University's "high employment rate after graduation." The university also offers "distance education programs" that allows students to attend "completely online" and to participate in "intensive labs" and lectures via the Internet for those who want to pursue their educations without giving up their full-time jobs. Whichever path students choose, everyone praises the "low cost" and says, "You will not find a better education for the same amount of money." Students also understand that with those reasonable tuitions come some compromises. While there are quite a few nice buildings, such as the previously mentioned aviation department, students remark that the general education buildings are "a tad outdated." (Since this printing, several buildings have been renovated/constructed.)

Life
Opinions range on the size and options for scenic hang outs in the city of Grand Forks, with some calling it a "pretty decent-sized town," and others saying, "The town offers little to do." Most people tend to make their own fun, and "partying" seems to be fairly prevalent. Most students tend to stay inside as the weather can get "freezing cold" during the winter months. Weekend programming, put together by various student organizations, holds events every Friday and Saturday night, and most students try "to attend every UND Weekend Programming [event]." Hockey games are another event that everyone raves about, saying they are "a blast to go to, whether you like hockey or not." There is also a new "state-of-the-art" Wellness Center that is "extremely popular," and it offers a lot of free classes for students. While many students choose to live off-campus, a decent amount of students complain about the "lack of parking" for those who commute.

Student Body
A "typical" student at University of North Dakota is "someone who goes to class, but also balances their time being involved in organizations." Most are usually involved in numerous student groups, but they always make sure to have the time to "work out and hang with friends." Students seem to mostly come from one of two places: either "rural North Dakota or from the Twin Cities." Many notice "a divide along those lines." Most are Caucasian, leading some students to cite the University's need to draw in a slightly "more diverse" crowd.

FINANCIAL AID: 701-777-3121 • E-MAIL: UND.ADMISSIONS@UND.EDU • WEBSITE: WWW.UND.EDU

THE PRINCETON REVIEW SAYS

Admissions

Very important factors considered include: GPA, standardized test scores. *Important factors considered include:* Rigor of secondary school record. *Other factors considered include:* Recommendation(s). SAT or ACT required; SAT and SAT Subject Tests or ACT recommended; ACT with or without Writing component accepted. TOEFL required of all international applicants. *Academic units required:* 4 English; 3 mathematics; 3 science; (3 science lab); 3 social studies. *Academic units recommended:* 1 foreign language.

Financial Aid

The Princeton Review suggests that all financial aid forms be submitted as soon as possible after January 1. Federal Work-Study Program available. Institutional employment available. Off-campus job opportunities are excellent.

The Inside Word

As a potential incoming student, the University of North Dakota is ready and willing to help you apply; the website has applications broken down by student type, and for those unable to schedule a visit in person, there is also a virtual tour of campus. You'll also find admissions guidelines to help you see if you would be accepted for admission: The higher your GPA, the lower your SAT and ACT scores can be and vice-versa. However, the school says that everyone should apply for admission, even if you don't meet these standards, since your application will be reviewed by a committee that may make the decision based on other factors.

THE SCHOOL SAYS "..."

From the Admissions Office

"More than 11,000 undergraduate students come to the University of North Dakota each year, from every state in the nation and nearly seventy countries. They're impressed by our academic excellence, more than 200 programs, our dedication to the liberal arts mission, and alumni success record. More than seventy percent of the University's new students rank in the top half of their high school classes, with more than one-third in the top quarter. As the oldest and most diversified institution of higher education in the Dakotas, Montana, Wyoming, and western Minnesota, UND is a comprehensive teaching and research university. Yet the University provides individual attention that may be missing at very large universities. UND graduates are highly regarded among prospective employers. Representatives from more than 200 regional and national companies recruit UND students every year. Our campus is approximately 98 percent accessible.

"Students applying for admission to UND are required to take either the ACT or SAT unless they are 25 or older. The ACT writing component is not a requirement for admission, and SAT results considered include only the math and critical reading sections."

SELECTIVITY

Admissions Rating	75
# of applicants	4,735
% of applicants accepted	71
% of acceptees attending	57

FRESHMAN PROFILE

Range ACT Composite	21–26
Minimum paper TOEFL	525
Average HS GPA	3.33
% graduated top 10% of class	15
% graduated top 25% of class	39
% graduated top 50% of class	71

DEADLINES

Regular Decision	
Priority	3/01
Nonfall registration?	Yes

APPLICANTS ALSO LOOK AT AND OFTEN PREFER

University of Minnesota—Twin Cities;
University of Wisconsin-Madison

FINANCIAL FACTS

Financial Aid Rating	75
Annual in-state tuition	$6,159
Annual out-of-state tuition	$16,444
Room and board	$6,586
Required fees	$1,349
Books and supplies	$1,000

UNIVERSITY OF NOTRE DAME

220 MAIN BUILDING, NOTRE DAME, IN 46556 • ADMISSIONS: 574-631-7505 • FAX: 574-631-8865

CAMPUS LIFE

Quality of Life Rating	68
Fire Safety Rating	94
Green Rating	95
Type of school	Private
Affiliation	Roman Catholic
Environment	City

STUDENTS

Total undergrad enrollment	8,466
% male/female	53/47
% from out of state	92
% frosh from public high school	42
% frosh live on campus	100
% ugrads live on campus	80
% African American	4
% Asian	6
% Caucasian	71
% Hispanic	10
% Native American	<1
% international	4
# of countries represented	87

SURVEY SAYS . . .

Everyone loves the Fighting Irish
Great food on campus
School is well run
Student publications are popular

ACADEMICS

Academic Rating	84
% students returning for sophomore year	99
% students graduating within 4 years	90
% students graduating within 6 years	95
Calendar	Semester
Student/faculty ratio	11:1
Profs interesting rating	79
Profs accessible rating	85

Most classes have 10–19 students.
Most lab/discussion sessions have
10–19 students.

MOST POPULAR MAJORS
finance; psychology; political science

STUDENTS SAY " . . ."

Academics

Notre Dame has many traditions, including a "devotion to undergraduate education" you might not expect from a school with such an athletic reputation. Professors here are, by all accounts, "wonderful": "Not only are they invested in their students," they're "genuinely passionate about their fields of study," "enthusiastic and animated in lectures," and "always willing to meet outside of class to give extra help." Wary that distance might breed academic disengagement, professors ensure "large lectures are broken down into smaller discussion groups once a week to help with class material and…give the class a personal touch." For its part, "the administration tries its best to stay on top of the students' wants and needs." They make it "extremely easy to get in touch with anyone." Like the professors, administrators try to make personal connections with students. For example, "our president (a priest), as well as both of our presidents emeritus, make it a point to interact with the students in a variety of ways—teaching a class, saying mass in the dorms, etc." Overall, "while classes are difficult," "students are competitive against one another," and "it's necessary to study hard and often, [but] there's also time to do other things."

Life

Life at Notre Dame is centered around two things—"residential life" and "sports." The "dorms on campus provide the social structure" and supply undergrads with tons of opportunities to get involved and have fun." "During the school week" students "study a lot, but on the weekends everyone seems to make up for the lack of partying during the week." The school "does not have any fraternities or sororities, but campus is not dry, and drinking/partying is permitted within the residence halls." The administration reportedly tries "to keep the parties on campus due to the fact that campus is such a safe place and they truly do care about our safety." In addition to parties the dorms are really competitive in the Interhall Sport System, and "virtually every student plays some kind of sport [in] his/her residence hall." Intercollegiate sports, to put it mildly, "are huge." "If someone is not interested in sports upon arrival, he or she will be by the time he or she leaves." "Everybody goes to the football games, and it's common to see 1,000 students at a home soccer game." Beyond residential life and sports, "religious activities," volunteering, "campus publications, student government, and academic clubs round out the rest of ND life."

Student Body

Undergrads at Notre Dame report "the vast majority" of their peers are "very smart" "white kids from upper- to middle-class backgrounds from all over the country, especially the Midwest and Northeast." The typical student "is a type-A personality that studies a lot, yet is athletic and involved in the community. They are usually the outstanding seniors in their high schools," the "sort of people who can talk about the BCS rankings and Derrida in the same breath." Additionally, something like "85 percent of Notre Dame students earned a varsity letter in high school." "Not all are Catholic" here, though most are, and it seems that most undergrads "have some sort of spirituality present in their daily lives." "ND is slowly improving in diversity concerning economic backgrounds, with the university's policy to meet all demonstrated financial need." As things stand now, those who "don't tend to fit in with everyone else hang out in their own groups made up by others like them (based on ethnicity, sexual orientation, etc.)."

FINANCIAL AID: 574-631-6436 • E-MAIL: ADMISSIONS@ND.EDU • WEBSITE: WWW.ND.EDU

THE PRINCETON REVIEW SAYS

Admissions

Very important factors considered include: Rigor of secondary school record. *Important factors considered include:* Class rank, GPA, standardized test scores, application essay, extracurricular activities, recommendation(s), talent/ability, volunteer work, alumni/ae relations, character/personal qualities. *Other factors considered include:* First generation, racial/ethnic status, work experience, level of applicant's interest, religious affiliation. SAT or ACT required; ACT with or without Writing component accepted. TOEFL required of all international applicants. *Academic units required:* 4 English; 3 mathematics; 2 science; (2 science lab); 2 foreign language; 2 history; 3 academic electives. *Academic units recommended:* 4 English; 4 mathematics; 4 science; (2 science lab); 4 foreign language; 4 history.

Financial Aid

Students should submit: FAFSA, CSS/Financial Aid PROFILE, Noncustodial PROFILE, Business/Farm Supplement. The Princeton Review suggests that all financial aid forms be submitted as soon as possible after January 1. *Need-based scholarships/grants offered:* Federal Pell, SEOG, State scholarships/grants, private scholarships, the school's own gift aid. *Loan aid offered:* Direct Subsidized Stafford Loans, Direct Unsubsidized Stafford Loans, Direct PLUS loans, Federal Perkins Loans. Applicants will be notified of awards beginning 3/28. Off-campus job opportunities are fair.

The Inside Word

Notre Dame is one of the most selective colleges in the country. Almost everyone who enrolls is in the top 10 percent of their graduating class and possesses test scores in the highest percentiles. But, as the student respondents suggest, strong academic ability isn't enough to get you in here. The school looks for students with other talents, and seems to have a predilection for athletic achievement. Legacy students get a leg up but are by no means assured of admission.

THE SCHOOL SAYS " . . ."

From the Admissions Office

"Notre Dame is a Catholic university, which means it offers unique opportunities for academic, ethical, spiritual, and social service development. The First Year of Studies program provides special assistance to our students as they make the adjustment from high school to college. The first-year curriculum includes many core requirements, while allowing students to explore several areas of possible future study. Each residence hall is home to students from all classes; most will live in the same hall for all their years on campus. An average of 93 percent of entering students will graduate within five years.

"The highest critical reading score and the highest math score from either test will be accepted; the writing component score is not required. The ACT is also accepted (with or without writing component) in lieu of the SAT."

SELECTIVITY

Admissions Rating	98
# of applicants	17,647
% of applicants accepted	22
% of acceptees attending	53
# offered a place on the wait list	1,521
% accepting a place on wait list	53
% admitted from wait list	0

FRESHMAN PROFILE

Range SAT Critical Reading	660–750
Range SAT Math	680–770
Range SAT Writing	650–750
Range ACT Composite	32–34
Minimum paper TOEFL	560
Minimum web-based TOEFL	250
% graduated top 10% of class	90
% graduated top 25% of class	98
% graduated top 50% of class	100

DEADLINES

Early action	
Deadline	11/1
Notification	12/21
Regular	
Deadline	1/1
Notification	4/10
Nonfall registration?	Yes

APPLICANTS ALSO LOOK AT AND OFTEN PREFER
Princeton University; Stanford University

AND SOMETIMES PREFER
Cornell University; Duke University; Georgetown University; Northwestern University

AND RARELY PREFER
Boston College; University of Illinois at Urbana-Champaign; University of Michigan—Ann Arbor

FINANCIAL FACTS

Financial Aid Rating	93
Annual tuition	$45,730
Room and board	$13,224
Required fees	$507
Books and supplies	$1,050
% needy frosh rec. need-based scholarship or grant aid	95
% needy UG rec. need-based scholarship or grant aid	95
% needy frosh rec. non-need-based scholarship or grant aid	54
% needy UG rec. non-need-based scholarship or grant aid	48
% needy frosh rec. need-based self-help aid	74
% needy UG rec. need-based self-help aid	83
% frosh rec. any financial aid	70
% UG rec. any financial aid	81
% frosh need fully met	99
% ugrads need fully met	100
Average % of frosh need met	100
Average % of ugrad need met	100

UNIVERSITY OF OKLAHOMA

1000 ASP AVENUE, NORMAN, OK 73019-4076 • ADMISSIONS: 405-325-2252 • FAX: 405-325-7124

CAMPUS LIFE
Quality of Life Rating	91
Fire Safety Rating	86
Green Rating	80
Type of school	Public
Affiliation	No Affiliation
Environment	City

STUDENTS
Total undergrad enrollment	21,359
% male/female	49/51
% from out of state	30
% frosh live on campus	82
% ugrads live on campus	31
# of fraternities (% ugrad men join)	30 (23)
# of sororities (% ugrad women join)	18 (28)
% African American	5
% Asian	6
% Caucasian	63
% Hispanic	9
% Native American	4
% international	4
# of countries represented	129

SURVEY SAYS . . .
School is well run
Great off-campus food
Campus feels safe
Athletic facilities are great
Everyone loves the Sooners
Frats and sororities are popular

ACADEMICS
Academic Rating	75
% students returning for sophomore year	84
% students graduating within 4 years	35
% students graduating within 6 years	66
Calendar	Semester
Student/faculty ratio	17:1
Profs interesting rating	74
Profs accessible rating	73

Most classes have 10–19 students.
Most lab/discussion sessions have 20–29 students.

MOST POPULAR MAJORS
multi-/interdisciplinary studies; registered nusing; psychology

STUDENTS SAY ". . ."

Academics
Students "just swell with school pride" when they talk about the University of Oklahoma. They note, for example, that this "dynamic," "affordable," and "very research-oriented" institution reels in a slew of national merit scholars. They extol the "extensive" study abroad program. The meteorology program is "outstanding." "The engineering facilities are fantastic," and the campus as a whole is "gorgeous" and "well-kept." "The library is beautiful," reports a journalism major. "I could live in there." Like at any similar "big-time university," "the education here is what you make of it." "Anyone who truly wants to learn and achieve can find all sorts of opportunities." Then again, "if you just want to get by," you can "take easy blow-off classes." The faculty runs the gamut as well. "Most professors are great," relates an industrial engineering major. They "know what they are talking about," and they're "approachable." Professors "usually lecture more than they promote discussions." "The best can keep you riveted until the very end of the class period," promises an economics major. Others are "dry" and "overeager" teaching assistants "could use some work." Also, lower-level courses are often "huge," and they tend occur in "ancient coliseum-type" spaces.

Life
"There are tons of organizations" on OU's campus, and "there's no way you could possibly be bored." "From the Indonesian Student Association to the Bocce Ball League of Excellence, there's a group for" you. "The programming board here brings in a lot of great acts and keeps us very entertained in the middle of Oklahoma," adds one student. "School spirit is rampant," and intercollegiate athletics are insanely popular—particularly football. "Not everyone likes Sooner football," but it sure seems that way. Students at OU "live and breathe football" "to the point of near-frightening cultism." Game days in the fall are "an unforgettable experience," because "the campus goes into a frenzy." Fraternities and sororities are also "a large part of social life." Some students insist that the Greek system isn't a dominant feature of the OU landscape. "You hardly notice their presence" if you're not involved, they say, and "The majority of students aren't involved." Other students disagree. "Greek life is really big, unfortunately," they tell us. "It feels as though everyone here is Greek," and "there is a division" between the students who pledge and the students who don't. The "friendly and cute little town" of Norman is reportedly an ideal place to spend a day when not in class. Right next to campus is an area "full of" boutique shops and "a fine selection of bars and restaurants." "Norman is such a great town," gushes one student. "It's not too little to be boring but not too big to be impersonal."

Student Body
The typical student here is "pretty laid-back," "very good at prioritizing," "in some sort of organization or club," and "from Oklahoma or Texas." That student also "loves football," has "a penchant for fun," and has "no outrageous features." OU is home to "a wide variety of students with different political, religious, and economic backgrounds" though, and "there are plenty of options for every major and lifestyle." A lot of students come from a "suburban background" while "many come from small towns." There's also a "quite impressive" contingent of international students. Many students are "vaguely to devoutly Christian." Politically, "the atmosphere on campus tends to be conservative," but the left is well-represented. "We have a ton of liberals," relates one student, "and they are very much liberal." "There are the fraternity dudes and sorority girls" dressed in "North Face apparel and Nike shorts." "You have your partiers, hardcore studiers, and those in between who may lean one way or the other."

FINANCIAL AID: 405-325-5505 • E-MAIL: ADMREC@OU.EDU • WEBSITE: WWW.OU.EDU

THE PRINCETON REVIEW SAYS

Admissions

Very important factors considered include: Class rank, GPA, rigor of secondary school record, standardized test scores. *Important factors considered include:* Application essay, recommendation(s). *Other factors considered include:* Extracurricular activities, interview, talent/ability, volunteer work, work experience, alumni/ae relations, level of applicant's interest. SAT or ACT required; ACT with or without Writing component accepted. TOEFL required of all international applicants. *Academic units required:* 4 English; 3 mathematics; 3 science; (3 science lab); 2 social studies; 1 history; 2 academic electives. *Academic units recommended:* 4 mathematics; 4 science; 2 foreign language; 1 computer science.

Financial Aid

Students should submit: FAFSA. The Princeton Review suggests that all financial aid forms be submitted as soon as possible after January 1. *Need-based scholarships/grants offered:* Federal Pell, SEOG, State scholarships/grants, private scholarships, the school's own gift aid, United Negro College Fund. *Loan aid offered:* Direct Subsidized Stafford Loans, Direct Unsubsidized Stafford Loans, Direct PLUS loans, Federal Perkins Loans, College/university loans from institutional funds. Federal Work-Study Program available. Institutional employment available. Off-campus job opportunities are excellent.

The Inside Word

Like at a lot of large public schools, the admissions process at the University of Oklahoma is a fairly standardized affair that favors state residents. Students who graduate in the top half of their high school class and have decent grades in college prep courses and solid standardized test scores, stand a good chance at admission. Also worth noting: national merit scholars get a lot of perks here including a sweet scholarship package.

THE SCHOOL SAYS "..."

From the Admissions Office

"Ask yourself some significant questions. What are your ambitions, goals, and dreams? Do you desire opportunity, and are you ready to accept challenge? What do you hope to gain from your educational experience? Are you looking for a university that will provide you with the tools, resources, and motivation to convert ambitions, opportunities, and challenges into meaningful achievement? To effectively answer these questions you must carefully seek out your options, look for direction, and make the right choice. The University of Oklahoma combines a unique mixture of academic excellence, varied social cultures, and a variety of campus activities to make your educational experience complete. At OU, comprehensive learning is our goal for your life. Not only do you receive a valuable classroom learning experience, but OU is also one of the finest research institutions in the United States. This allows OU students the opportunity to be a part of technology in progress. It's not just learning, it's discovery, invention, and dynamic creativity, a hands-on experience that allows you to be on the cutting edge of knowledge. Make the right choice and consider the University of Oklahoma!

"The SAT (or ACT) will be used when considering freshman applicants for admission. The writing component of either test is not required of students and is not used in determining admission to the university. The student's best composite score from any one test will be used."

SELECTIVITY

Admissions Rating	83
# of applicants	10,991
% of applicants accepted	80
% of acceptees attending	46
# offered a place on the wait list	1,815
% accepting a place on wait list	100
% admitted from wait list	90

FRESHMAN PROFILE

Range SAT Critical Reading	500–630
Range SAT Math	530–650
Range ACT Composite	23–29
Minimum paper TOEFL	550
Minimum web-based TOEFL	79
Average HS GPA	3.59
% graduated top 10% of class	33
% graduated top 25% of class	64
% graduated top 50% of class	92

DEADLINES

Regular	
Deadline	4/1
Notification	Rolling
Nonfall registration?	Yes

FINANCIAL FACTS

Financial Aid Rating	81
Annual in-state tuition	$3,957
Annual out-of-state tuition	$16,146
Room and board	$8,718
Required fees	$4,959
Books and supplies	$848
% needy frosh rec. need-based scholarship or grant aid	83
% needy UG rec. need-based scholarship or grant aid	79
% needy frosh rec. non-need-based scholarship or grant aid	14
% needy UG rec. non-need-based scholarship or grant aid	11
% needy frosh rec. need-based self-help aid	90
% needy UG rec. need-based self-help aid	00
% frosh rec. any financial aid	79
% UG rec. any financial aid	88
% UG borrow to pay for school	50
Average cumulative indebtedness	$22,140
% frosh need fully met	18
% ugrads need fully met	14
Average % of frosh need met	63
Average % of ugrad need met	57

UNIVERSITY OF OREGON

1217 UNIVERSITY OF OREGON, EUGENE, OR 97403-1217 • ADMISSIONS: 541-346-3201 • FAX: 541-346-5815

STUDENTS SAY ". . ."

Academics

If the University of Oregon excels at anything, it is in providing students with a wealth of academic opportunities. Indeed, students feel it is "a perfect place for someone seeking a well-rounded liberal arts secondary education," a school that has "all of the creative perks of a small learning environment with all of the excitement of a big school." Sports are a big deal here, "but there is also an emphasis on rigorous academics." Business, architecture, ecology, international studies, and political science all win accolades, but journalism is "pretty much the crown jewel of our academic programs." If there is a chink in UO's armor, it is the "inability for some students to get the classes they need." With such a wide array of fields of study available, some students find that essential classes are only available at difficult hours. Students also give mixed grades to the professors, who range from "remarkable" and "really passionate" educators who "are invested in their students" to a few "quite terrible" teachers who "are not dedicated to the students." Those attending UO should be self-motivating, since "the weight falls on the students to create relationships with professors." It is worth the effort, though, as "doing so can open many doors." When it all clicks—and many students report that once that once they were focused on their major things began to fall into place—students have enjoyed an education that "deeply altered the way I see things."

Life

Eugene, Oregon, is not going to give the nation's big cities a run for their money, but students here like it that way. When the weather is nice, students can be found outside "playing Frisbee, football, soccer, or just lounging in the grass," and when the rainy weather of the Pacific Northwest forces people indoors, "you find students in coffee shops on campus and off, studying, visiting, or relaxing." Music, hiking, and other outdoor activities are also popular pastimes. Indeed, the scenery proves a draw for many. "The coast is an hour away, hiking trails and mountains are everywhere, and you can even drive or take a bus up to Portland to get some city life." Greek life is growing on campus but does not dominate the school, and despite prohibitions on drinking in the dorms, students manage it anyway. "We are a dry campus," one attendee notes, "but that doesn't stop students." With the gorgeous scenery and wealth of things to do, it's no wonder students think that "life at school is pretty great."

Student Body

What kind of student attends the University of Oregon? The typical answer is that there is no typical answer. "You have your hipsters, hippies, jocks, athletes, drunks, nerds, and every other cliché you can think of"—students from "dreadlocked hippies to straight-laced conservatives, and everything else in between." That diversity in the student body means, "if you're willing to put forth any sort of effort into meeting people, you'll find a group" who will click with you. "No matter who you are," another student agrees, "there are programs and clubs on campus to take part in." Greek or non-Greek does make a difference. Students say there is a "huge divide between Greek-life and the rest of the student body." But overall, University of Oregon students are "friendly, open-minded, and generally environmentally/socially conscious." In other words, "there are all sorts of students at Oregon, and it is pretty diverse."

FINANCIAL AID: 800-760-6953 • E-MAIL: UOADMIT@UOREGON.EDU • WEBSITE: WWW.UOREGON.EDU

THE PRINCETON REVIEW SAYS

Admissions

Very important factors considered include: GPA, rigor of secondary school record. *Important factors considered include:* Standardized test scores. *Other factors considered include:* Class rank, application essay, extracurricular activities, first generation, geographical residence, racial/ethnic status, recommendation(s), state residency, talent/ability, volunteer work, work experience. SAT or ACT required; SAT and SAT Subject Tests or ACT required for some; ACT with Writing component required. TOEFL required of all international applicants. *Academic units required:* 4 English; 3 mathematics; 3 science; 3 social studies; 2 foreign language. *Academic units recommended:* (1 science lab).

Financial Aid

Students should submit: FAFSA. The Princeton Review suggests that all financial aid forms be submitted as soon as possible after January 1. *Need-based scholarships/grants offered:* Federal Pell, SEOG, State scholarships/grants, private scholarships, the school's own gift aid. *Loan aid offered:* Direct Subsidized Stafford Loans, Direct Unsubsidized Stafford Loans, Direct PLUS loans, Federal Perkins Loans, College/university loans from institutional funds. Federal Work-Study Program available. Institutional employment available. Off-campus job opportunities are good.

The Inside Word

No need to worry about elaborate written statements and mile-long academic résumés. Maintain a 3.0 or better GPA in a college prep curriculum and your ticket to UO is all but written. Even substandard test scores can be overlooked for applicants who meet that requirement. There is further leniency for less than stellar grades if personal circumstances got in the way of academic achievement; applicants for whom this applies should make the school aware when applying.

THE SCHOOL SAYS "..."

From the Admissions Office

"At the UO, you'll be part of a community dedicated to making a difference in the world and you'll find the inspiration and resources you'll need to succeed. You'll attend classes alongside students from all fifty states and ninety-five countries, and learn from people whose cultural, ethnic, political, and religious perspectives differ from your own. You'll have opportunities to participate in leading edge research and study with renowned faculty. You'll graduate with the critical thinking skills and professional preparation necessary to succeed in an increasingly global job market. Set in a 295-acre arboretum, the UO is literally green. Academic and outdoor programs will bring you into forests, mountains, rivers, and lakes. The cutting-edge Lewis Integrative Science Building earned a 'platinum' certification from the U.S. Green Building Council's Leadership in Energy and Environmental Design program; the new student union and recreation center are both on track for the same distinction. You'll have access to nationally recognized programs in sustainable architecture, psychology, geography, economics, education, and business. With a student/teacher ratio of nineteen to one and average class size of twenty students, you'll find a campus that meets your individual needs. You'll also have the benefits of a premier research university: 269 academic programs, excellent academic facilities, and more than 250 student organizations. To be eligible for freshman admission, submit your official high school transcript and SAT or ACT scores, graduate from an accredited high school, and write an essay."

SELECTIVITY

Admissions Rating	82
# of applicants	21,938
% of applicants accepted	74
% of acceptees attending	24
# offered a place on the wait list	1,337
% accepting a place on wait list	42
% admitted from wait list	65

FRESHMAN PROFILE

Range SAT Critical Reading	490–620
Range SAT Math	500–620
Range SAT Writing	490–610
Range ACT Composite	22–28
Minimum paper TOEFL	500
Average HS GPA	3.60
% graduated top 10% of class	25
% graduated top 25% of class	64
% graduated top 50% of class	94

DEADLINES

Deadline	11/1
Notification	12/15
Regular	
Priority	11/1
Deadline	1/15
Nonfall registration?	Yes

FINANCIAL FACTS

Financial Aid Rating	68
Annual in-state tuition	$8,220
Annual out-of-state tuition	$28,305
Room and board	$11,109
Required fees	$1,483
Books and supplies	$1,050
% needy frosh rec. need-based scholarship or grant aid	51
% needy UG rec. need-based scholarship or grant aid	58
% needy frosh rec. non-need-based scholarship or grant aid	38
% needy UG rec. non-need-based scholarship or grant aid	30
% needy frosh rec. need-based self-help aid	71
% needy UG rec. need-based self-help aid	75
% frosh rec. any financial aid	70
% UG rec. any financial aid	68
% UG borrow to pay for school	49
Average cumulative indebtedness	$24,540
% frosh need fully met	10
% ugrads need fully met	8
Average % of frosh need met	41
Average % of ugrad need met	50

UNIVERSITY OF THE PACIFIC

3601 PACIFIC AVENUE, STOCKTON, CA 95211 • ADMISSIONS: 209-946-2211 • FAX: 209-946-2413

STUDENTS SAY ". . ."

Academics

Educational diversity and strong academic programs bring many students to the University of the Pacific in Stockton, California. The school "provides an array of opportunities to suit anyone." "The accelerated programs in dentistry, law, and pharmacy" are a big hit, as well as the "amazing co-op program for engineers" and the "prestigious speech and language pathology program." The "four year guarantee" for some majors and the time and money saved by finishing earlier than other schools' programs is the deciding factor for many. "The Elementary Education program appealed to me because I would get my teaching credential and degree in four years, rather than five or six." Another reason people choose Pacific is the appeal of "very small" and "intimate" classes. One student says this allows for "the proper and necessary attention that I need in order to succeed academically." "Professors know you by name, and they are very involved and helpful." This "emphasis on close relationships between staff and students" shows that Pacific is "a school that truly cares about each student's education." A good deal of students describe professors as "extremely challenging," but also "extremely motivating." "They encourage me and push me to put 110 percent effort in everything inside and outside the classroom." Another student confirms that each class is "manageable but requires effort." If needed, assistance is readily available. "There is always someone around who can help you and plenty of tutors." "There are so many resources in place to help students succeed, that it's practically impossible not to do well." Although the cost may seem high, several students did benefit from "a lot of financial aid."

Life

Students love the "gorgeous and well-maintained" campus, but the surrounding city of Stockton does not get rave reviews. One student describes the University of the Pacific as a "nice school in an unlikely neighborhood." One student does not recommend "walking around certain parts of campus late at night," but adds, "We have great campus police and a STRIPE program that can transport you wherever you want on golf carts if you call them and let you know where you are." Students say the campus is fairly self-contained, with "a movie theater that shows free movies on the weekends for all Pacific students. We also have an on-campus grocery store and a cafeteria that is open until 1:00 A.M." Since there is no strong pull to leave campus, "students tend to resort to joining fraternities to give them something to do. It isn't always partying though. Pacific is not usually considered a party school since the campus "drug and alcohol policy is extremely strict." A lot of frats on campus are professional ones (i.e. pharmacy fraternities) that are committed to giving back to the community and hosting health fairs." Students say, "Student life varies widely by major." "Some majors are a lot more difficult than others, so not everyone studies." Keeping active and fit are also popular. "Our gym is very nice and hygienic. We also have a swimming pool with open hours and several soccer fields for recreational use."

Student Body

Some students agree that there is "a wide gap between the 'serious' students and the 'not serious' students." This may explain the seemingly contradictory observations that "people seem to party a lot" and that there is "not much time for anything but studying." Student comments suggest that the typical student "is involved in multiple organizations on campus, gets good grades, finds time for fun on the weekends, [and] stays late in the library even if they are just socializing." Pacific's size lends itself to a "friendly atmosphere." The "small campus contributes to a small town ambiance where you know everyone." One downside to this is that "student life becomes very cliquey, almost like high school."

FINANCIAL AID: 209-946-2421 • E-MAIL: ADMISSIONS@PACIFIC.EDU • WEBSITE: WWW.PACIFIC.EDU

THE PRINCETON REVIEW SAYS

Admissions

Very important factors considered include: Rigor of secondary school record. *Important factors considered include:* GPA, standardized test scores, application essay, extracurricular activities, first generation, recommendation(s). *Other factors considered include:* Class rank, geographical residence, talent/ability, volunteer work, work experience, alumni/ae relations, character/personal qualities, level of applicant's interest. SAT or ACT required; ACT with or without Writing component accepted. TOEFL required of all international applicants. *Academic units recommended:* 4 English; 2 social studies; 2 foreign language; 1 history; 1 academic elective; 1 visual/performing arts.

Financial Aid

Students should submit: FAFSA. The Princeton Review suggests that all financial aid forms be submitted as soon as possible after January 1. *Need-based scholarships/grants offered:* Federal Pell, SEOG, State scholarships/grants, private scholarships, the school's own gift aid. *Loan aid offered:* Direct Subsidized Stafford Loans, Direct Unsubsidized Stafford Loans, Direct PLUS loans, Federal Perkins Loans.

The Inside Word

While many factors are considered on applications, competition throughout California is intense. Exceptional performance in honors and advanced placement courses will help you stand out in the crowd.

THE SCHOOL SAYS "..."

From the Admissions Office

"One of the most concise ways of describing the University of the Pacific is that it is 'a major university in a small college package.' Our 3,877 undergraduates get the personal attention that you would expect at a small, residential college. But they also have the kinds of opportunities offered at much larger institutions, including more than ninety majors and programs; hundreds of student organizations; drama, dance, and musical productions; sixteen NCAA Division I athletic teams; and two dozen club and intramural sports. We offer undergraduate major programs in the arts, sciences and humanities, business, education, engineering, international studies, music, pharmacy, and health sciences. Some of the unique aspects of our academic programs include the following: We have the only independent, coed, nonsectarian liberal arts and sciences college located between Los Angeles and central Oregon; we have the only undergraduate professional school of international studies in California—and it's the only one in the nation that actually requires you to study abroad; we have the only engineering program in the West that requires students to complete a year's worth of paid work experience as part of their degree; our Conservatory of Music focuses on performance but also offers majors in music management, music therapy, and music education; and we offer several accelerated programs in business, dentistry, dental hygiene, education, law, engineering, and pharmacy. Our beautiful New England–style main campus is located in Stockton (population: about 300 thousand) and is within two hours or less of San Francisco, Santa Cruz, Yosemite National Park, and Lake Tahoe. SAT Subject Tests recommended: mathematics, chemistry (natural science majors only)."

SELECTIVITY

Admissions Rating	89
# of applicants	14,222
% of applicants accepted	73
% of acceptees attending	9
# offered a place on the wait list	1,100
% accepting a place on wait list	42
% admitted from wait list	7

FRESHMAN PROFILE

Range SAT Critical Reading	500–640
Range SAT Math	530–680
Range SAT Writing	500–640
Range ACT Composite	22–29
Minimum paper TOEFL	475
Minimum web-based TOEFL	150
Average HS GPA	3.47
% graduated top 10% of class	36
% graduated top 25% of class	68
% graduated top 50% of class	90

DEADLINES

Early action	
Deadline	11/15
Notification	1/15
Regular	
Priority	11/15
Deadline	1/15
Nonfall registration?	Yes

APPLICANTS ALSO LOOK AT AND OFTEN PREFER

University of California—Davis; University of California—Berkeley

AND SOMETIMES PREFER

University of California—Davis; University of California—Berkeley; University of California—Los Angeles; University of Southern California

FINANCIAL FACTS

Financial Aid Rating	66
Annual tuition	$39,290
Room and board	$12,336
Required fees	$520
Books and supplies	$1,710
% needy frosh rec. need-based scholarship or grant aid	97
% needy UG rec. need-based scholarship or grant aid	96
% needy frosh rec. need-based self-help aid	90
% needy UG rec. need-based self-help aid	93
% frosh rec. any financial aid	91
% UG rec. any financial aid	83
% frosh need fully met	7
% ugrads need fully met	7

UNIVERSITY OF PENNSYLVANIA

34TH & SPRUCE STREETS, PHILADELPHIA, PA 19104 • ADMISSIONS: 215-898-7507 • FAX: 215-898-9670

CAMPUS LIFE

Quality of Life Rating	89
Fire Safety Rating	78
Green Rating	82
Type of school	Private
Affiliation	No Affiliation
Environment	Metropolis

STUDENTS

Total undergrad enrollment	9,712
% male/female	50/50
% from out of state	82
% frosh from public high school	60
% frosh live on campus	97
% ugrads live on campus	54
# of fraternities (% ugrad men join)	36 (30)
# of sororities (% ugrad women join)	13 (27)
% African American	7
% Asian	19
% Caucasian	45
% Hispanic	10
% Native American	<1
% international	11
# of countries represented	104

SURVEY SAYS . . .
Students are happy
Great library
School is well run
Students love Philadelphia, PA
Great off-campus food
Athletic facilities are great
Lots of beer drinking
Hard liquor is popular
Frats and sororities are popular
Student publications are popular

ACADEMICS

Academic Rating	89
% students returning for sophomore year	98
% students graduating within 4 years	88
% students graduating within 6 years	96
Calendar	Semester
Student/faculty ratio	6:1
Profs interesting rating	76
Profs accessible rating	81
Most classes have 10–19 students.	

MOST POPULAR MAJORS
finance; economics; nursing

STUDENTS SAY " . . . "

Academics

At the University of Pennsylvania, students share an intellectual curiosity and top-notch resources but don't "buy into the stigma of being an Ivy League school." Students here are "very passionate about what they do outside the classroom" and the "flexible core requirements." The university is composed of four undergraduate schools (and "a library for pretty much any topic"). "You can take courses in any of the schools, including graduate-level courses." Luckily, there's a vast variety of disciplines available to students: "I can take a course in old Icelandic and even another one about the politics of food," says a student. Wharton, Penn's highly regarded, "highly competitive undergraduate business school" attracts "career-oriented" students who don't mind a "strenuous course load." There are "more than enough" resources, funding, and opportunity here for any student to take advantage of, and "Penn encourages students to truly take advantage of it all!" Professors can "sometimes seem to be caught up more in their research than their classes," but all "are incredibly well-versed in their subject (as well as their audience)." If you're willing to put in the time and effort, your professors "will be happy to reciprocate." In general, the instructors here are "very challenging academically" and are "always willing to offer their more than relevant life experience in class discussion."

Life

Penn students don't mind getting into intellectual conversations during dinner—"Politics and religion come up often, but so does baseball, types of wine, and restaurants"—but some "partying is a much higher priority here than it is at other Ivy League schools." "Campus is split between the downtown club scene and the frat/bar scene, depending on your preference." However, when it comes down to midterms and finals, "people get really serious and…buckle down and study." There's easy access to downtown Philadelphia, yet "still the comfortable feeling of having our own campus," giving students plenty of access to restaurants (BYO restaurants in Philly are "a huge hit"), shopping, concerts, and sports games, as well as plain old "hanging out with hallmates playing Mario Kart." "It's the perfect mix between an urban setting a traditional college campus." The school provides plenty of guest speakers, cultural events, clubs, and organizations for students to channel their energies (all of which "makes the campus feel smaller"), and seniors can even attend "Feb Club" in the month of February, which is essentially an event every night. The weekend buses to/from New York and D.C. "are always packed." It's a busy life at Penn, and "people are constantly trying to think about how they can balance getting good grades academically and their weekend plans."

Student Body

This "determined" bunch "is either focused on one specific interest, or very well-rounded." Pretty much everyone "was an overachiever ('that kid') in high school," and some students "are off-the-charts brilliant," making everyone here "sort of fascinated by everyone else." Everyone has "a strong sense of personal style and his or her own credo," but no group deviates too far from the more mainstream stereotypes. There's a definite lack of "emos" and hippies. There's "the career-driven Wharton kid who will stab you in the back to get your interview slot" and "the nursing kid who's practically nonexistent," but on the whole, there's tremendous school diversity, with "people from all over the world of all kinds of experiences of all perspectives."

FINANCIAL AID: 215-898-1988 • E-MAIL: INFO@ADMISSIONS.UPENN.EDU • WEBSITE: WWW.UPENN.EDU

THE PRINCETON REVIEW SAYS

Admissions

Very important factors considered include: GPA, rigor of secondary school record, standardized test scores, application essay, recommendation(s), character/personal qualities. *Important factors considered include:* Class rank, extracurricular activities, talent/ability. *Other factors considered include:* First generation, geographical residence, interview, racial/ethnic status, state residency, volunteer work, work experience, alumni/ae relations, level of applicant's interest. SAT and SAT Subject Tests or ACT required; ACT with Writing component required. TOEFL required of all international applicants. *Academic units recommended:* 4 English; 4 mathematics; 3 science; (3 science lab); 2 social studies; 4 foreign language; 3 history.

Financial Aid

Students should submit: FAFSA, Institution's own financial aid form, CSS/Financial Aid PROFILE, Noncustodial PROFILE, Business/Farm Supplement. The Princeton Review suggests that all financial aid forms be submitted as soon as possible after January 1. *Need based scholarships/grants offered:* Federal Pell, SEOG, State scholarships/grants, private scholarships, the school's own gift aid. *Loan aid offered:* Federal Nursing Loans, College/university loans from institutional funds. Applicants will be notified of awards beginning 4/1. Federal Work-Study Program available. Institutional employment available. Off-campus job opportunities are excellent.

The Inside Word

After a small decline four cycles ago, applications are once again climbing at Penn—the fifth increase in six years. The competition in the applicant pool is formidable. Applicants can safely assume that they need to be one of the strongest students in their graduating class in order to be successful.

THE SCHOOL SAYS "..."

From the Admissions Office

"Founded by Benjamin Franklin in 1740 to push the frontiers of knowledge, teaching, and problem solving to benefit society, Penn combines opportunities for practical training with foundations in the liberal arts and sciences all in one institution. A community that reflects the diversity of our world, with one of the largest international undergraduate student population in the Ivy League, our students and faculty work toward the shared goal of enacting change by questioning, thinking, and doing—often across traditional academic disciplines. The integration of knowledge and learning is created through access to four undergraduate schools: the College of Arts & Sciences, the School of Engineering & Applied Science, the Wharton School of Business, and the School of Nursing. Penn offers more than ninety majors, eighty minors, and the ability to earn more than one degree in four years.

"Penn believes that learning is only realized when put to use. The Penn community thrives on the open exchange of ideas and shared learning experiences, engaging students to access courses in twelve graduate schools, collaborate with faculty on research, and actively participate in over 450 clubs and organizations. Education through engagement is made possible by Penn's extensive partnerships for transformative civic outreach—around the world and close to our Philadelphia campus. More than 150 Academically Based Community-Service courses link Penn students to work in the community.

"Penn understands that the best minds should have access to the finest education, regardless of their families' ability to pay. To achieve this, Penn practices need-blind admissions, meets 100 percent of demonstrated financial need, and provides a no-loan aid package for all undergraduates receiving financial aid. Our goal is to allow students to pursue their aspirations without assuming a burden of debt, which is why we provide students the opportunity to graduate debt-free."

SELECTIVITY

Admissions Rating	99
# of applicants	31,282
% of applicants accepted	12
% of acceptees attending	63
# offered a place on the wait list	2,816
% accepting a place on wait list	62
% admitted from wait list	3
# of early decision applicants	4,817
% accepted early decision	25

FRESHMAN PROFILE

Range SAT Critical Reading	670–760
Range SAT Math	690–780
Range SAT Writing	690–780
Range ACT Composite	30–34
Average HS GPA	3.91
% graduated top 10% of class	94
% graduated top 25% of class	99
% graduated top 50% of class	100

DEADLINES

Early decision	
Deadline	11/1
Notification	12/15
Regular	
Deadline	1/1
Notification	4/1
Nonfall registration?	No

FINANCIAL FACTS

Financial Aid Rating	94
Annual tuition	$40,594
Room and board	$12,922
Required fees	$5,296
Books and supplies	$1,190
% needy frosh rec. need-based scholarship or grant aid	98
% needy UG rec. need-based scholarship or grant aid	99
% needy frosh rec. non-need-based scholarship or grant aid	0
% needy UG rec. non-need-based scholarship or grant aid	0
% needy frosh rec. need-based self-help aid	100
% needy UG rec. need-based self-help aid	100
% frosh rec. any financial aid	50
% UG rec. any financial aid	47
% UG borrow to pay for school	36
Average cumulative indebtedness	$19,798
% frosh need fully met	100
% ugrads need fully met	100
Average % of frosh need met	100
Average % of ugrad need met	100

CAMPUS LIFE

Quality of Life Rating	94
Fire Safety Rating	82
Green Rating	90
Type of school	Public
Affiliation	No Affiliation
Environment	Metropolis

STUDENTS

Total undergrad enrollment	18,304
% male/female	50/50
% from out of state	26
% frosh live on campus	97
% ugrads live on campus	44
# of fraternities (% ugrad men join)	20 (10)
# of sororities (% ugrad women join)	16 (9)
% African American	5
% Asian	8
% Caucasian	77
% Hispanic	3
% Native American	<1
% international	3
# of countries represented	42

SURVEY SAYS . . .

Students are happy
Students love Pittsburgh, PA
Great off-campus food
Athletic facilities are great
Everyone loves the Panthers

ACADEMICS

Academic Rating	81
% students returning for sophomore year	91
% students graduating within 4 years	64
% students graduating within 6 years	80
Calendar	Semester
Student/faculty ratio	14:1
Profs interesting rating	72
Profs accessible rating	74

Most classes have 10–19 students.
Most lab/discussion sessions have 20–29 students.

MOST POPULAR MAJORS

psychology; finance; nursing

STUDENTS SAY "..."

Academics

A few of the most common words students at The University of Pittsburgh use to describe their alma mater are: "value," "research," "academics," and "home." This "top research university" offers a "world class education" in a city some describe as "a halfway point between the town I grew up in and the big city urban life I hope to have in the future." Students extol the presence of strong programs across the undergraduate schools at Pitt as well as the plethora of research opportunities available through the proximity to University of Pittsburgh Medical School (UPMC). As one would expect from a large research university "all professors are experts in their fields, some just are better teachers than others." There is a general sentiment that "if you're willing to work hard, professors won't let you fall behind the material." Some professors go so far as to hold "office hours somewhere that students actually like to go--places like Panera or the Einstein's Bagels on campus--so that students get a chance to hang out with their professors. Pitt is the kind of place where if you make the "effort to talk to [professors], it will open huge doors for you."

Life

When asked to summarize their school, many students simply state "hail to Pitt!" And hail they certainly do! This positivity extends not only to the "famous speakers," "big time sports," and the "bar and party scene" found on campus but to the equally "vibrant cultural scene with theater and music" of Pittsburgh ensuring that "there is never a shortage of things to do on a weekend." A not so inconsequential perk of attending Pitt is "free transportation on Port Authority buses, and free admission to Carnegie Museums." A typical student "spends time in the library doing homework or chatting with friends" during their weekdays and "once Sunday rolls around." Though a senior assures us, "Pitt students know how to have a good time!" While "there's a lot to get involved in on campus, there is nothing overbearing about certain clubs or Greek Life." Students do love the food in Pittsburgh but say campus options could be "healthier," "cheaper" and have more options for those with "modified diets (ie: vegan, gluten-free.)" Internet is another complaint but Pitt is addressing the issues.

Student Body

With such diversity of programs, a student from North Carolina points out that Pitt draws students from places like "China, Germany, Canada, as well as from the 50 states." However, since the school is a public university, the majority of students do come from Pennsylvania. But with 18,000 students, Pitt "has a diversity of students so one can always find their niche." They often achieve this by finding a "club that fits their personality, qualities and hobbies." One pre-med student advises that "often, the nerds ARE the athletes and everyone can't be stereotyped into what they seem." Greek life "is small at Pitt, but it definitely has a strong presence." Those people looking for a party can find one, but "not everyone parties all weekend," and most people just "like to hang out."

FINANCIAL AID: 412-624-7488 • E-MAIL: OAFA@PITT.EDU • WEBSITE: WWW.PITT.EDU

THE PRINCETON REVIEW SAYS

Admissions

Very important factors considered include: GPA, rigor of secondary school record, standardized test scores. *Important factors considered include:* Application essay. *Other factors considered include:* Class rank, extracurricular activities, first generation, geographical residence, racial/ethnic status, recommendation(s), state residency, talent/ability, volunteer work, work experience, character/personal qualities, level of applicant's interest. SAT or ACT required; ACT with Writing component required. TOEFL required of all international applicants. *Academic units required:* 4 English; 3 mathematics; 3 science; (3 science lab); 2 social studies; 2 foreign language; 3 academic electives. *Academic units recommended:* 4 English; 4 mathematics; 4 science; (4 science lab); 3 social studies; 3 foreign language; 5 academic electives.

Financial Aid

Students should submit: FAFSA. The Princeton Review suggests that all financial aid forms be submitted as soon as possible after January 1. *Need-based scholarships/grants offered:* Federal Pell, SEOG, State scholarships/grants, private scholarships, the school's own gift aid, federal nursing scholarships. *Loan aid offered:* Direct Subsidized Stafford Loans, Direct Unsubsidized Stafford Loans, Direct PLUS loans, Federal Perkins Loans, Federal Nursing Loans, State Loans, College/university loans from institutional funds. Federal Work-Study Program available. Institutional employment available. Off-campus job opportunities are excellent.

The Inside Word

University of Pittsburgh operates on a rolling admission policy, which means the school offers admission to any student applying at any time until the admissions office is notified by the dean that admission is closed, so the earlier you apply, the more likely you are to get in. Applicants can also visit the school's website or call the school to schedule a visit to campus. For those looking for financial aid, five out of ten incoming freshman who apply for need-based aid receive it. However the school also offers a range of other types of financial aid, including the University Academic scholarship, which is a merit-based aid that offers students anything from $2,000 per year to full tuition and room and board. To be eligible, interested students need to have the application for the scholarship completed by January 15.

THE SCHOOL SAYS "..."

From the Admissions Office

"The University of Pittsburgh is one of sixty-two members of the Association of American Universities, a prestigious group whose members include the major research universities of North America. There are more than 450 degree programs available at the sixteen Pittsburgh campus schools (one offering only undergraduate degree programs, six offering graduate degree programs, and eight offering both) and four regional campuses, allowing students a wide latitude of choices, both academically and in setting and style, size, and pace of campus. In its most recent review, the National Research Council, the most respected evaluator of academic programs in the United States, ranked a number of Pitt's programs among the top in their respective fields, including the Departments of Philosophy and History and Philosophy of Science. The University Center for International Studies (UCIS) is a leader in international programs with internationally recognized centers specializing in Asian, Latin American, European, Russian/East European, and global studies. UCIS also houses a center focused on the European Union that the European Commission has designated a European Union Center of Excellence. Pitt has a notable record of high achieving graduates—since 1995 Pitt undergraduates have won four Rhodes scholarships, nine Marshall scholarships, eleven Truman scholarships, seven Udall scholarships, one Gates Cambridge scholarship, two Churchill scholarship, and 51 Goldwater scholarships. Pitt is ranked by the National Science Foundation as among America's top five universities in total federal science and engineering research and development support."

SELECTIVITY

Admissions Rating	94
# of applicants	27,634
% of applicants accepted	54
% of acceptees attending	26
# offered a place on the wait list	1,738
% accepting a place on wait list	28
% admitted from wait list	60

FRESHMAN PROFILE

Range SAT Critical Reading	580–670
Range SAT Math	600–690
Range SAT Writing	570–670
Range ACT Composite	26–31
Minimum paper TOEFL	600
Minimum web-based TOEFL	100
Average HS GPA	3.97
% graduated top 10% of class	53
% graduated top 25% of class	86
% graduated top 50% of class	99

DEADLINES

Nonfall registration?	Yes

APPLICANTS ALSO LOOK AT AND OFTEN PREFER

Boston University; Carnegie Mellon University; University of Pennsylvania; New York University

AND SOMETIMES PREFER

Pennsylvania State University—University Park; University of Maryland; College Park; The Ohio State University

FINANCIAL FACTS

Financial Aid Rating	68
Annual in-state tuition	$16,240
Annual out-of-state tuition	$26,246
Room and board	$10,700
Required fees	$860
Books and supplies	$1,152
% needy frosh rec. need-based scholarship or grant aid	71
% needy UG rec. need-based scholarship or grant aid	67
% needy frosh rec. non-need-based scholarship or grant aid	6
% needy UG rec. non-need-based scholarship or grant aid	5
% needy frosh rec. need-based self-help aid	82
% needy UG rec. need-based self-help aid	85
% frosh rec. any financial aid	58
% UG rec. any financial aid	57
% UG borrow to pay for school	69
Average cumulative indebtedness	$34,623
% frosh need fully met	13
% ugrads need fully met	12
Average % of frosh need met	55
Average % of ugrad need met	54

UNIVERSITY OF PUGET SOUND

1500 NORTH WARNER STREET CMB 1062, TACOMA, WA 98416-1062 • ADMISSIONS: 253-879-3211 • FAX: 253-879-3993

CAMPUS LIFE

Quality of Life Rating	88
Fire Safety Rating	75
Green Rating	94
Type of school	Private
Affiliation	No Affiliation
Environment	City

STUDENTS

Total undergrad enrollment	2,539
% male/female	43/57
% from out of state	76
% frosh from public high school	73
% frosh live on campus	99
% ugrads live on campus	64
# of fraternities (% ugrad men join)	3 (26)
# of sororities (% ugrad women join)	4 (35)
% African American	1
% Asian	7
% Caucasian	75
% Hispanic	7
% Native American	<1
% international	0
# of countries represented	9

SURVEY SAYS . . .

Lab facilities are great
Students are friendly
Easy to get around campus

ACADEMICS

Academic Rating	92
% students returning for sophomore year	87
% students graduating within 4 years	68
% students graduating within 6 years	78
Calendar	Semester
Student/faculty ratio	12:1
Profs interesting rating	95
Profs accessible rating	96

Most classes have 10–19 students.
Most lab/discussion sessions have
  10–19 students.

MOST POPULAR MAJORS

psychology; business/commerce; biology

STUDENTS SAY ". . ."

Academics

The University of Puget Sound is "the ideal learning environment with plenty of opportunity for both academic and personal growth." Students are encouraged to "branch out and go beyond their comfort zone in class and outside of class," and the school is "all about having involving intellectual exchanges of ideas…in the relaxed but conscientious cultural setting of the Pacific Northwest." "The academic culture requires a lot of hard work without being competitive," and the "laid-back culture" belies an "excellent and engaging science program," "nationally acclaimed" orientation program, good financial aid, and small, discussion-based classes. "Come as you are, work hard, do what you love, and expect the support of the entire student body and staff," says a student.

The professors at UPS are "fantastic, "passionate, engaging, and completely devoted to helping students learn, improve, and achieve." Most of the professors "are very focused on ensuring that the students are not only able to understand the topics discussed in class, but can also apply them practically in broader and interdisciplinary discussions." "Going to a small school means that you can learn things about professors from other students ahead of time," says a student of avoiding the few bad apple teachers. There is "a wide variety of classes" available in a large amount of subject areas, though the smaller ones tend to fill up quickly and it can be a struggle to get into some classes.

In this "open, intellectually critical, and socially engaging environment," academics come first and "it really shows." "The University of Puget Sound is a place to work hard without being miserable," says a biochemistry major. "It is almost impossible to lose interest when every professor brings their own area of expertise into the classroom and endorses an understanding of real world application," says another student.

Life

The "stunning" campus is located "in a unique part of the country" and is in a "nice neighborhood" that is both close to the waterfront and major metropolitan areas. "Classes take up a lot of time" but students make time for pleasure on the weekends, and like "to hang out at the cellar, the student-run pizza restaurant" or tale frequent backpacking and hiking trips ("Puget Sound Outdoors, a student-run organization, organizes trips every weekend"). A lot of people tend to relax with friends at off-campus houses, and "most parties are house parties, or the occasional frat party/Greek function." Most of the students are "in some way involved with a sports team, either varsity rec or intramural," and "there are always a lot of things going on on campus, like concerts or lectures or student-run events like a market."

People here "ponder life and things they are passionate" about quite often, and "everyone is very socially/politically active and active in different clubs on campus that promote community service." "Students here hold deep conversations and climb mountains daily (both figuratively and literally)," sums up one witty student. Many also find their way to downtown Tacoma with a group of friends and eat at some of the great restaurants, go to the art museums, or "go swing dancing."

Student Body

Puget Sound is "a place of fantastic tolerance" where students "accept, embrace, and applaud each other's differences." However, students admit that since many students are "middle-class white kids from semi-privileged to privileged backgrounds," a bit more diversity is needed. The "liberal student body" is "friendly and socially-minded" and made up of "talented people who are trying to change the world" (and "there are a lot of hipsters, as well"). Studies are a priority, but everyone at UPS "knows how to balance work, study, and relaxation very well." The "Pacific Northwest Lifestyle" is prevalent, meaning the typical student is "into the outdoors, wears very casual clothing, [and] has a relaxed demeanor."

FINANCIAL AID: 253-879-3214 • E-MAIL: ADMISSION@PUGETSOUND.EDU • WEBSITE: WWW.PUGETSOUND.EDU

THE PRINCETON REVIEW SAYS
Admissions
Very important factors considered include: GPA, rigor of secondary school record, application essay, character/personal qualities. *Important factors considered include:* Standardized test scores, extracurricular activities, recommendation(s), talent/ability, alumni/ae relations. *Other factors considered include:* Class rank, first generation, interview, racial/ethnic status, volunteer work, work experience, level of applicant's interest. SAT or ACT required; ACT with Writing component recommended. TOEFL required of all international applicants. *Academic units recommended:* 4 English; 3 social studies; 3 history; 1 visual/performing arts.

Financial Aid
Students should submit: FAFSA. The Princeton Review suggests that all financial aid forms be submitted as soon as possible after January 1. *Need-based scholarships/grants offered:* Federal Pell, SEOG, State scholarships/grants, private scholarships, the school's own gift aid. *Loan aid offered:* Direct Subsidized Stafford Loans, Direct Unsubsidized Stafford Loans, Direct PLUS loans, Federal Perkins Loans. Applicants will be notified of awards beginning 3/15. Federal Work-Study Program available. Institutional employment available. Off-campus job opportunities are excellent.

The Inside Word
Puget Sound supplies students with detailed information about the selection process, which can help alleviate some of that college application angst. While academic background is the primary consideration of every admissions committee (and that includes both grades and the rigor of the classes in which those grades were obtained), Puget Sound considers the whole candidate, and demonstrated interest in a particular issue or extracurricular activity will strengthen any application. Applicants can count on a considerate and caring attitude before, during, and after the review process.

THE SCHOOL SAYS "..."
From the Admissions Office
"We're a classic, forward-thinking and entrepreneurial liberal arts college with a renowned School of Music and an innovative business and leadership program. Our 2,600 students are proudly unclassifiable and universally kind. Our professors win a metric ton of teaching awards and do research with students that pushes the figurative envelope. We're ambitious and modest. We're collaborative and independent minded. We're rooted in the pioneering Pacific Northwest and in love with the world. None of these things are contradictions. All of them make sense. They add up to an education that is perfectly suited to this vast, brave, unclassifiable world."

SELECTIVITY
Admissions Rating	87
# of applicants	4,588
% of applicants accepted	85
% of acceptees attending	17
# of early decision applicants	160
% accepted early decision	85

FRESHMAN PROFILE
Range SAT Critical Reading	570–670
Range SAT Math	550–660
Range SAT Writing	550–670
Range ACT Composite	25–30
Minimum paper TOEFL	550
Minimum web-based TOEFL	213
% graduated top 10% of class	26
% graduated top 25% of class	51
% graduated top 50% of class	89

DEADLINES
Early decision	
Deadline	11/15
Notification	12/15
Regular	
Priority	1/15
Deadline	1/15
Notification	4/1
Nonfall registration?	Yes

APPLICANTS ALSO LOOK AT AND RARELY PREFER
The College of Idaho; Gonzaga University

FINANCIAL FACTS
Financial Aid Rating	82
Annual in-state tuition	$45,200
Annual out-of-state tuition	$11,180
% needy frosh rec. need-based scholarship or grant aid	99
% needy UG rec. need-based scholarship or grant aid	99
% needy frosh rec. non-need-based scholarship or grant aid	22
% needy UG rec. non-need-based scholarship or grant aid	11
% needy frosh rec. need-based self-help aid	66
% needy UG rec. need-based self-help aid	77
% frosh rec. any financial aid	96
% UG rec. any financial aid	94
% UG borrow to pay for school	61
Average cumulative indebtedness	$30,215
% frosh need fully met	26
% ugrads need fully met	18
Average % of frosh need met	71
Average % of ugrad need met	74

UNIVERSITY OF REDLANDS

1200 EAST COLTON AVENUE, REDLANDS, CA 92373 • ADMISSIONS: 909-748-8074 • FAX: 909-335-4089

STUDENTS SAY "..."

Academics

The University of Redlands is a smallish liberal arts college in Southern California that offers "great financial aid" and "emphasizes a balanced, broad education." "Small class sizes provide a more hands-on learning experience" and "personal attention." Class discussions are "often spicy and provoking." Professors are "friendly," "always prepared," and "willing to help you with anything." Some students call the coursework here "demanding." Whatever the case, there are "endless academic opportunities," and Redlands has the "resources for just about anything" you can conjure up to study. Through the College of Arts and Sciences (CAS), the majority of students follow a conventional undergraduate curriculum, declaring majors and minors. About 200 students choose the innovative approach of the Johnston Center for Integrative Studies. They design their own majors, work with professors to create contracts for their courses, and receive narrative evaluations of their work (instead of letter grades). Other academic highlights at Redlands include an impressive school of music, an uncommon major in communicative disorders, and excellence across the hard sciences. The study abroad program is also awesome. Some 40 percent of these undergrads take coursework in places far-flung, either for a traditional semester or during the fairly unique May Term, an intensive four-week period when students focus on one class. As far as complaints, red tape is pretty annoying—especially for a school this size. "Any bureaucratic task takes a million years to accomplish." Also, "a lot of courses aren't offered every year," and the ones that are available tend to "fill up fast."

Life

No one could deny that the Redlands campus "has incredible aesthetic appeal" and eye-popping scenery. It's also "bustling with fun people and tons of activities." "The whole campus is full of creativity." "There are programs and things to do every night, usually so much that you end up overbooking yourself and having to run from one thing to another in order to be everywhere you want to be." Though some note, "Some of the facilities are really old and outdated." This doesn't flag students' enthusiasm. "There is a lot of school spirit," and intercollegiate sports are popular. The Greek system, which consists of a handful of sororities and fraternities that are "not nationally affiliated," is pretty popular. However, "the party scene is only one part of life on campus and does not take over social life by any means." "There's a real spectrum of hard partiers and stone-cold sober people." The town of Redlands is "quirky" but "a bit isolated." Critics gripe that "there is not a lot to do" off campus. Devotees of the surrounding area tell us that there's "an excellent downtown" "with coffee shops, restaurants, and bars." "If you give the town half a chance," they maintain, "it actually has some cool features." In addition, the school sponsors a wealth of outdoor adventures and "rents out equipment such as snowboards, backpacks, sleeping bags, and anything else you would need in the wilderness." Students also take "trips up to Joshua Tree and Big Bear" or, for more urban fare, trek to Los Angeles.

Student Body

Students at Redlands are "passionate." They have a "sense of wonder and enthusiasm" and "a huge variety of interests." As a whole, students are "quite liberal" politically. Most students are "fairly involved in many aspects of school," and they promise that "everyone can find a niche somewhere on campus." The undergraduate population melds pretty well. There's "no separation of athletes, geeks, Greeks, etc." To the extent that there's any division, it's between Johnston students and students in the CAS. Johnston students—the ones who make their own majors and get evaluations instead of grades—definitely "pride themselves on their uniqueness," and they can be "eccentric." "There are colorful characters on both sides of the spectrum," though, and students assure us that any segregation is self-imposed. "I really don't see a line between the CAS and Johnston," observes one student. "It is only there for those who want it to be."

FINANCIAL AID: 909-748-8047 • E-MAIL: ADMISSIONS@REDLANDS.EDU • WEBSITE: WWW.REDLANDS.EDU

THE PRINCETON REVIEW SAYS

Admissions

Very important factors considered include: GPA, rigor of secondary school record, recommendation(s), talent/ability, character/personal qualities. *Important factors considered include:* Standardized test scores, application essay. *Other factors considered include:* Extracurricular activities, first generation, geographical residence, interview, racial/ethnic status, state residency, volunteer work, work experience, alumni/ae relations. SAT or ACT required; ACT with Writing component recommended. TOEFL required of all international applicants. *Academic units required:* 4 English; 3 mathematics; 2 science; (1 science lab); 2 social studies; 2 foreign language. *Academic units recommended:* 4 English; 4 mathematics; 3 science; (1 science lab); 2 social studies; 3 foreign language; 1 history.

Financial Aid

Students should submit: FAFSA, State aid form. The Princeton Review suggests that all financial aid forms be submitted as soon as possible after January 1. *Need-based scholarships/grants offered:* Federal Pell, SEOG, State scholarships/grants, private scholarships, the school's own gift aid. *Loan aid offered:* Federal Perkins Loans, College/university loans from institutional funds. Applicants will be notified of awards beginning 2/28. Federal Work-Study Program available. Off-campus job opportunities are fair.

The Inside Word

The admit rate here is reasonably high and students with above-average high school records and respectable standardized test scores should consider the school a target. Candidates who are interested in pursuing the self-designed programs available through the Johnston Center will find the admissions process to be distinctly more personal. Note, though, that you have to be admitted as a regular student in the CAS first.

THE SCHOOL SAYS "..."

From the Admissions Office

"We've created an unusually blended curriculum of the liberal arts and pre-professional study because we think education is about learning how to think and learning how to do. For example, our environmental studies students have synthesized their study of sociology, biology, and economics to develop an actual resource management plan for the local mountain communities. Our creative writing program encourages internships with publishing or television production companies. We educate managers, poets, environmental scientists, teachers, musicians, and speech therapists to be reflective about culture and society so that they can better understand and improve the world they'll enter upon graduation.

"First-year students applying for admission are required to submit the results of either the SAT or the ACT. We do not require the writing section of either test."

SELECTIVITY

Admissions Rating	86
# of applicants	4,668
% of applicants accepted	67
% of acceptees attending	21
# offered a place on the wait list	159
% accepting a place on wait list	77
% admitted from wait list	15

FRESHMAN PROFILE

Range SAT Critical Reading	510–610
Range SAT Math	520–620
Range ACT Composite	23–27
Minimum paper TOEFL	550
Minimum web-based TOEFL	213
Average HS GPA	3.66
% graduated top 10% of class	35
% graduated top 25% of class	65
% graduated top 50% of class	96

DEADLINES

Early action	
Deadline	11/15
Notification	12/31
Regular	
Priority	1/15
Nonfall registration?	Yes

APPLICANTS ALSO LOOK AT AND OFTEN PREFER
Occidental College; Chapman University

AND SOMETIMES PREFER
University of San Diego; Loyola Marymount University; UC Santa Barbara

AND RARELY PREFER
UC Riverside; Whittier

FINANCIAL FACTS

Financial Aid Rating	88
Annual tuition	$40,990
Room and board	$12,314
Required fees	$300
Books and supplies	$1,710
% needy frosh rec. need-based scholarship or grant aid	100
% needy UG rec. need-based scholarship or grant aid	99
% needy frosh rec. non-need-based scholarship or grant aid	74
% needy UG rec. non-need-based scholarship or grant aid	57
% needy frosh rec. need-based self-help aid	84
% needy UG rec. need-based self-help aid	91
% frosh rec. any financial aid	94
% UG rec. any financial aid	94
% UG borrow to pay for school	71
Average cumulative indebtedness	$32,231
% frosh need fully met	31
% ugrads need fully met	25
Average % of frosh need met	87
Average % of ugrad need met	85

UNIVERSITY OF RHODE ISLAND

NEWMAN HALL, KINGSTON, RI 02881 • ADMISSIONS: 401-874-7100 • FAX: 401-874-5523

CAMPUS LIFE
Quality of Life Rating	69
Fire Safety Rating	81
Green Rating	92
Type of school	Public
Affiliation	No Affiliation
Environment	Village

STUDENTS
Total undergrad enrollment	13,008
% male/female	46/54
% from out of state	41
% frosh live on campus	91
% ugrads live on campus	44
# of fraternities (% ugrad men join)	11 (12)
# of sororities (% ugrad women join)	9 (15)
% African American	5
% Asian	3
% Caucasian	68
% Hispanic	9
% Native American	<1
% international	2
# of countries represented	52

SURVEY SAYS . . .
Great library
Frats and sororities are popular
Student publications are popular
Lots of beer drinking
Hard liquor is popular

ACADEMICS
Academic Rating	73
% students returning for sophomore year	81
% students graduating within 4 years	41
% students graduating within 6 years	60
Calendar	Semester
Student/faculty ratio	16:1
Profs interesting rating	67
Profs accessible rating	69

Most classes have 20–29 students.
Most lab/discussion sessions have
10–19 students.

MOST POPULAR MAJORS
nursing; kinesiology; psychology

STUDENTS SAY " . . ."

Academics
The University of Rhode Island "is a school that challenges me to think big and outside the box," says one student. URI is known for having "excellent science programs," including a "marine biology program [that] is one of the best in the Northeast." Other stand-out majors include "nursing, pharmacy, and engineering." Praise for teachers and staff garners varied reactions, as this student notes, "You have bad mixed in with good, but I will say that the good professors are top-notch." As far as transitioning to the workplace, a sophomore says, "URI has impressive programs that help get your career started as soon as possible and also act as a bridge to graduate school." Another student observes that the staff is also "great at helping freshmen transferring from home to college, and there are lots of different programs offered to help students excel academically." Overall, URI is known to have a solid liberal ideology with "openness to creative and critical exploration." This engineering major finds the environment to be rather "forward-thinking [with an] emphasis on today's global workforce." URI is described as providing a "great sense of community" with a philosophical message that students should be connected to the world around them.

Life
The school's proximity to the beach and to other major cities like Providence and Boston make it appealing to students from all over the Northeast. "I think its beauty is definitely a strength, and the location near the beach is great," says a communication major. If fine dining is meaningful to your quality of life, it's worth noting that URI's dining hall has "won a national award the past two years in a row." There are complaints about the dry campus. One senior says, "Because we have a dry campus, people usually live in the surrounding neighborhoods, so you can travel to your friends' houses and party." Others say that students who live nearby still choose to stay on campus during weekends, since this is where their social life is centered. Life isn't all about "getting wasted," chides one sophomore. "Sometimes we get together [to] make dinner and just have a movie night inside our apartment." Students are said to have a "two brain track" in terms of serious attention to study followed by equal attention to "relaxing and having a good time." One student says, "Basketball games are really fun to watch," and "Newport cliff walks are popular during the nice weather." Greek life is a big part of URI's campus yet many students don't feel obliged to pledge; still they enjoy the Greek life's social offerings, "which accounts for the majority of on-campus activities."

Student Body
URI, as an affordable state school, naturally attracts a large percentage of Rhode Islanders. Rumor has it that this group "sticks to their friends from high school," yet one undergrad observes, "Rhody-borns are so afraid of college turning into another four years of high school that we go searching for new people to meet." As far as categorizing a "typical student," undergrads are reluctant to stereotype. "URI is diverse, and the students cannot be generalized into a certain type." Campus diversity is strong, and most groups intermingle without issue. One junior sums it up: "Just like any other college, some come to party and some come to learn, but in the end they are all good people."

FINANCIAL AID: 401-874-7530 • E-MAIL: ADMISSION@URI.EDU • WEBSITE: WWW.URI.EDU

THE PRINCETON REVIEW SAYS

Admissions

Very important factors considered include: GPA, rigor of secondary school record. *Important factors considered include:* Class rank, standardized test scores, application essay. *Other factors considered include:* Extracurricular activities, first generation, geographical residence, racial/ethnic status, recommendation(s), state residency, talent/ability, volunteer work, work experience, alumni/ae relations, character/personal qualities, level of applicant's interest. SAT or ACT required; ACT with or without Writing component accepted. TOEFL required of all international applicants. *Academic units required:* 4 English; 3 mathematics; 2 science; 2 social science; 2 foreign language; 5 academic electives.

Financial Aid

Students should submit: FAFSA. The Princeton Review suggests that all financial aid forms be submitted as soon as possible after January 1. *Need-based scholarships/grants offered:* Federal Pell, SEOG, State scholarships/grants, private scholarships, the school's own gift aid. *Loan aid offered:* Direct Subsidized Stafford Loans, Direct Unsubsidized Stafford Loans, Direct PLUS loans, Federal Perkins Loans, Federal Nursing Loans, College/university loans from institutional funds. Federal Work-Study Program available. Institutional employment available. Off-campus job opportunities are good.

The Inside Word

Early decision deadline is December 1. Don't forget to apply to URI's merit-based scholarships, which are open to international students as well. Remember if you're a resident of another New England state (besides Rhode Island) you may be eligible, depending on your major, for discounted tuition.

THE SCHOOL SAYS "..."

From the Admissions Office

"The University of Rhode Island offers a wide range of merit scholarships to students who have demonstrated academic success in a challenging college preparatory curriculum. You may be eligible for these awards if you have earned a GPA of 3.2/4.0, as well as SATs of 1050+ (critical reading and math) or ACT of 23+, and have demonstrated leadership and involvement in your school and/or community. To be considered for our highest scholarships, we recommend that you apply by our December 1 Early Action deadline.

"We also strongly recommend that students interested in engineering, nursing, and the doctorate in pharmacy apply by December 1 as spaces are limited in these programs.

1. The latest test scores we will consider for scholarship review are the November SATs and the October ACT.

2. We consider the single highest score on each section of the SAT (and ACT) across test dates, so there is no need to use "Score Choice."

3. The SAT critical reading, writing and math scores are used for admission evaluation. Currently, only the critical reading and math scores are used for scholarship consideration in addition to the other criteria lised above.

4. Merit Scholarships are four-year awards, renewable each semester as long as you maintain continuous full-time enrollment (12 credits per semester) and a minimum GPA of 2.8.

5. Unlike "Early Decision," Early Action is non-binding. You will not have to commit to URI until May 1."

SELECTIVITY	
Admissions Rating	76
# of applicants	20,907
% of applicants accepted	76
% of acceptees attending	21
# offered a place on the wait list	1,431
% accepting a place on wait list	31
% admitted from wait list	62

FRESHMAN PROFILE	
Range SAT Critical Reading	490–590
Range SAT Math	510–620
Range SAT Writing	490–590
Range ACT Composite	22–27
Minimum paper TOEFL	550
Minimum web-based TOEFL	213
Average HS GPA	3.30
% graduated top 10% of class	19
% graduated top 25% of class	47
% graduated top 50% of class	83

DEADLINES	
Early action	
Deadline	12/1
Notification	1/31
Regular	
Deadline	2/1
Notification	3/31
Nonfall registration?	Yes

APPLICANTS ALSO LOOK AT AND RARELY PREFER

Carnegie Mellon University; Occidental College; University of Maryland; Baltimore County

FINANCIAL FACTS	
Financial Aid Rating	83
Annual in-state tuition	$10,878
Annual out-of-state tuition	$26,444
Room and board	$11,160
Required fees	$1,572
Books and supplies	$1,200
% needy frosh rec. need-based scholarship or grant aid	84
% needy UG rec. need-based scholarship or grant aid	80
% needy frosh rec. non-need-based scholarship or grant aid	14
% needy UG rec. non-need-based scholarship or grant aid	8
% needy frosh rec. need-based self-help aid	82
% needy UG rec. need-based self-help aid	76
% frosh rec. any financial aid	91
% UG rec. any financial aid	86
% UG borrow to pay for school	77
Average cumulative indebtedness	$31,141
% frosh need fully met	97
% ugrads need fully met	91
Average % of frosh need met	64
Average % of ugrad need met	59

UNIVERSITY OF RICHMOND

SARAH BRUNET HALL, 28 WESTHAMPTON WAY, RICHMOND, VA 23173 • ADMISSION: 804-289-8640 • FAX: 804-287-6003

CAMPUS LIFE

Quality of Life Rating	91
Fire Safety Rating	81
Green Rating	93
Type of school	Private
Affiliation	No Affiliation
Environment	City

STUDENTS

Total undergrad enrollment	2,893
% male/female	48/52
% from out of state	80
% frosh from public high school	57
% frosh live on campus	99
% ugrads live on campus	87
# of fraternities (% ugrad men join)	7 (13)
# of sororities (% ugrad women join)	7 (22)
% African American	6
% Asian	6
% Caucasian	58
% Hispanic	7
% Native American	<1
% international	9
# of countries represented	74

SURVEY SAYS . . .

Classroom facilities are great
Lab facilities are great
Career services are great
School is well run
Great financial aid
Great food on campus
Great off-campus food
Athletic facilities are great
Lots of beer drinking

ACADEMICS

Academic Rating	95
% students returning for sophomore year	94
% students graduating within 4 years	82
% students graduating within 6 years	85
Calendar	Semester
Student/faculty ratio	8:1
Profs interesting rating	88
Profs accessible rating	93

Most classes have 10–19 students.
Most lab/discussion sessions have
10–19 students.

MOST POPULAR MAJORS

business administration; psychology; political
science

STUDENTS SAY ". . ."

Academics

The University of Richmond provides "the resources of a large university with the personal attention of a small college" and just "a hint of Southern charm." Financial aid is "generous." Facilities are "outstanding." "Students have access to state-of-the-art technologies and research labs that normally only graduate students would be able to work with." Among the sixty or so undergraduate majors, students call our attention to the "great business program" and the "excellent pre-med program." "Another of Richmond's strengths is its study abroad programs." Every year, a few hundred Richmond students take classes in more than thirty countries or complete a summer internship in one of six countries. The "core liberal arts program" here is reasonably broad and pretty much all coursework is "rigorous." "There are no easy classes," "and there is a significant amount of homework." The degree of difficulty notwithstanding, though, faculty members are overwhelmingly "brilliant," "insightful, accommodating," and "extremely accessible." "They genuinely care about their students and they make themselves totally available," gushes a political science major. "We're a school where professors know all of their students' names," expounds an English major, "and where the president of the university stops and talks to you on the way to your next class."

Life

This "gorgeous, peaceful, and isolated" suburban campus comes complete with "glistening lake in the center of it." During the week, "students get down to business" academically. "Everybody is in the library." However, "every single student is involved with an extracurricular activity or two" as well, "and since there aren't 20,000 students here, everyone has a chance to make a difference." A solid contingent of students plays intercollegiate or intramural sports or is "extremely invested" in a club sport. Fraternities and sororities also play a "very big" social role. However, some students "really dislike Greek life," and they insist that the Greek system "does not dominate the social scene." Other students flatly assert, "Greek life rules the Richmond campus." Parties are popular at the "frat lodges" (essentially an edifice containing a large dance floor with an area to serve beer, a deck, and a backyard). For those looking for a more intimate scene, apartment parties are also popular. "There are concerts, sporting events, movies, and just groups of friends doing a wide variety of things" as well. Off campus, "Richmond contains so many options for things to do and meaningful places to volunteer. The city itself contains so much history." Though some believe the university should be "more involved in the greater Richmond community."

Student Body

About 80 percent of the students at Richmond come from out of state. "A large percentage of the students here are attending on scholarship or with a very generous financial aid package," and "more and more, the school is starting to diversify from its stereotype as just rich white kids" "who seem to have unlimited spending budgets." There's also a "growing number of" international students. Nevertheless, "Richmond is pretty homogenous." The typical student is "from 'outside Philly' or 'outside Boston'" or is a "Mid-Atlantic prep school kid" "who probably owns several pairs of Sperrys." Many students "dress well" and "obviously care about their physical appearance." There are "lots of Polos, button-downs, and sundresses." Otherwise, these "clean cut," and (if they don't mind saying so themselves) "good looking" students are "ambitious," "friendly," "outgoing," "overcommitted," and usually a little stressed." There's also "a great mixture of nerds and athletes," and "everyone brings their own sense of individuality."

FINANCIAL AID: 804-289-8438 • E-MAIL: ADMISSION@RICHMOND.EDU • WEBSITE: WWW.RICHMOND.EDU

THE PRINCETON REVIEW SAYS

Admissions

Very important factors considered include: GPA, rigor of secondary school record. *Important factors considered include:* Class rank, if submitted, standardized test scores, application essay, first generation, talent/ability, character/personal qualities. *Other factors considered include:* Extracurricular activities, recommendation(s), volunteer work, work experience, alumni/ae relations. SAT or ACT required; SAT and SAT Subject Tests or ACT considered if submitted; ACT with or without Writing component accepted. TOEFL required of all international applicants. *Academic units required:* 4 English; 3 mathematics; 2 science; (2 science lab); 2 foreign language; 2 history. *Academic units recommended:* 4 English; 4 mathematics; 4 science; (4 science lab); 4 foreign language; 4 history.

Financial Aid

Students should submit: FAFSA for federal aid, CSS/Financial Aid PROFILE, Noncustodial PROFILE for institutional aid. Regular filing deadline is 2/15. The Princeton Review suggests that all financial aid forms be submitted as soon as possible after January 1. *Need-based scholarships/grants offered:* Federal Pell, SEOG, State scholarships/grants, private scholarships, the school's own gift aid. *Loan aid offered:* Direct Subsidized Stafford Loans, Direct Unsubsidized Stafford Loans, Direct PLUS loans, Federal Perkins Loans. Applicants will be notified of awards beginning 4/1. Federal Work-Study Program available. Institutional employment available. Off-campus job opportunities are excellent.

The Inside Word

While the University of Richmond remains a little bit of a safety school for students with loftier goals, the standardized test scores and grades of incoming students at Richmond are tremendous and most undergraduates here finished in the top quarter of their high school classes. Note also the pile of financial aid that's available here to students with exceptional credentials.

THE SCHOOL SAYS "..."

From the Admissions Office

"University of Richmond is one of less than one percent of colleges that is need blind and meets 100% of demonstrated financial need. University of Richmond combines the characteristics of a small college with the dynamics and resources of a large university. Our unique size, beautiful suburban campus and outstanding facilities offer students an extraordinary range of opportunities for intellectual achievement and personal growth. While faculty-student interaction and dialogue are at the forefront of the academic experience, research, internships and international experiences are important components of students' lives. Richmond is committed to providing students with rigorous academics and experiential learning. The university offers funding for undergraduate research, summer fellowships and internships. Our global approach to education shines through our many study-abroad and language immersion programs. We are committed to diversity and believe in leveraging its benefits in all aspects of college life. The student body is composed of scholars from a variety of backgrounds. One in five undergraduates is a domestic student of color; one in six is the first in his or her family to attend college; one in ten is an international student; and more than 80 percent hail from outside of Virginia."

SELECTIVITY

Admissions Rating	96
# of applicants	9,825
% of applicants accepted	31
% of acceptees attending	26
# offered a place on the wait list	4,129
% accepting a place on wait list	40
% admitted from wait list	6
# of early decision applicants	752
% accepted early decision	45

FRESHMAN PROFILE

Range SAT Critical Reading	590–690
Range SAT Math	620–720
Range SAT Writing	600–690
Range ACT Composite	28–31
Minimum paper TOEFL	550
Minimum web-based TOEFL	80
% graduated top 10% of class	64
% graduated top 25% of class	93
% graduated top 50% of class	99

DEADLINES

Early decision	
Deadline	11/15
Notification	12/15
Regular	
Deadline	1/15
Notification	4/1
Nonfall registration?	No

APPLICANTS ALSO LOOK AT AND OFTEN PREFER

Brown University; Duke University; Georgetown University; Princeton University;

AND SOMETIMES PREFER

Boston College; College of William and Mary; Wake Forest University; University of Virginia

AND RARELY PREFER

Davidson College; Elon University; Emory University

FINANCIAL FACTS

Financial Aid Rating	95
Annual tuition	$46,680
Room and board	$10,790
Required fees	$0
Books and supplies	$1,100
% needy frosh rec. need-based scholarship or grant aid	98
% needy UG rec. need-based scholarship or grant aid	99
% needy frosh rec. non-need-based scholarship or grant aid	14
% needy UG rec. non-need-based scholarship or grant aid	14
% needy frosh rec. need-based self-help aid	84
% needy UG rec. need-based self-help aid	83
% frosh rec. any financial aid	57
% UG rec. any financial aid	66
% UG borrow to pay for school	51
Average cumulative indebtedness	$22,225
% frosh need fully met	85
% ugrads need fully met	82
Average % of frosh need met	100
Average % of ugrad need met	100

UNIVERSITY OF ROCHESTER

300 WILSON BOULEVARD, ROCHESTER, NY 14627 • ADMISSIONS: 585-275-3221 • FAX: 585-461-4595

CAMPUS LIFE

Quality of Life Rating	85
Fire Safety Rating	88
Green Rating	81
Type of school	Private
Affiliation	No Affiliation
Environment	Metropolis

STUDENTS

Total undergrad enrollment	6,032
% male/female	48/52
% from out of state	58
% frosh from public high school	74
% frosh live on campus	99
% ugrads live on campus	82
# of fraternities (% ugrad men join)	16 (6)
# of sororities (% ugrad women join)	15 (8)
% African American	5
% Asian	10
% Caucasian	50
% Hispanic	6
% Native American	<1
% international	15
# of countries represented	89

SURVEY SAYS . . .

Students are friendly
Great off-campus food
Athletic facilities are great

ACADEMICS

Academic Rating	85
% students returning for sophomore year	96
% students graduating within 4 years	77
% students graduating within 6 years	85
Calendar	Semester
Student/faculty ratio	10:1
Profs interesting rating	74
Profs accessible rating	72

Most classes have 10–19 students.

MOST POPULAR MAJORS

economics; biology; psychology

STUDENTS SAY " . . ."

Academics

The University of Rochester's "innovative core curriculum, where there are essentially no required classes," is a strong draw for many students. This flexibility "is extremely rare and truly encourages personal exploration rather than conventional general education." "Instead of the college telling us what we have to study…students must chart out their own academic paths." Students agree this key difference ensures that "everyone is passionate about what they study because they get to choose every single class." The classes students have to choose from are described as "top-notch." As one student points out, "I definitely perceive the academics at University of Rochester as Ivy League caliber." U of R is highly regarded as a "cutting-edge research university." "There's a spirit of intellectual curiosity and student camaraderie at the U of R." Although the professors are highly praised for their "uniform brilliance," among other qualities, some students feel that "their intellectual know-how does not always translate into strong teaching skills." But most students focus on the strengths of their professors saying they "care about the subjects they teach and are constantly in the process of expanding knowledge in their fields. It is an honor to be influenced by and to influence such incredible minds." Students are also quick to mention the strong musical influence at the school. This "awesome music scene" is due to the Eastman School of Music, which "brings many interesting and world-famous performers to our little city." Of the many clubs on campus, the a cappella groups are "immensely popular" at U of R, with four different groups on campus that "easily sell out our biggest auditorium."

Life

Although the University of Rochester has several hot selling points for undergraduates, the weather is not high on the list. One student described the typical student as "nerdy and normally freezing!" Locals don't seem to complain though. They know that "being in western New York, we can get a lot of snow," and so they just add an extra layer of clothes. For others, there is simply too much else going on to notice. The more than 200 clubs available on campus are very popular. Students are "extremely involved" and are "a part of at least two or three clubs. And [a part means] they are actively involved and may even be on the executive board." Music, athletics, and studying in the library (which "is both a social and study place") are popular ways to spend time. Many students enjoy "getting off campus to bowl, ice skate, or go to the mall." Some students feel the school is "overly strict on fraternity parties as well as off-campus bar nights." Other students appreciate that vigilance, "because our campus is not situated in the safest area of the city, it is necessary that security is strict."

Student Body

Students at U of R strive to "be the best that you can be." The school's motto, "Meliora," is a Latin word meaning "ever better" and may "sum up what U of R is all about." As one student expounds, "Everyone on campus is doing something to change the world. This means that students are super involved in their own thing, but it also means that the school is supportive of you and how you wish to change the world." This "genuine and extremely passionate" view of their school and themselves creates a strong bond and sense of "community" among students. "Everyone here really loves learning; it's wonderful being at a place where everyone is a self-proclaimed nerd." "A typical student here is someone who took honors classes in high school and lots of AP classes and did amazing." "Most people here are also quirky, but in a friendly, cool way." Students tend to put academics first, which may explain why although many students participate in sports, athletics do not rule the school. The plus side to being a Division III school is that "it is not impossible to join a sports team and actually get playing time."

FINANCIAL AID: 585-275-3226 • E-MAIL: ADMIT@ADMISSIONS.ROCHESTER.EDU • WEBSITE: WWW.ROCHESTER.EDU

THE PRINCETON REVIEW SAYS

Admissions

Very important factors considered include: Rigor of secondary school record, recommendation(s), character/personal qualities. *Important factors considered include:* Standardized test scores, application essay, extracurricular activities, interview, talent/ability. *Other factors considered include:* Class rank, first generation, geographical residence, racial/ethnic status, volunteer work, work experience, alumni/ae relations, level of applicant's interest, SAT or ACT recommended; SAT and SAT Subject Tests or ACT required for some; ACT with or without Writing component accepted. TOEFL required of all international applicants.

Financial Aid

Students should submit: FAFSA, CSS/Financial Aid PROFILE, State aid form, Noncustodial PROFILE. The Princeton Review suggests that all financial aid forms be submitted as soon as possible after January 1. *Need-based scholarships/grants offered:* Federal Pell, SEOG, State scholarships/grants, the school's own gift aid. *Loan aid offered:* Direct Subsidized Stafford Loans, Direct Unsubsidized Stafford Loans, Direct PLUS loans, Federal Perkins Loans, Federal Nursing Loans. Applicants will be notified of awards beginning 4/1. Federal Work-Study Program available. Institutional employment available. Off-campus job opportunities are excellent.

The Inside Word

With nearly 5,300 undergrads, applicants to Rochester can expect a highly individualized academic experience—something that makes this school not only a great place to learn, but also an increasingly competitive institution when it comes to admissions. The most important consideration for admission is grades and standardized test scores, followed closely by the rigor of class work and recommendations. Keep in mind that Rochester is looking for students who will fit well within the school's academic environment and demonstrate a true interest in attending—that is, scheduling an interview could go a long way in increasing your odds.

THE SCHOOL SAYS "..."

From the Admissions Office

"Rochester believes that excellence requires freedom. In the Rochester Curriculum, students are free to select the courses that appeal to them most. There are no required subjects; students' interests drive their education. Students major in either sciences and engineering, humanities, or social sciences and complete a "cluster" of at least three related courses in each of the other two areas. Because Rochester is among America's smallest research universities, its students can pursue advanced studies and research in graduate courses, in arts and science or in any one of Rochester's nationally ranked schools of engineering, medicine, nursing, music, education, and business.

"Learning here takes place on a personal scale. Rochester remains one of the most collegiate among top research universities, with smaller classes and a nine to one student-faculty ratio—all within a university setting that attracts more than $400 million in research funding each year. Rochester faculty publish articles across the globe, win awards for their work, and collaborate with undergraduate students on a level that is rare in higher education.

"The expectation is that each student will live up to Rochester's motto, "Meliora" (ever better), recognizing that they are future leaders in industry, education, and culture. Navigating through world-renowned facilities and resources, a day in the life of two Rochester students—or any two days in the life of a single student—is never the same."

SELECTIVITY

Admissions Rating	97
# of applicants	16,261
% of applicants accepted	36
% of acceptees attending	23
# offered a place on the wait list	2,172
% accepting a place on wait list	37
% admitted from wait list	0
# of early decision applicants	569
% accepted early decision	54

FRESHMAN PROFILE

Range SAT Critical Reading	600–700
Range SAT Math	650–750
Range SAT Writing	620–700
Range ACT Composite	29–32
Minimum paper TOEFL	600
Minimum web-based TOEFL	100
Average HS GPA	3.80
% graduated top 10% of class	75
% graduated top 25% of class	97
% graduated top 50% of class	100

DEADLINES

Early decision	
Deadline	11/1
Notification	12/15
Regular	
Priority	12/1
Deadline	1/1
Notification	4/1
Nonfall registration?	Yes

FINANCIAL FACTS

Financial Aid Rating	93
Annual tuition	$44,580
Room and board	$13,128
Required fees	$792
Books and supplies	$1,290
% needy frosh rec. need-based scholarship or grant aid	100
% needy UG rec. need-based scholarship or grant aid	99
% needy frosh rec. non-need-based scholarship or grant aid	20
% needy UG rec. non-need-based scholarship or grant aid	16
% needy frosh rec. need-based self-help aid	79
% needy UG rec. need-based self-help aid	83
% frosh rec. any financial aid	84
% UG rec. any financial aid	82
% UG borrow to pay for school	65
Average cumulative indebtedness	$29,430
% frosh need fully met	92
% ugrads need fully met	91
Average % of frosh need met	97
Average % of ugrad need met	82

UNIVERSITY OF SAN DIEGO

5998 ALCALA PARK, SAN DIEGO, CA 92110-2492 • ADMISSIONS: 619-260-4506 • FAX: 619-260-6836

STUDENTS SAY ". . ."

Academics

This "academically challenging, Roman Catholic" institution couples "amazing academics" and "wonderful teachers and programs" with "great weather and a beautiful campus." As one liberal studies major notes, "I just felt an overwhelming sense of belonging the very first time I stepped on campus. I fell in love right away." USD "strives and puts into action ways to create a well-rounded student who is able to succeed out in the real world." Major draws to the curriculum here include "small class sizes, potential relationships with professors, and the caring nature of the faculty." The professors "are there for you and want you to do your best...I love that the classes are taught by instructors with PhDs rather than TAs. It is great having your professor know you personally." Beyond the picturesque coastal campus—"It is in San Diego"—"undergraduate research opportunities are great!" In addition, USD has a strong undergraduate business program. USD is all about "discovering one's passions in the classroom in order to fulfill them in the real world." Besides the high caliber academics, "it is vacation weather year round. I went to the beach and tanned in January; very few other college students can say that."

Life

Life at USD boasts "beauty and brains!" USD is a "laid-back school overlooking the ocean, so people are happy to be at school and in class every day." Many tout a picture of the campus as a "country club escape from the city with outstanding professors, a friendly student body, and a five-minute drive to the beach." It's a "beach town, so surfing, laying out, bathing suits, sunglasses, and flip-flops are very prevalent." Going to the beach "is easy, you can see the ocean from campus." A car "is not totally necessary, the campus is equipped with everything you need and we have Zipcar on campus!" "It's a very active and fit" community. Some note that they "would love to see more diversity on campus." "There is a big difference between students with scholarships and those who don't need scholarships to attend." Yet others note that there are "tremendous opportunities to get involved at USD, local community and abroad!" "San Diego is about working hard for what you want, but it has everything you need to enjoy your undergraduate years." At USD, "there is always something to do for fun." There "is a party scene, but it is not overbearing to the point where it is necessary to drink." A typical day in the life of a USD student "is to go to class, get a delicious breakfast burrito at La Paloma (served all day) and hit the beach for parties on the weekend." Those adventurers looking to relax "can go to the pool, beach, parties at the beach, downtown's Gaslamp District, and Sea World on the weekends." Plus, "you are only 1.5 hours away from Disneyland and Los Angeles and four hours from Las Vegas!" Surrounding San Diego is "an amazing city."

Student Body

USD "produces students who have a desire to pursue their dreams with philanthropy." In general, all students at USD are "motivated" and "looking to better themselves and achieve personal success." As one student says, "The students here are like the protagonists in a TV series." However, "don't let the students' good looks, high fashion, or athletic prowess and wealth fool you, these students had 4.0s in high school, have intense internships, compete for graduate and professional school spots, and are constantly serving the community." Others concede, the typical student "comes from substantial wealth, [is] white, has a strong work ethic, [and is] laid-back, athletic, outgoing, and friendly." Though, others note, "There are exceptions to the USD stereotype." Many students "receive financial aid" and thus join the leagues of those who "are very motivated to get good grades." Since USD is a Catholic school, "there are quite a few of us who are religious." Others note, "It feels a lot like high school...all the groups keep to themselves." Yet others say with the wealth of campus clubs, sporting events, internship, and community service opportunities, "there seems to be a niche for everyone."

FINANCIAL AID: 619-260-4514 • E-MAIL: ADMISSIONS@SANDIEGO.EDU • WEBSITE: WWW.SANDIEGO.EDU

THE PRINCETON REVIEW SAYS
Admissions

Very important factors considered include: GPA, rigor of secondary school record, standardized test scores. *Important factors considered include:* Class rank, application essay, extracurricular activities, recommendation(s), talent/ability, volunteer work, character/personal qualities, religious affiliation. *Other factors considered include:* First generation, geographical residence, interview, racial/ethnic status, work experience, alumni/ae relations, level of applicant's interest. SAT or ACT required; SAT and SAT Subject Tests or ACT considered if submitted; ACT with Writing component required. TOEFL required of all international applicants. *Academic units required:* 4 English; 3 mathematics; 3 science; (2 science lab); 2 social studies; 3 foreign language. *Academic units recommended:* 4 English; 4 mathematics; 4 science; (3 science lab); 3 social studies; 4 foreign language.

Financial Aid

Students should submit: FAFSA. Regular filing deadline is 3/2. The Princeton Review suggests that all financial aid forms be submitted as soon as possible after January 1. *Need-based scholarships/grants offered:* Federal Pell, SEOG, State scholarships/grants, private scholarships, the school's own gift aid, federal nursing scholarships. *Loan aid offered:* Direct Subsidized Stafford Loans, Direct Unsubsidized Stafford Loans, Direct PLUS loans, Federal-Perkins Loans, College/university loans from institutional funds. Federal Work-Study Program available. Institutional employment available. Off-campus job opportunities are good.

The Inside Word

USD offers a broad liberal arts core, small classes, and close interaction between students and professors. The dazzling campus and an unbeatable location are just gravy. As such, admission here is competitive. Solid test scores and outstanding grades should be a given for applicants.

THE SCHOOL SAYS "..."
From the Admissions Office

"The University of San Diego has received many local, regional, and national honors in its short, sixty-year history. We are known around the world for our beautiful campus, our outstanding faculty, our sustainability efforts, study abroad programs and the community service work done by our students. Recently, USD was selected as a "change maker" campus, one of only fourteen schools in the world so designated by the Ashoka Foundation. It is this honor that captures the spirit of USD and ties together all the others.

"We believe that the world's problems can be solved. We believe that the solution to these problems will not be found through a single discipline or focus. Instead, we know that the world's problems will be solved through innovation, collaboration, and compassion. USD was founded six decades ago with the principles of Catholic social teaching, a living tradition to work for socially just and peaceful societies and a mission to prepare generations of people changing the world for the better.

"We seek students who also believe in social innovation and change. Students at USD are bright, as our rapidly-growing student profile attests. But they also bring a passion for learning and making a difference. Through our strong liberal arts curriculum, international experiences, faculty and programs, we take that passion and turn it into a lifetime of making the world a better place."

SELECTIVITY
Admissions Rating	94
# of applicants	14,693
% of applicants accepted	49
% of acceptees attending	17
# offered a place on the wait list	1,791
% accepting a place on wait list	35
% admitted from wait list	1

FRESHMAN PROFILE
Range SAT Critical Reading	540–650
Range SAT Math	570–670
Range SAT Writing	550–660
Range ACT Composite	25–30
Minimum paper TOEFL	550
Minimum web-based TOEFL	213
Average HS GPA	3.88
% graduated top 10% of class	45
% graduated top 25% of class	91
% graduated top 50% of class	95

DEADLINES
Early action	
Deadline	
Regular	
Deadline	12/15
Nonfall registration?	Yes

APPLICANTS ALSO LOOK AT AND OFTEN PREFER
University of Southern California

AND SOMETIMES PREFER
Loyola Marymount University

AND RARELY PREFER
University of California—San Diego

FINANCIAL FACTS
Financial Aid Rating	76
Annual tuition	$40,900
Room and board	$11,910
Required fees	$492
Books and supplies	$1,710
% needy frosh rec. need-based scholarship or grant aid	97
% needy UG rec. need-based scholarship or grant aid	94
% needy frosh rec. non-need-based scholarship or grant aid	53
% needy UG rec. non-need-based scholarship or grant aid	43
% needy frosh rec. need-based self-help aid	76
% needy UG rec. need-based self-help aid	80
% frosh rec. any financial aid	75
% UG rec. any financial aid	72
% UG borrow to pay for school	51
Average cumulative indebtedness	$29,115
% frosh need fully met	12
% ugrads need fully met	14
Average % of frosh need met	72
Average % of ugrad need met	70

UNIVERSITY OF SAN FRANCISCO

2130 FULTON STREET, SAN FRANCISCO, CA 94117 • ADMISSIONS: 415-422-6563 • FAX: 415-422-2217

CAMPUS LIFE

Quality of Life Rating	82
Fire Safety Rating	60*
Green Rating	74
Type of school	Private
Affiliation	Jesuit Roman Catholic
Environment	Metropolis

STUDENTS

Total undergrad enrollment	6,392
% male/female	38/62
% from out of state	18
% frosh from public high school	52
% frosh live on campus	92
% ugrads live on campus	34
# of fraternities (% ugrad men join)	3 (1)
# of sororities (% ugrad women join)	5 (1)
% African American	3
% Asian	19
% Caucasian	31
% Hispanic	19
% Native American	<1
% international	18
# of countries represented	85

SURVEY SAYS . . .

Political activism is unpopular or nonexistent
Students love San Francisco, CA
Great off-campus food

ACADEMICS

Academic Rating	80
% students returning for sophomore year	87
% students graduating within 4 years	57
% students graduating within 6 years	69
Calendar	4/1/4
Student/faculty ratio	15:1
Profs interesting rating	79
Profs accessible rating	76

Most classes have 10–19 students.
Most lab/discussion sessions have
10–19 students.

MOST POPULAR MAJORS

registered nursing; psychology; financial
planning

STUDENTS SAY " . . . "

Academics

With its "Jesuit morals" and "close-knit" community, this "academically rigorous school" focuses on "promoting social justice, tolerance, and community spirit." USF "teaches its students about the importance of helping others and making a difference in today's society." The curriculum here not only focuses "a lot on education but on making students aware of issues in the world and, on a smaller scale, the local community." Classes here are about "educating minds and hearts to change the world." As one student notes, "I wanted to go to a small school in a big city that promotes important issues like social justice and community service." Many tout the school's "diversity" and "remarkable education." "Because the school is small, classes are too." "One-on-one attention from professors is common." "Professors are sincerely passionate about their subject and try to engage students and share their passion while ensuring learning and comprehension." "Most of the professors are really enthusiastic about their classes because most of them have already worked in the areas they're teaching and can enlighten us on their past failures and successes." "During my junior and senior semesters at USF, I began to really appreciate my professors of upper-division courses that are really devoted to their teachings."

Life

"People here love to go out and have a good time." Living in San Francisco, "there is always something to do." People "go out into the city to enjoy the beach, parks, downtown, city landmarks, club events, social justice groups, protests, and rallies for causes." When looking for a place to spend an idle-while afternoon, students "go to Golden Gate Park [or] take MUNI downtown." "There are too many places to eat!" Chinatown "is always fun; Fisherman's wharf and Pier 39 are always fun too." On campus, students are "very involved." This typical motto reverberates, "I have two on campus jobs, and I'm active in three clubs!" When it comes to socializing, "people think and discuss a lot of things; topics like religion, politics, international issues, [and] the environment." Using the gym "is also something to do since you get free membership to Koret Gym if you are a student at USF." On the weekend, for fun, students go to "the free festivals that are going on in the city…go shopping in downtown, hang out at the park, or check out a neighborhood or area I've never been to before with my friends." Those with an outdoors bent "enjoy going on bike rides through Golden Gate Park or to China Beach and watching the sunset." In general, life here is all about "managing my time in a way that I can get all my work done and still have time to hang out with friends." Dorms are generally well accommodated, but "like any other campus," students note, "The facilities in some of the building could be updated and the computer labs could be updated."

Student Body

A typical student at USF "cannot clearly be defined" as "the students at the University of San Francisco are from all walks of life"; "Students easily fit in to the school," which is "extremely diverse." Students "are very accepting of all cultures." True to their Jesuit values and passion for community service, students here call out the following attributes like roll call. Students are "outgoing, cheerful, fashionable, and active socially, politically, [and] environmentally." "Everyone is very friendly and tolerant," and "there are always new people to meet." While "there is no 'typical student'" at USF, "many students here are definitely involved in a green movement, sustainability, community service or international affairs." Those who are quick to affix a label cast the following stereotype, "Guys [at USF] are more of the grungy or hipster types. For girls, the school is a show…you find out quickly that many intend to see and be seen. Athletes [tend to] stick together." Whatever cues their fashion code may call for, the average student here "studies a lot [and is] always on the move helping out someone in need." "Ambitious goals" pervade student thinking, and everyone is "kind toward others." In essence, "San Francisco is home to a wide variety of people and, as such, so is USF."

FINANCIAL AID: 415-422-6303 • E-MAIL: ADMISSION@USFCA.EDU • WEBSITE: WWW.USFCA.EDU

THE PRINCETON REVIEW SAYS

Admissions

Very important factors considered include: GPA, rigor of secondary school record, standardized test scores, application essay. *Important factors considered include:* Class rank, extracurricular activities, recommendation(s), volunteer work, character/personal qualities. *Other factors considered include:* First generation, interview, racial/ethnic status, talent/ability, work experience, alumni/ae relations. SAT or ACT required; ACT with Writing component required. TOEFL required of all international applicants. *Academic units recommended:* 4 English; 3 mathematics; 2 science; (2 science lab); 3 social studies; 2 foreign language; 6 academic electives.

Financial Aid

Students should submit: FAFSA. The Princeton Review suggests that all financial aid forms be submitted as soon as possible after January 1. *Need-based scholarships/grants offered:* Federal Pell, SEOG, State scholarships/grants, private scholarships, the school's own gift aid, federal nursing scholarships. *Loan aid offered:* Direct Subsidized Stafford Loans, Direct Unsubsidized Stafford Loans, Direct PLUS loans, Federal Perkins Loans, Federal Nursing Loans, College/university loans from institutional funds. Federal Work-Study Program available. Institutional employment available. Off-campus job opportunities are excellent.

The Inside Word

The admissions committee at USF isn't purely numbers focused. They'll evaluate your full picture here, using your academic strengths and weaknesses along with your personal character strengths, essays, and recommendations to assess your suitability for admission. It's matchmaking. If you fit well in the USF community, you'll be welcome.

THE SCHOOL SAYS "..."

From the Admissions Office

"The University of San Francisco has experienced a significant increase in applications for admission over the past five years. We select applicants with strong academic credentials who will make the most of the university's academic opportunities, location in San Francisco, and its mission to educate minds and hearts to challenge the world. Community outreach and service to others, along with academic excellence, are characteristics that help distinguish those offered admission.

"The university has just completed a major upgrade to all administrative computer systems, including software that will help with student compatibility matching in residence halls.

"Applicants are required to take the SAT reasoning test (or the ACT with the writing section). The writing sections will be used for advising and placement purposes. SAT Subject Test scores will also be accepted."

SELECTIVITY

Admissions Rating	83
# of applicants	14,844
% of applicants accepted	61
% of acceptees attending	13
# offered a place on the wait list	801
%accepting a place on the wait list	33

FRESHMAN PROFILE

Range SAT Critical Reading	530–630
Range SAT Math	540–640
Range SAT Writing	530–630
Range ACT Composite	23–27
Minimum paper TOEFL	550
Minimum web-based TOEFL	79
Average HS GPA	3.61
% graduated top 10% of class	33
% graduated top 25% of class	71
% graduated top 50% of class	94

DEADLINES

Early decision	
Deadline	11/15
Notification	1/1
Early action	
Deadline	11/15
Notification	1/1
Regular	
Priority	1/15
Nonfall registration?	Yes

APPLICANTS ALSO LOOK AT AND OFTEN PREFER
University of California--Davis;Loyola Marymount University

AND SOMETIMES PREFER
University of California--Los Angeles; University of California--Berkeley

AND RARELY PREFER
University of La Verne; St. Louis University; University of Missouri--Columbia

FINANCIAL FACTS

Financial Aid Rating	69
Annual tuition	$40,996
Room and board	$13,320
Required fees	$454
Books and supplies	$1,600
% needy frosh rec. need-based scholarship or grant aid	94
% needy UG rec. need-based scholarship or grant aid	92
% needy frosh rec. non-need-based scholarship or grant aid	70
% needy UG rec. non-need-based scholarship or grant aid	49
% needy frosh rec. need-based self-help aid	81
% needy UG rec. need-based self-help aid	86
% UG rec. any financial aid	55
% UG borrow to pay for school	66
Average cumulative indebtedness	$29,054
% frosh need fully met	11
% ugrads need fully met	12
Average % of frosh need met	71
Average % of ugrad need met	64

UNIVERSITY OF SCRANTON

800 LINDEN STREET, SCRANTON, PA 18510-4699 • ADMISSIONS: 570-941-7540 FAX: 570-941-5928

STUDENTS SAY ". . ."

Academics

With "an outstanding record for admission to graduate programs, not only in law and medicine but also in several other fields," The University of Scranton is a good fit for ambitious students seeking "a Jesuit school in every sense of the word. If you come here, expect to be challenged to become a better person, to develop a strong concern for the poor and marginalized, and to grow spiritually and intellectually." The school manages to accomplish this without "forcing religion upon you, which is nice." Undergraduates also approve of the mandatory liberal-arts-based curriculum that "forces you to learn about broader things than your own major." Strong majors here include "an amazing occupational therapy program." "This is a great place for premeds and other sciences," students agree. While the workload can be difficult, "a tutoring center provides free tutoring for any students who may need it, and also provides work-study positions for students who qualify to tutor." Need more help? Professors "are extremely accessible. They will go to any lengths to help you understand material and do well," while administrators "are here for the students, and show that every day inside and outside of the classroom." Community ties here are strong; as one student points out, "the Jesuits live in our dorms, creating an even greater sense of community, because we don't view them as just priests, we view them as real people who can relate on our level."

Life

"There is a whole range of activities to do on the weekends" at The University of Scranton, including "frequent trips, dances, and movies that are screened for free." Students tell us "the school and student organizations provide plenty of options, such as retreats, talent shows, and other various activities." There are also "many intramurals to become involved in, and the varsity sports (specifically the women's) are very successful." Furthermore, "being a Jesuit school, social justice issues are huge. They are taught in the classroom, and students spend a lot of time volunteering." Hometown Scranton is big enough to provide "movie theaters, two malls, parks, a bowling alley, and a skiing/snowboarding mountain." In short, there are plenty of choices for the non-partier at Scranton. Many we heard from in our survey reported busy extracurricular schedules. But those seeking a party won't be disappointed here, either. Scranton undergrads "party a lot, but they balance it with studying. Parties are chances to go out, see people, dance, and drink if you want." You "can find a party any time of day, seven days a week" here, usually with a keg tapped and pouring. Few here feel the party scene is out of hand, however a typical student writes, "It's very different than at schools with Greek systems. It is a lot more laid-back, and all about everyone having a good time."

Student Body

While "the typical Scranton student is white, Catholic, and from the suburbs," students hasten to point out "within this sameness, there is much diversity. There are people who couldn't care at all about religion, and there are people who are deeply religious. Even in the Catholic atmosphere of the school, the school only requires that you learn about Catholicism as it stands. Theology classes…are prefaced with the idea that 'You do not have to believe this!'" Undergrads here are generally "friendly and welcoming. Cliques are pretty much nonexistent, and anyone who would be classified as 'popular' is only considered so because they are extremely friendly, outgoing, and seek out friendships with as many people as possible." Students tend to be on the Abercrombie-preppy side, with lots of undergrads of Italian, Irish, and Polish descent.

FINANCIAL AID: 570-941-7700 • E-MAIL: ADMISSIONS@SCRANTON.EDU • WEBSITE: WWW.SCRANTON.EDU

THE PRINCETON REVIEW SAYS

Admissions

Very important factors considered include: Class rank, GPA, rigor of secondary school record, standardized test scores. *Important factors considered include:* Extracurricular activities. *Other factors considered include:* Application essay, interview, recommendation(s), talent/ability, volunteer work, work experience, alumni/ae relations, character/personal qualities, level of applicant's interest. SAT or ACT required; ACT with or without Writing component accepted. TOEFL required of all international applicants. *Academic units required:* 4 English; 3 mathematics; 1 science; 2 foreign language; 2 history. *Academic units recommended:* 4 English; 4 mathematics; 2 science; 2 foreign language; 3 history.

Financial Aid

Students should submit: FAFSA. The Princeton Review suggests that all financial aid forms be submitted as soon as possible after January 1. *Need-based scholarships/grants offered:* Federal Pell, SEOG, State scholarships/grants, private scholarships, the school's own gift aid. *Loan aid offered:* Direct Subsidized Stafford Loans, Direct Unsubsidized Stafford Loans, Direct PLUS loans, Federal Perkins Loans. Federal Work-Study Program available. Institutional employment available. Off-campus job opportunities are good.

The Inside Word

Admission to Scranton gets harder each year. A steady stream of smart kids from the tristate area keeps classes full and the admit rate low. Successful applicants will need solid grades and test scores. As with many religiously affiliated schools, students should be a good match philosophically as well.

THE SCHOOL SAYS "..."

From the Admissions Office

"The University of Scranton is a Catholic and Jesuit university that is known for outstanding academic quality, a beautiful and technology-rich campus and a sense of community that helps students feel right at home. Our fifty-eight-acre hillside campus in northeastern Pennsylvania is just two hours from New York City and Philadelphia. Since 2008, we've invested nearly $204 million in campus improvements, either completed or under way. In 2011, Pilarz and Montrone Halls, which house nearly 400 upperclass students and a fitness center, opened. The new Loyola Science Center was completed in two phases in 2011 and 2012. A new $47 million center for rehabilitation education is scheduled for completion in 2015. Our location offers the best of both worlds—the city and the mountains. From campus, you can walk downtown to shop, watch a movie, visit a museum or see a show. The area also features minor league ice hockey and baseball, concerts, skiing, hiking, malls and shopping outlets.

"The university offers more than sixty majors, eighty clubs and organizations, and eighteen Division III athletic teams to the 3,834 undergraduate students in attendance. Scranton develops leaders in every sense through rigorous preparation in students' chosen fields coupled with a commitment to educating the whole person in the liberal arts tradition. Students extend their academic experience through participation in honors programs, internships, faculty-student research and study abroad, and the University provides excellent preparation for medical and other health professions doctoral programs, law school, graduate school, and post-graduate fellowships and scholarships.

"Students can apply online for free at scranton.edu/apply, or schedule a visit online at scranton.edu/visit, or by calling us at 1-888-SCRANTON."

SELECTIVITY

Admissions Rating	81
# of applicants	9,087
% of applicants accepted	75
% of acceptees attending	13
# offered a place on the wait list	647
% accepting a place on wait list	21
% admitted from wait list	58

FRESHMAN PROFILE

Range SAT Critical Reading	510–600
Range SAT Math	520–610
Range ACT Composite	22–27
Minimum paper TOEFL	550
Average HS GPA	3.37
% graduated top 10% of class	25
% graduated top 25% of class	59
% graduated top 50% of class	85

DEADLINES

Early action	
Deadline	11/15
Notification	12/15
Regular	
Priority	3/1
Deadline	3/1
Nonfall registration?	Yes

APPLICANTS ALSO LOOK AT AND OFTEN PREFER

Penn State University; Saint Joseph's University; University of Delaware; Quinnipiac University

AND SOMETIMES PREFER

Loyola Maryland; Temple University; Marist College; Fairfield University

FINANCIAL FACTS

Financial Aid Rating	73
Annual tuition	$39,556
Room and board	$13,566
Required fees	$400
Books and supplies	$1,200
% needy frosh rec. need-based scholarship or grant aid	97
% needy UG rec. need-based scholarship or grant aid	96
% needy frosh rec. non-need-based scholarship or grant aid	9
% needy UG rec. non-need-based scholarship or grant aid	6
% needy frosh rec. need-based self-help aid	83
% needy UG rec. need-based self-help aid	87
% frosh rec. any financial aid	95
% UG rec. any financial aid	91
% UG borrow to pay for school	76
Average cumulative indebtedness	$39,703
% frosh need fully met	12
% ugrads need fully met	10
Average % of frosh need met	68
Average % of ugrad need met	67

UNIVERSITY OF SOUTH CAROLINA—COLUMBIA

OFFICE OF UNDERGRADUATE ADMISSIONS, COLUMBIA, SC 29208 • ADMISSIONS: 803-777-7700 • FAX: 803-777-0101

CAMPUS LIFE

Quality of Life Rating	82
Fire Safety Rating	90
Green Rating	96
Type of school	Public
Affiliation	No Affiliation
Environment	City

STUDENTS

Total undergrad enrollment	23,028
% male/female	46/54
% from out of state	31
% frosh live on campus	94
% ugrads live on campus	36
# of fraternities (% ugrad men join)	22 (14)
# of sororities (% ugrad women join)	16 (31)
% African American	11
% Asian	3
% Caucasian	78
% Hispanic	4
% Native American	<1
% international	1
# of countries represented	115

SURVEY SAYS . . .

Great off-campus food
Athletic facilities are great
Lots of beer drinking
Everyone loves the Gamecocks
Frats and sororities are popular
Student publications are popular
Alumni active on campus

ACADEMICS

Academic Rating	76
% students returning for sophomore year	87
% students graduating within 4 years	53
% students graduating within 6 years	72
Calendar	Semester
Student/faculty ratio	17:1
Profs interesting rating	71
Profs accessible rating	73

Most classes have 20–29 students.
Most lab/discussion sessions have
20–29 students.

MOST POPULAR MAJORS
experimental psychology; nursing; criminal
justice

STUDENTS SAY ". . ."

Academics

An "affordable, large, and beautiful" public college with exuberant school spirit, University of South Carolina–Columbia offers "the perfect balance of education and fun" to more than 23,000 undergraduates. Choice is key to the USC experience. With 95 academic major programs to choose from, students praise the "diversity in classes, clubs, and events to get involved in," from science to the arts. Well-regarded programs at this "superior state school" include an "exceptional" marine science department, "one of the top-ranked business schools in the country," and a "highly rated and competitive" pharmacy program. First-year students should be prepared for the fact that "entry-level classes are extremely large," often incorporating "little to no discussion." Fortunately, the environment is far from impersonal, and most professors "seem to care immensely about how well each person is doing, even in classes of over 300 people." While you'll find "the good, the bad, and the ugly" on the teaching staff, the majority of "Professors are experts in their field and genuinely have a passion for sharing their knowledge with their students." A current student enthuses, "Some professors are so exceptional you want to take their class over and over again because you learn so much." Those who need extra assistance say the "academic help centers are excellent," including excellent tutoring programs "lead by students who were previously enrolled in the class." However, bureaucracy can be cumbersome at USC, and many would like to see "better organization of class registration and advisement" processes.

Life

USC's "historic southern vibe and lovely campus" make it a wonderful place to spend four years. Despite the school's considerable size, "students can find their niche in more than 400 organizations" on campus. Many undergraduates are "heavily involved in Greek life," but "there are tons of academic, sports, and community service groups to get involved with also." "School pride and traditions" are integral to the USC experience, especially on game day. Here, "football is a religion," and, throughout the fall semester, "the whole student body spends all day Saturday tailgating" at Williams-Brice Stadium. "Everyone likes to have a good time" at USC, and students "are constantly going out on the weekends (usually Thursday-Saturday nights)," when you'll find undergrads at house parties and Greek events, or out at Five Points, "a strip of restaurants and bars located in downtown near the school." With its vibrant, student-friendly community and beautiful South Carolina setting, "You have your choice of city life or country" at USC: "You can fish, camp, hunt and kayak one day, then the next you can hit the city, go to clubs, see a show, and sample local cuisine." Not to mention, the beautiful "weather almost always caters to outdoor activities."

Students

USC is filled with "outgoing" and "preppy" middle-class Southerners, who are "brought together by our common love for Carolina." In fact, many USC undergrads were "born and raised in South Carolina" and have been cheering on the Gamecocks since childhood. "Most of the students that attend are politically conservative" and many are religious—though a number of students point out that USC is far more politically and socially liberal than its South Carolina location might lead you to believe. Despite general similarities, you don't have to fit any mold to enjoy life at USC. A current student shares, "I am northern, not religious, and never go home to visit, and I still fit in fine; I am just not the norm." There is a lot of diversity in terms of clubs and interest groups, and "no matter what you're passionate about, there is a place for you at USC." The best way to find your niche is to "get involved with something and do it freshman year." Overall, the campus tends to be a friendly and welcoming place, where a "student can simply fit in by going to a football game and be[ing] surrounded by other Gamecocks." A current student tells us, "I love that I can strike up a conversation with anyone and everyone and 90 percent of the time, we'll become friends. Everyone is insanely happy at South Carolina."

UNIVERSITY OF SOUTH CAROLINA—COLUMBIA

FINANCIAL AID: 803-777-8134 • E-MAIL: ADMISSIONS-UGRAD@SC.EDU • WEBSITE: WWW.SC.EDU

THE PRINCETON REVIEW SAYS

Admissions

Very important factors considered include: GPA, application essay. *Important factors considered include:* Class rank, rigor of secondary school record. *Other factors considered include:* Standardized test scores, extracurricular activities, first generation, racial/ethnic status, recommendation(s), state residency, talent/ability, volunteer work, work experience, alumni/ae relations, character/personal qualities. SAT or ACT required; ACT with Writing component required. TOEFL required of all international applicants. *Academic units required:* 4 English; 4 mathematics; 3 science; (3 science lab); 2 social studies; 2 foreign language; 1 history; 1 academic elective; 1 visual/performing arts.

Financial Aid

Students should submit: FAFSA. The Princeton Review suggests that all financial aid forms be submitted as soon as possible after January 1. *Need-based scholarships/grants offered:* Federal Pell, SEOG, State scholarships/grants, private scholarships, the school's own gift aid, United Negro College Fund, federal nursing scholarships. *Loan aid offered:* Direct Subsidized Stafford Loans, Direct Unsubsidized Stafford Loans, Direct PLUS loans, Federal Perkins Loans, Federal Nursing Loans Applicants will be notified of awards beginning 4/1. Federal Work-Study Program available. Institutional employment available. Off-campus job opportunities are good.

The Inside Word

At University of South Carolina, as at most large schools, admissions decisions are based almost entirely on a prospective student's grades, test scores, and high school curriculum. A personal statement is not required, but is recommended. Applicants with a A-minus average and SAT section scores in the 1120–1280 range (or an ACT composite of 24–29) often get in. Higher standardized scores can offset a lower GPA, and vice versa.

THE SCHOOL SAYS "..."

From the Admissions Office

"In just six years, the number of annual undergraduate applicants to USC has doubled, making it more critical than ever for students to meet the university's priority application deadline. The University of South Carolina's national prominence in academics and research activities also has increased. USC is one of only thirty-five public research institutions to earn a designated status of 'very high research activity' by the Carnegie Foundation. As early as their freshman year, undergraduates are encouraged to compete for research grants. As South Carolina's flagship institution, USC offers more than 350 degree programs. More than 30,000 students seek baccalaureate, masters, or doctoral degrees. USC is known for its top-ranked academic programs, including its international business and exercise science programs—both rated number one nationally. Other notable programs include chemical and nuclear engineering; health education; hotel, restaurant, and tourism; marine science; law; medicine; nursing; and psychology, among others. USC is recognized for its pioneering efforts in freshman outreach, and the South Carolina Honors College is ranked number one in the country compared to all other honors colleges in public university settings. USC offers student support in such areas as career development, leadership training, research grants, pre-professional planning, and study abroad. On campus, students enjoy a state-of-the-art fitness center, an 18,000-seat arena, an 80,000-seat stadium, and more than 400 student organizations. Off campus, South Carolina's world-famous beaches and the Blue Ridge Mountains are each less than a three-hour drive away. The University of South Carolina is located in the state's capital city, making it a great place for internships and job opportunities."

SELECTIVITY

Admissions Rating	89
# of applicants	23,429
% of applicants accepted	61
% of acceptees attending	33

FRESHMAN PROFILE

Range SAT Critical Reading	540–640
Range SAT Math	560–650
Range ACT Composite	24–29
Minimum paper TOEFL	550
Minimum web-based TOEFL	210
Average HS GPA	4.00
% graduated top 10% of class	30
% graduated top 25% of class	67
% graduated top 50% of class	94

DEADLINES

Early action	
Deadline	10/15
Notification	12/20
Regular	
Priority	12/1
Deadline	12/1
Notification	3/15
Nonfall registration?	Yes

APPLICANTS ALSO LOOK AT AND OFTEN PREFER
The University of North Carolina at Chapel Hill

AND SOMETIMES PREFER
Clemson University

AND RARELY PREFER
Wake Forest University

FINANCIAL FACTS

Financial Aid Rating	80
Annual in-state tuition	$10,416
Annual out-of-state tuition	$28,128
Room and board	$8,909
Required fees	$400
Books and supplies	$994
% needy frosh rec. need-based scholarship or grant aid	44
% needy UG rec. need-based scholarship or grant aid	51
% needy frosh rec. non-need-based scholarship or grant aid	89
% needy UG rec. non-need-based scholarship or grant aid	64
% needy frosh rec. need-based self-help aid	90
% needy UG rec. need-based self-help aid	91
% frosh rec. any financial aid	96
% UG rec. any financial aid	87
% UG borrow to pay for school	46
Average cumulative indebtedness	$25,022
% frosh need fully met	30
% ugrads need fully met	27
Average % of frosh need met	75
Average % of ugrad need met	74

THE UNIVERSITY OF SOUTH DAKOTA

414 EAST CLARK, VERMILLION, SD 57069 • ADMISSIONS: 605-677-5434 • FAX: 605-677-6323

STUDENTS SAY ". . ."

Academics

With an honors program that is "the best-kept secret in the country" and professors who are "nearly always willing to go the extra mile for students," the University of South Dakota offers a "great student to faculty communicative experience at a reasonable price." Numerous departments garner praise from students, and the University boasts winners "almost every year for big scholarships like the Goldwater and Truman, competing with big, Ivy League, private colleges that charge quadruple the amount for the same education." While the nursing school is the most frequently praised, the "business, biology, premed, law, and psychology classes are very solid," and the "dental hygiene, music, and journalism schools" also stand out, with the most copious laurels heaped on the music department's professors who are "some of the best." All told, the wide selection of quality academics "gives students many options as far as majors go," and for students willing to throw themselves into their studies "the odds of getting into a professional or graduate program are good."

Life

"We work hard, so we can play hard," sums up the undergraduate philosophy at USD. "Although there is a lot of partying that happens, the students keep themselves occupied with school work, intramural sports, and hanging out with their friends." Vermillion's small size seems to be a double-edged sword; some insist that "the size of the town means no one is more than a 10-minute walk/bike ride away!" and that "since it is a smaller campus students have more opportunities to be involved in internships and various other activities." But the fact remains that "many of the upperclassmen live in the larger cities to the north and south." In general, "students have to make their own fun, which often involves partying or taking small road trips to other cities in the area." For those planning to roam further afield, "Vermillion is located very close to Yankton, Sioux City (IA), and Sioux Falls (all within an hour). They are bigger cities and offer everything a person would want to do (shopping, movies, entertainment)."

Student Body

A typical USD student "would be a conservative Midwesterner. He or she would be Caucasian" and would most likely have originated in "small towns in South Dakota, Iowa, and Nebraska." "Many people join a Greek system or are athletes or musicians. Those who do not fit into these three main groups seem to focus on their academics" and "[fit] in fine with the majority because of the open mindedness of most students." For example, "gay students are able to get along with the rest of student population." There's no denying that "partying is a definite part of the culture, though many of the 'smart' kids both party and work hard." Student organizations call out to many, and "it seems like every person on campus is part of at least one of them. It is a great way to meet new people and [to participate in] activities."

FINANCIAL AID: 605-677-5446 • E-MAIL: ADMISSIONS@USD.EDU • WEBSITE: WWW.USD.EDU

THE PRINCETON REVIEW SAYS

Admissions

Very important factors considered include: Class rank, GPA, rigor of secondary school record, standardized test scores. *Important factors considered include:* Alumni/ae relations. *Other factors considered include:* Application essay, extra-curricular activities, geographical residence, racial/ethnic status, recommendation(s), state residency, talent/ability, volunteer work, work experience, character/personal qualities. SAT and SAT Subject Tests or ACT required; ACT with or without Writing component accepted. TOEFL required of all international applicants. *Academic units required:* 4 English; 3 mathematics; 3 science; (3 science lab); 3 social studies. *Academic units recommended:* 4 mathematics; 4 science; 2 foreign language.

Financial Aid

Students should submit: FAFSA. The Princeton Review suggests that all financial aid forms be submitted as soon as possible after January 1. *Need-based scholarships/grants offered:* Federal Pell, SEOG, private scholarships, the school's own gift aid, federal nursing scholarships. *Loan aid offered:* Federal Perkins Loans, Federal Nursing Loans, College/university loans from institutional funds. Federal Work-Study Program available. Institutional employment available. Off-campus job opportunities are good.

The Inside Word

To be a candidate for general admission to USD, you must meet one of three general requirements: rank in the top 50 percent of your graduating class or obtain an ACT/SAT composite score of 21/990 or higher or have a minimum grade point average of at least 2.6 on a 4.0 scale in all high school courses. An applicant's high school curricula must also meet certain minimum requirements.

THE SCHOOL SAYS "..."

From the Admissions Office

"The University of South Dakota is the perfect fit for students looking for a smart educational investment. USD is South Dakota's only designated liberal arts university and is consistently rated among the top doctoral institutions in the country. Annually, USD awards scholarships to more than 800 first-year students, and more than 80 percent of USD students receive some form of financial aid through grants, loans, and work-study jobs.

"USD students earn the nation's most prestigious scholarships. Our quality of teaching and research prepares students to pursue their passions all over the world, at institutions such as Columbia, Johns Hopkins, The University of Chicago, and beyond. Fifty-nine students have been awarded prestigious Fulbright, Rhodes, National Science Foundation, Boren, Truman, Udall, Gilman, and Goldwater scholarships and grants for graduate study. Personal attention from our award-winning faculty and our welcoming environment makes students feel right at home.

"As the flagship liberal arts institution in South Dakota, USD—founded in 1862—has long been regarded as a leader in the state and the region. Notable undergraduate and postgraduate alumni include journalist Ken Bode, author and former news anchor Tom Brokaw, writer and Emmy Award–winner Dorothy Cooper Foote, U.S. Senator Tim Johnson, USA Today founder Al Neuharth, and U.S. Senator John Thune.

"Applicants are not required to take the writing test for either SAT or ACT. USD recommends taking the ACT over the SAT. Students who wish to send their SAT scores will have their scores converted to ACT scores for placement and scholarship consideration."

SELECTIVITY

Admissions Rating	69
# of applicants	3,606
% of applicants accepted	88
% of acceptees attending	42

FRESHMAN PROFILE

Range SAT Critical Reading	460–620
Range SAT Math	460–620
Range SAT Writing	430–580
Range ACT Composite	21–26
Minimum paper TOEFL	550
Minimum web-based TOEFL	220
Average HS GPA	3.36
% graduated top 10% of class	15
% graduated top 25% of class	38
% graduated top 50% of class	73

DEADLINES

Nonfall registration?	Yes

APPLICANTS ALSO LOOK AT AND OFTEN PREFER

University of Nebraska—Lincoln

FINANCIAL FACTS

Financial Aid Rating	86
Annual in-state tuition	$4,164
Annual out-of-state tuition	$6,246
Room and board	$7,089
Required fees	$3,858
Books and supplies	$1,100
% needy frosh rec. need-based scholarship or grant aid	44
% needy UG rec. need-based scholarship or grant aid	51
% needy frosh rec. non-need-based scholarship or grant aid	77
% needy UG rec. non-need-based scholarship or grant aid	51
% needy frosh rec. need-based self-help aid	83
% needy UG rec. need-based self-help aid	86
% frosh rec. any financial aid	94
% UG rec. any financial aid	81
% UG borrow to pay for school	75
Average cumulative indebtedness	$0
% frosh need fully met	57
% ugrads need fully met	58
Average % of frosh need met	73
Average % of ugrad need met	71

UNIVERSITY OF SOUTH FLORIDA

4202 EAST FOWLER AVENUE, TAMPA, FL 33620-9951 • ADMISSIONS: 813-974-3350 • FAX: 813-974-9689

CAMPUS LIFE

Quality of Life Rating	75
Fire Safety Rating	78
Green Rating	96
Type of school	Public
Affiliation	No Affiliation
Environment	Metropolis

STUDENTS

Total undergrad enrollment	30,376
% male/female	45/55
% from out of state	7
% frosh from public high school	95
% frosh live on campus	77
% ugrads live on campus	24
# of fraternities (% ugrad men join)	24 (8)
# of sororities (% ugrad women join)	23 (8)
% African American	11
% Asian	6
% Caucasian	55
% Hispanic	20
% Native American	<1
% international	3
# of countries represented	155

SURVEY SAYS . . .

Diverse student types on campus
Students get along with local community
Great off-campus food
Everyone loves the Bulls
Student publications are popular

ACADEMICS

Academic Rating	74
% students returning for sophomore year	89
% students graduating within 4 years	29
% students graduating within 6 years	57
Calendar	Semester
Student/faculty ratio	24:1
Profs interesting rating	69
Profs accessible rating	69

Most classes have 20–29 students.
Most lab/discussion sessions have
20–29 students.

MOST POPULAR MAJORS
psychology; business/commerce;
microbiology

STUDENTS SAY ". . ."

Academics

Conveniently located in Tampa, Florida, this top-tier state university attracts students for whom "price, diversity, and opportunities" are as important as a location that's "close to home." The University of South Florida "is all about community." One student says, "It was close to home, offered the degree that I wanted, offered me the most financial aid, and had many ties to the community and surrounding areas culturally and academically." USF may be huge, but this "does not affect the level of personal attention that students receive." Many here laud the honors program: "Classes are almost always discussion-based." In general, professors here "really want you to succeed." Students universally cheer, "The campus is beautiful!" Most of the professors "have worked twenty plus years in the field and are not strictly academia experienced, which results in more content-related discussions." Another adds, "Most professors, especially the business and philosophy related people, know their material and provide an open forum for learning." The College of Education has a sterling reputation for building "a caring community that expects excellence." With a large commuter population, there's a great diversity in the student body, "not just ethnically or culturally, but older students that bring experience and students from all socioeconomic levels." In addition, USF "is a top school for medical-related studies." USF offers the total package: "Fair tuition prices, a great city/location, excellent professors and [an excellent] learning atmosphere." USF is "doing everything within its capacity to provide the best education it can to every student, regardless of major, background, or ethnicity." This is an institution "dedicated to enriching their students and communities lives through eclectic methods."

Life

Life at USF "strongly promotes building a cohesive, comfortable community." The university enjoys "a diverse student population on a beautiful urban campus surrounded by a bustling city." Tampa "has a lot to offer for students. USF has so many clubs that each have various events, there is always something going on." Popular recreations include the "flea markets, poster sales, Patio Tuesdays (social event in the student center), clubs and organizations, free speech areas, residence hall parties, coffee houses, performances put on by the orchestras, bands, and theater, sports (Go Bulls!), guest speakers, etc." Many students enjoy the bustling club scene in Ybor City, a historic-district-turned-night-clubbing-district in Tampa's Latin Quarter where "there are a plethora of local bars and clubs to hang out at for fun."

Student Body

The USF student body is "a diverse mix socioeconomically, culturally, religiously, and racially." As one returning student testifies, "I am a nontraditional student in my fifties, and [I] feel completely comfortable in classes with students half my age. It's a very friendly school. All walks of life. I could not describe a typical student." USF "is a huge university." Every student "is completely different, so it's impossible to describe a 'typical' one." This makes for a welcome mix of professional and extracurricular interests; "So far, in every class it's been incredibly easy to get along with other classmates and everyone is really accepting of each other, no matter your background." As is often noted at many large universities with an active nightlife, "most people here have two personalities. One is extremely studious persona and the other is a party animal. Basically when it's time to let loose we let loose." On-campus students "are involved in campus and community activities, friendly, busy, and often have active social lives." There's "a strong sense of community fostered by club and organization involvement." USF "offers plenty of places to gather on campus." Despite the size of the school, social life is filled by "all sorts of activities and organizations that make it very easy to interact with people who share your views and interests."

FINANCIAL AID: 813-974-4700 • E-MAIL: ADMISSIONS@USF.EDU • WEBSITE: WWW.USF.EDU

THE PRINCETON REVIEW SAYS

Admissions

Very important factors considered include: GPA, rigor of secondary school record. *Important factors considered include:* Standardized test scores, first generation. *Other factors considered include:* Class rank, extracurricular activities, geographical residence, recommendation(s), state residency, talent/ability, volunteer work, work experience, character/personal qualities. SAT or ACT required; ACT with Writing component required. TOEFL required of all international applicants. *Academic units required:* 4 English; 4 mathematics; 3 science; (2 science lab); 3 social studies; 2 foreign language; 3 academic electives. *Academic units recommended:* 4 English; 4 mathematics; 3 science; (3 science lab); 3 social studies; 4 foreign language; 3 academic electives.

Financial Aid

Students should submit: FAFSA. The Princeton Review suggests that all financial aid forms be submitted as soon as possible after January 1. *Need-based scholarships/grants offered:* Federal Pell, SEOG, State scholarships/grants, private scholarships, the school's own gift aid. *Loan aid offered:* Direct Subsidized Stafford Loans, Direct Unsubsidized Stafford Loans, Direct PLUS loans, Federal Perkins Loans, College/university loans from institutional funds. Federal Work-Study Program available. Institutional employment available. Off-campus job opportunities are good.

The Inside Word

A traditional college-prep high school course load is required for admission to USF. Beyond making sure that you complete all prerequisite classes, however, keep two other things in mind when applying to USF. First, admissions decisions are made on a rolling basis, so the earlier one applies, the better his or her chance of acceptance since there are more unfilled seats early in the admissions cycle. Second, AP and international baccalaureate classes are looked on favorably in the admissions office, so if your school offers them, load up on them and do well.

THE SCHOOL SAYS "..."

From the Admissions Office

"Located in the Tampa Bay metropolitan area, USF is recognized as a top-50 public research university. USF takes great pride in its global faculty. Professors in all academic areas are responsible for discovering new solutions to existing and emerging problems. As an undergraduate at USF, you can participate actively in the creation of the knowledge that will be taught on other college campuses for decades to come. The faculty at USF is diverse as well.

"As students begin the application process, they should become familiar with USF's admission requirements. USF used extensive institutional research to validate that the high school GPA coupled with grade trends and the rigor of student's curriculum in high school are the most critical factors in student academic success at USF. Preference in admission, therefore, is given to students who complete at least three AP or IB courses, at least two college-level courses through dual enrollment, and additional coursework in math, science or foreign language beyond minimum requirements. SAT and ACT scores, while important, are less critical in USF's admission decisions when the high school GPA and rigor of curriculum are both strong. USF does use the SAT writing and the ACT English/writing components to make decisions, as scores of 550 and 24 respectively are additional indicators of potential for academic success. USF also takes into account special talents in and outside of the classroom as well as whether a student would be in the first generation of the family to attend college.

"With some of the best weather in the country, it's always a great time to visit USF. Campus tours, information sessions and tours of the residence halls are offered on weekdays throughout the year and on most Saturday mornings from September through April. Reservations are strongly encouraged."

SELECTIVITY

Admissions Rating	90
# of applicants	28,512
% of applicants accepted	45
% of acceptees attending	29

FRESHMAN PROFILE

Range SAT Critical Reading	530–620
Range SAT Math	550–640
Range SAT Writing	510–610
Range ACT Composite	23–28
Minimum web-based TOEFL	80
Average HS GPA	3.86
% graduated top 10% of class	36
% graduated top 25% of class	65
% graduated top 50% of class	76

DEADLINES

Regular	
Priority	3/1
Deadline	3/1
Notification	4/15
Nonfall registration?	Yes

APPLICANTS ALSO LOOK AT AND OFTEN PREFER
University of Florida

AND SOMETIMES PREFER
Florida State University; University of Central Florida

FINANCIAL FACTS

Financial Aid Rating	68
Annual in-state tuition	$4,559
Annual out-of-state tuition	$15,474
Room and board	$9,250
Required fees	$1,851
Books and supplies	$1,000
% needy frosh rec. need-based scholarship or grant aid	68
% needy UG rec. need-based scholarship or grant aid	67
% needy frosh rec. non-need-based scholarship or grant aid	92
% needy UG rec. non-need-based scholarship or grant aid	65
% needy frosh rec. need-based self-help aid	49
% needy UG rec. need-based self-help aid	61
% frosh rec. any financial aid	76
% UG rec. any financial aid	69
% UG borrow to pay for school	59
Average cumulative indebtedness	$22,719
% frosh need fully met	10
% ugrads need fully met	5
Average % of frosh need met	53
Average % of ugrad need met	47

UNIVERSITY OF SOUTHERN CALIFORNIA

OFFICE OF ADMISSION / JOHN HUBBARD HALL, LOS ANGELES, CA 90089-0911 • ADMISSIONS: 213-740-1111 • FAX: 213-821-0200

CAMPUS LIFE

Quality of Life Rating	78
Fire Safety Rating	95
Green Rating	87
Type of school	Private
Affiliation	No Affiliation
Environment	Metropolis

STUDENTS

Total undergrad enrollment	18,087
% male/female	49/51
% from out of state	31
% frosh from public high school	54
% frosh live on campus	99
% ugrads live on campus	33
# of fraternities (% ugrad men join)	37 (25)
# of sororities (% ugrad women join)	25 (19)
% African American	4
% Asian	23
% Caucasian	38
% Hispanic	14
% Native American	<1
% international	12
# of countries represented	118

SURVEY SAYS . . .
Everyone loves the Trojans
Frats and sororities are popular
Student publications are popular

ACADEMICS

Academic Rating	83
% students returning for sophomore year	96
% students graduating within 4 years	78
% students graduating within 6 years	91
Calendar	Semester
Student/faculty ratio	9:1
Profs interesting rating	77
Profs accessible rating	69

Most classes have 10–19 students.
Most lab/discussion sessions have 20–29 students.

STUDENTS SAY " . . . "

Academics

The University of Southern California boasts "a dynamic and culturally diverse campus located in a world-class city which is equally dynamic and culturally diverse." Everything related to cinema is "top notch." Among the other 150 or so majors here, programs in journalism, business, engineering, and architecture are particularly notable. The honors programs are "very good," too. One of the best perks about USC is its "large and enthusiastic alumni network." Becoming "part of the Trojan Family" is a great way to jump-start your career because USC graduates love to hire other USC graduates. "Almost everyone talks about getting job offers based solely on going to USC." "The school seems to run very smoothly, with few administrative issues ever being problematic enough to reach the awareness of the USC student community," says an international relations major. The top brass "is a bit mysterious and heavy handed," though. Also, "they milk every dime they can get from you." Academically, some students call the general education courses "a complete waste of time." There are a few "real narcissists" on the faculty as well as some professors "who seem to just be there because they want to do research." Overall, though, students report professors "make the subject matter come alive" and make themselves "very available" outside the classroom. "My academic experience at USC is fabulous," gushes an aerospace engineering major. "I would not choose any other school."

Life

On campus, life is "vibrant." There are more than 600 student organizations. Theatrical and musical productions are "excellent." School spirit is "extreme" and "infectious." "Football games are huge." "There is absolutely nothing that can top watching our unbelievable football team throttle the competition," says a merciless sophomore. "Drinking is a big part of the social scene" as well. "We definitely have some of the sickest parties ever," claims an impressed freshman. "Greek life is very big" and, on the weekends, a strong contingent of students "religiously" visits "The Row, the street lined with all the fraternity and sorority houses." Students also have "the sprawling city of Los Angeles as their playground." It's an "eclectic place with both high and low culture and some of the best shopping in the world." "Hollywood clubs and downtown bars" are popular destinations. Art exhibits, concerts, and "hip restaurants" are everywhere. However, "you need a car." Los Angeles traffic may be "a buzz kill" but students report that it's considerably preferable to the "absolutely terrible" public transportation system.

Student Body

The one thing that unites everyone here is "tons of Trojan pride." USC students are also "intensely ambitious" and, while there are some "complete slackers," many students hit the books "harder than they let on." Otherwise, students insist that, "contrary to popular belief, USC has immense diversity." "The stereotypical USC student is a surfer fraternity bro or a tan, trendy sorority girl from the O.C." You'll find plenty of those. Many students are also "extremely good looking." "No one cares what your orientation is," says a first-year student. There are "prissy Los Angeles types" and "spoiled" kids. In some circles, "family income and the brands of clothes you wear definitely matter." However, "though there are quite a few who come from mega wealth, there are also many who are here on a great deal of financial aid." There are "lots of nerds," too, and a smattering of "band geeks and film freaks."

FINANCIAL AID: 213-740-1111 • E-MAIL: ADMITUSC@USC.EDU • WEBSITE: WWW.USC.EDU

THE PRINCETON REVIEW SAYS

Admissions

Very important factors considered include: GPA, rigor of secondary school record, standardized test scores, application essay, recommendation(s). *Important factors considered include:* Extracurricular activities, talent/ability. *Other factors considered include:* Class rank, first generation, interview, racial/ethnic status, volunteer work, work experience, alumni/ae relations, character/personal qualities. SAT or ACT required; ACT with Writing component required. *Academic units required:* 4 English; 3 mathematics; 2 science; (2 science lab); 2 social studies; 2 foreign language; 3 academic electives. *Academic units recommended:* 4 English; 4 mathematics; 3 science; (3 science lab); 3 social studies; 3 foreign language; 3 academic electives.

Financial Aid

Students should submit: FAFSA, CSS/Financial Aid PROFILE, Noncustodial PROFILE, Business/Farm Supplement; Student/Parent Tax Information Form; Supplemental documents as requested. The Princeton Review suggests that all financial aid forms be submitted as soon as possible after January 1. *Need-based scholarships/grants offered:* Federal Pell, SEOG, State scholarships/grants, private scholarships, the school's own gift aid. *Loan aid offered:* Direct Subsidized Stafford Loans, Direct Unsubsidized Stafford Loans, Direct PLUS loans, Federal Perkins Loans, College/university loans from institutional funds. Applicants will be notified of awards beginning 4/1. Federal Work-Study Program available. Institutional employment available. Off-campus job opportunities are excellent.

The Inside Word

USC doesn't have the toughest admissions standards in California but it's up there. Your grades and test scores need to be outstanding to compete. Even if you are a borderline candidate, though, USC is certainly worth a shot. Few schools on the planet have a better alumni network and the "Trojan Family" really does create all kinds of opportunities for its members upon graduation.

THE SCHOOL SAYS "..."

From the Admissions Office

"One of the best ways to discover if USC is right for you is to walk around campus, talk to students, and get a feel for the area both as a place to study and a place to live. If you can't visit, we hold admission information programs around the country. Watch your mailbox for an invitation, or send us an e-mail if you're interested.

"Freshman applicants are required to submit a standardized writing exam. We will accept either the SAT or the ACT with its optional writing section."

SELECTIVITY

Admissions Rating	98
# of applicants	47,358
% of applicants accepted	20
% of acceptees attending	31

FRESHMAN PROFILE

Range SAT Critical Reading	620–720
Range SAT Math	660–760
Range SAT Writing	640–750
Range ACT Composite	29–33
Average HS GPA	3.73

DEADLINES

Regular	
Priority	12/1
Deadline	1/10
Notification	4/1
Nonfall registration?	Yes

APPLICANTS ALSO LOOK AT AND OFTEN PREFER

Columbia University; Duke University; Harvard College; Stanford University; Yale University; Brown University

AND SOMETIMES PREFER

University of California—Berkeley; Northwestern University; Princeton University; Cornell University; Washington University in St. Louis

AND RARELY PREFER

New York University; University of California—Los Angeles; University of California—San Diego; University of Michigan—Ann Arbor;

FINANCIAL FACTS

Financial Aid Rating	95
Annual tuition	$48,347
Room and board	$13,334
Books and supplies	$1,500
% needy frosh rec. need-based scholarship or grant aid	85
% needy UG rec. need-based scholarship or grant aid	90
% needy frosh rec. non-need-based scholarship or grant aid	58
% needy UG rec. non-need-based scholarship or grant aid	44
% needy frosh rec. need-based self-help aid	91
% needy UG rec. need-based self-help aid	94
% frosh rec. any financial aid	73
% UG rec. any financial aid	67
% UG borrow to pay for school	46
Average cumulative indebtedness	$29,136
% frosh need fully met	95
% ugrads need fully met	94
Average % of frosh need met	100
Average % of ugrad need met	100

THE UNIVERSITY OF TAMPA

401 WEST KENNEDY BOULEVARD, TAMPA, FL 33606-1490 • ADMISSIONS: 813-253-6211 • FAX: 813-258-7398

STUDENTS SAY ". . ."

Academics

The riverfront campus in Tampa, Florida, may be a big draw for The University of Tampa, but the school boasts more than an appealing location. It is a "great university in general with an exceptional business school," and students say that the academics "are hands-on and actually fun." The goal here is "preparing students to function as global citizens in specified career fields." Leading the way to help students achieve this goal are "very thorough" professors who "make themselves available for office hours so that students are able to do their best." Students here like the small class sizes, working with "professors that love what they teach," and the fact that "the student/teacher ratio is very good." Some complain that the professors "go too fast," making classes "hard to follow," but most students praise these educators as "very insightful and understanding when I had trouble in class." The university's business, nursing, communication, and education programs have all won acclaim, especially in preparing students for post-college careers. "I learn a lot about the subject and how it applies to the real-world," one student notes. "I never feel scared to ask questions and to comment about something we are discussing." All in all, one student summarizes, "The University of Tampa is a school that brings individuals from all around the world together with excellent classes, professors, athletics, clubs, and other extracurriculars."

Life

Pointing out that a university in Tampa, Florida, offers boundless opportunities when it comes to things to do is like pointing out the sky is blue. Boredom will never be an issue here. The Gulf of Mexico and its beaches are a short drive away. "Movies, malls, restaurants, and a lot of activities" provide entertainment when students are out of class. "Parties are great. Exploring the city and going to the beach are also great." Greek life thrives. So do sports, whether collegiate or professional (in addition to the native pro sports teams, dozens of major league baseball teams train here). Since most students "are very sociable," it's easy to make friend and meet new people. Students say, "Most of the time people are thinking about the weekend and the parties they will go to," but "no one pressures you." Overall, "Whether it's clubbing, the beach, scuba-diving, skydiving, we have it all here in paradise!"

Student Body

Friendly. Hardworking. The University of Tampa is home to "students from all over the world," a "very diverse" bunch "with different backgrounds [who] still mesh together fairly well." A friendly focus on fun ensures that "even though some cliques form, everyone fits in with each other." Students at Tampa should be prepared to embrace diversity, since there are "probably more international kids than in-state kids." Indeed, "our school is too diverse to even consider describing a typical student." For those who embrace the diversity—and most of the "smart, courteous" students here do—they will find that it "creates a really interesting and fun atmosphere to learn in and meet friends from all around the world." It is not difficult to find a place to fit in, nor is it difficult to be embraced by others. Though there are a few comments about some students being "spoiled and parent privileged," not everyone agrees. Other students say UT attendees support one another without reservation. "A fellow student will usually gladly help you out if need be." No matter how varied the student body, the tie that binds is a willingness to embrace fun.

FINANCIAL AID: 813-253-6219 • E-MAIL: ADMISSIONS@UT.EDU • WEBSITE: WWW.UT.EDU

THE PRINCETON REVIEW SAYS

Admissions

Very important factors considered include: GPA, rigor of secondary school record, standardized test scores. *Important factors considered include:* Application essay, recommendation(s), talent/ability. *Other factors considered include:* Class rank, extracurricular activities, first generation, interview, volunteer work, work experience, alumni/ae relations, character/personal qualities, level of applicant's interest. SAT or ACT required; ACT with Writing component recommended. TOEFL required of all international applicants. *Academic units required:* 4 English; 3 mathematics; 3 science; (2 science lab); 3 social studies; 2 foreign language; 3 academic electives.

Financial Aid

Students should submit: State aid form. The Princeton Review suggests that all financial aid forms be submitted as soon as possible after January 1. *Need-based scholarships/grants offered:* Federal Pell, SEOG, State scholarships/grants, private scholarships, the school's own gift aid. *Loan aid offered:* Direct Subsidized Stafford Loans, Direct Unsubsidized Stafford Loans, Direct PLUS loans, Federal Perkins Loans. Federal Work-Study Program available. Institutional employment available. Off-campus job opportunities are fair.

The Inside Word

Strong academic credentials are just the start for those seeking acceptance to UT. Applicants should be prepared to show that they've embraced active, hands-on learning. Participation in sports, internships, and other extracurriculars, as well as an educational background that embraces diversity, are all seen as big positives.

THE SCHOOL SAYS "..."

From the Admissions Office

"High school students may apply for admission after their junior year. Applicants are evaluated on many criteria; guidance counselor or teacher recommendations and an essay are not required if you have graduated high school and completed 17 or more college credit hours."

"A college preparatory curriculum is required, including a minimum of 18 academic units: four English courses, three sciences (two must be laboratory sciences), three mathematics, three social studies, two foreign languages and three academic electives. The incoming 2013-2014 class had an average (unweighted) GPA of 3.3, 1110 SAT (math and critical reading sections only) or a score of 24 on the ACT. Certain majors require separate departmental applications and/or requirements."

"The interdisciplinary Honors Program allows students to go beyond the classroom and regular coursework to study one-on-one with faculty through enrichment tutorials, Honors Abroad, internships, research and classroom-to-community outreach. One of the program's salient benefits is the Oxford Semester Abroad, awarded to UT's most qualified undergraduates each semester. Students are automatically considered for the Honors Program when they apply and are admitted to the University."

"While the University's facilities are state-of-the-art, our greatest features and benefits include our diverse student body (students from 50 states and 136 countries) and internships within walking distance of campus. UT's historic campus, coupled with our downtown, riverfront location, provides the perfect environment for academic enrichment and career preparation."

SELECTIVITY	
Admissions Rating	83
# of applicants	15,345
% of applicants accepted	52
% of acceptees attending	20
# offered a place on the wait list	1,290
% accepting a place on wait list	4
% admitted from wait list	100

FRESHMAN PROFILE	
Range SAT Critical Reading	480–570
Range SAT Math	500–580
Range SAT Writing	480–560
Range ACT Composite	21–26
Minimum paper TOEFL	550
Minimum web-based TOEFL	213
Average HS GPA	3.30
% graduated top 10% of class	18
% graduated top 25% of class	46
% graduated top 50% of class	84

DEADLINES	
Early action	
Deadline	5/1
Notification	12/15
Regular	
Priority	11/15
Nonfall registration?	Yes

FINANCIAL FACTS	
Financial Aid Rating	73
Annual tuition	$23,990
Room and board	$9,388
Required fees	$1,042
Books and supplies	$1,200
% needy frosh rec. need-based scholarship or grant aid	97
% needy UG rec. need-based scholarship or grant aid	97
% needy frosh rec. non-need-based scholarship or grant aid	99
% needy UG rec. non-need-based scholarship or grant aid	98
% needy frosh rec. need-based self-help aid	82
% needy UG rec. need-based self-help aid	84
% frosh rec. any financial aid	92
% UG rec. any financial aid	90
% UG borrow to pay for school	58
Average cumulative indebtedness	$31,742
% frosh need fully met	11
% ugrads need fully met	9
Average % of frosh need met	63
Average % of ugrad need met	62

THE UNIVERSITY OF TENNESSEE AT KNOXVILLE

320 STUDENT SERVICE BUILDING, KNOXVILLE, TN 37996-0230 • ADMISSIONS: 865-974-2184

CAMPUS LIFE

Quality of Life Rating	76
Fire Safety Rating	89
Green Rating	92
Type of school	Public
Affiliation	No Affiliation
Environment	City

STUDENTS

Total undergrad enrollment	20,948
% male/female	51/49
% from out of state	9
% frosh live on campus	93
% ugrads live on campus	37
# of fraternities (% ugrad men join)	24 (14)
# of sororities (% ugrad women join)	18 (21)
% African American	7
% Asian	3
% Caucasian	81
% Hispanic	3
% Native American	<1
% international	2
# of countries represented	113

SURVEY SAYS . . .
Students are happy
Students are friendly
Great off-campus food
Athletic facilities are great
Lots of beer drinking
Everyone loves the Vols; Lady Vols

ACADEMICS

Academic Rating	76
% students returning for sophomore year	86
% students graduating within 4 years	37
% students graduating within 6 years	68
Calendar	Semester
Student/faculty ratio	17:1
Profs interesting rating	67
Profs accessible rating	70

MOST POPULAR MAJORS
psychology; biological sciences; logistics and supply chain management

STUDENTS SAY ". . ."

Academics

The University of Tennessee "provides a family-like atmosphere full of opportunity and support!" Life at UT is all about "atmosphere, affordability, and school spirit." Many here tout "the school spirit and sense of community." In addition, the "in-state tuition and scholarship money" make "Tennessee a good deal for the amount you pay. I have fabulous teachers, great friends, fun activities to participate in, nice housing, a decent meal plan, and I pay $2,000 for all of it." "Although [UT is] a large school, you're not just a number; you're a face, a person, and a name." In general, "professors greatly appreciate an appetite to learn, and they welcome challenges that help us learn and grow as students." Most are "very intelligent, open to debate, well-versed on their topics, and willing to meet with students outside of class for any reason." One student says, "the majority of my experience with academia and professors has been diverse and excellent." UT embraces a classic liberal arts core dedicated to "helping students find their passions by providing a friendly and intellectually enriching environment to learn, lead, and grow." UT offers "many opportunities for involvement" and "sets a high standard for success." Attending UT "is about pursuing excellence in all areas of your life and using the knowledge you gain to prepare you for your future." It also "has a well-known medical program" and—for many—is "close to home."

Life

The typical UT student "loves all aspects of the university's life from its sports to its long-standing traditions." Students flock here for "family history, athletics, and to sing 'Rocky Top.'" "We love football just about as much as academics." However, academics here are just as intense as athletics. "Being a larger university, I have had many more opportunities than people I know at smaller schools in education as well as extracurriculars." "The University of Tennessee combines the best of all worlds: great education for a great price, sports, social life, and a ton of extracurriculars to choose from." In fact, many say, "there are so many clubs and groups that on a social level UT doesn't feel large at all." "There's also a great selection of food and a wonderful gym." Life at UT is all "about education, community, and becoming a true Tennessee volunteer." "There's a great sense of unity." The university "tries extremely hard to encourage acceptance of several kinds of diversity." A "LGBTQ Resource Center [recently] opened on campus." "There is also a large 'Stop Bias' program that is promoted." In general, there are "tons of clubs and organizations to get involved with if you are passionate about something." If pressed to note a campus flaw, students say UT is "stuck between a river and downtown Knoxville, so it now has no room to expand and way too many hills. So they've crammed all these buildings into too small of a space."

Student Body

"There is not one 'popular' group of students. We have athletes, artists, musicians, dancers, religious students, scientists, Greeks, volunteers, etc." In general a live-and-let-live atmosphere pervades this "friendly" "energetic," "personable" campus; "All students fit in extremely well." The Greek community here "is especially prevalent." Some wonder "how non-Greeks fit in." "The conservative, upper-class attitude is definitely the one with the strongest voice." However, others counter this stalwart image. "The best thing about being an average student here? If you don't want to conform, you don't have to." "Once you go beyond the surface and away from the jocks and sorority girls, there are all types of students at UT." Others enthusiastically concede, "The literary snob crowd is small, but it's here, they do cool stuff, and they welcome new folks all the time with open arms." A typical student "studies hard, but parties even harder at the appropriate times." Classical entrees to social life include "to become part of the Greek system here or be an athlete." Most students exhibit the hallmark "Southern hospitality" and are "industrious, honest, charitable, and compassionate."

THE UNIVERSITY OF TENNESSEE AT KNOXVILLE

FINANCIAL AID: 865-974-3131 • E-MAIL: ADMISSIONS@UTK.EDU • WEBSITE: WWW.UTK.EDU

THE PRINCETON REVIEW SAYS

Admissions

Very important factors considered include: GPA, rigor of secondary school record, standardized test scores. *Other factors considered include:* Class rank, application essay, extracurricular activities, first generation, geographical residence, racial/ethnic status, recommendation(s), state residency, talent/ability, volunteer work, work experience, alumni/ae relations, character/personal qualities, level of applicant's interest. SAT or ACT required; ACT with or without Writing component accepted. TOEFL required of all international applicants. *Academic units required:* 4 English; 4 mathematics; 3 science; (3 science lab); 1 social studies; 2 foreign language; 1 history; 1 visual/performing arts.

Financial Aid

Students should submit: FAFSA. The Princeton Review suggests that all financial aid forms be submitted as soon as possible after January 1. *Need-based scholarships/grants offered:* Federal Pell, SEOG, State scholarships/grants, private scholarships, the school's own gift aid. *Loan aid offered:* Direct Subsidized Stafford Loans, Direct Unsubsidized Stafford Loans, Direct PLUS loans, Federal Perkins Loans, State Loans, College/university loans from institutional funds. Applicants will be notified of awards beginning 3/15. Federal Work-Study Program available. Off-campus job opportunities are fair.

The Inside Word

UT must winnow through more than 13,000 freshman applications each year. That sort of volume doesn't allow for nuance. Students with above-average high school GPAs (achieved in a reasonable college prep curriculum) and above-average standardized test scores pretty much all make the cut. The school will consider additional evidence of an applicant's potential (school and community involvement, awards, essays, special talents, and recommendations) in making admissions decisions, particularly for marginal candidates.

THE SCHOOL SAYS "..."

From the Admissions Office

"The University of Tennessee, Knoxville, offers students the great program diversity of a major university, opportunities for research or original creative work in every degree program, and a welcoming campus environment. Nine colleges offer more than 170 undergraduate majors and concentrations to students from all fifty states and 100 foreign countries, and UT students can make the world their campus through study abroad programs. More than 400 clubs and organizations on campus allow students to further individualize their college experience in service, recreation, academics, and professional development. UT blends more than 200 years of history, tradition, and 'Volunteer Spirit' with the latest technology and innovation."

SELECTIVITY

Admissions Rating	91
# of applicants	14,396
% of applicants accepted	72
% of acceptees attending	41

FRESHMAN PROFILE

Range SAT Critical Reading	520–640
Range SAT Math	520–650
Range ACT Composite	24–29
Minimum paper TOEFL	523
Minimum web-based TOEFL	70
Average HS GPA	3.85
% graduated top 10% of class	52
% graduated top 25% of class	91
% graduated top 50% of class	100

DEADLINES

Regular	
Priority	11/1
Deadline	12/1
Notification	3/31
Nonfall registration?	Yes

APPLICANTS ALSO LOOK AT AND SOMETIMES PREFER

Clemson University; Vanderbilt University; University of South Carolina—Columbia

AND RARELY PREFER

University of Alabama—Tuscaloosa; University of Mississippi; Virginia Tech

FINANCIAL FACTS

Financial Aid Rating	73
Annual in-state tuition	$9,780
Annual out-of-state tuition	$27,970
Required fees	$1,414
% needy frosh rec. need-based scholarship or grant aid	96
% needy UG rec. need-based scholarship or grant aid	89
% needy frosh rec. non-need-based scholarship or grant aid	0
% needy UG rec. non-need-based scholarship or grant aid	0
% needy frosh rec. need-based self-help aid	99
% needy UG rec. need-based self-help aid	98
% frosh rec. any financial aid	63
% UG rec. any financial aid	59
% UG borrow to pay for school	53
Average cumulative indebtedness	$23,729
% frosh need fully met	28
% ugrads need fully met	21
Average % of frosh need met	67
Average % of ugrad need met	60

THE UNIVERSITY OF TEXAS AT AUSTIN

PO Box 8058, Austin, TX 78713-8058 • Admissions: 512-475-7440 • Fax: 512-475-7478

CAMPUS LIFE

Quality of Life Rating	87
Fire Safety Rating	76
Green Rating	97
Type of school	Public
Affiliation	No Affiliation
Environment	Metropolis

STUDENTS

Total undergrad enrollment	39,323
% male/female	48/52
% from out of state	5
% frosh live on campus	62
% ugrads live on campus	18
# of fraternities (% ugrad men join)	40 (15)
# of sororities (% ugrad women join)	32 (17)
% African American	4
% Asian	18
% Caucasian	48
% Hispanic	22
% Native American	<1
% international	5
# of countries represented	98

SURVEY SAYS . . .
Athletic facilities are great
Students love Austin, TX
Everyone loves the Longhorns
Student publications are popular
Political activism is popular

ACADEMICS

Academic Rating	77
% students returning for sophomore year	94
% students graduating within 4 years	51
% students graduating within 6 years	79
Calendar	Semester
Student/faculty ratio	18:1
Profs interesting rating	74
Profs accessible rating	69

Most classes have 10–19 students.
Most lab/discussion sessions have 10–19 students.

MOST POPULAR MAJORS
liberal arts; biology; business/commerce

STUDENTS SAY " . . ."

Academics

Students insist that the University of Texas at Austin has "everything you want in a college: academics, athletics, social life, location," and it's hard to argue with them. UT is "a huge school and has a lot to offer," meaning students have "an infinite number of possibilities open to them and can use them in their own way to figure out what they want for their lives." As one student tells us about arriving on campus, "I did not realize how much was available to me just as an enrolled student. There is free tutoring, gym membership, professional counseling, doctors visits, legal help, career advising, and many distinguished outside speakers. The campus is crawling with experts in every field you can imagine." Standout academic departments are numerous: from the sciences to the humanities to creative arts, UT makes a strong bid for the much-sought-after mantle of "Harvard of the south." Also, the school does a surprisingly good job of avoiding the factory-like feel of many large schools. One student observes: "Coming to a large university, there was a prejudgment that the huge classes will make it impossible to know your professor and vice versa. The university has dispelled that myth with professors who want to know you and [who] provide opportunities to get to know them." While professors "can vary greatly across a spectrum from 'I'm smarter than him' to 'I want to follow in his footsteps,'" "the class offerings at UT are generally vast and diverse, and students can often avoid taking the less-qualified professors with a little research."

Life

Life at UT Austin is "very relaxed…Students usually wear shorts and a t-shirt to class. When the weather gets cold, you might find students wearing the same shorts and t-shirt with a sweatshirt. Students and faculty frequently picnic all over campus. There are plenty of outdoor tables and grassy areas to sit." Undergrads "are often found throwing a Frisbee outside the tower or taking a nap under a tree. It's truly what you see in one of those cheesy brochures with everyone studying and smiling. Of course, the smiles aren't so bright during finals. We switch to an over-caffeinated, glazed-eye look instead." Hometown Austin "provides a social education that a college student newly out on his own would not find anywhere else," with "festivals or fairs of some kind going on downtown all the time" and "the infamous 6th Street with nightlife that dies down only after the bars close." Campus and the surrounding area offer "many hike-and-bike trails and fitness organizations. It's possible for students to train for marathons, half marathons, and triathlons while in school. Barton Springs pool is a natural spring that is very popular year-round. On any given Saturday you will find students throwing a football, going for a run, biking through the hills, kayaking in the river, having a late lunch at one of Austin's great restaurants, or just sleeping in."

Student Body

"Because of the huge Greek life at UT, a 'typical student' would be a sorority girl or fraternity boy," but—and it's a big but—such students "are hardly the majority, since UT is actually made of more 'atypical' people than most other schools. Everyone here has his own niche, and I could not think of any type of individual who would not be able to find one of his own." Indeed, "everyone at Texas is different! When you walk across campus, you see every type of ethnicity. There are a lot of minorities at Texas. Also, I see many disabled people, whom the school accommodates well. Everyone seems to get along. The different types of students just blend in together." Especially by Texas standards, "Austin is known for being 'weird.' If you see someone dressed in a way you've never seen before, you just shrug it off and say 'That's Austin!'"

THE UNIVERSITY OF TEXAS AT AUSTIN

FINANCIAL AID: 512-475-6203 • WEBSITE: WWW.UTEXAS.EDU

THE PRINCETON REVIEW SAYS
Admissions

Very important factors considered include: Class rank, rigor of secondary school record. *Important factors considered include:* Standardized test scores, application essay, extracurricular activities, talent/ability, volunteer work, work experience. *Other factors considered include:* First generation, racial/ethnic status, recommendation(s), state residency, character/personal qualities, level of applicant's interest. SAT or ACT required; ACT with Writing component required. TOEFL required of all international applicants. *Academic units required:* 4 language arts, 4 mathematics, 4 science, 3 ½ social studies, ½ economics, 1 physical education, 1 fine arts, 2 foreign language, ½ speech, 6 electives.

Financial Aid

Students should submit: FAFSA. The Princeton Review suggests that all financial aid forms be submitted as soon as possible after January 1. *Need-based scholarships/grants offered:* Federal Pell, SEOG, State scholarships/grants, private scholarships, the school's own gift aid. *Loan aid offered:* Direct Subsidized Stafford Loans, Direct Unsubsidized Stafford Loans, Direct PLUS loans, Federal Perkins Loans, State Loans. Federal Work-Study Program available. Off-campus job opportunities are fair.

The Inside Word

The university is required to automatically admit enough Texas applicants to fill 75 percent of available spaces set aside for students from Texas. The university will admit applicants from Texas who are in the top 7 percent of their high school class for the summer/fall 2014 and the spring 2015 entering freshman class. The rank needed for automatic admission for future classes will be announced each September. All students, including those eligible for automatic admission, should submit the strongest possible application to increase the likelihood of admission to the university and to their requested major. Admissions are quite competitive. Space for out-of-state students is limited, meaning they'll have even higher hurdles to clear.

THE SCHOOL SAYS "..."
From the Admissions Office

"For more than 125 years, students from all over the world have come to The University of Texas at Austin to obtain a first-class education. Recognized for research, teaching, and public service, the university boasts more than 130 undergraduate academic programs, hundreds of study abroad programs, outstanding student services, cultural centers, and volunteer and leadership opportunities designed to prepare students to make a difference in the world. Along with its nationally ranked athletic programs, the university's spirit is enhanced by cultural, artistic, and scientific opportunities that help to make Austin one of the most inviting destinations in the country. The Performing Arts Center hosts plays, Austin's opera and symphony, and visiting musical and dance groups. Students access more than eight million volumes in the university's seventeen libraries and study prehistoric fossils at the Texas Memorial Museum, Renaissance and Baroque paintings in the Blanton Museum, original manuscripts at the Ransom Center, and life in the 1960s at the Lyndon B. Johnson Library and Museum. Each year the university enrolls about 50,000 students from richly varied ethnic and geographic backgrounds. Every day graduates contribute to the world community as volunteers, teachers, journalists, artists, engineers, business leaders, scientists, and lawyers. With world-renowned faculty, top-rated academic programs, successful alumni, and such an enticing location, it's no surprise that The University of Texas at Austin ranks among the best universities in the world."

SELECTIVITY

Admissions Rating	94
# of applicants	38,161
% of applicants accepted	40
% of acceptees attending	47
# offered a place on the wait list	386
% accepting a place on wait list	73
% admitted from wait list	2

FRESHMAN PROFILE

Range SAT Critical Reading	550–670
Range SAT Math	590–710
Range SAT Writing	550–680
Range ACT Composite	25–31
Minimum paper TOEFL	550
Minimum web-based TOEFL	79
% graduated top 10% of class	75
% graduated top 25% of class	91
% graduated top 50% of class	98

DEADLINES

Regular	
Deadline	12/1
Notification	3/1
Nonfall registration?	Yes

FINANCIAL FACTS

Financial Aid Rating	79
Annual in tuition	$9,798
Annual out-of-state tuition	$33,842
Room and board	$11,362
Required fees	$0
Books and supplies	$750
% needy frosh rec. need-based scholarship or grant aid	91
% needy UG rec. need-based scholarship or grant aid	81
% needy frosh rec. non-need-based scholarship or grant aid	46
% needy UG rec. non-need-based scholarship or grant aid	26
% needy frosh rec. need-based self-help aid	62
% needy UG rec. need-based self-help aid	73
% UG rec. any financial aid	45
% UG borrow to pay for school	50
Average cumulative indebtedness	$25,300
% frosh need fully met	27
% ugrads need fully met	15
Average % of frosh need met	73
Average % of ugrad need met	64

THE UNIVERSITY OF TEXAS AT DALLAS

800 WEST CAMPBELL ROAD, RICHARDSON, TX 75080 • ADMISSIONS: 972-883-2270 • FAX: 972-883-2599

CAMPUS LIFE

Quality of Life Rating	76
Fire Safety Rating	92
Green Rating	90
Type of school	Public
Affiliation	No Affiliation
Environment	Metropolis

STUDENTS

Total undergrad enrollment	12,781
% male/female	57/43
% from out of state	3
% frosh from public high school	92
% frosh live on campus	56
% ugrads live on campus	26
# of fraternities (% ugrad men join)	10 (3)
# of sororities (% ugrad women join)	10 (2)
% African American	6
% Asian	27
% Caucasian	40
% Hispanic	17
% Native American	<1
% international	4
# of countries represented	106

SURVEY SAYS . . .
Lab facilities are great
Class discussions are rare
Great financial aid
Great off-campus food

ACADEMICS

Academic Rating	75
% students returning for sophomore year	89
% students graduating within 4 years	46
% students graduating within 6 years	63
Calendar	Semester
Student/faculty ratio	22:1
Profs interesting rating	71
Profs accessible rating	70

Most classes have 10–19 students.
Most lab/discussion sessions have 20–29 students.

MOST POPULAR MAJORS
biology; accounting; business/commerce

STUDENTS SAY ". . ."

Academics

Though nowhere near the size of some of its fellow state schools, UT Dallas provides its more than 12,000 undergraduates with a wealth of resources, financial aid, and opportunities, striving for "a future of talented and smart individuals." UTD has "one of the best tech schools around" and draws a good deal of students to its STEM programs (one student lovingly calls it "the nerd capital of the UT system"), causing a senior computer engineer to remark: "Engineering and the sciences for the win." The school is without many sports programs (notably football), but instead "emphasizes academics, which is what we are all here for."

Administration is responsive and invested in UTD's growing reputation, and the school "grows and changes year by year, continually getting better and better," with students acting as "a big part of that process." Someone is "always willing to help you with any problem you encounter," and the tutoring available also "really helps in understanding the material." They are dedicated to their students, this being apparent in "their open office hours and timely replies to e-mails."

Most of the professors "are very enthused about what they are teaching and genuinely want us to learn," and bring new topics to light through "very informative" discussion. "Their passion for their subject make it easy to love your classes!" says a student. "I get pushed academically, but I love it," says another. One of the shining benefits of UTD is the chance to get "actively involved with the faculty in research," which provides "several opportunities for honors, and ultimately allows you to prepare for a continued education after undergrad."

Life

The "well-kept campus" is "not too large," though "parking is a bit of an issue sometimes" and the "dining hall is pretty bad." There is a lot of studying going on, so "you can always find a group or just a lot of people hanging around on a specific area studying." "Some people practically build shrines to their GPA's and worship them on weekends," says one sophomore.

A lot of students commute (which makes life "pretty quiet") and there is no football team to rally around, so "it's hard to have a lot of school spirit"; however, "the social scene is definitely growing," and the Student Union acts as the "hub" for the entire school where "students can mingle and find friends." Computer labs also give many the chance to game and have fun (the video game culture is "strong"), and "there are usually always at least five to ten gamers in the room at once." The school provides "many things to do," with campus events like movies happening every week, and people often leave campus to seek more options, such as "movies, bowling, shopping, skating, concert, etc."

Student Body

There is "no clear majority of one race, creed, or background" at UT Dallas. Since most of the "exceptionally nice" and "very diverse" people are here for the sciences, there are "lots of smart people everywhere" and "everyone here is so open about the geeky side in everyone." Most agree that there could stand to be a bit more of a creative voice on campus and the school would do well to attract "more students to fine arts." Most students are "serious about their academics, but not too serious" and remember to take the time to relax; "video games/card games and…anime" are popular here, as are clubs and organizations.

FINANCIAL AID: 972-883-2941 • E-MAIL: INTEREST@UTDALLAS.EDU • WEBSITE: WWW.UTDALLAS.EDU

THE PRINCETON REVIEW SAYS

Admissions

Very important factors considered include: Rigor of secondary school record, class rank, GPA, standardized test scores. *Important factors considered include:* Application essay, recommendation(s). *Other factors considered include:* First generation, geographical residence, extracurricular activities, state residency, talent/ability, volunteer work, work experience, character/personal qualities, level of applicant's interest. SAT or ACT required; ACT with Writing component required. TOEFL required of all international applicants. *Academic units required:* 4 English; 4 mathematics; 3 science; (3 science lab); 3 social studies; 2 foreign language. *Academic units recommended:* 4 English; 4 mathematics; 3 science; (3 science lab); 4 social studies; 3 foreign language; 1 computer science; 1 visual/performing arts.

Financial Aid

Students should submit: FAFSA. The Princeton Review suggests that all financial aid forms be submitted as soon as possible after January 1. *Need-based scholarships/grants offered:* Federal Pell, FSEOG, TEACH, Iraq and Afghanistan Service Grant, State scholarships/grants, private scholarships, the school's own gift aid. *Loan aid offered:* Direct Subsidized Stafford Loans, Direct Unsubsidized Stafford Loans, Direct PLUS loans, Federal Perkins Loans, State Loans, University short-term loans from institutional funds. Federal Work-Study Program available. Institutional employment available. Off-campus job opportunities are excellent.

The Inside Word

UT Dallas is one of those by-the-numbers school for the majority of its admitted students. Texas law requires that prospective students are automatically admitted to the university as first-time freshmen if they graduated from an accredited Texas high school among the top 10 percent of their class, and then there is a separate set of numbers for students of good standing, including an SAT score of 1200 (math and reading) or an ACT score of 26. Students outside of these ranges are subject to a more traditional review based on individual strengths.

THE SCHOOL SAYS "..."

From the Admissions Office

"Founded in 1969, The University of Texas at Dallas has evolved into one of the top research institutions in Texas. UT Dallas provides some of the state's most-lauded business, engineering and science programs, and has also gained prominence for a breadth of educational paths, from arts and technology to audiology to biomedical engineering.

The University's faculty consists of more than 500 tenured and tenure-track members hailing from the world's best colleges and includes a Nobel laureate and members of the National Academy of Sciences and the National Academy of Engineering. In addition, UT Dallas is home to more than 50 centers, labs and institutes that facilitate undergraduate research, internships and collaborations with local industry.

UT Dallas students graduate with less debt than most college students in the country and are highly marketable upon graduation. UT Dallas graduates are recruited by 14 of the top 20 Fortune 500 companies and accepted into the top law and medical schools in the country."

SELECTIVITY

Admissions Rating	91
# of applicants	8,750
% of applicants accepted	59
% of acceptees attending	44

FRESHMAN PROFILE

Range SAT Critical Reading	550–670
Range SAT Math	600–700
Range SAT Writing	530–660
Range ACT Composite	25–31
Minimum paper TOEFL	550
Minimum web-based TOEFL	80
% graduated top 10% of class	38
% graduated top 25% of class	71
% graduated top 50% of class	91

DEADLINES

Regular	
Deadline	7/1
Nonfall registration?	Yes

FINANCIAL FACTS

Financial Aid Rating	78
Annual in-state tuition	$11,806
Annual out-of-state tuition	$30,378
Room and board	$9,240
Books and supplies	$1,200
% needy frosh rec. need-based scholarship or grant aid	90
% needy UG rec. need-based scholarship or grant aid	85
% needy frosh rec. non-need-based scholarship or grant aid	22
% needy UG rec. non-need-based scholarship or grant aid	7
% needy frosh rec. need-based self-help aid	72
% needy UG rec. need-based self-help aid	86
% frosh rec. any financial aid	80
% UG rec. any financial aid	70
% UG borrow to pay for school	43
Average cumulative indebtedness	$20,504
% frosh need fully met	36
% ugrads need fully met	16
Average % of frosh need met	78
Average % of ugrad need met	63

UNIVERSITY OF TORONTO

172 St. George Street, Toronto, ON M5R 0A3 • Admissions: 416-978-2190 • Fax: 416-978-7022

CAMPUS LIFE

Quality of Life Rating	67
Fire Safety Rating	71
Green Rating	66
Type of school	Public
Affiliation	No Affiliation
Environment	Metropolis

STUDENTS

Total undergrad enrollment	64,962
% male/female	44/56
% from out of state	8
% ugrads live on campus	15
% international	13
# of countries represented	166

SURVEY SAYS . . .

Class discussions are rare
Great library
Students love Toronto
Great off-campus food
Student publications are popular

ACADEMICS

Academic Rating	69
% students returning for sophomore year	91
% students graduating within 6 years	82
Calendar	Semester
Student/faculty ratio	10:1
Profs interesting rating	67
Profs accessible rating	64

STUDENTS SAY "..."

Academics

With "an excellent reputation and a huge selection of courses" as well as "a world-class city" to call home, the University of Toronto "provides expert knowledge in every field" to its 50,000-plus undergraduates and nearly 11,000 graduate students. True, it can be "hard to relate to the instructors given that the class sizes are so huge," and those looking for an intimate and supportive academic environment might not find a good fit at U of T. "The general attitude is one of professionalism and very little mercy [here]." Still, self-starters will find the limitless opportunities outweigh the drawbacks. As one student puts it, "Most of the professors are premier representatives of their respective industries." Another adds, "The fact that you are learning from Nobel Prize winners in a city full of adventures is unbeatable." "Excellent research facilities" are among the other assets here. The school also capitalizes on its location in the center of Toronto: "The city and the university draw on each other in a variety of ways—clinical opportunities and research flow in both directions." On top of that, industrious undergrads tell us, "The libraries and other research facilities here are excellent and contribute much to the overall academic experience."

Life

When they aren't hitting the books, University of Toronto students enjoy life in "one of the coolest cities in North America" where "there's always something new happening: the Toronto International Film Festival, skating in Nathan Phillips Square, etc." Students benefit from the fact that "the Royal Ontario Museum is on campus, a ton of pubs and art galleries are within walking distance, and a nightlife to suit just about any type of person" can be found in Toronto. When it comes to campus life, many students feel the school's spirit and unity is negatively affected by the large number of commuter students. "Off-campus students, of whom there are many, rarely participate in extracurricular activities," one student complains, "Interest in varsity sports is just pathetic" among all undergraduates. Others focus on the positives, pointing out the social and recreational opportunities available to those willing to look. A junior says, "Getting involved here takes some research in terms of navigating the 300 clubs and endless academic/research opportunities, but once I did some searching, I found several places where I fit in well and have fun." For those who live on campus, sororities and fraternities help nurture social bonds, and "most of the residential colleges have tons of events, from campus-wide capture the flag [games] to movie nights" or "intramural sports."

Student Body

At this large public school, the demographics on campus reflect those of surrounding Toronto, "one of the most diverse cities around." As one junior puts it, "It can be said that all students here have in common an excellent academic record prior to university. Beyond that, anything goes: There are huge variances in race, religion, sexual orientation, academic focus, postgraduate aspirations, socioeconomic background, disability, nationality, athleticism, and community involvement." A freshman chimes in, "On my floor alone there are kids from at least ten different countries and, even with the different cultures, we have blended together to make a big family." Most students say it's relatively easy to find a social group among like-minded individuals, despite the school's impressive size and diversity. According to one senior, "Most students will find a niche where they feel comfortable; there's a place for everyone."

FINANCIAL AID: 416-978-2190 • E-MAIL: ADMISSIONS.HELP@UTORONTO.CA • WEBSITE: WWW.UTORONTO.CA

THE PRINCETON REVIEW SAYS

Admissions

Very important factors considered include: Class rank, GPA, rigor of secondary school record, standardized test scores, first generation, level of applicant's interest. *Other factors considered include:* SAT and SAT Subject Tests or ACT required; ACT with Writing component required. TOEFL required of all international applicants.

Financial Aid

The Princeton Review suggests that all financial aid forms be submitted as soon as possible after January 1.

The Inside Word

University of Toronto takes a numbers-based approach to admissions. American students must submit not only high school transcripts and SAT/ACT scores but also results for three SAT Subject Tests/APs/IBs. Only those who perform well by all these metrics are likely to gain admission. Candidates should be aware that qualifications vary from program to program, and as an international student you'll have more paperwork to file. The University of Toronto is a recognized postsecondary institution for Federal Stafford Loans. All applicants are automatically considered for admission scholarships.

THE SCHOOL SAYS "..."

From the Admissions Office

"The University of Toronto is committed to being an internationally significant research university with undergraduate, graduate, and professional programs of study.

"For arts, science, commerce/management, concurrent teacher education, music, physical education, and health/kinesiology, U.S. Grade 12 in an accredited high school with a high grade point average and high scores on SAT Reasoning/ACT exams and a minimum of two appropriate SAT Subject Tests/APs/IBs (or a combination of SAT Subject Tests/APs/IBs covering different subjects) are required. English Grade 12/AP is required for all programs. Those seeking admission to science or commerce programs are strongly advised to complete AP Calculus.

"The minimum admission requirements are an excellent CGPA and Grade 12 GPA; scores of at least 1800 on SAT Reasoning and 26 on the ACT; no score below 500 on SAT Subject Tests. SAT scores below 500 in any part of the SAT Reasoning or Subject Tests are not acceptable.

"For engineering, applicants must present AP/IB Calculus, as well as AP/IB or SAT Subject Tests in both chemistry and physics. English Grade 12/AP is required for all programs. Applicants seeking admission to engineering after one year of university in the United States are required to present a GPA of at least 3.5 with two semesters of math, physics and chemistry. Refer to www.engineering.utoronto.ca for complete information."

SELECTIVITY	
Admissions Rating	61
# of applicants	67,955
% of applicants accepted	69
% of acceptees attending	18

FRESHMAN PROFILE	
Minimum paper TOEFL	600
Minimum web-based TOEFL	250

DEADLINES	
Regular	
Deadline	3/1
Nonfall registration?	No

FINANCIAL FACTS	
Financial Aid Rating	64

THE UNIVERSITY OF TULSA

800 SOUTH TUCKER DRIVE, TULSA, OK 74104 • ADMISSIONS: 918-631-2307 • FAX: 918-631-5003

CAMPUS LIFE
Quality of Life Rating	87
Fire Safety Rating	90
Green Rating	90
Type of school	Private
Affiliation	Presbyterian
Environment	Metropolis

STUDENTS
Total undergrad enrollment	3,394
% male/female	58/42
% from out of state	42
% frosh from public high school	75
% frosh live on campus	88
% ugrads live on campus	74
# of fraternities (% ugrad men join)	7 (21)
# of sororities (% ugrad women join)	9 (23)
% African American	5
% Asian	3
% Caucasian	55
% Hispanic	4
% Native American	4
% international	26
# of countries represented	73

SURVEY SAYS . . .
Students are friendly
Students get along with local community
Athletic facilities are great

ACADEMICS
Academic Rating	82
% students returning for sophomore year	90
% students graduating within 4 years	51
% students graduating within 6 years	69
Calendar	Semester
Student/faculty ratio	11:1
Profs interesting rating	80
Profs accessible rating	82
Most classes have 10–19 students.	
Most lab/discussion sessions have 20–29 students.	

MOST POPULAR MAJORS
petroleum engineering; business administration and management; mechanical engineering

STUDENTS SAY ". . ."

Academics
The University of Tulsa is a mid-size, private school that provides a superior learning environment and a myriad of academic opportunities to its 3,000 undergraduate students. Across disciplines, the academic experience is high quality and stimulating, incorporating "rigorous and invigorating lectures and well instructed lab periods." In addition to coursework, undergraduates benefit from unmatched "academic and professional opportunities reserved only for graduate students at other schools." A current student attests, "I had no trouble getting undergraduate research experience in biochemistry as early as sophomore year." Students rave about TU's outgoing professors, saying that "the faculty and staff at TU seem to take a personal interest in the students here. They are accessible and love to help students in any way possible, not only academically, but professionally and personally as well." How's this for involved? "I have even received a text message from a professor when I forgot to turn in a homework assignment," reports a sophomore. While course selection is occasionally limited by the school's size, "professors will frequently tailor independent study projects with students." When it comes to the administration, some students worry that they are too preoccupied with improving the college's rankings. Others insist that the administrative offices are just as student-friendly as the teaching staff. A sophomore shares, "I became involved in student government my third semester here, and I am so impressed by how accessible the administration is. The deans and president of the university really care about students."

Life
Student life at TU reflects the school's unequivocal emphasis on academics. Studious undergraduates agree that the University of Tulsa "is definitely not a big party school. Most of the students here are focused on studies." Nonetheless, there are plenty of opportunities for extracurricular involvement, and campus clubs range "from honor societies to multicultural groups to religious gatherings." The campus isn't too big, so students looking for leadership experience will be pleased to learn that "anyone can be involved and 'be someone' on campus." In addition to student clubs, "collegiate, intramural, and pick-up sports are really popular." About 20 percent of the campus is involved in a Greek organization, and "a lot of student life revolves strongly around sororities and fraternities." However, students reassure us that "even non-Greek students can visit the houses and hang out on a Friday night." If you don't feel like partying at fraternities, there's plenty more to do, on and off campus. A sophomore shares, "For fun my friends and I go bowling, explore the parks of Tulsa, watch movies, do arts and crafts, and go to the occasional party." While students readily admit that Tulsa isn't New York City, they appreciate the myriad of pleasures of their manageable mid-size city, which boasts "some really great restaurants and coffee shops around TU and in historic Tulsa."

Student Body
Defined in broad strokes, most TU undergraduates hail from affluent, Christian families in the Midwest. However, TU students insist that, while there are some similarities within the campus community, they cannot be summed up so easily. In addition to the array of "jocks, computer geeks, fashionistas, 'good' students, loners, and partygoers," The University of Tulsa has a "strong international community. Programs such as the petroleum engineering department attract a diverse international populace. One can hear five different languages simply walking to class!" Thanks, in part, to the international students, there is "a diverse religious life on campus, several activist groups that meet on campus, and countless student organizations." No matter what your background, "the majority of students I know at TU are very open and accepting of everyone else, regardless of religion, race, sexual orientation, athletic ability, major, and Greek affiliation." In fact, it's easy to feel at home on the TU campus. A junior explains, "Because the campus is small, even if you don't know somebody's name, you normally recognize their face from somewhere; this leads to a great sense of community."

FINANCIAL AID: 918-631-2526 • E-MAIL: ADMISSION@UTULSA.EDU • WEBSITE: WWW.UTULSA.EDU

THE PRINCETON REVIEW SAYS

Admissions

Very important factors considered include: GPA, rigor of secondary school record, standardized test scores. *Important factors considered include:* Class rank, application essay, interview, recommendation(s), level of applicant's interest. *Other factors considered include:* Extracurricular activities, first generation, racial/ethnic status, talent/ability, volunteer work, work experience, alumni/ae relations, character/personal qualities. SAT or ACT required; ACT with or without Writing component accepted. TOEFL required of all international applicants. *Academic units recommended:* 4 English; 4 mathematics; 3 science; (3 science lab); 3 social studies; 2 foreign language; 1 computer science; 1 visual/performing arts.

Financial Aid

Students should submit: FAFSA. The Princeton Review suggests that all financial aid forms be submitted as soon as possible after January 1. *Need-based scholarships/grants offered:* Federal Pell, SEOG, State scholarships/grants, private scholarships, the school's own gift aid. *Loan aid offered:* Direct Subsidized Stafford Loans, Direct Unsubsidized Stafford Loans, Direct PLUS loans, Federal Perkins Loans. Federal Work-Study Program available. Institutional employment available. Off-campus job opportunities are good.

The Inside Word

TU is a university with solid academic offerings, a strong sense of community, lots of student-faculty interaction, and attainable admission standards. The school's commitment to undergrads is clear. One of TU's most impressive programs, The Tulsa Undergraduate Research Challenge (TURC), allows undergrads to complete original research along with faculty.

THE SCHOOL SAYS "..."

From the Admissions Office

"The University of Tulsa is a private university with a comprehensive scope. Students choose from more than eighty majors offered through three undergraduate colleges—Arts and Sciences, Business Administration, and Engineering and Natural Sciences. Curricula can be customized with collaborative research, joint undergraduate and graduate programs, and an honors program, among others. Professors are equally committed to teaching undergraduates and to scholarly research. This results in extraordinary individual achievement, resulting in the nationally competitive scholarships students have won since 1995: fifty-one Goldwaters, forty-one National Science Foundation scholars, nine Trumans, seven Department of Defense scholars, nine Fulbrights, ten Phi Kappa Phi, nine Udalls, and five British Marshalls. Over the past decade over 1,000,000 square feet of facilities have been added costing over $250 million. These include athletic venues, 400 additional apartments, fitness center, Legal Information Center, literacy expansion and renovation, and a new performing arts center. Over 160 registered clubs, and interest groups, including intramural and recreational sports teams exist along with six fraternities and nine sororities. The 8,300 seat Reynolds Center is home to the standout Golden Hurricane NCAA Division I men's basketball team, campus events, and concerts. A forty-acre sports complex includes the fitness center and indoor tennis center that hosted the 2008 NCAA Division I Men's and Women's tennis finals. An outdoor freshman orientation program launches an entire first-year experience dedicated to developing students' full potential.

"Applicants are required to submit the SAT or ACT. The writing component is not required. For admission and scholarship review, the best composite score of submitted tests will be used."

SELECTIVITY

Admissions Rating	96
# of applicants	7,304
% of applicants accepted	41
% of acceptees attending	29

FRESHMAN PROFILE

Range SAT Critical Reading	560–710
Range SAT Math	570–690
Range ACT Composite	25–32
Minimum paper TOEFL	550
Minimum web-based TOEFL	80
Average HS GPA	3.80
% graduated top 10% of class	74
% graduated top 25% of class	90
% graduated top 50% of class	97

DEADLINES

Early action	
Deadline	11/1
Notification	11/25
Regular	
Priority	2/1
Nonfall registration?	Yes

APPLICANTS ALSO LOOK AT AND OFTEN PREFER

Texas Christian University; University of Oklahoma; Southern Methodist University; Saint Louis University

AND SOMETIMES PREFER

Trinity University; Baylor University; Tulane University; Washington University in St. Louis

AND RARELY PREFER

Texas A&M University—College Station; University of Kansas; University of Missouri

FINANCIAL FACTS

Financial Aid Rating	90
Annual tuition	$35,050
Room and board	$10,476
Required fees	$805
Books and supplies	$1,200
% needy frosh rec. need-based scholarship or grant aid	36
% needy UG rec. need-based scholarship or grant aid	47
% needy frosh rec. non-need-based scholarship or grant aid	100
% needy UG rec. non-need-based scholarship or grant aid	97
% needy frosh rec. need-based self-help aid	63
% needy UG rec. need-based self-help aid	70
% frosh rec. any financial aid	89
% UG rec. any financial aid	87
% UG borrow to pay for school	42
Average cumulative indebtedness	$34,610
% frosh need fully met	61
% ugrads need fully met	48
Average % of frosh need met	88
Average % of ugrad need met	82

UNIVERSITY OF UTAH

201 SOUTH 1460 EAST, ROOM 250 S, SALT LAKE CITY, UT 84112 • ADMISSIONS: 801-581-7281 • FAX: 801-585-7864

CAMPUS LIFE

Quality of Life Rating	65
Fire Safety Rating	90
Green Rating	94
Type of school	Public
Affiliation	No Affiliation
Environment	Metropolis

STUDENTS

Total undergrad enrollment	23,273
% male/female	55/45
% from out of state	19
% frosh from public high school	91
% frosh live on campus	45
% ugrads live on campus	13
# of fraternities (% ugrad men join)	10 (9)
# of sororities (% ugrad women join)	7 (11)
% African American	1
% Asian	5
% Caucasian	72
% Hispanic	9
% Native American	1
% international	7
# of countries represented	135

SURVEY SAYS . . .

Great library
Students get along with local community
Students love Salt Lake City, UT
Great off-campus food
Campus feels safe
Students are happy
Everyone loves the Utes
Student publications are popular

ACADEMICS

Academic Rating	65
% students returning for sophomore year	88
% students graduating within 4 years	24
% students graduating within 6 years	60
Calendar	Semester
Student/faculty ratio	13:1
Profs interesting rating	67
Profs accessible rating	64

Most classes have 10–19 students.
Most lab/discussion sessions have 10–19 students.

MOST POPULAR MAJORS

psychology; economics

STUDENTS SAY ". . ."

Academics

Nestled amid Salt Lake City's snowcapped mountains, the University of Utah is a large public school that offers extensive academic programs, ample research opportunities, and a surprisingly student-friendly atmosphere. No matter what your interests, you'll find like minds at The U. "I have studied everything from Tai Chi/Yoga movement and stage combat to differential equations and linear algebra," says a junior. "The one thing that has remained consistent throughout is the appreciation and dedication the people have for the topic they are involved in." The U is a research university that actually takes teaching seriously, and "every teacher that I've had shows incredible knowledge in their area, as well as personality and wit." "Classes are informative, challenging, and genuinely enjoyable." As is the case in many larger universities, "most general education courses are taught by grad students," whose teaching abilities can range from great to below average. "Ninety percent of my professors are fantastic; the ones that aren't are usually grad students," explains a junior. On this large campus, students have little contact with the school's administration and "there's definitely no hand-holding at the The U. If you're unsure of your major or career plans, it's easy to slip through the cracks." However, students assure us. "The administration puts student interests first whenever possible with a focus on keeping tuition low, creating a diverse environment, and providing opportunities and experience in order to prepare students to be productive citizens."

Life

While a large percentage of the undergraduate community at the University of Utah commutes to campus, there are still plenty of activities for the school's 4,000 resident students. There are many people "active in politics, environmental issues, and international issues," and, after hours, "the school holds different events throughout the year, such as Crimson Nights that feature activities such as bowling, crafts, games, food, and music." Socially, "Greek life is not as large as at other schools but is definitely a lot of fun and the best way to get to know more people your age." In addition, "during football season there are great tailgate parties with friends, drinks, and food." Right off campus, there are a range of great restaurants, and "the nightlife is hard to keep up with." There's always something good going on—whether it's at the bars and clubs downtown, or at small music venues." For outdoorsy types, The U is a paradise. "We have all four seasons and some of the best outdoors in the nation," explains one student. "Killer snow, amazing hills, mountains, lakes, and streams." In this natural wonderland, "hiking, biking, boating, snow-skiing, and snowboarding are just a few of the hundreds of activities available to students."

Student Body

Located in Salt Lake City, hometown to the Church of Jesus Christ of Latter Day Saints, The U has "plenty of social niches to fall into, and none of them are rigidly exclusive." A current student adds, "About half the student body is the typical Utah Mormon, and the other half is a mix of everything. The two halves usually stay separate but they get along." University of Utah students agree that "there is more diversity here than in any other part of the state." However, out-of-state students are uncommon, and "those of us not from Utah are definitely in the minority." While there are a number of residential students, a very large percentage of students also choose to commute to school while living with their parents or family. In addition, "there are a lot of older students and a lot of married students." Academically, however, U undergraduates are "independent, smart, and come to class ready to discuss ideas."

FINANCIAL AID: 801-581-6211 • E-MAIL: ADMISSIONS@SA.UTAH.EDU • WEBSITE: WWW.UTAH.EDU

THE PRINCETON REVIEW SAYS

Admissions

Very important factors considered include: GPA, rigor of secondary school record, standardized test scores. *Important factors considered include:* Talent/ability. *Other factors considered include:* Class rank, application essay, extracurricular activities, interview, racial/ethnic status, recommendation(s), character/personal qualities. SAT or ACT required; SAT and SAT Subject Tests or ACT considered if submitted; ACT with Writing component recommended. TOEFL required of all international applicants. *Academic units required:* 4 English; 2 mathematics; 3 science; (1 science lab); 2 foreign language; 1 history; 4 academic electives.

Financial Aid

Students should submit: FAFSA, Institution's own financial aid form. The Princeton Review suggests that all financial aid forms be submitted as soon as possible after January 1. *Need-based scholarships/grants offered:* Federal Pell, SEOG, State scholarships/grants, private scholarships, the school's own gift aid, federal nursing scholarships. *Loan aid offered:* Direct Subsidized Stafford Loans, Direct Unsubsidized Stafford Loans, Direct PLUS loans, Federal Perkins Loans, Federal Nursing Loans, State Loans, College/university loans from institutional funds. Applicants will be notified of awards beginning 4/15. Federal Work-Study Program available. Institutional employment available. Off-campus job opportunities are excellent.

The Inside Word

Admission is based primarily on the big three: Course selection, grades, and test scores. If you have a 3.0 GPA or better and average test scores, you're close to a sure bet for admission.

THE SCHOOL SAYS "..."

From the Admissions Office

"The University of Utah is a distinctive community of learning in the American West. Today's 30,819 students are from every state and 129 foreign countries. The university has research ties worldwide, with national standing among the top comprehensive research institutions. The university offers 100 undergraduate and more than ninety graduate degree programs. Nationally recognized honors and undergraduate research programs stimulate intellectual inquiry. Undergraduates collaborate with faculty on important investigations. In 2011–2012, the university's intercollegiate athletes began competing in the NCAA PAC-12 Conference. The football team has been nationally ranked for several years, as have our women's gymnastics and skiing teams. The university's location in Salt Lake City provides easy access to the arts, theater, Utah Jazz basketball, and hockey. Utah's great outdoors—skiing, hiking, and five national parks—are nearby. The university was the site for the opening and closing ceremonies and the Athletes Village for the 2002 Olympic Winter Games.

"Housing and residential education has greatly expanded the opportunity for students to live on campus with a new and wide variety of housing. Heritage Commons, constructed during the 2002 Olympics, is located in historic Fort Douglas on campus, and consists of twenty-one buildings, which accommodate more than 2,500 students. The university also has apartment housing available for students located minutes from campus in downtown Salt Lake City. In addition, a new housing complex recently opened for a 'living/learning community' that houses approximately 300 honors students.

"Applicants are required to submit ACT scores. SAT scores are also accepted, although ACT scores are preferred. Students are urged to take the ACT near the end of their junior year or early in the senior year of high school."

SELECTIVITY

Admissions Rating	75
# of applicants	11,354
% of applicants accepted	82
% of acceptees attending	34

FRESHMAN PROFILE

Range SAT Critical Reading	483–620
Range SAT Math	500–648
Range SAT Writing	480–610
Range ACT Composite	21–27
Minimum paper TOEFL	550
Average HS GPA	3.55
% graduated top 10% of class	21
% graduated top 25% of class	48
% graduated top 50% of class	83

DEADLINES

Regular	
Priority	12/1
Deadline	4/1
Nonfall registration?	Yes

FINANCIAL FACTS

Financial Aid Rating	64
% needy frosh rec. need-based scholarship or grant aid	82
% needy UG rec. need-based scholarship or grant aid	82
% needy frosh rec. non-need-based scholarship or grant aid	5
% needy UG rec. non-need-based scholarship or grant aid	2
% needy frosh rec. need-based self-help aid	91
% needy UG rec. need-based self-help aid	96
% frosh rec. any financial aid	59
% UG rec. any financial aid	61
% UG borrow to pay for school	41
Average cumulative indebtedness	$21,795
% frosh need fully met	17
% ugrads need fully met	9
Average % of frosh need met	67
Average % of ugrad need met	60

THE UNIVERSITY OF VERMONT

UNIVERSITY OF VERMONT ADMISSIONS, BURLINGTON, VT 05401-3596 • ADMISSIONS: 802-656-3370 • FAX: 802-656-8611

STUDENTS SAY ". . ."

Academics

At The University of Vermont—"a mid-sized university in a cute town that offers a quality education"—you'll get that quintessential college experience: a relaxed but academically-focused atmosphere amid big stone buildings and beautiful foliage. The school is "earthy with a touch of prep, strong outdoor ties, [and] a solid academic program," particularly in the sciences; the "ability to speak freely" is relished, and "UVM is about openness, acceptance, and sustainability while having fun." "The University of Vermont is focused on building a community from within its classrooms, rather than its Division I sports program." says a student. UVM is "not only aware of social-justice issues, it's a school that is actively involved in making change." The Rubenstein School (within UVM) is "an excellent environmental program known around the country" and is a huge draw; it's also "very easy" to switch schools (there is a "wide variety of majors") if you discover a new passion while you're here—which you very well might. Tuition increases have been small of late (less than 3% in 2013-14), which is one thing that the green students agree is essential to "sustainability." (True for all institutions of higher education.)

Faculty are overall much-lauded, but most agree that there can be some bad teachers: "You may get an amazing professor, or a professor that will lead you to your death." Small class sizes "allow for a more intimate learning experience," as do the resources available (such as a learning co-op, writing center, and career offices)."I am on a first-name basis with all of my professors and I feel comfortable talking to them at any time," says one senior environmental science major. The professors "can be tough on you, but it is reasonable." "As long as you try your hardest and put in the time, you can usually pass," says a student.

Life

As one might guess, the "landscape, scenery, and outdoor activities are plentiful" at UVM, and "it seems like at least half the school is involved in either the Ski & Snowboard Club, the Outing Club, or both." The Outing Club offers numerous outdoor trips every weekend, and people are pretty into "hiking, going down to Lake Champlain, or just hanging out on Church Street." "We are certainly academically based, yet you might not think it because people here are so independent, involved, and always have something fun going on or somewhere to be," says a junior.

The school has a huge campus, but "it is very easy to travel" and the school's "CATS buses help a huge amount, especially in bad weather!" There exists "a really good relationship with the Burlington community," and the music scene is really big: "lots of great bands come to Burlington, both on and off campus." Though not raging, students at UVM "know how to have a good time" in bars and at parties, and as far as pot use goes, one student summarizes: "It's Burlington, VT. You don't have to smoke, but you had better understand that 4/20 is a holiday." "There's something for everyone here, and it's just a lovely place to be!" says a happy student. However, some think that the meal plans "could really improve to be more flexible and better quality,"

Student Body

Students refer to the "Vermonter-ness", which encompasses a big focus on sustainability ("We compost and recycle as much as possible!"), a "liberal/left minded culture," and being "being green, healthy and happy." The "laid-back atmosphere" has "every kind of individual," all of whom are "passionate about their interests, supportive, and excited to do hands-on work to create positive changes within communities." "Racially, UVM is not diverse; but socially, it is heterogenous." Admittedly, there are a lot of hippies here, "but anyone can fit in." Everyone here is "dedicated to their studies, but in a non-competitive manner": instead of comparing exam grades, "students work together to study so that each student can do their best."

FINANCIAL AID: 802-656-5700 • E-MAIL: ADMISSIONS@UVM.EDU • WEBSITE: WWW.UVM.EDU

THE PRINCETON REVIEW SAYS

Admissions

Very important factors considered include: Rigor of secondary school record. *Important factors considered include:* Class rank, GPA, standardized test scores, application essay, state residency, character/personal qualities. *Other factors considered include:* Extracurricular activities, first generation, geographical residence, interview, racial/ethnic status, talent/ability, volunteer work, work experience, alumni/ae relations. SAT or ACT required; ACT with Writing component required. TOEFL required of all international applicants. *Academic units required:* 4 English; 3 mathematics; 2 science; (1 science lab); 3 social studies; 2 foreign language.

Financial Aid

Students should submit: FAFSA. The Princeton Review suggests that all financial aid forms be submitted as soon as possible after January 1. *Need-based scholarships/grants offered:* Federal Pell, SEOG, State scholarships/grants, private scholarships, the school's own gift aid, federal nursing scholarships. *Loan aid offered:* Direct Subsidized Stafford Loans, Direct Unsubsidized Stafford Loans, Direct PLUS loans, Federal Perkins Loans, Federal Nursing Loans, College/university loans from institutional funds. Applicants will be notified of awards beginning 3/31. Federal Work-Study Program available. Institutional employment available. Off-campus job opportunities are good.

The Inside Word

UVM is a very popular choice among out-of-state students, whom the school welcomes; more than half the student body originates from outside of Vermont. While admissions standards are significantly more rigorous for out-of-staters, solid candidates (B-plus/A-minus average, about a 600 on each section of the SAT) should do fine here. The school assesses applications holistically, meaning students who are weak in one area may be able to make up for it with strengths or distinguishing skills and characteristics in other areas.

THE SCHOOL SAYS "..."

From the Admissions Office

"Founded in 1791, the University of Vermont is among the oldest universities in the United States and one of the nation's premier small research universities. During much of its first century, the university was a private liberal college dedicated to undergraduate teaching. In 1868, it became Vermont's public land grant university and expanded its mission to include research and service.

"Today, UVM combines both elements of its heritage. Undergraduates work in small classes with faculty who are both mentors and world-class researchers. UVM's location in Vermont, known for its civic-mindedness, commitment to the environment, and essential values, strengthens the overall spirit of the university as a tolerant, enlightened, and unusually welcoming community. Not surprisingly, students are drawn to UVM from nearly every state (one third are from Vermont) and 50 countries.

"Academics at UVM are supplemented and deepened by a world of hands-on learning opportunities, from travel-study to service learning, and a wide array of internships in locations ranging from Vermont to China. Many students also assist faculty with their groundbreaking research in state-of-the-art facilities across campus, including UVM's highly-ranked medical school. The university is widely recognized for its environmental conscience, commitment to social justice, and global perspective. In recognition of this achievement outside the classroom, more than 105 UVM students have been selected as winners or finalists in the country's most competitive scholarships, such as the Truman, Fulbright, Udall and Goldwater.

"The University of Vermont is located in Burlington, one of America's liveliest small cities surrounded by idyllic countryside, the Green Mountains, and Lake Champlain. As the state's educational, medical, financial and cultural epicenter, Burlington is ranked one of the most desirable place to live and a top college town. In addition, Vermont's 'human scale' is often cited as offering UVM students unique opportunities to get involved and gain essential experience."

SELECTIVITY

Admissions Rating	86
# of applicants	22,381
% of applicants accepted	78
% of acceptees attending	14
# offered a place on the wait list	2,288
% accepting a place on wait list	24
% admitted from wait list	29

FRESHMAN PROFILE

Range SAT Critical Reading	540–640
Range SAT Math	540–650
Range SAT Writing	540–650
Range ACT Composite	24–29
Minimum paper TOEFL	550
Minimum web-based TOEFL	213
Average HS GPA	3.48
% graduated top 10% of class	33
% graduated top 25% of class	68
% graduated top 50% of class	96

DEADLINES

Early action	
Deadline	11/1
Notification	12/15
Regular	
Deadline	1/15
Notification	3/31
Nonfall registration?	Yes

FINANCIAL FACTS

Financial Aid Rating	70
Annual in-state tuition	$13,728
Annual out-of-state tuition	$34,656
Room and board	$10,402
Required fees	$1,990
Books and supplies	$1,200
% needy frosh rec. need-based scholarship or grant aid	98
% needy UG rec. need-based scholarship or grant aid	96
% needy frosh rec. non-need-based scholarship or grant aid	9
% needy UG rec. non-need-based scholarship or grant aid	5
% needy frosh rec. need-based self-help aid	71
% needy UG rec. need-based self-help aid	76
% frosh rec. any financial aid	89
% UG rec. any financial aid	82
% UG borrow to pay for school	60
Average cumulative indebtedness	$28,256
% frosh need fully met	14
% ugrads need fully met	11
Average % of frosh need met	67
Average % of ugrad need met	65

UNIVERSITY OF VIRGINIA

OFFICE OF ADMISSION, CHARLOTTESVILLE, VA 22906 • ADMISSIONS: 434-982-3200 • FAX: 434-924-3587

CAMPUS LIFE

Quality of Life Rating	88
Fire Safety Rating	76
Green Rating	97
Type of school	Public
Affiliation	No Affiliation
Environment	City

STUDENTS

Total undergrad enrollment	14,915
% male/female	45/55
% from out of state	27
% frosh from public high school	73
% frosh live on campus	100
% ugrads live on campus	41
# of fraternities (% ugrad men join)	27 (25)
# of sororities (% ugrad women join)	16(28)
% African American	6
% Asian	12
% Caucasian	61
% Hispanic	6
% Native American	<1
% international	6
# of countries represented	117

SURVEY SAYS . . .

Students are happy
School is well run
No one cheats
Students love Charlottesville, VA
Great off-campus food
Athletic facilities are great
Lots of beer drinking
Alumni active on campus
Active student government

ACADEMICS

Academic Rating	84
% students returning for sophomore year	97
% students graduating within 4 years	86
% students graduating within 6 years	93
Calendar	Semester
Student/faculty ratio	16:1
Profs interesting rating	80
Profs accessible rating	75

Most classes have 10–19 students.
Most lab/discussion sessions have
20–29 students.

MOST POPULAR MAJORS
business/commerce; psychology; biology

STUDENTS SAY ". . ."

Academics

There is much to love about the University of Virginia, one of the country's top public universities. Just to name a few: "Tradition, student self-governance, the honor system, the access to world renowned professors, [and] the beauty of the architecture." The school's affordable in-state tuition guarantees students access to "the perfect balance of world-class academics, a tradition of school spirit, and a great party scene." While there are a lot of opportunities at UVA, "no one is going to hold your hand and help you find what you're interested in." However, those who proactively seek out their own answers "find the UVA community is fully supportive of [their] passions, and there are tons of resources to pursue whatever interest you might have." The academic program is "definitely our greatest strength—no matter what you choose to major in, you will encounter great professors and stimulating courses," according to one student. Many of the school's most accomplished professors teach introductory and lower-level courses "to make themselves accessible to every student at UVA." Professors "want to get to know you as a person and are always helpful if you approach them with questions on content or other academic problems." Courses are "very flexible," and the faculty are "always coming up with new course options," though the class registration system is notoriously frustrating. The school has a "very strong honor system" that is run entirely by students (as are all extracurricular groups), so "it's rare to hear about someone's stuff being stolen or cheating on assignments." This autonomy is a huge boon to students' feelings toward their school, as is the universal "respect for tradition."

Life

Living on campus "is definitely a huge part of your first-year experience," and students all greatly appreciate "the unique history" and "hilarious and fun traditions" of the school (especially those upheld by the popular Greek system), "which help to foster a sense of community." The school offers a ton of resources, including "free counseling and psychological services, plenty of places to grab a bite to eat, a twenty-four-hour library, a movie theater, free transportation on both university and local transport services, a fabulous career services center, four gyms, and constant sporting events." "Whether I'm in the mood to go for a hike in the Blue Ridge Mountains or go shopping in the downtown mall, there is never a dull moment," says a student.

Most students instantly fall in love with the "accessible and charming" Charlottesville, with its "awesome, local, and iconic" food, "local quirky shops," "a thriving music scene, multicultural festivals," and "three great coffee places." On campus, the lawn or gardens "always sport students lounging and reading, people walking their dogs, townies with their kids, and professors and students having coffee." As for more traditionally collegiate forms of kicking back, UVA kids do enjoy "lots of drinking/partying," but "you can find people who don't like to if you try." "We put an incredible amount of effort into our academic lives, and then when the weekend comes we let loose like there's no tomorrow," says one student.

Student Body

The tough admissions standards mean that most all who attend here are "highly motivated, resourceful, [and] passionate about learning," and the student body does have a reputation as "a bunch of hard partying, politically aware, go-getters." There really is "a pervasive can-do attitude around UVA," and the "self-starter and very smart" students reflect that "with all the things we do only with support from each other." Almost 70 percent of students come from Virginia and are "typical preppy Southerners," and there are terrific town-gown relations; students here are also "really environmentally friendly and socially conscious." "We like to be activists and get involved in the community," says a student. You're also "practically an outcast if you don't join a student group...once you see the vast number of student groups around grounds, you'll find it hard not to join one—or maybe seventeen."

FINANCIAL AID: 434-982-6000 • E-MAIL: UNDERGRADADMISSION@VIRGINIA.EDU • WEBSITE: WWW.VIRGINIA.EDU

THE PRINCETON REVIEW SAYS

Admissions

Very important factors considered include: Class rank, GPA, rigor of secondary school record, first generation, racial/ethnic status, recommendation(s), state residency, alumni/ae relations. *Important factors considered include:* Standardized test scores, application essay, extracurricular activities, talent/ability, character/personal qualities. *Other factors considered include:* Geographical residence, volunteer work, work experience. SAT or ACT required; ACT with Writing component required. TOEFL required of all international applicants. *Academic units required:* 4 English; 4 mathematics; 2 science; 1 social studies; 2 foreign language. *Academic units recommended:* 5 mathematics; 4 science; 4 social studies; 5 foreign language.

Financial Aid

Students should submit: FAFSA, Institution's own financial aid form. The Princeton Review suggests that all financial aid forms be submitted as soon as possible after January 1. *Need-based scholarships/grants offered:* Federal Pell, SEOG, State scholarships/grants, private scholarships, the school's own gift aid, federal nursing scholarships. *Loan aid offered:* Federal Perkins Loans, Federal Nursing Loans, College/university loans from institutional funds. Applicants will be notified of awards beginning 4/5. Federal Work-Study Program available. Institutional employment available.

The Inside Word

As one of the premier public universities in the country, UVA holds its applicants to high standards. While admissions officers don't set minimum requirements, all viable candidates have stellar academic records. Intellectual ability is imperative, and prospective students are expected to have taken a rigorous course load in high school. Applicants should be aware that geographical location holds significant weight, as Virginia residents are given preference.

THE SCHOOL SAYS "..."

From the Admissions Office

"Admission to the University of Virginia is competitive. Students who stretch themselves and take rigorous courses in high school (honors-level, AP, A-level, IB, and DE courses, when offered) are more qualified for admission than those who do not. Many students applying to the University present solid academic credentials, but we are also looking beyond the numbers and are interested in a student's life and contributions outside of the classroom. Non-cognitive factors play a significant role in our review, and we are especially interested in students who exhibit strong leadership and personal qualities. Love of learning, the ability to think critically, analytically, and globally, strong writing skills, and the desire to make a difference in the world are also attributes of UVA students.

"SAT or ACT is required but neither is preferred. We strongly recommend that applicants take two SAT Subject Tests of their choice."

SELECTIVITY

Admissions Rating	98
# of applicants	29,021
% of applicants accepted	30
% of acceptees attending	40
# offered a place on the wait list	4,172
% accepting a place on wait list	62
% admitted from wait list	7
# of early decision applicants	13,645
% accepted early decision	28

FRESHMAN PROFILE

Range SAT Critical Reading	620–720
Range SAT Math	630–740
Range SAT Writing	620–720
Range ACT Composite	29–33
Average HS GPA	4.22
% graduated top 10% of class	92
% graduated top 25% of class	98
% graduated top 50% of class	99

DEADLINES

Early action	
Deadline	11/1
Notification	1/31
Regular	
Deadline	1/1
Notification	4/1
Nonfall registration?	No

APPLICANTS ALSO LOOK AT AND OFTEN PREFER

The College of William & Mary; Virginia Tech

AND SOMETIMES PREFER

Duke University; The University of North Carolina at Chapel Hill

AND RARELY PREFER

James Madison University

FINANCIAL FACTS

Financial Aid Rating	94
Annual in-state tuition	$10,016
Annual out-of-state tuition	$36,720
Room and board	$9,717
Required fees	$2,652
Books and supplies	$1,240
% needy frosh rec. need-based scholarship or grant aid	83
% needy UG rec. need-based scholarship or grant aid	82
% needy frosh rec. non-need-based scholarship or grant aid	10
% needy UG rec. non-need-based scholarship or grant aid	8
% needy frosh rec. need-based self-help aid	65
% needy UG rec. need-based self-help aid	62
% frosh rec. any financial aid	57
% UG rec. any financial aid	53
% UG borrow to pay for school	35
Average cumulative indebtedness	$21,875
% frosh need fully met	100
% ugrads need fully met	100
Average % of frosh need met	100
Average % of ugrad need met	100

UNIVERSITY OF WASHINGTON

1410 NORTHEAST CAMPUS PARKWAY, SEATTLE, WA 98195-5852 • ADMISSIONS: 206-543-9686

CAMPUS LIFE

Quality of Life Rating	78
Fire Safety Rating	94
Green Rating	99
Type of school	Public
Affiliation	No Affiliation
Environment	Metropolis

STUDENTS

Total undergrad enrollment	27,836
% male/female	48/52
% from out of state	14
% frosh from public high school	73
% frosh live on campus	65
% ugrads live on campus	25
# of fraternities (% ugrad men join)	32 (10)
# of sororities (% ugrad women join)	16 (9)
% African American	1
% Asian	14
% Caucasian	26
% Hispanic	3
% Native American	1
% international	5
# of countries represented	107

SURVEY SAYS . . .
Great library
Athletic facilities are great
Students love Seattle, WA
Great off-campus food
Everyone loves the Huskies
Student publications are popular
Students environmentally aware

ACADEMICS

Academic Rating	74
% students returning for sophomore year	93
% students graduating within 4 years	56
% students graduating within 6 years	80
Calendar	Quarter
Profs interesting rating	66
Profs accessible rating	66

Most classes have 20–29 students.
Most lab/discussion sessions have
20–29 students.

MOST POPULAR MAJORS
bioengineering; business/commerce;
computer science

STUDENTS SAY ". . ."

Academics

Students find "a great combination of high-powered academics, an excellent social life, and a wide variety of courses, all in the midst of the exciting Seattle life" at the University of Washington, the state's flagship institution of higher learning. UW offers "a lot of really stellar programs and the best bang for the buck, especially for in-state students or those in the sciences." Indeed, science programs "are incredible. The research going on here is cutting-edge and the leaders of biomedical sciences, stem cell research, etc. are accessible to students." Undergrads warn, however, that science programs are extremely competitive, "high pressure," and "challenging," with "core classes taught in lectures that seat more than 500 people," creating the sense that "professors don't seem to care too much whether you succeed." Pre-professional programs in business, law, nursing, medicine and engineering all earn high marks, although again with the caveat that the workload is tough and the hand-holding nominal. As one student puts it, "The University of Washington provides every resource and opportunity for its students to succeed. You just have to take advantage of them. No one will do it for you." For those fortunate enough to get in, the Honors Program "creates a smaller community of highly motivated students...It puts this school on top."

Life

UW students typically "have a good balance in their lives of education and fun." They "generally study hard and work in the libraries, but once the night-time hits, they look forward to enjoying the night with their friends." Between the large university community and the surrounding city of Seattle, undergrads have a near-limitless selection of extracurricular choices. As one student explains, "There are tons of options for fun in Seattle. Going down to Pike's Market on a Saturday and eating your way through is always popular. There are tons of places to eat on 'The Ave,'" the shopping district that abuts campus, "and the UVillage shopping mall is a five minute walk from campus with chain-store comfort available. Intramural sports are big for activities, and going to undergraduate theater productions is never a disappointing experience. During autumn or spring renting a canoe and paddling around lake Washington down by the stadium is fun." Husky football games "are amazing," and the Greek community "is very big" without dominating campus social life. In short, "the UW has anything you could want to do in your free time."

Student Body

"At such a large university, there is no 'typical' student," undergrads tell us, observing "one can find just about any demographic here and there is a huge variety in personalities." There "are quite a lot of yuppies, but then again, it's Seattle," and by and large "the campus is ultraliberal. Most students care about the environment, are not religious, and are generally accepting of other diverse individuals." Otherwise, "you've got your stereotypes: the Greeks, the street fashion pioneers, the various ethnic communities, the Oxford-looking grad students, etc." In terms of demographics, "the typical student at UW is white, middle-class, and is from the Seattle area," but "there are a lot of African American students and a very large number of Asian students." All groups "seem to socialize with each other."

Fax: 206-685-3655 • Financial Aid: 206-543-6101 • Website: www.washington.edu

THE PRINCETON REVIEW SAYS

Admissions

Very important factors considered include: GPA, rigor of secondary school record, application essay. *Important factors considered include:* Standardized test scores, extracurricular activities, first generation, talent/ability, volunteer work, work experience, character/personal qualities. *Other factors considered include:* State residency. SAT or ACT required; ACT with Writing component required. TOEFL required of all international applicants. *Academic units required:* 4 English; 3 mathematics; 2 science; (1 science lab); 3 social studies; 2 foreign language. *Academic units recommended:* 4 mathematics; 4 science; (3 science lab); 4 social studies; 3 foreign language; 1 history; 1 computer science; 1 visual/ performing arts.

Financial Aid

Students should submit: FAFSA. The Princeton Review suggests that all financial aid forms be submitted as soon as possible after January 1. *Need-based scholarships/grants offered:* Federal Pell, SEOG, State scholarships/grants, private scholarships, the school's own gift aid. *Loan aid offered:* Direct Subsidized Stafford Loans, Direct Unsubsidized Stafford Loans, Direct PLUS loans, Federal Perkins Loans, Federal Nursing Loans. Applicants will be notified of awards beginning 4/1. Federal Work-Study Program available. Institutional employment available. Off-campus job opportunities are excellent.

The Inside Word

In recent years, UW committed to a thorough review of all freshman applications, abandoning the previous process by which a formula was used to rank applicants according to high school GPA and standardized test scores. The new, holistic approach allows admissions officers to take into account a student's background, the degree to which he or she has overcome personal adversity, and such intangibles as leadership quality and special skills. The move has so far resulted in increased racial and socioeconomic diversity, a result praised by some and criticized by others, who regard the new system as a poorly disguised affirmative action program.

THE SCHOOL SAYS "..."

From the Admissions Office

"Are you curious about everything, from comet dust to computer game design, salmon to Salman Rushdie, ancient Rome to the atmospherics of Mars? Do you seek the freedom to chart your own course—and work on breakthrough research? Are you ready to cheer on the Division I Huskies and spend your weekends sea kayaking? Would you like to walk to class on a 700-acre stunning, ivy-covered campus, yet be only fifteen minutes from downtown Seattle? If the answers are yes, then the University of Washington may be the place for you. Offering more than 140 majors and 450 student organizations, the UW is looking for students who are both excited about the vast academic and social possibilities available to them and eager to contribute to the campus' cultural and intellectual life.

"We encourage you to take advantage of every opportunity in the application, especially the personal statement and activities summary, to tell us why Washington would be good fit for you and how you will contribute to the freshman class.

"Freshman applicants to the University of Washington are required to submit scores from either the SAT or ACT (with the writing component)."

SELECTIVITY

Admissions Rating	95
# of applicants	26,138
% of applicants accepted	59
% of acceptees attending	39
# offered a place on the wait list	2,334
% accepting a place on wait list	51
% admitted from wait list	49

FRESHMAN PROFILE

Range SAT Critical Reading	520–650
Range SAT Math	580–710
Range SAT Writing	450–650
Range ACT Composite	24–30
Minimum paper TOEFL	540
Minimum web-based TOEFL	207
Average HS GPA	3.75
% graduated top 10% of class	92
% graduated top 25% of class	98
% graduated top 50% of class	100

DEADLINES

Regular	
Deadline	12/1
Notification	3/31
Nonfall registration?	Yes

**APPLICANTS ALSO LOOK AT
AND OFTEN PREFER**
University of Southern California

AND SOMETIMES PREFER
Gonzaga University

AND RARELY PREFER
Washington State University; University of
Puget Sound; University of Colorado—Boulder

FINANCIAL FACTS

Financial Aid Rating	76
Annual in-state tuition	$11,305
Annual out-of-state tuition	$28,860
Room and board	$9,969
Required fees	$1,078
Books and supplies	$1,035
% needy frosh rec. need-based scholarship or grant aid	85
% needy UG rec. need-based scholarship or grant aid	85
% needy frosh rec. non-need-based scholarship or grant aid	13
% needy UG rec. non-need-based scholarship or grant aid	6
% needy frosh rec. need-based self-help aid	63
% needy UG rec. need-based self-help aid	75
% frosh rec. any financial aid	50
% UG rec. any financial aid	50
% UG borrow to pay for school	49
Average cumulative indebtedness	$20,800
% frosh need fully met	23
% ugrads need fully met	24
Average % of frosh need met	83
Average % of ugrad need met	82

UNIVERSITY OF WISCONSIN—MADISON

702 WEST JOHNSON STREET, SUITE 101, MADISON, WI 53715-1007 • ADMISSIONS: 608-262-3961 • FAX: 608-262-7706

CAMPUS LIFE
Quality of Life Rating	92
Fire Safety Rating	81
Green Rating	79
Type of school	Public
Affiliation	No Affiliation
Environment	City

STUDENTS
Total undergrad enrollment	29,504
% male/female	49/51
% from out of state	33
% frosh live on campus	92
% ugrads live on campus	25
# of fraternities (% ugrad men join)	26 (9)
# of sororities (% ugrad women join)	11 (8)
% African American	2
% Asian	6
% Caucasian	77
% Hispanic	5
% Native American	<1
% international	7
# of countries represented	144

SURVEY SAYS . . .
Students are happy
School is well run
Students are friendly
Students love Madison, WI
Great off-campus food
Athletic facilities are great
Lots of beer drinking
Hard liquor is popular
Everyone loves the Badgers
Alumni active on campus

ACADEMICS
Academic Rating	82
% students returning for sophomore year	95
% students graduating within 4 years	56
% students graduating within 6 years	84
Calendar	Semester
Student/faculty ratio	17:1
Profs interesting rating	76
Profs accessible rating	73

Most classes have 10–19 students.
Most lab/discussion sessions have
  20–29 students.

MOST POPULAR MAJORS
political science; biology; economics

STUDENTS SAY ". . ."

Academics

As a "nationally renowned" "top public university" that many call "the best college in the Midwest," the flagship of the University of Wisconsin system offers a "great school for [a] good price." UW Madison offers a stunning array of resources: over 5,000 classes, more than 2,000 professors, and a library system that boasts over fourteen million books and other artifacts. Students are encouraged to take advantage of their surroundings in Madison's ethos that "the whole great state of Wisconsin is at once the laboratory and the responsibility of this flagship campus." Students call their professors "the best of the best" in their fields, and love the way they facilitate "very independent learning": "Madison teaches you to become more competitive and self sufficient in reaching your goals." Undergraduates reveal that the bureacracy inherent in a large university becomes more manageable over the years. "As a junior (compared to freshman and sophomore year) I have found my classes to be devoted more to discussion as opposed to lecture." However, the quality of instructors is fairly persistent: "No matter what level the class is the professors are dedicated to helping their students." Some students report more mixed experiences with faculty, saying "professors range from being the bomb-diggity to the most horrible teacher I have ever had in my life" but nonetheless assert that "the classes are challenging (like 95 percent of the time)." Like any experience, though, what you put in is what you can expect to get out: "If you're willing to put in the work and use your resources you will can achieve any grade you want."

Life

Let its students put it to you this way: "Madison didn't get its top rank as a party school for our incredible chess matches." There's really no getting around the fact that Madison is a "huge party school" where "the weekends are a lavish display of hedonism." Halloween is a legendary party weekend on campus, and drinking is just "part of Wisconsin's lifestyle." Drinking, though, is hardly all there is to do, and "the university offers many substance-free activities and so does the surrounding community." Whether they're sober or not, undergrads brag that "Wisconsin students can have fun doing anything." Because of the region's Midwestern weather extremes, social life is somewhat impacted by the seasons: "When the weather is nice, it's lovely to just walk along State or Downtown and enjoy the weather, but during the winter, most people stay in and drink." Many students love to support "Badger Pride" by going "to football games," but again, there are enough other choices of activities to satisfy any taste: "I go on bike rides in the arboretum, or beer brewing seminars, or play guitar by one of the lakes, or go to protests at the State Capitol building." Overall, Madison's students seem happy to be there: "Just about every graduate will tell you UW gave them the best four years of their lives; partying, athletics (participating or watching), useful classes, just about everyone loves [it]."

Student Body

"Students don't really have to try to fit in" at Madison, because "there's a niche for everyone." In fact, "at Madison, the only thing that runs the same through each student is a drive to succeed, a passion to learn, and a love of Bucky!" While the university draws many natives from "some unpronounceable town in Wisconsin" and other homegrown Midwesterners, students "come from both coasts as well as the Midwest," and the school also attracts "a high number of international students." Indeed, student comments reflect that many region-local students chose Madison even among other options: "He/She beat out the rest of their high school class through wit and determination to become a Badger. They love football, beer, cheese, and brats." An attitude of "work hard, play hard" prevails on the "very diverse" campus, where "the typical student is very intelligent, hardworking, but also very social."

UNIVERSITY OF WISCONSIN—MADISON

FINANCIAL AID: 608-262-3060 • E-MAIL: ONWISCONSIN@ADMISSIONS.WISC.EDU • WEBSITE: WWW.WISC.EDU

THE PRINCETON REVIEW SAYS

Admissions

Very important factors considered include: Class rank, GPA, rigor of secondary school record. *Important factors considered include:* Standardized test scores, application essay, state residency. *Other factors considered include:* Extracurricular activities, first generation, racial/ethnic status, recommendation(s), talent/ability, volunteer work, work experience, alumni/ae relations, character/personal qualities, level of applicant's interest. SAT or ACT required; ACT with Writing component required. TOEFL required of all international applicants. *Academic units required:* 4 English; 4 mathematics; 3 science; 3 social studies; 3 foreign language; 2 academic electives. *Academic units recommended:* 4 English; 4 mathematics; 4 science; 4 social studies; 4 foreign language; 2 academic electives.

Financial Aid

Students should submit: FAFSA. The Princeton Review suggests that all financial aid forms be submitted as soon as possible after January 1. *Need-based scholarships/grants offered:* Federal Pell, SEOG, State scholarships/grants, private scholarships, the school's own gift aid. *Loan aid offered:* Direct Subsidized Stafford Loans, Direct Unsubsidized Stafford Loans, Direct PLUS loans, Federal Perkins Loans, Federal Nursing Loans. Federal Work-Study Program available. Institutional employment available. Off-campus job opportunities are excellent.

The Inside Word

UW-Madison strongly encourages applicants to use its online application, which now features new essay questions—consult the university's website for application tips. It's optional to supply a letter of recommendation, but if you can, do. Extracurricular activities are considered in addition to high school GPA and test scores, so it's a good idea to play them up in your essays.

THE SCHOOL SAYS "..."

From the Admissions Office

"UW-Madison is the university of choice for some of the best and brightest students. Our freshman class has an average ACT score of 28 and an average SAT of 1916. Almost 60 percent are from the top 10 percent of their high school class, and nearly all are from the top quarter.

"These factors combine to make admission to UW-Madison both competitive and selective. We consider academic record, course selection, strength of curriculum (honors, AP, IB, etc.), grade trend, class rank, results of the ACT/SAT, and non-academic factors. There is no prescribed minimum test score, GPA, or class rank criteria. Rather, we admit the best and most well-prepared students—students who have challenged themselves and who will contribute to Wisconsin's strength and diversity—for the limited space available.

"Each application is personally reviewed by our admission counselors. All domestic freshman applications completed by February 1 receive full and equal consideration. We offer two notification periods for domestic freshman applicants. To receive a decision during the First Notification Period, you must complete the application and submit all required materials (application fee, official high school transcript, official test scores, personal statements, and recommendations) postmarked by November 1. Admission decisions for these students will be made by the end of January. All students who complete their applications during the Second Notification Period (after November 1 but before the February 1 deadline) will have decision made on or by the end of March. All students receive equal consideration for admission whether they apply during the First or Second Notification Periods."

SELECTIVITY

Admissions Rating	94
# of applicants	29,675
% of applicants accepted	51
% of acceptees attending	42

FRESHMAN PROFILE

Range SAT Critical Reading	550–660
Range SAT Math	620–750
Range SAT Writing	590–680
Range ACT Composite	26–30
Minimum paper TOEFL	550
Minimum web-based TOEFL	80
Average HS GPA	3.81
% graduated top 10% of class	52
% graduated top 25% of class	89
% graduated top 50% of class	99

DEADLINES

Regular	
Deadline	2/1
Nonfall registration?	Yes

APPLICANTS ALSO LOOK AT AND OFTEN PREFER

University of Illinois at Urbana-Champaign; University of Minnesota-Twin Cities; University of Michigan-Ann Arbor; Marquette University

AND SOMETIMES PREFER

Northwestern University; University of Colorado-Boulder

FINANCIAL FACTS

Financial Aid Rating	84
Annual in-state tuition	$9,273
Annual out-of-state tuition	$25,523
Room and board	$8,354
Required fees	$1,130
Books and supplies	$1,200
% needy frosh rec. need-based scholarship or grant aid	80
% needy UG rec. need-based scholarship or grant aid	78
% needy frosh rec. non-need-based scholarship or grant aid	7
% needy UG rec. non-need-based scholarship or grant aid	7
% needy frosh rec. need-based self-help aid	76
% needy UG rec. need-based self-help aid	81
% UG borrow to pay for school	50
Average cumulative indebtedness	$25,664
% frosh need fully met	37
% ugrads need fully met	40
Average % of frosh need met	78
Average % of ugrad need met	80

UNIVERSITY OF WYOMING

DEPARTMENT 3435, LARAMIE, WY 82071 • ADMISSIONS: 307-766-5160 • FAX: 307-766-4042

STUDENTS SAY ". . ."

Academics

Why choose University of Wyoming? "Wyoming scholarships rock!" Hathaway Scholarships allow state residents to graduate virtually debt free, and financial aid for out-of-state students isn't too shabby, either. This allows students to get "an outstanding education for pennies on the dollar." This is a large university, though, which means "you have to make the commitment to do well." In other words, those grades aren't going to earn themselves! The business school, engineering school, and English departments all receive high marks from students, and the school's agricultural programs also have an excellent reputation. "They are on top of developing degree programs and courses focused on sustainability, green design, and climate change." There's "a 50/50 [split between] professors who love what they do and those who are just going with the flow," but "nine times out of ten they will go well out of their way to help you." Many faculty members "have real-world job experience that helps bring their lectures to life." Many students complain about the registration process, which favors athletes and members of the honors program, but others suggest that kicking up a fuss will get you into the classes you want, or they suggest applying for the honors program: "They pull in the best professors across campus, and the requirements are a piece of cake. Plus, you get free printing," semester-long book checkout at the library, and priority registration. (Conservatives take note: Some students describe the honors classes as "very biased and liberal.") "The new library is great and full of awesome resources," and study abroad resources are "absolutely amazing" as well.

Life

"Cowboy football is a blast! We may not have the best team or biggest crowd, but we make up for it in dedicated fans!" Supporting UW's Division I football team is a bit pastime in the fall. Winter in Laramie, Wyoming, may be freezing (student wish lists include reopening underground tunnels for travel between buildings, and/or "fire pits for staying warm on your way to your next class!"), but it's "a great town if you enjoy the outdoors," and "skiing, mountain biking, hiking, camping, fishing, mountain climbing, hunting are all popular activities." "People often say that there is nothing to do in Laramie but drink," and UW has its fair share of partying, though members of the large religious and nontraditional student populations are quick to point out that not everyone is searching for a house party every weekend. "The school offers a wide breadth of other activities from free ice skating to free movies, fly-fishing classes to a capella concerts, and many of these are run by students and are widely attended." Fort Collins and Denver, Colorado, are both about two and a half hours away by car, though if you're bringing a vehicle to campus, four-wheel drive is strongly recommended.

Student Body

"The majority of the students are Wyoming residents with a large portion of the rest coming from Colorado." Students tend to be "good-natured kids [who have] grown up on ranches or farms where a strong work ethic has been established," "usually nice with strong family values and a conservative upbringing." Politically, there seems to be a bit of a divide among students, which reflects the geography of the university: Laramie is considered a more liberal enclave in a traditionally conservative state. "The school creates an open-minded atmosphere within one of the most conservative states in the union," but on the other hand, "many of the Christian campus ministries are very outspoken." Students say, "We are not incredibly diverse ethnically, but we are diverse in so many other ways," and "every semester brings more and more minority and foreign students." There's "a huge amount of nontraditional students as well."

FINANCIAL AID: 307-766-2116 • E-MAIL: ADMISSIONS@UWYO.EDU • WEBSITE: WWW.UWYO.EDU

THE PRINCETON REVIEW SAYS

Admissions

Very important factors considered include: GPA, rigor of secondary school record, standardized test scores. *Important factors considered include:* Level of applicant's interest. *Other factors considered include:* Application essay, extracurricular activities, interview, recommendation(s), state residency, talent/ability, character/personal qualities. SAT or ACT required; ACT with or without Writing component accepted. TOEFL required of all international applicants. *Academic units required:* 4 English; 4 mathematics; 4 science; (3 science lab); 2 foreign language. *Academic units recommended:* 4 English; 4 mathematics; 4 science; (3 science lab); 2 foreign language.

Financial Aid

Students should submit: FAFSA. The Princeton Review suggests that all financial aid forms be submitted as soon as possible after January 1. *Need-based scholarships/grants offered:* Federal Pell, SEOG, State scholarships/grants, private scholarships, the school's own gift aid. *Loan aid offered:* Direct Subsidized Stafford Loans, Direct Unsubsidized Stafford Loans, Direct PLUS loans, Federal Perkins Loans. Federal Work-Study Program available. Institutional employment available. Off-campus job opportunities are good.

The Inside Word

The admissions process at UW is formula-driven. An unweighted high school GPA of 3.0 in a traditional college prep curriculum combined with some solid test scores (21 ACT or CR+M 980 SAT) will open the door to this university.

THE SCHOOL SAYS "..."

From the Admissions Office

"The University of Wyoming offers a personalized education for a fraction of the cost of other public universities. Located in Laramie, UW is regularly recognized as one of the nation's best college values. This comes as no surprise, as UW is a national research university offering countless academic opportunities.

"Explore 200+ programs of study through seven colleges and 3 specialized schools. From Engineering to Business, Performing Arts to Geology and Agricultural Economics to Nursing, we are sure you will find your program at UW.

"Over the past seven years, the UW campus has experienced incredible growth. 750 million dollars have been invested in new facilities including a new Business building, Creative Arts facility, UW Library and most recently the introduction of the NCAR supercomputer. The NCAR computer is a joint partnership between UW and the National Center for Atmospheric Research. Undergraduate students have access to all these facilities for instruction, internships and research.

"Set at 7,200 feet above sea level, UW and Laramie are in a pristine location to attend school and enjoy the outdoors. UW was recently recognized by Outside magazine as the 15th best college campus in the country for outdoor adventure. Just thirty miles from campus is over 2 million acres of national forest with peaks climbing over 12,000 feet. Campus life is exciting with 200+ student clubs and organizations as well as NCAA Division 1-A sports in the Mountain West conference."

SELECTIVITY

Admissions Rating	72
# of applicants	4,348
% of applicants accepted	96
% of acceptees attending	38

FRESHMAN PROFILE

Range SAT Critical Reading	480–620
Range SAT Math	510–620
Range ACT Composite	22–27
Minimum paper TOEFL	525
Minimum web-based TOEFL	71
Average HS GPA	3.48
% graduated top 10% of class	23
% graduated top 25% of class	50
% graduated top 50% of class	82

DEADLINES

Regular	
Priority	3/1
Deadline	8/10
Nonfall registration?	Yes

FINANCIAL FACTS

Financial Aid Rating	66
Annual in-state tuition	$3,240
Annual out-of-state tuition	$12,960
Room and board	$9,451
Required fees	$1,164
Books and supplies	$1,200
% needy frosh rec. need-based scholarship or grant aid	61
% needy UG rec. need-based scholarship or grant aid	69
% needy frosh rec. non-need-based scholarship or grant aid	83
% needy UG rec. non-need-based scholarship or grant aid	69
% needy frosh rec. need-based self-help aid	52
% needy UG rec. need-based self-help aid	61
% UG borrow to pay for school	48
Average cumulative indebtedness	$22,879
% frosh need fully met	24
% ugrads need fully met	16
Average % of frosh need met	63
Average % of ugrad need met	60

Ursinus College

Ursinus College, Collegeville, PA 19426 • Admissions: 610-409-3200 • Fax: 610-409-3662

STUDENTS SAY ". . ."

Academics

Set in Collegeville, Pennsylvania, this "small, close-knit college community" offers "an exceptional academic record" and "small-school atmosphere," which "provides accessibility to professors and successful students, enabling a better learning experience." This is "a campus filled with motivated students and professors who worked toward every student's success." "Academic integrity" is "high," "yet fostering leadership, community and personal growth [is] also extremely prided." The "greatest strengths" of Ursinus's program "are probably the focus on community service, the strength of the academic programs, and programs such as CIE (common intellectual experience, an entire class [where the focus is on] the whole campus reading and discussing the same books or movies." Ursinus is also known for its "strong biology and science program," which "allow students to maintain strong connections in other fields, from art to education." Classes "are small," and professors "are accessible and have extensive knowledge in their fields." The academic bar here is high. Professors expect "students to be engaged." They "tend to be very attentive to your performance in class and are available to help if you need it." While "[professors] expect a lot from you, and it is challenging," the workload is "very doable because of the relationships with professors and students." Overall, this small, rigorous program is "about creating free-thinking, intelligent, [and] contributing members of society" and "letting people be who they are without fear and while accomplishing learning beyond the classroom."

Life

During the week, "mostly everyone goes to class and then to the library or another study room to finish homework and study." "There is always something happening on campus, which is contrary to the big misconception about smaller schools." "Because the student population is low, everyone receives e-mails about everything going on." In addition, there "is a large athletic population, and games are highly attended." "Almost every night there is some party going on, and on weekends it can get crazy, but the drinking scene is easily avoidable." Others agree, "The school offers a lot of weekend activities for those of us who do not partake in drinking. They have movie nights, casino nights, game show nights, special dinners, [and] a lot of off campus events." While "the town [of Collegeville] is small, they are expanding and building upon it. Philadelphia is close as is King of Prussia, Phoenixville, Skippack, and Limerick so students have places to go off campus and have fun." "Most students stay on weekends and either attend a campus event or hang out with friends." "Partying does happen; it happens only Thursday through Saturday because most students are extremely serious about their academics."

Student Body

Ursinus students are "well-rounded, mature, and friendly." Everyone at Ursinus "has an interest in their academics as well as their social life." "Because of various requirements, students interact with all sorts of students with different majors, especially our CIE class, which requires a lot of introspection." Most students "can find a group of students they fit in with easily." The typical student "has a core group of friends, friends that they have classes with, many are involved with some kind of sport (intramural or collegiate), and many are involved with community service." While some tout the stereotypical badge of being "upper-middle- or middle-class, involved in a sport in some way"; however, by in large the student body here is "very open to other beliefs and opinions" and "willing to branch out into different areas other than their specified major." Overall, a "supportive and friendly" atmosphere pervades. Ursinus students "are all hard-working and must go above and beyond to compete academically." Students at Ursinus tend to balance their "very studious" academic aspirations "with an active and healthy extracurricular lifestyle." They're "outgoing to others [and] involved in campus and in the society." "Many students are athletes," and "About 20 percent of the campus is affiliated with a Greek organization." In a sentence, "Ursinus students are overachievers."

FINANCIAL AID: 610-409-3600 • E-MAIL: ADMISSIONS@URSINUS.EDU • WEBSITE: WWW.URSINUS.EDU

THE PRINCETON REVIEW SAYS

Admissions

Very important factors considered include: GPA, rigor of secondary school record. *Important factors considered include:* Class rank, application essay, extracurricular activities, recommendation(s), character/personal qualities. *Other factors considered include:* Standardized test scores, first generation, geographical residence, interview, racial/ethnic status, talent/ability, volunteer work, work experience, alumni/ae relations, level of applicant's interest. SAT or ACT with writing component considered if accepted. TOEFL required of all international applicants. *Academic units required:* 4 English; 3 mathematics; 2 science; (2 science lab); 4 social studies; 2 foreign language. *Academic units recommended:* 4 English; 4 mathematics; 4 science; (2 science lab); 4 social studies; 3 foreign language.

Financial Aid

Students should submit: FAFSA, Institution's own financial aid form, CSS/Financial Aid PROFILE. Regular filing deadline is 2/15. The Princeton Review suggests that all financial aid forms be submitted as soon as possible after January 1. *Need-based scholarships/grants offered:* Federal Pell, SEOG, State scholarships/grants, private scholarships, the school's own gift aid. *Loan aid offered:* Direct Subsidized Stafford Loans, Direct Unsubsidized Stafford Loans, Direct PLUS loans, Federal Perkins Loans. Applicants will be notified of awards beginning 4/1. Federal Work-Study Program available. Institutional employment available. Off-campus job opportunities are excellent.

The Inside Word

Ursinus has been test optional since 2011. But you'll still need a consistently excellent academic record to gain admission. If you're hoping to snag a scholarship, it's essential that you visit campus for an interview, and interviews are strongly encouraged anyway.

THE SCHOOL SAYS "..."

From the Admissions Office

"Located in suburban Philadelphia, the college boasts a beautiful 168-acre campus that features the Residential Village of renovated Victorian-style homes which house our students; a highly individualized academic experience; the nationally recognized Common Intellectual Experience first-year seminar; the Berman Museum of Art; and the Performing Arts Center. Ursinus is a member of the Centennial Conference along with Dickinson, Franklin & Marshall, Gettysburg, and Muhlenberg. Intercollegiate and intramural sports are very popular on campus. The academic environment is enhanced by a chapter of Phi Beta Kappa, an early assurance program to medical school with the Drexel University College of Medicine, and student exchanges both at home and abroad. The college offers student research carried out with the one-on-one attention Ursinus students receive from their professors. The Ursinus admission application requires submission of a graded high school paper."

SELECTIVITY

Admissions Rating	86
# of applicants	3,947
% of applicants accepted	66
% of acceptees attending	16
# offered a place on the wait list	65
% accepting a place on wait list	54
% admitted from wait list	20

FRESHMAN PROFILE

Range SAT Critical Reading	520–640
Range SAT Math	540–640
Range SAT Writing	530–640
Range ACT Composite	24–30
Minimum paper TOEFL	500
% graduated top 10% of class	33
% graduated top 25% of class	67
% graduated top 50% of class	92

DEADLINES

Early decision	
Deadline	1/15
Notification	2 weeks from submission
Early action	
Deadline	12/1
Notification	2 weeks from submission
Regular	
Priority	2/15
Notification	Rolling
Nonfall registration?	Yes

FINANCIAL FACTS

Financial Aid Rating	83
Annual tuition	$45,885
Room and board	$11,500
Required fees	$190
% needy frosh rec. need-based scholarship or grant aid	100
% needy UG rec. need-based scholarship or grant aid	100
% needy frosh rec. non-need-based scholarship or grant aid	19
% needy UG rec. non-need-based scholarship or grant aid	14
% needy frosh rec. need-based self-help aid	80
% needy UG rec. need-based self-help aid	84
% UG borrow to pay for school	80
Average cumulative indebtedness	35,903
% frosh need fully met	23
% ugrads need fully met	19
Average % of frosh need met	81
Average % of ugrad need met	81

VANDERBILT UNIVERSITY

2305 WEST END AVENUE, NASHVILLE, TN 37203 • ADMISSIONS: 615-322-2561 • FAX: 615-343-7765

CAMPUS LIFE

Quality of Life Rating	99
Fire Safety Rating	97
Green Rating	97
Type of school	Private
Affiliation	No Affiliation
Environment	Metropolis

STUDENTS

Total undergrad enrollment	6,794
% male/female	50/50
% from out of state	88
% frosh from public high school	64
% frosh live on campus	100
% ugrads live on campus	86
# of fraternities (% ugrad men join)	18 (26)
# of sororities (% ugrad women join)	16 (52)
% African American	8
% Asian	8
% Caucasian	61
% Hispanic	8
% Native American	<1
% international	6
# of countries represented	96

SURVEY SAYS . . .

Students are happy
Classroom facilities are great
Lab facilities are great
School is well run
Great financial aid
Students are friendly
Students involved in community service
Students love Nashville, TN
Great off-campus food
Campus feels safe
Lots of beer drinking
Hard liquor is popular
Frats and sororities are popular
Active student government

ACADEMICS

Academic Rating	91
% students returning for sophomore year	97
% students graduating within 4 years	87
% students graduating within 6 years	93
Calendar	Semester
Student/faculty ratio	8:1
Profs interesting rating	92
Profs accessible rating	88

Most classes have 10–19 students.
Most lab/discussion sessions have 10–19 students.

MOST POPULAR MAJORS

engineering science; social sciences; multi-/interdisciplinary studies

STUDENTS SAY ". . ."

Academics

The word "balance" is much used by students in describing Vanderbilt University, whether it is the "campus mixed with city, academics mixed with social life, small population mixed with big athletics," or the "unique balance [that] exists between social life and schoolwork." Students say this "balance" "makes [Vanderbilt] the best place to get a well-rounded college experience." As one student explains, "Everyone takes academics seriously, but everyone has other interests, too. No one is just a student. Everyone is involved in something." Another student says, "At Vanderbilt, I could [pursue] my interest in music while majoring in engineering, which was not the case in most other schools." The school is heavily influenced by the "incredible city" of Nashville. The "idyllic campus" is "only minutes away from being in the heart of the city," where people "are very social" and "like being involved." This correlates well with Vanderbilt students who "are very passionate about their extracurricular interests" and stay very "involved with organizations on campus and within the Nashville community. Within the more than 500 student organizations on campus, a student is hard-pressed not to find a few organizations that they can relate to." "The professors are engaging and love their jobs, which makes the students excited and eager to learn." Professors are "dedicated to the undergraduates" and "are always willing to meet with you outside of the classroom to discuss material from class or anything you want to. They make it clear that you are their first priority." "In the event that the class is too big, there are TAs who are more than willing to help." Besides the "truly enriching academic environment," there are many "opportunities that challenge me beyond the books," says a student. When asked about what improvements might be made to their school, many agreed, "Dining and parking are mediocre at best." "The lines at lunch can be really long, and not as many options are open on the weekends." Although vehicles do not seem essential to partake in Nashville and campus life, an improvement in "parking around campus" would be appreciated by students.

Life

"While courses are challenging and demanding, the environment is also fun." Students profess, "School comes first, but having a good time is a close second." "The social life is extremely fun and inclusive." "Greek life is large" here. For many freshman and sophomores, social life "revolves around frat parties." "Older students will go to parties at their friend's place and then go downtown to continue the night." One student explains, "There is [a] Greek scene at the school that offers one kind of Vanderbilt experience, then there are a whole lot of independents who have a different experience. Both groups seem to really enjoy their time here and interact frequently, but the experiences are different." "The campus is beautiful" and "the people—staff, students, professors—are warm and welcoming." "There are always free events going on around campus including everything from casino night, to free movies, to parties, to philanthropy events. There is never a lack of opportunities for fun on campus. On the weekends, people like to use our meal plan to eat off campus and ride our bus downtown to experience Nashville life." "There are so many unique local bars within walking distance!" On the whole, "people here are happy. I feel like I am either partying or doing homework, but it's a good mix."

Student Body

At Vanderbilt, "students hail from all over America and the world, but they all embrace the Southern spirit." A typical student is described as "extremely social," as well as "naturally very bright and motivated." Students stress the "atmosphere of individual achievement instead of competition. The students are academic...but at the same time they are not 'showy' about it." The main stereotype of a Vanderbilt student still is "preppy, wealthy, upper-class," and "involved in Greek life" is changing. "Geographic diversity has certainly expanded in the past ten years." "Students come from all over and the freshman experience does a good job making us a united class."

FINANCIAL AID: 800-288-0204 • E-MAIL: ADMISSIONS@VANDERBILT.EDU • WEBSITE: WWW.VANDERBILT.EDU

THE PRINCETON REVIEW SAYS

Admissions

Very important factors considered include: Class rank, GPA, rigor of secondary school record, standardized test scores, application essay, extracurricular activities, character/personal qualities. *Important factors considered include:* Recommendation(s), talent/ability. *Other factors considered include:* First generation, geographical residence, interview, racial/ethnic status, state residency, volunteer work, work experience, alumni/ae relations. SAT or ACT required; SAT and SAT Subject Tests or ACT considered if submitted; ACT with Writing component required. TOEFL required of all students whose high school instruction was not in English. *Academic units required:* 4 English; 3 mathematics; 3 science; (2 science lab); 2 social studies; 2 foreign language; 1 history; 3 academic electives. *Academic units recommended:* 4 English; 4 mathematics; 4 science; (3 science lab); 3 social studies; 2 foreign language; 1 history; 3 academic electives.

Financial Aid

Students should submit: FAFSA, CSS/Financial Aid PROFILE. The Princeton Review suggests that all financial aid forms be submitted as soon as possible after January 1. *Need-based scholarships/grants offered:* Federal Pell, SEOG, State scholarships/grants, private scholarships, the school's own gift aid. *Loan aid offered:* Direct Subsidized Stafford Loans, Direct Unsubsidized Stafford Loans, Direct PLUS loans, Federal Perkins Loans, Federal Nursing Loans, College/university loans from institutional funds. Applicants will be notified of awards beginning 4/1. Federal Work-Study Program available. Institutional employment available. Off-campus job opportunities are excellent.

The Inside Word

With a first year class of 1,600 and applications numbering approximately 31,000, competition for admission can be intense at this elite Nashville institution. Early decision is a popular route with about 40 percent of the class of 2016 being admitted in this fashion. But before you pull the trigger, take full advantage of Vandy's excellent admissions website featuring an extensive virtual tour and student blogs.

THE SCHOOL SAYS "..."

From the Admissions Office

"The Vanderbilt undergraduate experience is often described as uniquely balanced. Within the context of an outstanding academic landscape, students are encouraged to participate in a broad spectrum of campus organizations among a highly diverse population. Many students take classes in all four undergraduate schools, stretching their intellectual experience far beyond that of their declared major. Students typically live on campus all four years, beginning with a year at The Martha Rivers Ingram Commons, a living and learning residential community for first-year students. Opening in 2014, The Warren and Moore Residential Colleges will expand opportunities for upperclassmen to experience living-learning communities. Students take full advantage of Nashville, often participating in government-, business-, or education-related internships, and enjoying cultural offerings of the city, honored by The New York Times as America's next "it" city in 2013.

"Through Opportunity Vanderbilt, the university makes three commitments regarding financial aid:

1. Vanderbilt's admissions process is need-blind for all U.S. citizens and eligible non-citizens.

2. Vanderbilt meets 100 percent of a family's demonstrated financial need for all admitted students.

3. Financial aid awards do not include loans. Instead of offering need-based loans, Vanderbilt offers additional grant assistance.

"The admissions process is holistic—the student's complete academic and non-academic record is reviewed in conjunction with recommendations and personal essays. The audition is of primary importance for students applying to the Blair School of Music. Students admitted to Vanderbilt typically show exceptional academic accomplishment and are highly engaged in their communities, often serving in leadership roles."

SELECTIVITY

Admissions Rating	99
# of applicants	31,099
% of applicants accepted	13
% of acceptees attending	41
# of early decision applicants	3,181
% accepted early decision	22

FRESHMAN PROFILE

Range SAT Critical Reading	700–780
Range SAT Math	710–790
Range SAT Writing	680–770
Range ACT Composite	32–34
Minimum paper TOEFL	570
Average HS GPA 3.75 % graduated top 10% of class	88
% graduated top 25% of class	95
% graduated top 50% of class	98

DEADLINES

Early decision	
Deadline	11/1
Notification	12/15
Regular	
Priority	1/1
Deadline	1/1
Notification	4/1
Nonfall registration?	No

APPLICANTS ALSO LOOK AT AND OFTEN PREFER

Harvard College; Massachusetts Institute of Technology; Princeton University; Stanford University; Yale University

AND SOMETIMES PREFER

Brown University; Cornell University; Duke University; Georgetown University; Northwestern University; Rice University; The University of Chicago

AND RARELY PREFER

Emory University; Tulane University; University of Georgia; University of Michigan—Ann Arbor; Wake Forest University

FINANCIAL FACTS

Financial Aid Rating	99
% needy frosh rec. need-based scholarship or grant aid	90
% needy UG rec. need-based scholarship or grant aid	93
% needy frosh rec. non-need-based scholarship or grant aid	55
% needy UG rec. non-need-based scholarship or grant aid	42
% needy frosh rec. need-based self-help aid	39
% needy UG rec. need-based self-help aid	50
% frosh rec. any financial aid	60
% UG rec. any financial aid	65
% UG borrow to pay for school	22
Average cumulative indebtedness	$20,303
% frosh need fully met	100
% ugrads need fully met	100
Average % of frosh need met	100
Average % of ugrad need met	100

VASSAR COLLEGE

124 Raymond Avenue, Poughkeepsie, NY 12604 • Admissions: 845-437-7300 • Fax: 845-437-7063

STUDENTS SAY ". . ."

Academics

Vassar College is a small "academically challenging" school that offers a "perfect liberal arts feel" and seeks to broaden students' perspectives. The "strong sense of community" is apparent both in and out of the classroom, where the school drums home the idea that "it's all about being unique and letting your quirky characteristics shine." "We're asked to critically think about the world we live in and how our privilege plays into these systems," says a student. This freedom of character is a main reason why everyone here is "excited to be with each other, which creates this school spirit that isn't necessarily based on sports."

The lack of core requirements is "a great opportunity for students to explore anything they want before settling into a major." "Amazing" professors are "super accessible" and "fully engaged in the total Vassar community." "They are willing to meet you outside their office hours if they don't work for you," says a student. "My professors are…spectacular at illuminating difficult material," says a junior psychology major. Classes are all small and "most are very discussion-based"; students are "not competitive with each other, but with themselves," which creates a more relaxed environment despite the very high academics. Many do admit that there could stand to be "more sections of the most popular classes so that the most amount of people can be happy with their course selections."

Opportunities are there for students' voices to be heard, and "the administration is very willing to work with the student organization to accomplish goals," such as a ban on bottled water from dining services as a result of an initiative by the environmental group on campus. "Vassar students will do things in any way but the traditional way," says a sophomore. "No problem goes undiscussed." "Incredible" study abroad opportunities and a "beautiful campus" don't hurt, either.

Life

"When you get here it starts to feel like home very quickly," says a student of the "stunning" campus. "The vibe of the whole school is so chill," but does not hamper a "vibrant extracurricular scene." Vassar is "bursting at the seams with orgs": there are "a ton of intramural sports teams," nine a cappella groups, plenty of political organizations, a large performing arts contingent, and "basically anything else you can think of." "Close-knit dormitory communities" and an emphasis on being "hyper-socially aware" lead students to be "very politically conscious and deeply involved in volunteerism and activism."

New York City isn't far, so some people take advantage of that, and "there are always parties you can go to if you want to," but "there is nothing wrong with staying in and watching a movie or chatting with friends." There is no Greek life; intellectual conversations abound at all hours, and students spend "significant time thinking about the state of the world, what's going on within the campus community." There are always a decent amount of weekend activities such as "concerts, comedy shows, plays, dances, etc." Be warned: "transportation is limited to get off campus unless you own a car."

Student Body

The "left wing, artsy, intelligent," and "open-minded" individuals that make up the "eclectic" student body "thrive" in the "welcoming" environs of Vassar. The "very generous" amount of need-based financial aid that is awarded "allows for wide socioeconomic diversity," and "Freshman Orientation is a great way for people to make friends here." Many here are philosophically minded and "strive to be as politically correct as possible," and there is "a good amount of hipsters." "You can definitely find at least one other student for every obscure interest you have," assures a student.

FINANCIAL AID: 845-437-5230 • E-MAIL: ADMISSIONS@VASSAR.EDU • WEBSITE: WWW.VASSAR.EDU

THE PRINCETON REVIEW SAYS

Admissions

Very important factors considered include: Rigor of secondary school record. *Important factors considered include:* Class rank, GPA, standardized test scores, application essay, extracurricular activities, recommendation(s), talent/ability, character/personal qualities. *Other factors considered include:* First generation, geographical residence, interview, racial/ethnic status, volunteer work, work experience, alumni/ae relations. SAT and SAT Subject Tests or ACT required; ACT with Writing component required. TOEFL required of all international applicants. *Academic units recommended:* 4 English; 4 mathematics; 4 science; (3 science lab); 2 social studies; 4 foreign language; 2 history.

Financial Aid

Students should submit: FAFSA, CSS/Financial Aid PROFILE, Noncustodial PROFILE. Regular filing deadline is 2/15. The Princeton Review suggests that all financial aid forms be submitted as soon as possible after January 1. *Need-based scholarships/grants offered:* Federal Pell, SEOG, State scholarships/grants, private scholarships, the school's own gift aid. *Loan aid offered:* Direct Subsidized Stafford Loans, Direct Unsubsidized Stafford Loans, Direct PLUS loans, Federal Perkins Loans. Applicants will be notified of awards beginning 3/30. Federal Work-Study Program available. Institutional employment available. Off-campus job opportunities are fair.

The Inside Word

With acceptance rates hitting record lows, stellar academic credentials are a must for any serious Vassar candidate. Standardized test scores are required, but come second to high school transcripts. Once admissions officers see you meet their rigorous scholastic standards, they'll closely assess your personal essay, recommendations, and extracurricular activities. The college prides itself on selecting students who will add to the vitality of the campus. Demonstrating an intellectual curiosity that extends outside the classroom is as important as success within it.

THE SCHOOL SAYS "..."

From the Admissions Office

"Vassar presents a rich variety of social and cultural activities, clubs, sports, living arrangements, and regional attractions. Vassar is a vital, residential college community recognized for its respect for the rights and individuality of others.

"Candidates must submit either the SAT Reasoning Test and two SAT Subject Tests taken in different subject fields, or the ACT exam (the optional ACT writing component is required)."

SELECTIVITY

Admissions Rating	97
# of applicants	7,597
% of applicants accepted	24
% of acceptees attending	36
# offered a place on the wait list	1,274
% accepting a place on wait list	40
% admitted from wait list	16
# of early decision applicants	592
% accepted early decision	47

FRESHMAN PROFILE

Range SAT Critical Reading	660–750
Range SAT Math	650–730
Range SAT Writing	660–750
Range ACT Composite	30–33
Minimum paper TOEFL	600
Minimum web-based TOEFL	250
Average HS GPA	3.80
% graduated top 10% of class	66
% graduated top 25% of class	93
% graduated top 50% of class	99

DEADLINES

Early decision	
Deadline	11/15
Notification	12/15
Regular	
Deadline	1/1
Notification	4/1
Nonfall registration?	No

APPLICANTS ALSO LOOK AT AND OFTEN PREFER

Williams College; Harvard College; Amherst College; Yale University; Brown University

AND SOMETIMES PREFER

Wesleyan University; Columbia University; Tufts University

AND RARELY PREFER

New York University; Skidmore College

FINANCIAL FACTS

Financial Aid Rating	99
Annual tuition	$47,180
Room and board	$11,180
Required fees	$710
Books and supplies	$900
% needy frosh rec. need-based scholarship or grant aid	100
% needy UG rec. need-based scholarship or grant aid	99
% needy frosh rec. non-need-based scholarship or grant aid	0
% needy UG rec. non-need-based scholarship or grant aid	0
% needy frosh rec. need-based self-help aid	100
% needy UG rec. need-based self-help aid	100
% frosh rec. any financial aid	56
% UG rec. any financial aid	59
% UG borrow to pay for school	51
Average cumulative indebtedness	$16,365
% frosh need fully met	100
% ugrads need fully met	100
Average % of frosh need met	100
Average % of ugrad need met	100

VILLANOVA UNIVERSITY

AUSTIN HALL, 800 LANCASTER AVENUE, VILLANOVA, PA 19085 • ADMISSIONS: 610-519-4000 • FAX: 610-519-6450

STUDENTS SAY " . . ."

Academics

Known for being a basketball powerhouse, Villanova University (located in Pennsylvania) has developed an equally impressive reputation for academics. The school's admissions standards have continued to rise, and there is a "great support system" in place to help students achieve, between professors, advisors, tutors, research librarians, as well as a writing, math, and language learning center. Nova's career center and internship offices focus on getting students into jobs after college, and "the opportunities outside of the classroom really complement your education." "Villanova is full of resources for my success now, as a student, and will continue to be after I graduate as an alum," says a student. There is a real sense of community here, "stemming from service, school spirit around the basketball team, and everyone actively pursuing their own area of academic interest." The "passionate" professors are "true teachers and scholars," and they "go above and beyond their office hours." They are "easily accessible," and though some will seek you out, "it is mostly up to you to take advantage of them as a resource." "If you want to succeed, the community will do everything in its power to make sure you can do so," says a student. In addition to superior classroom quality (the faculty gets "fired up about what they teach"), there are "a lot of projects across majors that have real-world applications and are designed to help students in the long run." Classes are often a mixture of "lecture, discussion, individual/group projects, [and] fieldtrips." Villanova's "emphasis on service" is a point of praise for the student body, and everyone here embraces a sense of duty to make the world a better place. "We are the Nova Nation, built upon an unbreakable foundation of community," says a student.

Life

Many buildings are new or have been recently renovated, and "most residence halls are really impressive and kept up very well." Most of campus "has a focused atmosphere during the week," but come Thursday afternoon, "you can feel campus relax and people are more likely to go out," mainly off campus. During basketball season, "people get their work done early to flock to the [Pavillion] for games." Almost everyone is involved in at least one (but probably more) extracurricular activities and clubs, and "a ton of students get involved with intramurals or club sports teams, as well." The Campus Activity Team puts on different events over the weekend, including "a cinema that is always showing a movie," and the school also offers great service experiences, whether "week-long service break experiences all over the world, cheering on the athletes at Special Olympics Fall Festival, or driving into Philly to play with kids and help them with their studies." Formals are also "a big deal" on campus. For those who want to take a break from college life, the massive King of Prussia Mall is found nearby (with a free weekend shuttle), and it is "an easy short train ride to go to Philadelphia."

Student Body

This "outstanding community" is built on "a lot of mutual respect." People are "well-rounded," "very friendly," and "proud of Villanova," and most everyone here "dresses well" and is "extremely affable, professional, and an achiever." "Sometimes I think of Villanova as a school full of all the high school superstars," says one student. Balance is a skill that all Villanovans possess, and most are involved in some sort of volunteer activity; many also "party on the weekends, and show up ready to all of their classes." One can find a "very attractive student body" here, as well.

FINANCIAL AID: 610-519-4010 • E-MAIL: GOTOVU@VILLANOVA.EDU • WEBSITE: WWW.VILLANOVA.EDU

THE PRINCETON REVIEW SAYS

Admissions

Very important factors considered include: Class rank, GPA, rigor of secondary school record, standardized test scores. *Important factors considered include:* Application essay, extracurricular activities, recommendation(s), talent/ability, volunteer work, work experience, character/personal qualities. *Other factors considered include:* First generation, geographical residence, racial/ethnic status, state residency, alumni/ae relations, level of applicant's interest. SAT or ACT required; If ACT is taken, writing component required. TOEFL required of all international applicants. *Academic units required:* 4 English; 4 mathematics; 4 science; (2 science lab); 2 foreign language; 2 academic electives. *Academic units recommended:* 4 English; 4 mathematics; 4 science; (3 science lab); 4 foreign language; 2 academic electives.

Financial Aid

Students should submit: FAFSA, CSS/Financial Aid PROFILE, Noncustodial PROFILE. The Princeton Review suggests that all financial aid forms be submitted as soon as possible after January 1. *Need-based scholarships/grants offered:* Federal Pell, SEOG, State scholarships/grants, private scholarships, the school's own gift aid. *Loan aid offered:* Direct Subsidized Stafford Loans, Direct Unsubsidized Stafford Loans, Direct PLUS loans, Federal Perkins Loans, Federal Nursing Loans. Applicants will be notified of awards beginning 4/1. Federal Work-Study Program available. Institutional employment available. Off-campus job opportunities are excellent.

The Inside Word

Villanova's growing academic reputation means its application process is growing more competitive as well: 93 percent of the most recent admitted freshman class ranked in the top 20 percent of their high school graduating class. Although academic achievement is important, the university looks at the whole package when considering applicants and expects candidates to be well rounded. As a private university, Villanova is not exactly cheap, but the school offers a wide variety of scholarships and aid to qualifying students.

THE SCHOOL SAYS "..."

From the Admissions Office

"Villanova is the oldest and largest Catholic university in Pennsylvania, founded in 1842 by the Order of Saint Augustine. Students of all faiths are welcome. The university tends to attract students who are interested in volunteerism. Villanovans provide more than 200,000 hours of service annually and host the largest student-run Special Olympics in the nation. Villanova's scenic campus is located twelve miles west of Philadelphia. The university offers programs through four undergraduate colleges: Liberal Arts and Sciences, Engineering, Nursing, and the Villanova School of Business. There are 250 student organizations and 36 National Honor Societies at Villanova. Incoming freshmen can opt to be part of a Learning Community, through which student groups live together in specially-designated residence halls and learn together in courses and co-curricular programs. The university offers Naval and Marine Reserve Officers Training Corps (ROTC) programs and hundreds of options for studying abroad. Nova's alumni body is comprised of more than 111,000 people. Some prominent grads include: Maria Bello, Golden Globe-Nominated Actress; Robert J. McCarthy, COO of Marriott International Inc.; Madeline McCarthy Bell, President and COO, The Children's Hospital of Philadelphia; Robert Moran, President and COO of PetSmart(retired); James O'Donnell, CEO of American Eagle Outfitters(retired); and Dianna Sugg, Pulitzer Prize Recipient for Journalism.

"If you're looking to join Nova Nation, be prepared: The competition for admission is getting tougher every year."

SELECTIVITY

Admissions Rating	95
# of applicants	14,966
% of applicants accepted	49
% of acceptees attending	23
# offered a place on the wait list	4,541
% accepting a place on wait list	43
% admitted from wait list	18

FRESHMAN PROFILE

Range SAT Critical Reading	590–690
Range SAT Math	620–710
Range SAT Writing	600–690
Range ACT Composite	29–31
Minimum paper TOEFL	550
Average HS GPA	3.86
% graduated top 10% of class	60
% graduated top 25% of class	88
% graduated top 50% of class	99

DEADLINES

Early action	
Deadline	11/1
Notification	12/20
Regular	
Priority	12/15
Deadline	1/15
Notification	4/1
Nonfall registration?	No

APPLICANTS ALSO LOOK AT AND OFTEN PREFER

University of Notre Dame; Cornell University; Duke University; Georgetown University

AND SOMETIMES PREFER

Boston College; Bucknell University; University of Richmond; Vanderbilt University

AND RARELY PREFER

University of Delaware; Boston University; Drexel University; Fordham University; Lehigh University; Loyola University Maryland

FINANCIAL FACTS

Financial Aid Rating	77
Annual tuition	$43,840
Room and board	$11,856
Required fees	$740
% needy frosh rec. need-based scholarship or grant aid	93
% needy UG rec. need-based scholarship or grant aid	89
% needy frosh rec. non-need-based scholarship or grant aid	16
% needy UG rec. non-need-based scholarship or grant aid	25
% needy frosh rec. need-based self-help aid	85
% needy UG rec. need-based self-help aid	93
% frosh rec. any financial aid	66
% UG rec. any financial aid	70
% UG borrow to pay for school	55
Average cumulative indebtedness	$35,853
% frosh need fully met	20
% ugrads need fully met	17
Average % of frosh need met	81
Average % of ugrad need met	81

VIRGINIA POLYTECHNIC INSTITUTE AND STATE UNIVERSITY (VIRGINIA TECH)

UNDERGRADUATE ADMISSIONS, BLACKSBURG, VA 24061 • ADMISSIONS: 540-231-6267 • FAX: 540-231-3242

CAMPUS LIFE

Quality of Life Rating	99
Fire Safety Rating	83
Green Rating	98
Type of school	Public
Affiliation	No Affiliation
Environment	Town

STUDENTS

Total undergrad enrollment	23,928
% male/female	59/41
% from out of state	24
% frosh live on campus	98
% ugrads live on campus	37
# of fraternities	29
# of sororities	12
% African American	3
% Asian	8
% Caucasian	72
% Hispanic	5
% Native American	<1
% international	4
# of countries represented	113

SURVEY SAYS . . .

Students are happy
Lab facilities are great
Career services are great
School is well run
Students are friendly
Diverse student types on campus
Students get along with local community
Students involved in community service
Great food on campus
Great off-campus food
Campus feels safe
Athletic facilities are great
Lots of beer drinking
Everyone loves the Hokies
Intramural sports are popular
Alumni active on campus

ACADEMICS

Academic Rating	80
% students returning for sophomore year	91
% students graduating within 6 years	83
Calendar	Semester
Student/faculty ratio	16:1
Profs interesting rating	76
Profs accessible rating	81

Most classes have 20–29 students.
Most lab/discussion sessions have 20–29 students.

MOST POPULAR MAJORS
engineering; biology

STUDENTS SAY ". . ."

Academics

Virginia Tech is a school with a reputation as big as its campus. Known for its "beautiful campus, amazing community feel, top-notch engineering field," and as a "good value"—not to mention its renowned athletics—Virginia Tech offers "a perfect blend of challenging and fun, encompassed in an unparalleled community feel." That community feel is a big part of the attraction to this top-ranked school, with students saying they feel "more comfortable here than anywhere in the world." Students are here, of course, for an education at a well-respected research university. At Virginia Tech, that education is provided by "passionate professors who bring real-life examples and cases into their teachings." The school's size and correspondingly large teaching staff mean that at times "professors are hit-or-miss," with "a few who just see it as another job." Most, however, "are really there to help you know as much as you can," a group who are "are extremely helpful and devoted to their students." The best of this school's professors "really make students eager to learn." One student enthuses, "My professors here have changed the way I look at the world and have become some of my biggest heroes." But maybe another student sums it up best: "I would definitely say that my academic experience has been outstanding and that it has opened my eyes to even more possibilities.

Life

Living "in the middle of nowhere" may seem like a recipe for boredom, but members of VT's Hokie Nation make the most of this "perfect college town." After all, when "there are 30,000 people around you that are the same age as you, you find stuff to do." When not consumed with Virginia Tech football—you'll see more maroon and orange in a single day here than most people will see in a lifetime—students here do, well, a little bit of everything. "School-related and Greek-life functions are the main sources of weekend activities," students say, but deceptively quiet Blacksburg and the surrounding area offer plenty of other options. On weekends, students "go out to parties or downtown with friends, we go out to eat, we play tennis, lay out on the 'drillfield,' play in the snow when we have some, go on hikes, and go to the river." That's just a start. Students find "there is always something fun going on to do with your friends," including "bowling, movies, club sports, video games," and more. If you can't find it in Blacksburg, it's ten minutes away in Christiansburg. Students enjoy relaxing, getting into discussions, or having outdoor adventures in a pastoral setting. When autumn arrives, "football games dominate the social scene."

Student Body

Better be ready to be part of the Hokie Nation, because the "typical student is someone who has a love for all things Virginia Tech." Those who attend VT "are proud of our school," and "A typical student here wears Virginia Tech clothes practically every day." Indeed, "you will find them at every VT football game." But the student body is about more than cheering for the maroon and orange. These "middle-class, decent-looking" students study hard "but play harder." Education matters here, but maybe not as much as living life. "The typical student is serious about schoolwork," students say, "but also knows how to have a good time." Most of the student body are "white and from Virginia or North Carolina," a group who are "smart, approachable, and kind." "While we may be lacking in racial diversity," one student notes, "we have every personality type and quirk you could ever imagine." If you are "well-rounded, involved, and [have] lots of school spirit," you are likely to fit in at VT.

VIRGINIA POLYTECHNIC INSTITUTE AND STATE UNIVERSITY (VIRGINIA TECH)

FINANCIAL AID: 540-231-5179 • E-MAIL: VTADMISS@VT.EDU • WEBSITE: WWW.VT.EDU

THE PRINCETON REVIEW SAYS

Admissions

Very important factors considered include: GPA, rigor of secondary school record, standardized test scores. *Other factors considered include:* Extracurricular activities, first generation, geographical residence, racial/ethnic status, recommendation(s), state residency, talent/ability, volunteer work, work experience, alumni/ae relations, character/personal qualities, level of applicant's interest. SAT or ACT required; ACT with Writing component required. TOEFL required of all international applicants. *Academic units required:* 4 English; 3 mathematics; 2 science; (2 science lab); 1 social studies; 1 history; 4 academic electives. *Academic units recommended:* 4 mathematics; 3 science; 3 foreign language.

Financial Aid

Students should submit: FAFSA. The Princeton Review suggests that all financial aid forms be submitted as soon as possible after January 1. *Need-based scholarships/grants offered:* Federal Pell, SEOG, State scholarships/grants, private scholarships, the school's own gift aid. *Loan aid offered:* Direct Subsidized Stafford Loans, Direct Unsubsidized Stafford Loans, Direct PLUS loans, Federal Perkins Loans, College/university loans from institutional funds. Federal Work-Study Program available. Off-campus job opportunities are excellent.

The Inside Word

With some 20,000 applications pouring into the admissions office each year, it's no wonder that the game here is all about numbers, numbers, numbers. Your high school grades will be top priority, so maintain strong grades. Standardized tests also play a big role. Most solid performers will find that acceptance comes with few problems, though the school's competitive disciplines—engineering and architecture, for example—will demand a higher caliber of student.

THE SCHOOL SAYS "..."

From the Admissions Office

"Virginia Tech offers the opportunities of a large research university in a small-town setting. Undergraduates choose from more than seventy majors in seven colleges, including nationally ranked architecture, business, forestry, and engineering schools, as well as excellent computer science, biology, and communication studies, and architecture programs. Technology is a key focus, both in classes and in general. All first-year students are required to own a personal computer, each residence hall room has Ethernet connections, and every student is provided e-mail and Internet access. Faculty incorporate a wide variety of technology into class, utilizing chat rooms, online lecture notes, and multimedia presentations. The university offers cutting-edge facilities for classes and research, abundant opportunities for advanced study in the honors program, undergraduate research opportunities, study abroad, internships, and cooperative education. Students enjoy nearly 700 organizations which offer something for everyone. Tech offers the best of both worlds—everything a large university can provide and a small-town atmosphere.

"Freshman applicants must take the SAT or ACT with writing section. We will use the highest scores from any SAT or ACT test scores submitted."

SELECTIVITY

Admissions Rating	86
# of applicants	19,112
% of applicants accepted	70
% of acceptees attending	40
# offered a place on the wait list	1,863
% accepting a place on wait list	65
% admitted from wait list	0
# of early decision applicants	1,086
% accepted early decision	96

FRESHMAN PROFILE

Range SAT Critical Reading	540–640
Range SAT Math	580–680
Range SAT Writing	540–640
Minimum paper TOEFL	550
% graduated top 10% of class	41
% graduated top 25% of class	83
% graduated top 50% of class	98

DEADLINES

Early decision	
Deadline	11/1
Notification	12/15
Deadline	1/15
Notification	4/1
Nonfall registration?	Yes

APPLICANTS ALSO LOOK AT AND OFTEN PREFER

University of Virginia; The College of William & Mary

AND RARELY PREFER

The College of William & Mary; The University of North Carolina at Chapel Hill

FINANCIAL FACTS

Financial Aid Rating	73
Annual out-of-state tuition	$24,769
Room and board	$7,650
Required fees	$1,838
Books and supplies	$1,120
% needy frosh rec. need-based scholarship or grant aid	67
% needy UG rec. need-based scholarship or grant aid	70
% needy frosh rec. non-need-based scholarship or grant aid	49
% needy UG rec. non-need-based scholarship or grant aid	37
% needy frosh rec. need-based self-help aid	67
% needy UG rec. need-based self-help aid	74
% frosh rec. any financial aid	77
% UG rec. any financial aid	75
% UG borrow to pay for school	55
Average cumulative indebtedness	$26,925
% frosh need fully met	14
% ugrads need fully met	16
Average % of frosh need met	60
Average % of ugrad need met	64

VIRGINIA WESLEYAN COLLEGE

1584 WESLEYAN DRIVE, NORFOLK/VIRGINIA BEACH, VA 23502-5599 • ADMISSIONS: 757-455-3208 • FAX: 757-461-5238

CAMPUS LIFE

Quality of Life Rating	81
Fire Safety Rating	71
Green Rating	91
Type of school	Private
Affiliation	Methodist
Environment	Metropolis

STUDENTS

Total undergrad enrollment	1,385
% male/female	36/64
% from out of state	25
% frosh from public high school	86
% frosh live on campus	83
% ugrads live on campus	59
# of fraternities	4
# of sororities	4
% African American	23
% Asian	1
% Caucasian	59
% Hispanic	7
% Native American	<1
% international	1
# of countries represented	7

SURVEY SAYS . . .

Students get along with local community
Everyone loves the Marlins
Great off-campus food

ACADEMICS

Academic Rating	78
% students returning for sophomore year	67
% students graduating within 4 years	42
% students graduating within 6 years	48
Calendar	4/1/4
Student/faculty ratio	12:1
Profs interesting rating	86
Profs accessible rating	82

Most classes have 10–19 students.

MOST POPULAR MAJORS

business administration and management;
criminal justice; social sciences

STUDENTS SAY ". . ."

Academics

The strength of tiny Virginia Wesleyan College, located across 300 "beautiful" wooded acres in Norfolk, lies in its capability "to create a community feel and successfully bring new students into the fold seamlessly." Students love the college's compact size, which is "small enough that you can walk into a room and name at least five people whom you know and like, but big enough that it is not full of clones." In trying to give each student a devoted personal experience, the school makes students "feel welcome and proud to be a Marlin." "It is easy to get help in classes," due to the small student/faculty ratio and the fact that professors here "truly care about each student as individuals." The "very intelligent, innovative student tutors" also provide support for those who need it. These "scholarly relationships between educators and students" create a sort of academic "home away from home" for everyone who sets foot on campus, and most class sizes are so small that "professors can focus more on helping the students than just spitting out information." "Every professor I've had so far has been a character who loves what they teach and whose enthusiasm is catching," says one student. Lesson plans at VWC are "very well structured, but also allow for some variation," which "allows for students to think more in depth about every subject." The professors "welcome questions during the lecture" and "are focused on ensuring each student understands the material." "They never want to move on if their students do not understand," says a student.

Life

"Life at VWC is pleasant." The small size of the "quaint" campus means that "you can get anywhere you need in the matter of minutes, and anyone is willing to help you if you need any assistance." At this "very free-spirited" school, having fun "is simply a matter of how creatively you want to waste time and/or be productive," though be warned that campus security is "strict." People definitely "get involved" here (particularly with volunteering), and there are "plenty of school- and club-sponsored events that are very well-planned." A lot of people also go to "THE BEACH!" (both the Chesapeake Bay and the ocean are close) or head to the shopping malls, bars, and concert venues of Virginia Beach and Norfolk about ten minutes away; however, "unless you have a car, it can be difficult to get to things." On campus, many agree, "The cafeteria food is awful," but the formerly "shoddy" internet improved by leaps and bounds in the fall of 2012 with Wi-Fi installation in every dorm and tripled speed across the network. The school also could use more "entertainment areas for students, like a lounge for movies or games," particularly for commuters, who often feel "left out back." However, at night, the school is "very supportive of its adult students."

Student Body

Most students here "seem to care about their success here, and many of them care deeply about the community." There are "many student athletes," and most at VWC are "involved in several activities," including "some form of community service." The majority of students also lives on campus, and "everyone hangs out with everyone during the weekend." Though everyone here is undoubtedly "friendly," a few admit, "If you don't play a sport or aren't in a Greek organization, then it's harder to find friends."

Virginia Wesleyan College

FINANCIAL AID: 757-455-3345 • E-MAIL: ADMISSIONS@VWC.EDU • WEBSITE: WWW.VWC.EDU

THE PRINCETON REVIEW SAYS

Admissions

Very important factors considered include: GPA, rigor of secondary school record, level of applicant's interest. *Important factors considered include:* Standardized test scores, application essay, extracurricular activities, recommendation(s). *Other factors considered include:* First generation, interview, talent/ability, volunteer work, work experience, alumni/ae relations, character/personal qualities. SAT or ACT required for some; ACT with or without Writing component accepted. TOEFL required of all international applicants. *Academic units required:* 4 English; 3 mathematics; 2 science; (2 science lab); 2 foreign language; 1 history; 1 computer science. *Academic units recommended:* 4 English; 3 mathematics; 2 science; (2 science lab); 2 foreign language; 1 history; 4 academic electives; 1 computer science.

Financial Aid

Students should submit: FAFSA, State aid form. The Princeton Review suggests that all financial aid forms be submitted as soon as possible after January 1. *Need-based scholarships/grants offered:* Federal Pell, SEOG, State scholarships/grants, private scholarships, the school's own gift aid. *Loan aid offered:* Direct Subsidized Stafford Loans, Direct Unsubsidized Stafford Loans, Direct PLUS loans, Federal Perkins Loans. Federal Work-Study Program available. Institutional employment available. Off-campus job opportunities are good.

The Inside Word

Getting in isn't too difficult at Virginia Wesleyan. Prospective freshmen who present a 3.5 GPA on a 4.0 scale and who have taken a strong, college preparatory curriculum in high school can apply for test-optional admission. Admission is rolling, and decisions are usually released within two weeks of application submission.

THE SCHOOL SAYS ". . ."

From the Admissions Office

"Virginia Wesleyan College seeks to enroll qualified students from diverse social, religious, racial, economic, and geographic backgrounds. Admission is based solely on the applicant's academic and personal qualifications. Factors considered include the application essay, recommendations, standardized test scores, and extracurricular activities. Virginia Wesleyan requires either the SAT 1 or ACT scores. Although we do not require more than one SAT or ACT score, we do take the highest individual verbal and math scores from all of the tests taken. The college offers test optional admission to prospective freshmen who present a 3.5 GPA on a 4.0 scale and who have taken a strong, college preparatory curriculum in high school. A high school diploma is required (GED accepted) and TOEFL is required for all international applicants. Virginia Wesleyan considers applications on a rolling admissions basis. Applicants can typically expect notification within two to three weeks after we receive your completed application and supporting documents. While there is no specific deadline for admission, we encourage students to submit applications for Early Action by December 10 and for Wesleyan Scholarship consideration by January 1. Priority decisions for spring freshman applications is January 1; for fall freshman applications, March 1. Prospective students are encouraged to visit our beautiful 300-acre wooded campus for a tour and to meet with an admissions counselor. Learn more about admissions at www.vwc.edu."

SELECTIVITY

Admissions Rating	68
# of applicants	3,890
% of applicants accepted	86
% of acceptees attending	13

FRESHMAN PROFILE

Range SAT Critical Reading	450–560
Range SAT Math	440–550
Range SAT Writing	440–540
Range ACT Composite	19–24
Minimum paper TOEFL	550
Minimum web-based TOEFL	213
Average HS GPA	3.32
% graduated top 10% of class	13
% graduated top 25% of class	42
% graduated top 50% of class	80

DEADLINES

Regular	
Priority	3/1
Nonfall registration?	Yes

FINANCIAL FACTS

Financial Aid Rating	74
Annual tuition	$31,532
Room and board	$8,508
Required fees	$650
Books and supplies	$1,000
% needy frosh rec. need-based scholarship or grant aid	100
% needy UG rec. need-based scholarship or grant aid	99
% needy frosh rec. non-need-based scholarship or grant aid	18
% needy UG rec. non-need-based scholarship or grant aid	16
% needy frosh rec. need-based self-help aid	84
% needy UG rec. need-based self-help aid	82
% frosh rec. any financial aid	99
% UG rec. any financial aid	98
% UG borrow to pay for school	85
Average cumulative indebtedness	$36,445
% frosh need fully met	11
% ugrads need fully met	11
Average % of frosh need met	70
Average % of ugrad need met	65

WABASH COLLEGE

PO Box 352, Crawfordsville, IN 47933 • Admissions: 765-361-6225 • Fax: 765-361-6437

CAMPUS LIFE

Quality of Life Rating	81
Fire Safety Rating	86
Green Rating	78
Type of school	Private
Affiliation	No Affiliation
Environment	Village

STUDENTS

Total undergrad enrollment	896
% male/female	100/0
% from out of state	25
% frosh from public high school	89
% frosh live on campus	100
% ugrads live on campus	89
# of fraternities (% ugrad men join)	9 (60)
% African American	6
% Asian	1
% Caucasian	76
% Hispanic	6
% Native American	<1
% international	7
# of countries represented	8

SURVEY SAYS . . .

Lots of conservative students
Classroom facilities are great
Lab facilities are great
Career services are great
School is well run
No one cheats
Students are friendly
Easy to get around campus
Athletic facilities are great
Lots of beer drinking
Everyone loves the Little Giants
Intramural sports are popular
Frats and sororities are popular
Alumni active on campus
Active student government

ACADEMICS

Academic Rating	97
% students returning for sophomore year	85
% students graduating within 4 years	64
% students graduating within 6 years	69
Calendar	Semester
Student/faculty ratio	11:1
Profs interesting rating	98
Profs accessible rating	97

Most classes have 10–19 students.
Most lab/discussion sessions have fewer than 10 students.

MOST POPULAR MAJORS
biology; history; psychology

STUDENTS SAY " . . ."

Academics

A "small, personalized, rigorous, elite institution" with an all-male student body, "Wabash College is a powerful small school that changes lives." In a word, Wabash is all about "tradition." The men here "live by a Wabash motto: 'Think Critically, Act Responsibly, Live Humanely, and Lead Effectively.'" With a "95 percent acceptance rate into law school and a 90 percent acceptance rate into medical school," academics here are nothing to shake a stick at. Wabash is "a very challenging academic environment," "but you are provided with every opportunity needed to succeed and excel." Students flock here for the "devoted alumni network, strong, academically focused Greek system, small classes, personal professors, [and] emphasis on reading and writing." "One of the best things about Wabash is the opportunities it provides." The campus boasts "a state-of-the-art athletic center, an incredibly supportive faculty and staff, and an extensive alumni network." "Whether you strive for academic, athletic, community, or professional success, Wabash provides the means to achieve your goals." Professors here "are, generally speaking, the biggest selling point for Wabash." "They are world-class teachers [and] researchers." When not teaching, "professors are nearly always available, and most departments have a tutoring center led by upperclassmen open every night of the week if you need assistance." "Many of the professors are also active in the social life of the school and can be seen tailgating with students before games or participating in different student-run clubs." All members of this unique community tout the understanding that Wabash College "is a school where boys come to become men, and men come to become gentlemen."

Life

The campus as a whole "is incredibly intimate." "The depth of the relationships between students and faculty is incredible." Furthermore, "the type of scholastic discourse that takes place both within and outside of the classroom is unparalleled." The school has a strict "honesty policy, which most, if not everybody, take seriously." Must hold fast to the credo that "what makes this place special [is] the life blood of our school: exceptional men who wish to learn and lead." "We work hard at classes five days a week, but the upperclassmen often make time to go to the Neon Cactus at Purdue on Thursday." "Friday and Saturday are devoted to releasing the stress from the week with a lot of cold beer." "In the warm months, we grill outside and have drinks with professors. In the cold months, we hang out in the fraternity house talking about movies, or world events, or what the pledges did last week." The academic buildings are built around a grassy field, called the "mall," and "there are frequently pickup games of soccer or ultimate Frisbee." Some say that "the absence of women is hard to bear." "After a while, you begin to embrace the lifestyle." "When you are done with class you might go to ESH (Employment Self-Help), an on-campus job, or you might go relax with your friends at your fraternity."

Student Body

A typical Wabash student "is an athlete who is willing to work long hours to get good grades." "Studious, eager to learn and to get work done, [and] serious about school," students here are "almost treated like peers by professors." "Everyone at Wabash works very hard and benefits from the rigorous academic requirements." "Lower-class to upper-class backgrounds allow for a variety of perspectives and previous educations." Regardless of where they hail from, "students embrace the backgrounds of their classmates and work together to learn." Some say, "It's an all-male college, but that's where the universal attributes end." "There could stand to be some more ethnic diversity"; however, others say, "I think that's got more to with self-selection than anything else." "The library is packed Sunday through Thursday evening"; on the weekends, everyone "cuts loose and hangs out with friends." The most dominant social factor "is fraternity, followed by sports." The typical student is "from the Midwest, plays a sport, and will be going into business or grad school after graduation."

FINANCIAL AID: 765-361-6370 • E-MAIL: ADMISSIONS@WABASH.EDU • WEBSITE: WWW.WABASH.EDU

THE PRINCETON REVIEW SAYS

Admissions

Very important factors considered include: Class rank, GPA, rigor of secondary school record. *Important factors considered include:* Standardized test scores, extracurricular activities, interview, talent/ability, level of applicant's interest. *Other factors considered include:* Application essay, first generation, geographical residence, racial/ethnic status, recommendation(s), volunteer work, work experience, alumni/ae relations, character/personal qualities. SAT or ACT required; SAT and SAT Subject Tests or ACT considered if submitted; ACT with Writing component required. TOEFL required of all international applicants. *Academic units recommended:* 4 English; 4 mathematics; 2 science; (2 science lab); 2 social studies; 2 foreign language; 2 academic electives.

Financial Aid

Students should submit: FAFSA, CSS/Financial Aid PROFILE, Noncustodial PROFILE. Regular filing deadline is 3/1. The Princeton Review suggests that all financial aid forms be submitted as soon as possible after January 1. *Need-based scholarships/grants offered:* Federal Pell, State scholarships/grants, private scholarships, the school's own gift aid. *Loan aid offered:* Direct Subsidized Stafford Loans, Direct Unsubsidized Stafford Loans, Direct PLUS loans, College/university loans from institutional funds. Applicants will be notified of awards beginning 3/31. Institutional employment available. Off-campus job opportunities are good.

The Inside Word

Wabash is one of the few remaining all-male colleges in the country, and like the rest of the brotherhood, it has a small applicant pool. The pool is highly self-selected, and the academic standards for admission, while selective, aren't especially demanding. Graduating is a whole other matter. Don't consider applying if you're not ready to do the grueling work required for success here.

THE SCHOOL SAYS "..."

From the Admissions Office

"Wabash College is different—and distinctive—from other liberal arts colleges. Different in that Wabash is an outstanding college for men only. Distinctive in the quality and character of the faculty, in the demanding nature of the academic program, in the seriousness and maturity of the men who enroll, and in the richness of the traditions that have evolved throughout its 180-year history. Wabash is preeminently a teaching institution, and fundamental to the learning experience is the way faculty and students talk to each other—with mutual respect for the expression of informed opinion. For example, students who collaborate with faculty on research projects are considered their peers in the research—an esteem not usually extended to undergraduates. The college takes pride in the sense of community that such a learning environment fosters. But perhaps the single most striking aspect of student life at Wabash is personal freedom. The college has only one rule: 'The student is expected to conduct himself at all times, both on and off the campus, as a gentleman and a responsible citizen.' Wabash College treats students as adults, and such treatment attracts responsible freshmen and fosters their independence and maturity.

"For students seeking admission, Wabash will accept the SAT or the ACT. Wabash will use the student's best scores from either examination and will accept the SAT or ACT writing portions in place of an essay. Wabash does not require SAT Subject Tests."

SELECTIVITY

Admissions Rating	86
# of applicants	1,129
% of applicants accepted	70
% of acceptees attending	31
# offered a place on the wait list	36
% accepting a place on wait list	83
% admitted from wait list	10
# of early decision applicants	60
% accepted early decision	88

FRESHMAN PROFILE

Range SAT Critical Reading	498–610
Range SAT Math	530–640
Range SAT Writing	480–590
Range ACT Composite	22–28
Minimum paper TOEFL	550
Minimum web-based TOEFL	79
Average HS GPA	3.67
% graduated top 10% of class	33
% graduated top 25% of class	72
% graduated top 50% of class	93

DEADLINES

Early decision	
Deadline	11/15
Notification	11/30
Early action	
Deadline	12/1
Notification	12/19
Regular	
Priority	12/1
Nonfall registration?	Yes

APPLICANTS ALSO LOOK AT AND OFTEN PREFER
Indiana University—Bloomington; Purdue University- West Lafayette

AND SOMETIMES PREFER
Butler University; DePauw University; Hanover College

FINANCIAL FACTS

Financial Aid Rating	91
Annual tuition	$35,000
Room and board	$8,510
Required fees	$650
Books and supplies	$1,000
% needy frosh rec. need-based scholarship or grant aid	96
% needy UG rec. need-based scholarship or grant aid	98
% needy frosh rec. non-need-based scholarship or grant aid	37
% needy UG rec. non-need-based scholarship or grant aid	24
% needy frosh rec. need-based self-help aid	89
% needy UG rec. need-based self-help aid	88
% frosh rec. any financial aid	83
% UG rec. any financial aid	79
% UG borrow to pay for school	76
Average cumulative indebtedness	$30,118
% frosh need fully met	42
% ugrads need fully met	36
Average % of frosh need met	96
Average % of ugrad need met	95

WAGNER COLLEGE

PAPE ADMISSIONS BUILDING, STATEN ISLAND, NY 10301-4495 • ADMISSIONS: 718-390-3411 • FAX: 718-390-3105

STUDENTS SAY ". . ."

Academics

Wagner College, located on Staten Island, is a "tight-knit and fun, yet academically challenging," liberal arts school that operates under the Wagner Plan, combining a solid foundation in the liberal arts with practical and applied experiences like internships, with a commitment to service learning and community. The school is "in the perfect location with a surplus of unique resources" and is composed of "an excellent and vibrant community that supports its students every step of the way." The "commitment of the faculty and staff have for the student body is outstanding." Thanks to the plan, students are encouraged "to explore and reflect upon a myriad of subjects and issues." "Even though I am a biology major, I have the wonderful opportunity to explore interdisciplinary topics in the humanities and social sciences throughout my undergraduate career," says one student. The college's unique first-year program consists of a set of three classes with the same twenty-eight students, which "helps transition us from high school to college by progressively learning how to write college-level pieces as well as by engaging in a mandatory thirty-hour community service requirement." This "small, beautiful learning community" is guided by an "extremely attentive and competent" faculty. The professors "ask you to do your best and to push your limitations away" and are "extremely accessible outside of class." "The first time I was nervous about registration, my advisor sat down had lunch, and we registered together," says a student. "It is comforting that I can go to my professors whenever I need assistance with work." The school's science and physician's assistant programs are notably strong, as are the "fantastic" theater and musical programs. Students all universally agree that Wagner "lets you experience all different types of subjects by following the concept: learning by doing."

Life

At Wagner, students are "mostly concerned about their careers, whether they want to make it on Broadway or find the cure for cancer." There's plenty of school-run activities "through co-curricular programs and various clubs," so there are "countless things to do." Beyond all doubt, "the best thing to do…is to take advantage of New York City." The campus is just "a ferry ride away from Manhattan," and the majority of people takes the Wagner shuttle to the S.I. ferry ("all for free!") and goes to the city, whether to shop, eat, or go to a Broadway show. On weekends, there are "parties run by organizations from time to time" or in dorm rooms, since "there is no off-campus housing." Every year, the school has an event called Wagner Stock, where a famous musician or group comes to play. Food is a huge pain point here: Students want "more access to the dining hall in the late hours of the night," "more food options," and just better food in general.

Student Body

The student body here celebrates its "diverse" makeup but Division I athletics and the "great theater program" are very visible in this "small close community." But a student not in either of these programs can find their group through clubs and the major that they are in." Many students have "one major and a minor," and "half of them might study abroad for a semester and or have one or two internships before they graduate." Everyone basically goes about their own business, but "is very approachable." No one seems to have any trouble finding their own crowd, but even once that occurs, "different crowds frequently mingle and almost everyone gets along." "People just talk to everyone," says a student.

FINANCIAL AID: 718-390-3183 • E-MAIL: ADM@WAGNER.EDU • WEBSITE: WWW.WAGNER.EDU

THE PRINCETON REVIEW SAYS

Admissions

Very important factors considered include: Class rank, GPA, rigor of secondary school record. *Important factors considered include:* Application essay, extracurricular activities, interview, recommendation(s), talent/ability, character/personal qualities. *Other factors considered include:* Standardized test scores, volunteer work, work experience, level of applicant's interest. SAT or ACT required for some; ACT with or without Writing component accepted. TOEFL required of all international applicants. *Academic units required:* 4 English; 3 mathematics; 2 science; (1 science lab); 1 social studies; 2 foreign language; 3 history; 6 academic electives.

Financial Aid

Students should submit: FAFSA, State aid form. The Princeton Review suggests that all financial aid forms be submitted as soon as possible after January 1. *Need-based scholarships/grants offered:* Federal Pell, SEOG, State scholarships/grants, private scholarships, the school's own gift aid. *Loan aid offered:* Direct Subsidized Stafford Loans, Direct Unsubsidized Stafford Loans, Direct PLUS loans, Federal Perkins Loans, Federal Nursing Loans. Federal Work-Study Program available. Institutional employment available. Off-campus job opportunities are good.

The Inside Word

As far as grades and test scores, the profile of the average freshman class at Wagner is solid. Standardized tests are optional, and there is more value placed on the strength of your course work and your grades in those classes. The admissions staff here is dedicated to finding the right students for their school. Wagner is looking for students who like to be involved in community events, so make sure your application reflects your extracurriculars. An interview bodes well for serious applicants.

THE SCHOOL SAYS "..."

From the Admissions Office

"At Wagner College, we attract and develop active learners and future leaders. Wagner College has received national acclaim (*Time* magazine, American Association of Colleges and Universities) for its innovative curriculum, The Wagner Plan for the Practical Liberal Arts. At Wagner, we capitalize on our unique geography; we are a traditional, scenic, residential campus, which happens to sit atop a hill on an island overlooking lower Manhattan. Our location allows us to offer a program that couples required off-campus experiences (experiential learning), with 'learning community' clusters of courses. This program begins in the first semester and continues through the senior capstone experience in the major. Fieldwork and internships, writing-intensive reflective tutorials, connected learning, 'reading, writing, and doing': At Wagner College our students truly discover 'the practical liberal arts in New York City.'"

SELECTIVITY

Admissions Rating	83
# of applicants	2,942
% of applicants accepted	70
% of acceptees attending	21
# offered a place on the wait list	58
% accepting a place on wait list	71
% admitted from wait list	20
# of early decision applicants	68
% accepted early decision	87

FRESHMAN PROFILE

Range SAT Critical Reading	530–630
Range SAT Math	520–640
Range SAT Writing	520–620
Range ACT Composite	22–27
Minimum paper TOEFL	550
Minimum web-based TOEFL	217
Average HS GPA	89.10
% graduated top 10% of class	15
% graduated top 25% of class	73
% graduated top 50% of class	92

DEADLINES

Early decision	
Deadline	12/1
Notification	1/2
Regular	
Priority	12/15
Deadline	2/15
Nonfall registration?	Yes

APPLICANTS ALSO LOOK AT AND OFTEN PREFER

New York University; Fairfield University

AND SOMETIMES PREFER

Muhlenberg College; Ithaca College; Northeastern University

AND RARELY PREFER

Quinnipiac University; Marist College; Drew University

FINANCIAL FACTS

Financial Aid Rating	77
Annual tuition	$38,920
Room and board	$11,660
Required fees	$300
Books and supplies	$797
% needy frosh rec. need-based scholarship or grant aid	99
% needy UG rec. need-based scholarship or grant aid	99
% needy frosh rec. non-need-based scholarship or grant aid	0
% needy UG rec. non-need-based scholarship or grant aid	0
% needy frosh rec. need-based self-help aid	70
% needy UG rec. need-based self-help aid	79
% frosh rec. any financial aid	98
% UG rec. any financial aid	93
% frosh need fully met	27
% ugrads need fully met	23
Average % of frosh need met	76
Average % of ugrad need met	69

WAKE FOREST UNIVERSITY

PO Box 7305, Winston Salem, NC 27109 • Admissions: 336-758-5201 • Fax: 336-758-4324

STUDENTS SAY ". . ."

Academics

North Carolina's own Wake Forest University prepares students to lead lives that matter and a reputation for quality that affords its students "excellent placement into jobs and graduate schools." Students come to Wake Forest for an education of the entire person, and the school "practices intentional interactions between professors and students, students with each other, and students and their larger community." This grand scale plan for well-rounded grooming includes "opportunities to serve, to become a leader, and to become part of initiatives that are larger than you." Professors "demand a lot of work but love teaching and students," and classes "are not easy and good grades are tough to come by." "Professors often expect their class to be every student's focus, which is often very difficult," says one student. Fortunately, faculty "are extremely helpful and excited to be teaching or meeting with students one-on-one" and "ensure that students are comfortable with voicing their opinions." Indeed, "from the students to the faculty and staff to the administrators, everyone is open and greets everyone with a smile" here. "Overall I've had a fantastic academic experience with professors that have helped me discover my intellectual passions and have had a vested interest in my success," says a junior.

The small school atmosphere matched with the large school resources, availability, and reputation are "some of the greatest aspects of Wake Forest." "I feel that I could ask any professor I've had at Wake for a letter of recommendation, and they would know me personally enough to do so," says a student. There is a similarly "strong vision and support" from the administration and the alumni network, who back "crazy opportunities that meld ideas and people that just don't happen at other colleges." The school is committed to the teacher-scholar model, so not only do professors do cutting edge research, they let undergrads in on it. "Wake Forest is a campus where some of the most academically impressive and competitive students assemble, the community is an encouraging atmosphere evident to anyone who steps on the grounds, and the social life is unbeatable," says a student.

Life

Wake Forest students work extremely hard on weekdays, often spending hours in the library to complete work, but "absolutely let loose on weekends." The school's "vibrant social scene" and a schedule that is "always bustling with extracurricular activities" keeps the candle burning at both ends, and "parties, going to bars downtown, concerts, game nights, and chill hang outs at friends' houses" are other methods of fun. The D1 athletics—perhaps you've heard of them?—lend Wake Forest a "big-school sports feel at a small school"; and many students play intramural sports or exercise fairly regularly as "people are very conscious of their image" at this health-conscious university. A "large proportion" of the school is Greek, and therefore "a great deal of the conversations relate to other Greek organizations or issues/drama within said Greek organization." There are also organizations like the Student Union that "promote other fun aspects of campus life (i.e. Movie nights, guest speakers, campus carnivals, etc.)" Students take part in "lots of great traditions at Wake Forest, like our annual Shag on the Mag dance in the spring," "rolling the quad after a big athletic win," and dinner at the on-campus restaurant Shorty's. Philanthropy is a "HUGE part of the WFU experience," and there are several extremely large philanthropy events that happen throughout the year.

Student Body

The university is steeped in Southern traditions and hospitality that "most students fit into or learn to adhere to in their tenure as Wake Students," but the school "is also home to students from around the country and the world." In this "tight-knit, supportive community" nearly everybody is "intelligent, ambitious, [and] highly involved," not to mention "beautiful." "It's like a living J.Crew magazine," says one student. Most everyone here is "preppy, involved in greek life, [and] from the east coast (either north or south)." Thanks to a strong foundation of friendliness and acceptance among the student body, "people generally don't have any trouble fitting in here, and can usually easily find groups of people who share their interests."

FINANCIAL AID: 336-758-5154 • E-MAIL: ADMISSIONS@WFU.EDU • WEBSITE: WWW.WFU.EDU

THE PRINCETON REVIEW SAYS
Admissions

Very important factors considered include: Class rank, GPA, rigor of secondary school record, application essay, character/personal qualities. *Important factors considered include:* Extracurricular activities, interview, recommendation(s), talent/ability. *Other factors considered include:* Standardized test scores, first generation, geographical residence, racial/ethnic status, state residency, volunteer work, alumni/ae relations, level of applicant's interest, religious affiliation. SAT and SAT Subject Tests or ACT considered if submitted; ACT with Writing component required. TOEFL required of all international applicants. *Academic units required:* 4 English; 3 mathematics; 1 science; 2 social studies; 2 foreign language. *Academic units recommended:* 4 English; 4 mathematics; 4 science; 4 social studies; 4 foreign language.

Financial Aid

Students should submit: FAFSA, CSS/Financial Aid PROFILE, State aid form, Noncustodial PROFILE. Regular filing deadline is 2/1. The Princeton Review suggests that all financial aid forms be submitted as soon as possible after January 1. *Need-based scholarships/grants offered:* Federal Pell, SEOG, State scholarships/grants, private scholarships, the school's own gift aid. *Loan aid offered:* Direct Subsidized Stafford Loans, Direct Unsubsidized Stafford Loans, Direct PLUS loans, Federal Perkins Loans, State Loans, College/university loans from institutional funds. Federal Work-Study Program available. Institutional employment available. Off-campus job opportunities are excellent.

The Inside Word

Wake Forest's considerable application numbers afford admissions officers the opportunity to be rather selective. In particular, admissions officers remain diligent in their matchmaking efforts—finding students who are good fits for the school—and their hard work is rewarded by a high graduation rate. Candidates will need to be impressive in all areas to gain admission, since all areas of their applications are considered carefully. A relatively large number of qualified students find themselves on Wake Forest's wait list.

THE SCHOOL SAYS "..."
From the Admissions Office

"Wake Forest University has been dedicated to the liberal arts for over a century and a half; this means education in the fundamental fields of human knowledge and achievement. It seeks to encourage habits of mind that ask why, that evaluate evidence, that are open to new ideas, that attempt to understand and appreciate the perspective of others, that accept complexity and grapple with it, that admit error, and that pursue truth.

"Wake Forest is among a small, elite group of American colleges and universities recognized for their outstanding academic quality. It offers small classes taught by full-time faculty—not graduate assistants—and a commitment to student interaction with those professors. Students are provided ThinkPad computers. Classroom and residence halls are fully networked. Students are admitted based on the unique qualities they bring to our community. Wake Forest's generous financial aid program allows deserving students to enroll regardless of their financial circumstances.

"Wake Forest is the first top thirty national university in the United States to make standardized tests such as the SAT and ACT with writing optional in the admissions process. If applicants feel that their SAT or ACT with writing scores are a good indicator of their abilities, they may submit them and they will be considered in the admissions decision. If, however, a prospective student does not feel that their scores accurately represent their academic abilities, they do not need to submit them until after they have been accepted and choose to enroll. Wake Forest takes a holistic look at each applicant."

SELECTIVITY	
Admissions Rating	96
# of applicants	11,121
% of applicants accepted	35
% of acceptees attending	31

FRESHMAN PROFILE	
Range SAT Critical Reading	600–700
Range SAT Math	630–720
Range ACT Composite	28–31
Minimum paper TOEFL	600
Minimum web-based TOEFL	250
% graduated top 10% of class	76
% graduated top 25% of class	93
% graduated top 50% of class	99

DEADLINES	
Early decision	
Deadline	1/1
Early action	
Deadline	11/15
Notification	1/15
Regular	
Deadline	1/1
Notification	4/1
Nonfall registration?	No

APPLICANTS ALSO LOOK AT AND SOMETIMES PREFER
Duke University; Vanderbilt University; University of Virginia; The University of North Carolina at Chapel Hill

FINANCIAL FACTS	
Financial Aid Rating	92
Annual tuition	$44,200
Room and board	$12,000
Required fees	$542
Books and supplies	$1,100
% needy frosh rec. need-based scholarship or grant aid	83
% needy UG rec. need-based scholarship or grant aid	93
% needy frosh rec. non-need-based scholarship or grant aid	49
% needy UG rec. non-need-based scholarship or grant aid	69
% needy frosh rec. need-based self-help aid	66
% needy UG rec. need-based self-help aid	87
% frosh rec. any financial aid	39
% UG rec. any financial aid	34
% UG borrow to pay for school	38
Average cumulative indebtedness	$33,262
% frosh need fully met	89
% ugrads need fully met	67
Average % of frosh need met	100
Average % of ugrad need met	99

WARREN WILSON COLLEGE

PO Box 9000, Asheville, NC 28815-9000 • Admissions: 800-934-3536 • Fax: 828-298-1440

STUDENTS SAY ". . ."

Academics

Warren Wilson's unique approach to education is encapsulated in its "Triad program." This distinctive curriculum combines academics with "work and service." Though this program might demand more of your time, undergrads here speak quite highly of it. As one psych major shares, Triad "allows students to deepen their understanding of the world's needs and prepares them for a lifestyle of service beyond college." Additionally, it's an "active style of learning" that "really pushes students…to become well-rounded individuals." Undergrads are especially enthusiastic about the college's "environmental focus and strong science programs." There's "a working farm on campus that students run, and it [lends] excellent opportunity for hands-on experience." Undergrads also laud the "good creative writing department." Importantly, "the majority of the faculty are genuinely interested in the well-being of each and every student." Professors are "easy to talk to and highly available." This accessibility extends to the administration as well. As one impressed junior tells us, "We know our administration by first name, and if we want to talk to them, it's no problem to schedule an appointment or have the admin attend a student government meeting."

Life

Undergrads at Warren Wilson tend to lead hectic lives. Many concur that "students are really busy during the week" and therefore view the weekend as "a time for release." However, the intellectual debates don't just stop because it's leisure time. As one freshman shares, life often "revolves around political arguments and philosophical discussions held over cans of Pabst Blue Ribbon." Of course, activities extend beyond delightful and thought-provoking conversation. Students "greatly enjoy" the outdoors, and many can often be found "exploring trails, visiting the animals on the farm, swimming, kayaking, and canoeing on the Swannanoa River." Additionally, "fall soccer games, Friday night themed dance parties…and Thursday night contra dances" are all well attended. One senior adds that "poetry slams, talent shows, theatrical productions, and parties that are held in the common areas of the dorms" are all great fun. Students are also "very politically and environmentally active, and community service" is extremely popular. Venturing into downtown Asheville is common as well. The town center is only "a fifteen-minute ride from campus, and there is a bus that goes back and forth during specific hours." The "funky" area has "a great arts and music scene," and "there are lots of concerts, performances, restaurants and local stores to visit."

Student Body

Warren Wilson is a college that "is very open to the idea of individuality" and thus manages to attract "a wide range of students." Many undergrads proclaim their peers to be "dynamic people" who are all "atypical." As a sophomore proudly boasts, "The great thing about this school is that a person, in all their weirdness, is loved and embraced by the community." Of course, for all this diversity, some commonalities do seep through. The "vast majority of people who go here are liberal" and are concerned "with social justice issues." Indeed, the mantle "hippie" is frequently bandied about. While some might object to this stereotype, many undergrads are "committed to environmental awareness." A freshman notes that his fellow students "care about the outdoors, recycle, unplug appliances not in use, and would rather eat an organic salad than a steak." Additionally, most undergrads are hardworking and very industrious, constantly thinking of new projects to do and coming up with interesting ideas." But perhaps this math major sums up his peers best, "If you like people with weird haircuts, people with a different gender identity, vegans, feminists, and future organic farmers—or are one of these people—you will probably fit right in."

WARREN WILSON COLLEGE

FINANCIAL AID: 800-934-3536 • E-MAIL: ADMIT@WARREN-WILSON.EDU • WEBSITE: WWW.WARREN-WILSON.EDU

THE PRINCETON REVIEW SAYS

Admissions

Very important factors considered include: Rigor of secondary school record, standardized test scores, application essay, first generation, interview, volunteer work, work experience, character/personal qualities, level of applicant's interest. *Important factors considered include:* Class rank, GPA, recommendation(s). *Other factors considered include:* Extracurricular activities, state residency, talent/ability, alumni/ae relations. SAT or ACT required; ACT with or without Writing component accepted. TOEFL required of all international applicants. *Academic units required:* 4 English; 3 mathematics; 2 science; (2 science lab); 3 history. *Academic units recommended:* 2 foreign language.

Financial Aid

Students should submit: FAFSA, State aid form. The Princeton Review suggests that all financial aid forms be submitted as soon as possible after January 1. *Need-based scholarships/grants offered:* Federal Pell, SEOG, State scholarships/grants, the school's own gift aid. *Loan aid offered:* Direct Subsidized Stafford Loans, Direct Unsubsidized Stafford Loans, Direct PLUS loans, Federal Perkins Loans, College/university loans from institutional funds. Off-campus job opportunities are good.

The Inside Word

At Warren Wilson College, one's sense of social commitment is as vital to the admissions process as one's high school transcript—the college desires students who are actively engaged in their communities. Admissions officers are interested in applicants who seek to make connections and who understand how to apply what they learn in the classroom to outside projects and activities.

THE SCHOOL SAYS ". . ."

From the Admissions Office

"This book is *The Best 379 Colleges and* Warren Wilson College is a great college for many students. There are 3,500 colleges in the U.S., and there is a best place for everyone. The 'best college' is one that has the right size, location, programs, and above all, the right feel for you, even if it is not listed here. Warren Wilson College may be the best choice if you think and act independently, actively participate in your education, and want a college that provides a sense of community. Your hands will get dirty here, your mind will be stretched, and you'll not be anonymous. ICome explore our wonderful campus, meet our vibrant faculty, and learn all the different ways we might be right for you. However, if you want to be a part of an academic community that works and serves together, this might be exactly what you are looking for."

SELECTIVITY
Admissions Rating	72
# of applicants	1,214
% of applicants accepted	70
% of acceptees attending	18
# of early decision applicants	44
% accepted early decision	41

FRESHMAN PROFILE
Range SAT Critical Reading	530–660
Range SAT Math	480–590
Range SAT Writing	520–610
Range ACT Composite	23–27
Minimum web-based TOEFL	80
Average HS GPA	3.50
% graduated top 10% of class	22
% graduated top 25% of class	50
% graduated top 50% of class	81

DEADLINES
Early decision	
Deadline	11/16
Notification	12/1
Regular	
Deadline	1/31
Nonfall registration?	Yes

APPLICANTS ALSO LOOK AT AND OFTEN PREFER
Davidson College

AND SOMETIMES PREFER
University of Vermont

AND RARELY PREFER
University of North Carolina-Asheville; Guilford College

FINANCIAL FACTS
Financial Aid Rating	74
Annual tuition	$30,462
Room and board	$9,280
Required fees	$390
Books and supplies	$820
% needy frosh rec. need-based scholarship or grant aid	91
% needy UG rec. need-based scholarship or grant aid	91
% needy frosh rec. non-need-based scholarship or grant aid	24
% needy UG rec. non-need-based scholarship or grant aid	17
% needy frosh rec. need-based self-help aid	100
% needy UG rec. need-based self-help aid	100
% UG borrow to pay for school	44
Average cumulative indebtedness	$17,533
% frosh need fully met	11
% ugrads need fully met	14
Average % of frosh need met	73
Average % of ugrad need met	72

WASHINGTON COLLEGE

300 WASHINGTON AVENUE, CHESTERTOWN, MD 21620 • ADMISSIONS: 410-778-7700 • FAX: 410-778-7287

CAMPUS LIFE

Quality of Life Rating	76
Fire Safety Rating	97
Green Rating	67
Type of school	Private
Affiliation	No Affiliation
Environment	Rural

STUDENTS

Total undergrad enrollment	1,424
% male/female	42/58
% from out of state	48
% frosh from public high school	68
% frosh live on campus	99
% ugrads live on campus	85
# of fraternities (% ugrad men join)	4 (9)
# of sororities (% ugrad women join)	3 (14)
% African American	4
% Asian	2
% Caucasian	79
% Hispanic	4
% Native American	<1
% international	5
# of countries represented	36

SURVEY SAYS . . .

Lab facilities are great
Lots of beer drinking

ACADEMICS

Academic Rating	86
% students returning for sophomore year	81
% students graduating within 4 years	69
% students graduating within 6 years	71
Calendar	Semester
Student/faculty ratio	11:1
Profs interesting rating	92
Profs accessible rating	87

Most classes have 10–19 students.
Most lab/discussion sessions have 10–19 students.

MOST POPULAR MAJORS

psychology; business administration and management; biology

STUDENTS SAY ". . ."

Academics

Washington College is all about "gaining a distinctive and strong education in the liberal arts through personalized programs and hands-on experience." Located in small-town Chestertown, Maryland, this "small, tight-knit" community fosters a "high level of education" and an "intimate and personalized education experience." Washington College is a place where "students learn to think outside of the box while becoming better people and having the time of their lives." Centrally located between "three major employment markets: Washington, D.C., Philadelphia, and Baltimore," this "beautiful campus" "provides the perfect setting for a learning environment." "There are not as many distractions, but there is enough to keep you busy." Professors here are "highly educated, very personal, and willing to bend over backwards to ensure your education." Unlike at large research universities, faculty at Washington College are "here to teach, and they love to teach." The "attention given to the students by faculty is undeniable." The English and creative writing programs are among "the best in the country," earning Washington College a reputation "as a writing school," with the famous "Rose O'Neill Literary House, and the Sophie Kerr Prize." Students say all in one breath, "The professors are world-class, and the campus is beautiful. Also the Eastern Shore of Maryland is an incredible place to be."

Life

Living at Washington College "is as good as a college experience can get." "No matter what your interests are there is plenty to do." Some note that because of "the small-town environment, we have to make our own fun on weekends, but there's usually something on-campus to make it less of a challenge." "I personally love the environment and being outdoors. I spend a lot of time kayaking at our boat house on the Chester River, fishing on the Eastern Shore of Maryland, and supporting our athletic teams." "The school's rather small, so we know almost all of the athletes, so we're not only supporting a program, we're supporting our best friends." On campus, "there are plenty of student-run activities." When it comes to facilities, "the athletic department is great, and the dining hall is new and wonderful." For fun, students "often go to plays hosted by the drama department, attend interesting guest lectures, play Wii in the dorm rooms, play Frisbee on the campus green, play pool in the student center, go to movies, or stroll around Chestertown and the waterfront." We drink in the dorms and suites because almost everyone lives on campus." Washington College "is located within a rural town; however, we are not completely isolated. We are about forty minutes away from Annapolis." Students do warn, "Being in a rural town was hard at first."

Student Body

A typical Washington College student "is preppy—from the way they dress to the way that they interact with each other and their professors." It's "an athletic campus, as even non-athletes are generally fit and participate in intramural sports." Most students "come from a somewhat affluent background, and the majority study and work very hard, but they also party very hard on the weekends." Though some note "there is very little diversity on campus," others say while the campus "might lack in racial diversity, people have diverse morals, values, and political views." There seem to be "two major, distinct campus cultures: the athletic/Greek life people and the English/drama people. People generally gravitate to one or the other." "It isn't hard to find your 'place,' though." Most students are "involved in several different types of activities." Students "usually fit in by playing a sport or joining Greek life, but there is always a club for everyone." Others concur, Washington College is a "melting pot of individuals from different backgrounds, but the typical student is open-minded, ambitious, and extremely innovative." Athletes and burgeoning writers alike "have strong pride and love for our school."

FINANCIAL AID: 410-778-7214 • E-MAIL: ADM.OFF@WASHCOLL.EDU • WEBSITE: WWW.WASHCOLL.EDU

THE PRINCETON REVIEW SAYS

Admissions

Very important factors considered include: GPA, rigor of secondary school record, interview, level of applicant's interest. *Important factors considered include:* Class rank, standardized test scores, application essay. *Other factors considered include:* Extracurricular activities, first generation, geographical residence, recommendation(s), state residency, talent/ability, volunteer work, work experience, alumni/ae relations, character/personal qualities, SAT or ACT recommended; ACT with or without Writing component accepted. *Academic units required:* 4 English; 3 mathematics; 3 science; (2 science lab); 2 social studies; 2 foreign language; 2 history. *Academic units recommended:* 4 English; 4 mathematics; 4 science; (3 science lab); 2 social studies; 4 foreign language; 2 history.

Financial Aid

Students should submit: FAFSA. The Princeton Review suggests that all financial aid forms be submitted as soon as possible after January 1. *Need-based scholarships/grants offered:* Federal Pell, SEOG, State scholarships/grants, private scholarships, the school's own gift aid. *Loan aid offered:* Direct Subsidized Stafford Loans, Direct Unsubsidized Stafford Loans, Direct PLUS loans. Federal Work-Study Program available. Institutional employment available. Off-campus job opportunities are good.

THE SCHOOL SAYS "..."

From the Admissions Office

"Founded in 1782 under the patronage of George Washington as the first college of the new nation, Washington College has been dedicated to developing tomorrow's leaders for more than 230 years. We aim to expand your intellect and creativity through independent study and collaborative research with faculty. You'll receive a truly personalized education that stretches your talents and potential. Professors and staff also work hard to link students to real-world experience and networking through professional conferences and internships. No matter what path you choose, we promise to nurture your growth and transformation into an accomplished, curious and independent thinker. Our graduates enter the world challenged and inspired, ready to assume the responsibilities of informed citizenship. We're committed to helping you launch a life filled with purpose and passion.

"All this intellectual and emotional growth happens on a campus that has been through a physical transformation in the past several years: some $80 million in improvements that include a brand new Commons with food court, coffee shop, student center and game room, a totally renovated library and arts center, an expanded fitness center, and two new residence halls with geothermal heating. Our setting on the Chester River in historic Chestertown, close by the Chesapeake Bay, enriches our programs in history and ecology, and we award the largest undergraduate literary prize in the world, the Sophie Kerr Prize.

"Admission to Washington College is selective; decisions are based primarily on a student's record of academic achievement. Campus visits are strongly recommended."

SELECTIVITY

Admissions Rating	87
# of applicants	4,647
% of applicants accepted	66
% of acceptees attending	11
# offered a place on the wait list	306

FRESHMAN PROFILE

Range SAT Critical Reading	520–640
Range SAT Math	530–640
Range SAT Writing	510–610
Range ACT Composite	25–29
Average HS GPA	3.53
% graduated top 10% of class	33
% graduated top 25% of class	67
% graduated top 50% of class	88

DEADLINES

Early decision	
Deadline	11/1
Notification	12/1
Early action	
Deadline	12/1
Notification	12/20
Regular	
Priority	2/15
Nonfall registration?	Yes

FINANCIAL FACTS

Financial Aid Rating	91
Annual tuition	$40,384
Room and board	$9,442
Required fees	$736
Books and supplies	$1,250
% needy frosh rec. need-based scholarship or grant aid	99
% needy UG rec. need-based scholarship or grant aid	98
% needy frosh rec. non-need-based scholarship or grant aid	18
% needy UG rec. non-need-based scholarship or grant aid	15
% needy frosh rec. need-based self-help aid	82
% needy UG rec. need-based self-help aid	88
% frosh rec. any financial aid	95
% UG rec. any financial aid	93
% UG borrow to pay for school	65
Average cumulative indebtedness	$35,510
% frosh need fully met	61
% ugrads need fully met	55
Average % of frosh need met	94
Average % of ugrad need met	90

WASHINGTON & JEFFERSON COLLEGE

60 SOUTH LINCOLN STREET, WASHINGTON, PA 15301 • ADMISSIONS: 724-223-6025

STUDENTS SAY ". . ."

Academics

Washington & Jefferson College is a small, elite school known for its "academic rigor" and "prestigious reputation." In addition to two conventional semesters, the college also features a unique intercession period in January, "which allows for a month of focused learning on a topic that is often much different than something…offered during a semester, including travel and topics of specific interest to professors." Professors bring their passion to the classroom on a regular basis; students say that they are "very interactive and enjoy the small class sizes and getting to know each student's personality." "Professors are there because they love to teach and will go the extra mile for students." "They are very knowledgeable and are very accessible outside of class," and personal connections with professors "oftentimes leads to internships or research projects" for undergraduate students. In general, the college is excellent at providing students with ample opportunities to prepare for their futures. It boasts "a great reputation for graduate school preparation" and has an "impeccable record at placing students in medical, graduate, and law schools." Additionally, there are "so many opportunities with alumni relations." The study abroad office is also excellent, and there are many opportunities for students to develop their own research projects overseas or at home with funding from the Magellan Project. In short, students think that "a degree from Washington & Jefferson College is valuable." The academics here are "very demanding, but the opportunities that you will get both during and after your time there are unmatched."

Life

Student life at Washington & Jefferson College is a "good balance of schoolwork, athletics, and fun." The "beautiful, small campus" is home to a "friendly, warm," "family-like environment," where the emphasis is placed on the well-being of the students. It is "easy to get involved and be active in campus organizations." Greek life is extremely popular on campus, as are sports and club activities. Students "study hard during the week, but party hard on the weekends." "Parties are regular on weekends," but alternatively, the school also "provides multiple activities over the weekends—especially for students who do not drink." "There are always music, art, speakers, and events" on campus. "A lot of students…will attend these, but most are more likely to party for fun." Some students complain, "There needs to be more to do on campus on the weekends," and the school is trying to respond to this demand by "working hard to produce more student activities, such as bringing in great bands for concerts" to campus. Washington & Jefferson's home city of Washington "isn't ideal" for college students, but student services provides a shuttle to and from nearby Pittsburgh on the weekends, which can be "a great escape from the close-knit campus community."

Student Body

Students at Washington & Jefferson College tend to have "similar backgrounds, beliefs, and morals." A typical student "works hard in the classroom and is serious about getting good grades but likes to go out and have fun on weekends with friends." Students tend to be "athletic, sporty, smart," "well-off financially," and "relatively preppy." However, students are also noted for being very social, as well as "extremely friendly and helpful." Many students are a part of Greek life, and many are "student athletes who seem to balance sports and academics with much success." Some say, "It would be nicer to have more of a range of ethnic and social backgrounds" at the college, and the administration is making small but sure strides to increase diversity on campus. The typical student at W&J is focused on his or her course work; he or she is "also involved outside of the classroom in clubs, athletics, Greek Life, or one of a variety of other things the school has to offer." The students here "have a common goal to be successful in life," and with this goal in mind, everyone works together to form a tight-knit community and "gets along pretty well."

WASHINGTON & JEFFERSON COLLEGE

FAX : 724-223-6534 • FINANCIAL AID: 724-223-6019 • E-MAIL: ADMISSION@WASHJEFF.EDU • WEBSITE: WWW.WASHJEFF.EDU

THE PRINCETON REVIEW SAYS

Admissions

Very important factors considered include: Class rank, GPA, rigor of secondary school record, application essay, interview, recommendation(s), character/personal qualities. *Important factors considered include:* Standardized test scores, extracurricular activities. *Other factors considered include:* Geographical residence, racial/ethnic status, state residency, talent/ability, volunteer work, work experience, alumni/ae relations, level of applicant's interest. SAT and SAT Subject Tests or ACT considered if submitted; ACT with or without Writing component accepted. TOEFL required of all international applicants. *Academic units required:* 3 English; 3 mathematics; 1 science; (1 science lab); 2 foreign language; 6 academic electives. *Academic units recommended:* 4 English; 4 mathematics; 2 science; (2 science lab); 3 foreign language; 6 academic electives.

Financial Aid

Students should submit: FAFSA. The Princeton Review suggests that all financial aid forms be submitted as soon as possible after January 1. *Need-based scholarships/grants offered:* Federal Pell, SEOG, State scholarships/grants, private scholarships, the school's own gift aid. *Loan aid offered:* Direct Subsidized Stafford Loans, Direct Unsubsidized Stafford Loans, Direct PLUS loans, Federal Perkins Loans, College/university loans from institutional funds. Federal Work-Study Program available. Institutional employment available. Off-campus job opportunities are good.

The Inside Word

Washington & Jefferson College takes a well-rounded approach to admissions, reflecting the type of student the school aims to admit. Academic record, class rank, personal statement, and extracurricular activities are all thoroughly evaluated. Most prospective students are high work diligently to secure a spot at this prestigious institution. The lucky applicants who receive a fat letter in the mail are welcomed into a distinctive community that promises to broaden their horizons and to prepare them for a successful future.

THE SCHOOL SAYS "..."

From the Admissions Office

"At Washington & Jefferson College, the entire community is devoted to ensuring student success. In the last three years, 100 percent of W&J graduates taking the Pennsylvania bar exam passed, and we regularly see admission rates of 90 percent for graduates headed to medical and law school. The College has added $100 million in new facilities since 2002, including residence halls, athletic facilities, a state-of-the-art technology center, the Burnett Center (housing accounting, business, economics, education, entrepreneurial studies, and modern languages), and the new Swanson Science Center (dedicated to the physical sciences, including physics, chemistry, biochemistry, and bioinformatics). Unique to W&J is the Magellan Project, providing stipends for innovative internships, research fellowships, and independent study-travel programs, domestic or international. Alumni mentors help students attain valuable internships, and, upon graduation, assist with career placement. You dream it; we make it happen. Our students are balanced, goal-oriented, active, engaged, and involved and we look for applicants who demonstrate these qualities in every stage of the admissions process. If you are a student who thrives on academic rigor, wants a close personal relationship with top-notch faculty, and values being a member of a true college community, we encourage you to consider W&J. Finally, W&J recommends but does not require scores from the SAT (or ACT). If submitted, we will use the best scores from either test. Be sure to check out our new four-year Graduation Guarantee at washjeff.edu."

SELECTIVITY

Admissions Rating	90
# of applicants	7,176
% of applicants accepted	40
% of acceptees attending	11
# offered a place on the wait list	53
% accepting a place on wait list	43
% admitted from wait list	22
# of early decision applicants	22
% accepted early decision	50

FRESHMAN PROFILE

Range SAT Critical Reading	510–610
Range SAT Math	540–620
Range ACT Composite	23–27
Minimum paper TOEFL	580
Minimum web-based TOEFL	233
Average HS GPA	3.33
% graduated top 10% of class	37
% graduated top 25% of class	70
% graduated top 50% of class	94

DEADLINES

Early decision	
Deadline	12/1
Notification	12/15
Early action	
Deadline	1/15
Notification	2/15
Regular	
Priority	1/15
Deadline	3/1
Nonfall registration?	Yes

FINANCIAL FACTS

Financial Aid Rating	77
Annual tuition	$39,250
Room and board	$10,490
Required fees	$460
Books and supplies	$800
% needy frosh rec. need-based scholarship or grant aid	89
% needy UG rec. need-based scholarship or grant aid	86
% needy frosh rec. non-need-based scholarship or grant aid	93
% needy UG rec. non-need-based scholarship or grant aid	89
% needy frosh rec. need-based self-help aid	88
% needy UG rec. need-based self-help aid	87
% frosh rec. any financial aid	100
% UG rec. any financial aid	98
% UG borrow to pay for school	81
Average cumulative indebtedness	
% frosh need fully met	18
% ugrads need fully met	17
Average % of frosh need met	80
Average % of ugrad need met	76

WASHINGTON STATE UNIVERSITY

PO Box 641067, PULLMAN, WA 99164-1067 • ADMISSIONS: 509-335-5586 • FAX: 509-335-4902

CAMPUS LIFE

Quality of Life Rating	82
Fire Safety Rating	86
Green Rating	98
Type of school	Public
Affiliation	No Affiliation
Environment	Town

STUDENTS

Total undergrad enrollment	22,825
% male/female	49/51
% from out of state	8
% frosh from public high school	99
% frosh live on campus	85
% ugrads live on campus	26
# of fraternities (% ugrad men join)	25 (20)
# of sororities (% ugrad women join)	14 (25)
% African American	3
% Asian	5
% Caucasian	66
% Hispanic	11
% Native American	1
% international	4
# of countries represented	96

SURVEY SAYS . . .

Students are happy
Students are friendly
Students get along with local community
Campus feels safe
Athletic facilities are great
Lots of beer drinking
Everyone loves the Cougars
Intramural sports are popular
Student publications are popular
Alumni active on campus

ACADEMICS

Academic Rating	76
% students returning for sophomore year	80
% students graduating within 4 years	40
% students graduating within 6 years	65
Calendar	Semester
Student/faculty ratio	18:1
Profs interesting rating	74
Profs accessible rating	78
Most classes have 10–19 students.	

MOST POPULAR MAJORS

business administration and management; social sciences; nursing

STUDENTS SAY ". . ."

Academics

From the moment you arrive on the campus of Washington State, you sense that the university is a "tight-knit community." In turn, this helps to foster a "friendly atmosphere" and "great spirit," both of which permeate the school. As one happy undergrad shares, "Washington State University became part of my family once I [set] foot on this campus. Every staff member is so nice and very welcoming. It is home away from home." Another student quickly adds, "I felt like WSU wanted me to attend their school. They called, they encouraged, they gave information, and checked frequently about any questions I had." Academically, Washington State excels in the sciences, especially with their pre-veterinary and animal sciences programs. Undergrads also like to highlight the fantastic communications department. When it comes to professors, WSU students think theirs are top-notch. Indeed, many find their teachers to be "passionate about their material and eager to pass on their knowledge to students." Moreover, they "treat students respectfully, avoid condescension, and create an environment where students are able to learn not just 'what' but 'how.'" Another aspect undergrads appreciate is that their professors really "try [and] make you think outside the box." Perhaps most important, they are "incredibly friendly and accessible." As one relieved student shares, "There was never a point when I felt I could not go to a professor for additional help." A fellow undergrad succinctly states, "WSU is a place where you can live, laugh, and learn alongside some the best faculty and students in the world."

Life

Life at Washington State moves at a frenzied pace. Indeed, "every weekend there is a free movie at our Student Union building. On campus there [are] always advertisements for fun events put on by various clubs. The Student Entertainment Board brings in comedians and musicians for low costs. There are also often educational and interesting lectures by accomplished professors or outside people. Many residence halls have board games for the residents to use as well as at least one TV lounge and often a pool table." Moreover, Cougar spirit is alive and well in this student body, and many undergrads love to go out and root for various WSU sports teams. "Football Saturdays are a campus wide event. There is nothing quite like freezing your butt off watching your team, good or not. There are also Beasley Coliseum to watch basketball and Bohler Gym to watch volleyball." Certainly, it's an active campus in general. As one undergrad shares, "The Student Recreation Center or rec is superb and many people can be seen there on a daily basis not only to work out but also to attend fitness classes." In addition, "there are [plenty of] intramural and club sports...that students can be a part of." Further, "when the weather is nice, outdoor activities are really popular: Eco-Adventure trips with the Outdoor Recreation Center...the Pullman-Moscow bike trail, a trip to the dunes or the cliffs, or just lying in the grass outside Thompson Hall!"

Student Body

When asked to describe their peers, undoubtedly the first word that comes to mind for most WSU students is "friendly." Indeed, these "easygoing" undergrads strive to cultivate a campus where "everyone is welcome." Perhaps it's easy to do that given that "there's no 'typical' student" here. One undergrad expounds, "The thing about WSU is that there is a niche for everyone—seriously. I was [pleasantly] surprised by how many international students [are here.] [What's more,] there are people from all different sexual orientations, backgrounds, and ethnicities." A fellow student continues, "You are bound to find groups of people that you fit in with, whether its long boarding, going to church, academic clubs, charity groups, Greek community, and the list goes on. WSU facilitates a greatly diverse community and provides excellent support to anyone who seeks it."

FINANCIAL AID: 509-335-9711 • E-MAIL: ADMISSIONS@WSU.EDU • WEBSITE: WWW.WSU.EDU

THE PRINCETON REVIEW SAYS

Admissions

Very important factors considered include: GPA, standardized test scores. *Important factors considered include:* Rigor of secondary school record, grade trends. *Other factors considered include:* Extracurricular activities, recommendation(s), talent/ability, volunteer work, work experience. SAT or ACT required; ACT with or without Writing component accepted. English proficiency exam required of all international applicants. *Academic units required:* 4 English; 3 mathematics; 2 lab science; 3 social studies; 2 foreign language; 1 visual/performing arts. *Academic units recommended:* 4 English; 4 mathematics; 2 lab science; 3 social studies; 2 foreign language; 1 visual/performing arts or academic elective.

Financial Aid

Students should submit: FAFSA. The Princeton Review suggests that all financial aid forms be submitted as soon as possible after January 1. *Need-based scholarships/grants offered:* Federal Pell, SEOG, State scholarships/grants, private scholarships, the school's own gift aid, federal nursing scholarships. *Loan aid offered:* Direct Subsidized Stafford Loans, Direct Unsubsidized Stafford Loans, Direct PLUS loans, Federal Perkins Loans, Federal Nursing Loans. Applicants will be notified of awards beginning 4/15. Federal and State Work-Study Program available. Institutional employment available. Off-campus job opportunities are good.

The Inside Word

Admission to Washington State University requires successful completion of a college prep curriculum. In addition, the committee will consider standardized test scores. Applicants who are either in the top 10 percent of their class or have a minimum GPA of 3.5 are guaranteed admission.

THE SCHOOL SAYS "..."

From the Admissions Office

"At Washington State University, you work side-by-side with nationally renowned faculty who help you succeed. Many academic programs rank among the nation's best. Programs are designed to give you real-world experience through internships, community service, in-depth labs, and study abroad experiences. Plus, many disciplines encourage you to participate in faculty research or conduct your own. If you have top grades and a passion for learning, the highly acclaimed Honors College challenges you with interdisciplinary studies, rich classroom discussions, and research opportunities.

"The campus forms the heart of a friendly college town where faculty and fellow students help you achieve your greatest potential. More than 300 campus organizations connect you with others who share your interests. Each year employers return to campus seeking WSU graduates. WSU also has three non-residential urban campuses in Spokane, the Tri-Cities (Richland), and Vancouver.

"The priority date to apply for admission and the deadline to apply for scholarships is January 31. For your candidacy to be considered, you must complete the high school core curriculum and provide official scores from the SAT or ACT. If you apply by January 31 and are among the top 10 percent of your high school class or have at least a 3.5 GPA, you're assured admission."

SELECTIVITY

Admissions Rating	73
# of applicants	14,887
% of applicants accepted	82
% of acceptees attending	34

FRESHMAN PROFILE

Range SAT Critical Reading	450–570
Range SAT Math	460–580
Range SAT Writing	440–550
Range ACT Composite	19–25
Minimum paper TOEFL	520
Average HS GPA	3.29
% graduated top 10% of class	30
% graduated top 25% of class	52
% graduated top 50% of class	83

DEADLINES

Regular	
Priority	1/31
Nonfall registration?	Yes

APPLICANTS ALSO LOOK AT AND OFTEN PREFER

University of Washington

AND SOMETIMES PREFER

Gonzaga University; University of Oregon; Seattle University; University of Idaho

FINANCIAL FACTS

Financial Aid Rating	76
Annual out-of-state tuition	$23,966
Room and board	$10,524
Required fees	$1,426
% needy frosh rec. need-based scholarship or grant aid	75
% needy UG rec. need-based scholarship or grant aid	72
% needy frosh rec. non-need-based scholarship or grant aid	37
% needy UG rec. non-need-based scholarship or grant aid	29
% needy frosh rec. need-based self-help aid	58
% needy UG rec. need-based self-help aid	69
% frosh rec. any financial aid	72
% UG rec. any financial aid	68
% UG borrow to pay for school	59
Average cumulative indebtedness	$23,952
% frosh need fully met	18
% ugrads need fully met	23
Average % of frosh need met	70
Average % of ugrad need met	72

WASHINGTON UNIVERSITY IN ST. LOUIS

CAMPUS BOX 1089, ST. LOUIS, MO 63130-4899 • ADMISSIONS: 314-935-6000 • FAX: 314-935-4290

CAMPUS LIFE

Quality of Life Rating	98
Fire Safety Rating	94
Green Rating	97
Type of school	Private
Affiliation	No Affiliation
Environment	City

STUDENTS

Total undergrad enrollment	6,851
% male/female	50/50
% from out of state	93
% frosh from public high school	57
% frosh live on campus	100
% ugrads live on campus	78
# of fraternities (% ugrad men join)	11 (25)
# of sororities (% ugrad women join)	7 (25)
% African American	6
% Asian	17
% Caucasian	55
% Hispanic	6
% Native American	<1
% international	8
# of countries represented	84

SURVEY SAYS . . .

Students are happy
Classroom facilities are great
Lab facilities are great
Career services are great
School is well run
Students are friendly
Great food on campus
Great off-campus food
Dorms are like palaces
Campus feels safe
Active minority support groups

ACADEMICS

Academic Rating	93
% students returning for sophomore year	96
% students graduating within 4 years	88
% students graduating within 6 years	94
Calendar	Semester
Student/faculty ratio	8:1
Profs interesting rating	86
Profs accessible rating	84

Most classes have 10–19 students.
Most lab/discussion sessions have
10–19 students.

MOST POPULAR MAJORS

biology; engineering; business administration
and management

STUDENTS SAY ". . ."

Academics

Armed with a "fantastic reputation," Washington University offers undergraduates "unparalleled facilities and resources and a friendly and intellectual atmosphere." Students join a "supportive community" replete with "academic flexibility," a myriad of "research opportunities" and plentiful "merit scholarships." Moreover, Wash U.'s size is "big enough that [you] don't know everyone and...can meet new people often, but it is small enough that [you] recognize a lot of faces and know a considerable percentage of the people there." Academically, students are quick to praise the "strong" pre-med program, which provides excellent MCAT prep. Regardless of major, students warn us that no one should expect to breeze through classes here. Indeed, courses "are difficult." Thankfully, however, "with a good work ethic...they are manageable." Then again, it's also easy to be motivated when you're surrounded and supported by an "amazing" faculty. And these students greatly enjoy learning from professors who "are always engaged and passionate about what they're teaching." Further, many undergrads say it's quite evident that Wash U. professors are invested in the success of their students. A neuroscience major shares, "My professors work hard to make sure both that I fully grasp the material and that I understand its significance in relation to the course and my education as a whole." In the end, as an impressed anthropology major says, "Wash U. pulls out all the stops to make sure you have the best college experience possible, socially and academically."

Life

Boredom is practically nonexistent at Wash U. There's never a day that passes without some form of exciting entertainment. For example, "petting zoos, the carnival on the swamp, and a visiting orchestra are just a few things to look forward to each year." Certainly, extracurricular options abound and "anyone can find organizations on campus that pursue his/her interest." A freshman strongly agrees sharing, "Everyone gets involved with different student groups on campus, from environmental awareness groups to improv groups to butter-churning groups." Additionally, the Greek system is another "major source of entertainment for students." Though one sophomore stresses that "it doesn't [necessarily] dominate campus social life." And a freshman assures us that "there is no large divide between Greek and non-Greek students." Lastly, hometown St. Louis is a "really cool city for the people willing to explore it." Fortunately, the university makes it fairly easy to do so since "every student receives a UPass which covers most of the public transportation in the area." Undergrads can enjoy everything from "art galleries and museums to exquisite restaurants (like the Peruvian 'Mango') and a well-frequented stadium for the Cardinal's baseball games [as well as] other sports (like the Argentina vs. Bosnia soccer game this year!)."

Student Body

Wash U. undergrads agree that their school consistently manages to attract "motivated," "passionate" and "highly engaged" students. They are also quick to categorize their peers as "smart, moderately wealthy, a little bit nerdy, and extremely compassionate." And while most students are "hardworking and focused," a political science student highlights the fact that they are also "collaborative." Indeed, there's no place for cutthroat behavior here and "nobody wants to see their peers fail." Undergrads also tend to be "very socially aware and socially active." And though "people [might] joke about the typical Wash U student being pre-med and Jewish, but in reality...students are diverse in terms of their academic interests, religious inclinations, and cultural affiliations." Additionally, many undergrads boast that "the 'nice factor' advertised by the admissions department really is true: students are quick to smile, greet each other, hold the door, etc. All in all, "the Midwestern feel at Wash U makes it an extremely inclusive school, and a place where everyone is celebrated and welcome."

FINANCIAL AID: 888-547-6670 • E-MAIL: ADMISSIONS@WUSTL.EDU • WEBSITE: WUSTL.EDU

THE PRINCETON REVIEW SAYS

Admissions

Very important factors considered include: Class rank, GPA, rigor of secondary school record, standardized test scores, application essay, extracurricular activities, recommendation(s), talent / ability, volunteer work, work experience, character / personal qualities. *Other factors considered include:* First generation, geographical residence, interview, racial / ethnic status, alumni / ae relations, level of applicant's interest. SAT or ACT required; ACT with or without Writing component accepted. TOEFL required of all international applicants. *Academic units recommended:* 4 English; 4 mathematics; 4 science; (4 science lab); 4 social studies; 2 foreign language; 4 history.

Financial Aid

Students should submit: FAFSA, Institution's own financial aid form, CSS / Financial Aid PROFILE, Noncustodial PROFILE. Regular filing deadline is 2/1. The Princeton Review suggests that all financial aid forms be submitted as soon as possible after January 1. *Need-based scholarships/grants offered:* Federal Pell, SEOG, State scholarships/grants, private scholarships, the school's own gift aid. *Loan aid offered:* Direct Subsidized Stafford Loans, Direct Unsubsidized Stafford Loans, Direct PLUS loans, Federal Perkins Loans, State Loans, College/university loans from institutional funds. Applicants will be notified of awards beginning 4/1. Federal Work-Study Program available. Institutional employment available. Off-campus job opportunities are excellent.

The Inside Word

Washington University is highly selective and competition for admission is fierce. A strong transcript decorated with high-level classes is recommended. Course selection will also be important, depending on the school/major. For example, it's highly recommended that engineering candidates take the most challenging math program available. Additionally, along with any science / premed majors, they should have taken both chemistry and physics. Finally, students applying to the College of Architecture are highly encouraged to submit a portfolio (it is required of applicants to the College of Art).

THE SCHOOL SAYS "..."

From the Admissions Office

"Washington University in St. Louis is a research university that offers a unique environment for undergraduate students to learn and grow. Unparalleled curriculum flexibility and learning opportunities in a friendly and supportive community inspire undergraduates to explore their interests and develop new ones. Working with their advisors, undergraduates may choose a traditional single major, as many do. Others combine majors with minors, second majors, and pre-professional programs – all within their four-year undergraduate experience. We encourage our students to participate in internships, study abroad programs, research and scholarship, and more than 300 clubs and organizations, rounding out Washington University's commitment to help each student identify and pursue his or her passion. Visit campus and ask our students about their experiences at Washington University. As part of this commitment to help our students, Washington University offers a program that eliminates need-based loans as part of its undergraduate financial assistance awards to families of students with incomes of $75,000 or less. At Washington University, we take a personalized approach to financial assistance and encourage families to contact us to discuss any unique circumstances that might exist. This initiative and its goal of helping families with the most need will not lessen our desire, responsibility, or ability to work with all families to ensure they have the financial resources they need. Applicants are required to submit scores from either the SAT or ACT test. Applicants who submit scores from the ACT test may submit with or without the writing component."

SELECTIVITY

Admissions Rating	99
# of applicants	30,117
% of applicants accepted	16
% of acceptees attending	34
# of early decision applicants	2,029
% accepted early decision	27

FRESHMAN PROFILE

Range SAT Critical Reading	700–760
Range SAT Math	720–790
Range SAT Writing	700–770
Range ACT Composite	32–34
% graduated top 10% of class	95
% graduated top 25% of class	99
% graduated top 50% of class	100

DEADLINES

Early decision	
Deadline	11/15
Notification	12/15
Regular	
Deadline	1/15
Notification	4/1
Nonfall registration?	No

APPLICANTS ALSO LOOK AT AND OFTEN PREFER

Harvard College; Stanford University; University of Pennsylvania; Yale University; Princeton University

AND SOMETIMES PREFER

Duke University; Northwestern University; The University of Chicago; Cornell University; Rice University

AND RARELY PREFER

Tulane University; Tufts University; University of Michigan—Ann Arbor

FINANCIAL FACTS

Financial Aid Rating	97
Annual tuition	$45,700
Room and board	$14,377
Required fees	$767
Books and supplies	$960
% needy frosh rec. need-based scholarship or grant aid	96
% needy UG rec. need-based scholarship or grant aid	86
% needy frosh rec. non-need-based scholarship or grant aid	13
% needy UG rec. non-need-based scholarship or grant aid	7
% needy frosh rec. need-based self-help aid	69
% needy UG rec. need-based self-help aid	65
% frosh rec. any financial aid	55
% UG rec. any financial aid	52
% UG borrow to pay for school	32
Average cumulative indebtedness	$23,082
% frosh need fully met	100
% ugrads need fully met	100
Average % of frosh need met	100
Average % of ugrad need met	100

WEBB INSTITUTE

298 Crescent Beach Road, Glen Cove, NY 11542 • Admissions: 516-671-2213, ext. 107 • Fax: 516-674-9838

CAMPUS LIFE

Quality of Life Rating	95
Fire Safety Rating	79
Green Rating	60*
Type of school	Private
Affiliation	No Affiliation
Environment	Village

STUDENTS

Total undergrad enrollment	79
% male/female	81/19
% from out of state	70
% frosh from public high school	91
% frosh live on campus	100
% ugrads live on campus	100
% African American	0
% Asian	6
% Caucasian	86
% Hispanic	4
% Native American	0
% international	0
# of countries represented	0

SURVEY SAYS . . .

Students always studying
Students are happy
Classroom facilities are great
Lab facilities are great
Career services are great
Internships are widely available
Great financial aid
No one cheats
Students are friendly
Diverse student types on campus
Campus feels safe
Easy to get around campus
Very little drug use
Alumni active on campus
Active student government

ACADEMICS

Academic Rating	98
% students returning for sophomore year	86
% students graduating within 4 years	92
% students graduating within 6 years	96
Calendar	Semester
Student/faculty ratio	7:1
Profs interesting rating	89
Profs accessible rating	99

Most classes have 20–29 students.

STUDENTS SAY ". . ."

Academics

A "highly specialized" private academy, Webb Institute offers a single "prestigious" degree program in naval architecture and marine engineering. By all accounts, this tiny school does "an excellent job of preparing students with the technical skills, knowledge, and work ethic to succeed in the marine field." The "rigorous" academic program comes with a notoriously "heavy workload," as students master structural engineering, mechanical engineering, systems design, and other fields related to ship architecture. A current undergrad admits, "This is the hardest I've worked my whole life and passing with a C is considered a success." Most, however, welcome the challenge, saying the school excels at "fostering values of hard work, perseverance, leadership, honesty, and respect" in every student. Because Webb is "a college the size of a frat" (there are only about eighty undergraduates!), "you know everyone, professors and president included." Plus, "with no teaching assistants or graduate students, you always interact directly with the professor." "Tough but accessible," the school's eleven full-time faculty members are "highly knowledgeable and are willing to help students understand the material, even outside of class." They also "have significant work experience that they bring to the classroom to relate lessons to the real world." On top of that, students "gain job experience by working for two months every winter" via the "mandatory internship program," which means each "will graduate with eight months of work experience in the field." Students are prepared, and it shows: The school boasts an incredible "100 percent placement rate" post-graduation. Even better, all admitted U.S. citizens receive a "full scholarship" covering their tuition—they are only responsible for the costs of room, board, and supplies.

Life

Life at Webb is "four years of hard work and late nights," though students say, "If you manage your time well, it's not so bad": "Between projects and tests, we find time to enjoy ourselves, get exercise, and help out the community." When they aren't hitting the books, Webbies often "play basketball in the gym or 'frockey' (a Webb Frisbee game) on the tennis courts," or simply relax at school. Located "in a mansion on Long Island sound," the beautiful Webb campus "is full of scenic places to relax, both outdoors and in." Not surprisingly, maritime activities are also popular pastimes. On the weekends, many go "sailing or kayaking," or take "one of the school-funded motor boats on the Long Island Sound for some fishing or water skiing." Webb undergrads engage in more traditional college activities, too—"sports, movies, video games, drinking"—or "venture into NYC occasionally" for a night on the town. With such a small student body, though, students must be proactive if they want to maintain a balanced lifestyle. A current undergrad explains, "From volunteering, to sports, to parties on campus, students are the ones who make the opportunities come about." Even the school's popular sports teams have to "scour the mansion looking for extra players." But, students assure us, "All it takes is some initiative."

Students

There are students from "all different countries, races, states, and ages" at Webb, though the school predominantly attracts "nerdy white males with [an] affinity for boats." A current undergrad hollers, "We definitely want more women! Please!" Even so, "There is a wide range of personalities" at the school, from "quiet and reserved" to "awkward" to social. Thanks to the miniscule enrollment, the campus comes to feel like "one big family," with an "extremely close-knit bond between the whole student body." Admittedly, "when you spend all your time with the same twenty-four people, you tend to become pretty friendly with each other." Though a love for boats is the most obvious common denominator, Webbies also tend to be "smart and well-informed." Around campus, "conversations often turn to philosophy and debates about various subjects," like literature and politics.

WEBB INSTITUTE

FINANCIAL AID: 516-671-2213 • E-MAIL: ADMISSIONS@WEBB-INSTITUTE.EDU • WEBSITE: WWW.WEBB-INSTITUTE.EDU

THE PRINCETON REVIEW SAYS

Admissions

Very important factors considered include: Class rank, GPA, rigor of secondary school record, standardized test scores, interview, recommendation(s), character/personal qualities, level of applicant's interest. *Important factors considered include:* Extracurricular activities. *Other factors considered include:* Talent/ability, volunteer work, work experience. *Academic units required:* 4 English; 4 mathematics; 2 science; (2 science lab); 2 social studies; 4 academic electives.

Financial Aid

Students should submit: FAFSA, Institution's own financial aid form, Business/Farm Supplement. Regular filing deadline is 7/1. The Princeton Review suggests that all financial aid forms be submitted as soon as possible after January 1. *Need-based scholarships/grants offered:* Federal Pell, State scholarships/grants, private scholarships, the school's own gift aid. *Loan aid offered:* Direct Subsidized Stafford Loans, Direct Unsubsidized Stafford Loans, Direct PLUS loans. Applicants will be notified of awards beginning 8/1. Off-campus job opportunities are fair.

The Inside Word

Although the applicant pool is highly self-selecting, admission to Webb is ultra-tough. The admissions committee is dedicated to finding students who will excel in the school's rigorous program. To apply, prospective students must submit high-school transcripts indicating rank in class, two letters of recommendation, and SAT scores, plus SAT subject tests in mathematics level I or II. Applications and all supporting materials must be filed by October 15 for early decision and February 15 for regular decision.

THE SCHOOL SAYS "..."

From the Admissions Office

"Webb, the only college in the country that specializes in the engineering field of naval architecture and marine engineering, seeks young men and women of all races from all over the country who are interested in receiving an excellent engineering education with a full-tuition scholarship. Students don't have to know anything about ships, they just have to be motivated to study how mechanical, civil, structural, and electrical engineering come together with the design elements that make up a ship and all its systems. Being small and private has its major advantages. Every applicant is special and the President will interview all entering students personally. The student/faculty ratio is eight to one, and since there are no teaching assistants, interaction with the faculty occurs daily in class and labs at a level not found at most other colleges. The entire campus operates under the Student Organization's honor system that allows unsupervised exams and twenty-four-hour access to the library, every classroom and laboratory, and the shop and gymnasium. Despite a total enrollment of between eighty-five and ninety students and a demanding workload, Webb manages to field five intercollegiate teams. Currently more than 60 percent of the members of the student body play on one or more intercollegiate teams. Work hard, play hard and the payoff is a job for every student upon graduation. The placement record of the college is 100 percent every year.

"Freshman applicants must take the SAT. We also require scores from two SAT Subject Tests in math level 1 or 2 and either physics or chemistry."

SELECTIVITY

Admissions Rating	95
# of applicants	82
% of applicants accepted	38
% of acceptees attending	71
# of early decision applicants	10
% accepted early decision	30

FRESHMAN PROFILE

Range SAT Critical Reading	660–740
Range SAT Math	700–750
Range SAT Writing	620–710
Average HS GPA	3.90
% graduated top 10% of class	58
% graduated top 25% of class	42
% graduated top 50% of class	100

DEADLINES

Early decision	
Deadline	10/15
Notification	12/15
Regular	
Priority	10/15
Deadline	2/15
Nonfall registration?	No

APPLICANTS ALSO LOOK AT AND OFTEN PREFER

United States Coast Guard Academy; United States Naval Academy; University of Michigan—Ann Arbor

AND SOMETIMES PREFER

The Cooper Union for the Advancement of Science and Art; Virginia Tech

FINANCIAL FACTS

Financial Aid Rating	67
Annual tuition	$0
Room and board	$13,200
Required fees	$0
Books and supplies	$950
% needy frosh rec. need-based scholarship or grant aid	50
% needy frosh rec. non-need-based scholarship or grant aid	0
% needy UG rec. non-need-based scholarship or grant aid	0
% needy frosh rec. need-based self-help aid	0
% needy UG rec. need-based self-help aid	0
% frosh rec. any financial aid	17
% UG rec. any financial aid	25
% UG borrow to pay for school	33
Average cumulative indebtedness	$4,500
% frosh need fully met	0
% ugrads need fully met	0

WELLS COLLEGE

ROUTE 90, AURORA, NY 13026 • ADMISSIONS: 315-364-3264 • FAX: 315-364-3227

STUDENTS SAY ". . ."

Academics

Located in a beautiful area close to Ithaca, New York, Wells College has the availability of a larger college town without being directly in a largely populated area. The emphasis is on community, offering an outstanding classroom experience and innovative liberal arts curriculum that prepares students for leadership in a variety of fields. One student shares, "Even professors who are very busy with other academic work make time for students. Classroom discussion is always encouraged, and most professors seem to genuinely value students' opinions, concerns, and experiences." "I love my professors, and I love my classes. They can be challenging, but it's the best sort of challenge." Another student adds, "The professors here know you by name, and they know your strengths and weaknesses well enough to push you in all the right ways. They care about making your educational experience truly be your educational experience, not their own, and they care more about your personal growth than about the grade you get on their exam." A current student adds, "The campus community is great. It's a very safe, comfortable atmosphere, and the small size means no student is going to slip through the cracks." Most students appreciate the small-school environment, as this junior affirms; "I can get to know my professors one on and one and don't have to be just another number to them." Another student agrees, "Professors are great; they're approachable, engaging, and truly do care about the students' education. I am encouraged to explore and learn and expand my horizons."

Life

Aurora is a small town on Lake Cayuga in New York State. "When it's hot, we go swimming in the lake, and that's always fun. We sometimes go sailing, or we go for a drive to any of the hundreds of tiny museums, antique stores, and small wineries in the area. In the winter, we go sledding down the big hill that leads to the athletic center. It's a picturesque existence." Transportation can sometimes be an issue, but students know they don't have to get off campus to have fun, as this student tells us: "Occasionally, we get off campus to bigger towns for fun. Our school is definitely more education-based, but we know how to have fun in our own way." At Wells, students will find a community rich with traditions. One junior reveals, "The traditions on campus are superior and amazing!" In turn, they foster "a great sense of community." Another student shares, "We participate in silly contests and traditions and love every second of it! I participated in the May Day Dance in my freshman year, and I get dressed up and sing my heart out for Odd/Even every year!" Overall when asked why Wells is a good choice, one student tells us, "I received a good scholarship, I found the traditions fascinating, and I loved the level of academic engagement that I saw from sitting in on classes as a prospective student."

Student Body

Wells transitioned to a coed college in 2005, but the school has overcome any growing pains." This can partly be attributed to the fact the college "has a strong emphasis on community." Students say, "Everyone is important and has a place here." Another student adds, "Wells seems to attract friendly, eccentric people who are socially and politically conscious, academic-minded, and tolerant. It doesn't matter if you're a student, professor, or a member of the cleaning crew—we're all learning together, and not matter what happens, we've got each other's backs." In essence, Wells provides a community of learning with "great student diversity, everyone has their own unique traits, but above all, everyone is accepted." One sophomore sums it up nicely, stating, "The typical student is a focused, engaged student who enjoys learning and works hard. Students at Wells find themselves bonding over their similar interests, and they treat each other like family."

FINANCIAL AID: 315-364-3289 • E-MAIL: ADMISSIONS@WELLS.EDU • WEBSITE: WWW.WELLS.EDU

THE PRINCETON REVIEW SAYS

Admissions

Very important factors considered include: GPA, rigor of secondary school record, standardized test scores, extracurricular activities, recommendation(s). *Important factors considered include:* Application essay, interview. *Other factors considered include:* Class rank, talent/ability, volunteer work, work experience, alumni/ae relations, character/personal qualities, level of applicant's interest. SAT or ACT required; ACT with or without Writing component accepted. TOEFL required of all international applicants. *Academic units required:* 4 English; 3 mathematics; 2 science; (2 science lab); 1 social studies; 3 history; 2 academic electives. *Academic units recommended:* 4 mathematics; 3 science; (3 science lab); 2 social studies; 2 foreign language; 2 history; 3 academic electives.

Financial Aid

Students should submit: FAFSA. The Princeton Review suggests that all financial aid forms be submitted as soon as possible after January 1. *Need-based scholarships/grants offered:* Federal Pell, SEOG, State scholarships/grants, private scholarships, the school's own gift aid. *Loan aid offered:* Federal Perkins Loans. Federal Work-Study Program available. Institutional employment available. Off-campus job opportunities are poor.

The Inside Word

Wells is engaged in that age-old admissions game called matchmaking. There are no minimums or cutoffs in the admissions process here. But don't be fooled by the high admit rate. The admissions committee will look closely at your academic accomplishments. However, they will also give attention to your essay, recommendations, and extracurricular pursuits. The committee also recommends an interview; we suggest taking them up on it.

THE SCHOOL SAYS "..."

From the Admissions Office

"Wells College believes the twenty-first century needs well-educated individuals with the ability, self-confidence, and vision to contribute to an ever-changing world. Wells offers an outstanding classroom experience and innovative liberal arts curriculum that prepares students for leadership in a variety of fields, including business, government, the arts, sciences, medicine, and education. By directly connecting the liberal arts curriculum to experience and career development through internships, off-campus study, study abroad, research with professors, and community service, each student has an ideal preparation for graduate and professional school as well as for the twenty-first century."

SELECTIVITY

Admissions Rating	83
# of applicants	1,673
% of applicants accepted	71
% of acceptees attending	12
# offered a place on the wait list	57
% accepting a place on wait list	98
% admitted from wait list	102
# of early decision applicants	15
% accepted early decision	27

FRESHMAN PROFILE

Range SAT Critical Reading	500–630
Range SAT Math	480–600
Range SAT Writing	480–590
Range ACT Composite	22–27
Minimum paper TOEFL	550
Minimum web-based TOEFL	213
Average HS GPA	3.50
% graduated top 10% of class	31
% graduated top 25% of class	65
% graduated top 50% of class	91

DEADLINES

Early decision	
Deadline	12/15
Notification	1/15
Early action	
Deadline	12/15
Notification	2/1
Regular	
Priority	12/15
Deadline	3/1
Notification	4/1
Nonfall registration?	Yes

APPLICANTS ALSO LOOK AT AND OFTEN PREFER

Smith College; Mount Holyoke College; Hobart and William Smith Colleges

AND SOMETIMES PREFER

Alfred University

FINANCIAL FACTS

Financial Aid Rating	79
Annual tuition	$33,200
Room and board	$11,900
Required fees	$1,500
Books and supplies	$800
% needy frosh rec. need-based scholarship or grant aid	93
% needy UG rec. need-based scholarship or grant aid	93
% needy frosh rec. non-need-based scholarship or grant aid	13
% needy UG rec. non-need-based scholarship or grant aid	15
% needy frosh rec. need-based self-help aid	75
% needy UG rec. need-based self-help aid	69
% frosh rec. any financial aid	96
% UG rec. any financial aid	95
% UG borrow to pay for school	90
Average cumulative indebtedness	$26,207
% frosh need fully met	13
% ugrads need fully met	15
Average % of frosh need met	75
Average % of ugrad need met	78

WELLESLEY COLLEGE

BOARD OF ADMISSION, WELLESLEY, MA 02481-8203 • ADMISSIONS: 781-283-2270 • FAX: 781-283-3678

STUDENTS SAY "..."

Academics

This "rigorous" all-women's school in Massachusetts is one of the most selective liberal arts schools in the country, boasting notable alumnae such as Madeline Albright, Nora Ephron, and Hillary Rodham Clinton. Since Wellesley is all about "supporting women who will run the world," students are "very well taken care of here," finding themselves part of "a great community that encourages and frees women to find their inner strength." Coupled with "amazing financial aid," and study abroad opportunities, the college "is a supportive, engaging, and downright fun community." The "vibrant," "worldly, interesting" professors here are "top-of-the-line," and "they know so much about their fields [that] an A paper is hard to come by." Students embrace the fact that "they expect a lot from us"; such an atmosphere may not allow for slack classes, but "it does allow for an impressive amount of growth." These "masters of their fields" offer "an immense amount of resources and time" to their students, and "class lectures combine the perfect balance of lecture and discussion to keep them engaging." "If I am not in class, my professors will notice and care to make sure I am doing all right," says one student. Faculty members are also very open to having students help with their research. "My name will be published alongside the professor for whom I worked in her next book!" says one. Alumnae stick together, and Wellesley's support system and alumnae network "guarantee you a top spot in places you are interested in, or at least some guidance on how to get in there." There are plenty of resources available to students from the administration (such as "tons of grants, academic/health advising"), as well as the ability to cross register with MIT, Babson, and Olin, giving students access to a "rich array of courses" and classmates.

Life

The town of Wellesley is "cute, but there's nothing to do after 6:00 P.M." No matter what kind of scene you're into, most students "like to get off the Wellesley campus on the weekend, if not for partying then just for sanity." Many Wellesley women "enjoy going to parties at local coed schools like MIT, Harvard, Babson, and Olin"; going into Boston to "escape the intensity of the campus" (there is a bus that runs, though not as frequently as some would like) is also a great way to relax, see a movie, or grab a bite. If students decide to stay on campus, "organizations are really great about throwing engaging events, bringing off-campus speakers, and creating a fun environment close to home." Wellesley women love to "meet over food and discuss everything under the sun." A typical activity/discussion cycle runs as such: "class work, homework, midterms, politics, the future of the country, the environment, going to MIT to party, going to Harvard to party, music, social construction of gender, you name it." People "actually do a lot of academic things" for fun here, mostly involving extracurricular clubs that explore their interests.

Student Body

Students are "very intense and motivated" at Wellesley, but at the same time remain "passionate, active, and intelligent women." The term used on campus is "Wendy Wellesley," which is someone "who is on top of all their class work plus some extra material, is concerned with the world, has extreme (almost impossible) ambition, and can interact with people in an extremely thoughtful and confident manner." It can be "competitive" here, but "there is a strong belief in women's rights, which comes with women's college territory." "Students are stressed constantly, but mainly because they stress themselves out," says one woman of her "type-A, very hardworking, perfectionist" fellow students. Still, "students here really accept each other for all their quirks." The common denominator among all Wellesley students is that "we all strive to do our best and have a greater vision for the world beyond Wellesley."

WELLESLEY COLLEGE

FINANCIAL AID: 781-283-2360 • E-MAIL: ADMISSION@WELLESLEY.EDU • WEBSITE: WWW.WELLESLEY.EDU

THE PRINCETON REVIEW SAYS

Admissions

Very important factors considered include: GPA, rigor of secondary school record, standardized test scores, application essay, recommendation(s), character/personal qualities. *Important factors considered include:* Class rank, extracurricular activities, talent/ability. *Other factors considered include:* First generation, geographical residence, interview, racial/ethnic status, state residency, volunteer work, work experience, alumni/ae relations, level of applicant's interest. SAT and SAT Subject Tests or ACT required; ACT with Writing component required. *Academic units recommended:* 4 English; 4 mathematics; 3 science; (2 science lab); 4 social studies; 4 foreign language; 4 history.

Financial Aid

Students should submit: FAFSA, CSS/Financial Aid PROFILE, Noncustodial PROFILE. The Princeton Review suggests that all financial aid forms be submitted as soon as possible after January 1. *Need-based scholarships/grants offered:* Federal Pell, SEOG, State scholarships/grants, private scholarships, the school's own gift aid. *Loan aid offered:* Direct Subsidized Stafford Loans, Direct Unsubsidized Stafford Loans, Direct PLUS loans, Federal Perkins Loans, State Loans, College/university loans from institutional funds. Applicants will be notified of awards beginning 4/1. Federal Work-Study Program available. Institutional employment available. Off-campus job opportunities are excellent.

The Inside Word

When making an admissions decision, Wellesley considers a broad range of factors, including a student's academic record, the difficulty of her high school curriculum, participation in extracurricular activities, class rank, recommendations, personal essay, standardized test scores, leadership, and special talents (students may submit art, music, or theater supplements along with their applications). Personal interviews are highly recommended, but not required, though they can be a useful way to help you stand out in Wellesley's extraordinary applicant pool.

THE SCHOOL SAYS " . . ."

From the Admissions Office

"Widely acknowledged as the nation's best women's college, Wellesley College provides students with numerous opportunities on campus and beyond. With a long-standing commitment to and established reputation for academic excellence, Wellesley offers more than 1,000 courses in fifty-four established majors and supports 180 clubs, organizations, and activities for its students. The College is easily accessible to Boston, a great city in which to meet other college students and to experience theater, art, sports, and entertainment. Considered one of the most diverse colleges in the nation, Wellesley students hail from seventy countries and all fifty states.

"As a community, we are looking for students who possess intellectual curiosity: the ability to think independently, ask challenging questions, and grapple with answers. Strong candidates demonstrate both academic achievement and an excitement for learning. They also display leadership, an appreciation for diverse perspectives, and an understanding of the College's mission to educate women who will make a difference in the world.

"The SAT and two SAT Subject Tests or ACT with writing component are required. We strongly recommend that students planning to apply early decision complete the tests before the end of their junior year and no later than October of their senior year."

SELECTIVITY

Admissions Rating	97
# of applicants	4,765
% of applicants accepted	31
% of acceptees attending	43
# offered a place on the wait list	1,091
% accepting a place on wait list	54
% admitted from wait list	4
# of early decision applicants	304
% accepted early decision	54

FRESHMAN PROFILE

Range SAT Critical Reading	660–760
Range SAT Math	650–750
Range SAT Writing	670–760
Range ACT Composite	29–33

DEADLINES

Early decision	
Deadline	11/1
Notification	12/15
Regular	
Deadline	1/15
Notification	4/1
Nonfall registration?	No

APPLICANTS ALSO LOOK AT AND OFTEN PREFER

Brown University; Princeton University; Harvard College

AND SOMETIMES PREFER

Cornell University; Duke University; Georgetown University; New York University; Washington University in St. Louis; Middlebury College; The University of Chicago; Wesleyan University

AND RARELY PREFER

University of California—Berkeley; University of California—Los Angeles; Mount Holyoke College

FINANCIAL FACTS

Financial Aid Rating	98
Annual tuition	$44,802
Required fees	$276
Books and supplies	$2,050
% needy frosh rec. need-based scholarship or grant aid	100
% needy UG rec. need-based scholarship or grant aid	100
% needy frosh rec. non-need-based scholarship or grant aid	0
% needy UG rec. non-need-based scholarship or grant aid	0
% needy frosh rec. need-based self-help aid	91
% needy UG rec. need-based self-help aid	90
% frosh rec. any financial aid	58
% UG rec. any financial aid	61
% UG borrow to pay for school	60
Average cumulative indebtedness	$14,030
% frosh need fully met	100
% ugrads need fully met	100
Average % of frosh need met	100
Average % of ugrad need met	100

Wesleyan College (GA)

4760 Forsyth Road, Macon, GA 31210-4462 • Admissions: 478-477-1110 • Fax: 478-757-4030

CAMPUS LIFE

Quality of Life Rating	74
Fire Safety Rating	88
Green Rating	75
Type of school	Private
Affiliation	Methodist
Environment	City

STUDENTS

Total undergrad enrollment	648
% male/female	0/100
% from out of state	12
% frosh from public high school	81
% frosh live on campus	90
% ugrads live on campus	82
% African American	29
% Asian	1
% Caucasian	41
% Hispanic	4
% Native American	<1
% international	21
# of countries represented	27

SURVEY SAYS . . .
Classroom facilities are great
Lab facilities are great
Very little drug use
Alumni active on campus

ACADEMICS

Academic Rating	90
% students returning for sophomore year	69
% students graduating within 4 years	58
% students graduating within 6 years	64
Calendar	Semester
Student/faculty ratio	11:1
Profs interesting rating	86
Profs accessible rating	77

Most classes have fewer than 10 students.
Most lab/discussion sessions have fewer than 10 students.

MOST POPULAR MAJORS
business administration; psychology; international business

STUDENTS SAY "..."

Academics

To many of its students, the words "sisterhood" and "tradition" are synonymous with Wesleyan College. Founded in 1836, Wesleyan "was the first college [chartered] to offer degrees to women." This private women's college located in Macon, Georgia, is "all about community, academics, and faith." Students say, "Everyone develops into a big family." Although this "diverse college full of brilliant women [is] devoted to sisterhood and tradition," it still manages to "[balance] more modern ideas and practices." Students compliment the "academic rigor, supportive atmosphere, diverse student body, nice facilities, and excellent classroom environment." Professors and academics receive the most praise. "Professors are definitely the best part of Wesleyan. [They are] totally dedicated and engaging." With hardly a negative word against them on student surveys, these "excellent," "open-minded" professors teach "challenging" material, and although they tend to be "strict," they are also "nice" and "encourage critical thinking and looking at things from different perspectives." "The professors here actually care about you, so don't be surprised when you receive an e-mail asking why you were not in class the previous day!" Classes may be "challenging" but "the academic experience is worth the cost of tuition." "The atmosphere is very uplifting and supportive," and students ensure, "There is no failing unless you absolutely, positively strive to fail."

Life

Life at Wesleyan College is not one big party. Students are "very studious and competitive in the classroom." "Everyone came here to get a good education, and that's what drives most of us here." The campus is dry. If you stay on campus, "you have to make your own fun. "It is small and quiet, a good place to study without all the distractions." "Students are usually very busy with classes and most are involved with some kind of school club/organization, so people don't typically spend a lot of time off campus." "If on-campus facilities are closed—the gym, athletic building, barn, science or music building, academic center, etc.—then there are plenty of off-campus facilities, usually within walking distance." "The Macon area has many clubs in it so a lot of girls gather up large groups and hit the town on the weekends. There is a movie theatre five minutes up the road that plays all the latest movies." Although the campus "has lots of trees and good places to take walks," some students would like to see a few improvements. "Upgrades to buildings need to be done," and "the food (has improved drastically) but we need more [vegetarian and health] options."

Student Body

Students at Wesleyan "are all very different from places all over the world." "The great international population leads to diverse religious, ethnic, and cultural backgrounds." They are different "in terms of political views, religious affiliation, and sexual orientation," and they are "opinionated." Some are "young and vibrant ready to tackle the world, while some are older ladies with children and jobs but [all] take pride in their education." What ties these students together is academics, sisterhood, and honor code. "The sisterhood program is an amazing tool that helps those who need a support system." "By being assigned a big sister, we have an easier way of adjusting and meeting new people." "There are sisterhood pep rallies every two months, which unite the school as a whole." Unity is important at an all-women school. As noted by one student, "We are all female, so we bump heads occasionally." Due to all the positive comments on student surveys, most would probably echo this comment of a fellow student: "I have had an amazing four years here, and I don't want to leave!"

FINANCIAL AID: 478-757-5205 • E-MAIL: ADMISSION@WESLEYANCOLLEGE.EDU • WEBSITE: WWW.WESLEYANCOLLEGE.EDU

THE PRINCETON REVIEW SAYS

Admissions

Very important factors considered include: Rigor of secondary school record. *Important factors considered include:* Class rank, GPA, standardized test scores, extracurricular activities, interview, recommendation(s), talent/ability. *Other factors considered include:* Application essay, volunteer work, work experience, alumni/ae relations, level of applicant's interest. SAT or ACT required; ACT with or without Writing component accepted. TOEFL required of all international applicants. *Academic units required:* 4 English; 3 mathematics; 3 science; (2 science lab); 3 social studies; 2 foreign language. *Academic units recommended:* 4 English; 4 mathematics; 4 science; (3 science lab); 4 social studies; 4 foreign language; 2 academic electives.

Financial Aid

Students should submit: FAFSA, Institution's own financial aid form, State aid form. Regular filing deadline is 6/15. The Princeton Review suggests that all financial aid forms be submitted as soon as possible after January 1. *Need-based scholarships/grants offered:* Federal Pell, SEOG, State scholarships/grants, private scholarships, the school's own gift aid. *Loan aid offered:* Direct Subsidized Stafford Loans, Direct Unsubsidized Stafford Loans, Direct PLUS loans, Federal Perkins Loans, State Loans, College/university loans from institutional funds. Federal Work-Study Program available. Off-campus job opportunities are good.

The Inside Word

Wesleyan College values diversity. At this small college, you'll find students from more than twenty countries and twenty-one states, with a wide range of interests. To evaluate a student's qualitative characteristics, Wesleyan recommends that applicants submit a teacher recommendation and have a personal interview with the admissions staff (though neither is required). Students are also encouraged to submit samples of their creative work, such as poetry, music, or research projects.

THE SCHOOL SAYS ". . ."

From the Admissions Office

"Wesleyan College in Macon, Georgia was founded in 1836 as the first college in the world chartered to grant degrees to women. Today it is recognized as one of the nation's most diverse and affordable selective four-year liberal arts colleges. Located just 90 minutes south of Atlanta, the beautiful 200-acre wooded campus is listed in the National Register of Historic Places. Students value the College's rigorous academic programs, tradition of service, and reputation for excellence. An exceptional faculty teaches classes in seminar style. A student/faculty ratio of eleven-to-one ensures that students are known by name, not by a grade or a number. The acceptance rate of Wesleyan students into medical, law, business, and other graduate programs is exemplary. Undergraduate degrees are offered in thirty-two majors and twenty-nine minors including self-designed majors and interdisciplinary programs, plus eight pre-professional programs that include engineering, medicine, pharmacy, veterinary medicine, health sciences, dental, law, and theology. Fall semester 2013 the College welcomed its first cohort of students to the new Bachelor of Science in Nursing Program. Both men and women enroll in the Master of Education and accelerated Executive Master of Business Administration programs. Wesleyan has five NCAA Division III sports teams – soccer, basketball, tennis, softball, and volleyball, and an outstanding equestrian program which competes in Intercollegiate horse Show Association and Affiliated national Riding Commission events. Proud of it's longtime affiliation with The United Methodist Church, Wesleyan plans to open a new environmentally sustainable, $6 million chapel in the spring of 2015."

SELECTIVITY

Admissions Rating	86
# of applicants	779
% of applicants accepted	43
% of acceptees attending	35

FRESHMAN PROFILE

Range SAT Critical Reading	450–570
Range SAT Math	430–560
Range SAT Writing	420–540
Range ACT Composite	17–22
Minimum paper TOEFL	550
Minimum web-based TOEFL	213

DEADLINES

Early decision	
Deadline	11/15
Notification	12/15
Early action	
Deadline	2/15
Notification	3/15
Regular	
Priority	3/1
Deadline	6/1
Nonfall registration?	Yes

APPLICANTS ALSO LOOK AT AND OFTEN PREFER
Mercer University

AND SOMETIMES PREFER
University of Georgia; Emory University; Mercer University; Agnes Scott College

AND RARELY PREFER
Florida State University; University of Florida; Rhodes College

FINANCIAL FACTS

Financial Aid Rating	77
Annual tuition	$19,500
Room and board	$8,600
Required fees	$150
Books and supplies	$2,000
% needy frosh rec. need-based scholarship or grant aid	99
% needy UG rec. need-based scholarship or grant aid	98
% needy frosh rec. non-need-based scholarship or grant aid	10
% needy UG rec. non-need-based scholarship or grant aid	9
% needy frosh rec. need-based self-help aid	75
% needy UG rec. need-based self-help aid	80
% frosh rec. any financial aid	100
% UG rec. any financial aid	97
% UG borrow to pay for school	61
Average cumulative indebtedness	$31,776
% frosh need fully met	14
% ugrads need fully met	13
Average % of frosh need met	71
Average % of ugrad need met	71

WESLEYAN UNIVERSITY (CT)

70 WYLLYS AVENUE, MIDDLETOWN, CT 06459-0265 • ADMISSIONS: 860-685-3000 • FAX: 860-685-3001

CAMPUS LIFE

Quality of Life Rating	94
Fire Safety Rating	84
Green Rating	94
Type of school	Private
Affiliation	No Affiliation
Environment	Town

STUDENTS

Total undergrad enrollment	2,906
% male/female	48/52
% from out of state	92
% frosh from public high school	52
% frosh live on campus	100
% ugrads live on campus	99
# of fraternities (% ugrad men join)	9 (4
# of sororities (% ugrad women join)	4 (1)
% African American	7
% Asian	8
% Caucasian	53
% Hispanic	10
% Native American	<1
% international	9
# of countries represented	52

SURVEY SAYS . . .

Lots of liberal students
Students are happy
Classroom facilities are great
Lab facilities are great
No one cheats
Students are friendly
Diverse student types on campus
Students environmentally aware
Great food on campus
Great off-campus food
Dorms are like palaces
Athletic facilities are great
Theater is popular

ACADEMICS

Academic Rating	96
% students returning for sophomore year	95
% students graduating within 4 years	86
% students graduating within 6 years	92
Calendar	Semester
Student/faculty ratio	9:1
Profs interesting rating	93
Profs accessible rating	95

Most classes have 10–19 students.
Most lab/discussion sessions have
  10–19 students.

MOST POPULAR MAJORS
psychology; economics

STUDENTS SAY ". . ."

Academics

Tucked away in Middletown, Connecticut, Wesleyan University is a dynamic institution "committed [to] catering to its undergraduates." The school certainly attracts those with a high level of "intellectual interest and curiosity" and students "really engage their education in a meaningful way." Fortunately, there's a "lack of…competitive cutthroat [behavior which] really promotes a community of learning." Undergrads at Wesleyan also appreciate "the lack of core curriculum," which gives students the flexibility to really "explore new areas" and "obtain a broad education." Academics here are "very challenging" but students find their classes immensely "rewarding." This is wholly due to professors who are "always available and eager to speak with students, and have a terrific passion for their work." Many of them maintain "intimate relationships with students" and a junior tells us that "having a meal with a professor at their home is not a rare occurrence." While a few students find that "the administration is full of red tape," others insist that they are "generally very responsive to student needs" and "very invested in the happiness of the students." As one senior concludes, "I feel that the administration as well as faculty work hard to make Wesleyan a strong community where everyone's voice matters."

Life

Wesleyan students have eclectic interests and passions and the social scene really reflects that. An intellectual group, undergrads can frequently be found deep in conversation with their peers, discussing anything from "the ethics of grading [or] the rendering of astrophysics into tangible graphics [to] the analysis of the feminist meanings of a Spanish worksheet." Of course, you shouldn't let this deceive you. These students also know how to kick back and have fun. "From the traditional frat party, to a gathering at a program house, [to] a performance or movie with friends in somebody's living room, Wesleyan offers a variety of social scenes for students to get involved in." Activities certainly run the gamut. An African American studies major shares, "For fun, people go to performances, sporting events, lectures, protests, restaurants, open mics, parties, campus events, etc." On any given day these lucky students might enjoy "anything from an Indian dance festival to an open forum on the economic recession to a frat party that's also a charity event for a school in Kenya." Of course, Wesleyan students are also quite adept at making their own fun and they can be found "sledding on the snow, rolling down the hill, playing Duck Duck Goose, [and] having awesome corny dance parties."

Student Body

Undergrads at Wesleyan are fairly adamant about the fact that they cannot "be pigeon-holed." While many insist "there are no typical students," others concede that there "are a few traits that often connect [everyone]." Most people "are interested in engaging with the world around them, often in hopes of improving it." Indeed this is a "passionate" group who are very "socially-conscious, politically aware, and [into] activism." Moreover, Wesleyan students are "driven," "intellectually curious" and "eager to learn and experience new things." These are kids who are "serious about academics" but also know how to "relax and have fun." They are also "very proud to be part of a diverse community" and are always excited to "meet new people." Another commonality is that undergrads here tend to "have a variety of interests." As a Spanish and film studies double-major illustrates, "Your best friend might be captain of the football team and double-majoring in chemistry and art studio." Perhaps most importantly, students at Wesleyan "aren't afraid to associate with many different kinds of people." A content senior sums up, "Students here are committed to creating a strong and close-knit community made up of open-minded people."

WESLEYAN UNIVERSITY (CT)

FINANCIAL AID: 860-685-2800 • E-MAIL: ADMISSIONS@WESLEYAN.EDU • WEBSITE: WWW.WESLEYAN.EDU

THE PRINCETON REVIEW SAYS

Admissions

Very important factors considered include: Rigor of secondary school record. *Important factors considered include:* Class rank, GPA, standardized test scores, application essay, first generation, racial/ethnic status, recommendation(s), talent/ability, character/personal qualities. *Other factors considered include:* Extracurricular activities, geographical residence, interview, volunteer work, work experience, alumni/ae relations. SAT and SAT Subject Tests or ACT required; ACT with Writing component recommended. TOEFL required of all international applicants. *Academic units recommended:* 4 English; 4 mathematics; 4 science; (3 science lab); 4 social studies; 4 foreign language; 4 history.

Financial Aid

Students should submit: FAFSA, CSS/Financial Aid PROFILE, Noncustodial PROFILE. Regular filing deadline is 2/15. The Princeton Review suggests that all financial aid forms be submitted as soon as possible after January 1. *Need-based scholarships/grants offered:* Federal Pell, SEOG, State scholarships/grants, private scholarships, the school's own gift aid. *Loan aid offered:* Direct Subsidized Stafford Loans, Direct Unsubsidized Stafford Loans, Direct PLUS loans, Federal Perkins Loans, College/university loans from institutional funds. Applicants will be notified of awards beginning 4/1. Federal Work-Study Program available. Institutional employment available. Off-campus job opportunities are good.

The Inside Word

You want the inside word on Wesleyan admissions? Read *The Gatekeepers: Inside the Admissions Process at a Premier College*, by Jacques Steinberg. The author spent an entire admissions season at the Wesleyan admissions office. His book is a wonderfully detailed description of the Wesleyan admissions process (which is quite similar to processes at other private, highly selective colleges and universities).

THE SCHOOL SAYS "..."

From the Admissions Office

"Wesleyan faculty believe in an education that is flexible and affords individual freedom and that a strong liberal arts education is the best foundation for success in any endeavor. The broad curriculum focuses on essential communication skills and analytical abilities through course content and teaching methodology, allowing students to pursue their intellectual interests with passion while honing those capabilities. As a result, Wesleyan students achieve a very personalized but broad education. Wesleyan's Dean of Admission and Financial Aid, Nancy Hargrave Meislahn, describes the qualities Wesleyan seeks in its students: 'Our very holistic process seeks to identify academically accomplished and intellectually curious students who can thrive in Wesleyan's rigorous and vibrant academic environment; we look for personal strengths, accomplishments, and potential for real contribution to our diverse community.'

"Applicants will meet standardized testing requirements one of two ways: by taking the SAT plus two SAT Subject Tests of the student's choice or by taking the ACT (writing component recommended)."

SELECTIVITY

Admissions Rating	98
# of applicants	10,690
% of applicants accepted	20
% of acceptees attending	34
# offered a place on the wait list	2,144
% accepting a place on wait list	36
% admitted from wait list	10
# of early decision applicants	924
% accepted early decision	43

FRESHMAN PROFILE

Range SAT Critical Reading	650–740
Range SAT Math	660–750
Range SAT Writing	660–750
Range ACT Composite	30–33
Minimum paper TOEFL	600
Minimum web-based TOEFL	100
Average HS GPA	3.76
% graduated top 10% of class	67
% graduated top 25% of class	91
% graduated top 50% of class	99

DEADLINES

Early decision	
Deadline	11/15
Notification	12/15
Regular	
Deadline	1/1
Notification	4/1
Nonfall registration?	No

APPLICANTS ALSO LOOK AT AND OFTEN PREFER
Brown University; Yale University; Stanford University; Harvard University

AND SOMETIMES PREFER
Bowdoin College; Middlebury College; Northwestern University

AND RARELY PREFER
Oberlin College; New York University

FINANCIAL FACTS

Financial Aid Rating	97
Annual tuition	$47,702
Room and board	$13,226
Required fees	$270
Books and supplies	$1,300
% needy frosh rec. need-based scholarship or grant aid	94
% needy UG rec. need-based scholarship or grant aid	94
% needy frosh rec. non-need-based scholarship or grant aid	0
% needy UG rec. non-need-based scholarship or grant aid	0
% needy frosh rec. need-based self-help aid	95
% needy UG rec. need-based self-help aid	97
% frosh rec. any financial aid	47
% UG rec. any financial aid	48
% UG borrow to pay for school	45
Average cumulative indebtedness	$20,966
% frosh need fully met	100
% ugrads need fully met	100
Average % of frosh need met	100
Average % of ugrad need met	100

WEST VIRGINIA UNIVERSITY

ADMISSIONS OFFICE, MORGANTOWN, WV 26506-6009 • ADMISSIONS: 304-293-2121 • FAX: 304-293-3080

CAMPUS LIFE

Quality of Life Rating	79
Fire Safety Rating	95
Green Rating	84
Type of school	Public
Affiliation	No Affiliation
Environment	Town

STUDENTS

Total undergrad enrollment	22,757
% male/female	54/46
% from out of state	49
% frosh live on campus	84
% ugrads live on campus	24
# of fraternities (% ugrad men join)	17 (6)
# of sororities (% ugrad women join)	10 (5)
% African American	4
% Asian	2
% Caucasian	83
% Hispanic	4
% Native American	<1
% international	4

SURVEY SAYS . . .
Great off-campus food
Athletic facilities are great
Lots of beer drinking
Hard liquor is popular
Everyone loves the Mountaineers
Student publications are popular

ACADEMICS

Academic Rating	73
% students returning for sophomore year	77
% students graduating within 4 years	34
% students graduating within 6 years	57
Calendar	Semester
Student/faculty ratio	21:1
Profs interesting rating	73
Profs accessible rating	75

Most classes have 10–19 students.
Most lab/discussion sessions have 20–29 students.

MOST POPULAR MAJORS
engineering; health professions; business administration

STUDENTS SAY ". . ."

Academics

"One student reports that West Virginia University boasts "a relaxed, social, and extremely school-spirited environment," and that WVU's academics "challenge students in the classroom" and prepare them "to be successful in the next step of life after college." Another student praises the engineering program, which offers "many opportunities for seniors looking for jobs. I also like the fact that it is a big university, but being in Morgantown gives it a homey feel." Students find a happy medium that combines studying and socializing. "The school is all about connecting academics and leadership with incredible enthusiasm for school activities." "A wonderful experience with a good balance of academics and fun opportunities." "Great academic experience wrapped up in a fun college atmosphere." For in-state undergraduates, affordability is the key to choosing WVU. Many students are drawn to the "diversity of programs" offered at West Virginia University. With this variety of programs comes a "diversified faculty who bring a wide range of knowledge and experiences." Some students would prefer smaller classes because, as one student put it, "The large classes make it difficult to form solid teacher-student relationships." But another student offers a different perspective, "If you put forth any type of effort, you'll get to know your professors at WVU. Of course, with some of the bigger classes, you can sit in the back and go unnoticed, but that's a personal choice."

Life

There is no escaping the "pride" West Virginia University students feel for their school, many of whom say they were "born to be a Mountaineer." Whether it's describing their majors, the marching band, alumni, or the football and basketball teams, it seems unanimous that the "spirit of the university is outstanding." As one student states, "West Virginia University is all about combining such high academic standards with the atmosphere of Mountaineer pride, only something you can feel at a football game singing 'Country Roads' with 50,000 of your closest friends." "Fun" seems to best describe student life at WVU. Whether on campus at the "amazing student recreational center," which is "complete with weight room, indoor swimming pool, hot tubs, indoor track, indoor basketball and racquetball courts, ping-pong tables, and boxing equipment," at the Mountainlair student union watching free movies, or off campus exploring Morgantown, everyone seems to be having a good time. "One of the best things about Morgantown is downtown High Street. People always ask, 'you goin downtown tonight?'" This is referring to the very wide selection of bars, clubs, lounges, and restaurants that are located downtown, most concentrated along High Street. High Street starts at the south end of downtown and travels all the way up through the downtown campus. Some students would like to see an improvement in both parking and transportation, but the beauty of the area and the level of student assistance "outside the classroom with learning centers, free tutors, [and] group work areas" all get high marks.

Student Body

Students describe themselves as "outgoing" as well as "relaxed and social." School spirit is evident. "The typical student always has some piece of WVU apparel on, and that's usually sweatpants." "Students are very involved on campus with academics and various clubs and organizations. It is a very lively campus and there is always something going on. Although one student reports, "A lot of people here drink quite often," students also say that there is plenty to do on campus that doesn't include alcohol.

FINANCIAL AID: 304-293-5242 • E-MAIL: GO2WVU@MAIL.WVU.EDU • WEBSITE: WWW.WVU.EDU

THE PRINCETON REVIEW SAYS

Admissions

Very important factors considered include: GPA, standardized test scores. *Important factors considered include:* Rigor of secondary school record, state residency. *Other factors considered include:* Extracurricular activities, recommendation(s), talent/ability, work experience. SAT or ACT required; ACT with or without Writing component accepted. TOEFL required of all international applicants. *Academic units required:* 4 English; 4 mathematics; 3 science; (3 science lab); 3 social studies; 2 foreign language; 1 visual/performing arts.

Financial Aid

Students should submit: FAFSA, State aid form. Regular filing deadline is 3/1. The Princeton Review suggests that all financial aid forms be submitted as soon as possible after January 1. *Need-based scholarships/grants offered:* Federal Pell, SEOG, State scholarships/grants, private scholarships, the school's own gift aid. *Loan aid offered:* Direct Subsidized Stafford Loans, Direct Unsubsidized Stafford Loans, Direct PLUS loans, Federal Perkins Loans, Federal Nursing Loans. Federal Work-Study Program available. Institutional employment available. Off-campus job opportunities are good.

The Inside Word

While standards for general admission to WVU aren't especially rigorous, you'll find admission to its premier programs to be quite competitive. Admission to the College of Business and Economics, for example, requires a high school GPA of at least 3.75 and an SAT math score of at least 610. Programs in computer science, education, engineering, fine arts, forensics, journalism, medicine, and nursing all require fairly impressive credentials. If you're not admitted to the program of your choice, you may be able to transfer to it later if your grades are good enough, but it won't be easy.

THE SCHOOL SAYS "..."

From the Admissions Office

"From quality academic programs and outstanding, caring faculty, to incredible new facilities and a campus environment that focuses on students' needs, WVU is a place where dreams can come true. Our tradition of academic excellence attracts some of the region's best high school seniors. WVU has produced twenty-four Rhodes Scholars, thirty-five Goldwater Scholars, twenty-two Truman Scholars, six members of the USA Today's All-USA College Academic First Team, and two Udall Scholarship winners. Whether your goal is to be an aerospace engineer, reporter, physicist, athletic trainer, opera singer, forensic investigator, pharmacist, or CEO, WVU's 191 degree choices can make it happen. Unique student-centered initiatives help students experience true education beyond the classroom. The Mountaineer parents club connects more than 20,000 families, and a parents' helpline (800-WVU-0096) leads to a full-time parent advocate. A Student Recreation Center includes athletic courts, pools, weight/fitness equipment, and a fifty-foot indoor climbing wall. A major building program is creating new classrooms, labs, health-care facilities, an art museum, and a student wellness center. With programs for studying abroad, a Center from Black Culture and Research, and Office of Disability Services, and a student body that comes from every WV county, fifty states, and 100 different countries, WVU encourages diversity. WVU research funding has topped $174 million for the second consecutive year, making WVU a major research institution where undergraduates can participate. All applicants are required to take the ACT writing assessment as part of the ACT exam, or take the SAT to be considered for admission."

SELECTIVITY

Admissions Rating	72
# of applicants	16,079
% of applicants accepted	85
% of acceptees attending	36

FRESHMAN PROFILE

Range SAT Critical Reading	470–570
Range SAT Math	480–580
Range ACT Composite	21–26
Minimum paper TOEFL	550
Minimum web-based TOEFL	61
Average HS GPA	3.40
% graduated top 10% of class	20
% graduated top 25% of class	45
% graduated top 50% of class	79

DEADLINES

Regular	
Priority	3/1
Deadline	8/1
Nonfall registration?	Yes

APPLICANTS ALSO LOOK AT AND OFTEN PREFER

Virginia Tech; Pennsylvania State University—University Park; University of Maryland; College Park

AND SOMETIMES PREFER

James Madison University; University of Pittsburgh—Pittsburgh Campus

FINANCIAL FACTS

Financial Aid Rating	83
Annual in-state tuition	$6,456
Annual out-of-state tuition	$19,632
Books and supplies	$1,100
% needy frosh rec. need-based scholarship or grant aid	58
% needy UG rec. need-based scholarship or grant aid	59
% needy frosh rec. non-need-based scholarship or grant aid	83
% needy UG rec. non-need-based scholarship or grant aid	31
% needy frosh rec. need-based self-help aid	58
% needy UG rec. need-based self-help aid	66
% frosh rec. any financial aid	72
% UG rec. any financial aid	75
Average cumulative indebtedness	$29,149
% frosh need fully met	30
% ugrads need fully met	30
Average % of frosh need met	72
Average % of ugrad need met	75

WESTMINSTER COLLEGE (PA)

319 South Market Street, New Wilmington, PA 16172 • Admissions: 724-946-7100 • Fax: 724-946-6171

STUDENTS SAY "..."

Academics

Since 1852, Westminster College has remained intent crafting a personalized learning process for students, with the aim of turning out well-rounded individuals who "can live and affect the world around us in a positive way." The "challenging" liberal arts curriculum provides a broad foundation for academic study, and the school heavily stresses the application of what's learned by pushing students "to prepare themselves for the future using real life simulations." At this "very happy place," the administration always "keeps the interests of the students in mind," the classes are small, and "students get the attention they need." Westminster runs on personal relationships between faculty and students, and "Even the janitor knows your name." The low student/teacher ratio means the "extremely accessible and helpful" professors are devoted to ensuring that every last student understands the material, and "office doors are always open." This care extends far beyond the classroom, as professors love to see students involved in interesting activities outside of classes, and they "pretty much beg you to study abroad because they know it will be so beneficial for you as a person." "If you see some slacking there is always someone there, whether a classmate or professor, to bring you up," says one student. A few students do remark on the school's rather slow adoption of modern technology ("We just got wireless Internet this year"), but this is more than made up for by the "variety of courses," "student-teacher bonds," and "opportunities to get involved." "Contrary to popular belief, Westminster College, not Disneyland, is the happiest place on earth," says a student.

Life

"This school has so much going on that it is almost impossible to not be involved," says one student of the busy hive that is Westminster. There are more than 100 clubs and a wide range of activities offered, including "concerts, competitions, Humans versus Zombies, a Frisbee team, philosophy club, jazz band, flute choir, an equestrian team, an ice skating class, [and] karate class." The administration plan events all throughout the week ("Most people stay on campus on the weekends"), such as "movies on weekends, concerts on Friday or Saturday nights, sports events at least once a week, [and] special cuisine nights at the [cafeteria]." Located in the heart of Amish country, the dry town and campus "creates a great place to focus and learn" with "small-town appeal and charm that's irresistible." Greek life "is especially important for socialization," and many join it in some form or another (whether a social sorority or fraternity, or an honors society). Some students do choose to party off campus, but "it's far enough off of campus that you don't feel pressured to join in if you don't want to." Off-campus malls, restaurants, and cities "are not too far away," but "so much is happening on campus during the week and weekends that I do not see much need to go off-campus often."

Student Body

The typical Titan is "extremely friendly" and academically driven; students "know how to have fun but also know when to study and hit the books." Though the majority of Westminster students are white and Christian, "no one at Westminster is discriminatory towards other races, genders, religions, or sexual orientations." The student body is small enough that it can be called "tight-knit," and there's a lot of frequent interaction among students, because almost all who go to school here "get involved with a number of extracurricular activities" or "community service and philanthropic events." This easygoing crowd "gets along very well," and "just about everyone fits in to the mix somewhere." Many students say, "Westminster is your family," and "it is a quick and easy process to make friends and find a niche."

FINANCIAL AID: 724-946-7102 • E-MAIL: ADMIS@WESTMINSTER.EDU • WEBSITE: WWW.WESTMINSTER.EDU

THE PRINCETON REVIEW SAYS

Admissions

Very important factors considered include: GPA, rigor of secondary school record, standardized test scores, first generation, interview, level of applicant's interest. *Important factors considered include:* Class rank, application essay, recommendation(s), character/personal qualities. *Other factors considered include:* Extracurricular activities, racial/ethnic status, talent/ability, volunteer work, work experience, alumni/ae relations. SAT or ACT required; ACT with or without Writing component accepted. TOEFL required of all international applicants. *Academic units required:* 4 English; 3 mathematics; 2 science; (2 science lab); 2 social studies; 2 foreign language; 1 history; 3 academic electives.

Financial Aid

Students should submit: FAFSA, Institution's own financial aid form. The Princeton Review suggests that all financial aid forms be submitted as soon as possible after January 1. *Need-based scholarships/grants offered:* Federal Pell, SEOG, State scholarships/grants, private scholarships, the school's own gift aid. *Loan aid offered:* Direct Subsidized Stafford Loans, Direct Unsubsidized Stafford Loans, Direct PLUS loans, Federal Perkins Loans.

The Inside Word

Westminster offers both early action and rolling admissions (following the December 15 deadline). The school will accept either the SAT or ACT test scores and also has an organization of student volunteers dedicated to assisting the Office of Admissions in the recruitment of qualified students. Most of your competition will be from Pennsylvania, with the rest mostly coming from Ohio.

THE SCHOOL SAYS "..."

From the Admissions Office

"When you step onto the Westminster campus, you just know. Maybe it's the total strange who holds the door open for you. Maybe it's your professor from two years ago who still greets you by name. Whatever it is, you know it feels like home.

"Founded in 1852 and related to the Presbyterian Church (U.S.A.), Westminster College ranks first in the nation as 'Best College for Women in Science, Technology, Engineering and Math.' A top-tier liberal arts college and a national leader in graduation rate performance, Westminster is named to the President's Honor Roll for excellence in service learning.

"Nearly 1,600 undergraduate and graduate students benefit from individualized attention from dedicated faculty while choosing from 41 majors and nearly 100 organizations on the New Wilmington, Pa., campus. Visit Westminster.edu for more information."

SELECTIVITY

Admissions Rating	77
# of applicants	1,368
% of applicants accepted	71
% of acceptees attending	32

FRESHMAN PROFILE

Range SAT Critical Reading	470–570
Range SAT Math	480–590
Range ACT Composite	20–25
Minimum paper TOEFL	550
Minimum web-based TOEFL	213
Average HS GPA	3.40
% graduated top 10% of class	20
% graduated top 25% of class	55
% graduated top 50% of class	87

DEADLINES

Early action	
Deadline	11/15
Notification	11/15
Regular	
Deadline	4/15
Nonfall registration?	No

APPLICANTS ALSO LOOK AT AND OFTEN PREFER

Pennsylvania State University; University of Pittsburgh

AND SOMETIMES PREFER

Grove City College; Duquesne University

AND RARELY PREFER

Allegheny College; Washington & Jefferson College

FINANCIAL FACTS

Financial Aid Rating	81
Annual tuition	$29,150
Room and board	$9,200
Required fees	$1,160
Books and supplies	$1,000
% needy frosh rec. need-based scholarship or grant aid	100
% needy UG rec. need-based scholarship or grant aid	99
% needy frosh rec. non-need-based scholarship or grant aid	99
% needy UG rec. non-need-based scholarship or grant aid	97
% needy frosh rec. need-based self-help aid	79
% needy UG rec. need-based self-help aid	81
% frosh rec. any financial aid	
% UG rec. any financial aid	
% UG borrow to pay for school	83
Average cumulative indebtedness	$32,753
% frosh need fully met	20
% ugrads need fully met	17
Average % of frosh need met	80
Average % of ugrad need met	80

WESTMINSTER COLLEGE (UT)

1840 SOUTH 1300 EAST, SALT LAKE CITY, UT 84105 • ADMISSIONS: 801-832-2200 • FAX: 801-832-3101

STUDENTS SAY ". . ."

Academics

Located in Salt Lake City, Westminster College is "a small private college" with "an urban setting that has easy access to the outdoors." Winter sports are a major part of campus life, but if you are not already proficient on the hills, don't worry, "we have really awesome ski and snowboard classes here." The school is also known for its "outstanding" nursing program, which is perhaps "the best nursing program in the state." Westminster's small size provides students with "intimate classes" and "professors [who] truly care about their students." "I have never felt more comfortable on a college campus," one public health major says. However, "as a small school, Westminster is lacking in some resources," and some students wish the college was "adding more majors to choose from." "Westminster has a very personal culture" and "professors really get to know and care about their students." "I know all of my professors on a first name basis," one student says. "Professors are creative with their teaching methods" and they "focus on helping students to excel and do well in class and otherwise rather than getting published." While the majority of professors "are highly educated in their field, some are better than others at expressing their field." "Westminster gives great financial aid," and "the support staff is amazing! Any question, concern, doubt, general lack of know how, they answered, pacified, and educated." "To me, Westminster was the epitome of that whole 'college package,'" one student says of their decision to attend. "The campus was beautiful and up-to-date, there was a broad range of majors, the location was ideal, and yet it was set within this amazing local and collegiate community." Another puts it more succinctly: "I honestly believe that Westminster is nearly perfect."

Life

Westminster is a place where "everyone looks forward to a good snow day." Skiing and snowboarding are central features of student life, with "six resorts within a half hour drive of campus." Students here are all about "working hard and getting to ski to reward yourself for the hard work." Salt Lake City provides "many opportunities (professional, recreational, and cultural)" and the campus is only "fifteen minutes away from outdoor recreation areas." On campus, "there are awesome student association run events!" Activities range from "spontaneous cupcake wars to international fests to dances to community service projects and everything in between." "I love the small-campus feel and the fact that it has an amazing location in a safe neighborhood," a Communications major reports. "The atmosphere on campus is my favorite part of the school," says a neuroscience major. "It's a really friendly, open, fun place to be." Another student declares that "life is truly elevated at Westminster College."

Student Body

Students at Westminster are either "here to learn, or here to ski; often a combination of the two." The student body is not especially racially diverse, with most students being "white, in shape, environmentally friendly, etc." Still, "all students are unique and are individuals" and can be "anything from snow bro, hipster, intellectual, religious, atheist, or spoiled slacker." In regards to political views, "while it may be fair to call Utah a 'sea of conservatism,' SLC certainly is not. Westminster reflects SLC's more liberal leanings." "The community is close-knit and supportive" and "nearly everyone skis or snowboards" or at least likes to "hike, rock climb, [and] camp." Some students who are not big on outdoor sports can "feel like outsider[s]." As at many colleges, certain students "are more concerned about school while there are many who like to party and rely on their parents to pay their way while they slack off." Overall this "wonderful mix" of students is the "best-kept secret around." Westminster College is a place "where ski bums, overachievers and Mormons collide to make up an awesome, fun residential student body."

WESTMINSTER COLLEGE (UT)

FINANCIAL AID: 801-832-2502 • E-MAIL: ADMISSION@WESTMINSTERCOLLEGE.EDU • WEBSITE: WWW.WESTMINSTERCOLLEGE.EDU

THE PRINCETON REVIEW SAYS

Admissions

Very important factors considered include: Class rank, GPA, rigor of secondary school record, standardized test scores, application essay, extracurricular activities, first generation, geographical residence, interview, racial/ethnic status, recommendation(s), state residency, talent/ability, volunteer work, work experience, alumni/ae relations, character/personal qualities, level of applicant's interest, religious affiliation. SAT or ACT required; ACT with Writing component recommended. TOEFL required of all international applicants. *Academic units required:* 4 English; 2 mathematics; 3 science; 2 social studies; 2 foreign language; 1 history; 2 academic electives. *Academic units recommended:* 4 English; 3 mathematics; 3 science; 2 social studies; 3 foreign language; 1 history; 3 academic electives.

Financial Aid

Students should submit: FAFSA. The Princeton Review suggests that all financial aid forms be submitted as soon as possible after January 1. *Need-based scholarships/grants offered:* Federal Pell, SEOG, State scholarships/grants, private scholarships, the school's own gift aid. *Loan aid offered:* Direct Subsidized Stafford Loans, Direct Unsubsidized Stafford Loans, Direct PLUS loans, Federal Perkins Loans. Applicants will be notified of awards beginning 3/1. Federal Work-Study Program available. Institutional employment available. Off-campus job opportunities are excellent.

The Inside Word

Westminster accepts a solid majority of applicants it receives, so you don't have to have been the valedictorian to apply. Students with good grades and above national average test scores have a very strong chance of being accepted. Students who fall a little short in those categories can still impress the admissions office with extracurricular achievement, powerful essays, or other demonstrable talents.

THE SCHOOL SAYS "..."

From the Admissions Office

"Founded in 1875, Westminster College is a private, comprehensive, liberal arts college dedicated to students and their learning, and offers one of the most unique learning environments in the country. Located where the Rocky Mountains meet the vibrant city of Salt Lake, Westminster blends classroom learning with experiences derived from its unique location to help students develop skills and attributes critical for success in a rapidly changing world. Impassioned teaching and active learning are the hallmarks of the Westminster experience.

"Each application is read and reviewed individually by an admissions committee who takes into account both level of challenge in course work and grades received. Either the SAT or ACT exam is accepted. Writing ability will be assessed through the writing sections of the SAT, ACT, application essays, and in some cases, other writing samples such as graded papers.

"Westminster College has a rolling application deadline and will accept applications until the class is filled. To be eligible for the widest array of financial aid—and more than 97 percent of freshmen receive some financial aid—April 15 is the priority consideration deadline for fall semester, and May 15 is the deadline for on-campus housing applications."

SELECTIVITY
Admissions Rating	79
# of applicants	2,461
% of applicants accepted	75
% of acceptees attending	24

FRESHMAN PROFILE
Range SAT Critical Reading	500–610
Range SAT Math	500–610
Range ACT Composite	22–28
Minimum paper TOEFL	550
Average HS GPA	3.53
% graduated top 10% of class	23
% graduated top 25% of class	55
% graduated top 50% of class	88

DEADLINES
Regular	
Priority	2/1
Deadline	8/15
Nonfall registration?	Yes

APPLICANTS ALSO LOOK AT AND OFTEN PREFER
Brigham Young University (UT)

AND SOMETIMES PREFER
University of Utah; University of Idaho; Utah State University

FINANCIAL FACTS
Financial Aid Rating	82
Annual tuition	$28,992
Room and board	$8,208
Required fees	$508
Books and supplies	$1,000
% needy frosh rec. need-based scholarship or grant aid	100
% needy UG rec. need-based scholarship or grant aid	98
% needy frosh rec. non-need-based scholarship or grant aid	10
% needy UG rec. non-need-based scholarship or grant aid	9
% needy frosh rec. need-based self-help aid	88
% needy UG rec. need-based self-help aid	90
% frosh rec. any financial aid	97
% UG rec. any financial aid	92
% UG borrow to pay for school	60
Average cumulative indebtedness	$26,379
% frosh need fully met	22
% ugrads need fully met	21
Average % of frosh need met	81
Average % of ugrad need met	75

WHEATON COLLEGE (IL)

501 COLLEGE AVENUE, WHEATON, IL 60187 • ADMISSIONS: 630-752-5005 • FAX: 630-752-5285

STUDENTS SAY ". . ."

Academics
Wheaton College strives to cultivate students' knowledge and to "prepare them to enter the world as strong and capable individuals who serve Christ and His Kingdom." This "academically rigorous" and deeply religious liberal arts school is equally as interested in the character of each student, with a focus on "developing yourself in ways [that] will affect you long after you've left the school campus." Professors here are "the heart and soul of this campus," and they're "exceptional teachers who genuinely care for the academic and spiritual well-being of their students." They "attempt to connect with students in ways other than the material they are told to teach," and it's "not unusual to meet professors outside of class, whether that be for a meal, coffee, or fun activities." That's not to say that there aren't a few bad apples or that the grading isn't tough; professors "rarely curve," but they do provide "many mentoring and tutoring sessions" to those in need. There's a "serious integration of faith and learning" that "places a high emphasis on opening up our eyes to serious issues going on around the world." "When you see other people using their gifts for God and hear them encouraging you to do the same, it's inspiring," says one student. Class sizes at Wheaton are pleasantly small, and one-on-one interaction is very common through "internships, teaching assistants, research opportunities, and the 'Dine with a Mind' program." This student body that's truly "sincere about learning" goes on to form a "very close-knit network of graduates" that's easily accessible after graduation. Other than that, students laud the "successful career placement, top-notch music conservatory, [and] excellent science facilities."

Life
All Wheaton students adhere to a community covenant, which is a set of rules and regulations governing students that forbids things, such as drinking and smoking. While several students wish that the school was "more lenient in their punishment system," most are happy to comply and even claim that it "forces us to come up with super-creative ways to have fun." "Everyone has at least one costume—bring one if you come here because you will need it," says a mysterious student. Drink-wise, "Wheaton students don't need alcohol to have an awesome time," and food-wise, the school has what some students call the "greatest college food in the country." The train station is a few minutes' walk from campus, which can bring you to nearby Chicago, but most students "just find fun activities to do on campus…like bond with [students who live on their housing] floor or play campus-wide Sardines." The college offers lots of activities during the weekend and has tons of "random traditions," such as a "student 'Iron Chef' competition in the dining hall." Students here are very passionate about social justice issues and "just as likely to be found discussing theology or philosophy as the latest sports game." ESL tutoring, mentoring, and serving on spring break service trips are also popular extracurricular activities for Wheaties.

Student Body
Pretty much the entirety of Wheaton is composed of "academically strong, driven, and Christian students," and the phrase "type-A personality" is oft-used. The school draws students from all over the country (including "quite a lot of homeschooled and international students"), and the diversity isn't as strong as some students would like, though "they are making a lot of efforts to change that in the admissions office." Students at Wheaton "take their studies extremely seriously and work very hard to keep high grades," but most still get involved with student activities, ministries, and sports, and enjoy the groups of friends that form when people share a "common identity." In their downtime, people "have a respectful and creative sense of fun and do not waste their time." All in all, "most students find some way to fit in."

FINANCIAL AID: 630-752-5021 • E-MAIL: ADMISSIONS@WHEATON.EDU • WEBSITE: WWW.WHEATON.EDU

THE PRINCETON REVIEW SAYS

Admissions

Very important factors considered include: GPA, rigor of secondary school record, standardized test scores, application essay, interview, recommendation(s), character/personal qualities, religious affiliation. *Important factors considered include:* Extracurricular activities, talent/ability, volunteer work, work experience. *Other factors considered include:* Class rank, first generation, geographical residence, racial/ethnic status, state residency, alumni/ae relations, level of applicant's interest. SAT or ACT required. TOEFL required of all international applicants. *Academic units recommended:* 4 units English, 4 units math, 4 units science, 4 units social science, 3 units foreign language.

Financial Aid

Students should submit: FAFSA, Institution's own financial aid form. The Princeton Review suggests that all financial aid forms be submitted as soon as possible after January 1. *Need-based scholarships/grants offered:* Federal Pell, SEOG, State scholarships/grants, private scholarships, the school's own gift aid. *Loan aid offered:* Direct Subsidized Stafford Loans, Direct Unsubsidized Stafford Loans, Direct PLUS loans, Federal Perkins Loans. Federal Work-Study Program available. Institutional employment available. Off-campus job opportunities are excellent.

The Inside Word

Although Wheaton College looks for students who are strong academically, the college doesn't have any minimum requirements for GPA, class rank, or standardized test scores. The school does look for evidence of Christian faith when making its decision, and proof of Christian commitment is necessary for admission, but you'll also have to prove the quality of your high school courses.

THE SCHOOL SAYS "..."

From the Admissions Office

"At Wheaton, we're commited to being a community that fearlessly pursues truth, upholds an academically rigorous curriculum, and promotes virtue. The college takes seriously its impact on society. The influence of Wheaton is seen in fields ranging from government (the former speaker of the house) to sports (two NBA coaches) to business (the CEO of John Deere) to music (Metropolitan Opera National Competition winners) to education (over forty college presidents) to global ministry (Billy Graham). Wheaton seeks students who want to make a difference and are passionate about their Christian faith and rigorous academic pursuit.

"Applicants are required to submit results from the SAT or the ACT. Wheaton will use the highest of these scores from either test in evaluating a student's application."

SELECTIVITY

Admissions Rating	93
# of applicants	1,941
% of applicants accepted	70
% of acceptees attending	44
# offered a place on the wait list	382
% accepting a place on wait list	33
% admitted from wait list	36

FRESHMAN PROFILE

Range SAT Critical Reading	600–710
Range SAT Math	590–700
Range SAT Writing	600–700
Range ACT Composite	27–32
Minimum paper TOEFL	587
Average HS GPA	3.71
% graduated top 10% of class	58
% graduated top 25% of class	82
% graduated top 50% of class	97

DEADLINES

Early action	
Deadline	11/1
Notification	12/31
Regular	
Deadline	1/10
Notification	4/1
Nonfall registration?	No

APPLICANTS ALSO LOOK AT
AND SOMETIMES PREFER
Grove City College

AND RARELY PREFER
Baylor University; Calvin College; The College of William & Mary; Davidson College

FINANCIAL FACTS

Financial Aid Rating	84
Annual tuition	$31,900
Room and board	$8,820
Books and supplies	$1,120
% needy frosh rec. need-based scholarship or grant aid	100
% needy UG rec. need-based scholarship or grant aid	98
% needy frosh rec. non-need-based scholarship or grant aid	42
% needy UG rec. non-need-based scholarship or grant aid	36
% needy frosh rec. need-based self-help aid	76
% needy UG rec. need-based self-help aid	81
% frosh rec. any financial aid	75
% UG rec. any financial aid	73
% UG borrow to pay for school	55
Average cumulative indebtedness	$25,413
% frosh need fully met	23
% ugrads need fully met	21
Average % of frosh need met	88
Average % of ugrad need met	89

WHEATON COLLEGE (MA)

OFFICE OF ADMISSION, NORTON, MA 02766 • ADMISSIONS: 508-286-8251 • FAX: 508-286-8271

STUDENTS SAY ". . ."

Academics

This historic Massachusetts institution, originally founded in 1834 as a female seminary, is now a "small liberal arts college" that provides "a top notch education" for "high performing students." Wheaton is a school that "focuses strongly on creating the well-rounded, aware, worldly and accepting liberal arts graduate." Students love the "small class sizes" that engender a "close connection with faculty." These factors "are incredibly conducive to classroom discussion and cooperative learning in all subjects" and "students are expected to be present and participate in class." Students know that "if you work hard, you will succeed," and if you are struggling people will help you out. "There's an atmosphere of goodwill," a Psychology and Hispanic Studies student explains. "For example, if someone is having trouble in a class or looking for a summer job, help is always available and easily reachable." Another attraction is "the beautiful campus" that is located close to both Providence and Boston. The most common complaint among students is the dining and meal plans, which are "very limited," "could possibly be healthier" and in general are "awful." "It's understandable that it's hard to cater to the tastes of such a diverse community, but it'd be nice if things had a decent flavor to it," one student says. That said, "the food is probably the only issue" at this exciting college. There is a strong "sense of community" on campus, and "professors and students alike are all so friendly, genuine, helpful, motivated, and proactive people." You can tell people are comfortable here as they walk around campus "like any person you would see walking around their own house" and everyone is "very friendly and genuine." "Not only do students here value comfortable clothes, they get to know the campus well and get comfortable being in it," a Psychology major says. At the end of the day, "Wheaton is all about finding your passion and exploring avenues that you might never have thought to explore." One senior raves about their experience, telling potential applicants that Wheaton is "the most diverse, welcoming, accepting, and colorful place you'll ever live in."

Life

As a small school, "the party scene does not compare to a large university" and some suggest "the party scene at Wheaton is practically nonexistent." Instead, students enjoy the "active force" of the college's programming council that ensures "students will always have something to do on weekends." Students are very active in student groups and organizations, including the "over 100 clubs and organizations on campus that do programming in a regular basis." "The typical girl auditions for an a cappella group or a monologue/improv group," one student explains. "The typical male is either involved with a sport or finds a gaming clique." While there is a lot to do on campus, "the surrounding town (if you can call it that) consists of a CVS, Walgreens, two old-man bars, a bad Chinese place and a corner store." Consequentially, students often take trips to "Boston and Providence, which are extremely easy to get to" as "Providence is less than 30 minutes away, and Boston about an hour." Wheaton is a "close-knit community" with a "friendly and accepting campus culture." "People are truly passionate about their academic areas of interest and their hobbies" at Wheaton, and spend late nights debating "everything from politics to Harry Potter."

Student Body

Students at Wheaton "are independent thinkers and take pride in their individuality" while working "well together, no matter what social group you may be a part of." They might be best summed up as "quirky, but in all different ways." "Students usually fall into friend groups very fast," normally finding "a set of friends after first semester." "Students are generally liberal" and often "very New-England" and "smart, social, involved." Many students are "from the northeast, white and middle class," yet "the diversity is mind-bending" and there are plenty of "students of color, international students, queer students, various religious denominations." However, one student points out that "the student body is 60 percent female, and it is not uncommon at all to have a class where most students are women." The main feeling on campus is that of a "tight knit community" where anyone can come "and find a place to fit in or stand out.

WHEATON COLLEGE (MA)

FINANCIAL AID: 508-286-8232 • E-MAIL: ADMISSION@WHEATONCOLLEGE.EDU • WEBSITE: WWW.WHEATONCOLLEGE.EDU

THE PRINCETON REVIEW SAYS

Admissions

Very important factors considered include: GPA, rigor of secondary school record, application essay, extracurricular activities, first generation, talent/ability, character/personal qualities. *Important factors considered include:* Class rank, interview, recommendation(s), volunteer work, work experience, alumni/ae relations. *Other factors considered include:* Geographical residence, racial/ethnic status, state residency, level of applicant's interest. SAT and SAT Subject Tests or ACT considered if submitted; ACT with or without Writing component accepted. TOEFL required of all international applicants. *Academic units recommended:* 4 English; 4 mathematics; 3 science; (2 science lab); 3 social studies; 4 foreign language; 2 history.

Financial Aid

Students should submit: FAFSA, CSS/Financial Aid PROFILE, Noncustodial PROFILE, Business/Farm Supplement. Regular filing deadline is 2/1. The Princeton Review suggests that all financial aid forms be submitted as soon as possible after January 1. *Need-based scholarships/grants offered:* Federal Pell, SEOG, State scholarships/grants, private scholarships, the school's own gift aid. *Loan aid offered:* Direct Subsidized Stafford Loans, Direct Unsubsidized Stafford Loans, Direct PLUS loans, Federal Perkins Loans. Applicants will be notified of awards beginning 4/1. Federal Work-Study Program available. Institutional employment available. Off-campus job opportunities are good.

The Inside Word

Wheaton tells prospective students, "We want to get to know you, too. Not just your SAT scores, but what do you do for fun?" While the school certainly looks at the traditional measures like GPA and test scores, Wheaton wants to get a sense of you as an individual. The option of submitting a personal portfolio gives you a great opportunity to show Wheaton what makes you tick and what makes you unique.

THE SCHOOL SAYS ". . ."

From the Admissions Office

"We have been described as a place where world-changing ideas flourish. And we're okay with that. Our students come from all over the country and the world, and they definitely stand out from the crowd. In fact, Wheaton was placed on The Daily Beast/Newsweek's list of America's 25 Brainiac Schools, based on our students' success in winning the most prestigious scholarship awards. Over the past decade, more than 158 Wheaton students have won national and international scholarships, including the Rhodes, Marshall, Fulbright, Truman and Watson awards. Of course, we think our faculty are pretty amazing, too. They are world-class researchers, scholars and artists, who are also outstanding teachers and advisors. Wheaton faculty involve their students in original research and scholarship projects that help to create new knowledge, as well as incredible opportunities. Our Filene Center for Academic Advising and Career Services dedicates nearly $700,000 in stipends and fellowships each year to support internships and research. We also get our students connected to a worldwide alumni network that can help graduates to choose careers, find internships and get started on their first jobs. We are proud of what our graduates do as well as who they become."

SELECTIVITY

Admissions Rating	87
# of applicants	3,433
% of applicants accepted	73
% of acceptees attending	18
# offered a place on the wait list	254
% accepting a place on wait list	41
% admitted from wait list	18
# of early decision applicants	113
% accepted early decision	83

FRESHMAN PROFILE

Range SAT Critical Reading	560–670
Range SAT Math	550–670
Range ACT Composite	25–30
Minimum web-based TOEFL	90
Average HS GPA	3.30
% graduated top 10% of class	37
% graduated top 25% of class	70
% graduated top 50% of class	93

DEADLINES

Early decision	
Deadline	11/15
Notification	12/15
Early action	
Deadline	11/15
Notification	1/15
Regular	
Deadline	1/15
Notification	4/1
Nonfall registration?	Yes

APPLICANTS ALSO LOOK AT AND OFTEN PREFER

Bates College; Connecticut College

AND SOMETIMES PREFER

Skidmore College; University of Vermont

AND RARELY PREFER

Boston University; Clark University

FINANCIAL FACTS

Financial Aid Rating	91
Annual tuition	$44,780
Room and board	$11,500
Required fees	$294
Books and supplies	$940
% needy frosh rec. need-based scholarship or grant aid	98
% needy UG rec. need-based scholarship or grant aid	98
% needy frosh rec. non-need-based scholarship or grant aid	14
% needy UG rec. non-need-based scholarship or grant aid	8
% needy frosh rec. need-based self-help aid	93
% needy UG rec. need-based self-help aid	96
% frosh rec. any financial aid	93
% UG rec. any financial aid	84
% UG borrow to pay for school	61
Average cumulative indebtedness	$28,195
% frosh need fully met	52
% ugrads need fully met	38
Average % of frosh need met	93
Average % of ugrad need met	93

WHITMAN COLLEGE

345 BOYER AVENUE, WALLA WALLA, WA 99362 • ADMISSIONS: 509-527-5176 • FAX: 509-527-4967

CAMPUS LIFE

Quality of Life Rating	99
Fire Safety Rating	81
Green Rating	90
Type of school	Private
Affiliation	No Affiliation
Environment	Town

STUDENTS

Total undergrad enrollment	1,525
% male/female	43/57
% from out of state	64
% frosh from public high school	68
% frosh live on campus	100
% ugrads live on campus	67
# of fraternities (% ugrad men join)	4 (26)
# of sororities (% ugrad women join)	4 (42)
% African American	1
% Asian	6
% Caucasian	72
% Hispanic	8
% Native American	1
% international	3
# of countries represented	25

SURVEY SAYS . . .

Lots of liberal students
Students are happy
Classroom facilities are great
Lab facilities are great
Career services are great
School is well run
No one cheats
Students are friendly
Diverse student types on campus
Students environmentally aware
Great off-campus food
Dorms are like palaces
Campus feels safe
Easy to get around campus
Athletic facilities are great
Intramural sports are popular
Active student government

ACADEMICS

Academic Rating	98
% students returning for sophomore year	94
% students graduating within 4 years	80
% students graduating within 6 years	88
Calendar	Semester
Student/faculty ratio	9:1
Profs interesting rating	98
Profs accessible rating	98
Most classes have 10–19 students.	
Most lab/discussion sessions have 20–29 students.	

MOST POPULAR MAJORS
biology; psychology; English language and literature

STUDENTS SAY ". . ."

Academics

If learning can be both rigorous and laid-back at the same time, it happens at Whitman College in Walla Walla, WA. The "challenging" academics here are coupled with a "relaxed attitude" in order to give students "the best education possible without sacrificing all the fun one expects of college." Populated mainly by "intelligent, ambitious liberals with far-reaching goals," this somewhat idealistic school seeks to build critical thinking skills through "an earnest discourse about 'life, the universe, and everything.'" So no one starts off with a blank slate, all first-year students are required to take a course referred to as "Encounters" which is a two semester introduction to the liberal arts and the academic construction of knowledge. Distribution requirements ensure that all students get a breadth of courses, and a lack of TAs ensures that they get all the attention they need. Although there's always a dud or two in the mix, professors are "genuinely brilliant and interesting people" and "love to spend time with students outside of class," whether it be for academic help or just conversation. "It is not uncommon to have potlucks, classes, or movie night over at your professor's house with your class," says one student.

On the administrative side of things, bureaucracy and red tape are kept to a minimum in this chill environment through "effortless use of the 'system'" and the administration gets raves all around for its devotion to "maintaining quality student life," which is something of a rarity. "I have never heard of *any* college being as supportive as this place has been to me in just the past two years," says a student. "Whitman's president gave me a ride to campus one semester after I met him at the airport," says another. As one can imagine, all these things come together to form a student body that's "happy, well-balanced, and well-cared-for."

Life

Most people stay on campus for their fun, "especially first-years," and throughout this "bubble" the "sense of closeness and comradeship is very evident through attendance at student-run concerts, art shows, etc." Everything is within ten minutes' walking distance. Academics take precedence for almost everyone, but "most students find time to party on the weekends," due to a "lenient and fair" alcohol policy. Thanks to the campus activities board, "there's almost always something fun going on, whether or not a person chooses to drink," such as Drive-In Movie Night and Casino Night. With "four beautiful seasons," outdoor activities are also very popular, thanks to "a great gear rental program that gets people outside hiking, biking, kayaking, and rock-climbing," and "Frisbees are everywhere when it's warm." In fact, there's so much going on "if someone says they are bored, students laugh and wish they could relate."

Student Body

It's a sociable bunch at Whitman, where most students "are interested in trying new things and meeting new people" and "everyone seems to have a weird interest or talent or passion." The quirky Whitties "usually have a strong opinion about *something*," and one freshman refers to her classmates as "cool nerds." Diversity has risen steadily over the past several years, as the school has made an effort to recruit beyond the typical "mid- to upper-class and white" contingent. Everyone here is pretty outdoorsy and environmentally aware ("to the point where you almost feel guilty for printing an assignment"), and a significant number of students have won fellowships and scholarships such as the Fulbright, Watson, Truman, and Udall."

FINANCIAL AID: 509-527-5178 • E-MAIL: ADMISSION@WHITMAN.EDU • WEBSITE: WWW.WHITMAN.EDU

THE PRINCETON REVIEW SAYS

Admissions

Very important factors considered include: Rigor of secondary school record, application essay, character/personal qualities. *Important factors considered include:* GPA, standardized test scores, extracurricular activities, racial/ethnic status, recommendation(s), talent/ability. *Other factors considered include:* Class rank, first generation, geographical residence, interview, state residency, volunteer work, work experience, alumni/ae relations, level of applicant's interest. SAT or ACT required; ACT with Writing component required. TOEFL required of all international applicants. *Academic units recommended:* 4 English; 4 mathematics; 3 science; (3 science lab); 2 social studies; 2 foreign language; 2 history.

Financial Aid

Students should submit: FAFSA, CSS/Financial Aid PROFILE, Noncustodial PROFILE. Regular filing deadline is 2/1. The Princeton Review suggests that all financial aid forms be submitted as soon as possible after January 1. *Need-based scholarships/grants offered:* Federal Pell, SEOG, State scholarships/grants, private scholarships, the school's own gift aid. *Loan aid offered:* Direct Subsidized Stafford Loans, Direct Unsubsidized Stafford Loans, Direct PLUS loans, Federal Perkins Loans. Applicants will be notified of awards beginning 4/1. Federal Work-Study Program available. Institutional employment available. Off-campus job opportunities are good.

The Inside Word

Whitman's admissions committee emphasizes essays and extracurriculars more than SAT scores. The college cares much more about who you are and what you have to offer if you enroll than it does about what your numbers will do for the freshman academic profile. Whitman is a mega-sleeper. Educators all over the country know it as an excellent institution, and the college's alums support it at one of the highest rates of giving at any college in the nation. Students seeking a top-quality liberal arts college owe it to themselves to take a look.

THE SCHOOL SAYS "..."

From the Admissions Office

"Located in historic Walla Walla only 45 minutes by air or 4 hours by car from Seattle in sunny Southeastern Washington State, Whitman College offers a combination of a rigorous academic environment that is collaborative; a down-to-earth Northwest culture; and a vibrant, engaging campus life. Whitman is also distinguished by the following:

- 9 to 1 student-faculty ratio
- Capstone written and oral assessments in one's major field of study
- Numerous winners of Ford Foundation, Fulbright, Goldwater, National Science Foundation, Rhodes, and Watson fellowships and scholarships
- Science departments that have been recognized by the National Science Foundation as among the top fifty colleges per capita
- State of the art facilities including a library, computer labs and a health center open 24/7
- An indoor climbing wall custom designed by Entre Prises Climbing Walls USA and made up of hundreds of imprint and freeform panels.
- An undergraduate research conference in which over 200 students present their original research to the Whitman community
- NCAA-DIII athletics with 8 varsity sports and more than 15 club sports, including alpine skiing, Ultimate Frisbee, and lacrosse.
- A nationally recognized Outdoor Program, with adventures open to all students.
- Semester in the West, an experiential, on-the-road study of economic, cultural and environmental issues
- An 88 percent graduation rate, a 65 percent graduate school rate, and a 50 percent study abroad rate
- A charming campus defined by historic buildings, streams, bridges, gardens, and close proximity to award-winning Main St. Walla Walla."

SELECTIVITY	
Admissions Rating	95
# of applicants	2,586
% of applicants accepted	57
% of acceptees attending	27
# offered a place on the wait list	446
% accepting a place on wait list	33
% admitted from wait list	0
# of early decision applicants	163
% accepted early decision	77

FRESHMAN PROFILE	
Range SAT Critical Reading	610–730
Range SAT Math	610–693
Range SAT Writing	608–700
Range ACT Composite	28–32
Minimum paper TOEFL	560
Minimum web-based TOEFL	220
Average HS GPA	3.74
% graduated top 10% of class	61
% graduated top 25% of class	84
% graduated top 50% of class	97

DEADLINES	
Early decision	
Deadline	11/15
Notification	12/21
Regular	
Priority	11/15
Deadline	1/15
Notification	3/29
Nonfall registration?	Yes

APPLICANTS ALSO LOOK AT AND OFTEN PREFER
Pomona College; Stanford University; Middlebury College; Carleton College

AND SOMETIMES PREFER
Colorado College; Macalester College

AND RARELY PREFER
University of Washington

FINANCIAL FACTS	
Financial Aid Rating	91
Annual tuition	$44,440
Room and board	$11,228
Required fees	$360
Books and supplies	$1,400
% needy frosh rec. need-based scholarship or grant aid	100
% needy UG rec. need-based scholarship or grant aid	100
% needy frosh rec. non-need-based scholarship or grant aid	36
% needy UG rec. non-need-based scholarship or grant aid	28
% needy frosh rec. need-based self-help aid	81
% needy UG rec. need-based self-help aid	84
% frosh rec. any financial aid	81
% UG rec. any financial aid	82
% UG borrow to pay for school	49
Average cumulative indebtedness	$17,114
% frosh need fully met	53
% ugrads need fully met	50
Average % of frosh need met	93
Average % of ugrad need met	96

WHITTIER COLLEGE

13406 PHILADELPHIA STREET, WHITTIER, CA 90608 • ADMISSIONS: 562-907-4238 • FAX: 562-907-4870

CAMPUS LIFE

Quality of Life Rating	71
Fire Safety Rating	86
Green Rating	68
Type of school	Private
Affiliation	No Affiliation
Environment	Suburban

STUDENTS

Total undergrad enrollment	1,695
% male/female	44/56
% from out of state	19
% frosh live on campus	74
% ugrads live on campus	51
# of fraternities (% ugrad men join)	4 (9)
# of sororities (% ugrad women join)	5 (13)
% African American	6
% Asian	11
% Caucasian	36
% Hispanic	38
% Native American	1
% international	3
# of countries represented	30

SURVEY SAYS . . .
Great library
Diverse student types on campus
Great off-campus food
Student publications are popular
Lots of beer drinking
Hard liquor is popular

ACADEMICS

Academic Rating	79
% students returning for sophomore year	82
% students graduating within 4 years	64
% students graduating within 6 years	67
Calendar	4/1/4
Student/faculty ratio	13:1
Profs interesting rating	82
Profs accessible rating	79
Most classes have 10–19 students.	
Most lab/discussion sessions have 10–19 students.	

MOST POPULAR MAJORS
business; psychology; kinesiology and nurtrition science

STUDENTS SAY ". . ."

Academics

At tiny Whittier College in California, there's a proud emphasis placed on the interconnectedness of all of the liberal arts disciplines. Students are challenged to learn things relevant to their field and "encouraged to take courses in seemingly unrelated fields and then make connections to see how they actually all relate." In being allowed "to pursue their educations in a comfortable and friendly environment," students enjoy how the school allows for a "strengthening of student integrity" by providing a tight-knit community. Professors are "all passionate about their subject material," and their understanding and flexibility are spoken of highly; although "a course [may be] geared to a particular subject, the professors make it a point to relate the discipline to others we may be interested in, too." "All of your professors will know you by name, and not by number, because you matter to them." Aside from being knowledgeable and sincere, faculty also help students to "pursue larger goals in life," and encourage students "to take their own initiative in developing their goals and future." Small class sizes (and an "amazing" range of classes) at Whittier provide students with the opportunity to ask questions and to receive personalized attention, and teachers "make you feel welcome and always informed." Academics are "challenging, but not...difficult to where it is impossible." Whittier also offers a January term to help students graduate on time [or] early, and there's free tutoring to help with homework and studies. Internships, work study, and leadership are all available starting as a freshman, and it's "easy to travel abroad." Basically, "if you utilize the resources available on campus, you can truly make your own experience."

Life

When schoolwork is done, busy Whittier students "do their best to promote their own strengths in extracurricular activities." This is a true California school at heart, and "you can always find students laying out on the quad soaking up the beautiful Southern California sun." "On sunny days (which is basically everyday), I have seen slip-n-slides on the quad." The whole town "is supportive of Whittier College," and "there are several unique mom-and-pop shops and eateries throughout Uptown, along with a movie theater," all within walking distance. Still, a lot of students get out of Whittier by driving to Los Angeles or the nearby beach, and "getting a Disneyland annual pass is very popular." In recent years, housing has been overcrowded, resulting in some busy cafeterias and creative living arrangements. On weekends, some "like to party at the houses off campus that certain students rent out," but for those who don't, there are a "lot of on-campus activities are offered in the evening." "The school does not revolve around the 'party scene' like other campuses, although one does exist if it's desired," says a student. Societies, intramurals, and clubs on campus "are constantly organizing events" though some commuter students who aren't able to participate in these events speak of feeling disconnected from the Whittier community.

Student Body

Predictably, there are a number of California natives at Whittier, but those from out-of-state find themselves happily adopted. Students here are extremely friendly and "mostly fit in with their types," but there's a fair amount of cross-pollination among the groups because "everyone sort of meets each other in all the different classes." Everyone at Whittier "has a niche," and for the most part, "everyone respects, as well as embraces, each others' uniqueness." The Division III school is athletically inclined, and a fair number of people play sports, though "it's not 'that' athletic of a student body."

FINANCIAL AID: 562-907-4285 • E-MAIL: ADMISSION@WHITTIER.EDU • WEBSITE: WWW.WHITTIER.EDU

THE PRINCETON REVIEW SAYS

Admissions

Very important factors considered include: Rigor of secondary school record, application essay, level of applicant's interest. *Important factors considered include:* GPA, standardized test scores, extracurricular activities, interview, recommendation(s), talent/ability, volunteer work, character/personal qualities. *Other factors considered include:* Class rank, first generation, geographical residence, racial/ethnic status, state residency, work experience, alumni/ae relations. SAT or ACT required; ACT with Writing component required. TOEFL required of all international applicants. *Academic units required:* 3 English; 2 mathematics; 1 science; (1 science lab); 1 social studies; 2 foreign language. *Academic units recommended:* 4 English; 3 mathematics; 2 science; 2 social studies; 3 foreign language.

Financial Aid

Students should submit: FAFSA. Regular filing deadline is 6/30. The Princeton Review suggests that all financial aid forms be submitted as soon as possible after January 1. *Need-based scholarships/grants offered:* Federal Pell, SEOG, State scholarships/grants, private scholarships, the school's own gift aid. *Loan aid offered:* Direct Subsidized Stafford Loans, Direct Unsubsidized Stafford Loans, Direct PLUS loans, Federal Perkins Loans. Federal Work-Study Program available. Off-campus job opportunities are good.

The Inside Word

Whittier is looking for well-rounded students, and so activities and recommendations are just as important as scores and grades—the admissions office hates to focus just on numbers. Though 65 percent of students hail from California, no preference is given to state of origin. Through the Whittier Scholars program, students may construct a personalized major that fits academic and career goals.

THE SCHOOL SAYS "..."

From the Admissions Office

"Faculty and students at Whittier share a love of learning and delight in the life of the mind. They join in understanding the value of the intellectual quest, the use of reason, and a respect for values. They seek knowledge of their own culture and the informed appreciation of other traditions, and they explore the interrelatedness of knowledge and the connections among disciplines. An extraordinary community emerges from teachers and students representing a variety of academic pursuits, individuals who have come together at Whittier in the belief that study within the liberal arts forms the best foundation for rewarding endeavor throughout a lifetime.

"Whittier College is a vibrant, residential, four-year liberal arts institution where intellectual inquiry and experiential learning are fostered in a community that promotes respect for diversity of thought and culture. A Whittier College education produces enthusiastic, independent thinkers who flourish in graduate studies, the evolving global workplace, and life."

SELECTIVITY
Admissions Rating	78
# of applicants	4,380
% of applicants accepted	63
% of acceptees attending	16

FRESHMAN PROFILE
Range SAT Critical Reading	460–570
Range SAT Math	470–580
Range SAT Writing	470–580
Range ACT Composite	20–25
Minimum paper TOEFL	550
Minimum web-based TOEFL	230
Average HS GPA	3.47
% graduated top 10% of class	23
% graduated top 25% of class	44
% graduated top 50% of class	89

DEADLINES
Early action	
Deadline	11/15
Notification	12/30
Regular	
Priority	2/1
Nonfall registration?	Yes

APPLICANTS ALSO LOOK AT AND OFTEN PREFER
University of Redlands; Occidental College

AND SOMETIMES PREFER
Loyola Marymount University; Pitzer College

AND RARELY PREFER
Chapman University; Claremont McKenna College

FINANCIAL FACTS
Financial Aid Rating	75
Annual tuition	$41,246
Room and board	$12,046
Required fees	$665
Books and supplies	$650
% needy frosh rec. need-based scholarship or grant aid	91
% needy UG rec. need-based scholarship or grant aid	92
% needy frosh rec. non-need-based scholarship or grant aid	8
% needy UG rec. non-need-based scholarship or grant aid	8
% needy frosh rec. need-based self-help aid	85
% needy UG rec. need-based self-help aid	87
% frosh rec. any financial aid	92
% UG rec. any financial aid	89
% UG borrow to pay for school	74
Average cumulative indebtedness	$27,752
% frosh need fully met	12
% ugrads need fully met	11
Average % of frosh need met	72
Average % of ugrad need met	72

WILLAMETTE UNIVERSITY

900 STATE STREET, SALEM, OR 97301 • ADMISSIONS: 503-370-6303 • FAX: 503-375-5363

CAMPUS LIFE

Quality of Life Rating	89
Fire Safety Rating	97
Green Rating	98
Type of school	Private
Affiliation	Methodist
Environment	City

STUDENTS

Total undergrad enrollment	1,970
% male/female	44/56
% from out of state	72
% frosh from public high school	77
% frosh live on campus	95
% ugrads live on campus	66
# of fraternities (% ugrad men join)	4 (27)
# of sororities (% ugrad women join)	3 (28)
% African American	2
% Asian	7
% Caucasian	63
% Hispanic	10
% Native American	2
% international	1
# of countries represented	41

SURVEY SAYS . . .

Students are happy
Lab facilities are great
Students are friendly
Students environmentally aware
Easy to get around campus
Intramural sports are popular

ACADEMICS

Academic Rating	95
% students returning for sophomore year	86
% students graduating within 4 years	71
% students graduating within 6 years	78
Calendar	Semester
Student/faculty ratio	11:1
Profs interesting rating	94
Profs accessible rating	91

Most classes have 10–19 students.
Most lab/discussion sessions have
10–19 students.

MOST POPULAR MAJORS
biology; economics; psychology

STUDENTS SAY "..."

Academics

Traditional academics are strong at Willamette, but perhaps what stands out most is that "learning opportunities outside of the classroom are endless." Located right across the street from the Oregon state capitol, there are countless "leadership opportunities and student research opportunities." Professors here are "very willing to help students find internships, jobs and research opportunities." In the classroom, those same professors are "incredible resources" who "are all very dedicated to their classes rather than research or outside obligations," and who provide classes that "are interesting and varied." You will be challenged, but only with the goal of helping you succeed. As one student notes, "I have felt intellectually pushed outside my comfort zone while still being incredibly supported in all of my academic classes." Another noticed that "my professors are not looking to fail me or weed me out of classes; they just believe in me, and want me to excel." These educators "make their material relevant" and tend to be "passionate about their subject." Classes are "often discussion-based, not lecture-based, so students are not just regurgitating information they hear from a professor, but working with the material and exploring their own thoughts and ideas." Overall, the environment here "encourages growth and development, both inside and outside the classroom," which one student says is "unique to a small Liberal Arts school."

Life

"Lots of intellectual discussions," a thriving Greek life, pursuing "social justice" and "social causes," and just plain being busy are the core of life at Willamette. On this campus, "there is a lot of emphasis on how to make an impact on the community and the school as a whole." Indeed, "students are involved in a variety of organizations on campus and off that concern these types of issues," which is not difficult given the school's close proximity to Oregon's seat of government. Students here "often think about politics, civic duties, and volunteering," filling their time with "philanthropic events, house parties, or outdoor trips." This isn't limited to a minority of students, either. "Very few students only attend class; most have three or more activities they are involved in." Less intellectual pursuits are within range, though may be something of a drive. Portland and all its quirky culture (not to mention its thriving craft beer scene) is a close forty minutes away, while the Oregon coast and Mount Hood are about two hours away. But students don't need to venture far. "There is so much to see and do in the Willamette Valley that students have opportunities to do pretty much anything."

Student Body

Give the nature of life on campus, it should come as no surprise that "a typical Willamette student is excited to learn, to explore, and be an active participant within the community." Students here are "interested in helping others through academic tutoring and community service," a group who tend to be "accepting, politically involved, and civic minded." Individuals vary—"students embrace the idea of being unique and proud of it"—but almost all are "academically driven, balanced with social endeavors, and eager to mix in with other students." Most are "from the West Coast," "friendly and open," and, of course, very busy. "Almost all students are involved in multiple things." This common need to be doing things ensures students "share a friendliness that's evident the moment you step onto campus." As one student notes, to get the most out of Willamette, "you have to be willing to challenge yourselves and others, and be accepting of the community are a part of."

FINANCIAL AID: 503-370-6273 • E-MAIL: LIBARTS@WILLAMETTE.EDU • WEBSITE: WWW.WILLAMETTE.EDU

THE PRINCETON REVIEW SAYS

Admissions

Very important factors considered include: Class rank, GPA, rigor of secondary school record, standardized test scores, application essay. *Important factors considered include:* Interview, recommendation(s). *Other factors considered include:* extracurricular activities, first generation, geographical residence, racial/ethnic status, talent/ability, alumni/ae relations, character/personal qualities. SAT or ACT required; ACT with Writing component required. TOEFL required of all international applicants. *Academic units recommended:* 4 English; 4 mathematics; 3 science; (3 science lab); 1 social studies; 4 foreign language; 2 history; 2 academic electives.

Financial Aid

Students should submit: FAFSA. The Princeton Review suggests that all financial aid forms be submitted as soon as possible after January 1. *Need-based scholarships/grants offered:* Federal Pell, SEOG, State scholarships/grants, private scholarships, the school's own gift aid. *Loan aid offered:* Direct Subsidized Stafford Loans, Direct Unsubsidized Stafford Loans, Direct PLUS loans, Federal Perkins Loans. Federal Work-Study Program available. Institutional employment available. Off-campus job opportunities are excellent.

The Inside Word

Your academic record will play the biggest part when being evaluated as a prospective student, especially the rigor of your high school coursework, grade trends, and naturally, your grades themselves. An inconsistent high school performance will be seen unfavorably by admissions officers. Unsurprisingly, a record of community service and strong extracurricular activities will greatly enhance your application in the eyes of Willamette admissions officers, who look to see a habit of participation in something beyond the classroom in their students.

THE SCHOOL SAYS "..."

From the Admissions Office

"Willamette University is a place where talented faculty inspire students to examine issues critically, think creatively and act effectively. By leveraging our collaborative community and location in the Pacific Northwest, we challenge students to transform knowledge into action — the foundation of a successful career and a meaningful life."

"With a student-faculty ratio of 11:1, Willamette students can easily find a mentor. Eleven of the 24 Oregon Professors of the Year since 1990 are from Willamette — a record unmatched by any other school in the state."

"With the Oregon State Capitol located across the street, Willamette offers unparalleled access to state government — and numerous chances to explore and implement ideas through research and internships alongside policymakers and the state's top scientists and economists."

"Willamette's 305-acre Zena Forest and Farm provide unique outdoor classrooms and laboratories where students can perform scientific research, run an organic food farm, or find inspiration for their music and art. Willamette is also co-located with Tokyo International University of America, creating numerous chances to explore international culture through social, language and living exchanges."

"Our graduates go on to impressive careers and lives of achievement and meaning. Among Willamette's alumni are a Nobel Prize-winning economist, corporate presidents and CEOs, nationally recognized artists, 15 Oregon Supreme Court justices and numerous Fulbright Grant-winners."

SELECTIVITY

Admissions Rating	92
# of applicants	8,109
% of applicants accepted	58
% of acceptees attending	12
# offered a place on the wait list	48
% accepting a place on wait list	100
% admitted from wait list	17

FRESHMAN PROFILE

Range SAT Critical Reading	540–660
Range SAT Math	540–650
Range SAT Writing	535–640
Range ACT Composite	24–29
Minimum paper TOEFL	550
Minimum web-based TOEFL	213
Average HS GPA	3.69
% graduated top 10% of class	41
% graduated top 25% of class	75
% graduated top 50% of class	94

DEADLINES

Regular	
Priority	2/1
Nonfall registration?	Yes

APPLICANTS ALSO LOOK AT AND OFTEN PREFER
Whitman College

AND SOMETIMES PREFER
University of Puget Sound; Lewis & Clark College; University of Washington; Colorado College; Santa Clara University; Occidental College

AND RARELY PREFER
University of Oregon

FINANCIAL FACTS

Financial Aid Rating	89
Annual tuition	$41,990
Room and board	$10,380
Required fees	$315
Books and supplies	$950
% needy frosh rec. need-based scholarship or grant aid	99
% needy UG rec. need-based scholarship or grant aid	99
% needy frosh rec. non-need-based scholarship or grant aid	32
% needy UG rec. non-need-based scholarship or grant aid	18
% needy frosh rec. need-based self-help aid	81
% needy UG rec. need-based self-help aid	81
% frosh rec. any financial aid	
% UG rec. any financial aid	
% UG borrow to pay for school	64
Average cumulative indebtedness	$28,849
% frosh need fully met	38
% ugrads need fully met	39
Average % of frosh need met	86
Average % of ugrad need met	86

WILLIAM JEWELL COLLEGE

500 COLLEGE HILL, LIBERTY, MO 64068 • ADMISSIONS: 816-781-7700 • FAX: 816-415-5040

CAMPUS LIFE

Quality of Life Rating	88
Fire Safety Rating	81
Green Rating	62
Type of school	Private
Environment	Suburban

STUDENTS

Total undergrad enrollment	1,043
% male/female	43/57
% from out of state	38
% frosh from public high school	90
% frosh live on campus	98
% ugrads live on campus	83
# of fraternities (% ugrad men join)	3 (31)
# of sororities (% ugrad women join)	4 (31)
% African American	6
% Asian	1
% Caucasian	78
% Hispanic	4
% Native American	1
% international	3
# of countries represented	19

SURVEY SAYS . . .

Students are happy
Students are friendly
Students get along with local community
Students love Liberty, MO
Frats and sororities are popular

ACADEMICS

Academic Rating	89
% students returning for sophomore year	77
% students graduating within 4 years	50
% students graduating within 6 years	59
Calendar	Semester
Student/faculty ratio	10:1
Profs interesting rating	93
Profs accessible rating	90

Most classes have fewer than 10 students.
Most lab/discussion sessions have
 10–19 students.

MOST POPULAR MAJORS

nursing; biology; business administration
and management

STUDENTS SAY "..."

Academics

The minute students step onto campus at William Jewell, they are welcomed into an "amazing community" replete with "top-notch academics." As one senior gushes, "Everyone on campus makes you feel at home and the faculty and staff are some of the most genuine people you will ever meet." Moreover, as small liberal arts college, William Jewell "provides a superb education" that many undergrads here feel is "unmatched in the Midwest." After all, the college endeavors to transform undergrads into "critical thinkers" who are bound to achieve "success and find [their] passion." This is no doubt due in large part to the fact that "William Jewell provides a well-rounded education for its students and challenges them to step outside of their own perspectives." Though the college has many fantastic majors from which to choose, undergrads are especially quick to highlight "the strong science and pre-med program" along with the "well established" non-profit program. The nursing program also has a "great reputation." On the whole, undergrads speak very highly of their "amazingly dedicated" professors. Impressively, teachers here tend to be "great lecturers...who [also] excel in discussion formatted classes." Another senior adds, "The professors at William Jewell are very personable and willing to go the extra step to build a connection with each and every student. They are always finding the best way to reach out to their students and provide each student with the best chance of success." Overall, William Jewell offers a "rigorous set of programs that push you to the limits of your ability."

Life

Students here agree that "life at Jewell is a busy one." As one knowledgeable senior happily shares, "There are always campus activities going on whether that be sporting events or resident hall gatherings or even the occasional fraternity/sorority party." A junior specifies, "Student organizations often sponsors events like CU-At-the-Movies, Skate Night [and] Bowling Night where we get discounted prices to go out and have fun. We also play 'Gotcha!' (an assassin game), on campus every year and Browning Hall is playing Humans vs. Zombies this year." Additionally, "a number of students...are active in Greek life." Fortunately, we're assured that there's no pressure to join and independent students still feel included. Undergrads here also love to take advantage of the "Harriman-Jewell series [which] offers free tickets to students, and brings world-class arts and culture such as pianists (Emanuel Ax) and dance (Mark Morris Dance Group) to Kansas City." Speaking of KC, William Jewell is only a "twenty-minute drive away" from the heart of the city. As another senior brags, "Once downtown you can do just about anything. There is the Power & Light District with the Sprint Center, the Kaufman Center and just a few miles south you get into Westport where you can find numerous college/young adult students at any given time."

Student Body

Undergrads at William Jewell are a "laid back but focused" lot. Indeed, students are quick to define their peers as "driven" and "intelligent" people who are "committed to their education and community." Of course, some see the typical Jewell student as "a white, Protestant, upper-middle class, girl who loves Pinterest." Although a junior cautions that, "the population isn't as diverse as other schools I have been to," he also counters that, "everyone is pretty open and accepting of just about anyone." Fortunately, many find that "students fit in very easily." Overall, "no one really is ever left out of anything as long as they're putting the effort in to have friends and be a part of an organization as well as the Jewell community as a whole." Another junior adds that, "While most [undergrads] attend college straight out of high school, there is a growing number of non-traditional students especially in the nursing program." Finally, as one satisfied political science student succinctly states, "We have a high retention rate which tells me that students fit in well."

FINANCIAL AID: 816-415-5975 • E-MAIL: ADMISSION@WILLIAM.JEWELL.EDU • WEBSITE: WWW.JEWELL.EDU

THE PRINCETON REVIEW SAYS

Admissions

Very important factors considered include: Rigor of secondary school record. *Important factors considered include:* Class rank, GPA, standardized test scores, recommendation(s). *Other factors considered include:* Application essay, extra-curricular activities, first generation, interview, talent/ability, volunteer work, work experience, alumni/ae relations, character/personal qualities. SAT or ACT required; ACT with Writing component recommended. TOEFL required of all international applicants. *Academic units required:* 4 English; 3 mathematics; 3 science; (1 science lab); 3 social studies; 2 foreign language. *Academic units recommended:* 4 English; 4 mathematics; 3 science; (1 science lab); 3 social studies; 3 foreign language; 2 academic electives.

Financial Aid

Students should submit: FAFSA. The Princeton Review suggests that all financial aid forms be submitted as soon as possible after January 1. *Need-based scholarships/grants offered:* Federal Pell, SEOG, State scholarships/grants, the school's own gift aid. *Loan aid offered:* Federal Perkins Loans, Federal Nursing Loans. Federal Work-Study Program available. Institutional employment available. Off-campus job opportunities are excellent.

The Inside Word

Competition for admission is strong and candidates must demonstrate success with a rigorous course load. Of course, similar to most small colleges, Jewell is also looking for applicants who will complement the campus. Therefore, you can be assured that personal statements and recommendations will be closely assessed.

THE SCHOOL SAYS "..."

From the Admissions Office

"William Jewell College is committed to bringing together talented students and gifted faculty mentors within a vibrant community sparked by a rigorous and intentional liberal arts curriculum. A full range of personal and professional development experiences are presented by the selective national liberal arts college's location within the Kansas City metroplex of more than two million. The William Jewell College experience focuses on enhancing the student's ability to apply learning to complex ethical, scientific and cultural problems. The college places a high value on experiential learning and gives students the opportunity to 'live what they learn.' By completing the college's thirty-eight-hour liberal arts core plus three applied learning experiences, Jewell students can receive a second major in Applied Critical Thought and Inquiry. This means that all students can graduate with double majors and some with triple majors. The internationally recognized Oxbridge Honors Program combines British tutorial methods of instruction with opportunities for a year of study in Oxford or Cambridge. It is the only program of its kind in the nation. Jewell's undergraduate Nonprofit Leadership major is one of only thirteen nationwide and ranks among the top three in academic rigor. The Pryor Leadership Studies Program includes course work, community service projects and internships that help students enhance their leadership skills in a variety of settings. William Jewell students graduate equipped with deep content knowledge in their major(s), a host of social and real-world experiences, personal maturity and the intellectual habits of mind for success in a world of change and challenge."

SELECTIVITY

Admissions Rating	87
# of applicants	1,433
% of applicants accepted	58
% of acceptees attending	31

FRESHMAN PROFILE

Range SAT Critical Reading	498–670
Range SAT Math	510–645
Range ACT Composite	22–28
Minimum paper TOEFL	550
Minimum web-based TOEFL	213
Average HS GPA	3.69
% graduated top 10% of class	23
% graduated top 25% of class	58
% graduated top 50% of class	90

DEADLINES

Regular	
Priority	12/1
Deadline	8/15
Nonfall registration?	Yes

APPLICANTS ALSO LOOK AT AND OFTEN PREFER
University of Missouri

AND RARELY PREFER
Northwest Missouri State University

FINANCIAL FACTS

Financial Aid Rating	75
Annual tuition	$31,420
Room and board	$8,410
Books and supplies	$1,200
% needy frosh rec. need-based scholarship or grant aid	100
% needy UG rec. need-based scholarship or grant aid	94
% needy frosh rec. non-need-based scholarship or grant aid	100
% needy UG rec. non-need-based scholarship or grant aid	93
% needy frosh rec. need-based self-help aid	77
% needy UG rec. need-based self-help aid	79
% frosh rec. any financial aid	99
% UG rec. any financial aid	97
% UG borrow to pay for school	68
Average cumulative indebtedness	$29,178
% frosh need fully met	20
% ugrads need fully met	21
Average % of frosh need met	78
Average % of ugrad need met	79

WILLIAMS COLLEGE

PO Box 487, Williamstown, MA 01267 • Admissions: 413-597-2211 • Fax: 413-597-4052

STUDENTS SAY ". . ."

Academics

Williams College is a small bastion of the liberal arts "with a fantastic academic reputation." "Williams students tend to spend a lot of time complaining about how much work they have" but they say the academic experience is "absolutely incomparable." Classes are "small" and "intense." "The facilities are absolutely top-notch in almost everything." Research opportunities are plentiful. A one-month January term offers study abroad programs and a host of short pass/fail courses that are "a college student's dream come true." "The hard science departments are incredible." Economics, art history, and English are equally outstanding. Despite the occasional professor "who should not even be teaching at the high school level," the faculty at Williams is one of the best. Most professors "jump at every opportunity to help you love their subject." "They're here because they want to interact with undergrads." "If you complain about a Williams education then you would complain about education anywhere," wagers an economics major.

Life

Students at Williams enjoy a "stunning campus." "The Berkshire mountains are in the background every day as you walk to class" and opportunities for outdoor activity are numerous. The location is in "the boonies," though, and the surrounding "one-horse college town" is "quaint" at best. "There is no nearby place to buy necessities that is not ridiculously overpriced." Student life happens almost exclusively on campus. Dorm rooms are "large" and "well above par" but the housing system is "very weird." While some students like it, there is a general consensus that its creators "should be slapped and sent back to Amherst." Entertainment options include "lots of" performances, plays, and lectures. Some students are "obsessed with a capella groups." Intramurals are popular, especially broomball ("a sacred tradition involving a hockey rink, sneakers, a rubber ball, and paddles"). Intercollegiate sports are "a huge part of the social scene." For many students, the various varsity teams "are the basic social blocks at Williams." "Everyone for the most part gets along, but the sports teams seem to band together," explains a sophomore. Booze-laden parties" "and general disorder on weekends" are common. "A lot of people spend their lives between homework and practice and then just get completely smashed on weekends." Nothing gets out of hand, though. "We know how to unwind without being stupid," says a sophomore.

Student Body

The student population at Williams is not the most humble. They describe their peers as "interesting and beautiful" "geniuses of varying interests." They're "quirky, passionate, zany, and fun." They're "athletically awesome." They're "freakishly unique" and at the same time "cookie-cutter amazing." Ethnic diversity is stellar and you'll find all kinds of students including "the goth students," "nerdier students," "a ladle of environmentally conscious pseudo-vegetarians," and a few "west coast hippies." However, "a typical student looks like a rich white kid" who grew up "playing field hockey just outside Boston" and spends summers "vacationing on the Cape." Sporty students abound. "There definitely is segregation between the artsy kids and the athlete types but there is also a significant amount of crossover." "Williams is a place where normal social labels tend not to apply," reports a junior. "Everyone here got in for a reason. So that football player in your theater class has amazing insight on Chekhov and that outspoken environmental activist also specializes in improv comedy."

FINANCIAL AID: 413-597-4181 • E-MAIL: ADMISSION@WILLIAMS.EDU • WEBSITE: WWW.WILLIAMS.EDU

THE PRINCETON REVIEW SAYS

Admissions

Very important factors considered include: Class rank, GPA, rigor of secondary school record, standardized test scores, recommendation(s), talent/ability. *Important factors considered include:* Application essay, extracurricular activities, first generation, racial/ethnic status, alumni/ae relations, character/personal qualities. *Other factors considered include:* Geographical residence, volunteer work, work experience. SAT or ACT required; ACT with Writing component required. *Academic units recommended:* 4 English; 4 mathematics; 4 science; (3 science lab); 4 social studies; 4 foreign language.

Financial Aid

Students should submit: FAFSA, CSS/Financial Aid PROFILE, Noncustodial PROFILE. Regular filing deadline is 2/1. The Princeton Review suggests that all financial aid forms be submitted as soon as possible after January 1. *Need-based scholarships/grants offered:* Federal Pell, SEOG, State scholarships/grants, private scholarships, the school's own gift aid. *Loan aid offered:* Direct Subsidized Stafford Loans, Direct Unsubsidized Stafford Loans, Direct PLUS loans, Federal Perkins Loans, College/university loans from institutional funds. Applicants will be notified of awards beginning 4/1. Federal Work-Study Program available. Institutional employment available.

The Inside Word

As is typical of highly selective colleges, at Williams high grades and test scores work more as qualifiers than to determine admissibility. Beyond a strong record of achievement, evidence of intellectual curiosity, noteworthy non-academic talents, and a non-college family background are some aspects of a candidate's application that might make for an offer of admission. But there are no guarantees—the evaluation process here is rigorous. The admissions committee (the entire admissions staff) discusses each candidate in comparison to the entire applicant pool. The pool is divided alphabetically for individual reading; after weak candidates are eliminated, those who remain undergo additional evaluations by different members of the staff. Admission decisions must be confirmed by the agreement of a plurality of the committee. Such close scrutiny demands a well-prepared candidate and application.

THE SCHOOL SAYS "..."

From the Admissions Office

"Special course offerings at Williams include Oxford-style tutorials, where students (in teams of two) research and defend ideas, engaging in weekly debate with a faculty tutor. Half of Williams' students pursue study abroad at some point, with about thirty students annually spending at year at Oxford. Four weeks of winter study each January provide time for individualized projects, research, and novel fields of study. Students compete in thirty-two Division III athletic teams, perform in twenty-five musical groups, stage ten theatrical productions, and volunteer in thirty service organizations. The college receives several million dollars annually for undergraduate science research and equipment. The town offers two distinguished art museums, the Williams College Museum of Art and the Clark Art Institute, and 2,200 forest acres—complete with a treetop canopy walkway—for environmental research and recreation.

"Students are required to submit either the SAT or the ACT including the optional writing section. Applicants should also submit scores from any two SAT Subject Tests. To limit the debt obligations of its graduates, Williams maintains one of the lowest loan expectations of any college or university in the country. Often the aid packages of students whose families demonstrate high financial need are made up entirely of grants and a campus job—and do not include any loans."

SELECTIVITY

Admissions Rating	99
# of applicants	6,853
% of applicants accepted	18
% of acceptees attending	45
# offered a place on the wait list	1,227
% accepting a place on wait list	28
% admitted from wait list	13
# of early decision applicants	617
% accepted early decision	40

FRESHMAN PROFILE

Range SAT Critical Reading	670–770
Range SAT Math	660–770
Range SAT Writing	690–780
Range ACT Composite	30–34
% graduated top 10% of class	88
% graduated top 25% of class	98
% graduated top 50% of class	100

DEADLINES

Early decision	
Deadline	11/10
Notification	12/15
Regular	
Deadline	1/1
Nonfall registration?	No

APPLICANTS ALSO LOOK AT AND OFTEN PREFER

Harvard College; Yale University; Princeton University

AND SOMETIMES PREFER

Amherst College

AND RARELY PREFER

The University of Chicago; Middlebury College

FINANCIAL FACTS

Financial Aid Rating	90
Books and supplies	$800
% needy frosh rec. need-based scholarship or grant aid	99
% needy UG rec. need-based scholarship or grant aid	99
% needy frosh rec. non-need-based scholarship or grant aid	0
% needy UG rec. non-need-based scholarship or grant aid	0
% needy frosh rec. need-based self-help aid	100
% needy UG rec. need-based self-help aid	100
% frosh rec. any financial aid	49
% UG rec. any financial aid	52
% UG borrow to pay for school	29
Average cumulative indebtedness	$12,474
% frosh need fully met	100
% ugrads need fully met	100
Average % of frosh need met	100
Average % of ugrad need met	100

WITTENBERG UNIVERSITY

PO BOX 720, SPRINGFIELD, OH 45501 • ADMISSIONS: 937-327-6314 • FAX: 937-327-6379

CAMPUS LIFE

Quality of Life Rating	78
Fire Safety Rating	96
Green Rating	83
Type of school	Private
Affiliation	Lutheran
Environment	Town

STUDENTS

Total undergrad enrollment	1,776
% male/female	44/56
% from out of state	29
% frosh from public high school	80
% frosh live on campus	94
% ugrads live on campus	84
# of fraternities (% ugrad men join)	6 (25)
# of sororities (% ugrad women join)	5 (35)
% African American	8
% Asian	1
% Caucasian	92
% Hispanic	3
% Native American	<1
% international	2
# of countries represented	26

SURVEY SAYS . . .

Students are happy
Lab facilities are great
Students are friendly
Lots of beer drinking

ACADEMICS

Academic Rating	84
% students returning for sophomore year	74
% students graduating within 4 years	56
% students graduating within 6 years	63
Calendar	Semester
Student/faculty ratio	12:1
Profs interesting rating	94
Profs accessible rating	96

Most classes have 10–19 students.
Most lab/discussion sessions have
10–19 students.

MOST POPULAR MAJORS
business/commerce; biology; psychology

STUDENTS SAY " . . ."

Academics

Located in Springfield, Ohio, Wittenberg combines a "small school atmosphere" with "a wide horizon of learning opportunities." The school offers "high academic standards and a dedication to research" that makes "an environment where students can excel in the classroom and out." This "friendly, athletic campus" "offers a close-knit community where professors and students build professional and personal relationships." The school's motto is "Having Light, We Pass It On To Others." This is taken seriously by the "extremely engaging" professors who are "committed to helping students both in and out of the classroom." The "fabulous" teachers at Wittenberg are "always accessible and willing to help" and really get to know students "on a personal level." "I feel like I am learning from my best friends," one happy student reports. An Environmental Science student agrees, saying, "I have become very close to a few of my professors and have really come to enjoy my classroom experience." Some students say that "communication with the student body" and "upper level administration" "is not always the best." Still, a Communications major lavishes praise on the entire staff, "not only just teachers, but I would go as far to say even down to the maintenance and janitor crew." Part of the reason students love classes at Wittenberg is the small class sizes. This "means excellent attention paid to students." "The class sizes and student-teacher ratio makes it an ideal place to develop professional relationships" and these relationships "really elevates the learning environment and makes classes far more interesting than large schools." The "open-minded and encouraging" faculty really pushes "students to build our own ideas and projects." All in all, "the people, the faculty and students are very happy, connected, and welcoming community." This, combined with the "gorgeous campus" might explain the "high morale among the students." As a Psychology major explains, "Wittenberg is a place where students can develop themselves as a whole person—academically, professionally, and socially."

Life

Students are typically busy and even "often over-involved" at Wittenberg. Your average student might be "involved and overcommitted in at least 2 clubs and a sport or Greek life." "With over 100 student clubs and organizations, it is easy to find things to get involved in," one student explains. "Witt students generally know how to work hard and play hard" and "party every day." One student says that partying is so pervasive that "if you do not drink then you have no chance of fitting in." "The typical student is one who drinks constantly, and rarely ever gets in trouble for it," since, students say, the University is lax on enforcing drug and alcohol rules. Still, there are plenty of other activities to do on campus from "just hang[ing] out and spend[ing] time with each other" to "Witt Wednesday" in which "comedians or musicians come to entertain." "What don't we do?" one student says. One quirky, or even "downright surreal" part of campus life has to do with the crows. "Our crow-deterrent alarms, which are mounted on the roofs of every building, are triggered by students walking by," one student explains. "It's downright uncanny at night to hear crow death screams played from the rooftops as you walk back to your dorm." Students who love nature will enjoy "a reservoir to swim in, 2 playground/parks, and 3 national parks for hiking."

Student Body

This "beautiful school" is filled with "friendly," "outgoing," and "quirky people." "It is hard to describe a typical student because we are very diverse, but with that diversity we all are able to get in," an Environmental Science student says. If you had to generalize, most students are "white, from Ohio, [and] middle class," but "Wittenberg has a wonderful variety of students." Students tend to be "fun personalities, engaged, curious and eager to learn, smart." "All types of students here are welcomed in with ease" and everyone can "find at least one friend group." One student elaborates that these groups "are like amoebas that are constantly shifting, made up of many different people." Overall Wittenberg is a "tight-knit community" where all you have to do to make a friend is "step out and say hello!"

FINANCIAL AID: 937-327-7321 • E-MAIL: ADMISSION@WITTENBERG.EDU • WEBSITE: WWW.WITTENBERG.EDU

THE PRINCETON REVIEW SAYS

Admissions

Very important factors considered include: Class rank, GPA, rigor of secondary school record. *Important factors considered include:* Application essay, extracurricular activities, recommendation(s), talent/ability, volunteer work, character/personal qualities. *Other factors considered include:* Standardized test scores, first generation, interview, work experience, alumni/ae relations. SAT or ACT considered if submitted; ACT with or without Writing component accepted. TOEFL required of all international applicants. *Academic units required:* 4 English; 3 mathematics; 3 science; (2 science lab); 2 foreign language; 2 history. *Academic units recommended:* 4 English; 4 mathematics; 5 science; (2 science lab); 3 foreign language; 3 history.

Financial Aid

Students should submit: FAFSA. The Princeton Review suggests that all financial aid forms be submitted as soon as possible after January 1. *Need-based scholarships/grants offered:* Federal Pell, SEOG, State scholarships/grants, private scholarships, the school's own gift aid, United Negro College Fund. *Loan aid offered:* Direct Subsidized Stafford Loans, Direct Unsubsidized Stafford Loans, Direct PLUS loans, Federal Perkins Loans, College/university loans from institutional funds. Federal Work-Study Program available. Institutional employment available. Off-campus job opportunities are excellent.

The Inside Word

Wittenberg accepts both its own application and the common application, and the application fee is waived if you apply online. The university only requires a short personal statement instead of the traditional formal essay. Wittenberg has a fairly high acceptance rate, but students will still want to make sure all parts of their application are the best they can be.

THE SCHOOL SAYS ". . ."

From the Admissions Office

"At Wittenberg, you will experience an active and engaged learning environment, a setting where you can refine your definition of self yet gain exposure to the varied kinds of knowledge, people, views, activities, options, and ideas that add richness to our lives. Wittenberg is a university where students are able to thrive in a small campus environment with many opportunities for intellectual and personal growth in and out of the classroom. Campus life is as diverse as the interests of our students. Wittenberg attracts students from all over the United States and from many other countries. Historically, the university has been committed to geographical, educational, cultural, and religious diversity. With their varied backgrounds and interests, Wittenberg students have helped initiate many of the more than 125 student organizations that are active on campus. The students will be the first to tell you there's never a lack of things to do on or near the campus any day of the week, if you're willing to get involved.

"Wittenberg University is test score optional. Freshman applicants can choose to submit either ACT (with or without writing component) or SAT scores."

SELECTIVITY

Admissions Rating	73
# of applicants	5,160
% of applicants accepted	89
% of acceptees attending	12
# of early decision applicants	181
% accepted early decision	84

FRESHMAN PROFILE

Range SAT Critical Reading	520–620
Range SAT Math	520–620
Range ACT Composite	23–25
Minimum paper TOEFL	550
Average HS GPA	3.43
% graduated top 10% of class	22
% graduated top 25% of class	49
% graduated top 50% of class	81

DEADLINES

Early decision	
Deadline	11/15
Notification	12/15
Early action	
Deadline	12/1
Notification	1/1
Regular	
Priority	3/15
Nonfall registration?	Yes

APPLICANTS ALSO LOOK AT AND OFTEN PREFER

Miami University; Ohio Wesleyan University; The Ohio State University—Columbus; The College of Wooster Denison University; Ohio University-Athens

AND SOMETIMES PREFER

Capital University

FINANCIAL FACTS

Financial Aid Rating	86
Annual tuition	$37,230
Room and board	$9,932
Required fees	$800
Books and supplies	$1,000
% needy frosh rec. need-based scholarship or grant aid	100
% needy UG rec. need-based scholarship or grant aid	99
% needy frosh rec. non-need-based scholarship or grant aid	0
% needy UG rec. non-need-based scholarship or grant aid	0
% needy frosh rec. need-based self-help aid	95
% needy UG rec. need-based self-help aid	94
% frosh rec. any financial aid	100
% UG rec. any financial aid	99
% UG borrow to pay for school	69
Average cumulative indebtedness	$30,748
% frosh need fully met	27
% ugrads need fully met	28
Average % of frosh need met	83
Average % of ugrad need met	83

WOFFORD COLLEGE

429 North Church Street, Spartanburg, SC 29303-3663 • Admissions: 864-597-4130 • Fax: 864-597-4147

CAMPUS LIFE

Quality of Life Rating	85
Fire Safety Rating	82
Green Rating	74
Type of school	Private
Affiliation	Methodist
Environment	City

STUDENTS

Total undergrad enrollment	1,570
% male/female	52/48
% from out of state	44
% frosh from public high school	67
% frosh live on campus	96
% ugrads live on campus	93
# of fraternities (% ugrad men join)	7 (45)
# of sororities (% ugrad women join)	5 (58)
% African American	8
% Asian	3
% Caucasian	81
% Hispanic	3
% Native American	0
% international	2
# of countries represented	15

SURVEY SAYS . . .

Lots of conservative students
Students are happy
Classroom facilities are great
Lab facilities are great
Career services are great
School is well run
Students are friendly
Easy to get around campus
Athletic facilities are great
Lots of beer drinking
Frats and sororities are popular

ACADEMICS

Academic Rating	90
% students returning for sophomore year	90
% students graduating within 4 years	78
% students graduating within 6 years	82
Calendar	4/1/4
Student/faculty ratio	11:1
Profs interesting rating	92
Profs accessible rating	88

Most classes have 10–19 students.
Most lab/discussion sessions have
20–29 students.

MOST POPULAR MAJORS

biology; finance; business/
managerial economics

STUDENTS SAY "..."

Academics

Wofford's "excellent reputation with graduate programs" and "challenging" classes have established this South Carolina school as "a liberal arts college that provides an excellent education and opportunities to expand your horizon." Wofford is known as "a great and successful academic school," a community of learning where individuality, curiosity, and success are fostered every day" in large part thanks to a staff of educators that "challenges students to think and discuss their ideas in every class." Teachers here "expect a lot," but students don't have to go it alone. The "extremely knowledgeable, engaging, and helpful" professors are "willing to assist in any way they can," educators who "go over and beyond to help you achieve even the hardest goal." Even in popular-but-difficult courses like premed and government, Wofford's small campus means "it's easy to have interaction between teachers and students." "Many even give home or cell phone numbers," another student comments. "It is challenging," students say, "but the professors make it fun!" That same passion for learning extends to the student body. This is a campus "where all of the students look out for each other and help one another succeed."

Life

Greek life is a big deal at Wofford. Even those not directly involved in fraternities and sororities find that "the most popular destination on Friday and Saturday nights" is Fraternity Row, where there are "live bands, music, dancing, and much more that the students enjoy." "Greeks and non-Greeks are generally out, and there are often bands performing at the houses," though on Saturdays, "It closes at midnight, so then we go to the seniors' apartments." Though there is "a beautiful downtown area that students like to walk around and shop," staying close to school is not unusual since "the campus is very much its own small community." Indeed, "there is barely any need to get off campus." For those who want to escape the "Wofford Bubble," there is Spartanburg, which may be "lacking in interesting things to do," but "does have a good variety of restaurants." Even better, "a lot of the restaurants, bars, and shops will give you a discount if you are a Wofford student." For those disinclined to party or travel, "almost every day there is a school-sponsored event on campus. From painting on the lawn to an oyster roast, there is always something to do." But Wofford students are also hardworking students, so before and after all that, they "go to the library and the science center a lot."

Student Body

It should come as no surprise that "the frat scene is high" at Wofford, since "the typical Wofford student is very similar to the 'stereotypical' Southerner: polite, tied to tradition, friendly, welcoming, living life at a slower pace, and very passionate about their beliefs." Many students say they are "not involved in Greek life," but are "just as happy as the people who are." Students here are "preppy, studious, from South Carolina, and conservative." If that sounds limiting, students say it is not. Wofford students say, "While groups generally stick together, tolerance and acceptance is the norm." That is because, on campus, "it doesn't matter what club or group you are involved in, you will be included no matter what. I have been here for almost two years and have failed to meet an unkind student." Though the campus is predominantly white, "there is some diversity on campus," including significant populations of Asian American and African American students. Perhaps one student sums it up best when they say this school offers "a unique culture: diverse in background, ethnicity, and views, but united by the communal notion that at our essence, we are all Wofford."

FINANCIAL AID: 864-597-4160 • E-MAIL: ADMISSION@WOFFORD.EDU • WEBSITE: WWW.WOFFORD.EDU

THE PRINCETON REVIEW SAYS

Admissions

Very important factors considered include: GPA, rigor of secondary school record. *Important factors considered include:* Class rank, standardized test scores, application essay, extracurricular activities, talent/ability, volunteer work, character/personal qualities. *Other factors considered include:* First generation, geographical residence, interview, racial/ethnic status, recommendation(s), work experience, alumni/ae relations. SAT or ACT required; ACT with Writing component required. TOEFL required of all international applicants. *Academic units recommended:* 4 English; 4 mathematics; 3 science; (3 science lab); 3 social studies; 3 foreign language; 1 history; 1 academic elective; 1 computer science; 1 visual/performing arts.

Financial Aid

Students should submit: FAFSA. Regular filing deadline is 6/1. The Princeton Review suggests that all financial aid forms be submitted as soon as possible after January 1. *Need-based scholarships/grants offered:* Federal Pell, SEOG, State scholarships/grants, private scholarships, the school's own gift aid. *Loan aid offered:* Direct Subsidized Stafford Loans, Direct Unsubsidized Stafford Loans, Direct PLUS loans, Federal Perkins Loans. Applicants will be notified of awards beginning 4/1. Federal Work-Study Program available. Institutional employment available. Off-campus job opportunities are good.

The Inside Word

Wofford College distinguishes itself by providing its students with an extremely supportive environment. This concern extends to the applications it receives, each of which is given careful consideration. Students who have earned decent grades in challenging courses should find themselves with an opportunity to attend a school that is gaining a reputation as one of the South's premier liberal arts colleges.

THE SCHOOL SAYS "..."

From the Admissions Office

"A century ago, Wofford athletics team chose the Boston Terrier as their mascot. These beloved dogs are small, but they are full of intelligence and energy. Similarly, with an enrollment of about 1,600 students, Wofford is small, but campus life is ideal for learning and fun. In fact, the college's scores on the National Survey of Student Engagement (NSSE) have ranked with the best in the country for several years. According to the 2011 'Open Doors' study of participation in international programs, Wofford stands second among all the nation's liberal arts colleges. Our "new Urban" Village Housing for seniors and our environmental studies center have won architectural awards, and our entire historic campus is a national arboretum. Our athletics teams have won recent Southern Conference championships in football and basketball, and our quarterback and point guard in 2012 were members of Phi Beta Kappa. Wofford thus remains committed to its historic mission—turning out graduates who can make international connections and become difference makers in a variety of vocations and professions."

SELECTIVITY

Admissions Rating	89
# of applicants	2,718
% of applicants accepted	69
% of acceptees attending	22
# offered a place on the wait list	108
% accepting a place on wait list	48
% admitted from wait list	100
# of early decision applicants	82
% accepted early decision	80

FRESHMAN PROFILE

Range SAT Critical Reading	540–620
Range SAT Math	540–640
Range SAT Writing	520–620
Range ACT Composite	24–29
Minimum paper TOEFL	550
Minimum web-based TOEFL	213
Average HS GPA	3.54
% graduated top 10% of class	42
% graduated top 25% of class	77
% graduated top 50% of class	96

DEADLINES

Early decision	
Deadline	11/1
Notification	12/1
Early action	
Deadline	11/15
Notification	2/1
Regular	
Deadline	2/1
Notification	3/15
Nonfall registration?	Yes

APPLICANTS ALSO LOOK AT AND SOMETIMES PREFER
Furman University

AND RARELY PREFER
Clemson University; University of South Carolina—Columbia

FINANCIAL FACTS

Financial Aid Rating	88
Annual tuition	$35,515
Room and board	$10,280
Books and supplies	$1,200
% needy frosh rec. need-based scholarship or grant aid	94
% needy UG rec. need-based scholarship or grant aid	92
% needy frosh rec. non-need-based scholarship or grant aid	30
% needy UG rec. non-need-based scholarship or grant aid	29
% needy frosh rec. need-based self-help aid	59
% needy UG rec. need-based self-help aid	57
% frosh rec. any financial aid	93
% UG rec. any financial aid	94
% UG borrow to pay for school	49
Average cumulative indebtedness	$24,721
% frosh need fully met	40
% ugrads need fully met	41
Average % of frosh need met	75
Average % of ugrad need met	79

WORCESTER POLYTECHNIC INSTITUTE

ADMISSIONS OFFICE, BARTLETT CENTER, WORCESTER, MA 01609 • ADMISSIONS: 508-831-5286 • FAX: 508-831-5875

STUDENTS SAY "..."

Academics

The reputation of Worcester Polytechnic Institute amongst engineers around the country is impeccable, and rightfully so: this highly hands-on university in central Massachusetts has a "rigorous academic environment" and is focused on "creative collaboration in a non-competitive environment with a common goal of innovation." The campus "has a real excitement regarding knowledge," and while the majority of students choose to do engineering and math here, "there are opportunities to do humanities and business course as well."

One of the more unique aspects of the WPI curriculum is the project activity, which includes the Major Qualifying Project (MQP) and the Interactive Qualifying Project (IQP) for juniors and seniors, both of which are done with an advisor and often involve off-campus sponsorship. This, along with the grading system (students are awarded a grade of A, B, C, or No Record) "encourages cooperation among students rather than cut-throat competition." Classes run in a quarter system (three classes for each of the four seven-week terms), which means faculty is "forced to only teach us the most important material, without material that may be considered 'filler material.'"

The majority of professors are "very engaging" and "present material in better ways then just showing Powerpoint slides one after the other." As you get into higher level classes the subjects are more focused, and "almost all classes have a lab component." Students are "always helping one another, [and] everyone (including the professors) wants the students to succeed." The project-based learning and reputation of WPI gives students "the ability to work on real engineering projects around the world." As one sophomore puts it: "WPI won't teach you everything you need to know to be a good engineer, but they'll teach you where to find all the information you need to face any obstacle."

Life

WPI "does a great job of making sure we all fit in and have an awesome friend group," says a student. Worcester "isn't the greatest city," but "WPI is in a nice area." There is a great social life on campus as well as off campus, and "there is plenty to do for those eighteen and up as well as twenty-one and up." "It would literally take hours to describe all the amazing things they take place on campus," says a junior.

Students are academically engaged during the week "because it's practically a requirement at WPI," but know how to let go on weekends and occasional weeknights. With around 200 organizations and "a very active Social Committee" there is always something happening on campus, such as "free movies on weekends (post-theater but pre-DVD release)," "dances, fundraisers, activities, socials, concerts," LARPing, and robot competitions. "We definitely are a geeky campus," says a student. Now, "a geeky tech school is not the place someone would expect to find a flourishing Greek community," says a student. "But in fact the Panhellenic community on campus is excellent."

Student Body

"It's nice to know that no matter what you like, you're going to find a kindred spirit at WPI," says a student of the "rather smart," "open and friendly" crowd. The school is around 70 percent guys (and almost all of the student body is here for a STEM major) so fraternities and sports are popular (sororities and sports for girls, too), and all have a "nerdy side" that "brings us together." Still, don't get it wrong: WPI "is not a school full of Poindexters who never leave their rooms." "We have athletes, Greek life, theatre, and anything else you can find at any other school. However, we all have a common bond because of our love of math, science, and all things logical," says a student.

WORCESTER POLYTECHNIC INSTITUTE

FINANCIAL AID: 508-831-5469 • E-MAIL: ADMISSIONS@WPI.EDU • WEBSITE: WWW.WPI.EDU

THE PRINCETON REVIEW SAYS

Admissions

Very important factors considered include: GPA, rigor of secondary school record. *Important factors considered include:* Class rank, standardized test scores, extracurricular activities, recommendation(s), character/personal qualities. *Other factors considered include:* Application essay, first generation, geographical residence, interview, talent/ability, volunteer work, work experience, alumni/ae relations, level of applicant's interest. SAT and SAT Subject Tests or ACT considered if submitted; ACT with or without Writing component accepted. TOEFL required of all international applicants. *Academic units required:* 4 English; 4 mathematics; 2 science; (2 science lab). *Academic units recommended:* 4 science; 2 social studies; 2 foreign language; 1 history; 1 computer science.

Financial Aid

Students should submit: FAFSA, CSS/Financial Aid PROFILE, Noncustodial PROFILE. Regular filing deadline is 2/1. The Princeton Review suggests that all financial aid forms be submitted as soon as possible after January 1. *Need-based scholarships/grants offered:* Federal Pell, SEOG, State scholarships/grants, private scholarships, the school's own gift aid. *Loan aid offered:* Direct Subsidized Stafford Loans, Direct Unsubsidized Stafford Loans, Direct PLUS loans, Federal Perkins Loans, State Loans, College/university loans from institutional funds. Applicants will be notified of awards beginning 4/1. Federal Work-Study Program available. Institutional employment available. Off-campus job opportunities are good.

The Inside Word

WPI's high admission rate is the result of a self-selecting applicant pool; those who don't have a decent chance of getting in here rarely bother to apply. The relatively low rate of conversion of accepted students to enrollees is due to the fact that WPI is a 'safety' school for many applicants. Those who get in here and at MIT, CalTech, Cornell, or Carnegie Mellon usually wind up elsewhere.

THE SCHOOL SAYS "..."

From the Admissions Office

"Projects and research enrich WPI's academic program. WPI believes that in these times simply passing courses and accumulating theoretical knowledge is not enough to truly educate tomorrow's leaders. Tomorrow's professionals ought to be involved in project work that prepares them today for future challenges. Projects at WPI come as close to professional experience as a college program can possibly achieve. In fact, WPI works with more than 200 companies, government agencies, and private organizations each year. These groups provide opportunities where students get a chance to work in real, professional settings. Students gain invaluable experience in planning, coordinating team efforts, meeting deadlines, writing proposals and reports, making oral presentations, doing cost analyses, and making decisions.

Applicants are required to submit SAT or ACT scores, or in lieu of test scores may submit supplemental materials through WPI's Flex Path program. Students who choose the Flex Path are encouraged to submit examples of academic work or extracurricular projects that reflect a high level of organization, motivation, creativity and problem-solving ability."

SELECTIVITY

Admissions Rating	95
# of applicants	8,578
% of applicants accepted	52
% of acceptees attending	25
# offered a place on the wait list	1,938
% accepting a place on wait list	38
% admitted from wait list	0

FRESHMAN PROFILE

Range SAT Critical Reading	560–670
Range SAT Math	650–740
Range SAT Writing	570–670
Range ACT Composite	28–32
Minimum paper TOEFL	550
Minimum web-based TOEFL	213
Average HS GPA	3.85
% graduated top 10% of class	65
% graduated top 25% of class	92
% graduated top 50% of class	99

DEADLINES

Early action	
Deadline	11/1
Notification	12/20
Regular	
Deadline	2/1
Notification	4/1
Nonfall registration?	Yes

APPLICANTS ALSO LOOK AT AND OFTEN PREFER

Massachusetts Institute of Technology; Cornell University; Carnegie Mellon University; Brown University

AND SOMETIMES PREFER

Tufts University; Rensselaer Polytechnic Institute; Boston University; University of Rochester

AND RARELY PREFER

University of Massachusetts Amherst; University of Connecticut; Rochester Institute of Technology; Northeastern University

FINANCIAL FACTS

Financial Aid Rating	81
Annual tuition	$42,178
Room and board	$13,082
Required fees	$600
Books and supplies	$1,000
% needy frosh rec. need-based scholarship or grant aid	99
% needy UG rec. need-based scholarship or grant aid	95
% needy frosh rec. non-need-based scholarship or grant aid	42
% needy UG rec. non-need-based scholarship or grant aid	31
% needy frosh rec. need-based self-help aid	62
% needy UG rec. need-based self-help aid	60
% frosh rec. any financial aid	99
% UG rec. any financial aid	95
% frosh need fully met	46
% ugrads need fully met	37
Average % of frosh need met	71
Average % of ugrad need met	72

XAVIER UNIVERSITY OF LOUISIANA

ONE DREXEL DRIVE, NEW ORLEANS, LA 70125 • ADMISSIONS: 504-520-7388 • FAX: 504-520-7941

STUDENTS SAY " . . ."

Academics

One of the top Historically Black Colleges/Universities (HBCU), Xavier University of Louisiana prides itself on educating students in a range of subjects, to provide a "thriving underlying foundation, upon which students can achieve the very best for themselves." Though perhaps best known for its science departments, the New Orleans-based school has both a College of Arts and Sciences and a College of Pharmacy and requires "high academic standards" for all of majors across the board. Between its academic reputation and the emphasis placed on community leadership, no matter the reason that you go to XU, you leave "fully educated." "I was challenged academically, but not broken. The workload was not overwhelming," says a student. Small class sizes means great interaction with professors, and the ensuing "close-knit relationships" are cited by many as a major part of their satisfaction with the school. Also on that list? "The education you receive at XU, considering the extremely low tuition cost and financial aid opportunities for a private university, is unparalleled." Professors at XU are dedicated to ensuring that all students "are proficient, if not masters, in the materials taught," and they provide "an excellent foundation for further academic and career success." XU produces a tremendous number of graduates who go on to medical school and other professional schools in "the pursuit of success." Most faculty members are "almost always available in some form or fashion to help you with any questions you may have," and the school itself provides "multiple resources for any problems that need reinforcement." One exception, however, is the financial aid and fiscal services departments, which "have very little time to discuss things with students."

Life

Despite its location, XU "is by no means a party school." Because the student body is mostly composed of science majors, people "are always studying," and "study groups are a common thing." Students "will take occasional breaks," but for the most part, grades are the important thing at XU. "We are not a school that places as much emphasis on 'fun' as we do making sure we are productive and contributing citizens by the time we graduate," says a student. Though the school offers "lots of opportunities to volunteer," many students complain that there aren't enough social activities to keep students occupied, and school spirit suffers as a result. "We have a strong academic standing, but our campus life is pretty limited," says one student. The dry campus also enforces a curfew ("Sometimes it feels like a boarding school"), so the typical college experience and hair-letting-loose happens off-campus: "Campus is a place to work." Not everyone is familiar with the city (there's no off-campus housing associated with XU), so going out to movies, clubs, and shopping on weekends usually happens in groups. There's also a fair amount of interaction with neighboring schools like Tulane, Loyola, and Dillard. "There are so many things to do right around the corner from Xavier; I can see musicals, watch the Saints, see the Hornets play, salsa dance, get amazing Southern cuisine, listen to 'bounce' music, and learn how to dance, see parades and second lines," sums up a Big Easy lover.

Student Body

Studious, studious, studious. Most students are "very focused, driven, and destined for success," and unsurprisingly, you run into a lot of "aspiring" doctors and pharmacists. The majority of students are African American or Asian, and the female-to-male ratio is quite high. The student body as a whole has a "conservative mentality." It's "very easy" to make friends here, particularly through study groups, and the small campus means that "everyone recognizes everyone" and "gets along with each other."

FINANCIAL AID: 504-520-7835 • E-MAIL: APPLY@XULA.EDU • WEBSITE: WWW.XULA.EDU

THE PRINCETON REVIEW SAYS

Admissions

Very important factors considered include: GPA, rigor of secondary school record, standardized test scores, recommendation(s). *Important factors considered include:* Class rank, application essay. *Other factors considered include:* Extracurricular activities, interview, talent/ability, volunteer work, work experience, alumni/ae relations, character/personal qualities. SAT or ACT required; SAT and SAT Subject Tests or ACT considered if submitted; ACT with Writing component recommended. TOEFL required of all international applicants. *Academic units required:* 4 English; 2 mathematics; 1 science; 1 social studies; 8 academic electives. *Academic units recommended:* 4 mathematics; 3 science; 1 foreign language; 1 history.

Financial Aid

Students should submit: FAFSA. The Princeton Review suggests that all financial aid forms be submitted as soon as possible after January 1. *Need-based scholarships/grants offered:* Federal Pell, SEOG, State scholarships/grants, private scholarships, the school's own gift aid, United Negro College Fund. *Loan aid offered:* Direct Subsidized Stafford Loans, Direct Unsubsidized Stafford Loans, Direct PLUS loans, Federal Perkins Loans. Federal Work-Study Program available. Institutional employment available. Off-campus job opportunities are good.

Inside Word

This HBCU has a rolling admissions process, and applicants typically receive notification of the school's decision within one month of completed application submission. Campus visits are encouraged. If you want to be considered for scholarships, you'll need to include a strong personal statement that reflects evidence of leadership. Admission to the school's College of Pharmacy is separate from that of the College of Arts and Sciences and is subject to a different set of requirements.

THE SCHOOL SAYS "..."

From the Admissions Office

"You have made a great decision in planning to go to college. You will never regret it. It will help you reach your greatest potential as an individual and as a contributing member of our society. You will make another important decision when you select Xavier for your college education. For more than 80 years, Xavier has been expanding horizons, opening new worlds, enriching lives, developing leaders and sending graduates out to conquer their selected corner of the world. Xavier graduates have heeded the call of urban America, providing enlightened leadership in city government. They have served as mayors, headed municipal agencies, donned judicial robes. They have also served in state legislatures. In the health professions, Xavier is a national leader in providing graduates for schools of medicine and dentistry, including the country's top-ranked schools. College of Pharmacy graduates can be found in almost every state, serving in neighborhood pharmacies, in hospitals, and in the pharmaceutical industry. Xavier graduates are vital members of health care teams, while others conduct biomedical research.

"Xavier educators are found in classrooms of colleges and schools. They also serve as presidents, superintendents and principals. Business graduates rise quickly in the world of business and industry. Xavier alumni report the news on network television and in leading national publications. They perform on opera and concert stages in the music centers of the world. As lawyers and social scientists, they help right some of the wrongs of our society. They fulfill the Xavier tradition in leadership and service. Xavier seeks students to keep that tradition alive—students with great potential, who will not settle for less than high achievement, students who make a difference in the lives they touch. You can make your life count for something special by coming to Xavier."

SELECTIVITY

Admissions Rating	81
# of applicants	3,987
% of applicants accepted	64
% of acceptees attending	26
# offered a place on the wait list	172
% accepting a place on wait list	13
% admitted from wait list	35

FRESHMAN PROFILE

Range SAT Critical Reading	430–560
Range SAT Math	440–550
Range SAT Writing	420–520
Range ACT Composite	19–25
Minimum paper TOEFL	550
Minimum web-based TOEFL	220
Average HS GPA	3.33
% graduated top 10% of class	33
% graduated top 25% of class	60
% graduated top 50% of class	83

DEADLINES

Early action	
Deadline	1/15
Notification	2/15
Regular	
Priority	3/1
Deadline	7/1
Notification	10/15
Nonfall registration?	Yes

FINANCIAL FACTS

Financial Aid Rating	66
Annual tuition	$18,500
Room and board	$7,800
Required fees	$2,060
Books and supplies	$1,200
% needy frosh rec. need-based scholarship or grant aid	70
% needy UG rec. need-based scholarship or grant aid	69
% needy frosh rec. non-need-based scholarship or grant aid	91
% needy UG rec. non-need-based scholarship or grant aid	78
% needy frosh rec. need-based self-help aid	93
% needy UG rec. need-based self-help aid	96
% frosh rec. any financial aid	94
% UG rec. any financial aid	24
% UG borrow to pay for school	87
Average cumulative indebtedness	$25,566
% frosh need fully met	0
% ugrads need fully met	0
Average % of frosh need met	13
Average % of ugrad need met	13

XAVIER UNIVERSITY (OH)

3800 VICTORY PARKWAY, CINCINNATI, OH 45207-5311 • ADMISSIONS: 513-745-3301 • FAX: 513-745-4319

STUDENTS SAY ". . ."

Academics

Xavier University is a medium-sized Jesuit school where "professors genuinely want students to succeed" and "really care about their students." Classes offer "real life, unbiased discussion" in a "fast-paced" environment. The idea is simple: to get students thinking about their place in the world. "The professors, staff, and students at Xavier University are truly invested in the community, whether local, national, or international, and making it a better place." One student enthused, "I have come away from classes questioning (the world) almost every day at this university, and I think that's a wonderful thing." These efforts are spearheaded by educators "who have spent significant time working in their field" but who still "make students the priority over other commitments." These "wonderful" professors "invigorate their subjects" and make themselves readily available to students. In fact, "the majority of my professors give us their cell phone numbers so that we can access them outside the classroom, in case we have questions that emails cannot [answer]." At Xavier, teachers are rewarded for teaching well. "In order to gain tenure here, professors are graded predominantly on teaching performance rather than research like most other institutions." The result is that "at Xavier, students learn and grow into people that can make a change in the world—all while having a blast and making memories with friends that will last a lifetime."

Life

One need not be into the "party scene" to find a good time at Xavier. "At Xavier it is easy to find the perfect balance of academic and social life." Students here "do not feel too overwhelmed," so even though there is "never a dull moment," excitement tends to be low-key, centered around enjoying time with friends "talking about faith, politics, what's on TV, the whole spectrum" rather than going wild. Finding things to do outside the classroom is not difficult. "Xavier SAC hosts tremendous events for Xavier students to participate in," and downtown Cincinnati offers plenty of options, from "movie theaters and an awesome restaurant" to a new casino, along with "professional sports, Broadway shows, as well as the aquarium and zoo." School sports such as basketball often draw large groups together. "Everyone is alive with excitement for the games, which are in themselves amazing." Indeed, when it comes to hoops, "basketball season is the time of the year that we all look forward to." There are, of course, parties, though as one student says, "It's more of a drinking school than a partying school. With no big time football program on Saturdays, we like to just relax and have fun." Overall, "I am never bored at Xavier because I always have something to focus my time on."

Student Body

The "career-driven" students of Xavier are "dedicated to their studies, tend to work ahead, find the best internships, and really prepare for their career," but that does not mean they are not "very outgoing and friendly." One student claims, "I once had a professor comment that he has never seen so many hugs on a college campus." Students here are "involved in a variety of activities, work hard to achieve goals, and are concerned with the dignity of others." That sentiment is not universal on this largely Caucasian campus. Most students agree they feel a "diverse community atmosphere" at Xavier. Indeed, as one student says, "Xavier is accepting of people from all walks of life; there is a niche for everyone." Misgivings aside, the near universal sentiment is that students here are "hard working, intelligent, disciplined, and always looking to go the extra mile to help other people in any way they can."

XAVIER UNIVERSITY (OH)

FINANCIAL AID: 513-745-3142 • E-MAIL: XUADMIT@XAVIER.EDU • WEBSITE: WWW.XAVIER.EDU

THE PRINCETON REVIEW SAYS

Admissions

Very important factors considered include: Rigor of secondary school record. *Important factors considered include:* GPA, standardized test scores, application essay, extracurricular activities, recommendation(s), volunteer work, character/personal qualities. *Other factors considered include:* Class rank, first generation, talent/ability, work experience, alumni/ae relations, level of applicant's interest. SAT or ACT required; ACT with or without Writing component accepted. TOEFL required of all international applicants. *Academic units recommended:* 4 English; 3 mathematics; 3 science; 3 social studies; 2 foreign language; 5 academic electives.

Financial Aid

Students should submit: FAFSA. The Princeton Review suggests that all financial aid forms be submitted as soon as possible after January 1. *Need-based scholarships/grants offered:* Federal Pell, SEOG, State scholarships/grants, private scholarships, the school's own gift aid. *Loan aid offered:* Direct Subsidized Stafford Loans, Direct Unsubsidized Stafford Loans, Direct PLUS loans, Federal Perkins Loans. Federal Work-Study Program available. Institutional employment available. Off-campus job opportunities are excellent.

The Inside Word

There will be no major hurdles for above-average students when it comes to winning admission to Xavier. For others, it will take a little more legwork. Look to provide credible demonstrations of commitment to academics and Jesuit ideals of service, and a Catholic approach to academics if you want to win over admissions officers.

THE SCHOOL SAYS "..."

From the Admissions Office

"Founded in 1831, Xavier University is the fourth oldest of the twenty-eight Jesuit colleges and universities in the United States. The Jesuit tradition is evident in the university's core curriculum, degree programs, and involvement opportunities. Xavier is home to approximately 7,000 total students; 4,300 degree-seeking undergraduates. The student population represents more than forty-five states and forty-three foreign countries. Xavier offers more than eighty undergraduate academic majors and more than fifty minors in the College of Arts and Sciences; the Williams College of Business; and the College of Social Sciences, Health, and Education. Most popular majors include business, natural sciences, nursing, communication arts, education, psychology, biology, sport management/marketing, and pre-professional study. Other programs of note include University Scholars; Honors AB; Philosophy, Politics, and the Public; Army ROTC, study abroad, academic service-learning, and community engagement fellowship. There are more than 100 academic clubs, social and service organizations, and recreational sports activities on campus. Students participate in groups such as student government, campus ministry, performing arts, and intramural sports as well as one of the largest service-oriented Alternative Break clubs in the country. Xavier is a member of the Division I Big East Conference and fields teams in men's and women's basketball, cross-country, track, golf, soccer, swimming, and tennis, as well as men's baseball and women's volleyball.

"Xavier is situated on more than 180 acres in a residential area of Cincinnati, Ohio. The face of Xavier continues to change with the addition of the technology-based Conaton Learning Commons and Smith Hall, a new building for the Williams College of Business, both which opened in fall 2010, Fenwick Place which includes a 535-bed residence hall, a dining hall and offices that opened in fall 2011 and a new classroom building to open in fall 2015. Applicants must submit results from the SAT or ACT. The student's best score(s) from either test will be used. The writing portion of the SAT/ACT is not required and will not be used in admission and scholarship decisions."

SELECTIVITY

Admissions Rating	80
# of applicants	10,907
% of applicants accepted	70
% of acceptees attending	17
# offered a place on the wait list	118
% accepting a place on wait list	20
% admitted from wait list	92

FRESHMAN PROFILE

Range SAT Critical Reading	500–600
Range SAT Math	510–610
Range SAT Writing	490–590
Range ACT Composite	23–27
Minimum paper TOEFL	530
Minimum web-based TOEFL	71
Average HS GPA	3.62
% graduated top 10% of class	22
% graduated top 25% of class	54
% graduated top 50% of class	85

DEADLINES

Regular	
Priority	2/1
Nonfall registration?	Yes

APPLICANTS ALSO LOOK AT AND OFTEN PREFER
University of Notre Dame

AND SOMETIMES PREFER
Indiana University—Bloomington; Loyola The University of Chicago; Marquette University; Miami University; The Ohio State University Columbus; University of Dayton; University of Cincinnati

AND RARELY PREFER
University of Kentucky; Saint Louis University; Purdue University—West Lafayette

FINANCIAL FACTS

Financial Aid Rating	77
Annual tuition	$32,070
Room and board	$10,740
Required fees	$930
Books and supplies	$1,000
% needy frosh rec. need-based scholarship or grant aid	97
% needy UG rec. need-based scholarship or grant aid	96
% needy frosh rec. non-need-based scholarship or grant aid	16
% needy UG rec. non-need-based scholarship or grant aid	13
% needy frosh rec. need-based self-help aid	75
% needy UG rec. need-based self-help aid	79
% frosh rec. any financial aid	100
% UG rec. any financial aid	90
% UG borrow to pay for school	70
Average cumulative indebtedness	$30,540
% frosh need fully met	22
% ugrads need fully met	19
Average % of frosh need met	74
Average % of ugrad need met	72

YALE UNIVERSITY

PO BOX 208234, NEW HAVEN, CT 06520-8234 • ADMISSIONS: 203-432-9300 • FAX: 203-432-9392

CAMPUS LIFE

Quality of Life Rating	96
Fire Safety Rating	61
Green Rating	96
Type of school	Private
Affiliation	No Affiliation
Environment	City

STUDENTS

Total undergrad enrollment	5,430
% male/female	50/50
% from out of state	93
% frosh from public high school	55
% frosh live on campus	100
% ugrads live on campus	87
% African American	7
% Asian	16
% Caucasian	47
% Hispanic	10
% Native American	<1
% international	11
# of countries represented	118

SURVEY SAYS . . .

Students are happy
Classroom facilities are great
Internships are widely available
School is well run
Great financial aid
Students are friendly
Diverse student types on campus
Great off-campus food
Dorms are like palaces
Lots of beer drinking
Hard liquor is popular
Theater is popular
Student publications are popular
Active minority support groups

ACADEMICS

Academic Rating	96
% students returning for sophomore year	99
% students graduating within 4 years	89
% students graduating within 6 years	96
Calendar	Semester
Student/faculty ratio	6:1
Profs interesting rating	89
Profs accessible rating	85
Most classes have 10–19 students.	

MOST POPULAR MAJORS
economics; political science; history

STUDENTS SAY ". . ."

Academics

Listening to Yale students wax rhapsodic about their school, one can be forgiven for wondering whether they aren't actually describing the platonic form of the university. By their own account, students here benefit not only from "amazing academics and extensive resources" that provide "phenomenal in-and out-of-class education," but also from participation in "a student body that is committed to learning and to each other." Unlike some other prestigious, prominent research universities, Yale "places unparalleled focus on undergraduate education," requiring all professors to teach at least one undergraduate course each year. "[You know] the professors actually love teaching, because if they just wanted to do their research, they could have easily gone elsewhere." A residential college system further personalizes the experience. Each residential college "has a Dean and a Master, each of which is only responsible for 300 to 500 students, so administrative attention is highly specialized and widely available." Students further enjoy access to "a seemingly never-ending supply of resources (they really just love throwing money at us)" that includes "the twelve million volumes in our libraries." In short, "the opportunities are truly endless." "The experiences you have here and the people that you meet will change your life and strengthen your dreams," says one student. Looking for the flip side to all this? "If the weather were a bit nicer, that would be excellent," one student offers. Guess that will have to do.

Life

Yale is, of course, extremely challenging academically, but students assure us that "aside from the stress of midterms and finals, life at Yale is relatively carefree." Work doesn't keep undergrads from participating in "a huge variety of activities for fun. There are more than 400 student groups, including singing, dancing, juggling fire, theater…the list goes on. Because of all of these groups, there are shows on-campus all the time, which are a lot of fun and usually free or less than five dollars. On top of that, there are parties and events on campus and off campus, as well as many subsidized trips to New York City and Boston." Many here "are politically active (or at least politically aware)" and "a very large number of students either volunteer or try to get involved in some sort of organization to make a difference in the world." When the weekend comes around, "there are always parties to go to, whether at the frats or in rooms, but there's definitely no pressure to drink if you don't want to. A good friend of mine pledged a frat without drinking and that's definitely not unheard of (but still not common)." The relationship between Yale and the city of New Haven "sometimes leaves a little to be desired, but overall it's a great place to be for four years."

Student Body

A typical Yalie is "tough to define because so much of what makes Yale special is the unique convergence of different students to form one cohesive entity. Nonetheless, the one common characteristic of Yale students is passion—each Yalie is driven and dedicated to what he or she loves most, and it creates a palpable atmosphere of enthusiasm on campus." True enough, the student body represents a wide variety of ethnic, religious, economic, and academic backgrounds, but they all "thrive on learning, whether in a class, from a book, or from a conversation with a new friend." Students here also "tend to do a lot." "Everyone has many activities that they are a part of, which in turn fosters the closely connected feel of the campus." Undergrads tend to lean to the left politically, but for "those whose political views aren't as liberal as the rest of the campus…there are several campus organizations that cater to them."

FINANCIAL AID: 203-432-2700 • E-MAIL: STUDENT.QUESTIONS@YALE.EDU • WEBSITE: WWW.YALE.EDU

THE PRINCETON REVIEW SAYS

Admissions

Very important factors considered include: Class rank, GPA, rigor of secondary school record, standardized test scores, application essay, extracurricular activities, recommendation(s), talent/ability, character/personal qualities. *Other factors considered include:* First generation, geographical residence, interview, racial/ethnic status, state residency, volunteer work, work experience, alumni/ae relations, level of applicant's interest. SAT and SAT Subject Tests or ACT required; ACT with Writing component required. TOEFL required of all international applicants.

Financial Aid

Students should submit: FAFSA, CSS/Financial Aid PROFILE, Noncustodial PROFILE, Business/Farm Supplement. Regular filing deadline is 3/1. The Princeton Review suggests that all financial aid forms be submitted as soon as possible after January 1. *Need-based scholarships/grants offered:* Federal Pell, SEOG, State scholarships/grants, private scholarships, the school's own gift aid, United Negro College Fund. *Loan aid offered:* Direct Subsidized Stafford Loans, Direct Unsubsidized Stafford Loans, Direct PLUS loans, Federal Perkins Loans, State Loans, College/university loans from institutional funds. Applicants will be notified of awards beginning 4/1. Institutional employment available.

The Inside Word

Yale estimates that over three-quarters of all its applicants are qualified to attend the university, but less than 10 percent get in. That adds up to a lot of broken hearts among kids who, if admitted, could probably handle the academic program. With so many qualified applicants to choose from, Yale can winnow to build an incoming class that is balanced in terms of income level, racial/ethnic background, geographic origin, and academic interest. For all but the most qualified, getting in typically hinges on offering just what an admissions officer is looking for to fill a specific slot. Legacies (descendents of Yale grads) gain some advantage—although they still need exceptionally strong credentials.

THE SCHOOL SAYS "..."

From the Admissions Office

"The most important questions the admissions committee must resolve are 'Who is likely to make the most of Yale's resources?' and 'Who will contribute significantly to the Yale community?' These questions suggest an approach to evaluating applicants that is more complex than whether Yale would rather admit well-rounded people or those with specialized talents. In selecting a class of 1,300 from roughly 30,000 applicants, the admissions committee looks for academic ability and achievement combined with such personal characteristics as motivation, curiosity, energy, and leadership ability. The nature of these qualities is such that there is no simple profile of grades, scores, interests, and activities that will assure admission. Diversity within the student population is important, and the admissions committee selects a class of able and contributing individuals from a variety of backgrounds and with a broad range of interests and skills.

"Applicants for the entering class are required to take the SAT and two Subject Tests of their choice, or the ACT with the writing component."

SELECTIVITY

Admissions Rating	99
# of applicants	29,610
% of applicants accepted	7
% of acceptees attending	68

FRESHMAN PROFILE

Range SAT Critical Reading	700–800
Range SAT Math	710–790
Range SAT Writing	710–800
Range ACT Composite	32–35
Minimum paper TOEFL	600
Minimum web-based TOEFL	250
% graduated top 10% of class	95
% graduated top 25% of class	99
% graduated top 50% of class	100

DEADLINES

Early action	
Deadline	11/1
Notification	12/15
Regular	
Deadline	12/31
Notification	4/1
Nonfall registration?	No

FINANCIAL FACTS

Financial Aid Rating	99
Annual tuition	$42,300
Room and board	$13,000
Required fees	$0
Books and supplies	$1,200
% needy frosh rec. need-based scholarship or grant aid	100
% needy UG rec. need-based scholarship or grant aid	100
% needy frosh rec. non-need-based scholarship or grant aid	0
% needy UG rec. non-need-based scholarship or grant aid	0
% needy frosh rec. need-based self-help aid	74
% needy UG rec. need-based self-help aid	87
% frosh rec. any financial aid	51
% UG rec. any financial aid	52
% UG borrow to pay for school	16
Average cumulative indebtedness	$8,940
% frosh need fully met	100
% ugrads need fully met	100
Average % of frosh need met	100
Average % of ugrad need met	100

PART 4

INDEXES

If you'd like an expert to help you find, apply to, and get accepted at the right colleges for you, check out Collegewise, the admissions services division of The Princeton Review. Their college counselors work with students in person and online to make getting into college less stressful, and dare we say, maybe a little bit fun. Visit www.collegewise.com for more information.

Admissions services are also available through independent counselors, who are typically members of one of several professional organizations: Higher Education Consultants Association (www.hecaonline.org), Independent Educational Consultants Association (www.iecaonline.com), or National Association for College Admission Counseling (www.nacacnet.org). Should you consider seeking the services of an independent counselor, I encourage you to visit these organizations' websites for up-to-date information and listings.

Sincerely,

Robert Franek
Lead Author, *The Best 378 Colleges*
SVP—Publisher
The Princeton Review

ABOUT THE AUTHORS

Robert Franek is a graduate of Drew University and Vice President and Publisher for The Princeton Review. He has proudly been a part of the company since 1999. Robert comes to The Princeton Review with an extensive admissions background. In addition, he owns a walking tour business, leading historically driven, yet not boring, walking tours of his favorite town, New York City!

David Soto is a graduate of the Walter Cronkite School of Journalism at Arizona State University and Director of Content Development for The Princeton Review. He helps create a line of guidebook titles on various aspects of the admissions process, including college, graduate school, and career-related topics, as well as the company website which serves more than half of all college-bound students. He lives in Brooklyn, NY.

Kristen O'Toole is a graduate of Bates College and has an MFA from Columbia University. She has worked on The Princeton Review's admissions guidebooks in various capacities since 2008, and is currently Editor of these titles and related publishing projects.

INDEX OF SCHOOLS

INDEX OF SCHOOLS BY LOCATION

INDEX OF SCHOOLS BY TUITION

Price categories are based on figures the schools reported to us in early spring 2013 for tuition (out-of-state tuition for public schools) and do not include fees, room, board, transportation, or other expenses.

No Tuition

Berea College	102
College of the Ozarks	182
Deep Springs College	210
United States Air Force Academy	576
United States Coast Guard Academy	578
United States Merchant Marine Academy	580
United States Military Academy (West Point)	582
United States Naval Academy	584
Webb Institute	774

Less Than $10,000

Brigham Young University (UT)	114
McGill University	366
The University of South Dakota	716

$10,000—$15,000

City University of New York—City College	154
City University of New York—Queens College	158
Grove City College	274
Salisbury University	476
State University of New York—Purchase College	528
State University of New York—University at Albany	532
Truman State University	566
University of Louisiana at Lafayette	644
University of Wyoming	744

$15,000—$20,000

Angelo State University	70
California State University, Stanislaus	126
Christopher Newport University	148
City University of New York—Baruch College	150
City University of New York—Brooklyn College	152
City University of New York—Hunter College	156
The Evergreen State College	236
Flagler College	240
Florida State University	244
Hampton University	282
Howard University	300
Indiana University of Pennsylvania	308
Iowa State University	310
James Madison University	314
Montana Tech of the University of Montana	386
National University of Ireland Maynooth	394
North Carolina State University	404
Ohio University—Athens	418
Sonoma State University	498
State University of New York at Binghamton	522
State University of New York at Geneseo	524
State University of New York— College of Environmental Science and Forestry	526
State University of New York—Stony Brook University	530
Tuskegee University	572
University of Arkansas—Fayetteville	592
University of Houston	632
University of Idaho	634
University of Kentucky	642
University of Mary Washington	650
University of Minnesota—Twin Cities	662
University of Mississippi	664
University of Nebraska—Lincoln	670

University of New Orleans	676
The University of North Carolina at Asheville	678
The University of North Carolina at Greensboro	682
The University of North Dakota	684
University of Oklahoma	688
University of South Florida	718
Wesleyan College (GA)	780
West Virginia University	784
Xavier University of Louisiana	810

$20,000—$25,000

Arizona State University	72
Auburn University	76
The College of Idaho	178
The College of New Jersey	180
Colorado State University	192
Hillsdale College	292
Kansas State University	322
Louisiana State University	340
Missouri University of Science and Technology	382
New Jersey Institute of Technology	400
Portland State University	430
Rutgers, The State University of New Jersey—New Brunswick	464
Spelman College	504
Temple University	550
Texas A&M University—College Station	552
Thomas Aquinas College	556
The University of Alabama at Birmingham	586
The University of Alabama at Tuscaloosa	588
University of Central Florida	608
University of Cincinnati	612
University of Kansas	640
University of Louisville	646
University of Maryland—Baltimore County	652
University of Missouri	666
The University of Montana—Missoula	668
University of New Mexico	674
The University of Tampa	722
University of Utah	734
Virginia Polytechnic Institute and State University (Virginia Tech)	754
Washington State University	770

$25,000—$30,000

Alfred University	62
Becker College	92
Bradley University	110
Calvin College	128
Catawba College	136
College of Charleston	174
Duquesne University	226
Elon University	230
Emerson College	232
Florida Southern College	242
George Mason University	254
Georgia Institute of Technology	260
Le Moyne College	334
Marywood University	362
Miami University (OH)	370
Michigan Technological University	374
Nazareth College	396
New College of Florida	398

THE PRINCETON REVIEW NATIONAL COLLEGE COUNSELOR ADVISORY BOARD, 2014–2015

We thank the members of this board for their careful and considered input on our products and services.

Michael A. Acquilano, Director of College Guidance, Staten Island Academy, Staten Island, NY

Roland M. Allen, Director of College Counseling, St. Margaret's Episcopal School, San Juan Capistrano, CA

Carol I. Bernstein, Director of College Guidance, Chadwick School, Palos Verdes Peninsula, CA

Lee Bierer, Weekly Countdown to College Syndicated Columnist and Independent College Counselor, College Admission Strategies, Charlotte, NC

Marianne M. Borgmann, Director of Guidance, Cincinnati Hills Christian Academy, Cincinnati, OH

Vicki Brunnick, MA, LPC, Counselor/Scholarship Chair, Myers Park High School Charlotte, NC

Judy S. Fairfull, Guidance Department Head, Doherty Memorial High School, Worcester, MA, Worcester Public School District, MA

Meghan Farley, Co-Director of College Counseling, Pingree School, South Hamilton, MA

Maureen Ferrell, Director of College Counseling, The Summit Country Day School, Cincinnati, OH

Nancy Griesemer, MPA, Columnist for Examiner.com and Independent College Consultant, College Explorations, Oakton, VA

Chuck Gutman, College Counselor, Waukegan High School, Waukegan, IL

Troy B. Hammond, Director of University Counseling, Bayview Glen School, Toronto, Ontario, Canada

Ann R. Harris, PhD, Director of College Guidance, Parish Episcopal School, Dallas, TX

Ann Herbener, College Counselor, Papillion-La Vista High School, Papillion, NE

William Hirt, College Counselor, Professional Children's School, New York, NY

Tricia Georgi Howard, Director of College Counseling, St. Ursula Academy, Toledo, OH

Marilyn J. Kaufman, MEd, Independent College Counselor, President of College Admission Consultants, Dallas, TX

Geri Kellogg, LPC Counselor, J.J. Pearce High School, Richardson, TX

Helene Kunkel, College Advisor, Palisades Charter High School, Pacific Palisades, CA

Joanne Levy-Prewitt, College Admissions Advisor, Moraga, CA

Moira McKinnon, Director of College Counseling, Berwick Academy, South Berwick, ME

Susan S. Marrs, Director, College Counseling, Seven Hills School, Cincinnati OH

Bruce Richardson, Director of Guidance, Plano Senior High School, Plano, TX

Kimberly R. Simpson, Educational Consultant, Collegiate Admissions Consulting Services, LLC, Covington, LA

Chris Teare, Director of College Counseling, Antilles School, Saint Thomas, VI

Theresa Urist, Director of College Counseling, Prospect Hill Academy Charter School, Cambridge, MA

Michael Wilner, Educational Consultant and Founder, Wilner Education, Putney, VT

SCHOOL SAYS . . .

In this section you'll find advertisements directly from colleges with information they'd like you to consider about their schools. The editorial in these pages is entirely the responsibility of the colleges. It does not reflect any opinion of The Princeton Review about the schools, and The Princeton Review did not create the advertisements. The Princeton Review charges the schools a fee to offset the cost of printing their advertisements in this section.

The Princeton Review does not charge schools a fee to be profiled in this book, or in any of our books. The company has never required colleges, universities, or any institutions to pay a fee for their profiles or inclusions in our books.

For information about how we selected the 379 outstanding schools in this book, see page 21, "How and Why We Produce This Book."

SHAPE YOUR MIND

Adelphi University is committed to helping students succeed, with rich educational and practical experiences that influence their academic, professional and personal lives. Just 23 miles from Manhattan, Adelphi provides a vibrant academic and student life, including extraordinary study abroad, internship and community service opportunities.

Students flourish at Assumption College. Strong academic programs in the liberal arts, sciences, business and professional studies, rooted in the rich Catholic intellectual tradition, will provide you with the skills you'll need to excel.

But there's more to education than coursework. At Assumption we'll help you cultivate the character and personal values you'll need to meet the demands of a changing world. The campus community will challenge and support you to achieve more than you thought possible, and put you on the path to leading a life of meaning.

Find your light at Assumption, and learn how to share it with the world.

500 Salisbury Street
Worcester, MA 01609
www.assumption.edu
866.477.7776

GET THE FACTS

:: **42** majors and **47** minors in the liberal arts, sciences, business and professional studies

:: **2,000** undergraduates from 30 states and 12 countries

:: **90** percent of the students live on campus in guaranteed housing all four years

:: Founded in **1904,** Assumption is the fourth-oldest Catholic college in New England

:: Students can choose from more than **60** student clubs and organizations

:: **Recognized as a top tier school** by *U.S. News and World Report*

:: **23** top-performing NCAA Division II athletic teams

:: **11:1** student/faculty ratio

:: *Assumption Assurance* program provides **4-year tuition freeze** for the Class of 2019 at 2015-2016 tuition rate

:: Merit scholarships up to **$20,000** annually

:: Located in the 2nd-largest city in New England, Worcester has more than **30,000** college students overall

:: **Our Rome campus** turns the entire "Eternal City" into a living classroom

Worcester, MA | Rome, Italy

 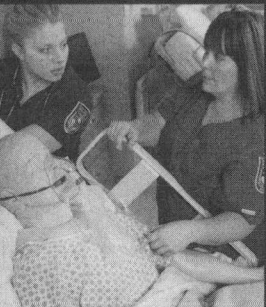 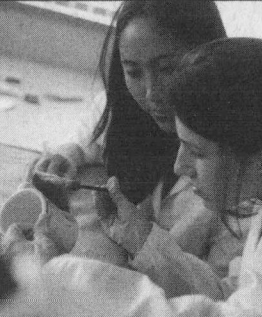  

Strength in

DIVERSITY

CSU Stanislaus. A close community that celebrates diversity.

California State University, Stanislaus is an exceptional public university that, because of its student-friendly size and commitment to excellence, is able to offer all the benefits of a private education. CSU Stanislaus offers baccalaureate degrees in the liberal arts, sciences, business and education, as well as teaching credentials, master's degree programs, and other professional studies.

Through a strong commitment to diversity and educational equity, CSU Stanislaus helps all students reach their full potential.

Learn more... **www.csustan.edu**

California State University|Stanislaus

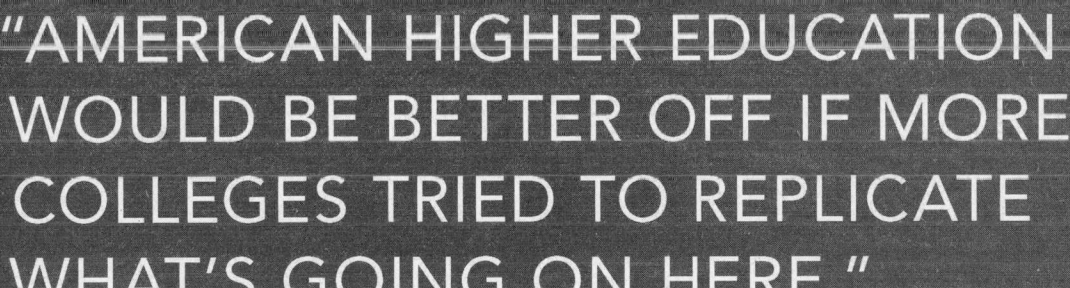

Convention isn't going to change the world.

"Suburban development and city planning are driving many of the issues that sustainability professionals must address. These issues require solutions from different areas, which is why we have faculty trained in geography, sociology, ecology, and so on, who are all part of one school of sustainability. We give our students the broader knowledge base needed to solve the serious challenges facing communities."

Michael Finewood, Ph.D.
Assistant Professor of Geography and Sustainability

falk.chatham.edu

chatham UNIVERSITY
FALK SCHOOL OF SUSTAINABILITY

Eden Hall Campus | Bachelor of Sustainability | Master of Sustainability | Master of Arts in Food Studies

CHRISTOPHER NEWPORT
UNIVERSITY

Meet Linda Oh, a biology major in CNU's
pre-dentistry program. As a Bonner Service Scholar
she completes at least 300 hours of service each year
working to inspire local youth and helping them overcome challenges.

LEADERSHIP. SERVICE. HONOR.
LEARN TO LEAD A LIFE OF SIGNIFICANCE

At Christopher Newport University our outstanding liberal arts
and sciences programs shape hearts and minds for a lifetime
of service. Your journey begins in the classroom, where you
will study with accomplished scholars of outstanding quality.

Outside the classroom you will join students like Linda in
fine-tuning your leadership skills by collaborating closely
with fellow CNU Captains and professors, to make a
lasting impact on campus, in the community and around
the globe. From mentoring inner-city youth and playing
the cello in the University Orchestra, like Linda, to groundbreaking research, CNU prepares you to do the work that
shapes, defines and enriches the world.

Learn today how you will serve the greater good.

Find out what it means to be a Captain.

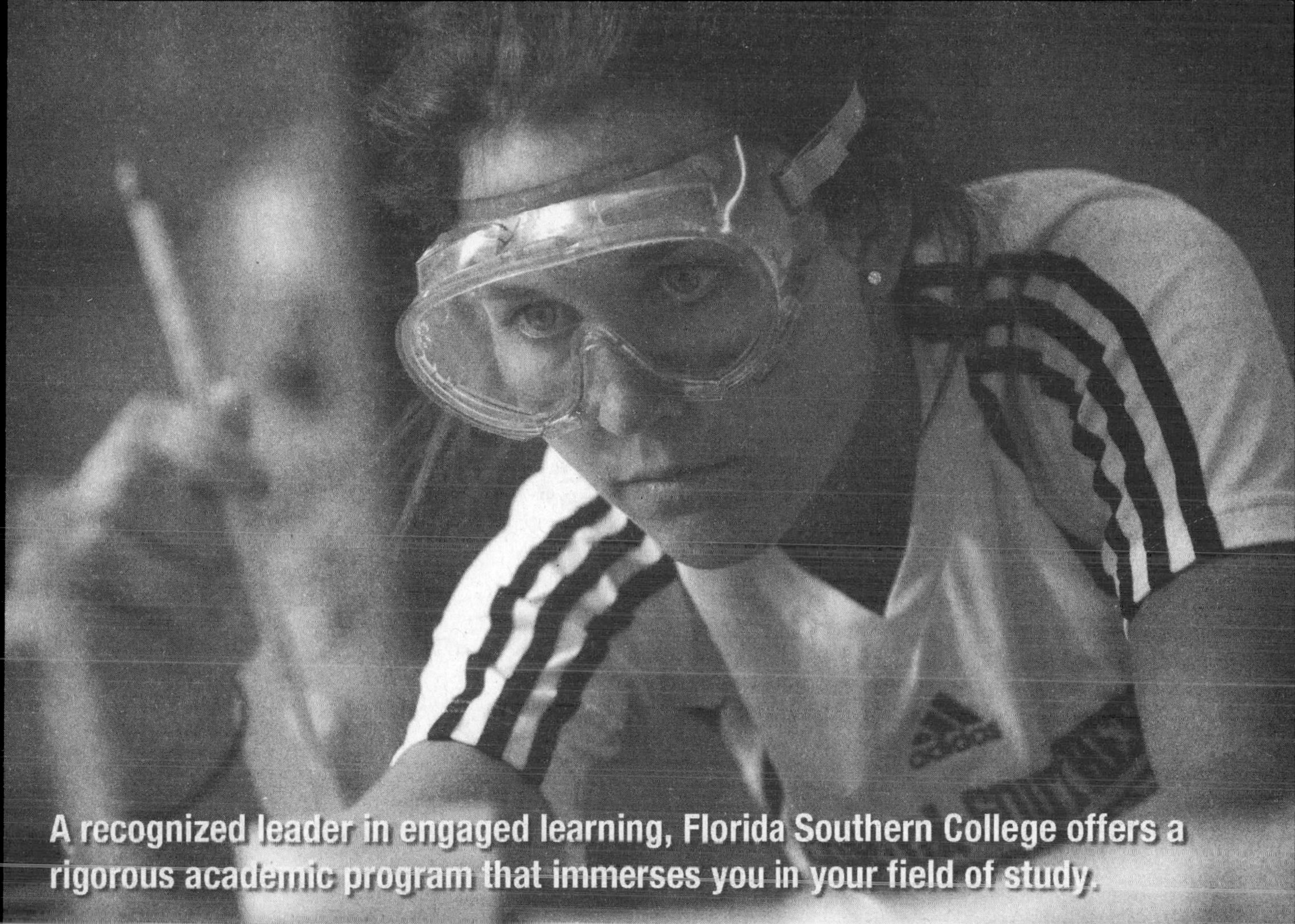

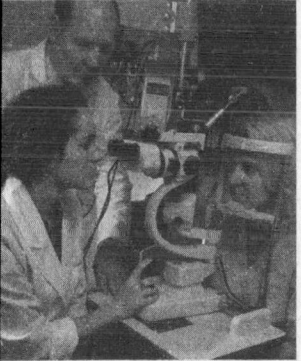

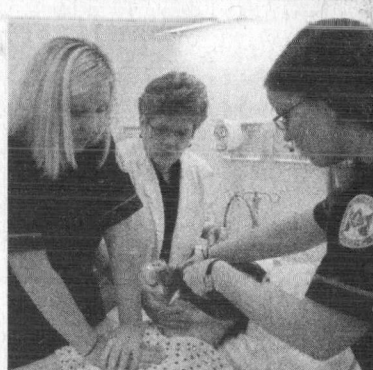

Discover a place where *faith*, *freedom* and *rigorous academics* lead to remarkable student outcomes.

#1
Top Value Private Liberal Arts College

91%
Freshman Retention Rate

96%
employed or enrolled in graduate school within six months of receiving their diplomas.

A Top Liberal Arts College where accepted students enroll.
US NEWS

A Best National Liberal Arts College.
US NEWS

Best Colleges Undergraduate Engineering Programs.
US NEWS

Top 13 percent of America's best colleges.
Princeton Review

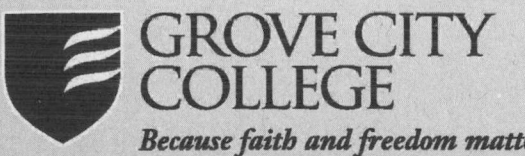

GROVE CITY COLLEGE
Because faith and freedom matter

Learn more about the Grove City College experience, or schedule a campus visit.
www.gcc.edu | 724-458-2100

NATIONAL UNIVERSITY OF IRELAND
MAYNOOTH

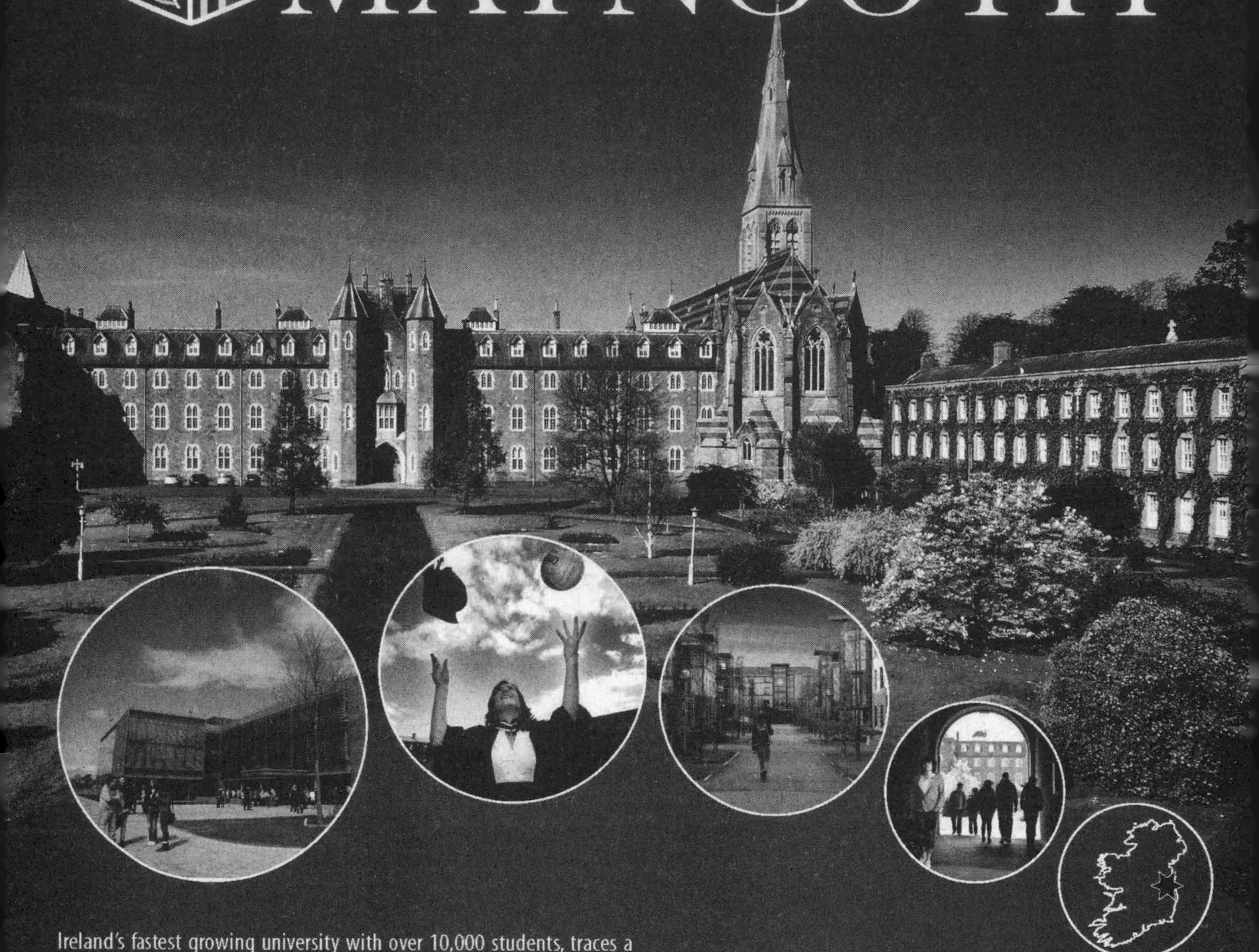

Ireland's fastest growing university with over 10,000 students, traces a tradition of academic excellence in the humanities and sciences back to 1795. Located in the town of Maynooth in a historical setting with a medieval castle at the gates of the university, National University of Ireland Maynooth is also only 25-minutes away from Dublin, Ireland's vibrant capital city. The University is adjacent to Ireland's 'silicon valley', with strong links to Intel, HP, Google and other giants of industry, leading to the best graduate employment records of any Irish university.

Walk in the footsteps of some of Ireland's greatest historical figures, while setting out on your own path to success, supported by some of the world's finest academics. Draw inspiration from our alumni John Hume, Nobel Peace Prizewinner; Brian Friel, internationally celebrated author and playwright; or Nicholas Callan, inventor of the 'Maynooth' battery and the induction coil which changed the study of modern electrical science.

STUDY WITH US

The National University of Ireland Maynooth offers the best of both worlds: a gateway to the leading minds of Ireland's past and a springboard for your future.

International Office
National University of Ireland Maynooth
www.nuim.ie/international

Tel: +353 1 708 3868
Fax: +353 1 708 6113
International.Office@nuim.ie

www.facebook.com/international.NUIM

http://pinterest.com/NUIM

THE FIRST INTERNATIONAL UNIVERSITY IN THE PRINCETON REVIEW

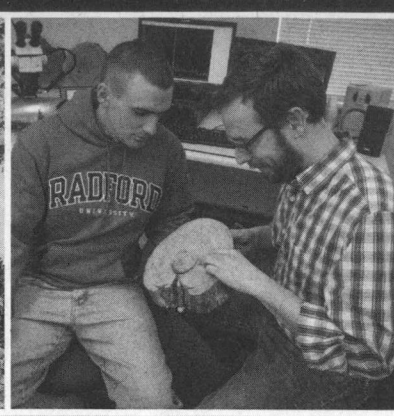

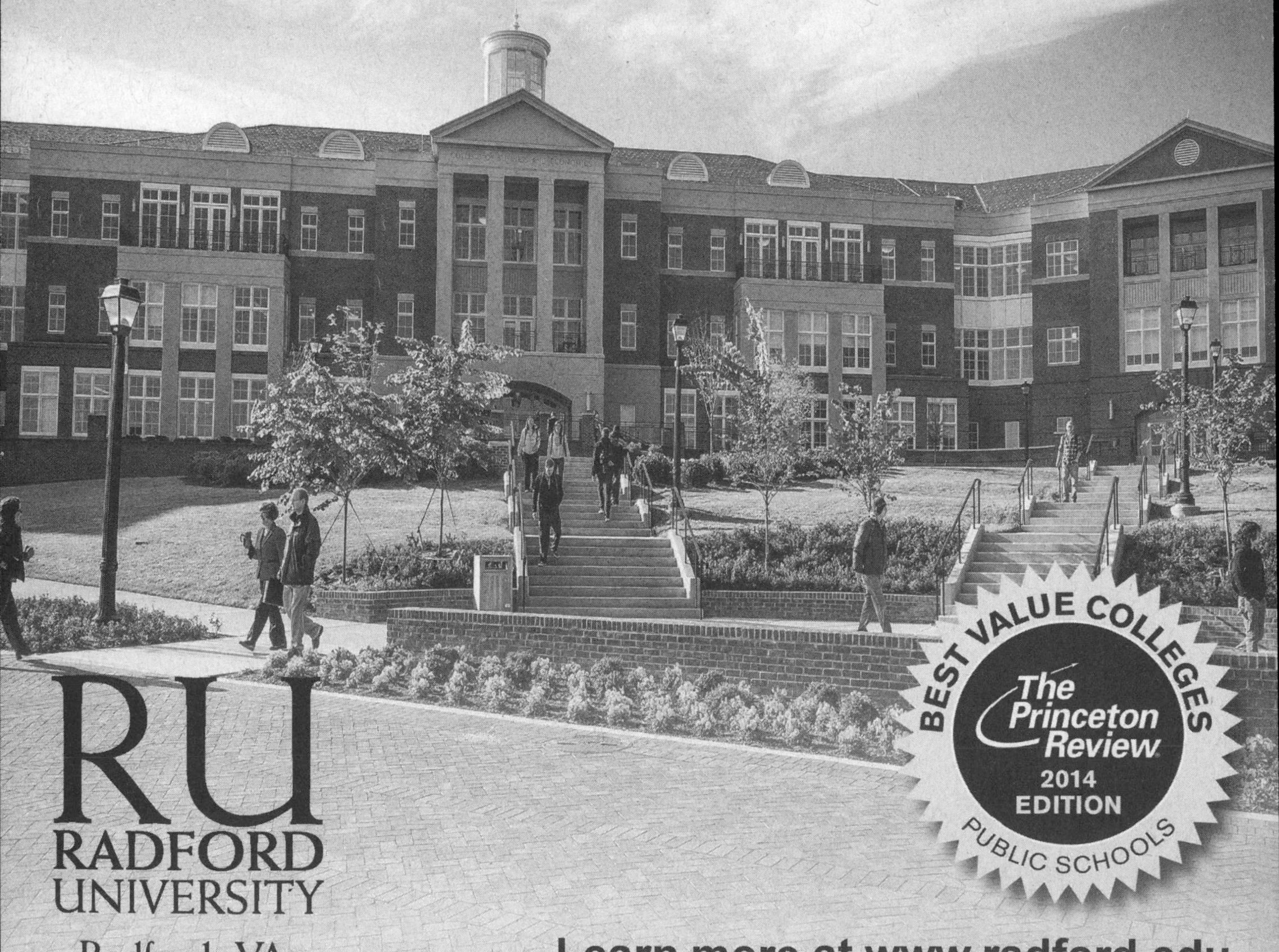

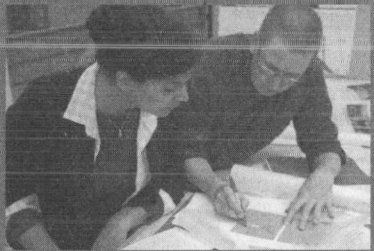

1889

Manchester, New Hampshire

A comprehensive
liberal arts education
where you'll gain true insight
into how the world works—
and how you can make
it work better.

The facts

97	18
Percent of students are awarded financial aid	Our average class size

98%	11:1	60
of 2013 graduates are employed, in school or engaged in service	Our student/ faculty ratio	Minutes to skiing, beaches, and Boston

VISIT US!
www.anselm.edu/visit

CONNECT WITH US!
social.anselm.edu

A green campus
in the Green Mountains

Major in environmental studies, biology, chemistry,
international relations or more than 30 other subjects
while making a difference in our world.

SAINT MICHAEL'S COLLEGE FOUNDED 1904

SMCVT.EDU · BURLINGTON, VERMONT

reporter
history buff
socialite

writer
dancer
foodie

environmentalist
mathematician
ideal roomie

artistic genius
rising star
born leader

filmmaker
linguist
explorer

IT'S EASY TO SPOT A PURCHASE STUDENT. THERE'S NO ONE ELSE LIKE THEM.

Purchase has a talent for attracting the multi-talented. Passionate, creative, driven and diverse, our students are (ironically) alike in their desire to make a difference, explore the possibilities and celebrate their individuality.

For more information call 914.251.6300 or visit purchase.edu/buildyourself.

Purchase College
STATE UNIVERSITY OF NEW YORK

UMass Boston

Boston's public research university

NOTED FOR

» New Honors College

» New School for the Environment

» Half a billion dollars in new facilities over the next three years

» New Integrated Science Center

» Dynamic learning environment

» Diverse, rich, global perspective

» Close proximity to Boston

» Quality education at a tremendous value

» Maintaining affordability with robust financial aid packages

» More than 175 academic programs

FOR MORE INFORMATION:
WWW.UMB.EDU | 617.287.6000
ENROLLMENT.INFO@UMB.EDU

UMASS BOSTON

14.353AM

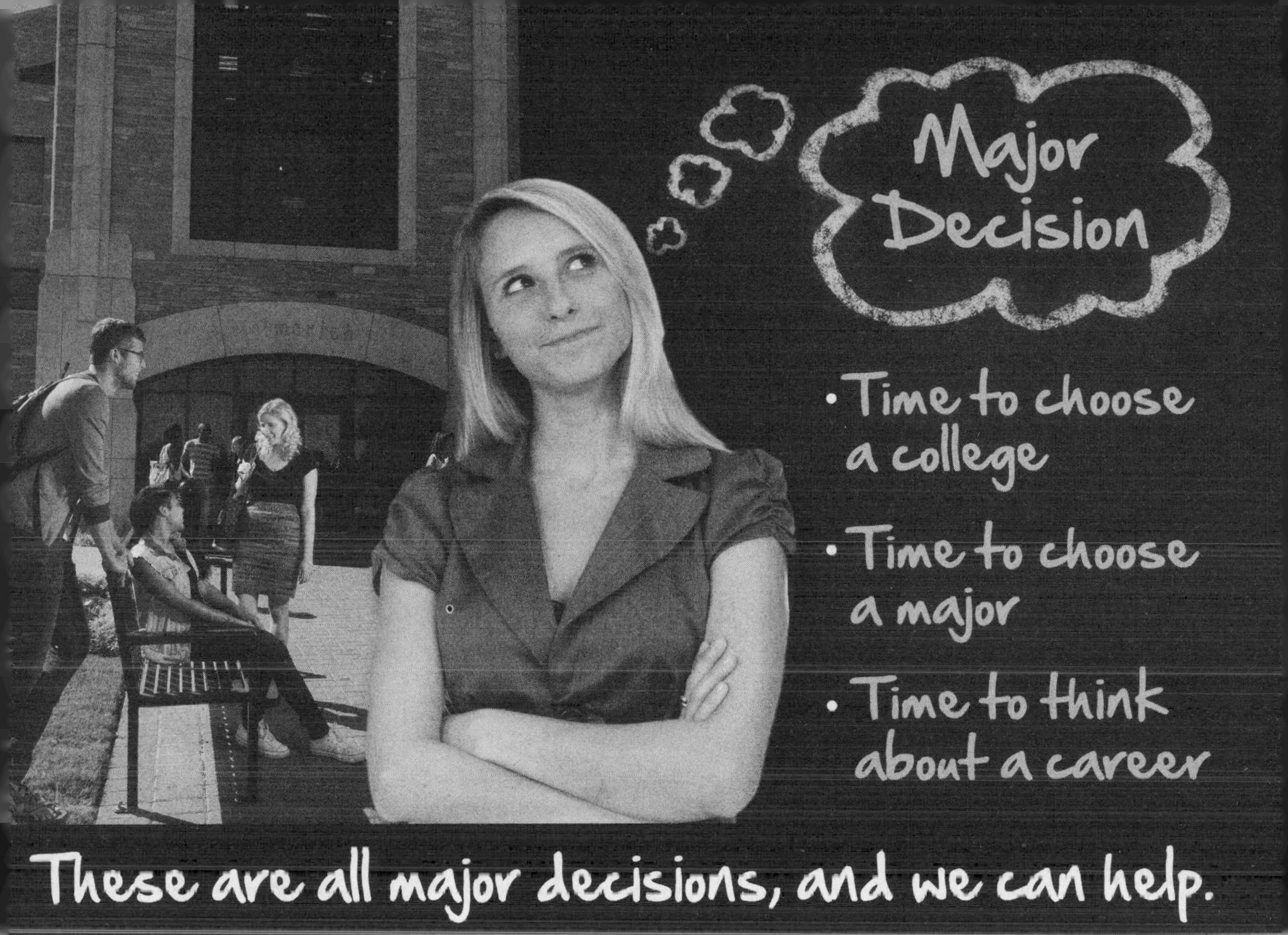
Major Decision
• Time to choose a college
• Time to choose a major
• Time to think about a career
These are all major decisions, and we can help.

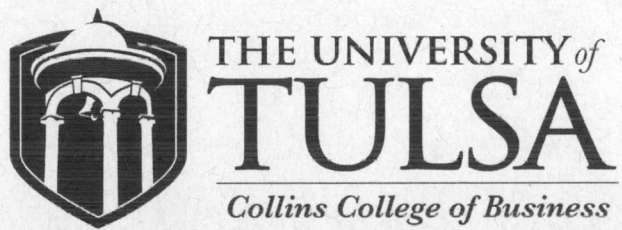

NOTES

NOTES

NOTES

NOTES

NOTES

NOTES

NOTES

NOTES

NOTES

WE KNOW APPLYING TO COLLEGES IS STRESSFUL.
Why Not Win $2,000 for It?

Participate in our 2015 "College Hopes & Worries Survey."

You might win our college scholarship prize!

The Princeton Review has conducted this survey of high school students applying to colleges and parents of applicants since 2005. Why? We're curious to know what concerns you the most about your application experiences and what your dream college would be.

Our survey has just 14 questions—way shorter than any college app. You can zip through it in less than three minutes. Plus, in addition to the $2,000 scholarship prize we'll give to one lucky participant chosen at random, we'll give another 25 participants (also chosen at random) a free copy of one of our college-related guidebooks. They can chose either *Paying for College Without Going Broke, If the U Fits: Expert Advice on Finding the Right College and Getting Accepted,* or *The Best Value Colleges.* In March 2015, about the time you'll (hopefully) be receiving college acceptance and financial aid award letters, we'll post the survey findings on our site and inform the scholarship winner and book winners. For more information, see "OFFICIAL RULES" below.

We know how exciting and how stressful college applications can be. We hope the information on our site and in our books helps you find, get in to, and get aid from the college best for you. We wish you great success in your applications and your college years ahead.

Official Rules:

Princeton Review 2015 "College Hopes & Worries Survey" Prize Sweepstakes

NO PURCHASE NECESSARY. OPEN TO RESIDENTS OF THE FIFTY UNITED STATES (AND WASHINTON, DC) THIRTEEN YEARS OF AGE AND OLDER ONLY.

1. HOW TO ENTER: To enter via the Internet, visit www.princetonreview.com/go/survey. LIMIT ONE ENTRY PER PERSON. All online entries must be received by 11:59 P.M. EDT on February 28, 2015. To enter without Internet access or answering the questionnaire, handwrite your name, complete address, and phone number on a postcard and mail to: The Princeton Review, 2014 College Hopes & Worries Survey, c/o Robert Franek, 317 Madison Ave. 5th Fl., New York, NY 10017. Mail-in entries must be received by February 21, 2015. Not responsible for lost, late, or misdirected mail.

2. ELIGIBILITY: Open to residents of the 50 United States and D.C., 13 years of age and older, except for employees of The Princeton Review ("Sponsor"), its affiliates, subsidiaries and agencies (collectively "Promotion Parties"), and members of their immediate family or persons living in the same household. Void where prohibited.

3. RANDOM DRAWINGS: A random drawing will be held on or about March 31, 2015. Odds of winning will depend upon the number of eligible entries received. Winner will be notified by e-mail/mail and/or telephone, at Sponsor's option and will be required to sign and return any required Affidavit of Eligibility, Release of Liability and Publicity Release within seven (7) days of attempted delivery or prize will be forfeited and an alternate winner may be selected. The return of any prize or prize notification as undeliverable may result in disqualification and an alternate winner may be selected.

4. PRIZES: One (1) Grand Prize: $2,000.00 Scholarship, awarded as a check. Twenty-Five (25) First Prizes: winner's choice of one of the following Princeton Review books: *Paying for College without Going Broke, If the U Fits,* or *The Best Value Colleges.* Approximate Retail Value: $19.00. Total prize value: $2,475.00. Limit one prize per family/household. All prizes will be awarded.

5. GENERAL RULES: All income taxes resulting from acceptance of prize are the responsibility of winner. By entering sweepstakes, entrant accepts and agrees to these Official Rules and the decisions of Sponsor, which shall be final in all matters. By accepting prize, winner agrees to hold Promotion Parties, their affiliates, directors, officers, employees and assigns harmless against any and all claims and liability arising out of use of prize. Acceptance also constitutes permission to the Promotion Parties to use winner's name and likeness for marketing purposes without further compensation or right of approval, unless prohibited by law. Promotion Parties are not responsible for lost or late mail, or for technical, hardware, or software malfunctions, lost or unavailable network connections, or failed, incorrect, inaccurate, incomplete, garbled, or delayed electronic communication whether caused by the sender or by any of the equipment or programming associated with or utilized in this sweepstakes, or by any human error which may occur in the processing of the entries in this sweepstakes. If, in the Sponsor's opinion, there is any suspected evidence of tampering with any portion of the promotion, or if technical difficulties compromise the integrity of the promotion, the Sponsor reserves the right to modify or terminate the sweepstakes in a manner deemed reasonable by the Sponsor, at the Sponsor's sole discretion. In the event a dispute arises as to the identity of a potentially winning online entrant, entries made by Internet will be declared made by the name on the online entry form. All federal and state laws apply.

6. WINNERS LIST: For the names of the winners, available after May 1, 2014, send a self-addressed, stamped (#10) envelope to: The Princeton Review, 2013 College Hopes & Worries Survey Contest Winners, c/o Robert Franek, 317 Madison Ave. 5th Fl., New York, NY 10017.

SPONSOR: TPR Education IP Holdings, LLC, Natick, MA 01760.

College Hopes & Worries Survey 2015

Mail to The Princeton Review, 2015 College Hopes & Worries Survey, c/o Robert Franek, 317 Madison Ave., 5th Fl., New York, NY 10017 (mailed entries must be received by February 20, 2014) or fill out online (online entries can be submitted between January 26 and February 28, 2015) at www.PrincetonReview.com/go/survey.

Name _____

Address (optional) _____

City / State / ZIP _____

Daytime phone _____

E-mail address_____

I am ____ a parent of a student ____ a student applying to attend college beginning in

____ Spring or Fall 2014 ____Spring or Fall 2015 ____ Later (indicate year:_____).

1   What would be your "dream" college? What college would you most like to attend (or see your child attend) if chance of being accepted or cost were not an issue? (Please write complete name of school e.g. "Oklahoma University," not initials such as "OU", which could also be an abbreviation for Ohio University.)

_____

2   How many colleges will you (your child) apply to?

____ 1 to 4

____ 5 to 8

____ 9 to 12

____ 13 or more

3   What is (or will be) the toughest part of your (your child's) college application experience? (Choose one.)

____ Researching colleges schools to apply to

____ Taking the SAT, ACT, or AP exams

____ Completing applications for admission and financial aid

____ Waiting for the decision letters and deciding which college to attend

4   Which college admission exam do you wish you (your child) could take if all of the following options were available? (Note the new, redesigned SAT won't be offered until spring of 2016, but imagine all three tests were current options as you make your answer choice. For more information about the differences between the current and the new redesigned SAT, go to www.princetonreview.com/satchanges.)

____ The ACT

____ The SAT

____ The new redesigned SAT

5   How would you rate the college application guidance and support you (your child) have (has) received from your (your child's) high school college advisor / guidance counselor?

____ Excellent

____ Good

____ Fair

____ Poor

6   What do you estimate your (or your child's) college degree will cost, including four years of tuition, room and board, fees, books and other expenses? (Choose one.)

____ More than $100,000

____ $75,000 to $100,000

____ $50,000 to 75,000

____ $25,000 to $50,000

____ Up to $25,000

7   How necessary will financial aid (education loans, scholarships, or grants) be to pay for your (your child's) college education? (Choose one.)

____ Extremely

____ Very

____ Somewhat

____ Not at all

8   What's your biggest concern about applying to or attending college? (Choose one.)

____ Won't get into first-choice college

____ Will get into first-choice college, but won't be able to attend due to high cost and/or insufficient financial aid

____ Level of debt I (my child) will take on to pay for the degree

____ Will attend a college I (my child) may regret

9   How would you gauge your stress level about the college application process? (Choose one.)

____ Very High

____ High

____ Average

____ Low

____ Very Low

10 Ideally, how far from home would you like the college you (your child) attend(s) to be? (Choose one.)

____ 0 to 250 miles

____ 250 to 500 miles

____ 500 to 1,000

____ 1,000 miles or more

11 When it comes to choosing the college you (your child) will attend, which of the following do you think it is most likely to be? (Choose one.)

____ College with best academic reputation

____ College with best program for my (my child's) career interests

____ College that will be the most affordable

____ College that will be the best overall fit

12 If you (your child) had a way to compare colleges based on their commitment to environmental "green" issues (e.g. practices concerning energy use, recycling, etc.), how much would this contribute to your (your child's) decision to apply to or attend a school?

____ Strongly

____ Very much

____ Somewhat

____ Not much

____ Not at all

13 What will be the biggest benefit of your (your child) getting a college degree?

____ The education overall

____ The experience: exposure to new ideas, places, and people

____ The potentially better job and higher income

14 On the whole, do you believe college will be "worth it" for you (your child)?

____ Yes

____ No

Optional: What advice would you give to college applicants or parents of applicants going through this experience next year?

_____

_____

_____

_____

_____

_____

_____

_____

_____

_____

_____

_____

_____

_____